D0890399

NATIONAL WATER SUMMARY
ON WETLAND RESOURCES

By U.S. Geological Survey

Judy D. Fretwell, John S. Williams,
and Phillip J. Redman, Compilers

United States Geological Survey
Water-Supply Paper 2425

U.S. DEPARTMENT OF THE INTERIOR
BRUCE BABBITT, Secretary

U.S. GEOLOGICAL SURVEY
Gordon P. Eaton, Director

UNITED STATES GOVERNMENT PRINTING OFFICE: 1996

For sale by the U.S. Government Printing Office
Superintendent of Documents, M.S. SSOP, Washington, D.C.   20402–9328

United States Geological Survey
National Water Summary
ISBN 0-607-85696-3

Foreword

National Water Summary on Wetland Resources is the eighth in a series of reports that describes the conditions, trends, availability, quality, and use of the water resources of the United States. This volume describes an often-overlooked water resource—wetlands. It gives a broad overview of wetland resources and includes discussions of the scientific basis for understanding wetland functions and values; legislation that regulates the uses of wetlands; wetland research, inventory, and evaluation; and issues related to the restoration, creation, and recovery of wetlands. In addition, it presents more-specific information—types and distribution, hydrologic setting, trends, and conservation—on the wetland resources of each State, the District of Columbia, Puerto Rico, the U.S. Virgin Islands, and several Pacific islands over which the United States has jurisdiction.

Wetlands serve as a transitional environment between water bodies and dry land and represent a significant part of the Nation's natural resources. They contain economically important timber, fuel, and food sources; provide esthetic and recreational opportunities; and influence the quantity, quality, and ecological status of water bodies, which include rivers, aquifers, lakes, reservoirs, and estuaries. Wetlands owe their existence, in part, to precipitation, streams, lakes, ground water, and oceans and, in return, perform important functions that affect the quantity and quality of these water resources. Although wetlands are best known for their function as habitat for birds, fish, and other wildlife, their less well known hydrologic and water-quality functions provide such benefits as reducing the severity of flooding and erosion by modifying the flow of water or improving water quality by filtering out contaminants.

Public and scientific views of wetlands have changed greatly over time. Only a few decades ago, wetlands were generally considered to be of little or no value. Those who eliminated wetlands through draining or filling were thought of as performing a public service. The role of the wetlands as a breeding ground for disease (primarily malaria) and their inability to be exploited for agricultural production caused them to be viewed as an economic "bad" rather than as a public "good," as they are viewed today. Because of new scientific knowledge, as well as a change in values (as manifested in our Nation's environmental laws), efforts to eliminate wetlands are viewed in a negative light by many. In fact, government and private citizens are making investments in the preservation, remediation, or creation of wetlands.

Although we now understand some of the benefits of wetlands and government agencies have established programs to protect them, wetland-protection policies remain a controversial public issue. In keeping with its mission, the U.S. Geological Survey (USGS) has prepared this report with the intent of informing public officials, scientists, and the general public about wetlands. Our purpose is to increase and help improve the understanding of this valuable resource and to provide the scientific information base upon which wise decisions regarding the classification, use, modification, or restoration of wetlands can be made. The hydrologic, biological, and economic consequences of these decisions are substantial and often politically contentious. The USGS takes no position on these issues but hopes to make a positive contribution to the process whereby these decisions are made.

The USGS is an earth science information agency. It collects, manages, and disseminates data; conducts interpretive scientific studies and research; and publishes the results of these efforts in many forms. The work of the USGS is organized into four thematic areas—resources, hazards, environment, and information management. Wetlands are addressed in each of these areas. For example, some wetlands play an integral role in water-resource availability because they are major discharge areas for some aquifers. Some wetlands relate to the hazards theme through their role in the mitigation of floods. Wetlands are affected by environmental changes, such as changes in the source or distribution of water, and, in turn, cause changes in the environment, such as shifts in vegetation or in habitat for birds, fish, and other animals; studies of these changes tie into the environmental theme. And, finally, with respect to the information management theme, the process of classifying, monitoring, and understanding wetlands is dependent upon the hydrologic, geologic, and topographic data collected by the USGS.

The USGS has taken this opportunity to draw on the expertise of the many agencies and organizations that have missions directly or indirectly related to wetlands to provide a broad background for government officials, water-resource managers, and the general public. You will note that many of the chapters of this volume have authors from other agencies with key roles in research, classification, or management of wetlands. Production of this volume was a team effort, just as management of wetlands is a team effort. We thank our colleagues in the many other agencies that helped make this report possible. I would like to pay special tribute to the late Dr. Edward T. LaRoe of the National Biological Service, coauthor of the chapter on research. He was a leading wetland researcher and played a pivotal role in the evolution of all biological research in the U.S. Department of the Interior.

Though this volume merely touches on the many and varied aspects of wetlands, it provides a starting place for further study and a base upon which to begin to understand the values of wetlands to the Nation. We hope it is useful, and we welcome your comments on this volume, as well as on our other products.

DIRECTOR

Hidden River near Homosassa Springs, Florida. *(Photograph by Judy D. Fretwell, U.S. Geological Survey.)*

There has been a lot said about the sacredness of our land which is our body, and the values of our culture which is our soul. But water is the blood of our tribes, and if its life-giving flow is stopped, or it is polluted, all else will die and the many thousands of years of our communal existence will come to an end.

Frank Tenorio, Governor, San Felipe Pueblo, 1978

Contents

Figures

Figures—Continued

Figures—Continued

In "State Summaries of Wetland Resources"—
Each State summary has photographs and maps showing—
1. A well-known wetland in the State.
2. Wetland distribution and physiography.
Some State summaries have other maps, diagrams, or photographs showing related wetland resources information.

Tables

In "State Summaries of Wetland Resources"—
Each State summary has a table that lists the wetland-related activities of Federal, State, and local government agencies and private organizations in the State.

Executive Summary, State Highlights and Introduction

Wetland in Bridgeport Valley, California; Sierra Nevada Mountains in the background.
(Photograph by Steve Van Denburgh, U.S. Geological Survey.)

This wetland is part of a local park near Madison, Wisconsin.
(Photograph by Patricia S. Greene.)

Executive Summary _____

This National Water Summary on Wetland Resources documents wetland resources in the United States. It presents an overview of the status of our knowledge of wetlands at the present time—what they are, where they are found, why they are important, and the controversies surrounding them, with an emphasis on their hydrology. The "State Summaries of Wetland Resources" part of this National Water Summary describes wetland resources in each State, the District of Columbia (combined with Maryland), Puerto Rico, the U.S. Virgin Islands, and the Western Pacific Islands. The following discussion is a summary of the two parts of this book—"Overview of Wetland Resources" and "State Summaries of Wetland Resources."

OVERVIEW OF WETLAND RESOURCES

The Overview of Wetland Resources part of this National Water Summary consists of three sections— "Technical Aspects of Wetlands," "Wetland Management and Research," and "Restoration, Creation, and Recovery of Wetlands"—that contain 11 articles providing information on many technical and societal aspects of wetland resources. The following text summarizes the many facts about wetland resources that these articles report.

Technical Aspects Of Wetland Resources

Wetlands began disappearing soon after permanent European colonization of the United States. More than one-half of the 221 million acres of wetlands that existed at that time have disappeared; only 103 million acres remain today. Early in this Nation's history, it was believed that wetlands presented obstacles to development and that wetlands should be eliminated. Federal laws provided incentives for "reclaiming" wetlands. Only recently people have begun to recognize wetland values and attempted to find ways to preserve them, including changing Federal laws. These attempts have slowed the rate of wetland loss, but losses continue today. The history of wetland losses in the conterminous United States from the time of the first permanent European settlement and changes in societal attitudes toward wetlands are documented in "History of Wetlands in the Conterminous United States."

Although there is controversy over the precise, legal definition of a wetland, wetlands are scientifically defined by their hydrology, vegetation, and soils. The many different types of wetlands, found in many different geographic settings, have different functions. Wetlands can be grouped according to these differences using a nationally consistent terminology (Cowardin and others, 1979) to identify mapping units for Federal and State wetland inventories and to determine wetland status and trends that can aid in planning and management of the resource. The different types of wetlands and the classification systems describing them are presented in "Wetland Definitions and Classifications in the United States."

An understanding of the basic hydrologic processes that control the formation, persistence, size, and functions of wetlands is necessary for determining appropriate protective measures for particular wetlands and for determining the success of those measures. The source and distribution of water is a major factor in the differences in wetland types and distribution across the country. Both a favorable geologic setting and an adequate and persistent supply of water are necessary for the existence of a wetland. Different wetlands receive water from different sources; ground water, streams, lakes, tides, snow, and rain. The source of water largely determines its quality, which in turn is largely responsible for wetland vegetation. The wetland vegetation affects the value of the wetland to animals and people. Wetlands provide many beneficial water-related functions. Some wetlands provide flood control, some provide water for aquifers, others feed streams, some modify climate, others improve water quality, some help maintain the salt balance necessary for estuarine life, and still others control erosion. "Wetland Hydrology, Water Quality, and Associated Functions" describes the different water-related factors that determine what types of wetlands will be established and what functions each will perform.

One of the best known functions of wetlands is as habitat for birds. About one-third of the North American bird species use wetlands for water, food, shelter, or breeding. About 138 of the 1,900 bird species in the conterminous United States are wetland dependent. For wetland-dependent birds, habitat loss or degradation usually translates to population loss. Some international treaties—The Migratory Bird Treaty and the Ramsar Convention—are partly responsible for much of the formal wetland protection in this country. "Wetlands as Bird Habitat" discusses the relation of birds and wetlands and the effects of wetland losses on birds, and describes some efforts to reduce wetland loss.

Wetland Management And Research

Many of the benefits that wetlands provide accrue primarily to the general public instead of the private landowner. Landowners usually have few incentives to conserve wetlands that fulfill the needs of the general public. The Government, therefore, provides incentives and regulates and manages some wetland resources to protect the resources from degradation and destruction. Despite current recognition of wetland benefits, potentially conflicting interests still exist, and disagreement on how to protect wetlands has led to differences in local, State, and Federal guidelines. Current wetland-protection regulation commonly requires that wetland loss to development be offset by replacing wetlands by means of mitigation. Section 404 of the Clean Water Act and the "Swampbuster" program are two major Federal vehicles of wetland protection. Coastal wetlands are provided some protection by the Coastal Zone Management Act and the Coastal Barriers Resources Act. Major Federal legislation and initiatives that affect wetlands are discussed in "Wetland Protection Legislation."

The recent understanding of wetland values and the benefits that they provide has been broadened by the research efforts. In 1992, wetland research was being done by 18 Federal agencies—12 of which had expenditures of $1 million or more—as part of their mission or responsibilities defined by Congress. In 1992, Federal wetland research expenditures totaled about $63 million. Ecological processes and functions differ with wetland type; therefore, research needs and techniques also differ. Types of Federal wetland research fall into one of the following broad categories: wetland processes, wetland functions, human-induced stresses, delineation and identification, and management. Research needs also differ among agencies; nevertheless, efforts are coordinated to share information and to avoid duplication. Disappearing coastal and bottom-land hardwood wetlands are among the major areas of research. These and other areas of research are discussed in "Wetland Research by Federal Agencies."

Wetland mapping is a prerequisite for wetland inventory, regulation, management, protection, and restoration. Maps are used to analyze wetland trends and the effects of projects, policies, and activities on wetlands. The U.S. Fish and Wildlife Service has a major responsibility for the mapping and inventory of the Nation's wetlands as mandated by legislation enacted in the past 40 years. This responsibility is satisfied through the agency's National Wetlands Inventory program by producing maps, establishing a wetland data base, publishing and distributing reports on the status and trends of wetlands in this country, and by providing other products related to the identification, mapping, and inventory of wetlands. To date, the National Wetlands Inventory has produced more than 43,300 maps, covering more than 83 percent of the conterminous United States, 28 percent of Alaska, and all of Hawaii and the U.S. Territories. Other Federal agencies with wetland mapping and inventory activities, specific to their missions, are the Natural Resources Conservation Service (formerly known as the Soil Conservation Service)—freshwater wetlands with the potential for agricultural conversion; the National Oceanic and Atmospheric Administration—coastal wetlands associated with marine resources; and the U.S. Geological Survey—geographically significant wetlands. More information can be found in "Wetland Mapping and Inventory."

Placing a value on wetlands facilitates decisions on which sites should be developed to ensure that the most valuable wetlands are preserved. The value of a wetland lies in the benefits that its habitat, water-quality, and hydrologic functions provide to the environment or to people. Economic value can be placed on some wetland products, but true value goes beyond money. Some wetland values extend beyond the perimeter of the wetland and provide benefits on a local, regional, or global scale. Several systems of wetland evaluation have been or are being developed to assign numerical values to wetland functions in order to allow for the comparison of the worth of one wetland to another. The article "Wetland Functions, Values, and Assessment" discusses three different wetland evaluation methods—the Federal Highway Administration's "Wetland Evaluation Technique," the U.S. Environmental Protection Agency's "Environmental Monitoring Assessment Program—Wetlands," and the U.S. Army Corps of Engineers' "Hydrogeomorphic Approach."

Restoration, Creation, And Recovery

For the past few centuries wetlands have been drained or altered to accommodate human needs. This continues to happen, although at a slower rate than in the past. As people have begun to recognize what is lost when wetlands are destroyed, efforts have been made to restore lost wetlands or to create new ones. Restoration and creation of wetlands can help maintain the quality of wetlands and their surrounding ecosystems, and at the same time accommodate the human need for development. Although indications are that some replacement can be successful, full functional replacement has not yet been demonstrated. This is, in part, because of the youth of most restoration and creation projects and, in part, because of the lack of followup on most projects. Scientific knowledge about wetland restoration and creation differs by wetland type, function, and location. We know most about intertidal salt marshes and know much less about replacing forested wetlands because of the time needed for woody vegetation to mature. The more complex the hydrology and ecology of a system, the more difficult it is to restore the system; complete restoration might be impossible in some systems. The ecosystems least likely to be replaced are bogs and fens that have developed over thousands of years. "Wetland Restoration and Creation" discusses what is involved in restoring and creating wetlands and chances of being successful.

In August 1992, Hurricane Andrew caused massive destruction in southern Florida and in Louisiana—two States with some of the largest wetland acreages in the country. The storm passed directly over the Florida Everglades—the largest wetland complex in the United States—and the Atchafalaya River Basin, La., which contains the largest hardwood swamp in the United States. Although there were some immediate detrimental effects on plants and animals, the long-term effects seem to have been minimal in Florida. In Louisiana, the hurricane may have hastened the coastal erosion and wetland deterioration processes that were already at work. "Effects of Hurricane Andrew (1992) on Wetlands in Southern Florida And Louisiana" describes the effects of this major hurricane on these wetlands.

The Great Midwest Flood of 1993, in the Mississippi and Missouri River Basins, was the most devastating flood in United States' history. The areal extent, intensity, and long duration makes this flood unique in the 20th century. Effects of the flood were both detrimental and beneficial to wetlands. Trees were uprooted, islands were eroded, many wetland plants were destroyed, and several bird species fledged few young. Massive sedimentation buried mussels; mammals displaced from the flood plain suffered higher than normal mortalities on highways and railroads; the floodwaters transported large amounts of contaminants and nutrients into and down streams; nuisance plants replaced native vegetation; and turbidity made it difficult for some fish to feed. Nevertheless, some fish spawn and feed on inundated flood plains when temperature rise accompanies flooding—which was the case in this flooding. Also, some fish habitat was improved by the creation of deep scour holes and massive underwater debris piles that provide cover. Effects of the flooding are discussed in "Effects of the Great Midwest Flood of 1993 on Wetlands."

STATE SUMMARIES OF WETLAND RESOURCES

State Summaries of Wetland Resources in this National Water Summary provides an overview of the wetland resources of the 50 States, the District of Columbia (combined with Maryland), Puerto Rico, the U.S. Virgin Islands, and several Pacific islands over whose wetlands the United States has some form of jurisdiction. (The term "State" is used in the following discussion for all these geographic areas.) The State summaries contain the following sections:

Types and Distribution

Wetlands in the United States are of many types. Some of the more familiar names for different kinds of wetlands are swamp, marsh, bog, playa, tideflat, prairie pothole, and pond. Examples of lesser known, local names for different wetland types are cienega, pocosin, muskeg, wet pine flatwoods, and willow carrs. The "Types and Distribution" section of each State summary contains a brief discussion of the wetland types in the State and relates the common, locally known wetland names to the classification system used by Federal agencies to identify and delineate wetlands (see the article "Wetland Definitions and Classifications in the United States" in this volume for an extensive discussion of wetland types and classification).

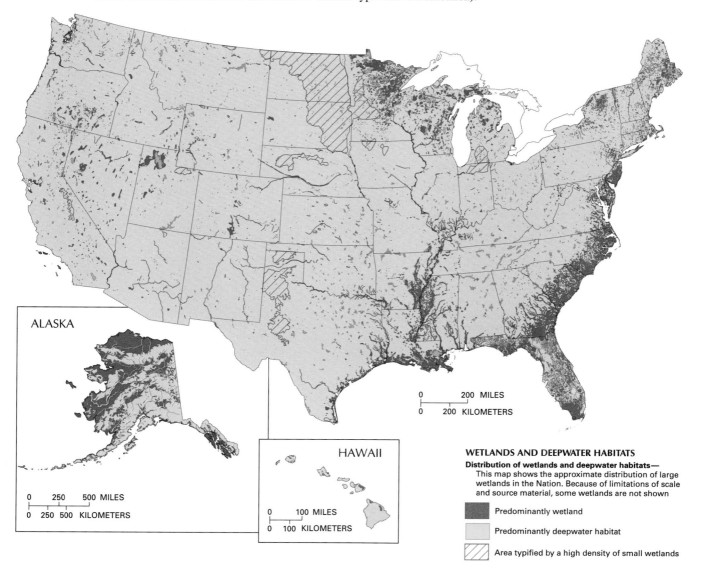

ALASKA

0   250   500 MILES
0 250 500 KILOMETERS

HAWAII

0   100 MILES
0 100 KILOMETERS

0   200 MILES
0   200 KILOMETERS

WETLANDS AND DEEPWATER HABITATS
Distribution of wetlands and deepwater habitats—
This map shows the approximate distribution of large wetlands in the Nation. Because of limitations of scale and source material, some wetlands are not shown

Predominantly wetland

Predominantly deepwater habitat

Area typified by a high density of small wetlands

The "Types and Distribution" section of each State summary also contains a brief discussion of wetland distribution in the State and a map that shows the general distribution of major wetlands. The State maps were derived from a national map that was compiled by the U.S. Fish and Wildlife Service (fig. 1). Because the data used to compile the map differ in reliability from State to State, the distribution of wetlands shown should be considered approximate. Also, because small areas physically cannot be represented at the scale at which the map was compiled, only relatively large wetlands are shown.

Example of table 1 used in each State summary (in this case Maryland and the District of Columbia) showing selected wetland-related activities of government agencies and private organizations within the State.

[Source: Classification of activities is generalized from information provided by agencies and organizations. ●, agency or organization participates in wetland-related activity; ..., agency or organization does not participate in wetland-related activity. MAN, management; REG, regulation; R&C, restoration and creation; LAN, land acquisition; R&D, research and data collection; D&I, delineation and inventory]

Agency or organization	MAN	REG	R&C	LAN	R&D	D&I
FEDERAL						
Department of Agriculture						
Consolidated Farm Service Agency	...	●	...	...	...	...
Natural Resources Conservation Service	...	●	●	...	●	●
Department of Commerce						
National Oceanic and Atmospheric Administration	●	●	...	...	●	●
Department of Defense						
Army Corps of Engineers	●	●	●	●	●	●
Department of the Interior						
Fish and Wildlife Service	●	...	●	●	●	●
Geological Survey	...	...	...	...	●	...
National Biological Service	...	...	...	...	●	...
National Park Service	●	...	●	●	●	●
Environmental Protection Agency	...	●	...	...	●	●
STATE						
Department of the Environment						
Water Management Administration	●	●	●	●	●	●
Department of Natural Resources						
Chesapeake Bay and Watershed Programs	●	...	●	...	●	●
Natural Heritage Program	●	...	...	...	●	...
Program Open Space	...	...	...	●	...	...
Office of State Planning	...	...	...	...	...	●
State Highway Administration	...	...	●	...	...	...
University of Maryland	...	...	...	...	●	...
DISTRICT OF COLUMBIA						
Department of Consumer and Regulatory Affairs	...	●	...	...	...	...
Department of Public Works	●	...	●	...	...	...
Metropolitan Council of Governments	...	●	...	...	...	...
Soil and Water Conservation District	●	...	●	...	...	...
SOME COUNTY AND LOCAL GOVERNMENTS	●	●	●	...	...	...
PRIVATE ORGANIZATIONS						
Chesapeake Bay Foundation	...	...	●	...	...	...
Environmental Concern, Inc.	...	...	●	...	●	...
Maryland Land Trust Alliance	●	...	...	...	●	...
The Nature Conservancy	●	...	...	...	●	...

Hydrologic Setting

Wetlands can form almost anywhere that water remains on or near the land surface for an extended period. Some wetlands are ephemeral, containing water for only a few weeks in spring, whereas others are permanently inundated. In arid regions, some wetlands are wet only in years when rainfall is much above normal.

The factors that determine where and when wetlands form include precipitation amount and timing, evaporation and transpiration rates, topography, and geologic characteristics (see "Wetland Hydrology, Water Quality, and Associated Functions" in this volume for a discussion of wetland hydrology). The "Hydrologic Setting" section of the State summaries provides an overview of the factors that determine wetland hydrology in each State.

Trends

The area of wetlands in the conterminous United States has decreased by about one-half since the founding of the Nation in the late 1700's (Dahl, 1990), and the decline is continuing. The "Trends" section of each State summary contains a brief accounting of wetland losses and gains and lists the major causes of wetland loss. (For a national perspective of wetland trends, see "History and Trends of Wetlands in the Conterminous United States" in this volume.)

Conservation

Wetland-conservation efforts are carried out by Federal, State, and local government agencies; many private organizations also work to conserve wetlands. The "Conservation" section of each State summary provides an account of the wetland-conservation activities on each of those levels. Included are primary Federal, State, and local regulations affecting wetlands, as well as a discussion of other aspects of wetland conservation, such as management, land acquisition, planning, mitigation, research, restoration and creation, delineation, inventory, education, and many more. (For a discussion of regulatory legislation pertaining to wetlands, see "Wetland Protection Legislation" in this volume.)

Each State summary contains a table (such as the accompanying table for Maryland and the District of Columbia) that lists selected wetland-related activities of Federal, State, and local government agencies and private organizations in the State. The information contained in the table and in the "Conservation" section was compiled in 1993; because of the often dynamic nature of government bureaucracies and agency responsibilities, the names of agencies and the activities listed for them can be considered reliable as of that date and no later.

References Cited

Cowardin, L.M., Carter, Virginia, Golet, F.C., and LaRoe, E.T., 1979, Classification of wetlands and deepwater habitats of the United States: U.S. Fish and Wildlife Service Report FWS/OBS–79/31, 131 p.

Dahl, T.E., 1990, Wetlands—Losses in the United States, 1780's to 1980's: Washington, D.C., U.S. Fish and Wildlife Service, 13 p.

State Summary Highlights

Following are a few notable facts about the wetlands of the 50 States, the District of Columbia, Puerto Rico, the Virgin Islands, and several islands of the Pacific Ocean, as reported in the State summaries:

Alabama

Wetlands cover about 10 percent of Alabama and range in size from small areas of less than an acre to the 100,000-acre forested tract in the Mobile-Tensaw River Delta. Most of the State's forested wetlands are bottom-land forests in alluvial flood plains. Coastal waters support extensive salt marshes. Wetland acreage in the area that is now Alabama has been reduced by about one-half in the last two centuries. Major causes of wetland loss or alteration have been agricultural and silvicultural conversions in the interior; dredging on the coast; industrial, commercial, and residential development; erosion; subsidence; and natural succession of vegetation.

Alaska

Alaska has more area covered by wetlands—about 170 million acres—than the other 49 States combined. More than 70,000 swans, 1 million geese, 12 million ducks, and 100 million shorebirds depend on Alaskan wetlands for resting, feeding, or nesting. Freshwater Alaskan wetlands include bogs, fens, tundra, marshes, and meadows; brackish and saltwater wetlands include flats, beaches, rocky shores, and salt marshes. Most of the State's freshwater wetlands are peatlands (wetlands that have organic soils), and cover as many as 110 million acres. Alaska's coastal wetlands are cooperatively protected and managed by local governments, rural regions, and the State.

Arizona

Less than 1 percent of Arizona's landscape has wetlands. Since the late 1800's, streams and wetlands throughout Arizona have been modified or drained, resulting in the loss of more than one-third of the State's original wetlands. The most extensive Arizona wetlands are in riparian zones and include oxbow lakes, marshes, cienegas, and bosques. Nonriparian wetlands include tinajas, playas, and caldera lakes. Extreme aridity and seasonally varying precipitation are the climatic characteristics that most significantly influence wetland formation and distribution in Arizona. Recreational use of wetlands provides economic benefits to the State.

Arkansas

About 8 percent of Arkansas is wetland. The most extensive areas are forested wetlands (swamps and bottom-land forests) along major rivers. Arkansas wetlands, especially those in the Mississippi River Valley, are a critical component of the series of wetlands along the Mississippi Flyway. Wetlands in the Cache-Lower White River system have been designated as one of nine "Wetlands of International Importance" in the United States. Arkansas has lost more wetland acres than any other inland State; most of the loss has been due to conversion to farmland. Arkansas has adopted a program that applies an antidegradation policy to substantial alteration of water bodies, including adjacent wetlands.

California

California's wetlands have significant economic and environmental value, providing benefits such as water-quality maintenance, flood and erosion attenuation, prevention of saltwater intrusion, and wildlife habitat. The Sacramento-San Joaquin Delta regularly harbors as much as 15 percent of the waterfowl on the Pacific Flyway. California has lost as much as 91 percent of its original wetlands, primarily because of conversion to agriculture. Flooded rice fields, which are converted wetlands, covered about 658,600 acres in the mid-1980's. Rice farmers, State and university researchers, and private organizations are cooperatively studying the feasibility of managing rice fields for migratory waterfowl habitat. Wetland protection is identified as a goal of The California Environmental Quality Act of 1970.

Colorado

Wetlands cover about 1 million acres of Colorado—1.5 percent of the State's area. Wetlands occur in all life and climatic zones, from the high mountains to the arid plains and plateaus. Wetland types in Colorado include forested wetlands, willow carrs, fens, marshes, alpine snow glades, and wet and salt meadows. Wetlands are vital to wildlife in the State, particularly in the arid regions. Colorado's wetland area has decreased by about one-half in the last two centuries, and losses are continuing due to a variety of land-development pressures; however, irrigation and changes in land-use practices have resulted in new wetlands, principally in the San Luis Valley and near Boulder.

Connecticut

Wetlands cover about 173,000 acres of Connecticut—5 percent of the State's land surface. Connecticut has lost an estimated one-third to three-fourths of its original wetlands over the 200-year period between the 1780's and 1980's. Forested wetlands, primarily red maple swamps, are the predominant wetland type, constituting 54 percent of the State's wetlands. Salt marshes, tidal flats, and beaches are the primary coastal wetlands. Wetland protection in Connecticut is carried out at the Federal, State, and (or) local government level, depending on the type and location of the wetland resource.

Delaware

Wetlands cover about 17 percent of Delaware. Wetlands in Delaware are diverse. Extensive estuarine wetlands line Delaware Bay and the Atlantic Ocean. Delmarva bays, which are seasonally flooded depressions in the Coastal Plain, contain marsh, shrub, and forest vegetation. More than one-half of Delaware's wetlands have been converted to nonwetland uses or otherwise altered since the 1780's. The State Wetlands Act controls development in tidal wetlands, and a proposed statute would establish a State-run nontidal-wetlands regulatory program. Delaware has established its own wetland classification, which has five categories that are based on a wetland's functions and values.

District of Columbia

The District of Columbia has about 250 acres of wetlands; all are palustrine or riverine. Most occur along the tidal reaches of the Potomac and Anacostia Rivers. About 87 percent of the District's wetlands have been drained or filled since the District was established in the 1790's. The National Park Service owns and maintains most wetlands in the District of Columbia. To alter wetlands, permits must be obtained from the U.S. Army Corps of Engineers and the Department of Consumer and Regulatory Affairs. Wetland conservation is accomplished on Federal and local levels and through the activities of private organizations.

Florida

Florida has about 11 million acres of wetlands, more than any of the other 47 conterminous States. The abundance of wetlands in Florida is due primarily to the low, flat terrain and plentiful rainfall. Most of Florida's wetlands are forested freshwater habitats on stream flood plains, in small depressions and ponds, and covering wet flatwoods. The Everglades, in southern Florida, is a large freshwater marsh that once received surface- and ground-water flows from the Kissimmee River-Lake Okeechobee Basin but which now depends on water releases from canals and water-retention areas. Florida has lost nearly one-half of its wetlands, primarily to agricultural drainage. The State protects wetlands by regulating development in wetland areas, acquiring wetlands and land adjacent to wetlands, and requiring local governments to produce long-range plans for wetland protection.

Georgia

Georgia has more than 7.7 million acres of wetlands. Georgia's wetlands are diverse, ranging from mountain seepage areas to estuarine tidal flats. This diversity is primarily due to the wide variety of landforms present, each of which can have different geologic and hydrologic characteristics. The greatest acreages of wetlands are in the coastal plain, where flood-plain wetlands are most extensive and tidal freshwater swamps and estuarine marshes meet. Most of Georgia's wetlands are forested freshwater habitats associated with streams. The Okefenokee Swamp in Georgia, one of the largest freshwater wetlands in the United States, is a mosaic of emergent marshes, aquatic beds, forested and scrub-shrub wetlands, and forested uplands.

Hawaii

Wetlands constitute less than 3 percent of the State, but they have had a major economic effect on Hawaiian society both before and after European contact. Wetlands are habitats for several species of birds and plants endemic to the Hawaiian Islands. Wetland formation in Hawaii is influenced by climate, topography, and geology; wetlands form where local hydrologic conditions favor water retention near the land surface. Although rainfall is high in many areas of the islands, steep topography and the high permeability of the volcanic rock that forms the islands result in rapid discharge of storm runoff to the ocean as surface-water and ground-water flow. Coastal wetland losses have been greatest on Oahu, where wetlands have been drained and filled for resort, industrial, and residential development.

Idaho

Most of Idaho's 386,000 acres of wetlands are in flood plains and riparian areas along streams and other water bodies. Since about 1860, when mining and farming began in the State, wetland acreage has decreased by 56 percent. The Idaho State Water Plan states that, insofar as is possible, the State should assume responsibility for wetland management and protection. Policy plans made by the Idaho Department of Fish and Game for 1991 to 2005 focus land-acquisition efforts on wetland areas where habitat protection is critical. Many private organizations and groups have participated in projects involving wetland acquisition and restoration.

Illinois

Wetlands cover about 3.5 percent of Illinois. The largest acreage of wetlands is in the bottom-land forests and swamps along the State's major rivers. Northeastern Illinois also has a large concentration of wetlands. Illinois has lost as much as 90 percent of its original wetlands over the last 200 years; most of the losses have been due to drainage for conversion to agricultural and other uses. The primary State law governing wetlands is the Interagency Wetland Policy Act of 1989, which sets a goal of no net loss of wetlands due to projects funded by the State. Wetlands can be owned and protected by the public as County Forest Preserve Districts.

Indiana

About 85 percent of Indiana's wetlands have been lost since the 1780's, primarily because of conversion to agricultural land. The current rate of wetland loss is about 1 to 3 percent of the remaining wetlands per year. Most of the wetlands remaining in Indiana, about 813,000 acres, are in the northeastern part of the State, including extensive wetlands in and near the Indiana Dunes National Lakeshore. The Department of Natural Resources is developing a State wetland conservation plan under a grant from the U.S. Environmental Protection Agency. Several River Basin Commissions are encouraging or pursuing wetland restoration as a flood-control measure with an added benefit of recreation potential.

Iowa

Iowa has diverse wetlands that include prairie-pothole marshes, swamps, sloughs, bogs, fens, and ponds. Wetlands cover about 1.2 percent of Iowa, but about 200 years ago more than 11 percent of the State's area was wetland. Conversion of wetlands to agricultural lands, largely in the prairie-pothole region, has been the primary cause of wetland loss. Wetland acreage has been slowly increasing since 1987 as a result of the Prairie Pothole Joint Venture, a cooperative Federal, State, county, and private-organization program. The Wetland Reserve Program of the 1990 Food, Agriculture, Conservation, and Trade Act has the potential to add a substantial number of additional acres.

Kansas

Kansas has about 435,000 acres of wetlands, which include sandhill pools along the Arkansas River, playa lakes in western Kansas, freshwater marshes such as those in Cheyenne Bottoms, and salt marshes such as those in Quivira National Wildlife Refuge. Kansas wetlands are important to migrating waterfowl and shore-birds, which depend on the few remaining wetlands in the Central Flyway. Kansas has lost about one-half its wetlands during the last 200 years, mostly due to conversion to cropland and depletion of surface and ground water due to irrigation withdrawals. Wetland preservation and restoration are being accomplished through cooperation among Federal and State agencies and private organizations.

Kentucky

Wetlands compose less than 2.5 percent of Kentucky's land area, but they have considerable environmental, socioeconomic, and esthetic value. Most Kentucky wetlands lie shoreward of rivers, lakes, and reservoirs and include cypress swamps, bottom-land hardwood forests, marshes, and ponds. More than one-half of Kentucky's original wetlands have been lost, primarily as a conversion to cropland and pastureland; most conversions have been in western Kentucky. The State fosters protection of wetlands through a system of registry and dedication agreements with private entities. Most of Kentucky's wetlands are privately owned.

Louisiana

Wetlands are a major source of income for the people of Louisiana, providing revenues from harvesting of fish and shellfish, trapping, and recreation. Most of the State's wetlands are freshwater swamps, but the area of coastal marsh is substantial: Louisiana's coastal marshes represent as much as 40 percent of the coastal marshes in the United States. Wetlands once covered more than one-half of the area that is now Louisiana, but wetland acreage has declined to less than one-third of the State's land surface over the last 200 years. The Louisiana Coastal Wetlands Conservation and Restoration Program implements specific projects to conserve, enhance, restore, and create coastal wetlands.

Maine

Maine's wetlands are diverse, ranging from inland swamps and peatlands to coastal salt marshes and mud flats. One-fourth of the State is wetland, and most wetlands are owned by individuals, timber companies, or other private landowners. Land-use changes have led to wetland losses. Early in Maine's history, expansion of fishing and farming communities along the coast resulted in the filling of many coastal wetlands. Wetlands along inland waterways were converted to agricultural use. Recent losses have been due to urbanization and other development. Wetland conservation in Maine is a combined effort by Federal, State, and local governments and private organizations and landowners.

Maryland

Maryland has about 591,000 acres of wetlands, one-half of which are tidal and one-half nontidal. Extensive estuarine wetlands exist on both sides of the Chesapeake Bay. The Delmarva Peninsula has many wetlands in Delmarva bays, topographic depressions whose wetness is controlled by the water table. About 64 percent of Maryland's wetlands have been converted to nonwetland uses since the 1780's. To obtain permits for altering wetlands in Maryland, a single State-Federal application is submitted to the Maryland Department of the Environment. Wetland conservation in Maryland is accomplished on the Federal, State, and local level and through the activities of private organizations.

Massachusetts

Wetlands cover about 590,000 acres of Massachusetts, about 12 percent of the State's area. Massachusetts has lost about 28 percent of its original wetlands since the 1780's. Agricultural and urban expansion have caused most of the losses. Forested wetlands, primarily red maple swamps, comprise more than one-half of the State's wetlands; estuarine and marine wetlands account for about one-fifth. Regulatory functions of wetland conservation in Massachusetts are performed at the Federal, State, and local government level, and private organizations are active in land acquisition and management, research, education, and policy review and planning.

Michigan

Wetlands cover about 15 percent of Michigan. They provide many benefits, including flood and erosion attenuation, water-quality maintenance, recreation, and wildlife habitat. Michigan's wetlands are largely associated with surface features that are the result of glaciation. Most Michigan wetlands are vegetated by forest or shrubs, but fresh marsh is abundant in coastal and inland areas. About one-half of the State's wetlands have been converted to other uses, primarily agriculture. The Goemaere-Anderson Wetland Protection Act of 1980 (Public Law 203) and other State statutes are the basis for Michigan's wetland-conservation program. The U.S. Environmental Protection Agency has oversight of the State program.

Minnesota

Minnesota has about 9.5 million acres of wetlands, about one-half the wetland acreage present in predevelopment times. Most wetland losses have been due to drainage for agriculture. Minnesota's wetlands are diverse, ranging from extensive northern peatlands to small prairie potholes. Minnesota has about 150,000 to 200,000 acres of wild rice beds. The centerpiece of Minnesota's efforts to protect wetlands is the Wetland Conservation Act of 1991, which sets a goal of no net wetland loss. The law fills the gap in wetland protection between larger, deepwater habitats that are already protected by Minnesota statute and agricultural wetlands that are addressed by the Federal "Swampbuster" provisions.

Mississippi

Wetlands occupy more than 13 percent of Mississippi. Bottom-land forests, swamps and freshwater marshes account for most of Mississippi's wetland acreage; coastal marshes also are extensive. Wetlands in Mississippi are a key part of the Lower Mississippi Valley Joint Venture program for the restoration of Mississippi Flyway waterfowl populations. Nearly three-fifths of the State's wetlands have been converted to nonwetland uses, primarily agriculture. Mississippi wetlands have been and continue to be a source of timber, and the cleared, fertile lands have become productive farmland. The Natural Heritage Program identifies and inventories priority wetlands.

Missouri

Missouri's wetlands occupy 643,000 acres, about 1.4 percent of the State's area. Swamps and other forested wetlands, marshes and fens, and shrub swamps constitute most of the wetland acreage. Missouri's location on the Mississippi Flyway makes the State a favored wintering area for hundreds of thousands of waterfowl and other birds, including bald eagles. Missouri has lost as much as 4.2 million acres (87 percent) of its original wetlands. Most wetland loss has been due to agricultural conversions, urban development, and flood-control measures. The State has developed a wetland-management plan to guide its efforts in the restoration and management of wetlands until the year 2000.

Montana

Wetlands cover only a small part of Montana, but their ecological and economic importance far outweighs their relative size. About 27 percent of the wetlands present before 1800 have been converted to other land uses, primarily cropland. Losses to cropland have been particularly great in north-central and eastern Montana, an area that is part of the Nation's most valuable waterfowl production area, the prairie pothole region of the northern Great Plains. Montana has no comprehensive wetland-protection program; however, the Water Quality Bureau of the Montana Department of Health and Environmental Sciences is developing enforceable water-quality and biological standards specific to Montana wetlands.

Nebraska

Nebraska has three wetland complexes recognized as being of international importance as migrational and breeding habitat for waterfowl and nongame birds: the Rainwater Basin wetlands in south-central and southeastern Nebraska, the Big Bend reach of the Platte River (directly north of the Rainwater Basin), and the Sandhills wetlands in north-central and northwestern Nebraska. Nebraska has lost about 1 million acres of wetlands in the last 200 years—about 35 percent of the State's original wetland acreage. Conversion to agricultural use was the primary cause for most of the losses, but urbanization, reservoir construction, highway construction, and other activities also contributed.

Nevada

Wetlands cover less than 1 percent of Nevada but are some of the most economically and ecologically valuable lands in the State. Benefits of wetlands include flood attenuation, bank stabilization, water-quality improvement, and fish and wildlife habitat. Desert wetlands include marshes in playa lakes, nonvegetated playas, and riparian wetlands; mountain wetlands include fens and other wetlands that form in small glacial lakes. More than one-half of Nevada's original wetlands have been lost, primarily due to conversion of wetlands to cropland and diversion of water for agricultural and urban use; many others have been seriously degraded by human activities. Some wetlands have been created by mine dewatering and sewage treatment.

New Hampshire

Wetlands occupy as much as 10 percent of New Hampshire and are an integral part of its natural resources. Swamps and peatlands comprise most of the State's wetlands. Many wetlands have been converted to nonwetland uses such as crop or pastureland. Others have been altered or degraded by urbanization, peat mining, timber harvesting, road building, all-terrain vehicle use, and other causes. New Hampshire regulates wetlands primarily through State law and the rules of the Wetlands Board; local conservation commissions have an advisory role in local wetland protection. During 1987 to 1993, the State acquired diverse wetlands by purchase and donation or protected wetlands through conservation easements.

New Jersey

New Jersey has about 916,000 acres of wetlands, most of which are in the coastal plain. Forested wetlands are the most common and widely distributed wetlands in the State. Salt marshes are the most common wetlands in coastal areas. Wetlands are ecologically and economically valuable to the State. Cranberry growing is a significant industry in New Jersey; more than 3,000 acres of cranberry bog wetlands were under private management in 1992. Between the 1780's and 1980's, New Jersey lost about 39 percent of its wetlands. Wetlands have been drained primarily for crop production and pasturage and filled for housing, transportation, industrialization, and landfills.

New Mexico

Wetlands cover about 482,000 acres (0.6 percent) of New Mexico; most are in the eastern and northern areas of the State. New Mexico's wetlands include forested wetlands, bottom-land shrublands, marshes, fens, alpine snow glades, wet and salt meadows, shallow ponds, and playa lakes. Riparian wetlands and playa lakes are especially valuable to migratory waterfowl and wading birds. New Mexico has lost about one-third of its wetlands, mostly due to agricultural conversion, diversion of water to irrigation, overgrazing, and urbanization. Other causes of loss or degradation have been mining, clear cutting, road construction, streamflow regulation, and invasion by nonnative plants.

New York

New York has about 2.4 million acres of wetlands. One-half of the 160 species identified as endangered or threatened by the Department of Environmental Conservation are wetland dependent. Counties in the Adirondack Mountains and those south and east of Lake Ontario have the largest percentages of wetland area; counties that make up New York City and Long Island, along the border with Pennsylvania, and in the Catskills have the smallest percentages. From the 1780's to 1980's, about 60 percent of New York's wetland area was lost, primarily because of conversion to agriculture and other land uses. Counties may facilitate wetland acquisition through the funding of bond acts.

North Carolina

About 5.7 million acres of North Carolina—17 percent of the State—is wetland. The Coastal Plain contains 95 percent of the State's wetlands. Before colonization by Europeans, North Carolina had about 11 million acres of wetlands. Nearly one-third of the wetland alterations in the Coastal Plain have occurred since the 1950's; most have resulted from conversion to managed forests and agriculture. The Roanoke River flood plain has one of the largest intact and least disturbed bottom-land hardwood forests in the mid-Atlantic region. About 70 percent of the rare and endangered plants and animals in the State are wetland dependent.

North Dakota

Wetlands once covered about 4.9 million acres of North Dakota—11 percent of the State. By the 1980's, the acreage had decreased to about 2.7 million acres, a loss of about 45 percent. Most of the losses have been caused by drainage for agricultural development. The rate of agricultural conversions in the future will likely depend on crop prices and other economic factors. Most of North Dakota's wetlands are prairie potholes, which provide nesting and feeding habitat for migratory waterfowl and wading birds. About one-half the Nation's duck population originates in the Prairie Pothole Region of North Dakota and other prairie States.

Ohio

Ohio's wetlands cover about 1.8 percent of the State. Swamps, wet prairies, coastal and embayment marshes, peatlands, and wetlands along stream margins and backwaters are the most common Ohio wetlands. Wetland area in Ohio has declined by 90 percent during the last 200 years, from about 5,000,000 acres to about 483,000 acres. Drainage of wetlands for agriculture has been the primary cause of wetland loss, but recreational use, fluctuating water levels, urban development, mining, logging, and fire also have contributed. Ohio designates all wetlands as State Resource Waters. As such, wetland water quality is protected from degradation that may interfere with designated uses.

Oklahoma

Wetlands cover about 950,000 acres (2 percent) of Oklahoma. Wetlands in Oklahoma include bottom-land hardwood forests and swamps; marshes and wet meadows; aquatic-bed wetlands characterized by submersed or floating plants in ponds, lakes, rivers, and sloughs; and sparsely vegetated wetlands such as intermittently flooded playa lakes. Most forested wetlands are in eastern Oklahoma, where precipitation is highest and evaporation lowest. Riparian wetlands and playa lakes in drier western Oklahoma are especially valuable to wildlife. Nearly two-thirds of Oklahoma's original wetlands have been lost as a result of agricultural conversions, channelization, impoundment, streamflow regulation, and other causes.

Oregon

Wetlands are economically and ecologically valuable to Oregon and can be found statewide. Oregon had nearly 1.4 million acres of wetlands as of the mid-1980's, a decline of more than one-third over the previous 200 years. Most of the losses were due to conversion to agricultural uses, primarily in the Willamette River Valley and Upper Klamath Basin. To improve the effectiveness and efficiency of Oregon's efforts to conserve, restore, and protect wetlands, the State has developed the Wetland Conservation Strategy. The strategy is based on the recommendations of advisory committees representing Federal, State, and local agencies and interest groups.

Pennsylvania

About 1.4 percent (404,000 acres) of Pennsylvania is covered by wetlands. Deciduous and forested wetlands are the most common types, followed by open water, marshes, shrub wetlands, and others. Wetlands are most densely distributed in the glaciated northwestern and northeastern parts of the State. Wetland area in Pennsylvania has decreased by more than one-half in the last 200 years. The primary causes of wetland loss or degradation have been conversion to cropland, channelization, forestry, mining, urban development, and the construction of ponds and impoundments. About 50 private conservancy organizations in the State work to protect and preserve natural lands, including wetlands, on a local level.

Puerto Rico

Wetlands in Puerto Rico are diverse, ranging from interior montane wetlands of the rain forest to intertidal mangrove swamps along the coast. Puerto Rico's wetlands are valuable natural resources that provide habitat for wildlife and a water supply for several large cities. Nearly all of Puerto Rico's wetlands have been modified by man—historically for sugar cane agriculture and more recently for housing development, transportation, tourist facilities, and other types of development. Wetland restoration efforts are underway at several locations throughout Puerto Rico; an example is the freshwater wetlands of Laguna Cartagena, once one of the most important waterfowl habitats on the island.

Rhode Island

Wetlands cover about 65,000 acres of Rhode Island, about 10 percent of the State's area. Forested wetlands, primarily red maple swamps, are the most abundant wetland type and account for nearly three-quarters of the State's wetlands. Once more common in Rhode Island, Atlantic white cedar wetlands are now found mostly in the southwestern part of the State. Wetlands are regulated primarily at the State-government level in Rhode Island; different agencies regulate coastal and freshwater wetlands. Local land-use controls are an additional wetland-protection measure. Many of Rhode Island's natural resources have been acquired and protected through cooperative efforts of private and public entities.

South Carolina

Nearly one-quarter of South Carolina is wetland—about 4.6 million acres. South Carolina's wetlands provide flood attenuation, erosion control, water-quality maintenance, recreational opportunities, and fish and wildlife habitat. South Carolina wetlands are important wintering areas for migratory waterfowl on the Atlantic Flyway. Wetlands in the State include wet pine flatwoods, pocosins, Carolina bays, beaver ponds, bottom-land forests, swamps, fresh and salt marshes, and tidal flats. About 80 percent of the wetlands are freshwater and forested. Wetland acreage in South Carolina has declined by more than one-quarter since the late 1700's, primarily as a result of human activities.

South Dakota

Wetlands occupy about 1.8 million acres (3.6 percent) of South Dakota. These wetlands are of great economic and esthetic value because they provide important habitat for wildlife (especially migratory waterfowl), hydrologic benefits that include water retention and flood attenuation, and numerous recreational opportunities. By far the most common wetland type in South Dakota is the prairie pothole, which occurs in glaciated eastern South Dakota. Wetland area in South Dakota has decreased by about 35 percent during the last 200 years— from about 2.7 million to about 1.8 million acres. Agricultural conversions, notably in the prairie pothole region, have accounted for most wetland losses.

Tennessee

Estimates of Tennessee's wetland area range from 640,000 to 1,400,000 acres. Although wetlands constitute a small percentage of Tennessee, they are ecologically and economically valuable to the State. Bottom-land forests are the most common Tennessee wetlands; they are most abundant in the flood plains of rivers in the western part of the State. Nearly three-fifths of Tennessee's original wetlands have been lost; major causes of loss or degradation in Tennessee have included agricultural conversions, logging, reservoir construction, channelization, sedimentation, and urbanization. The Tennessee Wetlands Acquisition Act of 1986 authorizes the acquisition of wetlands by use of real estate transfer taxes.

Texas

Wetlands cover about 7.6 million acres of Texas, 4.4 percent of the State's area. The most extensive wetlands are the bottom-land hardwood forests and swamps of East Texas; the marshes, swamps, and tidal flats of the coast; and the playa lakes of the High Plains. Wetlands provide flood attenuation, bank stabilization, water-quality maintenance, fish and wildlife habitat, and opportunities for hunting, fishing, and other recreational activities. Commercial fisheries benefit directly from coastal wetlands. Texas has lost about one-half of its original wetlands as a result of agricultural conversions, overgrazing, urbanization, channelization, water-table declines, construction of navigation canals, and other causes.

Utah

Wetlands cover only a small part of Utah but provide critical aquatic habitat in an arid environment as well as economic and other benefits. Utah wetlands include the shallows of small lakes, reservoirs, ponds, and streams; riparian wetlands; marshes and wet meadows; mud and salt flats; and playas. The largest wetlands in the State surround Great Salt Lake. Because of the importance of Great Salt Lake and its associated wetlands to migratory waterfowl and shorebirds, in 1991 the lake was designated a Hemispheric Reserve in the Western Hemisphere Shorebird Reserve Network. Streamflow regulation and agricultural, residential, industrial, and ski-area development have resulted in widespread wetland losses.

Vermont

Estimates of the area covered by wetlands in Vermont range from 4 to 6 percent of the State's total area. The largest wetlands are in the valleys of the northeast and in river flood plains and deltas in the Lake Champlain Valley. Vermont's wetlands provide flood and erosion control, water-quality maintenance, timber, and recreational opportunities. As much as 35 percent of Vermont's wetlands have been lost; major causes have been conversion to agriculture and residential and recreational development. The State is undertaking the Vermont Wetlands Conservation Strategy, a comprehensive review of current wetland conservation programs that will recommend actions to improve wetland conservation in Vermont.

U.S. Virgin Islands

Wetlands in the U.S. Virgin Islands comprise about 3 percent of the land surface. Wetlands are habitat for fish, shellfish, and birds, including endangered species such as the peregrine falcon and brown pelican. Freshwater is scarce in the islands, and wetlands there are mainly estuarine and marine types such as salt ponds, mangrove forests, sea grass beds, and coral reefs. Shoreline wetlands are vulnerable to destruction from construction of tourist facilities and water-dependent developments like marinas and to degradation by sedimentation and septic tank leachate. The Territorial Legislature adopted the Indigenous and Endangered Species Act of 1990, which establishes a policy of "no net loss of wetlands" to the maximum extent possible.

Virginia

Virginia has about 1 million acres of wetlands; one-quarter are tidal and three-quarters are nontidal. Forested wetlands (swamps) are the most common wetlands in the State. Both shores of the Chesapeake Bay have extensive estuarine wetlands. Conversion to nonwetland uses (agricultural, urban, industrial, and recreational), channelization and ditching, and other causes have resulted in the loss of about 42 percent of Virginia's wetlands since the 1780's. Development in wetlands is regulated in part by means of the Virginia Water Protection Permit. Local governments may adopt prescribed zoning ordinances and form citizen wetland boards to regulate their own tidal wetlands; the State retains an oversight and appellate role.

Washington

Wetlands cover only about 2 percent (939,000 acres) of Washington, but they benefit the State both ecologically and economically. Wetlands are nursery and feeding areas for anadromous fish such as salmon and steelhead trout. About 75 percent of the State's wetlands contain freshwater and include forested and shrub swamps, bogs, fens, marshes, wet prairies and meadows, vernal pools, and playas. About 25 percent are estuarine or marine and include marshes, tidal flats, beaches, and rocky shores. Estimates of wetland loss in Washington range from 20 to 50 percent; causes of loss or degradation include agricultural conversion, urban expansion, siting of ports and industries, logging, and invasion of nonnative plants and animals.

West Virginia

Wetlands constitute less than 1 percent of West Virginia's surface area but contribute significantly to the State's economic development and ecological diversity. Common West Virginia wetlands include swamps, peat bogs, marl wetlands, marshes, wet meadows, and ponds. The Canaan Valley and Meadow River wetlands together contain about 14 percent of the State's wetlands. The Canaan Valley wetland complex is the largest in the central Appalachian Mountains. West Virginia has lost about one-fourth of its original wetlands; primary causes have been agricultural conversions, channelization, pond and reservoir construction, and urbanization. Some wetlands have been created as a result of beaver activity.

Western Pacific Islands

Most of the wetlands in the Mariana, Samoan, Caroline, and Marshall Islands (referred to as the Western Pacific Islands in this report) are in coastal areas. Wetlands on the islands include mangrove swamps, marshes, and coral reefs. Wetlands are of economic importance on many islands because the staple food, taro, is grown in converted or constructed wetlands. On the larger islands, wetlands are important wildlife habitat. Available trend information indicates that on many islands there has been wetland loss or degradation due to agricultural conversion, urban expansion, or firewood cutting. Wetland activities on islands under United States jurisdiction are subject to Federal regulation.

Wisconsin

Wetlands cover more than 5 million acres (15 percent) of Wisconsin. Common wetlands include swamps and marshes in southern Wisconsin and peatlands in northern Wisconsin. Wetlands are most numerous in glaciated parts of the State; the unglaciated "driftless" section of southwestern Wisconsin has few wetlands, except in stream valleys filled with unconsolidated outwash and alluvium. Wetland acreage has decreased by nearly one-half over the last 200 years, primarily owing to agricultural development. In 1991 the State became the first to adopt water-quality standards for wetlands; the standards allow the State to control wetland development under section 401 of the Clean Water Act.

Wyoming

Wetlands cover about 1.25 million acres (2 percent) of Wyoming and are the most diverse ecosystems in the State's semiarid environment. The Laramie Plain Lakes wetland complex is home to the Wyoming toad, an endangered species. Trend information indicates that wetland acreage in Wyoming has decreased over time, primarily due to agricultural and urban development. However, agricultural diversions, whose original purpose was to flush salts and increase hay-meadow production, have enhanced wetlands along the Bear River; the Bear River wetland is one of the most productive and diverse bird habitats in Wyoming. The Wyoming Wetlands Act is the basis for wetland program development by the State.

Introduction

This volume, *National Water Summary on Wetland Resources*, is organized into two parts, a somewhat different format than the seven previous volumes (see inside front cover for previous volumes) in the *National Water Summary* series. (The "Hydrologic Conditions and Water-Related Events" included in the previous volumes are published separately, as U.S. Geological Survey Open-File Reports Numbers 96–107 and 96–145.)

This volume is the result of a coordinated effort to compile the most up-to-date information available on wetland resources. Although much has been written about the biological aspects of wetlands, much less has been written about the hydrology and the non-habitat functions of wetlands. This volume presents an overview of wetland resources from many different perspectives.

The first part of this volume, "Overview of Wetland Resources," discusses wetland resources from a national perspective and provides background information for the State summaries section. This section contains articles on the technical, management and research, and restoration, creation, and recovery aspects of wetland resources. These articles relate the history of wetlands in the United States; the definition of wetlands and a description of the U.S. Fish and Wildlife Service Classification System (Cowardin and others, 1979); hydrologic and water-quality factors that affect the distribution of wetlands and related functions commonly attributed to wetlands; the role of wetlands as habitat for birds; the roles of Federal agencies in wetland protection legislation and research; progress in inventory and mapping of wetlands; techniques for evaluating wetlands; human attempts to restore damaged wetlands and create new ones; and the recovery of wetlands following natural disasters.

The second part, "State Summaries of Wetland Resources," describes wetlands of each State, the District of Columbia (combined with Maryland), Puerto Rico, the U.S. Virgin Islands, and the Western Pacific Islands. Each State summary discusses wetlands in terms of value, types and distribution, hydrologic setting, and trends in acreage from predevelopment to modern times. Each State summary also provides an overview of public- and private-sector wetland-conservation efforts in that State and a table showing the wetland-related responsibilities of principal government agencies and private organizations within the State. Illustrations include a map depicting the areal distribution of principal wetlands and selected related features such as ecoregions, physiography, precipitation, runoff, evaporation, or other physical or climatic features that influence the presence or distribution of wetlands in that State. Some of the State summaries include a map or cross section depicting the hydrologic setting of wetlands and (or) a map showing predevelopment wetland distribution.

To supplement the information provided in this volume, bibliographic references are listed at the end of each article and State summary. An extensive list of suggested references for more information about topics discussed in the "Overview of Wetland Resources" is available in U.S. Geological Survey Open-File Report 96–169. This report also is available online at *http://h2o.usgs.gov/public/nwsum/bib/bib.html.* Most technical terms are defined in the glossary at the end of this volume, and a conversion table of water measurements precedes the glossary.

Horicon Marsh, Wisconsin, provides recreational opportunities. *(Photograph by Phillip J. Redman, U.S. Geological Survey.)*

Acknowledgments

Preparation of the *National Water Summary* requires compiling information from many individuals within the U.S. Geological Survey and various Federal and State agencies. The *National Water Summary on Wetland Resources* is the eighth in this series of U.S. Geological Survey Water-Supply Papers and it was prepared under the direction of Robert M. Hirsch, Chief Hydrologist. The report compilers gratefully acknowledge the assistance of water-resources agencies in each State in preparing and reviewing the State summaries of wetland resources. In addition, the following Federal agencies and other organizations contributed articles for this report:

- ManTech Environmental Technology, Incorporated
- U.S. Department Of Defense
    Army Corps Of Engineers
- U.S. Department Of the Interior
    Fish And Wildlife Service
    National Biological Service
- U.S. Environmental Protection Agency
- University Of Texas

In addition, the following Federal agencies and other organizations provided materials for this report:
- American Indian Resources Institute
- National Aeronautics and Space Administration
- U.S. Department of Commerce
    National Oceanic and Atmospheric Administration
- U.S. Department of the Interior
    National Park Service

Although individual acknowledgment of all reviewers, managers, illustrators, and typists who participated in the preparation of this report is not feasible, their cooperation and many contributions made this report possible. The following persons, however, deserve special mention:

The authors of the individual articles and the State summaries, who adhered to strict guidelines and whose names appear on the articles; David W. Moody and Richard W. Paulson, who had the vision for this report, made the contacts, and got it started; Virginia Carter, who provided technical guidance and reviewed every article; Katherine Walton-Day, Martha A. Hayes, Helen M. Light, Melanie R. Darst, and Benjamin F. McPherson, who prepared prototype State summaries, and D. Briane Adams, and Marcus C. Waldron, who helped coordinate the effort; Kenneth J. Lanfear, who provided managerial assistance; Jo Ann Macy, who provided managerial assistance and editorial review; Jack H. Green and Chester Zenone, who provided technical editorial review; Edith B. Chase, Elizabeth A. Ciganovich, and Mary A. Kidd, who provided editorial review and editorial assistance; Hyla Strickland, who provided editorial review and editorial assistance in the preparation of the State summaries; John M. Watson, who provided editorial review of the State summaries; and Susan Tufts-Moore, who provided editorial review for several Overview articles; Patricia S. Greene, Robert J. Olmstead, and Gregory J. Allord, who assisted with the design, coordination, and layout of the report and its illustrations; James O. Whitmer, Gina P. Barker, Timothy D. Covington, John M. Watermolen, Joel J. Skalet, and Alan M. Duran, who assisted with the graphics; Jamaica Pettit, who did typesetting and layout for the State summaries; Kimberley L. Fry, who provided general assistance with review and preparation of articles in the front part (Introduction and Overview sections) of the book; Helen F. Ipsaro and volunteer Judy G. Fry, who proofread the front-part articles; volunteers Katie Green, Joyce Ipsaro, and Uma Rao, who helped keep us organized.

References Cited

Cowardin, L.M., Carter, Virginia, Golet, F.C., and LaRoe, E.T., 1979, Classification of wetlands and deepwater habitats of the United States: U.S. Fish and Wildlife Service Report FGWS/OBS–79/31, 131 p.

Fry, K.L., comp., 1996, Supplemental reference list for the National Water Summary on Wetland Resources: U.S. Geological Survey Open-File Report, No. 96–169, 39 p.

McCabe, G.J., Crowe, Michael, Brown, W.O., and Fretwell, J.D., 1996, Hydrologic conditions and water-related events—Water Year 1992: U.S. Geological Survey Open-File Report No. 96–107, 1 sheet.

McCabe, G.J., Crowe, Michael, Brown, W.O., Fretwell, J.D., and Fry, K.L., 1996, Hydrologic conditions and water-related events—Water Year 1993: U.S. Geological Survey Open-File Report, No. 96–145, 1 sheet.

Overview of Wetland Resources

A restored wetland near Blackfoot River, Montana. *(Photograph by Kenneth J. Lanfear, U.S. Geological Survey.)*

Overview of Wetland Resources

Technical Aspects of Wetlands
History of Wetlands in the Conterminous United States

By Thomas E. Dahl[1] and Gregory J. Allord[2]

At the time of European settlement in the early 1600's, the area that was to become the conterminous United States had approximately 221 million acres of wetlands. About 103 million acres remained as of the mid-1980's (Dahl and Johnson, 1991). Six States lost 85 percent or more of their original wetland acreage—twenty-two lost 50 percent or more (Dahl, 1990) (fig. 2). Even today, all of the effects of these losses might not be fully realized.

Historical events, technological innovations, and values of society sometimes had destructive effects on wetlands. By examining the historical backdrop of why things happened, when they happened, and the consequences of what happened, society can better appreciate the importance of wetlands in water-resource issues. Society's views about wetlands have changed considerably—especially in the last half century. Interest in the preservation of wetlands has increased as the value of wetlands to society has become more fully understood. From a cultural standpoint, it is interesting to understand how changes in opinions and values came about, and what effects these changes had on wetland resources. From an ecological perspective, it is important to understand how the loss of wetlands affects fish, wildlife, and the environment as a whole.

EARLY 1600'S TO 1800—COLONIAL SETTLEMENT

Wetland drainage began with permanent settlement of Colonial America. Throughout the 1600's and 1700's, colonization was encouraged by European monarchs to establish footholds in North America. The effects of this colonization on the landscape became obvious in the early to mid-1700's.

Much of our knowledge of early wetlands comes from maps and other documents that survived over time. The origins of settlers influenced both where people settled and how they mapped and used natural resources. Few records exist because the original English, French, and Spanish settlements were established before the land was surveyed. Settlements in the North tended to be clustered, whereas communities in the South were more widely scattered because of the predominance of agriculture. Many different land surveying systems resulted in an incomplete patchwork of ownership that ultimately caused many legal problems due to boundary errors and overlapping claims (Garrett, 1988). It was not until 1785 that the Land Ordinance Act established the United States Public Land Survey, which required surveying and partitioning of land prior to settlement. Although not

Interest in the preservation of wetlands has increased as the value of wetlands has become more fully understood.

Figure 2. States with notable wetland loss, 1780's to mid-1980's. *(Source: Modified from Dahl, 1990.)*

EXPLANATION
Percent of wetlands lost, 1780's to mid-1980's

☐ Less than 50
▨ 50–85 (16 States)
▪ More than 85 (6 States)

---

[1] U.S. Fish and Wildlife Service.
[2] U.S. Geological Survey.

The original extent of wetland acreage and the effect of widespread drainage is evident in Washington County, N.C. Originally, wetlands covered over 186,000 acres or about 85 percent of the land area of Washington County. Large-scale drainage began as early as 1788 with the construction of a canal 6 miles long and 20 feet wide to drain the wetlands north and east of Phelps Lake (Washington County Historical Society, 1979). A system of cross ditches leading into the main canal was designed to drain up to 100,000 acres of wetlands so that rice and corn could be grown (Tant, 1981). Today, about 34 percent of Washington County's original wetland acreage remains in scattered tracts.

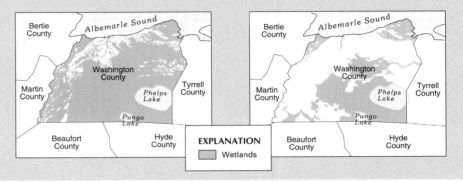

Figure 3. Extent of wetlands in Washington County, N. C., circa 1780 (left) and 1990 (right). *(Source: U.S. Fish and Wildlife Service, Status and Trends, unpub. data, 1994.)*

Technical advances facilitated wetland conversion.

Oil-powered dredge digging a 30-foot-wide ditch to drain wetlands near Carroll, Iowa. *(Photograph courtesy of National Archives, 8–D–2214–2570.)*

established to provide information on natural resources, surveys do provide some information about the distribution and location of wetlands.

During the 1700's, wetlands were regarded as swampy lands that bred diseases, restricted overland travel, impeded the production of food and fiber, and generally were not useful for frontier survival. Settlers, commercial interests, and governments agreed that wetlands presented obstacles to development, and that wetlands should be eliminated and the land reclaimed for other purposes. Most pioneers viewed natural resources from wetlands as things to be used without limit (Tebeau, 1980). The most productive tracts of land in fertile river valleys in parts of Virginia had been claimed and occupied before 1700. The resulting shortage of choice land stimulated colonists to move south to the rich bottom lands along the Chowan River and Albemarle Sound of North Carolina on the flat Atlantic coastal plain. Initially, settlements consisted primarily of shelters and subsistence farms on small tracts of land. To extend the productive value of available land, wetlands on these small tracts were drained by small hand-dug ditches. During the mid- to late 1700's, as the population grew, land clearing and farming for profit began to affect larger tracts of land; many coastal plain wetlands were converted to farmland (fig. 3). Once drained, these areas provided productive agricultural lands for growing cash crops.

Widespread wetland drainage was most prevalent in the southern colonies. In 1754, South Carolina authorized the drainage of Cacaw Swamp for agricultural use (Beauchamp, 1987). Similarly, areas of the Great Dismal Swamp in Virginia and North Caro-

lina were surveyed in 1763 so that land could be reclaimed for water transportation routes. Farming on large plantations was common practice in the South and necessitated some drainage or manipulation of wetlands.

By the 1780's, immigrants had settled along the fertile river valleys of the Northeast and as far south as present-day Georgia. Wetlands in these river valleys suffered losses with this settlement (fig. 4). Small towns and farms were established in the valleys along the rivers of Massachusetts, Connecticut, New York, and Pennsylvania. Settlement extended to the valleys beyond the Appalachian Mountains in Virginia and followed the major rivers inland through the Carolinas by 1800.

Figure 4. States with notable wetland loss, early 1600's to 1800.

1800 TO 1860—WESTWARD EXPANSION

The period between 1800 and 1860 was a time of growth in the United States. During these decades, numerous land acquisitions—the Louisiana Purchase (1803); Florida and eastern Louisiana ceded by Spain (1819); annexation of Texas (1845); the Oregon Com-

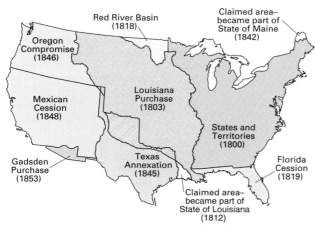

Figure 5. Major United States land acquisitions between 1800 and 1860. *(Source: U.S. Geological Survey, 1970.)*

promise (1846); and lands ceded from Mexico (1848)—greatly expanded the land area of the United States (Garrett, 1988) (fig. 5). With this land expansion, the population grew from 7.2 million in 1810 to 12.8 million in 1830 (U.S. Bureau of the Census, 1832). Land speculation increased with this rapid growth and marked a period when land and resources seemed to be available for the taking. It was a time of rapid inland movement of settlers westward into the wetland-rich areas of the Ohio and Mississippi River Valleys (fig. 2). Large-scale conversion of wetlands to farmlands started to have a real effect on the distribution and abundance of wetlands in the United States. Areas where notable wetland loss occurred between 1800 and 1860 are shown in figure 6.

Figure 6. States with notable wetland loss, 1800 to 1860.

Technical advances throughout the 1800's greatly facilitated wetland conversions. The opening of the Erie Canal in 1825 provided settlers with an alternative mode and route of travel from New York to the Great Lakes States, increasing migration of farmers to the Midwest. The canal also provided low-cost transportation of timber and agricultural products from the Nation's interior to eastern markets and seaports (McNall, 1952). Another innovation, the steam-powered dredge, allowed the channelizing or clearing of small waterways at the expense of adjacent wetlands. Between 1810 and 1840, new agricultural implements—plows, rakes, and cultivators—enabled settlers to break ground previously not considered for farming (McManis, 1964). Mechanical reapers introduced in the 1830's stimulated competition in, and furthered refinements of, farm equipment marketed

in the Midwest (Ross, 1956). These innovations ultimately took a toll on wetlands as more land was drained, cleared, and plowed for farming.

Wetland drainage continued. In the Midwest, the drainage of the Lake Erie marshes of Michigan and Ohio probably started about 1836. Cotton and tobacco farming continued to flourish in the Southern States and precipitated the additional drainage of thousands of acres of wetlands for conversion to cropland.

Wetlands also were being modified in other ways. The Horicon Marsh in Wisconsin was dammed and flooded in 1846 for a transportation route and to provide commercial fishing. Toward the middle of the century, lumbering was an important industry in the Midwest, supplying wood for construction and fuel for stoves and fireplaces. Much of the Nation's timber came from the swamp forests of Ohio, Indiana, and Illinois, which typically contained a mix of birch, ash, elm, oak, cottonwood, poplar, maple, basswood, and hickory.

In 1849, Congress passed the first of the Swamp Land Acts, which granted all swamp and overflow lands in Louisiana to the State for reclamation. In 1850, the Act was made applicable to 12 other States, and in 1860, it was extended to include lands in two additional States (Shaw and Fredine, 1956) (table 1). Although most States did not begin immediate large-scale reclamation projects, this legislation clearly set the tone that the Federal Government promoted wetland drainage and reclamation for settlement and development. This tone pervaded policy and land-use trends for the next century.

1860 TO 1900—AGRICULTURE MOVES WEST

The American Civil War (1861–65) affected wetlands because traversing swamps and marshes with heavy equipment presented major logistical problems for both armies. The design, engineering, and construction of transportation and communication networks were stimulated. Attention became focused on the development of routes around, through, or over water bodies and wetlands, and on production of accurate maps (fig. 7). These maps provided an early glimpse of some of the Nation's wetlands.

After the war, the Nation's attention focused on westward expansion and settlement. Railroads were important in the initial development of transportation routes. The railroads not only opened new lands, including wetlands, to development, but the railroad industry also was a direct consumer of wetland forest products. In the 1860's, more than 30,000 miles of railroad track existed in the United States (Stover, 1961). The railroads of Ohio consumed 1 million cords of wood annually just for fuel (Gordon, 1969). The additional quantity of wood used for ties is not known. From 1859 to 1885, intense timber cutting and land clearing eliminated many of Ohio's wetlands, including the Black Swamp (fig. 8).

The Black Swamp was in the northwestern corner of Ohio and was a barrier to travel and settlement.

Table 1. Acreage granted to the States under the authority of the Swamp Land Acts of 1849, 1850, and 1860

YEAR	STATE	ACRES
1849	Louisiana	9,493,456
1850	Alabama	441,289
	Arkansas	7,686,575
	California	2,192,875
	Florida	20,325,013
	Illinois	1,460,164
	Indiana	1,259,231
	Iowa	1,196,392
	Michigan	5,680,310
	Mississippi	3,347,860
	Missouri	3,432,481
	Ohio	26,372
	Wisconsin	3,360,786
1860	Minnesota	4,706,503
	Oregon	286,108
	TOTAL	**64,895,415**

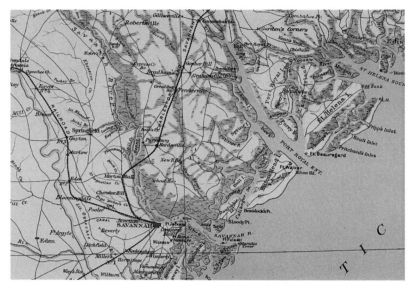

Figure 7. Confederate States of America map of Southeastern United States with wetlands depicted for strategic rather than natural resources value. *(Source: National Archives, Record Group 94, Civil War Atlas, Plate CXLIV.)*

As new kinds of machinery increased the ability to till more land, the conversion of wetlands to farmlands increased rapidly. Huge wheat farms, or "Bonanza Farms," were operating in the Dakota Territory (present-day North and South Dakota) by 1875. New mechanical seeders, harrowers, binders, and threshers, designed specifically for wheat production, were used to cultivate large tracts of land for these farms (Knue, 1988). Many wetlands were lost as a result of these operations.

Improvements in drainage technology greatly affected wetland losses in the East and the Midwest. As the use of steam power expanded, replacing hand labor for digging ditches and manufacturing drainage tiles, the production and installation of drainage tiles increased rapidly. By 1880, 1,140 factories located mainly in Illinois, Indiana, and Ohio manufactured drainage tiles that were used to drain wetlands for farming (Pavelis, 1987). By 1882, more than 30,000 miles of tile drains were operating in Indiana alone. By 1884, Ohio had 20,000 miles of public ditches designed to drain 11 million acres of land (Wooten and Jones, 1955).

Wetland conversion in the Central Valley of California began in the mid-1800's, when farmers began diking and draining the flood-plain areas of the valley for cultivation (fig. 9). Other States had notable losses of wetlands between 1860 and 1900 (fig. 10).

This forested wetland was estimated to have been 120 miles long and 40 miles wide, covering an area nearly equal in size to Connecticut (Gordon, 1969; Ohio Department of Natural Resources, 1988). The swamp, which was an elm-ash forested wetland typical of the region, contained a variety of commercially valuable trees (Eyre, 1980). Nothing was left of the Black Swamp by the end of the nineteenth century.

During the mid- to late 1880's, agriculture expanded rapidly westward along the major river systems. Several regions of abundant wetlands lay directly in the path of this expansion (Wooten and Jones, 1955), including:
- The prairie pothole wetlands of western Minnesota, northern Iowa, and North and South Dakota
- The bottom lands of Missouri and Arkansas in the lower Mississippi River alluvial plain
- The delta wetlands of Mississippi and Louisiana
- The gulf plains of Texas

By the 1860's, settlers started to farm and drain the prairie pothole region. At first, only a modest number of potholes were drained. By the late 1800's, however, the numbers had increased significantly.

1900 TO 1950—CHANGING TECHNOLOGY

The first half of the twentieth century was a time of ambitious engineering and drainage operations. Two World Wars, a rapidly growing population, and industrial growth fueled the demand for land as industry and agriculture propelled the United States to the status of a world leader. Technology was increasingly important in manipulation of the Nation's water resources. Two of the most notable projects that affected wetlands were California's Central Valley Project and the lock and dam system on the Mississippi River.

Although draining had begun one-half century earlier, wetland modification in the Central Valley accelerated early in the 20th century. By the 1920's, about 70 percent of the original wetland acreage had been modified by levees, drainage, and water-diversion projects (Frayer and others, 1989). In the 1930's,

HISTORIC WETLANDS	AREA IN ACRES	DATE DRAINED	SOURCE
Black Swamp	3,072,000	1859–1885	Ohio Dept. Nat. Res., 1988
Pickaway Plains	4,800	1821	Gordon, 1969
Scioto Marsh	16,000	1859, 1883	Gordon, 1969
Other marshes, Hardin County	9,000	1860's	Howe, 1900
Hog Creek Marsh	8,000	1868–1874	Gordon, 1969
Cranberry Marsh	1,000	Unknown	Gordon, 1969
Lake Erie Marshes	300,000	1936–1974	Bednarik, 1984
Dougan's Prairie	Unknown	1827	Middleton, 1917
TOTAL	**3,410,800**		

Figure 8. Location, estimated original acreage, and drainage date of Ohio's historic wetlands.

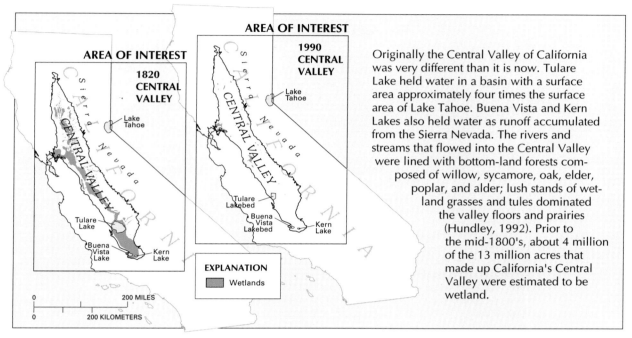

Originally the Central Valley of California was very different than it is now. Tulare Lake held water in a basin with a surface area approximately four times the surface area of Lake Tahoe. Buena Vista and Kern Lakes also held water as runoff accumulated from the Sierra Nevada. The rivers and streams that flowed into the Central Valley were lined with bottom-land forests composed of willow, sycamore, oak, elder, poplar, and alder; lush stands of wetland grasses and tules dominated the valley floors and prairies (Hundley, 1992). Prior to the mid-1800's, about 4 million of the 13 million acres that made up California's Central Valley were estimated to be wetland.

Figure 9. Wetlands of the Central Valley of California, circa 1820 (left) and 1990 (right). *(Source: U.S. Fish and Wildlife Service, Status and Trends, unpub. data, 1994.)*

large-scale flood-control projects, diversion dams, and water-control structures were being built on the tributary rivers entering the valley.

Wetland modification also continued farther east. Before the installation of the lock and dam system in 1924, the bottom lands of the Mississippi River corridor were primarily wooded islands separated by deep sloughs (Green, 1984). Hundreds of small lakes and ponds were scattered throughout extensive wooded areas. The river channel was subject to shifting sands and shallows, and changed constantly. Lake and dam structures were built to create a permanent navigable waterway. The water depth increased behind each dam to create a pool that extended upstream to the next dam. The first pool was filled in 1935 and the system was completed when the last pool was filled in 1959. The resulting changes to the river system eliminated large water-level fluctuations and helped stabilize water depth and flooding. Bottom lands no longer dried out in summer, and former hay meadows and wooded areas were converted to marshlands surrounding the pools. One type of wetland was

exchanged for another. Although some pools of the Upper Mississippi River have problems with silt deposition and restricted water circulation, these "created" wetland areas provide habitat for fur-bearing animals, waterfowl, and fish.

In other parts of the country, this era was marked by urban and agricultural expansion projects that drained both large and small wetlands. Some of the most ambitious projects were attempts to drain and cultivate Horicon Marsh in Wisconsin in 1904; commercial timber harvesting in southern Georgia, which began in 1908 as a precursor to attempts to drain the Okefenokee Swamp (Trowell, 1988); and in 1914, the draining of North Carolina's largest natural lake, Lake Mattamuskeet, to create farmland (U.S. Fish and Wildlife Service, undated). Early in the century, land developers dug drainage ditches in an attempt to drain a huge area for development in the vast peatlands north of Red Lake, Minn. (Glaser, 1987). On July 29, 1917, the Minneapolis Sunday Tribune ran a full page advertisement to attract homesteaders to the Red Lake area—"perhaps the last of the unsettled, uncut timberland in the middle of the country" (Wright, 1984). By 1930, nearly all of the prairie wetlands in Iowa, the southern counties of Minnesota, and the Red River Valley in North Dakota and Minnesota were drained (Schrader, 1955).

Attempts were underway to drain and farm large parts of The Everglades (a huge expanse of wetlands in southern Florida). By the 1930's, more than 400 miles of drainage canals were already in place (Lord, 1993). (See article "Wetland Resources of Florida" in the State Summaries section of this volume.) With the passage of the Sugar Act of 1934, additional wetlands in southern Florida were drained and put into sugarcane production. Sugarcane yields more than doubled from 410,000 to 873,000 tons between 1931 and 1941 (Clarke, 1977), largely at the expense of

Figure 10. States with notable wetland loss, 1860 to 1900.

Drainage tile operation, circa 1940's. Tiles provide a conduit for moving water from a wetland. *(Photograph courtesy of U.S. Department of Agriculture.)*

The Migratory Bird Hunting Stamp Act was one of the first pieces of legislation to initiate the process of acquiring and restoring America's wetlands.

wetland acreage. Severe flooding in southern Florida in the 1920's and again in the 1940's prompted the U.S. Army Corps of Engineers to build the Central and Southern Florida Project for flood control. This massive undertaking, which required levees, water-storage areas, channel improvements, and large pumps, caused additional large modification to The Everglades' environment (Light and Dineen, 1994).

Mechanized farm tractors had replaced horses and mules for farm labor during this half century. The tractors could be used more effectively than animals for drainage operations, and the old pasture land then became available for improvement and production of additional crops. In the Midwest and the North-central States, the use of tractors probably contributed to the loss of millions of acres of small wetlands and prairie potholes.

In the 1930's, the U.S. Government, in essence, provided free engineering services to farmers to drain wetlands; and by the 1940's, the Government shared the cost of drainage projects (Burwell and Sugden, 1964). Organized drainage districts throughout the country coordinated efforts to remove surface water from wetlands (Wooten and Jones, 1955). Figure 11 shows areas of notable wetland losses between 1900 and 1950.

Figure 11. States with notable wetland loss, 1900 to 1950.

In 1934, in stark contrast to these drainage activities, Congress passed the Migratory Bird Hunting Stamp Act. This Act was one of the first pieces of legislation to initiate the process of acquiring and restoring America's wetlands.

1950 TO PRESENT—CHANGING PRIORITIES AND VALUES

By the 1960's, most political, financial, and institutional incentives to drain or destroy wetlands were in place. The Federal Government encouraged land drainage and wetland destruction through a variety of legislative and policy instruments. For example, the Watershed Protection and Flood Prevention Act (1954) directly and indirectly increased the drainage of wetlands near flood-control projects (Erickson and others, 1979). The Federal Government directly subsidized or facilitated wetland losses through its many public-works projects, technical practices, and cost-shared drainage programs administered by the U.S. Department of Agriculture (Erickson, 1979). Tile and open-ditch drainage were considered conservation practices under the Agriculture Conservation Program—whose policies caused

wetland losses averaging 550,000 acres each year from the mid-1950's to the mid-1970's (Office of Technology Assessment, 1984). Agriculture was responsible for more than 80 percent of these losses (Frayer and others, 1983). Figure 12 shows States with notable wetland losses between 1950 and 1990.

Figure 12. States with notable wetland loss, 1950 to 1990.

Since the 1970's, there has been increasing awareness that wetlands are valuable areas that provide important environmental functions. Public awareness of, and education about, wetlands has increased dramatically since the early 1950's. Federal policies, such as the "Swampbuster," have eliminated incentives and other mechanisms that have made the destruction of wetlands technically and economically feasible. New laws, such as the Emergency Wetland Resources Act of 1986, also curtail wetland losses. (See article "Wetland Protection Legislation" in this volume for information on legislation affecting wetlands.) Some of the more ambitious drainage projects of earlier years have been abandoned. Now, places like Lake Mattamuskeet, Horicon Marsh, and the Okefenokee Swamp, which once were targeted for drainage, have become National Wildlife Refuges that provide wetland habitat for a variety of plants and animals.

The effects of the Federal policy reversal on the rate of wetland loss are not clear. Estimates indicate that wetland losses in the conterminous United States from the mid-1970's to the mid-1980's were about 290,000 acres per year (Dahl and Johnson, 1991). This is about one-half of the losses that occurred each year in the 1950's and '60's. The preceding numbers do not include degraded or modified wetlands. Although the estimate above reflects a declining rate of loss, land development continues to destroy wetlands.

From about 1987 to the present, Federal efforts to restore wetlands have increased. Although there is no precise number for all of the wetland acres restored, the U.S. Fish and Wildlife Service (1991) estimated that between 1987 and 1990 about 90,000 acres were added to the Nation's wetland inventory.

Attempts are underway now to restore some of The Everglades. The remaining Everglades comprise about 2,300 square miles, three-fifths of which is impounded in managed water-conservation areas (Lord, 1993). This wetland system currently is experiencing mercury contamination and other water-quality problems, water-supply and diversion controversies, declining wildlife populations, increasing pressure from tourism, urban and agricultural expansion, and influx of nuisance plants.

The magnitude of environmental alterations in Florida, with numerous conflicting interests, exemplifies the dilemma of managing water resources and wetlands. What initially seemed to be a matter of water removal turned into an extremely complex and costly issue involving water-use objectives at all levels of government (Tebeau, 1980).

Today there are more than 100 dams within the California Central Valley drainage basins and thousands of miles of water-delivery canals. Water is diverted for irrigation, hydroelectric power, and municipal and industrial water supplies. Only 14 percent of the original wetland acreage remains. The Tulare Lake Basin has been virtually drained, leaving only remnant wetland areas and a dry lakebed, and Buena Vista and Kern Lakes rarely contain water (fig. 9).

Currently (1994), manipulation of water levels in wetlands rather than the complete removal of water as in the past, is a trend that affects wetlands. Partial drainage or lowering of the water levels to allow for certain uses is becoming prevalent in some parts of the country. Effects of this type of management are uncertain.

EXAMPLE OF CHANGING ATTITUDES—HORICON MARSH

The history of the Horicon Marsh in Wisconsin is an example of how people's attitudes toward wetlands have changed through time (fig. 13). Horicon Marsh was dammed, flooded, and renamed Lake Horicon in 1846. At that time, it was the largest manmade lake in the world (about 4 miles wide by 14 miles long) (Wisconsin Department of Natural Resources, 1990). Lake Horicon was used for commercial transportation and for commercial fishing. In 1869, the dam was removed and the land returned to marsh. In 1883, two sportsmen's clubs, which leased the marsh area, reported that 500,000 ducks hatched annually in the marsh. They also reported that 30,000 muskrats and mink were trapped in the southern half of the marsh. Huge flocks of geese also were reported (Freeman, 1948). In 1904, attempts were made to drain the marsh and sell the reclaimed land for truck farms. Lawsuits resulting from inadequate drainage halted the reclamation effort.

In 1921, local conservationists began efforts to protect Horicon Marsh as a game refuge, and the State of Wisconsin created the Horicon Marsh Wildlife Refuge in July 1927. Later, to avoid legal confrontations with the local farmers, the State bought property and (or) water rights to the southern half of the refuge and the Federal Government purchased rights to the northern half. In 1990, Horicon Marsh was added to the sites recognized by the Convention on Wetlands of International Importance especially as Waterfowl Habitat.

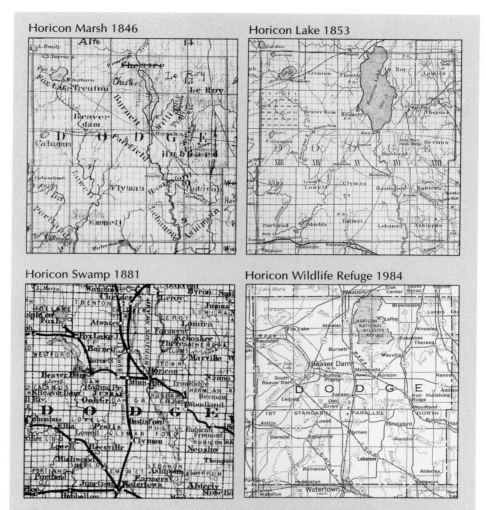

Figure 13. Horicon Marsh, Wis., evolved from original marsh (1846), to lake (1853), to swamp (1881), to wildlife refuge (1984). *(Source: Sequence is left to right, top to bottom, Historical Society of Wisconsin negative number WHi (X3) 50111, WHi (X3) 50212, WHi (X3) 50113; U.S. Geological Survey, 1984.)*

Estimates indicate that today slightly more than 100 million acres of wetlands remain in the conterminous United States. Although the rate of wetland conversion has slowed in recent years, wetland losses continue to outdistance wetland gains.

References Cited

Beauchamp, K.H., 1987, A history of drainage and drainage methods, *in* Pavelis, G.A., ed., Farm drainage in the United States—History, status, and prospects: Washington, D.C., Economic Research Service, U.S. Department of Agriculture, Miscellaneous Publication no. 1455, p. 13–29.

Bednarik, K.E., 1984, Saga of the Lake Erie marshes, *in* Hawkins, A.S., Hanson, R.C., Nelson, H.K., and Reeves, H.M., eds., Flyways—Pioneering waterfowl management in North America: Washington, D.C., U.S. Fish and Wildlife Service, p. 423–430.

Burwell, R.W., and Sugden, L.G., 1964, Potholes—Going, going..., *in* Linduska, J.P., ed., Waterfowl tomorrow: Washington, D.C., U.S. Fish and Wildlife Service, p. 369–380.

Clarke, M.J., 1977, An economic and environmental assessment of the Florida Everglades sugarcane industry: Baltimore, Md., Johns Hopkins University, 140 p.

Dahl, T.E., 1990, Wetlands—Losses in the United States, 1780's to 1980's: Washington, D.C., U.S. Fish and Wildlife Service Report to Congress, 13 p.

Dahl, T.E., and Johnson, C.E., 1991, Wetlands—Status and trends in the conterminous United States, mid-1970's to mid-1980's: Washington, D.C., U.S. Fish and Wildlife Service, 22 p.

Erickson, R.E., 1979, Federal programs influencing wetlands, Seventh Annual Michigan Landuse Policy Conference: East Lansing, Mich., Michigan State University, 246 p.

Erickson, R.E., Linder, R.L., and Harmon, K.W., 1979, Stream channelization (p.l. 83-566) increased wetland losses in the Dakotas: Wildlife Society Bulletin, v. 7, no. 2, p. 71–78.

Eyre, F.H., 1980, Forest cover types of the United States and Canada: Washington, D.C., Society of American Foresters, 148 p.

Frayer, W.E., Monahan, T.J., Bowden, D.C., and Graybill, F.A., 1983, Status and trends of wetlands and deepwater habitats in the conterminous United States, 1950's to 1970's: Fort Collins, Colo., Colorado State University, 31 p.

Frayer, W.E., Peters, D.D., and Pywell, H.R., 1989, Wetlands of the California Central Valley—Status and Trends—1939 to mid 1980's: Portland, Oreg., U.S. Fish and Wildlife Service, 28 p.

Freeman, A.E., and Bussewitz, W.R., 1948, History of Horicon: Horicon, Wis., undated, 126 p.

Garrett, W.E., ed., 1988, Historical atlas of the United States: Washington, D.C., National Geographic Society, 289 p.

Glaser, P.H., 1987, The ecology of patterned boreal peatlands of northern Minnesota—A community profile: U.S. Fish and Wildlife Service, Report 85 (7.14), 98 p.

Gordon, R.B., 1969, The natural vegetation of Ohio in pioneer days: Columbus, Ohio, Bulletin of the Ohio Biological Survey, v. III, no. 2, Ohio State University, 113 p.

Green, W.E., 1984, The great river refuge, *in* Hawkins, A.S., Hanson, R.C., Nelson, H.K., and Reeves, H.M., eds., Flyways—Pioneering waterfowl management in North America: Washington, D.C., U.S. Fish and Wildlife Service, p. 431–439.

Howe, Henry, 1900, Historical collections of Ohio: Cincinnati, Ohio, Ohio centennial edition, Published by the State of Ohio, v. 1, p. 881.

Hundley, Norris, Jr., 1992, The great thirst—Californians and water, 1700's–1990's: Berkeley, Calif., University of California Press, 551 p.

Knue, Joseph, 1988, Of time and prairie—100 years of people and wildlife in North Dakota—Observations in change: Bismarck, N. Dak., North Dakota State Game and Fish Department, 106 p.

Light, S.S., and Dineen, J.W., 1994, Water control in The Everglades—A historical perspective, *in* Davis, S.M., and Ogden, J.C., eds., Everglades—The ecosystem and its restoration: Delray Beach, Fla., St. Lucie Press, p. 47–84.

Lord, L.A., 1993, Guide to Florida environmental issues and information: Winter Park, Fla., Florida Conservation Foundation, 364 p.

McManis, D.R., 1964, The initial evaluation and utilization of the Illinois prairies, 1815–1840: Chicago, Ill., University of Chicago, Department of Geography Research Paper no. 94, 109 p.

McNall, N.A., 1952, An agricultural history of the Genesee Valley, 1790–1860: Philadelphia, Pa., University of Pennsylvania Press, 276 p.

Middleton, E.P., 1917, History of Champaign County, Ohio, its people, industries and institutions: Indianapolis, Ind., B.E. Bowen and Co., Inc., 116 p.

Office of Technology Assessment, 1984, Wetlands—Their use and regulation: Washington, D.C., U.S. Congress, OTA-0-206, 208 p.

Ohio Department of Natural Resources, 1988, Ohio wetlands priority conservation plan—An addendum to the 1986 Ohio statewide comprehensive outdoor recreation plan: Office of Outdoor Recreation Services, 67 p.

Pavelis, G.A., ed., 1987, Farm drainage in the United States—History, status, and prospects: Economic Research Service, U.S. Department of Agriculture, Miscellaneous Pub. No. 1455, 170 p.

Ross, E.D., 1956, Retardation in farm technology before the power age: Agricultural History 30, p. 11–18.

Schrader, T.A., 1955, Waterfowl and the potholes of the north central states, *in* The yearbook of agriculture 1955: Washington, D.C., U.S. Department of Agriculture, 84th Congress, 1st Session, House Document no. 32, p. 596–604.

Shaw, S.P., and Fredine, C.G., 1956, Wetlands of the United States—Their extent and their value to waterfowl and other wildlife: Washington, D.C., U.S. Fish and Wildlife Service Circular 39, 67 p.

Stover, J.F., 1961, American railroads: Chicago, Ill., University of Chicago Press, 310 p.

Tant, P.L., 1981, Soil survey of Washington County, North Carolina: Washington, D.C., U.S. Soil Conservation Service, 99 p.

Tebeau, C.W., 1980, A history of Florida: Coral Gables, Fla., University of Miami Press, 527 p.

Trowell, C.T., 1988, Exploring the Okefenokee—Roland M. Harper in the Okefenokee Swamp, 1902 and 1919: Douglas, Ga., North Georgia College, Research Paper no. 2, 89 p.

U.S. Bureau of the Census, 1832, Return of the whole number of persons within the several districts of the U.S., 1830: Washington, D.C.

U.S. Fish and Wildlife Service, 1991, United States Department of the Interior budget justification—Fiscal year 1992: Washington, D.C., 121 p.

_____Undated, Mattamuskeet National Wildlife Refuge: Swan Quarter, N.C., (Brochure).

U.S. Geological Survey, 1984, Wisconsin State base map: U.S. Geological Survey, scale 1:500,000.

Washington County Historical Society, 1979, Historic Washington County: Plymouth, N.C., 31 p.

Wisconsin Department of Natural Resources, 1990, Wetlands/wonderlands—Wisconsin natural resources: Madison, Wis., Wisconsin Department of Natural Resources, 16 p.

Wooten, H.H., and Jones, L.A., 1955, The history of our drainage enterprises, *in* The yearbook of agriculture, 1955: Washington, D.C., U.S. Department of Agriculture, 84th Congress, 1st Session, House Document no. 32, p. 478–498.

Wright, H.E., Jr., 1984, Red Lake peatland—Its past and patterns: Minneapolis, Minn., University of Minnesota, James Ford Bell Museum of Natural History, v. 1, 7 p.

FOR ADDITIONAL INFORMATION: Thomas E. Dahl, National Wetlands Inventory, 9720 Executive Center Drive, Suite 101 - Monroe Building, St. Petersburg, FL 33702; Gregory J. Allord, U.S. Geological Survey, 505 Science Drive, Madison, WI 53711

Technical Aspects of Wetlands

Wetland Definitions and Classifications in the United States

By Ralph W. Tiner[1]

"Wetland" is a generic term for all the different kinds of wet habitats—implying that it is land that is wet for some period of time, but not necessarily permanently wet. Wetlands have numerous definitions and classifications in the United States as a result of their diversity, the need for their inventory, and the regulation of their uses. This article provides an overview of wetland definitions and classification systems of major wetland types in the United States. It also introduces the U.S. Fish and Wildlife Service (FWS) classification system (Cowardin and others, 1979) that is used throughout this volume.

Wetlands typically occur in topographic settings where surface water collects and (or) ground water discharges, making the area wet for extended periods of time. Examples of some of these topographic settings, and some common names for wetland types associated with them are:
- Depressions (swales, sloughs, prairie potholes, Carolina bays, playas, vernal pools, oxbows, and glacial kettles)
- Relatively flat depositional areas that are subject to flooding (intertidal flats and marshes, coastal lowlands, sheltered embayments, shorelines, deltas, and flood plains)
- Broad, flat areas that lack drainage outlets (interstream divides and permafrost muskegs)
- Sloping terrain associated with springs, seeps, and drainageways; and relatively flat or sloping areas adjacent to bogs and subject to expansion by accumulation of peat
- Open water bodies (floating mats and submersed beds)

Cross sections of some typical wetland landscapes and the position of the wetland relative to specific topographic features are shown in figure 14.

All areas considered to be wetlands must have enough water at some time during the year to stress plants and animals that are not adapted to life in water or saturated soils. A variety of wetland plant communities and soil types have developed in the United States because of regional differences in hydrologic regimes, climate, soil-forming processes, and geologic settings. Consequently, many terms, such as "marsh," "bog," "fen," "swamp," "pocosin," "pothole," "playa," "salina," "vernal pool," "bottom-land hardwood swamp," "river bottom," "lowland," and others are applied to different types of wetlands across the country.

WETLAND DEFINITIONS

Wetlands have been defined for specific purposes, such as research studies, general habitat classification, natural resource inventories, and environmental regulations. Before the beginning of wetland-protection laws in the 1960's, wetlands were broadly defined by scientists working in specialized fields (Lefor and Kennard, 1977). A botanist's definition would emphasize plants; a soil scientist would focus on soil properties; and a hydrologist's definition would emphasize fluctuations of the water table.

Nonregulatory Definition

The FWS developed a nonregulatory, technical definition that could have several uses, ranging from wetland protection to scientific investigations. This definition emphasizes three important attributes of wetlands: (1) hydrology—the degree of flooding or soil saturation; (2) vegetation—plants adapted to grow in water or in a soil or substrate that is occasionally oxygen deficient due to saturation (hydrophytes); and (3) soils—those saturated long enough during the growing season to produce oxygen-deficient conditions in the upper part of the soil, which commonly includes the major part of the root zone of plants (hydric soils) (Cowardin and others, 1979; Tiner, 1991). To supplement this

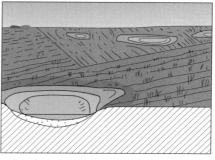
Isolated depressions

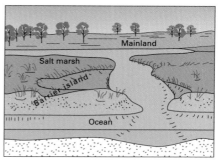
Sheltered embayments

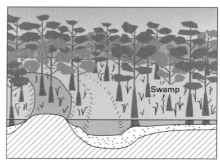
Flood plains

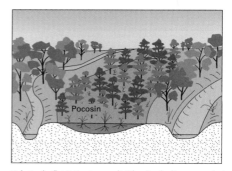
Relatively flat interstream divides (including pocosins)

Figure 14. Cross sections of selected wetland landscapes showing typical positions of wetlands relative to topographic features.

[1] U.S. Fish and Wildlife Service.

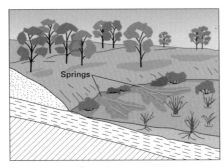

Seepage areas and springs

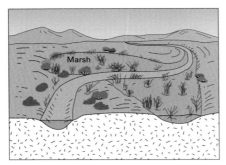

Basins with streams

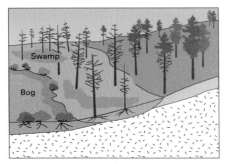

Blanket bogs in boreal and arctic regions

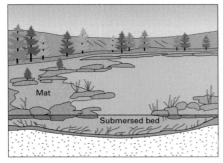

Open water bodies with floating mats and
submersed beds

Figure 14. Cross sections of selected wetland
landscapes showing typical positions of
wetlands relative to topographic features.
—Continued.

definition and to help identify wetlands in the United States, the FWS prepared a list of wetland plants (Reed, 1988). In addition, the Soil Conservation Service[1] (SCS) developed a list of hydric soils (U.S. Soil Conservation
Service, 1991).

On the basis of plant and soil conditions, wetlands typically fall into one
of three categories: (1) areas with hydrophytes and hydric soils (marshes,
swamps, and bogs); (2) areas without soils but with hydrophytes (aquatic
beds and seaweed-covered rocky shores); and (3) areas without soil and
without hydrophytes (gravel beaches and tidal flats) that are periodically
flooded. The FWS definition generally does not include permanent deepwater areas as wetlands. However, permanent shallow waters that commonly
support aquatic beds and emergent plants (erect, rooted, nonwoody plants
that are mostly above water) are classified as wetlands.

Regulatory Definitions as Compared to Nonregulatory Definitions

In the 1960's and 1970's, State and Federal environmental laws gave some
protection to wetlands. On the basis of different interests to be protected,
however, each governing body developed a different definition of wetlands.
Examples of some of these definitions are given in table 2. Only wet soils
vegetated with hydrophytes are considered as wetlands by the three Federal
agencies involved with regulation—the SCS, the U.S. Environmental Protection Agency (EPA), and the U.S. Army Corps of Engineers (Corps). The
FWS uses a nonregulatory definition that is broader and includes aquatic beds
in shallow freshwater and naturally nonvegetated areas. In the context of vegetated wetlands, all four agency definitions are conceptually the same in that
they include hydrology, vegetation, and soils.

Most States have developed regulatory definitions to protect certain wetlands from exploitation. Therefore, State definitions are much broader than
any of the Federal definitions. The State definitions tend to emphasize the
presence of certain plants for identification purposes (table 2). However, the
States did not produce a comprehensive list of "wetland plant species,"
making it difficult to use vegetation consistently to identify the limits of wetlands (Tiner, 1989 and 1993a).

WETLAND CLASSIFICATION

"Wetland classification," as used in this article, refers to the designation of different wetland types on the basis of hydrology, vegetation, and soils.
The Federal Government's early attempts to classify wetlands were motivated
largely by agricultural interests that sought to convert wetlands to cropland.
The first classification systems put wetlands into a few general categories
on the basis of location—river swamps, lake swamps, and upland swamps
(Wright, 1907). Other classification systems were related to the degree of
inundation—permanent swamps, wet grazing land, periodically overflowed
land, and periodically swampy land (Dachnowski, 1920).

Later wetland classifications developed from a need to differentiate wetlands from other land-cover types for regional and national planning purposes,
or because of ecological interest. Martin and others (1953) developed a "*Classification of Wetlands in the United States*" to serve as a framework for the
1954 national inventory to assess the amount and types of wetland waterfowl habitat. Although this system is still in use, the inadequate definition
of wetland types has led to inconsistencies in application across the country
(Cowardin and others, 1979).

When the FWS began a review of existing wetland inventories in 1974,
they found more than 50 classification schemes (U.S. Fish and Wildlife Service, 1976). The only one of these that was nationally based was that of Martin
and others (1953). Subsequently, the FWS worked with several prominent
wetland scientists and mapping experts to identify necessary elements for a
new classification system based on the concept of ecosystems (Sather, 1976).
Four key objectives were established:
- Identify ecologically similar habitat units
- Classify these units systematically to facilitate resource-management
  decisions
- Identify units for inventory and mapping purposes
- Provide uniformity in concept and terminology throughout the country

---

[1] The SCS became the Natural Resources
Conservation Service in 1994.

Table 2. Examples of wetland definitions used by Federal and State agencies in the United States

Organization (reference)	Wetland definition
FEDERAL	
U.S. Fish and Wildlife Service (Cowardin and others, 1979)	"Wetlands are lands transitional between terrestrial and aquatic systems where the water table is usually at or near the surface or the land is covered by shallow water. For the purposes of this classification wetlands must have one or more of the following three attributes: (1) at least periodically, the land supports predominantly hydrophytes; (2) the substrate is predominantly undrained hydric soil; and (3) the substrate is nonsoil and is saturated with water or covered by shallow water at some time during the growing season of each year."
U.S. Army Corps of Engineers (33 CFR 328.3) U.S. Environmental Protection Agency (40 CFR 230.3)	"Wetlands are those areas that are inundated or saturated by surface or groundwater at a frequency and duration sufficient to support, and that under normal circumstances do support, a prevalance of vegetation typically adapted for life in saturated soil conditions. Wetlands generally include swamps, marshes, bogs, and similar areas."
U.S. Soil Conservation Service (National Food Security Act Manual 1988) (The Act is commonly known as the "Swampbuster")	"Wetlands are defined as areas that have a predominance of hydric soils and that are inundated or saturated by surface or ground water at a frequency and duration sufficient to support, and under normal circumstances do support, a prevalence of hydrophytic vegetation typically adapted for life in saturated soil conditions, except lands in Alaska identified as having high potential for agricultural development and a predominance of permafrost soils."
STATE	
Connecticut (CT General Statutes, Sections 22a–36 to 45, inclusive, 1972, 1987)	"Wetlands mean land, including submerged land which consists of any of the soil types designated as poorly drained, very poorly drained, alluvial, and floodplain by the National Cooperative Soils Survey, as may be amended from time to time, by the Soil Conservation Service of the United States Department of Agriculture. Watercourses are defined as rivers, streams, brooks, waterways, lakes, ponds, marshes, swamps, bogs, and all other bodies of water, natural or artificial, public or private."
Connecticut (CT General Statutes, Sections 22a–28 to 35, inclusive 1969)	"Wetlands are those areas which border on or lie beneath tidal waters, such as, but not limited to banks, bogs, salt marshes, swamps, meadows, flats or other low lands subject to tidal action, including those areas now or formerly connected to tidal waters, and whose surface is at or below an elevation of one foot above local extreme high water." (Also includes a list of plants capable of growing in tidal wetlands.)
Rhode Island Coastal Resources Management Council (RI Coastal Resources Management Program as amended June 28, 1983)	"Coastal wetlands include salt marshes and freshwater or brackish wetlands contiguous to salt marshes. Areas of open water within coastal wetlands are considered a part of the wetland. Salt marshes are areas regularly inundated by salt water through either natural or artificial water courses and where one or more of the following species predominate:" (8 indicator plants listed). "Contiguous and associated freshwater or brackish marshes are those where one or more of the following species predominate:" (9 indicator plants listed).
Rhode Island Department of Environmental Management (RI General Law, Sections 2–1–18 et seq.)	Fresh water wetlands are defined to include, "but not limited to marshes; swamps; bogs; ponds; river and stream flood plains and banks; areas subject to flooding or storm flowage; emergent and submergent plant communities in any body of fresh water including rivers and streams and that area of land within fifty feet (50') of the edge of any bog, marsh, swamp, or pond." Various wetland types are further defined on the basis of hydrology and indicator plants, including bog (15 types of indicator plants), marsh (21 types of indicator plants), and swamp (24 types of indicator plants plus marsh plants).
New Jersey (Pinelands Protection Act, N.J. STAT. ANN. Section 13:18–1 to 13:29.)	"Wetlands are those lands which are inundated or saturated by water at a magnitude, duration and frequency sufficient to support the growth of hydrophytes. Wetlands include lands with poorly drained or very poorly drained soils as designated by the National Cooperative Soils Survey of the Soil Conservation Service of the United States Department of Agriculture. Wetlands include coastal wetlands and inland wetlands, including submerged lands." "Coastal wetlands are banks, low-lying marshes, meadows, flats, and other lowlands subject to tidal inundation which support or are capable of supporting one or more of the following plants:" (29 plants are listed). "Inland wetlands" are defined as including, but not limited to, Atlantic white cedar swamps (15 plants listed), hardwood swamps (19 plants specified), pitch pine lowlands (10 plants listed), bogs (12 plants identified), inland marshes (6 groups of plants listed), lakes and ponds, and rivers and streams.
New Jersey (Coastal Wetland Protection Act - N.J. STAT. ANN. Section 13:18–1 to 13:9A–10)	"Coastal wetlands" are "any bank, marsh, swamp, meadow, flat or other low land subject to tidal action in the Delaware Bay and Delaware River, Raritan Bay, Sandy Hook Bay, Shrewsbury River including Navesink River, Shark River, and the coastal inland waterways extending southerly from Manasquan Inlet to Cape May Harbor, or at any inlet, estuary, or those areas now or formerly connected to tidal areas whose surface is at or below an elevation of 1 foot above local extreme high water, and upon which may grow or is capable of growing some, but not necessarily all, of the following:" (19 plants are listed.) Coastal wetlands exclude "any land or real property subject to the jurisdiction of the Hackensack Meadowlands Development Commission...."
Massachusetts (MA General Law Chapter 131, Section 40)	"The term 'freshwater wetlands' shall mean wet meadows, marshes, swamps, bogs, areas where groundwater, flowing or standing surface water or ice provides a significant part of the supporting substrate for a plant community for at least five months of the year; emergent and submergent plant communities in inland waters; that portion of any bank which touches any inland waters." Various wetland types are further defined on the basis of hydrology and indicator plants and include bogs (19 types of indicator plants), swamps (22 types of plants), wet meadows (12 types of plants), and marshes (22 types of indicator plants).

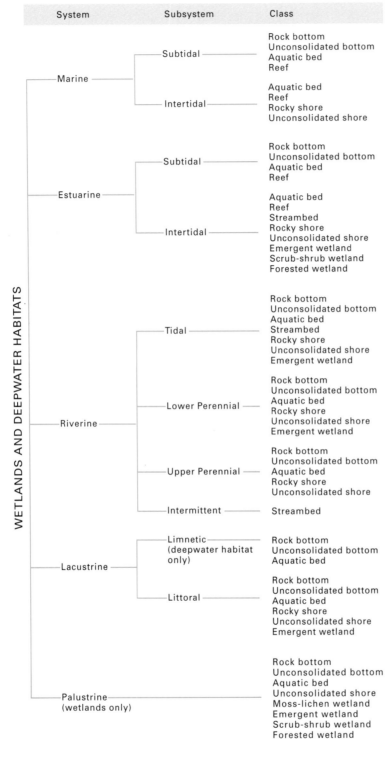

Figure 15. Classification hierarchy of wetlands and deepwater habitats showing systems, subsystems, and classes. *(Source: Cowardin and others, 1979).*

On the basis of these objectives, the FWS developed a new wetland classification system. The system was extensively field tested and reviewed by public and private sectors before being published as "Classification of Wetlands and Deepwater Habitats of the United States" (Cowardin and others, 1979). Since its publication, the system has become the national and international standard for identifying and classifying wetlands (Mader, 1991; Gopal and others, 1982).

THE U.S. FISH AND WILDLIFE SERVICE WETLAND CLASSIFICATION SYSTEM

A synopsis of the FWS wetland classification system is presented here. Each of the State summaries in this volume gives a general summary of the system, and a more comprehensive discussion can be found in Cowardin and others (1979). The system described here proceeds from general to specific, as shown in figure 15.

System.— Each system represents "a complex of wetlands and deepwater habitats, that share the influence of similar hydrologic, geomorphologic, chemical, or biological factors" (Cowardin and others, 1979, p. 4). Five systems are defined:
- Marine—open ocean and its associated coastline
- Estuarine—tidal waters of coastal rivers and empayments, salty tidal marshes, mangrove swamps, and tidal flats
- Riverine—rivers and streams
- Lacustrine—lakes, reservoirs, and large ponds
- Palustrine—marshes, wet meadows, fens, playas, potholes, pocosins, bogs, swamps, and small shallow ponds

The overwhelming majority of the Nation's wetlands fall within the Palustrine System; most of the remaining wetlands are in the Estuarine System.

Subsystem.—Each system, except the Palustrine, is divided into subsystems (fig. 15). The Marine and Estuarine Systems have two subsystems that are defined by tidal water levels: subtidal—continuously submersed areas; and intertidal—alternately flooded and exposed to air. The Lacustrine System has two subsystems that are defined by water depth: littoral—the shallow-water zone where wetlands extend from the lakeshore to a depth of 6.6 feet below low water or to the extent of nonpersistent emergent plants such as arrowheads, pickerelweed, wild rice, or bulrush, if they grow beyond that depth; and limnetic—the deepwater zone where low water is deeper than 6.6 feet (deepwater habitat). The Riverine System has four subsystems that represent different reaches of a flowing freshwater system: tidal—water levels subject to tidal fluctuations; lower perennial—permanent, slow-flowing waters having a well-developed flood plain; upper perennial—permanent, fast-flowing waters having very little or no flood plain; and intermittent—streambeds with flowing water for only part of the year.

Classes.—Each subsystem is divided into classes, which describe the general appearance of the wetland or deepwater habitat in terms of the dominant vegetative form, or composition of the substrate (table 3). For areas where vegetation covers 30 percent or more of the surface, five vegetative classes are

Table 3. Classes and subclasses of wetlands and deepwater habitats as defined by Cowardin and others (1979)

Class	Brief description	Subclasses
Rock bottom	Generally permanently flooded areas with bottom substrates consisting of at least 75 percent stones and boulders and less than 30 percent vegetative cover.	Bedrock; rubble
Unconsolidated bottom	Generally permanently flooded areas with bottom substrates consisting of at least 25 percent particles smaller than stones and less than 30 percent vegetative cover.	Cobble-gravel; sand; mud; organic
Aquatic bed	Generally permanently flooded areas that are vegetated by plants growing principally on or below the water surface.	Algal; aquatic; rooted vascular; floating vascular
Reef	Characterized by elevations above the surrounding substrate and interference with normal wave flow; they are primarily subtidal.	Coral; mollusk; worm
Streambed	Channel whose bottom is completely dewatered at low water periods.	Bedrock; rubble; cobble-gravel; sand; mud; organic; vegetated
Rocky shore	Wetlands characterized by bedrock stones or boulder with areal coverage of 75 percent or more and with less than 30 percent coverage by vegetation.	Bedrock; rubble
Unconsolidated shore	Wetlands having unconsolidated substrates with less than 75 percent coverage by stones, boulders, and bedrock and less than 30 percent native vegetative cover.	Cobble-gravel; sand; mud; organic; vegetated
Moss-lichen wetland	Wetlands dominated by mosses or lichens where other plants have less than 30 percent coverage.	Moss; lichen
Emergent wetland	Wetlands dominated by erect, rooted, herbaceous hydrophytes.	Persistent; nonpersistent
Scrub-shrub wetland	Wetlands dominated by woody vegetation less than 20 feet (6 meters) tall.	Deciduous; evergreen; dead woody plants
Forested wetland	Wetlands dominated by woody vegetation 20 feet (6 meters) or taller.	Deciduous; evergreen; dead woody plants

used—aquatic bed, moss-lichen wetland, emergent wetland, scrub-shrub wetland, and forested wetland. Aquatic beds may be either wetlands or deepwater habitats, depending on water depth.

Six other classes are used where vegetation generally is absent and where substrate and degree of flooding are distinguishing features—rock bottom, unconsolidated bottom, reef, streambed, rocky shore, and unconsolidated shore. Areas that are nonvegetated and permanently flooded are classed as either rock bottom or unconsolidated bottom. Areas that are periodically flooded are classed as streambed, rocky shore, or unconsolidated shore. Reefs are found in both permanently flooded (deepwater habitats) and periodically flooded tidal areas (wetlands).

Subclass.—Each class is divided further into subclasses (table 3) to define the substrate in non-vegetated areas or the dominant vegetation in vegetated areas. In vegetated areas, the subclasses are—persistent or nonpersistent emergents, mosses and lichens, or broad-leaved deciduous, needle-leaved deciduous, broad-leaved evergreen, needle-leaved evergreen, and dead woody plants. In nonvegetated areas the subclasses are—bedrock, rubble, cobble-gravel, mud, sand, and organic.

Dominance Type.—Below the subclass, dominance type can be applied to specify the dominant plant or animal in the wetland. This level allows one to distinguish between distinct plant communities (red maple forested wetland and pin oak forested wetland, or a tussock-sedge-dominated emergent wetland and cattail-dominated emergent wetland). In this way, individual wetlands can be grouped in ecologically similar units.

Modifiers.—The classification system also uses modifiers to describe hydrologic, chemical, and soil characteristics, and the effects of humans on the wetlands. The four specific modifiers used are—water regime, water chemistry, soil, and special. These modifiers can be applied to classes, subclasses, and dominance types.

The water-regime modifiers describe flooding or soil saturation and are divided into two main groups—tidal and nontidal. Tidal modifiers can be subdivided into two general categories—salt- and brackish-water and freshwater. The nontidal modifier—inland freshwater and saline—defines conditions where runoff, ground-water discharge or recharge, evapotranspiration, wind, and lake seiches (oscillation of the water) cause water-level changes. Both tidal and nontidal modifiers are briefly defined in table 4.

Water-chemistry modifiers are divided into two categories: salinity and pH. The salinity modifiers have been further divided into two groups: haline for estuarine and marine tidal areas dominated by sodium chloride and saline for nontidal areas dominated by salts other than sodium chloride. The salinity and

The FWS classification system has become the national and international standard for identifying and classifying wetlands.

Table 4. Water regime modifiers as defined by Cowardin and others (1979)

Group	Water type	Water regime and definition
Tidal	Salt- and brackish-water areas	Subtidal — Permanently flooded tidal waters
		Irregularly exposed — Exposed less often than daily by tides
		Regularly flooded — Daily tidal flooding and exposure to air
		Irregularly flooded — Flooded less often than daily and typically exposed to air
	Freshwater	Permanently flooded — Permanently flooded by tides and river overflow but with tidal fluctuation in water levels
		Semipermanently flooded — Flooded most of the growing season by river overflow but with tidal fluctuation in water levels
		Regularly flooded — Daily tidal flooding and exposure to air
		Seasonally flooded — Flooded irregularly by tides and river overflow
		Temporarily flooded — Flooded irregularly by tides and for brief periods during growing season by river overflow
Nontidal	Inland freshwater and saline areas	Permanently flooded — Flooded throughout the year in all years
		Intermittently exposed — Flooded year-round except during extreme droughts
		Semipermanently flooded — Flooded throughout the growing season in most years
		Seasonally flooded — Flooded for extended periods in the growing season, but surface water is usually absent by the end of the growing season
		Saturated — Surface water is seldom present, but the substrate is saturated to the surface for most of the growing season
		Temporarily flooded — Flooded for only brief periods during the growing season, with the water table usually well below the soil surface for most of the season
		Intermittently flooded — The substrate is usually exposed and only flooded for variable periods without detectable seasonal periodicity (may be upland in some situations)
		Artificially flooded — Duration and amount of flooding is controlled by pumps or siphons in combination with dikes or dams

The FWS wetland classification system has provided a uniformity of wetland terminology.

fluctuations in salinity of water in a wetland and the type of salt causing the salinity determines what plant and animal species the wetland can support. The pH modifiers identify waters that are acid (pH less than 5.5), circumneutral (pH 5.5–7.4), and alkaline (pH greater than 7.4).

Soil modifiers are divided into two categories— organic and mineral. In general, if a soil has 20 percent or more organic matter by weight in the upper 16 inches, it is considered an organic soil. If it has less than this amount, it is a mineral soil.

Special modifiers are used to describe human or beaver activities. These modifiers are: excavated, impounded (obstruct outflow of water), diked (obstruct inflow of water), partly drained, farmed, and artificial (materials deposited by humans to create or modify a wetland).

Although an extensive treatment of wetlands is beyond the scope of this article, it would be incomplete without examples of the classification of some of the different wetland types. In figure 16, some of the major wetland types are listed by their common names and then classified by the FWS system. The variety of wetlands and their locations also are illustrated. For further information on wetland types, see

Mitsch and Gosselink (1986), Niering (1984), Tiner (1984, 1987, 1993b), and Wilen and Tiner (1993).

CONCLUSIONS

The FWS wetland classification system places ecologically similar habitats into a hierarchal system that permits wetland classification down to dominance types, which are based on dominant plants or substrates. The system can be used to identify units for inventory and mapping for Federal and State wetland inventories. It also has provided a uniformity of wetland terminology. The FWS uses this classification to determine wetland status and trends—information useful to resource managers and planners at all levels of government.

Since the 1954 inventory by the FWS, wetlands have changed because of natural and human-related activities. Wetland characteristics and values have become better defined, more widely known, and more appreciated. As a result, Federal and State legislation has been passed to protect wetlands, and some States have completed wetland surveys (Cowardin and others, 1979) to aid in protecting and managing this resource.

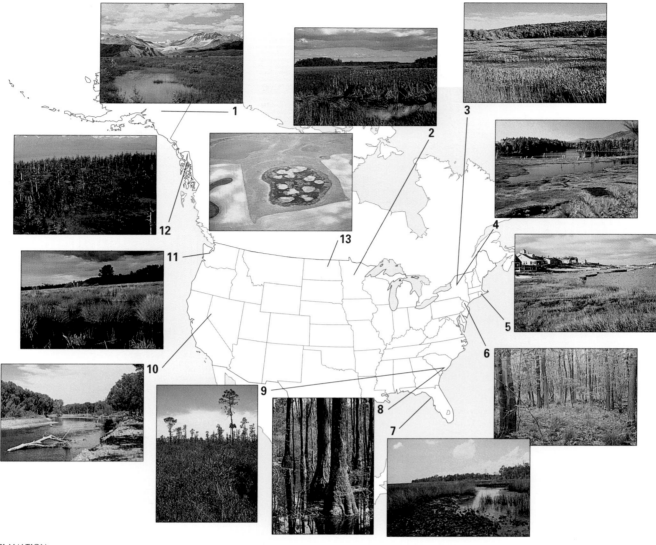

EXPLANATION

Number	General wetland type	Location	System	Subsystem	Class	Subclass	Water regime
1	Willow swamp	Alaska Range east of Paxon, Alaska	Palustrine	—	Scrub-shrub	Broad-leaved deciduous	Seasonally flooded
2	Cattail marsh	Near Brainerd, Minn.	Palustrine	—	Emergent	Persistent	Seasonally flooded
3	Inland lakeshore marsh	Lake Durant, N.Y.	Lacustrine	Littoral	Emergent	Nonpersistent	Permanently flooded
4	Floating bog	Adirondacks, N.Y.	Palustrine	—	Scrub-shrub	Broad-leaved evergreen	Saturated
5	Salt marsh	Nantucket, Mass.	Estuarine	Intertidal	Emergent	Persistent	Tidal, Irregularly flooded
6	Maple-ash swamp	Sussex County, N.J.	Palustrine	—	Forested	Broad-leaved deciduous	Seasonally flooded
7	Brackish marsh	Cedar Key, Fla.	Estuarine	Intertidal	Emergent	Persistent	Tidal, Irregularly flooded
8	Cypress-gum swamp	Francis Marion National Forest, S.C.	Palustrine	—	Forested	Needle/broad-leaved deciduous	Semipermanently flooded
9	Pocosin	Francis Marion National Forest, S.C.	Palustrine	—	Scrub-shrub	Broad-leaved evergreen	Saturated
10	Cottonwood riparian forest	Near Reno, Nev.	Palustrine	—	Forested	Broad-leaved deciduous	Temporarily flooded
11	Wet meadow	Nisqually, Wash.	Palustrine	—	Emergent	Persistent	Seasonally flooded
12	Black spruce bog	Juneau, Alaska	Palustrine	—	Forested	Needle-leaved evergreen	Saturated
13	Prairie pothole	Devil's Lake area, N. Dak.	Palustrine	—	Emergent	Nonpersistent	Semipermanently flooded

Figure 16. Examples of the classification for major wetland types in the United States, following Cowardin and others (1979). *(Note that there are no subsystems for the Palustrine System. Photograph 1 by David Dahl; 4 by Bill Zinni; 12 by Jon Hall; all others by Ralph W. Tiner. All photographers are with the U.S. Fish and Wildlife Service.)*

References Cited

Cowardin, L.M., Carter, Virginia, Golet, F.C., and LaRoe, E.T., 1979, Classification of wetlands and deepwater habitats of the United States: U.S. Fish and Wildlife Service Report FWS/OBS–79/31, 131 p.

Dachnowski, A.P., 1920, Peat deposits in the United States and their classification: Soil Science, v. 10, no. 6, p. 453–456.

Gopal, Brij, Turner, R.E., Wetzel, R.G., and Whigham, D.F., 1982, Wetlands—Ecology and management, in Proceedings of the First International Wetlands Conference, September 10–17, 1980, New Delhi, India: Jaipur, India, National Institute of Ecology and International Scientific Publications, 514 p.

Lefor, M.W., and Kennard, W.C., 1977, Inland wetland definitions: Storrs, Conn., University of Connecticut., Institute of Resources, Report 28, 63 p.

Mader, S.F., 1991, Forested wetlands classification and mapping—A literature review: New York, N.Y., National Council of the Paper Industry for Air and Stream Improvement, Inc., Technical Bulletin no. 606, 99 p.

Martin, A.C., Hotchkiss, Neil, Uhler, F.M., and Bourn, W.S., 1953, Classification of wetlands of the United States: Washington D.C., U.S. Fish and Wildlife Service Special Scientific Report, Wildlife, no. 20, 14 p.

Mitsch, W.J., and Gosselink, J.G., 1986, Wetlands: New York, N.Y., Van Nostrand Reinhold Co., Inc., 539 p.

Niering, W.A., 1984, Wetlands: New York, N.Y., Alfred A. Knopf, Inc., 638 p.

Reed, P.B., Jr., 1988, National list of plant species that occur in wetlands—National summary: Washington, D.C., U.S. Fish and Wildlife Service Biological Report, v. 88, no. 24, 244 p.

Sather, J.H., ed., 1976, National wetland classification and inventory workshop, July 20–23, 1975, College Park, Md., University of Maryland, Proceedings: Washington, D.C., U.S. Fish and Wildlife Service Report, 358 p.

Tiner, R.W., 1984, Wetlands of the United States—Current status and recent trends: Washington, D.C., U.S. Fish and Wildlife Service Report, 59 p.

_____1987, A field guide to coastal wetland plants of the northeastern United States: Amherst, Mass., University of Massachusetts Press, 285 p.

_____1989, Wetland boundary delineation, in Majumdar, S.K., Brooks, R.P., Brenner, F.J., and Tiner, R.W., Jr., eds., Wetlands ecology and conservation—Emphasis in Pennsylvania: Easton, Pa., Pennsylvania Academy of Sciences, p. 231–248.

_____1991, The concept of a hydrophyte for wetland identification: BioScience, v. 41, no. 4, p. 236–247.

_____1993a, Using plants as indicators of wetland: Philadelphia, Pa., Academy of Natural Sciences of Philadelphia, Proceedings, v. 144, p. 240–253.

_____1993b, Field guide to coastal wetland plants of the southeastern United States: Amherst, Mass., University of Massachusetts Press, 328 p.

U.S. Fish and Wildlife Service, 1976, Existing state and local wetland surveys (1965–1975), v. II, Narrative: Washington, D.C., U.S. Fish and Wildlife Service, Office of Biological Services Report, 453 p.

U.S. Soil Conservation Service, 1991, Hydric soils of the United States: Washington, D.C., in cooperation with the National Technical Committee for Hydric Soils, U.S. Department of Agriculture, Miscellaneous publication 1491.

Wilen, B.O., and Tiner, R.W., 1993, Wetlands of the United States, in Whigham, D.F., Dykyjová, Dagmar, and Hejny, Slavomil, eds., Wetlands of the world I: Dordrecht, Netherlands, Kluwer Academic Publishers, p. 515–636.

Wright, J.O., 1907, Swamp and overflowed lands in the United States: Washington, D.C., U.S. Department of Agriculture, Office of Experiment Stations, Circular 76, 23 p.

FOR ADDITIONAL INFORMATION: Ralph W. Tiner, U.S. Fish and Wildlife Service, 300 Westgate Center Drive, Hadley, MA 01035

Technical Aspects of Wetlands
Wetland Hydrology, Water Quality, and Associated Functions

By Virginia Carter[1]

The formation, persistence, size, and function of wetlands are controlled by hydrologic processes. Distribution and differences in wetland type, vegetative composition, and soil type are caused primarily by geology, topography, and climate. Differences also are the product of the movement of water through or within the wetland, water quality, and the degree of natural or human-induced disturbance. In turn, the wetland soils and vegetation alter water velocities, flow paths, and chemistry. The hydrologic and water-quality functions of wetlands, that is, the roles wetlands play in changing the quantity or quality of water moving through them, are related to the wetland's physical setting.

Wetlands are distributed unevenly throughout the United States because of differences in geology, climate, and source of water (fig. 17). They occur in widely diverse settings ranging from coastal margins, where tides and river discharge are the primary sources of water, to high mountain valleys where rain and snowmelt are the primary sources of water. Marine wetlands (those beaches and rocky shores that fringe the open ocean) are found in all coastal States. Estuarine wetlands (where tidal saltwater and inland freshwater meet and mix) are most plentiful in Alaska and along the southeastern Atlantic coast and the gulf coast. Alaska has the largest acreage of estuarine wetlands in the United States, followed by Florida and Louisiana.

Inland (nontidal) wetlands are found in all States. Some States, such as West Virginia, have few large wetlands, but contain many small wetlands associated with streams. Other States, such as Nebraska, the Dakotas, and Texas, contain many small isolated wetlands—the lakes of the Nebraska Sandhills, the prairie potholes, and the playa lakes, respectively. Northern States such as Minnesota and Maine contain numerous wetlands with organic soils (peatlands), similar in origin and hydrologic and veg-

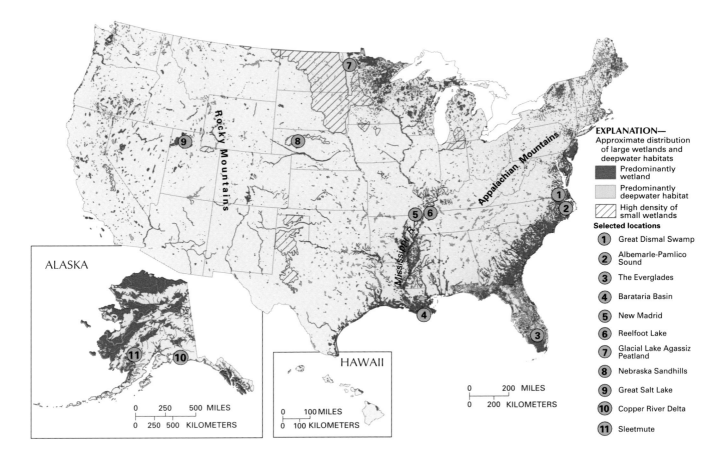

EXPLANATION—
Approximate distribution of large wetlands and deepwater habitats

- Predominantly wetland
- Predominantly deepwater habitat
- High density of small wetlands

Selected locations

1. Great Dismal Swamp
2. Albemarle-Pamlico Sound
3. The Everglades
4. Barataria Basin
5. New Madrid
6. Reelfoot Lake
7. Glacial Lake Agassiz Peatland
8. Nebraska Sandhills
9. Great Salt Lake
10. Copper River Delta
11. Sleetmute

Figure 17. Major wetland areas in the United States and location of sites mentioned in the text. (*Source: Data from T.E. Dahl, U.S. Fish and Wildlife Service, unpub. data, 1991.*)

[1] U.S. Geological Survey.

Typical prairie pothole wetland in North Dakota. *(Photograph by Virginia Carter, U.S. Geological Survey.)*

Glacial Lake Agassiz peatland, Minnesota. *(Photograph by Virginia Carter, U.S. Geological Survey.)*

etative characteristics to the classic bog and fen peatlands of northern Europe. However, peatlands are by no means limited to Northern States—they occur in the Southeastern and Midwestern United States wherever the hydrology and chemical environment are conducive to the accumulation of organic material.

Wetlands occur on flood plains—for example, the broad bottom-land hardwood forests and river swamps (forested wetlands) of southern rivers and many of the narrow riparian zones along streams in the Western United States. Wetlands are commonly associated with lakes or can occur as isolated features of the landscape. They can form large complexes of open water and vegetation such as The Everglades of Florida, the Okefenokee Swamp of Georgia and Florida, the Copper River Delta of Alaska, and the Glacial Lake Agassiz peatland of Minnesota.

HYDROLOGIC PROCESSES IN WETLANDS

Hydrologic processes occurring in wetlands are the same processes that occur outside of wetlands and collectively are referred to as the hydrologic cycle. Major components of the hydrologic cycle are precipitation, surface-water flow, ground-water flow, and evapotranspiration (ET). Wetlands and uplands continually receive or lose water through exchange with the atmosphere, streams, and ground water. Both a favorable geologic setting and an adequate and persistent supply of water are necessary for the existence of wetlands.

The wetland water budget is the total of inflows and outflows of water from a wetland. The components of a budget are shown in the equation in figures 18 and 19. The relative importance of each component in maintaining wetlands varies both spatially and

Figure 18. Components of the wetland water budget. (P + SWI + GWI = ET + SWO + GWO + ΔS, where P is precipitation, SWI is surface-water inflow, SWO is surface-water outflow, GWI is ground-water inflow, GWO is ground-water outflow, ET is evapotranspiration, and ΔS is change in storage.)

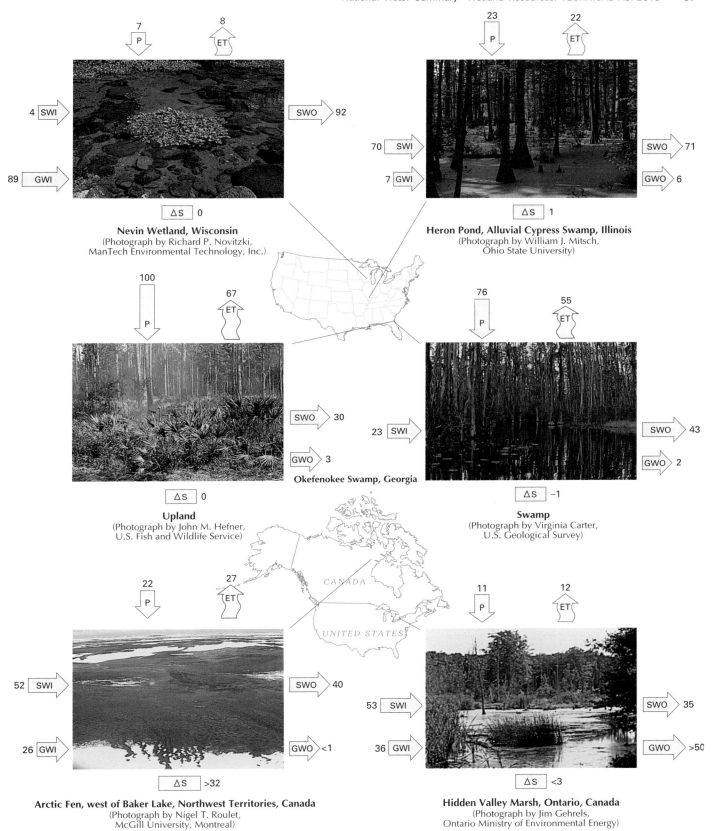

Figure 19. Water budgets for selected wetlands in the United States and Canada. (P + SWI + GWI = ET + SWO + GWO + ΔS, where P is precipitation, SWI is surface-water inflow, SWO is surface-water outflow, GWI is ground-water inflow, GWO is ground-water outflow, ET is evapotranspiration, and ΔS is change in storage. Components are expressed in percentages. Abbreviations used: < = less than; > = greater than.) (*Sources from left to right and top to bottom: Novitzki, 1978; Roulet and Woo, 1986; Rykiel, 1984; Rykiel, 1984; Mitsch and Gosselink, 1993; and Gehrels and Mulamoottil, 1990.*)

temporally, but all these components interact to create the hydrology of an individual wetland.

The relative importance of each of the components of the hydrologic cycle differs from wetland to wetland (fig. 19). Isolated basin wetlands, typified by prairie potholes and playa lakes, receive direct precipitation and some runoff from surrounding uplands, and sometimes receive ground-water inflow. They lose water to ET; some lose water that seeps to ground water, and some overflow during periods of excessive precipitation and runoff. These wetlands range from very wet to dry depending on seasonal and long-term climatic cycles. Wetlands on lake or river flood plains also receive direct precipitation and runoff and commonly receive ground-water inflow. In addition, they can be flooded when lakes or rivers are high. Water drains back to the lake or river as floodwaters recede. Wet and dry cycles in these wetlands commonly are closely related to lake and river water-level fluctuations. Coastal wetlands, while also receiving direct precipitation, runoff, and ground-water inflow, are strongly influenced by tidal cycles. Peatlands with raised centers may receive only direct precipitation or may be affected by ground-water inflow also. Surface-water inflows affect only the edges of these wetlands.

Determining water budgets for wetlands is imprecise because as the climate varies from year to year so does the water balance. The accuracy of individual components depends on how well they can be measured and the magnitude of the associated errors (Winter, 1981; Carter, 1986). However, water budgets, in conjunction with information on the local geology, provide a basis for understanding the hydrologic processes and water chemistry of a wetland, understanding its functions, and predicting the effects of natural or human-induced hydrologic alterations. Each of the components is discussed below.

> *Water budgets provide a basis for understanding hydrologic processes of a wetland.*

Precipitation

Precipitation is any form of water, such as rain, snow, sleet, hail, or mist, that falls from the atmosphere and reaches the ground. Precipitation provides water for wetlands directly and indirectly. Water is provided for a wetland directly when precipitation falls on the wetland or indirectly when precipitation falls outside the wetland and is transported to the wetland by surface- or ground-water flow. For example, snow that falls on wetland basins provides surface-water flow to wetlands during spring snowmelt. Snowmelt may also recharge ground water, sustaining ground-water discharge to wetlands during summer, fall, and winter.

The distribution of precipitation across the United States is affected by major climatic patterns. In North America, maximum rainfall is found on the western slopes of mountain ranges in the West, along the east coast, and in Hawaii. Tropical areas such as Florida and Puerto Rico also receive large quantities of precipitation. By contrast, precipitation is minimal in the continental interior where the atmosphere is dry; the driest part of North America is the southwestern desert. Wetlands are most abundant in areas with ample precipitation.

Evapotranspiration

The loss of water to the atmosphere is an important component of the wetland water budget. Water is removed by evaporation from soil or surfaces of water bodies and by transpiration by plants (fig. 20). The combined loss of water by evaporation and transpiration is termed evapotranspiration (ET). Solar radiation, windspeed and turbulence, relative humidity, available soil moisture, and vegetation type and density affect the rate of ET. Evaporation can be measured fairly easily, but ET measurements, which require measuring how much water is being transpired by plants on a daily, weekly, seasonal, or yearly basis, are much more difficult to make. For this reason scientists use a variety of formulas to estimate ET and there is some controversy regarding the best formula and the accuracy of these estimates (Gehrels and Mulamoottil, 1990; Carter, 1986; Dolan and others, 1984; Idso, 1981).

Evapotranspiration is highly variable both seasonally and daily (Dolan and others, 1984). ET losses from wetlands vary with plant species, plant density, and plant status (whether the plants are actively growing or are dormant). Seasonal changes in ET also relate to the water-table position (Ingram, 1983) (more water evaporates from the soil or is transpired by plants when the water table is closer to land surface) and also to temperature changes (more water evaporates or is transpired in hot weather than in cold). Daily ET rates are controlled chiefly by the energy available to evaporate water—there is generally less at night and on cool, cloudy days.

Surface Water

Surface water may be permanently, seasonally, or temporarily present in a wetland. Surface water is supplied to wetlands through normal streamflow, flooding from lakes and rivers, overland flow, ground-water discharge, and tides. Ground water discharged into wetlands also becomes surface water. Surface-water outflow from wetlands is greatest during the wet season and especially during flooding. Surface water may flow in channels or across the surface of a wetland. Flow paths and velocity of water over the surface of a wetland are affected by the topography and vegetation within the wetland.

Streamflow from wetlands that have a large component of ground-water discharge tends to be more evenly distributed throughout the year than stream-

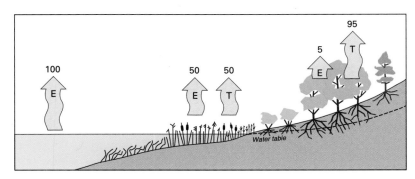

Figure 20. Percentage of transpiration and evaporation from various wetland components. (E, evaporation; T, transpiration.)

flow from wetlands fed primarily by precipitation (fig. 21).This is because ground-water discharge tends to be relatively constant in quantity compared with precipitation and snowmelt.

In coastal areas, tides provide a regular and predictable source of surface water for wetlands, affecting erosion, deposition, and water chemistry. The magnitude of daily high and low tides is affected by the relative position of the sun and the moon—highest and lowest tides usually occur during full or new moons. Where tidal circulation is impeded by barrier islands (for example, in the Albemarle-Pamlico Sound in North Carolina, where tides are primarily wind-driven) or dikes and levees, tidal circulation may be small or highly modified. Strong winds and storms can cause extreme changes in sea level, flooding both wetlands and uplands.

Ground Water

Ground water originates as precipitation or as seepage from surface-water bodies. Precipitation moves slowly downward through unsaturated soils and rocks until it reaches the saturated zone. Water also seeps from lakes, rivers, and wetlands into the saturated zone. This process is known as ground-water recharge and the top of the saturated zone is known as the water table. Ground water in the saturated zone flows through aquifers or aquifer systems composed of permeable rocks or other earth materials in response to hydraulic heads (pressure). Ground water can flow in shallow local aquifer systems where water is near the land surface or in deeper intermediate and regional aquifer systems (fig. 22). Differences in hydraulic head cause ground water to move back to the land surface or into surface-water bodies; this process is called ground-water discharge. In wetlands that are common discharge areas for different flow systems, waters from different sources can mix. Ground-water discharge occurs through wells, seepage or springs, and directly through ET where the water table is near the land surface or plant roots reach the water table. Ground-water discharge will influence the water chemistry of the receiving wetland whereas ground-water recharge will influence the chemistry of water in the adjacent aquifer.

Wetlands most commonly are ground-water discharge areas; however, ground-water recharge also occurs. Ground-water recharge or discharge in wetlands is affected by topographic position, hydrogeology, sediment and soil characteristics, season, ET, and climate and might not occur uniformly throughout a wetland. Recharge rates in wetlands can be much slower than those in adjacent uplands if the upland soils are more permeable than the slightly permeable clays or peat that usually underlie wetlands.

The accumulation and composition of peat in wetlands are important factors influencing hydrology and vegetation. It was long assumed that the discharge of ground water through thick layers of well-decomposed peat was negligible because of its low permeability, but recent studies have shown that these layers can transmit ground water more rapidly than previously thought (Chason and Siegel, 1986). Peatland type (fen or bog) and plant communities are affected by the chemistry of water in the surface lay-

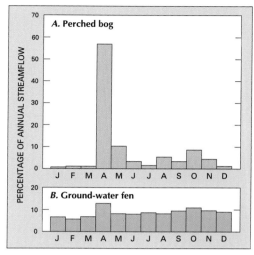

Figure 21. Monthly streamflow from two wetlands in northern Minnesota; **A**, a perched bog whose inflow component is primarily precipitation, and **B**, a fen whose inflow component is primarily ground water. *(Source: Modified from Boelter and Verry, 1977.)*

ers of the wetland; the source of water (precipitation, surface water, or ground water) controls the water chemistry and determines what nutrients are available for plant growth. Ground-water flow in extensive peatlands such as the Glacial Lake Agassiz peatland in Minnesota may be controlled by the development of ground-water mounds (elevated water tables fed by precipitation) in raised bogs where ground water moves downward through mineral soils before discharging into adjacent fens (Siegel, 1983; Siegel and Glaser, 1987). Movement of the ground water through mineral soils increases the nutrient content of the water.

Coastal wetlands and shallow embayments represent the lowest point in regional and local ground-water flow systems; ground water discharges into these areas, sometimes in quantities large enough to affect the chemistry of estuaries (Valiela and Costa, 1988;

The hydrology of a wetland is largely responsible for the vegetation of the wetland.

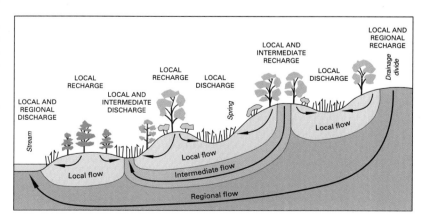

Figure 22. Ground-water flow systems. Local ground-water flow systems are recharged at topographic highs and discharged at immediately adjacent lows. Regional ground-water flow systems are recharged at the major regional topographic highs and discharged at the major regional topographic lows. Intermediate flow systems lie between the other two systems. *(Source: Modified from Winter, 1976.)*

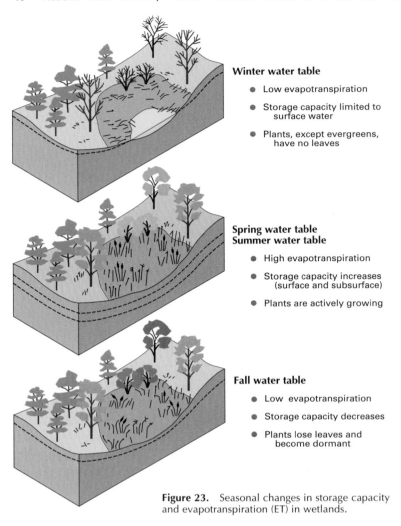

Winter water table
- Low evapotranspiration
- Storage capacity limited to surface water
- Plants, except evergreens, have no leaves

Spring water table
Summer water table
- High evapotranspiration
- Storage capacity increases (surface and subsurface)
- Plants are actively growing

Fall water table
- Low evapotranspiration
- Storage capacity decreases
- Plants lose leaves and become dormant

Figure 23. Seasonal changes in storage capacity and evapotranspiration (ET) in wetlands.

Valiela and others, 1990). The quantity of ground water discharged varies throughout the tidal cycle, affecting the water chemistry of the wetland soils (Harvey and Odum, 1990; Valiela and others, 1990).

Storage

Storage in a wetland consists of surface water, soil moisture, and ground water. Storage capacity refers to the space available for water storage—the higher the water table, the less the storage capacity of a wetland. Some wetlands have continuously high water tables, but generally, the water table fluctuates seasonally in response to rainfall and ET. Storage capacity of wetlands is lowest when the water table is near or at the surface—during the dormant season when plants are not transpiring, following snowmelt, and (or) during the wet season (fig. 23). Storage capacity increases during the growing season as water tables decline and ET increases. When storage capacity is high, infiltration may occur and the wetland may be effective in retarding runoff. When water tables are high and storage capacity is low, any additional water that enters the wetland runs off the wetland rapidly.

The vegetation affects the value of the wetland to animals and people.

SOME EFFECTS OF HYDROLOGY ON WETLAND VEGETATION

The hydrology of a wetland is largely responsible for the vegetation of the wetland, which in turn affects the value of the wetland to animals and people. The duration and seasonality of flooding and (or) soil saturation, ground-water level, soil type, and drainage characteristics exert a strong influence on the number, type, and distribution of plants and plant communities in wetlands. Although much is known about flooding tolerance in plants, the effect of soil saturation in the root zone is less well understood. Golet and Lowry (1987) showed that surface flooding and duration of saturation within the root zone, while not the only factors influencing plant growth, accounted for as much as 50 percent of the variation in growth of some plants. Plant distribution is also closely related to wetland water chemistry; the water may be fresh or saline, acidic or basic, depending on the source(s).

HYDROGEOLOGIC SETTINGS

The source and movement of water are very important for assessing wetland function and predicting how changes in wetlands will affect the associated basin. Linkages between wetlands, uplands, and deepwater habitats provide a framework for protection and management of wetland resources. Water moving into wetlands has chemical and physical characteristics that reflect its source. Older ground water generally contains chemicals associated with the rocks through which it has moved; younger ground water has fewer minerals because it has had less time in contact with the rocks. Which processes can and will occur within the wetland are determined by the characteristics of the water entering and the characteristics of the wetland itself—its size, shape, soils, plants, and position in the basin.

Because wetlands occur in a variety of geologic and physiographic settings, attempts have been made to group or classify them in such a way as to identify similarities in hydrology. For example, Novitzki (1979, 1982) developed a hydrologic classification for Wisconsin wetlands based on topographic position and surface water-ground water interaction; Gosselink and Turner (1978) grouped freshwater wetlands according to hydrodynamic energy gradients; and Brinson (1993) developed a hydrogeomorphic classification for use in evaluating wetland function. (See the articles "Wetland Definitions and Classifications in the United States" and "Wetland Functions, Values, and Assessment" in this volume.) Wetlands, like lakes, are associated with features where water tends to collect. They are commonly found in topographic depressions, at slope breaks, in areas of stratigraphic change, and in permafrost areas (fig. 24) (Winter and Woo, 1990).

Topographic Depressions

Most wetlands occur in or originate in topographic depressions—these include lakes, wetland basins, and river valleys (fig. 24A). Depressions may be formed by movement of glaciers and water; action of wind, waves, and tides; and (or) by processes associated with tectonics, subsidence, or collapse.

Glacial movement.—Glaciers shaped the landscape of many of the Northern States and caused wetlands to form in mountainous areas such as the Rocky Mountains and the northern Appalachians. As the glaciers advanced over the Northern United States they gouged and scoured the land surface, making numerous depressions, depositing unsorted glacial materials, and burying large ice masses. As the climate warmed, the glaciers retreated, leaving behind the depressions and the large masses of buried ice. As the temperatures continued to warm, the ice masses melted to form kettle holes. In many cases, water filled the depressions and kettle holes, forming lakes. As the lakes filled with sediments, they were replaced by wetlands.

Water movement.—Wetlands also are formed by the movement of water as it flows from upland areas toward the coast. The flow characteristics of water are partly determined by the slope of the streambed. On steeply sloping land, water generally flows rapidly through relatively deep, well-defined channels. As the slope decreases, the water spreads out over a wider area and channels usually become shallower and less defined. Shallow channels tend to meander or move back and forth across the flood plain. The changes in flow path sometimes result in oxbow lakes and floodplain wetlands. When the river floods, the isolated oxbow lakes begin to fill with sediment, providing an excellent place for more wetlands to form. Obstruction to the normal flow of water also can cause the water to change course and leave gouges in front of or channels around the obstruction, or can cause water to be impounded behind the obstruction. Many lakes and wetlands are formed behind dams made by humans or beavers.

Wind, wave, and tidal action.—Wetlands are common in areas of sand dunes caused by wind, waves, or tides. Wetlands formed in the depressions between sand dunes are found in the Nebraska Sandhills, along the shoreline of the Great Lakes, and on barrier islands and the seaward margins of coastal States. In coastal States, tides, waves, and wind cause the movement of sand barriers and the closing of inlets, which often result in the formation of shallow lagoons with abundant associated emergent wetlands.

Tectonic activities.—Tectonic activity is responsible for depression wetlands such as Reelfoot Lake on the Mississippi River flood plain in Tennessee caused by the 1812 New Madrid earthquake. Earthquakes result when two parts of the Earth's crust move relative to each other, causing displacement of land. When this occurs, depressions may result along the lines of displacement or the flow paths of rivers may be changed, leaving isolated bodies of water. When a source of water coincides with these depressions, wetlands can form.

Subsidence and collapse features.—Land subsidence and collapse also can form depressions in which wetlands and lakes occur. In some areas, especially in the Southwest, pumping of ground water has caused the land above an aquifer to sink, forming depressions where water collects and wetlands develop. In karst topography (landscapes resulting from the solution of carbonate rocks such as limestone), such as is found in Florida, wetlands form in sinkholes. Collapse of volcanic craters produces

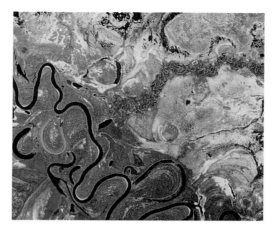

Infrared color photograph of oxbow lakes in the drainage area of Hoholitna River near Sleetmute, Alaska. *(Photograph courtesy of National Aeronautics and Space Administration.)*

Lotus in Reelfoot Lake, Tennessee. *(Photograph by Virginia Carter, U.S. Geological Survey.)*

Coastal marsh along San Francisco Bay, California. *(Photograph by Virginia Carter, U.S. Geological Survey.)*

This recently collapsed sinkhole, in central Florida, provides an ideal spot for a wetland to form. *(Photograph by Terry H. Thompson, U.S. Geological Survey.)*

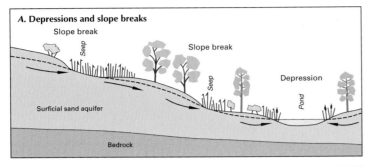

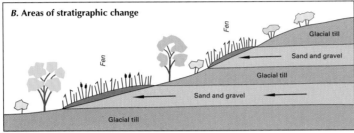

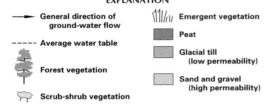

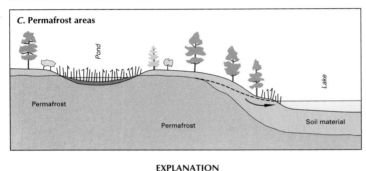

EXPLANATION

→ General direction of ground-water flow

〰 Emergent vegetation

---- Average water table

■ Peat

🌲 Forest vegetation

▨ Glacial till (low permeability)

☁ Scrub-shrub vegetation

▢ Sand and gravel (high permeability)

Figure 24. Cross sections showing principal hydrogeologic settings for wetlands; *A,* slope break and depression, *B,* area of stratigraphic change, and *C,* permafrost area.

calderas that fill with water and sediment and contain lakes or wetlands.

Slope Breaks

The water table sometimes intersects the land surface in areas where the land is sloping. Where there is an upward break or change in slope, ground water moves toward the water table in the flatter landscape (fig. 24A) (Roulet, 1990; Winter and Woo, 1990). Where ground water discharges to the land surface, wetlands form on the lower parts of the slope. Constant ground-water seepage maintains soil saturation and wetland plant communities. The Great Dismal Swamp of Virginia and North Carolina is maintained by seepage of ground water at the slope break at the bottom of an ancient beach ridge that runs along the western edge (Carter and others, 1994).

Areas of Stratigraphic Change

Where stratigraphic changes occur near land surface, the layering of permeable and less-permeable rocks or soils affects the movement of ground water. When water flowing through the more permeable rock encounters the less permeable rock, it is diverted along the surface of the less permeable rock to the land surface. The continual seepage that occurs at the surface provides the necessary moisture for a wetland (fig. 24B). Fens in Iowa form on valley-wall slopes where a thin permeable horizontal layer of rock is sandwiched between two less permeable layers and continual seepage from the permeable layer causes the formation of peat (Thompson and others, 1992).

Permafrost Areas

Permafrost is defined as soil material with a temperature continuously below 32°F (Fahrenheit) for more than 1 year (Brown, 1974); both arctic and subarctic wetlands in Alaska are affected by permafrost (figs. 24C and 25). Permafrost has low permeability and infiltration rates. As a result, recharge through permafrost is extremely slow (Ford and Bedford, 1987). In areas covered by peat, organic silt, or dense vegetation, permafrost is commonly close to the surface. In areas covered by lakes, streams, and ponds, permafrost can be absent or at great depth below the surface-water body. The surface or active layer of permafrost thaws during the growing season. In areas where permafrost is continuous, there is virtually no hydraulic connection between ground water in the surface layer and ground water below the permafrost zone. The imperviousness of the frozen soil slows drainage and causes water to stand in surface depressions, forming wetlands and shallow lakes.

In discontinuous permafrost areas (fig. 25), unfrozen zones on south-facing slopes (in the northern hemisphere) and under lakes, wetlands, and large rivers provide hydraulic connections between the surface and the ground water below the permafrost zone. Ground-water discharge to wetlands from deeper aquifers can occur through the unfrozen zone (Williams and Waller, 1966; Kane and Slaughter, 1973). In discontinuous permafrost regions, whether a slope faces away from or toward the sun can determine the presence or absence of permafrost and thus influence the location and distribution of wetlands (Dingman and Koutz, 1974). Permafrost is sensitive to factors that upset the thermal equilibrium. Thermokarst features (depressions in the land surface caused by thawing and subsequent settling of the land) may be caused by regional climatic change or human activities. These depressions formed by local thawing of permafrost are usually filled with wetlands.

WATER QUALITY IN WETLANDS

The water chemistry of wetlands is primarily a result of geologic setting, water balance (relative proportions of inflow, outflow, and storage), quality of inflowing water, type of soils and vegetation, and human activity within or near the wetland. Wetlands

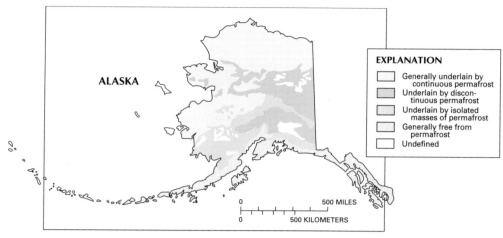

Figure 25. Continuous, discontinuous, and sporadic permafrost areas of Alaska. *(Source: Modified from Ford and Bedford, 1987.)*

dominated by surface-water inflow and outflow reflect the chemistry of the associated rivers or lakes. Those wetlands that receive surface-water or ground-water inflow, have limited outflow, and lose water primarily to ET have a high concentration of chemicals and contain brackish or saline (salty) water. Examples of such wetlands are the saline playas, wetlands associated with the Great Salt Lake in Utah, and the permanent and semipermanent prairie potholes. In contrast, wetlands that receive water primarily from precipitation and lose water by way of surface-water outflows and (or) seepage to ground water tend to have lower concentrations of chemicals. Wetlands influenced strongly by ground-water discharge have water chemistries similar to ground water. In most cases, wetlands receive water from more than one source, so the resultant water chemistry is a composite chemistry of the various sources.

Plants can serve as indicators of wetland chemistry. In tidal wetlands, the distribution of salty water influences plant communities and species diversity. In freshwater wetlands, pH (a measure of acidity or alkalinity) and mineral and nutrient content influence plant abundance and species diversity.

HYDROLOGIC AND WATER-QUALITY FUNCTIONS OF WETLANDS

Wetland hydrologic and water-quality functions are the roles that wetlands play in modifying or controlling the quantity or quality of water moving through a wetland. An understanding of wetland functions and the underlying chemical, physical, and biological processes supporting these functions facilitates the management and protection of wetlands and their associated basins.

The hydrologic and water-quality functions of wetlands are controlled by the following:
- Landscape position (elevation in the drainage basin relative to other wetlands, lakes, and streams)
- Topographic location (depressions, flood plains, slopes)
- Presence or absence of vegetation
- Type of vegetation

- Type of soil
- The relative amounts of water flowing in and water flowing out of the wetland
- Local climate
- The hydrogeologic framework
- The geochemistry of surface and ground water

Although broad generalizations regarding wetland functions can be made, effectiveness and magnitude of functions differ from wetland to wetland.

Natural functions of wetlands can be altered or impaired by human activity. Although slow incremental changes in the natural landscape can lead to small changes in wetlands, the accumulation of these small changes can permanently alter the wetland function (Brinson, 1988). Some of the major hydrologic and water-quality functions of wetlands—(1) flood storage and stormflow modification, (2) ground-water recharge and discharge, (3) alterations of precipitation and evaporation, (4) maintenance of water quality, (5) maintenance of estuarine water balance, and (6) erosion reduction—are discussed below.

Flood Storage and Stormflow Modification

Wetlands associated with lakes and streams store floodwaters by spreading water out over a large flat area. This temporary storage of water decreases runoff velocity, reduces flood peaks, and distributes stormflows over longer time periods, causing tributary and main channels to peak at different times. Wetlands with available storage capacity or those located in depressions with narrow outlets may store and release water over an extended period of time. In drainage basins with flat terrain that contains many depressions (for example, the prairie potholes and playa lake regions), lakes and wetlands store large volumes of snowmelt and (or) runoff. These wetlands have no natural outlets, and therefore this water is retained and does not contribute to local or regional flooding.

A strong correlation exists between the size of flood peaks and basin storage (percentage of basin area occupied by lakes and wetlands) in many drainage basins throughout the United States (Tice, 1968;

The effectiveness and magnitude of a function varies from wetland to wetland.

Hains, 1973; Novitzki, 1979, 1989; Leibowitz and others, 1992). Novitzki (1979, 1989) found that basins with 30 percent or more areal coverage by lakes and wetlands have flood peaks that are 60 to 80 percent lower than the peaks in basins with no lake or wetland area. Wetlands can provide cost-effective flood control, and in some instances their protection has been recognized as less costly than flood-control measures such as reservoirs or dikes (Carter and others, 1979). Loss of wetlands can result in severe and costly flood damage in low-lying areas of a basin.

Not all wetlands are able to store floodwaters or modify stormflow; some, in fact, add to runoff. Downstream wetlands, such as those along the middle and lower reaches of the Mississippi River and its tributaries, are more effective at reducing downstream flooding than are headwater wetlands, largely as a result of larger storage capacities (Ogawa and Male, 1986). Runoff from wetlands is strongly influenced by season, available storage capacity, and soil permeability. Wetlands in basin headwaters are commonly sources of runoff because they are ground-water discharge areas. Wetlands in Alaska that are underlain by permafrost have little or no available storage capacity; runoff is rapid and flood peaks are often very high.

Ground-Water Recharge and Discharge

Ground-water recharge and discharge are hydrologic processes that occur throughout the landscape and are not unique functions of wetlands. Recharge and discharge in wetlands are strongly influenced by local hydrogeology, topographic position, ET, wetland soils, season, and climate. Ground-water discharge provides water necessary to the survival of the wetland and also can provide water that leaves the wetland as streamflow. Most wetlands are primarily discharge areas; in these wetlands, however, small amounts of recharge can occur seasonally.

Recharge to aquifers can be especially important in areas where ground water is withdrawn for agricultural, industrial, and municipal purposes. Wetlands can provide either substantial or limited recharge to aquifers. Much of the recharge to the Ogallala aquifer in West Texas and New Mexico is from the 20,000 to 30,000 playa lakes rather than from areas between lakes, ephemeral streams, and areas of sand dunes (Wood and Osterkamp, 1984; Wood and Sanford, 1994). Recharge takes place through the bottoms of some streams, especially in karst topography and in the arid West. Some recharge also takes place when floodwater moves across the flood plain and seeps down into the water-table aquifer. Cypress domes in Florida and prairie potholes in the Dakotas also are thought to contribute to ground-water recharge (Carter and others, 1979). Ground-water recharge from a wetland can be induced when aquifer water levels have been drawn down by nearby pumping.

Most estuarine wetlands are discharge areas rather than recharge areas, primarily because they are on the low topographic end of local and regional ground-water flow systems. As the tide rises, water is temporarily stored on the surface of the wetland and in the wetland soils, where it mixes with the discharging freshwater. The water moves back into the estuary or tidal river as the tide ebbs. Precipitation fall-

ing on nontidal freshwater wetlands on barrier islands may recharge the shallow freshwater aquifer overlying the deeper salty water.

Alterations of Precipitation and Evaporation

Wetlands can influence local or regional weather and climate in several ways. Wetlands tend to moderate seasonal temperature fluctuations. During the summer, wetlands maintain lower temperatures because ET from the wetland converts latent heat and releases water vapor to the atmosphere. In the winter, the warmer water of the wetland prevents rapid cooling at night; warm breezes from the wetland surface may prevent freezing in nearby uplands. Wetlands also modify local atmospheric circulation and thus affect moisture convection, cloud formation, thunderstorms, and precipitation patterns. Therefore, when wetlands are drained or replaced by impermeable materials, significant changes in weather systems can occur.

Maintenance of Water Quality

Ground water and surface water transport sediments, nutrients, trace metals, and organic materials. Wetlands can trap, precipitate, transform, recycle, and export many of these waterborne constituents, and water leaving the wetland can differ markedly from that entering (Mitsch and Gosselink, 1993; Elder, 1987). Wetlands can maintain good quality water and improve degraded water.

Water-quality modification can affect an entire drainage basin or it may affect only an individual wetland. Water chemistry in basins that contain a large proportion of wetlands is usually different from that in basins with fewer wetlands. Basins with more wetlands tend to have water with lower specific conductance and lower concentrations of chloride, lead, inorganic nitrogen, suspended solids, and total and dissolved phosphorus than basins with fewer wetlands. Generally, wetlands are more effective at removing suspended solids, total phosphorus, and ammonia during high-flow periods and more effective at removing nitrates at low-flow periods (Johnston and others, 1990). Novitzki (1979) reported that streams in a Wisconsin basin, which contained 40 percent wetland and lake area, had sediment loads that were 90 percent lower than in a comparable basin with no wetlands. Wetlands may change water chemistry sequentially; that is, upstream wetlands may serve as the source of materials that are transformed in downstream wetlands. Estuaries and tidal rivers depend on the flow of freshwater, sediments, nutrients, and other constituents from upstream.

Wetlands filter out or transform natural and anthropogenic constituents through a variety of biological and chemical processes. Wetlands act as sinks (where material is trapped and held) for some materials and sources (from which material is removed) of others. For example, wetlands are a major sink for heavy metals and for sulfur, which combines with metals to form relatively insoluble compounds. Some wetland mineral deposits (bog iron, manganese) are or have been important metal reserves in the past. Organic carbon in the form of plant tissues and peat

Wetlands can influence weather and climate.

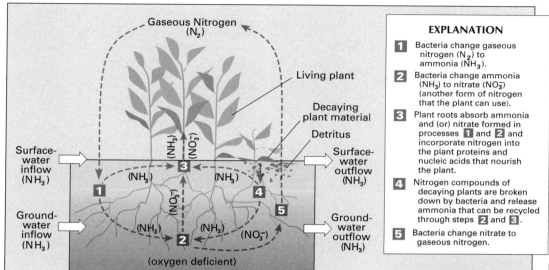

Figure 26. Simplified diagram of the nitrogen cycle in a wetland.

accumulates in wetlands creating a source of water-borne dissolved and particulate organic materials. Some materials, for example nutrients, are changed from one form to another as they pass through the wetland (fig. 26). Most stored materials in wetlands are immobilized as a result of prevailing water chemistry and hydrology, but any disturbance can result in release of those materials.

The water purification functions of wetlands are dependent upon four principal components of the wetland—substrate, water, vegetation, and microbial populations (Hammer, 1992; Hemond and others, 1987).

Substrates.—Wetland substrates provide a reactive surface for biogeochemical reactions and habitat for microbes. Wetland soils are the medium in which many of the wetland chemical transformations occur and the primary storage area of available chemicals for most plants (Mitsch and Gosselink, 1993). Organic or peat soils differ from mineral soils in their biogeochemical properties, including their ability to hold water and bind or immobilize mineral constituents.

Water.—Ground and surface waters transport solid materials and gases to the microbial and plant communities, remove the by-products of chemical and biological reactions from the wetlands, and maintain the environment in which the essential biochemical processes of wetlands occur. Flooding or soil saturation causes oxygen-deficient conditions that markedly influence many biological transformations.

Vegetation.—Wetland vegetation reduces the flow and decreases velocities of water, causing the deposition of mineral and organic particles and constituents attached to them, such as phosphorus or trace metals. Plants introduce oxygen to the generally oxygen-deficient soil environment through their roots, creating an oxidized root zone where bacterial transformations of nitrogenous and other compounds can occur (Good and Patrick, 1987). Plants also provide a surface for microbial colonization. Wetland plants remove small quantities of nutrients, trace metals, and other compounds from the soil water and incorporate

them into plant tissue, which may later be recycled in the wetland through decomposition, stored as peat, or transported from the wetland as particulate matter (Boyt and others, 1977; Tilton and Kadlec, 1979; Hammer, 1992).

Microbes.—The microbial community, which includes bacteria, algae, fungi, and protozoa, is responsible for most of the chemical transformations that occur in wetlands. In order to meet their metabolic needs, microbes use up oxygen; transform nutrients, manganese, and iron; and generate methane, hydrogen sulfide gas, and carbon dioxide.

Wetlands serve as short-term or long-term sediment sinks. Floodwater spreading out across a wetland decreases in velocity, and sediments settle out and are trapped within the wetland. Some of this sediment may be transported out of the wetland during future flooding. Sediment deposition in estuarine wetlands provides a constant input that is of special importance for maintenance of wetlands acreage during periods of sea-level rise (Bricker-Urso and others, 1989).

The ability of wetlands to filter and transform nutrients and other constituents has resulted in the construction and use of artificial wetlands in the United States and other countries to treat wastewater and acid mine drainage (Hammer, 1989, 1992; Wieder, 1989). However, individual wetlands have a limited capacity to absorb nutrients and differ in their ability to do so (Tiner, 1985). A wetland's effectiveness in improving water quality depends on hydrologic patterns, amount and type of vegetation, time of year, and the constituent of concern (Zedler and others, 1985).

Estuarine Water Balance

Estuaries receive freshwater from precipitation, ground-water discharge, streamflow, and overland flow. Ground water discharges through shallow-water sediments of the estuary or through marsh soils and can affect the nutrient balance and salinity of the

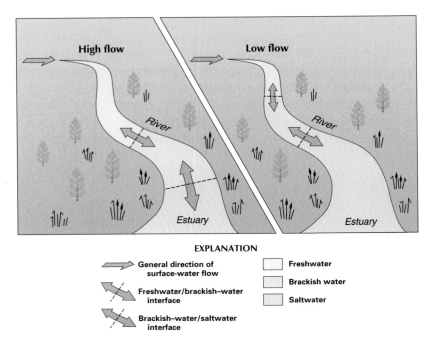

EXPLANATION

➡ General direction of surface-water flow

⤢ Freshwater/brackish–water interface

⤢ Brackish–water/saltwater interface

☐ Freshwater

☐ Brackish water

☐ Saltwater

Figure 27. Movement of the freshwater-saltwater interface in an estuary during periods of high flow and during periods of low flow.

and shallow vegetated wetlands protect shorelines in moderate and small storms if the water does not carry excessive amounts of abrasive floating debris. Wetland vegetation decreases water velocities through friction and causes sedimentation in shallow water areas and flood-plain wetlands, thus decreasing the erosive power of the water and building up natural levees. Trees are excellent riverbank stabilizers and have been planted to reduce erosion along United States shorelines. Other wetland plants such as bulrushes, reeds, cattails, cordgrass, and mangroves can also successfully withstand wave and current action.

When vegetation is removed, streambanks collapse and channels widen and (or) deepen; removal of wetland vegetation can turn a sediment sink into a sediment source. The dissipation of erosive forces by vegetation differs from wetland to wetland and depends upon vegetative composition and root structure, sediment type, and the frequency and intensity of water contact with the bank.

SUMMARY

Wetlands are complex ecosystems in which ground water and surface water interact, but because ground water cannot be directly observed, its role in the hydrology of wetlands is sometimes more difficult to understand than that of surface water. Many wetlands owe their existence not only to poor drainage at the site but also to the discharge of ground water at the site. The hydrology of a wetland determines what functions it will perform. Each wetland is unique, but those with similar hydrologic settings generally perform similar functions.

References Cited

Boelter, D.H., and Verry, E.S., 1977, Peatland and water in the northern Lake States: U.S. Department of Agriculture Forest Service General Technical Report NC-31, 22 p.

Boyt, F.L., Bayley, S.E., and Zoltek, John, Jr., 1977, Removal of nutrients from treated municipal wastewater by wetland vegetation: Journal of Water Pollution Control Federation, v. 49, no. 5, p. 789–799.

Bricker-Urso, Suzanne, Nixon, S.W., Cochran, J.K., Hirschberg, D.J., and Hunt, C.D., 1989, Accretion rates and sediment accumulation in Rhode Island salt marshes: Estuaries, v. 12, no. 4, p. 300–317.

Brinson, M.M., 1988, Strategies for assessing the cumulative effects of wetland alteration on water quality: Environmental Management, v. 12, no. 5, p. 655–662.

———1993, A hydrogeomorphic classification for wetlands: U.S. Army Corps of Engineers, Technical Report WRP-DE-4, 79 p.

Brown, R. J. E., 1974, Distribution and environmental relationships of permafrost: Canada National Committee for the Hydrologic Decade, p. 1–5.

Carter, Virginia, 1986, An overview of the hydrologic concerns related to wetlands in the United States: Canadian Journal of Botany, v. 64, no. 2, p. 364–374.

Carter, Virginia, Bedinger, M.S., Novitzki, R.P., and Wilen, W.O., 1979, Water resources and wetlands, *in* Greeson, P.E., Clark, J.R. and Clark, J.E., eds., Wetland functions and values—The state of our understanding: Minneapolis, Minnesota, Water Resources Association, p. 344–376.

Carter, Virginia, Gammon, P.T., and Garrett, M.K., 1994,

receiving waters (Valiela and others, 1978; Harvey and Odum, 1990). Estuarine salinity decreases during periods of high streamflow as the freshwater-saltwater interface moves down the estuary from the stream toward the sea (fig. 27). Estuarine salinity increases as streamflow decreases and the interface moves up the estuary. Estuarine plants and animals are well adjusted to these normal seasonal fluctuations in salinity. Water temporarily stored in floodplain wetlands upstream from the estuary deposits sediment and nutrients, and water leaving these wetlands exports decomposition products and organic detritus to the estuary. This temporary storage of water and the concurrent decrease in flow velocity aid in controlling the timing and size of the freshwater influx to the estuary. For example, the freshwater wetlands of the Barataria Basin in Louisiana serve as a major freshwater reservoir for maintenance of favorable salinities in the brackish zone, and the major pulse of materials to the estuary coincides with the arrival of migrant fish for growth and spawning. Leaves that fall in flood-plain wetlands are broken down and enriched by microbial action and produce high-quality food for detrital based food chains in the estuary. Alterations in the timing and quality of streamflow and associated suspended particulate and dissolved material, caused by dams or artificial drainage, can alter the chemistry of coastal waters and affect the organisms that inhabit them.

Wetlands reduce the erosive forces of wind and waves.

Erosion Reduction

Wetlands reduce shoreline erosion by stabilizing sediments and absorbing and dissipating wave energy (Hammer, 1992). The ability of wetlands to stabilize and protect shorelines depends on their capacity to reduce the erosive forces of wind and waves. Beaches

Ecotone dynamics and boundary determination in the Great Dismal Swamp, Virginia and North Carolina: Ecological Applications, v. 4, no. 1, p. 189–203.

Chason, D.B., and Siegel, D.I., 1986, Hydraulic conductivity and related physical properties of peat, Lost River Peatland, Northern Minnesota: Soil Science, v. 142, no. 2, p. 91–99.

Dingman, S.L., and Koutz, F.R., 1974, Relations among vegetation, permafrost, and potential insolation in Central Alaska: Arctic and Alpine Research, v. 6, no. 1, p. 37–42.

Dolan, T.J., Hermann, A.J., Bayley, Suzanne, and Zoltek, John, 1984, Evapotranspiration of a Florida, U.S.A., freshwater wetland: Journal of Hydrology, v. 74, p. 355–371.

Elder, J.F., 1987, Factors affecting wetland retention of nutrients, metals, and organic materials, in Kusler, J.A., and Brooks, Gail, eds., Wetland hydrology: National Wetland Symposium, 1987, Proceedings, p. 178–184.

Ford, Jesse, and Bedford, B.L., 1987, The hydrology of Alaskan wetlands, USA—A review: Arctic and Alpine Research, v. 19, no. 3, p. 209–229.

Gehrels, Jim, and Mulamoottil, George, 1990, Hydrologic processes in a southern Ontario wetland: Hydrobiologia, v. 208, p. 221–234.

Golet, F.C. and Lowry, D.J., 1987, Water regimes and tree growth in Rhode Island Atlantic white cedar swamps, in Laderman, A.D, ed., Atlantic white cedar wetlands: Boulder, Colo., Westview Press, p. 91–110.

Good, B.J., and Patrick, W.H., Jr., 1987, Root-water-sediment interface processes, in Reddy, K.R., and Smith, W.H., eds., Aquatic plants for water treatment and resource recovery: Orlando, Fla., Magnolia Publishing Company, p. 359–371.

Gosselink, J.G., and Turner, R.E., 1978, The role of hydrology in freshwater wetland ecosystems, in Good, R.E., Whigham, D.F., and Simpson, R.L., eds., Freshwater wetlands—Ecological processes and management potential: New York, Academic Press, p. 63–78.

Hains, C.F., 1973, Floods in Alabama—Magnitude and frequency, based on data through September 30, 1971: U.S. Geological Survey and Alabama Highway Dept., 38 p.

Hammer, D.A., 1989, Constructed wetlands for waste water treatment: Chelsea, Mich., Lewis Publishers, Inc., 831 p.

———1992, Creating freshwater wetlands: Chelsea, Mich., Lewis Publishers, 298 p.

Harvey, J.W., and Odum, W.E., 1990, The influence of tidal marshes on upland groundwater discharge to estuaries: Biogeochemistry, v. 10, p. 217–236.

Hemond, H.F., Army, T.P., Nuttle, W.K., and Chen, D.G., 1987, Element cycling in wetlands—Interactions with physical mass transport, in Hites, R.A., and Eisenreich, S.J., eds., Sources and fates of aquatic pollutants: Washington, D.C., American Chemical Society, Advances in Chemistry Series 216, p. 519–537.

Idso, S.B., 1981, Relative rates of evaporative water losses from open and vegetation covered water bodies: American Water Resources Bulletin, v. 17, no. 1, p. 46–48.

Ingram, H.A.P., 1983, Hydrology, in Gore, A.J.P., ed., Ecosystems of the world, 4A, Mores—Swamp, bog, fen and moor: New York, Elsevier Scientific Publishing Company, p. 67–158.

Johnston, C.A., Detenbeck, N.E., and Niemi, G.J., 1990, The cumulative effect of wetlands on stream water quality and quantity—A landscape approach: Biogeochemistry, v. 10, p. 105–141.

Kane, D.L., and Slaughter, C.W., 1973, Recharge of a central Alaska lake by subpermafrost groundwater: Second International Conference on Permafrost, Siberia, 1973, Proceedings, p. 458–468.

Leibowitz, S.G., Abbruzzese, Brooks, Adamus, P.R.,

Hughes, L.E., Iris, J.T., 1992, A synoptic approach to cumulative impact assessment—A proposed methodology, in McCannell, S.G., and Hairston, A.R., eds.: U.S. Environmental Protection Agency, EPA/600/R–92–167, 127 p.

Mitsch, W.J., and Gosselink, J.G., 1993, Wetlands: New York, Van Nostrand Reinhold, 722 p.

Novitzki, R.P., 1978, Hydrology of the Nevin Wetland near Madison, Wisconsin: U.S. Geological Survey Water-Resources Investigations 78–48, 25 p.

———1979, Hydrologic characteristics of Wisconsin's wetlands and their influence on floods, stream flow, and sediment, in Greeson, P.E., and Clark, J.R., eds., Wetland functions and values—The state of our understanding: Minneapolis, Minn., American Water Resources Association, 674 p.

———1982, Hydrology of Wisconsin wetlands: Wisconsin Geological Natural History Survey, Information Circular 40, 22 p.

———1989, Wetland hydrology, in Majumdar, S.K., Brooks, R.P., Brenner, F.J., and Tiner, R.W., Jr., eds., Chapter Five, Wetlands ecology and conservation—Emphasis in Pennsylvania: The Pennsylvania Academy of Science, p. 47–64.

Ogawa, Hisashi, and Male, J.W., 1986, Simulating of flood mitigation role of wetlands: Journal of Water Resources Planning and Management, v. 112, no. 1, p. 114–127.

Roulet, N.T., 1990, Hydrology of a headwater basin wetland—Groundwater discharge and wetland maintenance: Hydrological Processes, v. 4, p. 387–400.

Roulet, N.T., and Woo, Ming-ko, 1986, Hydrology of a wetland in the continuous permafrost region: Journal of Hydrology, v. 89, p. 73–91.

Rykiel, E. J., 1984, General hydrology and mineral budgets for Okefenokee Swamp—Ecological significance, in Cohen, A.D., Casagrande, D.J., Andrejko, M.J., and Best, G.R., eds., The Okefenokee Swamp—Its natural history, geology, and geochemistry: Los Alamos, N. Mex., Wetland Surveys, p. 212–228.

Siegel, D.I., 1983, Ground water and the evolution of patterned mires, glacial lake Agassiz peatlands, northern Minnesota: Journal of Ecology, v. 71, p. 913–921.

———1992, Groundwater hydrology, in Wright, H.E., Jr., Coffin, B.A., and Asseng, N.E., eds., The patterned peatlands of Minnesota: Minnesota, University of Minnesota Press, p. 163–172.

Siegel, D.I., and Glaser, P.H., 1987, Groundwater flow in a bog-fen complex, Lost River peatland, Northern Minnesota: Journal of Ecology, v. 75, p. 743–754.

Thompson, C.A., Bettis, E.A., III, and Baker, R.G., 1992, Geology of Iowa Fens: Journal of Iowa Academy of Science, v. 99, no. 2–3, p. 53–59.

Tice, R. H., 1968, Magnitude and frequency of floods in the United States: U.S. Geological Survey Water-Supply Paper 1672, 13 p.

Tilton, D. L., and Kadlec, R. H., 1979, The utilization of a fresh-water wetland for nutrient removal from secondarily treated waste water effluent: Journal of Environmental Quality, v. 8, no. 3, p. 328–334.

Tiner, R.W., Jr., 1985, Wetlands of New Jersey: Newton Corner, Mass., U.S. Fish and Wildlife Service, National Wetlands Inventory, 117 p.

Valiela, Ivan, and Costa, J.E., 1988, Eutrophication of Buttermilk Bay, a Cape Cod coastal embayment—Concentrations of nutrients and watershed nutrients and watershed nutrient budgets: Environmental Management, v. 12, no. 4, p. 539–553.

Valiela, Ivan, Costa, J.E., Foreman, Kenneth, Teal, J.M., Howes, Brian, and Aubrey, David, 1990, Transport of groundwater-borne nutrients from watersheds and their effects on coastal waters: Biogeochemistry, v. 10, p. 177–197.

Valiela, Ivan, Teal, J.M., Volkmann, Susanne, Shafer,

Deborah, and Carpenter, E.J., 1978, Nutrient and particulate fluxes in a salt marsh ecosystem—Tidal exchanges and inputs by precipitation and groundwater: Limnology and Oceanography, v. 23, no. 4, p. 708–812.

Wieder, R.K., 1989, A survey of constructed wetlands for acid coal mine drainage treatment in the eastern United States: Wetlands, v. 9, no. 2, p. 299–315.

Williams, J.R., and Waller, R.M., 1966, Ground water occurrence in permafrost regions of Alaska: National Research Council, p. 159–164.

Winter, T.C., 1976, Numerical simulation analysis of the interaction of lakes and ground water: U.S. Geological Survey Professional Paper 1001, 45 p.

_____1981, Uncertainties in estimating the water balance of lakes; Water Resources Bulletin, v. 17, no. 1, p. 82–115.

Winter, T.C., and Woo, Ming-Ko, 1990, Hydrology of lakes and wetlands: Surface Water Hydrology: The Geological Society of America, v. O-l, p. 159–187.

Wood, W.W., and Osterkamp, W.R., 1984, Recharge to the Ogallala aquifer from Playa Lake Basins on the Llano Estacado: Wetstone, G.A., ed., Ogallala Aquifer Symposium II, Lubbock, Texas, 1984, Proceedings, p. 337–349.

Wood, W.W., and Sanford, W.E., 1994, Recharge to the Ogallala: 60 years after C.V. Theis' analysis, *in* Urban, L.V., and Wyatt, A.W., eds., Playa Basin Symposium: Texas Tech University, Lubbock, Texas, 1994, 324 p.

Zedler, J.B., Huffman, Terry, Josselyn, Michael, eds., 1985, Pacific Regional Wetland Functions: Proceedings of a workshop held at Mill Valley, Calif., April 14–16, 1985, Amherst, Mass., The Environmental Institute, University of Massachusetts, Publication no. 90-3, 162 p.

FOR ADDITIONAL INFORMATION: Virginia Carter, U.S. Geological Survey, 430 National Center, Reston, VA 22092

Technical Aspects of Wetlands
Wetlands as Bird Habitat

By Robert E. Stewart, Jr.[1]

Figure 28. This wetland in California is habitat for migrating snow geese. *(Photograph by James R. Nelson, California Department of Fish and Game.)*

The value of a wetland to a specific bird species is affected by the presence of surface water and the duration and timing of flooding.

One of the best known functions of wetlands is to provide a habitat for birds (fig. 28). Humans have known of the link between birds and wetlands for thousands of years. Prehistoric people drew pictures of birds and wetlands on cave walls, scratched them onto rocks, and used them in the design of artifacts (fig. 29); and Native American lore provides accounts of bird hunts in wetlands. Wetlands are important bird habitats, and birds use them for breeding, nesting, and rearing young (fig. 30). Birds also use wetlands as a source of drinking water and for feeding, resting, shelter, and social interactions. Some waterfowl, such as grebes, have adapted to wetlands to such an extent that their survival as individual species depends on the availability of certain types of wetlands within their geographic range. Other species, such as the northern pintail or the American widgeon, use wetlands only during some parts of their lives.

Wetlands occupy only a small part of the landscape that is now the conterminous United States—11 percent in 1780 and just 5 percent in 1980 (Dahl and others, 1991). Nonetheless, they are important to birds. During the past 20 years, policies and programs that encourage altering, draining, or filling of wetlands have decreased, and policies that encourage wetland conservation and restoration have increased. (See article "Wetland Protection Legislation" in this volume.) Among the wetland attributes society seeks to protect and conserve are those that benefit wildlife, particularly migratory birds. This article discusses the benefits that wetlands provide for birds and the effects of wetland losses on birds.

Figure 29.   The importance of wetland birds to ancient people is portrayed in these two artifacts. The petroglyph at the left, created between A.D. 1300 and 1650, is located at Petroglyph National Monument near Albuquerque, N. Mex. The clay "duck pot" at the right, fired between 200 B.C. and A.D. 500, was unearthed at Hopewell Culture National Historical Park, Chillicothe, Ohio. *(Photographs courtesy of the National Park Service.)*

[1] National Biological Service.

The geographic location of a wetland may determine how and when birds will use it.

Figure 30. This baby heron will be raised in a wetland environment. *(Photograph courtesy of National Biological Service.)*

Figure 31. The raccoon is a wetland predator that eats eggs and preys on birds. *(Photograph courtesy of National Biological Service.)*

Figure 32. The American alligator is an effective and voracious predator of wetland birds in the South. *(Photograph courtesy of National Biological Service.)*

Figure 33. This American bittern, with its protective coloration, is well hidden in the vegetation. *(Photograph by James Leopold, National Biological Service.)*

WETLAND FACTORS THAT AFFECT BIRDS

The relation between wetlands and birds is shaped by many factors. These include the availability, depth, and quality of water; the availability of food and shelter; and the presence or absence of predators. Birds that use wetlands for breeding depend on the physical and biological attributes of the wetland. Birds have daily and seasonal dependencies on wetlands for food and other life-support systems.

The value of a wetland to a specific bird species is affected by the presence of surface water or moist soils and the duration and timing of flooding. Water might be present during the entire year, during only one or more seasons, during tidal inundation, or only temporarily during and after rainfall or snowmelt. At times water might not be present at the land surface, but might be close enough to the land surface to maintain the vegetation and foods that are needed by birds. Birds may use wetlands located in depressions in an otherwise dry landscape, along streams, or in tidally influenced areas near shorelines.

The availability or influence of water is a very important wetland feature to birds. It is not, however, the only feature that determines if birds will be present, how birds use the wetland, or how many kinds or numbers of birds may use the wetland. Other determining physical or biological factors include water depth and temperature, presence or absence of vegetation, patchiness or openness of vegetation, type of vegetation, foods, water chemistry, type of soils, and geographic or topographic location. Any variations in any of these wetland features will cause subtle, but distinct, differences in bird use.

Wetlands provide food for birds in the form of plants, vertebrates, and invertebrates. Some feeders forage for food in the wetland soils, some find food in the water column, and some feed on the vertebrates and invertebrates that live on submersed and emergent plants. Vegetarian birds eat the fruits, tubers, and leaves of wetland plants. Water temperatures influence food production. Invertebrate production in the water column may ultimately depend on water temperature and the ability of a wetland to produce algae. Cold water might not be a hospitable environment for small animals and plants that some wetland birds eat. However, water that is too warm also might not produce foods that some birds prefer.

Wetland vegetation provides shelter from predators and from the weather. The presence or absence of shelter may influence whether birds will inhabit a wetland or a nearby upland area. Predators are likely to abound where birds concentrate, breed, or raise their young. Wetlands form an important buffer or barrier to land-based predators and reduce the risk of predation to nesting or young birds. However, some predators, such as the raccoon (fig. 31), are well adapted to both wetland and upland environments, and take large numbers of both young and nesting birds. Mink forage for nesting or sleeping birds along the edges and interiors of wetlands. Other animals, such as the snapping turtle, the alligator (fig. 32), or the large-mouthed bass, are effective water-based predators of young birds, particularly young waterfowl. Snakes take their toll as well. Many bird species that are highly adapted to feeding in a wetland

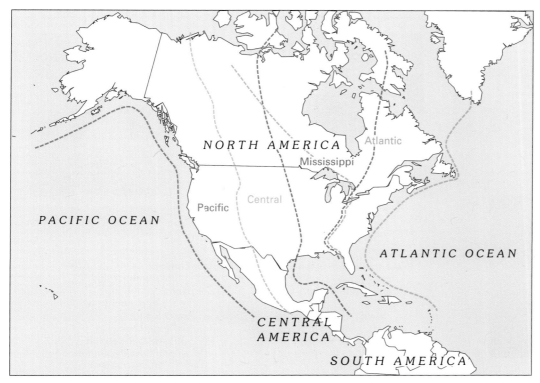

Figure 34. Major flyway corridors for migrating birds in the Western Hemisphere. *(Source: From U.S. Fish and Wildlife Service files.)*

environment also have genetic adaptations that lower their risk of becoming prey. One such example is the bittern (fig. 33), which has excellent protective coloration. The same vegetation that hides birds from predators also provides some shelter from severe weather. In spring, during cold and stormy weather, waterfowl such as canvasback ducks protect their young in the shelter of a marsh that is almost impenetrable to wind.

The geographic location of a wetland may determine how and when birds will use it or use adjacent habitat. In the northern latitudes or at high altitudes, some wetlands are covered with ice in the winter and are temporarily "out of service" for birds adapted to a water environment, but emergent vegetation might still offer shelter and food for some species. Birds that eat fish, aquatic invertebrates, or submersed vegetation cannot forage for food because of the ice cover. Some wetlands are on the migration path of waterfowl and other migratory birds and provide stopover locations for traveling birds (fig. 34). These birds might feed in agricultural fields during the day and return to the shelter of wetlands during the night.

The "prairie potholes" are a special type of wetland, found in the north-central part of the United States. These potholes are an example of a wetland type that is important to migrating waterfowl. Here the timing and duration of inundation and the salinity of the water are important factors in the production of plants and invertebrates used by birds. These, and many other wetland characteristics, are influenced by a number of things:

- Water-level fluctuations throughout the year, in response to rainfall and snowmelt, that maintain wetland zones such as wet meadows and marshes
- Short-term (years) and long-term (decades) climatic trends that cycle wetlands between a wet and dry state
- Interaction of surface and ground water
- Interaction of ground water with rocks and soils that influence salinity and other wetland water chemistry

THE IMPORTANCE OF WETLANDS TO BIRDS

Because of the great variety of wetlands, bird adaptation to and use of wetland environments differs greatly from species to species. Birds' use of wetlands during breeding cycles ranges widely. Some birds depend on wetlands almost totally for breeding, nesting, feeding, or shelter during their breeding cycles. Birds that need functional access to a wetland or wetland products during their life cycle, especially during the breeding season, can be called "wetland dependent" (table 5). Other birds use wetlands only for some of their needs, or they might use both wetland and upland habitats. Of the more than 1,900 bird species that breed in North America, about 138 species in the conterminous United States are wetland dependent (American Ornithologists' Union, 1983).

Many bird species use forested wetlands as well as forested uplands, feeding on the abundant insects associated with trees (fig. 35). These birds are not de-

Table 5. Wetland-dependent breeding birds of the conterminous United States, including federally endangered or threatened species and subspecies[1,2]

[Source: Data from American Ornithologists' Union, 1983; Niering, 1988; Ehrlich and others, 1992]

Green-backed heron. *(Photograph by Thomas A. Muir, National Biological Service.)*

This brown pelican is an endangered species. *(Photograph by Thomas A. Muir, National Biological Service.)*

Roseate spoonbill at a nesting rookery. *(Photograph by Ronald F. Paille, U.S. Fish and Wildlife Service.)*

Snowy egret on the nest. *(Photograph by David Hall, U.S. Fish and Wildlife Service.)*

Cranes and their allies
  Yellow rail
  Black rail
    [3] California black rail
  Clapper rail
    [4] Light-footed clapper rail
    [4] California clapper rail
    [4] Yuma clapper rail
  King rail
  Virginia rail
  Sora rail
  Purple gallinule
  Common moorhen
  American coot
  Limpkin
  Sandhill crane (facultative)
    [4] Mississippi sandhill crane
    [4] Whooping crane

Cuckoos
  Mangrove cuckoo

Grebes
  Least grebe
  Pied-billed grebe
  Horned grebe
  Red-necked grebe
  Eared grebe
  Western grebe

Herons and their allies
  American bittern
  Least bittern
  Great blue heron
    [4] Florida great white heron
  Great egret
  Snowy egret
  Little blue heron
  Tricolored heron
  Reddish egret
  Cattle egret
  Green-backed heron
  Black-crowned night heron
  Yellow-crowned night heron
  White ibis
  Glossy ibis
  White-faced ibis
  Roseate spoonbill
  [4] Wood stork

Kingfishers
  Belted kingfisher

Loons
  Common loon

Owls
  Short-eared owl

Perching birds
  Flycatchers
    Alder flycatcher
    Willow flycatcher
    Gray flycatcher
  Swallows
    Tree swallow
    Northern rough-winged swallow
    Bank swallow
  Wrens
    Sedge wren
    Marsh wren
  Dippers
    American dipper
  Vireos
    Black-whiskered vireo
  Warblers
    [4] Bachman's warbler
    Prothonotary warbler
    Swainson's warbler
    Northern waterthrush
    Louisiana waterthrush
    Connecticut warbler
    Common yellowthroat
  Sparrows
    Savannah sparrow
      [3] Belding's savannah sparrow
    LeConte's sparrow
    Sharp-tailed sparrow
    Seaside sparrow
      [5] Dusky seaside sparrow
      [4] Cape sable sparrow
    Lincoln's sparrow
    Swamp sparrow
  Blackbirds
    Red-winged blackbird
    Tricolored blackbird
    Yellow-headed blackbird
    Great-tailed grackle
    Boat-tailed grackle

Pelicans and their allies
  American white pelican
  Brown pelican
    [4] California brown pelican

The American avocet. *(Photograph courtesy of National Biological Service.)*

Colony of sandwich terns on the Chandeleur Islands, La. *(Photograph courtesy of National Biological Service.)*

These American wigeons will spend part of their lives in a wetland habitat and part in an upland environment. *(Photograph courtesy of National Biological Service.)*

Male wood ducks. *(Photograph by Thomas A. Muir, National Biological Service.)*

Double-crested cormorant
Olivaceous cormorant
Anhinga
Shorebirds, Gulls, and Alcids
Plovers, surfbirds, and turnstones
　Snowy plover
　Wilson's plover
　⁴ Piping plover
　Killdeer (facultative)
Oystercatchers
　American oystercatcher
　American black oystercatcher
Avocets and stilts
　Black-necked stilt
　American avocet
Sandpipers and allies
　Willet
　Spotted sandpiper
　Marbled godwit
　Common snipe
　American woodcock
　⁴ Eskimo curlew
Phalarope
　Wilson's phalarope
Gulls and terns
　Laughing gull
　Franklin's gull
　Little gull
　Heerman's gull (facultative)
　Ring-billed gull
　California gull
　Herring gull
　Western gull
　Great black-backed gull
　Gull-billed tern
　Caspian tern
　Royal tern
　Elegant tern
　Sandwich tern
　⁴ Roseate tern
　Common tern
　Forster's tern
　Least tern
　　⁴ California least tern
　Sooty tern
　Black tern
Skimmers
　Black skimmer

Vultures, Hawks, and Falcons
　Osprey
　American swallow-tailed kite
　⁴ Everglade snail kite
　⁴ Bald eagle
　Northern harrier
　Peregrine falcon
　　⁴ American peregrine falcon
Waterfowl
Swans
　Trumpeter swan
Geese
　Canada goose
Tree ducks
　Fulvous whistling duck
　Black-bellied whistling duck
Surface feeding ducks
　Wood duck
　Green-winged teal
　American black duck
　Mottled duck
　Mallard
　Northern pintail
　Blue-winged teal
　Cinnamon teal
　Northern shoveler
　Gadwall
　American wigeon
Bay ducks
　Canvasback
　Redhead
　Ring-necked duck
　Greater scaup
　Lesser scaup
Sea ducks
　Harlequin duck
　White-winged scoter
　Common goldeneye
　Barrow's goldeneye
　Bufflehead
Mergansers
　Hooded merganser
　Common merganser
　Red-breasted merganser
Stiff-tailed ducks
　Ruddy duck

¹ Table arranged by group, species, and subspecies. To facilitate the use of this table, order of presentation differs from that normally used.
² Does not include oceanic or pelagic birds.
³ Candidate for placement on endangered species list.
⁴ Federally endangered or threatened wetland-dependent bird species or subspecies.
⁵ Became extinct in 1987.

Figure 35. Prothonotary warblers feed on insects of forested wetlands and uplands alike. *(Photograph courtesy of National Biological Service.)*

Widespread draining and altering of wetlands has affected bird populations.

pendent on wetlands because they use both habitats equally well. Some birds, such as wood ducks, are found primarily in forested wetlands and are dependent on this wetland type.

Many migratory birds are wetland dependent, using wetlands during their migration and breeding seasons. Migratory birds may spend the winter in wetlands in the Southern United States, or farther south (fig. 34). Throughout winter, these birds use southern wetlands for food and nutrients to sustain them for their return trip north and the breeding season.

Not all wetlands are of equal value to waterfowl and other birds. An inventory in the conterminous United States during the early 1950's showed that of 74.4 million acres of wetlands, 8.8 million acres had a high value for waterfowl, 13.6 million acres were of moderate value, 24.1 million acres were of low value, and 27.9 million acres were of negligible value (Shaw and Fredine, 1956, p. 17). These categories were identified on a State-by-State basis and were ranked according to use by waterfowl, with "high" being most used. The primary focus of this inventory was waterfowl; thus these rankings might not reflect wetland values for other birds. Also, the inventory was for only natural wetlands that had been little altered by human activities. The three areas of highest value are the Mississippi River corridor southward from Cairo, Ill., and westward along the Texas gulf coast; the entire east coast from Maine southward through most of Florida; and the northern Midwest.

THE INFLUENCE OF WETLANDS ON WATERFOWL POPULATIONS

Considerable research has increased the understanding of wetlands' influence on the numbers of waterfowl that breed and their breeding success. However, the relation between wetlands and the population and propagation of various waterfowl species is not well understood. This relation depends on: (1) the number of wetlands in the area; (2) the wetlands' size and water depth; (3) whether the wetlands hold open water in the early spring or through late August; (4) the climate; and (5) the species of bird and the bird's adaptations to wetlands.

In the prairie pothole region in the late 1970's, for example, as the number of wetlands in an area increased, populations of dabbling ducks increased, but at a ratio of less than 1:1 (fig. 36). In the past 20 years, the duck-pothole ratio has decreased, possibly due to decreases in upland cover and increases in predation. Bellrose (1977) also found waterfowl densities and propagation to be related to the number of wetlands per square mile; generally, waterfowl densities and propagation increased as the number of wetlands increased. However, he found that mallard production decreased when the number of wetlands exceeded 12 per square mile.

Different waterfowl species adapt to different wetland types, inhabit different geo-

graphic areas, and nest at different times. The relation of many other species of birds to wetlands are undoubtedly just as complex.

EFFECTS OF WETLAND LOSS AND DEGRADATION ON BIRDS

About one-third of North American bird species use wetlands for food, shelter, and (or) breeding (Kroodsma, 1979). Thus, widespread draining and altering of wetlands has affected bird populations. Because most of the wetland drainage and alteration occurred between the 1930's and 1950, before scientific estimates of bird populations began, most estimates of population declines are inferred. Before the passage of the Migratory Bird Treaty Act in 1918, the reduction in waterfowl populations was blamed largely on excessive hunting and wetland drainage (Day, 1959). However, since 1930 most of the reduction has been attributed to the loss or degradation of wetlands (Bellrose and Trudeau, 1988) and the loss of suitable upland habitats that surround wetlands.

For most wetland-dependent birds, habitat loss in breeding areas translates directly into population losses. As wetlands are destroyed, some birds may move to other less suitable habitats, but reproduction tends to be lower and mortality tends to be higher. Hence, the birds that breed in these poorer quality habitats will not contribute to a sustainable population through the years (Pulliam and Danielson, 1991).

About one-half of the 188 animals that are federally designated as endangered or threatened are wetland dependent (Niering, 1988). Of these, 17 are bird species or subspecies (table 5). These birds are categorized as endangered or threatened because their populations are so low that the risk of their extinction is real and immediate. The circumstances that cause each species or subspecies to be endangered differ greatly.

Wetland loss due to draining, filling, or altering of surface-water and ground-water flow is a concern to many people. Wetland degradation also has a substantial effect on birds. Although wetland degradation is a serious problem, it is one that is more subtle and less understood than wetland losses. Degradation can take many forms:

- Amounts and periodicity of water supplies can be altered
- The quality of water flowing into and through a wetland can be modified
- The flows of sediments or freshwater to coastal marshes can be reduced
- Water levels can be stabilized in wetlands that otherwise would undergo beneficial drawdowns or water-table fluctuations
- Wetland vegetation may be altered by harvesting or by introducing exotic species, making it of little or no value to wetland-dependent birds

An example of wetland degradation is found in the Chesapeake Bay region. Nutrients and sediments entering the bay from agricultural, urban, and industrial areas have caused increased algal blooms, decreased invertebrate production, and lowered oxygen levels. This degradation has reduced the acreage of seagrasses that form an important link in the food

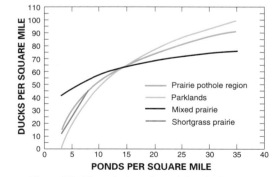

Figure 36. The relation of pond density increase to number of ducks. (Source: After Bellrose, 1977.)

chain for invertebrates, fish, and wetland-dependent birds. The decline in the canvasback duck population in this area is thought to be directly related to the decline in seagrasses.

Chemicals and sediments that move from agricultural areas into wetlands are two of the most pervasive sources of degradation. The shift in human populations from inland areas to coastal areas of the United States has caused problems in coastal wetlands through overloaded sewage treatment systems. The large and growing volume of industrial wastes that enter ground- and surface-water supplies also threatens to degrade wetlands. These threats, combined with habitat destruction, have a net negative effect on the population of wetland birds. Thus, if the amount and quality of wetland habitat is substantially reduced, populations of wetland-dependent birds in the area also can be expected to decrease.

SOME EFFORTS TO PRESERVE WETLAND BIRD HABITATS

Many people believe that ownership or management of wetlands by public conservation agencies, such as the U.S. Fish and Wildlife Service, and by private organizations, such as the Nature Conservancy or the National Audubon Society, offers the best assurance that the highest value wetlands will be maintained for future generations. (A discussion of the agencies and organizations that participate in management and conservation of wetlands in each State can be found in the State Summaries section of this report.)

A few early concerns for wetlands important to waterfowl are reflected in the creation of the first national wildlife refuge and in the establishment of the Federal Duck Stamp program. The first national wildlife refuge was created in 1903, by President Theodore Roosevelt, to protect a wetland—Pelican Island, Florida (U.S. Fish and Wildlife Service, [1995]). Concern for the loss of waterfowl led to the Federal Duck Stamp program that began in 1934 (Mitsch and Gosselink, 1993) and continues today. Duck stamps are sold to waterfowl hunters to provide money for the purchase or preservation of wetlands (fig. 37).

Several international treaties are partly responsible for much of the formal wetland protection in this country—the Migratory Bird Treaty and the Convention on Wetlands of International Importance especially as Waterfowl Habitat. "In 1918, the U[nited] S[tates] passed into law the Migratory Bird Treaty Act, ratifying a treaty with Great Britain, on behalf of Canada, that recognized the conservation responsibilities for more than 800 species of migratory birds shared by the two countries" (U.S. Fish and Wildlife Service, [1995]). Subsequent to that act, the United States developed the National Wildlife Refuge System consisting of 500 reserves—many of which are wetlands important to birds—comprising more than 90 million acres (fig. 38). The system has the highest ratio of wetlands to dry land in public ownership. The National Park Service manages the Everglades National Park and several preserves that also have high ratios of wetlands to dry lands.

The Convention on Wetlands of International

Figure 37. The purchase of duck stamps provides funds for the acquisition or protection of wetlands important to waterfowl. *(Source: U.S. Fish and Wildlife Service.)*

Importance especially as Waterfowl Habitat, more commonly known as the "Ramsar Convention" is an intergovernmental treaty for international cooperation for the conservation of wetland habitats. The U.S. Fish and Wildlife Service is responsible for implementation of the convention in the United States. A "List of Wetlands of International Importance" has been developed by the convention. Sites on this list are known as "Ramsar Sites" and are wetlands that convention members have a special obligation to preserve. There are 15 Ramsar sites in this country (fig. 38).

SUMMARY AND CONCLUSIONS

Human activities have caused shifts in wetland-dependent bird populations since European settlement of the United States, especially since the beginning of the 20th century. Many acres of wetlands were drained between the 1930's and 1950, well before any of the national bird surveys were begun. As a result, it is not possible to accurately determine the effects of habitat destruction on long-term wetland bird populations.

It is apparent that there have been many changes in the distribution and numbers of wetland birds. Wetlands on breeding, migratory, or wintering areas are all important to sustain bird populations. As the wetland habitats in these areas are drained or altered, the ability of these areas to sustain bird populations decreases. Each species of wetland-dependent bird has a unique and complex set of needs for wetland

About one-half of the 188 animals that are federally designated as endangered or threatened are wetland dependent.

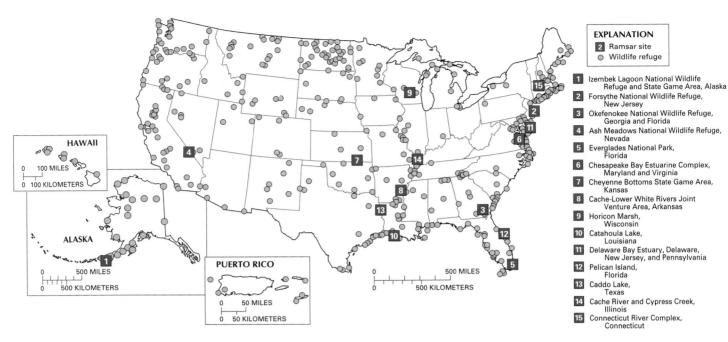

EXPLANATION
2 Ramsar site
• Wildlife refuge

1 Izembek Lagoon National Wildlife Refuge and State Game Area, Alaska
2 Forsythe National Wildlife Refuge, New Jersey
3 Okefenokee National Wildlife Refuge, Georgia and Florida
4 Ash Meadows National Wildlife Refuge, Nevada
5 Everglades National Park, Florida
6 Chesapeake Bay Estuarine Complex, Maryland and Virginia
7 Cheyenne Bottoms State Game Area, Kansas
8 Cache-Lower White Rivers Joint Venture Area, Arkansas
9 Horicon Marsh, Wisconsin
10 Catahoula Lake, Louisiana
11 Delaware Bay Estuary, Delaware, New Jersey, and Pennsylvania
12 Pelican Island, Florida
13 Caddo Lake, Texas
14 Cache River and Cypress Creek, Illinois
15 Connecticut River Complex, Connecticut

Figure 38.   Location of National Fish and Wildlife Refuge System reserves and Ramsar sites in the United States. *(Source: U.S. Fish and Wildlife Service, 1993, [1995].)*

habitats that makes it difficult to generalize about how loss or degradation of wetlands affects bird populations. It seems reasonable to expect, however, that as the numbers of wetlands in a region decline, so too will the numbers of wetland-dependent birds.

In some parts of the United States, extensive wetland losses have displaced birds from large areas. Continued wetland losses probably will cause continued losses of wetland birds. However, recent recognition of the wetland values, and the effects of their losses, have provided incentives to maintain and restore wetlands.

References Cited

American Ornithologists' Union, 1983, Check-list of North American Birds: Lawrence, Kans., Allen Press, Inc., 6th edition, 877 p.

Bellrose, F.C., 1977, Species distribution, habitats, and characteristics of breeding dabbling ducks in North America, *in* Bookhout, T.A., 1977, Waterfowl and wetlands—An integrated review: Proceedings of a symposium held at the 39th Midwest Fish and Wildlife Conference, Madison, Wis., La Crosse Printing Co., Inc, 152 p.

Bellrose, F. C., and Trudeau, N.M., 1988, Wetlands and their relationship to migrating and winter populations of waterfowl, v. I: Portland, Oreg., Timber Press, p. 183–194.

Dahl, T.E., and Johnson, C.E., 1991, Wetlands—Status and trends in the conterminous United States, mid-1970's to mid-1980's: Washington, D.C., U.S. Fish and Wildlife Service, 22 p.

Day, A.M., 1959, North American waterfowl: Harrisburg, Pa., Stackpole Co., 363 p.

Ehrlich, P.R., Dobkin, D.S., and Wheye, Darryl, 1992, Birds in jeopardy: Stanford, California, Stanford University Press, 260 p.

Kroodsma, D. E., 1979, Habitat values for nongame wetland birds, *in* Greeson, P.E., Clark, J.R., and Clark, J.E. eds., 1979, Wetland functions and values—The state of our understanding: Minneapolis, Minn., American Water Resources Association, p. 320–343.

Mitsch, W.J., and Gosselink, J.G., 1993, Wetlands: New York, Van Nostrand Reinhold, 722 p.

Niering, W.A., 1988, Endangered, threatened and rare wetland plants and animals of the continental United States, *in* Hook, D.D., McKee, W.H., Jr., Smith, H.K., and others, 1988, The ecology and management of wetlands—Volume I—The ecology of wetlands: Portland, Oreg., Timber Press, 592 p.

Pulliam, H.R., and Danielson, B.J., 1991, Sources, sinks and habitat selection—A landscape perspective on population dynamics: The American Naturalist, v. 137, p. 850–866.

Shaw, S.P., and Fredine, C.G., 1956, Wetlands of the United States—Their extent and their value to waterfowl and other wildlife: U.S. Fish and Wildlife Service, Circular 39, 67 p.

U.S. Fish and Wildlife Service, 1993, Annual report of lands under control of the U.S. Fish and Wildlife Service as of September 30, 1993: Division of Realty, 43 p.

U.S. Fish and Wildlife Service, [1995], Wetlands of International Importance—United States Participation in the "Ramsar" Convention, Ramsar, Iran, 1971, 11 p.

FOR ADDITIONAL INFORMATION: Robert E. Stewart, Jr., National Biological Service, Southern Science Center, 700 Cajundome Boulevard, Lafayette, LA 70506

Wetland Management and Research
Wetland Protection Legislation

By Todd H. Votteler[1] and Thomas A. Muir[2]

The people of the United States have begun to recognize that wetlands have numerous and widespread benefits. However, many of the goods and services wetlands provide have little or no market value. Because of this, the benefits produced by wetlands accrue primarily to the general public. Therefore, the Government provides incentives and regulates and manages wetland resources to protect the resources from degradation and destruction. Other mechanisms for wetland protection include acquisition, planning, mitigation, disincentives for conversion of wetlands to other land uses, technical assistance, education, and research.

Although many States have their own wetland regulations, the Federal Government bears a major responsibility for regulating wetlands. The five Federal agencies that share the primary responsibility for protecting wetlands include the Department of Defense, U.S. Army Corps of Engineers (Corps); the U.S. Environmental Protection Agency (EPA); the Department of the Interior, U.S. Fish and Wildlife Service (FWS); the Department of Commerce, National Oceanic and Atmospheric Administration (NOAA); and the Department of Agriculture, Natural Resources Conservation Service (NRCS) (formerly the Soil Conservation Service). Each of these agencies has a different mission that is reflected in the implementation of the agency's authority for wetland protection. The Corps' duties are related to navigation and water supply. The EPA's authorities are related to protecting wetlands primarily for their contributions to the chemical, physical, and biological integrity of the Nation's waters. The FWS's authorities are related to managing fish and wildlife—game species and threatened and endangered species. Wetland authority of NOAA lies in its charge to manage the Nation's coastal resources. The NRCS focuses on wetlands affected by agricultural activities.

States are becoming more active in wetland protection. As of 1993, 29 States had some type of wetland law (Want, 1993). Many of these States have adopted programs to protect wetlands beyond those programs enacted by the Federal Government. As more responsibility is delegated from the Federal Government to the States, State wetland programs are gaining in importance. Thus far, States have devoted more attention to regulating coastal wetlands than inland wetlands. The most comprehensive State programs include those of Connecticut, Rhode Island, New York, Massachusetts, Florida, New Jersey, and Minnesota (Mitsch and Gosselink, 1993). Many of these States regulate those activities affecting wetlands that are exempt from the Clean Water Act, Section 404 program. (For more information on specific State wetland protection programs, see the State Summary section of this volume.)

Despite the current recognition of wetland benefits, many potentially conflicting interests still exist, such as that between the interests of landowners and the general public and between developers and conservationists. Belated recognition of wetland benefits and disagreement on how to protect them has led to discrepancies in local, State, and Federal guidelines. Discrepancies in Federal programs are apparent in table 6, which shows programs that encourage conversion of wetlands and those that discourage conversion of wetlands. Conflicting interests are the source of much tension and controversy in current wetland protection policy. Although attempts are being made to reconcile some of these differences, many policies will have to be modified to achieve consistency.

Despite all the government legislation, policies, and programs, wetlands will not be protected if the regulations are not enforced. Perhaps the best way to protect wetlands is to educate the public of their benefits. If the public does not recognize the benefits of wetland preservation, wetlands will not be preserved. Protection can be accomplished only through the cooperative efforts of citizens.

FEDERAL WETLAND PROTECTION PROGRAMS AND POLICIES

The Federal Government protects wetlands directly and indirectly through regulation, by acquisition, or through incentives and disincentives as described in table 6. Section 404 of the Clean Water Act is the primary vehicle for Federal regulation of some of the activities that occur in wetlands. Other programs, such as the "Swampbuster" program and the Coastal Management and Coastal Barriers Resources Acts, provide additional protection. Coastal wetlands generally benefit most from the current network of statutes and regulations. Inland wetlands are more vulnerable than coastal wetlands to degradation or loss because current statutes and policies provide them less comprehensive protection. Several of the major Federal policies and programs affecting wetlands are discussed in the following few pages. Also discussed are some of the States' roles in Federal wetland policies.

The Clean Water Act

The Federal Government regulates, through Section 404 of the Clean Water Act, some of the activities that occur in wetlands. The Section 404 program originated in 1972, when Congress substantially amended the Federal Water Pollution Control Act and created a Federal regulatory plan to control the discharge of dredged or fill materials into wetlands and other waters of the United States. Discharges are commonly associated with projects such as channel construction and maintenance, port development, fills to create dry land for development sites near the water, and water-control projects such as dams and levees. Other kinds of activities, such as the straightening of river channels to speed the flow of water downstream

If the public does not recognize the benefits of wetland preservation, wetlands will not be preserved.

---

[1] University of Texas.
[2] National Biological Service.

Table 6. Federal programs that have significant effects on wetlands in the United States.   **A**, Regulations encouraging wetland conversion. **B**, Regulations discouraging or preventing wetland conversion.   **C**, Acquisitions discouraging or preventing wetland conversion.   **D**, Other policies and programs preventing or discouraging wetland conversion.

[Abbreviations: AFA, All Federal Agencies; ASCS, Agricultural Stabilization and Conservation Service; BLM, Bureau of Land Management; Corps, U.S. Army Corps of Engineers; CWS,Canadian Wildlife Service; DOD, Department of Defense; DOE, Department of Energy; DOI, Department of the Interior; DOT, Department of Transportation;

A, ENCOURAGING WETLAND CONVERSION

Program or Act	Implementing agency	Effect of program
Executive Order 12630, Constitutional Takings	AFA	Provides a review process for agencies to protect against unintentional "takings" of private property.
Federal-Aid Highway Act of 1968	DOT	Highway construction can affect wetlands at every stage. Wetlands are often prime sites for highways.
Federal Crop Insurance	USDA	Indirectly encourages farmers to place frequently inundated areas, including wetlands, into production.
Federal Livestock Grazing	USFS, BLM	Overgrazing promotes the loss of rlparian habitat.
Flood Control Act of 1944 (P.L. 78–534)	Corps	Authorized various flood-control projects resulting in wetland destruction.
National Flood Insurance Program	FEMA	Encourages development in flood plains, which contain wetlands, by providing low-cost Federal insurance.
Payment-in-Kind (PIK) Program	USDA	Indirectly encourages farmers to place previously unfarmed areas, including wetlands, into production.
Small Reclamation Projects Acts of 1956 (70 Stat. 1044)	DOI	Encourages State and local participation in small western reclamation projects, which can destroy riparian habitat.
Surface Mining Control and Reclamation Act (P.L. 95–87), (1977)	DOI	Establishes a program for regulating surface mining and reclaiming coal-mined lands, including wetlands, under the Office of Surface Mining, Reclamation, and Enforcement.
Surface Transportation Revenue Act of 1991 (P.L. 102–240)	DOT	Transportation projects directly and indirectly destroy wetlands.
U.S. Tax Code	IRS	Encourages farmers to drain and clear wetlands through tax deductions and credits for development activities.
Water Resources Development Act of 1976, 1986, 1988, 1990 (P.L.'s 94–587, 99–662, 100–676, 101—640)	Corps	Water development projects directly and indirectly destroy wetlands.

B, DISCOURAGING OR PREVENTING WETLAND CONVERSION—*Regulations*

Program or Act	Implementing agency	Effect of program
Comprehensive Environmental Response Compensation and Liability Act (Superfund) (P.L. 96–510) (1980)	AFA	Establishes liability of the U.S. Government for damages to natural resources over which the U.S. has sovereign rights. Requires the President to designate Federal officials to act as trustees for natural resources, and to conduct natural resource damage assessments.
* Coastal Barriers Resources Act (P.L. 96–348) (1982)	NOAA	Designates various undeveloped coastal barrier islands for inclusion in the Coastal Barrier Resources System. Designated areas are ineligible for Federal financial assistance that may aid development.
* Coastal Zone Management Act (P.L. 92–583) (1972)	NOAA	Provides Federal funding for wetlands programs in most coastal States, including the preparation of coastal zone management plans.
Estuary Protection Act (P.L. 90–454) (1968)	DOI	Authorized the study and inventory of estuaries, and the Great Lakes, and provided for management of designated estuaries between DOI and the States.
* Federal Water Pollution Control (P.L. 92–-500) (*Clean Water Act*) Section 404 (1972)	Corps, EPA FWS, NMFS	Regulates many activities that involve the disposal of dredged and fill materials in waters of the United States, including many wetlands.
Federal Water Project Recreation Act (P.L. 89–72) (1965)	DOI, Corps	Recreation and fish and wildlife enhancement must be considered by Federal water projects. Authorizes Federal funds for acquiring land for waterfowl refuges.
Fish and Wildlife Coordination Act of 1956	DOI	Authorizes the development and distribution of fish and wildlife information and the development of policies and procedures relating to fish and wildlife.
Migratory Bird Conservation Act (45 Stat. 1222) (1929)	FWS	Established a commission to approve the acquisition of migratory bird habitat.
National Wildlife Refuge Acts (numerous Acts)	FWS	Numerous statutes establish refuges, many of which contain significant wetland acreage.
National Environmental Policy Act of 1969 (P.L. 91–190)	AFA	Requires the preparation of an environmental impact statement of all major Federal actions significantly affecting the environment.
Ramsar Convention (Treaty), adopted 1973, enforced from 1975	FWS	Convention maintains a list of wetlands of international importance and encourages the wise use of wetlands.
Rivers and Harbors Act of 1938 (52 Stat. 802)	Corps	Provides that "due regard" be given to wildlife conservation in planning Federal water projects.
Rivers and Harbors Appropriation Act of 1899, Section 10 of the (30 Stat. 1151)	Corps	Prohibits the unauthorized obstruction or alteration of navigable waters.
Watershed Protection and Flood Prevention Act (68 Stat. 666) (1954)	FWS, NRCS	Authorizes the FWS to investigate wildlife conservation on NRCS small watershed projects.
Wild and Scenic Rivers Act, (P.L. 90–542) (1968)	DOI, USDA	Protects designated river segments from damming and other alterations without a permit.
Wilderness Act of 1964 (78 Stat. 890)	DOI, USDA	Requires review of Federal lands for inclusion in the National Wilderness Preservation System.

* Discussed in text.

Table 6 —Continued.

[Abbrevations—Continued. EPA, U.S. Environmental Protection Agency; FEMA, Federal Emergency Management Agency; FERC, Federal Energy Regulatory Commission; FmHA, Farmer's Home Administration; FWS, U.S. Fish and Wildlife Service; GSA, General Services Administration; IRS, Internal Revenue Service; NMFS, National Marine Fisheries Service; NOAA, National Oceanic and Atmospheric Administration; NPS, National Park Service; NRCS, Natural Resources Conservation Service; USCG, U.S. Coast Guard; USDA, U.S. Department of Agriculture; USFS, U.S. Forest Service]

C, DISCOURAGING OR PREVENTING WETLAND CONVERSION—*Acquisitions*

Program or Act	Implementing agency	Effect of program
Coastal Wetland Planning, Protection and Restoration Act (P.L. 101–646) (1990)	Corps, FWS EPA, NMFS	Provides for interagency wetlands restoration and conservation planning and acquisition in Louisiana, other coastal States, and the Trust Territories.
Emergency Wetlands Resources Act of 1986 (P.L. 99–645)	FWS	Pays debts incurred by FWS for wetlands acquisition, and provides additional revenue sources.
Federal Aid in Wildlife Restoration Act (1937) (Ch. 899, 50 Stat.917)	FWS	Provides grants to States for acquiring, restoring, and maintaining wildlife areas.
Fish and Wildlife Conservation Act (P.L. 96–366) (1980)	FWS	Identifies land and water in the Western Hemisphere critical for migratory nongame birds.
Land and Water Conservation Fund Act (1964) (P.L. 88–578)	FWS, NPS	Acquires wildlife areas.
Lea Act(62 Stat. 238) (1948)	FWS	Authorizes the acquiring and developing of various waterfowl management areas in California.
Migratory Bird Hunting and Conservation Stamps (1934) (Ch. 71, 48 Stat. 452)	FWS	Acquires wetland easements using revenues from fees paid by hunters for duck stamps.
North American Waterfowl Management Plan (1986)	FWS, CWS	Establishes a plan for managing waterfowl resources by various methods, such as acquiring wetlands.
North American Wetlands Conservation Act (1989) (P.L. 101–233)	FWS	Encourages public/private partnerships by providing matching grants to organizations for protecting, restoring, or enhancing wetlands.
Surface Transportation Revenue Act of 1991 (P.L. 102–240)	DOT	Authorizes funding for wetland mitigation banks for State departments of transportation.
Transfer of Certain Real Property for Wildlife Conservation Purposes Act (62 Stat. 240) (1948)	GSA, DOI	Allows the GSA to transfer property to DOI, or States, for wildlife conservation.
U.S. Tax Code Tax Reform Act of 1986 (P.L. 99–514)	IRS	Provides deductions for donors of wetlands and to some nonprofit organizations.
Water Bank Act (1970) (P.L. 91–559)	ASCS	Leases wetlands and adjacent uplands from farmers for waterfowl habitat for 10-year periods.
Wetlands Loan Act (1961) (P.L. 87–383)	FWS	Provides interest-free loans for wetland acquisition and easements.

D, DISCOURAGING OR PREVENTING WETLAND CONVERSION—*Other Policies and Programs*

Program or Act	Implementing agency	Effect of program
Endangered Species Act of 1973 (P.L. 93–205)	FWS	Provides for the designation and protection of wildlife, fish, and plant species that are in danger of extinction.
* Executive Order 11990, Protection of Wetlands (1977)	AFA	Requires Federal agencies to minimize impacts of Federal activities on wetlands.
* Executive Order 11988, Protection of Floodplains (1977)	AFA	Requires Federal agencies to minimize impacts of Federal activities on flood plains.
Executive Order 12580, Superfund Implementation (1987)	DOI	Directs DOI to develop rules for assessing damages under CERCLA (Comprehensive Environmental Response Compensation and Liabilities Act) as a natural resource trustee.
Federal Noxious Weed Act (P.L. 93–629) (1975)	DOI, USDA DOE, DOD	Authorizes controlling the spread of noxious weeds on Federal lands.
Federal Power Act (41 Stat. 1063) (1920)	FERC	FERC will cooperate with other Federal agencies in assessing proposed power projects, such as dams. FERC must consider protection of fish and wildlife resources.
Fish and Wildlife Coordination Act (1965) (P.L. 89–72)	FWS	Requires Federal agencies to consult with FWS before issuing permits for most water-resource projects.
Food, Agriculture, Conservation, and Trade Act of 1990 (P.L. 101–624)	NRCS	Wetland Reserve Program purchases perpetual nondevelopment easements on farmed wetlands. Subsidizes restoration of croplands to wetlands.
* Food Security Act of 1985 (*Swampbuster*) (P.L. 99–198)	ASCS, FWS, FmHA	"Swampbuster" program suspends agricultural subsidies for farmers who convert wetlands to agriculture. Conservation Easements program allows FmHA to eliminate some farm debts in exchange for long-term easements that protect wetlands and other areas.
National Wildlife Refuge System Administration Act of 1966 (P.L. 89–669)	DOI	Provides the guidelines for managing National Wildlife Refuges.
Nonindigenous Aquatic Nuisance Prevention and Control Act of 1990 (P.L. 101–646)	FWS, USCG, EPA, Corps, NOAA	Created a Federal program to prevent and control the spread of species that are aquatic nuisances.
Oil Pollution Act of 1990 (P.L. 101–380)	DOE, DOI, NOAA	Enhanced the response to oil spills and required natural resource damage assessments.
Tax Deductions for Conservation Easements (Section 6 of P.L. 96–541)	IRS	Allows taxpayers to take a deduction for a qualified real property interest contributed to a conservation organization for conservation purposes.
U.S. Tax Code Reform Act of 1986 (P.L. 99–514)	IRS	Eliminates incentives for clearing land. Deductible conservation expenditures must be consistent with wetlands protection. Capital gains on converted wetlands treated as income.
Water Resources Development Act of 1976, 1986, 1988, 1990, (P.L.'s 94–587, 99–662, 100–676, 101–640)	Corps	States that future mitigation plans for Federal water projects should include "in kind" mitigation for bottom-land hardwood forests.

and clearing land, are regulated as Section 404 discharges if they involve discharges of more than incidental amounts of soil or other materials into wetlands or other waters.

The Corps and the EPA share the responsibility for implementing the permitting program under Section 404 of the Clean Water Act. However, Section 404(c) of the Clean Water Act gives the EPA authority to veto the permit if discharge materials at the selected sites would adversely affect such things as municipal water supplies, shellfish beds and fishery areas, wildlife, or recreational resources. By 1991, the EPA had vetoed 11 of several hundred thousand permits since the Act was passed (Schley and Winter, 1992).

The review process for a Section 404 permit is shown in figure 39. After notice and opportunity for a public hearing, the Corps' District Engineer may issue or deny the permit. The District Engineer must comply with the EPA's Section 404(b)(1) Guidelines and must consider the public interest when evaluating a proposed permit. Four questions related to the guidelines are considered during a review of an application:

1. Is the proposed discharge the least damaging practical alternative?
2. Does the proposed discharge comply with other environmental standards or regulations?
3. Will the proposed discharge significantly degrade wetlands?
4. Have all the appropriate and practical steps been taken to minimize potential harm to the wetlands?

Wetland mitigation is often required, and if required, the permit applicant will need to develop a specific, detailed plan.

Through a public interest review, the Corps tries to balance the benefits an activity may provide against the costs it may incur. The criteria applied in this process are the relative extent of the public and private need for the proposed structure or work and the extent and permanence of the beneficial or detrimental effects on the public and private uses to which the area is suited. Some of the factors considered in the public interest review are listed in figure 39. Cumulative effects of numerous piecemeal changes are considered in addition to the individual effects of the projects.

The FWS, NOAA, and State fish and wildlife agencies, as the organizations in possession of most of the country's biological data, have important advisory roles in the Section 404 program. The FWS and NOAA (if a coastal area is involved) provide the Corps and the EPA with comments about the potential environmental effects of pending Section 404 permits. Other government agencies, industry, and the public are invited to participate through public notices of permit applications, hearings, or other information-collecting activities. However, the public interest review usually does not involve public comment unless the permit is likely to generate significant public interest or if the potential consequences of the permit are expected to be significant. All recommendations must be given full consideration by the Corps, but there is no requirement that they must be acted upon.

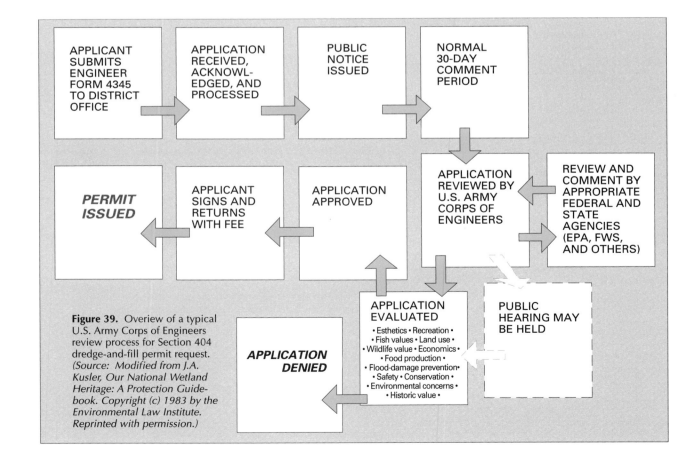

Figure 39. Overeiew of a typical U.S. Army Corps of Engineers review process for Section 404 dredge-and-fill permit request. *(Source: Modified from J.A. Kusler, Our National Wetland Heritage: A Protection Guidebook. Copyright (c) 1983 by the Environmental Law Institute. Reprinted with permission.)*

If the FWS or NOAA disagree with a permit approved by a District Engineer, they can request that the permit be reviewed at a higher level within the Corps. However, the Assistant Secretary of the Army has the unilateral right to refuse all requests for higher level reviews. The Assistant Secretary accepted the additional review of 16 of the 18 requested out of the total 105,000 individual permits issued between 1985 and 1992 (Schley and Winter, 1992).

Because many activities may cause the discharge of dredged and fill materials, and the potential effects of these activities differ, the Corps has issued general regulations to deal with a wide range of activities that could require a Section 404 permit. The Corps can forgo individual permit review by issuing general permits on a State, regional, or nationwide basis. General permits cover specific categories of activities that the Corps determines will have minimal effects on the aquatic environment, including wetlands. General permits are designed to allow activities with minimal effects to begin with little, if any, delay or paperwork. General permits authorize approximately 75,000 activities annually that might otherwise require a permit (U.S. Environmental Protection Agency, 1991); however, most activities in wetlands are not covered by general permits (Morris, 1991).

Not all dredge and fill activities require a Section 404 permit. Many activities that cause the discharge of dredged and fill materials are exempt from Section 404. The areas specifically exempted from Section 404 include: normal farming, forestry, and ranching activities; dike, dam, levee, and other navigation and transportation structure maintenance; construction of tem-

porary sedimentation basins on construction sites; and construction or maintenance of farm roads, forest roads, or temporary roads for moving mining equipment (Morris, 1991). In addition, the Corps' flood-control and drainage projects and other Federal projects authorized by Congress and planned, financed, and constructed by a Federal agency also are exempt from the Section 404 permitting requirements if an adequate environmental impact statement is prepared.

Not all methods of altering wetlands are regulated by Section 404. Common methods of altering wetlands are listed in table 7. Unregulated methods include: wetland drainage, the lowering of ground-water levels in areas adjacent to wetlands, permanent flooding of existing wetlands, deposition of material that is not specifically defined as dredged and fill material by the Clean Water Act, and wetland vegetation removal (Office of Technology Assessment, 1984).

State authority over the Federal Section 404 program is a goal of the Clean Water Act. Assumption of authority from the EPA has been completed only by Michigan and New Jersey. Under this arrangement, the EPA is responsible for approving State assumptions and retains oversight of the State Section 404 program, and the Corps retains the navigable waters permit program (Mitsch and Gosselink, 1993). States cannot issue permits over EPA's objection, but EPA has the authority to waive its review for selected categories of permit applications. Few States have chosen to assume the program, in part because few Federal resources are available to assist States and assumption does not include navigable waters (World Wildlife Fund, 1992).

The Clean Water Act regulates dredge and fill activities that would adversely affect wetlands.

Table 7. Methods of altering wetlands
[Source: The Conservation Foundation, 1988, p. 15]

PHYSICAL	
Filling	adding any material to raise the bottom level of a wetland or to replace the wetland with dry land
Draining	removing the water from a wetland by ditching, tiling, pumping, and so forth
Excavating	dredging and removing soil and vegetation from a wetland
Diverting water away	preventing the flow of water into a wetland by removing water upstream, lowering lake levels, or lowering ground-water tables
Clearing	removing vegetation by burning, digging, application of herbicide, scraping, mowing, or otherwise cutting
Flooding	raising water levels, either behind dams, by pumping, or otherwise channeling water into a wetland
Diverting or withholding sediment	trapping sediment by constructing dams, channels, or other types of projects, thereby inhibiting wetland regeneration in natural deposition areas such as deltas
Shading	placing pile-supported platforms or bridges over wetlands, causing vegetation to die because of a lack of adequate sunlight
Conducting activities in adjacent areas	disrupting the interactions between wetlands and adjacent land areas, or incidentally affecting wetlands through activities at adjoining sites
CHEMICAL	
Changing nutrient levels	increasing or decreasing nutrient levels within the local water and or soil system, forcing wetland plant community changes
Introducing toxics	adding toxic compounds to a wetland either intentionally (for example, herbicide treatment to reduce vegetation) or unintentionally, adversely affecting wetland plants and animals
BIOLOGICAL	
Grazing	consumption and compaction of vegetation by domestic or wild animals
Disrupting natural populations	reducing populations of existing species, introducing exotic species, or otherwise disturbing resident organisms

"Swampbuster"

The program that seeks to remove Federal incentives for the agricultural conversion of wetlands is part of the Food Security Act of 1985 and 1990, and is known as "Swampbuster." Swampbuster renders farmers who drained or otherwise converted wetlands for the purpose of planting crops after December 23, 1985, ineligible for most Federal farm subsidies. Through Swampbuster, Congress directed the U.S. Department of Agriculture (USDA) to slow wetland conversion by agricultural activities (U.S. Fish and Wildlife Service, 1992). The government programs that Swampbuster specifically affects are listed in Section 1221 of the Food Security Act. If a farmer loses eligibility for USDA programs under Swampbuster, he or she may regain eligibility during the next year simply by not using wetlands for growing crops. Swampbuster is administered by USDA's Consolidated Farm Service Agency. The NRCS and the FWS serve as technical consultants (World Wildlife Fund, 1992).

The Swampbuster was amended by the Food, Agriculture, Conservation, and Trade Act of 1990 to create the Wetland Reserve Program. The Wetland Reserve Program provides financial incentives to farmers to restore and protect wetlands through the use of long-term easements (usually 30-year or permanent). The program provides farmers the opportunity to offer a property easement for purchase by the USDA and to recieve cost-share assistance (from 50 to 75 percent) to restore converted wetlands. Landowners make bids to participate in the program. The bids represent the payment they are willing to accept for granting an easement to the Federal Government. The Consolidated Farm Service Agency ranks the bids according to the environmental benefit per dollar. Easements require that farmers implement conservation plans approved by the NRCS and the FWS. Enrollment in the pilot program was authorized for nine States. The program's goal is to enroll 1 million acres by 1995 (U.S. Fish and Wildlife Service, 1992). Funding for this program is appropriated annually by Congress (U.S. Army Corps of Engineers, 1994). Because 74 percent of United States' wetlands are on private land, programs that provide incentives for private landowners to preserve their wetlands, such as the Wetland Reserve Program, are critical for protecting wetlands (Council of Environmental Quality, 1989).

Coastal Wetlands Protection Programs

The 1972 Coastal Zone Management Act and the 1982 Coastal Barriers Resources Act protect coastal wetlands. The Coastal Zone Management Act encourages States (35 States and territories are eligible, including the Great Lakes States) to establish voluntary coastal zone management plans under NOAA's Coastal Zone Management Program and provides funds for developing and implementing the plans. The NOAA also provides technical assistance to States for developing and implementing these programs. For Federal approval, the plans must demonstrate enforceable standards that provide for the conservation and environmentally sound development of coastal resources. The program provides States with some control over wetland resources by requiring that Federal activities be consistent with State coastal zone man-

"Swampbuster" removes Federal incentives for the agricultural conversion of wetlands.

The Coastal Zone Management Program provides States with some control over wetland resources.

agement plans, which can be more stringent than Federal standards (World Wildlife Fund, 1992, p. 87). A State also can require that design changes or mitigation requirements be added to Section 404 permits to be consistent with the State coastal zone management plan. The Coastal Zone Management Act has provided as much as 80 percent of the matching-funds grants to States to develop plans for coastal management that emphasize wetland protection (Mitsch and Gosselink, 1993). Some States pass part of the grants on to local governments. The Act's authorities are limited to wetlands within a State's coastal zone boundary, the definition of which differs among States. As of 1990, 23 States had federally approved plans.

The 1982 Coastal Barriers Resources Act denies Federal subsidies for development within undeveloped, unprotected coastal barrier areas, including wetlands, designated as part of the Coastal Barrier Resources System. Congress designates areas for inclusion in the Coastal Barriers Resource System on the basis of some of the following criteria (Watzin, 1990):

- Size
- Development status
- Composition
- Wind, wave, and tidal energies
- Associated aquatic habitat, including adjacent wetlands

In addition, States, local governments, and conservation organizations owning lands that were "otherwise protected" could have their lands added to this system until May 1992. ("Otherwise protected" lands are areas within undeveloped coastal barriers that were already under some form of protection.) Once in the Coastal Barriers Resources System, these areas are rendered ineligible for almost all Federal financial subsidies for programs that might encourage development. In particular, these lands no longer qualify for Federal flood insurance, which discourages development because coastal lands are frequently subject to flooding and damage from hurricanes and other storms. The FWS is responsible for mapping these areas and approves lands to be included in the system. The purposes of the Coastal Barrier Resources Act are to minimize the loss of human life, to reduce damage to fish and wildlife habitats and other valuable resources, and to reduce wasteful expenditure of Federal revenues (Watzin, 1990). In the future, eligible surplus government land will be included if approved by the FWS. About 95 percent of the 788,000 acres added to the system in 1990 along the Atlantic and Gulf coasts consists of coastal wetlands and near-shore waters (World Wildlife Fund, 1992).

Flood-Plain and Wetland Protection Orders

Executive Orders 11988, *Floodplain Management*, and 11990, *Protection of Wetlands*, were signed by President Carter in 1977. The purpose of these Executive Orders was to ensure protection and proper management of flood plains and wetlands by Federal agencies. The Executive Orders require Federal agencies to consider the direct and indirect adverse effects of their activities on flood plains and wetlands. This requirement extends to any Federal action within a flood plain or a wetland except for routine maintenance of existing Federal facilities and structures. The Clinton administration has proposed revising Executive Order 11990 to direct Federal agencies to consider wetland protection and restoration planning in the larger scale watershed/ecosystem context.

WETLAND DELINEATION STANDARDS

The Corps published, in 1987, the *Corps of Engineers Wetland Delineation Manual*, a technical manual that provides guidance to Federal agencies about how to use wetland field indicators to identify and delineate wetland boundaries (U.S. Army Corps of Engineers, 1987). In January of 1989, the EPA, Corps, SCS, and FWS adopted a single manual for delineating wetlands under the Section 404 and Swampbuster programs—*The Federal Manual for Identifying and Delineating Jurisdictional Wetlands* (commonly referred to as the "1989 Manual"). The "1989 Manual" establishes a national standard for identifying and delineating wetlands by specifying the technical criteria used to determine the presence of the three wetland characteristics: wetland hydrology, water-dependent vegetation, and soils that have developed under anaerobic conditions (U.S. Environmental Protection Agency, 1991).

In 1991, the President's Council on Competitiveness proposed revisions to the 1989 Manual because of some concern that nonwetland areas were regularly being classified as wetlands (Environmental Law Reporter, 1992a). The proposed 1991 Manual was characterized by many wetland scientists as politically based rather than scientifically based. In September of 1992, Congress authorized the National Academy of Science to conduct a $400,000 study of the methods used to identify and delineate wetlands (Environmental Law Reporter, 1992b). On August 25, 1993, the Clinton administration's wetland policy, proclaimed that, "Federal wetlands policy should be based upon the best science available" (White House Office of Environmental Policy, 1993) and the 1987 Corps Manual is the sole delineation manual for the Federal Government until the National Academy of Sciences completes its study (White House Office of Environmental Policy, 1993).

MITIGATION

Mitigation is the attempt to alleviate some or all of the detrimental effects arising from a given action. Wetland mitigation replaces an existing wetland or its functions by creating a new wetland, restoring a former wetland, or enhancing or preserving an existing wetland. This is done to compensate for the authorized destruction of the existing wetland. Mitigation commonly is required as a condition for receiving a permit to develop a wetland.

Wetland mitigation can be conducted directly on a case-by-case onsite basis, or through a banking system. Onsite mitigation requires that a developer create a wetland as close as possible to the site where a wetland is to be destroyed. This usually involves a one-to-one replacement.

A mitigation bank is a designated wetland that is created, restored, or enhanced to compensate for future wetland loss through development. It may be and usually is located somewhere other than near the site to be destroyed and built by someone other than the developer. The currency of a mitigation bank is the mitigation credit. "Mitigation banks require systems for valuing the compensation credits produced and for determining the type and number of credits needed as compensation for any particular project. ***Mitigation bank credit definitions are an attempt to identify those features [of wetland] which allow reasonable approximations of replacement" (U.S. Army Corps of Engineers, 1994, p. 63). Wetland evaluation methods have been developed or are being developed to address the problem of evaluating two different wetlands so that the degradation of one can be offset by the restoration, enhancement, or creation of the other and to assign either a qualitative or quantitative value to each wetland. When buying the credits, developers pay a proportionate cost toward acquiring, restoring, maintaining, enhancing, and monitoring the mitigation bank wetland. Banks cover their costs by selling credits to those who develop wetlands, or by receiving a taxpayer subsidy.

Several problems are associated with wetland mitigation. The concept of wetland compensation may actually encourage destruction of natural wetlands if people believe that wetlands can be easily replaced. A 1990 Florida Department of Environmental Regulation study examined the success of wetland creation projects and found that the success rate of created tidal wetlands was 45 percent, whereas the success rate for created freshwater wetlands was only 12 percent. (Redmond, 1992). Figure 40 shows the relative success of wetland mitigation projects overall in south Florida. The apparent factor controlling the lower success rate for freshwater wetlands was the difficulty in duplicating wetland hydrology, that is, water-table fluctuations, frequency and seasonality of flooding, and ground-water/surface-water interactions.

A study of wetland mitigation practices in eight States revealed that in most of the States, more wetland acreage was destroyed than was required to be created or restored, resulting in a net loss of acreage when mitigation was included in a wetlands permit (Kentula and others, 1992). Less than 55 percent of the permits included monitoring of the project by site visit. A limited amount of information exists about the number of acres of wetlands affected by mitigation or the effectiveness of particular mitigation techniques because of the lack of followup. Several studies in Florida reported that as many as 60 percent of the required mitigation projects were never even started (Lewis, 1992). In addition, the mitigation wetland commonly was not the same type of wetland that was destroyed, which resulted in a net loss of some wetland types. (See article "Wetland Restoration and Creation" in this volume.)

RECENT PRESIDENTIAL WETLAND PROTECTION INITIATIVES

In his 1988 Presidential address and in his 1990 budget address to Congress, President Bush echoed the recommendations of the National Wetland Policy Forum. The Forum was convened in 1987 by the Conservation Foundation at the request of EPA. The short-

> *"Federal wetlands policy should be based upon the best science available."*

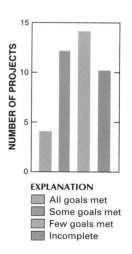

Figure 40. Status of 40 wetland mitigation projects in south Florida. The average age of the projects was less than 3 years. *(Source: Modified from Mitsch and Gosselink, 1993.)*

EXPLANATION
- All goals met
- Some goals met
- Few goals met
- Incomplete

term recommendation of the forum was to decrease wetland losses and increase wetland restoration and creation—the concept of "no net loss"—as a national goal. This implied that when wetland loss was unavoidable, creation and restoration should replace destroyed wetlands (Mitsch and Gosselink, 1993).

On August 25, 1993, President Clinton unveiled his new policy for managing America's wetland resources. The program was developed by the Interagency Working Group on Federal Wetlands Policy, a group chaired by the White House Office on Environmental Policy with participants from the EPA, the Corps, the Office of Management and Budget, and the Departments of Agriculture, Commerce, Energy, Interior, Justice, and Transportation. The Administration's proposals mix measures that tighten restrictions on activities affecting wetlands in some cases and relax restrictions in other areas. The Clinton policy endorses the goal of "no net loss" of wetlands; however, it clearly refers to "no net loss" of wetland acreage rather than "no net loss" of wetland functions.

The President's wetland proposal would expand Federal authority under the Section 404 program to regulate the draining of wetlands in addition to regulating dredging and filling of wetlands. Other proposed changes to the Federal permitting program include the requirement that most Section 404 permit applications be approved or disapproved within 90 days, and the addition of an appeal process for applicants whose permits are denied. The EPA and the Corps are directed to relax regulatory restrictions that cause only minor adverse effects to wetlands such as activities affecting very small areas.

The Clinton policy calls for avoiding future wetland losses by incorporating wetland protection into State and local government watershed-management planning. This new policy also significantly expands the use of mitigation banks to compensate for federally approved wetland development or loss.

Clinton's proposals relaxed some of the current restrictions on agricultural effects on wetlands and increased funding for incentives to preserve and restore wetlands on agricultural lands. The administration policy excluded 53 million acres of "prior converted croplands" from regulation as wetlands. Also, authority over wetland programs affecting agriculture was shifted from the FWS to the NRCS and proposed increased funding for the Wetlands Reserve Program, which pays farmers to preserve and restore wetlands on their property.

> *"No net loss" of wetlands is a national goal.*

References Cited

Conservation Foundation, 1988, Protecting America's wetlands—An action agenda: Washington, D.C., The Conservation Foundation, p. 15.

Council of Environmental Quality, 1989, Environmental trends: Washington, D.C., Office of the President, Council of Environmental Quality, p. 152.

Environmental Law Reporter, 1992a, Agencies working to resolve controversy, official says: Washington, D.C., Bureau of National Affairs, v. 23, no. 13, p. 924.

_____1992b, Reilly favors return to 1987 manual, cites emerging consensus on delineation: Washington, D.C., Bureau of National Affairs, v. 23, no. 17, p. 1,260.

Kentula, Mary, Sifneos, Jean, Brooks, Robert, Gwin, Stephanie, Holland, Cindy, and Sherman, Arthur, 1992, An approach to decisionmaking in wetland restoration and creation: U.S. Environmental Protection Agency, EPA/600/R–92/150, 151 p.

Kusler, J.A., 1983, Our national wetland heritage—A protection guidebook: Washington, D.C., Environmental Law Institute, p. 62.

Lewis, Roy, 1992, Why Florida needs mitigation banking: National Wetlands Newsletter, v. 14, no. 1, p. 7.

Mitsch, W.J., and Gosselink, J.G., 1993, Wetlands: New York, Van Nostrand Reinhold Company, 722 p.

Morris, Marya, 1991, Wetland protection—A local government handbook: Chicago, Ill., American Planning Association, 31 p.

Office of Technology Assessment, 1984, Wetlands—Their use and regulation: Washington, D.C., OTA–O–206, p. 168–169.

Redmond, Ann, 1992, How successful is mitigation?: Washington, D.C., National Wetlands Newsletter, v. 14, no. 1, p. 5–6.

Schley, Terry, and Winter, Linda, 1992, New 404(q) MOA— diluting EPA's role: Washington, D.C., National Wetlands Newsletter, Environmental Law Institute, v. 14, no. 6, p. 8.

U.S. Army Corps of Engineers, 1987, Corps of Engineers wetlands delineation manual: Vicksburg, Miss., U.S. Army Corps of Engineers Technical Report Y–87–1, p. 1.

_____1994, National wetland mitigation banking study— Wetland mitigation banking: Washington, D.C., Environmental Law Institute, IWR Report 94–WMB–6, 178 p.

U.S. Environmental Protection Agency, 1991, Proposed revisions to the Federal manual for delineating wetlands: Washington, D.C., Office of Wetlands, Oceans, and Watersheds, p. 1–4.

U.S. Fish and Wildlife Service, 1992, Digest of Federal resource laws of interest to the U.S. Fish and Wildlife Service: Washington, D.C., U.S. Fish and Wildlife Service, Office of Legislative Services, p. 26.

Want, William, 1993, Law of wetlands regulation: Deerfield, Ill., Clark Boardman Callaghan, p. 13-2.

Watzin, M.C., 1990, Coastal Barrier Resources System mapping process, *in* Federal coastal wetland mapping program: Washington, D.C., U.S. Fish and Wildlife Service Biological Report 90 (18), p. 21–26.

White House Office of Environmental Policy, 1993, Protecting America's wetlands—A fair, flexible, and effective approach: the White House, Office of Environmental Policy, p. 15.

World Wildlife Fund, 1992, Statewide wetlands strategies— A guide to protecting and managing the resource: Washington, D.C., Island Press, 268 p.

FOR ADDITIONAL INFORMATION: Todd H. Votteler, 4312 Larchmont Avenue, Dallas, TX 75205; Thomas A. Muir, U.S. Geological Survey, 413 National Center, Reston, VA 22092

Wetland Management and Research
Wetland Research by Federal Agencies

By Richard E. Coleman[1], Edward T. LaRoe[2], and Russell F. Theriot[1]

Because wetlands were drained and filled for farming and building purposes during the last several hundred years, more than half of the original wetlands in the United States have been lost (Frayer and others, 1983). Only during the last quarter century has society begun to understand the value of wetlands and the particular benefits that they provide. (See the article "History of Wetlands in the Conterminous United States" in this volume.) This understanding has been broadened by the concerted efforts of many public and private researchers. This article addresses the research contributions of Federal agencies: which agencies are involved in wetland research, why they are involved, and the nature of their research.

In an effort to develop a strategy for preventing the further loss of wetlands, the Committee on Earth and Environmental Sciences established a Wetlands Research Subcommittee to determine the status of wetland research being conducted by Federal agencies. These efforts resulted in an unpublished report that presented a national inventory and data base of ongoing research and addressed future research needs (Wetlands Research Subcommittee, unpub. data, 1992). Data presented in the following few pages are drawn largely from these findings.

During 1992, Federal wetland research expenditures were about $63 million. A total Federal investment of more than $250 million is distributed over the lifetime of the existing projects. The amount of Federal research spending per State is depicted in figure 41.

THE REASONS FOR FEDERAL INVOLVEMENT IN WETLAND RESEARCH

Scientists from many organizations, including those in the private sector, those from colleges and universities, and those from public institutions, are engaged in wetland research. Typically, each organization has its own reasons for being involved in wetland research. Federal wetland research may be done because it is part of an agency's mission, is part of an agency's responsibilities as outlined by the Congress, or is otherwise in the national interest.

When research is mission oriented, it is part of the basic work of an agency. Mission-oriented Federal agency wetland research generally is done for one of five reasons:

1. Ownership—The agency owns and is responsible for managing wetlands. The agency is the steward of its land.
2. Public trust responsibilities—An agency may be responsible for ensuring the long-term survival of certain fish and other wildlife resources, which are

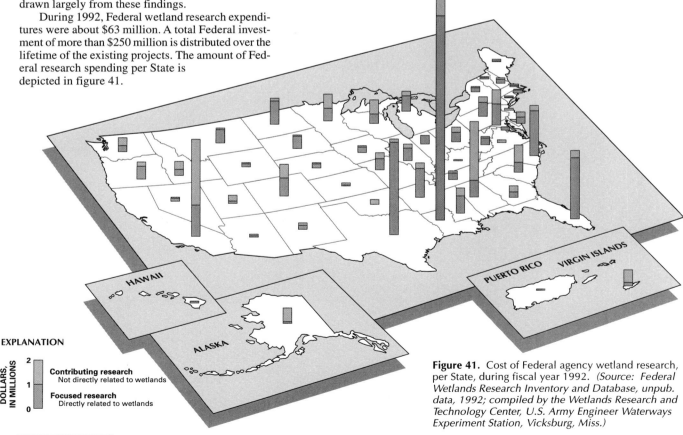

EXPLANATION

DOLLARS, IN MILLIONS

Contributing research
Not directly related to wetlands

Focused research
Directly related to wetlands

Figure 41. Cost of Federal agency wetland research, per State, during fiscal year 1992. *(Source: Federal Wetlands Research Inventory and Database, unpub. data, 1992; compiled by the Wetlands Research and Technology Center, U.S. Army Engineer Waterways Experiment Station, Vicksburg, Miss.)*

[1] U.S. Army Corps of Engineers.
[2] National Biological Service.

held in trust for the public. Wetlands form critical habitat and are part of the ecological system on which many of these species depend.

3. Regulatory responsibilities—Because wetlands provide so many benefits to society, activities that adversely affect them may be subject to regulation. Some agencies, therefore, have regulatory authority over wetlands.

4. Development activities—Federal agencies have an obligation to avoid projects or actions that may adversely affect wetlands, to minimize the negative effects of their activities on wetlands, and to mitigate unavoidable wetland losses. These requirements apply to all Federal agencies, but those regularly involved in large-scale development projects support specific wetland research activities.

5. Science—Agencies that have missions directly related to science may conduct or support research on wetlands.

Although many different levels of government may have mission-oriented research, Federal agency wetland research activities relate to congressionally mandated responsibilities. Most significant among these are provisions that relate to:

• Interstate commerce—Wetlands are part of the entire physical landscape, from river headwaters to the sea. They form parts of water bodies that provide shipping, transportation, and navigation. Some wetlands are used as routes for trade in interstate commerce, and wetland products are used in interstate trade. What happens to wetlands in one State can affect wetland activities, benefits, and uses in another State.

• International treaties—The benefits and uses of wetlands are the subject of international treaties, such as the Ramsar Convention of 1971 and the Migratory Bird Treaty, which are the exclusive domain of the Federal Government. International efforts that result from those treaties, such as efforts between Canada, Mexico, and the United States to restore declining wetland-dependent waterfowl populations, have an essential Federal element. (See article "Wetlands as Bird Habitat" in this volume.)

There is also an intrinsic national interest in wetland research. Where wetland questions or issues are widespread or shared by jurisdictions, or affect the national health, safety, or welfare, Congress may determine that there is a national interest that justifies Federal agency research.

TYPES OF FEDERAL WETLAND RESEARCH

The Federal Wetlands Research Inventory and Database reported in 1992 that 18 Federal agencies were conducting some wetland research (Wetlands Research Subcommittee, unpub. data, 1992). Two types of research were included in the inventory—focused and contributing. Focused research is specifically designed to investigate wetlands or some component thereof; contributing research provides some information about wetlands but is not directly related to wetlands.

Research categories also were identified by the Inventory and Database. These categories were defined by the subject of the wetland research being conducted, and were listed in five topical areas:

1. Wetland processes—Research to address factors that affect the type, location, size, and functions of wetlands.

2. Wetland functions—Research to determine the role wetlands play and the benefits they provide.

3. Human-induced stresses—Research to improve ways of detecting or quantifying the effects of

> *The understanding of wetlands as a valued resource has been broadened by the concerted efforts of many public and private researchers.*

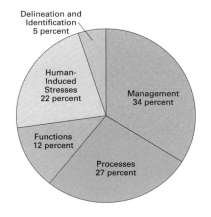

AGENCY		RESEARCH CATEGORY				
		PROCESSES	FUNCTIONS	HUMAN-INDUCED STRESSES	DELINEATION AND IDENTIFICATION	MANAGEMENT
Army Corps of Engineers	Corps	$ 1,072,000	$ 438,000	$ 154,000	$ 364,000	$ 4,818,000
Agricultural Research Service	ARS	814,000	0	65,000	0	909,000
Bureau of Mines	BOM	316,000	49,000	0	0	0
Bureau of Reclamation	BOR	25,000	25,000	0	0	150,000
Department of Energy	DOE	2,698,000	2,126,000	2,195,000	1,279,000	2,110,000
Federal Highway Administration	FHA	77,000	39,000	29,000	347,000	100,000
Minerals Management Service	MMS	500,000	0	0	0	0
National Oceanic and Atmospheric Administration	NOAA	287,000	2,144,000	523,000	100,000	165,000
National Park Service	NPS	1,046,000	0	194,000	0	531,000
National Science Foundation	NSF	269,000	0	0	0	0
Office of Surface Mining	OSM	0	0	0	0	147,000
Smithsonian Institute	SMI	847,000	100,000	32,000	88,000	1,000
Soil Conservation Service*	SCS	32,000	0	0	0	2,014,000
Tennessee Valley Authority	TVA	55,000	167,000	70,000	0	2,674,000
U.S. Environmental Protection Agency	EPA	150,000	586,000	0	0	2,320,000
U.S. Fish and Wildlife Service	FWS	2,366,000	1,027,000	7,039,000	771,000	4,916,000
U.S. Forest Service	USFS	213,000	409,000	13,000	0	412,000
U.S. Geological Survey	USGS	6,534,000	844,000	3,456,000	118,000	1,567,000

* Became the Natural Resources Conservation Service in 1994.

Figure 42. Summary of Federal agency wetland research expenditures by research category during 1992. (*Source: Federal Wetlands Research Inventory and Database, unpub. data, 1992; compiled by the Wetlands Research and Technology Center, U.S. Army Engineer Waterways Experiment Station, Vicksburg, Miss.*)

stress on wetlands, or of determining stress thresholds of wetlands.

4. Wetland delineation and identification—Research on methods and techniques to identify wetlands and delineate wetland boundaries.
5. Management—Research to develop tools and technologies to maintain, restore, and construct wetlands.

Figure 42 depicts the expenditures on Federal research in each of these categories in 1992. Individual research studies may span several of these categories; however, these categories represent a convenient way to describe existing research activities.

In addition to distinguishing the type of research, it also is useful to distinguish the type of wetland being studied. Because ecological processes and functions differ with the type of wetland, research needs and techniques also differ. Disappearing coastal and bottom-land hardwood wetlands are among the major areas of research. Figure 43 shows Federal expenditures for research on different types of wetlands. (See article "Wetland Definitions and Classification in the Conterminous United States" for an explanation of wetland types.)

AGENCY ROLES AND RESPONSIBILITIES

Federal wetland research is conducted throughout the Nation. Twelve agencies listed in the Wetland Research Subcommittee's report and discussed below have wetland research expenditures of $1 million or more. Although not discussed below, other agencies with less funding that also contribute to wetland research are the Department of the Interior's Bureau of Mines, Bureau of Reclamation, Minerals Management Service, and Office of Surface Mining; the Federal Highway Administration's Department of Transportation; and the National Science Foundation.

Department of the Interior

Wetland research activities in the Department of the Interior relate to its responsibilities as the primary steward of America's natural resources. The Department of the Interior performs basic scientific research on wetland processes and functions and applied focused research on human-induced stresses, delineation and identification, and management of wetlands. The Department assumes ownership and management responsibilities for wetlands through the U.S. Fish and Wildlife Service (FWS) and the National Park Service, and scientific research responsibilities through the activities of the U.S. Geological Survey (USGS) and the National Biological Service (NBS). Research funding for the Department was greater than $30.5 million in 1992 (figs. 42–43).

U.S. Fish and Wildlife Service: The FWS has stewardship responsibilities for fish and other wildlife (such as migratory birds, anadromous fish, and endangered species), their habitats, and for wildlife refuges. As a major Federal landowner, the FWS protects and manages wetlands and associated habitats on more than 90 million acres of national wildlife refuges and provides advice about and technical support for regulatory activities and trust species to other Federal, State, and private landowners. The FWS, through the National Wetlands Inventory program, provides detailed wetland maps for the Nation, and also reports to Congress every 10 years the status and trends of the Nation's wetlands. (See article "Wetland Mapping and Inventory" in this volume.) Research focuses on improved methods and tools for identifying and delineating different wetland types.

U.S. Geological Survey: The USGS provides geologic, hydrologic, and topographic information to assist Federal, State, and local governments, the private sector, and individual citizens in making management decisions about the use of land and water

What happens to wetlands in one State can affect wetland activities, benefits, and uses in another State.

AGENCY		WETLAND TYPES*				
		MARINE	ESTUARINE	RIVERINE	PALUSTRINE	LACUSTRINE
Army Corps of Engineers	Corps	$ 0	$ 1,750,000	$ 1,529,000	$ 2,036,000	$ 824,000
Agricultural Research Service	ARS	0	20,000	1,053,000	650,000	65,000
Bureau of Mines	BOM	0	0	0	0	0
Bureau of Reclamation	BOR	0	0	50,000	50,000	100,000
Department of Energy	DOE	153,000	418,000	1,855,000	2,640,000	406,000
Federal Highway Administration	FHA	5,000	5,000	2,000	193,000	0
Minerals Management Service	MMS	250,000	250,000	0	0	0
National Oceanic and Atmospheric Administration	NOAA	193,000	2,925,000	66,000	35,000	0
National Park Service	NPS	7,000	818,000	428,000	480,000	58,000
National Science Foundation	NSF	0	170,000	13,000	86,000	0
Office of Surface Mining	OSM	0	0	0	64,000	0
Smithsonian Institute	SMI	420,000	355,000	267,000	26,000	0
Soil Conservation Service	SCS	184,000	806,000	323,000	352,000	268,000
Tennessee Valley Authority	TVA	0	0	84,000	531,000	2,084,000
U.S. Environmental Protection Agency	EPA	150,000	225,000	736,000	1,421,000	270,000
U.S. Fish and Wildlife Service	FWS	428,000	2,949,000	5,202,000	4,033,000	3,564,000
U.S. Forest Service	USFS	0	0	102,000	945,000	0
U.S. Geological Survey	USGS	1,482,000	3,587,000	2,606,000	2,880,000	1,963,000

* Descrepancies in total expenditures occur because some agencies did not include constructed wetlands when reporting these figures.

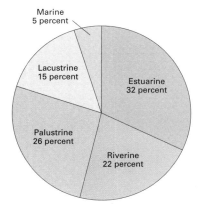

Figure 43. Summary of Federal agency wetland research expenditures by wetland type during 1992. *(Sources: Federal Wetlands Research Inventory and Database, unpub. data, 1992; compiled by the Wetlands Research and Technology Center, U.S. Army Engineer Waterways Experiment Station, Vicksburg, Miss.)*

Core sample being collected by the U.S. Geological Survey at a fen in Minn., tells the sediment history of this particular wetland. *(Photograph by Nancy Rybicki, U.S. Geological Survey.)*

The National Biological Service collects turtlegrass near Chandeleur Islands, La., to study the effects of water quality on the plant. *(Photograph courtesy of The National Biological Service.)*

The National Biological Service collects bulltongue in a marsh near Lake Salvador, La., for use in greenhouse experiments in salinity and flooding tolerance. *(Photograph courtesy of The National Biological Service.)*

resources. The USGS's wetland research activities are an important part of the agency's activities. Research focuses on the geology, chemistry, hydrology, and biology of wetlands and their interactions. Studies are conducted in selected wetlands to determine the processes responsible for the formation and evolution of wetlands and to increase understanding of wetland functions. Some specific topics that hydrologic studies address are ground-water/surface-water interactions; the role of wetlands in water-quality improvement; the relation between flood-plain wetlands, riverine and estuarine hydrology, and water quality; and the relation of light and water chemistry to aquatic plant distribution in tidal waters.

National Park Service: Wetland research by the National Park Service is primarily issue driven; it is management-oriented and focuses on protecting resources, mitigating the effects of human actions on wetlands, and restoring natural wetland functions where they have been disturbed by past or ongoing human activities.

National Biological Service: The NBS was established in October 1993 and, therefore, was not included in the report by the Wetland Research Subcommittee and not included in the graphs in figures 42–43. However, it is a large player in research being done on wetlands and, therefore, is included in this discussion. The NBS inventories and monitors wetlands and conducts biological research on many aspects of wetlands; in fact, most activities of the NBS are wetland related. It provides biological information and research support to management agencies within the Federal Government.

Department of Energy

The Department of Energy's role in and responsibilities toward wetland research are related to its compliance with environmental regulations. The Department does this by assessing the environmental effects of its activities on lands, including wetlands, under its jurisdiction, and by operating and developing facilities in ways that maintain and enhance environmental quality while providing efficient energy production, transmission, and use. Research focuses on supporting these activities. Research funding was about $10.3 million in 1992 (figs. 42–43).

Department of Defense

Wetland research activities of the Department of Defense result primarily from legislation pertaining to the mission of the U.S. Army Corps of Engineers (Corps). The Army, through the Corps, is assigned responsibility for much of the Nation's water-resource development activities, including efforts to protect, conserve, restore, and establish new wetlands. In performing its development mission, such as keeping waterways open by dredging or building levees to protect cities from flooding, the Corps directly affects wetlands and must consider the effects of its activities. The Corps has established a formal Wetlands Research Program to support its wetland-related responsibilities. This program is designed to include both basic and applied research that emphasize the Corps strengths in engineering design and construction, stewardship, and management. Research funding for the Corps in 1992 was about $6.5 million (figs. 42–43).

Department of Agriculture

The Department of Agriculture performs wetland research through several of its agencies; the Natural Resources Conservation Service (formerly known as the Soil Conservation Service), the Agricultural Research Service, and the U.S. Forest Service. Research funding for the Department of Agriculture was about $4.5 million in 1992 (figs. 42–43).

Natural Resources Conservation Service: The Natural Resources Conservation Service assists other Federal, State, and local governments in resource conservation activities that include wetland protection. Their authority covers mainly lands with high potential for conversion to agricultural uses.

The Natural Resources Conservation Service's plant materials centers develop new varieties of plants and the technology for using plants to solve soil and water-conservation problems. They also provide for the commercial production of these plants. Some of the centers conduct investigations on how to reestablish marsh vegetation along eroding tidal shores in the mid-Atlantic States and the Gulf Coast States from Alabama to Mexico. Projects are underway at other centers to develop new varieties of plants and encourage plant reproduction, to develop techniques for establishing and maintaining restored and created freshwater wetlands, and to design and construct wetlands that act as biological filters of agricultural runoff.

Economic Research Service: Although the Economic Research Service is not one of the agencies listed in the Wetland Research Subcommittee report, its research is integral to oversight of the Wetland Reserve Program by the Natural Resources Conservation Service (see the article "Wetland Protection Legislation" in this volume), and is, therefore, mentioned in this discussion. The Economic Research Service conducts cost and benefit comparison studies to determine effective economic incentives associated with wetland conservation or destruction. Because the Wetland Reserve Program is voluntary, research focuses on identifying costs that limit farmers' participation.

Agricultural Research Service: The Agricultural Research Service's mission includes development of technology needed to ensure maintenance of environmental quality and natural resources. Their research supports implementation of Federal agricultural legislation and development of new agricultural practices that produce less off-site contamination. Many programs indirectly contribute to national wetland goals by improving management of basins that drain into wetlands.

U.S. Forest Service: The U.S. Forest Service conducts research to support improved management of Federal, State, and private forests; the research comprises efforts to describe ecosystem dynamics and to develop improved technology for restoring and rehabilitating forested wetlands. Research is conducted on the role of flowing water in sustaining chemical, physical, and biological processes integral to the functioning of wetland and riparian ecosystems. The For-

The U.S. Army Corps of Engineers collects water-level data at a bottom-land hardwood wetland located along the Cache River, Ark. *(Photograph courtesy of the U.S. Army Corps of Engineers.)*

The U.S. Army Corps of Engineers dewatered this freshwater wetland at a restoration site at Kenilworth Marsh in Maryland to facilitate planting. Dewatering was achieved by building temporary dikes made from water-filled tubes designed by the Corps for this purpose. *(Photograph courtesy of the U.S. Army Corps of Engineers.)*

est Service also conducts studies of technological improvements used for reforesting wetland and riparian sites, which involves understanding how tree species adapt to flooding. Other areas of study include establishing understory vegetation, restoring wetland hydrology, and rehabilitating fish and other wildlife habitat.

Department of Commerce

The Department of Commerce conducts its research through the National Oceanic and Atmospheric Administration. In 1992, funding for research by the Department was about $3 million (figs. 42–43).

National Oceanic and Atmospheric Administration: The National Oceanic and Atmospheric

National Marine Fisheries Service scientists study the effects of oyster-shell reefs on sedimentation and use by marine organisms in this created wetland at Swansboro Marsh, N.C. *(Photograph by David L. Meyer, National Marine Fisheries Service.)*

The information derived from broad-scope, individual agency research may complement that of other agencies.

Administration's (NOAA) mission is to manage our ocean and coastal resources, describe and predict changes in the Earth's oceans and atmosphere, and promote its global stewardship through scientific research and service. Three of NOAA's five organizations are directly involved in wetland research: the National Marine Fisheries Service, the National Ocean Service, and the Office of Oceanic and Atmospheric Research. NOAA also has a relevant agency-wide program, the Coastal Ocean Program, which supports management of the coastal ocean environment.

The Coastal Ocean Program is intended to provide scientific products that support coastal ocean management through improved understanding and prediction of environmental quality, fishery resources, and coastal hazards. One of the Coastal Ocean Program's component programs seeks to understand and quantify the relation between estuarine habitat and coastal ocean productivity. Initial re-search has been focused on locating and determining rates of loss of seagrasses, emergent marshes, and adjacent uplands using satellite and aerial photography. Research is being conducted on the functional attributes of these habitats and their capability of being restored.

National Marine Fisheries Service: This organization is the Federal steward of the Nation's living marine resources, from 200 miles offshore (the seaward extent of the Nation's assessment of mineral and energy sources) to the freshwater tributaries used by anadromous species for spawning. National Marine Fisheries Service's scientists conduct basic and applied research to advance understanding of wetland habitat functioning in response to natural and human-induced environmental changes, to develop improved techniques for habitat restoration and assessment, and to support the habitat permit review process. The National Marine Fisheries Service's Restoration Center develops and implements habitat restoration plans that seek to restore, replace, or acquire the equivalent of the resources determined to have been injured by releases of oil or hazardous substances to the environment.

National Ocean Service: This organization administers programs that provide support for managing marine environments. It manages a national network of marine sanctuaries and estuarine research reserves. The estuarine research reserves, throughout the National Estuarine Research Reserves System, are established, managed, and maintained with the help of State authorities to assure their long-term protection. Research activities are used to facilitate management of wetlands. Priorities change biennially and have included nonpoint-source pollution (1993–94) and habitat restoration (1994–95).

Office of Oceanic and Atmospheric Research: This organization is responsible for conducting research that improves understanding and prediction of oceanic and atmospheric conditions. This includes investigating processes that regulate wetland ecosystem structure and production, the responses of these systems to natural and human-induced conditions, and the effects of global climate and other atmospheric conditions on marine resources and ecosystems.

U.S. Environmental Protection Agency

Research needs within the U.S. Environmental Protection Agency (EPA) are extensive. The Wetlands Research Program of the EPA is an applied research program that primarily provides technical support to improve the Agency's ability to carry out its regulatory responsibilities. Three components of the Wetlands Research Program are the Wetland Function Project, the Characterization and Restoration Project, and the Landscape Function Project. Detailed studies of individual wetlands conducted to understand better the processes within wetlands that contribute to wetland functions and wetland responses to environmental stressors are carried out through the Wetland Function Project. Studies of the characteristics of groups of wetlands that compare the functions of natural, restored, and created wetlands within similar geographic settings are carried out through the Characterization and Restoration Project. Research is con-

National Marine Fisheries Service scientists, using a drop sampler, collect aquatic organisms in a salt marsh on Galveston Island, Tex. This is often done to assess damages following an oil spill. *(Photograph by Lawrence P. Rozas, National Marine Fisheries Service.)*

ducted on the interactions of wetlands with other ecosystems and on the cumulative effects of human activities on wetland functions through the Landscape Function Project. In 1992, EPA's funding for wetland research was about $3 million (figs. 42–43).

Tennessee Valley Authority

The Tennessee Valley Authority (TVA) is a resource management agency created by the Tennessee Valley Authority Act of 1933. Its research focuses on both natural and constructed wetlands. Natural-wetlands research is directed toward protecting and enhancing aquatic bed, emergent, and riparian forested wetlands and the wildlife populations dependent on them. Constructed-wetlands research is directed toward designing and operating constructed wetlands to solve specific waste-management or environmental problems and examining the basic mechanics and physiology of these systems. Wetland research is conducted in the field, in laboratories, and at a unique 32-celled physical model at a constructed-wetland research facility in Muscle Shoals, Ala. In 1992, funding for research was about $3 million (figs. 42–43).

Smithsonian Institution

Smithsonian research on wetlands is focused on the biota, hydrology, and functions of wetlands. Aerial photographs, remote sensing, and Geographic Information Systems are used to extend research results from specific sites to larger regions and to relate wetlands to their drainage basins. Research support comes directly from Congress, from Smithsonian trust funds, and from extramural grants and contracts. Funding for research in 1992 was about $1 million (figs. 42–43).

COORDINATION OF RESEARCH AMONG FEDERAL AGENCIES

Federal agencies conduct wetland research to execute their congressionally mandated missions. Generally these research efforts fall within well-defined limits. By necessity, some agencies conduct research with a broad range of activities. The information derived from broad-scope, individual agency research may complement that of other agencies.

Federal agencies have special obligations, as stewards of public monies, to get the most out of research dollars. Effective coordination is essential to assure that agencies efficiently budget and use research funds, to ensure that research is not duplicated by two or more agencies (and money wasted), and to ensure that the "best science" is achieved. Federal agencies involved in wetland research use formal and informal coordination mechanisms to achieve these goals.

Informal coordination takes many forms. It includes scientists from each agency communicating directly with scientists in other agencies about matters of common interest. It also includes many adhoc committees and working groups organized to accomplish general coordination as well as specific research objectives. Among the adhoc committees is the Federal Interagency Coordination Committee on Wetlands

Local teachers work in cooperation with U.S. Environmental Protection Agency scientists to measure elevations and create site maps on this restored wetland in Portland, Oreg. *(Photograph courtesy of the U.S. Environmental Protection Agency.)*

Research and Development, a voluntary group that meets annually in Washington, D.C., to present the status of agency research programs and discuss areas of potential interaction. This Committee developed the first National Summary of Ongoing Wetlands Research by Federal Agencies (U.S. Army Engineer Waterways Experiment Station, 1992). All Federal agencies that perform wetland research are invited to these meetings. Another voluntary adhoc committee, the Forested Wetlands Research and Development Interagency Coordination Committee, formed working groups and developed a multiyear interagency research proposal for work in forested wetlands in Southern States. The Corps, the NBS, and the FWS provide funds for this research; and the EPA, Agricultural Research Service, and Natural Resources Conservation Service actually do the research.

Federal agencies also use informal scientific reviews of individual projects and entire programs for coordination. The purpose of these reviews is to expose a project or program to external review and comment, as well as to provide a forum for exchanging views and ideas about each participating agency's project or program. The wetland research programs operated by the Corps, FWS, and EPA, and projects of the NBS's National Wetland Research Center and Cooperative Research Units Center regularly receive external peer review. Several Federal agencies regularly hold interagency planning meetings to discuss new wetland research goals and projects, solicit comments, and explore areas for potential partnerships and cooperation.

Agencies with responsibilities for regulating and managing Federal lands, which include wetlands, conduct workshops, seminars, and other informal meetings to facilitate effective interaction and coordination of their research. Professional societies, scientific literature, agency publications, newsletters, bulletins, and topical conferences also offer mechanisms for coordination and information exchange.

More formal coordination is achieved through exchange agreements, in which scientists may be exchanged from one agency to another for specific pe-

Federal agencies have special obligations, as stewards of public monies, to get the most out of research dollars.

riods to provide needed expertise. As an example, the Wetlands Classification System developed by the FWS was prepared with full-time assistance of scientists from the Corps and the Soil Conservation Service, and the authors of the report defining the system (Cowardin and others, 1979) included representatives from the FWS, the USGS, and NOAA. Written agreements such as Memorandums of Agreement or Memorandums of Understanding also are used to facilitate cooperation between agencies that share mutual objectives. Reimbursable and shared funding may be used to leverage available research dollars and take advantage of specific expertise available in some agencies and lacking in others.

Formal coordination may be required by specific legislative or administrative decisions, such as the Clinton administration's decisions relating to implementation of the Breaux Bill, which requires agencies to coordinate in assessing damages and implementing corrective mechanisms in south Louisiana's coastal wetlands.

ACKNOWLEDGMENTS

Representatives of Federal agencies listed herein contributed to this report. The authors are particularly grateful to the following: Robert E. Stewart, Jr., NBS;

Mon S. Yee, Natural Resources Conservation Service; Doug Ryan, U.S. Forest Service; David Correll, Smithsonian Institute; Mary E. Kentula, EPA; David A. Seyler, USGS; Clive Jorgensen, Department of Energy; and Joel Wagner, National Park Service.

References Cited

Cowardin, L.M., Carter, Virginia, Golet, F.C., and LaRoe, E.T., 1979, Classification of wetlands and deepwater habitats of the United States: U.S. Fish and Wildlife Service, Report FWS/OBS–79/31, 131 p.
Frayer, W.E., Monahan, T.J., Bowden, D.C., and Graybill, F.A., 1983, Status and trends of wetlands and deepwater habitats in the conterminous United States, 1950's to 1970's: Fort Collins, Colorado State University, p. 32.
U.S. Army Engineer Waterways Experiment Station, 1992, National summary of ongoing wetlands research by Federal agencies: Vicksburg, Miss., Prepared by the Wetlands Research Program, 69 p.

FOR ADDITIONAL INFORMATION: Wetlands Research Program (CEWES–EP–W), U.S. Army Engineer Waterways Experiment Station, 3909 Hall Ferry Rd., Vicksburg, MS 39180

Wetland Management and Research
Wetland Mapping and Inventory

By Bill O. Wilen[1], Virginia Carter[2], and J. Ronald Jones[2]

Wetland maps are a prerequisite for wetland inventory and for wetland development planning, management, protection, and restoration. Maps provide information on wetland type, location, and size. Detailed wetland maps are necessary for analysis of the effect of projects at specific sites and for providing baseline spatial data for the assessment of the effects of national policies and activities. Wetland maps are used by local, State, and Federal agencies, as well as by private industry and organizations. They are used for many purposes, including the development of comprehensive resource management plans, environmental impact assessments, natural resource inventories, habitat surveys, and the analysis of trends in wetland status.

Several Federal agencies map wetlands in support of their Congressional mandate. These include the U.S. Department of the Interior, U.S. Fish and Wildlife Service (FWS); the U.S. Department of Agriculture, Natural Resources Conservation Service (NRCS); and the U.S. Department of Commerce, National Oceanic and Atmospheric Administration (NOAA). The FWS has the primary responsibility for mapping and inventory of all the wetlands of the United States. The wetland maps produced by other agencies serve different purposes and generally involve cooperation with the FWS.

THE U.S. FISH AND WILDLIFE SERVICE'S MAPPING AND INVENTORY ACTIVITIES

The FWS National Wetlands Inventory is responsible for the mapping and inventory of wetlands throughout the United States. The Emergency Wetlands Resources Act of 1986 and amendments to it in 1988 and 1992 define the responsibilities of the

National Wetlands Inventory. (See the article "Wetland Protection Legislation" in this volume for more information on this and other wetland legislation.)

History and Status of the National Wetlands Inventory

In 1906, and again in 1922, the U.S. Department of Agriculture inventoried the wetlands of the United States to identify those that could be drained and converted to other uses (Wilen and Tiner, 1993). In 1954, the first nationwide wetland survey by the FWS covered about 40 percent of the conterminous United States and focused on important waterfowl wetlands. This survey was not comprehensive by today's standards, but it stimulated public interest in the conservation of waterfowl wetlands (Shaw and Fredine, 1956). (See the article "Wetlands as Bird Habitat" in this volume.)

After the earlier inventories, and in response to passage of the Emergency Wetlands Resources Act and its amendments, the FWS established the National Wetlands Inventory. The program is designed to (1) produce detailed maps on the characteristics and extent of the Nation's wetlands, (2) construct a national wetlands data base, (3) disseminate wetland maps and digital data, (4) report results of State wetland inventories, (5) report to Congress every 10 years on the status and trends of the Nation's wetlands, and (6) assemble and distribute related maps, digital data, and reports.

The National Wetlands Inventory has produced more than 50,800 maps covering 88 percent of the conterminous United States, 30 percent of Alaska, and all of Hawaii and the U.S. Territories (fig. 44) Priorities for mapping have been based on the needs of the FWS, other Federal agencies, and State agen-

Wetland maps are a prerequisite for wetland inventory, planning, management, protection, and restoration.

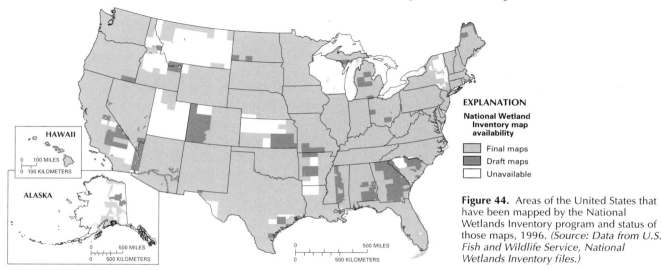

EXPLANATION

National Wetland Inventory map availability

- Final maps
- Draft maps
- Unavailable

Figure 44. Areas of the United States that have been mapped by the National Wetlands Inventory program and status of those maps, 1996. *(Source: Data from U.S. Fish and Wildlife Service, National Wetlands Inventory files.)*

[1] U.S. Fish and Wildlife Service.
[2] U.S. Geological Survey.

cies. To date, mapping has been concentrated on the coastal zone (including the Great Lakes), prairie wetlands, playa lakes, flood plains of major rivers, and areas that reflect goals of the North American Waterfowl Management Plan (U.S. Fish and Wildlife Service, 1976). As a practical matter, priorities have been based on the availability of funding and the availability of high-quality aerial photographs. The National Wetlands Inventory produced maps at a rate of about 5 percent of the conterminous United States and about 2 percent of Alaska annually through 1995—about 3,200 1:24,000-scale maps in the conterminous United States and about 60 1:63,360-scale maps in Alaska.

To date, almost 18,800 maps, representing 29 percent of the United States, have been digitized.

The National Wetlands Inventory has published a series of documents on the trends in wetland losses and gains. The first of these reports was "Status and Trends of Wetlands and Deepwater Habitats in the Conterminous United States, 1950's to 1970's" (Frayer and others, 1983). In the Emergency Wetlands Resources Act of 1986 and subsequent amendments, Congress directed the National Wetlands Inventory to (1) update and improve the information contained in this report by 1990 and at 10-year intervals thereafter and (2) estimate the number of acres of wetland habitat in each State in the 1780's and the 1980's and calculate the percentage of loss in each State. In response to this directive, the National Wetlands Inventory published a 1990 report to Congress titled "Wetlands— Losses in the United States, 1780's to 1980's" (Dahl, 1990).

The National Wetlands Inventory also is preparing a geographically referenced digital data base for wetlands so that wetland information can be placed in geographic information systems (GIS) for use with computers. These digital maps and information are easily transmitted over the Internet. To date, almost 18,800 maps, representing 29 percent of the United States, have been digitized (fig. 45). Statewide data bases have been digitized for Delaware, Hawaii, Indiana, Maryland, Illinois, New Jersey, Washington, Iowa, Minnesota, and West Virginia. Digitization is in progress for Florida, North Carolina, South Carolina, South Dakota, and Virginia. Wetland digital data are available for parts of 35 other States.

In addition to wetland maps and status and trend reports, the National Wetlands Inventory produces special items related to the identification, mapping, and inventory of wetlands. The "National List of Plant Species that Occur in Wetlands" (Reed, 1988) is an important tool for identifying wetlands on the basis of their vegetation. A computerized data base for wetland plants, developed by the National Wetlands Inventory, also lists plants found in wetlands and ranks their affinity to the wetland environment. This information is important for determining whether an area is really a wetland. Additionally, the National Wetlands Inventory has contributed to a list of hydric soils (soils found in wetlands) (U.S. Soil Conservation Service, 1991). Many published State wetland reports, including "Wetlands of Maryland" (Tiner and Burke, 1995), "Wetlands of Connecticut" (Metzler and Tiner, 1992), and "Status of Alaska Wetlands" (Hall, Frayer, and Wilen, 1994), contain wetland inventory results and other important information. Finally, in cooperation with the U.S. Geological Survey (USGS), the National Wetlands Inventory has published a map (scale of 1 inch equals 50 miles) showing the locations of major wetland complexes in the conterminous United States, Hawaii, and Puerto Rico (Dahl, 1991) and a map (scale of 1 inch equals 40 miles) of Alaska's wetland resources (Hall, 1991).

OTHER FEDERAL AGENCIES' MAPPING AND INVENTORY ACTIVITIES

Natural Resources Conservation Service.—The NRCS (formerly the Soil Conservation Service) conducts its wetland inventory under the auspices of the wetland conservation provision (nicknamed "Swampbuster") of the Food Security Act of 1985. This Act provides for the reduction of a farmer's program benefits if wetlands are converted to agricultural production. In order to implement this act, the mapping of the NRCS is focused on freshwater wetlands that have a high potential for agricultural conversion, such as those adjacent to or lying within the boundaries of existing agricultural fields.

The NRCS does not produce a standard map product. Many delineations are made on 1:660-scale

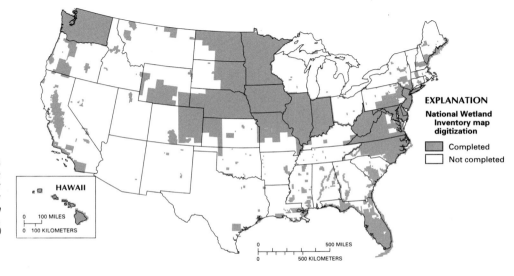

Figure 45. Areas of the conterminous United States and Hawaii where wetland data have been digitized by the National Wetlands Inventory program, 1996. (Source: Data from U.S. Fish and Wildlife Service, National Wetlands Inventory files.)

HAWAII

0   100 MILES
0   100 KILOMETERS

EXPLANATION

National Wetland Inventory map digitization

Completed

Not completed

0   500 MILES
0   500 KILOMETERS

The "Swampbuster" discourages the conversion of wetlands to cropland. This wetland, which was converted to cropland at one time, has been restored. *(Photograph courtesy of the U.S. Fish and Wildlife Service.)*

The National Oceanic and Atmospheric Administration delineates coastal wetland and upland habitats, such as this coastal wetland at Chincoteague National Wildlife Refuge on Assateague Island, Va. *(Photograph by Judy D. Fretwell, U.S. Geological Survey.)*

black-and-white aerial photographs; others are made on soil-survey base maps at scales that range from 1:10,000 to 1:64,000 (Teels, 1990). Information sources for this program include recent and historical aerial photographs, such as those regularly acquired by the U.S. Department of Agriculture, National Wetlands Inventory maps from the FWS, U.S. Department of Agriculture crop history records, and field verifications.

National Oceanic and Atmospheric Administration.—The NOAA has developed the Coastal Wetland Habitat Change Program in order to delineate coastal wetland habitats and adjacent uplands and plains to monitor changes in these habitats on a cycle of 1 to 5 years. The basis for monitoring will be a data base describing the areal extent and distribution of coastal wetlands in the conterminous United States. The program will help to determine the linkages between estuarine and marine wetlands, as well as the distribution, abundance, and health of living marine resources.

U.S. Geological Survey.—The USGS compiles, produces, and disseminates topographic, hydrologic, and geologic maps and digital data related to wetlands. The standard USGS 1:24,000-scale topographic map commonly is used as a base for wetland mapping by other Federal, State, and local agencies. However, because USGS maps depict wetlands as unbounded symbols (fig. 46), the maps cannot be used to establish exact boundaries for wetlands. Intermediate-scale (1:100,000) and large-scale maps (scales of 1:24,000 or greater) are used for project planning. Large-scale maps known as orthophoto quadrangles, which are made by manipulation of aerial photographs to achieve a positionally accurate photographic base map, are used as a base for State wetland mapping.

COORDINATION OF FEDERAL WETLAND MAPPING EFFORTS

Differing needs of various Federal agencies can require different types of maps or different map scales. However, many needs can be satisfied by common products, and efforts are being made to standardize maps and map products whenever possible or practical. Federal digital wetland mapping is coordinated by the Wetlands Subcommittee of the Federal Geographic Data Coordination group in an effort to meet requirements established by the Office of Management and Budget. The Office of Management and Budget requires agencies to develop a national digital spatial information resource in collaboration with State and local governments and the private sector. This requirement is for the purposes of (1) promoting the development, maintenance, and management of a national digital wetland data base; (2) encouraging the development and implementation of standards, exchange formats, specifications, procedures, and guidelines; (3) promoting interaction among other Federal, State, and local government agencies that have interests in the generation, collection, use, and transfer of wetland spatial data; (4) maintaining and disseminating information on the type and availability of wetland spatial data; and (5) promoting the concept of effective wetland management.

> *Efforts are made to standardize maps and map products whenever possible or practical.*

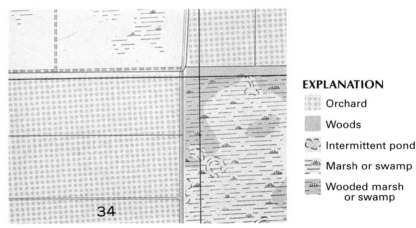

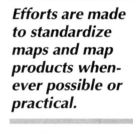

EXPLANATION

Orchard

Woods

Intermittent pond

Marsh or swamp

Wooded marsh or swamp

Figure 46. Unbounded symbols on a U.S. Geological Survey topographic map show the general location of wetlands.

PRODUCING NATIONAL WETLANDS INVENTORY MAPS

Most natural-resource inventories make use of aerial photographs or satellite images combined with field verification. The National Wetlands Inventory uses the best and most appropriate aerial photographs available for mapping wetlands. The principal data source in the early 1980's was the 1:80,000-scale, high-altitude, black-and-white aerial photography acquired by the USGS for topographic mapping and production of orthophoto quadrangles. After the USGS began its National High-Altitude Photography Program, 1:58,000-scale color-infrared photographs for the entire country became available; the National Wetlands Inventory uses these photographs extensively. In 1987, the USGS replaced the National High-Altitude Photography Program with the National Aerial Photography Program, which produces 1:40,000-scale color-infrared photographs; the National Wetlands Inventory uses these photographs as well. In some cases, the National Wetlands Inventory uses supplementary photography, such as some 1:60,000-scale color-infrared photographs of the prairie pothole region of the northern Great Plains, which were acquired from the National Aeronautics and Space Administration.

Stereoscopic color-infrared photographs are best for identifying and delineating wetlands. Color, texture, and pattern are important features of wetland vegetation and background soils. A combination of vegetation factors produce a specific response or signature on the photograph (Wilen and Pywell, 1992). These vegetation factors include leaf size, shape,

The National Wetlands Inventory uses the best and most appropriate aerial photographs available for mapping wetlands.

structure, and arrangement; branching pattern; height; growth habit; and color. Determining the boundary of a wetland is the most difficult part of mapping. Normally, transitions are found at the boundary from upland vegetation to wetland vegetation, from nonhydric to hydric (wetland) soils, and from land that is not flooded to areas that are subject to flooding or saturation. On color-infrared photographs, water generally shows as a distinctive black and blue-black color because of its lack of reflectance. Wetlands that have canopy openings and contain standing water exhibit this signature along with assorted wetland-vegetation signatures. Saturated soils show darker tones because of the nonreflectance of the soil-water component. Even when wetland basins are dry, the silt, clay, and other fine-grained materials hold more water than the upland soils hold, which results in a distinctive dark color because of the lack of infrared reflectance.

Vegetation characteristics help to identify wetlands. Wetland vegetation generally is more dense, more crowded, and more concentrated than upland vegetation. Wetland vegetation normally exhibits a higher degree of lushness, vigor, and intensity than does upland vegetation. Even wheat grown in a dry wetland basin has a distinctive signature; it is more vigorous because of extra moisture in the basin. Dead and dying vegetation in flooded wetland basins also has distinctive signatures. When physiographic positions are associated with the vegetative characteristics described above, wetland locations become more obvious on an aerial photograph (fig. 47).

Patterns, or the repetition of the spatial arrangement, of vegetative types also provide important clues in the identification of wetlands. Basins that have a semipermanently flooded center may have a seasonally flooded band around the center and a temporarily flooded outer band. Patterns are not restricted to vegetation—they can include drainage patterns and land-use patterns. Unplanted basins in farm fields might indicate wetlands; land-cover patterns such as ridges and swales help separate uplands and wetlands. When wetlands are being mapped, the photointerpreter closely checks areas indicated by swamp symbols as wetlands on USGS topographic maps and NRCS soil survey maps to ensure their possible inclusion as wetlands; such areas are considered wetlands unless strong evidence indicates otherwise.

A typical National Wetlands Inventory map consists of wetland boundaries added to a black-and-white version of a 1:24,000-scale USGS topographic base map. Wetlands are classified according to guidelines developed by Cowardin and others (1979). (See article "Wetland Definitions and Classifications in the United States" in this volume.) These wetland classifications are shown on the map as alpha-numeric codes that are identified in a map explanation at the bottom of the map. Many steps are involved in the production of a wetland map from selecting the sites for field verification to delineation, quality control, and production of the final map product (fig. 48). All National Wetlands Inventory photointerpreters are trained extensively in wetland identification, the FWS wetland classification system, and the field identification of wetland plants and soils in order to ensure the best quality, most accurate maps.

 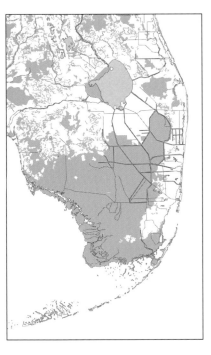

Figure 47. Wetland features such as water, vegetation, and soil are identified on an aerial photograph by their signatures (left), and these signatures are used to produce wetland maps (right). *(Source: U.S. Geological Survey, 1995 (left); T.E. Dahl, U.S. Fish and Wildlfie Service, unpub. data, 1992 (right).)*

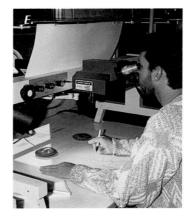

STEPS IN PRODUCING NATIONAL WETLANDS INVENTORY MAPS

1. Determine project area.

2. Obtain source materials.

3. Prepare source materials (photo *A*).

4. Review photo interpretation and plan field trip (photo *B*).

5. Conduct a field reconnaissance of study area.

6. Make photo interpretation (photo *C*).

7. Check photointerpretation (quality control) (photo *D*).

8. Transfer photointerpreted data to base map (photo *E*).

9. Check transferred information (quality control).

10. Prepare copy of draft map for review.

11. Conduct review of draft maps.

12. Make changes to draft map manuscript (photo *F*).

13. Conduct final quality-control checks.

14. Produce final map for distribution (photo *G*).

15. Digitize the final map (photo *H*).

Figure 48. The sequence of steps in producing National Wetlands Inventory maps. *(Photographs A and E by Judy D. Fretwell, U.S. Geological Survey; all other photographs by Donald W. Woodard, U.S. Fish and Wildlife Service.)*

HOW AND WHERE TO GET NATIONAL WETLANDS INVENTORY MAPS

Maps of the National Wetlands Inventory can be acquired from 33 State-run distribution centers, 6 USGS Earth Science Information Center regional offices, or by calling the USGS national toll-free number: 1-800-USA-MAPS. Maps can also be viewed at the Library of Congress and the Federal Depository Library System and downloaded cost-free through the National Wetlands Inventory Home Page on the Internet at http://www.nwi.fws.gov. The six regional USGS Earth Science Information Centers provide online computer links to the National Wetlands Inventory map data base, which contains current information about the availability and production history of National Wetlands Inventory maps and digital data. Digital data are available in Digital Line Graph 3 (DLG3) optional or Geographic Resources Analysis Support System (GRASS) formats; latitude and longitude, State Plane Coordinates, or Universal Transverse Mercator (UTM) coordinate systems; and 9-track, 8-mm, or 1/4-inch cassettes in UNIX-TAR or ASCII tape formats. Other products available at cost include acreage statistics by quadrangle, county, or study area and color-coded wetland maps.

References Cited

Cowardin, L.M., Carter, Virginia, Golet, F.C., and LaRoe, E.T., 1979, Classification of wetlands and deepwater habitats of the United States: U.S. Fish and Wildlife Service, Biological Services Program Report FWS/OBS–79/31, 131 p.

Dahl, T.E., 1990, Wetlands–Losses in the United States, 1780's to 1980's: Washington, D.C., U.S. Fish and Wildlife Service, Report to Congress, 21 p.

———1991, Wetland resources of the United States: U.S. Fish and Wildlife Service National Wetlands Inventory map, scale 1:3,168,000.

Frayer, W.E., Monahan, T.J., Bowden, D.C., and Graybill, F.A., 1983, Status and trends of wetlands and deepwater habitats in the conterminous United States, 1950's to 1970's: Fort Collins, Colo., Colorado State University, 32 p.

Hall, J.V., 1991, Wetland resources of Alaska: U.S. Fish and Wildlife Service National Wetlands Inventory map, scale 1:2,500,000.

Hall, J.V., Frayer, W.E., and Wilen, B.O., 1994, Status of Alaska wetlands: Anchorage, Alaska, U.S. Fish and Wildlife Service, 33 p.

Metzler, K.J., and Tiner, R.W., 1992, Wetlands of Connecticut: State Geological and Natural History Survey of Connecticut in cooperation with the U.S. Fish and Wildlife Service National Wetlands Inventory, Report of Investigations no. 13, 115 p.

Reed, P.B., Jr., 1988, National list of plant species that occur in wetlands—1988 national summary: U.S. Fish and Wildlife Service Biological Report 88 (24), 244 p.

Shaw, S.P., and Fredine, C.G., 1956, Wetlands of the United States—Their extent and their value to waterfowl and other wildlife: U.S. Fish and Wildlife Service Circular 39, 67 p.

Teels, B.M., 1990, Soil Conservation Service's wetland inventory, in Kiraly, S.J., Cross, F.A., and Buffington, J.D., eds., Federal coastal wetland mapping programs; a report by the National Ocean Pollution Policy Board: Washington, D.C., U.S. Fish and Wildlife Service Biological Report 90 (18), p. 93–103.

Tiner, R.W., and Burke, D.G., 1995, Wetlands of Maryland: Annapolis, Md., Maryland Department of Natural Resources, Water Resource Administration, in cooperation with U.S. Fish and Wildlife Service, National Wetlands Inventory, 193 p.

U.S. Fish and Wildlife Service, 1976, Existing state and local wetland surveys (1965–1975), v. II, Narrative: Washington, D.C., U.S. Fish and Wildlife Service, Office of Biological Services Report, 453 p.

U.S. Geological Survey, 1995, South Florida Satellite Image Map, 1993: Reston, Va., U.S. Geological Survey, 1 sheet, scale 1:500,000.

U.S. Soil Conservation Service, 1991, Hydric soils of the United States: U.S. Soil Conservation Service in cooperation with the National Technical Committee for Hydric Soils, Miscellaneous Publication No.1491, 3d ed., unnumbered pages.

Wilen, B.O., and Pywell, H.R., 1992, Remote sensing of the Nation's wetlands, National Wetlands Inventory, in Proceedings: Forest Service Remote Sensing Applications Conference, 4th biennial, Orlando, Fla., unnumbered pages.

Wilen, B.O., and Tiner, R.W., 1993, Wetlands of the United States, in Whigham, D.F., Dykyjová, Dagmar, and Hejny, Slavomil, eds., Wetlands of the world I—Inventory, ecology, and management: Dordrecht, The Netherlands, Kluwer Academic Publishers, p. 515–636.

FOR ADDITIONAL INFORMATION: Bill O. Wilen, U.S. Fish and Wildlife Service, National Wetlands Inventory, 4401 N. Fairfax Drive, Room 400 Arlington, VA 22203; Virginia Carter, U.S. Geological Survey, 430 National Center, Reston, VA 22092

Wetland Management and Research
Wetland Functions, Values, and Assessment

By Richard P. Novitzki[1], R. Daniel Smith,[2] and Judy D. Fretwell[3]

Wetlands, or the lack thereof, were a significant factor in the severe flooding in the Upper Mississippi and Missouri River Basins in the summer of 1993 (Parrett and others, 1993) (fig. 49). Damages associated with the flooding were undoubtedly worse than they would have been if flood-plain wetlands had still been in place. Human modification of the original wetlands (a common practice in the early part of this century) had destroyed the ability of the wetlands to modify flooding. (See the article "Effects of the Great Midwest Flood of 1993 on Wetlands" in this volume.) Flood control, however, is only one of the values that wetlands have for society. In order to protect wetlands, the public first must recognize the values of wetlands. People need to understand what is lost when a wetland is changed into an agricultural field, a parking lot, a dump, or a housing development. Understanding the functions of wetlands will make it easier to evaluate wetlands when other uses are considered.

RECOGNITION OF WETLAND FUNCTIONS AND THEIR VALUES

In the 1970's, scientists, ecologists, and conservationists began to articulate the values of wetlands. At a wetland conference in 1973, wetlands were acknowledged to be an important part of the hydrologic cycle (Helfgott and others, 1973). In 1977, participation at the first National Wetland Protection Symposium—attended by more than 700 people—demonstrated a growing interest in the value of wetlands and the need to protect them (Kusler and Montanari, 1978). At a Wetland Values and Management Confer-

ence in 1981, scientists defined the unique qualities of wetlands and developed a list of wetland functions (Richardson, 1981). In addition to the more commonly recognized habitat functions of wetlands, the scientists described hydrologic and water-quality functions. During the 1980's, participants at many more conferences and symposia expanded the understanding and appreciation of the values of wetlands (Kusler and Riexinger, 1986).

WETLAND FUNCTIONS DEFINED

Wetland functions are defined as a process or series of processes that take place within a wetland. These include the storage of water, transformation of nutrients, growth of living matter, and diversity of wetland plants, and they have value for the wetland itself, for surrounding ecosystems, and for people. Functions can be grouped broadly as habitat, hydrologic, or water quality, although these distinctions are somewhat arbitrary and simplistic. For example, the value of a wetland for recreation (hunting, fishing, bird watching) is a product of all the processes that work together to create and maintain the wetland.

Not all wetlands perform all functions nor do they perform all functions equally well. The location and size of a wetland may determine what functions it will perform. For example, the geographic location may determine its habitat functions, and the location of a wetland within a watershed may determine its hydrologic or water-quality functions (fig. 50). Many factors determine how well a wetland will perform these functions: climatic conditions, quantity and quality of water entering the wetland, and disturbances or al-

Not all wetlands perform all functions nor do they perform all functions equally well.

Wetlands are among the most productive habitats in the world.

Figure 49. Flooding in the Upper Mississippi River Basin, summer 1993. *(Photograph © Cameron Davidson, 1993.)*

[1] ManTech Environmental Technology, Inc.
[2] U.S. Army Corps of Engineers.
[3] U.S. Geological Survey.

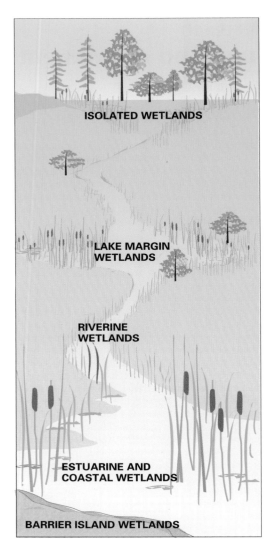

CHARACTERISTICS AND FUNCTIONS OF WETLANDS

Isolated Wetlands
1. Waterfowl feeding and nesting habitat
2. Habitat for both upland and wetland species of wildlife
3. Floodwater retention area
4. Sediment and nutrient retention area
5. Area of special scenic beauty

Lake Margin Wetlands
1. See "isolated wetlands" above
2. Removal of sediment and nutrients from inflowing waters
3. Fish spawning area

Riverine Wetlands
1. See "isolated wetlands" above
2. Sediment control, stabilization of river banks
3. Flood conveyance area

Estuarine and Coastal Wetlands
1. See "isolated wetlands" above
2. Fish and shellfish habitat and spawning areas
3. Nutrient source for marine fisheries
4. Protection from erosion and storm surges

Barrier Island Wetlands
1. Habitat for dune-associated plant and animal species
2. Protection of backlying lands from high-energy waves
3. Scenic beauty

Figure 50. Wetland functions depend upon the location of the wetland within a watershed. *(Source: Modified from J.A. Kusler, Our National Heritage: A Protection Guidebook. Copyright (c) 1983 by the Environmental Law Institute. Reprinted by permission.)*

Timber harvest in a bottom-land forested wetland. *(Photograph by R. Daniel Smith, U.S. Army Engineer Waterways Experiment Station.)*

Hay harvest in a prairie wetland. *(Photograph by Richard P. Novitzki, ManTech Environmental Technology, Inc.)*

teration within the wetland or the surrounding eco-system. Wetland disturbances may be the result of natural conditions, such as an extended drought, or human activities, such as land clearing, dredging, or the introduction of nonnative species.

Perhaps wetlands are best known for their habitat functions, which are the functions that benefit wildlife. Habitat is defined as the part of the physical environment in which plants and animals live (Lapedes, 1976), and wetlands are among the most productive habitats in the world (Tiner, 1989). They provide food, water, and shelter for fish, shellfish, birds, and mammals, and they serve as a breeding ground and nursery for numerous species. Many endangered plant and animal species are dependent on wetland habitats for their survival. (See the article "Wetlands as Bird Habitat" in this volume.) Hydrologic functions are those related to the quantity of water that enters, is stored in, or leaves a wetland. These functions include such factors as the reduction of flow velocity, the role of wetlands as ground-water recharge or discharge areas, and the influence of wetlands on atmospheric processes. Water-quality functions include the trapping of sediment, pollution control, and the biochemical processes that take place as water enters, is stored in, or leaves a wetland. (See article "Wetland Hydrology, Water Quality, and Associated Functions" in this volume for more information on hydrologic and water-quality functions.)

WETLAND VALUES DEFINED

If something has "value," then it is worthwhile, beneficial, or desirable. The value of a wetland lies in the benefits that it provides to the environment or to people, something that is not easily measured. Wetlands can have ecological, social, or economic values. Wetland products that have an economic value, such as commercial fish or timber, can be assigned a monetary value. True wetland value, however, goes beyond money. How much value does one place on the beauty of a wetland or its archeological significance? Wetland values are not absolute. What is valuable and important to one person may not be valuable to another person. As an example, the value of a wetland as duck habitat may be important to the hunter or birdwatcher but not to the farmer who owns the land.

"While wetland functions are natural processes of wetlands that continue regardless of their perceived value to humans, the value people place on those functions in many cases is the primary factor determining whether a wetland remains intact or is converted for some other use" (National Audubon Society, 1993). In addition, values assigned to wetland functions may change over time as society's perceptions and priorities change. The values that benefit society as a whole tend to change slowly; however, the values assigned by individuals or small groups are arbitrary, and most are subject to rapid and frequent change and may even conflict. For example, timber production may be improved by draining a wetland site, whereas waterfowl production may be improved by impounding more water. Society may have to resolve conflicts regarding the management or preservation of wetlands and their functions. Furthermore,

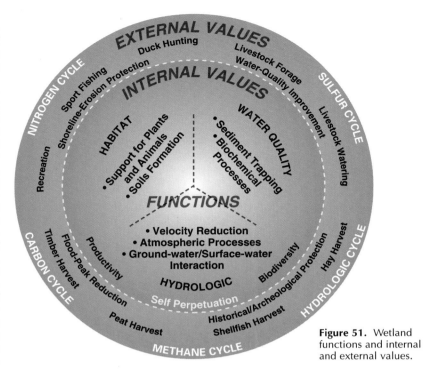

Figure 51. Wetland functions and internal and external values.

society may have to choose among wetland functions that benefit individuals or small groups, that are of value to most of society, or that are important to the maintenance of the wetland itself.

Wetland functions have value on several levels—internal, local, regional, and global. All wetland functions are internal, but the values or benefits of wetland functions can be internal or external to the wetland (fig. 51). Functions that provide internal values are the functions that maintain or sustain the wetland and are essential to the continued existence of the wetland. Conversely, many functions have external values that extend beyond the wetland itself. On a local scale, wetlands affect adjacent or nearby ecosystems, for example, by reducing flooding in downstream communities or by removing nutrients from wastewater. However, the broadest influence of wetland functions is global. Wetlands are now thought to have a significant effect on air quality, which is influenced by the nitrogen, sulfur, methane, and carbon cycles. In addition, migrating birds are dependent upon wetlands as they travel.

PURPOSE OF WETLAND ASSESSMENT

Many times when decisions are made about development of an area, such as the selection of a site for a large commercial or industrial facility, the choice of sites is not between a wetland or an upland, but between wetlands. In areas that have many wetlands, all alternative sites or routes for roads for a major facility may involve the destruction or alteration of wetlands. In such cases, legal requirements commonly exist that require the replacement of destroyed wetlands. Even when a choice must be made between a wetland site and an upland site, the upland site may have great value to the community. Managers, planners, regulators, and even the general public have long

A system of wetland assessment is necessary to ensure that the most valuable wetlands are protected.

felt the need to have in place a system of assessment or evaluation that would make the choices clearer and ensure that the most valuable wetlands are preserved. Such an evaluation system could be based entirely or partly on wetland function if values could be assigned to individual functions.

Wetland assessment methods have been or are being developed that assign numerical values to wetland functions. Some methods assign values on the basis of the benefits to the wetland itself by considering the question: How important is this function in terms of maintaining this particular wetland? Other methods assign values on the basis of the benefits to surrounding ecosystems or to humans. The types of questions considered in this approach are as follows: How important is this function to environmental quality downstream? How does this function benefit society? This latter assessment method allows for the comparison of the worth of one wetland to that of another wetland.

The development of a single method for assessing the functions of wetlands or for assigning values to the functions of wetlands is not a simple task. Indeed, probably no one method will satisfy all needs. However, assessing each function of a wetland and then assigning a value to each function is a step toward the protection of sensitive wetlands. Furthermore, an evaluation system that provides the basis for comparing wetlands would facilitate mitigation for unavoidable wetland losses, would provide a tool for determining the success (or failure) of programs and policies intended to protect or manage wetland resources, and would assist in identifying long-term trends in the condition of wetland resources.

WETLAND ASSESSMENT METHODS

The three wetland assessment methods described herein are representative of the methods that are available or are being used by wetland managers and planners. The Wetland Evaluation Technique was devel-

oped for the Federal Highway Administration and has been used widely. It assigns values to specific functions of individual wetlands. The Environmental Monitoring Assessment Program—Wetlands was developed by the Environmental Protection Agency. It is presented here as an example of a program that focuses on determining the ecological condition of a population of wetlands in a region. It does this by comparing the function of a statistical sample of wetlands to reference wetlands in the region. The Hydrogeomorphic approach is being developed by the U.S. Army Corps of Engineers for assessing wetland functions. It combines features of the other two methods by measuring the functions of individual wetlands and also by comparing them to functions performed by other wetlands.

Wetland Evaluation Technique (WET)

The WET is a comprehensive approach for evaluating individual wetlands that was developed in 1983 (Adamus, 1983; Adamus and Stockwell, 1983) and revised in 1987 under the auspices of the U.S. Army Corps of Engineers (Adamus and others, 1987). The WET considers wetland functions to be the physical, chemical, and biological characteristics of a wetland. It assigns wetland values to the characteristics that are valuable to society. The following functions are assigned values by WET:

- Ground-water recharge
- Ground-water discharge
- Floodflow alteration
- Sediment stabilization
- Sediment/toxicant retention
- Nutrient removal/transformation
- Production export
- Wildlife diversity/abundance
- Aquatic diversity/abundance
- Recreation
- Uniqueness/heritage

The recreational pleasures of a wetland are captured in this photo at Horicon Marsh, Wis. *(Photograph by Phillip J. Redman, U.S. Geological Survey.)*

The WET evaluates functions and values in terms of effectiveness, opportunity, social significance, and habitat suitability. Effectiveness assesses the capability of a wetland to perform a particular function. For example, a wetland that has no outlet is assigned a high value for sediment retention, whereas a wetland just downstream from a dam is assigned a low value. Opportunity assesses the potential for a wetland to perform a specific function; for example, a wetland in a forested area that has no potential sediment sources would be assigned a low opportunity value for sediment retention. Social significance assesses the value of a wetland in terms of special designations (does it have endangered species?), potential economic value (is it used regularly for recreational activities?), and strategic location (is it in a State where very few wetlands of its type remain?). The WET uses "predictors" that relate to the physical, chemical, and biological characteristics of the function being evaluated. As an example, the presence or absence of a constricted outlet from a wetland could be used to predict whether the wetland might be effective in storing floodwaters. In addition, WET can be used to assess the habitat suitability for waterfowl and wetland-dependent birds, fish, and invertebrates.

The WET approach was designed to provide a balance between costly, site-specific studies and the "best professional judgment" approach, which is less costly but lacks reproducibility. The WET method is intended to be used by any environmental professional, so that an engineer can evaluate biological functions or a biologist can evaluate hydrologic functions. First, information resources are obtained for the wetland, the area surrounding the wetland, and the area downstream from the wetland. Then a series of questions is answered about the wetland's watershed, topography, vegetation, and other features. By progressing next through a series of flow charts (or an available computer software package), an evaluation can assign a probability rating of "high," "moderate," or "low" to each of the functions listed above (except

for recreation) and a habitat suitability rating for waterfowl, fish, and other wildlife (Adamus, 1988). The probability rating is an estimate of the "likelihood" that a wetland will perform a function on the basis of its characteristics. It does not estimate the degree or magnitude to which a function is performed. Recreation is not evaluated because no scientific basis exists for making an objective assessment without extensive data collection at the site.

The WET approach probably has been applied to nearly every type of wetland in every State; however, it has proved to be unwieldy to use. For most users, the need to be able to apply this method to every wetland in every part of the United States makes the system unnecessarily cumbersome. For example, most users are interested in a local area and prefer not to enter data repeatedly for local characteristics that are unlikely to change, as is required in the WET approach. In order to refine the method for specific regions and to refine the thresholds among the low, medium, and high values, Adamus (1988) intended that regional versions and five different levels of WET be developed, neither of which has happened. Despite its shortcomings, however, WET continues to be used by those who are familiar with it. Furthermore, much of the data generated by its application could be used to create data bases that would simplify its use and would improve its regional application.

Environmental Monitoring Assessment Program—Wetlands (EMAP—Wetlands)

In 1988, the Environmental Protection Agency initiated the Environmental Monitoring Assessment Program (EMAP) in order to provide improved information on the status and trends in the condition of the Nation's ecological resources. The wetlands part of EMAP was intended to develop an approach for assessing the condition (how well a wetland is performing its functions) of different types of wetlands in a region and in the Nation as a whole (Novitzki,

EMAP—Wetlands identifies "indicators" of condition, standardizes methods of measurement, and establishes a national network.

Sheep foraging at a wetland near Bridgeport, Calif. *(Photograph by A.S. Van Denburgh, U.S. Geological Survey.)*

1994; Novitzki and others, 1994). The near-term objectives of the program were to conduct research in order to identify "indicators" of wetland condition, to standardize methods of measurement, and to establish a national network for monitoring wetlands at regional scales and over long periods (decades). In some places, it is impossible or impractical to measure wetland functions directly; therefore, characteristics or "indicators" are measured, and these indicate how well certain functions are being performed by the wetland. For example, the number of waterfowl per acre can be calculated from actual field measurements and then can be used as an indicator of how well a wetland is performing its waterfowl habitat function.

The HGM approach represents a combination of the WET and EMAP—Wetlands approaches

The EMAP—Wetlands program was intended to have three phases. First, pilot studies were to be conducted to evaluate the ability of selected indicators to make a distinction between healthy and degraded wetlands. Next, regional demonstrations were to be conducted by using some of the best indicators from the pilot studies. These demonstrations would confirm the ability of the program to assess the condition of a specific type of wetland in a specific region. Finally, the program would be implemented to monitor the condition of a specific wetland type in a region. Only Phase I has been conducted.

Data from pilot and demonstration studies in Phase I are being analyzed to develop preliminary indices of signs of the health of a wetland. One index will be for biological integrity, which combines indicators of healthy plant and animal communities. Biological characteristics of the sampled wetlands will be compared with those of the most unaltered wetlands of the same type in the region, known as reference wetlands. This comparison is based on the assumption that the least altered wetlands have sustainable biological integrity.

Other likely indices will be related to the following: habitat integrity (how does the population of waterfowl, finfish, or shellfish in sampled wetlands compare with that in reference wetlands?), hydrologic integrity (how similar is the hydrologic regime in the sampled wetlands to that in reference wetlands?), and water-quality improvement (how do sediment trapping and other water-quality processes in sampled wetlands compare with those in reference wetlands?). Wetland health may be evaluated either by similarity (how similar are sampled wetlands to reference wetlands?) or by biological criteria (are the sampled wetlands above or below a level determined from measurements obtained in the reference wetlands?). The comparison of the condition of sampled wetlands with the condition of reference wetlands provides a means for telling the difference between changes that result from long-term changes in climate (both sampled wetlands and reference wetlands will be affected) and changes that happen because of management actions, regulatory policy, or other human factors that affect wetlands (only the sampled wetlands will be affected).

Pilot studies of salt marshes in the Gulf of Mexico and prairie pothole wetlands of the Midwest have been completed. Results of these studies have been evaluated to identify the indicators that most effectively reveal the difference between healthy and degraded wetlands. In the salt marshes, the indicators that seem to hold the greatest promise (Turner and Swenson, 1994) are as follows:
- Ratio of vegetated areas to open water
- Number of plant species (or the diversity of plant species)
- Biomass (production of plant material per unit area)
- Amount of organic matter in soil
- Salinity

Serene beauty is provided by this restored wetland in Montana. *(Photograph by Edith B. Chase, U.S. Geological Survey.)*

In prairie pothole wetlands, indicators of the health of a wetland that seem to hold the greatest promise at the local level (L.M. Cowardin, U.S. Fish and Wildlife Service, oral commun., 1994) are:

- Amount of developed land in the surrounding upland
- Rates of increase and decrease in the number of water-filled basins or in the area of water surface between April (spring thaw) and August (end of summer)
- Ratio of temporary to seasonal to semipermanent wetlands

At the level of the individual wetland ecosystem, other promising indicators (L.M. Cowardin, oral commun., 1994) are:

- Diversity of plant species
- Number and types of species of large invertebrates
- Range of water-level fluctuation
- Sedimentation rate

Hydrogeomorphic Approach (HGM)

In 1990, the U.S. Army Corps of Engineers began developing the Hydrogeomorphic Approach (HGM) as a way to provide a foundation for assessing the physical, chemical, and biological functions of wetlands (Brinson, 1993; Smith and others, 1995). The program, still being developed, is intended to revise and simplify the WET approach described above (Adamus and others, 1987), as well as make it more applicable to specific regions. The WET procedure develops a profile of specific characteristics (predictors) for an individual wetland, and these are used to assess the degree of effectiveness of the different functions of the wetland. The HGM approach compares the characteristics of a specific wetland with the characteristics of a group of wetlands (reference wetlands) in the region, and this information is used to assess the degree to which the individual wetland is performing selected functions. Thus, the HGM approach represents a combination of the WET and EMAP—Wetlands approaches. Wetland characteristics to be evaluated by HGM are limited to those that are important in the specific region and hydrogeomorphic setting. Hence, different characteristics will be identified and evaluated for different hydrogeomorphic settings, such as closed basins in the Midwest (for example, prairie pothole wetlands), river-edge wetlands in the Southeast (for example, bottom-land hardwood wetlands), and coastal wetlands (for example, salt marshes).

In the HGM approach, local wetland scientists or managers identify the functions that are performed by wetlands in a specific hydrogeomorphic setting in that region. Also, they identify wetland characteristics (indicators), such as plant communities, plant species, and density of stems, that suggest whether or not a wetland is performing a specific function, such as slowing the flow velocity of floodwater. Next, the value of each function is determined by measuring the degree to which that function is likely to be performed. This is based on the characteristics of the indicators. For example, if lines of debris are selected as an indicator that a wetland has been flooded, their altitude may be used to determine how deep the water may have been during flooding and thus how much water may be stored in the wetland. The nature of the debris lines also may suggest the velocity of the water as it moved through the wetland. For example, small leaves and twigs suggest slow-moving water, small branches suggest somewhat swifter water, and large branches and tree trunks suggest very high velocities. Sediment deposits observed at the site may suggest the depositional characteristics. For example, no sediment deposits suggest little deposition, thin silt deposits suggest that slow-moving water was sustained for long periods, and gravel and cobble deposits might suggest that water was flowing rapidly when it entered the site but then slowed significantly at the site.

A wetland assessment provided by the HGM approach will likely be a "site profile" that lists the site characteristics that are related to identified wetland functions. This profile then will be compared with characteristics of the reference wetlands (all wetlands in the region in the same geomorphic class) in order to rank the site. A data base that contains profiles of wetland characteristics (indicators of wetland functions) for each wetland type (hydrogeomorphic class) will be established for each region. These data will define the range of characteristics found in these wetlands.

At present (1995), the HGM approach is in development and has not been released to the public. Field tests of this assessment method have been conducted in river-edge wetlands in the Pacific Northwest, the Northeast, the Rocky Mountains, the Southwest, and the Southeast; in coastal wetlands in the Pacific Northwest, the North and South Atlantic States, and the gulf coast States; and in closed-basin wetlands in the Midwest. Data and insights derived from these tests are being compiled and will be evaluated in regional workshops. Following those evaluations, manuals of draft HGM methods will be prepared and presented for comment and review in regional workshops.

CONCLUSIONS

If any hope remains for preserving the Nation's wetland resources, it depends upon obtaining public support. Public support can be won if scientists can explain clearly how wetlands function, how they interact with their surroundings, and how their functions can benefit society. Wetlands have come under intensive scientific study only during the last two decades. Techniques of wetland evaluation will improve as scientists gather more information about the processes that take place in wetlands and about the similarities and differences among the functions of different types of wetlands. In order to develop public support and to encourage enlightened policy decisions and regulations, it is critical to create and maintain a data base of wetland characteristics in which the data are reliable, comparable, and repeatable at periodic intervals in order to monitor long-term trends.

More than one approach to wetland evaluation is possible, as illustrated by the examples discussed above. Wetland functions and their values to humans and other living matter may be assessed for an individual wetland by using approaches such as WET or

It is critical to create and maintain a data base of wetland characteristics in which the data are reliable, comparable, and repeatable.

HGM. After this, they can be compared with other natural wetlands in a region by using the HGM approach. Both WET and HGM can be used to determine the amount of mitigation required to off-set unavoidable wetland loss, as well as to evaluate the degree of success of individual mitigation projects. (See article "Wetland Protection Legislation" in this volume for further discussion of mitigation.) The EMAP—Wetlands approach suggests that it might be possible to examine the condition (pristine or degraded) of a population of wetlands in a specified area. Periodic reevaluation of this population of wetlands might be used to determine trends in their condition and to identify the effects of broad policy decisions (such as "no net loss"), programs (such as mitigation banking where wetlands are created or restored to offset losses of other wetlands), or natural phenomena (such as climate change).

References Cited

Adamus, P.R, 1983, FHWA Assessment method, *v. 2 of* Method for wetland functional assessment: Washington, D.C., U.S. Department of Transportation, Federal Highway Administration Report no. FHWA–IP–82–24, 134 p.

———1988, The FHWA/Adamus (WET) method for wetland functional assessment., *in* Hook, D.D., McKee, W.H., Jr., Smith, H.K., Gregory, James, Burrell, V.G., Jr., DeVoe, M.R., Sojka, R.E., Gilbert, Stephen, Banks, Roger, Stolzy, L.H., Brooks, Chris, Mathews, T.D., and Shear, T.H., Management, use, and value of wetlands, *v. 2 of* The ecology and management of wetlands: Portland, Oreg., Timber Press, p. 128–133.

Adamus, P.R., Clairain, E.J., Jr., Smith, R.D., and Young, R.E., 1987, Wetland Evaluation Technique (WET), *v. 2 of* Methodology: Vicksburg, Miss., U.S. Army Corps of Engineers, Waterways Experiment Station, Operational Draft Technical Report, 206 p. + appendixes.

Adamus, P.R., and Stockwell, L.T., 1983, Critical review and evaluation concepts, *v. 1 of* Method for wetland functional assessment: Washington, D.C., U.S. Department of Transportation, Federal Highway Administration Report no. FHWA–IP–82–23, 176 p.

Brinson, M.M., 1993, Hydrogeomorphic classification for wetlands: Washington, D.C., U.S. Army Corps of Engineers, Wetlands Research Program Technical Report WRP–DE–4, 79 p.

Helfgott, T.B., Lefor, M.W., and Kennard, W.C., 1973, First Wetland Conference: Storrs, Conn., University of Connecticut, Institute of Water Resources, Report 21, Proceedings, 199 p.

Kusler, J.A., 1983, Our national wetland heritage—A protection guidebook: Washington, D. C., Environmental Law Institute, p. 4.

Kusler, J.A., and Montanari, J.H., 1978, National Wetland Protection Symposium: U.S. Fish and Wildlife Service, Office of Biological Services, FWS/OBS–78–97, Proceedings, 255 p.

Kusler, J.A., and Riexinger, Patricia, eds., 1986, National Wetland Assessment Symposium: Albany, N.Y., Association of State Wetland Managers, Proceedings, 331 p.

Lapedes, D.N., ed., 1976, McGraw-Hill dictionary of scientific and technical terms: New York, McGraw-Hill Book Company, 1634 p.

National Audubon Society, 1993, Saving wetlands—A citizen's guide for action in the Mid-Atlantic region: Camp Hill, Pa., National Audubon Society, 130 p.

Novitzki, R.P., 1994, EMAP—Wetlands—A program for assessing wetland condition, *in* Mitsch, W.J., ed., Global wetlands—Old World and New: New York, Elsevier Science Publishers, p. 691–709.

Novitzki, R.P., Rosen, B.H., McAllister, L.S., Ernst, T.L., Huntley, B.E., and Dwire, K., 1994, EMAP—Wetlands—Research strategy for the assessment of wetland condition: Corvallis, Oreg., U.S. Environmental Protection Agency, Environmental Research Laboratory, 149 p.

Parrett, Charles, Melcher, N.B., and James, R.W., Jr., 1993, Flood discharges in the upper Mississippi River basin, 1993: U.S. Geological Survey Circular 1120–A, 14 p.

Richardson, Brandt, ed., 1981, Selected proceedings of the Midwest Conference on Wetland Values and Management: Navarre, Minn., Freshwater Society, 660 p.

Smith, R.D., Ammann, Alan, Bartoldus, C., and Brinson, M.M., 1995, An approach for assessing wetland functions using hydrogeomorphic classification, reference wetlands, and functional indices: Vicksburg, Miss., U.S. Army Engineers Waterways Experiment Station, Technical Report TRWRP–DE 10, [100 p.]

Tiner, R.W., 1989, Wetlands of Rhode Island: Newton Corner, Mass., U.S. Fish and Wildlife Service, National Wetlands Inventory, 71 p., appendix.

Turner, R.E., and Swenson, E.M., 1994, Indicator development for evaluating estuarine emergent conditions—salt marsh pilot—technical narrative (draft final report): Baton Rouge, La., Louisiana State University, v. 1, 65 p.

FOR ADDITIONAL INFORMATION: Richard P. Novitzki, ManTech Environmental Technology, Inc., 1600 S.W. Western Blvd., Corvallis, OR 97333; R. Daniel Smith, U.S. Army Engineer Waterways Experiment Station, 3909 Halls Ferry Road, Vicksburg, MS 39180; Judy D. Fretwell, U.S. Geological Survey, 407 National Center, Reston, VA 22092

Restoration, Creation, and Recovery of Wetlands

Wetland Restoration and Creation

Mary E. Kentula[1]

The benefits of restoration of degraded or destroyed wetlands and creation of new wetlands has only recently been recognized. As the population has expanded across the Nation during the past few centuries, wetlands have been drained and altered to accommodate human needs. These changes to wetlands have directly, or indirectly, brought about changes in the migratory patterns of birds, local climate, and the makeup of plant and animal populations. In the past, people used wetland plants and animals for shelter and food. More recently, people have become more aware of other benefits that wetlands provide—water-quality improvement, flood attenuation, esthetics, and recreational opportunities. Now, it is recognized that numerous losses are incurred when a wetland is damaged or destroyed. Restoration and creation can help maintain the benefits of wetlands and their surrounding ecosystems, and at the same time accommodate the human need for development.

Wetland restoration rehabilitates a degraded wetland or reestablishes a wetland that has been destroyed. Restoration takes place on land that has been, or still is, a wetland. A term commonly associated with restoration is "enhanced." An enhanced wetland is an existing wetland that has been altered to improve a particular function, usually at the expense of other functions. For example, enhancing a site to increase its use by a particular species of bird commonly limits its use as habitat for other species. (For information on functions of wetlands see the articles "Wetland Hydrology, Water Quality, and Associated Functions" and "Wetland Functions, Values, and Assessment" in this volume.)

Wetland creation is the construction of a wetland on a site that never was a wetland. This can be done only on a site where conditions exist that can produce and sustain a wetland. Consequently, creation is more difficult than restoration. A term commonly associated with wetland creation is "constructed." A constructed wetland is a wetland created specifically for the purpose of treating wastewater, stormwater, acid mine drainage, or agricultural runoff (Hammer, 1989). As used in this article, "project wetland" refers to restored or created wetlands. (For a more complete discussion of the meaning of these terms and others associated with restoration and creation, see Lewis, 1990.)

CHALLENGES OF RESTORATION AND CREATION

Ecological issues and physical limitations are important factors to consider when planning for wetland restoration or creation. The relative merits of destroying the function of an existing wetland, or other ecosystem, in exchange for another wetland function involves the consideration of numerous questions such as: (1) Which is more important, the existing or the replacement function? (2) Will the proposed wetland increase wildlife diversity? (3) Is the increased diversity worth the loss of habitat of any endangered species? Questions of this type always arise during planning for wetland restoration and creation.

A well-documented example of a physical limitation associated with restoring a wetland can be seen along the shoreline of the Salmon River Estuary, Oreg. (Frenkel and Morlan, 1990, 1991). In the past, many high marsh wetlands along the Pacific coast were diked to remove them from tidal action. After the area was diked, the wetlands dried up and the land was used for pasture. In 1978, in an effort to restore the Salmon River Estuary to its original condition, two dikes were removed to allow the original wetlands to reestablish themselves. However, after 10 years, the resulting wetlands (fig. 52) were not typical of other high marshes along the estuary. The land behind the dikes had subsided over time, and the restored wetlands were more typical of wetlands at lower elevations nearer the estuary (low marsh). Although the wetlands continue to evolve as sediments are trapped and deposited by the vegetation (thus raising the elevation), it might take another 50 years for the restored wetlands to become similar again to the original high marsh (Frenkel and Morlan, 1991). The time required and the ability to develop a fully functional soil system in project wetlands may be major determinants of the eventual acceptance or rejection of restoration and creation as management options.

It is difficult to make a definitive statement about the ability to replace wetland functions. Goals for restoration and creation projects seldom are stated and information on the existing functions of the wetlands seldom are documented. This is due, in part, to the difficulty and expense of quantifying wetland functions. Also, responsible monitoring during construction and after completion of the project wetland is uncommon. Most information available on project wetlands is in the form of qualitative case studies.

> *Wetland alterations have brought about changes in the migratory patterns of birds, local climate, and make up of plant and animal populations.*

> *Restoration and creation can help maintain the benefits of wetlands and accommodate the human need for development.*

Figure 52. View of a restored salt marsh in the Salmon River Estuary on the Oregon coast. *(Photograph courtesy of the EPA Wetlands Research Program.)*

[1] U.S. Environmental Protection Agency (EPA).

DESIGNING FOR SUCCESS

Much of the written material on wetland restoration and creation deals with "project design." Project design considers a large number of site-specific, interdependent factors that determine the structure and function of a wetland. Although there is no "cookbook" for restoring or creating wetlands, documents describing general approaches to restoration and creation and the conditions conducive to project success are available (Garbisch, 1986; Marble, 1990; Pacific Estuarine Research Laboratory, 1990; Hammer, 1992; Maynord and others, 1992). Elements common to wetland project design are site-selection criteria, hydrologic analysis, water source and quality, substrate augmentation and handling, plant material selection and handling, buffer zones placement, and long-term management. A brief overview of each element is presented here in a sequence similar to that followed in project planning.

Site selection.—Sites for project wetlands often are selected on the basis of available land, or on policies that require wetlands to be restored or created to compensate for nearby wetland losses (mitigation). A wetland's structure, function, and ability to persist over time are greatly influenced by its location. Wetlands in settings with limited human influence can differ greatly in structure and function from wetlands in settings dominated by human activities. Therefore, the present and projected land uses of the surrounding area are a consideration when selecting the site. The characteristics of existing wetlands, in the same general area, or in an area with similar land uses, can be used as models for what might be expected of the project wetland. Benefits that extend beyond the wetland itself can be derived from the placement of a wetland if care is taken in site selection. For example, restoration of riverbank wetlands between agricultural land and a stream can improve downstream water quality (Olson, 1992).

Hydrologic analysis.—Hydrologic conditions probably are the most important determinants of the type of wetland that can be established and what wetland processes can be maintained (Mitsch and Gosselink, 1993). Elements of site hydrology that are important to maintaining a wetland are inflows and outflows of ground water and surface water, the resulting water levels, and the timing and duration of soil saturation or flooding.

One factor influencing hydrology is the configuration of the basin (depression) containing the wetland.

The position of the basin surface relative to the water table influences the degree of soil saturation and flooding. To ensure that standing water is present year round, many project wetlands are excavated so that the deepest part of the basin is below the lowest anticipated water level. The slope of the basin banks determines how much of the site will be vegetated and by what kinds of plants (fig. 53). This is because the slope determines how far the substrate (soil or rock material that forms the surface of the basin) will be from water and how much of the substrate has the necessary conditions of wetness for specific plant species (Hollands, 1990). The ability to maintain the desired plant community, therefore, is ultimately dependent on the hydrology of the site. In a properly constructed freshwater marsh, the lowest point of the wetland will be inundated to a depth and for a period long enough that emergent vegetation can persist, but not so long as to destroy the plants.

Water source and quality.—Although it is commonly acknowledged that site hydrology is a major determinant of the success or failure of wetland restoration or creation, the influence of water quality often is ignored. Inputs of chemicals from the surrounding landscape can overwhelm a wetland's ability to improve water quality and can change the characteristics of the site. For example, deicing salts are used extensively along highways and, if they enter a wetland, can alter the productivity and composition of its plant community, possibly favoring nuisance species such as purple loosestrife (Niering, 1989).

Substrate augmentation and handling.—Wetlands are characterized by hydric soils, which develop as a result of an area being saturated, flooded, or ponded long enough during the growing season to develop anaerobic (oxygen-deficient) conditions (U.S. Soil Conservation Service, 1991) (fig. 54). Most of the chemical reactions in wetlands take place in the soils, where most chemicals are stored (Mitsch and Gosselink, 1993). The soils of project wetlands are receiving increased attention as studies link substrate characteristics to ecological function. Although a created wetland may be structurally similar to a natural wetland, its hydrology may differ greatly from that of the natural wetland if the permeability of the substrates differ (O'Brien, 1986). In addition to differences in permeability, soils in project wetlands commonly have a smaller amount of organic matter than soils in similar natural wetlands. Because organic matter in soils stores nutrients that are critical to plant growth (Pa-

Benefits can extend beyond the wetland if care is taken in site selection.

Hydrologic conditions probably are the most important determinants of wetland types and processes.

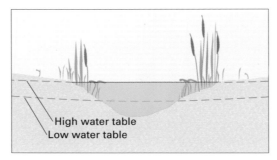
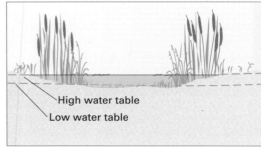

High water table
Low water table

High water table
Low water table

Figure 53. The relative position of a basin substrate, the water table, and differences in vegetation resulting from the degree of basin slope.

cific Estuarine Research Laboratory, 1990), the smaller amounts of organic matter in soils of project wetlands may limit plant growth (Langis and others, 1991). Augmenting, or mulching, the substrate of project wetlands with materials from a "donor" wetland can increase soil organic matter and provide a source of needed plant species, microbes, and invertebrates. Mulching makes the substrate more conducive to rapid revegetation by reducing the evaporation of pore water, runoff, soil loss and erosion, and surface compaction and crusting (Thornburg, 1977). Mulching also can cause problems such as the introduction of unwanted plant species.

Plant material selection and handling.—Vegetation is the most striking visual feature of a wetland. Because of the unique and stressful conditions that develop in wetlands, varying from long periods of flooding to periodic drying, plants and animals found there have developed distinctive mechanisms to deal with these stresses and conditions. It is important to recognize the constraints of this unique environment when planning a project wetland. Plant communities established in project wetlands will fare better if they closely resemble communities in similar, local wetlands. To increase the likelihood of successful colonization, Garbisch (1986) suggests that project managers:

- Select herbaceous species that rapidly stabilize the substrate and that have potential value for fish and wildlife
- Select species that are adaptable to a broad range of water depths. A survey of vegetation at wetlands of the type being created or restored can identify the conditions of "wetness" needed by species
- Avoid choosing only those species that are foraged by wildlife expected to use the site—muskrats and geese have been known to denude sites
- Avoid committing significant areas of the site to species that have questionable potential for successful establishment

In addition, Stark (1972) suggests the selection of "low maintenance" vegetation.

Buffer zone placement.—Protective measures are needed for many restored and created wetlands, particularly in urbanized areas. This protection can take the form of an undeveloped, vegetated band around the wetland; a fence or barrier; or a lake or sediment basin. This buffer between the wetland and surrounding land is desirable; however, the characteristics of an appropriate vegetated buffer are not well defined. Although composition is important, width is the most frequently cited characteristic of an adequate buffer zone. Requirements for both composition and width are dependent upon the adjacent land uses, their potential effect on the functions of the wetland, and the requirements of the animals that will use the wetland and buffer area. Buffers are used to:

- Deter predators from entering wetlands
- Trap and prevent undesirable materials from entering the wetland through runoff from the surrounding landscape
- Provide habitat for wildlife that depend on uplands in addition to wetlands for part of their life cycle

Long-term management.—Careful monitoring of newly established wetlands and the ability to make mid-course corrections are critical to long-term suc-

Figure 54. Scientist checking to see if a soil sample has the unique coloration typical of wetland (hydric) soils. *(Photograph courtesy of the EPA Wetlands Research Program).*

Chemicals from the surrounding landscape can overwhelm a wetland's ability to improve water quality.

cess. However, few project sponsors have been willing to assume long-term responsibility for managing these new systems (Kusler and Kentula, 1990b). Because of this, project wetlands that are designed to be self-sustaining or self-managing will have the best chance of survival. The installation of control structures, such as tide gates or pumps, that will require maintenance and are subject to vandalism could be disadvantageous to the life of the project wetland.

EVALUATION OF SUCCESS

One of the most vexing aspects of wetland restoration and creation projects is defining success, primarily because there is no generally accepted definition. This is true for many reasons—lack of clearly stated objectives, lack of long-term monitoring (Kusler and Kentula, 1990b), and the subjective point of view of the definer (Roberts, 1993). The vast majority of project wetlands are ecologically young—10 years of age or less. The lack of information on ecologically mature projects limits the ability to predict whether or not the functions of project wetlands can replace the functions of natural wetlands. Nevertheless, the results of ongoing research and good professional judgment can be used to provide insight into the selection of projects that have a high probability of success.

Various attempts have been made to define success criteria for wetland projects. The earliest criteria assumed that if conditions were correct for the establishment of wetland vegetation, then other ecological functions would either be present or develop over time. Now, it is known that a site "green" with vegetation does not necessarily mean success, and the standards by which projects are judged are more likely to be tied to wetland functions.

The Wetlands Research Program of the U.S. Environmental Protection Agency (EPA) is developing an approach to establish quantitative performance crite-

Plants in project wetlands fare better if they closely resemble those in similar, local wetlands.

ria for project wetlands. In this approach, groups of natural wetlands serve as reference sites against which project wetlands are judged. For example, Zedler (1993) uses reference data from natural marshes being used by clapper rails (an indigenous bird species) to define criteria that can be used to judge the suitability of restored and created habitat for the birds. Older project wetlands also are used as reference sites against which to judge newer project wetlands, both to verify that development is as expected and to identify developmental patterns that may have resulted from changes in project design (Kentula and others, 1992). This approach is designed to produce results that are regionally applicable to wetland protection and management.

One tool for comparing the characteristics of project wetlands with similar, naturally occurring wetlands is a performance curve (fig. 55). Functions in a group of restored wetlands can be expected to increase gradually with time to a point of maturity at which time the level of function has stabilized. The mean level of function in mature project wetlands is generally less than that for natural wetlands. Rate and time of maturation and functional level at maturity will differ from project to project, depending on the type of wetland being restored. The curve provides information on when to monitor, how restored wetlands typically develop, and when project goals have been met. Changes in the characteristics of project wetlands can be expected in response to the maturation process, but also in response to changes in the environment. Information on the development of project wetlands and similar natural wetlands helps managers determine whether an observed change is typical for a particular year or stage of development.

Over time, successful project wetlands can be expected to become similar to comparable natural wetlands. A comparison of plant diversity on project wetlands and similar natural wetlands in Oregon (Kentula and others, 1992), Connecticut (Confer and Niering,

1992), and Florida (Brown, 1991) showed that, although the level of diversity differs with each project, diversity tends to be higher on each project wetland than on its natural counterpart. The type of wetland studied was a pond with a fringe of freshwater marsh (fig. 56). If a project wetland develops as hoped and expected, after 2 to 5 years it probably will have a plant diversity greater than or equal to that of similar natural wetlands. As competition for space and resources increases and the plants more completely cover the site, the diversity usually decreases and the plant community tends to become more like that of a mature site.

STATUS OF THE SCIENTIFIC KNOWLEDGE OF RESTORATION AND CREATION

Current scientific knowledge about successful wetland restoration and creation has been documented in "Wetland Creation and Restoration: The Status of the Science" (Kusler and Kentula, 1990a). Although the literature on wetland restoration and creation has increased since the publication of that book, the general assessment presented still applies. Key points from the Executive Summary (Kusler and Kentula, 1990b) are discussed below. (Additional information on restoration of aquatic systems, including wetlands, can be found in a recent publication by the National Research Council Committee on Restoration of Aquatic Ecosystems, 1992.)

The status of scientific knowledge about wetland restoration and creation differs by wetland function, type, and location. It is still uncertain if the full suite of functions provided by a particular wetland type can be replaced. Full functional replacement has not yet been demonstrated. In the case of specific functions, the most is known about replacement of flood storage and waterfowl habitat, and the least is known about water-quality-improvement and ground-water-associated functions. The more complex the hydrology and ecology of a system, the more difficult it is to restore the system. Complete restoration might be impossible in some systems.

With respect to types and locations of wetlands, the most is known about restoration and creation of intertidal salt marshes along the coasts of the United States, in particular, the tall cordgrass marshes of the Atlantic coast. However, these salt marshes comprise only about 5 percent of the total wetland area of the Nation and are only a small part of the marine and estuarine wetlands.

Much less is known about restoration and creation of inland freshwater wetlands, such as ponds, forested wetlands, or bogs and fens. Among these wetlands, most is known about restoration and creation of those dominated by open water, such as ponds, and the associated herbaceous vegetation. Much less is known about replacing forested wetlands because of the time needed for woody vegetation to mature. Experts agree, however, that the ecosystems that are least likely to be successfully replaced are bogs and fens. These are the wetlands with deep organic soils that have developed over thousands of years and that have hydrologic conditions that are difficult, if not impossible, to duplicate.

> *It is still uncertain if a full suite of wetland functions can be replaced.*

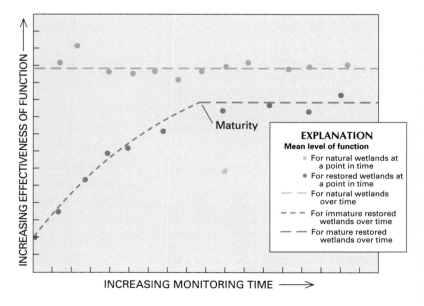

Figure 55. Typical performance curve illustrating the comparison of groups of natural wetlands and restored wetlands of the same type and similar size in the same land-use setting. *(Source: Modified from Kentula and others, 1992.)*

FEDERAL AGENCY RESEARCH ON WETLAND RESTORATION AND CREATION

Several Federal agencies have missions, and therefore conduct research activities, that involve wetlands. This section presents a brief overview of Federal research on wetland restoration and creation. [For more information on wetland research by Federal agencies, see the publications of the Wetlands Research Program of the U.S. Army Corps of Engineers (Corps) and the article "Wetland Research by Federal Agencies" in this volume.] The Corps has been leading an effort to provide a reference source on current wetland research being conducted by Federal agencies. The first edition (U.S. Army Corps of Engineers, Wetlands Research Program, 1992) presents information provided by the Corps, the EPA, the Soil Conservation Service (renamed Natural Resources Conservation Service in October 1994), the Forest Service, the National Marine Fisheries Service, the U.S. Fish and Wildlife Service, the Bureau of Reclamation, and the U.S. Geological Survey. The Corps surveyed over 25 agencies in 1993. To complement the Corps' reference source, the U.S. Fish and Wildlife Service is maintaining the Wetland Creation/Restoration data base to provide a current compilation of the published literature. A hard copy of the bibliographic material contained in the digital data base also has been produced (Schneller-McDonald and others, 1989).

Federal agencies' research into wetland restoration and creation generally falls into two categories—design implementation and performance evaluation. Major contributions on project design have been made by agencies involved in large-scale development, like the Corps (Maynord and others, 1992) and the Federal Highway Administration (Marble, 1990). The EPA has focused its research on evaluation to support the agency responsibilities under Section 404 of the Clean Water Act (Zedler and Kentula, 1986; Leibowitz and others, 1992). Agencies responsible for stewardship of living resources, such as the National Marine Fisheries Service, have produced information that will increase their effectiveness in management (Thayer, 1992).

The Natural Resources Conservation Service and the U.S. Fish and Wildlife Service probably will contribute the most information on practical, low-cost approaches to wetland restoration under the 1990 Farm Bill (Food, Agriculture Conservation and Trade Act of 1990—(P.L. 101–624) and the Wetland Reserve Program. Under these programs, thousands of wetland acres previously converted to agriculture have been restored to wetlands. To support these efforts, both agencies have produced guidelines for their field personnel who are working with the farmers to restore wetlands (U.S. Soil Conservation Service, 1992; Wenzel, 1992). (For more information on legislation affecting wetlands, see the article "Wetland Protection Legislation" in this volume.)

CONCLUSIONS

Wetland restoration and creation is more an art than a science, and functional replacement of wetlands has not been conclusively demonstrated. At the same time, the growing body of literature and experience is

Figure 56.   This pond with a fringe of marsh in Portland, Oreg., is a restored wetland and is an example of the type of freshwater project wetland most common in this country. *(Photograph courtesy of the EPA Wetlands Research Program.)*

increasing the ability to discern which projects have a high probability of restoring or replacing damaged or lost ecosystems. Two factors that most limit the effective use of restoration and creation are: (1) lack of information on ecologically mature restored and created wetlands, and on the maturation process; and (2) the limited number of well designed and well constructed project wetlands that can be used as models.

In general, restoration is likely to be more successful than creation. Restoration of a damaged or destroyed wetland will have a greater chance of establishing the range of prior wetland functions, including critical habitat. Also, chances are greater for the long-term persistence of a restored wetland than for one created where none existed before.

Ecosystems that are least likely to be successfully replaced are bogs and fens.

Restoration is likely to be more successful than creation.

References Cited

Brown, M.T., 1991, Evaluating constructed wetlands through comparisons with natural wetlands: Corvallis, Oreg., U.S. Environmental Protection Agency, Environmental Research Laboratory, EPA/600/3–91/058, 37 p.

Confer, S.R., and Niering, W.A., 1992, Comparison of created and natural freshwater emergent wetlands in Connecticut: Wetlands Ecology and Management, v. 2, no. 3, p. 143–156.

Frenkel, R.E., and Morlan, J.C., 1990, Restoration of the Salmon River salt marshes—Retrospect and perspective: U.S. Environmental Protection Agency, Region 10, 142 p.

_____1991, Can we restore our salt marshes? Lessons from the Salmon River, Oregon: Northwest Environmental Journal, v. 7, p. 119–135.

Garbisch, E.W., Jr., 1986, Highways and wetlands—Compensating wetland losses: McLean, Va., Federal Highway Administration, Office of Implementation, Contract Report DOT–FH–11–9442, 60 p.

Hammer, D.A., ed., 1989, Constructed wetlands for wastewater treatment—Municipal, industrial, and agricultural: Chelsea, Mich., Lewis Publishers, Inc., 831 p.

Hammer, D.A., 1992, Creating freshwater wetlands: Chelsea, Mich., Lewis Publishers, Inc., 298 p.

Hollands, G.G., 1990, Regional analysis of creation and restoration of kettle and pothole wetlands, *in* Kusler, J.A., and Kentula, M.E., eds., Wetland creation and restoration—The status of the science: Washington, D.C., Island Press, p. 281–298.

Kentula, M.E., Brooks, R.P., Gwin, S.E., Holland, C.C., Sherman, A.D., and Sifneos, J.C., 1992, An approach to improving decision making in wetland restoration and creation: Washington, D.C., Island Press, 151 p.

Kusler, J.A., and Kentula, M.E., eds., 1990a, Wetland creation and restoration—The status of the science: Washington, D.C., Island Press, 591 p.

Kusler, J.A., and Kentula, M.E. , 1990b, Executive summary, *in* Kusler, J.A., and Kentula, M.E., eds., Wetland creation and restoration—The status of the science: Washington, D.C., Island Press, p. xvii–xxv.

Langis, Rene, Zalejko, M.K., and Zedler, J.B., 1991, Nitrogen assessments in a constructed and natural salt marsh of San Diego Bay: Ecological Applications v.1, p. 40–51.

Leibowitz, S.G., Preston, E.M., Arnaut, L.Y., Detenbeck, N.E., Hagley, C.A., Kentula, M.E., Olson, R.K., Sanville, W.D., and Sumner, R.R., 1992, Wetland research plan—An integrated risk-based approach: Corvallis, Oreg., U.S. Environmental Protection Agency, Environmental Research Laboratory, EPA/600/R–92/060, 123 p.

Lewis, R.R., Jr., 1990, Wetland restoration/creation/enhancement terminology—Suggestions for standardization, *in* Kusler, J.A., and Kentula, M.E., eds., Wetland creation and restoration—The status of the science: Washington, D.C., Island Press, p. 417–423.

Marble, A.D., 1990, A guide to wetland functional design: McLean, Va., Federal Highway Administration Report Number FHWA–IP–90–010, 222 p.

Maynord, S.T., Landin, M.C., McCormick, J.W., Davis, J.E., Evans, R.A., and Hayes, D.F., 1992, Design of habitat restoration using dredged material at Bodkin Island, Chesapeake Bay, Maryland: Vicksburg, Miss., U.S. Army Corps of Engineers, Waterways Experiment Station, Wetlands Research Program Technical Report WRP–RE–3, 33 p. + tables and figures.

Mitsch, W.J., and Gosselink, J.G., 1993, Wetlands (second edition): New York, Van Nostrand Reinhold Company, Inc., 722 p.

National Research Council Committee on Restoration of Aquatic Ecosystems—Science, Technology, and Public Policy, 1992, Restoration of aquatic ecosystems— Science, technology, and public policy: Washington, D.C., National Academy Press, 552 p.

Niering, W.A., 1989, Effects of stormwater runoff on wetland vegetation: Proceedings of the Stormwater Conference, Southborough, Mass., New England Institute for Environmental Studies, p. 1–38.

O'Brien, A.L., 1986, Hydrology and the construction of a mitigating wetland, *in* Larson, J.S., and Neill, Christopher, eds., Mitigating freshwater wetland alterations in the glaciated northeastern United States—An assessment of the science base: Amherst, Mass., Environmental Institute, University of Massachusetts, Publication 87–1, p. 83–200.

Olson, R.K., ed., 1992, Special Issue—The role of created and natural wetlands in controlling nonpoint source pollution: Ecological Engineering, v. 1, no. 1/2, p. 1–170.

Pacific Estuarine Research Laboratory, 1990, A manual for assessing restored and natural coastal wetlands with examples from southern California: LaJolla, Calif., California Sea Grant Report Number T–CSGCP–021, 105 p.

Roberts, L., 1993, Wetlands trading is a losing game, say ecologists: Science, v. 260, no. 5116, p. 1,890–1,892.

Schneller-McDonald, Karen, Ischinger, L.S., and Auble, G.T., 1989, Wetland creation and restoration—Description and summary of the literature: Washington, D.C., U.S. Fish and Wildlife Service Biological Report 89, 66 p. + database records.

Stark, Nellie, 1972, Low maintenance vegetation—Wildland shrubs, their biology and utilization: Washington, D.C., U.S. Department of Agriculture, Forest Service, General Technical Report INT–1.

Thayer, G.W., ed., 1992, Restoring the Nation's marine environment: College Park, Md., Maryland Sea Grant College, 716 p.

Thornburg, A., 1977, Use of vegetation for stabilization of shorelines of the Great Lakes, *in* the Proceedings of the Workshop on the Role of Vegetation in Stabilization of the Great Lakes Shoreline: Ann Arbor, Mich., Great Lakes Basin Commission, p. 39–53.

U.S. Army Corps of Engineers, Wetlands Research Program, 1992, National summary of ongoing wetlands research by Federal agencies (1992): Vicksburg, Miss., U.S. Army Corps of Engineers, Waterways Experiment Station, 69 p.

U.S. Soil Conservation Service, 1991, Soils—Hydric soils of the United States: Washington, D.C., U.S. Department of Agriculture, Soil Conservation Service Miscellaneous Publication Number 1491.

_____1992, Field handbook, Chapter 13—Wetland restoration, enhancement, and creation: Washington, D.C., U.S. Department of Agriculture, Soil Conservation Service, 79 p.

Wenzel, T.A., 1992, Minnesota wetland restoration guide: Minneapolis, Minn., Minnesota Board of Water and Soil Resources.

Zedler, J.B., 1993, Canopy architecture of natural and planted cordgrass marshes—Selecting habitat evaluation criteria: Ecological Applications, v. 3, no. 1, p. 123–138.

Zedler, J.B., and Kentula, M.E., 1986, Wetlands research plan: Corvallis, Oreg., U.S. Environmental Protection Agency, Environmental Research Laboratory, EPA/600/3–86/009, 118 p.

FOR ADDITIONAL INFORMATION: Mary E. Kentula, Wetlands Research Program, U.S. Environmental Protection Agency, Environmental Research Laboratory, Corvallis, OR 97333

Restoration, Creation and Recovery of Wetlands
Effects of Hurricane Andrew (1992) on Wetlands in Southern Florida and Louisiana

By John K. Lovelace[1] and Benjamin F. McPherson[1]

Hurricane Andrew was a small but powerful storm that caused massive destruction along a path through southern Florida and south-central Louisiana in late August 1992 (fig. 57). Rainfall associated with Andrew was light for a hurricane because of the small size and rapid forward movement of the storm. However, rainfall totals of more than 7 inches were recorded for the storm period in southeastern Florida and Louisiana; a high of 11.9 inches was recorded in Hammond, La. (Rappaport, 1992). Maximum sustained windspeeds of 141 mph (miles per hour), with gusts of 169 mph, were recorded on August 24, just before landfall in Florida (Rappaport, 1992). A storm surge of about 17 feet above sea level was recorded at Biscayne Bay, Fla. (fig. 58) and about 9 feet near Terrebonne Bay in south-central Louisiana (fig. 59).

Hurricane Andrew originated in the North Atlantic Ocean, moved westward over the Bahamas, and made landfall near the southern tip of Florida on the morning of August 24. After passing over the Florida Everglades, the storm proceeded in a northwesterly direction across the Gulf of Mexico and made landfall in south-central Louisiana at Point Chevreuil on the morning of August 26. Andrew deteriorated rapidly after landfall in Louisiana and was downgraded to a tropical depression on August 27. The remnants of Andrew proceeded on a northeasterly path, producing severe weather throughout the Southeastern States (Rappaport, 1992).

Hurricane Andrew moved across southern Florida at an average forward speed of 18 mph (National Oceanic and Atmospheric Administration, 1992). As it crossed southern Florida, Andrew left a path of destruction 25 miles wide and 60 miles long (Gore, 1993).

Andrew left a path of destruction 25 miles wide and 60 miles long

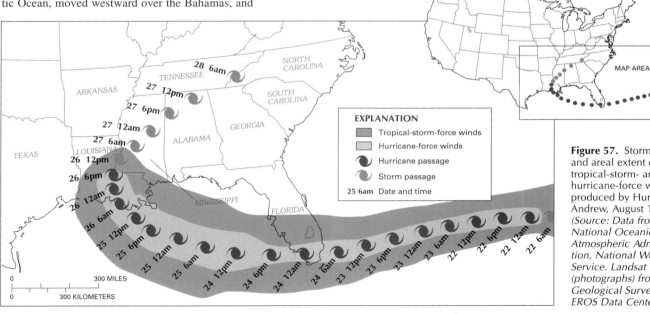

Figure 57. Storm path and areal extent of tropical-storm- and hurricane-force winds produced by Hurricane Andrew, August 1992. *(Source: Data from National Oceanic and Atmospheric Administration, National Weather Service. Landsat images (photographs) from U.S. Geological Survey, EROS Data Center.)*

August 23, 1992 4:53 pm   *August 24, 1992 4:41 pm*   *August 25, 1992 4:29 pm*   *August 26, 1992 4:17 pm*

[1] U.S. Geological Survey.

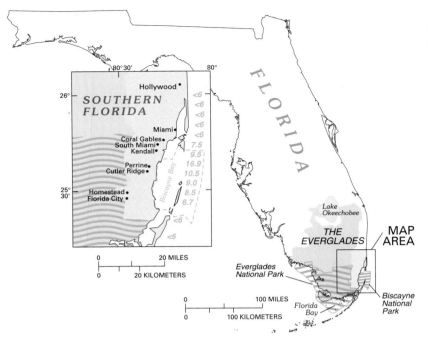

Figure 58. Storm-surge elevations, in feet above sea level, at selected points along the coast of Florida; < indicates less than. *(Source: Data from U.S. Geological Survey files.)*

Hurricane Andrew passed through the heart of the largest wetlands in the United States, the Florida Everglades. (See article "Florida Wetland Resources" in the State Summaries part of this volume.) Perhaps the most dramatic effect of the storm's passage through these wetlands was the major structural damage to trees caused by the strong winds. The storm passed directly over Biscayne National Park and Everglades National Park, knocking down or severely damaging mangrove trees on about 70,000 acres of wetlands in the two parks. Within the storm's path, virtually all large trees located in hammock areas (islands of dense, tropical undergrowth), typically hardwoods, were defoliated and about 25 percent of the trees were windthrown or badly broken. About one-fourth of the royal palms and one-third of the pine trees in Everglades National Park were broken or damaged by the winds (fig. 60). Damage to woody vegetation was most severe near the eye of the storm where winds were the strongest (Davis and others, 1994). However, within 20 days surviving trees and shrubs had sprouted new growth (Alper, 1992).

The storm appeared to have only minor effects on the interior freshwater wetlands of The Everglades, which are composed mainly of sawgrass. Nearly all post-storm (August 28 to September 17, 1992) water-quality properties sampled by the South Florida Water Management District were within the range of pre-storm values. These properties included

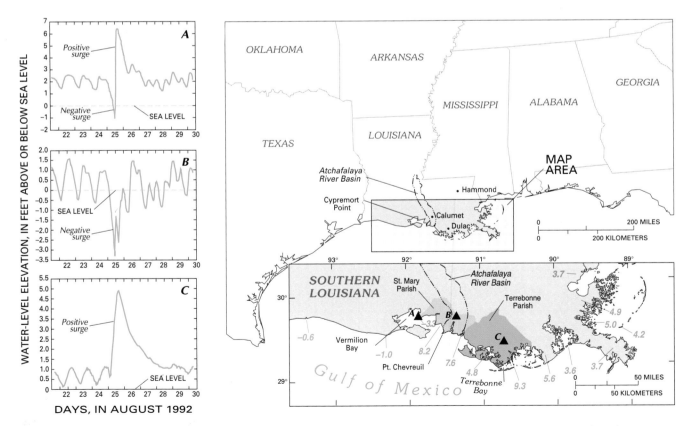

Figure 59. Storm-surge elevations, in feet above or below sea level, at selected points along the coast of Louisiana. Graphs indicate water levels at sites *A*, Vermilion Bay, near Cypremont Point; *B*, Wax Lake outlet, at Coleman; *C*, Houma Navigation Canal, at Dulac. *(Source: Data from U.S. Geological Survey files.)*

turbidity, color, ammonia, and dissolved phosphate. Wind-heaped, vegetative marsh debris was evident along the edges of some forested islands, and the characteristic periphyton mat (group of stalkless micro-organisms that live attached to surfaces projecting from the bottom of freshwater bodies) was absent or altered in structure. However, much of The Everglades' marsh appeared undamaged by the storm. A significant effect of the wind in the freshwater wetlands was the destruction of, or damage to, about 80 percent of the hydrologic and meteorologic monitoring stations located along the storm's path (Davis and others, 1994).

The hurricane had little effect on wildlife in The Everglades. Thirty-two deer wearing radio collars for a National Park Service study survived the hurricane, and the releafing of vegetation provided them with food and cover. Adult alligators appeared unaffected, but nests and young may have been adversely affected. Most wading birds survived; estimates of pre- and post-storm populations were similar, and about normal for the late-summer wet season (Davis and others, 1994).

In the marine environment, the major effects of the hurricane were changes in nearshore water quality, patches of intense bottom scouring, and beach overwash. Dramatically increased turbidity persisted in some areas for at least 30 days, particularly in western Biscayne Bay where mangrove peat soils continued to break down and enter the water. In northeastern Florida Bay, at the southern edge of the affected area, concentrations of ammonia, dissolved phosphate, and dissolved organic carbon increased dramatically. Phytoplankton (microscopic drifting aquatic plants) blooms added to the increased turbidity and, combined with low dissolved-oxygen concentrations, could have had severe effects on fish and invertebrate populations. In addition, fuel from hundreds of damaged boats and marina fuel tanks in Biscayne Bay continued to discharge into the water for at least 27 days after the hurricane had passed (Davis and others, 1994).

In Louisiana, the storm surge produced significant flooding in a few populated areas in the southern part of the State. However, there was no major flooding of inland rivers. The greatest surge was east of the point of landfall, where the counterclockwise rotation of winds, combined with forward motion of the hurricane, pushed water northward (fig. 59). Andrew also produced a negative surge of as much as 3 feet below sea level along the coast from about 10 miles west of landfall to the Texas State line, as the counterclockwise winds west of the hurricane's eye pushed water away from the shore. Because the hurricane was moving in a northwesterly direction at the time of landfall, areas near landfall experienced a negative surge as the hurricane was to the southeast, then a positive surge as the hurricane moved past and was to the west.

After making landfall in Louisiana, Hurricane Andrew curved back towards the northeast, passing over the Atchafalaya River Basin, which contains the largest hardwood swamp (1.5 million acres) in the United States, and Louisiana's largest palustrine wetland. (See article "Louisiana Wetland Resources " in this volume.) In parts of the basin, the storm severely

Figure 60. Hammock (top) and pine forest (bottom) in Everglades National Park, Fla., after Hurricane Andrew, September 1992. *(Photographs by Benjamin F. McPherson, U.S. Geological Survey.)*

damaged trees, primarily willows and some cypress. Near the coast, about 80 percent of the trees were knocked down; about 20 miles inland, the estimates were about 30 percent. With the loss of trees, an estimated 50 to 75 percent of the young squirrels in the area, those produced during the second litter of the year, died. The storm had little effect on deer (David Morrison, Louisiana Department of Wildlife and Fisheries, oral commun., 1993).

In the Atchafalaya River Basin, an estimated 182 million freshwater fish perished because of the resuspension of anaerobic bottom materials in the water column (fig. 61). Most of the fish probably died during the first 24 hours after the storm as toxic hydrogen sulfide was released from bottom sediments, and decaying organic matter consumed dissolved oxygen, causing fish to asphyxiate (Gary Tilyou, Louisiana Department of Wildlife and Fisheries, oral commun., 1993). After the storm, U.S. Geological Survey personnel measured dissolved-oxygen concentrations of less than 1 mg/L throughout most of the basin, in an area extending northward more than 60 miles from the coast (Charles Demas, U.S. Geological Survey, oral commun., 1993). Dissolved-oxygen concentrations in the upper water column of larger water bodies in the Atchafalaya River Basin generally range from 3 to 6 mg/L during summer months (Dennis K. Demecheck, U.S. Geological Survey, oral commun., 1994). During the 2 weeks follow-

Hurricane Andrew passed through the heart of the largest wetlands in the United States.

Figure 61. Dead fish in the Atchafalaya River Basin, La., September 2, 1992. *(Photograph by Charles R. Demas, U.S. Geological Survey.)*

An estimated 9.4 million saltwater fish valued at $7.8 million were killed by the storm.

ing the hurricane, fishkills were caused primarily by the movement of water containing low concentrations of dissolved oxygen into previously unaffected water (Gary Tilyou, Louisiana Department of Wildlife and Fisheries, oral commun., 1993). The value of freshwater fish killed was about $160 million, most of which was attributed to the estimated 29,000 paddlefish that died. (The paddlefish is an endangered species and its valuation is based on the $2,500 per-fish fine for killing paddlefish.) Estimates of the number of other species killed (in millions) include shad, 100; bream, 23; crappie, 7; largemouth bass, 5; fresh-water drum, 11; buffalo, 12; catfish, 11; and carp, 1 (Harry Blanchet, Louisiana Department of Wildlife and Fisheries, oral commun., 1993).

In the coastal waters, an estimated 9.4 million saltwater fish valued at $7.8 million were killed by the storm. The exact causes of death are uncertain, but popular theories include suffocation, caused by clogging of gills by sediment, and gas-bubble disease, caused by the formation of nitrogen bubbles in the fish's bloodstream due to increased pressure. Most of the fish were found along a band of coastline about 5 miles long, just southeast of the point of landfall. Species killed (in millions) include menhaden, 5.7; mullet, 0.9; croaker, 0.9; spotted sea trout, 0.2; sea catfish, 0.4; black drum, 0.03; and red drum, 0.02 (Harry Blanchet, Louisiana Department of Wildlife and Fisheries, oral commun., 1993).

Large segments of Louisiana's coastal marsh, primarily in Terrebonne and St. Mary Parishes, were damaged. About 40 percent of the Nation's tidal wetlands are located on Louisiana's gulf coast (S.J. Williams, 1993). A substantial part of these wetlands is composed of fresh and intermediate marsh (Chabreck and Linscombe, 1978). Much of this marsh is "floatant" (a floating type of marsh). The marsh is said to float because partially decomposed organic matter and intertwining plant roots form a dense mat that rises and falls with the water level. The roots of the plants that make up the mat are unattached, or only partly attached, to the bottom (Lee Foot, U.S. Fish and Wildlife Service, oral commun., 1993).

The marsh suffered substantial damage caused by wind, tide, and wave action. Three specific kinds of damage were identified:
- Compressed marsh, where a net decrease in surface area results from the marsh being pushed together, somewhat like an accordion closing
- Marsh balls, which are created by the marsh being piled, rolled, or otherwise deformed to create large mounds (resulting in decreased surface area)

- Sediment deposition in thicknesses of as much as 10 inches, but averaging less than 1 inch, which killed vegetation and sank part of the floating marsh

Other damage was attributed to vegetative scour, which resulted from large areas of attached plants having their roots torn from the bottom, and salt burn, which occurred when saline (salty) water from the Gulf of Mexico was pushed into freshwater areas, killing and damaging salt-sensitive plants (Lee Foot, U.S. Fish and Wildlife Service, oral commun., 1993).

About 25 square miles of coastal wetlands in Louisiana are being lost every year due to coastal erosion and wetland deterioration. Hurricane Andrew probably caused substantial immediate loss of coastal wetlands and possibly has hastened the erosion and deterioration processes already at work (Dunbar and others, 1992).

References Cited

Alper, Joe, 1992, Everglades rebound from Andrew: Science, v. 257, p. 1,852–1,854.
Chabreck, R.H., and Linscombe, Greg, 1978, Vegetative type map of the Louisiana coastal marshes: Louisiana Department of Wildlife and Fisheries, New Orleans, La., 1 sheet.
Davis, G.E., Loope, L.L., Roman, C.T., Smith, G., and Tilmont, J.T., compilers, 1994, Assessment of Hurricane Andrew impacts on natural and archeological resources of Big Cypress National Preserve, Biscayne National Park, and Everglades National Park, 15–24 September 1992: National Park Service, 158 p.
Dunbar, J.B., Britsch, L.D., and Kemp, E.B., III, 1992, Land loss rates, report 3, Louisianna coastal plain: U.S. Army Corps of Engineers Technical Report GL–90–2, p. 27.
Gore, Rick, 1993, Andrew aftermath: National Geographic, v. 183, no. 4, p. 2–37.
National Oceanic and Atmospheric Administration, 1992, Special climate summary, Hurricane Andrew: National Oceanic and Atmospheric Administration, Southeast Regional Climate Center, Columbia, S.C., 7 p.
Rappaport, Edward, 1992, Preliminary report, Hurricane Andrew, 16–28 August 1992: National Oceanic and Atmospheric Administration, National Weather Service, National Hurricane Center, Coral Gables, Fla., 28 p.
Williams, S.J., Penland, Shea, and Roberts, H.H., 1993, Processes affecting coastal wetland loss in the Louisiana deltaic plain, *in* Magoon, O.T., Wilson, W.S., Converse, Hugh, and Tobin, L.T., eds., Coastal Zone '93–Proceedings of the Eighth Symposium on Coastal and Ocean Management, July 19–23, 1993, New Orleans, La.: New York, American Society of Civil Engineers, v. 1, p. 211–219.

FOR ADDITIONAL INFORMATION: John K. Lovelace, U.S. Geological Survey, Louisiana District, 3535 S. Sherwood Forest Blvd., Suite 120, Baton Rouge, LA 70816; Benjamin F. McPherson, U.S. Geological Survey, Tampa Subdistrict, 4710 Eisenhower Blvd., Suite B–5, Tampa, FL 33634

Restoration, Creation, and Recovery of Wetlands
Effects of the Great Midwest Flood of 1993 on Wetlands

By James R. Kolva[1]

The Great Midwest Flood of 1993 was the "most devastating flood in modern United States history" with economic damages near $20 billion. More than 50,000 homes were damaged or destroyed. The areal extent, intensity, and long duration of the flooding makes this event unique in the 20th century (National Oceanic and Atmospheric Administration, 1994). At least 38 people lost their lives as a result of this extreme flood (Interagency Floodplain Management Task Force, 1994).

Significant flooding in the Upper Mississippi River Basin began in mid-June and persisted into early August 1993. The areal extent of this flooding included southern Minnesota, southwestern Wisconsin, Iowa, western Illinois, northern Missouri, southern North Dakota, and eastern parts of South Dakota, Nebraska, and Kansas (fig. 62).

Record flood-peak discharge was recorded at 39 streamflow-gaging stations in the Upper Mississippi River Basin. Fifteen other gaging stations recorded peak discharges exceeding previous maximum known regulated discharges (Parrett and others, 1993). The recurrence interval of the peak discharge at 40 stations exceeded the 100-year flood (one-percent chance of occurring in any given year).

Near-record and record precipitation in June and July, falling on soil already saturated by as much as twice normal early spring rains, caused these record floods. Precipitation for the period January–July 1993 totaled more than 20 inches in most of the flooded area and more than 40 inches in parts of northeastern Kansas and east-central Iowa (Wahl, Vining, and Wiche, 1993). Many areas received more precipitation in those 7 months than is normally received during the entire year.

The Great Midwest Flood of 1993 was unique not only because of the record high water levels and flows and the wide areal extent, but also because of the long duration of flooding. Many rivers were above flood stage for several months. The long period of inundation had significant effects on agricultural land and wetlands.

The flood effects on wetlands varied in both the short term and long term. In the Upper Mississippi National Wildlife Refuge, the flooding lasted 14 weeks—from April through mid-August. "This prolonged inundation of bottom-land hardwood forest and backwater wetlands caused many tree tip-overs, scoured out ground cover and tree regeneration sites, eroded islands, destroyed emergent/submergent vegetation beds, impacted project dikes, and thus destroyed most of the moist soil plants at three sites," according to James Lennartson of the U.S. Fish and Wildlife Service. The effects on wildlife populations also were severe. Many birds, including green-backed herons and red-shouldered hawks, fledged few young

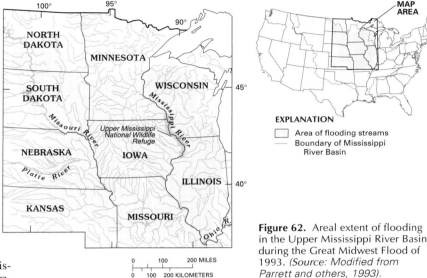

Figure 62. Areal extent of flooding in the Upper Mississippi River Basin during the Great Midwest Flood of 1993. *(Source: Modified from Parrett and others, 1993).*

due to flooded foraging areas. Substrate disturbance and massive sedimentation affected freshwater mussel populations. Mussels were found buried by 1 to 2 feet of sand. Mammals were displaced from the flood plain and suffered higher than normal mortality rates on adjacent roads and railroad tracks (James Lennartson, U.S. Fish and Wildlife Service, written commun., 1994). Fishes that rely on sight to find their food were handicapped because of the increased turbidity.

The flooding, however, had some short-term benefits. Many fish feed and spawn on inundated flood plains. "Ideal conditions for spring spawning fishes occur during years in which flood and temperature rise are coupled" (Scientific Assessment and Strategy Team, 1994). The evidence, particularly in the lower Missouri River flood plain, "***indicates that the magnitude and timing of the 1993 flood provided appropriate temperature and discharge cues for spawning river-floodplain fishes" (Scientific Assessment and Strategy Team, 1994).

The long-term effects of the floods are still being evaluated. Fish habitat may have been improved by creation of deep scour holes and massive underwater debris piles which provide more cover (James Lennartson, oral commun., 1994). Greater-than-normal sedimentation on flood plains and in wetland ponds may have introduced contaminants and excess nutrients into those areas. Exotic plants such as purple loosestrife have colonized disturbed areas and displaced native vegetation (Susan Hassletine, U.S. Fish and Wildlife Service, oral commun., 1994). Purple loosestrife colonies also have been observed at higher elevations than normal, probably because seeds were carried by the extremely high floodwaters to these

...the "most devastating flood in modern United States history"...

...a historically unprecedented hydrometeorological event...

[1] U.S. Geological Survey.

This perimeter levee surrounding the Clarence Cannon National Wildlife Refuge, Mo., damaged during the 1993 flooding, allowed excessive water to enter the refuge. *(Photograph courtesy of U.S. Fish and Wildlife Service.)*

These prairie grasses (foreground) and trees (background) were killed by the excessive water resulting from the long-term flooding of the Mississippi River in the summer of 1993. *(Photograph courtesy of U.S. Fish and Wildlife Service.)*

locations (James Lennartson, oral commun., 1994). Flood debris on flood plains has caused access problems for people at some places, but provides good wildlife cover. Open wetland aquatic vegetation appeared to be back to normal condition during the summer of 1994 (Susan Hassletine, oral commun., 1994).

Wetlands commonly mitigate the effects of floods. Wetland areas can be filled with and temporarily store floodwaters so that flood effects on agricultural and residential areas are lessened. However, wetlands have been steadily dissappearing or converted to other uses throughout the flood-affected area for the last two centuries (see "History of Wetlands in the Conterminous United States" in this volume). These wetlands include the river flood plains and the upland prairie potholes.

Many upland prairie pothole wetlands are closed flow systems, which fill with rain and melting snow and then slowly evaporate or drain through the ground-water system. Thus, they are ideal retention basins during and after intense rains because they "do not normally contribute to stream flow by runoff, except during storms large enough to make the depressions fill and spill" (Scientific Assessment and Strategy Team, 1994). This seems to have been the case in the flood of 1993. All available storage capacity of the wetlands was exceeded, and usually noncontributing areas did contribute to runoff (Interagency Floodplain Management Task Force, 1994). In modeling done by the Scientific Assessment and Strategy Team (1994), upland wetlands simulated decreased flooding in a 1-year event by 9–23 percent, but only by 5–10 percent in a 100-year event. Flood-plain wetlands decreased flooding 5–6 percent for 1-year floods and only 2–3 percent for the 100-year storms.

The Executive Summary of the Report of the Interagency Floodplain Management Review Committee to the Administrative Floodplain Management Task Force (1994) states the effect that wetlands had on the Great Midwest Flood of 1993:

The loss of wetlands and upland cover and the modification of the landscape throughout the basin over the last century and a half significantly increased runoff. *** Although upland watershed treatment and restoration of upland and bottom-land wetlands can reduce flood stages in more frequent floods (25 years and less), it is questionable whether they would have significantly altered the 1993 conditions (Interagency Floodplain Management Task Force, 1994).

In conclusion, the Great Midwest Flood of 1993 was a historically unprecedented hydrometeorological event in area affected, severity of the effects, and duration of the effects. Wetlands were affected beneficially and detrimentally in the short and long term. The historical loss of wetlands from the basin increased the severity of the flood, but even if all presettlement wetlands had still existed, the flood would probably still have set records and caused billions of dollars in damages.

References Cited

Interagency Floodplain Management Task Force, 1994, Report to the Administration Floodplain Management Task Force—Sharing the Challenge: Floodplain Management into the 21st Century, 191 p.

National Oceanic and Atmospheric Administration, 1994, Natural disaster survey report, The Great Flood of 1993, [281 p.].

Parrett, Charles, Melcher, N.B., and James, R.W., Jr., 1993, Flood disharges in the Upper Mississippi River Basin, *in* Floods in the Upper Mississippi River Basin, 1993: U.S. Geological Survey Circular 1120–A, 14 p.

Scientific Assessment and Strategy Team, 1994, Preliminary report to the Interagency Floodplain Management Review Committee of the Administration Floodplain Management Task Force—Science for floodplain management into the 21st century.

Wahl, K.L., Vining, K.C., and Wiche, G.J., 1993, Precipitation in the Upper Mississipi River Basin—January 1 through July 31, 1993, *in* Floods in the Upper Mississippi River Basin, 1993: U.S. Geological Circular 1120–B, 13 p.

FOR ADDITIONAL INFORMATION: James R. Kolva, U.S. Geological Suevey, Utah District, 1745 West 1700 South, Salt Lake City, UT 84104

State Summaries
of Wetland Resources

Horicon Marsh, Wisconsin, provides recreational
opportunities for outdoor enthusiasts.
(Photograph by Phillip J. Redman, U.S. Geological Survey.)

State Summaries of Wetland Resources

Alabama
Wetland Resources

Wetlands cover about 10 percent of Alabama and range in size from small areas of less than an acre scattered throughout the State to a large forested tract of more than 100,000 acres in the Mobile–Tensaw River Delta (fig. 1). Wetlands are a valuable resource because they can reduce flood stages, stabilize banks, and improve water quality. Alabama's wetlands also are important nesting, breeding, nursing, and feeding grounds for many species of fish, birds, and other wildlife and are a vital habitat for rare and endangered plants and animals and for migrating waterfowl (Shaw and Fredine, 1956). Some of the spring-fed wetlands in the State are home to threatened or endangered species such as the watercress darter, coldwater darter, and pygmy sculpin. Commercial and recreational fisheries are sustained in large part by species that spend at least part of their life cycle in wetlands. The State's wetlands and adjacent waters also are used for recreational activities such as hunting, boating, bird watching, and photography and for research and education.

TYPES AND DISTRIBUTION

Wetlands are lands transitional between terrestrial and deepwater habitats where the water table usually is at or near the land surface or the land is covered by shallow water (Cowardin and others, 1979). The distribution of wetlands and deepwater habitats in Alabama is shown in figure 2A; only wetlands are discussed herein.

Wetlands can be vegetated or nonvegetated and are classified on the basis of their hydrology, vegetation, and substrate. In this summary, wetlands are classified according to the system proposed by Cowardin and others (1979), which is used by the U.S. Fish and Wildlife Service (FWS) to map and inventory the Nation's wetlands.

At the most general level of the classification system, wetlands are grouped into five ecological systems: Palustrine, Lacustrine, Riverine, Estuarine, and Marine. The Palustrine System includes only wetlands, whereas the other systems comprise wetlands and deepwater habitats. Wetlands of the systems that occur in Alabama are described below.

System	Wetland description
Palustrine	Nontidal and tidal-freshwater wetlands in which vegetation is predominantly trees (forested wetlands); shrubs (scrub-shrub wetlands); persistent or nonpersistent emergent, erect, rooted herbaceous plants (persistent- and nonpersistent-emergent wetlands); or submersed and (or) floating plants (aquatic beds). Also, intermittently to permanently flooded open-water bodies of less than 20 acres in which water is less than 6.6 feet deep.
Lacustrine	Nontidal and tidal-freshwater wetlands within an intermittently to permanently flooded lake or reservoir larger than 20 acres and (or) deeper than 6.6 feet. Vegetation, when present, is predominantly nonpersistent emergent plants (nonpersistent-emergent wetlands), or submersed and (or) floating plants (aquatic beds), or both.
Riverine	Nontidal and tidal-freshwater wetlands within a channel. Vegetation, when present, is same as in the Lacustrine System.
Estuarine	Tidal wetlands in low-wave-energy environments where the salinity of the water is greater than 0.5 part per thousand (ppt) and is variable owing to evaporation and the mixing of seawater and freshwater.
Marine	Tidal wetlands that are exposed to waves and currents of the open ocean and to water having a salinity greater than 30 ppt.

The FWS estimates that wetlands cover from 2.3 million to 3.1 million acres in Alabama (J.M. Hefner, U.S. Fish and Wildlife Service, written commun., 1992). Palustrine forested wetlands such as cypress and gum swamps, mixed hardwood forests, and wet pine flatwoods account for most of that acreage.

Most of the State's forested wetlands are bottom-land forests in alluvial flood plains. Cypress and tupelo gum commonly predominate in the permanently or seasonally flooded areas (swamps), whereas other trees such as swamp oak, water hickory, red maple, magnolia, sweetgum, and sycamore are more common in less frequently inundated areas. The loss of bottom-land forest has been extensive throughout the Southeastern United States; in some regions, only a small percentage of the original hardwood forests remains (Mitsch and Gosselink, 1986). Alabama has conserved a large tract of its bottom-land forest along approximately 50 miles of the Mobile–Tensaw River Delta.

Other palustrine wetlands, such as shrub swamps (scrub-shrub wetlands) and seepage bogs (emergent wetlands), exist as small, isolated wetlands in the Coastal Plain of Alabama (fig. 2B). These wetlands typically are associated with ground-water seepage in swales or near the bottom of slopes. Seepage bogs support a unique and diverse flora, including at least 20 species of carnivorous plants such as pitcher plants, sundews, butterworts, and bladderworts. The bogs also are home to several species of orchids and a variety of sedges (Mohlenbrock, 1992). Fresh marshes, emergent wetlands

Figure 1. Cypress trees and marsh in the Mobile–Tensaw River Delta. A large tract of delta wetlands has been designated a National Natural Landmark by the National Park Service. *(Photograph by Benjamin F. McPherson, U.S. Geological Survey.)*

vegetated primarily by sedges, rushes, and grasses, commonly fringe ponds, reservoirs, and fresh tidal reaches of coastal rivers.

Although not as abundant as palustrine wetlands, lacustrine and riverine wetlands constitute a significant proportion of Alabama's freshwater wetlands. There are few natural lakes in the State, but impoundments on most of the larger rivers have created many acres of lacustrine wetlands in the shallows of the reservoirs. These wetlands can be nonvegetated (unconsolidated-bottom wetlands), vegetated by emergent plants such as American lotus and golden club that are not visible above the water surface during part of the year (nonpersistent-emergent wetlands), or vegetated by plants such as water lily or pondweed that grow on or below the water surface (aquatic-bed wetlands).

Like lacustrine wetlands, riverine wetlands are nonvegetated or vegetated by nonpersistent emergent or submersed plants. Vegetated riverine wetlands are most common in slow-flowing reaches of Coastal Plain rivers. Whereas many riverine wetlands have been converted to deepwater habitat by impoundment, riverine wetlands are still present in the shallows of the remaining streams and rivers that have not been impounded. Rocky shoals are riverine rock-bottom wetlands that were once more common upstream from the Fall Line in most of the State's rivers before they were impounded. These wetlands are now present only in the Cahaba River system (which remains largely unimpounded) and in a few tributaries of other, now-impounded rivers. Rocky shoals, primarily in the Cahaba River and the Little Cahaba River (a tributary), support stands of the Cahaba lily, a spider lily that grows only in the rocky-shoal habitat (Cahaba River Society, 1992).

Estuarine marshes (emergent wetlands) are extensive in Alabama's coastal waters. Salt marshes form along tidally influenced river reaches, on deltas, and on the shores of estuaries and bays. Salt marshes that are greatly influenced by seawater, such as those on

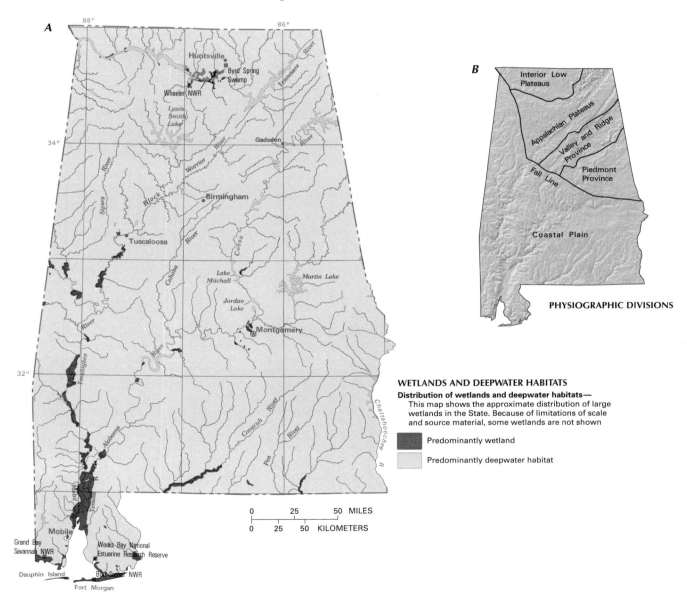

Figure 2. Wetland distribution in Alabama and physiography of the State. **A**, Distribution of wetlands and deepwater habitats. **B**, Physiography. *(Sources: A, T.E. Dahl, U.S. Fish and Wildlife Service, unpub. data, 1991. B, Physiographic divisions from Fenneman, 1946; landforms data from EROS Data Center.)*

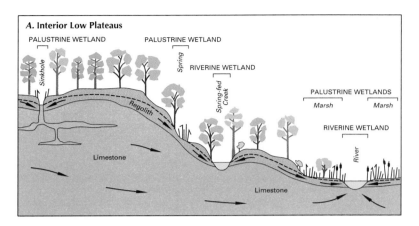

A. Interior Low Plateaus

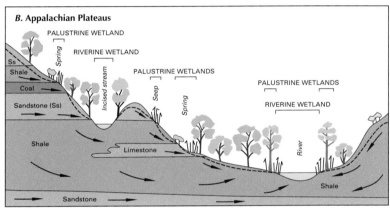

B. Appalachian Plateaus

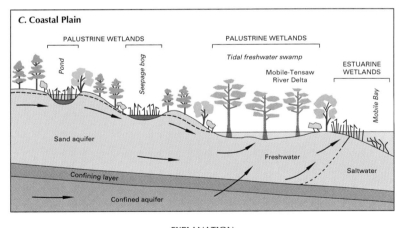

C. Coastal Plain

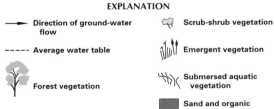

EXPLANATION

→ Direction of ground-water flow

----- Average water table

Forest vegetation

Scrub-shrub vegetation

Emergent vegetation

Submersed aquatic vegetation

Sand and organic deposits

Figure 3. Generalized geohydrologic setting of wetlands in three physiographic provinces of Alabama. *A*, Appalachian Plateaus. *B*, Interior Low Plateaus. *C*, Coastal Plain.

Little Dauphin Island and the Fort Morgan peninsula, are vegetated predominantly by dense stands of black needlerush in areas that are flooded during extreme high tides and by smooth cordgrass in areas that are flooded more regularly (Stout, 1979). In contrast, coastal marshes in less saline habitats have a greater diversity of emergent plants (Stout, 1990). Field and others (1991) estimated that coastal salt marshes cover 25,500 acres in southern Alabama.

Beds of submersed aquatic vegetation grow in the shallow waters of Mobile Bay and adjacent estuaries; they are usually inundated except during low tide (Stout, 1990). Only the zone of these aquatic beds exposed during mean low tide is considered to be wetland by the FWS National Wetland Inventory; most estuarine aquatic beds are in deepwater habitats.

HYDROLOGIC SETTING

Wetlands form where there is a persistent water supply at or near the land surface. The location and persistence of the supply is controlled by factors such as precipitation, evapotranspiration, topography, soil type, geology, runoff, and, near the coast, tides. Plentiful rainfall, about 55 inches per year statewide (Jeffcoat and Mooty, 1986), is an important factor contributing to wetland formation and maintenance in Alabama. Wetlands commonly form in topographically low areas, in areas of impeded drainage, and at locations where the water table intersects the land surface. The movement of ground water into wetlands is controlled by hydraulic gradients (which are primarily determined by topography), recharge from precipitation, regional geologic structure, joints and fractures in the bedrock, and aquifer porosity, permeability, and thickness.

For the purpose of discussing wetland hydrology, Alabama can be divided into two geohydrologic regions that are separated by the Fall Line (fig. 2B). The Fall Line is a regional topographic feature that marks the boundary between the ancient, resistant crystalline rocks of the northern part of the State and the younger, softer sediments to the south.

The region north of the Fall Line in Alabama lies in four physiographic provinces—the Interior Low Plateaus, the Appalachian Plateaus, the Valley and Ridge, and the Piedmont (fig. 2B). This region has diverse topography; altitudes range from 200 to 2,400 feet above sea level. Wetlands in this region are commonly associated with rivers, reservoirs, and impoundments (as in Wheeler National Wildlife Refuge) or with springs, seeps, and solution features such as caves and sinkholes (fig. 3A and 3B). Most of the once-common rocky-shoal habitat has been destroyed by channelization and damming of rivers, except in the Cahaba River Basin and a few tributaries of other rivers (Cahaba River Society, 1992). Most of the major springs in the State are in the Interior Low Plateaus and Valley and Ridge Province, where carbonate rocks predominate. These rocks characteristically are fractured and cavernous and readily transmit ground water to the land surface (Chandler and Moore, 1987). Isolated wetlands have formed near springs and seeps and in sinkholes throughout the northern part of the State. Byrd Spring Swamp (also known as Byrd Spring Lake), a 650-acre wetland containing tupelo gum and other bottom-land hardwoods, is a notable example of a wetland that is spring fed from a karst cave system (U.S. Fish and Wildlife Service, 1992).

The region south of the Fall Line in Alabama—the Coastal Plain—has a gentle slope on which rivers and streams have developed broad flood plains shaped by wide seasonal fluctuations in river levels. Wetlands have formed over extensive areas on these flood plains in response to an abundant supply of water from river flooding and ground-water sources. The hydrology of flood-plain wetlands is typically dominated by river water levels that respond to basinwide climatic conditions (Winter and Woo, 1990). In late winter and early spring, annual flooding by rivers and streams can inundate the entire flood plain to depths of several feet or more. Natural levees along rivers and streams trap water in the flood plain and reduce surface runoff (Hofstetter, 1983). Water trapped in flood-plain wetlands is lost primarily by evapotranspiration and as ground-water recharge (Winter and Woo, 1990). During much of the year, water levels in the flood plains are at or below the land surface, except in ponds, depressions, and sloughs, which can retain surface water year round.

Wetlands on flood plains also are sustained by ground water (fig. 3C). A rise in river stage causes water to go into bank storage, which results in a rise in ground-water levels in the flood plain. Ground-water inflow from adjacent uplands also can be an important source of water to flood-plain wetlands because flood plains are topographically low and are a natural place for discharge from ground-water flow systems (Winter and Woo, 1990).

On flood plains near the coast, river discharge combined with tidal action causes flooding and temporary storage of freshwater in large areas of wetlands, such as those in the Mobile–Tensaw River Delta (fig. 3C). The temporary storage affects the timing and size of freshwater influx into Mobile Bay, which is critical in maintaining optimal salinities in the bay. Temporary storage of freshwater in the delta wetlands also improves the quality of the water that flows into the bay by reducing nutrient and sediment loads and by increasing organic detrital loads that serve as a food source for many estuarine organisms (Dardeau and others, 1990; Stout, 1990).

Estuarine wetlands form where freshwater and saltwater mix and can be subject to widely varying salinity caused by tidal fluctuations and by seasonal and annual differences in freshwater input that result from climate variation. Plants and animals of estuarine wetlands must be adapted to constantly changing hydrologic, salinity, and nutrient-availability regimes. Owing to the differing physiological tolerances of wetland plants and animals, wetland communities develop in identifiable zones in response to those factors.

TRENDS

Alabama has lost as much as 50 percent of its wetlands in the last 200 years (Dahl, 1990). In predevelopment times, wetlands covered about 7.6 million acres of the area that is now Alabama. Recent estimates of the remaining wetland acreage in Alabama range from 2.3 million to 3.1 million acres (J.M. Hefner, U.S. Fish and Wildlife Service, written commun., 1992) to about 3.8 million acres (U.S. Department of Agriculture, 1985). Differences in the estimates possibly reflect differences in inventory terminology or techniques.

Alabama lost about 10 percent of its interior wetlands from 1956 through 1979 (U.S. Fish and Wildlife Service, 1992). Primary causes for the loss of the interior wetlands were agricultural conversion of wetlands to croplands, conversion of bottom-land hardwood forests to pine culture, and inundation caused by reservoir construction.

Alabama lost about 69 percent of its coastal freshwater marsh and 29 percent of its estuarine marsh from 1955 through 1979. Primary reasons for the loss of these coastal wetlands were industrial

and commercial development, residential development, erosion and subsidence, and natural succession from wetlands to uplands (Roach and others, 1987). Much of the loss of coastal wetlands occurred in the Mobile Bay area, where the loss was due to direct and indirect effects of dredging (Duke and Kruczynski, 1992). Stout (1979) estimated that about 6,000 acres of marshland in the bay have been destroyed and about 2,200 acres of marshland created by deposition of dredged material. Cumulative effects of alterations of all kinds on the Mobile Bay ecosystem resulted in a loss of more than 10,000 acres of emergent estuarine marsh and probably more than 50 percent of the submerged aquatic vegetation in the bay between 1955 and 1979 (Watzin and others, in press).

The FWS recently evaluated wetland changes in upper Mobile Bay (Watzin and others, in press). The evaluation revealed no additional loss of estuarine-marsh acreage since 1979 and reported a substantial (75 percent) increase in freshwater marsh from 1979 to 1988. The increase in freshwater marsh was attributed to growth of emergent vegetation in disposal areas and ditches and to mapping errors in earlier inventories. About 1,200 acres (2.7 percent) of forested wetlands in the upper Mobile Bay area were lost or converted to scrub-shrub wetlands between 1979 and 1988. A major cause of the conversions was clearcutting associated with timber harvest. Losses were due largely to creation of impoundments and commercial development.

Wetland regulations currently (1993) in effect generally allow wetland destruction only when mitigated by wetland enhancement or creation. The effectiveness of these measures in slowing wetland loss will depend upon enforcement of and compliance with the mitigation requirements. The effectiveness of wetland mitigation in sustaining the ecological functions of wetlands remains in question (Stout, 1979; Alabama Department of Environmental Management, 1992).

CONSERVATION

Many government agencies and private organizations participate in wetland conservation in Alabama. The most active agencies and organizations and some of their activities are listed in table 1.

Federal wetland activities.—Development activities in Alabama wetlands are regulated by several Federal statutory prohibitions and incentives that are intended to slow wetland losses. Some of the more important of these are contained in the 1899 Rivers and Harbors Act; the 1972 Clean Water Act and amendments; the 1985 Food Security Act; the 1990 Food, Agriculture, Conservation, and Trade Act; the 1986 Emergency Wetlands Resources Act; and the 1972 Coastal Zone Management Act.

Section 10 of the Rivers and Harbors Act gives the U.S. Army Corps of Engineers (Corps) authority to regulate certain activities in navigable waters. Regulated activities include diking, deepening, filling, excavating, and placing of structures. The related section 404 of the Clean Water Act is the most often-used Federal legislation protecting wetlands. Under section 404 provisions, the Corps issues permits regulating the discharge of dredged or fill material into wetlands. Permits are subject to review and possible veto by the U.S. Environmental Protection Agency (EPA), and the FWS has review and advisory roles. Section 401 of the Clean Water Act grants to States and eligible Indian Tribes the authority to approve, apply conditions to, or deny section 404 permit applications on the basis of a proposed activity's probable effects on the water quality of a wetland.

Most farming, ranching, and silviculture activities are not subject to section 404 regulation. However, the "Swampbuster" provision of the 1985 Food Security Act and amendments in the 1990 Food, Agriculture, Conservation, and Trade Act discourage (through financial disincentives) the draining, filling, or other alteration of wetlands for agricultural use. The law allows exemptions from penalties in some cases, especially if the farmer agrees to restore the

Table 1. Selected wetland-related activities of government agencies and private organizations in Alabama, 1993

[Source: Classification of activities is generalized from information provided by agencies and organizations. •, agency or organization participates in wetland-related activity; ..., agency or organization does not participate in wetland-related activity. MAN, management; REG, regulation; R&C, restoration and creation; LAN, land acquisition; R&D, research and data collection; D&I, delineation and inventory]

Agency or organization	MAN	REG	R&C	LAN	R&D	D&I
FEDERAL						
Department of Agriculture						
Consolidated Farm Service Agency		•				
Forest Service	•		•	•	•	•
Natural Resources Conservation Service		•	•		•	•
Department of Commerce						
National Oceanic and Atmospheric Administration	•	•			•	•
Department of Defense						
Army Corps of Engineers	•	•	•	•	•	•
Military reservations	•					
Department of the Interior						
Fish and Wildlife Service	•		•	•	•	•
Geological Survey					•	
National Biological Service					•	
National Park Service	•				•	
Environmental Protection Agency		•			•	•
Tennessee Valley Authority	•				•	
STATE						
Department of Conservation and Natural Resources	•	•	•	•	•	•
Department of Economic and Community Affairs					•	
Department of Environmental Management	•	•			•	
Geological Survey of Alabama					•	•
Marine Environmental Sciences Consortium					•	•
SOME COUNTY AND LOCAL GOVERNMENTS		•				
PRIVATE ORGANIZATIONS						
The Nature Conservancy	•			•		
Coastal Land Trust	•			•		

altered wetland or other wetlands that have been converted to agricultural use. The Wetlands Reserve Program of the 1990 Food, Agriculture, Conservation, and Trade Act authorizes the Federal Government to purchase conservation easements from landowners who agree to protect or restore wetlands. The Consolidated Farm Service Agency (formerly the Agricultural Stabilization and Conservation Service) administers the Swampbuster provisions and Wetlands Reserve Program. The Natural Resources Conservation Service (formerly the Soil Conservation Service) determines compliance with Swampbuster provisions and assists farmers in the identification of wetlands and in the development of wetland protection, restoration, or creation plans.

The 1986 Emergency Wetlands Resources Act and the 1972 Coastal Zone Management Act and amendments encourage wetland protection through funding incentives. The Emergency Wetland Resources Act requires States to address wetland protection in their Statewide Comprehensive Outdoor Recreation Plans to qualify for Federal funding for State recreational land; the National Park Service provides guidance to States in developing the wetland component of their plans. Coastal States that adopt coastal-zone management programs and plans approved by the National Oceanic and Atmospheric Administration (NOAA) are eligible for Federal funding and technical assistance through the Coastal Zone Management Act.

Federal agencies are responsible for the proper management of wetlands on public land under their jurisdiction. In Alabama, the U.S. Forest Service manages wetlands in five National Forests, which contain 636,476 acres of land and more than 400 miles of rivers (Alabama Department of Economic and Community Affairs, 1991). The FWS manages 55,000 acres on five National Wildlife Refuges in the State, of which about 29,000 acres are wetlands

(Frank Dukes, U.S. Fish and Wildlife Service, oral commun., 1992). The Corps manages 14 impoundments in the State and more than 100 public-use areas (U.S. Army Corps of Engineers, 1981). Military bases in Alabama cover an area of about 400,000 acres, some of which contain wetlands. The Sanctuaries and Reserves Division of NOAA, in cooperation with the State of Alabama, manages the Weeks Bay National Estuarine Research Reserve. The Tennessee Valley Authority (TVA) maintains 3,750 acres of managed wetlands in northern Alabama (Wes James, Tennessee Valley Authority, oral commun., 1993). The Wildlife and Natural Heritage Resources Section of TVA develops and implements conservation and management strategies to ensure protection of wildlife and natural heritage resources on TVA lands and promotes protection and enhancement of such resources elsewhere in the region. The Natural Heritage Resources Section, in cooperation with State wildlife-management agencies and the FWS, operates projects that provide critical wetland habitats that support migratory waterfowl and other important wetland species.

Although it does not manage wetlands, EPA's wetland-research programs facilitate wetland management and conservation in Alabama. The EPA, in cooperation with State and other Federal agencies, is assessing coastal wetlands in the State as part of its Gulf of Mexico Program. The EPA and FWS are conducting a demonstration project that will map changes in wetlands in Mobile Bay and the lower Mobile–Tensaw River Delta.

State wetland activities.—Although Alabama currently (1993) has no comprehensive wetland-protection program, the State is assessing the need for a wetlands policy. Several State agencies actively participate in aspects of Federal programs, and some wetlands are protected under State programs.

The Alabama Department of Economic and Community Affairs is responsible for planning policies that protect the State's water resources, including wetlands. The Department's newly formed Office of Water Resources has initiated a 3-year study to be completed in 1995 that will address protection of wetlands and other water resources in the State. The Department also addresses wetland issues in its Statewide Comprehensive Outdoor Recreation Plan in response to section 303 of the Federal Emergency Wetlands Resources Act of 1986.

The Alabama Department of Environmental Management manages wetlands in Alabama's coastal zone through its regulatory authority under the Alabama Coastal Zone Management Act and through its authority to issue section 401 water-quality certification. The Department identifies wetlands and submersed grassbeds as coastal resources for which effects from any regulated uses must be considered. This activity includes review of all State and Federal permitting activities for the coastal zone of the State and primarily, in the case of wetlands, section 404 dredge-and-fill permits and Rivers and Harbors Act navigable-water permits issued by the Corps (Alabama Department of Environmental Management, 1992). Alabama's Coastal Zone Management program defines the coastal zone as that part of the State where the land surface is less than 10 feet above sea level. However, Rathbun and others (1987) reported that approximately 28 percent of Alabama's coastal wetlands are in areas that are higher than 10 feet and, thus, are excluded from protection under the Coastal Zone Management program.

Mitigation for wetland losses caused by approved projects is required in the coastal zone. A review of some of these coastal mitigation projects indicated that, of 14 projects, 6 could not be evaluated, 3 were successful, 2 were partially successful, and 3 were failures (Alabama Department of Environmental Management, 1992).

The Department of Environmental Management regulates dredge-and-fill activities in wetlands that are not in Alabama's coastal zone solely through the State's authority to issue section 401 water-quality certification under the Clean Water Act and through the Nonpoint Source Discharge Management Program. Other activities that might affect wetlands, such as draining or logging operations that do not result in significant wetland fill, are not regulated. Wetland waters are considered to be waters of the State in the Alabama Water Pollution Control Act but are not defined or protected by the act for their inherent value (Alabama Department of Environmental Management, 1992).

The Alabama Department of Conservation and Natural Resources comments on section 404 permit applications and on local land-use issues to call attention to potential effects on wildlife. The Department manages, regulates, and acquires land (including wetlands) for wildlife-management areas, State parks, and for other State recreational lands. The Department also will administer a new program, "Forever Wild," that has the objective of acquiring land for protection, recreation, education, and scientific research.

Private wetland activities.—Private organizations in Alabama are important advocates for wetlands. These organizations inform the public on wetland issues, organize citizen networks, and lobby for wetland protection. The Alabama Conservancy, the Coastal Land Trust, the Sierra Club, the National Audubon Society, the Alabama Wildlife Federation, and the Cahaba River Society are involved in State wetland issues.

The Nature Conservancy is active in the acquisition and protection of wetlands in Alabama. The Nature Conservancy, along with the Coastal Land Trust, acquired 18,000 acres of wetlands in the Mobile–Tensaw River Delta. Most of this acreage has been sold to the Corps as part of its Tennessee–Tombigbee Waterway mitigation project and will be managed by the State. The Nature Conservancy has been instrumental in the purchase and preservation of several other wetland areas in the State, including the Bon Secour National Wildlife Refuge, the Weeks Bay National Estuarine Research Reserve, several small (2- to 35-acre) pitcher plant bogs in northern Alabama, and a 156-acre tract in southern Alabama that is primarily pine savannah containing some wetlands. The Nature Conservancy also has been requested by the FWS to assist in the establishment of the Grand Bay Savannah National Wildlife Refuge in southwestern Alabama and southern Mississippi. This proposed 13,000-acre refuge will have substantial wetland acreage (Stratton Bull, The Nature Conservancy of Alabama, written commun., 1993).

References Cited

Alabama Department of Economic and Community Affairs, 1991, Alabama Statewide Comprehensive Outdoor Recreation Plan: Montgomery, Alabama Department of Economic and Community Affairs, 146 p. and appendix.

Alabama Department of Environmental Management, 1992, Water-quality report to Congress: Montgomery, Alabama Department of Environmental Management, 105 p. and appendix.

Cahaba River Society, 1992, It's almost lily time!: Cahaba River Society newsletter, May/June 1992, 16 p.

Chandler, R.V., and Moore, J.D., 1987, Springs in Alabama: Alabama Geological Survey Circular 134, 95 p.

Cowardin, L.M., Carter, Virginia, Golet, F.C., and LaRoe, E.T., 1979, Classification of wetlands and deepwater habitats of the United States: U.S. Fish and Wildlife Service Report FWS/OBS–79/31, 131 p.

Dahl, T.E., 1990, Wetlands—Losses in the United States, 1780's to 1980's: Washington, D.C., U.S. Fish and Wildlife Service Report to Congress, 13 p.

Dahl, T.E., Johnson, C.E., and Frayer, W.E., 1991, Status and trends of wetlands in the conterminous United States, mid-1970's to mid-1980's: Washington, D.C., U.S. Fish and Wildlife Service Report to Congress, 28 p.

Dardeau, M.R., Shipp, R.L. and Wallace, R.K., 1990, Faunal components, *in* Mobile Bay—Issues, resources, status, and management—Proceedings of a seminar held November 17, 1988: Washington, D.C., National Oceanic and Atmospheric Administration, Estuary-of-the-Month Seminar Series no. 15, p. 89–114.

Duke, Thomas, and Kruczynski, W.L., eds., 1992, Status and trends of emergent and submerged vegetated habitats, Gulf of Mexico, USA: The Environmental Protection Agency, Gulf of Mexico Program, 161 p.

Fenneman, N.M., 1946, Physical divisions of the United States: Washington, D.C., U.S. Geological Survey special map, scale 1:7,000,000.

Field, D.W., Reyer, A.J., Genovese, P.V., and Shearer, B.D., 1991, Coastal wetlands of the United States—An accounting of a valuable national resource: Washington, D.C., National Oceanic and Atmospheric Administration and U.S. Fish and Wildlife Service cooperative report, 59 p.

Hofstetter, R.H., 1983, Wetlands of the United States, *in* Gore, A.J.P., ed., Ecosystems of the world; 4B, Mires—Swamp, bog, fen and moor: Regional studies, Amsterdam, Elsevier Scientific Publishing Co., p. 201–244.

Jeffcoat, H.H., and Mooty, W.S., 1986, Alabama surface-water resources, *in* U.S. Geological Survey, National water summary 1985—Hydrologic events and surface-water resources: U.S. Geological Survey Water-Supply Paper 2300, p. 131–136.

Mitsch, W.J., and Gosselink, J.G., 1986, Wetlands: New York, Van Nostrand Reinhold Company, 537 p.

Mohlenbrock, R.H., 1992, Conecuh bogs, Alabama: Natural History, v. 101, no. 3, p. 60–62.

Rathburn, C.E., Watzin, M.C., Johnston, J.B., and O'Neil, P.E., 1987, Areal extent of wetlands above and below the 10-foot contour line in Alabama: U.S. Fish and Wildlife Service, National Wetland Research Center Open-File Report 86–3, 9 p.

Roach, E.R., Watzin, M.C., Scurry, J.D., and Johnston, J.B., 1987, Wetland changes in coastal Alabama, *in* Lowery, T.A., ed., Proceedings of Symposium on the Natural Resources of the Mobile Bay Estuary, Mobile, Ala., February 10–12, 1987: Mobile, Ala., Auburn University, Alabama Sea Grant Extension Service and Alabama Cooperative Extension Service, p. 92–101.

Shaw, S.P., and Fredine, C.G., 1956, Wetlands of the United States—Their extent and their value to waterfowl and other wildlife: U.S. Fish and Wildlife Service Circular 39, 67 p.

Stout, J.P., 1979, Marshes of the Mobile Estuary—Status and evaluation, *in* Loyacano, H.A., Jr., and Smith, J.P., eds., Proceedings of the Symposium on the Natural Resources of the Mobile Bay Estuary, Mobile, Ala., 1979: Mobile, Ala., U.S. Army Corps of Engineers, Mobile District, p. 113–122.

_____1990, Estuarine habitats, *in* Mobile Bay—Issues, resources, status, and management—Proceedings of a seminar held in Washington, D.C., November 17, 1988: National Oceanic and Atmospheric Administration, Estuary-of-the-Month Seminar Series no. 15, p. 63–88.

U.S. Army Corps of Engineers, 1981, Environmental data inventory, State of Alabama: Mobile, Ala., U.S. Army Corps of Engineers, 325 p.

U.S. Department of Agriculture, 1985, Status and conditions of land and water resources in Alabama, 1982: Auburn, Ala., U.S. Department of Agriculture, 140 p.

U.S. Fish and Wildlife Service, 1992, Regional wetlands concept plan, Emergency Wetlands Resources Act, Southeast Region: Atlanta, U.S. Fish and Wildlife Service, 259 p.

Watzin, M.C., Tucker, Sandy, and South, Celeste, in press, Environmental problems in the Mobile Bay ecosystem—The cumulative effects of human activities: Mobile, Ala., Mississippi–Alabama Sea Grant Consortium Publication.

Winter, T.C., and Woo, Ming-Ko, 1990, Hydrology of lakes and wetlands, *in* Wolman, M.G., and Riggs, H.C., eds., Surface water hydrology: Boulder, Colo., Geological Society of America, The Geology of North America, v. O–1, p. 159–187.

FOR ADDITIONAL INFORMATION: District Chief, U.S. Geological Survey, 520 19th Avenue, Tuscaloosa, AL 35401; Regional Wetland Coordinator, U.S. Fish and Wildlife Service, 1875 Century Building, Atlanta, GA 30345

Prepared by
Benjamin F. McPherson,
U.S. Geological Survey

Alaska
Wetland Resources

Alaska has more area covered by wetlands—approximately 170 million of its 367 million acres—than the total area of wetlands in the other 49 States combined (Dahl, 1990). Alaska has a wide variety of topographic, geologic, climatic, and hydrologic conditions that contribute to the variety of wetland complexes in the State. Alaska's wetland complexes differ in size, function, and type, and they include types that are rare in other States, such as vast expanses of treeless tundra (fig. 1) in northern Alaska and extensive black spruce peatlands, or muskegs, elsewhere in the State.

Wetlands are sociologically, ecologically, and economically important to Alaska. Wetlands provide the resources for people in rural Alaskan villages to survive (Ellanna and Wheeler, 1990)—almost all subsistence hunting, fishing, trapping, and food gathering occurs on or adjacent to wetlands. Many mammals, fish, and birds within the State depend on some type of wetland for breeding, nesting, rearing young, or feeding. Alaska's wetlands provide recreational opportunities and support related businesses for people who hunt, observe, and photograph wildlife.

Alaska has seven wetland complexes that are important for their water-habitat value (Tiner, 1984): Yukon–Kuskokwim Delta, Izembek Lagoon, Yukon Flats, Teshekpuk Lake, upper Alaska Peninsula, Copper River Delta, and upper Cook Inlet. In general, wetlands in Alaska that have the highest value for waterfowl are coastal salt marshes and wetlands in and adjacent to lakes that have extensive periods of drawdown or that fluctuate with river flow (Lensink and Derksen, 1990).

During spring and fall migrations, huge flocks of waterfowl (ducks, geese, and swans) and shorebirds (dowitchers, godwits, plovers, turnstones, sandpipers, curlews, snipe, phalaropes, and yellowlegs) stop at wetland areas in Alaska. More than 70,000 swans, 1 million geese, 12 million ducks, and 100 million shorebirds depend on Alaskan wetlands for resting, feeding, or nesting (King and Lensink, 1971). During years of drought in prairie States and Provinces of Canada, birds displaced from their traditional breeding areas fly northward to wetlands in Alaska.

Alaska wetlands provide forage for large mammals such as caribou, moose, and musk oxen. They also provide food and habitat for beaver, muskrat, mink, and land otter. Rocky coastal beaches serve as rookeries (areas where breeding and pupping occur) and resting areas for marine mammals such as seal, sea lion, and walrus. Alaska wetlands sustain some of the world's richest commercial, sport, and subsistence fisheries. Almost 90 percent of wild salmon caught in the United States are caught in Alaskan waters. These fish rely on palustrine and riverine wetlands to provide food, cover, and spawning areas during their life in inland waters, and they pass through riverine, estuarine, and marine wetlands on their migration to and from the ocean. Resident freshwater and estuarine fish also depend on wetland habitat.

Wetlands in Alaska have important hydrologic and water-quality functions, including flow regulation, erosion control, sediment retention, nutrient uptake, and contaminant removal. Many wetlands have limited flood-control or water-storage functions during snowmelt because their soils are seasonally or perennially frozen, limiting absorption of runoff. However, several characteristics of wetlands help reduce peak flows, even when soils are frozen (Post, 1990). Water is detained behind hummocks and within depressions, ponds, and lakes, and the velocity of the water is slowed by vegetation. The mosses, peats, and mineral soils of wetlands can become dryer during winter, and during snowmelt these materials are able to absorb some meltwater. Following snowmelt, wetlands have a greater capacity for streamflow regulation because the capacity of the soils to store water increases: higher temperatures increase the thickness of unfrozen soils and increase evaporation and plant transpiration, which help lower the water table.

Wetland plants help control the erosion of mineral soils by decreasing wind and water velocities near the ground and by holding soil particles together with their roots. In permafrost areas, vegetation also reduces erosion by preventing the warming and thawing of ice-rich soils. In flood plains, wetland vegetation removes some suspended sediment from floodwaters by slowing water velocities.

Wetlands in Alaska transform and retain nutrients and toxic compounds. Nutrients and contaminants attach to the organic and fine mineral soils. Plants, phytoplankton, fungi, and bacteria use the nutrients and degrade some of the contaminants.

TYPES AND DISTRIBUTION

Wetlands are lands transitional between terrestrial and deepwater habitats where the water table usually is at or near the land surface or the land is covered by shallow water (Cowardin and others, 1979). The distribution of wetlands and deepwater habitats in Alaska is shown in figure 2A; only wetlands are discussed herein.

Wetlands can be vegetated or nonvegetated and are classified on the basis of their hydrology, vegetation, and substrate. In this summary, wetlands are classified according to the system proposed by Cowardin and others (1979), which is used by the U.S. Fish and Wildlife Service (FWS) to map and inventory the Nation's wetlands. At the most general level of the classification system, wetlands are grouped into five ecological systems: Palustrine, Lacustrine, Riverine, Estuarine, and Marine. The Palustrine System includes only wetlands, whereas the other systems comprise wetlands and deepwater habitats. Wetlands of the systems that occur in Alaska are described on page 3.

Figure 1. Tundra on the Arctic coastal plain southwest of the Kavik River. Willow thickets are present along the meandering stream. *(Photograph by F.C. Golet, U.S. Fish and Wildlife Service.)*

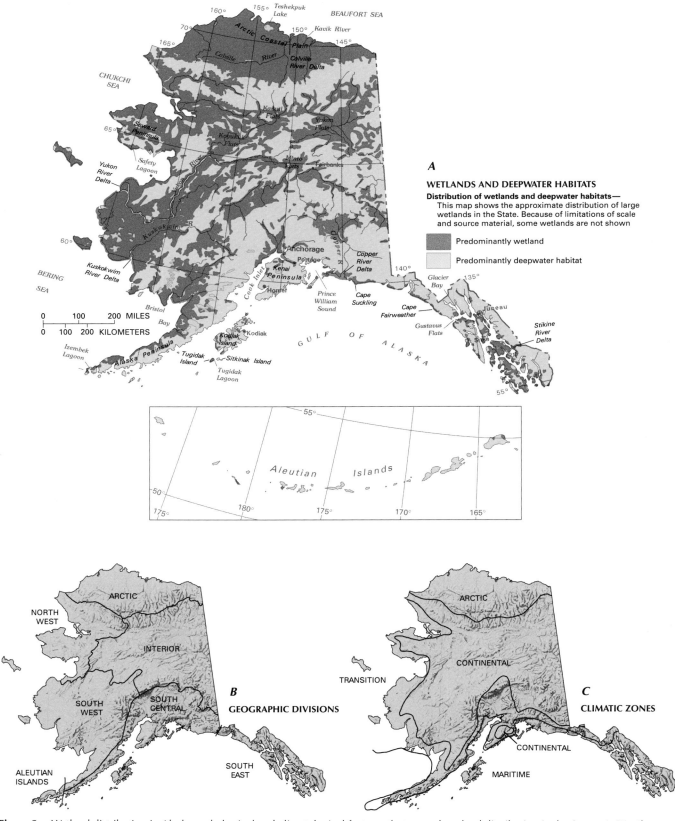

Figure 2. Wetland distribution in Alaska and physical and climatological features that control wetland distribution in the State. **A**, Distribution of wetlands and deepwater habitats. **B**, Geographic divisions. **C**, Climatic zones. (*Sources: A, T.E. Dahl, U.S. Fish and Wildlife Service, unpub. data, 1991. B, Geographic divisions modified from Lamke, 1986; landforms data from EROS Data Center. C, Hartman and Johnson, 1978.*)

System	Wetland description
Palustrine	Nontidal and tidal-freshwater wetlands in which vegetation is predominantly trees (forested wetlands); shrubs (scrub-shrub wetlands); persistent or nonpersistent emergent, erect, rooted herbaceous plants (persistent- and nonpersistent-emergent wetlands); mosses and lichens (moss-lichen wetland); or submersed and (or) floating plants (aquatic beds). Also, intermittently to permanently flooded open-water bodies of less than 20 acres in which water is less than 6.6 feet deep.
Lacustrine	Nontidal and tidal-freshwater wetlands within an intermittently to permanently flooded lake or reservoir larger than 20 acres and (or) deeper than 6.6 feet. Vegetation, when present, is predominantly nonpersistent emergent plants (nonpersistent-emergent wetlands), or submersed and (or) floating plants (aquatic beds), or both.
Riverine	Nontidal and tidal-freshwater wetlands within a channel. Vegetation, when present, is same as in the Lacustrine System.
Estuarine	Tidal wetlands in low-wave-energy environments where the salinity of the water is greater than 0.5 part per thousand (ppt) and is variable owing to evaporation and the mixing of seawater and freshwater.
Marine	Tidal wetlands that are exposed to waves and currents of the open ocean and to water having a salinity greater than 30 ppt.

Wetlands and deepwater habitats in Alaska are being inventoried by the FWS. As of December 1992, about 25 percent of the State had been mapped to determine acreage of the wetland types within the classification system of Cowardin and others (1979). Wetlands also have been inventoried in some of Alaska's urban areas by the U.S. Army Corps of Engineers (Corps). Maps showing wetland areas for parts of Anchorage, Fairbanks, Juneau, and the Kenai Peninsula are available. The Natural Resource Conservation Service and Alaska Department of Natural Resources Soil and Water Conservation Districts also have mapped wetlands in some parts of south-central and interior Alaska having agricultural and potentially agricultural lands. The FWS 170-million-acre estimate for wetland area in Alaska (Dahl, 1990) is based on soil surveys, land-cover maps, National Wetland Inventory maps, and preliminary results of statistical surveys conducted by the National Wetland Inventory.

The Joint Federal–State Land Use Planning Commission for Alaska (1973), Batten and Murray (1982), Lee and Hinckley (1982), Batten (1990), and Viereck and others (1992) describe Alaska's wetland vegetation. Many plants in Alaska grow well in a wide range of climate, soil, and water conditions. Some species dominate plant communities on both wet and dry soils, sometimes making it difficult to differentiate Alaska wetlands from uplands solely on the basis of vascular-plant communities.

Palustrine System.— Most of Alaska's wetlands are palustrine. Palustrine wetlands in Alaska include both peatlands (wetlands that have organic soils) and nonpeatlands. Peatlands, also known as mires, occur throughout Alaska and cover an estimated 27 to 110 million acres (Northern Technical Services and EKONO, Inc., 1980; Dachnowski-Stokes, 1941), depending on the peatland definition and inventory techniques used. In general, a peatland is a moss-lichen, emergent, scrub-shrub, or forested wetland containing more than 12 inches of a wet organic soil (peat) consisting of partly to well-decomposed plants. However, definitions of peatland differ in the thickness of peat required. Peat forms when the rate of plant production exceeds the rate of decomposition, usually under water-saturated conditions. Poor air circulation, low levels of oxygen, and cool ground water within the saturated soil inhibit the activity of soil bacteria and fungi, so dead plant material decomposes slowly. Some peatlands in Alaska are underlain by poorly permeable silt, clay, well-decomposed peat, or bedrock, which contribute to the water-holding capacity of those sites. Throughout Alaska, peat is commonly several feet thick in topographic depressions and in poorly drained lowlands.

Bogs and fens are peatlands that generally have a water table near the surface and ground-cover vegetation that is predominantly mosses. Sedges, heath shrubs, and trees commonly grow above the moss layer. In Alaska, sphagnum and feather mosses commonly dominate the ground cover in flat peatlands having rain and snow as the predominant sources of water (bogs), whereas brown mosses, grasses, and sedges are more prevalent on low-gradient slopes having some internal drainage or ground-water inflow (fens). A moss-floored peatland containing black spruce trees found primarily on cold, wet, poorly drained soils is commonly referred to as muskeg. A muskeg can be either a bog or a fen, depending on the source of water. Bogs and fens underlain by permafrost are extensive in wet, low-relief areas near the Yukon and Kuskokwim Rivers in interior Alaska, where they cover about 9 million acres (Joint Federal–State

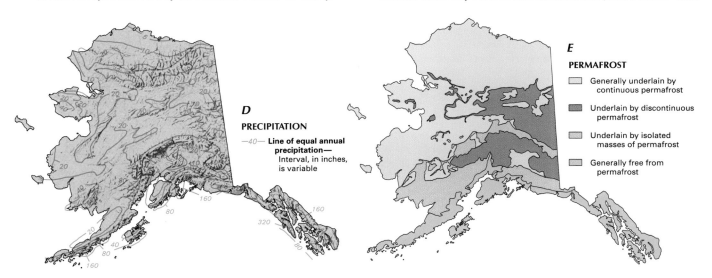

Figure 2. **Continued.** *D*, Average annual precipitation. *E*, Permafrost distribution. (*Sources: D, Lamke, 1986. E, Ferrians, 1965.*)

Land Use Planning Commission for Alaska, 1973). In southeastern Alaska, where the terrain is mountainous, fens are more abundant than bogs. Bogs and fens in southeastern Alaska form at the edges of mountain slopes and on adjacent lowlands. There, the wetlands are not underlain by permafrost but are commonly underlain by bedrock at a shallow depth.

Tundra, marshes, and meadows form in wet areas over mineral or organic soils. Tundra is characterized by treeless terrain covered by mosses, lichens, grasses, sedges, and low shrubs (mostly emergent, moss-lichen, or scrub-shrub wetland). Permafrost commonly is present at a shallow depth. Tundra occurs where summers are not warm enough for tree growth and is most extensive in northern Alaska and above treeline in mountains throughout the State. Three general types of tundra communities exist—wet, moist, and alpine. The Joint Federal–State Land Use Planning Commission for Alaska (1973) estimated that wet tundra covers about 33 million acres, moist tundra about 66 million acres, and alpine tundra about 85 million acres. Most lowland tundra remains wet or moist throughout the short thawing season because it is underlain by permafrost. However, only a small part of alpine tundra in higher mountain regions is considered wetland.

Freshwater marshes (emergent wetlands) are periodically inundated by standing or slowly moving water. Marshes in Alaska contain sedges, rushes, marestail, and other aquatic plants. The vegetation shows a distinct zonation according to water depth and frequency of exposure. Marshes are distinguished from bogs and fens by the general absence of moss, heath-type shrubs, and peat. Marshes are common around the margins of lakes, ponds, and rivers, in wet depressions and oxbows, on flood plains, in deltas, and on gently sloping benches receiving water from steeper slopes above. Wet meadows (emergent wetlands) occupy seasonally flooded sites that dry out late in the growing season, although soils typically remain saturated. Wet meadows are covered predominantly by herbaceous emergent plants, usually sedges, and are present on flood plains, lakeshores, and poorly drained lowlands throughout the State.

Palustrine wetlands within braided stream channels are commonly dominated by woody plants and perennial herbs. Willow and alder are the predominant plants in riparian scrub-shrub wetlands adjacent to Alaska's many rivers. Cottonwood predominates in riparian forested wetlands. Ponds commonly contain aquatic beds with water lilies, pondweeds, and submersed aquatic plants.

Lacustrine System.—Alaska has hundreds of thousands of lakes which together cover more than 5 million acres (Joint Federal–State Land Use Planning Commission for Alaska, 1973), but estimates of the area covered by wetlands within these lakes are not available. Lakes are abundant in lowlands underlain by permafrost, in oxbows along braided and meandering rivers, in depressions in glacial-drift deposits, and in mountain valleys dammed by glacial moraines. Many lakes in Alaska contain aquatic beds in deeper water and emergent aquatic plants in shallower water, commonly grading into surrounding palustrine and riverine wetlands.

Lacustrine wetlands used extensively by waterfowl are characteristically in lakes having gradually sloping shorelines and extensive shallow areas; profuse growth of submersed aquatic plants; a border of palustrine wetlands vegetated by emergent plants such as sedges, cattails, and bulrush; an extensive band of grassland around the lake; an abundance of aquatic insects; and a lake bottom composed of mineral soil (Lensink and Derksen, 1990). Those characteristics are common in lakes that have long periods of gradually receding water levels or that are connected to a river. In the Yukon Flats, such lakes have the highest density of nesting waterfowl in interior Alaska, and they support a breeding population of more than 1 million ducks.

Riverine System.—Wetlands within river channels include bars and flats of mud, sand, or gravel. Alaska has tens of thousands of rivers, streams, and creeks, but estimates of riverine wetland acreage are not available. Riverine wetlands provide critical spawning and rearing habitat for resident fish and for fish that migrate from the ocean to spawn. Many riverine wetlands are subject to annual or periodic inundations caused by snowmelt, glacier melt, and summer rainfall. Vegetated wetlands in low-gradient channels include submersed and floating aquatic plants and nonpersistent emergent plants such as buckbean, pendent grass, and cinquefoil. Vegetated wetlands in high-gradient mountain streams are dominated by submersed aquatic mosses.

Estuarine System.—Estuarine wetlands cover about 2 million acres in Alaska (Hall, 1988). Nonvegetated estuarine wetlands include flats, beaches, and rocky shores, which cover about 1.7 million acres and are most abundant (about 874,000 acres) in northwestern and southwestern Alaska. Tidal flats are mud and sand shores that appear to lack vegetation; however, a rich layer of microscopic plants such as diatoms, blue-green algae, and dinoflagellates typically covers the sediments. Intertidal sand and mud flats bordering the Yukon–Kuskokwim Delta cover about 130,000 acres and in places are more than 6 miles wide. A series of barrier islands protects large areas of nonvegetated tidal flats in the Copper River Delta. More than 20,000 acres of tidal flats occur on the seaward edge of the Colville River Delta on the Beaufort Sea Coast. Extensive tidal flats not associated with major river deltas include Gustavus Flats near the mouth of Glacier Bay, intertidal lagoons of Tugidak and Sitkinak Islands south of Kodiak Island, and vast mudflats in upper Cook Inlet.

Vegetated estuarine wetlands cover about 345,000 acres in Alaska (Hall, 1988). The most common type of estuarine vegetated wetland is the salt marsh (emergent wetland). Salt marshes containing sedges and grasses occur in tidally flooded, low-energy areas, such as gently sloping shores close to the mouths of rivers or behind barrier islands and beaches. Large salt-marsh complexes occur along the 500-mile shoreline of the Yukon–Kuskokwim Delta (about 162,000 acres), on the outer edge of the Copper River Delta, and in the upper Cook Inlet area. Several million migrating shorebirds and waterfowl use these coastal salt marshes for feeding and resting.

Vegetated estuarine wetlands also include aquatic beds of algae and eelgrass. Rocky materials in tidal flats along the Aleutian Islands, in the western Gulf of Alaska, and in southeastern Alaska provide habitat for algae. During fall, nearly the entire world's population of Steller's eiders and emperor geese gather in aquatic-bed wetlands in lagoons along the upper Alaska Peninsula. Izembek Lagoon near the tip of the Alaska Peninsula contains one of the largest eelgrass beds in the world, more than 84,000 acres. This lagoon serves as an international crossroad for migratory waterfowl and shorebirds from Asia, the mid-Pacific, and North America. Safety Lagoon on Seward Peninsula and Tugidak Lagoon on Tugidak Island are other large eelgrass beds important to migrating waterfowl.

Marine System.—Marine wetlands, which border the open ocean and are exposed to high-energy waves, cover about 46,000 acres in Alaska (Hall, 1988). Nonvegetated marine wetlands are generally sand and cobble-gravel shores or rocky shores. Most of the 250-mile coastline between Cape Suckling and Cape Fairweather in the northern part of the Gulf of Alaska is sand beach, whereas most of the coast along the Aleutian Island chain is bedrock and boulder rocky shores. Vegetated marine wetlands occur primarily as algal aquatic beds colonizing rocky shores of the Alaska Peninsula and shores adjacent to the Gulf of Alaska.

HYDROLOGIC SETTING

Wetlands are present wherever topographic, climatic, and hydrologic conditions favor the retention of water. Low relief, permafrost, a general abundance of precipitation relative to evaporation and plant transpiration, short cool summers, poorly permeable rocks near the land surface, and large tidal fluctuations help form and maintain extensive wetlands in Alaska. Wetland characteristics continuously change with changes in climate, water supply, soil moisture, salinity, maturation of vegetation communities, tectonic activity, fire, ice scour, glacier advance and retreat, and human activities such as draining and filling.

Alaska has seven broad, generally recognized geographic regions (fig. 2B). These regions are Southeast, Aleutian Islands, South-central, Southwest, Northwest, Arctic, and Interior Alaska. Alaska has four climatic zones—Maritime, Transition, Continental, and Arctic (fig. 2C). The State's high mountain ranges, extensive coastline, vast size—one-sixth the total area of the United States—and long north-to-south distance are the principal causes for the great differences in climate. From the northern part of the Arctic Zone to the southern part of the Maritime Zone, average annual precipitation ranges from about 5 to 320 inches (fig. 2D), and average annual temperature ranges from 10 to 45 degrees Fahrenheit. Two-thirds of the annual precipitation occurs from September through March in the Maritime Zone and from June through November in the Continental and Arctic Zones. In the Transition Zone, seasonal precipitation patterns are not sharply defined, fluctuate from year to year, and can resemble those of either the Maritime or Continental Zones.

Spring snowmelt supplies the most input to the annual water budget in most Alaskan wetlands. Snowmelt is generally confined to a short time period during spring but produces considerable runoff because it can represent the precipitation accumulated for most of the year. During summer, local rain or the melting of snow and glacier ice in upland areas replenishes the water supply of many wetlands. In much of the Southeast and South-central regions of Alaska, precipitation greatly exceeds evaporation.

Many wetlands throughout Alaska are underlain by poorly permeable materials, such as decomposed peat, bedrock, silt, clay, seasonally frozen soils, or permafrost, that do not readily allow water from snowmelt or rain to pass through. Permafrost, soil having a temperature below freezing for 2 years or more, helps form and maintain wetlands in the Northwest, Arctic, and Interior regions. The extent and thickness of the permafrost decrease southward from a continuous layer as much as several hundred feet thick in the Arctic region to areas generally free of permafrost in the South-central and Southeast regions (fig. 2E). In the Arctic coastal plain, thawed soils in the summer commonly are no more than 3-feet thick, limiting the rooting depth of plants and the infiltration of water. Long winters, cool summers, and the presence of permafrost maintain vast wet expanses under the same precipitation conditions that would produce only deserts in regions having temperate climates.

Alaska has about 34,000 miles of shoreline. Extremely large tidal fluctuations occur daily in southeastern Alaska, Prince William Sound, Cook Inlet, and Bristol Bay, forming expansive tidal flats and salt marshes. The diurnal fluctuation during spring tides is about 40 feet vertically in upper Cook Inlet near Anchorage. In coastal areas having little topographic relief, such as those in the Southwest, Northwest, and Arctic regions, storm surges push seawater inland several miles and affect the types and growth of plants.

Alaska's large rivers form extensive deltas. The Yukon–Kuskokwim Delta is one of the world's largest and supports more than 10 million acres of wetland. The deltas of the Colville, Copper, and Stikine Rivers also support vast wetlands. Expansive wetlands, such as the Yukon, Minto, Kanuti, and Koyukuk Flats, also occur adjacent to rivers flowing through large areas of low relief.

Tectonic activities affect the hydrology of Alaska's wetlands. During the 1964 earthquake, the Copper River Delta was uplifted 6 to 13 feet, and the Portage area, which is 40 miles southeast of Anchorage, subsided as much as 8 feet. In the Copper River Delta, some wetlands that were salt marshes before the earthquake have become freshwater systems. Also, in some areas, salt marshes have migrated seaward almost a mile. Kodiak Island and parts of southeastern Alaska are rising because glaciers whose weight had formerly caused land subsidence are melting. The relative fall in sea level is presumably modifying wetlands above the tidal zone and creating wetlands within the new tidal zone.

The productivity of many Alaska wetlands is affected by fires. Fires occur only infrequently in coastal areas, allowing as much as several tens of feet of peat to accumulate in some bogs and fens in southeastern Alaska. Fires, common in interior Alaska, rid marshes of dead grass, sedges, and shrubs and make new shoots available for waterfowl and mammals. Burning of vegetation and peat releases minerals and nutrients from organic litter, usually potassium, calcium, phosphorus, magnesium, chloride, and nitrogen. However, where permafrost is present, a severe fire may cause the relative abundance of plant species to change, especially if the fire removes the insulating organic layer, which in turn causes the top of the permafrost to lower. If the burned area remains undisturbed, wetland conditions will eventually return, but it can take 50 to 100 years to complete the cycle.

Sea ice and glaciers also affect Alaska wetlands. Sea ice scours the coast and limits the establishment of vegetation in intertidal and subtidal areas of the Bering, Chukchi, and Beaufort Seas. Advancing glaciers can cover wetlands, whereas retreating glaciers provide new areas where wetlands can form.

TRENDS

Information on historical wetland gains and losses in Alaska is limited. Estimates of wetland losses for the entire State range from about 80,000 to 200,000 acres, or about 0.05 to 0.15 percent of the historic wetland area (Senner, 1989; Dahl, 1990). Senner (1989), using existing quantitative data and aerial photographic interpretation techniques, estimated the following wetland losses through 1986 by activity: petroleum-related development, about 30,000 acres; mining, about 13,000 acres; infrastructure (roads, harbors, airports, and railroads), about 13,000 acres; development (residential, recreational, and commercial), about 13,000 acres; agriculture, about 8,500 acres; construction of military facilities (mostly roads and airfields), about 2,400 acres; and timber, less than 2,000 acres. Wetland losses have generally occurred in urban areas (Anchorage, Juneau, Fairbanks), around villages and communities, and in large industrial developments such as oil fields, transportation corridors, and industrial sites. As much as 50 percent of the wetlands in low-lying areas of Anchorage have been filled since 1945 (Alaska Department of Natural Resources, 1992). Any additional industrial, commercial, and residential development within areas that are predominantly wetland, such as in the Southwest, Northwest, and Arctic regions, might result in further draining or filling of wetlands.

CONSERVATION

Many government agencies and private organizations participate in wetland conservation in Alaska. The most active agencies and organizations and some of their activities are listed in table 1.

Federal wetland activities.—Development activities in Alaska wetlands are regulated by several Federal statutory prohibitions and incentives that are intended to slow wetland losses. Some of the more important of these are contained in the 1899 Rivers and Harbors Act; the 1972 Clean Water Act and amendments; the 1985 Food Security Act; the 1990 Food, Agriculture, Conservation, and Trade Act; the 1986 Emergency Wetlands Resources Act; and the 1972 Coastal Zone Management Act.

Section 10 of the Rivers and Harbors Act gives the Corps authority to regulate certain activities in navigable waters. Regulated activities include diking, deepening, filling, excavating, and plac-

Table 1. Selected wetland-related activities of government agencies and private organizations in Alaska, 1993

[Source: Classification of activities is generalized from information provided by agencies and organizations. •, agency or organization participates in wetland-related activity; ..., agency or organization does not participate in wetland-related activity. MAN, management; REG, regulation; R&C, restoration and creation; LAN, land acquisition; R&D, research and data collection; D&I, delineation and inventory]

Agency or organization	MAN	REG	R&C	LAN	R&D	D&I
FEDERAL						
Department of Agriculture						
Consolidated Farm Service Agency	...	•	...	...	...	...
Forest Service	•	...	•	•	•	•
Natural Resources Conservation Service	...	•	•	...	•	•
Department of Commerce						
National Oceanic and Atmospheric Administration	•	•	...	...	•	...
Department of Defense						
Army Corps of Engineers	•	•	•	...	•	•
Military reservations	•	...	•	•	•	•
Department of the Interior						
Bureau of Land Management	•	...	•	•	•	•
Bureau of Mines	...	...	•	...	•	•
Fish and Wildlife Service	•	...	•	•	•	•
Geological Survey	...	...	...	...	•	...
Minerals Management Service	...	...	...	...	•	...
National Biological Service	...	...	...	...	•	...
National Park Service	•	...	•	•	•	•
Environmental Protection Agency	...	•	...	...	•	•
NATIVE ALASKAN REGIONAL AND VILLAGE CORPORATIONS	•	...	•	•	...	...
STATE						
Department of Environmental Conservation	...	•	...	...	•	...
Department of Fish and Game	•	•	•	•	•	•
Department of Natural Resouces	•	•	•	•	•	•
Department of Transportation and Public Facilities	...	...	•	•	...	...
University of Alaska	•	...	...	...	•	...
SOME BOROUGH AND LOCAL GOVERNMENTS	•	•	•	•	•	•
PRIVATE ORGANIZATIONS						
Ducks Unlimited	•	...	...	•	•	...
The Nature Conservancy	•	...	...	•	•	•

ing of structures. The related section 404 of the Clean Water Act is the most often-used Federal legislation protecting wetlands. Under section 404 provisions, the Corps issues permits regulating the discharge of dredged or fill material into wetlands. Permits are subject to review and possible veto by the U.S. Environmental Protection Agency (EPA), and the FWS has review and advisory roles. Section 401 of the Clean Water Act grants to States and eligible Indian Tribes the authority to approve, apply conditions to, or deny section 404 permit applications on the basis of a proposed activity's probable effects on the water quality of a wetland.

Most farming, ranching, and silviculture activities are not subject to section 404 regulation. However, the "Swampbuster" provision of the 1985 Food Security Act and amendments in the 1990 Food, Agriculture, Conservation, and Trade Act discourage (through financial disincentives) the draining, filling, or other alteration of wetlands for agricultural use. The law allows exemptions from penalties in some cases, especially if the farmer agrees to restore the altered wetland or other wetlands that have been converted to agricultural use. The Wetlands Reserve Program of the 1990 Food, Agriculture, Conservation, and Trade Act authorizes the Federal Government to purchase conservation easements from landowners who agree to protect or restore wetlands. The Consolidated Farm Service Agency (formerly the Agricultural Stabilization and Conservation Service) administers the Swampbuster provisions and Wetlands Reserve Program. The Natural Resources Conservation Service (formerly the Soil Conservation Service) determines com-

pliance with Swampbuster provisions and assists farmers in the identification of wetlands and in the development of wetland protection, restoration, or creation plans.

The 1986 Emergency Wetlands Resources Act and the 1972 Coastal Zone Management Act and amendments encourage wetland protection through funding incentives. The Emergency Wetland Resources Act requires States to address wetland protection in their Statewide Comprehensive Outdoor Recreation Plans to qualify for Federal funding for State recreational land; the National Park Service (NPS) provides guidance to States in developing the wetland component of their plans. Coastal States that adopt coastal-zone management programs and plans approved by the National Oceanic and Atmospheric Administration are eligible for Federal funding and technical assistance through the Coastal Zone Management Act.

Many large tracts of land in Alaska are managed by Federal agencies including the Bureau of Land Management (about 90 to 100 million acres), the FWS (16 wildlife refuges covering about 77 million acres), the NPS (parks and preserves covering about 50 million acres), the U.S. Forest Service (2 National Forests covering about 24 million acres), and the U.S. Department of Defense (about 2 million acres). Because wetlands in Alaska are widespread, almost all of these tracts contain some wetland. Thus, these agencies directly or indirectly manage, inventory, or collect data on wetlands. Many agencies are restoring and enhancing fish and wildlife habitats in wetlands that they manage. Reclamation of old mining sites, riverbanks trampled by fishermen, or other disturbed areas can include revegetation and wetland restoration. Some agencies also are acquiring new lands containing wetlands. Governmental and nongovernmental groups and individuals have input into the management plans for these Federal tracts.

Native Alaskan regional and village corporation wetland activities.—The Alaska Native Claims Settlement Act in 1971 allocated about 44 million acres to Native Alaskan regional and village corporations. Much of this land contains wetlands.

State wetland activities.—Development activities in Alaska wetlands are regulated by several State agencies. If the wetland is in a coastal area, a section 404 permit application is submitted to the Corps and also to the Alaska Division of Governmental Coordination, which coordinates the review of permit applications by the Alaska Department of Environmental Conservation, Alaska Department of Fish and Game, and Alaska Department of Natural Resources. The Division of Governmental Coordination also determines whether a proposed coastal activity is consistent with the standards of the Alaska Coastal Management Program and with local management policies and plans. State-agency reviews of permit applications for activities outside of coastal areas are not coordinated by the Division.

The Department of Environmental Conservation certifies permit applications for compliance with State water-quality standards under section 401 of the Clean Water Act and compliance with other State laws and regulations. Pursuant to section 305(b) of the Clean Water Act, the Department submits to the EPA and the U.S. Congress a biennial assessment of the State's water quality, including that in wetlands (Alaska Department of Environmental Conservation, 1992).

Under Title 16 of the Alaska statutes, the Department of Fish and Game has discretion to approve, deny, or issue conditional permits for activities affecting fish and wildlife and their habitats within State critical-habitat areas (about 1.4 million acres), game refuges (about 1.3 million acres), and game sanctuaries (about 94,000 acres), many of which contain wetlands. Outside of such areas, The Department's role is limited to activities affecting anadromous-fish habitat.

The Department of Natural Resources Division of Parks and Outdoor Recreation is the lead agency developing State Comprehensive Outdoor Recreation Plans for Alaska. Pursuant to the requirements of the Emergency Wetlands Resources Act of 1986, the plan (Alaska Department of Natural Resources, 1992) prioritizes wetland protection by wetland type and function and outlines criteria used for the selection of high-recreational-value wetlands for possible acquisition. The Department of Natural Resources Soil and Water Conservation Districts help private landowners determine whether the landowner's rural properties contain wetlands and whether a proposed activity requires permits from Federal and State agencies.

As a result of the 1959 Alaska Statehood Act, Alaska gained selection rights to about 105 million acres from the Federal Government. So far, the State has received title to about 85 million acres. The State also owns about 65 million acres of submersed lands that include the land between mean high tide and 3 miles offshore and the land under many large lakes and rivers. Most State lands are managed by the Department of Natural Resources, including about 3 million acres in State parks and about 2 million acres in State forests. The University of Alaska owns some wetlands and has several academic departments researching wetlands and fish and wildlife that use wetlands.

Regional, borough, and local wetland activities.—The Alaska Coastal Management Act established the Alaska Coastal Management Program, which is described by the Alaska Division of Governmental Coordination (1990, 1991) and Kyle (1982). The act allows local governments, rural regions, and the State to cooperatively protect and manage Alaska's coastal resources, including wetlands. The coastal zone includes all marine waters and submersed lands extending offshore to the 3-mile limit of State jurisdiction and inland areas affecting coastal waters and resources. Many communities are along the coast or along a major river within the coastal zone. Thirty-three coastal communities or regions have formed districts to work with the Alaska Coastal Policy Council and to prepare Coastal Management Plans that guide development in their local areas. These district plans influence local, State, and Federal decisions on development within the district, including the issuance of section 404 permits.

Anchorage, Juneau, Homer, Kodiak, and Sitka have wetland-management plans designating critical wetlands where little or no development is allowed, as well as less valuable wetlands that may be available for development. These plans aid project planning, decrease the number of permit applications, and expedite review of approvable projects.

General permits can be issued by the Corps to authorize specified activities within an area, such as a coastal district. They can be administered by a local government and eliminate the need for individual evaluation.

Private wetland activities.—Alaska has many private-interest groups that keep the public informed on wetland issues, organize citizen networks, and lobby either for or against wetland-protection measures. The Nature Conservancy helps government agencies and private landowners identify rare and important ecological communities, protects valuable habitats and natural systems through acquisition or purchase, and assists governmental agencies and other conservation organizations in their land-preservation efforts. Ducks Unlimited has helped government agencies acquire, enhance, and protect wetlands used by waterfowl in the Anchorage, Fairbanks, and the Copper River Delta areas. The Alaska Center for the Environment, Anchorage Waterways Council, National Audubon Society, National Wildlife Federation, Sierra Club, Southeast Alaska Conservation Association, and Trustees for Alaska are a few of the organizations engaged in activities to protect Alaska's wetlands, including programs to educate the public about wetland issues. The Alaska Wetlands Coalition opposes potential developmental constraints and is lobbying for the State to be exempt from portions of section 404 regulations because of the abundance of wetlands in the State.

References Cited

Alaska Department of Environmental Conservation, 1992, Alaska water quality assessment, 1992: Juneau, Alaska Department of Environmental Conservation, Division of Environmental Quality, Water Quality Management Section, 57 p.
Alaska Department of Natural Resources, 1992, Alaska's outdoor legacy—Statewide Comprehensive Outdoor Recreation Plan, 1992–1996, Public review draft: Anchorage, Alaska Department of Natural Resources, Division of Parks and Outdoor Recreation, 100 p.
Alaska Division of Governmental Coordination, 1990, Alaska coastal management program—Annual report, Fiscal year 1989: Juneau, Division of Governmental Coordination, 29 p.
_____1991, Alaska coastal management program—Statutes and regulations, September 1991: Juneau, Division of Governmental Coordination, 105 p.
Batten, A.R., 1990, A synopsis of Alaska wetland vegetation, in Alaska—Regional wetland functions, Proceedings of a workshop, Anchorage, Alaska, May 28–29, 1986: University of Massachusetts at Amherst, The Environmental Institute Publication 90–1, p. 23–44.
Batten, A.R., and Murray, D.F., 1982, A literature survey on the wetland vegetation of Alaska: U.S. Army Engineer Waterways Experiment Station Technical Report Y–82–2, 222 p.
Cowardin, L.M., Carter, Virginia, Golet, F.C., and LaRoe, E.T., 1979, Classification of wetlands and deepwater habitats of the United States: U.S. Fish and Wildlife Service Report FWS/OBS–79/31, 131 p.
Dachnowski-Stokes, A.P., 1941, Peat resources in Alaska: U.S. Department of Agriculture Technical Bulletin 769, 82 p.
Dahl, T.E., 1990, Wetlands—Losses in the United States, 1780's to 1980's: Washington, D.C., U.S. Fish and Wildlife Service Report to Congress, 13 p.
Ellanna, L.J., and Wheeler, P.C., 1990, Subsistence use of wetlands in Alaska, in Alaska—Regional wetland functions, Proceedings of a workshop, Anchorage, Alaska, May 28–29, 1986: University of Massachusetts at Amherst, The Environmental Institute Publication 90–1, p. 85–103.
Ferrians, O.J., Jr., 1965, Permafrost map of Alaska: U.S. Geological Survey Miscellaneous Geologic Investigations Series Map I–445, scale 1:2,500,000.
Hall, J.V., 1988, Alaska coastal wetlands survey: Anchorage, U.S. Fish and Wildlife Service, 34 p.
Hartman, C.W., and Johnson, P.R., 1978, Environmental atlas of Alaska: Fairbanks, University of Alaska, Institute of Water Resources, 101 p.
Joint Federal–State Land Use Planning Commission for Alaska, 1973, Major ecosystems of Alaska: Washington, D.C., U.S. Geological Survey map, scale 1:2,500,000.
King, J.G., and Lensink, C.J., 1971, An evaluation of Alaskan habitat for migratory birds: U.S. Department of the Interior, Bureau of Sport Fisheries and Wildlife Administrative Report, 74 p.
Kyle, A.D., 1982, Local planning for wetlands management—A manual for districts in the Alaska Coastal Management Program: Juneau, Alaska Office of Coastal Management, 89 p.
Lamke, R.D., 1986, Alaska surface-water resources, in U.S. Geological Survey, National water summary 1985—Hydrologic events and surface-water resources: U.S. Geological Survey Water-Supply Paper 2300, p. 137–144.
Lee, L.C., and Hinckley, T.M., 1982, Impact of water level changes on woody riparian and wetland communities—The Alaska region: U.S. Fish and Wildlife Service Report FWS/OBS–82/22, v. IX, 212 p.
Lensink, C.J., and Derksen, D.V., 1990, Evaluation of Alaska wetlands for waterfowl, in Alaska—Regional wetland functions, Proceedings of a workshop, Anchorage, Alaska, May 28–29, 1986: University of Massachusetts at Amherst, The Environmental Institute Publication 90–1, p. 45–84.
Northern Technical Services and EKONO, Inc., 1980, Peat resource estimation in Alaska: Anchorage, Northern Technical Services, v. 1, 107 p. (contract report prepared for the U.S. Department of Energy).
Post, R.A., 1990, Effects of petroleum operations in Alaskan wetlands—A critique: Alaska Department of Fish and Game Technical Report 90–3, 112 p.
Senner, R.G.B., 1989, Effects of petroleum operations in Alaskan wetlands: Anchorage, Robert Senner and Company, 138 p.

Tiner, R.W., Jr., 1984, Wetlands of the United States—Current status and recent trends: Washington, D.C., U.S. Fish and Wildlife Service, 59 p.

Viereck, L.A., Dyrness, C.T., Batten, A.R., and Wenzlick, K.J., 1992, The Alaska vegetation classification: U.S. Forest Service, General Technical Report PNW–GTR–286, 278 p.

FOR ADDITIONAL INFORMATION: District Chief, U.S. Geological Survey, 4230 University Drive, Suite 201, Anchorage, AK 99508; Regional Wetland Coordinator, U.S. Fish and Wildlife Service, 1011 East Tudor Road, Anchorage, AK 99503

Prepared by
Roy L. Glass,
U.S. Geological Survey

Arizona
Wetland Resources

L ess than 1 percent of Arizona's landscape has wetlands (Arizona State Parks, 1989). Since the late 1800's, streams and wetlands throughout Arizona have been drained or modified, resulting in the loss of more than one-third of the State's original wetlands (Dahl, 1990). Despite their limited extent, wetlands are a valuable resource for the State's people and wildlife.

Benefits derived from the State's wetlands include flood control, streambank stabilization, water-quality improvement, water supply, wildlife habitat, recreation, and education. Riparian wetlands can lessen the severity of floods by retaining stormwater and releasing it slowly. Riparian vegetation can stabilize streambanks and reduce erosion. Wetlands can improve water quality by decreasing the sediment and pollutant load in the water that filters through the wetland (Carter, 1986). Rivers, lakes, and artificial stock ponds are sources of water for public supply, irrigation, and livestock use.

Wetlands are among the most valuable wildlife habitats in Arizona (Arizona State Parks, 1989). The variety and concentration of wildlife in wetlands are the result of abundant water, diverse vegetation (which provides adequate cover), and the dynamic and transitional nature of constantly changing water levels. Wetlands provide essential habitat for many waterfowl and other birds (including shorebirds and tropical migrants), amphibians, fish, and mammals. Some of the threatened or endangered species that depend directly or indirectly on Arizona wetlands include the bald eagle, humpback chub, Apache trout, Gila topminnow, Yuma clapper rail, Hualapai Mexican vole, and ocelot (Arizona State Parks, 1989).

Recreational use of wetlands benefits the State economically. Arizona's streams and wetlands offer diverse recreational experiences, including boating, hunting and fishing, camping, hiking, and wildlife watching. During 1978, in more than 46,000 visits to just three wetlands in southern Arizona, nonresident wildlife watchers generated more than $5 million in tourist revenue, or approximately $12,370 per acre (Arizona State Parks, 1989). Some wetlands, such as Montezuma Well (fig. 1), also are of historical, archeological, and cultural interest and provide opportunities for education and research. Many Arizona tourist attractions are prehistoric and historic settlements that developed around streams and wetland areas that provided fish, game, and water.

Figure 1. Montezuma Well, a lacustrine spring-fed wetland/deepwater habitat that has formed in a sinkhole. Located in a semiarid basin, this wetland was one of the few sources of water for prehistoric inhabitants of the area. *(Photograph by Eleanor Robbins, U.S. Geological Survey.)*

TYPES AND DISTRIBUTION

Wetlands are lands transitional between terrestrial and deepwater habitats where the water table usually is at or near the land surface or the land is covered by shallow water (Cowardin and others, 1979). The distribution of wetlands and deepwater habitats in Arizona is shown in figure 2A; only wetlands are discussed herein.

Wetlands can be vegetated or nonvegetated and are classified on the basis of their hydrology, vegetation, and substrate. In this summary, wetlands are classified according to the system proposed by Cowardin and others (1979), which is used by the U.S. Fish and Wildlife Service (FWS) to map and inventory the Nation's wetlands. At the most general level of the classification systm, wetlands are grouped into five ecological systems: Palustrine, Lacustrine, Riverine, Estuarine, and Marine. The Palustrine System includes only wetlands, whereas the other sytems comprise wetlands and deepwater habitats. Wetlands of the systems that occur in Arizona are described below.

System	Wetland description
Palustrine	Wetlands in which vegetation is predominantly trees (forested wetlands); shrubs (scrub-shrub wetlands); persistent or nonpersistent emergent, erect, rooted, herbaceous plants (persistent- and nonpersistent-emergent wetlands); or submersed and (or) floating plants (aquatic beds). Also, intermittently to permanently flooded open-water bodies of less than 20 acres in which water is less than 6.6 feet deep.
Lacustrine	Wetlands within an intermittently to permanently flooded lake or reservoir. Vegetation, when present, is predominantly nonpersistent emergent plants (nonpersistent-emergent wetlands), or submersed and (or) floating plants (aquatic beds), or both.
Riverine	Wetlands within a channel. Vegetation, when present, is same as in the Lacustrine System.

Palustrine wetlands are represented in Arizona by riparian wetlands that include oxbow lakes, marshes, cienegas, and bosques and nonriparian wetlands such as tinajas. Palustrine wetlands also include artificially created wetlands such as farm ponds and cattle stock ponds. Riparian wetlands are in a transitional zone between the stream or lake and the dry desert upland. These habitats, the most extensive Arizona wetland habitat type, form as a result of consistently wet surface or subsurface conditions. Oxbow lakes are former river channels that are sustained by floodwater from the nearby main stem of a river. Cienegas are riparian spring-fed marshes that are surrounded by upland and characterized by permanently saturated, organic soils (Arizona State Parks, 1989). Cottonwood and willow bosques (forests) are largely restricted to the flood plains of perennial and intermittent streams. The forests are sustained by winter and spring flooding. Some streams are sustained by ground-water pumpage and have provided a scattering of aquatic communities in arid parts of Arizona that were once devoid of surface water. Tinajas, also known as rock pools, are small depressions scoured in bedrock by boulders moved by flash floods (Arizona State Parks, 1988).

Lacustrine wetlands in Arizona include playas and caldera lakes. Playas, also referred to as sinks or sinkholes, are dry, unvegetated lakebeds in closed basins. The surface water of playa lakes comes from direct precipitation and runoff; over time, the surface water evaporates and leaves tightly compacted fine sediments that compose the lake bottom. During wetter years, these areas can be flooded. Caldera lakes are formed by the collapse of basalt crust over a volcanic vent.

Riverine wetlands in Arizona occur in perennial, ephemeral, and intermittent streams. Perennial streams contain flowing water throughout the entire year. Intermittent streams are streams that flow seasonally. Ephemeral streams, called washes, flow occasionally and only as a result of surface runoff from precipitation.

HYDROLOGIC SETTING

Extreme aridity and seasonally varying precipitation are the climatic characteristics that most significantly affect wetland formation and distribution in Arizona. The State's few perennial streams arise mainly at higher altitudes, where there is more moisture and lower evaporation rates. As these streams descend to the desert plains, evaporative losses and seepage to the ground-water system greatly reduce or eliminate surface flows.

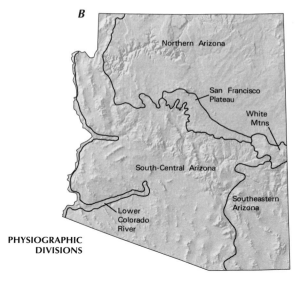

PHYSIOGRAPHIC DIVISIONS

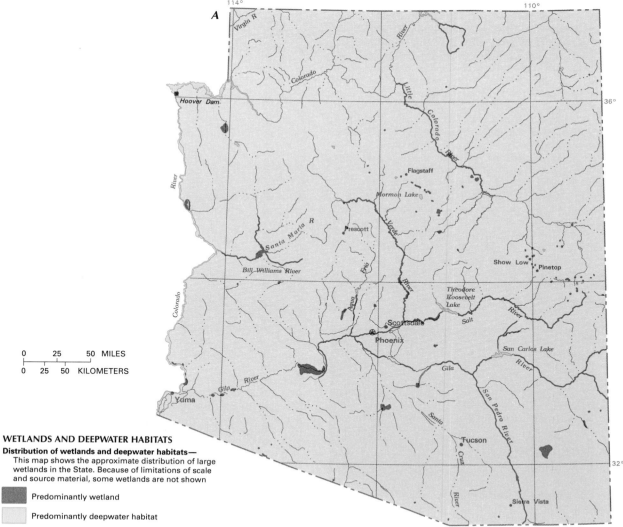

WETLANDS AND DEEPWATER HABITATS

Distribution of wetlands and deepwater habitats—
This map shows the approximate distribution of large wetlands in the State. Because of limitations of scale and source material, some wetlands are not shown

■ Predominantly wetland

☐ Predominantly deepwater habitat

Figure 2. Wetland distribution in Arizona and physiography of the State. **A**, Distribution of wetlands and deepwater habitats. **B**, Physiography. *(Sources: A, T.E. Dahl, U.S. Fish and Wildlife Service, unpub. data, 1991. B, Physiographic divisions from Brown, 1985; landforms data from EROS Data Center.)*

Most wetlands in Arizona require more moisture than that provided by local precipitation. Such moisture is available in drainages and their flood plains (riparian zones) (fig. 3), on poorly drained lands, and in and near other wet areas such as ponds, margins of lakes, and springs and their outflows.

Arizona can be divided into six physiographically distinct regions for purposes of discussing wetland hydrology (fig. 2B). These six regions are the (1) White Mountains, (2) the San Francisco Plateau, (3) Northern Arizona, (4) South-Central Arizona, (5) Southeastern Arizona, and (6) the Lower Colorado River.

White Mountains.—The White Mountains region is the wettest part of the State; precipitation averages more than 23 inches per year, of which more than 50 percent falls as snow (Brown, 1985). Snow is the main source for most of Arizona's perennial streams. Most of the vegetated wetlands in the region are above 8,000 feet in the cold boreal or subalpine climatic zone (Arizona State Parks, 1989). Many of the wetlands have been flooded by reservoirs. The water in these reservoirs typically is clear and promotes abundant aquatic vegetation (Brown, 1985). Reservoir wetlands in the White Mountains region are the nesting habitat of more than 70 percent of the waterfowl present in Arizona (Brown, 1985). Playas are present east of Show Low, below 5,500 feet in altitude (Arizona State Parks, 1989). Riparian wetlands in the region are on flood plains of high-altitude creeks and other drainages.

San Francisco Plateau.—Annual precipitation in the San Francisco Plateau region averages about 19 inches, and about 75 percent falls as snow (Arizona State Parks, 1989). Because of a permeable substrate of basalt and cinder, the San Francisco Plateau has few perennial streams. Most wetlands are in intermountain grasslands or open woodlands and have a seasonal water regime that depends on winter precipitation and snowmelt. Palustrine emergent, scrub-shrub, and forested wetlands form around caldera lakes. Caldera lakes typically are found at altitudes between 6,900 and 7,200 feet (Arizona State Parks, 1989). An example is Mormon Lake, which is southeast of Flagstaff and is the State's largest natural water body.

Northern Arizona.—The Northern Arizona region has a cold-temperate to boreal climate (Arizona State Parks, 1988). At least four types of palustrine wetlands exist in this region. These wetlands include small seasonal lakes in the southern part of the Northern Arizona region, tule-fringed sinkholes (emergent wetland), marshes of the Little Colorado River and a few of its tributaries, and riparian forested wetlands (Brown, 1985; Platts and Jensen, 1986).

South-Central Arizona.—The South-Central Arizona region has a warm-temperate to tropical-subtropical climate (Arizona State Parks, 1988). Most of the wetlands in this region have disappeared during the 20th century because of large-scale surface-water diversions and extensive ground-water pumping required to support municipal and agricultural development. Oxbow lakes and associated marshes were once fairly common in the flood plains of the major rivers in this area, particularly along the lower Verde, Salt, and Gila Rivers. Most of the wetlands in this part of the State are directly associated with the free-flowing, unmodified stream segments in the more mountainous regions and with ephemeral and intermittent streams at lower altitudes. Forested wetlands are common in this region.

Southeastern Arizona.—Summer precipitation in Southeastern Arizona is more predictable than in other parts of the State and generally exceeds winter precipitation. Historical accounts of this area describe many extensive ponds and shallow grassy marshes (Arizona State Parks, 1989). Channelization and ground-water withdrawals have drained most of the marshes, and those that remain have been stripped of vegetation and reduced in size. Seasonal playa lakes are common in this region. A few cienegas and other marshes exist in the northern part of the region, but similar wetlands have disappeared or have been eliminated in the eastern part of the region (Arizona State Parks, 1989). Many of the cienegas and marshes are directly connected to linear riparian corridors associated with streams. Wetlands in the region occur at altitudes between 3,200 and 4,600 feet (Arizona State Parks, 1989).

Lower Colorado River.—The Lower Colorado River region has a tropical-subtropical climate (Arizona State Parks, 1988). In the extreme northwestern part of the region, wetlands are directly associated with the Colorado River and the Virgin River. Historically, oxbow lakes and associated marshes were common in this area. Construction of Hoover Dam in 1935, however, eliminated the natural fluctuations of the Colorado River, which deprived many oxbow lakes of their major source of water. The result has been a decrease in wetlands associated with oxbow lakes.

TRENDS

Arizona's landscape was not always as dry as it is today. Little more than a century ago, Arizona had a natural river-drainage system that flowed year-round and spanned nearly every part of the State (Arizona State Parks, 1989). Perennial streams sustained the Native American and Hispanic cultures that occupied the State and provided water for a fledgling Anglo-American pioneer community. Arizona has lost many of its natural wetlands as the increasing requirements of agriculture, mining and other industry, and cities have resulted in the modification of the State's aquatic landscape. All the major rivers and many of the lesser streams have been impounded, regulated, and diverted (Arizona State Parks, 1989). Many other perennial streams and wetlands have disappeared because ground-water pumping has drained the aquifers, and other land-use practices have altered the hydrology of the drainage basins. Some of these changes were implemented for flood control, water storage, and hydroelectric power. Others changes resulted from land-use practices and water-management actions (Arizona State Parks, 1989). Regardless of the causes, the restructuring of Arizona's stream and wetland systems has affected the natural extent and distribution of these resources. The result has been greatly diminished opportunities for stream- and wetland-based recreation and degraded open-space quality in and around urban communities. Further, diminished natural-runoff re-

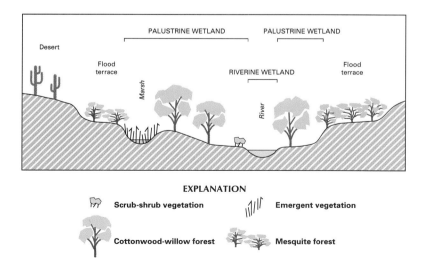

EXPLANATION

Scrub-shrub vegetation   Emergent vegetation

Cottonwood-willow forest   Mesquite forest

Figure 3. Hydrologic setting of wetlands in riparian areas of the Sonoran Desert. *(Source: Arizona State Parks, 1988.)*

tention caused by wetland alteration or destruction has led to faster rising streams and higher flood peaks; these conditions have eliminated native fish and wildlife species in some areas.

Dahl (1990) estimates that, from predevelopment times until the 1980's, wetland acreage in Arizona decreased by more than one-third. Harvesting of trees for fuel and building supplies, overgrazing, conversion to croplands, inundation by impoundments, desiccation caused by diversions, invasion of nonnative plant species, plant eradication for increased water yield and flood control, floodplain development for urban needs, sand and gravel mining, and channelization and flood control have directly affected riparian wetlands. Losses of nonflowing surface water and aquatic habitat in cienegas also have been extensive.

Trends that will affect the future of wetlands in Arizona are the increasing population and urbanization; the changing attitudes about land-, water-, and riparian-resource uses; the diversifying economy; and the shifting and increasingly complex patterns of water use. The population and urbanization trends can be expected to affect stream and wetland resources because the demand for wetland recreation will continue to increase, and municipal development will increase pressure to encroach on riparian areas for residential, commercial, and industrial activities.

CONSERVATION

Many government agencies and private organizations participate in wetland conservation in Arizona. The most active agencies and organizations and some of their activities are listed in table 1.

Federal wetland activities.—Development activities in Arizona wetlands are regulated by several Federal statutory prohibitions and incentives that are intended to slow wetland losses. Some of the more important of these are contained in the 1899 Rivers and Harbors Act; the 1972 Clean Water Act and amendments; the 1985 Food Security Act; the 1990 Food, Agriculture, Conservation, and Trade Act; and the 1986 Emergency Wetlands Resources Act.

Section 10 of the Rivers and Harbors Act gives the U.S. Army Corps of Engineers (Corps) authority to regulate certain activities in navigable waters. Regulated activities include diking, deepening, filling, excavating, and placing of structures. The related section 404 of the Clean Water Act is the most often-used Federal legislation protecting wetlands. Under section 404 provisions, the Corps issues permits regulating the discharge of dredged or fill material into wetlands. Permits are subject to review and possible veto by the U.S. Environmental Protection Agency, and the FWS has review and advisory roles. Section 401 of the Clean Water Act grants to States and eligible Indian Tribes the authority to approve, apply conditions to, or deny section 404 permit applications on the basis of a proposed activity's probable effects on the water quality of a wetland.

Most farming, ranching, and silviculture activities are not subject to section 404 regulation. However, the "Swampbuster" provision of the 1985 Food Security Act and amendments in the 1990 Food, Agriculture, Conservation, and Trade Act discourage (through financial disincentives) the draining, filling, or other alteration of wetlands for agricultural use. The law allows exemptions from penalties in some cases, especially if the farmer agrees to restore the altered wetland or other wetlands that have been converted to agricultural use. The Wetlands Reserve Program of the 1990 Food, Agriculture, Conservation, and Trade Act authorizes the Federal Government to purchase conservation easements from landowners who agree to protect or restore wetlands. The Consolidated Farm Service Agency (formerly the Agricultural Stabilization and Conservation Service) administers the Swampbuster provisions and Wetlands Reserve Program. The Natural Resources Conservation Service (formerly the Soil Conservation Service) determines compliance with Swampbuster provisions and assists farmers in the identification of wetlands and in the development of wetland protection, restoration, or creation plans.

The 1986 Emergency Wetlands Resources Act encourages wetland protection through funding incentives. The act requires States to address wetland protection in their Statewide Comprehensive Outdoor Recreation Plans to qualify for Federal funding for State recreational land; the National Park Service provides guidance to States in developing the wetland component of their plans.

State wetland activities.—The Arizona Game and Fish Department is responsible for the management of fish and wildlife throughout the State except within Indian reservations (Arizona State Parks, 1989). The Department of Environmental Quality is responsible for setting, monitoring, and enforcing water-quality standards for all navigable waters, their major tributaries, and all ground water of the State. The Department of Water Resources has authority for general control and supervision of the waters in Arizona and the appropriation and distribution of such waters.

Through the actions of the Game and Fish Department, Department of Environmental Quality, Department of Water Resources, and State Parks, the State has taken steps to conserve streams and wetlands and promote their recreational use but has not established

Table 1. Selected wetland-related activities of government agencies and private organizations in Arizona, 1993

[Source: Classification of activities is generalized from information provided by agencies and organizations. •, agency or organization participates in wetland-related activity; ..., agency or organization does not participate in wetland-related activity. MAN, management; REG, regulation; R&C, restoration and creation; LAN, land acquisition; R&D, research and data collection; D&I, delineation and inventory]

Agency or organization	MAN	REG	R&C	LAN	R&D	D&I
FEDERAL						
Department of Agriculture						
Consolidated Farm Service Agency	...	•	...	...	...	...
Forest Service	•	...	•	•	•	•
Natural Resources Conservation Service	...	•	•	...	•	•
Department of Defense						
Army Corps of Engineers	•	•	•	...	•	...
Military reservations	•	...	...	...	...	...
Department of the Interior						
Bureau of Land Management	•	...	•	...	•	...
Bureau of Reclamation	•	...	•	...	•	...
Fish and Wildlife Service	•	...	•	...	•	•
National Biological Service	...	...	...	...	•	...
Geological Survey	...	...	...	...	•	...
National Park Service	•	...	•	...	•	•
Environmental Protection Agency	...	•	...	...	•	...
TRIBAL						
Some Indian tribes	•	...	...	...	...	•
STATE						
Department of Environmental Quality	•	•	•	...	•	...
Department of Water Resources	...	•	...	...	•	...
Game and Fish Department	•	•	•	...	•	...
Outdoor Coordinating Commission	•	...	...	...	...	...
State parks	•	...	•	...	...	...
COUNTY AND LOCAL						
Counties	•	...	•	...	...	•
Municipalities	•	...	...	...	...	•
Salt River Project	•	...	...	...	•	...
PRIVATE ORGANIZATIONS						
Desert Fishes Council	...	...	...	...	•	•
Ducks Unlimited	•	...	...	...	...	...
Johnson Historical Museum of the Southwest	•	...	...	•	...	...
National Audubon Society	•	...	...	...	•	...
Arizona Riparian Council	•	...	...	...	•	•
Arizona Wildlife Federation	•	...	...	...	...	...
The Arizona Nature Conservancy	•	...	...	•	•	•
Whittell Trust	...	...	...	...	•	...

a comprehensive policy pertaining to these resources. The Riparian Area Advisory Committee, made up of agencies, associations, citizen groups, and academia, currently (1993) is working on a full report to the Governor that will address a statewide policy and recommendations.

County and local wetland activities.—The framework exists within county and city governments to incorporate wetland areas as assets to the local community. Local governments can establish policies to protect wetlands by restricting nearby development and land uses. Arizona municipalities that have programs or policies to facilitate the protection of wetlands and riparian areas include Scottsdale, Prescott, Tucson, Sierra Vista, Show Low, and Pinetop.

The quasi-public Salt River Project's activities have major implications for streams and wetlands in Arizona (Arizona State Parks, 1989). The reservoirs and irrigation projects that the Project administers have inundated or otherwise drastically altered tens of thousands of acres of native riparian areas and hundreds of miles of free-flowing streams (Arizona State Parks, 1989). In recent years, however, the Project has been active in the Arizona Riparian Council and in work to establish methods of measuring and permitting critical instream flows. Additionally, the Project's environmental policy includes protection of aquatic ecology and cooperation with Federal, State, and local agencies responsible for environmental protection.

Private wetland activities.—Programs from private groups focus mainly on the acquisition and management of stream and riparian areas, education and information exchange, wetland restoration, and advocacy for wetland recreation and conservation. The Nature Conservancy, an international nonprofit organization, seeks to protect rare plants and animals by preserving the habitats they need to survive—critical lands in the United States and beyond our borders. The Arizona Riparian Council provides an important communication channel for professionals working in the area of riparian-habitat management. Through the work of its subcommittees, the Council has begun to address coordination and consistency problems within the existing decentralized statewide riparian-management system.

References Cited

Arizona State Parks, 1988, Chapter 3—Wetlands resources in Arizona—An addendum to 1983 statewide comprehensive outdoor recreation plan: Phoenix, Arizona State Parks, p. 29–60.

_____1989, Arizona rivers, streams, and wetlands study, *in* 1989 Statewide comprehensive outdoor recreation plan: Phoenix, Arizona State Parks, 244 p.

Brown, D.E., 1985, Arizona wetlands and waterfowl: Tucson, University of Arizona Press, 169 p.

Carter, Virginia, 1986, An overview of the hydrologic concerns related to wetlands in the United States: Canadian Journal of Botany, v. 64, p. 364–374.

Cowardin, L.M., Carter, Virginia, Golet, F.C., and LaRoe, E.T., 1979, Classification of wetlands and deepwater habitats of the United States: U.S. Fish and Wildlife Service Report FWS/OBS–79/31, 131 p.

Dahl, T.E., 1990, Wetlands—Losses in the United States, 1780's to 1980's: Washington, D.C., U.S. Fish and Wildlife Service Report to Congress, 13 p.

Platts, W.S., and Jensen, Sherman, 1986, Wetland/riparian ecosystems of the Great Basin/desert and montane region—An overview, *in* Great Basin/Desert and Montane Regional Wetland Functions —Proceedings of a workshop held at Logan, Utah, February 27–28, 1986: The Environmental Institute, University of Massachusetts at Amherst Publication 90–4, p. 1–22.

FOR ADDITIONAL INFORMATION: District Chief, U.S. Geological Survey, 375 South Euclid Avenue, Tucson, AZ 85719; Regional Wetland Coordinator, U.S. Fish and Wildlife Service, 500 Gold Avenue, SW, Room 4012, Albuquerque, NM 87103

Prepared by
L.K. Ham, U.S. Geological Survey, and
S.K. Bulmer and Tanna Thornburg,
Arizona State Parks

Arkansas
Wetland Resources

Wetlands occupy about 8 percent of the land surface in Arkansas (Dahl, 1990) and are an important but threatened resource. Historically, wetlands occupied a much larger area of the State and greatly influenced early economic development. At the time the first Europeans settled in the area, wetlands occupied about 28 percent of what is now Arkansas. These wetlands consisted largely of vast bottom-land forests and swamps bordering the Mississippi River and other rivers and streams. The forested wetlands contained abundant bottom-land trees such as cypress, tupelo gum, sycamore, birch, cottonwood, and several species of oak that provided a source of timber for domestic and economic development. As the forests were cleared and the wetlands were drained, the fertile bottom land was opened up to agriculture, which eventually became the mainstay of the local economy. The loss of wetlands to agriculture and urbanization and the associated loss of wildlife habitat have slowed but continue to be a major concern (Arkansas Department of Pollution Control and Ecology, 1992).

Wetlands provide critical habitat for many important plants and animals in Arkansas. Seven endangered species and three threatened species of plants and animals inhabit wetlands in the State (Curtis James, U.S. Fish and Wildlife Service, written commun., 1993). Some of the endangered or threatened species of animals and plants in Arkansas that rely on wetlands sometime during their lives include the bald eagle, the red-cockaded woodpecker, the grey bat, the pink mucket pearly mussel, the fat pocketbook pearly mussel, and the pondberry.

Arkansas bottom-land forested wetlands provide important habitats for many species of fish. Seasonal flooding of river flood plains provides access to new or expanded food supplies during periods of increased energy needs of fish at critical stages in their reproductive and growth cycles (Jack Kilgore, John Baker, and R.D. Smith, U.S. Army Corps of Engineers, unpub. data, 1993).

Wetlands in Arkansas, especially those in the Mississippi River Valley, are a critical component of the series of wetland habitats along the Mississippi Flyway, which is used by millions of migratory birds each year. The management board of the Lower Mississippi Valley Joint Venture for the restoration of Mississippi Flyway waterfowl populations considers the protection and preservation of wetlands in Arkansas to be a key to the success of their program (Lower Mississippi Valley Joint Venture Management Board, 1990). Wetlands in the Cache–Lower White River system (fig. 1) in the Mississippi Flyway have been designated as one of nine "Wetlands of International Importance" in the United States under provisions of the Convention on Wetlands of International Importance Especially as Wildlife Habitat (Arkansas Department of Pollution Control and Ecology, 1992), which is known informally as the Ramsar Convention after Ramsar, Iran, where the convention was held in 1971.

Wetlands modify the water quality and hydrology of conterminous water bodies by serving as nutrient, sediment, and sediment-related toxic-materials traps. For example, Kleiss (1993), in a study on the Cache River in eastern Arkansas, found that there was a substantial decrease in suspended sediment and nitrate loads in the river after it passed through a wetland. Wetlands also mitigate the severity of floods and droughts by serving as floodways and reservoirs for surface waters and recharge-discharge areas for ground water (Mitsch and Gosselink, 1993). Wetlands in Arkansas also provide recreational opportunities for hunting, fishing, bird watching, and boating to thousands of people each year.

TYPES AND DISTRIBUTION

Wetlands are lands transitional between terrestrial and deepwater habitats where the water table usually is at or near the land surface or the land is covered by shallow water (Cowardin and others, 1979). The distribution of wetlands and deepwater habitats in Arkansas is shown in figure 2A; only wetlands are discussed herein.

Wetlands can be vegetated or nonvegetated and are classified on the basis of their hydrology, vegetation, and substrate. In this summary, wetlands are classified according to the system proposed by Cowardin and others (1979), which is used by the U.S. Fish and Wildlife Service (FWS) to map and inventory the Nation's wetlands. At the most general level of the classification system, wetlands are grouped into five ecological systems: Palustrine, Lacustrine, Riverine, Estuarine, and Marine. The Palustrine System includes only wetlands, whereas the other systems comprise wetlands and deepwater habitats. Wetlands of the systems that occur in Arkansas are described below.

System	Wetland description
Palustrine	Wetlands in which vegetation is predominantly trees (forested wetlands); shrubs (scrub-shrub wetlands); persistent or nonpersistent emergent, erect, rooted, herbaceous plants (persistent- and nonpersistent-emergent wetlands); or submersed and (or) floating plants (aquatic beds). Also, intermittently to permanently flooded open-water bodies of less than 20 acres in which water is less than 6.6 feet deep.
Lacustrine	Wetlands within an intermittently to permanently flooded lake or reservoir. Vegetation, when present, is predominantly nonpersistent emergent plants (nonpersistent-emergent wetlands), or submersed and (or) floating plants (aquatic beds), or both.
Riverine	Wetlands within a channel. Vegetation, when present, is same as in the Lacustrine System.

Most of the wetlands in Arkansas are palustrine forested, scrub-shrub, and nonvegetated wetlands (Arkansas Department of Pollution Control and Ecology, 1992; U.S. Fish and Wildlife Service, 1992). The most extensive areas of wetlands in the State lie along the major rivers, such as the lower Mississippi, Arkansas, Red, White, and Little Rivers and their principal tributaries in the Mis-

Figure 1. Black Swamp, a wetland along the Cache River. The Cache–Lower White River wetlands have been designated "Wetlands of International Importance" under the provisions of the 1971 Ramsar Convention. *(Photograph by Ed Morris, U.S. Geological Survey.)*

sissippi Alluvial Plain, South Central Plains, and Arkansas Valley Ecoregions (fig. 2A and 2B). Other wetlands are scattered throughout the State and are associated with springs and seeps in the Ouachita Mountains and Ozark Highlands. Arkansas has 7 National Wildlife Refuges, 1 National Scenic River System, 1 National Forest, 17 State wildlife management areas, and 6 State parks that contain significant wetland areas.

The larger wetlands in Arkansas generally are forested wetlands associated with the flood plains of rivers such as the Saline, Ouachita, and Little Rivers and Bayou Dorcheat. Mixed forested and scrub-shrub wetlands border the Cache, Black, and St. Francis Rivers and Taylor Bay. Little Bayou Meto is lined by an example of a mixed forested and emergent wetland, which is uncommon in Arkansas. Smaller wetlands with unique features include Centerville Pondberry and Coffee Prairie. These two wetlands contain plant species of special concern to the State. Coffee Prairie has been identified by The Nature Conservancy and the Natural Heritage Commission as deserving of priority protection (U.S. Fish and Wildlife Service, 1992).

HYDROLOGIC SETTING

The existence of wetlands depends on geologic and hydrologic conditions that favor the retention of water and on hydrologic processes that allow the water to accumulate (Winter and Woo, 1990). Wetland hydrology involves complex water-flow patterns that are affected by regional and local geology, topography, soil characteristics, and climate. Water in small wetlands can be supplied by local shallow ground-water flow systems, surface waters, or precipitation. In the mountainous areas of northern and western Arkansas, wetlands typically are small and associated with springs. Larger wetlands in southern and eastern Arkansas commonly receive water from local and regional ground-water flow systems and surface water. Surface water collects in topographic lows, and ground water commonly discharges in these areas. The rate at which water percolates downward from these wetlands to ground-water systems or upward from ground-water systems to the wetlands is a function of local hydraulic conditions and geologic characteristics.

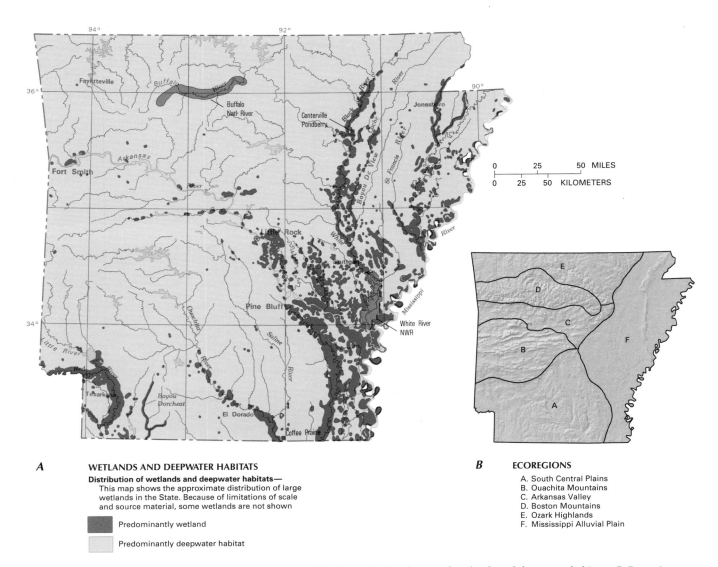

A   WETLANDS AND DEEPWATER HABITATS
Distribution of wetlands and deepwater habitats—
This map shows the approximate distribution of large wetlands in the State. Because of limitations of scale and source material, some wetlands are not shown

Predominantly wetland

Predominantly deepwater habitat

B   ECOREGIONS
A. South Central Plains
B. Ouachita Mountains
C. Arkansas Valley
D. Boston Mountains
E. Ozark Highlands
F. Mississippi Alluvial Plain

Figure 2. Wetland distribution in Arkansas and ecoregions of the State. **A**, Distribution of wetlands and deepwater habitats. **B**, Ecoregions. *(Sources: A, T.E. Dahl, U.S. Fish and Wildlife Service, unpub. data, 1991. B, Ecoregions from Omernik, 1987; landforms data from EROS Data Center.)*

In some parts of the State, seasonal fluctuations in precipitation result in seasonal differences in the flooded area of wetlands. However, precipitation in the State is abundant and averages from 40 to 56 inches per year. No season is without at least moderate amounts of precipitation (Freiwald, 1985); therefore, seasonal variations in the water content of most wetlands in the State are small.

Major wetlands in Arkansas are closely associated with the State's large river flood plains, and most are influenced by the Mississippi River. In the northeastern and eastern parts of the State, many streams flow through channels cut into alluvium—sands, silts, and clays—deposited by the Mississippi River. These streams include the Black, White, St. Francis, and Cache Rivers and Bayou Deview (Arkansas Department of Pollution Control and Ecology, 1992).

The flood plain of the Mississippi River is an area of little topographic relief that has been subjected to frequent flooding. This frequent flooding has resulted in the establishment of large stands of water-tolerant bottom-land trees and the development of backwater swamps associated with such hydrologic conditions (fig. 3A, 3B, and 3C). The continued survival of these forested and scrub-shrub wetlands depends on continued seasonal flooding and dewatering cycles. Disruption of the flooding and dewatering cycle can adversely affect plant and animal communities in wetlands and alter the size and type of the wetlands. When the flooding cycle is prevented, such as when wetland areas are leveed or ditched and drained, the water-tolerant plant species commonly are replaced by less water-tolerant trees and shrubs. Once the threat of flooding is reduced, these areas often are cleared for agriculture. When wetlands are drained or cleared, they can no longer trap sediments and sediment-bound contaminants, remove nutrients from flood waters, or provide off-channel storage to lessen the severity of floods. Also, nursery habitat for certain species of fish and invertebrates is greatly restricted when wetlands are drained. This can result in lower fish and invertebrate populations. Conversely, in forested wetlands subjected to permanent flooding, such as occurs when a river is dammed, the establishment of new trees will cease and the existing trees will die. Eventually, the forested wetland will be replaced by open water.

TRENDS

The area that is now Arkansas began losing wetlands shortly after the arrival of European settlers and has lost more wetland acres than any inland State in the Nation (Scott Yaich, U.S. Fish and Wildlife Service, written commun., 1993). Wetland loss in Arkansas from the 1780's to the 1980's was about 72 percent (Dahl, 1990), and many remaining wetlands have been altered from their natural state. Arkansas originally contained about 9,848,600 acres of wetlands before the arrival of European settlers. By 1937, wetland area in the State had decreased to about 4,900,000 acres (U.S. Fish and Wildlife Service, 1992). The rate of wetland loss increased after World War II owing to the increased availability of mechanized equipment. Wetland loss was about 36 percent of the remaining wetland area from 1957 to 1967 but decreased to about 14 percent from 1977 to 1985 (Arkansas Department of Pollution Control and Ecology, 1992). Holder (1969) estimated that 90 percent of the wetland loss in the last 40 years was due to the expansion of soybean production. By 1993, more than 90 percent of Arkansas' original bottom-land forested wetlands had been converted to upland or other types of wetlands (Scott Yaich, U.S. Fish and Wildlife Service, written commun., 1993). The 72-percent wetland loss reported by Dahl (1990) represents total wetland loss in the State but does not account for conversion of natural wetlands to some other type of wetland or the creation of artificial wetlands. For example, some of the State's remaining wetland acreage includes small farm ponds, which are not high-quality wetland habitat (Scott Yaich, U.S. Fish

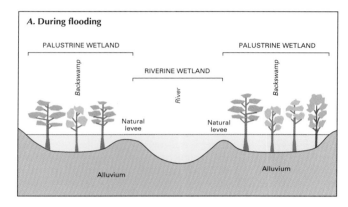

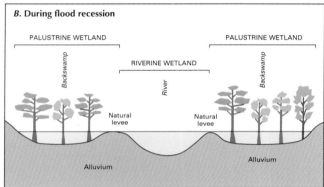

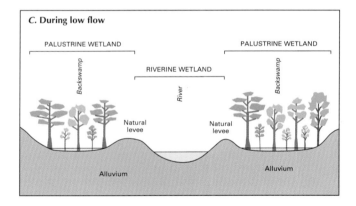

Figure 3. Surface hydrologic interaction between a river and forested wetlands in the flood plain. *A*, During flooding. *B*, During flood recession. *C*, During low flow; note establishment of new trees.

and Wildlife Service, written commun., 1993).

Almost all of the cleared lands in the major wetland areas of the State were being farmed in the 1990's, although many of these areas are considered marginal for crop production because of the flooding hazard (U.S. Fish and Wildlife Service, 1992). Some of these marginal farmlands reverted to scrub-shrub wetlands when farming operations were discontinued.

Even though the rate of wetland loss has declined in recent years, Arkansas continues to lose wetlands. Continuing threats to the remaining, primarily forested wetlands of the State as identified by FWS (1992) include (1) drainage and flood protection, (2) dredging and stream channelization, (3) conversion of forested wetland to scrub-shrub, emergent, or open-water wetlands, (4) alteration of drainage patterns, (5) construction of dikes and levees, and (6) discharge of pollutants.

Much of the historical wetland loss within Arkansas has been a result of Federal legislation. In 1850, the U.S. Congress passed the Swamp Land Act, which granted to Arkansas 7,686,575 acres of swamp and overflow lands considered unfit for cultivation. The objective of the act was to help control floods in the Mississippi River Valley and encourage the drainage and clearing of these "sub marginal" lands for agriculture by allowing sale of these lands to private individuals for development (Shaw and Fredine, 1971). Congress passed the Flood Control Act of 1928 in response to the disastrous 1927 floods in the Mississippi Valley. This act removed the requirement for local interests to pay one-half of the cost of levee construction on the Mississippi River. The passage of this bill resulted in the accelerated construction of a vast network of levees along the Mississippi River and its tributaries. The net effect of this and other flood-control acts was the conversion of thousands of acres of wetlands to agriculture due to the removal of the threat of frequent flooding (Arkansas Department of Pollution Control and Ecology, 1992).

CONSERVATION

Many government agencies and private organizations participate in wetland conservation in Arkansas. The most active agencies and organizations and some of their activities are listed in table 1.

Federal wetland activities.—Development activities in Arkansas wetlands are regulated by several Federal statutory prohibitions and incentives that are intended to slow wetland losses. Some of the more important of these are contained in the 1899 Rivers and Harbors Act; the 1972 Clean Water Act and amendments; the 1985 Food Security Act; the 1990 Food, Agriculture, Conservation, and Trade Act; and the 1986 Emergency Wetlands Resources Act.

Section 10 of the Rivers and Harbors Act gives the U.S. Army Corps of Engineers (Corps) authority to regulate certain activities in navigable waters. Regulated activities include diking, deepening, filling, excavating, and placing of structures. The related section 404 of the Clean Water Act is the most often-used Federal legislation protecting wetlands. Under section 404 provisions, the Corps issues permits regulating the discharge of dredged or fill material into wetlands. Permits are subject to review and possible veto by the U.S. Environmental Protection Agency, and the FWS has review and advisory roles. Section 401 of the Clean Water Act grants to States and eligible Indian Tribes the authority to approve, apply conditions to, or deny section 404 permit applications on the basis of a proposed activity's probable effects on the water quality of a wetland.

Most farming, ranching, and silviculture activities are not subject to section 404 regulation. However, the "Swampbuster" provision of the 1985 Food Security Act and amendments in the 1990 Food, Agriculture, Conservation, and Trade Act discourage (through financial disincentives) the draining, filling, or other alteration of wetlands for agricultural use. The law allows exemptions from penalties in some cases, especially if the farmer agrees to restore the altered wetland or other wetlands that have been converted to agricultural use. The Wetlands Reserve Program of the 1990 Food, Agriculture, Conservation, and Trade Act authorizes the Federal Government to purchase conservation easements from landowners who agree to protect or restore wetlands. The Consolidated Farm Service Agency (formerly the Agricultural Stabilization and Conservation Service) administers the Swampbuster provisions and Wetlands Reserve Program. The Natural Resources Conservation Service (formerly the Soil Conservation Service) determines compliance with Swampbuster provisions and assists farmers in the identification of wetlands and in the development of wetland protection, restoration, or creation plans.

The 1986 Emergency Wetlands Resources Act encourages wetland protection through funding incentives. The act requires

Table 1. Selected wetland-related activities of government agencies and private organizations in Arkansas, 1993

[Source: Classification of activities is generalized from information provided by agencies and organizations. •, agency or organization participates in wetland-related activity; ..., agency or organization does not participate in wetland-related activity. MAN, management; REG, regulation; R&C, restoration and creation; LAN, land acquisition; R&D, research and data collection; D&I, delineation and inventory]

Agency or organization	MAN	REG	R&C	LAN	R&D	D&I
FEDERAL						
Department of Agriculture						
Consolidated Farm Service Agency	...	•	...	...	...	...
Forest Service	•	...	•	...	...	•
Natural Resources Conservation Service	...	•	•	...	...	•
Department of Defense						
Army Corps of Engineers	...	•	...	•	...	•
Department of the Interior						
Fish and Wildlife Service	•	...	•	•	•	•
Geological Survey	...	...	...	...	•	...
National Biological Service	...	...	...	...	•	...
National Park Service	•	...	•	...	•	...
Environmental Protection Agency	...	•	...	...	•	...
STATE						
Department of Pollution Control and Ecology	•	•	...	...	...	•
Forestry Commission	•	•	•	...	•	•
Game and Fish Commission	•	•	•	•	...	•
Natural Heritage Commission	•	...	...	•	...	•
Soil and Water Conservation Commission	•	•	•	...	...	...
PRIVATE						
Ducks Unlimited	...	...	...	•	...	•
National Audubon Society	•	...	...	...	•	•
The Nature Conservancy	•	...	•	•	...	•

States to address wetland protection in their Statewide Comprehensive Outdoor Recreation Plans to qualify for Federal funding for State recreational land; the National Park Service (NPS) provides guidance to States in developing the wetland component of their plans.

The FWS administers seven National Wildlife Refuges, including the 154,000-acre White River National Wildlife Refuge located along the lower White River in Arkansas. The FWS also administers wetland-acquisition programs and advises Federal and State agencies responsible for wetland conservation. Other Federal agencies that have management or monitoring responsibilities for wetlands in Arkansas include the NPS, the U.S. Forest Service (FS), and the U.S. Geological Survey (USGS). The FS is responsible for the management of wetlands in the State's National Forests. Buffalo National River, a segment of the Buffalo River under the jurisdiction of the NPS, has some small wetland areas associated with the river. The USGS collects information on the quantity and quality of many of the Nation's water resources, including its wetlands.

State wetland activities.—Arkansas has a Natural and Scenic Rivers program and a Natural Heritage program. These two programs designate extraordinary and ecologically sensitive areas, including wetlands, within the State. A technical review committee made up of representatives from State agencies makes recommendations to the Governor on section 404 permits. The State has adopted a program administered by the Arkansas Department of Pollution Control and Ecology that applies an antidegradation policy to substantial alterations of a water body, including associated wetlands. In addition, the Arkansas Soil and Water Conservation Commission and the Arkansas Forestry Commission have extensive responsibilities concerning the management of the State's wetlands.

The Arkansas Game and Fish Commission, the State's lead wildlife agency, has a long-standing commitment to protect wetlands within the Mississippi River Valley because of the area's importance to wildlife, particularly to migratory birds. The Arkansas Game and Fish Commission owns or controls more than 174,000 acres in 14 wildlife management areas within the Mississippi River Valley, much of which consists of wetlands. The Arkansas Game and Fish Commission and the Arkansas Natural Heritage Commission are committed to additional investment in the Mississippi River Valley and have begun developing comprehensive plans for these activities. The Game and Fish Commission has developed the Cache–Lower White Rivers Joint Venture under the North American Waterfowl Management Plan. The objective of this program is to protect bottom-land habitat in the Cache River and lower White River Basins, which constitute the second-largest area of contiguous bottom-land habitat in the Mississippi River Valley, second only to the Atchafalaya River Basin in Louisiana. In 1990, protected Federal and State lands in the Joint Venture were designated "Wetlands of International Significance" under the provisions of the 1971 Ramsar Convention, which produced an international agreement for cooperation in the conservation of wetland habitats.

In 1988, the Natural Heritage Commission, in cooperation with the Arkansas Chapter of The Nature Conservancy, began to develop the White River–Lower Arkansas River Megasite plan (Lynch and others, 1992). This plan presents a landscape-level design inventory of an ecologically intact, biologically diverse bottom-land system that includes more than 550,000 acres. More than 280,000 acres in this habitat system are public lands. The boundaries of this habitat system differ somewhat from those of the high-priority waterfowl habitat defined by the Cache–Lower White Rivers Joint Venture, although both are in the Mississippi River Valley.

Regional and private wetland activities.—The Arkansas Chapter of The Nature Conservancy is involved in an effort to protect and restore the forested wetlands of the Mississippi River Alluvial Plain in Arkansas as part of a coordinated effort to protect wetlands of that region in seven States. The National Audubon Society and Ducks Unlimited also are involved in the protection and restoration of wetlands and the critical wildlife habitats they contain.

More than 50 percent of the remaining bottom-land forests in the Mississippi River Valley are in private ownership and much of these forests are commercial timberlands owned by the forest-products industry. Most of these commercial timberlands are a critical part of the Lower White–Lower Arkansas River Megasite plan because they occupy key locations contiguous with and connecting public lands within the system.

References Cited

Arkansas Department of Pollution Control and Ecology, 1992, Wetlands, Chapter 4 of water quality inventory report, 1992: Little Rock, Arkansas Department of Pollution Control and Ecology, p. 45–48.

Cowardin, L.M., Carter, Virginia, Golet, F.C., and LaRoe, E.T., 1979, Classification of wetlands and deepwater habitats of the United States: U.S. Fish and Wildlife Service Report FWS/OBS–79/31, 131 p.

Dahl, T.E., 1990, Wetlands—Losses in the United States, 1780's to 1980's: U.S. Fish and Wildlife Service Report to Congress, 13 p.

Freiwald, D.A., 1985, Average annual precipitation and runoff for Arkansas, 1951–80: U.S. Geological Survey Water-Resources Investigations Report 84–4363, scale 1:1,000,000.

Holder, Trusten, 1969, Disappearing wetlands in eastern Arkansas: Little Rock, Arkansas Planning Commission, 71 p.

Kleiss, B.A., 1993, An ecosystem study of bottom land hardwood wetlands associated with the Cache River, eastern Arkansas, *in* Landin, M.C., ed., Wetlands, Proceedings of the 13th Annual Conference Society of Wetland Scientists, New Orleans, La.: Utica, Miss., Society of Wetland Scientists, South Central Chapter, p. 31–37.

Lower Mississippi Valley Joint Venture Management Board, 1990, Conserving waterfowl and wetlands: Vicksburg, Miss., North American Waterfowl Management Plan, Lower Mississippi Valley Joint Venture, 32 p.

Lynch, J.M., Baker, W.W., Foti, Tom, and Peacock, Lance, 1992, The White River-lower Arkansas River megasite—A landscape conservation design project: Little Rock, Arkansas Natural Heritage Commission and the Arkansas Nature Conservancy, 81 p.

Mitsch, W.J., and Gosselink, J.G., 1993, Wetlands (2d ed.): New York, Van Nostrand Reinhold Company, 722 p.

Omernik, J. M., 1987, Ecoregions of the United States—Map supplement: Annals of the Association of American Geographers, v. 77, no. 1, scale 1:2,500,000.

Shaw, S.P., and Fredine, C.G., 1971, Wetlands of the United States—Their extent and their value to waterfowl and other wildlife: U.S. Fish and Wildlife Service Circular 39, 67 p.

U.S. Fish and Wildlife Service, 1992, Regional wetlands concept plan—Emergency wetlands resources act, southeast region: Atlanta, Ga., U.S. Fish and Wildlife Service, 259 p.

Winter, T.C., and Woo, Ming-Ko, 1990, Hydrology of lakes and wetlands: *in* Wolman, M.G., and Riggs, H.C., eds., Surface water hydrology: Boulder, Colo., Geological Society of America, The geology of North America, v. O–1, chap. 8, p. 159–187.

FOR ADDITIONAL INFORMATION: District Chief, U.S. Geological Survey, 401 Hardin Road, Little Rock, AR 72211; Regional Wetland Coordinator, U.S. Fish and Wildlife Service, 1875 Century Building, Suite 200, Atlanta, GA 30345

Prepared by
Charles R. Demas and Dennis K. Demcheck,
U.S. Geological Survey

California
Wetland Resources

California has about 454,000 acres of nonagricultural wetlands; more than 90 percent of the State's wetlands have been drained, mostly for agricultural purposes. Before significant agricultural conversion began, about 5 million acres of wetlands supported lush aquatic vegetation and provided habitat for hundreds of species of fish and wildlife as well as food, clothing, protection from predators, and transportation for native Americans.

California's wetlands provide stopover, wintering, and breeding habitat for vast numbers of waterfowl (fig. 1). The Sacramento–San Joaquin River Delta is the largest remaining wetland area in the State. The delta's wetlands regularly harbor as much as 15 percent of the waterfowl on the Pacific Flyway, the bird-migration corridor extending from the southern tip of South America to Alaska. Although significantly reduced in size since predevelopment times, wetlands in the delta are a source of large amounts of plant and algal materials that are the basis of complex food systems in the wetlands themselves and downstream in the estuaries of San Francisco Bay.

California's wetlands have significant environmental and economic value for humans and wildlife. Wetlands provide temporary storage of floodwaters, reducing downstream damage, and serve as buffers against erosion. Marshes in the Sacramento–San Joaquin River Delta and many coastal marshes act as freshwater barriers to seawater intrusion of aquifers. Wetlands also trap sediment and absorb many waterborne pollutants and excess nutrients. Wetlands provide fish and wildlife habitat; inland wetlands are excellent habitat for bass, catfish, bluegill, sunfish, crappie, geese, ducks, wading birds, and many species of amphibians. Wetlands offer recreational and educational activities, as well as opportunities for scientific studies.

TYPES AND DISTRIBUTION

Wetlands are lands transitional between terrestrial and deepwater habitats where the water table usually is at or near the land surface or the land is covered by shallow water (Cowardin and others, 1979). The distribution of wetlands and deepwater habitats in California is shown in figure 2A; only wetlands are discussed herein.

Wetlands can be vegetated or nonvegetated and are classified on the basis of their hydrology, vegetation, and substrate. In this

summary, wetlands are classified according to the system proposed by Cowardin and others (1979), which is used by the U.S. Fish and Wildlife Service (FWS) to map and inventory the Nation's wetlands. At the most general level of the classification system, wetlands are grouped into five ecological systems: Palustrine, Lacustrine, Riverine, Estuarine, and Marine. The Palustrine System includes only wetlands, whereas the other systems comprise wetlands and deepwater habitats. Wetlands of the systems that occur in California are described below.

System	Wetland description
Palustrine	Nontidal and tidal-freshwater wetlands in which vegetation is predominantly trees (forested wetlands); shrubs (scrub-shrub wetlands); persistent or nonpersistent emergent, erect, rooted herbaceous plants (persistent- and nonpersistent-emergent wetlands); or submersed and (or) floating plants (aquatic beds). Also, intermittently to permanently flooded open-water bodies of less than 20 acres in which water is less than 6.6 feet deep.
Lacustrine	Nontidal and tidal-freshwater wetlands within an intermittently to permanently flooded lake or reservoir larger than 20 acres and (or) deeper than 6.6 feet. Vegetation, when present, is predominantly nonpersistent emergent plants (nonpersistent-emergent wetlands), or submersed and (or) floating plants (aquatic beds), or both.
Riverine	Nontidal and tidal-freshwater wetlands within a channel. Vegetation, when present, is same as in the Lacustrine System.
Estuarine	Tidal wetlands in low-wave-energy environments where the salinity of the water is greater than 0.5 part per thousand (ppt) and is variable owing to evaporation and the mixing of seawater and freshwater.
Marine	Tidal wetlands that are exposed to waves and currents of the open ocean and to water having a salinity greater than 30 ppt.

The FWS National Wetland Inventory currently (1993) is mapping California's wetlands and compiling statewide acreage data. However, that inventory is not scheduled to be completed until the late 1990's, and there are no other systematically compiled data concerning statewide wetland acreage. Dahl (1990), on the basis of Central Valley (fig. 2B) acreage data in Frayer and others (1989) and approximations by the FWS, estimated that California had 454,000 acres of wetlands in the mid-1980's—0.4 percent of the State's area.

Frayer and others (1989) reported the results of a systematic survey of Central Valley and Sacramento–San Joaquin River Delta wetlands conducted in the mid-1980's. The study indicated that there were about 378,800 acres of freshwater and estuarine nonagricultural wetlands and 658,600 acres of flooded rice fields, most of which are converted wetlands. Field and others (1991) reported that the coastal counties of California had about 198,500 acres of palustrine, estuarine, and marine wetlands on the basis of interpretation of aerial photography done from the mid-1970's to the mid-1980's. Acreage data for the alluvial basins of northern California, montane wetlands in the Sierra Nevada and Cascade Range, and desert wetlands in southern California are not yet available.

The 378,800 acres of nonagricultural wetlands in the Central Valley and Sacramento–San Joaquin River Delta includes approximately 318,900 acres of palustrine wetlands and 59,900 acres of

Figure 1. Suisun Marsh provides habitat to many kinds of waterfowl. Agricultural and urban encroachment has reduced and continues to threaten valuable wetlands. *(Photograph courtesy of the Bureau of Reclamation.)*

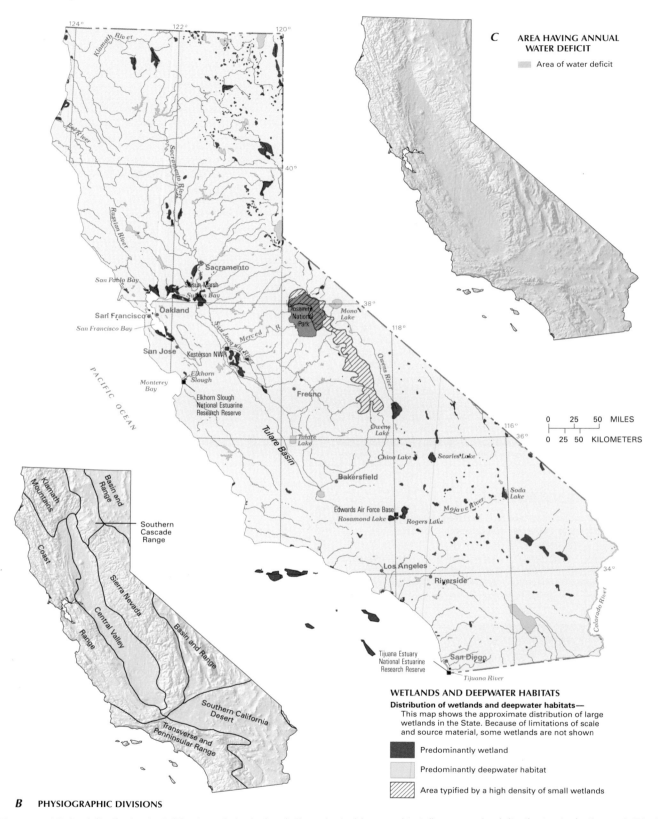

C **AREA HAVING ANNUAL WATER DEFICIT**

  ▨ Area of water deficit

B **PHYSIOGRAPHIC DIVISIONS**

WETLANDS AND DEEPWATER HABITATS

Distribution of wetlands and deepwater habitats—
This map shows the approximate distribution of large wetlands in the State. Because of limitations of scale and source material, some wetlands are not shown

  ■ Predominantly wetland

  ▨ Predominantly deepwater habitat

  ▨ Area typified by a high density of small wetlands

Figure 2. Wetland distribution in California and physical and climatological features that influence wetland distribution in the State. *A*, Distribution of wetlands and deepwater habitats. *B*, Physiography. *C*, Moisture balance. *(Sources: A, T.E. Dahl, U.S. Fish and Wildlife Service, unpub. data, 1991. B, Physiographic divisions modified from Fenneman, 1946; landforms from EROS Data Center. C, Modified from Thomas and Phoenix, 1976.)*

estuarine wetlands (Frayer and others, 1989). The palustrine wet-lands are of three types: (1) Those associated with or adjacent to rivers—primarily overflowed lands, sloughs, and bypasses; (2) those associated with grasslands—mainly on the alluvial fans of the eastern and western slopes of the valley, which contain numerous vernal pools during normal-precipitation years; and (3) marshes—mainly in the central lowlands of the Sacramento and San Joaquin River drainage basins and the Tulare Basin. The Central Valley's estuarine wetlands are in the Suisun Marsh in the westernmost part of the Sacramento–San Joaquin River Delta.

On the basis of data from Field and others (1991), most wetlands in California's coastal counties, which are primarily in the Coast Ranges, are classified as palustrine. Of the 198,500 coastal wetland acres, 46,700 acres are fresh marsh (palustrine emergent wetlands), 77,800 acres are palustrine forested or scrub-shrub wetlands, 21,700 acres are salt marsh (estuarine emergent wetlands), and 52,200 acres are tidal flats (estuarine unconsolidated-shore wetlands), which are mostly nonvegetated. (The acreages for individual wetland types do not total 198,500 because of rounding.)

The mountains of California contain palustrine, lacustrine, and riverine wetlands. These wetlands have not been inventoried to date (1993) because of their isolated and widely different topographic and ecological settings. Construction of reservoirs on the upland reaches of creeks and major rivers in the Sierra Nevada and Cascade Range has created additional wetland acreage. Palustrine wetlands of the Sierra, Cascades, and parts of the Coast Ranges are emergent wetlands commonly called bogs or meadows and forested or scrub-shrub wetlands called swamps. These wetlands are typically small, sometimes only a few thousand square feet, and exist randomly among coniferous forests at altitudes generally higher than 3,000 to 3,500 feet.

The desert basins of southeastern California contain lacustrine and palustrine wetlands referred to as playas, which are lakebeds that are intermittently flooded. Rogers, Soda, Searles, China, and Rosamond Lakes are large playas. The typical playa is nonvegetated except where fissures and sinklike depressions provide intermittent sources of water by pooling rainfall and overland flow. In unusually wet years and for periods following them, plants whose roots reach the water table, such as saltbrush, rabbitbrush, tamarisk, and mesquite, grow in areas of shallow ground water and around dry springs (C.J. Londquist, U.S. Geological Survey, written commun., 1993).

Mono Lake, a saline lake remnant of a much larger ice-age lake in the Basin and Range east of the central Sierra Nevada (fig. 2B), supports an abundance of brine shrimp and brine flies that are a significant food source for eared grebes, avocets, plovers, sandpipers, gulls, ducks, and phalaropes (Bakker, 1984). Because of the high salinity of the lake water, only salt-tolerant plants such as stinkweed, goosefoot, and salt or alkali grass grow around the lake.

In the Southern California Desert near the California–Mexico border is a type of palustrine desert wetland known popularly as an "oasis." These emergent, scrub-shrub, and forested wetlands support willow, catclaw, mesquite, cottonwood, tamarisk, reeds, arrowwood, and in some places, sedges, tules, and cattails. But the most distinctive plants of the oases are the native fan palms (Bakker, 1984).

HYDROLOGIC SETTING

To understand the existence of once vast natural wetlands in a State that has an average annual precipitation of about 20 inches and is commonly considered to be semiarid to arid, California's hydrography and topography must be examined. Most of the State has a natural annual water deficit (fig. 2C). However, in the areas having a natural water surplus, precipitation ranges from 40 to as much as 90 inches per year, most of that being snowfall in the Sierra Nevada,

Cascade Range, and Klamath Mountains. Annual precipitation amounts can differ widely from year to year because of variability in the Pacific storm track.

Mountain ranges induce precipitation at the higher altitudes and create "rain shadows" (dry areas) in the leeward valleys and plains. In California, nearly continuous ranges of coastal mountains extend from the Oregon border to Mexico, and these ranges are paralleled by the southern Cascade Range and the Sierra Nevada about 150 miles farther inland (fig. 2B). Between the two ranges, in the rain shadow of the Coast Ranges, lies the Central Valley, nearly 400 miles long and 70 miles wide. In the rain shadow of the southern Cascade Range, the Sierra Nevada, and the coastal mountains of southern California are the Basin and Range and Southern California Desert physiographic provinces.

Central Valley wetlands.—Streams originating in the Sierra Nevada carry 95 percent of the runoff entering the Central Valley. Before hydrologic modification associated with agriculture, much of the southern Sierra Nevada runoff flowed into the internally drained Tulare Basin, creating several large freshwater lakes that existed for more than 2,000,000 years (Page, 1986). The largest, Tulare Lake, formed a large lacustrine wetland extending over 600 square miles. Streams flowing in the trough of the Central Valley typically have low gradients and almost imperceptible natural levees. Consequently, before the rivers were contained by irrigation and flood-control projects, flood plains were wide, and in many years the entire valley was inundated by floodwater. Overbank flooding created thousands of acres of marshland and tens of thousands of vernal pools. Despite flood-control projects since the mid-1850's, overbank flooding still can occur in wet years.

In the years before flood-control and irrigation projects, shallow water tables supported large areas of wetlands on the valley floor. However, as a result of agricultural drainage, ground-water withdrawal, building of upland diversion dams, and flood-control projects, the original flow paths of water into the Central Valley and most of California's other alluvial basins have been altered, and the valley's hydrology is now generally as shown in figure 3A. Floods no longer regularly cover the valley floors but are diverted to cropland, stored, or channeled. Ground-water levels under the valley floors have been drawn down to such an extent that recharge is primarily from irrigation, and discharge is mainly to large centers of ground-water pumping (Bertoldi and others, 1991). Most of the valley's wetlands are now sustained by controlled application of water (Frayer and others, 1989).

Many wildlife refuges in the Central Valley use irrigation drain water either as a part or as the total source of water. Until 1986, 1,200 acres of ponds in the Kesterson National Wildlife Refuge (fig. 2A) were partly sustained by agricultural drain water from the west side of the San Joaquin Valley. In 1983, the FWS discovered an unusually high incidence of deformed or dead birds in the refuge. Studies of the drain water entering the ponds and of the water in the ponds showed that the deformities were caused by high concentrations of selenium in the drain water. The Bureau of Reclamation (BOR) implemented a plan to mitigate the effects of the drain water at the refuge by stemming the flow of agricultural drain water into the refuge and eliminating all aquatic habitat in the areas of the contaminated ponds. Surface water is now imported into the refuge.

Estuarine wetlands.—California's estuaries have a high degree of variability in their physical and hydrologic environment. For most of the year, coastal estuaries, such as the Suisun Marsh below the confluence of the Sacramento and San Joaquin Rivers (and the Sacramento–San Joaquin Delta wetlands under natural conditions) are sustained by brackish to saline water. In the wet season during winter, they can become completely fresh. In addition, streamflow varies substantially, from none in many years to floods in wet years.

There is little emergent wetland acreage remaining in the Sacramento–San Joaquin River Delta. After World War I, nearly all delta marshland had been transformed to the series of improved channels and leveed islands that exist to the present (fig. 3B). The delta soils are predominantly organic peat, and in agricultural use have oxidized extensively, causing land surfaces to subside to more than 15 feet below sea level within the leveed islands (California Department of Water Resources, 1993) so that emergent wetlands can exist only on the margins of the delta.

Three of California's estuarine wetlands have attracted national and international attention. The largest of these wetland areas is the complex system of over 1,000 miles of waterways in the Sacramento–San Joaquin River Delta and three bays within a 1,200-square-mile area of central California. The bays, beginning with the most landward, are Suisun, San Pablo, and the largest, San Francisco. About 70 percent of California's water supply originates in the Sierras, flows through the Central Valley into the bay-delta system, then discharges into the Pacific Ocean at San Francisco Bay.

Two other, smaller estuarine wetlands, Elkhorn Slough on Monterey Bay and the Tijuana River estuary at San Diego, have been included in the National Oceanic and Atmospheric Administration's (NOAA) National Estuarine Research Reserves. Such reserves are defined as "classes of ecosystems worthy of research and education, yet different enough to warrant selection as a distinct regional type" (Zedler and others, 1992). The recent geologic factors that shape these estuaries are the forces of slowly rising sea level, which

causes inland migrations of the estuaries, and tectonic uplift, which partly offsets the effects of a rising sea level. Deep submarine canyons and unusual shoreline configurations affect the size and condition of both estuaries. Longshore drifting and currents have not been measured, but the effects are well known. Beach erosion has caused landward movement of the estuarine shorelines and subsequent salinity changes. After decades of study at the Tijuana National Estuarine Research Reserve, restoration programs are underway.

Montane wetlands.—The most common types of montane wetlands in California are meadows, which are palustrine wetlands with persistent emergent vegetation (fig. 3C and 3D). Meadows in California have been best studied in the Sierras, where they are estimated to compose about 10 percent of the total area (Ratliff, 1985). At higher altitudes, glacial cirques commonly contain small pools or lakes known as tarns. Meadows can develop when tarns fill with sediment, peat, or both.

California's mountains are geomorphologically dynamic because of glaciation, tectonic uplift, and volcanic eruptions in the recent geologic past. Dynamic features include glacially scoured depressions, moraines, and till and outwash deposits resulting from landslides and mudflows and from volcanic debris and lava flows that impede the movement of water from precipitation and snowmelt, leading to the formation of wetlands. Impoundments can form

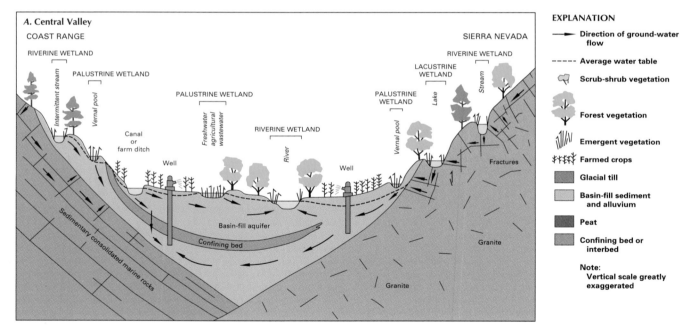

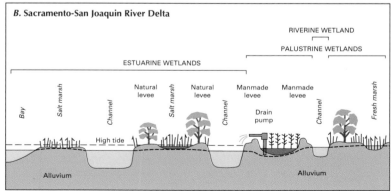

Figure 3. Generalized hydrologic setting of wetlands in California. **A**, Central Valley. **B**, Sacramento–San Joaquin River Delta.

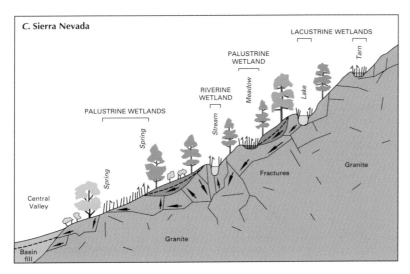

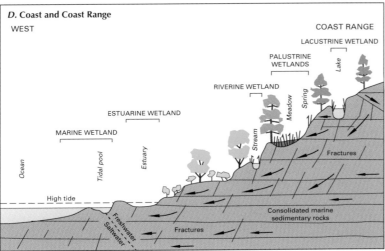

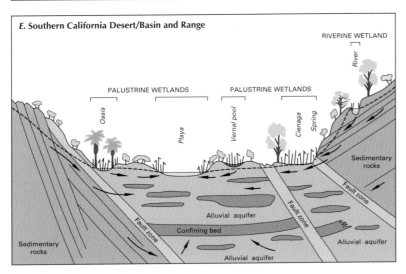

Figure 3.   Continued.   Generalized hydrologic setting of wetlands in California. *C*, Sierra Nevada. *D*, Coast and Coast Ranges. *E*, Southern California Desert and Basin and Range.

as a result of landslides or mining, road construction, and other human activities. Beavers create wetlands as a result of dam building. An example of a landslide-created wetland can be found in Mirror Lake at the base of Half Dome in Yosemite National Park. The lake is filling with sediment, and vegetation is becoming established.

Meadows form in several topographic positions: depressions in valley bottoms, on glacially gouged surfaces, in glacial moraines with surface depressions where water is held, and on slight to moderate slopes where ground water discharges into fine-textured soils (commonly glacial or landslide deposits) at a rate greater than it can be released to streams and the atmosphere.

Meadows can have a range of hydrologic characteristics, from seasonally wet from snowmelt to saturated throughout the year. A single meadow can have several different hydrologic regimes, each supporting different vegetative communities (Ratliff, 1985). Meadows can be hydrologically dependent on both surface and ground water. Recent studies indicate that ground water is more important to meadow wetlands than previously thought (Akers, 1986; Winter and Woo, 1990).

The present hydrologic condition of meadows in the Sierras, and likely elsewhere in California, ranges from slightly to highly altered; however, no systematic evaluation has been reported. Grazing of livestock since the mid-1850's disturbed many meadows enough to cause erosion, which in turn affected the hydrologic regime and the vegetative communities. More recently, intensive recreational use has contributed to degraded meadow conditions as well. Restoration of meadow vegetation to support grazing by livestock and wildlife requires that the hydrologic regime first be restored (Ratliff, 1985).

Southern California Desert/Basin and Range Wetlands.—Southeastern California from the Mexico border to the eastern flank of the Sierra Nevada lies in the rain shadow of the mountain ranges to the west. Precipitation is very low and temperatures are very high. Water for wetlands typically is supplied by mountain front creeks, springs, seeps, pools, and in more recent times, irrigation canals (fig. 3E). The largest wetlands in the region are playas, which typically are dry much of the year. Playas receive water from intermittent surface flows and from direct precipitation during infrequent storms. Water leaves playas through evaporation and transpiration because there is no surface drainage. Elsewhere, isolated springs and seeps support generally small marshes (cienagas) and other wetlands, such as oases. Where the water supply is relatively persistent but drainage is limited, saline wetlands can form.

California's population is concentrated and increasing in the southern part of the State. The growing demand for water and recreational activities (Bureau of Land Management, 1980) affects water resources and desert lands, especially wetland and riparian areas. Ground-water pumping in the western Mojave Desert has caused fissures in playas at Edwards Air Force Base, and riparian vegetation has been adversely affected by declining ground-water levels. Increased amounts of water diverted for urban uses decreases the amount supporting wetlands. Recreational activities and grazing have damaged riparian vegetation, contributing to a general decline in the quantity and quality of riparian wetlands.

Owens Valley, a closed basin at the base of the Sierra Nevada's eastern escarpment, historically received runoff from the mountains that supported flow in the Owens River. This surface-water flow maintained Owens Lake and a ground-water level close to the ground surface of the valley floor. Diversions of surface water and ground water to Los Angeles since 1970 virtually eliminated wetlands dependent on surface water in the river and lake. However, ground-water-dependent vegetation on the valley floor has survived a lowering of the water table by several feet by extending the root systems (Sorenson and others, 1991). Its longer term survival and reproduction have not been studied.

TRENDS

The earliest estimates of wetland acreage in California are those documented by the California State Engineers Surveys dating between 1868 and 1886 (Hall, 1887). At that time, William H. Hall recorded nearly 5.2 million acres of land as swamps, lakes, bogs, and river overflow areas, most of which were located in the Central Valley. Dahl (1990) estimated that about 5 million acres of wetlands existed before large-scale agricultural conversions began. Of the original 5 million acres, nearly 4 million were palustrine, lacustrine, and riverine wetlands in the Central Valley, 700,000 were estuarine wetlands, 65,000 were palustrine and lacustrine wetlands of the Coast Ranges, 120,000 were palustrine, lacustrine, and riverine wetlands of the Cascade Range and Sierra Nevada, and 15,000 acres were riverine or palustrine wetlands of the interior basins and ranges.

Significant wetland loss in California began in about 1850. In that year, the National Swamp and Overflowed Land Act conveyed all swamp and overflowed land, including delta marshes, from Federal ownership to the State of California. In 1866, the California Legislature formed the Board of Swamp and Overflowed Land Commissioners to manage reclamation projects and proceeds from sales of swampland by the State. In 1869, the board relinquished its authority to individual county boards of supervisors. By about 1870, nearly all of California's wetlands were in private ownership, and subsidies were established to aid private developers in reclaiming swamplands (California Department of Water Resources, 1993).

Between 1850 and 1920, about 70 percent of California's wetland acreage was modified or converted to upland, largely by levee and drainage projects (Dennis and others, 1984). Nearly all of the reclaimed land was put into agriculture, helping to make California the leading agricultural State in the Nation by 1887. The diversion and redistribution of Sierran runoff water into the valley continued vigorously so that by 1939, 85 percent of the wetlands had been lost. By 1940, Tulare Lake, which had in post-European-settlement history covered as much as 1,000 square miles, had been completely drained. Between 1938 and the early 1970's, construction of large-scale irrigation systems had modified more than 90 percent of the original wetlands.

Although losses of wetlands have been large, some changes in land-use practices since about 1980 have caused increases or improvements in wetland habitats. Since 1939, a switch from pastureland and row-crop farming to flooded rice paddies in the Sacramento Valley and parts of the San Joaquin Valley has increased palustrine wetlands by 41,000 acres (Frayer, 1989). Rice farmers, in conjunction with university and State researchers and private organizations, are developing methods to flood rice paddies during critical periods of occupation by migratory waterfowl. If these methods are perfected, several hundred thousand acres could be returned to seasonal wetland-habitat status while continuing to be used as agricultural lands.

CONSERVATION

Many government agencies and private organizations participate in wetland conservation in California. The most active agencies and organizations and some of their activities are listed in table 1.

Federal wetland activities.—Development activities in California wetlands are regulated by several Federal statutory prohibitions and incentives that are intended to slow wetland losses. Some of the more important of these are contained in the 1899 Rivers and Harbors Act; the 1972 Clean Water Act and amendments; the 1985 Food Security Act; the 1990 Food, Agriculture, Conservation, and Trade Act; the 1986 Emergency Wetlands Resources Act; and the 1972 Coastal Zone Management Act.

Table 1. Selected wetland-related activities of government agencies and private organizations in California, 1993

[Source: Classification of activities is generalized from information provided by agencies and organizations. •, agency or organization participates in wetland-related activity; ..., agency or organization does not participate in wetland-related activity. MAN, management; REG, regulation; R&C, restoration and creation; LAN, land acquisition; R&D, research and data collection; D&I, delineation and inventory]

Agency or organization	MAN	REG	R&C	LAN	R&D	D&I
FEDERAL						
Department of Agriculture						
Consolidated Farm Service Agency	...	•	...	...	...	...
Forest Service	•	...	•	•	•	•
Natural Resources Conservation Service	...	•	...	•	•	•
Department of Commerce						
National Oceanic and Atmospheric Administration	•	•	...	...	•	...
Department of Defense						
Army Corps of Engineers	...	•	•	...	•	•
Military reservations	•	...	...	...	...	...
Department of the Interior						
Bureau of Land Management	•	...	•	•	•	•
Bureau of Reclamation	•	...	•	...	...	...
Fish and Wildlife Service	•	•	•	•	•	...
Geological Survey	...	...	...	...	•	•
National Biological Service	...	...	...	...	•	•
National Park Service	•	...	•	...	•	•
Environmental Protection Agency	...	•	...	...	•	•
STATE						
Environmental Protection Agency						
State Water Resources Control Board	...	•	...	...	...	...
Regional Water-Quality Control Board	...	•	...	...	•	•
Resources Agency						
California Coastal Commission	...	•	...	...	•	...
Department of Conservation	...	•	...	...	•	...
Department of Fish and Game	•	•	•	•	•	...
Department of Parks and Recreation	•	...	•	...	•	...
Department of Water Resources	•	•	...	...	•	...
San Francisco Bay Conservation and Development Commission	...	•	•	•	•	...
State Reclamation Board	...	•	...	...	...	...
State Lands Commission	•	•	...	•	...	...
State Coastal Conservancy	...	...	•	•	...	...
Wildlife Conservation Board	...	...	•	•	...	...
SOME COUNTY AND LOCAL GOVERNMENTS						
Local planning authorities	...	...	...	•	...	•
Reclamation districts	•	•	•	•	...	•
Resource conservation districts	•	•	•	•	•	•
Water districts	•	...	•	•	...	...
PRIVATE						
California Waterfowl Association	•	...	•	...	•	...
Ducks Unlimited	•	...	•	•	...	...
Farmlands and Open-Space Foundation	...	...	•	...	•	...
National Audubon Society	•	...	...	...	•	...
Pacific Flyway Project	•	...	...	...	•	...
Sierra Club	...	...	...	...	•	•
The Nature Conservancy	•	...	•	•	•	...
Trust for Public Land	•	...	...	•	•	•

Section 10 of the Rivers and Harbors Act gives the U.S. Army Corps of Engineers (Corps) authority to regulate certain activities in navigable waters. Regulated activities include diking, deepening, filling, excavating, and placing of structures. The related section 404 of the Clean Water Act is the most often-used Federal legislation protecting wetlands. Under section 404 provisions, the Corps issues permits regulating the discharge of dredged or fill material into wetlands. Permits are subject to review and possible veto by the U.S. Environmental Protection Agency (EPA), and the FWS has review and advisory roles. Section 401 of the Clean Water Act grants to States and eligible Indian Tribes the authority to approve, apply conditions to, or deny section 404 permit applications on the basis of a proposed activity's probable effects on the water quality of a wetland.

Most farming, ranching, and silviculture activities are not subject to section 404 regulation. However, the "Swampbuster" provision of the 1985 Food Security Act and amendments in the 1990 Food, Agriculture, Conservation, and Trade Act discourage (through financial disincentives) the draining, filling, or other alteration of wetlands for agricultural use. The law allows exemptions from penalties in some cases, especially if the farmer agrees to restore the altered wetland or other wetlands that have been converted to agricultural use. The Wetlands Reserve Program of the 1990 Food, Agriculture, Conservation, and Trade Act authorizes the Federal Government to purchase conservation easements from landowners who agree to protect or restore wetlands. The Consolidated Farm Service Agency (CFSA, formerly the Agricultural Stabilization and Conservation Service) administers the Swampbuster provisions and Wetlands Reserve Program. The Natural Resources Conservation Service (NRCS, formerly the Soil Conservation Service) determines compliance with Swampbuster provisions and assists farmers in the identification of wetlands and in the development of wetland protection, restoration, or creation plans.

The 1986 Emergency Wetlands Resources Act and the 1972 Coastal Zone Management Act and amendments encourage wetland protection through funding incentives. The Emergency Wetlands Resources Act requires States to address wetland protection in their Statewide Comprehensive Outdoor Recreation Plans to qualify for Federal funding for State recreational land; the National Park Service provides guidance to States in developing the wetland component of their plans. Coastal States that adopt coastal-zone management programs and plans approved by NOAA are eligible for Federal funding and technical assistance through the Coastal Zone Management Act.

The EPA has authority, through the National Pollution Discharge System, National Pretreatment Program, Ocean Dumping/Dredging and Fill Program, and the Clean Water Act, to certify that permitted use of the State's waters is consistent with established water-quality objectives. Under the Clean Water Act, the EPA's San Francisco Bay-Estuary Project has a 5-year-program objective to develop a comprehensive management plan that would set operational standards for nearly 700,000 acres of estuarine and marine wetlands.

The U.S. Department of Agriculture, through local conservation districts and the NRCS, administers the Federal Water Bank program with assistance from the CFSA and the State of California. The major objective of this program is to restore, preserve, enhance, or improve wetland habitat in important migratory waterfowl nesting and breeding areas.

The NOAA administers the Coastal Zone Management Act, whose purpose is to increase awareness and understanding of the coastal environment and to increase the ability of States' coastal-zone-management programs to address problems. NOAA funding under the act assists California in coastal-plan development, including wetlands. Grants have been awarded to the California Coastal Plan and San Francisco Bay Plan. NOAA also administers the National Estuarine Research Reserve program, which provides site acquisition for preservation, research, and education.

The FWS manages approximately 225,000 acres of land on 34 National Wildlife Refuges, Wildlife Management Areas, National Fish Hatcheries, or other wildlife facilities. Wetlands on these holdings are among the most important habitat along the entire Pacific Flyway. Through the American Waterfowl Management Plan, the FWS administers the Central Valley Joint Habitat Venture, which comprises private organizations and other public agencies that have pooled their resources to help meet a target of restoring and maintaining the diversity, distribution, and abundance of waterfowl at 1970's levels.

State wetland activities. — California has no single agency that implements an integrated plan for management of wetland resources, nor does the State have a wetlands-management policy. The Governor's Office sets broad environmental goals for the State. The Governor's Office of Planning and Research has no regulatory authority but has substantial influence in guiding administration policy and is the clearinghouse for all documents promulgated under the California Environmental Quality Act of 1970. This act establishes the basic charter for protection of California's environment. A major policy under the act is the maintenance of fish and wildlife populations, and the protection of wetlands is identified as a significant goal.

The California Environmental Protection Agency administers four boards that set standards, control pollution, and improve the quality of the environment throughout the State. The State Water Quality Control Board administers the system of water rights and, through a series of nine Regional Water Quality Control Boards, is responsible for implementing section 108 of the Clean Water Act, which is a mandate to control nonpoint pollution. The boards also implement the provisions of the Porter-Cologne Act of 1969. These provisions provide for assessment reports identifying surface-water bodies that would not meet water-quality standards without nonpoint-source controls and allow for the development and implementation of best-management practices for control of nonpoint sources of pollution.

Several departments and commissions, operating within the overall administration of the Resources Agency of the State of California, have primary responsibility for the enhancement and protection of wetland habitats. The Fish and Game Commission sets policy for the Department of Fish and Game. The Department has legislative authority to preserve, protect, and manage California's fish, game, and native plants, without respect to their economic value, and administers provisions of the State Endangered Species Act. The Department is responsible for wildlife management, collecting and managing data for waterfowl and nongame wildlife, disease research, wetland enhancement, and habitat development and management on 76 State-owned designated wildlife areas, ecological reserves, and other public lands. The Department of Fish and Game Stream or Lake Alteration Agreements are required for activities that result in changes in natural conditions in streams, lakes, channels, or crossings.

The San Francisco Bay Conservation and Development Commission is authorized by the McAteer–Petris Act to analyze, plan, and regulate development activities in San Francisco Bay and along its shoreline. The Commission implements the San Francisco Bay Plan and the Suisun Marsh Protection Plan. The Commission also regulates dredging and filling in the bay, and in sloughs, marshes, certain creeks, and tributaries within 100 feet of the bay. The plan is subject to Coastal Zone Management Agency consistency review as a component of California's Coastal Plan, which is administered by the Commission. The Suisun Marsh Preservation Act was enacted in 1977 to establish policies and programs in the Suisun Marsh Protection Plan. Local governments and districts must prepare local protection programs to bring their policies and ordinances into conformity with the provisions of the act.

The Department of Water Resources is authorized by the Delta

Protection Act of 1988 to approve levee improvement in wetlands of the Sacramento–San Joaquin Delta. The Department is responsible for the State Water Project pumping facilities in the delta. The Department, as authorized by Delta Flood Protection Act of 1988, is involved in a levee-improvement program for flood protection that overlaps the North Delta Water Management Plans for widening channels, the South Delta Water Management Plans, and the Los Banos Grandes projects. The Department represents the State in Corps and BOR flood-control and water-development projects.

County and local wetland activities.—Resource Conservation Districts are authorized by Division 9 of the California Public Resources Code to assist the State in conserving soil and water resources, including wetlands. There are about 400 water, reclamation, and drainage districts in California, another 300 park and open-space districts, and 110 public-utility districts governed by Division 9 authority for conservation.

In addition to special districts, county and city governments are required to have a general plan that has mandated elements including open space/conservation, safety, land use, and water circulation (Government Code, Section 65000 et seq.). There are no regional requirements for plan consistency among the counties and cities. The conservation element of the general plan must address the conservation, development, and utilization of natural resources, including water and its hydraulic force, forests, soils, rivers, and other waters, harbors, fisheries, wildlife, minerals, and other natural resources. The open-space element defines provisions for open space for the preservation of natural resources, the managed production of resources, outdoor recreation, and public health and safety.

Private wetland activities.—Duck hunting clubs own most of the nonagricultural Central Valley and Suisun Bay wetlands and manage these areas for waterfowl. Ducks Unlimited is a major participant in the Joint Venture program of the FWS, in which public and private organizations cooperate to preserve wetlands. The Nature Conservancy, California Waterfowl Association, Pacific Flyway Project, Trust for Public Land, Solano County Farmlands and Open Space Foundation, Sierra Club, and National Audubon Society have acquired sensitive lands for preservation and restoration.

References Cited

Akers, J.P., 1986, Ground water in the Long Meadows area and its relation with that in the General Sherman Tree area, Sequoia National Park, California: U.S. Geological Survey Water-Resources Investigations Report 85–4178, 15 p.

Bakker, E.S., 1984, An island called California—An ecological introduction to its natural communities: Berkeley, University of California Press, 484 p.

Bertoldi, G.L., Johnston, R.H., and Evenson, K.D., 1991, Ground water in the Central Valley, California—A summary report: U.S. Geological Survey Professional Paper 1401–A, 44 p.

Bureau of Land Management, 1980, California Desert Conservation Area Plan: Riverside, Calif., Bureau of Land Management, Desert District, 173 p.

California Department of Water Resources, 1993, Sacramento–San Joaquin delta atlas: Sacramento, California Department of Water Resources, 121 p.

Cowardin, L.M., Carter, Virginia, Golet, F.C., and LaRoe, E.T., 1979, Classification of wetlands and deepwater habitats of the United States: U.S. Fish and Wildlife Service Report, FWS/OBS–79/31, 131 p.

Dahl, T.E., 1990, Wetlands—Losses in the United States, 1780's to 1980's: Washington, D.C., U.S. Fish and Wildlife Service Report to Congress, 13 p.

Dennis, N.B., Marcus, M.L., and Hill, H., 1984, Status and trends of California wetlands—Report to the California Assembly Resources Subcommittee: Sacramento, The California Assembly, 125 p.

Fenneman, N.M., 1946, Physical divisions of the United States: Washington, D.C., U.S. Geological Survey special map, scale 1:7,000,000.

Field, D.W., Reyer, A.J., Genovese, P.V., and Shearer, B.D., 1991, Coastal wetlands of the United States: Rockville, Md., National Oceanic and Atmospheric Administration and U.S. Fish and Wildlife Service cooperative publication, 59 p.

Frayer, W.E., Peters, D.D., and Pywell, H.R., 1989, Wetlands of the California Central Valley—Status and trends, 1939–1980's: Portland, Oreg., U.S. Fish and Wildlife Service Report, 29 p.

Hall, W.H., 1887, Topographical and irrigation maps of the Great Central Valley of California, embracing the Sacramento, San Joaquin, Tulare and Kern Valleys and the bordering foothills for California: Sacramento, California Department of Engineering, scale about 1:380,160, 2 sheets.

Page, R.W., 1986, Geology of the fresh ground-water basin of the Central Valley, California, with textural maps and sections: U.S. Geological Survey Professional Paper 1401–C, 53 p.

Ratliff, R.D., 1985, Meadows in the Sierra Nevada of California—State of knowledge: U.S. Forest Service General Technical Report PSW–84, 52 p.

Sorenson, S.K., Dileanis, P.D., and Branson, F.A., 1991, Soil water and vegetation responses to precipitation and changes in depth to ground water in Owens Valley, California: U.S. Geological Survey Water-Supply Paper 2730–G, 54 p.

Thomas, H.E., and Phoenix, D.A., 1976, Summary appraisals of the Nation's ground-water resources, California region: U.S. Geological Survey Professional Paper 813–E, 51 p.

Winter, T.C., and Woo, Ming-Ko, 1990, Hydrology of lakes and wetlands, *in* Wolman, M.G., and Riggs, H.C., eds., Surface water hydrology: Boulder, Colo., Geological Society of America, The Geology of North America, v. O–1, p. 159–187.

Zedler, J.B., Nordby, C.S., and Kus, B.E., 1992, The ecology of Tijuana estuary, California—A national estuarine research reserve: Washington, D.C., National Oceanic and Atmospheric Administration Office of Coastal Resource Management, 151 p.

FOR ADDITIONAL INFORMATION: District Chief, U.S. Geological Survey, Room W–2233, Federal Building, 2800 Cottage Way, Sacramento, CA 95825; Regional Wetland Coordinator, U.S. Fish and Wildlife Service, 911 N.E. 11th Avenue, Portland, OR 97232

Prepared by
G.L. Bertoldi and Walter C. Swain,
U.S. Geological Survey

Colorado
Wetland Resources

Wetlands cover only about 1.5 percent of Colorado but are ecologically and economically valuable to the State. Wetlands provide important wildlife habitat—during some part of their life cycle, as much as 90 percent of the State's fish and wildlife depend on riparian habitats that include wetlands (Redelfs, 1980), and wetlands provide stopover and breeding grounds to migratory waterfowl. Wetlands also provide flood attenuation, bank stabilization, and water-quality improvement (fig. 1). Colorado's tourist industry benefits from the scenic beauty of the State's wetlands and deepwater habitats and from the opportunities they afford for recreational activities that include hunting, fishing, bird watching, nature photography, camping, hiking, and boating. Because wetland vegetation generally is more lush and productive than that in uplands, some wetlands are considered prime grazing land. Peat is mined from wetlands for use as a garden soil amendment. In the past, much of the State's mineral wealth was mined from placer gold and heavy-mineral deposits in riparian zones. These benefits are provided by diverse wetlands distributed across Colorado's plains, mountains, and deserts.

TYPES AND DISTRIBUTION

Wetlands are lands transitional between terrestrial and deepwater habitats where the water table usually is at or near the land surface or the land is covered by shallow water (Cowardin and others, 1979). The distribution of wetlands and deepwater habitats in Colorado is shown in figure 2A; only wetlands are discussed herein.

Wetlands can be vegetated or nonvegetated and are classified on the basis of their hydrology, vegetation, and substrate. In this summary, wetlands are classified according to the system proposed by Cowardin and others (1979), which is used by the U.S. Fish and Wildlife Service (FWS) to map and inventory the Nation's wetlands. At the most general level of the classification system, wetlands are grouped into five ecological systems: Palustrine, Lacustrine, Riverine, Estuarine, and Marine. The Palustrine System includes only wetlands, whereas the other systems comprise wetlands and deepwater habitats. Wetlands of the systems that occur in Colorado are described below.

System	Wetland description
Palustrine	Wetlands in which vegetation is predominantly trees (forested wetlands); shrubs (scrub-shrub wetlands); persistent or nonpersistent emergent, erect, rooted, herbaceous plants (persistent- and nonpersistent-emergent wetlands); or submersed and (or) floating plants (aquatic beds). Also, intermittently to permanently flooded open-water bodies of less than 20 acres in which water is less than 6.6 feet deep.
Lacustrine	Wetlands within an intermittently to permanently flooded lake or reservoir. Vegetation, when present, is predominantly nonpersistent emergent plants (nonpersistent-emergent wetlands), or submersed and (or) floating plants (aquatic beds), or both.
Riverine	Wetlands within a channel. Vegetation, when present, is same as in the Lacustrine System.

There is no current (1993) estimate of statewide wetland acreage in each of the systems. Inventories of wetland and open-water areas conducted in the 1950's estimated that 3 percent was river-

ine, 14 percent was mixed lacustrine and palustrine, and 83 percent was palustrine (U.S. Fish and Wildlife Service, 1955; 1960). Palustrine wetlands in Colorado include forested wetlands in riparian areas and near springs and seeps; scrub-shrub wetlands, such as willow carrs (thickets) and bottomland shrublands; emergent wetlands, such as marshes, fens, alpine snow glades, and wet and salt meadows; and aquatic-bed wetlands in ponds and lakes (Colorado Department of Natural Resources, 1992).

Wetlands occupy about 1 million acres (1.5 percent) of Colorado (Dahl, 1990). In the Great Plains (fig. 2B), wetlands occur in the flood plains of the South Platte and Arkansas Rivers and in scattered locations throughout the plains. Wetlands generally are sparsely distributed in the Colorado Plateaus and Wyoming Basin. In the Southern and Middle Rocky Mountains, wetlands occur primarily in high mountain valleys and intermountain basins.

HYDROLOGIC SETTING

Wetlands form where there is a persistent water supply at or near the land surface. The location and persistence of the supply is a function of interdependent climatic, physiographic, and hydrologic factors such as precipitation and runoff patterns, evaporation, topography, and configuration of the water table.

Precipitation (fig. 2C) and runoff rates differ annually and with season and location. The average annual precipitation in Colorado ranges from about 7 inches in the San Luis Valley to about 60 inches in some mountainous areas. Most runoff occurs in spring and early summer and is greatest in the mountains. Greater precipitation and runoff in the mountains are the principal reasons for the greater acreage of wetlands in the intermountain basins than in other regions of the State. In the mountains, melting snow is the primary source of runoff, whereas in the eastern plains, runoff is mostly from rainfall (Petsch, 1986). The timing and volume of runoff affect the establishment and function of riparian wetlands. High streamflow, which results from snowmelt in the mountains during spring and early summer, is essential for the maintenance of normally func-

Figure 1. Wetland in Tennessee Park, about 4 miles northwest of Leadville. This wetland receives acidic mine drainage and was the subject of a study to determine the capacity of wetlands to improve the chemical quality of such drainage. *(Photograph by Katherine Walton-Day, U.S. Geological Survey.)*

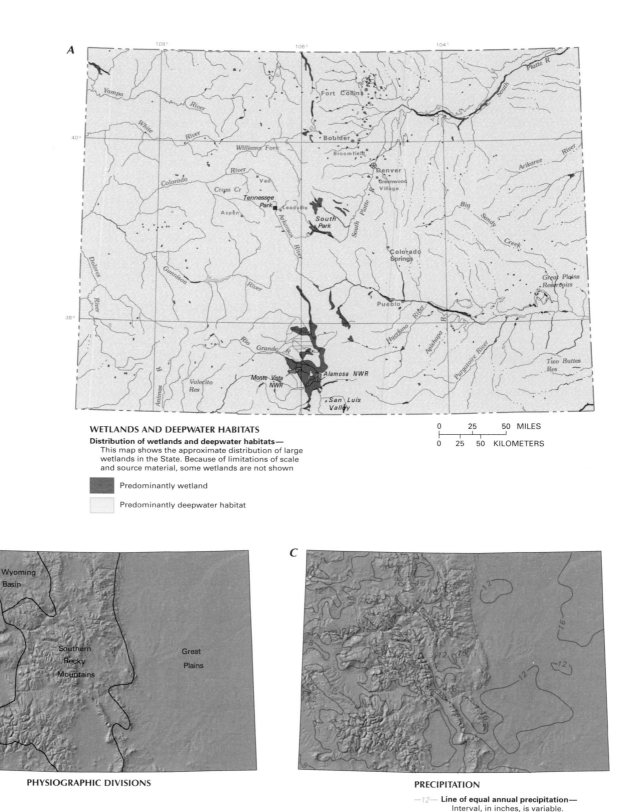

WETLANDS AND DEEPWATER HABITATS

Distribution of wetlands and deepwater habitats—
This map shows the approximate distribution of large
wetlands in the State. Because of limitations of scale
and source material, some wetlands are not shown

Predominantly wetland

Predominantly deepwater habitat

0   25   50 MILES
0   25   50 KILOMETERS

PHYSIOGRAPHIC DIVISIONS

PRECIPITATION

—12— **Line of equal annual precipitation—**
Interval, in inches, is variable.

Figure 2. Wetland distribution in Colorado and physical and climatological features that control wetland distribution in the State. **A**, Distribution of wetlands and deepwater habitats. **B**, Physiography. **C**, Annual precipitation. *(Sources: A, T.E. Dahl, U.S. Fish and Wildlife Service, unpub. data, 1991. B, Physiographic divisions from Fenneman, 1946; landforms data from EROS Data Center. C, Petsch, 1986.)*

tioning riparian ecosystems. Water-control projects such as reservoirs or irrigation canals, which reduce seasonal streamflow variation and eliminate periodic flooding, can adversely affect many streamside-wetland functions (Cooper, 1988).

Evaporation generally is greatest in eastern Colorado (fig. 2D). Evaporation decreases with altitude and is least in the mountains. Local evaporation patterns can affect wetland development. For example, on the windward side of ridges above timberline, strong winds redistribute snow to the leeward side and increase evaporation (Windell and others, 1986). The result is a dry environment on the windward side, whereas on the leeward side, accumulated snow melts slowly and creates a moist environment conducive to development of alpine wetlands.

In most of Colorado, evaporation exceeds precipitation annually, and, except in mountainous areas, there is a net statewide annual moisture deficit that inhibits wetland formation. The moisture deficit prevents the formation of bogs, which are emergent wetlands that have organic soils and receive moisture only from precipitation. In mountainous areas, where there is sufficient moisture for bog formation, steep topography and shifting stream channels prevent their development (Cooper, 1986).

Ground-water discharge from springs, shallow water tables, or both maintain wetlands in many areas of Colorado. The results of a study of wetlands in a river basin in the eastern plains indicated that most wetlands were along springfed streams that have perennial flow in reaches 1–2 miles in length (Cooper and Cottrell, 1989). In the intermountain basins, ground water is an important determinant of wetland location. Wetlands in the San Luis Valley (fig. 2A), an intermountain basin, are hydrologically supported by springs or ground-water mounds that form during spring and summer runoff (Cooper and Severn, 1992).

Climatic, topographic, and hydrologic characteristics differ among and sometimes within physiographic provinces. Colorado's diverse physiography results in diverse hydrologic settings for wetland formation.

In the Great Plains, wetlands occur in riparian zones of perennial streams, in oxbow lakes (abandoned stream meanders), in isolated depressions that have permanent or seasonal water supply, in playa lakes (primarily in the southern part of the region), and in association with reservoirs or channelized streams, rivers, and irrigation ditches.

In the Colorado Plateaus and Wyoming Basin, wetlands occur along perennial and intermittent streams, in oxbow lakes, around reservoirs, in springs and seeps, and where there is a shallow water table. Because of their semiarid to arid climate, these regions have a lower density and acreage of wetlands than does the rest of the State. As a result, the region's wetlands are disproportionately valuable to wildlife.

In the Rocky Mountains, wetlands form in two physiographically and climatically distinct settings: mountain valleys and intermountain basins. Mountain valleys generally are geologically young and, therefore, steep. The valleys have been shaped either by running water over their entire length or by glaciers at higher altitude and running water at lower altitude. Wetlands in mountain valleys occur in both glaciated and nonglaciated parts of the valleys in locations from cliff faces to valley floors. Glaciation (fig. 2E) in the alpine zone of some mountain valleys formed large cirque basins in which remnant glaciers or late-melting snow maintain spring, seep, and snowbed wetlands. Cirque lakes, or tarns, formed by glacial scouring, collect meltwater and attenuate downhill flow. Also in the alpine zone, ponds form in depressions behind slumping saturated soils or in depressions caused by the weight of accumulated snow. Below cirque basins, glaciated, steep-sided, U-shaped valleys have broad, flat floors and relatively low-gradient streams. Wetlands form on saturated cliff faces, at the sloping floor near the sides of the valley, in oxbow lakes, in glacial kettle ponds, in depressions on the surface of glacial moraines, in lakes created by terminal or lateral moraines, in landslide-formed lakes, in or near seeps and springs, and in beaver ponds. In steep, V-shaped, nonglaciated parts of mountain valleys, wetlands occur as narrow riparian wetlands, in or near springs and seeps, and in beaver ponds (Windell and others, 1986).

Intermountain basins, which were formed by tectonic forces, are filled by sediments derived from erosion of the surrounding mountains. The large, flat valleys are drained by low-gradient meandering streams and rivers. Wetlands in the intermountain basins form along these streams and rivers, in natural and constructed impoundments, in oxbow lakes, and in areas having a shallow water table maintained by underlying aquifers, annual flooding, or impermeable substrates (Windell and others, 1986).

The San Luis Valley is an intermountain basin in southern Colorado. Throughout much of the valley, the water table is shal-

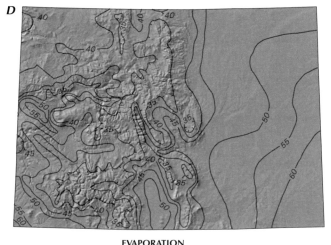

EVAPORATION

—40— **Line of equal free-water-surface evaporation**—Interval, 5 inches

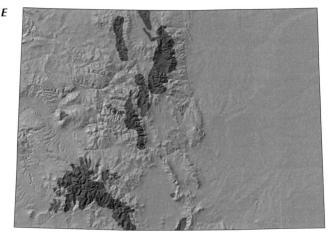

GLACIATION

▨ Glacial extent during most recent glacial maximum

Figure 2.   Continued.   Wetland distribution in Colorado and physical and climatological features that control wetland distribution in the State. **D**, Annual free-water-surface evaporation. **E**, Extent of most recent glaciation. *(Sources: D, Farnsworth and others, 1982. E, Montagne, 1972.)*

low or at land surface, creating large areas of wetlands that have diverse vegetation (Cooper and Severn, 1992). Wetlands in the valley provide habitat for resident and migratory waterfowl and enhance water quality. The valley hosts endangered whooping cranes during migration and has the State's largest concentration of wintering bald eagles (U.S. Fish and Wildlife Service, 1990). The State's largest National Wildlife Refuges, Alamosa and Monte Vista, are located there. Ground water is used to irrigate the valley and augment surface-water flow in the Rio Grande. Recently, developers have sought to export ground water from the valley to urban areas. The State Engineer's office estimated that this project could cause permanent water-table drawdown of several feet over large areas in the northern valley (Cooper and Severn, 1992). Such declines could decrease wetland acreage by reducing the area of saturated or inundated soil and the duration of inundation in emergent wetlands (Cooper and Severn, 1992). Redelfs (1980) reported that changes in irrigation practices since the early 1970's already have reduced wetland acreage in the valley by 40 to 50 percent and have caused loss or drastic alteration of high-quality wetlands. The issue of new ground-water development illustrates the conflicts that occur frequently between development and wetland-conservation interests in the State.

Studies of wetland function have been conducted in a few Colorado wetlands. Rovey and others (1986) concluded that vegetation and water levels of wetlands in the Cross Creek area were dependent on stream hydrology. However, in another study of Cross Creek wetlands, Sundeen and others (1989) determined that the hydrology of those wetlands was largely independent of streams that flowed through them. Ruddy and Williams (1991) reached a similar conclusion about wetlands in the Williams Fork. Cooper (1990), in a study of wetland vegetation in South Park, delineated stands of rare vegetation whose main range is in wetlands of boreal and arctic Canada and Alaska. A study of the water-quality function of a subalpine wetland in the upper Arkansas River basin (indicated that the wetland removed iron from a stream affected by acidic mine drainage that flowed through the wetland (Walton-Day, 1991). An upper-montane wetland has been intensively studied to determine the processes that caused elevated uranium concentrations (Owen, 1990), and reconnaissance work has been conducted in many other such wetlands (Owen and others, 1992). Although these investigations of natural processes have added to what is known of Colorado's wetlands, the functions and values of the State's wetlands remain largely unstudied (Cooper and Severn, 1992).

TRENDS

The FWS has estimated that, from the 1780's to the 1980's, wetland area in Colorado decreased by 50 percent—from about 2 million to about 1 million acres (Dahl, 1990). In agricultural areas, conversion to cropland, dewatering for irrigation purposes, and overgrazing by livestock contribute to wetland losses. In urban areas, wetland losses are due to encroachment by residential and commercial construction, channelization, dewatering for municipal and industrial purposes, and contamination from inadequately treated sewage and industrial waste. In other areas, losses have been caused by ski-resort development, transmountain water diversions, drainage, river channelization, burning, clear cutting, mining and related activities that produce toxic acidic or alkaline drainage, peat mining, placer mining, water disposal, mine-tailing deposition, erosion and sedimentation, accidents such as drilling-mud spills or tailing-dam failures, sand and gravel mining, road and railroad construction, dams and reservoirs, and acidic precipitation (U.S. Fish and Wildlife Service, 1990, p. 9; Windell and others, 1986).

Some land-use practices have created new wetlands or enlarged existing ones. Leaking ditches, uncapped flowing wells, and seeps and return flows associated with irrigation have increased wetland acreage or improved wetland habitat, notably in the San Luis Val-

ley (Windell and others, 1986), but also in other regions of the State (Hopper, 1968; Rector and others, 1979). Gravel-pit construction also has increased wetland acreage, and gravel mining and agricultural activities are totally or partially responsible for two-thirds of the wetlands inventoried in the Boulder, Colo., area (Cooper, 1988). Reservoir construction has undoubtedly increased the acreage of lacustrine wetlands.

CONSERVATION

Many government agencies and private organizations participate in wetlands conservation in Colorado. The most active agencies and organizations and some of their activities are listed in table 1.

Federal wetland activities. — Development activities in Colorado wetlands are regulated by several Federal statutory prohibitions and incentives that are intended to slow wetland losses. Some of the more important of these are contained in the 1899 Rivers and Harbors Act; the 1972 Clean Water Act and amendments; the 1985 Food Security Act; the 1990 Food, Agriculture, Conservation, and Trade Act; and the 1986 Emergency Wetlands Resources Act.

Section 10 of the Rivers and Harbors Act gives the U.S. Army Corps of Engineers (Corps) authority to regulate certain activities in navigable waters. Regulated activities include diking, deepening, filling, excavating, and placing of structures. The related section 404 of the Clean Water Act is the most often-used Federal legislation protecting wetlands. Under section 404 provisions, the Corps issues permits regulating the discharge of dredged or fill material into wetlands. Permits are subject to review and possible veto by the U.S. Environmental Protection Agency (EPA), and the FWS has review and advisory roles. Section 401 of the Clean Water Act grants to States and eligible Indian Tribes the authority to approve, apply conditions to, or deny section 404 permit applications on the basis of a proposed activity's probable effects on the water quality of a wetland.

Most farming, ranching, and silviculture activities are not subject to section 404 regulation. However, the "Swampbuster" provision of the 1985 Food Security Act and amendments in the 1990 Food, Agriculture, Conservation, and Trade Act discourage (through financial disincentives) the draining, filling, or other alteration of wetlands for agricultural use. The law allows exemptions from penalties in some cases, especially if the farmer agrees to restore the altered wetland or other wetlands that have been converted to agricultural use. The Wetlands Reserve Program of the 1990 Food, Agriculture, Conservation, and Trade Act authorizes the Federal Government to purchase conservation easements from landowners who agree to protect or restore wetlands. The Consolidated Farm Service Agency (formerly the Agricultural Stabilization and Conservation Service) administers the Swampbuster provisions and Wetlands Reserve Program. The National Resources Conservation Service (formerly the Soil Conservation Service) determines compliance with Swampbuster provisions and assists farmers in the identification of wetlands and in the development of wetland protection, restoration, or creation plans.

The 1986 Emergency Wetlands Resources Act encourages wetland protection through funding incentives. The act requires States to address wetland protection in their Statewide Comprehensive Outdoor Recreation Plans to qualify for Federal funding for State recreational land; the National Park Service provides guidance to States in developing the wetland component of their plans.

State wetland activities. — Although Colorado currently (1993) has no comprehensive wetlands-protection program, the State is assessing the need for a wetlands policy. Several State agencies actively participate in aspects of Federal programs, and some wetlands are protected under State programs.

The Water Quality Control Division of the Department of Health reviews section 404 permit applications to ensure compli-

Table 1. Selected wetland-related activities of government agencies and private organizations in Colorado, 1993

[Source: Classification of activities is generalized from information provided by agencies and organizations. •, agency or organization participates in wetland-related activity; ..., agency or organization does not participate in wetland-related activity. MAN, management; REG, regulation; R&C, restoration and creation; LAN, land acquisition; R&D, research and data collection; D&I, delineation and inventory]

Agency or organization	MAN	REG	R&C	LAN	R&D	D&I
FEDERAL						
Department of Agriculture						
Consolidated Farm Service Agency	...	•	...	...	...	...
Forest Service	•	...	•	•	•	•
Natural Resources Conservation Service	...	•	•	...	•	•
Department of Defense						
Army Corps of Engineers	•	•	•	•	•	•
Military reservations	•	...	...	...	...	...
Department of the Interior						
Bureau of Land Management	•	...	•	•	•	•
Bureau of Reclamation	•	...	•	...	•	•
Fish and Wildlife Service	•	...	•	•	•	•
Geological Survey	...	...	...	...	•	...
National Biological Service	...	...	...	...	•	...
National Park Service	•	...	•	•	•	•
Environmental Protection Agency	...	•	•	...	•	•
Native American Tribes						
Southern Ute	•	•	•	...	•	•
Ute Mountain	...	•	...	...	...	•
STATE						
Department of Agriculture	...	...	...	...	•	...
Department of Health						
Hazardous Materials and Waste Management Division	...	•	...	...	...	...
Water Quality Control Commission	...	•	...	...	...	...
Water Quality Control Division	...	•	•	...	...	...
Department of Highways	...	...	...	•	•	•
Department of Natural Resources						
Division of Parks and Outdoor Recreation						
Colorado Natural Areas Program	•	...	...	...	•	•
Division of Wildlife	•	•	•	•	•	•
Land Commissioners	•	...	...	...	...	...
Division of Minerals and Geology	...	...	•	•	...	...
State Forest Service	...	...	•	•	...	...
SOME COUNTY AND LOCAL GOVERNMENTS	...	•	...	...	...	...
PRIVATE ORGANIZATIONS						
Ducks Unlimited	•	...	•	...	•	•
The Nature Conservancy	•	...	•	•	•	•

ance with State water-quality laws. A permit is not issued by the Corps without certification of such compliance by the Division. Pursuant to section 305(b) of the Clean Water Act, the Division submits to the EPA and the U.S. Congress a biennial assessment of the State's surface-water quality, including that of wetlands.

The Colorado Department of Natural Resources has diverse wetland responsibilities. The Department's Division of Parks and Outdoor Recreation develops the Statewide Comprehensive Outdoor Recreation Plan. Pursuant to the requirements of the Emergency Wetlands Resources Act of 1986, the most recent plan (Colorado Department of Natural Resources, 1992) prioritizes wetland protection by wetland type and function. The Division's Colorado Natural Areas Program identifies and seeks protection for unique natural areas in the State. A "natural area" designation results in a maintenance agreement among landowners, the Colorado Natural Areas Program, and other interested parties. By 1992, about 5,000 acres of wetland were in designated natural areas (J.J. Coles, Colorado Natural Areas Program, oral commun., 1992). The Colorado Natural Areas Program has compiled inventories of plants and animals and plant associations of special concern in environments that include wetlands. The Division of Wildlife reviews section 404 per-

mit applications and some local land-use issues to assess potential adverse effects on wildlife. Also, the Division regulates construction activities that affect streams and riparian areas, acquires wetlands through sales of Federal duck-hunting permits, and conducts habitat-improvement projects on public and private lands.

The activities of a few State agencies include restoration of former wetlands or creation of new wetlands. The Department of Highways uses best management practices to avoid or minimize disturbances to wetlands caused by highway maintenance and construction. Unavoidable damage to wetlands is mitigated through wetland restoration or creation. The Department has data-collection and monitoring programs to facilitate compliance with section 404 permitting requirements and to assess the effectiveness of mitigation projects. The Division of Minerals and Geology creates wetlands to treat water from abandoned mines. The State Forest Service helps private landowners develop or augment wetlands.

County and local wetland activities. — Most regulation of development activities in Colorado's wetlands is accomplished through Federal and State laws. However, Eagle and Pitkin Counties (which contain the towns of Vail and Aspen, respectively) and the cities of Boulder, Broomfield, Fort Collins, and Greenwood Village have adopted their own ordinances or guidelines to protect wetlands or to mitigate unavoidable wetland losses.

Private wetland activities. — Ducks Unlimited owns more than 2,200 acres of wetlands statewide (Ducks Unlimited, 1992). The Nature Conservancy owns about 1,600 acres (A.T. Carpenter, The Nature Conservancy, written commun., 1992). Other organizations that participate in wetland-protection activities in the State include the Colorado Native Plant Society, the Colorado Riparian Association, the Colorado Wildlife Federation, the Grand Canyon Trust, High Country Citizen's Alliance, the Sierra Club, Colorado Trout Unlimited, the Colorado Cattleman's Association, and Colorado Earth First! (Chew, 1991).

References Cited

Bureau of Land Management, 1991, Riparian-wetlands initiative for the 1990's: Bureau of Land Management Report BLM/WO/GI–91/001+4340, 50 p.

Chew, M.K., 1991, Bank balance—Managing Colorado's riparian areas: Fort Collins, Colorado State University Cooperative Extension Bulletin 553A, 49 p.

Colorado Department of Natural Resources, 1992, Statewide comprehensive outdoor recreation plan, draft of section IX, SCORP wetlands amendment: Denver, Colorado Department of Natural Resources, Division of Parks and Outdoor Recreation, 8 p.

Cooper, D.J., 1986, Ecological studies of wetland vegetation, Cross Creek Valley, Holy Cross Wilderness, Sawatch Range, Colorado: Boulder, Colo., Holy Cross Wilderness Defense Fund, Technical Report 2, 25 p. [Available from Holy Cross Wilderness Defense Fund, 1130 Alpine, Boulder, CO 80304.]

———1988, Advance identification of wetlands in the city of Boulder Comprehensive Planning Area: Boulder, Colo., Boulder Planning Department, 53 p.

———1990, Ecological studies in South Park, Colorado—Classification, functional analysis, rare species inventory, and the effects of removing irrigation (Contract report prepared for the U.S. Environmental Protection Agency, Region VIII, and the Park County Commission): Fairplay, Colo., Park County Commission, 94 p. [Available from Librarian, U.S. Geological Survey, Colorado District, Box 25046, MS 415, Denver Federal Center, Bldg. 53, Denver, CO 80225.]

Cooper, D.J., and Cottrell, T.R., 1989, An ecological characterization and functional evaluation of wetlands in the Cherry Creek Basin—Cherry Creek Reservoir upstream to Franktown (Contract report prepared for the U.S. Environmental Protection Agency, Region VIII, and the city of Greenwood Village): Golden, Colorado School of Mines, 57 p.

Cooper, D.J., and Severn, Craig, 1992, Wetlands of the San Luis Valley, Colorado—An ecological study and analysis of the hydrologic regime, soil chemistry, vegetation and the potential effects of a water table drawdown (Contract report prepared for the State of Colorado Division of Wildlife, U.S. Fish and Wildlife Service, and Rio Grande Water Conservation District [Colo.]): Denver, Colorado Division of Wildlife, 158 p. [Available from Librarian, U.S. Geological Survey, Colorado District, Box 25046, MS 415, Denver Federal Center, Bldg. 53, Denver, CO 80225.]

Cowardin, L.M., Carter, Virginia, Golet, F.C., and LaRoe, E.T., 1979, Classification of wetlands and deepwater habitats of the United States: U.S. Fish and Wildlife Service Report FWS/OBS–79/31, 131 p.

Dahl, T.E., 1990, Wetlands—Losses in the United States, 1780's to 1980's: Washington, D.C., U.S. Fish and Wildlife Service Report to Congress, 13 p.

Ducks Unlimited, 1992, Homework—Stockpiling wildlife does not work, preserving the habitat resource does!: Wild Dawn, v. 2, no. 4, p. 6–7.

Farnsworth, R.K., Thompson, E.S., and Peck, E.L., 1982, Evaporation atlas for the contiguous 48 United States: National Oceanic and Atmospheric Administration Technical Report NWS 33, 27 p.

Fenneman, N.M., 1946, Physical divisions of the United States: Washington, D.C., U.S. Geological Survey special map, scale 1:7,000,000.

Hopper, R.M., 1968, Wetlands of Colorado: Colorado Department of Game, Fish, and Parks Technical Publication 22, 89 p.

Montagne, J.M., 1972, Glaciation during the Wisconsin stage, in Rocky Mountain Association of Geologists, 1972, Geologic Atlas of the Rocky Mountain Region: Denver, Hirschfeld Press, p. 259.

Owen, D.E. (chair), 1990, Session G—Multidisciplinary studies of a mountain fen, Society of Wetland Scientists, 11th annual meeting, Final Program, Breckenridge, Colo., June 4–6, 1990: Society of Wetland Scientists, p. 54, 56–58, 61, 70.

Owen, D.E., Otton, J.K., Hills, F.A., and Schumann, R.R., 1992, Uranium and other elements in Colorado Rocky Mountain wetlands—A reconnaissance study: U.S. Geological Survey Bulletin 1992, 33 p.

Petsch, H.E., Jr., 1986, Colorado surface-water resources, in U.S Geological Survey, National water summary 1985—Hydrologic events and surface-water resources: U.S. Geological Survey Water-Supply Paper 2300, p. 167–174.

Rector, C.D., Mustard, E.W., and Windell, J.T., 1979, Lower Gunnison Basin wetland inventory and evaluation: U.S. Soil Conservation Service, Bureau of Reclamation, Colorado Division of Wildlife, and University of Colorado cooperative publication, 90 p.

Redelfs, A.E., 1980, Wetlands values and losses in the United States: Stillwater, Oklahoma State University, M.S. thesis, 144 p.

Rovey, E.W., Kraeger-Rovey, Catherine, and Cooper, D.J., 1986, Hydrological and ecological processes in a Colorado Rocky Mountain wetland, in Kane, D.L., ed., Proceedings of the Symposium on Cold Regions Hydrology, Fairbanks, Alaska, 1986: Bethesda, Md., American Water Resources Association, p. 93–100.

Ruddy, B.C., and Williams, R.S., Jr., 1991, Hydrologic relations between streamflow and subalpine wetlands in Grand County, Colorado: U.S. Geological Survey Water-Resources Investigations Report 90–4129, 53 p.

Sundeen, K.D., Leaf, C.F., and Bostrom, G.M., 1989, Hydrologic functions of sub-alpine wetlands in Colorado, in Fisk, D.W., ed., Proceedings of the Symposium on Wetlands—Concerns and Successes, Tampa, Fla., September 17–22, 1989: Bethesda, Md., American Water Resources Association, p. 401–413.

U.S. Fish and Wildlife Service, 1955, Wetlands inventory—Colorado: Albuquerque, N. Mex., U.S. Fish and Wildlife Service, Report by the Office of River Basin Studies, 19 p., 16 pls.

_____1960, Inventory of permanent water areas of importance to waterfowl in the state of Colorado: Albuquerque, N. Mex., U.S. Fish and Wildlife Service and Colorado Department of Game and Fish cooperative publication, 9 p.

_____1990, Regional wetlands concept plan—Emergency wetlands resources act: Lakewood, Colo., U.S. Fish and Wildlife Service, 90 p., 4 apps.

Walton-Day, Katherine, 1991, Hydrology and geochemistry of a natural wetland affected by acid mine drainage, St. Kevin Gulch, Lake County, Colorado: Golden, Colorado School of Mines, Ph.D. dissertation #T–4033, 299 p.

Windell, J.T., Willard, B.E., Cooper, D.J., and others, 1986, An ecological characterization of Rocky Mountain montane and subalpine wetlands: U.S. Fish and Wildlife Service Biological Report 86(11), 298 p.

FOR ADDITIONAL INFORMATION: District Chief, U.S. Geological Survey, Building 53, Box 25046, Mail Stop 415, Denver Federal Center, Denver, CO 80225; Regional Wetland Coordinator, U.S. Fish and Wildlife Service, Fish and Wildlife Enhancement, P.O. Box 25486, Denver Federal Center, Denver, CO 80225

Prepared by
Katherine Walton-Day,
U.S. Geological Survey

Connecticut
Wetland Resources

Connecticut's diverse wetlands are valued for the environmental and economic benefits they provide, such as wildlife habitat, water-quality improvement, flood and erosion control, recreation, hunting, trapping, and esthetic beauty. Wetlands provide food, shelter, and breeding and nursery grounds for fish, shellfish, birds, and other wildlife, many of whose populations are threatened or endangered. The quality of water that passes through wetlands is typically enhanced by physical and biochemical processes. Undeveloped floodplain wetlands along the Connecticut River and other rivers in the State provide natural storage that helps regulate floodwaters. Because wetlands are valuable to the people of Connecticut, the Federal and State governments own and protect several wetlands, such as Robbins Swamp (fig. 1).

TYPES AND DISTRIBUTION

Wetlands are lands transitional between terrestrial and deep-water habitats where the water table usually is at or near the land surface or the land is covered by shallow water (Cowardin and others, 1979). The distribution of wetlands and deepwater habitats in Connecticut is shown in figure 2A; only wetlands are discussed herein.

Wetlands can be vegetated or nonvegetated and are classified on the basis of their hydrology, vegetation, and substrate. In this summary, wetlands are classified according to the system proposed by Cowardin and others (1979), which is used by the U.S. Fish and Wildlife Service (FWS) to map and inventory the Nation's wetlands. At the most general level of the classification system, wetlands are grouped into five ecological systems: Palustrine, Lacustrine, Riverine, Estuarine, and Marine. The Palustrine System includes only wetlands, whereas the other systems comprise wetlands and deepwater habitats. Wetlands of the systems that occur in Connecticut are described below.

System	Wetland description
Palustrine	Nontidal and tidal-freshwater wetlands in which vegetation is predominantly trees (forested wetlands); shrubs (scrub-shrub wetlands); persistent or nonpersistent emergent, erect, rooted herbaceous plants (persistent- and nonpersistent-emergent wetlands); or submersed and (or) floating plants (aquatic beds). Also, intermittently to permanently flooded open-water bodies of less than 20 acres in which water is less than 6.6 feet deep.
Lacustrine	Nontidal and tidal-freshwater wetlands within an intermittently to permanently flooded lake or reservoir larger than 20 acres and (or) deeper than 6.6 feet. Vegetation, when present, is predominantly nonpersistent emergent plants (nonpersistent-emergent wetlands), or submersed and (or) floating plants (aquatic beds), or both.
Riverine	Nontidal and tidal-freshwater wetlands within a channel. Vegetation, when present, is same as in the Lacustrine System.
Estuarine	Tidal wetlands in low-wave-energy environments where the salinity of the water is greater than 0.5 part per thousand (ppt) and is variable owing to evaporation and the mixing of seawater and freshwater.

According to a survey conducted in the early 1980's by the Connecticut Department of Environmental Protection on contract to the FWS National Wetland Inventory (Metzler and Tiner, 1992), wetlands covered about 172,500 acres, or about 5 percent, of Connecticut at that time. Wetlands were defined on the basis of aerial-photo interpretation of visible vegetation types and hydrology. Evaluations of the accuracy of the National Wetland Inventory maps for Vermont and Massachusetts, which were produced using the same techniques as for the Connecticut inventory, indicated that the 1:24,000-scale maps had accuracies of 91 percent and greater than 95 percent, respectively, in those States (Metzler and Tiner, 1992). Wetland area and density are greatest in the eastern part of the State (fig. 2B). Palustrine wetlands are by far the most common wetland type in the State, followed by estuarine wetlands (fig. 2C); together, they constitute about 99 percent, by area, of the State's wetlands. The combined area of lacustrine and riverine wetlands makes up the remaining 1 percent of wetland acreage. A description of Connecticut's most common wetland types follows.

Palustrine wetlands.—Vegetated palustrine wetlands in Connecticut include ponds and shallow lakes in which the dominant vegetation is floating or submersed (aquatic-bed wetlands); freshwater marshes, fens, and bogs dominated by herbaceous plants (emergent wetlands); and bogs and swamps dominated by shrubs or trees (scrub-shrub or forested wetlands). Palustrine forested wetlands constitute 54 percent of the State's wetlands (Metzler and Tiner, 1992) and consist primarily of red maple swamps with some evergreen forested wetlands. Red maple grows in most inland wetlands because it tolerates a wide range of flooding and soil-saturation conditions. The vegetation found with red maple, in the understory and intermixed or codominating in the canopy, differs according to nutrient conditions and water regime. Evergreen forested wetlands are commonly vegetated by Atlantic white cedar in eastern Connecticut (Metzler and Tiner, 1992) and hemlock or black spruce in western Connecticut (Messier, 1980).

Lacustrine and riverine wetlands.—Although present throughout the State, lacustrine and riverine wetlands comprise only a small percentage of Connecticut's wetland area. These freshwater wetlands generally are restricted to the channel or the shallow zone between the shore and deepwater habitat. If vegetated, they have only aquatic-bed or nonpersistent emergent vegetation. Riverine wetlands are most abundant in the freshwater tidal areas of the Connecticut and Housatonic River (Metzler and Tiner, 1992). Shallow wetlands ad-

Figure 1. Robbins Swamp, near Canaan. This 1,000-acre forested wetland is the largest inland wetland in Connecticut. The wetland provides wildlife habitat, outdoor recreation, and other benefits. Parts are owned by the State and The Nature Conservancy. *(Photograph by Ellen M. Ramsey, The Nature Conservancy.)*

jacent to rivers or lakes are classified as palustrine wetlands if there is persistent emergent vegetation present.

Estuarine wetlands.—Estuarine wetlands consist of salt and brackish marshes (emergent and scrub-shrub wetlands) that have developed in protected coves and embayments along the coast and estuaries adjacent to Long Island Sound. Sparsely vegetated estuarine flats and beaches, alternately flooded by tide or exposed to air, also are present.

HYDROLOGIC SETTING

Wetlands occur in geologic, topographic, and hydrologic settings that enhance the accumulation and retention of ground water, surface water, or both for extended periods of time. Hydrologic processes are the primary factors determining the existence of wetlands; even if the geologic and topographic settings are favorable for wetland formation, unfavorable hydrologic conditions can inhibit wet-

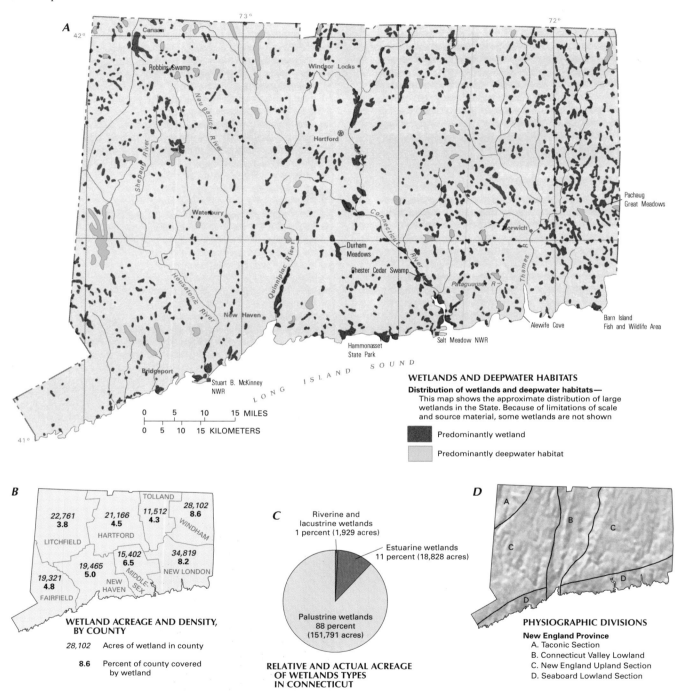

Figure 2. Wetland distribution in Connecticut and physical features that control wetland distribution in the State. **A**, Distribution of wetlands and deepwater habitats. **B**, Wetland acreage and density, by county. **C**, Relative and actual acreage of wetland types in the early 1980's for Connecticut. **D**, Physiography. *(Sources: A, T.E. Dahl, U.S. Fish and Wildlife Service, unpub. data, 1991. B and C, Data from Metzler and Tiner, 1992. D, Physiographic divisions from Fenneman, 1938; landforms data from EROS Data Center.)*

land formation (Winter, 1988). On an annual basis, precipitation exceeds evapotranspiration losses in Connecticut, resulting in an annual moisture surplus. Hydrology, therefore, favors the formation of wetlands throughout the State, and wetland location is determined primarily by geologic and topographic controls.

Connecticut's physical features—created by geologic forces over millions of years, erosion and deposition from recent glaciation, and human activities—combined with present-day hydrologic conditions, determine the distribution of wetlands in the State. Connecticut can be divided into four physiographic divisions based upon general topographic relief: the Taconic, the Connecticut Valley Lowland, the New England Upland, and the Seaboard Lowland Sections of the New England Province (fig. 2D). Topographic relief generally increases from the southeast to northwest corners of the State. Major lowland areas include the Seaboard Lowland, Connecticut Valley Lowland, and, in the New England Upland and Taconic Sections, deep valleys formed of weathered, calcareous bedrock. Connecticut was completely covered by ice during the last glaciation; the ice margin reached its maximum extent at Long Island, New York. Glaciation did little to change the preglacial, fluvially eroded bedrock topography except for locally deepening bedrock hollows and river valleys (Schafer and Hartshorn, 1965). Large quantities of sediment were produced and deposited over bedrock throughout the State. This sediment either was deposited on upland hilltops and slopes as till or was eroded and reworked by glacial meltwater and deposited as stratified drift (sorted and layered glacial sediments). Stratified drift was deposited in topographically low areas—major lowlands such as the Connecticut Valley Lowland and in stream and river valleys throughout the State. Many wetlands in Connecticut occur in the depressions, deepened valleys, and lowlands in which stratified drift was deposited.

Inland wetlands.—During deglaciation, a series of large glacial lakes occupied the Connecticut Valley Lowland, and smaller lakes occurred along many river valleys throughout the State (Schafer and Hartshorn, 1965). Extensive areas of flat, slowly permeable stratified drift were deposited on the bottom of these lakes. The generally low relief and poorly permeable substrate of these areas retain surface water or slow its drainage, leading to the formation and maintenance of wetlands. Owing to the low slope of these areas, small drainage obstructions can form large wetlands. Sources of water can be ground-water discharge, surface runoff, or direct precipitation.

Wetlands occur in small and large valleys throughout Connecticut. Some wetlands occupy the depressions, or kettles, left by melting ice blocks in stratified drift. Wetlands also have formed in areas modified by the recent erosion and deposition of rivers—in abandoned river channels, behind levees and overbank sediments adjacent to rivers, and in backswamp areas. In the New England Upland and Taconic Sections, the hilly topography of upland areas of till or bedrock generally does not retain surface runoff. Wetlands form primarily in isolated depressions where surface runoff and ground-water discharge collect. The depressions may have no outflow or have drainage controlled by bedrock sills, stratified drift, beaver dams, or manmade structures. Seepage wetlands may form where the water table intersects the land surface, such as on concave slopes and at breaks in slope; however, the wetlands are perennial only if ground-water discharge is perennial (Winter, 1988).

The position of a wetland in the landscape determines the nutrient status and vegetative characteristics of the wetland (Damman and French, 1987). Water that has moved through soil and subsurface materials carries nutrients that encourage plant growth. Wetlands in upland till and bedrock depressions are primarily areas of discharge from nutrient-poor, local ground-water flow systems, whereas wetlands in lowland stratified-drift valleys receive discharge from more nutrient-enriched ground-water flow systems (Winter, 1988). Wetlands in the New England Upland and Taconic

Sections, which are underlain by metamorphosed calcareous rocks, are distinct from those in the more widespread acidic bedrock areas of the State. Soils and ground water derived from calcareous rocks are rich in nutrients, resulting in wetlands such as Robbins Swamp that support a lush and diverse flora (Dowhan and Craig, 1976).

As vegetation became established after glacial retreat and developed in response to the warming climate, open-water areas filled with sediment or organic matter to become wetlands or remained lakes with wetlands fringing open water. Studies of upland wetlands in northeastern Connecticut have shown that wetlands have developed over many divergent paths in the time since deglaciation (Thorson, 1990, 1992; Thorson and Harris, 1991). Postsettlement agricultural and industrial practices, rather than natural ecological factors, determined the present-day character of all previously existing wetlands. In addition, many wetlands were formed since settlement as a result of the effects of colonial land use and the construction of cattle-watering sites, ice ponds, and mill ponds for water-powered industries.

Tidal wetlands.—Wetlands in coastal areas of Connecticut have water-level fluctuations that are driven largely by ocean tides. Tidal wetlands form a continuum from estuarine to tidal riverine to palustrine wetlands. The effects of wave energy and salinity on the wetlands diminish along this continuum, although not necessarily at the same rate. Tidal effects are present in the Connecticut River as far as Windsor Locks near the Massachusetts border, whereas wetlands have graded from salt and brackish to freshwater before reaching Hartford. Tidal wetlands receive freshwater input from upland areas through ground-water discharge, stream overflow, and hillslope runoff. Regional ground-water discharge is greatest near the break in slope between upland and coastal areas, and intermediate and local ground-water flow systems increase in importance in low areas (Winter, 1988). Floodwater resulting from high tides or stormflows may be temporarily stored on the wetland surface. The drainage of floodwater and hillslope runoff from the wetland surface is slowed by the low slope of coastal areas. Major areas of tidal wetlands are shown along major portions of the Housatonic, Quinnipiac, and Connecticut Rivers in figure 2A.

The major factors affecting the development and persistence of tidal wetlands are the postglacial rise of sea level relative to the land, the tidal regime, the supply of sediments to the wetland, and the ability of plants to survive submergence by saltwater (Redfield, 1972). Unless the submergence of tidal wetlands by rising sea level is counteracted by the vertical accretion of the wetland by sediment deposition and plant accumulation, the wetland will drown and become a deepwater habitat. When the glaciers melted, the sea rose and encroached upon land, inundating many stream and river valleys to form estuaries. Tidal wetlands either have migrated inland along estuaries, river valleys, and coastal slopes or the wetlands have been completely inundated. Salt-marsh peats, as much as 12.5 feet thick, overlie freshwater peats in parts of the Pataguanset River valley and indicate the change in wetland type in response to changing sea levels 4,000 years ago (Orson and others, 1987). Presently, tidal wetlands exist in a narrow setting between rising sea level and expanding coastal development. As sea level continues to rise, the migration of these wetlands inland is hindered by historic alteration of coastal-margin wetlands and by present development.

TRENDS

The FWS has estimated that Connecticut lost 74 percent of its original wetlands over the 200-year period between the 1780's and the 1980's (Dahl, 1990). The FWS estimate is based on the assumption that Connecticut originally had about 670,000 acres of wetlands. However, Metzler and Tiner (1992) discuss some of the limitations of the methods used in the FWS inventory to estimate predevelopment and recent wetland acreage when applied to Connecticut. They believe that statewide wetland losses of one-third to one-half are more realistic (Metzler and Tiner, 1992). The Connecticut Department of Environmental Protection estimates losses of 40 to 50 percent for freshwater wetlands and 65 percent for coastal wetlands.

Some tidal wetlands have been created through the effects of human activities. Barske (1988) describes the development of 700 acres of salt marsh at the mouth of the Housatonic River through the accumulation of sediment, the result of upstream deforestation and other activities. Often, however, human activities lead to the degradation of tidal wetlands. The elimination or restriction of tidal flow commonly results in reduced salinity, lowered water tables, subsidence of wetlands peats, and conversion of wetland vegetation to less salt-tolerant species (Roman and others, 1984; Rozsa, 1988). Roman and others (1984) estimate that 10 percent of Connecticut's salt marshes are subject to tidal-flow restriction. Loss of upstream freshwater wetlands, separation of watercourses and remaining upstream wetlands from downstream areas by a railroad right-of-way, and loss of downstream tidal marshes have all contributed to a reduction of productivity in Alewife Cove, an estuary on Long Island Sound (Welsh and others, 1976). Several degraded coastal wetlands in Connecticut are the site of restoration projects. The U.S. Army Corps of Engineers (Corps), in cooperation with the Connecticut Department of Environmental Protection, is working to identify and restore salt marshes that have been degraded as a result of tidal-flow restriction.

CONSERVATION

Many government agencies and private organizations participate in wetland conservation in Connecticut. The most active agencies and organizations and some of their activities are listed in table 1.

Table 1. Selected wetland-related activities of government agencies and private organizations in Connecticut, 1993

[Source: Classification of activities is generalized from information provided by agencies and organizations. ●, agency or organization participates in wetland-related activity; ..., agency or organization does not participate in wetland-related activity. **MAN**, management; **REG**, regulation; **R&C**, restoration and creation; **LAN**, land acquisition; **R&D**, research and data collection; **D&I**, delineation and inventory]

Agency or organization	MAN	REG	R&C	LAN	R&D	D&I
FEDERAL						
Department of Agriculture						
Consolidated Farm Service Agency	...	●	...	...	...	...
Forest Service	...	...	...	...	...	●
Natural Resources Conservation Service	...	...	●	...	●	●
Department of Commerce						
National Oceanic and						
Atmospheric Administration	●	●	...	...	...	...
Department of Defense						
Army Corps of Engineers	●	●	●	●	●	●
Military reservations	●	...	...	...	...	...
Department of the Interior						
Fish and Wildlife Service	●	...	●	●	●	●
National Biological Service	...	...	...	...	●	...
Environmental Protection Agency	...	●	...	...	...	●
STATE						
Department of Environmental Protection	●	●	●	●	●	●
Department of Transportation	●	...	●	●	●	●
University of Connecticut	...	...	...	...	●	...
TOWN AND CITY CONSERVATION COMMISSIONS	...	●	●	...	...	●
PRIVATE ORGANIZATIONS						
Connecticut Audubon Society	●	...	...	●	●	●
Ducks Unlimited	...	...	...	...	●	●
The Nature Conservancy	●	...	...	●	●	●

Federal wetland activities.—Development activities in Connecticut wetlands are regulated by several Federal statutory prohibitions and incentives that are intended to slow wetland losses. Some of the more important of these are contained in the 1899 Rivers and Harbors Act; the 1972 Clean Water Act and amendments; the 1985 Food Security Act; the 1990 Food, Agriculture, Conservation, and Trade Act; the 1986 Emergency Wetlands Resources Act; and the 1972 Coastal Zone Management Act.

Section 10 of the Rivers and Harbors Act gives the Corps authority to regulate certain activities in navigable waters. Regulated activities include diking, deepening, filling, excavating, and placing of structures. The related section 404 of the Clean Water Act is the most often-used Federal legislation protecting wetlands. Under section 404 provisions, the Corps issues permits regulating the discharge of dredged or fill material into wetlands. Permits are subject to review and possible veto by the U.S. Environmental Protection Agency, and the FWS has review and advisory roles. Section 401 of the Clean Water Act grants to States and eligible Indian Tribes the authority to approve, apply conditions to, or deny section 404 permit applications on the basis of a proposed activity's probable effects on the water quality of a wetland.

Most farming, ranching, and silviculture activities are not subject to section 404 regulation. However, the "Swampbuster" provision of the 1985 Food Security Act and amendments in the 1990 Food, Agriculture, Conservation, and Trade Act discourage (through financial disincentives) the draining, filling, or other alteration of wetlands for agricultural use. The law allows exemptions from penalties in some cases, especially if the farmer agrees to restore the altered wetland or other wetlands that have been converted to agricultural use. The Wetlands Reserve Program of the 1990 Food, Agriculture, Conservation, and Trade Act authorizes the Federal Government to purchase conservation easements from landowners who agree to protect or restore wetlands. The Consolidated Farm Service Agency (formerly the Agricultural Stabilization and Conservation Service) administers the Swampbuster provisions and Wetlands Reserve Program. The Natural Resources Conservation Service (formerly the Soil Conservation Service) determines compliance with Swampbuster provisions and assists farmers in the identification of wetlands and in the development of wetland protection, restoration, or creation plans.

The 1986 Emergency Wetlands Resources Act and the 1972 Coastal Zone Management Act and amendments encourage wetland protection through funding incentives. The Emergency Wetland Resources Act requires States to address wetland protection in their Statewide Comprehensive Outdoor Recreation Plans to qualify for Federal funding for State recreational land; the National Park Service (NPS) provides guidance to States in developing the wetland component of their plans. Coastal States that adopt coastal-zone management programs and plans approved by the National Oceanic and Atmospheric Administration are eligible for Federal funding and technical assistance through the Coastal Zone Management Act.

Federal agencies are responsible for the proper management of wetlands on public lands under their jurisdiction. The FWS protects and manages wetlands in two National Wildlife Refuges—the Stewart B. McKinney National Wildlife Refuge and the Salt Meadow National Wildlife Refuge. The Corps manages and conserves forests, water, fish, wildlife, wetlands, and recreation areas for multiple uses at dams, reservoirs, and parks located throughout the State.

State wetland activities.—Tidal wetlands are protected under the Tidal Wetlands Act of 1969 and the Coastal Management Act of 1979. Activities in tidal wetlands are regulated at the State level with exemptions for mosquito control, conservation, navigation, and emergency activities. Tidal wetlands are defined by the State as areas that border or lie beneath tidal waters and that contain certain plant species. About 15,000 acres of tidal salt marsh and 7,000 acres of brackish and freshwater tidal wetlands are regulated under this statute (Lefor and Tiner, 1972).

Nontidal freshwater wetlands are protected under the Inland Wetlands and Watercourses Act of 1972. Inland wetlands are regulated according to State standards by local inland wetlands and watercourses commissions. Permits are required for all activities within wetlands with exemptions for agricultural activities, construction and maintenance of water-supply systems, certain conservation and recreation uses, and the enjoyment and maintenance of residential property. Inland wetlands are defined by soil type—poorly drained, very poorly drained, flood-plain, or alluvial soils as delineated by the National Cooperative Soil Survey. Rivers, streams, waterways, and other natural and artificial water bodies are regulated under this statute as watercourses. On the basis of the State's wetland definition, 15 to 20 percent of Connecticut's land is subject to regulation as inland wetlands (Metzler and Tiner, 1992).

Under section 401 of the Federal Clean Water Act, any activity that results in a discharge, including that of fill into wetlands or State waters that requires a federal permit, must also obtain a section 401 water-quality certification stating that the activity will not violate State surface-water-quality standards. Many activities exempted under the Inland Wetlands and Watercourses Act are in the Department of Environmental Protection's jurisdiction under the section 401 certification program; however, normal maintenance and improvement of agricultural lands remain exempt from State and Federal authority. Use of the antidegradation provisions of State surface-water-quality standards on wetlands provides enhanced wetland protection. Antidegradation provisions provide for the protection of existing wetland functions and the level of water quality necessary to maintain and protect those functions. No degradation is allowed in areas designated as "outstanding national resource waters," such as National Wildlife Refuges, National Parks, State parks, wildlife areas, and other areas of ecological significance. The Water Resources Division of the Department of Environmental Protection is responsible for section 401 certifications in Connecticut.

The Department of Environmental Protection is the primary environmental and conservation agency in Connecticut. The Department owns more wetland acreage in Connecticut than does the Federal Government (Metzler and Tiner, 1992). Numerous wetlands are protected in State parks, State forests, and wildlife-management areas throughout the State. Chester Cedar Swamp and Pachaug Great Meadows are partly State-owned wetlands and are designated as National Natural Landmarks by the NPS. The State owns significant portions of wetlands at Robbins Swamp, Durham Meadows, Barn Island Fish and Wildlife Areas, and Hammonasset State Park (Metzler and Tiner, 1992). Wetlands are acquired through the Recreation and Natural Heritage Act and sale of the new Connecticut Waterfowl Hunting Stamp. Funds derived from the stamp will be used solely for wetland acquisition or improvements.

Development projects that cause unavoidable wetlands degradation or loss are required to mitigate or compensate for wetland loss by replacing or providing a substitute wetland resource. The Connecticut State Department of Transportation has been involved in wetlands creation and mitigation projects as a way to offset the long-term effects of highway construction. Wetlands, created and restored as a part of the design, permit, and construction process, have provided lost wetland functions with varying success (Butts, 1988). The Department of Transportation has acquired about 200 acres of wetlands in compensation for wetlands lost through development projects; most of this land has remained under the Department's management. The Department provides funds for wetland-related research primarily at the University of Connecticut.

Local wetland activities.—Inland wetland and watercourse commissions and coastal-area zoning and planning commissions are responsible for planning and regulating wetland-related activities at the town or municipal level. Inland wetland and watercourse commissions regulate activities through permitting under the Inland Wetland and Watercourses Act. Coastal-area zoning and planning commissions balance development and the preservation of environmental values in coastal areas under the Coastal Management Act. The act provides commissions with planning, research, and permitting authority. Education, training, support, and final authority are provided to commissions by the Department of Environmental Protection's Wetland Program.

Private wetland activities.—Private organizations in Connecticut are active in land acquisition and management, research, education, and policy review and planning. The Nature Conservancy protects about 1,800 acres of wetlands within the 9,000 acres of land under its ownership. Ducks Unlimited provides technical and financial assistance to Federal and State agencies in order to protect waterfowl habitat in Connecticut.

References Cited

Barske, Philip, 1988, Man and nature—Willing or unwilling partners, *in* Lefor, M.W., and Kennard, W.C., eds., Proceedings of the 4th Wetlands Conference, November 15, 1986: University of Connecticut Institute of Water Resources Report 34, p. 91–99.

Butts, M.P., 1988, Status of wetland creation/mitigation projects on State highway projects in Connecticut, *in* Lefor, M.W., and Kennard, W.C., eds., Proceedings of the 4th Wetlands Conference, November 15, 1986: University of Connecticut Institute of Water Resources Report 34, p. 13–18.

Cowardin, L.M., Carter, V., Golet, F.C., and LaRoe, E.T., 1979, Classification of wetlands and deepwater habitats of the United States: U.S. Fish and Wildlife Service Report FWS/OBS–79/31, 131 p.

Dahl, T.E., 1990, Wetlands—Losses in the United States, 1780's to 1980's: Washington, D.C., U.S. Fish and Wildlife Service Report to Congress, 13 p.

Damman, A.W.H., and French, T.W., 1987, The ecology of peat bogs of the glaciated northeastern United States—A community profile: U.S. Fish and Wildlife Service Biological Report 85(7.16), 100 p.

Dowhan, J.J., and Craig, R.J., 1976, Rare and endangered species of Connecticut and their habitats: Connecticut Geological and Natural History Survey Report of Investigations no. 6, 137 p.

Fenneman, N.M., 1938, Physiography of Eastern United States: New York, McGraw–Hill, 714 p.

Lefor, M.W., and Tiner, R.W., 1972, Tidal wetlands survey of the State of Connecticut—Report of the consultant biologists for the period December 22, 1969 to June 30, 1972: Storrs, Biological Sciences Group, University of Connecticut, 113 p.

Messier, S.N., 1980, The plant communities of the acid wetlands of northwestern Connecticut: Storrs, University of Connecticut, M.S. thesis, 98 p.

Metzler, K.J., and Tiner, R.W., 1992, Wetlands of Connecticut: State Geological and Natural History Survey of Connecticut Report of Investigations no. 13, 115 p.

Orson, R.A., Warren, R.S., and Niering, W.A., 1987, Development of a tidal marsh in a New England river valley: Estuaries, v. 10, p. 20–27.

Redfield, A.C., 1972, Development of a New England salt marsh: Ecological Monographs, v. 42, p. 201–237.

Roman, C.T., Niering, W.A., and Warren, R.S., 1984, Salt marsh vegetation change in response to tidal restriction: Environmental Management, v. 8, p. 141–150.

Rozsa, Ronald, 1988, An overview of wetland restoration projects in Connecticut, *in* Lefor, M.W., and Kennard, W.C., eds., Proceedings of the 4th Wetlands Conference, November 15, 1986: University of Connecticut Institute of Water Resources Report 34, p. 1–11.

Schafer, J.P., and Hartshorn, J.H., 1965, The Quaternary of New England, *in* Wright, H.E., Jr., and Frey, D.G., eds., The Quaternary of the United States: Princeton, N.J., Princeton University Press, p. 113–128.

Thorson, R.M., 1990, Development of small upland wetlands—A stratigraphic study in northeastern Connecticut: Storrs, University of Connecticut School of Engineering, Final Report JHR 90–191, 285 p.

_____1992, Remaking the wetlands in Lebanon, Connecticut—Cultural and natural changes in the postglacial epoch: Storrs, University of Connecticut School of Engineering, Final Report JHR 92–215, 157 p.

Thorson, R.M., and Harris, S.L., 1991, How "natural" are inland wetlands?—An example from the Trail Wood Audubon Sanctuary in Connecticut, USA: Environmental Management, v. 15, p. 675–687.

Welsh, B.L., Herring, J.P., Bessette, Diane, and Read, Luana, 1976, The importance of an holistic approach to ecosystem management and planning, _in_ Lefor, M.W., Kennard, W.C., and Helfgott, T.B., eds., Proceedings of the 3rd Wetlands Conference, June 14, 1975: University of Connecticut Institute of Water Resources Report 26, p. 16–33.

Winter, T.C., 1988, A conceptual framework for assessing cumulative impacts on the hydrology of nontidal wetlands: Environmental Management, v. 12, p. 605–620.

FOR ADDITIONAL INFORMATION: District Chief, U.S. Geological Survey, Ribicoff Federal Building, 450 Main Street, Room 525, Hartford, CT 06103; Regional Wetlands Coordinator, U.S. Fish and Wildlife Service, 300 Westgate Center Drive, Hadley, MA 01035

Prepared by
Sandra L. Harris,
U.S. Geological Survey

Delaware
Wetland Resources

Wetlands cover about 17 percent of Delaware (Tiner and Finn, 1986). These wetlands support rich biotic communities in freshwater, brackish-water, and saltwater settings across the State. Some of the most familiar wetlands in Delaware are the tidal marshes along Delaware Bay (fig. 1).

Wetlands have many chemical, physical, and biological functions. In Delaware, wetlands trap waterborne sediments, nutrients, and toxic chemicals by filtering inflowing water and storing or transforming the filtrate. Coastal-zone and flood-plain wetlands mitigate the effects of flooding caused by runoff and tides by reducing flow velocity, storing water temporarily, and releasing it gradually. Vegetation in riparian wetlands maintains stream channels by stabilizing the land surface, and tidal wetlands act as buffers against storm tides and waves, thus impeding erosion. One of the most important functions of wetlands is habitat for waterfowl, terrestrial and aquatic animals, and a wide variety of plant life. Wetlands provide food, shelter, resting and feeding places on migration routes, breeding areas, and nurseries for many animals including species of particular economic interest in Delaware such as muskrat, fish, ducks, and geese. Many rare and endangered plant species are adapted to hydrologic conditions present only in wetlands, especially freshwater wetlands.

Delaware's wetlands have considerable recreational and economic value. They provide outdoor educational and recreational opportunities, including activities such as bird watching, hiking, and canoeing. In addition, wetlands in Delaware support the hunting, fur trapping, commercial and sport fishing, lumbering, and tourist industries.

TYPES AND DISTRIBUTION

Wetlands are lands transitional between terrestrial and deepwater habitats where the water table usually is at or near the land surface or the land is covered by shallow water (Cowardin and others, 1979). The distribution of wetlands and deepwater habitats in Delaware is shown in figure 2A; only wetlands are discussed herein.

Wetlands can be vegetated or nonvegetated and are classified on the basis of their hydrology, vegetation, and substrate. In this summary, wetlands are classified according to the system proposed by Cowardin and others (1979), which is used by the U.S. Fish and Wildlife Service (FWS) to map and inventory the Nation's wetlands. At the most general level of the classification system, wetlands are grouped into five ecological systems: Palustrine, Lacustrine, Riverine, Estuarine, and Marine. The Palustrine System includes only wetlands, whereas the other systems comprise wetlands and deepwater habitats. Wetlands of the systems that occur in Delaware are described below.

System	Wetland description
Palustrine	Nontidal and tidal-freshwater wetlands in which vegetation is predominantly trees (forested wetlands); shrubs (scrub-shrub wetlands); persistent or nonpersistent emergent, erect, rooted herbaceous plants (persistent- and nonpersistent-emergent wetlands); or submersed and (or) floating plants (aquatic beds). Also, intermittently to permanently flooded open-water bodies of less than 20 acres in which water is less than 6.6 feet deep.
Lacustrine	Nontidal and tidal-freshwater wetlands within an intermittently to permanently flooded lake or reservoir larger than 20 acres and (or) deeper than 6.6 feet. Vegetation, when present, is predominantly nonpersistent emergent plants (nonpersistent-emergent wetlands), or submersed and (or) floating plants (aquatic beds), or both.
Riverine	Nontidal and tidal-freshwater wetlands within a channel. Vegetation, when present, is same as in the Lacustrine System.
Estuarine	Tidal wetlands in low-wave-energy environments where the salinity of the water is greater than 0.5 part per thousand (ppt) and is variable owing to evaporation and the mixing of seawater and freshwater.
Marine	Tidal wetlands that are exposed to waves and currents of the open ocean and to water having a salinity greater than 30 ppt.

Palustrine wetlands are the most abundant wetlands in Delaware, comprising 132,000 acres in 1983, or about 59 percent of the wetland area in the State (Tiner, 1985). Palustrine wetlands are distributed throughout the State in topographic depressions and in riparian zones along rivers and streams. In 1983, estuarine wetlands covered 89,800 acres in Delaware, or about 40 percent of the wetland area in the State. Estuarine wetlands occur along the shores of Delaware Bay and the Delaware River and behind the barrier beaches of the Atlantic Coast. Other types of wetland comprise less than 1 percent of Delaware's wetland area. In 1983, the State had about 650 acres of riverine wetland, 140 acres of lacustrine wetland, and 540 acres of marine wetland (mostly beaches and sandbars along the Atlantic Coast).

Delaware is a small State, but it contains many different types of wetlands. The plant composition of vegetated wetlands is determined by factors such as climate, soil type, ground-water and surface-water chemistry, salinity, and the extent and duration of flooding. The predominant vegetation or specific location of a Delaware wetland frequently determines its common name. For example, inland bays are natural coastal features that contain both palustrine and estuarine emergent wetlands, and such wetlands occur in Rehoboth, Indian River, and Little Assawoman Bays. Palustrine and estuarine emergent wetlands can be found in impoundments modified by constructed levees and managed by water-control structures. Salt and brackish marshes are predominantly estuarine emergent wetlands characterized by vegetation tolerant of brackish to salty

Figure 1. Estuarine wetlands on Cedar Creek at Slaughter Beach, Delaware. These are tidal wetlands typical of those found along Delaware Bay. *(Photograph by Evelyn M. Maurmeyer, Coastal and Estuarine Research, Inc.)*

water; small scrub-shrub wetlands commonly are associated with the landward margins of salt marshes. Interdunal swales (dune slacks) are topographic depressions among sand dunes on the Atlantic Coast that contain palustrine emergent or scrub-shrub wetlands. Palustrine forested wetlands in Delaware include Atlantic white cedar swamps, cypress swamps, and flood-plain forests, both tidal and nontidal. Delmarva bays (small, closed topographic depressions) commonly contain seasonally flooded palustrine emergent, scrub-shrub, or forested wetlands. Delmarva bays and associated wetlands also are known as whale wallows; loblollies; flatwoods depressions; and intermittent, temporary, vernal, woodland, or coastal-plain ponds.

The Delaware Department of Natural Resources and Environmental Control has established five wetland categories for the State based on relative functions and values of the State's wetlands. Category I wetlands provide exceptional value or unique biotic assemblages and include Delmarva bays, dune slacks, Atlantic white cedar swamps, and cypress swamps. Category II wetlands are those generally considered permanently to seasonally wet or those that provide significant habitat or biotic values. Category III wetlands include temporarily flooded wetlands and all wetlands not included in another category. Category IV wetlands consist of farmed wetlands. Category V wetlands are all wetlands created from nonwetland areas for purposes other than mitigation and include drainage ditches, farm ponds, stormwater-retention basins, and borrow pits.

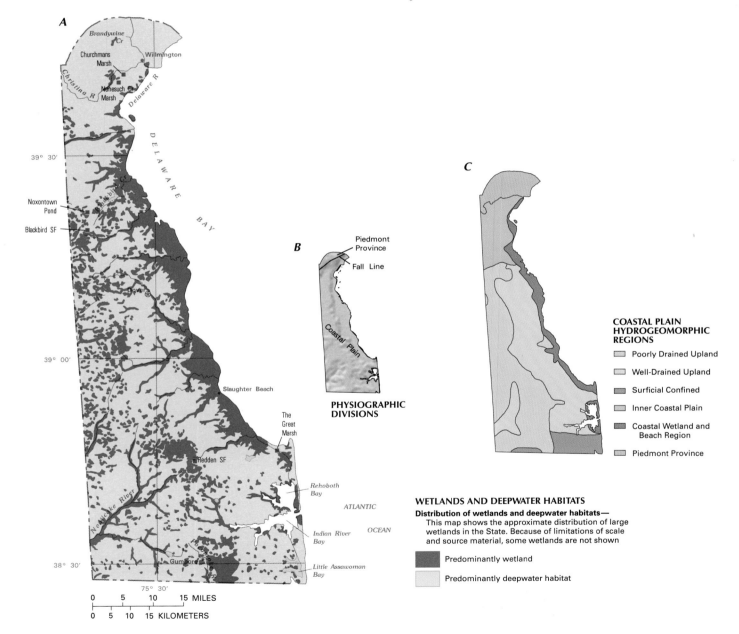

Figure 2.   Wetland distribution in Delaware and physical features that control wetland distribution in the State. **A**, Distribution of wetlands and deepwater habitats. **B**, Physiography. **C**, Hydrogeomorphic regions in the Coastal Plain of Delaware. *(Sources: A, T.E. Dahl, U.S. Fish and Wildlife Service, unpub. data, 1991. B, Landforms data from EROS Data Center; divisions from Spoljarik and Jordan, 1966. C, Shedlock and others, 1993.)*

HYDROLOGIC SETTING

In Delaware, water in small, nontidal wetlands is supplied by direct precipitation, surface runoff from precipitation, and localized, shallow ground-water-flow systems recharged by precipitation. Larger wetlands (tidal and nontidal) also can interact with regional ground-water-flow systems. The primary source of water in tidal wetlands is tidal inundation, although runoff and ground-water discharge can be important secondary sources. Water from surface runoff can collect in topographic lows, where ground water commonly discharges after periods of greater-than-normal precipitation. These hydrologic conditions are conducive to the formation and maintenance of wetlands.

Abundant precipitation (an annual average of 43 inches) (Simmons, 1986) and extensive tidal zones in Delaware Bay and the Atlantic Ocean provide ample water for wetlands in Delaware. Fluctuations in local precipitation and evapotranspiration rates combine with local differences in geology, topography, soil characteristics, and tides to create transient or seasonal changes in the local interactions of ground water and surface water in wetlands (Winter, 1992; Phillips and Shedlock, 1993). In general, mid-October to early April (nongrowing season) is a period of ground-water recharge, with high rates of precipitation and low rates of evapotranspiration. Mid-April to mid-October (growing season) is characterized by high rates of evapotranspiration and declining water levels (Johnston, 1973).

Delaware is in two physiographic provinces: the Coastal Plain and the Piedmont Province (fig. 2B). Geology, topography, and soils in the two provinces differ considerably; the types and distribution of wetlands in each province reflect this difference. Figure 3A–3C is a generalization of wetland hydrology in Delaware.

Coastal Plain.— Ninety-three percent of Delaware, including more than 94 percent of its wetland area, is in the Coastal Plain. All of the estuarine wetlands in the State are in this relatively flat province (Tiner, 1987), which rises from below sea level only to about 100 feet above sea level. The Coastal Plain is underlain by an extensive and locally complex surficial aquifer that has a wide range of depth, porosity, and permeability (Andres, 1987; Talley, 1987). Wetlands in the Coastal Plain generally intersect the surficial aquifer.

Coastal Plain wetlands are supported by precipitation, surface runoff, flooding from streams, and ground-water discharge. Recharge of the ground-water system in the Coastal Plain is mainly by infiltration of precipitation in interstream areas (Heath, 1984), and discharge results from evapotranspiration and by seepage to streams, estuaries, wells, ditches, and the ocean. Both local and regional ground-water flow may help sustain wetlands, especially in low-lying areas near the coast, which contain extensive, mainly emergent wetlands. Forested wetlands occur primarily in bottom lands along stream channels, especially in headwater areas. The width of these forested wetlands in streamside and upland areas commonly has been reduced by ditching and the conversion of land to agricultural use.

Regional differences in the configuration and geohydrologic properties of sedimentary deposits in the Coastal Plain are reflected by differences in topography, soils, degree of stream incision, the configuration of the water table, and the paths of ground-water flow. These characteristics, which affect the distribution of wetlands in the landscape, have been used to divide the Coastal Plain on the Delmarva Peninsula into hydrogeomorphic regions (Shedlock and others, 1993). In Delaware, there are five hydrogeomorphic regions (fig. 2C): the Poorly Drained Upland, the Well-Drained Upland, the Surficial Confined, the Inner Coastal Plain, and the Coastal Wetland and Beach. Each of these regions contains wetlands.

The Poorly Drained Upland lies along the drainage divide separating the Chesapeake Bay drainage basin to the west from the drainage basins of Delaware Bay and the Atlantic Ocean. This region is hummocky, has low relief, and has many seasonally flooded forested wetlands and small, sluggish streams in poorly defined, low-gradient, shallowly incised valleys (fig. 3A) (Shedlock and others, 1993). About 43 percent of the region is forested, including the topographic depressions, which have poorly drained soils and typically contain wetlands. Forests are interspersed with agricultural fields that are in areas of higher elevation than the forests. The water table in this region is shallow and has a relatively large seasonal fluctuation. Local ground-water-flow patterns are directly affected by the depth of the water table and can differ with seasonal precipitation, even to the extent of changing direction, so that wetlands where ground water is discharged in wet periods can become areas of ground-water recharge during dry periods (Phillips and Shedlock, 1993). Typical wetlands in this region are seasonally saturated, forested wetlands. Examples include the wetlands in Redden State Forest, which have poorly defined topographic boundaries (typical of the southern part of this region), and the small wetlands in Blackbird State Forest, which are contained within Delmarva bays (typical of the northern part of this region).

The Well-Drained Upland occurs in a north-south trending band in eastern Delaware and in an area in the southern part of the State around the headwaters of the Nanticoke River. This region is flat to gently rolling and has higher relief than the Poorly Drained Upland (fig. 3A). Streams are deeply incised, particularly tidal streams and their tributaries. About 28 percent of the Well-Drained Upland is forested, primarily in riparian (streamside) zones, which include most of the wetlands in the region. The rest of the region is covered by agricultural fields. Typical wetlands in the region include the palustrine forested wetlands along the Nanticoke River.

The Coastal Wetland and Beach region extends southward along the coast of Delaware from the Delaware River to the Delaware-Maryland border. This region is very flat and has dunes along the Atlantic Coast (fig. 3A). The surficial aquifer is composed of a variety of sediments that were deposited in several coastal settings, including beach, dune, and tidal marsh. The water table is generally within a few feet of the land surface because of geohydrologic conditions and because the land-surface altitude is near sea level. Wetlands in this region have complex hydrology because of the geologic setting and because of the interactions between tides and ground-water discharge. Extensive wetlands in low-lying areas form as shallow embayments, salt marshes, and tidal and nontidal freshwater marshes and swamps. Examples of wetlands in the Coastal Wetland and Beach region include the large marshes in Indian River Bay, the Great Marsh (an extensive tidal marsh along Delaware Bay), and the freshwater and brackish tidal marshes along Blackbird Creek.

The Surficial Confined region occupies two small areas of southern Delaware. The landscape is flat, except for a number of low, sandy ridges (relict dunes) that rise above their surroundings (fig. 3B). This region is physiographically similar to the Poorly Drained Upland. Geohydrologic conditions in the upper sand unit of the aquifer are the cause of the poor drainage conditions and widespread presence of wetlands in the Surficial Confined region (Shedlock and others, 1993). Extensively ditched agricultural lands have been converted from former wetland. About 55 percent of the area in this region is still in large tracts of woodlands that occur in uplands between streams and in wetlands in riparian zones. Examples of wetlands in the Surficial Confined region include the remnant of a large cypress swamp located east of Gumboro and the forested wetlands along the Pocomoke River.

The Inner Coastal Plain is in northern Delaware. There is considerable topographic relief in this region, and streams are well incised in their lower reaches (fig. 3C). Land use in this region is heterogeneous. There has been considerable development of the northeastern section, which is mostly urban. The northwestern section of the region is forested, and the southern section has mixed agricultural and residential usage. Wetlands in the Inner Coastal Plain occur in riparian zones, especially in the tidal reaches of the Christina River, in forested areas, and in small, discontinuous areas. Examples of wetlands in the region include Churchman's Marsh, a tidal emergent wetland; Nonesuch Creek Marsh, an emergent wetland whose tidal flow is restricted by tide gates; and the small, nontidal, palustrine wetlands around Noxontown Pond.

Piedmont Province.—The Piedmont Province occupies the northern 6 percent of the State and contains only 2 percent of Delaware's total wetland area (Tiner and Finn, 1986). The gently rolling hills of this province range in altitude from near sea level to about 450 feet. The Piedmont Province is underlain by folded and faulted igneous and metamorphic bedrock overlain by a regolith of variable thickness. Regolith, which underlies the land surface nearly everywhere in this province, is a layer of unconsolidated, mostly fine-grained material composed of fragmental, weathered bedrock and alluvium overlying unweathered bedrock. Wetlands in the Piedmont Province occur along riparian valleys and other low areas of the ground surface, which commonly occur over fracture zones in the bedrock. Water is more likely to collect and be discharged in these depressions than in other areas because fracture zones are major pathways of ground-water movement (Heath, 1984).

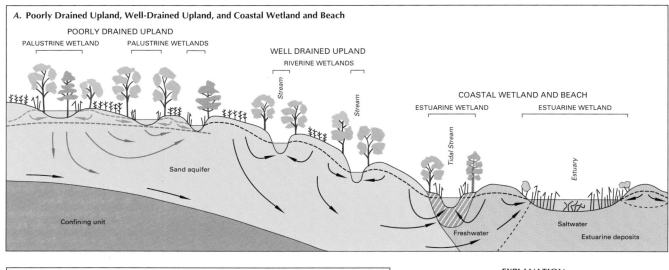

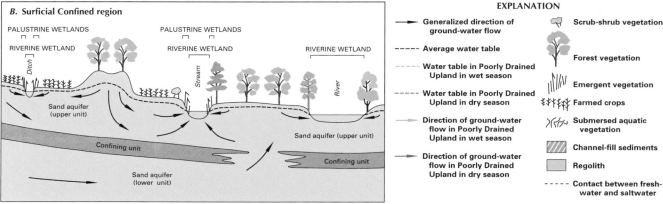

EXPLANATION

Generalized direction of ground-water flow

- - - - Average water table

- - - - Water table in Poorly Drained Upland in wet season

- - - - Water table in Poorly Drained Upland in dry season

Direction of ground-water flow in Poorly Drained Upland in wet season

Direction of ground-water flow in Poorly Drained Upland in dry season

Scrub-shrub vegetation

Forest vegetation

Emergent vegetation

Farmed crops

Submersed aquatic vegetation

Channel-fill sediments

Regolith

- - - - Contact between fresh-water and saltwater

Note: Vertical scale greatly exaggerated

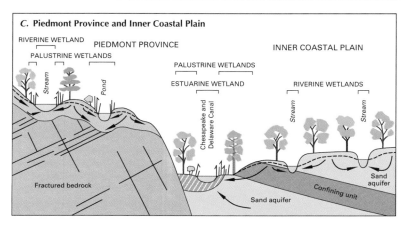

Figure 3. Geohydrologic setting of wetlands in Delaware. *A*, Poorly Drained Upland, Well-Drained Upland, and Coastal Wetland and Beach. *B*, Surficial Confined region. *C*, Piedmont Province and Inner Coastal Plain.

Recharge of the ground-water system in the Piedmont Province is by infiltration of precipitation, mostly in the uplands (Heath, 1984); however, most precipitation in this province is transported to surface depressions and streams by overland runoff. In forested areas, water seeps into the soil layer and moves through it laterally to discharge into streams and, by evapotranspiration, into the atmosphere. Some water moves below the soil zone to the water table in the regolith. The water seeps from the regolith into the underlying bedrock or discharges to surface-water bodies (fig. 3C). Much of the ground water available to wetlands in this region is stored in the regolith (Metzgar, 1973).

Types of wetlands in the Piedmont Province include flood-plain emergent marshes, seeps, and excavated farm ponds. Notable among wetlands in this province are the forested wetlands along Brandywine Creek.

TRENDS

In the 1780's, about 480,000 acres (36 percent) of Delaware was wetland (Dahl, 1990). By the mid-1980's, 223,000 wetland acres remained—a loss of about 54 percent since the 1780's. The estimated annual loss of all types of wetland between 1955 and 1981 was 1,600 acres (Tiner, 1987). Both human activities that adversely affect water quality and natural phenomena have contributed to widespread wetland loss and degradation.

Major causes of vegetated nontidal wetland loss have been channelization and ditching (about 55 percent), direct conversion to agriculture (28 percent), urbanization (12 percent), and pond creation (5 percent) (Tiner, 1987). Major causes of vegetated tidal wetland loss have been urbanization (63 percent), inundation by submersion, dredging, or impoundment (24 percent), and pond creation (6 percent). Small areas of wetland have been formed in recent times, especially by inadvertent flooding during road construction, by pond construction and, most recently, by the establishment of compensatory wetland-mitigation sites. Properly managed shallow ponds and impoundments do not usually result in wetland losses but rather in conversions from drier to wetter types of wetlands; they can even yield net increases in wetland value with the change in function. New wetlands also have formed on washover fans and flood tidal deltas along coastal areas as well as on former upland areas inundated by rising sea levels.

Implementation of the 1973 State Wetlands Act and the 1972 Federal Clean Water Act markedly reduced the rate of human-caused tidal wetland loss. The estimated annual tidal wetland loss between 1954 and 1973 was 444 acres (Lesser, 1971); between 1973 and 1979 the estimated annual rate of tidal-wetland loss was 20 acres (Hardisky and Klemas, 1983). Recent rates of nontidal-wetland loss have not been accurately quantified.

CONSERVATION

Many government agencies and private organizations participate in wetland conservation in Delaware. The most active agencies and organizations and some of their activities are listed in table 1.

Federal wetland activities.—Development activities in Delaware wetlands are regulated by several Federal statutory prohibitions and incentives that are intended to slow wetland losses. Some of the more important of these are contained in the 1899 Rivers and Harbors Act; the 1972 Clean Water Act and amendments; the 1985 Food Security Act; the 1990 Food, Agriculture, Conservation, and Trade Act; the 1986 Emergency Wetlands Resources Act; and the 1972 Coastal Zone Management Act.

Section 10 of the Rivers and Harbors Act gives the U.S. Army Corps of Engineers (Corps) authority to regulate certain activities in navigable waters. Regulated activities include diking, deepening, filling, excavating, and placing of structures. The related section 404

of the Clean Water Act is the most often-used Federal legislation protecting wetlands. Under section 404 provisions, the Corps issues permits regulating the discharge of dredged or fill material into wetlands. Permits are subject to review and possible veto by the U.S. Environmental Protection Agency, and the FWS has review and advisory roles. Section 401 of the Clean Water Act grants to States and eligible Indian Tribes the authority to approve, apply conditions to, or deny section 404 permit applications on the basis of a proposed activity's probable effects on the water quality of a wetland.

Most farming, ranching, and silviculture activities are not subject to section 404 regulation. However, the "Swampbuster" provision of the 1985 Food Security Act and amendments in the 1990 Food, Agriculture, Conservation, and Trade Act discourage (through financial disincentives) the draining, filling, or other alteration of wetlands for agricultural use. The law allows exemptions from penalties in some cases, especially if the farmer agrees to restore the altered wetland or other wetlands that have been converted to agricultural use. The Wetlands Reserve Program of the 1990 Food, Agriculture, Conservation, and Trade Act authorizes the Federal Government to purchase conservation easements from landowners who agree to protect or restore wetlands. The Consolidated Farm Service Agency (formerly the Agricultural Stabilization and Conservation Service) administers the Swampbuster provisions and Wetlands Reserve Program. The Natural Resources Conservation Service (formerly the Soil Conservation Service) determines compliance with Swampbuster provisions and assists farmers in the identification of wetlands and in the development of wetland protection, restoration, or creation plans.

The 1986 Emergency Wetlands Resources Act and the 1972 Coastal Zone Management Act and amendments encourage wetland

Table 1. Selected wetland-related activities of government agencies and private organizations in Delaware, 1993

[Source: Classification of activities is generalized from information provided by agencies and organizations. •, agency or organization participates in wetland-related activity; ..., agency or organization does not participate in wetland-related activity. MAN, management; REG, regulation; R&C, restoration and creation; LAN, land acquisition; R&D, research and data collection; D&I, delineation and inventory]

Agency or organization	MAN	REG	R&C	LAN	R&D	D&I
FEDERAL						
Department of Agriculture						
Consolidated Farm Service Agency	...	•	...	...	...	...
Natural Resources Conservation Service	...	•	•	...	•	...
Department of Commerce						
National Oceanic and						
Atmospheric Administration	...	...	•	...	•	•
Department of Defense						
Army Corps of Engineers	...	•	•	...	•	•
Department of the Interior						
Fish and Wildlife Service	•	...	•	•	•	•
Geological Survey	...	...	...	...	•	...
National Biological Service	...	...	...	...	•	...
National Park Service	•	...	•	•	•	•
Environmental Protection Agency	...	•	...	...	...	...
STATE						
Delaware Geological Survey	...	...	...	...	•	...
Department of Natural Resources and						
Environmental Control	•	•	•	•	...	•
State Highway Administration	...	•	•	...	•	•
University of Delaware						
College of Marine Studies	...	...	...	...	•	•
SOME COUNTY AND LOCAL GOVERNMENTS	•	•	...	•	...	•
PRIVATE ORGANIZATIONS						
The Nature Conservancy	•	...	...	•	•	...
Delaware Wild Lands, Inc.	•	...	•	•	...	...
Delaware Nature Society	•	...	•	•	•	...
Ducks Unlimited	•	...	•	•	...	...

protection through funding incentives. The Emergency Wetland Resources Act requires States to address wetland protection in their Statewide Comprehensive Outdoor Recreation Plans to qualify for Federal funding for State recreational land; the National Park Service provides guidance to States in developing the wetland component of their plans. Coastal States that adopt coastal-zone management programs and plans approved by the National Oceanic and Atmospheric Administration are eligible for Federal funding and technical assistance through the Coastal Zone Management Act.

State wetland activities.—Delaware's State Wetlands Act, enacted in 1973, protects coastal tidal wetlands, including some freshwater wetlands along tidal rivers, and requires a permit from the Department of Natural Resources and Environmental Control for many activities in these wetlands. A proposed freshwater (nontidal) wetlands statute would establish a State-run nontidal-wetlands regulatory program based on five categories of wetlands. This would be part of a comprehensive statewide management program and is intended to result in the assumption of authority for the Federal section 404 program by the State. The Department of Natural Resources and Environmental Control also administers section 401 of the Federal Clean Water Act, providing regulatory control in wetland areas in terms of effects on surface-water-quality standards. The coastal-zone management program in Delaware bars the development of heavy manufacturing industry within 2 miles of the State's coastline where wetlands are abundant, while allowing the development of light industry and the expansion of preexisting industry under a permit system. Permits are also required for substantial changes to the character of beach or open-water areas. The Subaqueous Lands Act and the Beach Preservation Act regulate activities in tidal and nontidal subaqueous navigable waters and within the coastal dune systems along the Atlantic Ocean and Delaware Bay.

Private wetland activities.—Private organizations with interests in wetlands in Delaware are active in the development of regulations, policy planning, advocacy, land acquisition and management, environmental education, and research. A few of the many such organizations in the State are The Nature Conservancy, the Delaware Nature Society, Delaware Wild Lands, Inc., the Sierra Club, Ducks Unlimited, and the Brandywine Conservancy.

References Cited

Andres, A.S., 1987, Geohydrology of the northern coastal area, Delaware: Delaware Geological Survey Hydrologic Map Series no. 5, scale 1:24,000.

Cowardin, L.M., Carter, Virginia, Golet, F.C., and LaRoe, E.T., 1979, Classification of wetlands and deepwater habitats of the United States: U.S. Fish and Wildlife Service Report FWS/OBS–79/31, 131 p.

Dahl, T.E., 1990, Wetlands—Losses in the United States, 1780's to 1980's: Washington, D.C., U.S. Fish and Wildlife Service Report to Congress, 13 p.

Hardisky, M.A., and Klemas, Vytautas, 1983, Tidal wetlands natural and human-made changes from 1973 to 1979 in Delaware—Mapping techniques and results: Environmental Management, v. 7, no. 4, p. 339–344.

Heath, R.C., 1984, Ground-water regions of the United States: U.S. Geological Survey Water-Supply Paper 2242, 78 p.

Johnston, R.H., 1973, Hydrology of the Columbia (Pleistocene) deposits of Delaware: Delaware Geological Survey Bulletin 14, 78 p.

Lesser, C.A., 1971, Memorandum to Secretary Austin N. Heller from Charles Lesser RE 1971 wetland inventory (corrected): Dover, Del., Department of Natural Resources and Environmental Control, 3 p.

Metzgar, R.G., 1973, Wetlands in Maryland: Maryland Department of State Planning Publication 157, 80 p.

Phillips, P.J., and Shedlock, R.J., 1993, Hydrology and chemistry of groundwater and seasonal ponds in the Atlantic Coastal Plain in Delaware, U.S.A.: Journal of Hydrology, v. 141, p. 157–178.

Shedlock, R.J., Hamilton, P.A., Denver, J.M., and Phillips, P.J., 1993, Multiscale approach to regional ground-water quality assessment of the Delmarva Peninsula, *in* Alley, W.M., ed., Multiscale approach to regional ground-water quality assessment: New York, Van Nostrand Reinhold & Co., p. 563–587.

Simmons, R.H., 1986, Delaware surface-water resources, *in* U.S. Geological Survey, National water summary 1985—Hydrologic events and surface-water resources: U.S. Geological Survey Water-Supply Paper 2300, p. 181–186.

Spoljaric, Nenad, and Jordan, R.R., 1966, Generalized geologic map of Delaware: Newark, Del., Delaware Geological Survey map, scale 1:296,075.

Talley, J.H., 1987, Geohydrology of the southern coastal area: Delaware Geological Survey Hydrologic Map Series no. 7, scale 1:24,000.

Tiner, R.W., 1985, Wetlands of Delaware: Newton Corner, Mass., U.S. Fish and Wildlife Service and Delaware Department of Natural Resources and Environmental Control cooperative publication, 77 p.

_____1987, Mid-Atlantic wetlands—A disappearing natural treasure: Newton Corner, Mass., U.S. Fish and Wildlife Service and U.S. Environmental Protection Agency cooperative publication, 28 p.

Tiner, R.W., and Finn, J.T., 1986, Status and recent trends of wetlands in five mid-Atlantic states—Delaware, Maryland, Pennsylvania, Virginia, and West Virginia: Newton Corner, Mass., U.S. Fish and Wildlife Service, National Wetlands Inventory Project technical report, 40 p.

Winter, T.C., 1992, A physiographic and climatic framework for hydrologic studies of wetlands, *in* Robarts, R.D., and Bothwell, M.L., eds., Proceedings of the Symposium on Aquatic Ecosystems in Semi-Arid Regions, 1990: Saskatoon, Saskatchewan, Environment Canada, The National Hydrology Research Institute Symposium Series no. 7, p. 127–147.

FOR ADDITIONAL INFORMATION: District Chief, U.S. Geological Survey, 208 Carroll Building, 8600 LaSalle Road, Towson, MD 21286; Regional Wetland Coordinator, U.S. Fish and Wildlife Service, 300 Westgate Center Drive, Hadley, MA 01035

Prepared by
Martha A. Hayes,
U.S. Geological Survey

Florida
Wetland Resources

Wetlands covered more than one-half of Florida, approximately 20.3 million acres, in predevelopment times. Although only about one-half of the original wetlands remain, Florida still has more wetlands than any of the other 47 conterminous States (Dahl, 1990). Wetlands in Florida are diverse and include types that are rare in other States, such as mangrove swamps and hydric hammocks. Associations of warm-temperate and subtropical wetlands not found elsewhere are common in Florida, a prime example being the unique complex of extensive sawgrass marshes and other wetlands known as The Everglades (fig. 1).

Florida's wetlands have considerable economic and environmental value. In river basins, flood-plain wetlands reduce downstream flood damages by retaining overflows in backwater ponds and depressions. Organic soils in many wetlands can store large quantities of water and release it slowly to plants during drought. Wetlands can filter out and accumulate pollutants from surface water—some cypress depressions in Florida have been used specifically for wastewater treatment (Dierberg and Brezonik, 1984). Many rare or endangered plant and animal species, such as the insectivorous white-top pitcherplant and the snail kite, live in Florida wetlands. Wetlands provide breeding and feeding grounds for resident and migratory birds. Coastal wetlands such as salt marshes, mangrove swamps, and seagrass beds are nursery areas for sea turtles and economically important species such as shrimp, blue crab,

oyster, mullet, spotted seatrout, and red drum (Tiner, 1984; Palik and Kunneke, 1984).

In the past, wetlands were considered obstacles to the development of the State. Widespread destruction and degradation of wetlands, however, resulted in drastic losses of wildlife, water shortages, and water-quality problems (Frayer and Hefner, 1991). Today, Florida's wetlands are considered important resources and are protected by laws that preserve their esthetic and ecological value.

TYPES AND DISTRIBUTION

Wetlands are lands transitional between terrestrial and deepwater habitats where the water table usually is at or near the land surface or the land is covered by shallow water (Cowardin and others, 1979). The distribution of wetlands and deepwater habitats in Florida is shown in figure 2A; only wetlands are discussed herein.

Wetlands can be vegetated or nonvegetated and are classified on the basis of their hydrology, vegetation, and substrate. In this summary, wetlands are classified according to the system proposed by Cowardin and others (1979), which is used by the U.S. Fish and Wildlife Service (FWS) to map and inventory the Nation's wetlands. At the most general level of the classification system, wetlands are grouped into five ecological systems: Palustrine, Lacustrine, Riverine, Estuarine, and Marine. The Palustrine System includes only wetlands, whereas the other systems comprise wetlands and deepwater habitats. Wetlands of the systems that occur in Florida are described below.

System	Wetland description
Palustrine	Nontidal and tidal-freshwater wetlands in which vegetation is predominantly trees (forested wetlands); shrubs (scrub-shrub wetlands); persistent or nonpersistent emergent, erect, rooted herbaceous plants (persistent- and nonpersistent-emergent wetlands); or submersed and (or) floating plants (aquatic beds). Also, intermittently to permanently flooded open-water bodies of less than 20 acres in which water is less than 6.6 feet deep.
Lacustrine	Nontidal and tidal-freshwater wetlands within an intermittently to permanently flooded lake or reservoir larger than 20 acres and (or) deeper than 6.6 feet. Vegetation, when present, is predominantly nonpersistent emergent plants (nonpersistent-emergent wetlands), or submersed and (or) floating plants (aquatic beds), or both.
Riverine	Nontidal and tidal-freshwater wetlands within a channel. Vegetation, when present, is same as in the Lacustrine System.
Estuarine	Tidal wetlands in low-wave-energy environments where the salinity of the water is greater than 0.5 part per thousand (ppt) and is variable owing to evaporation and the mixing of seawater and freshwater.
Marine	Tidal wetlands that are exposed to waves and currents of the open ocean and to water having a salinity greater than 30 ppt.

Lacustrine and riverine wetlands are not addressed in this report. They constitute a relatively small part of Florida's wetlands and were not distinguished from deepwater habitats by the FWS National Wetlands Inventory (Frayer and Hefner, 1991).

Palustrine System.—Eighty-seven percent of Florida's wetlands are in the Palustrine System. Palustrine forested wetlands cover 5.5

Figure 1. Sawgrass marsh and tree islands in the Everglades–Big Cypress region of southern Florida. *(Photograph courtesy of Florida State Archives.)*

million acres, nearly one-half the acreage of all Florida wetlands (Frayer and Hefner, 1991). These wetlands, which are widely distributed throughout the State, fringe rivers and lakes, line small drainages and sloughs, form in small depressions and ponds, and cover wet flatwoods. The predominant trees can be pines, hardwoods, or cypress.

Pine flatwoods, the most common ecological community in Florida, are distributed statewide. These communities are on flat land and have poorly drained, acidic, sandy soils that commonly are underlain by a clay or organic hardpan. Pine flatwoods can be a mixture of both wetland and upland communities that are difficult to delineate. Discrepancies between present-day estimates of 8.2 and 11.0 million acres of remaining wetlands in Florida (Frayer and Hefner, 1991; Kautz, 1991) might be due primarily to difficulties inherent in distinguishing wet from dry flatwoods. Wet flatwoods can grade into dry flatwoods with imperceptible changes in eleva-

tion. In many areas, numerous seasonal ponds, small streams, and other wetlands are embedded within the larger pine-flatwoods matrix. In wet flatwoods, soils can remain saturated through much of the rainy season, and there can be standing water for 1 to 2 months every year. During the dry season, however, high evapotranspiration from sandy soils and an impermeable hardpan preventing upward movement of ground water result in dry conditions that can persist for months (Abrahamson and Hartnett, 1990).

Palustrine forested wetlands in which mixed hardwoods predominate cover about 2 million acres of Florida (Kautz, 1991) and comprise many wetland types. Bottom-land hardwood forests on river flood plains are most common in the northern part of the State, reaching their greatest extent in the alluvial flood plains of the panhandle (Wharton and others, 1977). Tree diversity can be high in alluvial flood plains: a study of the flood-plain forest bordering the Apalachicola River (Leitman and others, 1984) recorded 47 tree

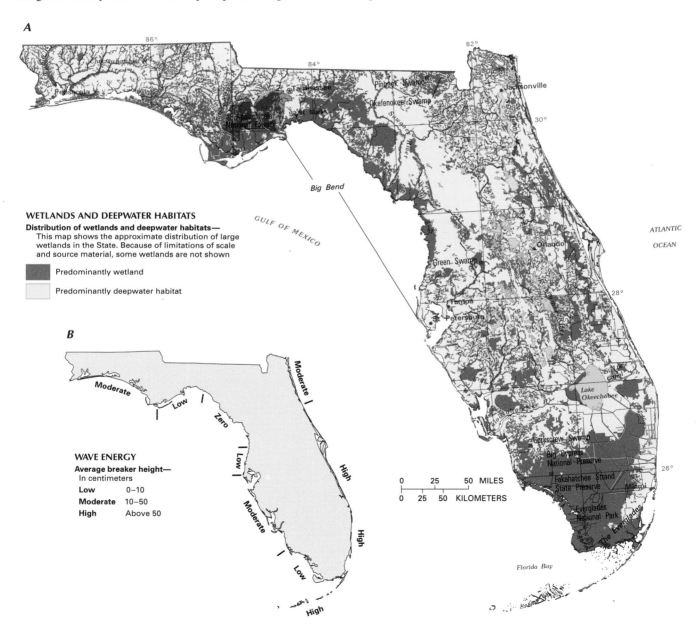

Figure 2.   Distribution of wetlands and deepwater habitats in Florida and physical and climatological features that control wetland distribution in the State. **A**, Distribution of wetlands and deepwater habitats. **B**, Wave height along the Florida coast. *(Sources: A, T.E. Dahl, U.S. Fish and Wildlife Service, unpub. data, 1991. B, Carlton, 1977.)*

species and 5 major tree communities. Blackwater streams, which are common in Florida, are dark colored owing to the presence of organic acids from decaying vegetation. The Suwannee River, which has characteristics of both blackwater and spring-fed streams, has an extensive flood-plain forest in its lower reaches. Bay swamps, black gum swamps, and other mixed-hardwood wetlands that form in depressions are common throughout Florida. These forested wetlands often are mixed with shrub bogs (scrub-shrub wetlands) as in the Apalachicola National Forest and in Pinhook Swamp, the southern extension of the Okefenokee Swamp in Florida (Wharton and others, 1977). Shrub bogs are depressional wetlands that have acidic, organic soils and that typically are dominated by titi, gallberry, fetterbush, and other evergreen shrubs (U.S. Soil Conservation Service, 1989). Hydric hammocks, which form on poorly drained soils or soils saturated by near-surface water tables and in which evergreen oaks such as live oak and swamp laurel oak predominate, are rare outside Florida (Vince and others, 1989). Exotic tree species such as melaleuca have invaded wetlands in southern Florida to such an extent that some authors consider wetlands in which they are the predominant vegetation to belong to a distinct forested-wetland type (Wharton and others, 1977; Ewel, 1990).

Palustrine forested wetlands in which cypress predominates cover about 1.6 million acres in Florida (Kautz, 1991). Cypress domes are small, isolated, depressional wetlands that have convex silhouettes when viewed from a distance. They are acidic, stillwater swamps that have standing water at least part of the year, and many have a permanent central pond. The Green Swamp in west-central Florida has a high density of cypress domes in a pine-flatwoods matrix (McPherson, 1979). Large swamps in which cypress predominates commonly ring lakes or line watercourses. Cypress strands are linear cypress swamps along watercourses. Fakahatchee Strand State Preserve in southwestern Florida contains an outstanding example of a cypress strand; the wetland harbors rare orchids,

palms, and the endangered Florida panther (Grow, 1989). Cypress scrub is a drier community of stunted cypress found primarily in southern Florida on nutrient-poor, calcium-carbonate-rich soils or shallow sand over limestone. Big Cypress National Preserve has large areas of cypress scrub in which mature cypress trees usually are less than 20 feet tall.

Palustrine emergent wetlands such as freshwater marshes and wet prairies cover 2.9 million acres of Florida (Frayer and Hefner, 1991). Freshwater marshes are concentrated in southern Florida, where about 1.6 million acres remained in 1973, including 624,000 acres of sawgrass marshes (Odum and Brown, 1977). Other major marsh systems include those in the Kissimmee and St. Johns River flood plains (Kushlan, 1990). Freshwater marshes are inundated most of the year, have thick accumulations of organic materials, and burn infrequently. Wet prairies usually are inundated for less than one-half of the year, have less organic accumulation, and burn more frequently—every 1–3 years if fuel is sufficient. Fires maintain both wetland types by limiting the invasion of woody vegetation and retarding the accumulation of organic matter (Kushlan, 1990).

Estuarine and Marine Systems.—Florida has about 1.4 million acres of estuarine and marine intertidal wetlands along 1,200 miles of coastline. About 12 percent of Florida's wetlands are estuarine, and less than 1 percent are marine. Tides cycle terrestrial sediments, nutrients, and detritus through coastal wetlands, making them highly productive ecological communities (Florida Natural Areas Inventory and Division of State Lands, 1990). The most common coastal wetlands are salt marshes, mangrove swamps, and seagrass beds.

Salt marshes are emergent wetlands that develop along low-wave-energy coastlines and in estuaries. Wave energy (fig. 2*B*), salinity, frequency of inundation, and tidal range vary along the coasts, resulting in substantial differences in the areal extent and plant-species composition of these marshes. The most extensive

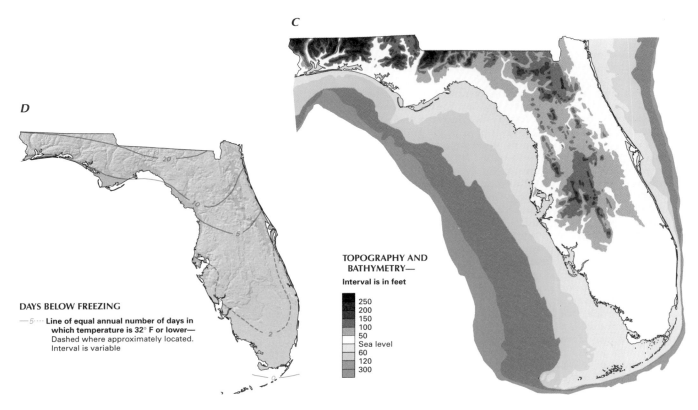

C

D

DAYS BELOW FREEZING

—5··· **Line of equal annual number of days in which temperature is 32° F or lower—** Dashed where approximately located. Interval is variable

TOPOGRAPHY AND BATHYMETRY—

Interval is in feet

250
200
150
100
50
Sea level
60
120
300

Figure 2.   Continued.   Distribution of wetlands and deepwater habitats in Florida and physical and climatological features that control wetland distribution in the State. **C**, Topography of Florida and bathymetry of adjacent offshore waters. **D**, Average annual number of days in which temperature is 32°F or lower. *(Sources: C, Fernald, 1981. D, Conway and Liston, 1990.)*

development of salt marshes occurs in the Big Bend region of the gulf coast (fig. 2A).

Mangrove swamps replace salt marshes along southern coastal areas that generally are subject to low-energy waves. Mangroves are salt-tolerant trees that colonize shallow, subtropical marine and estuarine waters. Tropical storms commonly damage or destroy mangroves before they reach their maximum height (Odum and McIvor, 1990), and most mangrove swamps are classified as scrub-shrub wetlands because the trees typically are less than 20 feet tall.

Seagrass beds are colonies of several species of rooted vascular plants that typically live totally submersed in saltwater. Most of Florida's seagrass beds are in Florida Bay at the southern tip of the State and in the Gulf of Mexico offshore from the Big Bend. In this report, only the shallowest zone of seagrass communities, in which shoal grass predominates, are considered to be wetlands; extensive seagrass beds below the intertidal zone are considered to be in deep-water habitats.

HYDROLOGIC SETTING

Many factors contribute to the abundance of wetlands in Florida, the most important of which are the low, flat terrain and plentiful rainfall. Most of the State's wetlands are in flat areas below 50 feet above sea level that extend from the coast inland for many miles (fig. 2A and 2C). Runoff and drainage in these wetlands are slow as a result of the low relief. The flat landscape and the impermeable strata underlying wetland soils commonly result in lateral flow of water on or near the land surface. Some wetlands are drained by low-gradient stream systems, as in the upper St. Johns River basin, which has extensive freshwater marshes and where the average velocity of the river is only 0.3 foot per second (Heath and Conover, 1981). Near the coast, water levels in freshwater wetlands along these streams are affected by tidal fluctuations. Close to the mouth of the streams, the transition from freshwater to saltwater causes major changes in the structure and composition of estuarine wetlands (Florida Department of Natural Resources, 1988).

Except along the southeastern coast, the land slopes gradually into the Gulf of Mexico and Atlantic Ocean. The shallow water offshore diminishes the energy of incoming waves, resulting in small, low-energy breakers onshore. Two areas on the gulf coast receive low-wave energy favorable to the development of tidal marshes, seagrass beds, and mangrove swamps (fig. 2B). The near-zero wave-energy coastline from north of Tampa to St. Marks is a result of the shallow offshore waters and a protected location in Florida's Big Bend. One of few coastal areas in the world subject to so little wave action, this part of the coast has the second-largest area of seagrass beds in the Gulf of Mexico (Zieman and Zieman, 1989), large areas of coastal marsh, and extensive hydric hammocks just landward of coastal salt marshes (Vince and others, 1989).

Rainfall in Florida averages 53 inches per year and is greatest during the warm season from June through September. Southern Florida has a subtropical climate characterized by two seasons—dry and rainy—rather than by the four seasons typical of temperate climates to the north. As a result, wetlands in southern Florida are affected by greater extremes of hydrologic conditions than those in the rest of the State. Wet prairies, wet pine flatwoods, and scrub cypress forests that are saturated or inundated in the rainy season can be severely dehydrated in the dry season in late winter and early spring when rainfall is relatively low and temperatures and evapotranspiration rates remain relatively high (Jordan, 1984).

Opposite conditions exist in northern Florida, where flooding and replenishment of water in swamps and flood plains is greatest in the late winter and early spring. Winter evapotranspiration is substantially lower than that in southern Florida because temperatures are near or below freezing on many days and much of the vegetation is dormant. Summer rainfall exceeds winter rainfall in

northern Florida, but the difference is not as great as in southern Florida because of a secondary rainfall peak in February and March. In adjacent States to the north, this secondary winter-spring peak is more pronounced and in some areas is the primary peak. Most of the drainage basins of the larger northern Florida rivers such as the Apalachicola, Choctawhatchee, Escambia, and Suwannee are in Georgia and Alabama. Therefore, rainfall patterns in those States have a significant effect on the hydrology of these rivers and their flood-plain wetlands. The broad flood plains of these rivers have topographic features and tree communities that have been shaped by wide fluctuations in river levels. During the annual flooding in late winter and early spring, water depths on the flood plain of 15–20 feet are not unusual. However, in the rest of the year, these flood plains are mostly dry except for ponds, depressions, and sloughs that retain water year round.

Southern Florida has a nearly freeze-free climate (fig. 2D). Wetlands along the southern coasts support plant species that generally do not thrive in the cooler climate of northern Florida coasts (Odum and others, 1982). For example, mangroves are killed back by freezes, which are more common in northern Florida, and some seagrass species are better adapted to the warm waters of the southern coasts. Wetlands in southern Florida commonly are invaded by nonnative tropical species that alter native-species associations; two such nonnative species, melaleuca and Brazilian pepper, have become predominant in many southern Florida wetlands. The near absence of frost in southern Florida that enables some tropical species to thrive also limits the distribution of some temperate wetland species. Pond pine, several hollies, titis, some of the tupelos, many bottom-land hardwood tree species, and several species of marsh plants grow only in the central and northern regions of the State.

Early travelers to southern Florida encountered a vast freshwater marsh that covered most of the peninsula from Lake Okeechobee south. This wetland, now known as The Everglades, covered about 2.9 million acres and was predominantly peatland covered by tall sawgrass growing in shallow water. Associated plant communities included pond apple swamps south of the lake, sloughs with aquatic vegetation, wet prairies, tree islands, and mangrove swamps bordering Florida Bay. The Everglades was part of the larger Kissimmee–Lake Okeechobee–Everglades Basin, which extended as a single drainage basin from present-day Orlando to Florida Bay, about two-thirds the length of the Florida peninsula (fig. 3A). The Kissimmee River meandered across a 2-mile-wide flood plain south to Lake Okeechobee, a shallow water body of 470,000 acres. When the lake was full, water sometimes overflowed the southern rim into The Everglades. Water in The Everglades moved slowly to the south by sheet flow in what Douglas (1947) called the River of Grass. Much of the land was inundated during the rainy season in normal years, and, during years of heavy rains, all but the highest tree islands were flooded. During floods, water moved with enough force to cause tree islands to develop an alignment pattern parallel to the lines of surface-water flow (Parker, 1974). During the dry season, ground-water levels generally were close to the land surface, but during some years, severe drought lowered water levels well below the land surface and fires swept over the land, burning vegetation and peat. Seasonally varying flows of freshwater from The Everglades into Florida Bay had an important influence on the salinity of the bay and contributed to the productivity of coastal wetlands and fisheries.

Significant drainage of The Everglades began in the early 1880's and continued through the 1960's. By the late 1920's, five canals connected Lake Okeechobee to the Atlantic Ocean. During the hurricanes of 1926 and 1928, Lake Okeechobee overflowed, killing thousands of people and destroying crops. In response to these disasters, a 38-foot-high dike was constructed around the southern shore of the lake, and canals were enlarged to increase drainage (Blake, 1980). The Central and Southern Florida Flood

Control Project of 1948 authorized construction of a complex drainage and water-management system comprising canals, levees, pumps, and control structures. Lake Okeechobee and three water-conservation areas (WCA's; fig. 3B) became reservoirs for flood protection during the wet season and for agricultural irrigation and recharge of ground water in urban wellfields during the dry season (Klein and others, 1975). Most of the 800,000 acres of the Everglades Agricultural Area was drained to grow sugar cane and other crops. About 50 percent of the original Everglades was eliminated by the early 1990's. The remaining 50 percent is preserved in WCA–1 (Loxahatchee National Wildlife Refuge), WCA–2, WCA–3, and

Everglades National Park, which was established in 1947 on 1.4 million acres at the southwestern end of the drainage basin.

Alterations of The Everglades by drainage and development have had severe environmental consequences. About 40 percent of the water that originally flowed southward from Lake Okeechobee into The Everglades is now diverted westward to the Gulf of Mexico by the Caloosahatchee Canal and eastward to the Atlantic Ocean by the St. Lucie Canal (fig. 3B). Seawater intrusion into the surficial aquifer has occurred as far as 6 miles inland in some areas (VanArman and others, 1984). Lowered water tables have resulted in oxidation of drained peat and damaging peat fires that have low-

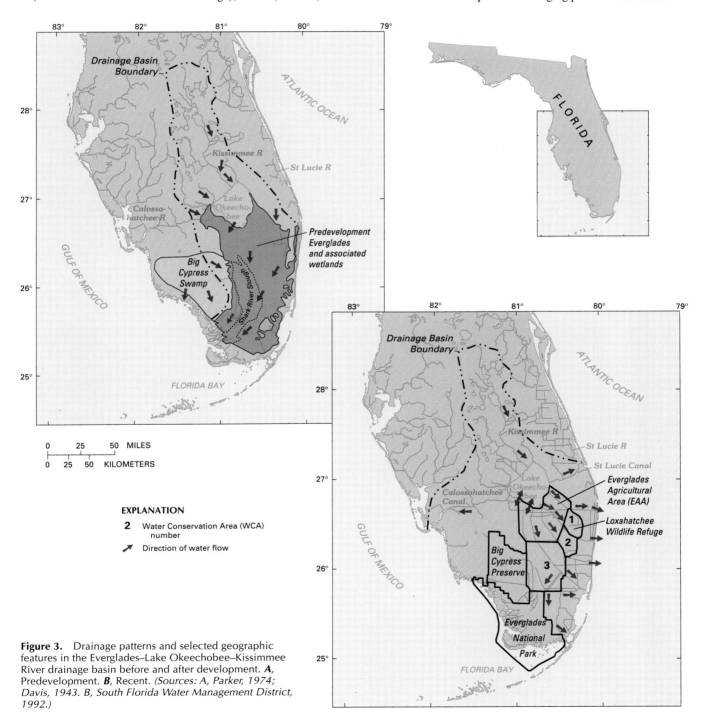

Figure 3. Drainage patterns and selected geographic features in the Everglades–Lake Okeechobee–Kissimmee River drainage basin before and after development. **A**, Predevelopment. **B**, Recent. *(Sources: A, Parker, 1974; Davis, 1943. B, South Florida Water Management District, 1992.)*

ered the land surface more than 5 feet in some agricultural areas (Davis, 1943; Duplaix, 1990). Using the WCA's as reservoirs has resulted in conditions that are often too dry or too wet to maintain natural communities (McPherson, 1973). South of Lake Okeechobee, populations of wood storks and other wading birds decreased by almost 95 percent from 1870 to 1973 as a direct result of hydrologic alterations (Crowder, 1974; Kushlan and others, 1975). Drainage and land clearing have increased opportunities for exotic plants such as melaleuca to become established in dense stands that exclude native species. Water pumped into canals from agricultural lands can have high levels of phosphorus and other nutrients. As a result, sawgrass, which is adapted to a low-nutrient environment (Davis, 1991), is being replaced by cattails in the northern Everglades, particularly in WCA–2, where nutrient loading is a problem (South Florida Water Management District, 1992).

The magnitude of environmental alterations of The Everglades has produced public concern and countermeasures to protect this significant wetland. The 570,000-acre Big Cypress National Preserve adjacent to Everglades National Park was established in 1974. The Everglades was designated a "Wetland of International Importance" by the Federal Government. State and Federal agencies working cooperatively have developed plans that call for acquisition of parts of Shark River Slough and the remaining Everglades east of Everglades National Park and reestablishment of water flows along historic flow paths. Preliminary plans also have been made to restore the once-meandering Kissimmee River, which was reduced from 90 to 52 miles in length by channelization in the 1960's. The State, as part of the settlement of a lawsuit filed by the Federal Government, has agreed to enforce a plan to greatly reduce nutrient loading from the Everglades Agricultural Area. Federal legislation has assured minimum flows to Everglades National Park, and attempts are being made to distribute water based on historic seasonal-flow models. However, as water-demand patterns in southern Florida become more complex, difficulties in providing water of the proper quantity and quality at the proper time to remaining natural areas of The Everglades will increase. Because of the extensive water-control system, water-management decisions have replaced natural events as the driving force controlling the function and evolution of The Everglades.

TRENDS

Wetlands covered more than one-half of Florida before development began (Hampson, 1984; Dahl, 1990). The Swamp Land Acts of the mid-1800's transferred 20.3 million acres of "swamp and overflowed" lands from Federal to State ownership (Shaw and Fredine, 1956), and that was the acreage assumed by the FWS National Wetlands Inventory for Florida's predevelopment (1780's) wetlands (Dahl, 1990). In 1906, the U.S. Department of Agriculture conducted the first inventory of the Nation's wetlands. The survey reported 19.8 million acres of wetlands in Florida excluding coastal lands overflowed by tidewater, indicating that wetland losses in Florida probably were minimal before the 1900's (Shaw and Fredine, 1956).

Wetland losses were greater in the early 1900's than in the period between 1930 and the mid-1950's owing to the lack of funds available for drainage projects during the Great Depression and World War II. By the mid-1950's, 15.3 million acres of wetlands remained (Shaw and Fredine, 1956). Most of the losses were due to agricultural drainage in the St. Johns River valley, on the lower east coast, in the Kissimmee River and Everglades region around Lake Okeechobee, and scattered in the west-central peninsula (Gray and others, 1924; U.S. Bureau of the Census, 1952; Blake, 1980). Between the mid-1950's and mid-1970's, wetland losses were extensive in The Everglades, where 1.5 million acres of primarily wet prairies and freshwater marshes were drained for agriculture and real estate development (Odum and Brown, 1977). Moderate drainage was conducted from the mid- to late 1950's in northern Florida to

enhance pine timber production. The rate of wetland losses for all of Florida slowed to 26,000 acres annually between the mid-1970's and mid-1980's; losses due to agriculture still were greatest, and losses to urbanization were second in importance (Frayer and Hefner, 1991).

Recent estimates of the wetland acreage remaining in Florida differ by almost 3 million acres; most of the difference is in the forested-wetland category. Wetlands delineated in figure 2A and reported by the FWS total 11 million acres (Frayer and Hefner, 1991). The Florida Game and Fresh Water Fish Commission, using 1985–89 Landsat Thematic Mapper imagery, estimated that about 8.2 million acres of wetlands remain (Kautz, 1991). Hampson (1984) estimated that about 8.3 million acres of wetlands existed in Florida in 1973. These two estimates are lower than the FWS estimate probably because they exclude most of Florida's wet pine flatwoods, one of the most common natural communities in the State. The Game and Fresh Water Fish Commission estimate also excluded some mixed-hardwood wetlands in areas where they could not be easily distinguished from upland hardwoods (J.M. Hefner, U.S. Fish and Wildlife Service, written commun., 1993).

Wetlands regulations and legislation in effect today generally allow wetlands destruction only when mitigated by wetlands enhancement, preservation, or creation. The effectiveness of these measures in slowing wetland loss is currently under evaluation (Frayer and Hefner, 1991). A recent report on the success of mitigation indicated that the ecological success rate for completed projects was low—for one-third of all permitted projects, the required mitigation had never been attempted (Florida Department of Environmental Regulation, 1991).

CONSERVATION

Many government agencies and private organizations participate in wetlands conservation in Florida. The most active agencies and organizations and some of their activities are listed in table 1.

Federal wetland activities.—Development activities in Florida wetlands are regulated by several Federal statutory prohibitions and incentives that are intended to slow wetland losses. Some of the more important of these are contained in the 1899 Rivers and Harbors Act; the 1972 Clean Water Act and amendments; the 1985 Food Security Act; the 1990 Food, Agriculture, Conservation, and Trade Act; the 1986 Emergency Wetlands Resources Act; and the 1972 Coastal Zone Management Act.

Section 10 of the Rivers and Harbors Act gives the U.S. Army Corps of Engineers (Corps) authority to regulate certain activities in navigable waters. Regulated activities include diking, deepening, filling, excavating, and placing of structures. The related section 404 of the Clean Water Act is the most often-used Federal legislation protecting wetlands. Under section 404 provisions, the Corps issues permits regulating the discharge of dredged or fill material into wetlands. Permits are subject to review and possible veto by the U.S. Environmental Protection Agency (EPA), and the FWS has review and advisory roles. Section 401 of the Clean Water Act grants to States and eligible Indian Tribes the authority to approve, apply conditions to, or deny section 404 permit applications on the basis of a proposed activity's probable effects on the water quality of a wetland.

Most farming, ranching, and silviculture activities are not subject to section 404 regulation. However, the "Swampbuster" provision of the 1985 Food Security Act and amendments in the 1990 Food, Agriculture, Conservation, and Trade Act discourage (through financial disincentives) the draining, filling, or other alteration of wetlands for agricultural use. The law allows exemptions from penalties in some cases, especially if the farmer agrees to restore the altered wetland or other wetlands that have been converted to agricultural use. The Wetlands Reserve Program of the 1990 Food, Agriculture, Conservation, and Trade Act authorizes the Federal Government to purchase conservation easements from landowners who agree to protect or restore wetlands. The Consolidated Farm

Service Agency (formerly the Agricultural Stabilization and Conservation Service) administers the Swampbuster provisions and Wetlands Reserve Program. The Natural Resources Conservation Service (formerly the Soil Conservation Service) determines compliance with Swampbuster provisions and assists farmers in the identification of wetlands and in the development of wetland protection, restoration, or creation plans.

The 1986 Emergency Wetlands Resources Act and the 1972 Coastal Zone Management Act and amendments encourage wetland protection through funding incentives. The Emergency Wetland Resources Act requires States to address wetland protection in their Statewide Comprehensive Outdoor Recreation Plans to qualify for Federal funding for State recreational land; the National Park Service provides guidance to States in developing the wetland component of their plans. Coastal States that adopt coastal-zone management programs and plans approved by the National Oceanic and Atmospheric Administration are eligible for Federal funding and technical assistance through the Coastal Zone Management Act.

State wetland activities.—The Department of Environmental Protection is the principal State agency that issues permits for development activities in wetlands. The Henderson Wetlands Act of 1984 gave the Department of Environmental Regulation (now called the Department of Environmental Protection) expanded jurisdiction over the issuance of permits for dredge-and-fill activities affecting wetlands. The Department of Environmental Protection evaluates the potential effects on wetlands before granting permits and seeks mitigation of unavoidable losses by enhancement, preservation of unaffected wetlands, or wetlands creation. Pursuant to section 305(b) of the Clean Water Act, the Department of Environmental Protection submits to the EPA and the U.S. Congress a biennial assessment of the State's surface-water quality, including that of wetlands. The Department of Environmental Protection has general oversight authority for the five water-management districts, which have authority to levy local taxes and regulatory authority over isolated wetlands within district boundaries. Authorization to use wetlands that are part of sovereign submerged lands is required from the Department of Environmental Protection. These lands, which lie under navigable waters, are held in trust for all the citizens of Florida. The Department of Environmental Protection has designated portions of these submerged lands as aquatic preserves, which are carefully managed.

Since 1963, the State of Florida has administered land-acquisition programs that have preserved many wetlands and areas adjacent to water bodies. Much of the land purchased for preservation, as well as parks and other State-owned properties, is managed by the Department of Environmental Protection; however, a substantial amount of publicly owned wetlands are managed by the water-management districts, the Game and Fresh Water Fish Commission, and the Division of Forestry. Historically, land-management programs were designed for recreation, to develop specific resources such as timber, or to favor a few important game animals or endangered species. Partly as a result of citizen input and involvement, ecosystem-management techniques such as prescribed burning are now widely used to maintain the natural character of wetlands and other ecological communities. Since the early 1970's, ecosystem maintenance as a land-management goal has gained favor in Florida as the best strategy to ensure long-term protection of plant and animal species as well as sustainable resources for people.

Regional, county, and local wetland activities.—Florida's Comprehensive Planning Act of 1985, administered by the Department of Community Affairs, requires local governments to produce long-range plans for the development and conservation of resources. Policies for wetlands protection are required elements of all plans. Some city and county governments have strong regulatory or land-acquisition programs that provide wetlands protection beyond that which is required by the State. Others, particularly in the largely rural northern part of the State, are less able to develop strong local protection programs owing to funding limitations; thus, the State and water-management districts have the largest roles in wetland protection in those areas.

Private wetland activities.—Private organizations in Florida have important roles as advocates of wetland conservation and protection. Florida has many private-interest groups that keep the public informed on wetland issues, organize citizen networks, and lobby for wetland-protection measures. The National Audubon Society, The Nature Conservancy, and the Trust for Public Lands have purchased wetlands in Florida for preservation. Some of these lands have been transferred to State or Federal ownership; others are preserved in private ownership, such as Corkscrew Swamp, an Audubon sanctuary. Other groups, such as the Florida Wildlife Federation and the Sierra Club, conduct wetland-protection activities that include programs to educate the public about wetland issues.

Table 1. Selected wetland-related activities of government agencies and private organizations in Florida, 1993

[Source: Classification of activities is generalized from information provided by agencies and organizations. •, agency or organization participates in wetland-related activity; ..., agency or organization does not participate in wetland-related activity. MAN, management; REG, regulation; R&C, restoration and creation; LAN, land acquisition; R&D, research and data collection; D&I, delineation and inventory]

Agency or organization	MAN	REG	R&C	LAN	R&D	D&I
FEDERAL						
Department of Agriculture						
Consolidated Farm Service Agency		•				
Forest Service	•		•	•	•	•
Natural Resources Conservation Service		•	•		•	•
Department of Commerce						
National Oceanic and Atmospheric Administration	•	•			•	
Department of Defense						
Army Corps of Engineers	•	•	•		•	•
Military reservations	•					
Department of the Interior						
Fish and Wildlife Service	•		•	•	•	•
Geological Survey					•	
National Biological Service					•	
National Park Service	•		•	•	•	•
Environmental Protection Agency		•			•	•
STATE						
Department of Agriculture and Consumer Services						
Division of Forestry	•					
Department of Community Affairs		•				
Department of Environmental Protection	•	•	•	•	•	•
Game and Fresh Water Fish Commission	•	•			•	•
University of Florida Center for Wetlands					•	
Other State university programs					•	
REGIONAL, COUNTY, AND LOCAL						
Water Management Districts	•	•	•	•	•	•
Regional Planning Councils		•				
Some County and City Governments	•	•	•			
PRIVATE ORGANIZATIONS						
National Audubon Society				•		
The Nature Conservancy	•			•		
Trust for Public Lands				•		

References Cited

Abrahamson, W.G., and Hartnett, D.C., 1990, Pine flatwoods and dry prairies, *in* Myers, R.L., and Ewel, J.J., eds., Ecosystems of Florida: Orlando, University of Central Florida Press, p. 103–149.

Blake, N.M., 1980, Land into water, water into land—A history of water management in Florida: Tallahassee, University Presses of Florida, 344 p.

Carlton, J.M., 1977, A survey of selected coastal vegetation communities of Florida: Florida Department of Natural Resources, Florida Marine Research Publication 30, 40 p.

Conway, McKinley, and Liston, L.L., eds., 1990, The weather handbook: Norcross, Ga., Conway Data, Inc., 548 p.

Cowardin, L.M., Carter, Virginia, Golet, F.C., and LaRoe, E.T., 1979, Classification of wetlands and deepwater habitats of the United States: U.S. Fish and Wildlife Service Report FWS/OBS –79/31, 131 p.

Crowder, J.P., 1974, Some perspectives on the status of aquatic wading birds in South Florida: U.S. Bureau of Sport Fisheries and Wildlife Report PB–231 216, 12 p.

Dahl, T.E., 1990, Wetlands—Losses in the United States, 1780's to 1980's: Washington, D.C., U.S. Fish and Wildlife Service Report to Congress, 13 p.

Davis, J.H., 1943, The natural features of southern Florida: The Florida Geological Survey Bulletin 25, 311 p.

Davis, S.M., 1991, Sawgrass and cattail nutrient flux—Leaf turnover, decomposition, and nutrient flux of sawgrass and cattail in the Everglades: Aquatic Botany, v. 40, p. 203–224.

Dierberg, F.E., and Brezonik, P.L., 1984, The effect of wastewater on the surface water and groundwater quality of cypress domes, *in* Ewel, K.C., and Odum, J.T., eds., Cypress Swamps: Gainesville, University Presses of Florida, p. 83–101.

Douglas, M.S., 1947, The Everglades—River of grass: New York, Rhinehart, 406 p.

Duplaix, Nicole, 1990, South Florida water—Paying the price: National Geographic, v. 178, no. 1, p. 89–113.

Ewel, K.C., 1990, Swamps, *in* Myers, R.L., and Ewel, J.J., eds., Ecosystems of Florida: Orlando, University of Central Florida Press, p. 281–322.

Fernald, E.A., ed., 1981, Atlas of Florida: Tallahassee, The Florida State University Foundation, Inc., 276 p.

Florida Department of Environmental Regulation, 1991, Report on the effectiveness of permitted mitigation: Tallahassee, Florida Department of Environmental Regulation, 59 p.

Florida Department of Natural Resources, 1988, Wetlands in Florida—An addendum to Florida's Comprehensive Outdoor Recreation Plan: Tallahassee, Florida Department of Natural Resources, 91 p.

Florida Natural Areas Inventory and Division of State Lands, 1990, Guide to the natural communities of Florida: Tallahassee, Florida Department of Natural Resources, 111 p.

Frayer, W.E., and Hefner, J.M., 1991, Florida wetlands—Status and trends, 1970's to 1980's: Atlanta, U.S. Fish and Wildlife Service, 31 p.

Gray, L.C., Baker, O.E., Marschner, F.J., and Weitz, B.O., 1924, The utilization of our lands for crops, pasture and forests, *in* U.S. Department of Agriculture, Agriculture yearbook—1923: Washington, D.C., U.S. Government Printing Office, 1,284 p.

Grow, Gerald, 1989, Florida parks—A guide to camping in nature (4th ed.): Tallahassee, Fla., Longleaf Publications, 260 p.

Hampson, P.S., 1984, Wetlands in Florida: Tallahassee, Florida Bureau of Geology Map Series 109, scale 1:2,000,000.

Heath, R.C., and Conover, C.S., 1981, Hydrologic almanac of Florida: U.S. Geological Survey Open-File Report 81–1107, 239 p.

Jordan, C.L., 1984, Florida's weather and climate—Implications for water, *in* Fernald, E.A., and Patton, D.J., eds., Water resources atlas of Florida: Tallahassee, Florida State University, p. 18–35.

Kautz, R.S., 1991, Space age habitat mapping: Florida Wildlife, v. 45, no. 73, p. 30–33.

Klein, Howard, Armbruster, J.T., McPherson, B.F., and Freiberger, J.J., 1975, Water and the south Florida environment: U.S. Geological Survey Water-Resources Investigations 24–75, 165 p.

Kushlan, J.A., 1990, Freshwater marshes, *in* Myers, R.L., and Ewel, J.J., Ecosystems of Florida: Orlando, University of Central Florida Press, p. 324–363.

Kushlan, J.A., Ogden, J.C., and Higer, A.L., 1975, Relation of water level and fish availability to wood stork reproduction in southern Everglades, Florida: U.S. Geological Survey Open-File Report 75–434, 56 p.

Leitman, H.M., Sohm, J.E., and Franklin, M.A., 1984, Wetland hydrology and tree distribution of the Apalachicola River flood plain, Florida: U.S. Geological Survey Water-Supply Paper 2196, 52 p.

McPherson, B.F., 1973, Vegetation in relation to water depth in Conservation Area 3, Florida: U.S. Geological Survey Open-File Report 73–0173, 60 p.

———1979, Land cover map of the Green Swamp area, Central Florida: U.S. Geological Survey Miscellaneous Investigations Series Map I–1134, scale 1:63,360.

Odum, H.T., and Brown, Mark, eds., 1977, Carrying capacity for man and nature in South Florida: Gainesville, Fla., National Park Service and University of Florida Center for Wetlands cooperative publication, 886 p.

Odum, W.E., and McIvor, C.C., 1990, Mangroves, *in* Myers, R.L., and Ewel, J.J., Ecosystems of Florida: Orlando, University of Central Florida Press, p. 517–548.

Odum, W.E., McIvor, C.C., and Smith, T.J., III, 1982, The ecology of the mangroves of South Florida—A community profile: U.S. Fish and Wildlife Service Report FWS/OBS–81/24, 144 p.

Palik, T.F., and Kunneke, J.T., 1984, Northwestern Florida ecological characterization—An ecological atlas: U.S. Fish and Wildlife Service Report FWS/OBS–82/47.1, 302 p.

Parker, G.G., 1974, Hydrology of the pre-drainage system of the Everglades in South Florida, *in* Gleason, P.J., ed., Environments of South Florida—Present and past: Miami, Fla., Miami Geological Society, Memoir 2, p. 718–727.

Shaw, S.P., and Fredine, C.G., 1956, Wetlands of the United States—Their extent and their value to waterfowl and other wildlife: U.S. Fish and Wildlife Service Circular 39, 67 p., 1 map.

South Florida Water Management District, 1992, Surface water improvement and management plan for the Everglades: West Palm Beach, South Florida Water Management District Support Information Document, 472 p.

Tiner, R.W., Jr., 1984, Wetlands of the United States—Current status and recent trends: Washington, D.C., U.S. Fish and Wildlife Service, 59 p.

U.S. Bureau of the Census, 1952, United States census of agriculture, 1950, v. 4—Drainage of agricultural lands: Washington, D.C., U.S. Government Printing Office, 307 p.

U.S. Soil Conservation Service, 1989, Twenty-six ecological communities of Florida (revised ed.): Gainesville, Florida Chapter Soil and Water Conservation Society, 286 p.

VanArman, Joel; Nealon, Dennis; Burns, Scott; Jones, Brad; Smith, Lisa; MacVicar, Thomas; Yamsura, Margaret; Federico, Anthony; Bucca, Jane; Knapp, Michael; and Gleason, Patrick, 1984, South Florida Water Management District, *in* Fernald, E.A., and Patton, D.J., eds., Water resources atlas of Florida: Tallahassee, Florida State University, p. 138–157.

Vince, S.W., Humphrey, S.R., and Simons, R.W., 1989, The ecology of hydric hammocks—A community profile: U.S. Fish and Wildlife Service Biological Report 85(7.26), 81 p.

Wharton, C.H.; Odum, H.T.; Ewel, K.C.; Duever, M.J.; Lugo, Ariel; Boyt, Rene; Bartholemew, J.; DeBellevue, E.B.; Brown, S.; Brown, M.; and Duever, L.C., 1977, Forested wetlands of Florida—Their management and use: Gainesville, University of Florida, 348 p.

Zieman, J.C., and Zieman, R.T., 1989, The ecology of the seagrass meadows of the west coast of Florida—A community profile: U.S. Fish and Wildlife Service Biological Report 85(7.25), 155 p.

FOR ADDITIONAL INFORMATION: District Chief, U.S. Geological Survey, 227 N. Bronough St., Suite 3015, Tallahassee, FL 32301; Regional Wetland Coordinator, U.S. Fish and Wildlife Service, 1875 Century Building, Suite 200, Atlanta, GA 30345

Prepared by
Melanie R. Darst, Helen M. Light, and Benjamin F. McPherson,
U.S. Geological Survey

Georgia
Wetland Resources

Georgia has more than 7.7 million acres of wetlands—about one-fifth of the surface area of the State (Hefner and others, 1994.) Most wetlands in Georgia have been adversely affected by human activities, but coastal salt marshes and a large area of preserved wilderness in the Okefenokee Swamp remain relatively undisturbed. One of the few remaining old-growth cypress-tupelo forests in the Southeast is on the lower Altamaha River flood plain (fig. 1).

Wetlands provide many economic and ecological benefits. Flood-plain wetlands dissipate the energy of floods, reduce erosion, and stabilize the streamside environment. Wetlands filter water entering rivers and coastal marsh systems, removing sediment and pollutants. Annual flooding moves leaf litter and other terrestrial organic detritus from the flood plain into the main channel, providing a primary source of food for stream and estuarine organisms. Wetlands bordering many streams in Georgia are important habitat corridors for wildlife. Amid the pine plantations and farms covering most of the uplands, wetland corridors connect areas that provide food, shelter, and water for many species of animals. During low-water periods, flood-plain ponds and backwaters contribute to biological diversity in stream ecosystems by providing still-water habitats for fish, amphibians, reptiles, and aquatic invertebrates. Biological productivity in estuarine emergent wetlands is higher than on most agricultural lands (Teal and Teal, 1969). Such coastal wetlands are essential to the life cycles of many commercially harvested species such as clams, shrimp, blue crab, and mullet (Tiner, 1984).

In addition to their ability to remove undesirable chemicals and support wildlife, wetlands are valued by tourists and Georgians for their recreational uses and natural beauty. Sidney Lanier, a native of Georgia, described a vista of coastal marshland in his poem "The Marshes of Glynn":

A league and a league of marsh-grass, waist-high,
  broad in the blade,
Green, and all of a height, and unflecked with a light
  or a shade,
Stretch leisurely off, in a pleasant plain,
To the terminal blue of the main.

TYPES AND DISTRIBUTION

Wetlands are lands transitional between terrestrial and deepwater habitats where the water table usually is at or near the land surface or the land is covered by shallow water (Cowardin and others, 1979). The distribution of wetlands and deepwater habitats in Georgia is shown in figure 2A; only wetlands are discussed herein.

Wetlands can be vegetated or nonvegetated and are classified on the basis of their hydrology, vegetation, and substrate. In this summary, wetlands are classified according to the system proposed by Cowardin and others (1979), which is used by the U.S. Fish and Wildlife Service (FWS) to map and inventory the Nation's wetlands. At the most general level of the classification system, wetlands are grouped into five ecological systems: Palustrine, Lacustrine, Riverine, Estuarine, and Marine. The Palustrine System includes only wetlands, whereas the other systems comprise wetlands and deepwater habitats. Wetlands of the systems that occur in Georgia are described below.

System	Wetland description
Palustrine	Nontidal and tidal-freshwater wetlands in which vegetation is predominantly trees (forested wetlands); shrubs (scrub-shrub wetlands); persistent or nonpersistent emergent, erect, rooted herbaceous plants (persistent- and nonpersistent-emergent wetlands); or submersed and (or) floating plants (aquatic beds). Also, intermittently to permanently flooded open-water bodies of less than 20 acres in which water is less than 6.6 feet deep.
Lacustrine	Nontidal and tidal-freshwater wetlands within an intermittently to permanently flooded lake or reservoir larger than 20 acres and (or) deeper than 6.6 feet. Vegetation, when present, is predominantly nonpersistent emergent plants (nonpersistent-emergent wetlands), or submersed and (or) floating plants (aquatic beds), or both.
Riverine	Nontidal and tidal-freshwater wetlands within a channel. Vegetation, when present, is same as in the Lacustrine System.
Estuarine	Tidal wetlands in low-wave-energy environments where the salinity of the water is greater than 0.5 part per thousand (ppt) and is variable owing to evaporation and the mixing of seawater and freshwater.
Marine	Tidal wetlands that are exposed to waves and currents of the open ocean and to water having a salinity greater than 30 ppt.

About 95 percent of Georgia's wetlands are palustrine. Estuarine and marine wetlands comprise approximately 4 percent of the State's wetland acreage. Lacustrine and riverine wetlands are not addressed in this report because they constitute a relatively small part of the State's wetlands and are generally fringe areas between palustrine wetlands and deepwater habitats.

Figure 1. Old-growth gum-cypress forest on the Altamaha River flood plain. *(Photograph by C.H. Wharton, Clayton, Ga.)*

Palustrine System.—Forested wetlands constitute about 83 percent of all palustrine wetlands in Georgia (J.M. Hefner, U.S. Fish and Wildlife Service, oral commun., 1993). Large tracts of second-growth bottom-land hardwoods and tupelo-cypress forests exist along many Georgia rivers. Most of these rivers can be characterized as either alluvial or blackwater streams.

Alluvial streams such as the Altamaha, Oconee, Ocmulgee, Savannah, Flint, and Chattahoochee Rivers carry large amounts of sediment. Their flood plains have mineral soils and diverse topographic features such as flats, ridges, backswamps, and oxbow lakes. Flats and ridges support forests of mixed bottom-land hardwood species; backswamps generally have canopies of tupelo and cypress. The alluvial river with the greatest average discharge in Georgia is the Altamaha River, which has a flood plain 3- to 5-miles wide along some reaches. The Altamaha River drainage basin includes about one-fourth of the State and extends from Atlanta to the Atlantic coast. The basin has many small streams and two large rivers, the Oconee and Ocmulgee Rivers, which join to form the Altamaha River.

Blackwater streams such as the Ogeechee, Satilla, and St. Marys Rivers generally contain water that is dark or tea colored because of a high content of tannins and other organic acids. Blackwater streams usually have low velocities and carry little sediment. Their flood plains have less topographic relief and are usually narrower than flood plains of alluvial streams. Blackwater river flood-plain wetlands have canopies of tupelo, cypress, and other tree species tolerant of wet organic soils.

Forested palustrine wetlands in Georgia that are not associated with stream systems include cypress domes, gum swamps, limesinks, Carolina bays, wet pine flatwoods, and hydric hammocks. Isolated cypress swamps and cypress domes occur primarily below the Fall Line (fig. 2B), the area of transition between the higher topographic relief of the piedmont to the north and the flatter topography of the coastal plain to the south. Cypress domes are circular depressional wetlands forested by pond cypress trees that grow taller in the center of the wetland and thus create a dome-shaped canopy. Gum swamps are depressional wetlands in which swamp

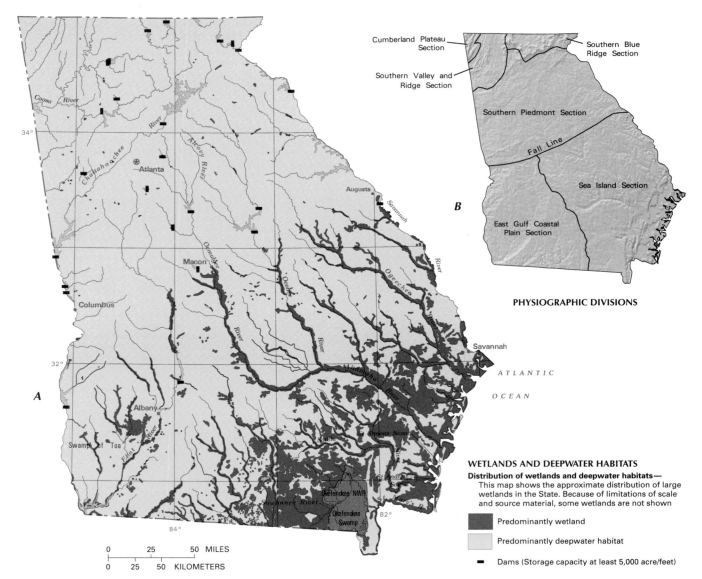

Figure 2. Wetland distribution in Georgia and physiography of the State. **A**, Distribution of wetlands and deepwater habitats. **B**, Physiography. *(Sources: A, T.E. Dahl, U.S. Fish and Wildlife Service, unpub. data, 1991. B, Physiographic divisions from Clark and Zisa, 1976; landforms data from EROS Data Center.)*

tupelo is the predominant tree. The northwestern part of the Okefenokee Swamp contains large tracts of gum swamp. Limesinks are depressional wetlands formed by the dissolution or collapse of underlying limestone. Limesinks differ widely in size, depth, and average length of time they are inundated or have saturated soils. The Swamp of Toa in southwestern Georgia is the most extensive limesink area in Georgia. Many of the limesinks are connected to ground-water aquifers and serve as recharge areas (Kalla and others, 1993). The Swamp of Toa is a mosaic of wetland and upland habitats that support rare plant and animal species such as chaffseed and blind cave salamander. Limesink depressions called sagponds are distinctive wetlands because they occur in mountainous northwestern Georgia yet contain relict populations of lowland plants (Wharton, 1977). Sagponds differ in wetness from intermittently to permanently flooded. Carolina bays, a wetland type unique to the Southeastern United States coastal plain, are oval depressions that have acidic, commonly peaty soils (Wharton, 1977). The predominant vegetation in these wetlands generally is leathery-leaved, evergreen, or semideciduous shrubs like fetterbush, titi, and zenobia. More than 1,000 Carolina bays, occupying an area of about 250,000 acres, have been mapped in Georgia (Wharton, 1977). Wet pine flatwoods forested by old-growth slash or pond pine grow mostly in southeastern Georgia and have soils that are saturated during part of the growing season. Small patches of wet pine flatwoods can be interspersed among upland pine forests. Hydric hammocks are a rare wetland type that exists in some areas of coastal Georgia. Semievergreen bottom-land hardwood species such as swamp laurel oak are the predominant vegetation (Vince and others, 1989).

Approximately 17 percent of Georgia's palustrine wetlands are nonforested (J.M. Hefner, U.S. Fish and Wildlife Service, oral commun., 1993). These nonforested wetlands are primarily fresh marshes associated with streams or isolated water bodies. In these wetlands, emergent vegetation such as giant cutgrass, wild rice, pickerelweed, and arrow arum are the predominant plants (Wharton, 1978). More than 20 percent of the Okefenokee Swamp is emergent marshes and aquatic beds. Herb bogs occur on sloping ground or in slight depressions in pine uplands (Wharton, 1978) and have abundant herbaceous plants, including orchids, insectivorous plants (such as pitcher plants), and a variety of wildflowers, but have few or no trees. The absence of a tree canopy in herb bogs might be due to the high frequency of fires and the nutrient-poor, shallow soils and underlying hardpan clays.

Estuarine and Marine Systems.—Most of Georgia's coastal wetlands are located in estuaries at the mouths of rivers. Salt marshes in which the predominant emergent plant species is smooth cordgrass are the most common estuarine wetlands (Wiegert and Freeman, 1990). Smooth cordgrass marshes are flooded daily by tides and are exposed to mostly low-energy waves. These marshes fringe the sounds that are between the mainland and offshore barrier islands. The largest area of estuarine wetlands in Georgia surrounds St. Andrews and St. Simons Sounds. This wetland has more than 110,000 acres of salt marshes (Field and others, 1991). Tidal flats are estuarine wetlands that are regularly exposed and flooded by tides. These flats generally are devoid of rooted vegetation but are important foraging areas for shorebirds. Georgia's marine wetlands comprise the intertidal zone of barrier-island ocean beaches.

HYDROLOGIC SETTING

The abundance of wetlands in Georgia is primarily due to high rainfall statewide and relatively flat topography in the southern part of the State. Annual rainfall in the State averages about 50 inches (Carter and Hopkins, 1986). The largest streams in Georgia originate in or near the mountainous northeastern part of the State, which has high precipitation and runoff. Flood-plain wetlands develop along stream borders in areas of low topographic relief, where stream

velocities are slower. Width of flood plains along rivers and the occurrence of isolated depressional wetlands between rivers increase as the land flattens toward the coast. Coastal areas have the greatest acreage of wetlands (fig. 2A).

The great diversity of Georgia wetlands is a result of the State's diverse physiography. Clark and Zisa (1976) divided Georgia into six physiographic sections (fig. 2B). Three of the sections, the Cumberland Plateau, Southern Valley and Ridge, and Southern Blue Ridge, are in northern Georgia and are the areas with the greatest topographic relief. Many of the wetlands in these sections are mountain seeps and bogs that are too small and scattered to be shown in figure 2A. Narrow wetlands border some streams. Depressional wetlands are rare, except for sagponds, which exist in some areas of the Coosa River Valley of the Southern Valley and Ridge Section and in the Cumberland Plateau Section.

The Southern Piedmont Section of Georgia lies between the more mountainous sections and the coastal plain. This section has a broad zone of gently rolling hills that are geologically similar to the Blue Ridge Mountains but have less relief as a result of stream erosion (Wharton, 1978). Flood plains are wider and better developed in the Southern Piedmont Section than in the more mountainous Southern Blue Ridge and Southern Valley and Ridge Sections to the north. Some depressional wetlands such as gum swamps exist in the Southern Piedmont Section, but cypress domes are absent.

The two physiographic sections that form the coastal plain in southern Georgia are the East Gulf Coastal Plain and Sea Island Sections (fig. 2B). These sections lie southeast of the Fall Line and include more than one-half the land area of Georgia. Topographic relief is lower, runoff is slower, and depressional features are more common in these two sections than in the Southern Piedmont Section.

Streams in the East Gulf Coastal Plain Section in southwestern Georgia trend north-south and drain into the Gulf of Mexico. Karst topography, which is created by dissolution of porous limestone near the land surface, prevails in parts of this section and is characterized by numerous limesinks and other depressional features.

The Sea Island Section contains the greatest extent of wetlands in Georgia. Flood-plain wetlands along rivers are more extensive in this section than in any other physiographic section. A schematic cross section of an alluvial flood plain in Georgia is shown in figure 3. The topographic features shown in the cross section were formed by deposition and removal of sediments by flowing water. Most areas of an active flood plain are flooded at least annually. The driest part of a flood plain is generally the natural levee adjacent to the river. Levees and flats, which drain rapidly after floods recede, are covered by canopies of bottom-land hardwoods such as live oak, water oak, sweetgum, overcup oak, water hickory, and swamp laurel oak. The wettest part of the flood plain, the backswamp, commonly is farthest from the river and adjacent to the uplands. Backswamps generally hold water after floods recede and are sometimes permanently saturated. Tupelo gum and cypress are the dominant trees because of their ability to tolerate long periods of flooding.

Rivers in the Sea Island Section flow southeastward toward the Atlantic coast, with the exception of the Suwanee River, which flows into the Gulf of Mexico. In their lower reaches, tidal freshwater swamps are flooded by a combination of tidal fluctuations and high seasonal freshwater flows. Estuaries at the river mouths are fringed by extensive marshes. Georgia's concave coastline, situated between the jutting Florida peninsula to the south and the outward-curving South Carolina coastline to the north, provides coastal wetlands in this area some protection from tropical storms. A series of large barrier islands protects estuaries from high-energy waves and provides shallowly inundated shorelines for the development of salt marshes. Tidal ranges are greater on the Georgia coast than along the other Southeastern Atlantic coastal States. This large tidal range (6–9 feet) influences both the inland extent and topography of salt marshes (Wiegert and Freeman, 1990).

The Sea Island Section also contains the largest acreages of isolated inland wetlands such as wet pine flatwoods, cypress swamps, gum swamps, and Carolina bays. Land-surface slopes are gentle in many areas within this section, and ground water is commonly near the land surface. Typically, there is a hardpan layer in the subsurface soil that prevents rapid infiltration during rainy periods, creating seasonally wet soils. During periods of little rainfall, these same areas can be very dry. Plants adapted to a wide range of moisture conditions, such as gallberry and saw palmetto, are common in these seasonally wet areas.

The Okefenokee Swamp, located in the southern part of the Sea Island Section (fig. 2B), covers approximately 440,000 acres in Georgia and is one of the largest freshwater wetlands in the United States. The swamp is a unique area containing a mosaic of emergent marshes, aquatic beds, forested and scrub-shrub wetlands, and forested uplands. The Okefenokee Swamp is located on a large terrace that once might have been a shallow marine lagoon. When sea level declined, the terrace was isolated by a sand ridge along the eastern edge. The swamp ecosystem appears to have developed in the depression within the last 7,000 years (Laerm and Freeman, 1986). The swamp has few inflowing streams and, therefore, primarily depends on rainfall for water (Rykiel, 1984). Headwaters of the Suwannee and St. Marys Rivers are in the swamp. Water depths average about 2 feet over an uneven layer of peat composed of plant material that has accumulated over thousands of years. Impermeable sediments underlying the peat keep most of the water from percolating into the ground. In severe drought, fires can burn the exposed peat, lowering the elevation of the swamp floor.

Major fires probably burn large areas of the Okefenokee Swamp every 25 to 30 years (Izlar, 1984a). When normal hydrologic conditions return, the swamp floor is again inundated, and those areas where the peat was reduced hold deeper water in which aquatic plants such as water lilies grow. If fires are suppressed, swamp-floor levels can become high enough to support other types of wetlands such as an emergent marsh vegetated by maidencane, sedges, iris, and other plants. Accumulated plant material contributes to the buildup of peat until trees like red maple can grow or until fire again reduces the amount of peat on the floor of the swamp.

The Okefenokee Swamp provides habitat for 36 species of fish, 37 species of amphibians, 66 species of reptiles, and 48 species of mammals (Laerm and others, 1984). Among the inhabitants of the swamp are rare animal and plant species such as round-tailed muskrat, sandhill crane, woodstork, and hooded pitcher plants. A reported 232 species of birds inhabit in the swamp during some part of the year; 120 of these species are permanent residents (Sanders, 1987).

The Okefenokee Swamp was preserved by its own inhospitableness for many years. In the 1890's a canal was dug through the ridge on the eastern border to drain the swamp for logging and development. Drainage was unsuccessful, but eventually about 90 percent of the marketable cypress was removed (Izlar, 1984b). Some pioneers managed to establish homesites in the swamp, but it was a place where only a few could make a living. The Okefenokee National Wildlife Refuge, created in 1937, includes approximately 85 percent of the swamp. After devastating fires in the 1950's, an earthern dam, or sill, was built on the Suwannee River to raise water levels in the swamp. This sill has affected water levels over approximately one-fourth of the swamp area. Since the installation of the sill, scientific studies have clarified the role of natural fire in rejuvenating the swamp, and wildlife managers are now considering allowing the sill to degenerate over time (Yin and Brook, 1992).

TRENDS

The FWS National Wetlands Inventory recently reported that Georgia had about 7.7 million acres of wetlands as of the 1980's (Hefner and others, 1994). This estimate was based on the results of a sampling procedure that used aerial photography. Another estimate, based on satellite imagery, classified approximately 4.3 million acres in Georgia as wetland (J.R. Bozeman, Georgia Department of Natural Resources, written commun., 1992). The largest discrepancy between these surveys was in the estimates of palustrine forested wetlands (J.M. Hefner, U.S. Fish and Wildlife Service, oral commun., 1993). The discrepancies between estimates of wetland acreages could have resulted from differences in accuracy and resolution between aerial photography and satellite imagery and in interpretive techniques used for each method (Federal Geographic Data Committee, 1992).

Because estimates of current wetland acreages in Georgia do not agree, estimates of losses are difficult to substantiate. Dahl (1990) reported wetland losses of approximately 23 percent for Georgia from the 1780's to 1980's, the lowest percentage of loss among the Southeastern States. Wetland losses throughout the Southeast have been caused primarily by drainage for farming and forestry operations (Hefner and Brown, 1985). Palustrine forested wetlands along streams and isolated swamps of the coastal plain probably have been the most affected. Between the mid-1970's and mid-1980's, more than 100,000 acres of freshwater forested wetlands in Georgia were destroyed, mostly because of conversion to land uses such as agriculture (Dahl and others, 1991). Nearly 500,000 acres of palustrine forested wetlands were converted during the same time period to scrub-shrub or emergent freshwater wetlands (Hefner and others, 1994). Loss of estuarine marshes has slowed since 1970 when Georgia began protecting those wetlands from development.

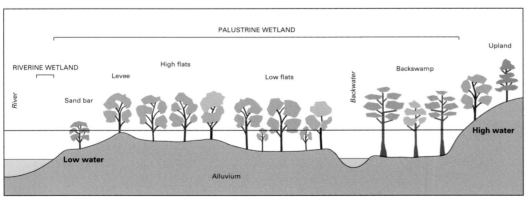

EXPLANATION

—— **High water**

—— **Low water**

Forest vegetation

Figure 3. Schematic cross section of an alluvial river flood plain in Georgia.

CONSERVATION

Many government agencies and private organizations participate in wetland conservation in Georgia. The most active agencies and organizations and some of their activities are listed in table 1.

Federal wetland activities. — Development activities in Georgia wetlands are regulated by several Federal statutory prohibitions and incentives that are intended to slow wetland losses. Some of the more important of these are contained in the 1899 Rivers and Harbors Act; the 1972 Clean Water Act and amendments; the 1985 Food Security Act; the 1990 Food, Agriculture, Conservation, and Trade Act; the 1986 Emergency Wetlands Resources Act; and the 1972 Coastal Zone Management Act.

Section 10 of the Rivers and Harbors Act gives the U.S. Army Corps of Engineers (Corps) authority to regulate certain activities in navigable waters. Regulated activities include diking, deepening, filling, excavating, and placing of structures. The related section 404 of the Clean Water Act is the most often-used Federal legislation protecting wetlands. Under section 404 provisions, the Corps issues permits regulating the discharge of dredged or fill material into wetlands. Permits are subject to review and possible veto by the U.S. Environmental Protection Agency, and the FWS has review and advisory roles. Section 401 of the Clean Water Act grants to States and eligible Indian Tribes the authority to approve, apply conditions to, or deny section 404 permit applications on the basis of a proposed activity's probable effects on the water quality of a wetland.

Most farming, ranching, and silviculture activities are not subject to section 404 regulation. However, the "Swampbuster" provision of the 1985 Food Security Act and amendments in the 1990 Food, Agriculture, Conservation, and Trade Act discourage (through financial disincentives) the draining, filling, or other alteration of wetlands for agricultural use. The law allows exemptions from penalties in some cases, especially if the farmer agrees to restore the altered wetland or other wetlands that have been converted to agricultural use. The Wetlands Reserve Program of the 1990 Food, Agriculture, Conservation, and Trade Act authorizes the Federal Government to purchase conservation easements from landowners who agree to protect or restore wetlands. The Consolidated Farm Service Agency (formerly the Agricultural Stabilization and Conservation Service) administers the Swampbuster provisions and Wetlands Reserve Program. The Natural Resources Conservation Service (formerly the Soil Conservation Service) determines compliance with Swampbuster provisions and assists farmers in the identification of wetlands and in the development of wetland protection, restoration, or creation plans.

The 1986 Emergency Wetlands Resources Act and the 1972 Coastal Zone Management Act and amendments encourage wetland protection through funding incentives. The Emergency Wetland Resources Act requires States to address wetland protection in their Statewide Comprehensive Outdoor Recreation Plans to qualify for Federal funding for State recreational land; the National Park Service provides guidance to States in developing the wetland component of their plans. Coastal States that adopt coastal-zone management programs and plans approved by the National Oceanic and Atmospheric Administration are eligible for Federal funding and technical assistance through the Coastal Zone Management Act.

State wetland activities. — The Georgia Department of Natural Resources is the principal State agency reviewing development activities in wetlands. Georgia has a coastal regulatory program and requires a State permit for development activities in coastal marshes. A similar program for regulating activities in freshwater wetlands does not exist. The Georgia Water Quality Control Act and section 401 of the Federal Clean Water Act provide indirect protection of freshwater wetlands in some instances. Under these two acts, the Environmental Protection Division of the Department of Natural Resources must certify, for both freshwater and estuarine areas, that wetland activities will not degrade water quality (Wagner and others, 1989).

In 1970, Georgia enacted the Coastal Marshlands Protection Act to protect and conserve estuarine marshlands. Since that time, permits issued by the Department of Natural Resources' Coastal Resources Division have allowed less than 600 acres of jurisdictional marshlands to be filled by nonexempt activities. Total coastal marshland losses, however, have been much higher as a result of filling for public works projects, which are exempt. For example, the estimated loss of tidal wetlands resulting from the construction of Interstate 95 through Georgia is approximately 4,000 acres (Georgia Department of Natural Resources, 1992).

Nonregulatory programs include acquisition of wetlands as part of wildlife-management areas and public fishing areas by the Department of Natural Resources' Game and Fish Division. Total wetland acreage owned by the State is estimated to exceed 57,000 acres. Wetland acquisitions are a priority of the Preservation 2000 program of 1991. Recent wetland tracts acquired with Preservation 2000 funds include approximately 7,000 acres of tidal salt marshes on two coastal barrier islands and approximately 6,000 acres of flood-plain swamp on the lower Altamaha River. Small areas of wetlands also have been enhanced, restored, or constructed by the Department of Natural Resources for mitigation, wastewater treatment, or waterfowl habitat management (Georgia Department of Natural Resources, 1992).

Table 1. Selected wetland-related activities of government agencies and private organizations in Georgia, 1993

[Source: Classification of activities is generalized from information provided by agencies and organizations. ●, agency or organization participates in wetland-related activity; ..., agency or organization does not participate in wetland-related activity. MAN, management; REG, regulation; R&C, restoration and creation; LAN, land acquisition; R&D, research and data collection; D&I, delineation and inventory]

Agency or organization	MAN	REG	R&C	LAN	R&D	D&I
FEDERAL						
Department of Agriculture						
Consolidated Farm Service Agency	...	●	...	...	...	...
Forest Service	●	...	●	●	●	●
Natural Resources Conservation Service	...	●	●	...	●	●
Department of Commerce						
National Oceanic and Atmospheric Administration	●	●	...	...	●	...
Department of Defense						
Army Corps of Engineers	●	●	●	...	●	●
Military reservations	●	...	...	...	...	...
Department of the Interior						
Fish and Wildlife Service	●	...	●	●	●	●
Geological Survey	...	...	...	...	●	...
National Biological Service	...	...	...	...	●	...
National Park Service	●	...	●	●	●	●
Environmental Protection Agency	...	●	...	...	●	●
STATE						
Department of Community Affairs	...	●	...	...	...	...
Department of Natural Resources						
Coastal Resources Division	●	●	●	...	●	●
Environmental Protection Division	...	●	●	...	...	...
Game and Fish Division	●	...	●	●	●	...
Parks, Recreation, and Historic Sites Division	●	...	●	●	...	...
Department of Transportation	...	...	●	...	...	...
Georgia Forestry Commission	●	...	●	...	...	...
REGIONAL, COUNTY, AND LOCAL						
Regional Development Centers	...	●	...	...	...	...
Some county and city governments	●	●	●	...	...	...
PRIVATE ORGANIZATIONS						
The Nature Conservancy of Georgia	●	...	...	●	●	●
Georgia Wildlife Federation	...	...	...	●	...	...
Trust for Public Lands	...	...	...	●	...	...

Regional, county, and local wetland activities.— "Growth Strategies Legislation" adopted in 1989 requires county and local governments to formulate planning and land-use control programs that include steps to protect wetlands (Georgia Department of Natural Resources, 1992). Guidelines for these county and local protection plans are being developed by the Department of Natural Resources, the Department of Community Affairs, and Regional Development Centers.

Private wetland activities.— Many private organizations in Georgia such as the Georgia Conservancy, the Sierra Club, and the National Wildlife Federation lobby for wetland-protection measures, participate in litigation involving wetland issues, and comment on State and Federal permits allowing wetland alterations. The Nature Conservancy of Georgia and the Georgia Wildlife Federation are acquiring river flood plains for preservation, primarily along the Altamaha and Alcovy Rivers, respectively.

References Cited

Carter, R.F., and Hopkins, E.H., 1986, Georgia surface-water resources, *in* U.S. Geological Survey, National water summary 1985—Hydrologic events and surface-water resources: U.S. Geological Survey Water-Supply Paper 2300, p. 195–200.

Clark, W.Z., Jr., and Zisa, A.C., 1976, Physiographic map of Georgia: Atlanta, Ga., Department of Natural Resources, scale 1:2,000,000.

Cowardin, L.M., Carter, Virginia, Golet, F.C., and LaRoe, E.T., 1979, Classification of wetlands and deepwater habitats of the United States: U.S. Fish and Wildlife Service Report FWS/OBS–79/31, 131 p.

Dahl, T.E., 1990, Wetlands—Losses in the United States, 1780's to 1980's: Washington, D.C., U.S. Fish and Wildlife Service Report to Congress, 13 p.

Dahl, T.E., Johnson, C.E., and Frazer, W.E., 1991, Wetlands—Status and trends in the conterminous United States, mid-1970's to mid-1980's: Washington, D.C., U.S. Fish and Wildlife Service Report to Congress, 22 p.

Federal Geographic Data Committee, 1992, Application of satellite data for mapping and monitoring wetlands: U.S. Geological Survey Federal Geographic Data Committee Technical Report 1, 44 p.

Field, D.W., Reyer, A.J., Genovese, P.V., and Shearer, B.D., 1991, Coastal wetlands of the United States: Washington, D.C., National Oceanic and Atmospheric Administration and U.S. Fish and Wildlife Service cooperative report, 59 p.

Georgia Department of Natural Resources, 1992, Water quality in Georgia, 1990–1991: Atlanta, Georgia Department of Natural Resources, 69 p.

Hefner, J.M., and Brown, J.D., 1985, Wetland trends in the southeastern United States: Wetlands, v. 4, p. 1–12.

Hefner, J.M., Wilen, B.O., Dahl, T.E., and Frayer, W.E., 1994, Southeast wetlands—Status and trends, mid-1970's to mid-1980's: Atlanta, Ga., U.S. Fish and Wildlife Service, 32 p.

Izlar, R.L., 1984a, Some comments on fire and climate in the Okefenokee swamp-marsh complex, *in* Cohen, A.D., Casagrande, D.J., Andrejko, M.J., and Best, G.R., eds., The Okefenokee Swamp—Its natural history, geology, and geochemistry: Los Alamos, N. Mex., Wetland Surveys, p. 70–85.

———1984b, A history of Okefenokee logging operations — A bourbon and branch water success story, *in* Cohen, A.D., Casagrande, D.J.,

Andrejko, M.J., and Best, G.R., eds., The Okefenokee Swamp—Its natural history, geology, and geochemistry: Los Alamos, N. Mex., Wetland Surveys, p. 5–17.

Kalla, P.I., Fasselt, Veronica, Rigdon, T.A., and Bowling, S.M., 1993, Advance identification of wetlands in Georgia, *in* Hatcher, K.J., ed., Proceedings of the 1993 Georgia Water Resources Conference, Athens, Ga., April 20–21, 1993: Athens, The University of Georgia, Institute of Natural Resources, p. 345–348.

Laerm, Joshua, and Freeman, B.J., 1986, Fishes of the Okefenokee Swamp: Athens, The University of Georgia Press, 118 p.

Laerm, Joshua, Freeman, B.J., Vitt, L.J., and Logan, L.E., 1984, Checklist of vertebrates of the Okefenokee Swamp, *in* Cohen, A.D., Casagrande, D.J., Andrejko, M.J., and Best, G.R., eds., The Okefenokee Swamp—Its natural history, geology, and geochemistry: Los Alamos, N. Mex., Wetland Surveys, p. 682–691.

Rykiel, E.J., Jr., 1984, General hydrology and mineral budgets for Okefenokee Swamp—Ecological significance, *in* Cohen, A.D., Casagrande, D.J., Andrejko, M.J., and Best, G.R., eds., The Okefenokee Swamp—Its natural history, geology, and geochemistry: Los Alamos, N. Mex., Wetland Surveys, p. 212–228.

Sanders, Sigrid, 1987, Studying the many faces of the Okefenokee Swamp: Athens, The University of Georgia, Research Reporter, v. 15, no. 4, p. 7–11.

Teal, John, and Teal, Mildred, 1969, Life and death of the salt marsh: New York, National Audubon Society and Ballantine Books, Inc., 274 p.

Tiner, R.W., Jr., 1984, Wetlands of the United States—Current status and recent trends: Washington, D.C., U.S. Fish and Wildlife Service, 59 p.

U.S. Fish and Wildlife Service, 1992, Regional wetlands concept plan—Emergency Wetlands Resources Act, southeast region: Atlanta, Ga., U.S. Fish and Wildlife Service, 259 p.

Vince, S.W., Humphrey, S.R., and Simons, R.W., 1989, The ecology of hydric hammocks—A community profile: U.S. Fish and Wildlife Service Biological Report 85(7.26), 81 p.

Wagner, Wendy, Carr, David, and Kellett, Katie, 1989, A citizen's guide to protecting wetlands in Georgia: Charlottesville, Va., Southern Environmental Law Center, 90 p.

Wharton, C.H., 1977, The natural environments of Georgia: Georgia Department of Natural Resources Bulletin 114, 227 p.

———1978, Physiography and biota of Georgia: BioScience, v. 28, no. 5, p. 336–339.

Wiegert, R.G., and Freeman, B.J., 1990, Tidal salt marshes of the southeast Atlantic coast—A community profile: U.S. Fish and Wildlife Service Biological Report 85(7.29), 70 p.

Yin, Zhi-Yong, and Brook, G.A., 1992, The impact of the Suwannee River sill on the surface hydrology of Okefenokee Swamp, U.S.A.: Journal of Hydrology, v. 136, no. 1–4, p. 193–217.

FOR ADDITIONAL INFORMATION: District Chief, U.S. Geological Survey, Peachtree Business Center, Suite 130, 3089 Amwiler Road, Atlanta, GA 30360; Regional Wetland Coordinator, U.S. Fish and Wildlife Service, 1875 Century Building, Suite 200, Atlanta, GA 30345

Prepared by
Melanie R. Darst and Helen M. Light,
U.S. Geological Survey

Hawaii
Wetland Resources

Wetlands constitute less than 3 percent of the State of Hawaii but have had a major economic effect on the development of Hawaiian society both before and after European contact. Native Hawaiian communities depended on wetlands for cultivation of taro and other staple food crops and for coastal fisheries. After the arrival of European and Asian immigrants, wetlands were used for rice and watercress cultivation. These agricultural uses of wetlands continue to the present, although their economic importance has declined because of demographic shifts and increased importation of food.

Wetlands provide important waterfowl and shorebird habitat. Endemic and endangered species that rely on Hawaiian wetlands include the Hawaiian stilt, Hawaiian coot, Hawaiian gallinule, and Hawaiian duck (Hawaii Department of Land and Natural Resources, 1988). Wetlands also are used by migratory shorebirds such as the Pacific golden plover and waterfowl such as the pintail duck (Hawaii Department of Land and Natural Resources, 1988). Some endemic Hawaiian plants are found only in wetlands (Vogl and Henrickson, 1971; Elliot, 1981).

In recent years, recreational, educational, and scientific uses of wetlands have increased. The Waimanu Valley on the island of Hawaii (figs. 1 and 2A) is managed as a part of the National Estuarine Research Reserve system for such purposes.

Wetlands can improve water quality (Hemond and Benoit, 1988) and reduce flooding (Carter, 1986). Wetlands in Pearl Harbor are being considered for use as sediment traps by the U.S. Navy (Stephanie Aschmann, U.S. Navy, oral commun., 1992). The Kawainui Marsh is an example of a wetland managed for flood protection.

TYPES AND DISTRIBUTION

Wetlands are lands transitional between terrestrial and deepwater habitats where the water table usually is at or near the land surface or the land is covered by shallow water (Cowardin and others, 1979). The distribution of wetlands and deepwater habitats in Hawaii is shown in figure 2A; only wetlands are discussed herein.

Wetlands can be vegetated or nonvegetated and are classified on the basis of their hydrology, vegetation, and substrate. In this summary, wetlands are classified according to the system proposed by Cowardin and others (1979), which is used by the U.S. Fish and Wildlife Service (FWS) to map and inventory the Nation's wetlands. At the most general level of the classification system, wetlands are grouped into five ecological systems: Palustrine, Lacustrine, Riverine, Estuarine, and Marine. The Palustrine System includes only wetlands, whereas the other systems comprise wetlands and deepwater habitats. Wetlands of the systems that occur in Hawaii are described below.

System	Wetland description
Palustrine	Nontidal and tidal-freshwater wetlands in which vegetation is predominantly trees (forested wetlands); shrubs (scrub-shrub wetlands); persistent or nonpersistent emergent, erect, rooted herbaceous plants (persistent- and nonpersistent-emergent wetlands); or submersed and (or) floating plants (aquatic beds). Also, intermittently to permanently flooded open-water bodies of less than 20 acres in which water is less than 6.6 feet deep.
Lacustrine	Nontidal and tidal-freshwater wetlands within an intermittently to permanently flooded lake or reservoir larger than 20 acres and (or) deeper than 6.6 feet. Vegetation, when present, is predominantly nonpersistent emergent plants (nonpersistent-emergent wetlands), or submersed and (or) floating plants (aquatic beds), or both.
Riverine	Nontidal and tidal-freshwater wetlands within a channel. Vegetation, when present, is same as in the Lacustrine System.
Estuarine	Tidal wetlands in low-wave-energy environments where the salinity of the water is greater than 0.5 part per thousand (ppt) and is variable owing to evaporation and the mixing of seawater and freshwater.
Marine	Tidal wetlands that are exposed to waves and currents of the open ocean and to water having a salinity greater than 30 ppt.

On the basis of mapping by the FWS National Wetland Inventory, wetland area in Hawaii has been estimated to be 110,810 acres (Hawaii Department of Land and Natural Resources, 1988). The estimate includes areas of mixed wetlands and upland rain forest (Dennis Peters, U.S. Fish and Wildlife Service, written commun., 1993). Almost 90 percent of the wetland area is palustrine wetlands (Hawaii Department of Land and Natural Resources, 1988). The FWS survey did not include marine wetlands, which are small and are not considered in this report. About 70 percent of Hawaiian wetlands are 5 acres or less, 20 percent are between 5 and 25 acres, and the remaining 10 percent are larger than 25 acres (Hawaii Department of Land and Natural Resources, 1988).

Figure 1. Estuarine wetland in Waimanu Valley on the island of Hawaii. *(Photograph by B.R. Hill, U.S. Geological Survey.)*

Palustrine wetlands.—The largest wetlands in the State are palustrine wetlands on the windward (northeastern) mountain slopes on the islands of Kauai, Maui, and Hawaii. These are primarily emergent and scrub-shrub wetlands and are known locally as bogs. Palustrine emergent wetlands also are present upstream from some coastal, estuarine wetlands.

Lacustrine wetlands.—Only a few lacustrine wetlands exist in the Hawaiian Islands. Lake Waiau is a small natural lake near the summit of Mauna Kea on the island of Hawaii. A number of small lakes occupy topographic depressions on Niihau. Several reservoirs are located on Kauai, Oahu, Molokai, and Maui.

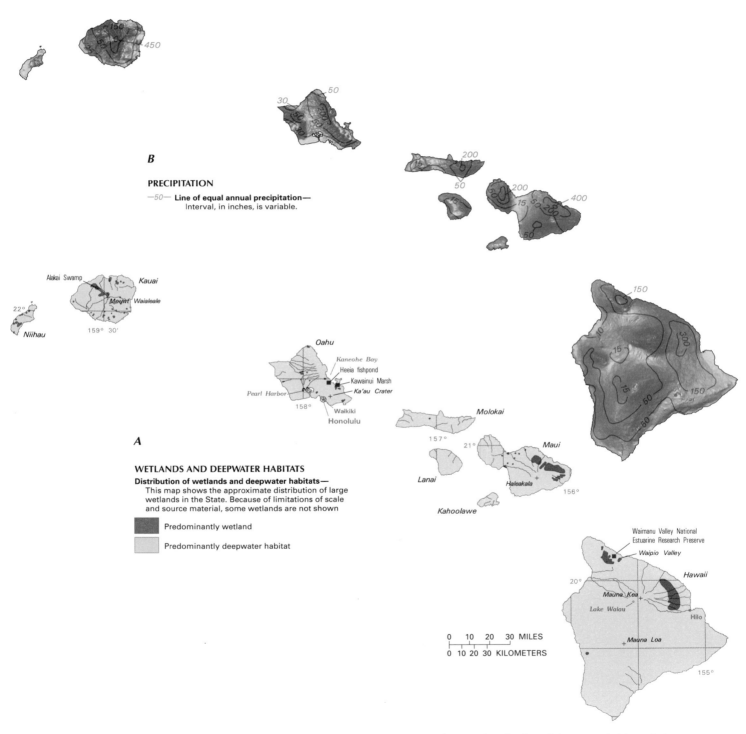

B

PRECIPITATION

—50— **Line of equal annual precipitation—**
Interval, in inches, is variable.

A

WETLANDS AND DEEPWATER HABITATS

Distribution of wetlands and deepwater habitats—
This map shows the approximate distribution of large wetlands in the State. Because of limitations of scale and source material, some wetlands are not shown

Predominantly wetland

Predominantly deepwater habitat

Figure 2. Wetland distribution and average annual precipitation in Hawaii. **A**, Distribution of wetlands and deepwater habitats. **B**, Average annual precipitation. (*Sources: A, T.E. Dahl, U.S. Fish and Wildlife Service, unpub. data, 1991. B, Lee and Valenciano, 1986.*)

Riverine wetlands.—Riverine wetlands in the State are in all four subsystems of the FWS classification: Tidal, Lower Perennial, Upper Perennial, and Intermittent. A total of 376 perennial streams and more than 100 intermittent streams were identified in Hawaii in a recent survey by the Hawaii Cooperative Park Service Unit (1990).

Estuarine wetlands.—Estuarine emergent wetlands are present at the mouths of many rivers, usually along the wet, windward shores of the major islands. Forested estuarine wetlands also have formed because of the introduction of mangrove in some coastal areas on Oahu and Molokai.

Anchialine pools are a unique type of estuarine wetland. These pools form in collapsed lava tubes and have a subsurface connection to the ocean. Therefore, the pools are affected by tidal action, although they are rarely, if ever, inundated by seawater. These wetlands pools average about 1 acre in area (Hawaii Department of Land and Natural Resources, 1988) and support populations of endemic shrimp. Anchialine pools were not included in the FWS National Wetlands Inventory maps; the Hawaii Department of Land and Natural Resources (1988) estimated that the pools have a total area of about 700 acres.

Fishponds constructed by native Hawaiians along the shores of the islands are another type of estuarine wetland. The ponds are formed by walls built of stone. Although artificial, these ponds are economically and culturally important and support several plant and animal species (Hawaii Department of Land and Natural Resources, 1988). Heeia fishpond on Oahu is an example of one such pond that is now preserved because of its cultural importance.

HYDROLOGIC SETTING

Hydrologic conditions on the Hawaiian islands are largely determined by climate and topography. When moisture-laden air masses moving with the trade winds reach the volcanic mountains that form the islands, the air masses are forced up the slopes, where they cool in the higher altitudes and release their moisture. Because of this climatic phenomenon, known as the orographic effect, rainfall is more plentiful on the windward sides of the islands (fig. 2*B*) (Blumenstock and Price, 1961). On the highest mountains (Haleakala on Maui, maximum altitude of 10,021 feet; Mauna Kea and Mauna Loa on Hawaii, maximum altitudes of 13,796 and 13,078 feet, respectively), the trade winds move around the peaks, and the

maximum rainfall is at altitudes of 2,000 to 4,000 feet; on the lower mountain ranges, the trade winds move over the mountains, and the rainfall maximums are at or near the crests (Blumenstock and Price, 1961). Rainfall gradients on the larger islands are high; average annual totals can range from greater than 200 inches to as little as 10 inches within 10 miles (fig. 2*B*). Geographically, evaporation is inversely proportional to rainfall and is less variable; the maximum annual pan-evaporation rate is about 106 inches, and the minimum is about 17 inches (Hawaii Department of Land and Natural Resources, 1973). Runoff averages about 40 percent of rainfall (Takasaki, 1978). Ground water on each island occurs primarily as a basal lens of freshwater floating on denser saltwater (fig. 3) (Valenciano, 1985). These floating freshwater lenses are known in Hawaii as basal ground water. The upper extent of a lens, the basal water table, is generally less than 100 feet above sea level (Takasaki, 1978; Valenciano, 1985).

Despite large amounts of rainfall in some areas, wetlands are not extensive in the Hawaiian islands because of the generally steep topography and the high permeability of bedrock (Elliot, 1981). Most water falling as rain travels rapidly to the ocean as surface-water and ground-water flow (Takasaki, 1978). Wetlands form only where local hydrologic conditions favor retention of water near the land surface (fig. 3).

Water is more likely to accumulate where precipitation is high and evaporation is low. In Hawaii, extensive bogs are confined to areas where rainfall exceeds 150 inches annually (fig. 2*A* and 2*B*). These areas are at altitudes between 1,500 and 5,000 feet on windward slopes. On the basis of limited pan-evaporation data, evaporation in these areas ranges from 50 to 95 inches annually (Hawaii Department of Land and Natural Resources, 1973).

Wetlands commonly form only where the water table intersects the land surface. Topography and water-table configuration determine the extent of areas where the land surface and water table intersect. Most of the land surface of the islands is many hundreds of feet above the basal water table. Therefore, basal ground water supports only a narrow zone of estuarine and palustrine wetlands near the shore, where the water table and the land surface intersect (fig. 3).

Many of Hawaii's estuarine wetlands have developed over geologic time as a result of gradual subsidence of the islands and the resulting rise in sea level relative to the land surface (Macdonald and others, 1970). The relative rise in sea level reduced the gradi-

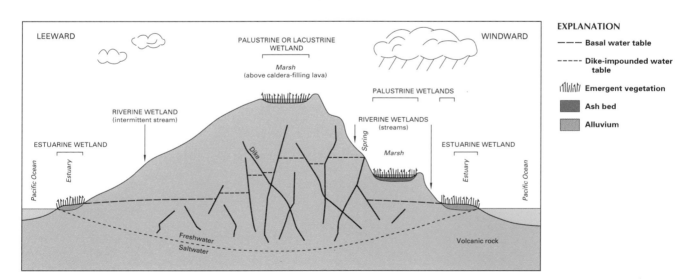

Figure 3. Generalized cross section of a Hawaiian island showing hydrologic and geologic features that affect wetland distribution. *(Source: Modified from Takasaki, 1978.)*

ent of streams entering the ocean. Sediments carried by the streams were deposited near the stream mouths, and the accumulated deposits were colonized by wetland vegetation. Wetlands in Pearl Harbor on Oahu and in Waimanu and Waipio Valleys on the island of Hawaii are examples of this process.

Topography affects the retention of surface runoff during rainstorms. On the steep, highly eroded slopes of Oahu, runoff is rapid; water does not accumulate at the land surface, and wetlands are rare (fig. 2A). On the younger islands of Maui and Hawaii, stream erosion has not progressed to the same extent as on Oahu, and much of the gently sloping surface of the original volcanic domes is still intact. On Kauai, caldera filling has resulted in nearly flat areas near

Table 1. Selected wetland-related activities of government agencies and private organizations in Hawaii, 1993

[Source: Classification of activities is generalized from information provided by agencies and organizations. ●, agency or organization participates in wetland-related activity; ..., agency or organization does not participate in wetland-related activity. MAN, management; REG, regulation; R&C, restoration and creation; LAN, land acquisition; R&D, research and data collection; D&I, delineation and inventory]

Agency or organization	MAN	REG	R&C	LAN	R&D	D&I
FEDERAL						
Department of Agriculture						
Consolidated Farm Service Agency	...	●	...	...	...	...
Forest Service	...	...	●	...	●	...
Natural Resources Conservation Service	...	...	●	●	...	●
Department of Commerce						
National Oceanic and Atmospheric Administration	●	●	...	...	●	...
Department of Defense						
Army Corps of Engineers	●	●	●	...	●	●
Marine Corps	●	...	...	...	...	...
Navy	●	...	●	...	●	...
Department of the Interior						
Fish and Wildlife Service	●	...	●	●	...	●
Geological Survey	...	...	...	...	●	...
National Biological Survey	...	...	...	...	●	...
National Park Service	●	...	●	●	●	...
Environmental Protection Agency	...	●	...	...	...	...
STATE						
Department of Health						
Office of Environmental Quality Control	...	●	...	...	...	...
Department of Land and Natural Resources						
Commission on Water Resource Management	...	●	...	...	...	...
Division of Forestry and Wildlife	●	●	●	●	●	●
Division of Water and Land Development	...	●	...	...	●	...
Division of Land Management	...	...	...	●	...	...
Office of Conservation and Environmental Affairs	...	●	...	...	...	...
Office of State Planning						
Coastal Zone Management Program	●	...	...	...	...	...
University of Hawaii						
Environmental Center	...	...	...	...	●	...
Water Resources Research Center	...	...	...	...	●	...
COUNTY						
City and County of Honolulu						
Department of Land Utilization	...	●	...	...	...	...
County of Hawaii						
Planning Department	...	●	...	...	...	...
County of Kauai						
Planning Department	...	●	...	...	...	...
County of Maui						
Planning Department	...	●	...	...	...	...
PRIVATE ORGANIZATIONS						
Ducks Unlimited	...	...	...	●	...	...
Hawaii Audubon Society	●	...	...	...	...	...
National Audubon Society	...	...	●	...	●	...
Native Hawaiian Plant Society	...	...	...	...	●	...
Outdoor Circle	...	...	...	...	●	●
The Nature Conservancy	●	...	●	●	●	...

the summit of Mount Waialeale. The extensive bogs on Kauai, Maui, and Hawaii occupy gently sloping mountainsides where rainfall is retained at the land surface (Fosberg, 1961, p. 21; van't Woudt and Nelson, 1963 p. 23; Vogl and Henrickson, 1971, p. 479).

Geologic heterogeneities, including andesitic lava flows, volcanic dikes, ash beds, soils, and alluvium, can restrict infiltration of rainfall, resulting in surface saturation. The extensive bogs on the islands of Kauai, Maui, and Hawaii have formed on soils, ash layers, or andesitic lava less permeable than the underlying basaltic lava (Stearns and Macdonald, 1942, 1946; Macdonald and others, 1960).

Low-permeability clay layers underlie many bogs in Hawaii. These clays result from weathering of bedrock in high-rainfall areas that have abundant plant remains on the forest floor. The organic acids derived from decaying plants cause rapid chemical weathering of bedrock. Although the characteristic clay layers have been considered a factor in bog development (Skottsberg, 1940; Fosberg, 1961; van't Woudt and Nelson, 1963; Vogl and Henrickson, 1971), the clay might actually be a result rather than a cause of impeded drainage (Wentworth and others, 1940).

Not much is known concerning the hydrologic functions of Hawaiian wetlands. Coastal wetlands are generally in ground-water discharge zones, and upland bogs are generally in ground-water recharge zones, but the importance of wetlands in controlling rates of ground-water movement is not known. A study of the Alakai Swamp on Kauai indicated that recharge from the swamp to the basal aquifer was not significant (van't Woudt and Nelson, 1963). Storage of surface runoff in bog peat (partially decomposed plant material) might supply streamflow following rains (Skottsberg, 1940; van't Woudt and Nelson, 1963). The bog in the Ka'au Crater on Oahu was formerly used as a water-supply reservoir (Elliot, 1981). When bog peat is completely saturated, bogs can act as sources of overland flow during rainstorms and might increase runoff (van't Woudt and Nelson, 1963). Coastal wetlands can reduce flooding because of their capacity to store surface runoff.

TRENDS

The Hawaii Department of Land and Natural Resources (1988) estimated that total wetland acreage in Hawaii before European contact in 1778 was 110,000 acres. Wetland area was about 114,000 acres in 1900 because of increased wetland agriculture as rice production became important. Since then, wetland agricultural acreage has declined by about 10,000 acres to a remnant of 420 acres used for taro and watercress production.

According to a recent FWS report (Dahl, 1990), Hawaii has lost about 7,000 acres of wetlands since the 1780's. These losses were in coastal estuarine and palustrine wetlands at altitudes less than 1,000 feet (Andy Yuen, U.S. Fish and Wildlife Service, written commun., 1992). Estimates of predevelopment wetland area (58,800 acres) and recent wetland area (51,800 acres) used by Dahl (1990) to compute losses are lower than those reported by the Department of Land and Natural Resources (1988) because Dahl's (1990) estimates do not include some areas of mixed wetland and rain forest at altitudes greater than 1,000 feet that were included in the Department's estimates (Andy Yuen, U.S. Fish and Wildlife Service, written commun., 1992). On the basis of the Department's estimates of 110,000 original wetland acres and Dahl's (1990) estimate of 7,000 acres lost, Hawaii has lost about 6 percent of its original wetlands.

Coastal wetland losses have been greatest on Oahu, where most of the population of the State resides. Maps and aerial photographs of the Honolulu area before 1940 show many agricultural and coastal wetlands that no longer exist. Much of the resort area of Waikiki was wetland before the dredging of the Ala Wai Canal. Many other wetlands have been partly or completely filled for industrial and residential developments. The FWS has estimated that 58 percent of wetlands in the Kaneohe Bay area were lost between 1927 and 1978 (Andy Yuen, U.S. Fish and Wildlife Service, written commun., 1992).

The most extensive wetlands in the State are in remote mountainous areas removed from agricultural and urban areas (fig. 2A). These wetlands are not presently threatened by human activities but are being degraded by trampling and rooting by feral animals, particularly pigs, and by the introduction of exotic plants (Elliot, 1981).

CONSERVATION

Many government agencies and private organizations participate in wetland conservation in Hawaii. The most active agencies and organizations and some of their activities are listed in table 1.

Federal wetland activities.—Development activities in Hawaii wetlands are regulated by several Federal statutory prohibitions and incentives that are intended to slow wetland losses. Some of the more important of these are contained in the 1899 Rivers and Harbors Act; the 1972 Clean Water Act and amendments; the 1985 Food Security Act; the 1990 Food, Agriculture, Conservation, and Trade Act; the 1986 Emergency Wetlands Resources Act; and the 1972 Coastal Zone Management Act.

Section 10 of the Rivers and Harbors Act gives the U.S. Army Corps of Engineers (Corps) authority to regulate certain activities in navigable waters. Regulated activities include diking, deepening, filling, excavating, and placing of structures. The related section 404 of the Clean Water Act is the most often-used Federal legislation protecting wetlands. Under section 404 provisions, the Corps issues permits regulating the discharge of dredged or fill material into wetlands. Permits are subject to review and possible veto by the U.S. Environmental Protection Agency, and the FWS has review and advisory roles. Section 401 of the Clean Water Act grants to States and eligible Indian Tribes the authority to approve, apply conditions to, or deny section 404 permit applications on the basis of a proposed activity's probable effects on the water quality of a wetland.

Most farming, ranching, and silviculture activities are not subject to section 404 regulation. However, the "Swampbuster" provision of the 1985 Food Security Act and amendments in the 1990 Food, Agriculture, Conservation, and Trade Act discourage (through financial disincentives) the draining, filling, or other alteration of wetlands for agricultural use. The law allows exemptions from penalties in some cases, especially if the farmer agrees to restore the altered wetland or other wetlands that have been converted to agricultural use. The Wetlands Reserve Program of the 1990 Food, Agriculture, Conservation, and Trade Act authorizes the Federal Government to purchase conservation easements from landowners who agree to protect or restore wetlands. The Consolidated Farm Service Agency (formerly the Agricultural Stabilization and Conservation Service) administers the Swampbuster provisions and Wetlands Reserve Program. The Natural Resources Conservation Service (formerly the Soil Conservation Service) determines compliance with Swampbuster provisions and assists farmers in the identification of wetlands and in the development of wetland protection, restoration, or creation plans.

The 1986 Emergency Wetlands Resources Act and the 1972 Coastal Zone Management Act and amendments encourage wetland protection through funding incentives. The Emergency Wetland Resources Act requires States to address wetland protection in their Statewide Comprehensive Outdoor Recreation Plans to qualify for Federal funding for State recreational land; the National Park Service (NPS) provides guidance to States in developing the wetland component of their plans. Coastal States that adopt coastal-zone management programs and plans approved by the National Oceanic and Atmospheric Administration are eligible for Federal funding and technical assistance through the Coastal Zone Management Act.

Several Federal agencies manage wetlands as wildlife refuges and other conservation areas. The FWS manages about 1,400 acres of refuge lands in Hawaii. The U.S. Navy and Marine Corps also manage wetland refuges. Other wetlands are managed by the NPS.

State wetland activities.—Hawaii has no laws specifically relating to wetland protection, but chapter 205A of the Hawaii Revised Statutes provides for regulation of coastal areas, including wetlands, in conjunction with the Federal Coastal Zone Management Act and Clean Water Act. Under the provisions of these and other laws, several State and county agencies regulate the use of wetlands in Hawaii (table 1). The Office of State Planning's Coastal Zone Management Program provides wetlands policy guidance. Policy is enforced through regulation by the county planning departments, which have permitting authority for designated Special Management Areas. These areas generally are within 300 feet of the shoreline but can extend much farther inland. The Office of Conservation and Environmental Affairs of the Department of Land and Natural Resources has permitting authority for all designated conservation lands, which can include upland as well as coastal wetlands. The Department of Health and the Coastal Zone Management Program make determinations of consistency with Federal laws for permits issued by the Corps. The Commission on Water Resource Management, a part of the Department of Land and Natural Resources, has authority to regulate channel alterations and enforce instream-flow standards. The Office of Hawaiian Affairs acts as an advocate for native Hawaiian concerns relating to wetlands. An effort to review State wetland policies is under way; this effort is being coordinated by the Office of Environmental Quality Control in the Department of Health.

The Division of Forestry and Wildlife of the Department of Land and Natural Resources is the principal State wetland-management agency. The Division manages wildlife refuges and other wetlands. The wetlands in Waimanu Valley on the island of Hawaii are included in the Waimanu National Estuarine Research Reserve, which is administered by the Department of Land and Natural Resources in cooperation with the National Oceanic and Atmospheric Administration. Hydrologic data are collected in this reserve by the U.S. Geological Survey in cooperation with the Department.

Private wetland activities.—Several private organizations engage in wetland activities (table 1) in Hawaii. The Nature Conservancy manages wetlands within its preserve system. Other groups, including the National and Hawaii Audubon Societies and Ducks Unlimited, are involved in efforts to acquire wetlands for conservation purposes. In addition, many other organizations take advocacy roles before government agencies in matters concerning wetlands. These include the Native Hawaiian Legal Corporation, the Sierra Club Legal Defense Fund, the Kawainui Heritage Foundation, and the National and Hawaii Audubon Societies.

References Cited

Blumenstock, D.I., and Price, Saul, 1961, Climates of the States—Hawaii: U.S. Department of Commerce, Environmental Science Services Administration, climatography of the States 60–51, 27 p.

Carter, Virginia, 1986, An overview of the hydrologic concerns related to wetlands in the United States: Canadian Journal of Botany, v. 64, p. 364–374.

Cowardin, L.M., Carter, Virginia, Golet, F.C., and LaRoe, E.T., 1979, Classification of wetlands and deepwater habitats of the United States: U.S. Fish and Wildlife Service Report FWS/OBS–79/31, 131 p.

Dahl, T.E., 1990, Wetlands—Losses in the United States, 1780's to 1980's: Washington, D.C., U.S. Fish and Wildlife Service Report to Congress, 13 p.

Elliot, M.E., 1981, Wetlands and wetland vegetation of the Hawaiian Islands: Honolulu, University of Hawaii, M.A. thesis, 228 p.

Fosberg, F.R., 1961, Guide to excursion III: Honolulu, Tenth Pacific Science Congress and University of Hawaii, 207 p.

Hawaii Cooperative Park Service Unit, National Park Service, 1990, A preliminary appraisal of Hawaii's stream resources: National Park Service Report R84, 294 p.

Hawaii Department of Land and Natural Resources, 1973, Pan evaporation in Hawaii 1894–1970: Hawaii Department of Land and Natural Resources Report R51, 82 p.

———1988, State recreation functional plan technical reference document and State comprehensive outdoor recreation plan, wetlands resources plan addendum: Honolulu, Hawaii, Department of Land and Natural Resources, variously paged.

Hemond, H.F., and Benoit, Janina, 1988, Cumulative impacts on water quality functions of wetlands: Environmental Management, v. 12, no. 5, p. 636–653.

Lee, Reuben, and Valenciano, Santos, 1986, Hawaii surface-water resources, *in* U.S. Geological Survey, National water summary 1985—Hydrologic events and surface-water resources: U.S. Geological Survey Water-Supply Paper 2300, p. 201–206.

Macdonald, G.A., Abbott, A.T., and Peterson, F.L., 1970, Volcanoes in the sea—The geology of Hawaii: Honolulu, University of Hawaii Press, 517 p.

Macdonald, G.A., Davis, D.A., and Cox, D.C., 1960, Geology and ground-water resources of the island of Kauai, Hawaii: Hawaii Division of Hydrography Bulletin 13, 212 p.

Skottsberg, Carl, 1940, Report on Hawaiian bogs—Proceedings of the Sixth Pacific Science Congress, July 24–August 12, 1939, Berkeley, Stanford, and San Francisco: Berkeley, University of California Press, v. 4, p. 659–661.

Stearns, H.T., and Macdonald, G.A., 1942, Geology and ground-water resources of the island of Maui, Hawaii: Territory of Hawaii Division of Hydrography Bulletin 7, 344 p.

———1946, Geology and ground-water resources of the island of Hawaii: Territory of Hawaii Division of Hydrography Bulletin 9, 363 p.

Takasaki, K.J., 1978, Summary appraisals of the nation's ground-water resources—Hawaii region: U.S. Geological Survey Professional Paper 813–M, 29 p.

Valenciano, Santos, 1985, Hawaii ground-water resources, *in* U.S. Geological Survey, National water summary 1984—Hydrologic events, selected water-quality trends, and ground-water resources: U.S. Geological Survey Water-Supply Paper 2275, p. 185–191.

van't Woudt, B.D., and Nelson, R.E., 1963, Hydrology of the Alakai Swamp, Kauai, Hawaii: Hawaii Agricultural Experiment Station Bulletin 132, 30 p.

Vogl, R.J., and Henrickson, James, 1971, Vegetation of an alpine bog on East Maui, Hawaii: Pacific Science, v. 25, p. 475–483.

Wentworth, C.K., Wells, R.C., and Allen, V.T., 1940, Ceramic clay in Hawaii: The American Mineralogist, v. 25, no. 1, p. 2–33.

FOR ADDITIONAL INFORMATION: District Chief, U.S. Geological Survey, 677 Ala Moana Boulevard, Suite 415, Honolulu, HI 96813; Regional Wetland Coordinator, U.S. Fish and Wildlife Service, 911 NE 11th Avenue, Portland, OR 97232

Prepared by
B.R. Hill,
U.S. Geological Survey

Idaho
Wetland Resources

Although Idaho's wetlands account for less than 1 percent of the State's area, its many small and isolated wetlands are essential to the functioning of diverse ecosystems in deserts, plains, and mountains (fig. 1). Wetlands provide vital habitat for waterfowl, migratory birds, fish, and other wildlife. More than 75 percent of Idaho's wildlife depend on wetlands during some part of their life cycle (Idaho Department of Fish and Game, 1990). Wetlands enhance the water quality of lakes and streams by removing nutrients and pollutants from influent water. During floods, wetlands store floodwater temporarily, slow water velocities, and reduce bank erosion.

Cities, small communities, and farms commonly were settled next to or near riparian (streamside) wetlands because of the availability of water and shade. Wetland vegetation generally is more lush and productive than that in uplands; livestock benefit from shade and forage provided by healthy wetlands. Idaho's development was enhanced by extracting large quantities of gold and other metals from streambeds and riparian zones along streams. Idaho's wetlands benefit an increasing population and a large tourism industry by providing unique scenery and recreational opportunities.

TYPES AND DISTRIBUTION

Wetlands are lands transitional between terrestrial and deepwater habitats where the water table usually is at or near the land surface or the land is covered by shallow water (Cowardin and others, 1979). The distribution of wetlands and deepwater habitats in Idaho is shown in figure 2A; only wetlands are discussed herein.

Wetlands can be vegetated or nonvegetated and are classified on the basis of their hydrology, vegetation, and substrate. In this summary, wetlands are classified according to the system proposed by Cowardin and others (1979), which is used by the U.S. Fish and Wildlife Service (FWS) to map and inventory the Nation's wetlands. At the most general level of the classification system, wetlands are grouped into five ecological systems: Palustrine, Lacustrine, Riverine, Estuarine, and Marine. The Palustrine System includes only wetlands, whereas the other systems comprise wetlands and deepwater habitats. Wetlands of the systems that occur in Idaho are described below.

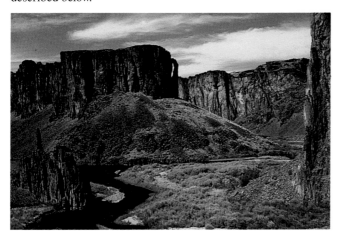

Figure 1. The Tules, a wetland in an abandoned meander channel of the Owyhee River. Tules is a name commonly used for stands of bulrush or cattail. *(Photograph by R.K. Moseley, Idaho Department of Fish and Game.)*

System	Wetland description
Palustrine	Wetlands in which vegetation is predominantly trees (forested wetlands); shrubs (scrub-shrub wetlands); persistent or nonpersistent emergent, erect, rooted, herbaceous plants (persistent- and nonpersistent-emergent wetlands); or submersed and (or) floating plants (aquatic beds). Also, intermittently to permanently flooded open-water bodies of less than 20 acres in which water is less than 6.6 feet deep.
Lacustrine	Wetlands within an intermittently to permanently flooded lake or reservoir. Vegetation, when present, is predominantly nonpersistent emergent plants (nonpersistent-emergent wetlands), or submersed and (or) floating plants (aquatic beds), or both.
Riverine	Wetlands within a channel. Vegetation, when present, is same as in the Lacustrine System.

Dahl (1990) estimated that wetlands occupy about 386,000 acres in Idaho. Most of the State's wetlands are in flood plains and riparian areas along streams and other water bodies. These are palustrine wetlands that include swamps (forested wetland); scrub-shrub wetlands that also contain smaller acreages of marsh, wet meadow, and seeps (emergent wetlands); and a few small ponds.

Many of the State's wetlands are in National Wildlife Refuges managed by the FWS. The Bear Lake National Wildlife Refuge (NWR) in southeastern Idaho includes about 17,600 acres of wetland-upland complex consisting of marsh, open water, and grasslands. Other wetlands in southeastern Idaho—Oxford Slough in the Bear River Basin and Grays Lake in the Snake River Basin—also have extensive emergent wetlands; about 13,000 acres of the original lakebed at Grays Lake NWR is being restored to marsh by the FWS. Camas NWR and State refuges at Market and Mud Lakes in eastern Idaho also have marshes. Other refuges in the Snake River Basin are Minidoka NWR, which predominantly consists of scrub-shrub wetlands along the shores of Lake Walcott on the Snake River; Deer Flat NWR, which includes Lake Lowell Reservoir (about 11,600 acres of wetlands and deepwater habitat); and 109 islands in the Snake River. Notable emergent wetlands are at Camas Prairie Centennial Marsh and C.J. Strike Reservoir. In the northern Rocky Mountains, the Kootenai NWR contains about 2,800 acres of wetlands on the flood plain of the Kootenai River. The mud flats along the Pack River and delta marshes along the Clark Fork are among the larger wetlands in northern Idaho. Small bogs, which are emergent wetlands that have organic soils and receive moisture only from precipitation, also are present in northern Idaho (Bureau of Reclamation, 1992).

Wetlands in Idaho's mountains are mostly alpine meadows (emergent wetlands) in flood plains and small shallow lakes and marshes in intermontane basins. In Idaho's plains, most wetlands are associated with river systems, although locally, high water tables sustain small wetlands, and during wet years, playas can be filled by surface-water runoff. Lacustrine wetlands are present in Idaho's lakes and reservoirs; riverine wetlands are present in river channels.

HYDROLOGIC SETTING

Wetlands are present where there is a persistent water supply at or near the land surface. The location and persistence of the supply are functions of interdependent climatic, physiographic, and

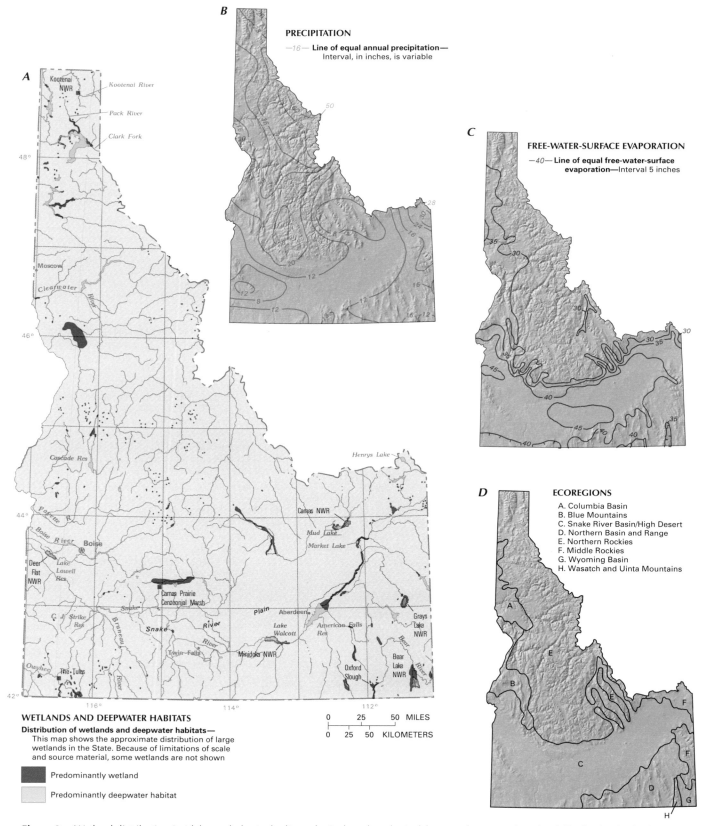

WETLANDS AND DEEPWATER HABITATS

Distribution of wetlands and deepwater habitats—
This map shows the approximate distribution of large wetlands in the State. Because of limitations of scale and source material, some wetlands are not shown

▪ Predominantly wetland

▫ Predominantly deepwater habitat

B

PRECIPITATION

—16— **Line of equal annual precipitation—**
Interval, in inches, is variable

C

FREE-WATER-SURFACE EVAPORATION

—40— **Line of equal free-water-surface evaporation—**Interval 5 inches

D

ECOREGIONS

A. Columbia Basin
B. Blue Mountains
C. Snake River Basin/High Desert
D. Northern Basin and Range
E. Northern Rockies
F. Middle Rockies
G. Wyoming Basin
H. Wasatch and Uinta Mountains

Figure 2. Wetland distribution in Idaho and physical, climatological, and ecological features that control wetland distribution in the State. *A*, Distribution of wetlands and deepwater habitats. *B*, Precipitation. *C*, Annual free-water-surface evaporation. *D*, Ecoregions. (*Sources: A, T.E. Dahl, U.S. Fish and Wildlife Service, unpub. data, 1991. B, Kjelstrom, 1986. C, Farnsworth and others, 1982. D, Omernik, 1987; landforms data from EROS Data Center.*)

hydrologic factors such as precipitation and runoff patterns, evaporation potential, topography, and configuration of the water table. Surface water collects in topographic lows, which can be either ground-water recharge or discharge areas. Soil composition determines the rate at which water is recharged or discharged.

Precipitation is affected by topography and ranges statewide from less than 10 inches per year on much of the Snake River Plain in southern Idaho to more than 60 inches per year in mountainous areas that are headwaters of the Clearwater River (fig. 2B). Greater precipitation in the mountains accounts in large part for the greater wetland acreage in the intermontane basins than on the plains in southern Idaho. Most of the water that supplies wetlands is from spring snowmelt, either as direct runoff or indirectly as recharge to the ground-water system. The timing and volume of runoff affect the establishment and functions of wetlands. Although mountainous areas have sufficient precipitation to supply wetlands, steep topography and shifting stream channels can prevent wetland development. Runoff in the Snake River Basin in southern Idaho is highly regulated by dams; runoff in most other river basins is regulated to some degree (Kjelstrom, 1986). Storage has decreased spring floodflows downstream from reservoirs, and wetland vegetation on the flood plain that normally receives moisture during floods must rely mostly on precipitation and shallow ground water for moisture. Diversions and scant precipitation deplete streamflow; as a result, water quality could be degraded, possibly resulting in changes in wetland functions and wildlife value (Kjelstrom and others, 1991).

Evaporation in the State generally increases from north to south (fig. 2C). Superimposed on this pattern are topographic complexities that cause evaporation to decrease with altitude. Evaporation from surface water ranges from 25 to 35 inches during the growing season and from 30 to 45 inches annually (Farnsworth and others, 1982). In Idaho, except for some high mountainous areas, potential evaporation exceeds precipitation during the growing season and wetland development is inhibited. The moisture deficit generally prevents the formation of bogs.

The hydrologic setting and functions of wetlands in Idaho differ regionally because of differences in climate, soils, geology, vegetation, and physiography. Omernik (1987) related these characteristics in order to develop regional patterns that were used to define ecoregions (fig. 2D).

In the Middle and Northern Rockies Ecoregions, mountain ranges are separated by valleys and, in places, broad basins (Pacific Northwest River Basins Commission, 1969; Omernik and Gallant, 1986). The alluvial and outwash deposits in the valleys are porous and permeable and can store and yield large volumes of water. Wetlands appear where less permeable rocks crop out or trap water and establish springs and seeps.

The Snake River Basin/High Desert Ecoregion (fig. 2D) is a gently sloping, semiarid plain that contains small wetlands and playas. Most wetlands are along the banks of the Snake River and its tributaries; many are emergent wetlands vegetated by sedges and rushes or are forested and scrub-shrub wetlands dominated by alder, willow, and cottonwood (Omernik and Gallant, 1986).

The Snake River and southern tributaries, such as the Bruneau and Owyhee Rivers, have cut deep canyons into the plain and generally are at a lower altitude than the regional water table; therefore, the river and its tributaries receive perennial inflow from ground water (Kjelstrom, 1992). Small streams are generally at a higher altitude than the regional water table and flow intermittently in response to surface runoff from precipitation and snowmelt. Shrub and grassland vegetation extends to the banks of intermittent and ephemeral streams. Water held near the surface by low-permeability rock can maintain small wetlands. Where the Snake River first crosses the Idaho–Oregon border, broad valleys have developed along the Snake, Boise, and Payette Rivers. Wetland acreage has in-

creased in the broad river valleys because cropland irrigation recharges aquifers and ground water maintains summer and fall base flows in streams and drains.

In the Columbia Basin and Blue Mountains Ecoregions, wetlands receive ground water from glacial outwash and alluvial deposits along streams. However, these types of deposits commonly are higher in altitude than the water table and thus cannot retain sufficient moisture for wetland development. Wetlands also could develop where loess and other windblown deposits are present, but wetland growth is inhibited because the soil is easily eroded. At lower altitudes, wetlands are grazed by livestock; wet meadows on the upper mountain slopes are summer grazing grounds (Pacific Northwest River Basins Commission, 1969).

The Northern Basin and Range Ecoregion in southeastern Idaho consists of broad basins between low mountain ranges. Hundreds of springs throughout the area provide water for many wetlands. Large wetland areas along the Bear River and most of its tributaries are generally in direct hydraulic connection with ground water (Kjelstrom, 1986). Most of the desert shrubland is grazed or cleared and used for irrigated agriculture, which has decreased wetland vegetation and degraded water quality of nearby wetlands.

TRENDS

Starting in 1805, explorers, pioneers, and trappers followed the waterways through Idaho. The first effects on wetlands occurred between 1818 and 1827 when beaver were virtually eliminated by trapping (Idaho Department of Fish and Game, 1990). Storage of water behind beaver dams creates wetlands, provides water for vegetation during dry periods, and decreases downstream bank erosion. Since about 1860, when mining and farming activities began, wetlands in Idaho have decreased 56 percent—from about 877,000 acres to about 386,000 acres (Dahl, 1990). In Idaho, agricultural practices account for most of the human-caused wetland losses; residential and commercial development accounts for most of the remaining losses (Idaho Department of Parks and Recreation, 1987). Of the 19.5 million acres of non-Federal land in Idaho—about one-third of the State—approximately 33 percent is cropland. Cropland increased by about 400,000 acres from 1967 to 1982. During that time, nearly 10,000 acres of farmland per year were converted to urban uses (Soil Conservation Service, 1984). Many small wetlands within farmlands were filled for urban use. In agricultural areas, conversion to cropland, dewatering for irrigation purposes, contamination from nutrients in irrigation-return flow, and overgrazing by livestock contributed to wetland loss or degradation. Livestock grazing in wetlands is a complex issue because most of the public land is grazed, and, although much of the riparian area on public lands has been adversely affected, riparian areas are commonly the primary and sometimes the only water supply for livestock that graze on arid rangeland. Results of an inventory of about 250 miles of National Forest riparian areas indicated that no single grazing strategy was effective for all areas (Clary and Webster, 1989). In urban areas, wetland losses are attributable to encroachment by residential and commercial construction, channelization for drainage, and dewatering for municipal and industrial purposes.

Loss of wetlands also can be attributed to dam and reservoir construction, mining activities, ground-water pumping, river channelization, erosion and sedimentation, and road and railroad construction. From 1860 to the 1930's, placer mining along many miles of streambeds damaged adjacent wetlands. Tailings from hard-rock mining and toxic acidic or alkaline drainage have degraded other wetlands.

Short-term causes of wetland degradation are wildfires, plant diseases, extremes in weather, and defoliation by cyclic species such as jackrabbits, tent caterpillars, and grasshoppers (Thomas, 1986). Prolonged droughts, such as the one from 1987 to 1992, have temporarily reduced the area or functions of some wetlands.

Some land-use practices have created new wetlands or enlarged existing ones. Leaking irrigation ditches, uncapped flowing wells, seeps, irrigation tailwater, and irrigation-return flows have increased wetland acreage and improved wetland habitat, notably in southern Idaho. Excavation of gravel pits and construction of reservoirs also have increased wetland acreage. However, such increases are small compared to losses.

Ratti and Kadlec (1992) estimated that about 91,000 acres of wetlands are protected in the National Wildlife Refuge system or by the State. Federal laws and State and local planning and regulatory programs are being used to identify and protect the remaining wetlands.

CONSERVATION

Many government agencies and private organizations participate in wetland conservation in Idaho. The most active agencies and organizations and some of their activities are listed in table 1.

Federal wetland activities.—Development activities in Idaho wetlands are regulated by several Federal statutory prohibitions and incentives that are intended to slow wetland losses. Some of the more important of these are contained in the 1899 Rivers and Harbors Act; the 1972 Clean Water Act and amendments; the 1985 Food Security Act; the 1990 Food, Agriculture, Conservation, and Trade Act; and the 1986 Emergency Wetlands Resources Act.

Section 10 of the Rivers and Harbors Act gives the U.S. Army Corps of Engineers (Corps) authority to regulate certain activities in navigable waters. Regulated activities include diking, deepening,

Table 1. Selected wetland-related activities of government agencies and private organizations in Idaho, 1993

[Source: Classification of activities is generalized from information provided by agencies and organizations. •, agency or organization participates in wetland-related activity; ..., agency or organization does not participate in wetland-related activity. **MAN**, management; **REG**, regulation; **R&C**, restoration and creation; **LAN**, land acquisition; **R&D**, research and data collection; **D&I**, delineation and inventory]

Agency or organization	MAN	REG	R&C	LAN	R&D	D&I
FEDERAL						
Department of Agriculture						
Consolidated Farm Service Agency	...	•	...	...	...	...
Forest Service	•	...	•	•	•	•
Natural Resources Conservation Service	...	•	•	...	•	•
Department of Defense						
Army Corps of Engineers	•	•	•	...	•	•
Military reservations	•	...	...	...	...	...
Department of the Interior						
Bureau of Land Management	•	...	•	•	•	•
Bureau of Reclamation	...	...	•	•	•	•
Fish and Wildlife Service	•	...	•	•	•	•
Geological Survey	...	...	...	...	•	...
National Biological Service	...	...	...	...	•	...
National Park Service	•	...	...	...	•	...
Environmental Protection Agency	...	•	...	...	•	•
STATE						
Department of Agriculture	...	...	...	...	•	...
Department of Fish and Game	•	•	•	•	•	•
Department of Health and Welfare						
Division of Environmental Quality	...	•	•	...	...	...
Department of Parks and Recreation	•	...	...	...	•	•
Department of Transportation	...	...	•	...	•	...
Department of Water Resources	•	•	...	...	...	...
SOME COUNTY AND LOCAL GOVERNMENTS	...	•	...	...	...	...
PRIVATE ORGANIZATIONS						
Ducks Unlimited	...	...	•	•	...	...
The Nature Conservancy	•	...	•	•	...	...

filling, excavating, and placing of structures. The related section 404 of the Clean Water Act is the most often-used Federal legislation protecting wetlands. Under section 404 provisions, the Corps issues permits regulating the discharge of dredged or fill material into wetlands. Permits are subject to review and possible veto by the U.S. Environmental Protection Agency (EPA), and the FWS has review and advisory roles. Section 401 of the Clean Water Act grants to States and eligible Indian Tribes the authority to approve, apply conditions to, or deny section 404 permit applications on the basis of a proposed activity's probable effects on the water quality of a wetland.

Most farming, ranching, and silviculture activities are not subject to section 404 regulation. However, the "Swampbuster" provision of the 1985 Food Security Act and amendments in the 1990 Food, Agriculture, Conservation, and Trade Act discourage (through financial disincentives) the draining, filling, or other alteration of wetlands for agricultural use. The law allows exemptions from penalties in some cases, especially if the farmer agrees to restore the altered wetland or other wetlands that have been converted to agricultural use. The Wetlands Reserve Program of the 1990 Food, Agriculture, Conservation, and Trade Act authorizes the Federal Government to purchase conservation easements from landowners who agree to protect or restore wetlands. The Consolidated Farm Service Agency (formerly the Agricultural Stabilization and Conservation Service) administers the Swampbuster provisions and Wetlands Reserve Program. The Natural Resources Conservation Service (formerly the Soil Conservation Service) (NRCS) determines compliance with Swampbuster provisions and assists farmers in the identification of wetlands and in the development of wetland protection, restoration, or creation plans.

The 1986 Emergency Wetlands Resources Act encourages wetland protection through funding incentives. The act requires States to address wetland protection in their Statewide Comprehensive Outdoor Recreation Plans to qualify for Federal funding for State recreational land; the National Park Service (NPS) provides guidance to States in developing the wetland component of their plans.

The U.S. Forest Service manages about 20 million acres of National Forest in Idaho and is assessing a process to evaluate the value and function of each wetland (Bureau of Reclamation, 1992). From 1964 to 1980, forested wetlands were further protected by the designation of about 4 million acres as wilderness areas.

The Bureau of Land Management (BLM) manages about 12 million acres, of which about 69,000 acres are riparian wetlands (Bureau of Reclamation, 1992). Waterfowl-habitat management areas have been designated on 68 sites within BLM lands, and habitat-improvement projects have been completed on 2,000 acres. In the 1970's, the BLM began protecting riparian areas by fencing stream segments, planting willows and other woody species, building check dams, and introducing beavers (Thomas, 1988). Intensive inventories of conditions, objectives, plans, and restoration will be made on 10,400 acres from 1991 to 1995 (Bureau of Land Management, 1991).

The FWS manages six National Wildlife Refuges and one waterfowl-production area. The agency is conducting numerous research and education projects involving wetland enhancement and conservation.

The NPS manages about 85,000 acres in Idaho. To date (1993), no estimates of wetland acreage on those lands have been made.

The Bureau of Reclamation (BOR) is carrying out cooperative research projects that demonstrate how wetlands and riparian habitat can be preserved and enhanced as part of an overall water-resources management plan. Most BOR wetland-restoration and development projects are multipurpose, but all projects enhance waterfowl habitat in accordance with the North American Waterfowl Management Plan of 1986. Research projects near American Falls Reservoir are designed to determine the effectiveness of small wetland-area impoundments on wetland plant communities, to improve quality of irrigation-return flow, and to enhance waterfowl habitat by developing a large wetland area on the north side of the reservoir (Bureau of Reclamation, 1992).

The NRCS will provide technical assistance to the BOR in the design and operation of a nutrient and sediment-control system adjacent to Cascade Reservoir (P.H. Calverley, Soil Conservation Service, written commun., 1992). Three shallow, vegetated wetland cells and one deepwater pond will be used to improve the water quality of irrigation-return flow. The NRCS Aberdeen Plant Materials Center, in cooperation with several Federal and State agencies, will conduct a long-term project to assemble, evaluate, select, and release for commercial production several improved varieties of riparian wetland plant species (P.H. Calverley, Soil Conservation Service, written commun., 1992).

The National Water Quality Assessment study of the upper Snake River Basin by the U.S. Geological Survey will address the effects of long-term water use on ground- and surface-water quality. Several wetland areas are within the basin.

State wetland activities.—The Idaho State Water Plan states that, insofar as is possible, the State should assume responsibility for wetland management and protection (Idaho Water Resource Board, 1992). Policy plans made by the Idaho Department of Fish and Game for 1991–2005 focus land-acquisition efforts on wetland areas where habitat protection is critical. Some activities administered by the department in the last 5 years include (1) the development or protection of about 500 blocks of wetland habitat and nearly 1,500 waterfowl nesting structures (Habitat Improvement Program); (2) mitigation for about 11,000 acres of wetland area lost to construction of several reservoirs (Wildlife Mitigation Program); (3) acquisition of about 4,300 acres of wetland habitat by use of waterfowl-stamp funds (State Duck Stamp Program); (4) identification of more than 200 valuable wetlands for protection (Idaho National Heritage Program); (5) encouragement of local participation and volunteer efforts to address nonpoint sources of pollution (Antidegradation Program); and (6) the publication and dissemination of several leaflets and guides dealing with waterways, riparian areas, wetlands, and aquatic biota (Aquatic Education Program) (Groen, 1991).

The Division of Environmental Quality of the Department of Health and Welfare reviews section 404 permit applications to ensure compliance with State water-quality laws. A permit is not issued by the Corps without certification of compliance by the division. Pursuant to section 305(b) of the Clean Water Act, the division submits to the EPA and the U.S. Congress a biennial assessment of the State's surface-water quality, including that in wetlands.

Idaho's Statewide Comprehensive Outdoor Recreation Plan was completed by the Department of Parks and Recreation and adopted by the Governor in January 1988. The Department is responsible for maintaining lists of wetlands and endangered plant species under the plan. The Idaho Wetlands Conservation Priority Plan, prepared by the Department, calls for the identification of wetlands warranting priority consideration for protection (Howard, 1991). One of the wetlands identified for priority protection is The Tules (fig. 1), which consists of about 160 acres in an abandoned meander channel of the Owyhee River. The Department also manages about 580 miles of nationally designated wild and scenic rivers that include riparian wetland.

The Idaho Department of Water Resources issues and manages surface- and ground-water rights and administers diverse activities that can affect wetlands. The Idaho Department of Transportation analyzes alternative roadway locations and uses construction techniques to lessen the degradation or loss of wetlands. When loss or degradation occurs, mitigation in the form of restoration or other compensation is required. A wetland bank in Idaho (Tiedemann, 1991) may be used when mitigation of unavoidable impacts caused by construction is not possible; compensation may be made by the offsite creation, restoration, or enhancement of wetlands. The University of Idaho and the Idaho Water Resources Research Institute are conducting projects to assess the effectiveness of constructed wetlands supplied by irrigation-return flow near Twin Falls and by sewer effluent from an aquaculture facility near Moscow. Also, the institute, in cooperation with the Idaho Bureau of Mines, is conducting projects to evaluate wetland design for the reduction of heavy metals in runoff from mine-waste sites. The University of Idaho's Cooperative Extension System is conducting research on pollutant and sediment runoff from several small parcels of land on which different grazing practices are used.

County and local wetland activities.—Most development in Idaho's wetlands is regulated by Federal and State laws. However, some city and county governments have ordinances and planning and zoning regulations that protect wetland areas and functions. Guidance and assistance to farmers and other landowners for wetland conservation are provided by the University of Idaho's Cooperative Extension System.

Private wetland activities.—The Nature Conservancy and Ducks Unlimited have participated in several projects involving acquisition and restoration of wetlands. Other organizations that participate in wetland-protection activities in the State include The National Wetlands Policy Forum, National Wildlife Federation, Wildlife Council, National Audubon Society, Pheasants Forever, Sierra Club, and Idaho Conservation League. Many other groups have formed to restore and preserve specific wetland areas. For example, the Henrys Lake Foundation was formed by summer homeowners, local ranchers, and business owners to restore the fishery in Henrys Lake. Money was raised to exclude livestock from the riparian area along a tributary stream (Chaney and others, 1990). In 1986, a group of ranchers in south-central Idaho formed the Beaver Committee with the aim of restoring riparian wetlands, reducing soil erosion, and improving the productivity of land for livestock grazing. About 100 beavers have been relocated to 25 creeks (High Country News, Paonia, Colo., August 24, 1992, p. 1, 10–12). In Boise, citizen groups protested the residential development of a riparian area in the Boise foothills. As a result, a land exchange between the city of Boise and the developer will preserve 100 acres of wetlands.

References Cited

Bureau of Land Management, 1991, Riparian-wetland initiative for the 1990's: Bureau of Land Management Report BLM/WO/GI–91/001+4340, 50 p.

Bureau of Reclamation, 1992, Idaho river systems management study, wetlands report: Denver, Bureau of Reclamation, 155 p.

Chaney, J.E., Elmore, Wayne, and Platts, W.S., 1990, Livestock grazing on western riparian areas: Eagle, Idaho, Northwest Resource Information Center, Inc., 45 p. [2d printing.]

Clary, W.P., and Webster, B.F., 1989, Managing grazing of riparian areas in the intermountain region: U.S. Forest Service, Intermountain Research Station General Technical Report INT–263, 11 p.

Cowardin, L.M., Carter, Virginia, Golet, F.C., and LaRoe, E.T., 1979, Classification of wetlands and deepwater habitats of the United States: U.S. Fish and Wildlife Service Report FWS/OBS–79/31, 131 p.

Dahl, T.E., 1990, Wetlands—Losses in the United States, 1780's to 1980's: Washington, D.C., U.S. Fish and Wildlife Service Report to Congress, 13 p.

Farnsworth, R.K., Thompson, E.S., and Peck, E.L., 1982, Evaporation atlas for the contiguous 48 United States: National Oceanic and Atmospheric Administration Technical Report NWS 33, 27 p.

Groen, Cal, 1991, A look at the players—Federal and State roles, Idaho Department of Fish and Game role in wetlands protection, *in* Wetlands protection in Idaho—Living with "no net loss": Boise, University of Idaho, Idaho Water Resources Research Institute, [about 140] p.

Howard, Jake, 1991, The role of the Idaho Department of Parks and Recreation in wetlands protection, *in* Wetlands protection in Idaho—Living with "no net loss": Boise, University of Idaho, Idaho Water Resources Research Institute, [about 140] p.

Idaho Department of Fish and Game, 1990, Between land and water—The wetlands of Idaho: Idaho Department of Fish and Game, Nongame Wildlife Leaflet no. 9, 12 p.

Idaho Department of Parks and Recreation, 1987, Idaho wetlands conservation priority plan—An addendum to the 1983 statewide comprehensive outdoor recreation plan: Boise, Idaho Department of Parks and Recreation, 13 p.

Idaho Water Resource Board, 1992, Idaho State water plan: Boise, Idaho Department of Water Resources, 56 p.

Kjelstrom, L.C., 1986, Idaho surface-water resources, *in* U.S. Geological Survey, National water summary 1985 — Hydrologic and surface-water resources: U.S. Geological Survey Water-Supply Paper 2300, p. 207 – 214.

———1992, Streamflow gains and losses in the Snake River and groundwater budgets for the Snake River Plain, Idaho and eastern Oregon: U.S. Geological Survey Open-File Report 90–172, 71 p.

Kjelstrom, L.C., and others, 1991, Idaho floods and droughts, *in* U.S. Geological Survey, National water summary 1988–89—Hydrologic events and floods and droughts: U.S. Geological Survey Water-Supply Paper 2375, p. 255–262.

Omernik, J.M., 1987, Ecoregions of the conterminous United States—Map supplement: Annals of the Association of American Geographers, v. 77, no. 1, scale 1:7,500,000.

Omernik, J.M., and Gallant, A.L., 1986, Ecoregions of the Pacific Northwest: U.S. Environmental Protection Agency Report EPA/600/3–86/033, 39 p.

Pacific Northwest River Basins Commission, 1969, Columbia-North Pacific region comprehensive framework study of water and related lands, appendix II—The region: Vancouver, Wash., Pacific Northwest River Basins Commission, 147 p.

Ratti, J.T., and Kadlec, J.A., 1992, Concept plan for the preservation of wetland habitat of the intermountain west—North American Waterfowl Management Plan: Portland, Oreg., U.S. Fish and Wildlife Service, 146 p.

Soil Conservation Service, 1984, Idaho's soil and water—Condition and trends: Boise, Soil Conservation Service, 24 p.

Thomas, A.E., 1986, Riparian protection/enhancement in Idaho: Rangelands, v. 8, no. 5, p. 224–227.

———1988, Seen a riparian lately? Good ones are green!: Idaho Wildlife, v. 8, no. 5, p. 6–9.

Tiedemann, R.B., 1991, Development and use of a wetland bank as a mitigation alternative in Idaho, *in* Wetlands protection in Idaho—Living with "no net loss": Boise, University of Idaho, Idaho Water Resources Research Institute, [about 140] p.

FOR ADDITIONAL INFORMATION: District Chief, U.S. Geological Survey, 230 Collins Road, Boise, ID 83702; Regional Wetland Coordinator, U.S. Fish and Wildlife Service, 911 NE 11th Avenue, Portland, OR 97232

Prepared by
L.C. Kjelstrom,
U.S. Geological Survey

Illinois
Wetland Resources

The diverse wetlands of Illinois, which cover about 3.5 percent of the State, have resulted from the interaction of geologic events, human activities, and hydrologic conditions. The State contains several ecologically significant wetlands. Two examples are Beall Woods on the Wabash River in eastern Illinois and the swamps along the Cache River in the southern part of the State. Beall Woods is one of the last near-virgin stands of wet bottom-land forest in the State, and the Cache River swamps (fig. 1) are among the few bald cypress/tupelo gum swamps remaining in southern Illinois. Core samples from some of the larger bald cypress trees indicate ages of more than 1,000 years. The Cache River swamps also are home to a colony of nesting great blue herons (Barickman, 1992).

Wetlands have many fish and wildlife, environmental-quality, and socioeconomic values (Tiner, 1984). Illinois wetlands provide feeding, spawning, and nursery grounds for catfish, sunfish, northern pike, muskie, and walleye. Common birds, such as ducks, turkeys, and owls, and threatened or endangered species, such as American bittern, upland sandpiper, Henslow's sparrow, and northern harrier, use Illinois wetlands for feeding and nesting sites (Barickman, 1992). Deer, muskrat, rabbits, beaver, and other fur-bearers use wetlands as a source of food and shelter. Numerous reptile and amphibian species also live in the wetlands of Illinois.

The environmental quality of aquatic habitats is enhanced by wetlands. Wetlands absorb nutrients and remove heavy metals and other contaminants from waters moving through them. Wetlands reduce turbidity and sediment loading and thereby slow the siltation of harbors and navigable rivers and streams (Tiner, 1984).

In addition to the habitat and environmental-quality values of wetlands, they also have socioeconomic benefits such as flood- and storm-damage protection, erosion control, public water supply, and production of economically important natural species (Tiner, 1984). Illinois is one of five States whose combined production of peat accounts for over 75 percent of the peat mined in the United States. Wetlands also are the site for many recreational and educational activities including hunting and fishing, nature study, boating, painting and drawing, and photography.

Figure 1. Swamp along the Cache River in southern Illinois. *(Photograph by Michael R. Jeffords, Illinois Natural History Survey.)*

TYPES AND DISTRIBUTION

Wetlands are lands transitional between terrestrial and deepwater habitats where the water table usually is at or near the land surface or the land is covered by shallow water (Cowardin and others, 1979). The distribution of wetlands and deepwater habitats in Illinois is shown in figure 2A; only wetlands are discussed herein.

Wetlands can be vegetated or nonvegetated and are classified on the basis of their hydrology, vegetation, and substrate. In this summary, wetlands are classified according to the system proposed by Cowardin and others (1979), which is used by the U.S. Fish and Wildlife Service (FWS) to map and inventory the Nation's wetlands. At the most general level of the classification system, wetlands are grouped into five ecological systems: Palustrine, Lacustrine, Riverine, Estuarine, and Marine. The Palustrine System includes only wetlands, whereas the other systems comprise wetlands and deepwater habitats. Wetlands of the systems that occur in Illinois are described below.

System	Wetland description
Palustrine	Wetlands in which vegetation is predominantly trees (forested wetlands); shrubs (scrub-shrub wetlands); persistent or nonpersistent emergent, erect, rooted, herbaceous plants (persistent- and nonpersistent-emergent wetlands); or submersed and (or) floating plants (aquatic beds). Also, intermittently to permanently flooded open-water bodies of less than 20 acres in which water is less than 6.6 feet deep.
Lacustrine	Wetlands within an intermittently to permanently flooded lake or reservoir. Vegetation, when present, is predominantly nonpersistent emergent plants (nonpersistent-emergent wetlands), or submersed and (or) floating plants (aquatic beds), or both.
Riverine	Wetlands within a channel. Vegetation, when present, is same as in the Lacustrine System.

As of the 1980's, 3.5 percent of Illinois, or about 1.25 million acres, was wetland (Dahl, 1990; Suloway and others, 1992). Most of the State's wetlands are either palustrine emergent wetlands such as marshes and wet prairies or palustrine forested wetlands such as bottom-land hardwood forests and bald cypress swamps. Also, open-water palustrine wetlands—primarily farm ponds—are present throughout the State (Hubbell, 1987).

On the basis of frequency of occurrence, the largest concentration of wetlands in Illinois is in the northeast. The largest acreage of wetlands in Illinois is along the State's major river systems (Hubbell, 1987). Marshes, wet prairies, and bogs (palustrine emergent, scrub-shrub, or forested wetlands) are most common in the northeastern part of the State, and bottom-land forests (palustrine forested wetlands) and swamps (palustrine scrub-shrub or forested) are present along Illinois rivers.

Dominant plants of marshes are sedges, cattails, and bulrushes. Wet prairie dominants include sedges, cordgrass, and blue flag iris. Silver maple, cottonwood, box elder, red maple, black willow, sycamore, and bald cypress are characteristic of bottom-land hardwood forests and swamps in the State.

Federally listed endangered species of Illinois wetlands include the eastern prairie white-fringed orchid and decurrent false aster.

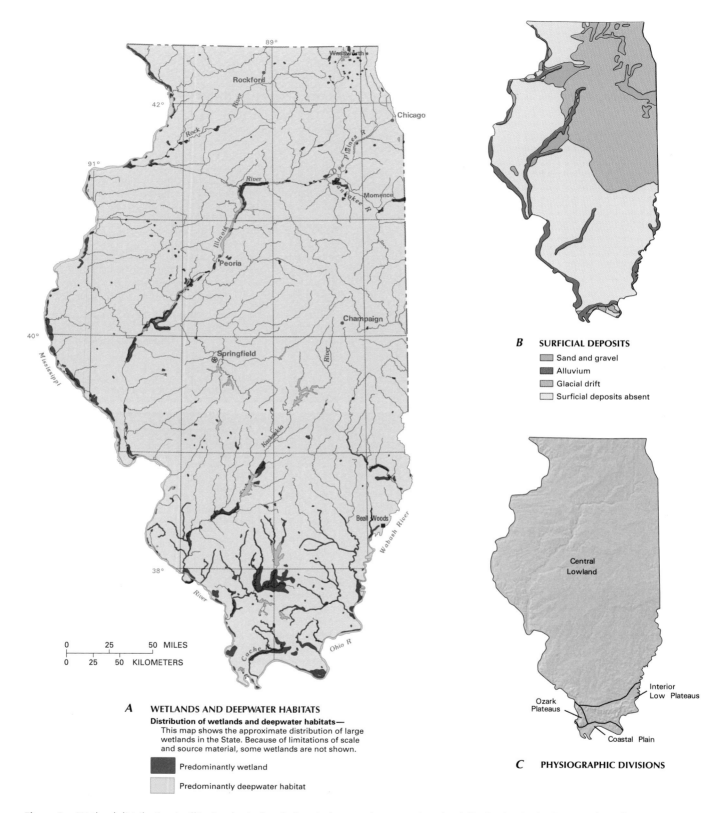

Figure 2. Wetland distribution in Illinois, physical and climatic features that control wetland distribution in the State, and trends in development of agricultural land. **A**, Distribution of wetlands and deepwater habitats. **B**, Surficial deposits. **C**, Physiography. *(Sources: A, T.E. Dahl, U.S. Fish and Wildlife Service, unpub. data, 1991. B, Voelker and Clarke, 1988; C, Physiographic divisions from Fenneman, 1946; landforms data from EROS Data Center)*

In addition, bald eagles and least terns use bottom lands for habitat (Jerry Bade, U.S. Fish and Wildlife Service, oral commun., 1993). The State of Illinois also maintains a list of endangered species. As of February, 1994, the State list contained 415 endangered species (E) and 96 threatened species (T)—about 40 percent of which are wetland dependent. Among the State-listed endangered or threatened wetland-plant species are white lady's slipper (E), queen-of-the-prairie (T), water elm (E), and marsh speedwell (T). State-listed animal species include the Illinois chorus frog (T), the Illinois mud turtle (E), sandhill crane (E), black tern (E), bluehead shiner (E), and river otter (E) (Susan Lauzon, Illinois Department of Conservation, oral commun., 1994).

HYDROLOGIC SETTING

Wetlands are present where the geohydrology and physiography favor the retention of water for extended periods. The location of wetlands in Illinois is strongly affected by its geologic history. Aquifers underlying wetlands in the State are composed of sedimentary and metamorphic rocks of various ages overlain by glacial drift. Glacial scouring and subsequent glacial melting at the end of the last ice age left depressions in the glacially derived sediments, or drift, deposited by the glaciers. Glacial drift covers a large area of the State (fig. 2B) and ranges in thickness from a few to several hundred feet (Sherrill and others, 1984). The geologic history of the State has significantly shaped its physiography. Most of Illinois lies in the Central Lowland physiographic province (fig. 2C), where the relatively flat topography is due to glaciation. The greatest relief is present where surface drainage has cut into the glacial deposits and, in some locations, into the underlying bedrock.

In Illinois, average annual precipitation (fig. 2D) ranges from about 34 inches per year in the north to 48 inches per year in the extreme south (Wendland and others, 1992). About three-fourths of the precipitation that reaches the land surface is returned to the atmosphere by evaporation and plant transpiration (LaTour and

Ackermann, 1990). The remaining precipitation recharges the ground- and surface-water systems. Recharge to the shallow ground-water system takes place in interstream areas of the surficial-drainage system. Aquifers overlain by confining units composed of silt and clay are recharged by precipitation entering areas where the aquifers crop out and by slow percolation downward through the

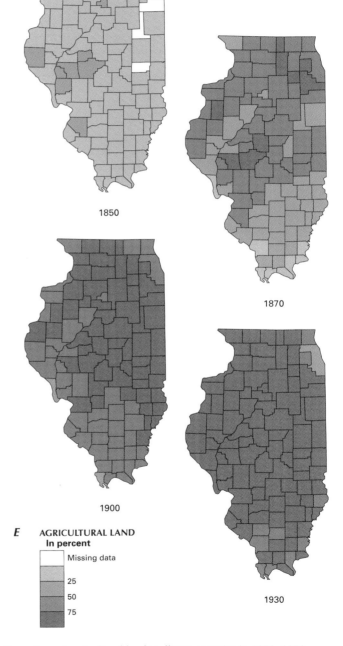

D **PRECIPITATION**

—40— **Line of equal average annual precipitation** — Interval, in inches, is variable

1850

1870

1900

1930

E **AGRICULTURAL LAND In percent**

◻ Missing data

25

50

75

Figure 2. Continued. *D*, Average annual precipitation, 1961–90. *E*, Percentage of agricultural land in Illinois counties in 1850, 1870, 1900, and 1930. *(Sources: D, Wendland and others, 1992. E, Data from U.S. Census Office, 1853, 1872, 1901; U.S. Census Bureau, 1932.)*

confining units. Water returns to the surface as base flow to streams, ponds, and lakes. Ground water moves through shale and dolomite aquifers in fractures or solution channels. Wetlands develop along streams and near glacially formed lakes where ground water discharges.

In the Central Lowland, wetlands are associated with groundwater discharge into depressions in the extensive glacial drift. In areas of high precipitation, low surface-water gradients coupled with the low permeability of fine-grained surficial deposits can result in poor drainage of glacial depressions. The resulting accumulation of water contributes to wetland formation. Ground-water discharge to streams in the Central Lowland also provides sites for wetland establishment.

In the Ozark Plateaus, Interior Low Plateaus, and Coastal Plain, ground water from drift or underlying bedrock discharges primarily to streams, as in the Cache River area and the wetlands along the Mississippi River. Wetlands also can form where clay or other fine sediments form a poorly permeable layer that holds water at or near the land surface, providing a suitable habitat for wetland vegetation.

TRENDS

Illinois once had vast expanses of wetlands but has lost as much as 90 percent of them (by area) since the 1780's (Dahl, 1990; S.P. Havera, Illinois Natural History Survey, written commun., 1993)— sixth in the Nation in terms of percentage loss. A notable example of this loss is the Great Kankakee Swamp (also known as the Grand Marsh). One of the largest marsh-swamp basins in the United States, in the 1830's, this wetland contained more than 1 million acres of wet prairie and marshes (Mitsch and others, 1979). It is now represented in Illinois by a relatively small tract of wetlands along the Kankakee River near Momence.

Wetlands in the State have been drained and filled since settlement by Europeans began in the 1600's. Of about 8,212,000 acres of wetlands that were present in the 1780's (Havera, 1992), only about 1,254,500 acres remained in the 1980's (Dahl, 1990; Suloway and others, 1992). About 6,000 acres remain undisturbed (White, 1978). Rates of loss in the State are estimated to be between 4,000 and 6,000 acres per year (Illinois Department of Conservation, undated).

In Illinois, the major cause of wetland loss has been artificial drainage—primarily to make lands suitable for crop production. The number of drained acres in Illinois increased from about 100,000 in the 1870's to nearly 5 million by 1920. Most of the wetland loss occurred between 1890 and 1930 (S.P. Havera, Illinois Natural History Survey, written commun., 1993). At the end of that period, about 17 percent of land in the State was in drainage districts (Illinois Tax Commission, 1941), and 27 percent of agricultural land had been drained either through district activities or by private action (U.S. Census Bureau, 1981). The percentages of agricultural land in each Illinois county for the years 1850, 1870, 1900, and 1930 are shown in figure 2E. The rapid and substantial growth in agriculture and the associated expansion of drainage districts in the State during that period paralleled the decline in wetland acreage as more and more land was drained for farming.

Agricultural expansion was not the sole reason for the decline in wetland acreage. The draining of wetlands for housing, transportation, industry, and landfills; stream channelization and dredging for navigation; and reservoir, harbor, and marina construction have also reduced wetland acreage. In addition to acreage loss caused by these activities, wetlands have been degraded by point and nonpoint discharges to surface waters. These discharges are associated with agricultural, industrial, municipal, and urban runoff, which add contaminants and sediment to surface waters.

Some wetland acreage has been added through the construction of ponds and reservoirs and through planned wetland construction. In Wadsworth, 35 miles north of Chicago, Wetlands Research, Inc., a nonprofit corporation, is coordinating the Des Plaines River Wetlands Demonstration Project. Since 1983, 50 acres of wetlands have been constructed (Wetlands Research, Inc., 1993). Also, the Cache River Wetlands Project, a joint effort of the Illinois Department of Conservation, the FWS, The Nature Conservancy, and Ducks Unlimited, has the primary goal of acquiring and restoring between 55,000 and 60,000 acres of contiguous wetland-upland complexes. The impoundment of streams and farm-pond construction, as well as natural processes, also can result in the creation of wetlands.

CONSERVATION

Many government agencies and private organizations participate in wetland conservation in Illinois. The most active agencies and organizations and some of their activities are listed in table 1.

Federal wetland activities.—Development activities in Illinois wetlands are regulated by several Federal statutory prohibitions and incentives that are intended to slow wetland losses. Some of the more important of these are contained in the 1899 Rivers and Harbors Act; the 1972 Clean Water Act and amendments; the 1985 Food Security Act; the 1990 Food, Agriculture, Conservation, and Trade Act; the 1986 Emergency Wetlands Resources Act; and the 1972 Coastal Management Act.

Table 1. Selected wetland-related activities of government agencies and private organizations in Illinois, 1993

[Source: Classification of activities is generalized from information provided by agencies and organizations. •, agency or organization participates in wetland-related activity; ..., agency or organization does not participate in wetland-related activity. **MAN**, management; **REG**, regulation; **R&C**, restoration and creation; **LAN**, land acquisition; **R&D**, research and data collection; **D&I**, delineation and inventory]

Agency or organization	MAN	REG	R&C	LAN	R&D	D&I
FEDERAL						
Department of Agriculture						
Consolidated Farm Service Agency	...	•	...	...	...	...
Forest Service	•	...	•	•	•	•
Natural Resources Conservation Service	...	•	•	...	•	•
Department of Commerce						
National Oceanic and Atmospheric Administration	...	...	•	...	...	...
Department of Defense						
Army Corps of Engineers	...	•	•	•	•	•
Military reservations	•	...	...	...	...	...
Department of the Interior						
Fish and Wildlife Service	•	...	•	•	•	•
Geological Survey	...	...	...	...	•	...
National Biological Service	...	...	...	...	•	...
National Park Service	•	...	•	•	•	•
Environmental Protection Agency	...	•	...	...	•	•
STATE						
Department of Agriculture	...	•	...	•	•	...
Department of Conservation	•	•	•	•	•	...
Department of Energy and Natural Resources	...	...	...	...	•	•
Department of Mines and Minerals	...	•	...	...	...	...
Department of Transportation	...	•	•	...	•	...
Environmental Protection Agency	•	•	•	...	•	...
Pollution Control Board	...	•	...	...	...	...
SOME COUNTY AND LOCAL GOVERNMENTS	...	•	...	•	...	...
PRIVATE						
Ducks Unlimited	...	...	•	•	•	•
The Nature Conservancy	•	...	•	•	•	•

Section 10 of the Rivers and Harbors Act gives the U.S. Army Corps of Engineers (Corps) authority to regulate certain activities in navigable waters. Regulated activities include diking, deepening, filling, excavating, and placing of structures. The related section 404 of the Clean Water Act is the most often-used Federal legislation protecting wetlands. Under section 404 provisions, the Corps issues permits regulating the discharge of dredged or fill material into wetlands. Permits are subject to review and possible veto by the U.S. Environmental Protection Agency, and the FWS has review and advisory roles. Section 401 of the Clean Water Act grants to States and eligible Indian Tribes the authority to approve, apply conditions to, or deny section 404 permit applications on the basis of a proposed activity's probable effects on the water quality of a wetland.

Most farming, ranching, and silvicultural activities are not subject to section 404 regulation. However, the "Swampbuster" provision of the 1985 Food Security Act and amendments in the 1990 Food, Agriculture, Conservation, and Trade Act discourage (through financial disincentives) the draining, filling, or other alteration of wetlands for agricultural use. The law allows exemptions from penalties in some cases, especially if the farmer agrees to restore the altered wetland or other wetlands that have been converted to agricultural use. The Wetlands Reserve Program of the 1990 Food, Agriculture, Conservation, and Trade Act authorizes the Federal Government to purchase conservation easements from landowners who agree to protect or restore wetlands. The Consolidated Farm Service Agency (formerly the Agricultural Stabilization and Conservation Service) administers the Swampbuster provisions and Wetlands Reserve Program. The Natural Resources Conservation Service (formerly the Soil Conservation Service) determines compliance with Swampbuster provisions and assists farmers in the identification of wetlands and in the development of wetland protection, restoration, or creation plans.

The 1986 Emergency Wetlands Resources Act and the 1972 Coastal Zone Management Act and amendments encourage wetland protection through funding incentives. The Emergency Wetland Resources Act requires States to address wetland protection in their Statewide Comprehensive Outdoor Recreation Plans to qualify for Federal funding for State recreational land; the National Park Service provides guidance to States in developing the wetland component of their plans. Coastal and Great Lakes States that adopt coastal-zone management programs and plans approved by the National Oceanic and Atmospheric Administration are eligible for Federal funding and technical assistance through the Coastal Zone Management Act.

Illinois has six National Wildlife Refuges with a combined area of nearly 100,000 acres. Goodwin and Niering (1975) evaluated a number of Illinois wetlands for possible registration as National Natural Landmarks. Their list includes nine additional wetland areas comprising about 7,000 acres.

State wetland protection.—The primary State law governing wetlands is the Interagency Wetland Policy Act of 1989, which sets a goal of no net loss of wetlands due to projects funded by the State. The act is administered through the Illinois Wetland Management Program of the Illinois Department of Conservation. There is also a Floodplain Management Statute under which the Illinois Department of Transportation issues permits for developments in the 100-year flood plain and for dredging and filling public water bodies. Most regulation of wetlands on private lands takes place at the local level. Wetlands can be owned and protected by the public as County Forest Preserve Districts.

County and local wetland protection.—Counties and municipalities can protect wetlands and other sensitive natural areas either by acquiring them or by enacting ordinances for their protection. Protection and acquisition are carried out to protect public health, safety, and welfare. One Illinois county has established two wetland banks. These banks have allowed the county to maintain no net loss of wetlands within its boundaries and to provide additional alternatives to developers for compliance with the mitigation requirements of the section 404 program. Two additional counties are investigating a similar banking concept that requires replacement of wetlands lost as a result of filling or dredging with wetlands of like kind and quality. Several municipalities in Illinois have specific ordinances protecting wetlands (M.E. Hubbell, Illinois Department of Conservation, oral commun., 1993).

References Cited

Barickman, Gene, 1992, Illinois wetlands: The Illinois Steward, Spring 1992, p. 1–5.
Cowardin, L.M., Carter, Virginia, Golet, F.C., and LaRoe, E.T., 1979, Classification of wetlands and deepwater habitats of the United States: U.S. Fish and Wildlife Service Report FWS/OBS–79/31, 131 p.
Dahl, T.E., 1990, Wetlands—Losses in the United States, 1780's to 1980's: Washington, D.C., U.S. Fish and Wildlife Service Report to Congress, 13 p.
Fenneman, N.M., 1946, Physical divisions of the United States: U.S. Geological Survey special map, scale 1:7,000,000.
Goodwin, R.H., and Niering, W.A., 1975, Inland wetlands of the United States evaluated as potential registered natural landmarks: National Park Service Natural History Theme Studies no. 2, 550 p.
Havera, S.P., 1992, Waterfowl of Illinois—Status and management, Final Federal aid performance report: Cooperative Waterfowl Research W–88–R, 1,035 p.
Hubbell, M.E., 1987, Inventory of Illinois wetlands—The Illinois wetland management program, in Singh, K.P., Lee, M.T., and Knapp, H.V., eds., Proceedings of the American Water Resources Association Illinois section annual conference, Champaign, Ill., April 28–29, 1987: Champaign, Ill., American Water Resources Association Illinois section, p. 199–204.
Illinois Department of Conservation, undated, A public guide to Illinois wetlands: Springfield, Illinois Department of Conservation, no pagination.
Illinois Tax Commission, 1941, Drainage district organization and finance, 1879–1937: Springfield, Illinois Tax Commission, 213 p.
LaTour, J.K., and Ackermann, W.C., 1990, Illinois water supply and use, in U.S. Geological Survey, National water summary 1987—Hydrologic events and water supply and use: U.S. Geological Survey Water-Supply Paper 2350, p. 235–242.
Mitsch, W.J., Hutchison, M.D., and Paulson, G.A., 1979, The Momence wetlands of the Kankakee River in Illinois—An assessment of their value: Illinois Institute of Natural Resources Document 79/17, 55 p.
Sherrill, M.G., Lazaro, T.R., and Harbison, L.L., 1985, Illinois ground-water resources, in U.S. Geological Survey, National water summary 1984—Hydrologic events, selected water-quality trends, and ground-water resources: U.S. Geological Survey Water-Supply Paper 2275, p. 199–204.
Suloway, L.B., Hubbell, M.E., and Erickson, Ronald, 1992, Analysis of the wetland resources of Illinois, v. 1—Overview and general results, Report to the Department of Energy and Natural Resources: Springfield, Ill., Department of Energy and Natural Resources, 35 p.
Tiner, R.W., Jr., 1984, Wetlands of the United States—Current status and trends: Washington, D.C., U.S. Fish and Wildlife Service, 59 p.
U.S. Census Bureau, 1932, Fifteenth census of the United States: 1930: Washington, D.C., U.S. Department of Commerce, 1,385 p.
———1981, 1978 Census of Agriculture, v. 1, State and County Data, pt. 13—Illinois: Washington, D.C., U.S. Department of Commerce, 717 p.
U.S. Census Office, 1853, Seventh census of the United States, taken in the year 1850: Washington, D.C., U.S. Census Office, 1,022 p.
———1872, Ninth census of the United States, taken in the year 1870, 3 volumes: Washington, D.C., U.S. Census Office, 2,326 p.
———1901, Twelfth census of the United States, taken in the year 1900: Washington, D.C., U.S. Census Office, 1,006 p.
Voelker, D.C., and Clarke, R.P., 1988, Illinois ground-water quality, in U.S. Geological Survey, National water summary 1986—Hydrologic events

and ground-water quality: U.S. Geological Survey Water-Supply Paper 2325, p. 237–244.

Wendland, W.M., Kunkel, K.E., Conner, Glen, and others, 1992, Mean 1961–1990 temperature and precipitation over the upper midwest: Illinois State Water Survey Research Report 92–01, 27 p.

Wetlands Research, Inc., 1993, "Living laboratory" offers unique research opportunities to improve environmental quality: Chicago, Ill., Wetlands Research, Inc., 11 p.

White, John, 1978, Illinois Natural Areas Inventory—Survey methods and results: Urbana, Ill., Illinois Natural Areas Inventory Technical Report v. 1, 426 p.

FOR ADDITIONAL INFORMATION: District Chief, U.S. Geological Survey, 102 East Main Street, 4th Floor, Urbana, IL 61801; Regional Wetland Coordinator, U.S. Fish and Wildlife Service, BHW Federal Building, 1 Federal Drive, Fort Snelling, MN 55112

Prepared by
Thomas H. Barringer and Gary O. Balding,
U.S. Geological Survey

Indiana
Wetland Resources

Wetlands cover about 813,000 acres of Indiana (Rolley, 1991)—about 3.5 percent of the State. These wetlands support rich biotic communities in freshwater settings across the State, especially in the north and southwest (fig. 1).

Wetlands have many chemical, physical, and biological functions. Wetlands trap waterborne sediments, nutrients, and toxic chemicals by filtering them out of inflowing water and storing or transforming them. The capacity of wetlands to trap sediment is particularly important in Indiana because surface erosion is a persistent, long-term result of intensive agricultural activity. Riparian (streamside) wetlands lessen the severity of floods by storing water temporarily and releasing it gradually, thus reducing flow velocity and delaying and attenuating flood peaks. Vegetation in riparian wetlands helps to maintain stream channels by stabilizing the land surface, and wetlands around lakes act as buffers to erosion from waves.

Wetlands provide habitat for waterfowl, fish, other terrestrial and aquatic animals, and a wide variety of plant life. Wetlands provide resting and feeding places on migration routes, as well as food, shelter, breeding areas, and nurseries for many animals, including species of economic interest in Indiana such as muskrat, fish, ducks, and geese. The State has listed 128 wetland-dependent plant species and over 60 wetland-dependent animal species as endangered, threatened, or of special concern (Indiana Department of Natural Resources, 1989).

In Indiana, wetlands have considerable recreational, educational, and economic value. Common activities in and surrounding wetlands are bird-watching, hiking, fishing, hunting, swimming, and boating. Wetlands are important to the fur trapping, lumbering, and tourist industries, which benefit the economy of the State.

TYPES AND DISTRIBUTION

Wetlands are lands transitional between terrestrial and deepwater habitats where the water table usually is at or near the land surface or the land is covered by shallow water (Cowardin and others, 1979). The distribution of wetlands and deepwater habitats in Indiana is shown in figure 2A; only wetlands are discussed herein.

Wetlands can be vegetated or nonvegetated and are classified on the basis of their hydrology, vegetation, and substrate. In this summary, wetlands are classified according to the system proposed by Cowardin and others (1979), which is used by the U.S. Fish and Wildlife Service (FWS) to map and inventory the Nation's wetlands. At the most general level of the classification system, wetlands are grouped into five ecological systems: Palustrine, Lacustrine, Riverine, Estuarine, and Marine. The Palustrine System includes only wetlands, whereas the other systems comprise wetlands and deepwater habitats. Wetlands of the systems that occur in Indiana are described below.

System	Wetland description
Palustrine	Wetlands in which vegetation is predominantly trees (forested wetlands); shrubs (scrub-shrub wetlands); persistent or nonpersistent emergent, erect, rooted, herbaceous plants (persistent- and nonpersistent-emergent wetlands); or submersed and (or) floating plants (aquatic beds). Also, intermittently to permanently flooded open-water bodies of less than 20 acres in which water is less than 6.6 feet deep.
Lacustrine	Wetlands within an intermittently to permanently flooded lake or reservoir. Vegetation, when present, is predominantly nonpersistent emergent plants (nonpersistent-emergent wetlands), or submersed and (or) floating plants (aquatic beds), or both.
Riverine	Wetlands within a channel. Vegetation, when present, is same as in the Lacustrine System.

Most Indiana wetlands have been filled or drained. Palustrine wetlands, which are the most abundant wetlands remaining in the State, are distributed throughout Indiana in topographic depressions, between agricultural fields, and in riparian zones along rivers, streams, and lakes. Palustrine forested wetlands are the most common wetlands in Indiana.

In the early to mid-1980's, palustrine forested wetlands covered about 504,000 acres, or approximately 62 percent of the wetland area of the State (Rolley, 1991). Palustrine emergent wetlands covered about 143,000 acres (18 percent of total wetland area), and scrub-shrub wetlands covered about 42,000 acres (5 percent). Lacustrine and riverine wetlands covered about 99,000 acres (12 percent). The remaining 3 percent of the wetland area in the State contained mixed or undetermined types of wetland.

Most of the wetlands in Indiana are in the north and along river flood plains in the south, particularly the southwest (Rolley, 1991). The northeastern part of the State contains most of Indiana's natural lakes and numerous small, isolated wetlands. The northwestern part of the State includes the Indiana Dunes National Lakeshore, which is on the southern shore of Lake Michigan. Most streams and rivers in Indiana flow to the southwest, where many wetlands are located in the river flood plains of the largest river systems (Indiana Department of Natural Resources, written commun., 1993). Wetlands in the rest of the State consist of small, widely scattered wetlands and narrow wetland bands along rivers and streams and around reservoirs (Indiana Department of Environmental Management, 1991).

Indiana has many types of wetlands, most of which are vegetated. The plant composition of vegetated wetlands is determined by factors such as climate, soil type, ground- and surface-water chemistry, and the extent and duration of flooding. The predominant vegetation or specific location of a wetland frequently deter-

Figure 1. Cowles Bog in the Great Marsh, Indiana Dunes National Lakeshore. *(Photograph by R.J. Shedlock, U.S. Geological Survey.)*

mines its common name. Familiar common names for some Indiana wetlands include marsh, wet prairie, swamp, slough, bottom-land hardwood forest, flatwood, bog, fen, kettle, pothole, dune swale, muck flat, and sinkhole pond. Marshes and wet prairies are palustrine emergent wetlands that contain grasses, sedges, or cattails. Swamps, sloughs, and bottom-land hardwood forests are palustrine forested and scrub-shrub wetlands typically found along rivers. Flatwoods are palustrine forested wetlands that form on level, poorly drained soils where the water table is shallow. Bogs and fens are palustrine wetlands that are generally located in depressions in once-glaciated areas of Indiana; these wetlands generally contain grasses, other soft-stemmed plants, and peat deposits. Kettles and potholes are emergent and scrub-shrub wetlands that formed in depressions left after large blocks of ice that were embedded in glacially deposited sediments melted. Dune swales are topographic depressions among sand dunes near Lake Michigan that contain palustrine emergent or scrub-shrub wetlands. Sinkhole ponds are lacustrine wetlands located in plugged sinkholes in areas where limestone bedrock is at or near the surface.

HYDROLOGIC SETTING

The wetlands of Indiana are formed and maintained by water from precipitation, surface-water runoff, and local and regional ground-water flow systems. Wetlands generally are in topographic lows, where water from surface runoff collects and where ground water commonly discharges after periods of heavy precipitation. Fluctuations in local precipitation and evapotranspiration rates combined with local differences in geology, topography, and soil characteristics cause transient or seasonal changes in the way that ground water and surface water interact in a wetland (Meyboom, 1966; Wilcox, 1986; Winter, 1992; Phillips and Shedlock, 1993).

Precipitation in Indiana varies seasonally and geographically. Precipitation falls throughout the year but is greatest from March through July (Crompton, 1986). Annual average precipitation ranges from about 36 inches in the northeastern part of the State to about 44 inches in the south-central part. Combined loss from evaporation and transpiration is nearly uniform across the State and averages 26 inches annually. Annual surface-water runoff averages about

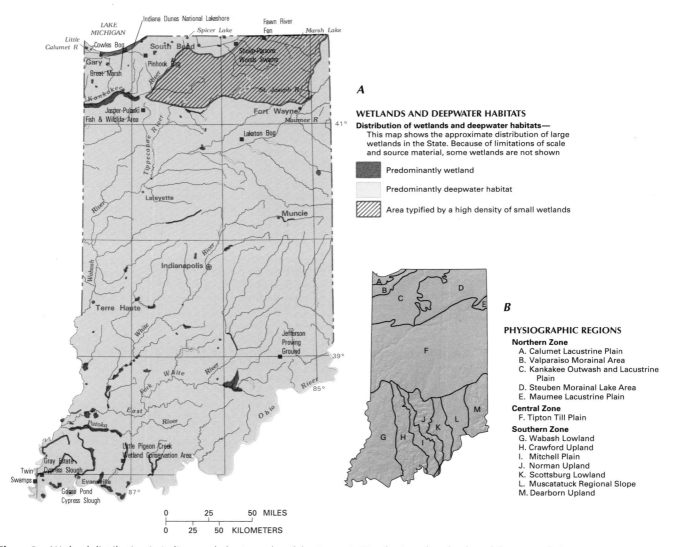

Figure 2.   Wetland distribution in Indiana and physiography of the State. *A,* Distribution of wetlands and deepwater habitats. *B,* Physiography. *(Sources: A, T.E. Dahl, U.S. Fish and Wildlife Service, unpub. data, 1991. B, Physiographic divisions modified from Schneider, 1966; landforms data from EROS Data Center.)*

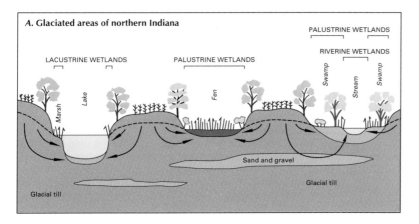

A. Glaciated areas of northern Indiana

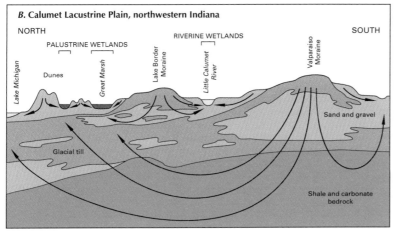

B. Calumet Lacustrine Plain, northwestern Indiana

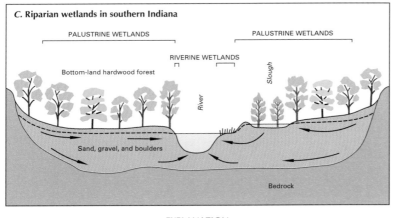

C. Riparian wetlands in southern Indiana

EXPLANATION

→ Direction of ground-water flow

----- Average water table

Forest vegetation

Scrub-shrub vegetation

Emergent vegetation

Farmed crops

Organic deposits

Note: Vertical scale greatly exaggerated

Figure 3. Generalized geohydrologic setting of common wetland types in Indiana. *A*, Wetlands in glaciated areas of northern Indiana. *B*, Wetlands in the Calumet Lacustrine Plain of northwestern Indiana. *C*, Riparian wetlands in bedrock areas of southern Indiana. *(Sources: A, Modified from Hartke and others, 1975. B, Modified from Shedlock and others, 1993. C, Modified from Gallaher and Price, 1966.)*

9.0 inches, and about 3.5 inches recharges the ground-water system (Clark, 1980). The abundant precipitation is conducive to the formation and maintenance of wetlands, which were once extensive in Indiana. However, agricultural tile drains, ditches, and straightened drainages have substantially reduced the retention of water and, hence, reduced wetland area in many parts of the State.

Indiana can be divided into three broad physiographic zones based on surficial and bedrock geology (fig. 2*B*). The northern zone consists of glacial moraine and areas reworked by water from ancient and present Lake Michigan. The central zone is a flat depositional plain of low relief. The physiography of the southern zone varies and is largely controlled by underlying bedrock. Wetland hydrology differs among and within these zones.

In the northern physiographic zone, different local depositional conditions during glacial advances and retreats have resulted in a complex surficial aquifer largely composed of till. Till is a heterogeneous mixture of clay, silt, sand, gravel, and boulders that is deposited directly by and underneath a glacier. The surficial aquifer in the northern zone is connected to deeper aquifer systems in places where the till is thin or missing (Shedlock and others, 1993). Wetlands in this zone generally are in low, poorly drained areas that have standing water (fig. 3*A*).

The northern zone has five physiographic units: the Valparaiso Morainal Area, the Steuben Morainal Lake Area, the Calumet Lacustrine Plain, the Kankakee Outwash and Lacustrine Plain, and the Maumee Lacustrine Plain (fig. 2*B*). Most of the wetlands that remain in Indiana are in the Valparaiso Morainal Area and the Steuben Morainal Lake Area. These physiographic units have irregular topography and as much as 200 feet of relief; numerous small, poorly integrated streams; and many closed depressions containing lakes and wetlands, including kettles, fens, and bogs. Water is supplied to these wet areas by precipitation, surface-water runoff and, except in bogs, shallow ground-water flow (fig. 3*A*). Notable wetlands in these areas are Spicer Lake, Marsh Lake, Laketon Bog, Pinhook Bog, and Fawn River Fen.

The Calumet Lacustrine Plain, Kankakee Outwash and Lacustrine Plain, and Maumee Lacustrine Plain have flat terrain and once contained extensive wetlands in glacial lakes and outwash plains. Land in these physiographic units has been nearly completely ditched and drained. Remaining wetlands in these units are mainly in riparian areas. The exception is the Calumet Lacustrine Plain, which contains extensive wetlands in and around the Indiana Dunes National Lakeshore (fig. 3*B*). In the Calumet Lacustrine Plain, major changes in the level of Lake Michigan occurred as the glaciers receded. Shoreline dune complexes formed sequentially approximately parallel to the modern lakeshore. Each new dune line prevented drainage from the south from reaching the lake directly, resulting in the development of a complex wetland system. The wetland system includes Cowles Bog (fig. 1), the largest peatland in Indiana. Peatlands form in depressions where there is poor drainage, standing water, and water chemistry not conducive to plant decay. Plant remains eventually fill the original depression and sometimes rise above the surrounding land surface, forming a peat mound.

Cowles Bog, which is sustained in part by ground water and therefore is by definition a fen, is an example of this process (Wilcox and others, 1986; Shedlock and others, 1993). The wetlands in the Indiana Dunes are the only wetlands in the State where a detailed long-term study (Shedlock and others, 1993) has been completed. The hydrology of both the riparian and the sand-dune wetlands in the Calumet Lacustrine Plain is controlled by precipitation and ground-water flow, primarily in shallow flow systems.

The central physiographic zone (fig. 2B) consists of one unit—the Tipton Till Plain, which is a nearly flat to gently rolling glacial plain of sandy and silty outwash sediments. At the extreme western edge of the plain, the Wabash River and its tributaries have cut as deep as 150 feet through the glacial deposits into bedrock. The Tipton Till Plain has been almost entirely drained for agricultural purposes. Remaining wetlands are in stream channels, along the edges of reservoirs, and in small, shallow depressions between agricultural fields. These wetlands are maintained by precipitation and local and regional ground-water flow.

The southern physiographic zone (fig. 2B) was partly covered by glaciers. There, the surficial aquifer consists of regolith and sedimentary deposits of glacial origin. Regolith is unconsolidated, mostly fine-grained material composed of fragmental, weathered bedrock and alluvium overlying unweathered bedrock. The southern zone has seven physiographic units: the Wabash Lowland, the Crawford Upland, the Mitchell Plain, the Norman Upland, the Scottsburg Lowland, the Muscatatuck Regional Slope, and the Dearborn Upland. Topography and soils differ considerably among the units and are primarily controlled by the type of underlying bedrock.

Most of the wetlands in the southern physiographic zone are in riparian areas along streams and rivers. These wetlands are maintained by precipitation and local shallow flow systems (fig. 3C). Some of the largest remaining wetlands in Indiana are in the Wabash and Scottsburg Lowlands and on the Muscatatuck Regional Slope. These wetlands are in the flood plains, confluences, and backwater areas of the Wabash, Patoka, White, and Ohio Rivers and their tributaries. Notable among these are the flatwoods in the tributaries of the East Fork of the White River, located in the Jefferson Proving Grounds; Little Pigeon Creek Wetland Conservation Area; Twin Swamps; and the Gray Estate and Goose Pond Cypress Sloughs. Unusual wetlands in this zone include those in the Wabash Lowland that have formed in long, narrow surface depressions between spoil piles in areas mined for coal. Also unusual are the sinkhole wetlands and ponds in the Mitchell Plain, formed where vertical solution zones in the carbonate bedrock have become plugged with soil and other debris, and water from precipitation and surface runoff has collected. Additionally, the Jasper–Pulaski Fish and Wildlife Area is a congregating area and migratory rest stop for eastern greater sandhill cranes.

TRENDS

In the 1780's, before settlement by Europeans, wetlands covered about 5.6 million acres (24 percent) of Indiana (Indiana Department of Natural Resources, 1989). At that time, and continuing to the present in some communities, wetlands were categorized as wastelands that could be made more useful by filling and draining. Federal and State laws encouraged these activities (Read, 1993). By the early 1980's, more than 85 percent of the original wetlands in Indiana had been destroyed, and only about 813,000 acres of wetlands remained (Rolley, 1991). About 85 percent of vegetated-wetland losses resulted from conversion of wetlands for agricultural purposes (Indiana Department of Natural Resources, 1989).

Agricultural, industrial, and residential-development interests in Indiana still encourage stream channelization and ditching, drain-

ing, filling, diking, dredging, and damming of wetlands. In addition to the direct loss of wetlands, the biological value of many natural wetlands has been degraded by contamination by excess nutrients, sediments, and toxic chemicals as well as by the spread of nonnative plant species that can eliminate native species. The loss and degradation of wetlands and resulting adverse effects on fish and wildlife populations have reduced recreational opportunities and the economic benefits that outdoor recreation can bring to local communities (Indiana Department of Natural Resources, written commun., 1993).

About 1 to 3 percent of Indiana's remaining wetlands are lost each year, primarily because of drainage for agricultural purposes (Indiana Division of Fish and Wildlife, written commun., 1993). A survey of wetlands in the northern one-third of Indiana indicated that by 1987, more than 10 percent of the wetlands in aerial photographs taken between 1981 and 1984 of the northern physiographic zone and Wabash River watershed had been drained (Indiana Department of Natural Resources, 1989).

Construction of flood-control reservoirs in the 1960's and 1970's doubled the acreage of open water by permanently flooding riparian zones along rivers. Lacustrine wetlands replaced the naturally occurring riverine and palustrine wetlands in the process. In fact, approximately 70 percent of existing lacustrine wetlands and 13 percent of palustrine wetlands in Indiana developed as the result of damming or excavation (Rolley, 1991). In addition, some new wetlands have formed in reclaimed and unreclaimed spoil areas in coal-mining zones. However, wetland losses in Indiana have been far greater than wetland gains.

To slow the rate of wetland loss, recent State and Federal laws require or encourage wetland protection or creation. For example, wetlands have been created by the establishment of compensatory wetland mitigation sites, especially for transportation-related projects. Regulations require that 3 acres be created for each acre destroyed, but the actual success rate is probably much lower (Indiana Department of Natural Resources, 1989). The Indiana tax code encourages wetland protection for sites larger than 10 acres. Some farmers have used provisions in Federal wetlands-related legislation to consolidate existing wetlands and create new ones (Indiana Department of Natural Resources, 1989). Some municipalities are invoking waste- and stormwater-management regulations to encourage the protection and development of wetlands. River Basin Commissions, notably those of the Kankakee, Maumee, and St. Joseph Rivers, are encouraging or pursuing wetland restoration as a flood-control measure that would have the added benefit of recreation potential. In addition, the Indiana Department of Natural Resources, FWS, and the Natural Resources Conservation Service (NRCS; formerly known as the Soil Conservation Service) have restored more than 600 wetlands totaling 3,000 acres and constructed many other wetlands under the Partners for Wildlife program. Wetland protection efforts are adversely affected by limited public understanding of wetland values, lack of information on wetland distribution and abundance in the State, and insufficient and unenforced legislation (Indiana Department of Natural Resources, written commun., 1993).

CONSERVATION

Many government agencies and private organizations participate in wetland conservation in Indiana. The most active agencies and organizations and some of their activities are listed in table 1.

Federal wetland activities.—Development activities in Indiana wetlands are regulated by several Federal statutory prohibitions and incentives that are intended to slow wetland losses. Some of the more important of these are contained in the 1899 Rivers and Harbors Act; the 1972 Clean Water Act and amendments; the 1985 Food

Table 1. Selected wetland-related activities of government agencies and private organizations in Indiana, 1993

[Source: Classification of activities is generalized from information provided by agencies and organizations. •, agency or organization participates in wetland-related activity; ..., agency or organization does not participate in wetland-related activity. **MAN**, management; **REG**, regulation; **R&C**, restoration and creation; **LAN**, land acquisition; **R&D**, research and data collection; **D&I**, delineation and inventory]

Agency or organization	MAN	REG	R&C	LAN	R&D	D&I
FEDERAL						
Department of Agriculture						
Consolidated Farm Service Agency	...	•	...	...	...	...
Natural Resources Conservation Service	...	•	•	...	•	•
Department of Commerce						
National Oceanic and Atmospheric						
Administration	...	•	...	...	...	...
Department of Defense						
Army Corps of Engineers	...	•	•	...	•	•
Department of the Interior						
Fish and Wildlife Service	•	•	•	•	•	•
Geological Survey	...	...	...	...	•	...
National Biological Service	...	...	...	...	•	...
National Park Service	•	...	•	•	•	•
Environmental Protection Agency	...	•	...	...	•	•
STATE						
Department of Environmental Management	•	•	...	...	...	•
Department of Natural Resources	•	•	•	•	•	•
Indiana Geological Survey	...	...	...	...	•	...
Indiana University						
School of Public and Environmental Affairs	...	...	...	...	•	•
Purdue University						
Department of Forestry and Natural Resources	...	...	...	...	•	•
State Highway Administration	...	...	...	...	•	•
SOME COUNTY AND LOCAL GOVERNMENTS	•	•	...	•	...	•
PRIVATE ORGANIZATIONS						
Ducks Unlimited	•	...	•	•	•	...
Hoosier Environmental Council	•	...	...	...	...	...
Izaak Walton League	•	...	•	•	...	...
Save the Dunes Council	•	...	•	...	...	...
Sierra Club	...	...	...	...	•	...
The Nature Conservancy	•	...	•	•	...	...

Security Act; the 1990 Food, Agriculture, Conservation, and Trade Act; the 1986 Emergency Wetlands Resources Act; and the 1972 Coastal Zone Management Act.

Section 10 of the Rivers and Harbors Act gives the U.S. Army Corps of Engineers (Corps) authority to regulate certain activities in navigable waters. Regulated activities include diking, deepening, filling, excavating, and placing of structures. The related section 404 of the Clean Water Act is the most often-used Federal legislation protecting wetlands. Under section 404 provisions, the Corps issues permits regulating the discharge of dredged or fill material into wetlands. Permits are subject to review and possible veto by the U.S. Environmental Protection Agency (EPA), and the FWS has review and advisory roles. Section 401 of the Clean Water Act grants to States and eligible Indian Tribes the authority to approve, apply conditions to, or deny section 404 permit applications on the basis of a proposed activity's probable effects on the water quality of a wetland.

Most farming, ranching, and silviculture activities are not subject to section 404 regulation. However, the "Swampbuster" provision of the 1985 Food Security Act and amendments in the 1990 Food, Agriculture, Conservation, and Trade Act discourage (through financial disincentives) the draining, filling, or other alteration of wetlands for agricultural use. The law allows exemptions from penalties in some cases, especially if the farmer agrees to restore the altered wetland or other wetlands that have been converted to agri-

cultural use. The Wetlands Reserve Program of the 1990 Food, Agriculture, Conservation, and Trade Act authorizes the Federal Government to purchase conservation easements from landowners who agree to protect or restore wetlands. The Consolidated Farm Service Agency (formerly the Agricultural Stabilization and Conservation Service) administers the Swampbuster provisions and Wetlands Reserve Program. The NRCS determines compliance with Swampbuster provisions and assists farmers in the identification of wetlands and in the development of wetland protection, restoration, or creation plans.

The 1986 Emergency Wetlands Resources Act and the 1972 Coastal Zone Management Act and amendments encourage wetland protection through funding incentives. The Emergency Wetland Resources Act requires States to address wetland protection in their Statewide Comprehensive Outdoor Recreation Plans to qualify for Federal funding for State recreational land; the National Park Service provides guidance to States in developing the wetland component of their plans. Coastal and Great Lakes States that adopt coastal-zone management programs and plans approved by the National Oceanic and Atmospheric Administration are eligible for Federal funding and technical assistance through the Coastal Zone Management Act.

State wetland activities.—Currently (1993), no Indiana law specifically regulates activities in wetlands, although the Department of Natural Resources is developing a State wetland conservation plan under a grant from the EPA. The scheduled completion date for the plan is mid-1995. Regulation and management of Indiana wetlands are performed under the Indiana Water Pollution Control Law, sections 401 and 404 of the Federal Clean Water Act, the Indiana Flood Control Act, the Indiana Preservation of Lakes Statute, the Indiana Nature Preserves Act, and the Indiana Wetland Conservation Program. The Indiana Department of Environmental Management and the Indiana Department of Natural Resources are the principal State agencies that administer the laws and associated permit programs.

The Indiana Water Pollution Control Law gives the Department of Environmental Management authority to protect wetlands, which are defined as "waters of the State" for this purpose. Section 401 of the Federal Clean Water Act authorizes the Department of Environmental Management's water-quality certification program. Corps section 404 dredge-and-fill applications are reviewed both by the Department of Environmental Management to determine whether the proposed activities will adversely affect water quality and by the Department of Natural Resources for comment on potential environmental impacts and habitat disturbance. The Indiana Flood Control Act requires a Construction in the Floodway Permit from the Department of Natural Resources in order to construct within the floodway of a river or stream and its adjacent wetlands. The Indiana Preservation of Lakes Statute requires a permit from the Department of Natural Resources to change the water level or alter the shoreline or bed of a public freshwater lake. The Indiana Nature Preserves Act established the Division of Nature Preserves within the Department of Natural Resources; the Division is responsible for the inventory, acquisition, dedication, management, and protection of significant natural areas throughout the State, including wetlands, but the program's strict criteria eliminate many wetlands from consideration. The Division of Fish and Wildlife of the Department of Natural Resources administers the Indiana Wetland Conservation Program, which also protects and manages "significant" wetlands in 20 areas (totaling 5,409 acres) acquired by donation, by purchase, or as compensation for loss resulting from permit violation.

Other State wetland-management activities of the Division of Fish and Wildlife include several projects in partnership with Federal, other State, and private agencies to conserve and restore wetlands for wildlife habitat. In addition, the Division administers recreation and conservation areas directly and performs management activities in about 364,000 acres, mostly lakes and rivers.

County and local wetland activities.—Several counties are developing wetland programs. For example, LaGrange County in northeastern Indiana is developing a water-treatment process that uses created wetlands to protect its natural lakes and streams.

Private wetland organization activities.—Several private organizations in Indiana are active in the development of wetland regulations, policy planning, advocacy, land acquisition and management, environmental education, and research. A few of the many private organizations active in wetlands issues in the State are The Nature Conservancy, whose primary wetland activities are acquisition, preservation, and management of wetland areas and associated watersheds; the Sierra Club, which has established the Wetlands Project, an information network to connect individuals, groups, and agencies working on wetland conservation and restoration; Ducks Unlimited, which supports the conservation and creation of waterfowl habitat; and the Izaak Walton League, the Save the Dunes Council, and the Hoosier Environmental Council, which support public education and efforts to enact wetland protection legislation.

References Cited

Clark, G.D., ed., 1980, The Indiana water resource: Indianapolis, Indiana Department of Natural Resources, v. I, 508 p.; v. II, 94 p.

Cowardin, L.M., Carter, Virginia, Golet, F.C., and LaRoe, E.T., 1979, Classification of wetlands and deepwater habitats of the United States: U.S. Fish and Wildlife Service Report FWS/OBS–79/31, 131 p.

Crompton, E.J., 1986, Indiana surface-water resources, *in* U.S. Geological Survey, National water summary 1985—Hydrologic events and surface-water resources: U.S. Geological Survey Water-Supply Paper 2300, p. 223–228.

Gallaher, J.T., and Price, W.E., Jr., 1966, Hydrology of the alluvial deposits in the Ohio River valley in Kentucky: U.S. Geological Survey Water-Supply Paper 1818, 80 p.

Hartke, E.J., Hill, J.R., and Reshkin, Mark, 1975, Environmental geology of Lake and Porter Counties, Indiana—An aid to planning: Indiana Department of Natural Resources, Indiana Geological Survey Special Report 11, Environmental Study 8, 57 p.

Indiana Department of Environmental Management, 1991, Indiana 305(b) report, 1990–1991: Indianapolis, Ind., Office of Water Management, p. 1–20.

Indiana Department of Natural Resources, 1989, Wetlands...Indiana's endangered natural resource, an appendix to Indiana outdoor recreation 1989—An assessment and policy plan: Indianapolis, Ind., Department of Natural Resources, Division of Outdoor Recreation, 19 p.

Meyboom, Peter, 1966, Unsteady groundwater flow near a willow ring in hummocky moraine: Journal of Hydrology, v. 4, p. 38–62.

Phillips, P.J., and Shedlock, R.J., 1993, Hydrology and chemistry of groundwater and seasonal ponds in the Atlantic Coastal Plain in Delaware, U.S.A.: Journal of Hydrology, v. 141, p. 157–178.

Read, C.J., 1993, Swamped, *in* Werner, P., ed., The wetlander: Indianapolis, Ind., Sierra Club Wetlands Project, v. 2, no. 1, p. 5.

Rolley, R.E., 1991, Indiana's wetland inventory: Department of Natural Resources, Division of Fish and Wildlife, Wildlife Management and Research Notes 532, 6 p.

Schneider, A.F., 1966, Physiography, *in* Lindsey, A.A., ed., Natural features of Indiana: Indianapolis, Indiana Academy of Science, p. 40–56.

Shedlock, R.J., Wilcox, D.A., Thompson, T.A., and Cohen, D.A., 1993, Interactions between ground water and wetlands, southern shore of Lake Michigan, USA: Journal of Hydrology, v. 141, p. 127–155.

Wilcox, D.A., 1986, The effects of deicing salts of water chemistry in Pinhook Bog, Indiana: Water Resources Bulletin, v. 22, no. 1, p. 57–65.

Wilcox, D.A., Shedlock, R.J., and Hendrickson, W.H., 1986, Hydrology, water chemistry and ecological relations in the raised mound of Cowles Bog: Journal of Ecology, v. 74, p. 1,103–1,117.

Winter, T.C., 1992, A physiographic and climatic framework for hydrologic studies of wetlands, *in* Robarts, R.D., and Bothwell, M.L., eds., Proceedings of the Symposium on Aquatic Ecosystems in Semi-Arid Regions, 1990: Saskatoon, Saskatchewan, Environment Canada, The National Hydrology Research Institute Symposium Series 7.

FOR ADDITIONAL INFORMATION: District Chief, U.S. Geological Survey, 5957 Lakeside Boulevard, Indianapolis, IN 46278; Regional Wetland Coordinator, U.S. Fish and Wildlife Service, BHW Federal Building, 1 Federal Drive, Fort Snelling, MN 55111

Prepared by
Martha A. Hayes,
U.S. Geological Survey

Iowa
Wetland Resources

Wetlands provide many benefits, such as attenuating flood-peak discharges, stabilizing streambanks, and improving water quality by trapping suspended sediment and accumulating or transforming some types of chemical contaminants. Wetlands also are valuable for fish and wildlife habitat. Publicly owned wetland areas provide diverse recreational opportunities.

Wetlands cover about 1.2 percent of Iowa. However, about 200 years ago more than 11 percent of the State was wetlands (Dahl, 1990), and they were once a conspicuous feature on the prairie landscape (fig. 1). Fertile soils and abundant wildlife associated with the prairie and its wetlands were attractions for early settlers. However, when farming became a way of life for the settlers, wetlands came to be considered obstacles. Today, wetlands are considered by many residents to be valuable resources and important reminders of Iowa's natural heritage.

TYPES AND DISTRIBUTION

Wetlands are lands transitional between terrestrial and deepwater habitats where the water table usually is at or near the land surface or the land is covered by shallow water (Cowardin and others, 1979). The distribution of wetlands and deepwater habitats in Iowa is shown in figure 2A; only wetlands are discussed herein.

Wetlands can be vegetated or nonvegetated and are classified on the basis of their hydrology, vegetation, and substrate. In this summary, wetlands are classified according to the system proposed by Cowardin and others (1979), which is used by the U.S. Fish and Wildlife Service (FWS) to map and inventory the Nation's wetlands. At the most general level of the classification system, wetlands are grouped into five ecological systems: Palustrine, Lacustrine, Riverine, Estuarine, and Marine. The Palustrine System includes only wetlands, whereas the other systems comprise wetlands and deepwater habitats. Wetlands of the systems that occur in Iowa are described below.

System	Wetland description
Palustrine	Wetlands in which vegetation is predominantly trees (forested wetlands); shrubs (scrub-shrub wetlands); persistent or nonpersistent emergent, erect, rooted, herbaceous plants (persistent- and nonpersistent-emergent wetlands); or submersed and (or) floating plants (aquatic beds). Also, intermittently to permanently flooded open-water bodies of less than 20 acres in which water is less than 6.6 feet deep.
Lacustrine	Wetlands within an intermittently to permanently flooded lake or reservoir. Vegetation, when present, is predominantly nonpersistent emergent plants (nonpersistent-emergent wetlands), or submersed and (or) floating plants (aquatic beds), or both.
Riverine	Wetlands within a channel. Vegetation, when present, is same as in the Lacustrine System.

Dahl (1990) estimated that Iowa has about 421,900 wetland acres. Several types of wetlands are present throughout Iowa. Prairie-pothole marshes (emergent wetlands), swamps (forested wetlands), sloughs, bogs (emergent wetlands), wet meadows (emergent wetlands), fens (emergent and scrub-shrub wetlands), and small ponds are examples of palustrine wetlands. The Lacustrine System includes large oxbows, natural lakes, and reservoirs. The Riverine System includes streams and rivers.

Prairie-pothole marshes are a familiar type of Iowa wetland. These wetlands occur in the area of latest glaciation of Iowa (fig. 2B). Most of the naturally occurring lakes in Iowa also are in this area. Bishop (1981) estimated that there are about 36,500 acres of natural and artificial prairie-pothole marshes in Iowa.

Other wetlands in Iowa are associated with rivers in the interior and on the eastern and western borders of the State. The wetlands formerly associated with the Missouri River are examples of wetlands that have been lost due to channelization, whereas many of the wetlands along the Mississippi River were created as a result of lock and dam construction (Iowa Department of Natural Resources, 1988). About 380,000 acres of wetlands are associated with the rivers and streams of Iowa; most, about 324,785 acres, are along the rivers that border the State (Bishop, 1981). Small wetlands occur in scattered areas throughout Iowa where ground-water discharge maintains a supply of water that allows wetland vegetation to develop or where poor surface drainage results in ponding of water.

HYDROLOGIC SETTING

Wetlands form in areas where there is persistent water at or near the land surface. Palustrine wetlands in Iowa occur mainly in shallow depressions on the land surface. Lacustrine and riverine wetlands occur within deeper water lakes or within the channels of streams, respectively.

The interaction between surface water and ground water within palustrine wetlands is complex. Winter (1989) describes several hydrologic settings of wetlands in the northern prairie, including wetlands in the area of the most recent glaciation in Iowa (fig. 2B). Most of the northern-prairie wetlands occur in depressions on the land surface. These depressions, which occur at various positions on the landscape (fig. 3), were formed by processes related to glacial advances and deposition, slumping, deformation, and collapse as ice melted (Prior, 1991). The landscape where these depressions occur is characterized by glacial deposits that are low in permeability and that have a gradual regional land-surface slope. The depressions do not contribute to surface runoff unless the water they contain breaches local drainage divides separating them from adjacent depressions (Winter, 1989).

Figure 1. Prairie-pothole marsh at Freda Haffner Kettlehole State Preserve, Iowa. *(Photograph by Jean Prior, Iowa Department of Natural Resources.)*

Ponded water in northern-prairie wetlands usually is continuous with the water table in the glacial deposits (fig. 3). Wetlands in relatively high topographic positions (fig. 3) recharge ground water through the infiltration of rainfall, snowmelt, and local surface runoff. Discharge is through evapotranspiration and lateral and downward ground-water flow. These topographically higher wetlands depend on adequate precipitation to maintain their supply of water and are among the first wetland areas to dry up during drought.

Ground water from elevated sources can discharge to lower areas (fig. 3). The lower depressions also can receive surface runoff. Water in these depressions occurs either as ponded water or as ground water just below the land surface. Discharge typically is by evapotranspiration. Topographically low wetlands are less susceptible to short-term drought because ground water can continue to flow to them as long as the adjacent water table is higher.

Some depressions occur at intermediate positions on the landscape (fig. 3). Ground water can enter these depressions from higher areas and exit by reinfiltrating to ground water. In some wetlands on level land that normally receive ground-water discharge, an increase in water level to above the water table results in recharge to the ground-water system until evapotranspiration lowers the water level in the wetland and ground-water discharge resumes.

Palustrine wetlands in the flood plains of rivers occur in depressions and other low-lying areas, such as meander scars and stream channels. Water sources for these wetlands include precipitation, ground-water discharge, and stream overflows. Water loss from these wetlands is by evapotranspiration and ground-water flow.

Fens and seeps are wetlands that form on hillslopes where ground-water discharge maintains a source of water to wetland vegetation (Prior, 1991). These wetlands form at the hillside exposures of permeable materials that transmit ground water to the land surface (Thompson and others, 1992). Fens and seeps are similar to springs except that the small flow rates do not result in surface runoff.

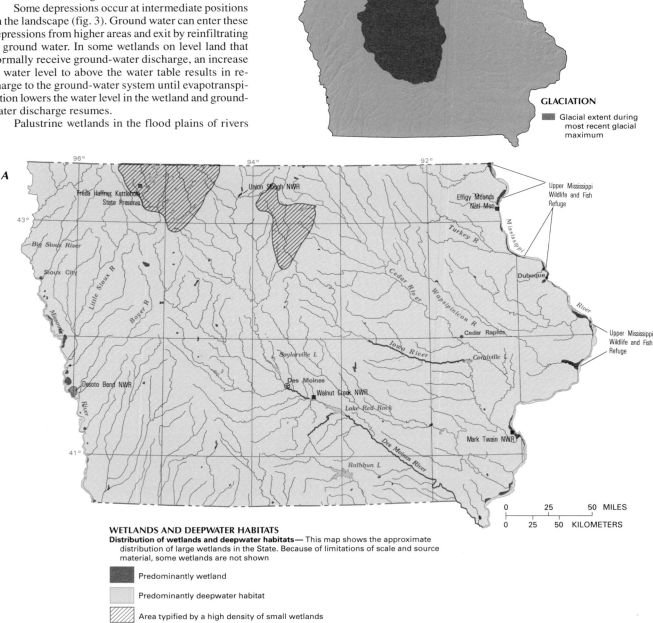

Figure 2. Wetland distribution in Iowa and extent of most recent glaciation. *A*, Distribution of wetlands and deepwater habitats. *B*, Extent of most recent glaciation. *(Sources: A, T.E. Dahl, U.S. Fish and Wildlife Service, unpub. data, 1991. B, Prior, 1991.)*

TRENDS

The FWS has estimated that Iowa lost 89 percent of its wetland area—more than 3.5 million acres—between the 1780's and the 1980's (Dahl, 1990). This percentage ranks third in the Nation for loss of wetlands; only California and Ohio have had greater percentage losses. The number of acres lost during the same time period was exceeded by 15 other States.

The Iowa Department of Natural Resources estimates that about 97.5 percent of Iowa's presettlement wetlands has been lost; 36,852 acres remain (Iowa Department of Natural Resources, 1990). The large difference in the wetland-area estimates by different agencies probably is due, in part, to differences in classification criteria. However, both estimates indicate the large magnitude of wetland loss that has occurred in Iowa during the past 200 years.

The primary cause of wetland loss has been agricultural development (Iowa Department of Natural Resources, 1990). Prairie potholes have been converted to farmland by draining. The drainage has been accomplished by constructing ditches to remove ponded water and installing subsurface drainage tile to lower the water table (Bishop, 1981). Some drained wetlands can be restored by removal or modification of the drainage system.

Wetland losses on flood plains are the result of stream channelization, flood control, and filling. Channelization can produce shorter, higher gradient stream segments, which results in a declining water table beneath the flood plain. Flood control, either by construction of reservoirs or dikes, reduces the potential for streams to overflow and recharge flood-plain depressions. Filling eliminates the depressions in which water accumulates. The Missouri River near Sioux City, Iowa, is an example of a stream segment that has been channelized and straightened. At Sioux City, the stream-water level has been lowered about 9 feet by channelization and construction of a reservoir on the Missouri River about 60 miles upstream. Buchmiller (1986) showed that water levels in wetlands on the flood plain responded directly to changes in the water level of the Missouri River.

The trend in wetland loss might be reversing. The Iowa Department of Natural Resources reported an increase of 1,852 wetland acres between 1987 and 1990 as a result of a five-State joint Federal, State, county, and private-organization program (Iowa Department of Natural Resources, 1990). The program, Prairie Pothole Joint Venture, hopes to acquire 2,000 acres of land in Iowa and restore 150 wetland areas per year (Iowa Department of Natural Resources, 1992). Many wetland acres are potential additions under the Wetlands Reserve Program of the 1990 Food, Agriculture, Conservation, and Trade Act. The Wetlands Reserve Program was created to purchase easements on private land to protect wetlands that otherwise can be lost to agricultural development.

Additional increases in wetland area are occurring as a result of reservoir construction in Iowa. Small soil-conservation structures and recreational reservoirs have been constructed in steep, typically well-drained terrain that originally might not have contained wetlands. The impoundment of water behind these structures can lead to increases in palustrine and lacustrine wetlands. However, the number of additional acres resulting from impoundment is expected to be small compared to the potential additions under the Wetlands Reserve Program (Jim Ayen, Soil Conservation Service, oral commun., 1992).

CONSERVATION

Many government agencies and private organizations participate in wetland conservation in Iowa. The most active agencies and organizations and some of their activities are listed in table 1.

Federal wetland activities.—Development activities in Iowa wetlands are regulated by several Federal statutory prohibitions and incentives that are intended to slow wetland losses. Some of the more important of these are contained in the 1899 Rivers and Harbors Act; the 1972 Clean Water Act and amendments; the 1985 Food Security Act; the 1990 Food, Agriculture, Conservation, and Trade Act; and the 1986 Emergency Wetlands Resources Act.

Section 10 of the Rivers and Harbors Act gives the U.S. Army Corps of Engineers (Corps) authority to regulate certain activities in navigable waters. Regulated activities include diking, deepening, filling, excavating, and placing of structures. The related section 404 of the Clean Water Act is the most often-used Federal legislation protecting wetlands. Under section 404 provisions, the Corps issues permits regulating the discharge of dredged or fill material into wetlands. Permits are subject to review and possible veto by the U.S. Environmental Protection Agency (EPA), and the FWS has review and advisory roles. Section 401 of the Clean Water Act grants to States and eligible Indian Tribes the authority to approve, apply conditions to, or deny section 404 permit applications on the basis of a proposed activity's probable effects on the water quality of a wetland.

Most farming, ranching, and silviculture activities are not subject to section 404 regulation. However, the "Swampbuster" provision of the 1985 Food Security Act and amendments in the 1990 Food, Agriculture, Conservation, and Trade Act discourages (through financial disincentives) the draining, filling, or other alteration of wetlands for agricultural use. The law allows exemptions from penalties in some cases, especially if the farmer agrees to restore the altered wetland or other wetlands that have been converted to agricultural use. The Wetlands Reserve Program of the 1990 Food, Agriculture, Conservation, and Trade Act authorizes the Federal Government to purchase conservation easements from landowners who agree to protect or restore wetlands. The Consolidated Farm Service Agency (formerly the Agricultural Stabilization and Conservation Service) administers the Swampbuster provisions and Wetlands Reserve Program. The Natural Resources Conservation Service (formerly the Soil Conservation Service) determines compliance with Swampbuster provisions and assists farmers in the identification of wetlands and in the development of wetland protection, restoration, or creation plans.

The 1986 Emergency Wetlands Resources Act encourages wetland protection through funding incentives. The act requires States to address wetland protection in their Statewide Comprehensive Outdoor Recreation Plans to qualify for Federal funding for State recreational land; the National Park Service provides guidance to States in developing the wetland

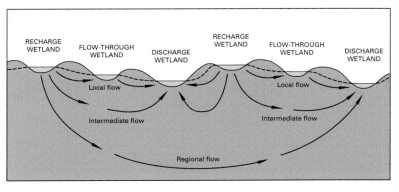

EXPLANATION

→ **Direction of ground-water flow**   ----- **Average water table**

Figure 3. Subsurface hydrology of northern-prairie wetlands. *(Source: Modified from Winter, 1992.)*

Table 1. Selected wetland-related activities of government agencies and private organizations in Iowa, 1993

[Source: Classification of activities is generalized from information provided by agencies and organizations. ●, agency or organization participates in wetland-related activity; ..., agency or organization does not participate in wetland-related activity. MAN, management; REG, regulation; R&C, restoration and creation; LAN, land acquisition; R&D, research and data collection; D&I, delineation and inventory]

Agency or organization	MAN	REG	R&C	LAN	R&D	D&I
FEDERAL						
Department of Agriculture						
Consolidated Farm Service Agency	...	●	●	...	...	...
Natural Resources Conservation Service	...	●	●	...	●	●
Department of Defense						
Army Corps of Engineers	●	●	●	...	●	●
Department of the Interior						
Fish and Wildlife Service	●	...	●	●	●	●
Geological Survey	...	...	...	...	●	...
National Biological Service	...	...	...	...	●	...
National Park Service	●	...	●	...	...	●
Environmental Protection Agency	...	●	●	...	●	...
STATE						
Department of Natural Resources						
Energy and Geological Resources Division	...	...	...	●	...	...
Environmental Protection Division	...	●	...	...	...	...
Fish and Wildlife Division	●	...	●	●	●	●
Parks, Recreation, and Preserves Division	●	...	...	...	...	...
Department of Transportation	●	...	●	●	...	...
Iowa State University						
Leopold Center for Sustainable Agriculture	...	...	...	...	●	...
University of Iowa						
Hygienic Laboratory	...	...	...	...	●	...
SOME COUNTY AND LOCAL GOVERNMENTS	●	...	●	●	...	●
PRIVATE ORGANIZATIONS						
Ducks Unlimited	...	...	●	●	...	...
Iowa Natural Heritage Foundation	●	...	●	●	...	●
Pheasants Forever	...	...	●	●	...	...
The Nature Conservancy	●	...	●	●	●	●

component of their plans.

In addition to its regulatory responsibilities, EPA provides financial assistance for special studies, development of wetland inventories, and other resource-management tools. Technical assistance is available to agencies and the public for wetland-delineation training, project consultation, and public education. The EPA oversees the State's development and implementation of water-quality standards that apply to surface waters, including wetlands. Two agencies have responsibilities for management of most Federal wetlands in Iowa. The Corps has responsibility for about 217,000 acres of land that includes wetlands in areas of Federal flood-control projects. The principal areas of these wetlands are along the Mississippi River and the four interior flood-control reservoirs in Iowa (Lake Red Rock, Saylorville Lake, Coralville Lake, and Rathbun Lake). The FWS manages land at five National Wildlife Refuges (NWR) that contain wetlands: Upper Mississippi River Wildlife and Fish Refuge, Mark Twain NWR, Union Slough NWR, Desoto Bend NWR, and Walnut Creek NWR. The NPS manages a small amount of wetland area at Effigy Mounds National Monument.

State wetland activities.—The principal wetlands-management agency in Iowa is the Iowa Department of Natural Resources. The Department manages more than 250,000 acres of public and some privately owned wetlands. The Department also is responsible for implementing Federal wetlands initiatives, such as the North American Waterfowl Management Plan. The Environmental Protection Division of the Department of Natural Resources is responsible for State regulatory actions. The State directly regulates wetlands under provisions of section 401 of the Clean Water Act, and some wetlands are protected for certain uses of water (Iowa Department of Natural Resources, 1990). The Iowa Department of Transporta-

tion manages small areas of wetlands within highway rights-of-way. The Department also identifies wetland areas that might be affected by construction projects and can acquire land and create additional wetlands to mitigate wetland loss resulting from construction projects.

County and local wetland activities.—Wetland management, restoration and creation, land acquisition, and delineation and inventory are being conducted by some county and local governments. The principal agencies involved are the county conservation boards. The extent of activity differs from one county to another.

Private wetland activities.—Several nonprofit private organizations are involved in wetland activities in Iowa. Ducks Unlimited, the Iowa Natural Heritage Foundation, and Pheasants Forever are partners with Federal, State, and local governments in raising funds for wetland acquisition and restoration. Although land is acquired by these organizations, typically it is sold or transferred to public agencies for management purposes. The Nature Conservancy also is active in acquiring land for preservation of endangered plant and animal species as well as ecologically unique habitats. Some of these land acquisitions contain wetlands.

References Cited

Bishop, R.A., 1981, Iowa's wetlands: Proceedings of the Iowa Academy of Science, v. 88, no. 1, p. 11–16.

Buchmiller, R.C., 1986, Hydrologic reconnaissance and summary of existing data on surface and ground-water resources in the Missouri River valley in Woodbury and Monona Counties, Iowa, 1985: U.S. Geological Survey Open-File Report 86–144, 21 p.

Cowardin, L.M., Carter, Virginia, Golet, F.C., and LaRoe, E.T., 1979, Classification of wetlands and deepwater habitats of the United States: Washington, D.C., U.S. Fish and Wildlife Service Report, FWS/OBS–79/31, 131 p.

Dahl, T.E., 1990, Wetlands—Losses in the United States, 1780's to 1980's: Washington, D.C., U.S. Fish and Wildlife Service Report to Congress, 13 p.

Iowa Department of Natural Resources, 1988, Iowa wetlands protection plan—A supplement to the Iowa statewide comprehensive outdoor recreation plan: Des Moines, Iowa Department of Natural Resources, 11 p.

_____1990, Water quality in Iowa during 1988 and 1989: Des Moines, Iowa Department of Natural Resources, p. 3–69 and 3–70.

_____1992, Iowa prairie pothole joint venture 1991 status report: Des Moines, Iowa Department of Natural Resources, 4 p.

Prior, J.C., 1991, Landforms of Iowa: Iowa City, University of Iowa Press, 153 p.

Thompson, C.A., Bettis III, E.A., and Baker, R.G., 1992, Geology of Iowa fens: Journal of Iowa Academy of Science, v. 99, no. 2–3, p. 53–59.

Winter, T.C., 1989, Hydrologic studies of wetlands in the northern prairie, *in* van der Valk, Arnold, ed., Northern prairie wetlands: Ames, Iowa State University Press, p. 16–54.

Winter, T.C., 1992, A physiographic and climatic framework for hydrologic studies of wetlands, *in* Robarts, R.D., and Bothwell, M.L., eds., Proceedings of the Symposium on Aquatic Ecosystems in Semi-arid Regions—Implications for resource management: Saskatoon, Saskatchewan, Environment Canada, The National Hydrology Research Institute Symposium Series 7, p. 127–148.

FOR ADDITIONAL INFORMATION: District Chief, U.S. Geological Survey, P.O. Box 1230, Iowa City, IA 52244; Regional Wetland Coordinator, U.S. Fish and Wildlife Service, BHW Building, 1 Federal Drive, Fort Snelling, , MN 55111

Prepared by
Robert C. Buchmiller,
U.S. Geological Survey

Kansas
Wetland Resources

Kansas once was covered by an estimated 841,000 acres of wetlands; of that area about 435,400 acres, or 0.8 percent of the State's area, remain (Dahl, 1990). Wetlands in Kansas represent some of the last aquatic areas available for wildlife and plants. Wetlands provide habitat for many species of birds, fish, mammals, reptiles, and invertebrates. Kansas wetlands are particularly important to migratory waterfowl and shorebirds, which depend on the few remaining wetlands in the Central Flyway for food, water, and cover during their seasonal migrations. Cheyenne Bottoms (fig. 1), a large freshwater marsh in central Kansas, is considered the most important migration staging point for shorebirds in North America (Wentz, 1988). Cheyenne Bottoms also provides habitat for five nationally threatened or endangered species—bald eagle, peregrine falcon, least tern, piping plover, and whooping crane (Kansas Biological Survey and Kansas Geological Survey, 1987).

Kansas wetlands are valuable for their hydrologic functions. By attenuating flood peaks and storing floodwaters, wetlands can protect adjacent and downstream property from flood damage and help control erosion. Wetlands also have important water-quality functions, including silt removal, mineral uptake, and nutrient transformation. Kansas wetlands also are important for recreation, tourism, and esthetic and educational benefits.

TYPES AND DISTRIBUTION

Wetlands are lands transitional between terrestrial and deepwater habitats where the water table usually is at or near the land surface or the land is covered by shallow water (Cowardin and others, 1979). The distribution of wetlands and deepwater habitats in Kansas is shown in figure 2A; only wetlands are discussed herein.

Figure 1. Blue-winged teal at Cheyenne Bottoms in central Kansas. *(Photograph by Mike Blair, Kansas Department of Wildlife and Parks.)*

Wetlands can be vegetated or nonvegetated and are classified on the basis of their hydrology, vegetation, and substrate. In this summary, wetlands are classified according to the system proposed by Cowardin and others (1979), which is used by the U.S. Fish and Wildlife Service (FWS) to map and inventory the Nation's wetlands. At the most general level of the classification system, wetlands are grouped into five ecological systems: Palustrine, Lacustrine, Riverine, Estuarine, and Marine. The Palustrine System includes only wetlands, whereas the other systems comprise wetlands and deepwater habitats. Wetlands of the systems that occur in Kansas are described below.

System	Wetland description
Palustrine	Wetlands in which vegetation is predominantly trees (forested wetlands); shrubs (scrub-shrub wetlands); persistent or nonpersistent emergent, erect, rooted, herbaceous plants (persistent- and nonpersistent-emergent wetlands); or submersed and (or) floating plants (aquatic beds). Also, intermittently to permanently flooded open-water bodies of less than 20 acres in which water is less than 6.6 feet deep.
Lacustrine	Wetlands within an intermittently to permanently flooded lake or reservoir. Vegetation, when present, is predominantly nonpersistent emergent plants (nonpersistent-emergent wetlands), or submersed and (or) floating plants (aquatic beds), or both.
Riverine	Wetlands within a channel. Vegetation, when present, is same as in the Lacustrine System.

Palustrine wetlands in Kansas include ephemeral wetlands; marshes; emergent wetlands in ground-water seeps, prairies, and oxbows; and forested wetlands in riparian areas. Ephemeral wetlands typically are flooded only seasonally; examples are sandhill pools located in the Arkansas River Valley in south-central Kansas and playa lakes scattered throughout the southwestern part of the State. Marshes occur in low-lying areas associated with river systems, terraces, and valley basins. Examples of fresh marshes are the Marais des Cygnes Wildlife Area in east-central Kansas, Jamestown Wildlife Area in north-central Kansas, and Cheyenne Bottoms. Salt marshes generally are limited to central Kansas. The largest salt marsh in the State is Quivira National Wildlife Refuge, which is located along Rattlesnake Creek. Areas saturated by fresh ground-water seepage are discontinuously distributed throughout the State. An example of an emergent wetland in a ground-water seep is the 11-acre Muscotah Marsh in northeastern Kansas. Prairie wetlands occur on nearly level soils on flood plains along rivers, streams, and creeks throughout most of the State. The Ninnescah River Basin wetlands, associated with the North and South Forks Ninnescah Rivers in south-central Kansas, include examples of prairie wetlands as well as riparian woodlands. Forested wetlands are located within riparian woodlands and forests along major rivers in both the eastern and western parts of the State (Lauver, 1989; Monda, 1992a).

Lacustrine wetlands in Kansas are primarily in impoundments. The Flint Hills National Wildlife Refuge at John Redmond Reservoir and Kirwin National Wildlife Refuge at Kirwin Reservoir are wetlands that have developed around lake headwater areas. These areas include both lacustrine wetlands and palustrine wetlands (persistent emergent, scrub-shrub, and forested wetlands along the shore or in backwater areas).

Riverine wetlands are most common in the eastern and central parts of the State. They include the beds of shallow, intermittent streams and areas less than 6.6 feet deep in perennial streams.

HYDROLOGIC SETTING

The availability of water to sustain wetlands depends on climatic, hydrologic, and physiographic factors as well as historic and present land use. Moisture is unevenly distributed across the State. Average annual precipitation in Kansas ranges from less than 16 inches in the west to more than 40 inches in the southeast (Jordan, 1986). In contrast, average annual evaporation potential increases from east to west, ranging from less than 44 inches in the northeast to more than 68 inches in the southwest (Farnsworth and others, 1982). Runoff is poorly sustained in the western and central parts of Kansas because of sparse precipitation, conservation practices, and withdrawals of water from streams and associated alluvial aquifers, primarily for irrigation. As a result, water deficits can occur during many seasons and years in these parts of the State.

Differences in topography and geology separate Kansas into broad physiographic divisions (fig. 2B). In the Great Plains of western Kansas, surface-water resources are scarce. Wetlands in these areas depend on water from precipitation and, in some areas, streamflow or shallow ground water. In the Central Lowland of eastern Kansas, surface water is more dependable. Water in streams, flood plains, and alluvial aquifers sustains many prairie wetlands and riparian woodlands and forests. In the Ozark Plateaus, one of the wettest and most densely forested areas in Kansas, the abun-

dant rainfall and high humidity create conditions favorable to wetlands (Spanbauer, 1988).

Wetlands in Kansas are temporarily, seasonally, semipermanently, or permanently flooded, depending on moisture availability. The playa lakes in southwestern Kansas are among the most temporary of palustrine wetlands, occurring in areas of low precipitation and high evaporation. Playas are sustained entirely by precipitation and surface drainage. These shallow basins drain areas as large as 2,000 acres but are flooded only after heavy rainfall or snowmelt in the spring. The clay soils of the playas tend to prevent seepage losses; most water loss is due to evaporation.

Sinks and shallow basins are other types of temporarily flooded wetlands in Kansas; they are mostly in the Great Plains region. The McPherson Valley Wetlands, a series of shallow lakes that historically covered a 126-square-mile area south of McPherson, are sinks caused by dissolution of underlying salt formations. The McPherson Valley Wetlands originally included several large, and many small, shallow marshes and two natural lakes (Wilson, 1992). Only one permanently flooded lake remains, along with a few shallow pools and marshes that were not drained. These areas are important for migratory waterfowl. Ongoing restoration of the McPherson Valley Wetlands is intended to reestablish and protect the seasonally and permanently flooded pools (Wilson, 1992).

Sandhill pools — depressions between the low dunes along the Arkansas River northeast of Hutchinson — become filled with water during the rainy season (Schoewe, 1949). Sandhill pools are poorly drained because of their nearly impervious subsoil. These wetlands can remain flooded, given a seasonally high water table, or can vanish during years of low precipitation (Lauver, 1989).

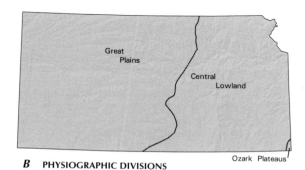

B   PHYSIOGRAPHIC DIVISIONS

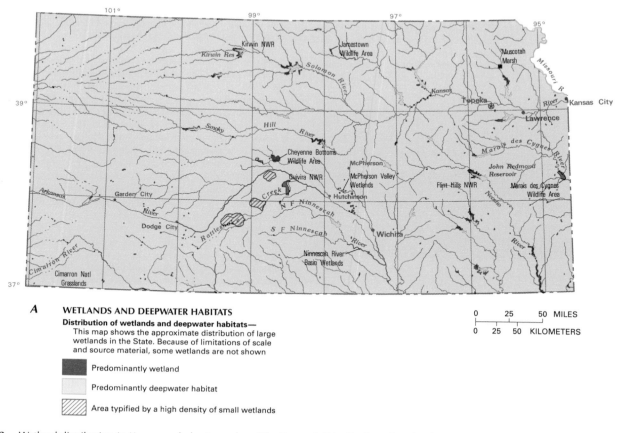

A   WETLANDS AND DEEPWATER HABITATS

Distribution of wetlands and deepwater habitats—
This map shows the approximate distribution of large wetlands in the State. Because of limitations of scale and source material, some wetlands are not shown

   Predominantly wetland

   Predominantly deepwater habitat

   Area typified by a high density of small wetlands

Figure 2. Wetland distribution in Kansas and physiography of the State. *A,* Distribution of wetlands and deepwater habitats. *B,* Physiography. *(Sources: A, T.E. Dahl, U.S. Fish and Wildlife Service, unpub. data, 1991. B, Physiographic divisions from Fenneman, 1946; landforms data from EROS Data Center.)*

Wetlands associated with riparian woodlands and forests can be flooded temporarily or seasonally, depending on the characteristics of streams with which they are associated. Riparian forested wetlands are located primarily along the Missouri, Kansas, Marais des Cygnes, and Neosho Rivers in the Central Lowland, where precipitation and runoff are sufficient to sustain streamflows and evaporation rates are relatively low. In prairie wetlands, drainage is poor, and the deep, alluvial soils remain saturated for most of the growing season (Monda, 1992a). In some years, prairie wetlands along flood plains in eastern Kansas may be inundated for several days at a time (Lauver, 1989).

Salt flats are seasonally inundated wetlands occurring on nearly level ground or within slight depressions. Salinity is high because of saline ground-water discharge or concentration of dissolved constituents by evaporation. Salt flats are located in central Kansas, where naturally saline ground water discharges to surface streams and pools. Soils in salt flats are saturated but contain standing water only after heavy precipitation (Monda, 1992a).

Fresh and salt marshes form in low-lying areas that have deep, poorly drained soils. Marshes range from semipermanently to permanently flooded (Monda, 1992a). Salt marshes are restricted to salty seepage areas that often contain brackish or stagnant water (Lauver, 1989). Quivira National Wildlife Refuge is sustained by water from Rattlesnake Creek. Downstream reaches of the stream and the marsh itself are natural ground-water discharge areas for underlying saltwater-bearing formations (Sophocleous, 1992).

Ground-water discharge is a vital source of moisture for some wetlands in Kansas. Localized artesian conditions cause soils in the Muscotah Marsh to be saturated by ground-water seepage. Within the Cimarron National Grasslands in southwestern Kansas, a ripar-

ian wetland on the flood plain of the Cimarron River is sustained by moisture from ground-water storage when the river is not flowing. The Cimarron River rarely flows, but when floods occur, the riparian areas are recharged and support new growth of woody vegetation. Controlled grazing on the Cimarron National Grasslands, which is managed by the U.S. Forest Service, ensures that some trees will remain among the sagebrush and grasses.

The disappearance of nearly one-half of the State's wetlands has increased the importance of those that remain. Migratory birds formerly had access to many wetlands as well as to shallow, braided river channels throughout central Kansas for foraging and resting. Draining of these wetlands and the depletion of streamflows in major streams such as the Arkansas River have left only Cheyenne Bottoms and Quivira National Wildlife Refuge as major stopover places in Kansas. Keeping those areas viable requires manipulation of the hydrologic system to ensure a consistent water supply.

The Kansas Department of Wildlife and Parks manages the 19,857-acre Cheyenne Bottoms Wildlife Area (fig. 3). Several adverse hydrologic conditions have had to be overcome to maintain shallow water in Cheyenne Bottoms—inadequate precipitation, declining flows in streams flowing into the area, periodic flooding, and high evaporation and transpiration losses. Evaporation and transpiration account for about 95 percent of the water lost from the wetland (Kansas Biological Survey and Kansas Geological Survey, 1987). In some years, losses can exceed the amount of water entering the basin and result in an overall deficit and increased salinity (Zimmerman, 1990).

The management strategy addressing these problems has focused on water storage, supplementation, and drainage. In the 1950's, diked pools were constructed to enhance storage, and dams

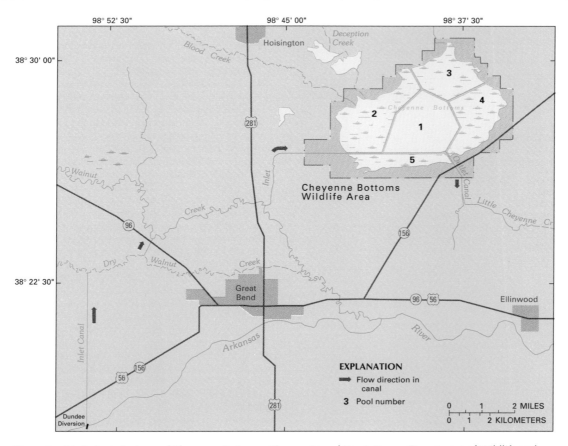

Figure 3. Hydrologic features of Cheyenne Bottoms. *(Source: Laurel Yasui, Kansas Department of Wildlife and Parks, written commun., 1992.)*

and ditches were built to divert water from the Arkansas River through Dry Walnut and Walnut Creeks to supplement natural flows from Blood and Deception Creeks. Ongoing activities at Cheyenne Bottoms include construction of additional dikes in pool 1 to create a deeper pool that will decrease evaporation relative to the volume of water stored; installation of pumping stations to facilitate water transfer among pools; level ditches dug through dense stands of cattails in silted areas of pool 4 to decrease water depth, provide varied habitat, and allow access to inner waters; and improvements to the canal from the Arkansas River to the marsh to reduce evaporation and seepage losses (Grover, 1992).

The Kansas Department of Wildlife and Parks holds water rights for 20,000 acre-feet per year from Walnut Creek and 30,000 acre-feet per year from the Arkansas River, but by the 1980's less than 20 percent of the legally protected amount of water was available (Karl Grover, Kansas Department of Wildlife and Parks, written commun., 1993). Declining flows in the Arkansas River and Walnut Creek have resulted from lower water tables caused primarily by ground-water withdrawals for irrigation, and from decreased runoff due to soil and water conservation practices such as terracing, construction of water impoundments, and conservation tillage (Kansas Biological Survey and Kansas Geological Survey, 1987; Zimmerman, 1990).

Recognition of the dependence of Cheyenne Bottoms on a managed hydrologic system resulted in legal action to protect the senior water right on Walnut Creek. In 1992, the Chief Engineer of the State Division of Water Resources established an Intensive

Table 1. Selected wetland-related activities of government agencies and private organizations in Kansas, 1993

[Source: Classification of activities is generalized from information provided by agencies and organizations. ●, agency or organization participates in wetland-related activity; ..., agency or organization does not participate in wetland-related activity. MAN, management; REG, regulation; R&C, restoration and creation; LAN, land acquisition; R&D, research and data collection; D&I, delineation and inventory]

Agency or organization	MAN	REG	R&C	LAN	R&D	D&I
FEDERAL						
Department of Agriculture						
Consolidated Farm Service Agency	...	●	...	...	...	...
Forest Service	●	...	●	●	●	●
Natural Resources Conservation Service	...	●	●	...	●	●
Department of Defense						
Army Corps of Engineers	●	●	●	...	●	●
Military reservations	●	...	...	...	...	...
Department of the Interior						
Bureau of Land Management	●	...	...	...	...	●
Fish and Wildlife Service	●	●	●	●	●	●
Geological Survey	...	...	...	...	●	...
National Biological Service	...	...	...	...	●	...
Environmental Protection Agency	...	●	...	...	●	●
STATE						
Biological Survey	...	...	...	...	●	●
Conservation Commission	...	●	...	...	...	...
Corporation Commission	...	●	...	...	...	...
Department of Agriculture						
Division of Water Resources	...	●	...	...	...	...
Department of Health and Environment	...	●	...	...	●	●
Department of Wildlife and Parks	●	●	●	●	●	●
Geological Survey	...	...	...	...	●	...
Water Office	●	●	...	...	...	...
PRIVATE						
Baker University	...	...	●	●	●	...
Ducks Unlimited	●	...	●	●	...	...
Kansas Wildscape Federation	...	...	...	●	...	...
Kansas Wildlife Foundation	●	...	●	●	...	...
National Audubon Society	...	...	...	...	●	...
Sierra Club	...	...	...	...	●	...
The Nature Conservancy	●	...	●	●	●	...

Groundwater Use Control Area in the Walnut Creek Basin, thus limiting water withdrawals by all irrigators, municipalities, and industries therein. The intent of the restrictions is to restore aquifer recharge and base flow to Walnut Creek.

TRENDS

According to FWS estimates, Kansas lost 405,600 acres, or 48 percent, of its wetlands between the 1780's and 1980's (Dahl, 1990). In 1890, the State sold 12 major salt marshes in central Kansas, some more than 1,000 acres in size. Many of these wetlands were drained and converted to agricultural uses shortly thereafter (Monda, 1992b). Draining and conversion to cropland have caused most of the wetland losses in Kansas; 40 percent of the losses occurred between 1955 and 1978 (Tiner, 1984). Most areas drained were shallow, palustrine wetlands such as the McPherson Valley Wetlands and the playa lakes. Only about 500 acres remain of the original 9,000-plus acres in the McPherson Valley Wetlands (Wilson, 1992), and about 70 percent of the original playa lakes are gone (Kansas Department of Wildlife and Parks, 1992a). Remaining wetlands, despite regulations protecting them, continue to be adversely affected by agricultural runoff of chemicals and sediment from surrounding croplands (Kansas Department of Wildlife and Parks, 1991). Other causes of wetland loss include depletion of surface and ground water, primarily as a result of irrigation withdrawals. Construction of flood-control structures and modifications to stream channels can result in drainage of wetlands or alteration of streamflows entering wetlands. Urban, industrial, and transportation-system development also can be detrimental to wetlands (Kansas Department of Wildlife and Parks, 1991).

CONSERVATION

Many government agencies and private organizations participate in wetland conservation in Kansas. The most active agencies and organizations and some of their activities are listed in table 1.

Federal wetland activities.—Development activities in Kansas wetlands are regulated by several Federal statutory prohibitions and incentives that are intended to slow wetland losses. Some of the more important of these are contained in the 1899 Rivers and Harbors Act; the 1972 Clean Water Act and amendments; the 1985 Food Security Act; the 1990 Food, Agriculture, Conservation, and Trade Act; and the 1986 Emergency Wetlands Resources Act.

Section 10 of the Rivers and Harbors Act gives the U.S. Army Corps of Engineers (Corps) authority to regulate certain activities in navigable waters. Regulated activities include diking, deepening, filling, excavating, and placing of structures. The related section 404 of the Clean Water Act is the most often-used Federal legislation protecting wetlands. Under section 404 provisions, the Corps issues permits regulating the discharge of dredged or fill material into wetlands. Permits are subject to review and possible veto by the U.S. Environmental Protection Agency (EPA), and the FWS has review and advisory roles. Section 401 of the Clean Water Act grants to States and eligible Indian Tribes the authority to approve, apply conditions to, or deny section 404 permit applications on the basis of a proposed activity's probable effects on the water quality of a wetland.

Most farming, ranching, and silviculture activities are not subject to section 404 regulation. However, the "Swampbuster" provision of the 1985 Food Security Act and amendments in the 1990 Food, Agriculture, Conservation, and Trade Act discourages (through financial disincentives) the draining, filling, or other alteration of wetlands for agricultural use. The law allows exemptions from penalties in some cases, especially if the farmer agrees to restore the altered wetland or other wetlands that have been converted to agricultural use. The Wetlands Reserve Program of the 1990 Food, Agriculture, Conservation, and Trade Act authorizes the Federal

Government to purchase conservation easements from landowners who agree to protect or restore wetlands. The Consolidated Farm Service Agency (formerly the Agricultural Stabilization and Conservation Service) (CFSA) administers the Swampbuster provisions and Wetlands Reserve Program. The Natural Resources Conservation Service (formerly the Soil Conservation Service) (NRCS) determines compliance with Swamp-buster provisions and assists farmers in the identification of wetlands and in the development of wetland protection, restoration, or creation plans.

The 1986 Emergency Wetlands Resources Act encourages wetland protection through funding incentives. The act requires States to address wetland protection in their Statewide Comprehensive Outdoor Recreation Plans to qualify for Federal funding for State recreational land; the National Park Service provides guidance to States in developing the wetland component of their plans.

Several Federal agencies provide technical and financial assistance for efforts to restore, enhance, or create wetlands and to educate the public about wetlands. The CFSA, through the Wetland Reserve Program, pays for easements on land where the owners are restoring and protecting wetlands. The Corps provides assistance for infrastructure restoration that affects wetlands and for some fish and wildlife habitat-restoration activities. The Corps also supports educational efforts through its interpretive programs and video library. The EPA provides financial and technical assistance for development of wetland inventories, project consultation, and public education. The EPA also oversees the development and implementation of State water-quality regulations that apply to surface waters, including wetlands. The FWS, through the Partners for Wildlife Program, offers technical advice and partial compensation to landowners who restore, enhance, or create wetlands.

State wetland activities. — State wetlands programs are distributed among many agencies. The Wetland and Riparian Areas Project is a cooperative effort that coordinates State programs for wetland and riparian areas, assists land managers, and promotes public awareness of wetland vaues and functions (Monda, 1992b). The project is coordinated through the Kansas Water Office as a multi-agency effort with grant funding from the EPA.

The Department of Wildlife and Parks manages most of the 22,265 acres of State-owned wetlands in Kansas. The agency has acquired, by purchase or lease, additional acreage in the playa-lakes region and the McPherson Valley Wetlands through Federal funding from FWS and, as part of the five-State Playa Lakes Joint Venture, from the North American Waterfowl Management Plan (Kansas Department of Wildlife and Parks, 1992b). The North American Waterfowl Management Plan is a multinational program for restoring waterfowl breeding populations by habitat acquisition and enhancement. Through its Wildlife Habitat Improvement Program, the Department of Wildlife and Parks provides financial and technical assistance to landowners who improve or develop wildlife habitat on private lands.

The Kansas Department of Health and Environment addresses wetland protection through its nonpoint-source pollution-control programs, Clean Lakes projects, and Lake and Wetland Monitoring Program. Water-quality regulations for wetlands are included within antidegradation policies and are used to protect wetlands through Clean Water Act section 401 water-quality certification and section 404 permit review (Kansas Department of Health and Environment, 1992). Any action involving a discharge of dredged or fill material into a wetland in Kansas must receive a section 401 water-quality certification from the Department of Health and Environment as well as a section 404 permit from the Corps. The Department may approve, make its approval conditional, or deny certification on the basis of water-quality criteria.

Several State agencies administer programs that affect wetlands through regulation of State waters. The Kansas Department of Agriculture's Division of Water Resources is responsible for review and approval of flood-plain zoning ordinances. The Division also regulates placement of fill and construction of levees within the 100-year flood plain, dam construction, stream obstruction, and channel modifications. The State Water Project's Environmental Coordination Act requires that various State agencies, including the Department of Wildlife and Parks, State and Extension Forestry, the Kansas Corporation Commission, and the State Historical Society, review applications to the Division of Water Resources for modification of streams and flood plains to determine potential adverse effects on wetlands, fish, and wildlife. These agencies may recommend acceptable alternatives to proposed modifications. The Kansas Water Office coordinates the manipulation of lake levels in Federal reservoirs through its Pool Level Management program, which can benefit waterfowl by controlling habitat access. The Kansas Water Office monitors minimum desirable streamflows established for 23 Kansas streams through the Minimum Desirable Streamflow program, thus protecting fish, wildlife, and water quality. The Kansas Water Office also oversees water-resource planning and management in Kansas through its administration of the State Water Plan. The Kansas Corporation Commission protects the State's fresh and other usable waters through regulation of drilling operations, surface-pond construction, and oil-and-gas spill cleanup.

The Kansas Biological Survey is involved in wetland activities through research on aquatic ecosystems, identification of Kansas Natural and Scientific areas, and development of models to evaluate the health of rivers, streams, and wetlands. The Kansas Geological Survey conducts geohydrologic studies related to wetlands in the State, such as the evaluation of the stream-aquifer system in the Rattlesnake Creek Basin, which includes Quivira National Wildlife Refuge.

The State Conservation Commission administers the Riparian and Wetland Protection Program, in which county conservation districts develop comprehensive plans to protect and restore riparian and wetland areas. Assistance from the Commission and the Department of Wildlife and Parks, along with funding from existing local, State, and Federal programs, is used to demonstrate the water-quality and flood-prevention benefits of riparian and wetland areas to landowners.

The Kansas State and Extension Forestry, through the Forestry Stewardship Program, provides technical assistance to landowners in proper management of riparian forests. Forest Stewardship Plans are developed by District Foresters, with participation by landowners, the Department of Wildlife and Parks, and the NRCS. Landowners who follow the plan are eligible for financial assistance through the Stewardship Incentive Program, which provides cost-share funding for riparian and wetland protection and improvements such as tree planting and maintenance, streambank stabilization, and preservation of fish and wildlife habitat.

Private wetland activities.—The Kansas chapter of Ducks Unlimited is involved in wetland-habitat conservation. Through its Matching Aid to Restore States Habitat program, Ducks Unlimited has provided the Department of Wildlife and Parks with matching funds that have been used, as of 1993, to purchase or lease 1,926 acres for wetland-habitat development. Another 916 acres of existing wetlands have benefited from additional development and restoration.

Baker University is involved in preservation and research at three natural areas in northeastern Kansas that contain wetland and riparian areas. The Nature Conservancy has cooperated with the FWS in the acquisition of 6,000 acres adjacent to the Marais des Cygnes Wildlife Area, and is building a 5,437-acre preserve near Cheyenne Bottoms.

Education and advocacy are as important to wetland protection as are regulation and land acquisition. The Kansas Wildlife Federation influences wetland activities in Kansas through education of its members and the public and lobbying of state legislators.

The Kansas Wildlife Federation was instrumental in securing funding for the Kansas Biological Survey and Kansas Geological Survey study of Cheyenne Bottoms and contributed financially to the lawsuit concerning enforcement of State water laws in the Walnut Creek Basin. The Kansas chapters of the Sierra Club and the National Audubon Society also are involved in education and advocacy regarding wetland issues.

References Cited

Carney, Edward, 1992, Water quality values, *in* Monda, M.J., ed., Wetland and riparian areas in Kansas—Resources in need of conservation: Topeka, Kansas Department of Wildlife and Parks, p. 24–25.

Cowardin, L.M, Carter, Virginia, Golet, F.C., and LaRoe, E.T., 1979, Classification of wetlands and deepwater habitats of the United States: U.S. Fish and Wildlife Service Report FWS/OBS–79/31, 131 p.

Dahl, T.E., 1990, Wetlands—Losses in the United States, 1780's to 1980's: Washington, D.C., U.S. Fish and Wildlife Service, 13 p.

Farnsworth, R.K., Thompson, E.S., and Peck, E.L., 1982, Evaporation atlas for the contiguous 48 United States: National Oceanographic and Atmospheric Administration Technical Report NWS 33, 27 p.

Fenneman, N.M., 1946, Physical divisions of the United States: Washington, D.C., U.S. Geological Survey special map, scale 1:7,000,000.

Grover, Karl, 1992, Cheyenne Bottoms renovation: Kansas Wildlife and Parks, v. 49, no. 2, p. 28–32.

Jordan, P.R., 1986, Kansas surface-water resources, *in* U.S. Geological Survey, National water summary 1985—Hydrologic events and surface-water resources: U.S. Geological Survey Water-Supply Paper 2300, p. 237–244.

Kansas Biological Survey and Kansas Geological Survey, 1987, Cheyenne Bottoms—An environmental assessment: Kansas Geological Survey Open-File Report 87–5, 719 p.

Kansas Department of Health and Environment, 1992, Kansas water quality assessment (305(b) report): Topeka, Kansas Department of Health and Environment, 58 p.

Kansas Department of Wildlife and Parks, 1991, A plan for Kansas wildlife and parks—Strategic plan: Topeka, Kansas Department of Wildlife and Parks, 158 p.

_____1992a, The playa—Oasis of the plains: Pratt, Kansas Department of Wildlife and Parks video, running time 14:23.

_____1992b, Playa Lakes Management Plan for the Playa Lakes Joint Venture of the North American Waterfowl Management Plan: Pratt, Kansas Department of Wildlife and Parks, 12 p.

Lauver, C.L., 1989, Preliminary classification of the natural communities of Kansas: Kansas Biological Survey Report 50, 21 p.

Monda, M.J., ed., 1992a, Classification of wetland and riparian areas in Kansas: Topeka, Kansas Department of Wildlife and Parks, 30 p.

_____1992b, Wetland and riparian areas in Kansas—Resources in need of conservation: Topeka, Kansas Department of Wildlife and Parks, 63 p.

Schoewe, W.H., 1949, The geography of Kansas—Part II, physical geography: Transactions of Kansas Academy of Sciences, v. 52, no. 3, p. 261–333.

Sophocleous, Marios, 1992, Stream-aquifer modeling of the lower Rattlesnake Creek basin with emphasis on the Quivira National Wildlife Refuge: Kansas Geological Survey Open-File Report 92–10, 29 p.

Spanbauer, M.K., 1988, Little Balkans: Kansas Wildlife and Parks, v. 45, no. 4, p. 6–10.

Tiner, R.W., Jr., 1984, Wetlands of the United States—Current status and recent trends: Washington, D.C., U.S. Fish and Wildlife Service, 59 p.

Wentz, W.A., 1988, An introduction to Cheyenne Bottoms: Kansas Wildlife and Parks, v. 45, no. 4, p. 30–31.

Wilson, Bert, 1992, McPherson Valley Wetlands: Kansas Wildlife and Parks, v. 49, no. 6, p. 21–25.

Zimmerman, J.L., 1990, Cheyenne Bottoms—Wetland in jeopardy: Lawrence, University Press of Kansas, 197 p.

FOR ADDITIONAL INFORMATION: District Chief, U.S. Geological Survey, 4821 Quail Crest Place, Lawrence, KS 66049; Regional Wetland Coordinator, U.S. Fish and Wildlife Service, Fish and Wildlife Enhancement, P.O. Box 25486, Denver Federal Center, Denver, CO 80225

Prepared by
Joan F. Kenny,
U.S. Geological Survey

Kentucky
Wetland Resources

Wetlands compose less than 2.5 percent of the surface area of Kentucky, but these fragile and finite ecosystems have considerable environmental, socioeconomic, and esthetic value. Axe Lake Swamp (fig. 1) is an example of a scenic wetland in the western part of the State.

Wetlands contribute to the maintenance of good water quality and can improve degraded waters by reducing suspended-sediment concentrations, removing nutrients, and processing various organic and inorganic compounds (Tiner, 1984). A wetland can attenuate flood peaks and then release the stored water slowly, reducing the environmental impacts of floods and, in some parts of the State, increasing ground-water recharge. Wetlands are among the world's most productive ecosystems, efficiently converting solar energy and inorganic nutrients to biomass that supports many terrestrial and aquatic food webs. Wetlands in Kentucky support a diverse community of aquatic plants (Beal and Thieret, 1986), including rare and endangered species that do not exist elsewhere. Wetlands are vital habitat for many species of waterfowl and other migratory birds and are spawning and nursery grounds for many species of game and nongame fishes. Wetlands are home for many amphibian and reptile species, as well as for several game and nongame mammals.

Recreational opportunities such as hunting, fishing, hiking, nature observation and photography, camping, and canoeing abound in Kentucky wetlands, affording enjoyment to State residents and visitors. Recent research on the ecological function of wetlands has led to several innovative programs in the State for the use of constructed wetlands to treat residential, agricultural, and acidic mine wastewaters.

Figure 1. Axe Lake Swamp, a forested wetland in western Kentucky. *(Photograph courtesy of the Kentucky State Nature Preserves Commission.)*

TYPES AND DISTRIBUTION

Wetlands are lands transitional between terrestrial and deepwater habitats where the water table usually is at or near the land surface or the land is covered by shallow water (Cowardin and others, 1979). The distribution of wetlands and deepwater habitats in Kentucky is shown in figure 2*A*; only wetlands are discussed herein.

Wetlands can be vegetated or nonvegetated and are classified on the basis of their hydrology, vegetation, and substrate. In this summary, wetlands are classified according to the system proposed by Cowardin and others (1979), which is used by the U.S. Fish and Wildlife Service (FWS) to map and inventory the Nation's wetlands. At the most general level of the classification system, wetlands are grouped into five ecological systems: Palustrine, Lacustrine, Riverine, Estuarine, and Marine. The Palustrine System includes only wetlands, whereas the other systems comprise wetlands and deepwater habitats. Wetlands of the systems that occur in Kentucky are described below.

System	Wetland description
Palustrine	Wetlands in which vegetation is predominantly trees (forested wetlands); shrubs (scrub-shrub wetlands); persistent or nonpersistent emergent, erect, rooted, herbaceous plants (persistent- and nonpersistent-emergent wetlands); or submersed and (or) floating plants (aquatic beds). Also, intermittently to permanently flooded open-water bodies of less than 20 acres in which water is less than 6.6 feet deep.
Lacustrine	Wetlands within an intermittently to permanently flooded lake or reservoir. Vegetation, when present, is predominantly nonpersistent emergent plants (nonpersistent-emergent wetlands), or submersed and (or) floating plants (aquatic beds), or both.
Riverine	Wetlands within a channel. Vegetation, when present, is same as in the Lacustrine System.

Most Kentucky wetlands are palustrine and include areas lying shoreward of rivers and lakes, such as bald cypress swamps, bottom-land hardwood forests, emergent wetlands, and small ponds. The alluvial flood plains of the Ohio and Mississippi Rivers and their tributaries in the Western Kentucky Coal Field and Mississippi Embayment physiographic regions (fig. 2*B*) contain most of the State's wetlands. Wetland vegetation in those regions is mostly bottom-land hardwood forest associated with scrub-shrub and emergent species. Lacustrine wetlands in Kentucky are limited to reservoirs and a few small natural lakes such as Metropolis Lake and Swan Lake and are the least abundant type in the State. Riverine wetlands also are not abundant in Kentucky, but they are particularly important in the eastern part of the State, where they provide habitat for rare and endangered species, protect against shoreline erosion, and convey floodwaters (Kentucky Division of Water, 1990).

The greatest areal extent of wetlands of all types in Kentucky is in the Western Kentucky Coal Field. The Clear Creek wetlands, located in the Tradewater River Basin, are the largest in this area and are the most disturbed by human activities. Clear Creek forms intermittent channels through marshes of cattail and other emergent plants, bottom-land hardwood forests, bald cypress swamps, and scattered dead forests. Submersed peat-moss mats can be found in the deeper waters (Hill, 1983). The Clear Creek Basin also contains the only vegetated riverine wetlands in the Western Kentucky Coal Field, including both aquatic-bed and nonpersistent-emergent wetlands. Pondweed, coontail, and water milfoil grow on or below the water surface, along with emergent species such as lizard's tail and smartweed (Mitsch and others, 1983). The extensive wetlands of Cypress Creek, which are adjacent to the creek channel, are composed of well-developed stands of bald cypress, bottom-land hardwood forests, and cattail communities (Taylor, 1985). The area supports a diverse plant and animal community, including waterfowl and many nongame species such as the bald eagle. The Pond Creek–Henderson Sloughs wetland system lies in the northern part of the Western Kentucky Coal Field and has been adversely affected by oil-well brines. This area is characterized by a mosaic of bald cypress swamps and bottom-land hardwood forests, scrub-shrub vegetation, and open-water emergent vegetation. Wetlands in this area lie within the Mississippi flyway and provide valuable habitat and feeding grounds for migratory waterfowl.

In the Mississippi Embayment, there are extensive areas of wetlands dominated by bald cypress swamps or bottom-land hardwood forests. Terrapin Creek State Nature Preserve is a temporarily to permanently flooded cypress swamp that contains several perennial springs. The area supports a number of fish species found no-

where else in the State. Axe Lake Swamp State Nature Preserve consists of a bald cypress swamp and bottom-land hardwood forest within the Ohio River flood plain and constitutes a part of the largest contiguous swamp in Kentucky. The swamp supports eight plant and animal species that are rare in the State and provides wintering habitat for thousands of waterfowl. Also located in the Mississippi Embayment are Metropolis Lake, Murphy's Pond, and Swan Lake, three wetlands that are classified as "Outstanding Resource Waters" by the Kentucky Natural Resources and Environmental Protection Cabinet.

Wetlands in the central and eastern parts of the State are sparse and scattered. Swamp forests occur on poorly drained flats and in shallow depressions in the upper Green River Basin in the Mississippian Plateaus. Vegetation includes swamp white oak, buttonbush, lizard's tail, and sedges (Hoagland and Jones, 1992). At least a dozen swamps associated with abandoned river channels or sinking creeks (creeks that disappear through a "swallow hole" into solution channels in the underground limestone bedrock) are located in the Inner and Outer Bluegrass regions and the Knobs (Bryant, 1978; Meijer and others, 1981). This type of forested wetland, which occurs on moderately wet upland flats, is now rare in the Bluegrass and the Knobs. Another example of Bluegrass-region wetlands is in the Sinking Creek Basin (Meijer, 1976). Vegetation includes stands of bald cypress, swamp white oak, sedges, and rushes. The karst area near Mammoth Cave in the Mississippian Plateaus has depressional wetlands on sandstone ridges that contain water for 9 to 10 months during most years. There are also scattered emergent wetlands with organic soils in the Cumberland Plateau. Sphagnum moss is present at many of these sites in dense mats as much as a foot thick, in association with shrubs, sedges, and ferns (Mark Evans, Kentucky State Nature Preserves Commission, oral commun., 1992). Common or characteristic plant species include spicebush, common alder, cinnamon fern, and net-veined chain-fern.

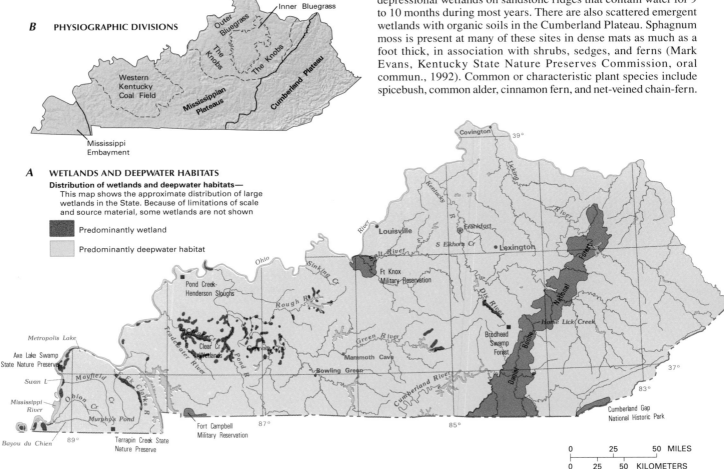

Figure 2.   Wetland distribution in Kentucky and physiography of the State. *A*, Distribution of wetlands and deepwater habitats. *B*, Physiography. *(Sources: A, T.E. Dahl, U.S. Fish and Wildlife Service, unpub. data, 1991. B, Physiographic divisions modified from McDowell, 1986; landforms data from EROS Data Center.)*

HYDROLOGIC SETTING

The types and distribution of wetlands in Kentucky are determined principally by factors that include climate, topography, hydrology, geology, and soil type. Wetlands occur most commonly in areas where precipitation exceeds evapotranspiration and runoff or where there are perennial sources of ground water. Seasonally, precipitation is least from August through October; during these months, ground-water inflows help to maintain saturation in wetland soils.

The greatest areal extent of wetlands in Kentucky is in the Western Kentucky Coal Field. The region grades from rolling hills in the south and east to flat flood plains in the northern areas near the Ohio River. Extensive bottom-land hardwood wetlands in this part of the State are the result of a shallow water table, poorly drained soils, and frequent overbank flooding following seasonal precipitation (Harker and others, 1981). Bottom-land hardwood forest, either seasonally flooded or temporarily flooded, is the major wetland type (Mitsch and others, 1983). Valleys of major streams and their tributaries are wide, flat, and filled with thick alluvium or glacial de-

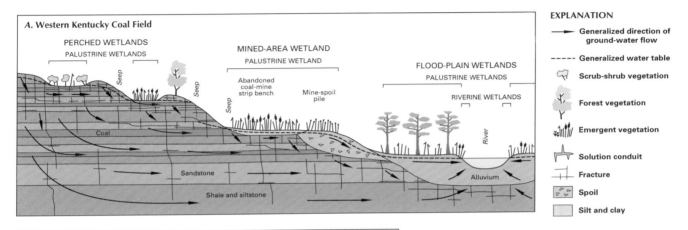

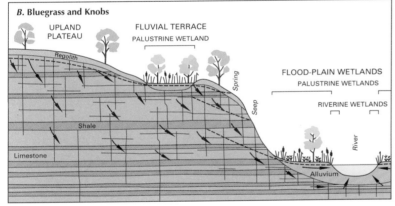

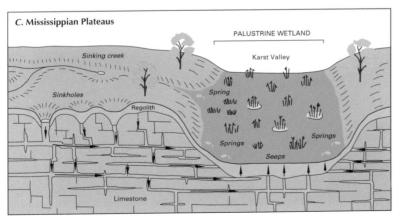

Figure 3. Generalized geohydrologic setting of representative wetlands in Kentucky. *A,* Western Kentucky Coal Field. *B,* Fractured bedrock and terrace deposits in the Inner and Outer Bluegrass regions and the Knobs. *C,* Karst terrane in the Mississippian Plateaus.

posits (fig. 3*A*). The associated flood plains contain many riparian wetlands. Soils near the Green, Pond, Tradewater, and Rough Rivers are thick and not well drained. The gentle slope of the Tradewater River and many of its tributaries (less than 1 foot per mile) results in floods that peak and subside slowly, fostering storage in associated alluvial wetlands. Base flow in streams and water in wetlands commonly are sustained by discharge of ground water from permeable limestone (Quinones and others, 1983). Many areas within the Western Kentucky Coal Field have been altered by strip mining, which has changed drainage characteristics. Swamp forests are left as stands of dead timber following disruption of the natural hydrology. Many of these areas are in transition to persistent-emergent or aquatic-bed wetlands. Abandoned coal-mine strip benches typically contain topographic depressions in which small wetlands form, and seepage through mine-spoil piles commonly supports wetlands on or below the piles.

Far western Kentucky is in the Mississippi Embayment. The region has low relief and is characterized by gently rolling uplands and wide, shallow valleys. Extensive bottom-land hardwood forests are found along Mayfield and Obion Creeks and Bayou de Chien. Much of the flood plain of these streams is composed of unconsolidated alluvium underlain by saturated sand and gravel. Other areas within the Mississippi Embayment have extensive deposits of loess or glacially derived outwash. The water table generally is shallow, and the region has some of the most productive aquifers in the State (Davis and others, 1973). Much of western Kentucky is subject to flooding by the Mississippi and Ohio Rivers, sometimes for prolonged periods. This periodic inundation is a primary source of water for riparian wetlands.

Wetlands in the central and eastern parts of the State generally are associated with karst terrane or are located on poorly drained flood plain or upland soils. Swamp forests in the Knobs and the Bluegrass region grow along the Green, Licking, Dix, and Kentucky Rivers and also occur on high-level terrace deposits at elevations of 600 to 1,000 feet (fig. 3B). Forested wetlands in the Knobs have formed on alluvium or low-permeability shale, whereas Bluegrass-region forested wetlands typically are in alluvium underlain by limestone and shale. Brodhead Swamp Forest, located in the Mississippian Plateaus, is in a sinkhole basin underlain by limestone and drained in the subsurface. The wetland is fed by several intermittent springs as well as by surface runoff (Hannan and Lassetter, 1982) and typically contains surface water for 11 months of the year. At other locations in the Mississippian Plateaus, wetlands form in sinkholes and karst valleys that are subject to flooding (fig. 3C). In the karst area surrounding Mammoth Cave, shallow depressional wetlands are sustained by the surficial aquifer on the tops of sandstone ridges. An underlying layer of compact, poorly permeable soil holds water in the soil at the surface. Scattered emergent wetlands with organic soils form at the base of gentle to steep slopes in valleys, ravines, and canyons in the southeastern Cumberland Plateau. These midelevation wetlands are fed by acidic ground-water seepage from stratified and fractured bedrock aquifers.

TRENDS

Wetlands are sensitive to changes in normal patterns of water storage and movement (Mitsch and Gosselink, 1986). Changes in hydrologic conditions, such as those associated with resource development or other human activities, commonly result in wetland loss or degradation. On the basis of the distribution of hydric soils as described by the Kentucky Division of Conservation (1982), Kentucky once had more than 1.6 million acres of wetlands. By 1977, about 929,000 acres (58 percent) of the State's original wetlands had been lost, primarily through drainage and subsequent conversion to cropland and pastureland. Losses were greatest in western Kentucky, amounting to 52 percent of the State's bottomland hardwood forests. By 1990, Kentucky's remaining wetland acreage was estimated to be between 387,000 acres (John Hefner, U.S. Fish and Wildlife Service, written commun., 1993) and 650,000 acres (Kentucky Division of Water, 1992), representing a total State loss of about 60 to 76 percent since predevelopment times.

Only 20 percent of the remaining naturally occurring wetlands in Kentucky are forested. In addition to losses from logging and conversion to agricultural land, the disproportionate loss of bottomland hardwoods might have been due to stream channelization. As flood frequency and duration are reduced, long-term changes in species composition occur; typically, riparian species are lost.

The FWS estimated that, as of 1983, losses of wetlands in Kentucky were continuing at a rate of about 3,600 acres annually (Tiner, 1984). The primary cause of wetland loss in the State has been conversion of bottom-land hardwood forests for agricultural use. Although loss due to agricultural conversion continues, the rate has declined because of changes in government subsidy programs, declining agricultural-commodity prices, and the overall scarcity of remaining forested wetlands. Other hydrologic alterations, such as channelization for flood control, highway construction, and modifications associated with industrial and commercial development, continue to adversely affect wetland resources in Kentucky. However, the loss due to those causes also is declining in response to expansion and enforcement of regulations.

Surface coal mining disturbs as much as 4,000 acres per year of the more than 2.9 million acres of land in the Western Kentucky Coal Field region (Mitsch and others, 1983). More than 114,000 acres of wetlands, principally bottom-land hardwood forests, could eventually be affected. Owing to the economic importance of coal,

conflicts of interest arise between advocates of wetland protection and advocates of resource development. In addition to loss, wetlands also can be degraded by water pollution. Acidic mine drainage from coal-mining activities is common in the Western Kentucky Coal Field region, and water having low pH and high sulphur or iron concentrations causes severe damage to plant and animal communities (U.S. Fish and Wildlife Service, 1992). In the Mississippi Embayment, nonpoint-source inputs of nutrients, pesticides, and sediments can exceed the capacity of wetlands to absorb, filter, and transform those pollutants to less harmful forms, resulting in degradation or loss of wetlands. Other pollutants such as industrial wastewater and pesticides have deleterious short-term and long-term effects on wetlands.

CONSERVATION

Many government agencies and private organizations participate in wetland conservation in Kentucky. The most active agencies and organizations and some of their activities are listed in table 1.

Federal wetland activities.—Development activities in Kentucky wetlands are regulated by several Federal statutory prohibitions and incentives that are intended to slow wetland losses. Some of the more important of these are contained in the 1899 Rivers and Harbors Act; the 1972 Clean Water Act and amendments; the 1985

Table 1. Selected wetland-related activities of government agencies and private organizations in Kentucky, 1993

[Source: Classification of activities is generalized from information provided by agencies and organizations. •, agency or organization participates in wetland-related activity; ..., agency or organization does not participate in wetland-related activity. **MAN**, management; **REG**, regulation; **R&C**, restoration and creation; **LAN**, land acquisition; **R&D**, research and data collection; **D&I**, delineation and inventory]

Agency or organization	MAN	REG	R&C	LAN	R&D	D&I
FEDERAL						
Department of Agriculture						
Consolidated Farm Service Agency	...	•	...	...	...	...
Forest Service	...	•	...	•	•	•
Natural Resources Conservation Service	...	•	...	•	•	•
Department of Defense						
Army Corps of Engineers	•	•	•	...	...	•
Military reservations	•	...	...	...	•	•
Department of the Interior						
Fish and Wildlife Service	•	...	•	•	•	...
Geological Survey	...	...	...	...	•	...
National Biological Survey	...	...	...	...	•	...
National Park Service	•	...	...	...	•	...
Office of Surface Mining	...	•	•	...	•	...
Environmental Protection Agency	...	•	...	...	•	•
Tennessee Valley Authority	•	...	•	...	•	•
STATE						
Geological Survey	...	...	...	...	•	•
Natural Resources and Environmental Protection Cabinet						
Division of Conservation	...	...	...	...	•	•
Division of Water	...	•	...	...	•	...
Surface Mining Reclamation and Enforcement	...	•	•	...	•	...
State Nature Preserves Commission	•	...	•	•	...	•
Tourism Cabinet						
Fish and Wildlife Resources	•	•	...	•	•	...
Transportation Cabinet	•	•	•	•	•	•
Water Resources Research Institute	...	...	•	...	•	•
PRIVATE ORGANIZATIONS						
Ducks Unlimited	•	...	•	•	...	•
Kentucky Resources Council	...	•	...	...	•	•
The Nature Conservancy	•	...	•	•	•	•
Riverfields	•	...	•	•	•	•

Food Security Act; the 1990 Food, Agriculture, Conservation, and Trade Act; and the 1986 Emergency Wetlands Resources Act.

Section 10 of the Rivers and Harbors Act gives the U.S. Army Corps of Engineers (Corps) authority to regulate certain activities in navigable waters. Regulated activities include diking, deepening, filling, excavating, and placing of structures. The related section 404 of the Clean Water Act is the most often-used Federal legislation protecting wetlands. Under section 404 provisions, the Corps issues permits regulating the discharge of dredged or fill material into wetlands. Permits are subject to review and possible veto by the U.S. Environmental Protection Agency (EPA), and the FWS has review and advisory roles. Section 401 of the Clean Water Act grants to States and eligible Indian Tribes the authority to approve, apply conditions to, or deny section 404 permit applications on the basis of a proposed activity's probable effects on the water quality of a wetland.

Most farming, ranching, and silviculture activities are not subject to section 404 regulation. However, the "Swampbuster" provision of the 1985 Food Security Act and amendments in the 1990 Food, Agriculture, Conservation, and Trade Act discourages (through financial disincentives) the draining, filling, or other alteration of wetlands for agricultural use. The law allows exemptions from penalties in some cases, especially if the farmer agrees to restore the altered wetland or other wetlands that have been converted to agricultural use. The Wetlands Reserve Program of the 1990 Food, Agriculture, Conservation, and Trade Act authorizes the Federal Government to purchase conservation easements from landowners who agree to protect or restore wetlands. The Consolidated Farm Service Agency (formerly the Agricultural Stabilization and Conservation Service) administers the Swampbuster provisions and Wetlands Reserve Program. The Natural Resources Conservation Service (formerly the Soil Conservation Service) determines compliance with Swampbuster provisions and assists farmers in the identification of wetlands and in the development of wetland protection, restoration, or creation plans.

The 1986 Emergency Wetlands Resources Act encourages wetland protection through funding incentives. The act requires States to address wetland protection in their Statewide Comprehensive Outdoor Recreation Plans to qualify for Federal funding for State recreational land; the National Park Service (NPS) provides guidance to States in developing the wetland component of their plans.

The EPA Wetlands Planning Unit has initiated an Advance Identification project in the Western Kentucky Coal Field. The project is a joint initiative between the EPA, the Corps, and the State and includes wetlands in four counties. The goals of the project are to increase public and industry awareness of wetland values and to generate information on wetland resources for regulatory agencies making permit decisions. The EPA has also awarded the Kentucky Natural Resources and Environmental Protection Cabinet, Division of Water, a project funded by the EPA State/Tribal Wetland Development Grant Program. The goal of this project is to collect biological, chemical, and physical data from minimally degraded wetland sites to develop biological standards for the assessment of wetland health.

The FWS Regional Wetlands Concept Plan (U.S. Fish and Wildlife Service, 1992) identified areas of wetlands in Kentucky that warrant protection because of their resource value, vulnerability, and scarcity. Among them are approximately 6,000 acres in the Cypress Creek area of the Western Kentucky Coal Field. This tract is recognized as habitat for several State-listed threatened or endangered species, contains five archeological sites, and is recognized as an important wetland area by the Kentucky State Nature Preserves Commission.

Several other Federal agencies conduct wetland-related activities in the State. The Forest Service (FS) is inventorying wetlands in the Daniel Boone National Forest. The FS manages wetlands for

waterfowl and has constructed approximately 100 acres of new wetlands as a part of their nationwide "Taking Wings Initiative." The Department of Defense has asked the FWS to identify all wetlands on Fort Knox and Fort Campbell Military Reservations and to conduct a survey of threatened and endangered species in wetlands on these properties. The NPS has inventoried wetlands in the four NPS properties in Kentucky. Cumberland Gap National Historic Park is working with the Kentucky State Nature Preserves Commission to study midelevation peatlands that are located within park boundaries. Fed by acidic seeps, these wetlands support a mixed community of shrub and emergent plants as well as scattered dense mats of sphagnum moss.

State wetland activities. — Kentucky has not adopted specific wetland regulations (Aldy, 1992). Wetlands are specifically defined in State water-quality standards and regulatory statutes. The State administers the Clean Water Act section 401 water-quality certification program, and wetlands are included in the definition of surface waters. The Kentucky Division of Water is the point of contact for administering the State water-quality certification review process of section 404 permit applications (Hannan and others, 1986). The Kentucky Natural Resources and Environmental Protection Cabinet has assembled an interagency working group to explore mitigation options to curtail the loss of Kentucky's bottom-land hardwood forests.

Although the FWS has not yet completed its inventory of Kentucky's wetlands, under a Memorandum of Agreement, the Kentucky Department of Fish and Wildlife Resources has provided funds to the Kentucky Division of Water to digitize all the FWS National Wetlands Inventory maps for Kentucky. The digitized information will become a part of the Kentucky Natural Resources and Environmental Protection Cabinet's geographic information system. In addition to having an active wetlands-acquisition program, the Kentucky Department of Fish and Wildlife Resources offers technical guidance in wetland identification and restoration to landowners and developers. The Department also participates in the New Madrid Wetlands Project, a four-State initiative to protect important waterfowl habitat in the lower Mississippi River valley. The proposal, developed to further the goals of the North American Waterfowl Management Plan, includes acquisition and management of 39,000 acres of wetlands in Kentucky.

The Kentucky State Nature Preserves Commission has recommended several wetlands for conservation and protection (Hannan and others, 1986). These areas were chosen on the basis of the presence of threatened or endangered species, the presence of critical habitat or an Outstanding Resource Water (as designated by the Kentucky Natural Resources and Environmental Protection Cabinet), and the imminence of destruction or alteration. They also manage a number of existing wetland preserves and foster the protection of other wetlands in the State through a system of registry and dedication agreements with private individuals.

Private wetland activities. — Most of Kentucky's wetlands are privately owned. The Nature Conservancy is active in land acquisition and stewardship of wetlands in Kentucky. The group also participates in joint management, along with various State agencies and private individuals, of several wetlands in the Mississippi Embayment as well as the Horse Lick Creek wetland system in the Knobs. The Kentucky Resources Council is an environmental advocacy organization that provides legal and technical support to local government and public interest groups to ensure the full and fair implementation of the Clean Water Act with respect to wetlands in the State. Riverfields is a group of concerned private citizens that owns and manages two wetland areas, including bottom-land hardwood forest in the alluvial flood plain of the Ohio River near Louisville. They strongly emphasize public education in their activities.

References Cited

Aldy, J.E., Jr., 1992, Trends in wetland regulation and the future of Kentucky's wetlands program: Frankfort, Kentucky Natural Resources and Environmental Protection Cabinet, 115 p.

Beal, E.O., and Thieret, J.W., 1986, Aquatic and wetland plants of Kentucky: Kentucky Nature Preserves Commission, Scientific and Technical Series 5, 314 p.

Bryant, W.S., 1978, Unusual forest type, hydro-mesophytic, for the Inner Bluegrass Region of Kentucky: Castanea, v. 43, p. 129–137.

Cowardin, L.M., Carter, Virginia, Golet, F.C., and LaRoe, E.T., 1979, Classification of wetlands and deepwater habitats of the United States: U.S. Fish and Wildlife Service Report FWS/OBS–79/31, 131 p.

Davis, R.W., Lambert, T.W., and Hansen, A.J., Jr., 1973, Subsurface geology and ground-water resources of the Jackson Purchase region, Kentucky: U.S. Geological Survey Water-Supply Paper 1987, 66 p.

Hannan, R.R., Fisher, W.L., Justis, Catherine, and Cicerello, R.R., 1986, Wetland protection strategies for Kentucky: Frankfort, Technical Report of the Kentucky Nature Preserves Commission, 146 p.

Hannan, R.R., and Lassetter, J.S., 1982, The vascular flora of the Brodhead Swamp Forest, Rockcastle County, Kentucky: Transactions of the Kentucky Academy of Science, v. 43, p. 43–49.

Harker, D.F., Jr., Warren, M.L., Camburn, K.E., and Cicerello, R.R., 1981, Aquatic biota and water-quality survey of the Western Kentucky Coalfield: Frankfort, Technical Report of the Kentucky Nature Preserves Commission, 896 p.

Hill, P.L., Jr., 1983, Wetland-stream ecosystems of the Western Kentucky Coalfield—Environmental disturbance and the shaping of aquatic community structure: Louisville, Kentucky, University of Louisville, Ph.D. dissertation, 290 p.

Hoagland, B.W., and Jones, R.L., 1992, Wetland and riparian flora of the upper Green River basin, south-central Kentucky: Transactions of the Kentucky Academy of Science, v. 53, p. 141–153.

Kentucky Division of Water, 1990, 1990 Kentucky report to Congress on water quality: Frankfort, Kentucky Natural Resources and Environmental Protection Cabinet, 187 p.

———1992, 1992 Kentucky report to Congress on water quality: Frankfort, Kentucky Natural Resources and Environmental Protection Cabinet, 187 p.

Kentucky Environmental Quality Commission, 1992, State of Kentucky's environment—A report of progress and problems: Frankfort, Kentucky Environmental Quality Commission, 332 p.

Kentucky Division of Conservation, 1982, Kentucky soil and water conservation program, Part 1—Overview and appraisal of soil and water resources: Frankfort, Kentucky Natural Resources and Environmental Protection Cabinet, Division of Conservation, 46 p.

McDowell, R.C., 1986, The Geology of Kentucky—A text to accompany the geologic map of Kentucky: U.S. Geological Survey Professional Paper 1151–H, 76 p.

Meijer, Willem, 1976, Notes on the flora of the Sinking Creek system and Elkhorn source areas in the Inner Bluegrass region of Kentucky: Transactions of the Kentucky Academy of Science, v. 37, p. 77–84.

Meijer, Willem, Campbell, J.J.N., Setser, Howard, and Meade, L.E., 1981, Swamp forests on high terrace deposits in the Bluegrass and Knobs Regions of Kentucky: Castanea, v. 46, p. 122–135.

Mitsch, W.J., and Gosselink, J.G., 1986, Wetlands: New York, Van Nostrand Reinhold, 539 p.

Mitsch, W.J., Taylor, J.R., Benson, K.B., and Hill, P.L., Jr., 1983, Atlas of wetlands in the principal coal surface mining region of western Kentucky: U.S. Fish and Wildlife Service Report FWS/OBS–82/72, 134 p.

Quinones, Fred, York, K.L., and Plebuch, R.O., 1983, Hydrology of Area 34, Eastern region, Interior Coal Province, Kentucky, Indiana, and Illinois: U.S. Geological Survey Water-Resources Investigations Report 82–638, 32 p.

Taylor, J.R., 1985, Community structure and primary productivity of forested wetlands in western Kentucky: Louisville, Kentucky, University of Louisville, Ph.D. dissertation, p. 11–39.

Tiner, R.W., Jr., 1984, Wetlands of the United States—Current status and recent trends: Washington, D.C., U.S. Fish and Wildlife Service, 59 p.

U.S. Fish and Wildlife Service, 1992, Regional wetlands concept plan—Emergency Wetlands Resources Act, Southeast Region: U.S. Fish and Wildlife Service, 259 p.

FOR ADDITIONAL INFORMATION: District Chief, U.S. Geological Survey, 2301 Bradley Avenue, Louisville, KY 40217; Regional Wetland Coordinator, U.S. Fish and Wildlife Service, 1875 Century Building, Suite 200, Atlanta, GA 80845

Prepared by
Kim H. Haag and Charles J. Taylor,
U.S. Geological Survey

Louisiana
Wetland Resources

Wetlands contribute to the economic, cultural, and ecological diversity of Louisiana. Presently, wetlands cover less than one-third of the State but are estimated to have covered about one-half of the State before the arrival of Europeans (Dahl, 1990). Wetlands have greatly influenced the cultural development of the State's inhabitants. American Indians occupied villages along these highly productive lands, as evidenced by the many shell mounds in these areas. Traditional Indian cultures still exist in Louisiana near the wetlands that influenced the development of their traditions. The Acadian (Cajun) culture developed in the isolation of southern Louisiana wetlands, and the popularity of Cajun cuisine today is directly related to the foods available from those areas. Major cities and towns such as New Orleans, Houma, Morgan City, and Lake Charles developed close to wetlands because of the wealth of natural resources available.

Wetlands are a major source of income for the people of Louisiana. Shellfish and finfish revenues from coastal and inland waters are estimated at $680 million annually (Keithly, 1991). In 1984, Louisiana was ranked first in the Nation in fisheries landings and second in fisheries value. In 1986, 28.6 percent of the commercial fish harvested in the Nation came from Louisiana; in 1991, that number dropped to 10.9 percent (The Advocate, Baton Rouge, April 18, 1993). The decline in Louisiana's commercial landings is believed to be related to coastal-wetland losses in the State. All of the commercially valuable fish species spend all or part of their life cycle in wetlands. Further, as recently as 1984, 40 percent of the Nation's wild furs and hides came from Louisiana wetlands (Louisiana Department of Wildlife and Fisheries, written commun., 1984). Louisiana wetlands also generate funds from recreational uses such as hunting, fishing, and bird watching. There are 17 National Wildlife Refuges, 28 State Wildlife Management and Refuge Areas, 7 State Parks, 1 National Park, and numerous State commemorative sites located entirely or partly within wetlands. In addition to these areas, The Nature Conservancy has two coastal preserves and five forested preserves in wetland areas (David Pashley, The Nature Conservancy, oral commun., 1993).

Ecologically, the rich diversity of plant and animal life in Louisiana wetlands is a priceless natural heritage for both the State and the Nation. State wetlands provide year-round habitat for eight endangered species and four threatened species. Many species of neotropical songbirds use Louisiana wetlands for resting and feeding habitat during migration. The State's wetlands provide winter habitat for many other species of birds, including the Arctic peregrine falcon and about one-half of the ducks, geese, and other waterfowl that use the Mississippi Flyway. Large numbers of waterfowl from the Central Flyway winter in the southwestern part of the State.

Wetlands in Louisiana are important in flood control and reduce the effects of storm surges associated with hurricanes. Wendell Curole of the Lafourche Parish Levee District has stated that 1 mile of marsh reduces a storm surge by 1 foot (The Advocate, Baton Rouge, April 18, 1993). As coastal wetlands are lost, this natural wetland function commonly is replaced by expensive storm surge projects (levees and gated structures) to protect coastal communities such as New Orleans and Houma. Wetlands also are being used as tertiary wastewater-treatment alternatives for small municipalities such as Thibodaux and, in general, serve as filters or traps for sediment, nutrients, and pollutants carried by water passing through them.

TYPES AND DISTRIBUTION

Wetlands are lands transitional between terrestrial and deepwater habitats where the water table usually is at or near the land surface or the land is covered by shallow water (Cowardin and others, 1979). The distribution of wetlands and deepwater habitats in Louisiana is shown in figure 2A; only wetlands are discussed herein.

Wetlands can be vegetated or nonvegetated and are classified on the basis of their hydrology, vegetation, and substrate. In this summary, wetlands are classified according to the system proposed by Cowardin and others (1979), which is used by the U.S. Fish and Wildlife Service (FWS) to map and inventory the Nation's wetlands. At the most general level of the classification system, wetlands are grouped into five ecological systems: Palustrine, Lacustrine, Riverine, Estuarine, and Marine. The Palustrine System includes only wetlands, whereas the other systems comprise wetlands and deepwater habitats. Wetlands of the systems that occur in Louisiana are described below.

Figure 1. A freshwater forested wetland on the shore of Lake Pontchartrain near La Branche. This wetland, which is near the New Orleans metropolitan area, is threatened by urban encroachment and runoff. *(Photograph by Dennis K. Demcheck, U.S. Geological Survey.)*

System	Wetland description
Palustrine	Nontidal and tidal-freshwater wetlands in which vegetation is predominantly trees (forested wetlands); shrubs (scrub-shrub wetlands); persistent or nonpersistent emergent, erect, rooted herbaceous plants (persistent- and nonpersistent-emergent wetlands); or submersed and (or) floating plants (aquatic beds). Also, intermittently to permanently flooded open-water bodies of less than 20 acres in which water is less than 6.6 feet deep.
Lacustrine	Nontidal and tidal-freshwater wetlands within an intermittently to permanently flooded lake or reservoir larger than 20 acres and (or) deeper than 6.6 feet. Vegetation, when present, is predominantly nonpersistent emergent plants (nonpersistent-emergent wetlands), or submersed and (or) floating plants (aquatic beds), or both.
Riverine	Nontidal and tidal-freshwater wetlands within a channel. Vegetation, when present, is same as in the Lacustrine System.

Estuarine .... Tidal wetlands in low-wave-energy environments where the salinity of the water is greater than 0.5 part per thousand (ppt) and is variable owing to evaporation and the mixing of seawater and freshwater.

Marine .... Tidal wetlands that are exposed to waves and currents of the open ocean and to water having a salinity greater than 30 ppt.

Palustrine wetlands, which include swamps, scrub-shrub wetlands, nontidal and tidal fresh marshes, and ponds, are the most common wetlands in Louisiana. Palustrine wetlands accounted for approximately 78 percent of the wetlands in Louisiana in the 1970's and are distributed statewide. The most common palustrine wetlands are swamps (forested wetlands) which contribute about 59 percent of the State's wetlands. Swamps in Louisiana are mostly cypress-tupelo gum swamps along the major rivers, bayous, and streams. In the 1970's, swamps had an area of between 5.6 and 6.8 million acres statewide, 3.0 million acres of which were in the Mississippi Alluvial Plain (fig. 2B) (Louisiana Department of Culture, Recreation and Tourism, 1988). Palustrine scrub-shrub wetlands are typically

associated with natural levees and spoil banks statewide. This type of wetland also has developed on some floating marshes in southern Louisiana. Nontidal and tidal fresh marshes are most common in southern Louisiana.

Coastal wetlands, mostly salt marshes (estuarine emergent wetlands), include about 2.5 million acres in Louisiana. About 40 percent of the State's coastal marshes are classified as fresh/intermediate (salinity 0.5–8.3 ppt, average 3.3 ppt), about 38 percent as brackish (salinity 1.0–18.4 ppt, average 8.0 ppt), and about 22 percent as saline (salinity greater than 18.4 ppt) (Louisiana Department of Culture, Recreation and Tourism, 1988; S.N. Gagliano, Coastal Environments, Inc., written commun. 1991). In the 1970's, coastal wetlands accounted for approximately 22 percent of the wetlands in Louisiana. Louisiana coastal marshes represent an estimated 35 to 40 percent of the coastal marshes and about 25 percent of all coastal wetlands in the conterminous United States. Coastal wetlands in Louisiana are in the Western Gulf Coastal Plain, Mississippi Alluvial Plain, and the Southern Coastal Plain ecoregions.

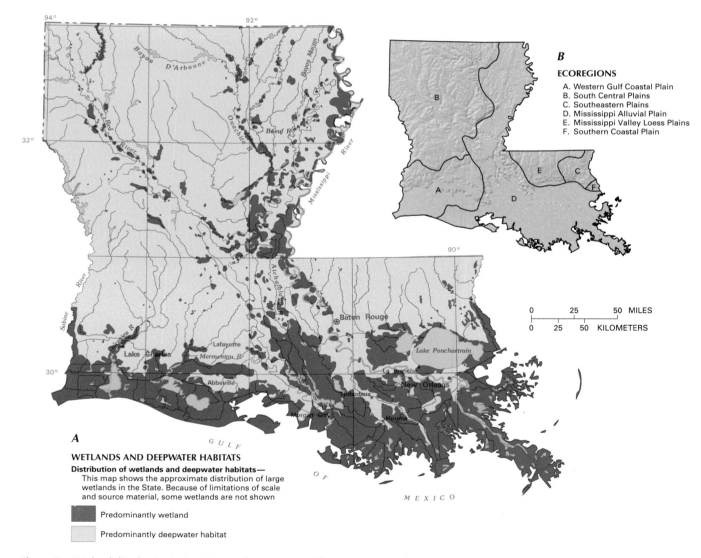

B
ECOREGIONS
A. Western Gulf Coastal Plain
B. South Central Plains
C. Southeastern Plains
D. Mississippi Alluvial Plain
E. Mississippi Valley Loess Plains
F. Southern Coastal Plain

A
WETLANDS AND DEEPWATER HABITATS
Distribution of wetlands and deepwater habitats—
This map shows the approximate distribution of large wetlands in the State. Because of limitations of scale and source material, some wetlands are not shown

Predominantly wetland

Predominantly deepwater habitat

Figure 2. Wetland distribution in Louisiana and ecoregions of the State. **A**, Distribution of wetlands and deepwater habitats. **B**, Ecoregions. *(Sources: A, T.E. Dahl, U.S. Fish and Wildlife Service, unpub. data, 1991. B, Omernik, 1987.)*

HYDROLOGIC SETTING

Wetland hydrology is affected by regional and local geology, topography, soil characteristics, and climate. Water in wetlands can come from either surface- or ground-water sources or from both. Wetlands can function as storage reservoirs for streams or sources of recharge for ground-water systems. Water in small nontidal wetlands is typically supplied by local shallow ground-water flow systems and localized runoff. Larger wetlands can receive discharge from or provide recharge to regional as well as local ground-water systems. Soils that underlie wetlands determine the rate at which water percolates downward to recharge the ground-water system or discharges from it. Precipitation in Louisiana, which averages between 50 to 60 inches per year (Newton, 1972), provides much of the surface-water runoff that maintains the State's wetlands.

Most wetlands in Louisiana are closely associated with the State's major rivers, bayous, and streams (fig. 2A). The Mississippi River and its shifting delta have created most of the State's estuarine and palustrine wetlands. The Mississippi River drains about 40 percent of the conterminous 48 States and parts of Canada (Craig and others, 1979). Large quantities of sediment were deposited annually in the Mississippi River flood plain and along coastal Louisiana before the installation of flood-control levees along the main channel of the river. The deposition of this sediment has resulted in the largest deltaic land mass in North America (Louisiana Department of Culture, Recreation and Tourism, 1988). Deltaic deposition at the mouth of the Mississippi River has been a dynamic process; several deltas have formed over the last 5,000 years (fig. 3). Older deltas have eroded and deteriorated as the next delta was formed (Coleman and Gagliano, 1964; Frazier, 1967).

The hydrology of swamps along rivers, bayous, and streams is characterized by annual cycles of flooding and dewatering. Plant communities in these swamps typically are dominated by cypress and tupelo gum trees. The value of these swamps to fish populations and overall aquatic productivity depends upon the renewal of nutrients and oxygenated water that takes place during these annual cycles. Reduced flooding can result in a conversion of swamps into bottom-land hardwood forests dominated by oak, hickory, and other hardwoods. Conversely, increased flooding or higher water tables can result in the conversion of bottom-land hardwood-forest wetlands to cypress-tupelo gum swamps. Excessive flooding, either in depth or duration, can result in the conversion of swamp to open-water, emergent, or scrub-shrub wetlands because of the lack of growth of new trees and the drowning of existing trees. The flood plain of the Atchafalaya River, the largest distributary of the Mississippi River, contains the best known example of a forested wetland in Louisiana. The Atchafalaya River swamp is the largest hardwood swamp in the country. The delta developing at the mouth of the Atchafalaya River is one of the few areas of the State where the shoreline (and associated marshland) is expanding.

The types of coastal wetlands (fresh, intermediate, brackish, and saline) and their distribution are dependent upon the availability of freshwater, frequency of storm-induced salinity maximums, and alterations to local hydrology caused by construction of oil- and gas-well access canals. All of these variables contribute to a continual advance and retreat of wetlands in the coastal areas of Louisiana.

TRENDS

Louisiana has lost about 46 percent of its wetlands (about 7.4 million acres) since the 1700's, when Europeans first began modifying the continent's geographic features (Dahl, 1990). Palustrine wetlands, primarily swamps, have decreased from an estimated 11.3 million acres to as little as 5.6 million acres in the 1970's. In the Mississippi Alluvial Plain, there has been a decline in palustrine wetlands from about 4.3 million acres in 1957 to about 3.0 million acres in 1977 (U.S. Fish and Wildlife Service, 1992). The decline in palustrine wetlands was due, in large part, to land clearing for agricultural purposes. Other causes of wetland loss include flood-control projects, oil and gas exploration, lignite and gravel mining, construction of catfish and crawfish ponds, dredging and filling for residential and commercial development, solid-waste disposal, and highway construction. The rate of loss of palustrine wetlands is

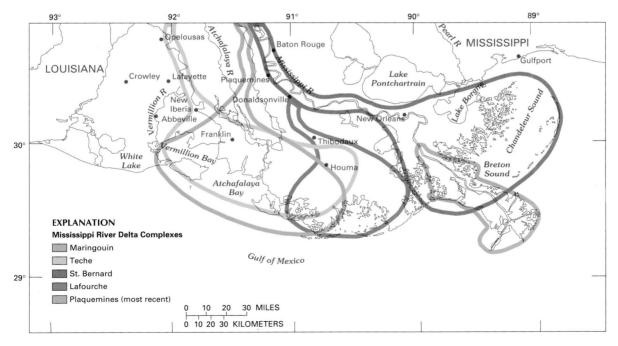

Figure 3. Prehistoric and present-day Mississippi River Delta complexes. *(Source: Kolb and Van Lopik, 1966.)*

thought to have been slowed by the "Swampbuster" provisions of the Food Security Act of 1985 and the 1990 Food, Agriculture, Conservation, and Trade Act, which provides for the purchase of wetlands from farmers. However, although palustrine wetland loss has slowed, it is still considered to be substantial.

Major causes of coastal wetland loss in Louisiana are a decrease in suspended-sediment load in the major streams due to dams and channelization and leveeing of the Mississippi River (Kesel, 1988, 1989); dredging of canals for oil and gas exploration, navigation, and pipeline installation; dredging, filling, and drainage for development; drainage for conversion to crop production or pasture; subsidence; erosion; marsh "eat-outs" by nutria; and hurricanes. About 8 percent of the State's coastal marshes have been dredged, creating canals and associated spoil banks. About one-half of the State's coastal marsh losses can be attributed to or related to canal construction (Scaife and others, 1983).

The overall balance between land gain (shoreline accretion) and land loss (shoreline erosion) in Louisiana has been one of net gain in wetland area over most of the last 5,000 years (Coleman and Gagliano, 1964) because of the abandonment of existing deltas and creation of new deltas by the Mississippi River. In the last 100 years, however, this trend has been reversed because of human alteration of the Mississippi River and the Louisiana coastal ecosystems. Construction of flood-control levees along the Mississippi River and its major tributaries and the dredging of canals in the Mississippi–Atchafalaya River Delta have deprived flood-plain and delta wetlands of sediment needed to prevent wetland loss caused by erosion or submergence.

Levee construction began as early as the 1700's in and near New Orleans; however, construction of levees on a large scale did not begin until after the disastrous flood of 1927. Dams constructed on the Missouri River and its tributaries in the mid-1950's trapped sediment and further reduced the sediment available to wetlands in southern Louisiana. Wetland loss was further accelerated by construction of navigation and oil- and gas-well access canals that exposed fresh and intermediate wetlands to more saline water and

disrupted historic north-south sheet-flow runoff in coastal areas.

Use of the Atchafalaya River Basin as a floodway and the extensive construction of access canals (and associated spoil banks) have resulted in the conversion of parts of the cypress-tupelo gum swamp in the basin to other types of wetlands. Wetlands created by these changes in the hydrologic system include bottom-land forests in areas of rapid deposition, scrub-shrub wetlands along spoil banks, and emergent wetlands at the mouth of the Atchafalaya and in open-water areas of the basin that have filled by sediment.

Coastal-wetland loss in Louisiana is a critical issue within the State. About 4 million acres of coastal wetlands existed in the State at the beginning of the 1900's (Dunbar and others, 1992). Since that time, the FWS estimates that more than 900,000 acres of these coastal wetlands have been lost (U.S. Fish and Wildlife Service, 1992). Seventy-three percent (654,000 acres) of the loss occurred between the 1950's and 1970's. The U.S. Army Corps of Engineers (Corps) has estimated that since 1930, 17.8 percent of the land in the southern coastal plain has been lost. (Dunbar and others, 1992). The highest coastal land-loss rates occurred from 1956 to 1974 (fig. 4), and the largest loss occurred along the present-day Mississippi River Delta (Dunbar and others, 1992). Estimated land-loss rates for the Louisiana coast during 1978 to 1987 range from about 40 to 64.5 square miles per year (U.S. Fish and Wildlife Service, 1992; Templet and Meyer-Arendt, 1986). Recent estimates indicate a slight decrease in erosion rates, which were estimated to be between 25 and 40 square miles per year in 1990. However, this decrease might be a result of the decreased availability of highly erodable organic sediments relative to more erosion-resistant soils that have a higher percentage of clays and silts, rather than to restoration efforts (S.M. Gagliano, Coastal Environments, Inc., oral commun., 1991). Dunbar and others (1992) reached similar conclusions and predicted that natural land-loss rates will continue to decrease slowly until a background rate of approximately 0.17 percent per year is reached.

Loss of coastal wetlands is closely associated with the loss of fisheries productivity and revenue. The conversion of wetlands to open water also represents a threat to oil and gas wells now located

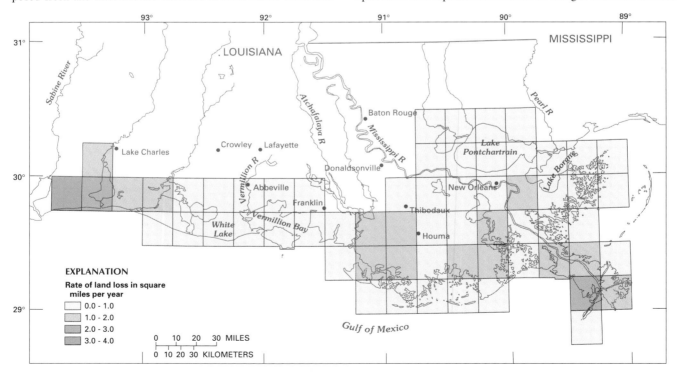

Figure 4.   Average coastal land-loss rates in Louisiana, 1956 to 1974. *(Source: Dunbar and others, 1992.)*

in the coastal wetlands. The State and Federal governments have recognized the problems associated with the loss of wetlands and have dedicated as much as $30 million annually for the mitigation of coastal wetland loss through the State Coastal Restoration Program and the Federal Coastal Wetlands, Planning, Protection, and Restoration Act of 1990.

CONSERVATION

Many government agencies and private organizations participate in wetland conservation in Louisiana. The most active agencies and organizations and some of their activities are listed in table 1.

Federal wetland activities.—Development activities in Louisiana wetlands are regulated by several Federal statutory prohibitions and incentives that are intended to slow wetland losses. Some of the more important of these are contained in the 1899 Rivers and Harbors Act; the 1972 Clean Water Act and amendments; the 1985 Food Security Act; the 1990 Food, Agriculture, Conservation, and Trade Act; the 1986 Emergency Wetlands Resources Act; and the 1972 Coastal Zone Management Act.

Section 10 of the Rivers and Harbors Act gives the Corps authority to regulate certain activities in navigable waters. Regulated activities include diking, deepening, filling, excavating, and placing

Table 1. Selected wetland-related activities of government agencies and private organizations in Louisiana, 1993

[Source: Classification of activities is generalized from information provided by agencies and organizations. •, agency or organization participates in wetland-related activity; ..., agency or organization does not participate in wetland-related activity. MAN, management; REG, regulation; R&C, restoration and creation; LAN, land acquisition; R&D, research and data collection; D&I, delineation and inventory]

Agency or organization	MAN	REG	R&C	LAN	R&D	D&I
FEDERAL						
Department of Agriculture						
Consolidated Farm Service Agency	...	•	...	...	...	...
Forest Service	•	...	...	•	...	•
Natural Resources Conservation Service	...	•	•	...	...	•
Department of Commerce						
National Oceanic and Atmospheric Administration	•	•	•	...	•	...
Department of Defense						
Army Corps of Engineers	...	•	...	•	...	•
Department of the Interior						
Fish and Wildlife Service	•	...	•	•	•	•
Geological Survey	•	...	...	...	•	...
Minerals Management Service	•	...	•	...	...	•
National Biological Service	•	...	...	...	•	...
National Park Service	•	...	•	•	•	...
Environmental Protection Agency	...	•	...	...	•	...
STATE						
Department of Agriculture	•	•	...	...	•	•
Department of Environmental Quality	...	•	•	...	•	•
Department of Health and Human Resources	...	•	...	...	•	...
Department of Natural Resources	•	•	•	...	•	...
Department of Transportation and Development	•	...	•	...	...	...
Department of Wildlife and Fisheries	•	•	•	•	...	•
Governor's Office of Coastal Activities	•	...	•	...	...	•
REGIONAL, PARISH, AND LOCAL						
Levee boards	•	•	...	•	...	•
Some parish governments	•	•	•	•	...	•
PRIVATE ORGANIZATIONS						
Coalition to Restore Coastal Louisiana	...	...	...	...	...	•
Gulf Coast Conservation Association	...	...	...	...	•	...
Lake Pontchartrain Basin Foundation	...	...	...	...	•	•
Louisiana Wildlife Federation	...	...	...	...	...	•
National Audubon Society	•	...	...	•	...	...
The Nature Conservancy	•	...	...	•	...	•

of structures. The related section 404 of the Clean Water Act is the most often-used Federal legislation protecting wetlands. Under section 404 provisions, the Corps issues permits regulating the discharge of dredged or fill material into wetlands. Permits are subject to review and possible veto by the U.S. Environmental Protection Agency, and the FWS has review and advisory roles. Section 401 of the Clean Water Act grants to States and eligible Indian Tribes the authority to approve, apply conditions to, or deny section 404 permit applications on the basis of a proposed activity's probable effects on the water quality of a wetland.

Most farming, ranching, and silviculture activities are not subject to section 404 regulation. However, the "Swampbuster" provision of the 1985 Food Security Act and amendments in the 1990 Food, Agriculture, Conservation, and Trade Act discourage (through financial disincentives) the draining, filling, or other alteration of wetlands for agricultural use. The law allows exemptions from penalties in some cases, especially if the farmer agrees to restore the altered wetland or other wetlands that have been converted to agricultural use. The Wetlands Reserve Program of the 1990 Food, Agriculture, Conservation, and Trade Act authorizes the Federal Government to purchase conservation easements from landowners who agree to protect or restore wetlands. The Consolidated Farm Service Agency (formerly the Agricultural Stabilization and Conservation Service) administers the Swampbuster provisions and Wetlands Reserve Program. The Natural Resources Conservation Service (formerly the Soil Conservation Service) determines compliance with Swampbuster provisions and assists farmers in the identification of wetlands and in the development of wetland protection, restoration, or creation plans.

The 1986 Emergency Wetlands Resources Act and the 1972 Coastal Zone Management Act and amendments encourage wetland protection through funding incentives. The Emergency Wetland Resources Act requires States to address wetland protection in their Statewide Comprehensive Outdoor Recreation Plans to qualify for Federal funding for State recreational land; the National Park Service (NPS) provides guidance to States in developing the wetland component of their plans. Coastal States that adopt coastal-zone management programs and plans approved by the National Oceanic and Atmospheric Administration are eligible for Federal funding and technical assistance through the Coastal Zone Management Act.

The Federal Government has been involved with wetlands in Louisiana dating back to the Swamp Land Act of 1849. This act granted to Louisiana all swamp and overflow lands then unfit for cultivation to help in controlling floods in the Mississippi River Valley by construction of levees and drains (Shaw and Fredine, 1971). Massive flooding by the Mississippi River in 1927 resulted in the Flood Control Act of 1928. This act provides comprehensive flood control for the lower Mississippi River Valley below Cairo, Ill., by authorizing the Corps to construct and maintain levees, floodways, channel modifications, and various control structures. Although the act provided much-needed relief from flooding, it has adversely affected the wetland resources in the Louisiana coastal zone.

In November 1990, Congress passed Public Law 101–646, the Coastal Wetlands Planning, Protection, and Restoration Act, which provides Federal funding (matched by State funding) for the planning and implementation of projects for the protection and restoration of coastal wetlands. The act directs the development of an annual priority-project list, ranked in order of cost effectiveness and consisting of small-scale projects that can be substantially completed within 5 years. The act also requires development of a comprehensive restoration plan for the entire Louisiana coast.

Large tracts of land, many containing wetlands, are managed by the FWS, U.S. Department of Defense, and the NPS. The plans for these lands are subject to a review process that allows local groups and individuals to have input into the planning process that determines the future direction management agencies pursue for economic, ecological, and recreational development of these lands.

State wetland activities.—The Louisiana Department of Wildlife and Fisheries Land Acquisition Program is funded primarily by duck-stamp and hunting-license revenues. Wetlands are given high priority in the acquisition of lands. The Department's Refuge Division manages almost 200,000 acres of coastal wetlands in four separate refuges. Providing waterfowl habitat is the primary purpose for these refuges. The Department's Natural Heritage Program's primary mission is the identification and indexing of unique natural habitats in Louisiana, which includes many wetlands. The Department also administers the Statewide Environmental Investigation program, which encourages mitigation of fish and wildlife habitat loss caused by local, State, or Federal development projects.

The Louisiana Department of Natural Resources' Coastal Management Division administers the Coastal Use Permitting Program. This program provides guidelines for the permitting of coastal-zone developmental activities in the least environmentally damaging manner. Coastal-use permits are required for any activity in the coastal zone except those specifically exempted by the Louisiana State Legislature. The Coastal Management Division Coastal Zone Program reviews Federal activities in the coastal zone to ensure consistency with State coastal-management plans.

The Louisiana Coastal Wetlands Conservation and Restoration Program is administered by the Office of Coastal Restoration and Management within the Department of Natural Resources. The program implements specific projects that are designed to conserve, enhance, restore, and create coastal vegetated wetlands through an annually updated priority plan approved by the Louisiana State Legislature. The program is funded from State oil and gas severance taxes placed in a Coastal Wetlands Conservation and Restoration Trust Fund.

Other State agencies actively involved in regulation or data collection in the coastal zone include the Department of Environmental Quality, Department of Agriculture, Department of Health and Human Resources, and the Department of Transportation and Development. For example, the Department of Environmental Quality is responsible for the enforcement of water-quality standards within the State's wetlands.

Regional, parish, and local wetland activities.—Parish governments in the Louisiana coastal zone have an interest in preserving and restoring wetlands. The Terrebonne Parish government (which contains Houma), for example, has a coastal-wetlands restoration program. Vermilion Parish (which contains Abbeville) has a Coastal Restoration Advisory Committee that participates in the Coastal Wetlands Planning, Protection, and Restoration Act process. Some city and parish governments have strong regulatory or land-acquisition programs that provide wetlands protection beyond that which is required by the State. Others are less able to develop strong local protection programs, owing to budgetary constraints.

Private wetland activities.—Private organizations in Louisiana are important as advocates of wetland conservation and protection. Louisiana has many private-interest groups that keep the public informed on wetland issues, organize citizen networks, and lobby for wetland-protection measures. The National Audubon Society and The Nature Conservancy have purchased wetlands in Louisiana for preservation.

References Cited

Coleman, J.M., and Gagliano, S.M., 1964, Cyclic sedimentation in the Mississippi River deltaic plain: Transactions of the Gulf Coast Association of Geological Societies, v. 14, p. 67–80.

Cowardin, L.M., Carter, Virginia, Golet, F.C., and LaRoe, E.T., 1979, Classification of wetlands and deepwater habitats of the United States: U.S. Fish and Wildlife Report FWS/OBS–79/31, 131 p.

Craig, N.J., Turner, R.E., and Day, J.W., 1979, Land loss in coastal Louisiana (USA): Environmental Management, v. 3, no. 2, p. 133–134.

Dahl, T.E., 1990, Wetlands—Losses in the United States, 1780's to 1980's: Washington D.C., U.S. Fish and Wildlife Service Report to Congress, 13 p.

Dunbar, J.B., Britsch, L.D., and Kemp, E.B., III, 1992, Land loss rates—Report 3, Louisiana Coastal Plain: U.S. Army Corps of Engineers Technical Report GL–90–2, 65 p.

Frazier, D.E., 1967, Recent deltaic deposits of the Mississippi River: Their development and chronology: Transactions of the Gulf Coast Association of Geological Societies, v. 17, p. 287–315.

Keithly, Walter, 1991, Louisiana seafood industry study—A summary: Louisiana Seafood Promotions and Marketing Board, 32 p.

Kesel, R.H., 1988, The decline in the suspended load of the lower Mississippi River and its influence on adjacent wetlands: Environmental Geology and Water Sciences, v. 11, no. 3, p. 271–281.

_____1989, The role of the Mississippi River in wetland loss in southeastern Louisiana, U.S.A.: Environmental Geology and Water Sciences, v. 13, no. 3, p. 183–193.

Kolb, C.R., and Van Lopik, J.R., 1966, Depositional environments of the Mississippi River deltaic plain, southeastern Louisiana, *in* Shirley, M.L. and Ragsdale, J.A., eds., Deltas: Houston Geological Society, p. 16–62.

Louisiana Department of Culture, Recreation and Tourism, 1988, Louisiana wetlands priority conservation plan: Baton Rouge, Louisiana Department of Culture, Recreation and Tourism, Office of State Parks, Division of Outdoor Recreation, 64 p.

Newton, M.B., Jr., 1972, Atlas of Louisiana: Louisiana State University, School of Geoscience Miscellaneous Publication 72–1, p. 10.

Omernik, J.M., 1986, Ecoregions of the United States—Map supplement: Annals of the Association of American Geographers, v. 77, no. 1, scale 1:7,500,000.

Scaife, W.W., Turner, R.E., and Costanza, R., 1983, Coastal Louisiana recent land loss and canal impacts: Environmental Management, v. 7, p. 433–442.

Shaw, S.P. and Fredine, C.G., 1971, Wetlands of the United States, their extent and their value to waterfowl and other wildlife: U.S. Fish and Wildlife Service Circular 39, 67 p.

Templet, P.H., and Meyer-Arendt, K.J., 1986, Louisiana wetland loss and sea level rise—A regional management approach to the problem, *in* Kusler, J.A., Quammen, M.L., and Brooks, Gail, eds., Proceedings of the National Wetland Symposium—Mitigation and Impacts and Losses, Oct. 8–10, 1986, New Orleans: Berne, N.Y., Association of State Wetland Managers, p. 230–237.

U.S. Fish and Wildlife Service, 1992, Regional wetlands concept plan; Emergency Wetlands Resources Act, Southeast Region: Atlanta, Ga., U.S. Fish and Wildlife Service, 249 p.

FOR ADDITIONAL INFORMATION: District Chief, U.S. Geological Survey, 3535 S. Sherwood Forest Boulevard, Suite 120, Baton Rouge, LA 70816; Regional Wetland Coordinator, U.S. Fish and Wildlife Service, 1875 Century Building, Suite 200, Atlanta, GA 30345

Prepared by
Charles R. Demas and Dennis K. Demcheck,
U.S. Geological Survey

Maine
Wetland Resources

Maine is rich in wetland resources. About 5 million acres, or one-fourth of the State, is wetland. Maine has a wide variety of wetlands, ranging from immense inland peatlands to salt marshes and mud flats along the coast.

Wetlands are an integral part of Maine's natural resources. Wetlands provide essential habitat for certain types of wildlife and vegetation, including rare and endangered species. They are used for timber and peat; hunting, fishing, and shellfishing; education and research; and bird, wildlife and plant observation, all of which boost tourism and the general economy. Wetlands also provide flood control, bank and shoreline-erosion control, sediment retention, water filtration, and nutrient uptake. In recognition of the importance of wetlands, many government and private organizations have worked to preserve wetlands and educate the public about wetland values. For example, the Maine Department of Conservation owns most of Maine's largest bog—the Great Heath (fig. 1), and wetlands in Acadia National Park and Rachel Carson National Wildlife Refuge are visited by thousands of people each year.

Figure 1. Fall foliage in an extensive dwarf-shrub community in Maine's Great Heath. A raised bog that has a coalesced dome, the Great Heath is Maine's largest continuous open bog. *(Photograph by Bob Johnston, Maine Geological Survey.)*

TYPES AND DISTRIBUTION

Wetlands are lands transitional between terrestrial and deepwater habitats where the water table usually is at or near the land surface or the land is covered by shallow water (Cowardin and others, 1979). The distribution of wetlands and deepwater habitats in Maine is shown in figure 2A; only wetlands are discussed herein.

Wetlands can be vegetated or nonvegetated and are classified on the basis of their hydrology, vegetation, and substrate. In this summary, wetlands are classified according to the system proposed by Cowardin and others (1979), which is used by the U.S. Fish and Wildlife Service (FWS) to map and inventory the Nation's wetlands. At the most general level of the classification system, wetlands are grouped into five ecological systems: Palustrine, Lacustrine, Riverine, Estuarine, and Marine. The Palustrine System includes only wetlands, whereas the other systems comprise wetlands and deepwater habitats. Wetlands of the systems that occur in Maine are described below.

System	Wetland description
Palustrine	Nontidal and tidal-freshwater wetlands in which vegetation is predominantly trees (forested wetlands); shrubs (scrub-shrub wetlands); persistent or nonpersistent emergent, erect, rooted herbaceous plants (persistent- and nonpersistent-emergent wetlands); or submersed and (or) floating plants (aquatic beds). Also, intermittently to permanently flooded open-water bodies of less than 20 acres in which water is less than 6.6 feet deep.
Lacustrine	Nontidal and tidal-freshwater wetlands within an intermittently to permanently flooded lake or reservoir larger than 20 acres and (or) deeper than 6.6 feet. Vegetation, when present, is predominantly nonpersistent emergent plants (nonpersistent-emergent wetlands), or submersed and (or) floating plants (aquatic beds), or both.
Riverine	Nontidal and tidal-freshwater wetlands within a channel. Vegetation, when present, is same as in the Lacustrine System.
Estuarine	Tidal wetlands in low-wave-energy environments where the salinity of the water is greater than 0.5 part per thousand (ppt) and is variable owing to evaporation and the mixing of seawater and freshwater.
Marine	Tidal wetlands that are exposed to waves and currents of the open ocean and to water having a salinity greater than 30 ppt.

Widoff (1988) estimated Maine's wetland area to be about 5,199,200 acres, whereas Tiner and Veneman (1989) classified 6,460,000 acres as wetland. The estimate by Tiner and Veneman (1989) was calculated from Natural Resources Conservation Service (NRCS, formerly the Soil Conservation Service) estimates of the distribution of hydric (wet) soils, and is considered high because it includes drained soils and hydric soils that occur in somewhat poorly drained areas that are not wetland. The estimate by Widoff (1988) is a compilation of earlier inventories. It estimates that wetlands in Maine comprise about 5,041,700 acres of palustrine, 87,500 acres of marine, and 70,000 acres of estuarine wetlands. Acreage for riverine and lacustrine wetlands is unknown.

The distribution of wetlands in Maine is influenced by physiography (fig. 2B). Many large wetlands occur in the Seaboard Lowland of eastern Maine. In the White Mountain Section of western Maine, wetlands occur primarily in narrow valleys separating mountains and foothills. Wetlands are distributed throughout the New England Upland of central and northern Maine but occur mainly in broad valleys between uplands of moderate relief. In many areas of the State, small wetlands are interrelated and form large wetland complexes.

Palustrine forested wetlands that have organic-rich mineral soils are commonly referred to as swamps, whereas wetlands that have organic soils over mineral soils are called peatlands. Widoff (1988) estimated that Maine contains at least 3,000,000 acres of wooded swamp. Swamps in southern Maine are dominated by hardwood communities similar to those in southern New England wetlands. Silver maple and black ash are characteristic in flood plains of major rivers, red maple swamps typically occur in poorly drained basins and along small streams, and black willow-alder swamps tend to dominate small watercourses and swales (Maine Natural Heritage Program, 1991). A few wetlands in southern Maine contain species at the northern extent of their range, such as Atlantic white cedar and black gum. Forested wetlands in northern Maine are dominated by communities similar to those in Canadian wetlands. For example, red spruce-balsam fir swamps typically occur in poorly drained basins and borders of streams; northern white cedar swamps occur in similar settings that have higher alkalinity; and black spruce, larch, and northern white cedar predominate in forested peatlands.

Palustrine scrub-shrub vegetation grows in most wetlands, generally as a transitional community to open water or upland, or between emergent wetlands and forested wetlands. Alder, willow, and sweet gale are characteristic of shrub swamps. Scrub-shrub vegetation in peatlands comprises predominantly broad-leaved evergreen shrubs such as leatherleaf, bog laurel, and labrador tea as well as stunted black spruce and larch. Peatlands that have large expanses of dwarf shrubs are referred to locally as heaths (Worley, 1981).

Peatlands (palustrine forested, scrub-shrub, emergent, and moss-lichen wetlands) occur throughout Maine and have been estimated to comprise about 700,000 acres (Widoff, 1988). The terms bog and fen are used to define peatland types in some classification systems (Davis and Anderson, 1991). Bogs are acidic, nutrient poor, and have a low species diversity, whereas fens are less acidic and have higher nutrient levels and species diversity. Typically, the herbaceous layer in bogs is dominated by sphagnum moss, whereas in fens it is dominated by sedges and mosses. Maine has numerous peatland types, including some that have a restricted distribution in the State (fig. 2C). For example, ribbed fens (fens that have lin-

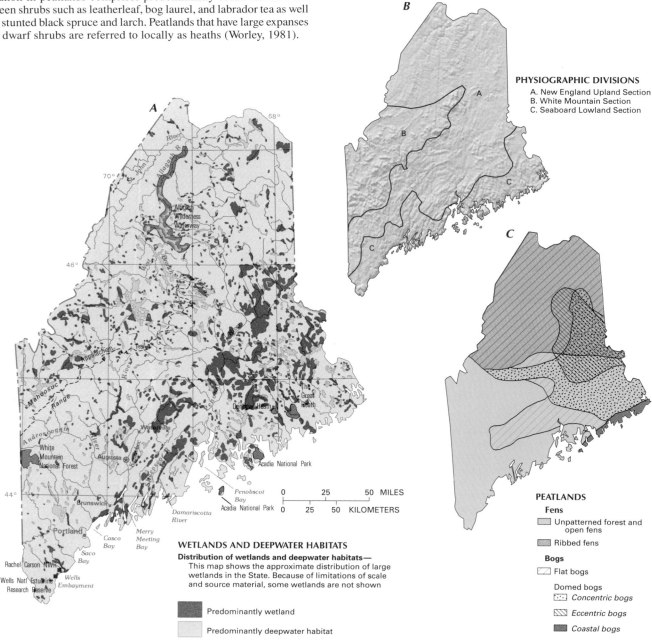

PHYSIOGRAPHIC DIVISIONS
A. New England Upland Section
B. White Mountain Section
C. Seaboard Lowland Section

WETLANDS AND DEEPWATER HABITATS

Distribution of wetlands and deepwater habitats—
This map shows the approximate distribution of large wetlands in the State. Because of limitations of scale and source material, some wetlands are not shown

⬛ Predominantly wetland

⬜ Predominantly deepwater habitat

PEATLANDS

Fens

⬜ Unpatterned forest and open fens

▨ Ribbed fens

Bogs

⬚ Flat bogs

Domed bogs

⬚ *Concentric bogs*

▨ *Eccentric bogs*

⬛ *Coastal bogs*

Figure 2. Wetland distribution, physiography, and distribution of peatland types in Maine. **A**, Distribution of wetlands and deepwater habitats. **B**, Physiography. **C**, Distribution of peatland types. *(Sources: A, T.E. Dahl, U.S. Fish and Wildlife Service, unpub. data, 1991. B, Physiographic divisions from Fenneman, 1946; landforms data from EROS Data Center. C, Davis and Anderson, 1991.)*

ear patterns created by ridges of peat and vegetation separated by elongate hollows or shallow pools) occur in northern and northwestern Maine (Sorenson, 1986); flat bogs occur in all but southwestern and southeastern Maine; and domed bogs (bogs that have raised surface profiles) occur in eastern Maine (Worley, 1981). Domed bogs exhibit different landforms, including concentric bogs (domed bogs that have ringing crescent-shaped pools), eccentric bogs (domed bogs on valley slopes), and coastal-plateau bogs (domed bogs that have flattened raised surfaces and steep margins). Coastal-plateau bogs and eccentric bogs are rare in the United States and reach their southern limit for the Northeastern United States in Maine (Davis and Anderson, 1991).

Palustrine emergent wetlands, commonly referred to as freshwater marshes, cover a small area in Maine relative to forested and scrub-shrub wetlands. In southern and central Maine, marshes are typically associated with lakes or slow streams. In general, cattails are characteristic of deeper water or permanently flooded marshes; grasses predominate in areas that have permanently saturated mineral soils, such as swales; and sedges typically occur in permanently saturated or seasonally flooded peatlands or areas that have muck soils.

Most of Maine's rivers and lakes have some areas that have slow reaches or shallow water where submersed, floating, or emergent aquatic vegetation is established. These wetlands are very important to the biological productivity of rivers and lakes. As a result of recent increases in beaver populations, many riverine and riparian palustrine wetlands have been flooded behind beaver dams. This flooding can be detrimental to existing wetlands but also can create wetlands that have high value to some wildlife, such as waterfowl.

Along Maine's coast the predominant wetlands are mud flats, rocky shores, beaches and bars, reefs, and aquatic beds (marine and estuarine wetlands). These habitats total about 125,500 acres (Widoff, 1988). Maine also has about 34,000 acres of salt and brackish marshes (estuarine emergent wetlands) (Widoff, 1988). Many salt and brackish marshes are small, and fringe creeks and indentations in the rocky coast. Jacobson and others (1987) divided Maine's coast into four physiographic subsections in which salt marshes differ in character and distribution. The southwestern coast is characterized by bays having sandy beaches behind which large salt marshes have developed, such as those of the Wells Embayment and Saco Bay. These are generally irregularly flooded marsh communities dominated by saltmeadow cordgrass and black grass. The south-central coast is characterized by fluvial marshes in the upper parts of narrow embayments, such as those of the Damariscotta and Sheepscot Rivers. This area of the coast also contains some tidally influenced freshwater wetlands (palustrine and riverine wetlands), such as those in Merry Meeting Bay at the confluence of the Kennebec and Androscoggin Rivers. The north-central coast, including Penobscot Bay, is a high-energy environment where marshes exist only as fringes bordering a few protected coves. The northeastern coast is characterized by narrow marshes that form along the base of coastal bluffs. These are generally regularly flooded marsh communities dominated by saltmarsh cordgrass.

HYDROLOGIC SETTING

Wetlands are hydrologic features that occur wherever climate and physiography favor the retention of water (Winter, 1992). Wetlands are found along rivers, lakes, and estuaries where flooding is likely to occur; in isolated depressions surrounded by upland where surface water collects; and on slopes and surface drainageways or where ground water discharges to the land surface in spring or seepage areas. Soil saturation favors the growth of wetland plants and the development of wetland soils. Water can be either present on the surface of wetlands, or it can keep underlying soils saturated near the surface with no surface water present (Tiner, 1991). The

timing and duration of the presence of water affects water chemistry, soil development, and plant communities in wetlands. Although wetness plays a large role in the determination of wetland type, many ecologic functions of wetlands depend upon other characteristics such as size, position of the wetland in a drainage network, or sources of water (Brinson, 1993). The type of wetland that develops in any particular setting is determined by complex interactions between hydrology and other factors such as climate, physiography, geology, biology, and site history.

Maine's climate provides moisture necessary for wetland formation and cool temperatures that allow peat to accumulate. Precipitation and fog are frequent. Most climatic variables that affect vegetation differ greatly across Maine, largely owing to the southwest-northeast orientation of mountains and coastline. For example, mean annual precipitation, potential evapotranspiration, mean annual temperature, and the frost-free period decrease from the coast to northwestern Maine (McMahon, 1990). Climatic conditions play a role in the unusual diversity of peatland types in Maine. For example, coastal-plateau bogs exist only in areas along Maine's northern coast where precipitation is high, fog is frequent, and temperature is moderate.

The distribution of wetlands in Maine is partly determined by physiography, glacial deposits, and the underlying bedrock. Areas of steep topography do not retain water long enough for wetlands to develop. Given favorable hydrologic conditions, wetlands form on drainage divides and near mountain tops. For example, several ridge-top subalpine bogs occur in the Mahoosuc Range (Johnson, 1985). Most of Maine's wetlands, however, are in lowlands, valleys, and depressions that have more favorable hydrologic conditions for wetlands.

Much of the low-lying area of Maine is covered by stratified clay, silt, sand, and gravel deposited during periods of glaciation by glacial meltwater in streams and lakes (Cameron, 1989). Most uplands are composed of bedrock mantled by glacial till, an unstratified mixture of clay, silt, sand, gravel, and boulders. Both till and fine-grained sediments (clay and silt) can restrict drainage and retain surface water. Thus, wetlands occur over till in central and northern Maine and at higher altitudes; over fine-grained glacial lake deposits in portions of some valleys of central Maine, such as the West Branch of the Penobscot; and over fine-grained marine deposits in the lowlands of coastal Maine and areas reaching inland along major river valleys.

Some Maine valleys contain deposits of coarse-grained stratified drift (sand and gravel). These coarse-grained deposits can transmit ground water to overlying wetlands. Some glacial landforms, such as ridges (eskers), hills (drumlins, kames, and moraines), depressions (kettles), and terraces and plains (outwash) can create conditions favorable for wetlands by disrupting drainage patterns, attenuating runoff, or retaining water. For example, in east-central Maine, numerous wetlands are found in kettles that formed when ice blocks buried by glacial outwash melted (Timson and Pickart, 1992). These kettles either filled with water to form kettle ponds or passed through several successional stages of infilling to become kettle-hole bogs. In other areas, eskers may block drainage and create areas of swampy terrain. On occasion, roads without adequate culverts can have similar effects.

Interactions between hydrology and vegetation can be illustrated by peatlands and coastal wetlands. In peatlands, vegetation patterns are determined largely by water chemistry and movement (Damman and French, 1987). For instance, bogs receive little input from runoff or ground water and rely on precipitation (including fog) and windblown dust as sources for water, nutrients, and minerals. Vegetation in bogs commonly occurs in concentric zones caused by the scarcity of nutrients and minerals available in the center of the bog and the increased availability of nutrients and minerals along bog margins. Fens also receive water from precipitation but rely on ground water and runoff for input of minerals and nutrients. Vegetation patterns in coastal wetlands respond to a wide range of physiographic, chemical, and biological processes that are influenced by tidal energy (Mitsch and Gosselink, 1986). For instance, the tidal range in Maine doubles from south to north, where it has a range of about 20 feet. In northeastern Maine, tidal flooding creates a sharp contrast between subtidal and terrestrial habitats and tends to compact and enhance the zonation of vegetation in Maine's salt marshes (Fefer and Shettig, 1980). As a result of high tidal energy, a shortage of sediment, and a steep, rocky coast, many coastal environments that are colonized by vegetation in other States occur as rocky shores and extensive mud flats in Maine.

TRENDS

Dahl (1990) estimated that Maine has lost about 20 percent of its wetlands since about the 1780's. However, this may be an overestimate because it was based on hydric soil mapping units (R.W. Tiner, Fish and Wildlife Service, written commun., 1993). Changes in land use have led to losses of both wetlands and contiguous upland fringes. The history of wetland loss in Maine is largely a history of the State's urban and agricultural development. Early in Maine's history, expansion of fishing and farming communities along the coast resulted in the filling of many coastal wetlands. Later, many flood-plain wetlands were filled or converted to agricultural use as development spread upstate along inland waterways. In the past few decades, most losses have been a consequence of development and urbanization (Widoff, 1988). Other factors that can destroy wetlands or affect wetland functions include road building, creation of reservoirs, agricultural activities, peat harvesting, timber harvesting, hydropower releases, inadequate bridge and culvert sizing, navigation improvements, and air or water pollution. Most Federal and State regulations focus on minimizing wetland losses from these and other sources. The cumulative effect of loss or alteration of wetlands in Maine is likely to be an important issue in the future.

CONSERVATION

Many government agencies and private organizations participate in wetland conservation in Maine. The most active agencies and organizations and some of their activities are listed in table 1.

Federal wetland activities. — Development activities in Maine wetlands are regulated by several Federal statutory prohibitions and incentives that are intended to slow wetland losses. Some of the more important of these are contained in the 1899 Rivers and Harbors Act; the 1972 Clean Water Act and amendments; the 1985 Food Security Act; the 1990 Food, Agriculture, Conservation, and Trade Act; and the 1986 Emergency Wetlands Resources Act.

Section 10 of the Rivers and Harbors Act gives the U.S. Army Corps of Engineers (Corps) authority to regulate certain activities in navigable waters. Regulated activities include diking, deepening, filling, excavating, and placing of structures. The related section 404 of the Clean Water Act is the most often-used Federal legislation protecting wetlands. Under section 404 provisions, the Corps issues permits regulating the discharge of dredged or fill material into wetlands. Permits are subject to review and possible veto by the U.S. Environmental Protection Agency, and the FWS has review and advisory roles. Section 401 of the Clean Water Act grants to States and eligible Indian Tribes the authority to approve, apply conditions to, or deny section 404 permit applications on the basis of a proposed activity's probable effects on the water quality of a wetland.

Most farming, ranching, and silviculture activities are not subject to section 404 regulation. However, the "Swampbuster" provision of the 1985 Food Security Act and amendments in the 1990 Food, Agriculture, Conservation, and Trade Act discourage (through financial disincentives) the draining, filling, or other alteration of

Table 1. Selected wetland-related activities of government agencies and private organizations in Maine, 1993

[Source: Classification of activities is generalized from information provided by agencies and organizations. •, agency or organization participates in wetland-related activity; ..., agency or organization does not participate in wetland-related activity. MAN, management; REG, regulation; R&C, restoration and creation; LAN, land acquisition; R&D, research and data collection; D&I, delineation and inventory]

Agency or organization	MAN	REG	R&C	LAN	R&D	D&I
FEDERAL						
Department of Agriculture						
Consolidated Farm Service Agency	...	•	...	...	...	...
Forest Service	•	...	•	•	•	•
Natural Resources Conservation Service	...	•	•	...	•	•
Department of Commerce						
National Oceanic and Atmospheric Administration	•	•	...	...	...	...
Department of Defense						
Army Corps of Engineers	...	•	•	•	•	...
Military reservations	•	...	...	...	...	...
Department of the Interior						
Fish and Wildlife Service	•	...	•	•	•	•
Geological Survey	...	...	...	...	•	...
National Biological Service	...	...	...	...	•	...
National Park Service	•	...	•	•	•	...
Environmental Protection Agency	...	•	...	...	•	•
STATE						
Department of Agriculture	•	...	•	...	...	...
Department of Conservation						
Bureau of Parks and Recreation	•	...	...	...	...	...
Bureau of Public Lands	...	...	...	•	...	...
Forest Bureau	•	...	...	...	...	...
Land Use Regulation Commission	•	•	...	...	...	•
Maine Geological Survey	•	...	...	...	•	•
Department of Economics and Community Development						
Natural Areas Program	...	...	...	...	...	•
Department of Environmental Protection	•	•	•	•	•	•
Department of Inland Fisheries and Wildlife	•	•	•	•	•	•
State Planning Office	...	...	...	•	...	...
State university programs	...	...	...	...	•	•
LOCAL						
Soil and Water Conservation Districts	...	...	•	...	...	•
Some county, town, and city governments	•	•	•	...	•	•
PRIVATE ORGANIZATIONS						
Maine Coast Heritage Trust	...	...	...	•	...	...
The Nature Conservancy	•	...	...	•	...	...
Private colleges and universities	...	...	...	...	•	•

wetlands for agricultural use. The law allows exemptions from penalties in some cases, especially if the farmer agrees to restore the altered wetland or other wetlands that have been converted to agricultural use. The Wetlands Reserve Program of the 1990 Food, Agriculture, Conservation, and Trade Act authorizes the Federal Government to purchase conservation easements from landowners who agree to protect or restore wetlands. The Consolidated Farm Service Agency (formerly the Agricultural Stabilization and Conservation Service) administers the Swampbuster provisions and Wetlands Reserve Program. The NRCS determines compliance with Swampbuster provisions and assists farmers in the identification of wetlands and in the development of wetland protection, restoration, or creation plans.

The 1986 Emergency Wetlands Resources Act and the 1972 Coastal Zone Management Act and amendments encourage wetland protection through funding incentives. The Emergency Wetland Resources Act requires States to address wetland protection in their Statewide Comprehensive Outdoor Recreation Plans to qualify for Federal funding for State recreational land; the National Park Service (NPS) provides guidance to States in developing the wetland component of their plans. Coastal States that adopt coastal-zone management programs and plans approved by the National Oceanic and Atmospheric Administration (NOAA) are eligible for Federal funding and technical assistance through the Coastal Zone Management Act.

Federal agencies manage many wetlands in Maine. The FWS manages wetlands in Waterfowl-Protection Areas, National Fish Hatcheries, and National Wildlife Refuges. Also, the FWS administers wetland-acquisition programs such as the Partners for Wildlife Program, which helps restore wetlands on private lands, and the North American Waterfowl Management Plan, a cooperative program that provides funding for purchasing wetlands and contiguous uplands. The NPS manages wetlands in Acadia National Park and along the Appalachian Trail and the Allagash River. The NPS has designated 15 sites as National Natural Landmarks in Maine, several of which are entirely wetland. Some of these are protected by the State, and others are protected voluntarily by individual landowners. Wetlands also are managed by the U.S. Forest Service in the White Mountain National Forest, and by NOAA at the Wells National Estuarine Research Reserve.

Federal agencies provide funding for research and inventory of Maine wetlands. The FWS has funded research on peatland ecology (Damman and French, 1987) and is funding a study of wetland trends in selected coastal areas in cooperation with the Gulf of Maine Council. The NPS is inventorying wetlands in Acadia National Park. The EPA funds the Casco Bay Estuary Project with the goal of minimizing adverse environmental impacts from the use and development of land and marine resources. The Wells National Estuarine Research Reserve is available for Federal, State, public, and private research projects. The U.S. Geological Survey (USGS), with cooperative funding from State agencies, has inventoried peatlands in Maine (Cameron, 1989) and studied the hydrology of Denbow Heath and the Great Heath (Nichols, 1983).

State wetland activities.—Maine protects wetlands primarily through administration of the Natural Resources Protection Act and the Mandatory Shoreland Zoning Act by the Maine Department of Environmental Protection and through activities of the Department of Conservation, Land Use Regulation Commission. The Natural Resources Protection Act protects freshwater and coastal wetlands, great ponds, rivers and streams, and other significant wildlife habitats. Any proposed alteration in or within 100 feet of protected areas requires a permit from the Department of Environmental Protection. Regulated wetlands include freshwater wetlands of 10 or more acres and coastal and flood-plain wetlands regardless of size. For regulatory purposes, the act establishes three classes of wetlands (Maine Department of Environmental Protection, 1990). Each class is assigned a value based on the wetland's functions. Class I wetlands receive the greatest protection owing to their biological functions. These are wetlands such as coastal wetlands; great ponds; and wetlands that provide habitat for endangered or threatened plants and animals, unique natural communities, or significant wildlife habitat as defined by the Maine Department of Inland Fisheries and Wildlife and the Atlantic Sea Run Salmon Commission. Class II wetlands are rated largely by hydrologic functions. These are wetlands such as large emergent marshes, (nonforested) peatlands, flood-plain wetlands, and wetlands within 250 feet of rivers, streams, lakes, or coastal wetlands. Class III wetlands include forested wetlands and wet meadows not located near open water. The act does not regulate the cutting of most forested wetlands.

The Mandatory Shoreline Zoning Act, administered by the Department of Environmental Protection, requires municipalities in coastal areas to establish land-use controls for all land areas within set distances of rivers, ponds, and wetlands. Land-use controls in the unorganized territories of northern Maine are established by the Land Use Regulation Commission. Zoning maps produced by the commission set buffers around scrub-shrub and emergent wetlands and also around streams and lakes. The Maine Department of Ag-

riculture, Bureau of Production and Marketing, assists by setting up best-management practices and reviewing permits for farming activities near great ponds and wetlands.

The Department of Environmental Protection also administers sections 305(b) and 401 of the Clean Water Act. Section 305(b) requires States to submit biennial water-quality-assessment reports to Congress and the EPA, a part of which specifically addresses water quality in wetlands. Section 401 requires State water-quality certification before a section 404 permit may be issued. Other laws administered by the Department that protect wetlands include the Dam Registration, Abandonment and Water Level Act and the Site Location of Development Law. The Department also works closely with other State and Federal agencies. For example, wetland losses due to road building are minimized through cooperation between the Maine Department of Transportation and the Department of Environmental Protection. The Corps has issued a Maine State Programmatic General Permit which allows permit work that would have otherwise required a Corps permit to be approved through the Department of Environmental Protection's permitting process.

Other State agencies manage, research, and inventory wetlands. The Department of Inland Fisheries and Wildlife may designate buffers around wetlands of high value, such as emergent wetlands, and around features such as deer yards or eagle nests, many of which are in or contiguous to wetland areas. The Department of Environmental Conservation, Maine Geological Survey, has inventoried Maine's peatland resources (Cameron and others, 1984) and coastal wetlands, has served as the lead agency for cooperative projects with the USGS, investigates surficial geology and coastal processes in wetland areas, and furnishes information such as FWS National Wetland Inventory maps to the public. The Maine Department of Economic and Community Development, Natural Areas Program, conducts an inventory and information-management program focused on endangered and rare plants and exemplary natural communities and has an official register of Maine Critical Areas and a mandate to effect voluntary conservation of these areas, more than 100 of which are wetlands. The program has published reports describing many of these critical areas.

State land acquisition is coordinated for all agencies by the Maine State Planning Office. In the last 5 years, the State Planning Office has purchased about 48,000 acres of land with a $35 million bond from the Land for Maine's Future Program funded by Maine voters in 1987. Several purchases were entirely wetland. Ownership of State lands is divided among three agencies—the Bureau of Parks and Recreation, the Bureau of Public Lands, and the Department of Inland Fisheries and Wildlife. The Bureau of Public Lands administers 450,000 acres of Public Reserved Lands, an estimated 5 percent of which are wetlands (Widoff, 1988). The Bureau of Parks and Recreation owns a few thousand acres of wetland within State parks and the Allagash Wilderness Waterway. Inland Fisheries and Wildlife manages about 32 major Wildlife Management Areas, many of which contain wetlands as their primary feature.

County and local wetland activities.—Municipalities are active in wetland protection in Maine. Under the Mandatory Shoreline Zoning Act, every municipality is empowered to adopt, administer, and enforce its own shoreland zoning ordinance and map. Some towns have imposed stricter regulations than the act requires. On the local level, town code enforcement officers often have first contact with individuals and developers whose activities in wetlands areas are regulated under the Natural Resources Protection Act and Mandatory Shoreline Zoning Act. The Department of Economics and Community Development, Office of Community Development, runs a Code Enforcement, Training, and Certification Program to train local code enforcement officers on State wetland rules and regulations.

Private wetland activities.—Private organizations perform complementary functions that cannot readily be accomplished by governmental agencies. For example, wetlands research is conducted in several academic departments at the University of Maine and at other colleges and universities in the State. Private organizations such as The Nature Conservancy can provide rapid action in purchase of property. The Maine Chapter of The Nature Conservancy owns 83 preserves, many which are entirely wetlands. The Maine Coast Heritage Trust is a land-conservation organization that facilitates donation of easements and land transactions for conservation purposes. Through their activities, some important natural areas that include wetlands have been designated as "forever wild." Other organizations involved with protection of Maine's wetlands or with some wetland holdings include 73 local land trusts, the Maine Audubon Society, the National Audubon Society, the Society for the Protection of New Hampshire Forests, the New England Wildflower Society, Ducks Unlimited, the Izaak Walton League, and many others. Individuals, timber companies, and other private landowners own most of Maine's wetlands, and many actively pursue wetland conservation.

References Cited

Brinson, M.M., 1993, Changes in the functioning of wetlands along environmental gradients: Wetlands, v. 13, no. 2, p. 65–74.

Cameron, C.C., 1989, Peat and its occurrence as a resource in Maine, *in* Tucker, R.D., and Marvinney, R.G., eds., Studies in Maine geology, v. 5: Augusta, Maine Department of Conservation, Maine Geological Survey, p. 125–146.

Cameron, C.C., Mullen, M.K., Lepage, C.A., and Anderson, W.A., 1984, Peat resources of Maine: Maine Geological Survey Bulletins 28–32.

Cowardin, L.M., Carter, Virginia, Golet, F.C., and LaRoe, E.T., 1979, Classification of wetlands and deepwater habitats of the United States: U.S. Fish and Wildlife Service Report FWS/OBS–79/31, 131 p.

Dahl, T.E., 1990, Wetlands—Losses in the United States, 1780's to 1980's: Washington D.C., U.S. Fish and Wildlife Service Report to Congress, 13 p.

Damman, A.W.H., and French, T.W., 1987, The ecology of peat bogs of the glaciated northeastern United States—A community profile: U.S. Fish and Wildlife Service Biological Report 85(7.16), 114 p.

Davis, R.B., and Anderson, D.S., 1991, The eccentric bogs of Maine—A rare wetland type in the United States: Maine State Planning Office, Critical Areas Program, Planning Report 93, 169 p.

Fefer, S.I., and Shettig, P.A. (principal investigators), 1980, An ecological characterization of coastal Maine (north and east of Cape Elizabeth): U.S. Fish and Wildlife Service Report FWS/OBS–80/29, v. 1–6.

Fenneman, N.M., 1946, Physical divisions of the United States: Washington D.C., U.S. Geological Survey special map, scale 1:7,000,000.

Jacobson, H.A., Jacobson, G.L., and Kelley, J.T., 1987, Distribution and abundance of tidal marshes along the coast of Maine: Estuaries, v. 10, no. 2, p. 126–131.

Johnson, C.W., 1985, Bogs of the northeast: Hanover, N.H., University Press of New England, 269 p.

Maine Department of Environmental Protection, 1990, Natural Resources Protection Act Wetland Protection Rules—Chapter 310: Augusta, Maine Department of Environmental Protection, 13 p.

Maine Natural Heritage Program, 1991, Natural landscapes of Maine—A classification of ecosystems and natural communities: Augusta, Department of Economic and Community Development, 77 p.

McMahon, J.S., 1990, The biophysical regions of Maine: Orono, University of Maine, M.S. thesis, 119 p.

Mitsch, W.J., and Gosselink, J.G., 1986, Wetlands: New York, Van Nostrand Reinhold, 539 p.

Nichols, W.J., Jr., 1983, Hydrologic data for the Great and Denbow Heaths in eastern Maine, October 1981–October 1982: U.S. Geological Survey Open-File Report 83–865, 34 p.

Sorenson, E.R., 1986, Ecology and distribution of ribbed fens in Maine: Augusta, Maine State Planning Office, Critical Areas Program, Planning Report 81, 171 p.

Timson, B.S., and Pickart, G., 1992, Inventory of glacial kettles, kettle-hole ponds, and kettle-hole bogs: Augusta, Maine State Planning Office, Critical Areas Program, 240 p.

Tiner, R.W., 1991, Maine wetlands and their boundaries—A guide for code enforcement officers: Augusta, Maine Department of Economic and Community Development, Office of Comprehensive Planning, 72 p.

Tiner, R.W., and Veneman, P.L., 1989, Hydric soils of New England: Amherst, Mass., University of Massachusetts Cooperative Extension, Revised Bulletin C–183R, 27 p.

Widoff, Lissa, 1988, Maine Wetlands Conservation Priority Plan: Augusta, Maine State Planning Office, Bureau of Parks and Recreation, 117 p.

Winter, T.C., 1992, A physiographic and climatic framework for hydrologic studies of wetlands, *in* Robarts, R.D., and Bothwell, M.L., eds., Aquatic ecosystems in semi-arid regions—Implications for resource management, 1992: Saskatoon, Saskatchewan, The National Hydrology Research Institute Symposium Series 7, Environment Canada, p. 127–148.

Worley, I.A., 1981, Maine Peatlands: Augusta, Maine State Planning Office, Critical Areas Program, Planning Report 73, 387 p.

FOR ADDITIONAL INFORMATION: District Chief, U.S. Geological Survey, 26 Ganneston Drive, Augusta, ME 04330; Regional Wetland Coordinator, U.S. Fish and Wildlife Service, 300 Westgate Center Drive, Hadley, MA 01035

Prepared by
David S. Armstrong,
U.S. Geological Survey

Maryland and the District of Columbia
Wetland Resources

Wetlands cover about 9.3 percent of Maryland and the District of Columbia. Many of these wetlands harbor unique and endangered species of plants and animals, and life is abundant in all of them. Some the most familiar wetlands in the region are the tidal marshes of the Chesapeake Bay (fig. 1).

Wetlands have many physical, chemical, and biological functions. For example, wetlands trap waterborne sediments, nutrients, and toxic chemicals by filtering them out of inflowing water and either storing or transforming them. Coastal-zone and flood-plain wetlands mitigate the effects of flooding from runoff and tides by reducing flow velocity, storing water temporarily, and releasing it gradually. Vegetation in riparian wetlands maintains stream channels by stabilizing the banks, and tidal wetlands impede erosion by storm surges and waves. One of the most important functions of wetlands is as habitat for waterfowl, wildlife, and a wide variety of plant life. Wetlands provide food, shelter, resting places on migration routes, breeding areas, and nurseries for many animals including species of economic importance in Maryland such as ducks, geese, oysters, blue crabs, and several kinds of finfish. Many rare and endangered plant species are adapted to conditions present only in wetlands.

Maryland's wetlands have considerable historic and economic value. Humans have inhabited Maryland's coastal wetlands for thousands of years, and unique cultures have developed there. Wetlands provide outdoor educational, recreational, and financial opportunities—hunting, commercial and sport fishing, bird watching, and tourism—all benefit Maryland's economy.

TYPES AND DISTRIBUTION

Wetlands are lands transitional between terrestrial and deepwater habitats where the water table usually is at or near the land surface or the land is covered by shallow water (Cowardin and others, 1979). The distribution of wetlands and deepwater habitats in Maryland and the District of Columbia is shown in figure 2A; only wetlands are discussed herein.

Wetlands can be vegetated or nonvegetated and are classified on the basis of their hydrology, vegetation, and substrate. In this summary, wetlands are classified according to the system proposed by Cowardin and others (1979), which is used by the U.S. Fish and Wildlife Service (FWS) to map and inventory the Nation's wetlands. At the most general level of the classification system, wetlands are grouped into five ecological systems: Palustrine, Lacustrine, Riverine, Estuarine, and Marine. The Palustrine System includes only wetlands, whereas the other systems comprise wetlands and deepwater habitats. Wetlands of the systems that occur in Maryland and the District of Columbia are described below.

System	Wetland description
Palustrine	Nontidal and tidal-freshwater wetlands in which vegetation is predominantly trees (forested wetlands); shrubs (scrub-shrub wetlands); persistent or nonpersistent emergent, erect, rooted herbaceous plants (persistent- and nonpersistent-emergent wetlands); or submersed and (or) floating plants (aquatic beds). Also, intermittently to permanently flooded open-water bodies of less than 20 acres in which water is less than 6.6 feet deep.
Lacustrine	Nontidal and tidal-freshwater wetlands within an intermittently to permanently flooded lake or reservoir larger than 20 acres and (or) deeper than 6.6 feet. Vegetation, when present, is predominantly nonpersistent emergent plants (nonpersistent-emergent wetlands), or submersed and (or) floating plants (aquatic beds), or both.
Riverine	Nontidal and tidal-freshwater wetlands within a channel. Vegetation, when present, is same as in the Lacustrine System.
Estuarine	Tidal wetlands in low-wave-energy environments where the salinity of the water is greater than 0.5 part per thousand (ppt) and is variable owing to evaporation and the mixing of seawater and freshwater.
Marine	Tidal wetlands that are exposed to waves and currents of the open ocean and to water having a salinity greater than 30 ppt.

Palustrine wetlands comprise most (57 percent) of the wetlands in Maryland and the District of Columbia, followed by estuarine wetlands (42 percent). Ninety percent of wetlands in Maryland and the District of Columbia are vegetated. The predominant vegetation or specific location of a wetland frequently determines its common name. Dune slacks are topographic depressions among sand dunes on the Eastern Shore (the part of Maryland on the Delmarva Peninsula) that contain palustrine emergent or scrub-shrub wetlands. Delmarva bays are topographic depressions on the Delmarva Peninsula that often contain seasonally flooded palustrine emergent, scrub-shrub, or forested wetlands. Swamps or swamp forests are palustrine tidal or nontidal forested wetlands. Seeps are small palustrine wetlands formed around springs; the pH of the water can be neutral, acidic (in sandstone), or alkaline (in carbonate rocks). Peatlands are palustrine emergent, scrub-shrub, or forested wetlands that have organic soils. A type of peatland called a bog in Maryland is permanently saturated by ground water and is, therefore, actually a fen. Seasonal sinkhole wetlands are seasonally wet palustrine emergent wetlands that form in sinkholes in areas underlain by limestone. Wet meadows are spring-fed palustrine emergent wetlands. Seagrass beds are estuarine aquatic-bed wetlands in which eelgrass commonly is the predominant vegetation. Riverine and lacustrine aquatic-bed wetlands, in which submersed aquatic vegetation such

Figure 1. Wetlands on the Eastern Shore of the Chesapeake Bay. Local variation in topography, soil characteristics, and hydrology are reflected in the vegetation patterns. *(Photograph by David F. Usher, U.S. Geological Survey.)*

as wild celery and hydrilla predominate, are known locally as SAV wetlands (for "submersed aquatic vegetation"). Salt and brackish marshes are estuarine emergent wetlands in which the predominant vegetation is tolerant of water that ranges from brackish to salty. Small scrub-shrub wetlands commonly are associated with salt marshes.

Maryland covers an area that extends from the Atlantic Ocean into the Appalachian Mountains. About 590,800 acres (9.3 percent) of Maryland's land area is wetland (R.W. Tiner, U.S. Fish and Wildlife Service, oral commun., 1992). Tidal and nontidal wetlands each comprise about one-half of the wetland acreage. The size and distribution of tidal wetlands are determined primarily by local topography and tidal range. The distribution of nontidal wetlands is determined by local topography, soil characteristics, and geohydrologic conditions. Tidal wetlands occur in or near the Chesapeake Bay and its tributaries or behind barrier islands on the Atlantic coast, whereas nontidal wetlands occur throughout the State. The most abundant wetland type in Maryland is palustrine forested wetland, which covers about 286,300 acres, nearly one-half the total wetland area in the State. Next most abundant is estuarine emergent wetland, covering about 203,400 acres. Maryland also has about 2,000 acres of riverine, 1,400 acres of lacustrine, and 700 acres of marine wetlands (mostly beaches and sand bars).

The District of Columbia has about 840 acres of wetlands (Guerrero, 1993); most are in the Coastal Plain along the Chesapeake and Ohio (C&O) Canal and the tidal reaches of the Potomac and Anacostia Rivers. Only a few acres of the District's wetlands are in the Piedmont Province. About 62 percent of the District's wetlands are riverine aquatic beds. Most of those are in the Anacostia River and the C&O Canal. About 34 percent of the District's wetlands are palustrine and are located along the Potomac and Anacostia Rivers and Rock Creek and on Theodore Roosevelt Island. Sixty percent of these palustrine wetlands are emergent, 16 percent are scrub-shrub, and 24 percent are forested. About 4 percent of the District's wetlands are lacustrine.

HYDROLOGIC SETTING

Maryland and the District of Columbia can be divided into three geohydrologic regions for purposes of discussing wetland hydrology: the Coastal Plain; a central region consisting of the Piedmont, Blue Ridge, and Valley and Ridge physiographic provinces; and the Appalachian Plateaus (fig. 2*B*).

Coastal Plain.—The relatively flat Coastal Plain physiographic province rises from below sea level to about 100 feet above sea level on the Delmarva Peninsula east of the Chesapeake Bay and to about 200 feet above sea level in southern Maryland west of the Chesapeake Bay (James, 1986). The Coastal Plain is underlain by unconsolidated sediments. More than 90 percent of Maryland's total wetland area, including all of its estuarine wetlands, is in this province (Tiner, 1987).

Recharge of the ground-water system in this region is mainly by infiltration of precipitation and occurs in interstream areas. Discharge occurs by seepage to streams, estuaries, and the ocean. Many Coastal Plain wetlands are in discharge areas of coastal and riparian zones. The low-lying areas of the Coastal Plain contain extensive wetlands in the form of seagrass beds, salt marshes, and tidal and nontidal freshwater marshes and swamps. These wetlands have complex hydrology; streamflow, ground-water flow, and tidal flow all are components. The many rivers and streams of the Coastal Plain have forested wetlands in the bottom lands along the channels. These wetlands are sustained by local and regional ground-water flow systems and overbank flooding during storms. The width of forested wetlands in streamside areas often is reduced by artificial draining and conversion of the land for agricultural use.

The Coastal Plain can be divided into two subregions of differing hydrology: the Eastern Shore and the area of the Coastal Plain west of the Chesapeake Bay. Inland, the Eastern Shore is poorly drained and has small depressional palustrine wetlands (Delmarva bays) and narrow bands of palustrine wetlands along ditches, streams, and rivers that drain areas from inland to the coasts (fig.

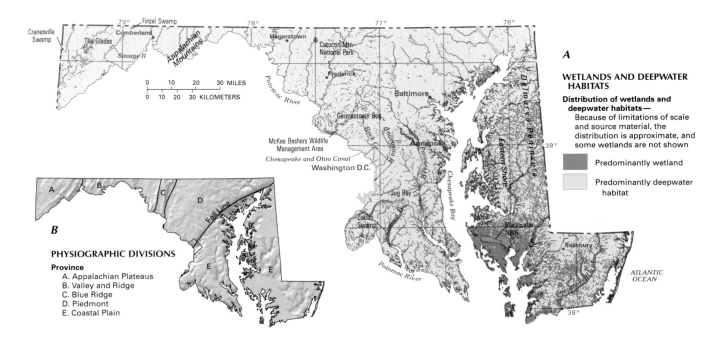

Figure 2. Wetland distribution in Maryland and the District of Columbia and physiography of the State and District. *A*, Distribution of wetlands and deepwater habitats. *B*, Physiography. *(Sources: A, T.E. Dahl, U.S. Fish and Wildlife Service, unpub. data, 1991. B, Physiographic divisions from Fenneman, 1946; landforms data from EROS Data Center.)*

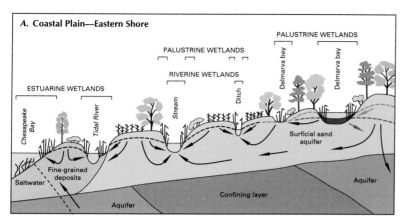

A. Coastal Plain—Eastern Shore

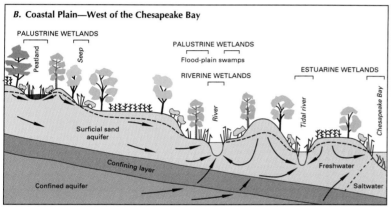

B. Coastal Plain—West of the Chesapeake Bay

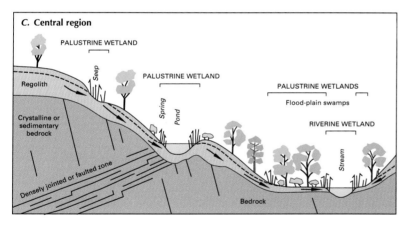

C. Central region

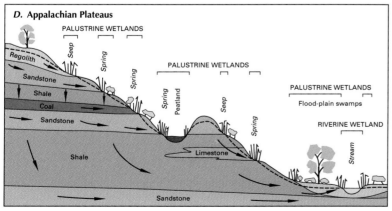

D. Appalachian Plateaus

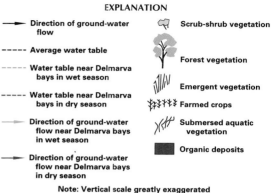

EXPLANATION

— Direction of ground-water flow

---- Average water table

---- Water table near Delmarva bays in wet season

---- Water table near Delmarva bays in dry season

— Direction of ground-water flow near Delmarva bays in wet season

— Direction of ground-water flow near Delmarva bays in dry season

Scrub-shrub vegetation

Forest vegetation

Emergent vegetation

Farmed crops

Submersed aquatic vegetation

Organic deposits

Note: Vertical scale greatly exaggerated

Figure 3. Generalized geohydrologic setting of wetlands in three regions of Maryland and the District of Columbia. *A*, Coastal Plain—Eastern Shore. *B*, Coastal Plain—west of the Chesapeake Bay. *C*, Central region. *D*, Appalachian Plateaus.

3*A*). Extensive estuarine marshes occur along the western shore of the peninsula and in the inland bays on the eastern shore of the peninsula.

Delmarva bays occur in several different settings, most commonly in the poorly drained center of the Delmarva Peninsula. Delmarva bays are connected to local shallow ground-water systems, which differ in areal extent, hydrochemistry, and degree of fluctuation of the water table (Hall and Malcom, 1990). Local flow patterns can vary seasonally because the depth of the water table around and below Delmarva bays is directly related to seasonal rainfall. Areas of ground-water discharge during wet seasons can be areas of ground-water recharge during dry seasons (fig. 3*A*) (Phillips and Shedlock, 1993).

West of the Chesapeake Bay, the geohydrology of the surficial aquifer is complex, and the local patterns of ground-water flow are not well understood. Patterns of ground-water flow shown in figure 3*B* are based on general geohydrologic principles described by Winter (1988, 1992). West of the bay, flood-plain swamps are abundant along rivers and streams. These wetlands are maintained by local and regional ground- and surface-water flow systems. In a few areas, peatlands, locally called bogs, occur in topographic lows. These wetlands are hydraulically connected to the local ground-water flow network. Seep wetlands occur along the Fall Line (fig. 2*B*), which marks the boundary between the sediments of the Coastal Plain and the higher altitude crystalline rocks of the Piedmont Province.

Maryland's Coastal Plain has many notable wetlands. The Pocomoke River swamp has extensive stands of bald cypress trees. In the Blackwater National Wildlife Refuge, brackish marshes grade into tidal freshwater marshes. Zekiah Swamp is a forested wetland that adjoins a freshwater emergent marsh along the Wicomico River. In the Jug Bay wetlands on the Patuxent River, tidal freshwater marshes grade into tidal and nontidal forested wetlands.

Central region.—The central region has considerably more topographic relief than the Coastal Plain. The gently rolling hills of the Piedmont Province are as much as 800 feet above sea level, and the mountains of the Blue Ridge Province rise to more than 1,600 feet. Altitudes in the Valley and Ridge Province range from about 400 feet in the valleys to about 1,500 feet on ridges (James, 1986). The central region is underlain by crystalline and consolidated sedimentary bedrock that has been subjected to considerable folding and faulting and that is overlain by a regolith of variable thickness. Regolith, which forms the land surface nearly everywhere, is a layer of unconsolidated, mostly fine-grained material composed of fragmental, weathered bedrock and alluvium overlying unweathered bedrock.

Recharge of the ground-water system in the central region is by infiltration of precipitation, mostly in the forested uplands. Most of the precipitation seeps into a thick, permeable soil layer, and most of that water moves laterally through the soil to surface depressions or streams. Water that moves below the soil zone enters the regolith, and much of that water seeps into the underlying bedrock. Ground water discharges from the regolith or bedrock by evapotranspiration, as seeps or springs, or directly into streams (fig. 3C). Much of the ground water available to wetlands in the region is held in the regolith (Metzgar, 1973).

Most of the wetlands in the central region are in valleys or other surface depressions. These topographic lows often indicate the presence of fracture zones in the bedrock. Fracture zones are more susceptible than unfractured zones to weathering and erosion, which allows the evolution of topographic depressions, and they are the major pathways of ground-water movement through bedrock (Heath, 1984). Water is more likely to be discharged into depressions than into other areas. For example, the source of water in the Germantown Bog is primarily ground water and, although no streams flow into this peatland, a stream flows out of it. Wetlands in the Piedmont Province include peatlands; flood-plain emergent marshes; chemically neutral, acidic, and alkaline seeps; seasonal sinkholes; and farm ponds. Wetlands in the Blue Ridge Province include isolated peatlands and forested wetlands in seepage areas smaller than 1 acre and surrounded by forest. Wetlands are rare in the Valley and Ridge Province, but those that are there include seeps, forested flood-plain wetlands, and wet meadows.

Notable wetlands in the Piedmont Province include the Germantown Bog (a fen rather than a true bog) and flood-plain marshes such as those in the McKee Beshers Wildlife Management Area. The isolated wetlands in the Blue Ridge Province, such as the acidic seeps in Catoctin Mountain National Park, are essential habitats for rare and endangered plants. Wetlands also provide important habitat in the Valley and Ridge Province, where the major wetlands are flood-plain swamps of the Potomac River and its tributaries and wet meadows in the area around Hagerstown.

Appalachian Plateaus.—The valleys and mountains of the Appalachian Plateaus range from 1,500 to 3,000 feet above sea level (James, 1986). The Appalachian Plateaus are characterized by severely eroded, flat-lying to gently folded shale, sandstone, coal, and limestone. The landscape consists of mountain crests, ridges, and hilltops that are formed of or capped by sandstone; wide, elongated valleys of intermediate altitude; and narrow, steep-sided valleys (Abbe, 1902).

Recharge of the ground-water system in this region is by infiltration of precipitation. Recharge primarily occurs in outcrop areas of sandstone formations in the uplands between streams (Heath, 1984). Discharge from the ground-water system is through seeps, springs, and streams (fig. 3D).

Most of the wetlands in this region are in wide valleys and topographic lows in shale beds and along contacts and bedding planes in the bedrock. Small wetlands are isolated from the surface-water system, but large wetlands drain into streams. For example, streams draining from Finzel Swamp (also known as Cranberry Swamp), a large peatland, are the headwaters for the Savage River. Peatlands are the largest wetland complexes in the Appalachian Plateaus; other wetland types in the region include seeps and flood-plain swamps. The peatlands generally are spring fed and have acidic water, although some are buffered by limestone. The predominant vegetation in many peatlands is shrubs and grasses, but some have open sphagnum mats. Notable wetlands in the Appalachian Plateaus are large peatlands such as Finzel Swamp, The Glades, and Cranesville Swamp, which is a classic northern peatland.

TRENDS

In the 1780's, about 1,650,000 acres, or 24 percent, of Maryland (Dahl, 1990) and about 8,700 acres, or 20 percent, of the District of Columbia (Department of Consumer and Regulatory Affairs, 1990) were wetland. At that time, and for 2 centuries thereafter, wetlands were regarded as a public nuisance — a source of disease and useful only if they could be turned into dry land (Maryland Conservation Commission, 1909). The influence of agricultural, tourism, recreational, and industrial interests led to the draining, dredging, filling, diking, and damming of wetland areas and to extensive stream channelization. These practices — in combination with other human activities such as forestry; mining; crop tillage; increased pesticide, herbicide, nutrient, and sediment loading from upland activities; urban development and pollution; natural impacts such as saltwater intrusion caused by sea-level rise and ground subsidence; wave-generated erosion; and hurricanes — have contributed to widespread wetland loss or degradation. About 590,800 wetland acres, or about 9.3 percent of the land surface, remain in Maryland (R.W. Tiner, U.S. Fish and Wildlife Service, oral commun., 1992) — a loss of about 64 percent since the 1780's.

When the District of Columbia was established in the 1790's, dredging and filling of wetlands to control disease and flooding began immediately. By the 1920's, most of the streams and springs that once drained into the Potomac and Anacostia Rivers were dry or enclosed in pipes (Williams, 1989). Most of the palustrine wetlands that those springs and streams supported have been covered by monuments, buildings, and parks. By 1992, only about 840 acres of wetlands, or about 10 percent of the wetland area in the 1780's, remained. The Department of Public Works and the U.S. Army Corps of Engineers (Corps) are directing wetland-restoration projects in the Anacostia River basin, where most of the District's remaining tidal wetlands are located.

CONSERVATION

Many government agencies and private organizations participate in wetland conservation in Maryland and the District of Columbia. The most active agencies and organizations and some of their activities are listed in table 1.

Federal wetland activities.—Development activities in Maryland and the District of Columbia wetlands are regulated by several Federal statutory prohibitions and incentives that are intended to slow wetland losses. Some of the more important of these are contained in the 1899 Rivers and Harbors Act; the 1972 Clean Water Act and amendments; the 1985 Food Security Act; the 1990 Food, Agriculture, Conservation, and Trade Act; the 1986 Emergency Wetlands Resources Act; and the 1972 Coastal Zone Management Act.

Section 10 of the Rivers and Harbors Act gives the Corps authority to regulate certain activities in navigable waters. Regulated activities include diking, deepening, filling, excavating, and placing of structures. The related section 404 of the Clean Water Act is the most often-used Federal legislation protecting wetlands. Under section 404 provisions, the Corps issues permits regulating the discharge of dredged or fill material into wetlands. Permits are subject to review and possible veto by the U.S. Environmental Protection Agency (EPA), and the FWS has review and advisory roles. Section

Table 1. Selected wetland-related activities of government agencies and private organizations in Maryland, 1993

[Source: Classification of activities is generalized from information provided by agencies and organizations. ●, agency or organization participates in wetland-related activity; ..., agency or organization does not participate in wetland-related activity. **MAN**, management; **REG**, regulation; **R&C**, restoration and creation; **LAN**, land acquisition; **R&D**, research and data collection; **D&I**, delineation and inventory]

Agency or organization	MAN	REG	R&C	LAN	R&D	D&I
FEDERAL						
Department of Agriculture						
Consolidated Farm Service Agency	...	●	...	...	...	...
Natural Resources Conservation Service	...	●	●	...	●	●
Department of Commerce						
National Oceanic and Atmospheric Administration	●	●	...	...	●	●
Department of Defense						
Army Corps of Engineers	●	●	●	●	●	●
Department of the Interior						
Fish and Wildlife Service	●	...	●	●	●	●
Geological Survey	...	...	...	...	...	...
National Biological Survey	...	...	...	...	●	...
National Park Service	●	...	●	●	●	●
Environmental Protection Agency	...	●	...	...	●	●
STATE						
Department of the Environment						
Water Management Administration	●	●	●	●	●	●
Department of Natural Resources						
Chesapeake Bay and Watershed Programs	●	...	...	●	●	●
Natural Heritage Program	●	...	...	●	●	●
Program Open Space	...	...	...	●	...	...
Office of State Planning	...	...	...	...	...	●
State Highway Administration	...	●	...	...	...	...
University of Maryland	...	...	...	...	●	...
DISTRICT OF COLUMBIA						
Department of Consumer and Regulatory Affairs	...	●	...	...	...	...
Department of Public Works	●	●	...	...	...	...
Metropolitan Council of Governments	...	●	...	...	...	...
Soil and Water Conservation District	●	●	●	...	...	...
SOME COUNTY AND LOCAL GOVERNMENTS	●	●	●	...	...	...
PRIVATE ORGANIZATIONS						
Chesapeake Bay Foundation	...	●	...	...	...	...
Environmental Concern, Inc.	...	●	●	...	●	...
Maryland Land Trust Alliance	●	...	...	●	...	...
The Nature Conservancy	●	...	...	●	...	...

pliance with Swampbuster provisions and assists farmers in the identification of wetlands and in the development of wetland protection, restoration, or creation plans.

The 1986 Emergency Wetlands Resources Act and the 1972 Coastal Zone Management Act and amendments encourage wetland protection through funding incentives. The Emergency Wetland Resources Act requires States to address wetland protection in their Statewide Comprehensive Outdoor Recreation Plans to qualify for Federal funding for State recreational land; the National Park Service (NPS) provides guidance to States in developing the wetland component of their plans. Coastal States that adopt coastal-zone management programs and plans approved by the National Oceanic and Atmospheric Administration are eligible for Federal funding and technical assistance through the Coastal Zone Management Act.

State wetland activities.— Maryland's Wetlands and Riparian Rights Act and Non-Tidal Wetlands Protection Act and Chapters 20 and 21 of the District of Columbia Code contain State-level requirements for construction activities in wetlands. To obtain permits for altering wetlands in Maryland, a joint State-Federal application must be submitted to the Maryland Department of the Environment's Water Resources Administration, which will route it to the appropriate regulatory agencies. The Department of the Environment administers the Maryland wetland-protection acts and is responsible for State compliance with section 305(b) of the Clean Water Act, which requires States to submit water-quality-assessment reports to Congress and the EPA biennially. These reports must specifically address water quality in wetlands. The Department of the Environment also administers section 401 of the Clean Water Act, which requires State water-quality certification before a section 404 permit may be issued.

Other regulatory activities are conducted by the Department of Natural Resources, the Office of State Planning, and the State Highway Administration. All activities in tidal wetlands are conducted under the Department of Chesapeake Bay and Watershed Programs; other activities are conducted by the Department's Natural Heritage and Greenways and Resource Planning Programs, by the Greenways Commission, by the Department of the Environment's Mining Program, and by the University of Maryland. The Maryland Natural Heritage Program supervises wetland management on State-owned lands and administers land-acquisition programs. The Department of Natural Resources' Greenways Program and the Greenways Commission work to maintain the integrity of natural areas and to integrate them with recreational use. The Mining Program has a small wetlands mitigation and restoration program in the Appalachian Plateaus region. Several academic departments and the Center for Environmental and Estuarine Studies at the University of Maryland conduct wetlands research.

Most wetlands in the District of Columbia are owned by the NPS, which maintains them and monitors wetland restoration and creation efforts along the Anacostia River. Permits for wetland alteration in the District of Columbia must be obtained from the Corps and the Department of Consumer and Regulatory Affairs.

County and local wetland activities.— County and local governments have enacted zoning restrictions on development in wetlands and created many conservation programs. Some counties (Baltimore, Harford, and Anne Arundel) have wetland programs. Prince Georges County has received partial authority from the State to implement the State Nontidal Wetland program. Other cooperative programs among State and local government agencies and private organizations coordinate regional programs and management and protection efforts, particularly around the District of Columbia and the Chesapeake Bay.

Private wetland activities.— Private organizations with interests in wetlands in Maryland and the District of Columbia are active primarily in regulation and policy planning, land acquisition and management, research, and adult and professional education.

401 of the Clean Water Act grants to States and eligible Indian Tribes the authority to approve, apply conditions to, or deny section 404 permit applications on the basis of a proposed activity's probable effects on the water quality of a wetland.

Most farming, ranching, and silviculture activities are not subject to section 404 regulation. However, the "Swampbuster" provision of the 1985 Food Security Act and amendments in the 1990 Food, Agriculture, Conservation, and Trade Act discourage (through financial disincentives) the draining, filling, or other alteration of wetlands for agricultural use. The law allows exemptions from penalties in some cases, especially if the farmer agrees to restore the altered wetland or other wetlands that have been converted to agricultural use. The Wetlands Reserve Program of the 1990 Food, Agriculture, Conservation, and Trade Act authorizes the Federal Government to purchase conservation easements from landowners who agree to protect or restore wetlands. The Consolidated Farm Service Agency (formerly the Agricultural Stabilization and Conservation Service) administers the Swampbuster provisions and Wetlands Reserve Program. The Natural Resources Conservation Service (formerly the Soil Conservation Service) determines com-

A few of the many organizations in the region are the Chesapeake Bay Foundation (regulation and policy planning), the Maryland Land Trust Alliance and The Nature Conservancy (land acquisition and management), Environmental Concern, Inc. (research and adult and professional education), and Alliance for the Chesapeake Bay (adult and professional education).

References Cited

Abbe, Cleveland, Jr., 1902, The physiography of Garrett County, *in* Maryland Geological Survey, Garrett County: Baltimore, Maryland Geological Survey, p. 27–54.

Cowardin, L.M., Carter, Virginia, Golet, F.C., and LaRoe, E.T., 1979, Classification of wetlands and deepwater habitats of the United States: U.S. Fish and Wildlife Service Report FWS/OBS–79/31, 131 p.

Dahl, T.E., 1990, Wetlands—Losses in the United States, 1780's to 1980's: Washington, D.C., U.S. Fish and Wildlife Service Report to Congress, 13 p.

Department of Consumer and Regulatory Affairs, 1990, 1990 Report to the U.S. Environmental Protection Agency and U.S. Congress pursuant to Section 305(b) Clean Water Act (P.L. 97–117): Washington, D.C., Department of Consumer and Regulatory Affairs, 123 p.

Fenneman, N.M., 1946, Physical divisions of the United States: Washington, D.C., U.S. Geological Survey special map, scale 1:7,000,000.

Guerrero, V.C., 1993, Inventory and status of wetlands in the District of Columbia: Washington, D.C., District of Columbia Department of Consumer and Regulatory affairs, 80 p.

Hall, Tom, and Malcom, Hope, 1990, Inventory of natural resource areas within the Chesapeake Bay region, v. 1—Maryland: Annapolis, Md., U.S. Fish and Wildlife Service, 24 p.

Heath, R.C., 1984, Ground-water regions of the United States: U.S. Geological Survey Water-Supply Paper 2242, 78 p.

James, R.W., Jr., 1986, Maryland and the District of Columbia surface-water resources, *in* U.S. Geological Survey, National water summary 1985—Hydrologic events and surface-water resources: U.S. Geological Survey Water-Supply Paper 2300, p. 265–270.

Maryland Conservation Commission, 1909, Reclamation of swamps, *in* Report for 1908–1909: Baltimore, Maryland Conservation Commission, p. 137–144.

Metzgar, R.G., 1973, Wetlands in Maryland: Annapolis, Maryland Department of State Planning Publication 157, 80 p.

Phillips, P.J., and Shedlock, R.J., 1993, Hydrology and chemistry of ground water and seasonal ponds in the Atlantic coastal plain in Delaware, U.S.A.: Journal of Hydrology, v. 141, p. 157–178.

Tiner, R.W., 1987, Mid-Atlantic wetlands—A disappearing natural treasure: Newton Corner, Mass., U.S. Fish and Wildlife Service and U.S. Environmental Protection Agency cooperative publication, 28 p.

Williams, G.P., 1989, Washington, D.C.'s vanishing springs and waterways, *in* Moore, J.E., and Jackson, J.S., eds., Geology, hydrology, and history of the Washington, D.C., area: Alexandria, Va., American Geological Institute, p. 76–94.

Winter, T.C., 1988, A conceptual framework for assessing cumulative impacts on the hydrology of nontidal wetlands: Environmental Management, v. 12, no. 5, p. 605–620.

———1992, A physiographic and climatic framework for hydrologic studies of wetlands, *in* Robarts, R.D., and Bothwell, M.L., eds., Proceedings of the Symposium on Aquatic Ecosystems in Semi-Arid Regions—Implications for resource management, 1990: Saskatoon, Saskatchewan, Environment Canada, The National Hydrology Research Institute Symposium Series 7, p. 127–147.

FOR ADDITIONAL INFORMATION: District Chief, U.S. Geological Survey, 208 Carroll Building, 8600 LaSalle Road, Towson, MD 21204; Regional Wetland Coordinator, U.S. Fish and Wildlife Service, 300 Westgate Center Drive, Hadley, MA 01035

Prepared by
Martha A. Hayes,
U.S. Geological Survey

Massachusetts
Wetland Resources

Wetlands cover about 11 percent of Massachusetts (Dahl, 1990) and are an important component of the State's water resources. Wetlands are valued and protected by the State for the environmental and economic benefits they provide, such as flood control, mitigation of storm damage, water-quality improvement, maintenance of ground-water supplies, wildlife habitat, and spawning and nursery habitat for many of the estuarine and marine fish and shellfish that support the State's sport-fishing and seafood industries (fig. 1). Most wetland functions are tied to the presence, movement, quality, and quantity of water in wetlands (Carter and others, 1979). For example, flood-plain wetlands along the Charles River provide natural storage and a reduction of floodwaters such that the least-cost solution to prevent future flooding was to acquire and protect the wetlands (U.S. Army Corps of Engineers, 1971). Massachusetts wetlands provide not only the functions and values for which they are protected by the State but other benefits such as scenic beauty and recreational opportunities. The benefits that Massachusetts' wetlands provide are a reflection of the diversity of the State's wetland resources.

TYPES AND DISTRIBUTION

Wetlands are lands transitional between terrestrial and deepwater habitats where the water table usually is at or near the land surface or the land is covered by shallow water (Cowardin and others, 1979). The distribution of wetlands and deepwater habitats in Massachusetts is shown in figure 2A; only wetlands are discussed herein.

Wetlands can be vegetated or nonvegetated and are classified on the basis of their hydrology, vegetation, and substrate. In this summary, wetlands are classified according to the system proposed by Cowardin and others (1979), which is used by the U.S. Fish and Wildlife Service (FWS) to map and inventory the Nation's wetlands. At the most general level of the classification system, wetlands are grouped into five ecological systems: Palustrine, Lacustrine, Riverine, Estuarine, and Marine. The Palustrine System includes only wetlands, whereas the other systems comprise wetlands and

Figure 1. Namskaket Marsh on Cape Cod. This wetland is the site of U.S. Geological Survey studies that monitor the development and fate of a wastewater plume moving toward this tidal wetland. *(Photograph courtesy of Kelsey-Kennard Photographers, Chatham, Mass.)*

deepwater habitats. Wetlands of the systems that occur in Massachusetts are described below.

System	Wetland description
Palustrine	Nontidal and tidal-freshwater wetlands in which vegetation is predominantly trees (forested wetlands); shrubs (scrub-shrub wetlands); persistent or nonpersistent emergent, erect, rooted herbaceous plants (persistent- and nonpersistent-emergent wetlands); or submersed and (or) floating plants (aquatic beds). Also, intermittently to permanently flooded open-water bodies of less than 20 acres in which water is less than 6.6 feet deep.
Lacustrine	Nontidal and tidal-freshwater wetlands within an intermittently to permanently flooded lake or reservoir larger than 20 acres and (or) deeper than 6.6 feet. Vegetation, when present, is predominantly nonpersistent emergent plants (nonpersistent-emergent wetlands), or submersed and (or) floating plants (aquatic beds), or both.
Riverine	Nontidal and tidal-freshwater wetlands within a channel. Vegetation, when present, is same as in the Lacustrine System.
Estuarine	Tidal wetlands in low-wave-energy environments where the salinity of the water is greater than 0.5 part per thousand (ppt) and is variable owing to evaporation and the mixing of seawater and freshwater.
Marine	Tidal wetlands that are exposed to waves and currents of the open ocean and to water having a salinity greater than 30 ppt.

The most recent inventory of Massachusetts wetlands, performed during 1975–77 by the FWS National Wetlands Inventory Project, mapped about 590,000 acres of wetlands in the State (Tiner, 1992). According to Metzler and Tiner (1992), the maps are at least 95 percent accurate. Palustrine wetlands are the most common wetland type in the State, followed by estuarine and marine wetlands (fig. 2B); all together, they constitute about 99 percent, by area, of the State's wetlands. The combined area of lacustrine and riverine wetlands makes up the remaining less than 1 percent of wetland acreage. A description of Massachusetts' most common wetland types follows.

Palustrine wetlands.—Vegetated palustrine wetlands in Massachusetts include ponds and shallow lakes in which the dominant vegetation is floating or submersed (aquatic-bed wetlands); freshwater marshes, fens, and bogs dominated by herbaceous plants (emergent wetlands); and bogs and swamps dominated by shrubs or trees (scrub-shrub or forested wetlands). Vernal pools are small, seasonally flooded wetlands that occur throughout Massachusetts. Because most vernal pools dry up, they are devoid of fish and thus provide a safe breeding habitat for many amphibian and invertebrate species.

Palustrine forested wetlands constitute 56 percent of the State's wetlands (Tiner, 1992) and consist primarily of red maple swamps with some evergreen forested wetlands. Red maple grows in most inland wetlands because it tolerates a wide range of flooding and soil-saturation conditions (Metzler and Tiner, 1992). The vegetation found with red maple, in the understory and intermixed or codominating in the canopy, differs according to nutrient conditions and water regime. Atlantic white cedar wetlands, the most common

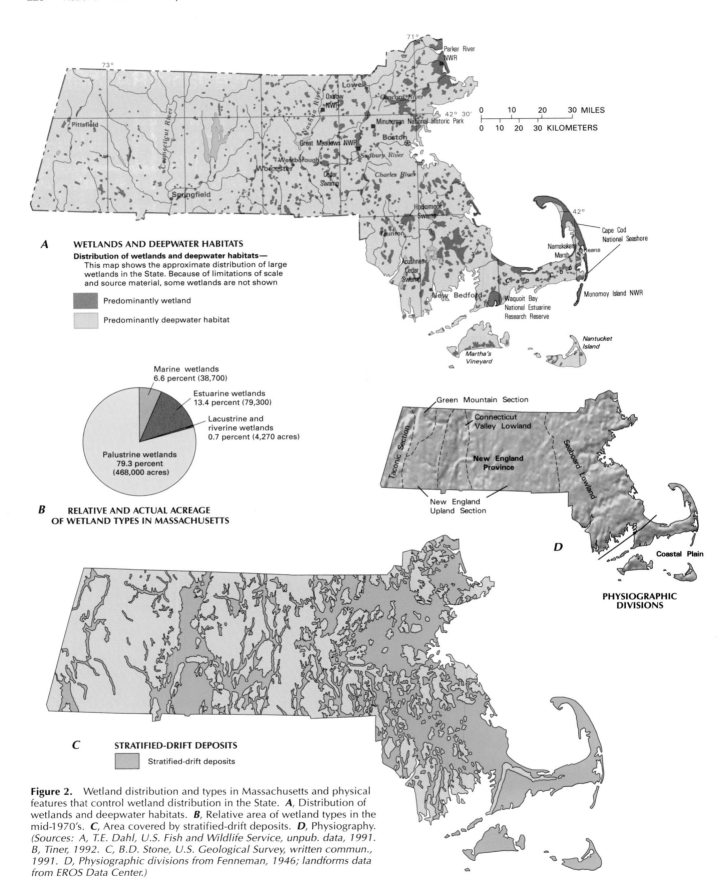

A   WETLANDS AND DEEPWATER HABITATS

Distribution of wetlands and deepwater habitats—
This map shows the approximate distribution of large wetlands in the State. Because of limitations of scale and source material, some wetlands are not shown

  Predominantly wetland

  Predominantly deepwater habitat

Marine wetlands
6.6 percent (38,700)

Estuarine wetlands
13.4 percent (79,300)

Lacustrine and
riverine wetlands
0.7 percent (4,270 acres)

Palustrine wetlands
79.3 percent
(468,000 acres)

B   RELATIVE AND ACTUAL ACREAGE
OF WETLAND TYPES IN MASSACHUSETTS

Green Mountain Section

Connecticut
Valley Lowland

**New England
Province**

Taconic Section

Seaboard Lowland

New England
Upland Section

D   Coastal Plain

**PHYSIOGRAPHIC
DIVISIONS**

C   STRATIFIED-DRIFT DEPOSITS

  Stratified-drift deposits

Figure 2.   Wetland distribution and types in Massachusetts and physical features that control wetland distribution in the State. **A**, Distribution of wetlands and deepwater habitats. **B**, Relative area of wetland types in the mid-1970's. **C**, Area covered by stratified-drift deposits. **D**, Physiography. *(Sources: A, T.E. Dahl, U.S. Fish and Wildlife Service, unpub. data, 1991. B, Tiner, 1992. C, B.D. Stone, U.S. Geological Survey, written commun., 1991. D, Physiographic divisions from Fenneman, 1946; landforms data from EROS Data Center.)*

evergreen forested wetlands, are concentrated south of Boston and form isolated wetlands in western and north-central Massachusetts and in the Connecticut River Valley (Sorrie and Woolsey, 1987).

Lacustrine and riverine wetlands.—Although present throughout the State, lacustrine and riverine wetlands comprise only a small percentage of Massachusetts' wetland area. These freshwater wetlands generally are restricted to the littoral zone between the shore and deepwater habitat and, if vegetated, have only aquatic-bed or nonpersistent emergent vegetation. The majority of riverine wetlands occur adjacent to the Connecticut River (Tiner, 1992). Wetlands in the shallows of rivers or lakes are classified as palustrine wetlands if there is persistent emergent vegetation present.

Estuarine and marine wetlands.—Estuarine and marine wetlands account for 20 percent of the State's total wetland acreage. In Massachusetts, marine wetlands consist of exposed intertidal flats and beaches and minor acreages of rocky shores and aquatic beds. Estuarine wetlands consist of salt and brackish marshes (emergent and scrub-shrub wetlands) that have developed behind coastal dunes and in protected coves and embayments along the coast and estuaries. These wetlands are commonly vegetated by grasses and aquatic plants. Sparsely vegetated estuarine flats and beaches, alternately flooded by tide or exposed to air, also are present.

HYDROLOGIC SETTING

Wetlands form in geologic, topographic, and hydrologic settings that enhance the accumulation and retention of ground water, surface water, or both for a period of time. Hydrologic processes are the primary factor determining the existence of wetlands; even if the geologic and topographic settings are favorable for wetland formation, unfavorable hydrologic conditions can inhibit wetland formation (Winter, 1988). On an annual basis, precipitation exceeds evapotranspiration losses in Massachusetts, resulting in an annual moisture surplus. Hydrology, therefore, favors the formation and maintenance of wetlands throughout the State, and wetland location is determined primarily by geologic and topographic controls.

Massachusetts was almost completely covered by ice during the last glaciation; the ice margin reached its maximum extent at Martha's Vineyard and Nantucket Island. Large quantities of glacial drift were deposited over bedrock throughout the State. This sediment was left in place as deposited from the ice as till or was eroded and reworked by glacial meltwater and deposited as stratified drift. Till is exposed at the land surface, primarily on upland hilltops and slopes. Stratified drift was deposited in topographically low areas where glacial meltwater collected—major lowlands such as the Coastal Plain Province, the Seaboard Lowland and Connecticut Valley Lowland Sections, and in stream and river valleys throughout the New England Upland, Green Mountain, and Taconic Sections (fig. 2C and 2D). Although stratified drift covers only 44 percent of Massachusetts, 68 percent of wetlands are underlain by this deposit (Motts and O'Brien, 1981). In general, the percentage of land containing wetlands decreases from east to west in the State; this decrease can be directly attributed to the distribution of stratified drift.

Inland wetlands.—Surficial materials of the Coastal Plain, which encompasses Cape Cod, Martha's Vineyard, and Nantucket Island, consist primarily of permeable stratified drift characterized by low relief. Despite the low relief, surface water does not collect in these areas because of the rapid infiltration of precipitation. Wetlands occur in the numerous kettle holes that intersect the ground-water table and receive water from ground-water discharge and precipitation. Kettle holes, closed topographic depressions, were created by the melting of stagnant ice blocks that were embedded in glacial sediments. Kettle holes pit the surface of stratified drift throughout the State. Because ground water moves relatively rapidly through the surficial materials of this area, plants in these wet-

lands are adapted to low-nutrient conditions. Kettle ponds in the Coastal Plain provide a habitat for plants that grow only on the exposed, sandy shores of nutrient-poor, acidic ponds and require seasonal water-table fluctuations (Henry Woolsey, Natural Heritage and Endangered Species Program, written commun., 1993).

Glacial lakes occupied the Connecticut Valley Lowland and Seaboard Lowland of Massachusetts, depositing extensive areas of flat, nearly impermeable stratified drift (Schafer and Hartshorn, 1965). Impermeable stratified drift that was deposited in a marine environment underlies areas of the Seaboard Lowland to the north of and surrounding Boston (Stone and Peper, 1982). These coastal areas were depressed by the weight of glacial ice to beneath even the lowered sea level but rose rapidly after deglaciation to expose marine sediments. The low relief and impermeable materials of these areas slow the drainage of surface-water, promoting the formation and maintenance of wetlands. Sources of water for these wetlands include precipitation, ground-water discharge, and river overflow. Slow drainage leads to acidic, low-nutrient conditions through the accumulation of plant metabolic wastes and through the gradual depletion of nutrients as water flows through the wetland. Because of the low slope, small drainage obstructions can form large wetlands—such as the 6,000-acre Hockomock Swamp near Taunton, the 1,500-acre Cedar Swamp near Westborough, and the 1,000-acre Acushnet Cedar Swamp near New Bedford.

Within the bedrock and till-covered hills of the New England Upland and Taconic Sections, wetlands occur primarily in depressions where surface runoff and ground-water discharge collect. The depressions have no outflow or have drainage controlled by bedrock sills, stratified drift, beaver dams, or manmade structures. Seepage wetlands can form where the ground-water table intersects or is close to the land surface—on concave slopes and at breaks in slope. However, these wetlands are permanently saturated only if ground-water discharge is perennial; otherwise, the wetlands are seasonally saturated for varying periods of time (Winter, 1988). Wetlands also form in river valleys, where they occupy kettle holes in stratified drift or areas modified by the erosion and deposition of rivers—in abandoned river channels, behind levees and overbank sediments adjacent to rivers, and in backswamp areas. As water moves through soil and surficial materials, it is enriched in nutrients for plant growth. The longer the flowpath beneath the surface, the more the water is enriched. Wetlands in upland till and bedrock depressions are primarily areas of discharge from nutrient-poor, local to intermediate ground-water flow systems, whereas wetlands in lowland valleys receive discharge from nutrient-enriched, intermediate and regional ground-water flow systems.

As vegetation became established after ice retreat and developed in response to the warming of climate, open-water areas filled with sediment and organic matter to become wetlands or remained lakes with wetland habitats fringing open water. Studies of upland wetlands in Connecticut have shown that wetlands developed over many divergent paths in the time since glaciation; however, all wetlands have been strongly affected by postsettlement agricultural and industrial practices (Thorson, 1990; Thorson and Harris, 1991). Many wetlands resulted from colonial agricultural practices and the creation of ice ponds and mill ponds for water-powered industries.

Beavers have created many wetlands in Massachusetts by flooding uplands and narrow river valleys. Beaver populations in Massachusetts have been successfully reestablished and now occupy all suitable habitats in the State (Thomas Decker, Massachusetts Division of Fisheries and Wildlife, oral commun., 1993). Beaver-created wetlands have many of the positive aspects associated with wetlands—including habitat for waterfowl and other wildlife, flood control, sediment control, fish production, and recreational and esthetic values—but the property damage beaver ponds may cause can result in conflict between beavers and humans (Decker and Cooper, 1991).

Tidal wetlands.—Tidal wetlands are present along coastal areas of the State in the Coastal Plain and the Seaboard Lowland. Tidal wetlands form a broad continuum from marine to estuarine, riverine, and palustrine wetlands. The effects of wave energy and salinity on the wetlands diminish along this continuum. Tidal wetlands receive freshwater from upland areas through ground-water discharge, stream overflow, and hillslope runoff. Regional ground-water discharge is greatest near the break in slope between upland and coastal areas, and intermediate and local ground-water flow systems increase in importance in areas that have less topographic relief (Winter, 1988). Floodwater resulting from high tides or stormflows may be temporarily stored in the wetland. The drainage of floodwater and hillslope runoff from the wetland surface is slowed by the low slope of coastal areas.

The major factors affecting the development and persistence of tidal wetlands are the rate of sea-level rise, the tidal regime, the supply of sediments to the wetland, and the ability of plants to survive submergence by saltwater (Redfield, 1972). Unless the submergence of tidal wetlands by rising sea level is counteracted by the vertical accretion of the wetland by sediment deposition and plant accumulation, the wetland will drown and become a deepwater habitat. As the last glacial ice melted and water was returned to the sea, sea level rose, encroaching upon land and submerging many stream and river valleys to form estuaries. Tidal wetlands either have migrated inland along estuaries, river valleys, and coastal slopes, or the wetlands have been completely submerged. Most existing saltwater wetlands in New England are younger than 4,000 years and might have thick freshwater deposits below saltwater peat (Redfield, 1972). Presently, tidal wetlands exist in a narrow setting between rising sea level and expanding coastal development. The migration of these wetlands inland, as sea level continues to rise, is hindered by the previous destruction of coastal-margin wetlands and by present development in low-lying uplands.

TRENDS

The FWS estimates that Massachusetts has lost 28 percent of its original wetlands over the 200-year period between the 1780's and the 1980's (Dahl, 1990). Agricultural and urban expansion in the Boston, Cape Cod, and Connecticut River Valley areas have caused many wetland losses (Motts and O'Brien, 1981). There are no statewide estimates of recent wetland losses or alteration; however, wetland losses and alterations continue in Massachusetts despite Federal and State regulation. In southeastern Massachusetts, about 1,300 acres of vegetated wetlands were either lost or altered from 1977 to 1986 through agriculture, development, and conversion of vegetated wetlands to open water (Tiner and Zinni, 1988).

Since 1978 there have been more than 51,000 permit applications submitted to the Department of Environmental Protection for work proposed in or near wetlands in the State. More than 9,000 applications were submitted in 1991; about one-third of these applications were from Cape Cod and the southeastern part of the State, one-third were for projects proposed in and around metropolitan Boston, and the remaining one-third were for projects in central and western Massachusetts (Massachusetts Division of Wetlands and Waterways, 1991).

CONSERVATION

Many government agencies and private organizations participate in wetland conservation in Massachusetts. The most active agencies and organizations and some of their activities are listed in table 1.

Federal wetland activities.—Development activities in Massachusetts wetlands are regulated by several Federal statutory prohibitions and incentives that are intended to slow wetland losses.

Table 1. Selected wetland-related activities of government agencies and private organizations in Massachusetts, 1993

[Source: Classification of activities is generalized from information provided by agencies and organizations. ●, agency or organization participates in wetland-related activity; ..., agency or organization does not participate in wetland-related activity. MAN, management; REG, regulation; R&C, restoration and creation; LAN, land acquisition; R&D, research and data collection; D&I, delineation and inventory]

Agency or organization	MAN	REG	R&C	LAN	R&D	D&I
FEDERAL						
Department of Agriculture						
Consolidated Farm Service Agency	...	●	...	...	...	...
Forest Service	...	●	...	...	...	●
Natural Resources Conservation Service	...	●	...	...	...	●
Department of Commerce						
National Oceanic and Atmospheric Administration	●	●	...	●	●	...
Department of Defense						
Army Corps of Engineers	...	●	●	●	●	●
Military reservations	●	...	...	...	...	...
Department of the Interior						
Fish and Wildlife Service	●	...	●	●	●	●
Geological Survey	...	...	...	...	●	...
National Biological Service	...	...	...	...	●	●
National Park Service	●	...	●	●	●	●
Environmental Protection Agency	...	●	...	●	...	●
STATE						
Department of Environmental Management	●	...	●	●	●	...
Department of Environmental Protection						
Division of Water Pollution Control	●	●	...	...	●	...
Division of Water Supply	●	●	...	...	●	...
Division of Wetlands and Waterways	...	●	●	...	●	●
Department of Fisheries, Wildlife and Environmental Law Enforcement	●	●	●	●	...	...
Massachusetts Environmental Policy Act Unit	...	●	...	...	...	...
Metropolitan District Commission	●	...	...	●	...	...
University of Massachusetts	...	...	...	...	●	...
TOWN AND CITY CONSERVATION COMMISSIONS	●	●	...	●	...	...
PRIVATE ORGANIZATIONS						
Ducks Unlimited	...	...	...	...	●	●
Massachusetts Audubon Society	●	...	●	●	●	●
The Nature Conservancy	●	...	...	●	●	●
The Trustees of Reservations	●	...	●	●	●	●

Some of the more important of these are contained in the 1899 Rivers and Harbors Act; the 1972 Clean Water Act and amendments; the 1985 Food Security Act; the 1990 Food, Agriculture, Conservation, and Trade Act; and the 1986 Emergency Wetlands Resources Act.

Section 10 of the Rivers and Harbors Act gives the U.S. Army Corps of Engineers (Corps) authority to regulate certain activities in navigable waters. Regulated activities include diking, deepening, filling, excavating, and placing of structures. The related section 404 of the Clean Water Act is the most often-used Federal legislation protecting wetlands. Under section 404 provisions, the Corps issues permits regulating the discharge of dredged or fill material into wetlands. Permits are subject to review and possible veto by the U.S. Environmental Protection Agency, and the FWS has review and advisory roles. Section 401 of the Clean Water Act grants to States and eligible Indian Tribes the authority to approve, apply conditions to, or deny section 404 permit applications on the basis of a proposed activity's probable effects on the water quality of a wetland.

Most farming, ranching, and silviculture activities are not subject to section 404 regulation. However, the "Swampbuster" provision of the 1985 Food Security Act and amendments in the 1990 Food, Agriculture, Conservation, and Trade Act discourage (through financial disincentives) the draining, filling, or other alteration of wetlands for agricultural use. The law allows exemptions from penalties in some cases, especially if the farmer agrees to restore the altered wetland or other wetlands that have been converted to agricultural use. The Wetlands Reserve Program of the 1990 Food, Agriculture, Conservation, and Trade Act authorizes the Federal Government to purchase conservation easements from landowners who agree to protect or restore wetlands. The Consolidated Farm Service Agency (formerly the Agricultural Stabilization and Conservation Service) administers the Swampbuster provisions and Wetlands Reserve Program. The Natural Resources Conservation Service (formerly the Soil Conservation Service) determines compliance with Swampbuster provisions and assists farmers in the identification of wetlands and in the development of wetland protection, restoration, or creation plans.

The 1986 Emergency Wetlands Resources Act and the 1972 Coastal Zone Management Act and amendments encourage wetland protection through funding incentives. The Emergency Wetland Resources Act requires States to address wetland protection in their Statewide Comprehensive Outdoor Recreation Plans to qualify for Federal funding for State recreational land; the National Park Service (NPS) provides guidance to States in developing the wetland component of their plans. Coastal States that adopt coastal-zone management programs and plans approved by the National Oceanic and Atmospheric Administration (NOAA) are eligible for Federal funding and technical assistance through the Coastal Zone Management Act.

Federal agencies are responsible for the proper management of wetlands on public lands under their jurisdiction. The FWS protects and manages wetlands in four National Wildlife Refuges in Massachusetts: approximately 3,300 acres of salt marsh and freshwater wetlands in the Parker River National Wildlife Refuge, 1,000 acres of flood-plain wetlands along the Nashua River within the Oxbow National Wildlife Refuge, flood-plain wetlands along 12 miles of the Concord and Sudbury Rivers of the Great Meadows National Wildlife Refuge, and 2,750 acres of marine, estuarine, and palustrine wetlands in the Monomoy Island National Wildlife Refuge. The NPS protects, manages, and studies many diverse wetlands in the Minuteman National Historic Park and the Cape Cod National Seashore. The Corps manages about 1,000 acres of wetlands at dams and reservoirs located throughout the State and 8,000 acres of wetlands in the Charles River Natural Valley Storage Project.

State wetland activities.—All State agencies that have responsibilities for wetland protection, management, and planning are managed by the Executive Office of Environmental Affairs chaired by the Secretary of Environmental Affairs. The principal authority of this office is to implement and oversee State policies that preserve, protect, and regulate natural resources and the environmental integrity of the Commonwealth of Massachusetts. The Water Resources Commission establishes statewide water-resources policies for agencies within the Executive Office of Environmental Affairs. In 1990, the Water Resources Commission adopted a policy of no net short-term loss of wetlands and a net long-term gain of wetlands; the policy incorporates the principles of avoidance or minimization of adverse impacts on wetlands and full compensatory mitigation for unavoidable wetland losses (Massachusetts Division of Wetlands and Waterways, 1991). Primary responsibility to implement this policy was delegated to the Department of Environmental Protection.

The Department of Environmental Protection's Division of Wetlands and Waterways implements two complementary programs for wetland protection—the Wetlands Protection Program and the Wetlands Conservancy Program. The Wetlands Protection Program functions primarily through permitting and enforcement by local conservation commissions. The program handles appeals and provides training, technical assistance, and enforcement support to conservation commissions. The Wetlands Conservancy Program is mapping the State's wetlands through aerial photography at a scale

of 1:5,000. The wetland maps will provide a detailed inventory of the extent and condition of the State's wetlands to be used to identify illegal wetland alterations and quantify wetland losses. In addition, important wetlands are selected for permanent deed restrictions prohibiting activities that impair wetland functions. At present (1993), 46,000 acres of coastal wetlands and 8,000 acres of inland wetlands are protected by deed restrictions.

The Department of Environmental Protection is integrating the 401 water-quality certification program with wetland permitting under the State's Wetland Protection Act. Under section 401 of the Federal Clean Water Act, any activity that results in a discharge, including that of fill into wetlands or State waters, that also requires a Federal permit must obtain a 401 water-quality certification stating that the activity will not result in violation of State surface-water-quality standards. Many activities exempted under the Wetland Protection Act will be in the Department of Environmental Protection's jurisdiction under the 401 certification program. Use of the anti-degradation provisions of State surface-water-quality standards on wetlands defined as "waters of the Commonwealth" provides enhanced wetland protection. Antidegradation provisions provide for the protection of existing uses in wetlands and the level of water quality necessary to maintain those uses. No degradation is allowed in areas designated as Outstanding National Resource Waters, such as National Wildlife Refuges, National Parks, State parks, wildlife areas, and other areas of ecological significance. Vernal pools that have been certified by the State are designated as Outstanding Resource Waters and therefore have added protection through section 401 and its antidegradation provisions.

The Department of Environmental Management is the primary land-management and natural-resource planning agency in the State. The Department is the largest landholder in Massachusetts, having 270,000 acres of State forests, parks, beaches, and wildlife areas that include wetlands. As a part of its land-stewardship plans, the Department oversees many activities and programs including research and data collection, land-resource inventory, coastal-dune restoration, and natural area programs. The Wildlands Program sets aside areas of State forests and parks that contain examples of unique plant communities or geologic formations in the State. The Office of Water Resources, within the Department of Environmental Management, is involved in two significant programs related to wetlands—the river-basin planning program and the watershed-protection and flood-prevention facilities program (Michael Gildesgame, Office of Water Resources, written commun., 1993). The river-basin planning program analyzes the water resources of each basin and develops recommendations for regional and community water-resources management that balance the consumptive needs of municipal, industrial, and commercial water withdrawals with the instream flow needed to maintain natural resources such as wetlands, wildlife, and fisheries. The 35-year-old cooperative Federal and State watershed-protection and flood-prevention facilities program maintains and preserves about 5,000 acres of open space associated with 32 flood-prevention facilities across the State. Installation of these structures has promoted the development of new wetlands and has enhanced wildlife habitat, public recreation, and water supply. The Waquoit Bay National Estuarine Research Reserve, located on the southern coast of Cape Cod, is cooperatively managed by the Department of Environmental Management and NOAA's Sanctuaries and Reserves Division. The 2,250-acre reserve was created under section 315 of the Federal Coastal Zone Management Act and has barrier beach, salt pond, salt marsh, and open-water habitats. The reserve serves as a natural laboratory and is the site of several interagency research projects.

The Department of Fisheries, Wildlife and Environmental Law Enforcement protects and manages the State's wild and living natural resources, including rare and endangered plant and animal species. Wetland protection is part of the overall mission of the Department—the protection of natural ecosystems. Critical wildlife habitats are protected by an aggressive land-acquisition program that emphasizes the natural corridors formed by rivers, streams, and their associated wetlands. The Natural Heritage and Endangered Species Program, which is funded primarily through voluntary income tax contributions, inventories rare- and endangered-species habitats in the State.

Local wetland activities.—The local conservation commissions of the 351 cities and towns in Massachusetts implement the State's Wetland Protection Act with jurisdiction over any work in, over, or adjacent to water bodies, wetlands, rivers, and streams within each municipality. No person may dredge, fill, or alter wetlands without notifying the local conservation commission in writing to explain the proposed work. In addition, cities and towns may enact local wetland bylaws, which can provide more stringent wetland and resource protection than that specified in the State's Wetland Protection Act. Commissions consist of three to seven volunteer members appointed directly by local elected authorities.

Private wetland activities.—Private organizations in Massachusetts are active in land acquisition and management, research, education, and policy review and planning. The Massachusetts Audubon Society owns 22,000 acres of land containing wetlands. The Trustees of Reservations owns and manages 18,000 acres of land in the State with historic, scenic, or ecological value. Ducks Unlimited provides technical and financial assistance to Federal and State agencies in order to protect waterfowl habitat in Massachusetts.

References Cited

Carter, Virginia, Bedinger, M.S., Novitzki, R.P., and Wilen, W.O., 1979, Water resources and wetlands, *in* Greeson, P.E., Clark, J.R., and Clark, J.E., eds., Wetlands functions and values—The state of our understanding—Proceedings of the National Symposium on Wetlands, November 1978: Minneapolis, Minn., American Water Resources Association, p. 344–376.

Cowardin, L.M., Carter, Virginia, Golet, F.C., and LaRoe, E.T., 1979, Classification of wetlands and deepwater habitats of the United States: U.S. Fish and Wildlife Service Report FWS/OBS–79/31, 131 p.

Dahl, T.E., 1990, Wetlands—Losses in the United States, 1780's to 1980's: Washington, D.C., U.S. Fish and Wildlife Service Report to Congress, 13 p.

Decker, Thomas, and Cooper, Jeanne, 1991, Evaluation of damage by beavers to highways and the economic costs to cities and towns in Massachusetts: Westboro, Massachusetts Division of Fisheries and Wildlife Technical Report, 14 p.

Fenneman, N.M., 1938, Physiography of Eastern United States: New York, McGraw–Hill, 714 p.

Massachusetts Division of Wetlands and Waterways, 1991, Wetlands white paper: Boston, Massachusetts Department of Environmental Protection, 64 p.

Metzler, K.J., and Tiner, R.W., 1992, Wetlands of Connecticut: Connecticut State Geological and Natural History Survey Report of Investigations No. 13, 115 p.

Motts, W.S., and O'Brien, A.L., 1981, Geology and hydrology of wetlands in Massachusetts: University of Massachusetts, Water Resources Research Center Publication 123, 147 p.

Redfield, A.C., 1972, Development of a New England salt marsh: Ecological Monographs, v. 42, p. 201–237.

Schafer, J.P., and Hartshorn, J.H., 1965, The Quaternary of New England, *in* Wright, H.E., Jr., and Frey, D.G., eds., The Quaternary of the United States: Princeton, N.J., Princeton University Press, p. 113–128.

Sorrie, B.A., and Woolsey, H.L., 1987, The status and distribution of Atlantic white cedar in Massachusetts, *in* Laderman, A.D., Atlantic white cedar wetlands: Boulder, Colo., Westview Press, p. 135–137.

Stone, B.D., and Peper, J.D., 1982, Topographic control of the deglaciation of eastern Massachusetts—Ice lobation and the marine incursion, *in* Larson, G.J., and Stone, B.D., eds., Late Wisconsinan glaciation of New England: Dubuque, Iowa, Kendall/Hunt Publishing Company, p. 145–163.

Thorson, R.M., 1990, Development of small upland wetlands—A stratigraphic study in northeastern Connecticut: University of Connecticut, School of Engineering Final Report JHR 90–191, 285 p.

Thorson, R.M., and Harris, S.L., 1991, How "natural" are inland wetlands? An example from the Trail Wood Audubon Sanctuary in Connecticut, USA: Environmental Management, v. 15, p. 675–687.

Tiner, R.W., Jr., 1992, Preliminary national wetland inventory report on Massachusetts' wetland acreage: Newton Corner, Mass., U.S. Fish and Wildlife Service National Wetlands Inventory Project, 5 p.

Tiner, R.W., Jr. and Zinni, William, Jr., 1988, Recent wetlands trends in southeastern Massachusetts: Newton Corner, Mass., U.S. Fish and Wildlife Service National Wetlands Inventory Project, 9 p.

U.S. Army Corps of Engineers, 1971, Charles River study, appendix H—Flood management plan formulation: Waltham, Mass., U.S. Army Corps of Engineers, 32 p.

Winter, T.C., 1988, A conceptual framework for assessing cumulative impacts on the hydrology of nontidal wetlands: Environmental Management, v. 12, p. 605–620.

FOR ADDITIONAL INFORMATION: District Chief, U.S. Geological Survey, 28 Lord Rd., Suite 280, Marlborough, MA 01752; Regional Wetlands Coordinator, U.S. Fish and Wildlife Service, 300 Westgate Center, Hadley, MA 01035

Prepared by
Sandra L. Harris,
U.S. Geological Survey

Michigan
Wetland Resources

Wetlands cover about 15 percent of Michigan. They are ecologically and economically valuable to the State. Wetlands provide shoreline protection as well as temporary flood storage. Wetlands protect water quality by removing excess nutrients and sediments from surface and ground water. Michigan's wetlands, such as Tobico Marsh shown in figure 1, provide important wildlife habitat and have a significant role in maintaining a high level of biological diversity. Most freshwater fish depend on wetlands at some stage in their life cycle. Birds use wetlands as migratory resting places, for breeding and feeding grounds, and as cover from predators. Wetlands, such as those in Seney National Wildlife Refuge, are a preferred habitat for muskrat, beaver, otter, mink, and raccoon. Some rare or threatened animals rely on wetlands, and 91 of 238 plant species listed as threatened or endangered by the State grow in wetland habitats (Cwikiel, 1992). Wetlands benefit the State's tourist and outdoor recreation industries by providing opportunities for activities such as hunting, fishing, trapping, hiking, canoeing, birdwatching, nature photography, and viewing wildflowers. Blueberries and wild rice are produced commercially in Michigan wetlands. In the early 1980's, Michigan was one of five States that together produced 75 percent of the peat mined in the United States.

TYPES AND DISTRIBUTION

Wetlands are lands transitional between terrestrial and deepwater habitats where the water table usually is at or near the land surface or the land is covered by shallow water (Cowardin and others, 1979). The distribution of wetlands and deepwater habitats in Michigan is shown in figure 2A; only wetlands are discussed herein.

Wetlands can be vegetated or nonvegetated and are classified on the basis of their hydrology, vegetation, and substrate. In this summary, wetlands are classified according to the system proposed by Cowardin and others (1979), which is used by the U.S. Fish and Wildlife Service (FWS) to map and inventory the Nation's wetlands. At the most general level of the classification system, wetlands are grouped into five ecological systems: Palustrine, Lacustrine, Riverine, Estuarine, and Marine. The Palustrine System includes only wetlands, whereas the other systems comprise wetlands and deepwater habitats. Wetlands of the systems that occur in Michigan are described below.

System	Wetland description
Palustrine	Wetlands in which vegetation is predominantly trees (forested wetlands); shrubs (scrub-shrub wetlands); persistent or nonpersistent emergent, erect, rooted, herbaceous plants (persistent- and nonpersistent-emergent wetlands); or submersed and (or) floating plants (aquatic beds). Also, intermittently to permanently flooded open-water bodies of less than 20 acres in which water is less than 6.6 feet deep.
Lacustrine	Wetlands within an intermittently to permanently flooded lake or reservoir. Vegetation, when present, is predominantly nonpersistent emergent plants (nonpersistent-emergent wetlands), or submersed and (or) floating plants (aquatic beds), or both.
Riverine	Wetlands within a channel. Vegetation, when present, is same as in the Lacustrine System.

There is no current (1993) estimate of statewide wetland acreage in each of the systems. However, the Michigan Department of Natural Resources has inventoried land cover and land use; the result is the Michigan Resource Inventory System (MIRIS). Wetland classifications were developed specifically for this inventory system. Classes of wetlands under this scheme are lowland conifers, 1,826,402 acres; lowland hardwoods, 2,484,430 acres; wooded wetland, 263,684 acres (palustrine forested wetlands under the Cowardin and others [1979] classification system); shrub/scrub wetland, 1,186,150 acres (palustrine scrub-shrub wetlands); aquatic-bed wetland, 60,863 acres (rooted and floating vascular aquatic-bed wetlands); emergent wetland, 419,061 acres (persistent- and nonpersistent-emergent wetlands; and unvegetated flats, 3,926 acres (unconsolidated-shore wetlands). The results of the MIRIS inventory are similar to the 1953 U.S. Fish and Wildlife Service inventory (U.S. Fish and Wildlife Service, 1955); wooded and scrub/shrub wetlands are the most common wetland types in Michigan. Emergent wetlands make up a relatively small percentage of the State's total wetlands.

Wetlands were estimated by Dahl (1990) to occupy about 5.6 million acres of Michigan in the mid-1980's. There are more than 6.2 million acres of wetlands classified under MIRIS. However, under the classification scheme for MIRIS, lowland conifers and lowland hardwoods are primarily wetlands but may also include some areas that would be defined as uplands based on regulatory definitions (Michigan Department of Natural Resources, 1992).

In 1972, the Department of Natural Resources conducted a shorelands inventory and identified 105,855 acres of Great Lakes coastal wetlands (Michigan Department of Natural Resources, 1973). It has been estimated that coastal wetland acreage in Michigan has been as much as 369,000 acres in the past (Jaworski and Raphael, 1978). Michigan coastal wetlands are distributed among the Great Lakes in the following proportions: 37 percent along Lake Huron; 28 percent along Lake Michigan; 16 percent along the St. Clair River, Lake St. Clair, and the Detroit River area; 13 percent along Lake Superior; and 6 percent along Lake Erie (Michigan Department of Natural Resources, 1992).

Figure 1. Tobico Marsh, a coastal wetland along the shore of Saginaw Bay. *(Photograph by Erin A. Lynch, U.S. Geological Survey.)*

Along Lake Michigan from Muskegon north to Empire, wetlands are associated with wide, low-gradient tributary mouths that extend inland for several miles. Beaver Island has extensive wetlands. The shoreline from Empire to the Straits of Mackinac contains few wetlands. The Upper Peninsula shoreline of Lake Michigan is composed of rocky points and headlands with sandy or marshy bay heads (Herdendorf and others, 1981).

Along the Lake Superior shoreline of Michigan, wetlands are most common along the Keweenaw Bay waterway and at tributary mouths in Marquette and Chippewa Counties. The Isle Royale shoreline and islands and the mainland shores of the St. Marys River contain wetlands (Herdendorf and others, 1981).

The Michigan shoreline of western Lake Erie consists of low-lying marshes (emergent wetland) and sand beaches (unconsoli-

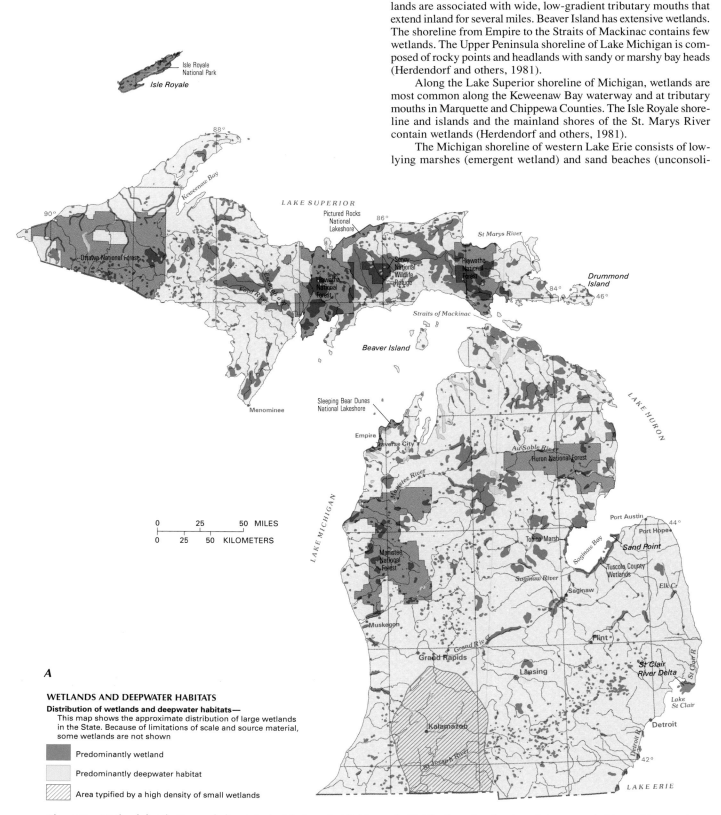

WETLANDS AND DEEPWATER HABITATS

Distribution of wetlands and deepwater habitats—
This map shows the approximate distribution of large wetlands in the State. Because of limitations of scale and source material, some wetlands are not shown

Predominantly wetland

Predominantly deepwater habitat

Area typified by a high density of small wetlands

Figure 2. Wetland distribution and climatological features in Michigan. **A**, Distribution of wetlands and deepwater habitats. *(Source: A, T.E. Dahl, U.S. Fish and Wildlife Service, unpub. data, 1991.)*

dated-shore wetland). The shoreline of Lake Huron from the Straits of Mackinac to Drummond Island generally consists of plains alternating with outcrops of limestone and dolomite. These plains are generally composed of clays and contain marshes. The beaches along the northern part of the Saginaw Bay are occasionally interrupted by wetlands. Most of the southeastern part of Saginaw Bay is marshy with shallow water inshore. From Sand Point to Port Austin the shore is composed of sand beaches with a bluff of uneven sand ridges. The sand ridges parallel the shoreline and alternate with wetlands. The area from Port Hope to the St. Clair River contains few wetlands. Along Lake St. Clair, the St. Clair River, and the Detroit River, the only extensive natural areas that have not been developed are the St. Clair River Delta wetlands and wetlands on islands at the mouth of the Detroit River (Herdendorf and others, 1981).

Approximately 18,000 acres of wetlands line Saginaw Bay (15 percent of the drainage basin) and comprise the largest remaining freshwater coastal wetland system in the Nation. Tobico Marsh (fig. 1) is an enclosed lagoon bordered on the east by a narrow coastal barrier at Saginaw Bay and on the west by sand ridges. Emergent wetlands occupy approximately 1,260 acres of Tobico Marsh. They contain many bird species and are attractive to waterfowl during migration. The Tuscola County Wetlands also are a part of the Saginaw Bay shoreline. They lie south of the Tobico Marsh and are confined to a relatively thin coastal and nearshore zone. In contrast to the Tobico Marsh, the Tuscola County Wetlands are open to wave action from Saginaw Bay. The wetlands occupy depressions within the premodern shoreline, clay flats, and lagoons at present lake level, and sandbars in the nearshore zone (Michigan Department of Natural Resources, 1993).

HYDROLOGIC SETTING

Wetlands form where there is a persistent water supply at or near the land surface. The location and persistence of the supply is a function of climatic, physiographic, and hydrologic factors such as precipitation and runoff patterns, evaporation potential, topography, and configuration of the water table. In Michigan, a favorable water budget coupled with impeded drainage promotes ample soil moisture for wetland development in depressions, many of which were formed by glaciation. Precipitation (fig. 2B) in the form of rain and snow averages approximately 31 inches annually. Lake-effect precipitation is prevalent in near-shore areas but also affects areas farther inland. Surface waters, including wetlands, are constantly replenished by precipitation. Runoff (fig. 2C) varies geographically and seasonally. It is greatest in areas where snowfall accumulation is heaviest (Miller and Twenter, 1986).

The topographic character of Michigan was largely determined by glaciation. Glacial lobes channeled through parts of the Great Lakes and deposited thick layers of drift material. The bulk of this drift accumulation may have been developed before the latest glacial period. Areas bordering the Lower Peninsula and in a broad belt extending southwest from the Saginaw River Basin beyond Lansing consist of flat drift deposits. Glacial lake waters covered much of these areas. There are more than 35,000 mapped lakes and ponds, and 36,350 miles of rivers and streams in Michigan (Sweat and Van Til, 1987). Nearly all of the lakes and associated wetlands in the lower peninsula occupy depressions in the surface of the glacial deposits. The Escanaba River Basin, in the center of the Upper Peninsula of Michigan, covers an area of 925 square miles. As much as 400 square miles of the southern part of the basin is covered by wetlands (Miller and Twenter, 1986). These wetlands are the remnants of an old glacial lake.

Kettle lake wetlands are common in upland areas within the Great Lakes Basin. Kettle lakes are formed by the incorporation of ice blocks in material that washed out from a melting glacial ice front. Where the melting ice block left a basin in the drift that penetrated the water table, kettle lakes were formed. These lakes differ in shape and size. In general, depth does not exceed 165 feet. The most common wetlands in kettle lakes are bogs. Kettle lakes can

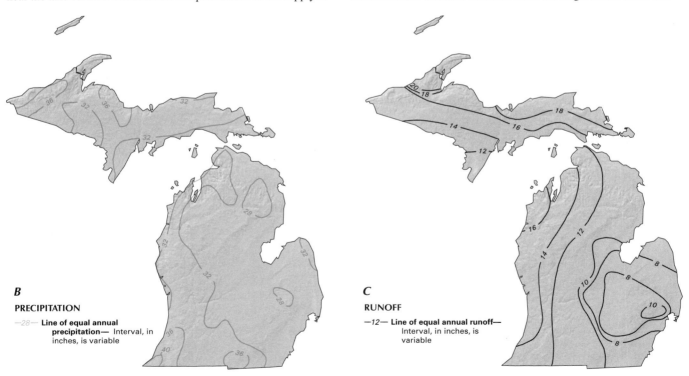

B

PRECIPITATION

—28— **Line of equal annual precipitation—** Interval, in inches, is variable

C

RUNOFF

—12— **Line of equal annual runoff—** Interval, in inches, is variable

Figure 2. Continued. Wetland distribution and climatological features in Michigan. **B**, Annual precipitation. **C**, Runoff. (*Sources: B and C, Miller and Twenter, 1986; landforms data from EROS Data Center.*)

eventually become bog lakes through a series of steps. First, the lake is fringed by floating mats of sedges that grow inward and encroach upon the open water. Eventually the mat covers the entire lake surface, and sphagnum moss and shrubs of the heath family become established. When growth exceeds decomposition, the lake basin begins to fill and peat deposits form. Ultimately, a succession of vegetation types may lead to a climax terrestrial forest (Herdendorf and others, 1981).

Freshwater coastal wetlands are extensive in Michigan. The occurrence, distribution, and diversity of coastal wetlands is, in part, determined by the morphology of the Great Lakes shoreline. Most Great Lakes wetlands develop in lagoons or flood ponds that form just landward of the shoreline. Glacial drift generally forms the upland boundaries, whereas barriers are created by water-laid sand, gravel, or cobble. Upland peninsulas formed by bedrock outcrops or resistant soil provide protection for shallow water areas cut into the shoreline. Riparian (streamside) wetlands extend inland along the flood plains and banks of tributary streams entering the lake basin. Their extent is a function of flood-plain width, which is greatest along larger streams with broad flood plains and least where streambanks are steep. It is difficult to distinguish between some riparian wetlands and those of embayed or barrier-lagoon systems because most tributary streams enter the lakes through lagoons and bays (Geis, 1985).

Sediments in the lagoon of the Tobico Marsh where emergent and submergent wetlands are present are composed of peats of variable consistency or a mixture of peat with fine sand. Tobico Marsh has one outlet — a small creek at the southern end of the marsh. During low water levels the lagoon is effectively sealed from Saginaw Bay. Because the lagoon becomes sealed and, therefore, lacks the flushing action that occurs in more open coastal wetlands, it could evolve into a peat bog (Herdendorf and others, 1981).

Coastal wetlands are, in general, younger than inland wetlands in Michigan because glacial ice receded from most of the Lower Peninsula approximately 12,000 years ago and the Great Lakes reached their present water levels less than 3,000 years ago. Therefore, coastal wetlands are at most 3,000 years old, whereas inland wetlands can be as old as 12,000 years. Coastal wetlands do not mature to the same extent as inland wetlands. Short-term, temporary water-level fluctuations and long-term, cyclic water-level changes can cause vegetation dieback, wetlands erosion, or lateral displacements of vegetative zones. These changes result in constant rejuvenation of coastal wetlands (Herdendorf and others, 1981).

TRENDS

The FWS has estimated that, from the 1780's to the 1980's, wetland area in Michigan decreased by 50 percent—from about 11.2 million to about 5.6 million acres (Dahl, 1990, p. 6). Most wetland loss in Michigan has been caused by drainage for agricultural purposes. Most drainage occurred before 1930. However, from 1934 through 1940, the Works Progress Administration and Federal Relief Agencies drained parts of Michigan to control malaria-carrying mosquitoes. Most drainage occurred in the southern one-third of the State—the area containing most of the important agricultural lands. Notations of bogs of 50 to 100 acres along Elk Creek and a swamp as far as the eye could see were in an 1852 diary entry of O.H. Perry describing a trip across the "thumb district" of eastern Michigan; most of these bogs have been drained. Industrialization has damaged wetlands along the Saginaw River and from the St. Clair River to Lake Erie. The moraine-till plain area of the central Lower Peninsula is the only other major area significantly damaged by drainage (U.S. Fish and Wildlife Service, 1955).

Approximately 37,000 acres of emergent marsh are thought to have existed around Saginaw Bay prior to development in the area. More than one-half of the basin's original wetlands have been drained, filled, altered, or destroyed (Michigan Department of Natu-

ral Resources, 1993). Since the 1850's, 9,420 acres of wetlands have been lost on the southeast coast of Saginaw Bay (Herdendorf and others, 1981).

CONSERVATION

Many government agencies and private organizations participate in wetland conservation in Michigan. The most active agencies and organizations and some of their activities are listed in table 1.

Federal wetland activities.—Development activities in Michigan wetlands are regulated by several Federal statutory prohibitions and incentives that are intended to slow wetland losses. Some of the more important of these are contained in the 1899 Rivers and Harbors Act; the 1972 Clean Water Act and amendments; the 1985 Food Security Act; the 1990 Food, Agriculture, Conservation, and Trade Act; the 1986 Emergency Wetlands Resources Act; and the 1972 Coastal Zone Management Act.

Section 10 of the Rivers and Harbors Act gives the U.S. Army Corps of Engineers (Corps) authority to regulate certain activities in navigable waters. Regulated activities include diking, deepening, filling, excavating, and placing of structures. The related section 404 of the Clean Water Act is the most often-used Federal legislation protecting wetlands. Under section 404 provisions, the Corps issues

Table 1.   Selected wetland-related activities of government agencies and private organizations in Michigan, 1993

[Source: Classification of activities is generalized from information provided by agencies and organizations. ●, agency or organization participates in wetland-related activity; ..., agency or organization does not participate in wetland-related activity. MAN, management; REG, regulation; R&C, restoration and creation; LAN, land acquisition; R&D, research and data collection; D&I, delineation and inventory]

Agency or organization	MAN	REG	R&C	LAN	R&D	D&I
FEDERAL						
Department of Agriculture						
Consolidated Farm Service Agency	...	●	...	...	...	...
Forest Service	●	...	●	...	●	●
Natural Resources Conservation Service	...	●	...	...	...	●
Department of Defense						
Army Corps of Engineers	●	●	●	●	●	●
Marine Reserve	...	...	...	●	...	...
National Guard	...	...	...	●	...	...
Department of the Interior						
Fish and Wildlife Service	●	...	●	●	●	●
Geological Survey	...	...	...	...	●	...
National Biological Service	...	...	...	...	●	...
National Park Service	●	...	●	●	●	●
Environmental Protection Agency	...	●	...	●	●	●
STATE						
Department of Natural Resources						
Fisheries Division	●	...	...	...	...	...
Forest Management Division	●	...	...	...	...	...
Land and Water Management Division	●	●	...	...	...	...
Surface Water Quality Division	●	●	...	...	...	...
Wildlife Division	...	...	●	●	...	...
Department of Transportation	...	...	●	...	...	...
SOME COUNTY AND LOCAL GOVERNMENTS	...	●	...	...	...	...
PRIVATE ORGANIZATIONS						
Clinton River Watershed Council	...	...	...	...	...	●
Detroit Audubon Society	...	...	...	●	...	...
Dow Chemical Company	...	...	●	...	...	...
Ducks Unlimited	...	...	●	●	...	...
Future Farmers of America	...	...	●	...	...	...
General Motors	...	...	●	...	...	...
Michigan Duck Hunters Association	...	...	●	...	...	...
Michigan Wildlife Habitat Foundation	...	...	●	...	...	...
The Nature Conservancy	●	...	●	●	●	●
Tipp of the Mitt Watershed Council	...	...	...	...	...	●
Waterfowl USA	...	...	●	●	...	...
Wetlands Conservation Association	...	...	●	...	...	...

permits regulating the discharge of dredged or fill material into wetlands. Permits are subject to review and possible veto by the U.S. Environmental Protection Agency (EPA), and the FWS has review and advisory roles. Section 401 of the Clean Water Act grants to States and eligible Indian Tribes the authority to approve, apply conditions to, or deny section 404 permit applications on the basis of a proposed activity's probable effects on the water quality of a wetland.

Most farming, ranching, and silviculture activities are not subject to section 404 regulation. However, the "Swampbuster" provision of the 1985 Food Security Act and amendments in the 1990 Food, Agriculture, Conservation, and Trade Act discourage (through financial disincentives) the draining, filling, or other alteration of wetlands for agricultural use. The law allows exemptions from penalties in some cases, especially if the farmer agrees to restore the altered wetland or other wetlands that have been converted to agricultural use. The Wetlands Reserve Program of the 1990 Food, Agriculture, Conservation, and Trade Act authorizes the Federal Government to purchase conservation easements from landowners who agree to protect or restore wetlands. The Consolidated Farm Service Agency (formerly the Agricultural Stabilization and Conservation Service) administers the Swampbuster provisions and Wetlands Reserve Program. The Natural Resources Conservation Service (formerly the Soil Conservation Service) determines compliance with Swampbuster provisions and assists farmers in the identification of wetlands and in the development of wetland protection, restoration, or creation plans.

The 1986 Emergency Wetlands Resources Act and the 1972 Coastal Zone Management Act and amendments encourage wetland protection through funding incentives. The Emergency Wetlands Resources Act requires States to address wetland protection in their Statewide Comprehensive Outdoor Recreation Plans to qualify for Federal funding for State recreational land; the National Park Service (NPS) provides guidance to States in developing the wetland component of their plans. Coastal and Great Lakes States that adopt coastal-zone management programs and plans approved by the National Oceanic and Atmospheric Administration are eligible for Federal funding and technical assistance through the Coastal Zone Management Act.

Federal agencies are responsible for the proper management of wetlands on public land under their jurisdiction. The U.S. Forest Service manages as much as 588,000 acres of wetlands in three National Forests in Michigan: Huron–Manistee (65,000 acres), Hiawatha (as much as 423,000 acres), and Ottawa National Forests (as much as 100,000 acres). The NPS manages approximately 3,600 acres of wetlands in Sleeping Bear Dunes National Lakeshore, as well as wetland acreage in Isle Royale National Park and Pictured Rocks National Lakeshore.

State wetland activities.—The Michigan Department of Natural Resources assumed administration of the section 404 wetlands program in October 1984. The principal statutory authority for the Michigan wetlands program is Public Act 203, the Goemaere-Anderson Wetland Protection Act of 1980. This act, in conjunction with several other State statutes and regulations, is the basis for Michigan's wetland conservation program. The act requires persons involved in the following activities to obtain a permit from the Michigan Department of Natural Resources: placing fill in a wetland; dredging or removal of soil or minerals from a wetland; constructing, operating, or maintaining any use or development in a wetland; and draining surface water from a wetland. The act also authorizes regulation of wetlands by local governments through wetland ordinances (Warbuch and others, 1990).

The EPA maintains Federal oversight of the State program, including veto authority. The EPA routinely reviews Public Notices for permit applications for "major discharges." Major discharges are defined, in part, as (1) greater than 10,000 cubic yards of fill; (2) discharges that contain toxic materials; and (3) discharges into areas determined to be unique, or where the waterway's commercial

value could be significantly reduced. The Corps retains jurisdiction over Rivers and Harbors Act and section 404 permitting in Great Lakes coastal areas, their connecting waterways, and major tributaries to the upstream limit of Federal navigability. In these areas, both a Corps and a Michigan Department of Natural Resources permit are required for activities in wetlands (Cwikiel, 1992).

Michigan currently (1993) is developing a Wetland Conservation Strategy. The strategy will focus on nonregulatory efforts throughout the State by (1) wetland education and outreach, (2) reclamation of wetlands to restore lost public benefits, (3) attention to wetland water-quality concerns, (4) coordination of existing wetland-management practices (including support of the North American Waterfowl Management Plan), and (5) identification and protection of Michigan's rare and unique wetlands. The strategy is due to be completed by January 1995.

County and local wetland activities.—In addition to their usual planning and zoning responsibilities, several municipalities in the following Michigan counties have adopted ordinances or guidelines to protect wetlands or to mitigate unavoidable wetland losses: Allegan, Antrim, Charlevoix, Cheboygan, Genesee, Grand Traverse, Ingham, Kalamazoo, Livingston, Monroe, Oakland, St. Clair, Washtenaw, and Wayne Counties.

Private wetland activities.—The Tipp of the Mitt Watershed Council offers a wetland-delineation service and a planning and zoning program to promote water-quality protection. The Wetlands Conservation Association is actively pursuing wetland restoration projects. The Wetlands Foundation of West Michigan assists with the design, funding, and permitting of projects that restore, enhance, or create wetlands primarily for habitat values.

Other organizations and industries that participate in wetland-protection activities in the State include Citizens for Alternatives to Chemical Contamination, Clean Water Action, Clinton River Watershed Council, Detroit Audubon Society, Dow Chemical Company, East Michigan Environmental Action Council, Environmental Protection Council of Oakland County, Friends of Rose Township, Friends of the Crystal River, Friends of the Rouge, Galien River Watershed Council, General Motors, Grand River Preservation Coalition, Huron River Watershed Council, Lake Michigan Federation, League of Women Voters of Michigan, Leelanau Conservancy Watershed Council, Michigan Audubon Society, Michigan Lake and Stream Associations Inc., Michigan United Conservation Clubs, Northern Michigan Environmental Action Council, Sierra Club Mackinac Chapter, Upper Peninsula Environmental Coalition, Water and Air Team for Charlevoix, and West Michigan Environmental Action Council. The activities of these groups are diverse and include participating in the planning and zoning process, serving as information clearinghouses, commenting on or assisting citizens in commenting on dredge and fill applications, engaging in or providing expert witnesses for wetland litigation, restoring wetlands, obtaining conservation easements, and many others.

References Cited

Cowardin, L.M., Carter, Virginia, Golet, F.C., and LaRoe, E.T., 1979, Classification of wetlands and deepwater habitats of the United States: U.S. Fish and Wildlife Service Report FWS/OBS–79/31, 131 p.

Cwikiel, Wilfred, 1992, Michigan wetlands—Yours to protect (2d ed.): Conway, Mich., Tipp of the Mitt Watershed Council, 84 p.

Dahl, T.E., 1990, Wetlands—Losses in the United States, 1780's to 1980's: Washington D.C., U.S. Fish and Wildlife Service, 13 p.

Geis, J.W., 1985, Environmental influences on the distribution and composition of wetlands in the Great Lakes Basin, *in* Prince, H.H, and D'Itri, F.M., eds., Coastal wetlands: Chelsea, Mich., Lewis Publishers, Inc., p. 15–31.

Herdendorf, C.E., Hartley, S.M., and Barnes, M.D., 1981, Fish and wildlife resources of the Great Lakes coastal wetlands within the United States—Volume one, Overview: Washington, D.C., Biological Services Program, U.S. Fish and Wildlife Service Report FWS/OBS–81/02–v. 1, 469 p.

Jaworski, Eugene, and Raphael, C.N., 1978, Fish, wildlife, and recreational values of Michigan's coastal wetlands: Lansing, Michigan Department of Natural Resources report, 209 p.

Michigan Department of Natural Resources, 1973, Shoreland inventory: Lansing, Mich., Division of Land and Resource Programs, 18 p.

_____1992, Water quality and pollution control in Michigan, 1992 report: Lansing, Michigan Department of Natural Resources, Surface Water Quality Division, Michigan 305(b) Report, v. 12, 307 p.

_____1993, Saginaw Bay national watershed initiative, Saginaw Bay watershed wetland facts: Lansing, Michigan Department of Natural Resources Communication Fact Sheet.

Miller, J.B., and Twenter, F.R., 1986, Michigan surface-water resources, in U.S. Geological Survey, National water summary 1985 — Hydrologic events and surface-water resources: U.S. Geological Survey Water-Supply Paper 2300, p. 277–284.

Sweat, M.J., and Van Til, R.L., 1987, Michigan water supply and use, in U.S. Geological Survey, National water summary 1987 — Hydrologic events and water supply and use: U.S. Geological Survey Water-Supply Paper 2350, p. 305–312.

U.S. Fish and Wildlife Service, 1955, Wetlands inventory of Michigan: Minneapolis, Minn., U.S. Fish and Wildlife Service, 41 p.

Warbuch, J.D., Wyckoff, M.A., and Williams, Kristine, 1990, Protecting inland lakes — A watershed management guidebook: Lansing, Mich., Planning and Zoning Center, Inc., in cooperation with Clinton River Watershed Council and the Michigan Department of Natural Resources, 192 p.

FOR ADDITIONAL INFORMATION: District Chief, U.S. Geological Survey, 6520 Mercantile Way, Suite 5, Lansing, MI 48911; Regional Coordinator, U.S. Fish and Wildlife Service, BHW Building, 1 Federal Drive, Fort Snelling, MN 55111

Prepared by
Erin A. Lynch and Marcus C. Waldron,
U.S. Geological Survey

Minnesota
Wetland Resources

Minnesota is famous for its many lakes; wetlands in the State, however, cover more than three times the area of lakes. About one-fifth of Minnesota is wetland. These wetlands provide numerous benefits to the people and wildlife of the State. Wetlands provide flood control by temporarily retaining stormwater runoff, and they reduce erosion of lakeshores and streambanks. Wetlands improve downstream water quality by capturing suspended particulates, dissolved nutrients, and contaminants such as heavy metals and agricultural pesticides. Wetlands provide essential habitat for waterfowl, furbearers, and other wildlife (Carter and others, 1979). Minnesota's wetlands also are especially valuable for their vegetation. Many of the State's rarest plant species and most distinctive plant communities are found only in wetlands (Coffin and Pfannmuller, 1988). Probably the rarest type of wetland in the State is a type of peatland called a calcareous fen (fig. 1).

TYPES AND DISTRIBUTION

Wetlands are lands transitional between terrestrial and deep-water habitats where the water table usually is at or near the land surface or the land is covered by shallow water (Cowardin and others, 1979). The distribution of wetlands and deepwater habitats in Minnesota is shown in figure 2A; only wetlands are discussed herein.

Wetlands can be vegetated or nonvegetated and are classified on the basis of their hydrology, vegetation, and substrate. In this summary, wetlands are classified according to the system proposed by Cowardin and others (1979), which is used by the U.S. Fish and Wildlife Service (FWS) to map and inventory the Nation's wetlands. At the most general level of the classification system, wetlands are grouped into five ecological systems: Palustrine, Lacustrine, Riverine, Estuarine, and Marine. The Palustrine System includes only wetlands, whereas the other systems comprise wetlands and deepwater habitats. Wetlands of the systems that occur in Minnesota are described below.

System	Wetland description
Palustrine	Wetlands in which vegetation is predominantly trees (forested wetlands); shrubs (scrub-shrub wetlands); persistent or nonpersistent emergent, erect, rooted, herbaceous plants (persistent- and nonpersistent-emergent wetlands); or submersed and (or) floating plants (aquatic beds). Also, intermittently to permanently flooded open-water bodies of less than 20 acres in which water is less than 6.6 feet deep.
Lacustrine	Wetlands within an intermittently to permanently flooded lake or reservoir. Vegetation, when present, is predominantly nonpersistent emergent plants (nonpersistent-emergent wetlands), or submersed and (or) floating plants (aquatic beds), or both.
Riverine	Wetlands within a channel. Vegetation, when present, is same as in the Lacustrine System.

Most Minnesota wetlands are categorized as palustrine because they have vegetation that remains standing all year. Most of these wetlands have an organic soil and are thus peatlands. A simplified definition of organic soil is one with an upper layer of partly decomposed plant material (peat) at least 12 inches (Wright and others, 1992) to 16 inches (Cowardin and others, 1979) thick. Peatlands cover about 6 million acres in Minnesota (Minnesota Department

of Natural Resources, 1984), although estimates range from about 5.2 million acres (Anderson and Craig, 1984) to about 7.2 million acres (Minnesota Department of Natural Resources, 1978) and depend on the definition chosen for organic soil and on data compilation methods. Palustrine wetlands on mineral soil cover about 3.5 million acres (Anderson and Craig, 1984). The total acreage of palustrine wetlands in Minnesota, both peatlands and mineral-soil wetlands, is thus about 9.5 million acres.

Peatlands can be categorized as either fens or bogs. Sometimes the word "bog" is informally applied to peatlands in general, but most peatlands in Minnesota are more properly called fens. Fens are peatlands that receive nutrients from ground water or runoff that has contacted mineral soil. Fens exist statewide but are more common in the north, where conditions are more favorable for peat accumulation. There are many different types of fens, corresponding to the wide range of possible hydrologic, climatic, and nutrient conditions. Open fens (persistent-emergent wetlands) in the conifer-hardwood forest zone (fig. 2B) commonly have sedge-dominated communities. Swamp-forest fens (forested or scrub-shrub wetlands) in this zone typically are covered by larch, black spruce, or northern white cedar, with an understory of low shrubs, sedges, and mosses (Glaser, 1992; Minnesota Department of Natural Resources, 1993). Fens in the prairie and deciduous forest-woodland zones typically have a scattered cover of shrubs such as willow and dogwood and a continuous ground cover of various sedges, grasses, and forbs (scrub-shrub or persistent-emergent wetlands). A rare type of these fens is a calcareous fen (fig. 1), which receives upwelling ground water rich in calcium carbonate.

Bogs are peatlands that receive nutrients only from precipitation and windblown dust. Consequently, bog water has low nutrient concentrations, and a continuous mat of sphagnum moss acidifies the water (Gorham and others, 1985). Bogs have a low diversity of species because few plants are adapted to these low-nutrient, acid conditions (Glaser and others, 1981; Glaser, 1992). Bogs in Minnesota typically are peat mounds covered by black spruce with an understory of broad-leaved evergreen shrubs and sphagnum moss (forested wetlands). Some bogs have a stunted tree and shrub community (scrub-scrub wetland) near the center. Nonforested patches of bog dominated by sedge (persistent-emergent wetlands) are less common but can occur where the peat is too wet for black spruce

Figure 1. Sioux Nation Fen. This type of wetland, a patterned calcareous fen, is rare in Minnesota. *(Photograph by James E. Almendinger, U.S. Geological Survey.)*

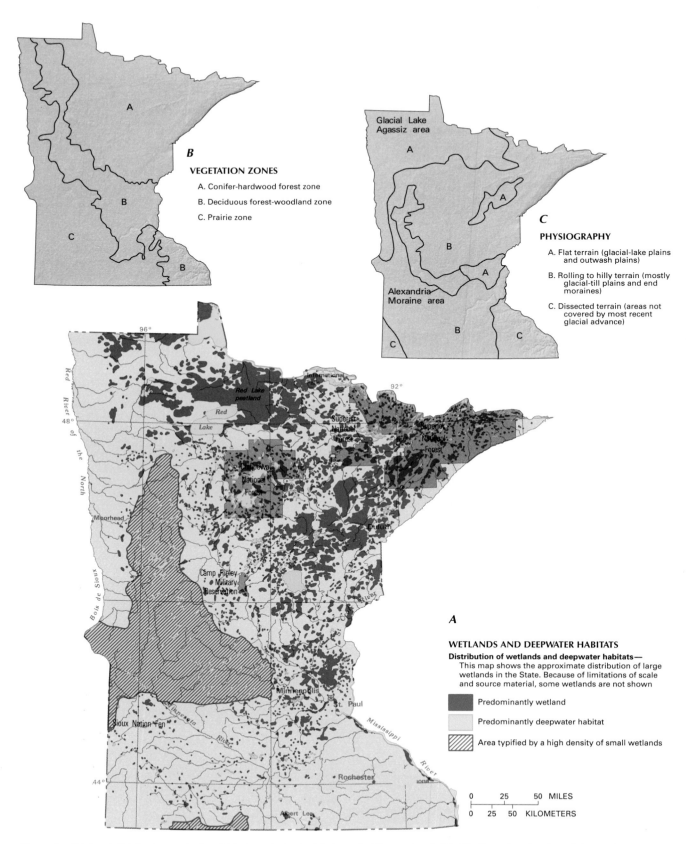

VEGETATION ZONES

A. Conifer-hardwood forest zone

B. Deciduous forest-woodland zone

C. Prairie zone

PHYSIOGRAPHY

A. Flat terrain (glacial-lake plains and outwash plains)

B. Rolling to hilly terrain (mostly glacial-till plains and end moraines)

C. Dissected terrain (areas not covered by most recent glacial advance)

WETLANDS AND DEEPWATER HABITATS

Distribution of wetlands and deepwater habitats—
This map shows the approximate distribution of large wetlands in the State. Because of limitations of scale and source material, some wetlands are not shown

Predominantly wetland

Predominantly deepwater habitat

Area typified by a high density of small wetlands

Figure 2. Wetland distribution and related biotic and physical features in Minnesota. **A**, Distribution of wetlands and deepwater habitats. **B**, Vegetation zones. **C**, Physiography. *(Sources: A, T.E. Dahl, U.S. Fish and Wildlife Service, unpub. data, 1991. B, Minnesota Department of Natural Resources, 1993. C, Adapted from Wright, 1972.)*

to grow, or where fire has removed the black spruce (Glaser, 1992; Minnesota Department of Natural Resources, 1993).

Palustrine wetlands on mineral soil are present statewide. In the western and southern parts of Minnesota, these wetlands commonly are called prairie potholes. These shallow depressions may have open water near the center surrounded by emergent marsh or wet meadow (persistent emergent wetland) in which broad-leaved sedges, grasses, and bulrushes predominate. In the eastern and northern parts of Minnesota, palustrine wetlands on mineral soil commonly are swamps (forested or scrub-shrub wetlands) in which either hardwood or conifer trees or shrubs predominate (Minnesota Department of Natural Resources, 1993).

Lacustrine and riverine wetlands commonly have beds of non-persistent-emergent, submersed, or floating aquatic plants. Most of the 3 million acres of Minnesota lakes are in the central and northeastern parts of the State. Probably the best known lacustrine wetlands are wild rice beds (nonpersistent-emergent wetlands), which occupy about 150,000 to 200,000 acres of shallow lakes (John Persell, Minnesota Chippewa Tribe, written commun., 1993).

HYDROLOGIC SETTING

The hydrology of wetlands is determined by climate, vegetation, physiography, and geology. Climate determines the net moisture supply, which is the difference between input of precipitation and loss by evaporation and plant transpiration. Physiography and geology influences not only the movement of water on and below the land surface but also the dissolved mineral content of the water.

Differences across Minnesota cause differences in vegetation and moisture supply. Average annual temperature, which influences evaporation and transpiration, ranges from about 36 °F (degrees Fahrenheit) in the north to about 46 °F in the south (Baker and Strub, 1965). Average annual precipitation ranges from about 20 inches in the west to about 30 inches in the east (Baker and others, 1967). These climatic gradients contribute to a diagonal zonation of major vegetation types and effective moisture, from the warm, dry prairie zone in the south and west to the cool, moist conifer-hardwood forest zone in the northeast (fig. 2B). Peatlands are more common in the conifer-hardwood forest zone than elsewhere in Minnesota, because the relatively cool and wet conditions help preserve the peat.

Seasonal and year-to-year changes in climate cause changes in the moisture supply. Some prairie potholes receive different amounts of snowmelt runoff and ground-water inputs from year to year and consequently change from shallow emergent marshes to open-water ponds persisting for several years (Eisenlohr and others, 1972; LaBaugh and others, 1987). Drought hinders peat accumulation because drying allows rapid microbial decomposition of the peat and makes it susceptible to fire. Peatlands consequently tend to be more common in the northeastern part of the State, which usually escapes severe drought (Borchert and Yaeger, 1968).

Physiography (fig. 2C) influences surface-water drainage and, consequently, wetland type and distribution. The last glacial advance did not cover the extreme southeastern and southwestern corners of the State. Wetlands are less common in these older areas because the naturally dissected terrain has few basins remaining. Most terrains in the State, however, were formed during the last glacial advance. Glacial-till plains and end moraines are gently rolling to hilly terrains that cover much of the State. The low infiltration capacity of the clayey soil of these terrains in west-central and southern Minnesota enhances overland runoff, which can collect in prairie potholes. The Alexandria Moraine area (fig. 2C) coincides with the statewide diagonal climate-vegetation zonation and forms the core of a region with a high density of wetlands intermixed with uplands (fig. 2A). Glacial-lake plains and outwash plains are relatively flat terrains where large peatlands can develop if the water table is high and the moisture supply is sufficiently large and constant. The lack of large peatlands on the western part of the Glacial Lake Agassiz area (fig. 2C) may be caused by the moisture supply being insufficient or variable.

Geology affects ground-water flow and chemistry. Ground-water discharge occurs where ground water seeps out of an aquifer into the wetland; ground-water recharge occurs where water from the wetland percolates into an aquifer (fig. 3A). Wetlands in the State commonly receive ground-water discharge, the amount and quality of which can affect the vegetation. Some prairie potholes are sites of naturally focused ground-water recharge, where overland runoff from the surrounding upland basin collects in the pothole before percolating into the surficial aquifer (LaBaugh and others, 1987).

The influence of hydrology, particularly ground-water hydrology, on wetlands is demonstrated by two examples. The first example is the Red Lake peatland in northwestern Minnesota. This peatland is a complex of fens and bogs with distinctive shapes and internal patterns related to slight differences in water chemistry and flow (Heinselman, 1963; Glaser and others, 1981; Glaser, 1992). Fens develop where upwelling ground water reaches the peatland surface and flows laterally through the upper layer of fibrous peat. A pat-

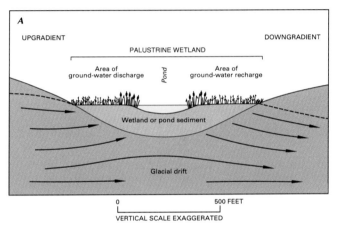

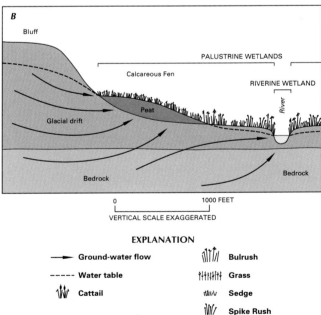

Figure 3. Hydrologic interaction between wetlands and ground water. *A*, Conceptual ground-water discharge and recharge in a wetland. *B*, Conceptual ground-water flow under a calcareous fen in the Minnesota River Valley.

terned fen sometimes develops in which the vegetation structure forms alternating ridges and troughs oriented at right angles to the direction of this slow surface flow. The ridges and troughs may be 10 to 50 feet wide (Heinselman, 1963), with the ridges occupied by low shrubs and the troughs by sedges or pools. The vast fens of the Red Lake peatland provide the regional setting atop which bogs can develop. Bogs in the Red Lake peatland have formed on peat mounds raised above the influence of upwelling ground water (Siegel and Glaser, 1987; Glaser, 1992; Siegel, 1992). The flow of fen water around the bogs can cause them to have a streamlined shape, rounded on the upgradient margin and extended to a long tail on the downgradient margin.

The second example of the influence of ground-water hydrology on wetlands is calcareous fens (fig. 3B), which are rare in Minnesota. Calcareous fens typically have significant amounts of upwelling ground water rich in calcium carbonate and surface slopes that drain excess water (Curtis, 1971; Eggers and Reed, 1987; Thompson and others, 1992). These wetlands can be found in the Minnesota River Valley on terraces at the base of the bluffs that form the valley wall. The high water table in the bluffs provides the necessary hydraulic pressure to force ground water to upwell at the fen. The fens generally lie above flood stages of the Minnesota River and slope toward the river, protecting against inundation from the river and providing drainage of excess water from the fen. As much as 25 feet of peat can accumulate over the zone of upwelling ground water. Calcareous fens are sensitive not only to activities such as ditching or filling but also to more subtle causes of degradation. For example, pumping nearby wells could lower the natural hydraulic pressures under the fen and reduce the amount of upwelling ground water, and changing the land use in the ground-water recharge area upgradient from the fen could change both the quantity and quality of the water available to the fen. Calcareous fens demonstrate that simply protecting the area of the wetland itself is not enough to ensure that the wetland will remain undamaged.

TRENDS

Most changes in Minnesota wetlands during the last 150 years have been caused by human activities. Estimates of wetland acreages before settlement of the area by Europeans in the mid-1800's range from about 15 to 18 million acres; as much as one-half (by area) of Minnesota's original wetlands might have been lost since presettlement times (Anderson and Craig, 1984; Tiner, 1984; Dahl, 1990). Most of the wetland loss has been the result of drainage for agriculture. By the early 1980's, more than 70 percent of Minnesota's originally poorly drained mineral soils in the prairie zone had been drained (Anderson and Craig, 1984). The loss of wetlands in the largely agricultural basin of the Minnesota River may cause increased flushing of water, nutrients, and soil from the uplands into the river ecosystem. The northern peatlands also have been affected by human activities. During the early 1900's, several northern counties went bankrupt as a result of funding the ditching of peatlands on the Glacial Lake Agassiz plain. Because of the flat landscape, the ditches were largely ineffective in draining the peatlands; however, ditching might have altered peatland vegetation hundreds of feet from the ditches (Glaser and others, 1981; Bradof, 1992). Small areas of peatland have been mined for horticultural purposes, logged for black spruce, or cultivated for specialty crops. The use of peat as a fuel, however, has not been economical to date (Keirstead, 1992).

Wetlands are sensitive to climate change also. About 7,000 years ago the water table in parts of Minnesota was as much as 20 feet lower than at present, and many prairie potholes were probably dry (Digerfeldt and others, 1992). The climate then became increasingly moist, and by 4,500 years ago peat began to form in the remnant Glacial Lake Agassiz plain (Glaser and others, 1981). Because

the western boundary of the Red Lake peatland is apparently controlled by the climatic moisture supply, the peatland might be diminished by warmer and drier climates resulting from natural climate cycles or, hypothetically, human-induced global warming. Such drier climates also could desiccate shallow prairie potholes, as in the past.

CONSERVATION

Many government agencies and private organizations participate in wetland conservation in Minnesota. The most active agencies and organizations and some of their activities are listed in table 1.

Federal wetland activities. — Development activities in Minnesota wetlands are regulated by several Federal statutory prohibitions and incentives that are intended to slow wetland losses. Some of the more important of these are contained in the 1899 Rivers and Harbors Act; the 1972 Clean Water Act and amendments; the 1985 Food Security Act; the 1990 Food, Agriculture, Conservation, and

Table 1. Selected wetland-related activities of government agencies and private organizations in Minnesota, 1993

[Source: Classification of activities is generalized from information provided by agencies and organizations. •, agency or organization participates in wetland-related activity; ..., agency or organization does not participate in wetland-related activity. MAN, management; REG, regulation; R&C, restoration and creation; LAN, land acquisition; R&D, research and data collection; D&I, delineation and inventory]

Agency or organization	MAN	REG	R&C	LAN	R&D	D&I
FEDERAL						
Department of Agriculture						
Consolidated Farm Service Agency	...	•	...	...	...	...
Forest Service	•	...	•	•	•	•
Natural Resources Conservation Service	...	•	•	...	...	•
Department of Commerce						
National Oceanic and Atmospheric Administration	...	•	...	...	...	...
Department of Defense						
Army Corps of Engineers	•	•	...	...	...	•
Department of the Interior						
Fish and Wildlife Service	•	...	•	...	•	•
Geological Survey	...	...	...	...	•	...
National Biological Service	...	...	...	...	•	...
National Park Service	•	...	...	...	•	•
Environmental Protection Agency	...	•	...	...	•	...
STATE						
Board of Water and Soil Resources	...	...	•	...	...	...
Department of Military Affairs	•	...	•	•	•	...
Department of Natural Resources						
Division of Fish and Wildlife	•	...	•	...	•	•
Division of Forestry	•	...	•	...	•	...
Division of Minerals	•	...	...	...	•	•
Division of Waters	•	...	•	...	•	•
Office of Planning	...	•	...	...	...	...
Department of Transportation	•	...	•	•	•	...
Environmental Quality Board	...	•	...	...	...	...
Pollution Control Agency	•	•	...	...	...	...
University of Minnesota	...	...	...	...	•	...
COUNTY AND LOCAL						
Counties and cities	•	•	...	...	•	...
Soil and water conservation districts	...	...	•	•	...	...
Townships	...	•	...	...	...	...
Watershed districts	•	...	•	•	•	...
SOVEREIGN NATIONS						
Native American tribes	•	...	...	...	•	•
PRIVATE ORGANIZATIONS						
Ducks Unlimited	...	...	•	...	•	...
Izaak Walton League	...	...	•	...	...	...
National Audubon Society	•	...	•	...	•	...
The Nature Conservancy	•	...	•	•	•	•

Trade Act; the 1986 Emergency Wetlands Resources Act; and the 1972 Coastal Zone Management Act.

Section 10 of the Rivers and Harbors Act gives the U.S. Army Corps of Engineers (Corps) authority to regulate certain activities in navigable waters. Regulated activities include diking, deepening, filling, excavating, and placing of structures. The related section 404 of the Clean Water Act is the most often-used Federal legislation protecting wetlands. Under section 404 provisions, the Corps issues permits regulating the discharge of dredged or fill material into wetlands. Permits are subject to review and possible veto by the U.S. Environmental Protection Agency (EPA), and the FWS has review and advisory roles. Section 401 of the Clean Water Act grants to States and eligible Indian Tribes the authority to approve, apply conditions to, or deny section 404 permit applications on the basis of a proposed activity's probable effects on the water quality of a wetland.

Most farming, ranching, and silviculture activities are not subject to section 404 regulation. However, the "Swampbuster" provision of the 1985 Food Security Act and amendments in the 1990 Food, Agriculture, Conservation, and Trade Act discourage (through financial disincentives) the draining, filling, or other alteration of wetlands for agricultural use. The law allows exemptions from penalties in some cases, especially if the farmer agrees to restore the altered wetland or other wetlands that have been converted to agricultural use. The Wetlands Reserve Program of the 1990 Food, Agriculture, Conservation, and Trade Act authorizes the Federal Government to purchase conservation easements from landowners who agree to protect or restore wetlands. The Consolidated Farm Service Agency (formerly the Agricultural Stabilization and Conservation Service) administers the Swampbuster provisions and Wetlands Reserve Program. The Natural Resources Conservation Service (formerly the Soil Conservation Service) determines compliance with Swampbuster provisions and assists farmers in the identification of wetlands and in the development of wetland protection, restoration, or creation plans.

The 1986 Emergency Wetlands Resources Act and the 1972 Coastal Zone Management Act and amendments encourage wetland protection through funding incentives. The Emergency Wetland Resources Act requires States to address wetland protection in their Statewide Comprehensive Outdoor Recreation Plans to qualify for Federal funding for State recreational land; the National Park Service (NPS) provides guidance to States in developing the wetland component of their plans. Coastal States that adopt coastal-zone management programs and plans approved by the National Oceanic and Atmospheric Administration are eligible for Federal funding and technical assistance through the Coastal Zone Management Act.

Federal agencies research wetlands and manage those on public land under their jurisdiction. The U.S. Forest Service (FS) is responsible for more than 2.8 million acres, with an unknown acreage of wetlands, in the Chippewa and the Superior National Forests and supports research in peatland ecology and hydrology. The NPS manages over 140,000 acres in Minnesota, with an unknown acreage of wetlands. The FWS manages about 500,000 acres, much of which is wetland, in 12 National Wildlife Refuges and numerous smaller waterfowl production areas in Minnesota. The Corps has wetland-management and restoration programs, especially in the Mississippi River lowlands. The EPA laboratory in Duluth is studying effects of sedimentation and agricultural chemicals on prairie potholes. The U.S. Geological Survey, with cooperative funding from State agencies, is studying the hydrology of small agricultural wetlands and calcareous fens.

State and local wetland activities.—The centerpiece of Minnesota's efforts to protect wetlands is the Wetland Conservation Act of 1991, which works toward a no-net-loss goal. The intent of the law is to avoid or minimize wetland losses; where wetland loss is unavoidable, the loss must be mitigated by replacement with a wetland of equal public value. The law also provides funds for per-

manent easements to some privately owned wetlands and for public education. The law promotes wetland preservation by allowing tax-exempt status for wetlands of high value. The law essentially fills the gap in wetland protection between larger, deepwater habitats, which are already protected by Minnesota statute, and agricultural wetlands that are already covered by the Federal "Swampbuster" provisions. The Board of Water and Soil Resources is the State agency responsible for promulgating rules to determine wetland value and to mitigate wetland losses, and local governmental units are responsible for carrying out the rules (table 1). Also included in the legislation are provisions to prohibit degradation of calcareous fens and to protect about 150,000 acres of ecologically significant peatlands.

The Department of Natural Resources has a variety of responsibilities concerning wetlands and administers about 5.3 million acres of State land, almost one-half of which may be wetlands, in addition to about 3 million acres of lakes. The Department's Division of Waters oversees permit applications for nearly all activities below the ordinary high-water level in the "protected waters and wetlands" of the State, which include virtually all water bodies that have open water or nonwoody vegetation, are deeper than about 6 inches, and are larger than 10 acres (2.5 acres in incorporated areas). The Department's Division of Fish and Wildlife acquires lands and currently (1993) manages over 700,000 acres, a significant portion of which are wetlands (Tom Landwehr, Minnesota Department of Natural Resources, oral commun., 1993). Within the Division of Fish and Wildlife, the Natural Heritage program identifies and classifies natural biologic communities, including wetlands; the Scientific and Natural Areas program acquires sites of ecological significance to the State, notably rare wetland types such as patterned fen and calcareous fen; and the Ecological Services section performs environmental reviews and will help develop a Statewide Comprehensive Wetland Conservation Plan. The Department of Natural Resources' Division of Forestry helps manage most State-owned land and also is chairing a public and private interagency committee to develop nonregulatory best-management practices to protect wetlands from forestry activities. The Department's Division of Minerals is responsible for applying the rules of the 1991 Wetland Conservation Act on lands from which metallic minerals or peats are mined. The Division of Minerals also sponsored a survey of peat deposits in the State, including their type, distribution, and thickness (Minnesota Department of Natural Resources, 1981). The Department of Natural Resources' Office of Planning is responsible for the State Comprehensive Outdoor Recreation Plan document required by Federal legislation and coordinates the environmental review process within the Department of Natural Resources.

Other State agencies also are involved with wetland protection or management. The Environmental Quality Board determines which activities affecting wetlands are subject to the environmental review process. The Water Quality Division of the Pollution Control Agency reviews permit applications for all discharges to wetlands and other waters of the State, pursuant primarily to sections 401 and 402 of the Federal Clean Water Act. The Pollution Control Agency also produces a biennial report monitoring statewide water quality, pursuant to section 305(b) of the act. The Department of Transportation is responsible for applying the Wetland Conservation Act rules to all State transportation projects that affect wetlands; this responsibility involves wetland impact assessment as well as wetland restoration and creation. The Department of Military Affairs manages the 53,000-acre Camp Ripley military reservation and has an active program of wetland management in cooperation with other State agencies.

Sovereign nation wetland activities.—Tribal councils of Native American people in Minnesota strive to create, restore, or enhance wetlands for waterfowl and wild rice production, particularly on reservations or on traditionally harvested lands. The U.S. Bureau of Indian Affairs helps provide funding for wetland projects through the Circle of Flight and Water Resources program.

Private wetland activities.—The National Audubon Society manages three wildlife sanctuaries that contain wetlands, conducts a public education program about wetlands, and is performing research for the EPA by investigating the effectiveness of past wetland-mitigation efforts. The Nature Conservancy actively seeks to purchase and protect ecologically significant wetlands. Ducks Unlimited provides funds for wetland restoration and for State or Federal agencies to purchase and manage wetlands for waterfowl production. The Izaak Walton League also provides funds for wetland restoration or creation. Private organizations that are involved in the protection of Minnesota wetlands include the Fish and Wildlife Legislative Alliance, Minnesota Conservation Federation, Minnesota Native Plant Society, Minnesota Waterfowl Association, Pheasants Forever, Project Environment Foundation, Sierra Club, Trout Unlimited, and others.

References Cited

Anderson, J.P., and Craig, W.J., 1984, Growing energy crops on Minnesota's wetlands—The land use perspective: Minneapolis, University of Minnesota Center for Urban and Regional Affairs, 95 p.

Baker, D.G., Haines, D.A., and Strub, J.H., Jr., 1967, Climate of Minnesota, part V—Precipitation facts, normals, and extremes: University of Minnesota Agricultural Experiment Station Technical Bulletin 254, 43 p.

Baker, D.G., and Strub, J.H., Jr., 1965, Climate of Minnesota, part III—Temperature and its application: St. Paul, University of Minnesota Agricultural Experiment Station Technical Bulletin 248, 63 p.

Borchert, J.R., and Yaeger, D.P., 1968, Atlas of Minnesota resources and settlement: St. Paul, Minnesota State Planning Agency, 262 p.

Bradof, K.L., 1992, Ditching of Red Lake peatland during the homestead era, *in* Wright, H.E., Jr., Coffin, B.A., and Aaseng, N.E., eds., The patterned peatlands of Minnesota: Minneapolis, University of Minnesota Press, p. 263–284.

Carter, Virginia, Bedinger, M.S., Novitzki, R.P., and Wilen, W.O., 1979, Water resources and wetlands, *in* Greeson, P.E., Clark, J.R., and Clark, J.E., eds., Wetland functions and values—The state of our understanding—Proceedings of the National Symposium on Wetlands, November 1978: Minneapolis, American Water Resources Association, p. 344–376.

Coffin, Barbara, and Pfannmuller, Lee, eds., 1988, Minnesota's endangered flora and fauna: Minneapolis, University of Minnesota Press, 473 p.

Cowardin, L.M., Carter, Virginia, Golet, F.C., and LaRoe, E.T., 1979, Classification of wetlands and deepwater habitats of the United States: U.S. Fish and Wildlife Service Report FWS/OBS–79/31, 131 p.

Curtis, J.T., 1971, The vegetation of Wisconsin: Madison, The University of Wisconsin Press, 657 p.

Dahl, T.E., 1990, Wetlands—Losses in the United States, 1780's to 1980's: Washington, D.C., U.S. Fish and Wildlife Service Report to Congress, 13 p.

Digerfeldt, Gunnar, Almendinger, J.E., and Björck, Svante, 1992, Reconstruction of past lake levels and their relation to groundwater hydrology in the Parkers Prairie sandplain, west-central Minnesota: Palaeogeography, Palaeoclimatology, Palaeoecology, v. 94, p. 99–118.

Eggers, S.D., and Reed, D.M., 1987, Wetland plants and plant communities of Minnesota and Wisconsin: St. Paul, U.S. Army Corps of Engineers, 201 p.

Eisenlohr, W.S., Jr., and others, 1972, Hydrologic investigations of prairie potholes in North Dakota, 1959–68: U.S. Geological Survey Professional Paper 585–A, 102 p., 3 pls.

Glaser, P.H., 1992, Vegetation and water chemistry, *in* Wright, H.E., Jr., Coffin, B.A., and Aaseng, N.E., eds., The patterned peatlands of Minnesota: Minneapolis, University of Minnesota Press, p. 15–26.

Glaser, P.H., Wheeler, G.A., Gorham, Eville, and Wright, H.E., Jr., 1981, The patterned mires of the Red Lake peatland, northern Minnesota—Vegetation, water chemistry and landforms: Journal of Ecology, v. 69, p. 575–599.

Gorham, Eville, Eisenreich, S.J., Ford, Jesse, Santelmann, M.V., 1985, The chemistry of bog waters, *in* Stumm, Werner, ed., Chemical processes in lakes: New York, John Wiley and Sons, p. 339–363.

Heinselman, M.L., 1963, Forest sites, bog processes, and peatland types in the Glacial Lake Agassiz region, Minnesota: Ecological Monographs, v. 33, no. 4, p. 327–374.

Keirstead, M.E., 1992, Management of Minnesota's peatlands and their economic uses, *in* Wright, H.E., Jr., Coffin, B.A., and Aaseng, N.E., eds., The patterned peatlands of Minnesota: Minneapolis, University of Minnesota Press, p. 285–299.

LaBaugh, J.W., Winter, T.C., Adomaitis, V.A., and Swanson, G.A., 1987, Hydrology and chemistry of selected prairie wetlands in the Cottonwood Lake area, Stutsman County, North Dakota, 1979–1982: U.S. Geological Survey Professional Paper 1431, 26 p.

Minnesota Department of Natural Resources, 1978, Peatlands—Minnesota, Wisconsin, Michigan: St. Paul, Minnesota Department of Natural Resources map, approximate scale 1:1,750,000.

_____1981, Minnesota peat program final report: St. Paul, Minnesota Department of Natural Resources Division of Minerals, 93 p.

_____1984, Recommendations for the protection of ecologically significant peatlands in Minnesota: St. Paul, Minnesota Department of Natural Resources, 57 p., 16 maps.

_____1993, Minnesota's native vegetation—A key to natural communities, version 1.5: St. Paul, Minnesota Department of Natural Resources Natural Heritage Program, 110 p.

Siegel, D.I., 1992, Groundwater hydrology, *in* Wright, H.E., Jr., Coffin, B.A., and Aaseng, N.E., eds., The patterned peatlands of Minnesota: Minneapolis, University of Minnesota Press, p. 163–172.

Siegel, D.I., and Glaser, P.H., 1987, Groundwater flow in a bog-fen complex, Lost River peatland, northern Minnesota: Journal of Ecology, v. 75, p. 743–754.

Thompson, C.A., Bettis, E.A., III, and Baker, R.G., 1992, Geology of Iowa fens: Journal of the Iowa Academy of Science, v. 99, no. 2–3, p. 53–59.

Tiner, R.W., Jr., 1984, Wetlands of the United States—Current status and recent trends: Washington, D.C., U.S. Fish and Wildlife Service, 59 p.

Wright, H.E., Jr., 1972, Physiography of Minnesota, *in* Sims, P.K., and Morey, G.B., eds., Geology of Minnesota, a centennial volume: Minneapolis, Minnesota Geological Survey, p. 561–578.

Wright, H.E., Jr., Coffin, B.A., and Aaseng, N.E., eds., 1992, The patterned peatlands of Minnesota: Minneapolis, University of Minnesota Press, 327 p.

FOR ADDITIONAL INFORMATION: District Chief, U.S. Geological Survey, 2280 Woodale Drive, Mounds View, MN 55112; Regional Wetland Coordinator, U.S. Fish and Wildlife Service, BHW Building, 1 Federal Drive, Fort Snelling, MN 55425

Prepared by
James E. Almendinger,
U.S. Geological Survey

Mississippi
Wetland Resources

Wetlands occupy more than 13 percent of the surface area in Mississippi (Dahl, 1990) and have greatly influenced the development of the State. The first European settlers found large tracts of bottom-land forests (forested wetlands) in the swamps bordering the Mississippi River and other river systems (fig. 1) and in the marshes (emergent wetlands) and swamps (forested and scrub-shrub wetlands) along the Gulf of Mexico. The forested wetlands in the alluvial plain of the Mississippi River provided timber resources of bald cypress, water oak, and tupelo gum that have been cleared and harvested continuously for the last 200 years. The cleared land opened up rich, fertile delta soils to agriculture (U.S. Fish and Wildlife Service, 1992).

Mississippi wetlands provide important habitat for several endangered and threatened species, including the bald eagle (Curtis James, U.S. Fish and Wildlife Service, written commun., 1993). Also, 5 National Wildlife Refuges, 6 National Forests, 1 National Seashore, 22 State Wildlife Management Areas, and 20 State parks contain wetland areas within their boundaries. Wetlands in Mississippi are a key part of the Lower Mississippi Valley Joint Venture program for the restoration of Mississippi Flyway waterfowl populations (Lower Mississippi Valley Joint Venture Management Board, 1990).

Wetlands trap suspended sediment, nutrients, and certain classes of pesticides and other organic contaminants (Boto and Patrick, 1979; Deason, 1989; German, 1989). Dissolved nutrients, sediments, and sediment-associated compounds such as trace metals, pesticides and other organic compounds, and bacteria are trapped or transformed during their passage through wetlands in receiving and outgoing waters (Kadlec and Kadlec, 1979). Inland wetlands provide flood storage, erosion control, outdoor recreation, water-quality improvement for surface water, recharge areas for ground water, and habitat for fish and wildlife. Coastal wetlands provide buffer areas to absorb storm surges and floods, outdoor recreation opportunities, water-quality improvement, and important habitat for nursery and feeding areas for fish and wildlife. Coastal wetlands in Mississippi are important in supporting a $50 million commercial and recreational fishery (U.S. Fish and Wildlife Service, 1992).

Figure 1. Flood-plain forest and wetlands on the lower Wolf River. *(Photograph by Dennis K. Demcheck, U.S. Geological Survey.)*

TYPES AND DISTRIBUTION

Wetlands are lands transitional between terrestrial and deepwater habitats where the water table usually is at or near the land surface or the land is covered by shallow water (Cowardin and others, 1979). The distribution of wetlands and deepwater habitats in Mississippi is shown in figure 2A; only wetlands are discussed herein.

Wetlands can be vegetated or nonvegetated and are classified on the basis of their hydrology, vegetation, and substrate. In this summary, wetlands are classified according to the system proposed by Cowardin and others (1979), which is used by the U.S. Fish and Wildlife Service (FWS) to map and inventory the Nation's wetlands. At the most general level of the classification system, wetlands are grouped into five ecological systems: Palustrine, Lacustrine, Riverine, Estuarine, and Marine. The Palustrine System includes only wetlands, whereas the other systems comprise wetlands and deepwater habitats. Wetlands of the systems that occur in Mississippi are described below.

System	Wetland description
Palustrine	Nontidal and tidal-freshwater wetlands in which vegetation is predominantly trees (forested wetlands); shrubs (scrub-shrub wetlands); persistent or nonpersistent emergent, erect, rooted herbaceous plants (persistent- and nonpersistent-emergent wetlands); or submersed and (or) floating plants (aquatic beds). Also, intermittently to permanently flooded open-water bodies of less than 20 acres in which water is less than 6.6 feet deep.
Lacustrine	Nontidal and tidal-freshwater wetlands within an intermittently to permanently flooded lake or reservoir larger than 20 acres and (or) deeper than 6.6 feet. Vegetation, when present, is predominantly nonpersistent emergent plants (nonpersistent-emergent wetlands), or submersed and (or) floating plants (aquatic beds), or both.
Riverine	Nontidal and tidal-freshwater wetlands within a channel. Vegetation, when present, is same as in the Lacustrine System.
Estuarine	Tidal wetlands in low-wave-energy environments where the salinity of the water is greater than 0.5 part per thousand (ppt) and is variable owing to evaporation and the mixing of seawater and freshwater.
Marine	Tidal wetlands that are exposed to waves and currents of the open ocean and to water having a salinity greater than 30 ppt.

In the mid-1980's, wetlands covered about 4,067,000 acres of Mississippi's 30,309,120 total land acres (Dahl, 1990). Palustrine wetlands in Mississippi include bogs, swamps, riverbank pioneer habitat, bottom-land forests, bayheads, coastal flatwoods, and savannahs (Ruple, 1992). Bottom-land forests (forested wetlands), swamps (forested or scrub-shrub wetlands), and fresh marshes (emergent wetlands) account for most of Mississippi's wetland acreage (U.S. Fish and Wildlife Service, 1992). The Mississippi Alluvial Plain (fig. 2B) has the greatest concentration of those wetlands, but significant expanses of wetlands occupy the flood plains of major rivers and their tributaries throughout the State.

Estuarine wetlands are the second-most common wetlands in Mississippi. Of about 77,500 acres of coastal marsh, 99 percent is estuarine, and 1 percent is fresh. There also are about 343,000 acres of mud flats and 9,000 acres of cypress-tupelo gum swamp (estuarine forested wetlands) (U.S. Fish and Wildlife Service, 1992).

HYDROLOGIC SETTING

The combination of hydrology, fire frequency, substrate and soil characteristics, and climate produces the characteristics that are unique to Mississippi's wetlands (Ruple, 1992). The existence of wetlands depends on geologic and physiographic conditions that favor the retention of water and on the hydrologic processes that allow the water to persist at a given site (Winter and Woo, 1990).

Wetland hydrology involves complex water-flow patterns that are affected by regional and local geology, topography, soil characteristics, and climate. Wetlands commonly form in topographic lows where ground-water discharge and runoff collect. Water in small wetlands typically is supplied by local shallow ground-water flow systems. Larger wetlands may interact with both local and regional ground-water flow systems.

Fire frequency, the time interval between fires on a wetland, is important in determining the successional state of a wetland (Ruple, 1992). In large part, fire frequency determines the kinds of vegetation present in a wetland and, therefore, the character of the wetland itself. For example, if a marsh or wet slough goes for decades without a fire, then the wetland typically develops into a scrub-shrub or hardwood forest. This succession happens because the lack of fire allows woody plants to replace herbaceous plants as the dominant vegetation present, changing the appearance of the wetland and the kinds of organisms using it (Ruple, 1992).

Soil composition determines the rate at which water percolates downward from a wetland to recharge the ground-water system or discharges from the ground-water system into a wetland. Fluctuations in local precipitation can combine with local variations in geology to create transient or seasonal changes in the interactions

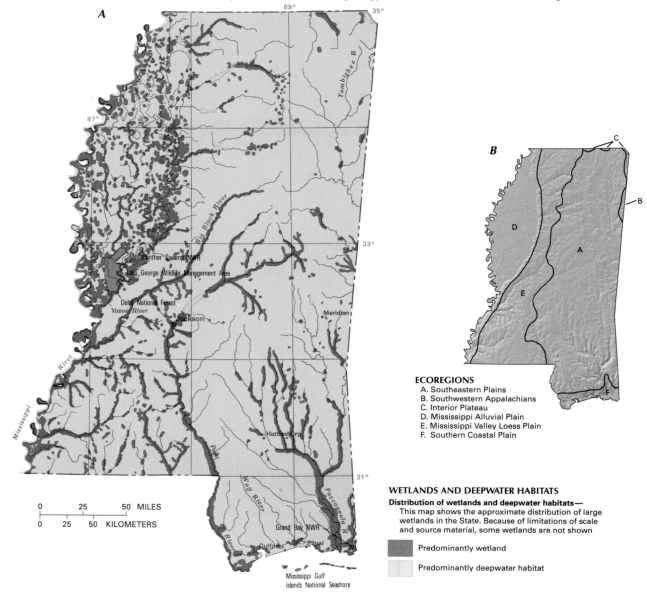

ECOREGIONS
A. Southeastern Plains
B. Southwestern Appalachians
C. Interior Plateau
D. Mississippi Alluvial Plain
E. Mississippi Valley Loess Plain
F. Southern Coastal Plain

WETLANDS AND DEEPWATER HABITATS
Distribution of wetlands and deepwater habitats—
This map shows the approximate distribution of large wetlands in the State. Because of limitations of scale and source material, some wetlands are not shown

■ Predominantly wetland
□ Predominantly deepwater habitat

Figure 2. Wetland distribution and ecoregions in Mississippi. **A**, Distribution of wetlands and deepwater habitats. **B**, Ecoregions. *(Sources: A, T.E. Dahl, U.S. Fish and Wildlife Service, unpub. data, 1991. B, Omernik, 1987.)*

of ground water and surface water. However, in Mississippi, precipitation is abundant, averaging 50 to 68 inches per year across the State (Lamonds and Boswell, 1986). These high annual rainfall averages minimize the transient or seasonal changes in the interactions of the ground and surface waters.

Most palustrine wetlands in Mississippi are closely associated with the State's major flood plains and are directly and indirectly affected by the Mississippi River. The flood plain of the Mississippi River is an area of relatively flat slope that has been subjected to frequent flooding. Flooding has resulted in the evolution of large areas of backwater swamps vegetated by water-tolerant trees such as cypress, tupelo gum, water oak, and red maple. The existence

and continued survival of these palustrine forested and palustrine scrub-shrub wetlands depends on whether these areas are able to undergo continued flooding and dewatering cycles. Disruption of the cycle can change the composition of the forest or shrub community or cause the disappearance of woody vegetation altogether, depending on the nature of the disruption. For example, when a forested or scrub-shrub wetland is leveed and drained, resulting in limited access for floodwaters, water-tolerant trees or shrubs are ultimately replaced by upland vegetation. Conversely, when a wetland is permanently flooded, such as by reservoir construction, recruitment of new trees or shrubs ceases, and the aging forest or scrub-shrub community eventually disappears.

The lower Yazoo River Basin contains one of the largest nearly contiguous forested wetlands remaining in Mississippi, comprising about 140,000 acres of bottom-land forest. The core of these forested wetlands includes the 60,000-acre Delta National Forest and the 27,000-acre Panther Swamp National Wildlife Refuge. The Yazoo River Basin supports threatened and endangered species such as the bald eagle, wood stork, Louisiana black bear, and pondberry. It also serves as a haven for migratory waterfowl and neotropical birds (Creasman and others, 1992). Wetlands, such as those associated with the Yazoo River Basin, directly affect the quality of the water that passes through them. The Yazoo River Basin wetlands have acted as traps for nutrients, suspended sediments, and pesticides in agricultural runoff within this intensively farmed region of the State, thus helping to maintain the water quality of streams and rivers. However, the result has been accelerated sediment deposition within the open-water areas and swamps, subsequent conversion of swamps to bottom-land forests, and uptake of pesticides by the wildlife that live in the basin (Mississippi Department of Environmental Quality, 1992).

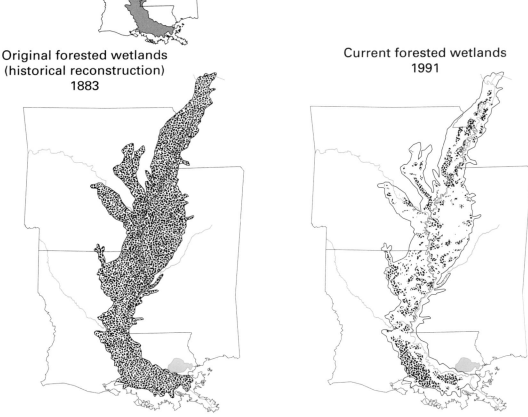

Figure 3. Reduction of forested wetlands in the Mississippi River Alluvial Plain, 1883–1991. *(Creasman and others, 1992).*

TRENDS

The Mississippi Alluvial Plain extends more than 700 miles from southern Illinois to the Gulf of Mexico. Historically, this area supported more than 21 million acres of forested wetlands in seven States (fig. 3). Conversion of the forest to agricultural use has reduced what was a vast wetland system to a scattered patchwork totaling about 4.9 million acres (Creasman and others, 1992).

Mississippi began losing wetlands shortly after the arrival of European settlers. In 1850, the U.S. Congress, with the objective of controlling floods in the Mississippi Valley, passed the second of the Swamp Land Acts, which granted to Mississippi 3,347,860 acres of swamp and overflow lands considered unfit for cultivation (Shaw and Fredine, 1971). The Flood Control Act of 1928 was passed by Congress as a result of the disastrous 1927 floods. The act provides comprehensive flood control for the lower Mississippi Valley downstream from Cairo, Ill. The act authorizes the U.S. Army Corps of Engineers (Corps) to construct and maintain levees, floodways, channel modifications, and various control structures. The passage of these and other flood-control acts resulted in the conversion of thousands of acres of wetlands to agriculture (Shaw and Fredine, 1971).

In 1937 there were about 1,750,000 acres of palustrine forested and palustrine scrub-shrub wetlands in Mississippi. By 1987 the area had decreased to about 600,000 acres (U.S. Fish and Wildlife Service, 1992)—a 66-percent reduction in those kinds of wetlands. Wetland loss in Mississippi from the 1780's to the 1980's was about 59 percent (Dahl, 1990). In 1992 the FWS reported that almost all of the cleared land in the major wetland areas was being farmed, although substantial areas were considered marginal for crop production because of the flood risks. Some of these marginal farmlands are reverting back to scrub-shrub wetlands as they remain fallow. Further, the rate of loss of bottom-land forests in Mississippi has recently decreased because of a decline in the agricultural economy and an increase in the recreational value of these forested wetlands. Threats to the remaining inland wetlands in Mississippi include drainage and flood-protection projects, dredging and stream channelization, alteration of drainage patterns, construction of dikes and levees, discharge of pollutants, erosion (U.S. Fish and Wildlife Service, 1992), and grazing. The introduction of nonnative plant or animal species, such as nutria (an aggressive herbivore), and the disturbance of resident fauna, such as removal of beaver populations, also are threats to Mississippi's remaining inland wetlands (Ruple, 1992).

Coastal wetland loss in Mississippi since 1930 exceeds 8,500 acres and has been primarily caused by industrial and urban development (U.S. Fish and Wildlife Service, 1992). Losses have decreased since passage of the Coastal Wetlands Protection Act in 1973. Continued threats to coastal wetlands in Mississippi include erosion from sea-level rise, subsidence, barrier-island migration, dredging and filling, discharge of pollutants, sedimentation, bulkheading, and alteration of water-exchange patterns between marshes and open water by installation of dikes and weirs (U.S. Fish and Wildlife Service, 1992).

CONSERVATION

Many government agencies and private organizations participate in wetland conservation in Mississippi. The most active agencies and organizations and some of their activities are listed in table 1.

Federal wetland activities.—Development activities in Mississippi wetlands are regulated by several Federal statutory prohibitions and incentives that are intended to slow wetland losses. Some of the more important of these are contained in the 1899 Rivers and Harbors Act; the 1972 Clean Water Act and amendments; the 1985

Table 1. Selected wetland-related activities of government agencies and private organizations in Mississippi, 1993

[Source: Classification of activities is generalized from information provided by agencies and organizations. •, agency or organization participates in wetland-related activity; ..., agency or organization does not participate in wetland-related activity. MAN, management; REG, regulation; R&C, restoration and creation; LAN, land acquisition; R&D, research and data collection; D&I, delineation and inventory]

Agency or organization	MAN	REG	R&C	LAN	R&D	D&I
FEDERAL						
Department of Agriculture						
Consolidated Farm Service Agency	...	•	...	...	...	...
Forest Service	•	...	•	...	•	•
Natural Resources Conservation Service	...	•	•	•	...	•
Department of Commerce						
National Oceanic and Atmospheric Administration	•	•	•	...	•	•
Department of Defense						
Army Corps of Engineers	...	•	•	...	...	•
Department of the Interior						
Fish and Wildlife Service	•	...	•	•	•	•
Geological Survey	...	...	...	...	•	...
National Biological Service	...	...	...	...	•	...
National Park Service	•	...	•	•	•	...
Environmental Protection Agency	...	•	...	...	•	•
STATE						
Department of Environmental Quality	•	•	...	...	...	...
Department of Wildlife, Fisheries, and Parks	•	•	•	•	•	•
Natural Heritage Program	...	...	...	...	...	•
COUNTY AND LOCAL						
Diamondhead	...	•	...	...	...	...
Jordan Rivers Shores	...	•	...	...	...	...
Timber Ridge	...	•	...	...	...	...
PRIVATE ORGANIZATIONS						
Ducks Unlimited	•	...	...	•	...	...
Eco-MS	...	...	...	...	...	•
Gulf Coast Conservation Association	...	...	...	...	...	•
Gulf Islands Conservancy, Inc.	...	...	...	...	...	•
Mississippi Coast Audubon Society	•	...	...	...	...	•
Mississippi Wildlife Federation	•	...	...	...	...	...
Save the Pascagoula, Inc.	•	...	...	...	...	...
Sierra Club, Mississippi Chapter	•	...	...	...	...	•
The Nature Conservancy, Mississippi Field Office	•	...	...	•	•	•

Food Security Act; the 1990 Food, Agriculture, Conservation, and Trade Act; the 1986 Emergency Wetlands Resources Act; and the 1972 Coastal Zone Management Act.

Section 10 of the Rivers and Harbors Act gives the Corps authority to regulate certain activities in navigable waters. Regulated activities include diking, deepening, filling, excavating, and placing of structures. The related section 404 of the Clean Water Act is the most often-used Federal legislation protecting wetlands. Under section 404 provisions, the Corps issues permits regulating the discharge of dredged or fill material into wetlands. Permits are subject to review and possible veto by the U.S. Environmental Protection Agency (EPA), and the FWS has review and advisory roles. Section 401 of the Clean Water Act grants to States and eligible Indian Tribes the authority to approve, apply conditions to, or deny section 404 permit applications on the basis of a proposed activity's probable effects on the water quality of a wetland.

Most farming, ranching, and silviculture activities are not subject to section 404 regulation. However, the "Swampbuster" provision of the 1985 Food Security Act and amendments in the 1990 Food, Agriculture, Conservation, and Trade Act discourage (through financial disincentives) the draining, filling, or other alteration of wetlands for agricultural use. The law allows exemptions from penalties in some cases, especially if the farmer agrees to restore the altered wetland or other wetlands that have been converted to agricultural use. The Wetlands Reserve Program of the 1990 Food,

Agriculture, Conservation, and Trade Act authorizes the Federal Government to purchase conservation easements from landowners who agree to protect or restore wetlands. The Consolidated Farm Service Agency (formerly the Agricultural Stabilization and Conservation Service) administers the Swampbuster provisions and Wetlands Reserve Program. The Natural Resources Conservation Service (formerly the Soil Conservation Service) determines compliance with Swampbuster provisions and assists farmers in the identification of wetlands and in the development of wetland protection, restoration, or creation plans.

The 1986 Emergency Wetlands Resources Act and the 1972 Coastal Zone Management Act and amendments encourage wetland protection through funding incentives. The Emergency Wetlands Resources Act requires States to address wetland protection in their Statewide Comprehensive Outdoor Recreation Plans to qualify for Federal funding for State recreational land; the National Park Service (NPS) provides guidance to States in developing the wetland component of their plans. Coastal and Great Lakes States that adopt coastal-zone management programs and plans approved by the National Oceanic and Atmospheric Administration (NOAA) are eligible for Federal funding and technical assistance through the Coastal Zone Management Act.

Several Federal agencies have wetland-management responsibilities. The NPS administers the Mississippi Gulf Islands National Seashore, a series of barrier islands in the Gulf of Mexico off Mississippi's coast that are fringed by estuarine and marine wetlands. The U.S. Geological Survey collects information on the quantity and quality of the Nation's water resources, including wetlands. NOAA's National Marine Fisheries Service and the Gulf of Mexico Fisheries Management Council prepare and approve plans and implement mechanisms concerning the management of fisheries in Mississippi estuarine and offshore waters including modifications to wetlands that could adversely affect juvenile fish stocks. NOAA's National Ocean Service, in cooperation with the National Marine Fisheries Service, has compiled an inventory of coastal wetlands. The U.S. Forest Service has an ongoing interest in the reforestation of bottom-land forests in the lower Mississippi River Valley. The EPA directs the Gulf of Mexico Program, which provides a forum for resolving complex environmental problems of the gulf from a regional perspective. The program promotes wetland management and restoration and use of wetlands in the treatment of wastewater by States that border the Gulf of Mexico.

State wetland activities.—The Mississippi Department of Wildlife, Fisheries, and Parks, which is governed by the Mississippi Commission on Wildlife, Fisheries, and Parks, is the primary State management agency for tidally influenced wetlands. As mandated by the Mississippi Coastal Wetlands Protection Law of 1973, the Department's Bureau of Marine Resources reviews and comments on all aspects of wetland protection.

The Mississippi Department of Environmental Quality is the primary State management agency for freshwater wetlands. The Department monitors and enforces many water-quality standards and regulations that directly affect wetlands. The Department's Office of Pollution Control requires section 401 water-quality certification of applicants seeking dredge and fill (section 404) permits from the Corps. During project review, the Office of Pollution Control attempts to prevent wetland losses by requesting that alternatives be considered. For unavoidable losses, the agency requests mitigation.

The Natural Heritage Program, authorized by the Mississippi Natural Heritage Act of 1978, identifies and inventories priority wetlands. The program requires that areas and species of biological significance or special concern to the State, including rare or threatened plants, be listed on the Mississippi Natural Registry.

County and local wetland activities.—Counties and cities review permit applications for projects that affect their inland and coastal wetlands. Typically, few comments are received from these agencies; however, some subdivisions have restrictions limiting development in adjacent coastal waters (Ruple, 1992).

Private and cooperative wetland activities.—Many citizen's groups and private organizations support efforts to protect Mississippi wetlands. Eco-MS is a coalition of about 35 environmental groups that support wetland protection efforts. The Gulf Islands Conservancy, Inc., the Gulf Coast Conservation Association, and the Mississippi Coast Audubon Society are dedicated to wetland protection in the Mississippi coastal area. The Mississippi Wildlife Federation and the Mississippi Chapter of the Sierra Club also actively support measures to protect wetlands statewide. The Nature Conservancy acquires and manages wetlands in Mississippi. More than 105,000 acres of wetlands along the Pascagoula River have been acquired by the State with the assistance of private organizations such as The Nature Conservancy and Save the Pascagoula, Inc. The Nature Conservancy, in conjunction with the FWS, is acquiring land to expand the Grand Bay National Wildlife Refuge. The Nature Conservancy also participates in the Mississippi Coastal Preserve Program.

In May 1986 an international commitment to conserving North America's waterfowl resources was pledged by signing of the North American Waterfowl Management Plan. Canada, the United States, and Mexico are the participants. The plan is a direct response to a continuing decline in waterfowl populations and the habitat upon which waterfowl and other wetland wildlife depend (Lower Mississippi Valley Joint Venture Management Board, 1990). Implementing the plan depends on the development of joint ventures and partnerships among Federal and State agencies and private organizations. The Lower Mississippi Valley Joint Venture is a cooperative effort by the FWS, The Nature Conservancy, Ducks Unlimited, and others to ensure the long-term success of waterfowl and wetland conservation in a seven-State area, including Mississippi.

References Cited

Boto, K.G., and Patrick, W.H., Jr., 1979, Role of wetlands in the removal of suspended sediments, *in* Greeson, P.E., Clark, J.R., and Clark, J.E., eds., Proceedings of the National Symposium on Wetlands, November 1978: Minneapolis, Minn., American Water Resources Association, p. 479–489.

Cowardin, L.M., Carter, Virginia, Golet, F.C., and LaRoe, E.T., 1979, Classification of wetlands and deepwater habitats of the United States: U.S. Fish and Wildlife Service Report FWS/OBS–79/31, 131 p.

Creasman, Lisa, Craig, Nancy Jo, and Swan, Mark, 1992, The forested wetlands of the Mississippi River—An ecosystem in crisis: Baton Rouge, La., The Nature Conservancy of Louisiana, 23 p.

Dahl, T.E., 1990, Wetlands—Losses in the United States, 1780's to 1980's: Washington, D.C., U.S. Fish and Wildlife Service Report to Congress, 13 p.

Deason, J.P., 1989, Impacts of irrigation drainwater on wetlands, *in* Fisk, D.W., ed., Wetlands—Concerns and successes: Bethesda, Md., American Water Resources Association, p. 127–138.

German, E.R., 1989, Removal of nitrogen and phosphorus in an undeveloped wetland area, central Florida, *in* Fisk, D.W., ed., Wetlands—Concerns and successes: Bethesda, Md., American Water Resources Association, p. 139–147.

Kadlec, R.H., and Kadlec, J.A., 1979, Wetlands and water quality, *in* Greeson, P.E., Clark, J.R., and Clark, J.E., eds., Proceedings of the National Symposium on Wetlands, November 1978: Minneapolis, Minn., American Water Resources Association, p. 436–456.

Lamonds, A.G., and Boswell, E.H., 1986, Mississippi surface-water resources, *in* U.S. Geological Survey, National water summary 1985—Hydrologic events and surface-water resources: U.S. Geological Survey Water-Supply Paper 2300, p. 295–300.

Lower Mississippi Valley Joint Venture Management Board, 1990, Conserving waterfowl and wetlands—The Lower Mississippi Valley Joint Venture: Vicksburg, Miss., North American Waterfowl Management Plan, 32 p.

Mississippi Department of Environmental Quality, 1992, Mississippi 1992 water quality assessment, Federal Clean Water Act Section 305(b) report: Mississippi Department of Environmental Quality, Office of Pollution Control, p. 93–104.

Omernik, J.M., 1987, Ecoregions of the conterminous United States — Map supplement: Annals of the Association of American Geographers, v. 77, no. 1, scale 1:7,500,000.

Ruple, David, ed., 1992, A citizen's guide for protecting wetlands in Mississippi: Mississippi Department of Wildlife, Fisheries, and Parks, 66 p.

Shaw, S.P., and Fredine, C.G., 1971, Wetlands of the United States, their extent and their value to waterfowl and other wildlife: U.S. Fish and Wildlife Service Circular 39, 67 p.

U.S. Fish and Wildlife Service, 1992, Regional wetlands concept plan — Emergency wetlands resources act, Southeast Region: Atlanta, Ga., U.S. Fish and Wildlife Service, 249 p.

Winter, T.C., and Woo, Ming-Ko, 1990, Hydrology of lakes and wetlands, *in* Wolman, M.G., and Riggs, H.C., eds., Surface water hydrology: Boulder, Colo., Geological Society of America, The Geology of North America, v. O–1, chap. 8, p. 159–187.

FOR ADDITIONAL INFORMATION: District Chief, U.S. Geological Survey, 100 W. Capitol Street, Suite 120, Jackson, MS 39269; Regional Wetland Coordinator, U.S. Fish and Wildlife Service, 1875 Century Building, Suite 200, Atlanta, GA 30345

Prepared by
Charles R. Demas and Dennis K. Demcheck,
U.S. Geological Survey

Missouri
Wetland Resources

Missouri wetlands occupy 643,000 acres, about 1.4 percent of the State's area (Dahl, 1990). Before the arrival of European settlers, wetlands occupied about 4.84 million acres, about 10.8 percent of what is now Missouri, and were a significant component of the landscape (Epperson, 1992).

Before European settlement, wetlands primarily were associated with the major rivers and streams, especially in the State's "bootheel" (southeastern area), which borders the Mississippi River. This area once contained about 50 percent of the State's wetlands and was nicknamed "swampeast" Missouri. Although they were considered impediments to progress, wetlands provided large economic benefits to the railroad companies that purchased and harvested the vast bottom-land forests of cypress, tupelo gum, and oak for timber (Epperson, 1992). After the commercial timber had been removed, these cleared wetlands were drained and converted to agricultural use, and they remain in that land-use category today.

Wetlands maintain water quality, mitigate flood effects, provide critical habitat for many rare and endangered plants and animals, and are a source of recreational activities such as birding, fishing, hunting, and ecotourism in unique areas such as Slaughter Sink and Grasshopper Hollow (fig. 1). Wetlands in Missouri provide critical habitat for 15 animal and 4 plant species that are endangered or threatened (Rick Hansen, U.S. Fish and Wildlife Service, written commun., 1993). Also within Missouri, a large number of wetland species are of special concern. Some of the endangered or threatened plants and animals associated with wetlands in Missouri include the eastern prairie fringed orchid, gray bat, Indiana bat, Ozark big bat, bald eagle, least tern, Neosho madtom, Ozark cavefish, and the Higgins eye pearly mussel.

Missouri's location on the Mississippi Flyway makes the State a favored wintering area for waterfowl and raptors. As many as 200,000 ducks, mainly mallard, but also pintail, green-winged teal, widgeon, gadwall, and shoveler, reside in the 21,600-acre Mingo National Wildlife Refuge in southeastern Missouri. As many as 200,000 geese and 300,000 ducks winter in the 6,890-acre Squaw Creek National Wildlife Refuge in northwestern Missouri. This refuge supports one of the largest wintering concentrations of bald eagles in the United States and harbors as many as 200 bird species at any given time. About 100 bald eagles winter in the 10,670-acre Swan Lake National Wildlife Refuge in north-central Missouri (Riley, 1979). Missouri has five National Wildlife Refuges, one National Scenic Riverway, one National Forest system, seven State wetland areas under the jurisdiction of the Missouri Department of Conservation in cooperation with the North American Waterfowl Plan, and four State parks that feature and preserve wetlands within their boundaries (Lower Mississippi Valley Joint Venture Management Board, 1990; Epperson, 1992).

TYPES AND DISTRIBUTION

Wetlands are lands transitional between terrestrial and deepwater habitats where the water table usually is at or near the land surface or the land is covered by shallow water (Cowardin and others, 1979). The distribution of wetlands and deepwater habitats in Missouri is shown in figure 2A; only wetlands are discussed herein.

Wetlands can be vegetated or nonvegetated and are classified on the basis of their hydrology, vegetation, and substrate. In this summary, wetlands are classified according to the system proposed by Cowardin and others (1979), which is used by the U.S. Fish and Wildlife Service (FWS) to map and inventory the Nation's wetlands. At the most general level of the classification system, wetlands are grouped into five ecological systems: Palustrine, Lacustrine, Riverine, Estuarine, and Marine. The Palustrine System includes only wetlands, whereas the other systems comprise wetlands and deepwater habitats. Wetlands of the systems that occur in Missouri are described below.

System	Wetland description
Palustrine	Wetlands in which vegetation is predominantly trees (forested wetlands); shrubs (scrub-shrub wetlands); persistent or nonpersistent emergent, erect, rooted, herbaceous plants (persistent- and nonpersistent-emergent wetlands); or submersed and (or) floating plants (aquatic beds). Also, intermittently to permanently flooded open-water bodies of less than 20 acres in which water is less than 6.6 feet deep.
Lacustrine	Wetlands within an intermittently to permanently flooded lake or reservoir. Vegetation, when present, is predominantly nonpersistent emergent plants (nonpersistent-emergent wetlands), or submersed and (or) floating plants (aquatic beds), or both.
Riverine	Wetlands within a channel. Vegetation, when present, is same as in the Lacustrine System.

Palustrine forested wetlands (swamps and other forested wetlands), palustrine emergent wetlands (marshes and fens), and palustrine scrub-shrub wetlands (shrub swamps) constitute most of the wetland acreage in Missouri (Epperson, 1992). Most of the State's wetlands are associated with rivers and streams (fig. 2A). The bootheel region is especially rich in wetlands.

Fens are small (0.5–10 acres), palustrine forested or emergent wetlands unique to areas where ground water, underground streams, and karst topography (resulting from limestone and dolomite rock dissolution) characterize the local hydrology and geology. In contrast to most other wetlands in Missouri, fens are created by ground water, not surface water (Epperson, 1992). These wetlands are located primarily along stream terraces and at the base of slopes in the Ozark Highlands (fig. 2B). Vegetation in fens primarily consists of grasses, sedges, and reeds; however, some are forested. Fens provide habitat for several unique plant and animal species, includ-

Figure 1. Grasshopper Hollow, a fen in the Ozark Highlands of Missouri. *(Photograph by Jane Epperson, Missouri Department of Natural Resources.)*

ing a disproportionate number of Missouri's rare and endangered plants and invertebrates (Mohlenbrock, 1993). Notable examples of fens include Grasshopper Hollow (fig. 1) and Slaughter Sink.

HYDROLOGIC SETTING

The existence of wetlands depends on specific topographic and geologic conditions that favor flooding or saturated soils and on the hydrologic processes that allow the water to persist (Winter and Woo, 1990). Wetland hydrology involves complex water-flow patterns that are affected by regional and local geology, topography, soil characteristics, and climate.

Wetlands in Missouri are a result of diverse surface- and ground-water conditions. Surface water collects in topographic lows, and ground water typically discharges there. Soil characteristics determine the rate at which water percolates downward to recharge the ground-water system or discharges from it. Fluctuations in lo-

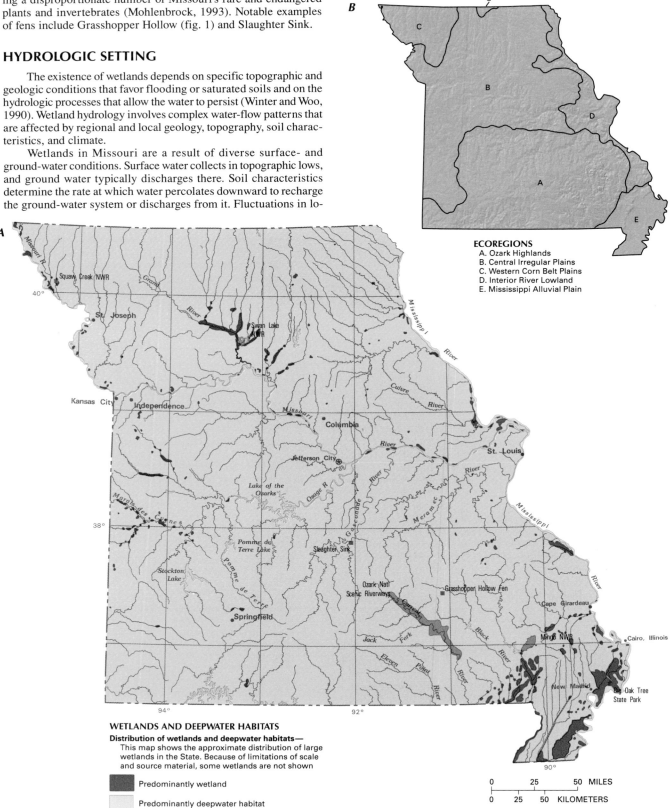

ECOREGIONS
A. Ozark Highlands
B. Central Irregular Plains
C. Western Corn Belt Plains
D. Interior River Lowland
E. Mississippi Alluvial Plain

WETLANDS AND DEEPWATER HABITATS

Distribution of wetlands and deepwater habitats—
This map shows the approximate distribution of large wetlands in the State. Because of limitations of scale and source material, some wetlands are not shown

Predominantly wetland

Predominantly deepwater habitat

Figure 2. Wetland distribution in Missouri and ecoregions of the State. **A**, Distribution of wetlands and deepwater habitats. **B**, Ecoregions. *(Sources: A, T.E. Dahl, U.S. Fish and Wildlife Service, unpub. data, 1991. B, Omernik, 1987.)*

cal precipitation can combine with local geologic differences to create transient or seasonal changes in the interactions of ground water and surface water. Average annual precipitation ranges from 36 to 48 inches per year across Missouri (Waite and Skelton, 1986). The extent of wetland areas located in parts of the State with lower annual precipitation rates, especially those associated with shallow ground-water systems and surface-water runoff, such as fens, depends on the timing and amounts of rainfall. Other wetland areas, such as those along major rivers, are less dependent on local rainfall patterns for their continued existence.

The largest wetlands in Missouri are closely associated with and are directly and indirectly affected by the Mississippi and Missouri Rivers and their tributaries. The flood plains created by the Mississippi and Missouri Rivers have resulted in an area of relatively flat slope that has been flooded frequently. The wetlands of the Missouri bootheel were formed as a result of the New Madrid earthquake (actually a series of earthquakes), which occurred in 1811. Lasting for several months, this catastrophe changed the course of the Mississippi River and greatly changed the topography of the Mississippi Alluvial Plain (McCaig and Boyce, 1988). All of the land from Cape Girardeau south to Arkansas sank from 10 to 50 feet, converting rich bootheel forests into swamp (Johnson and DeLano, 1990). The subsequent flooding in the subsided forested areas following the earthquakes resulted in the formation of large tracts of backwater swamps characterized by water-tolerant trees such as cypress, tupelo gum, water oak, and swamp red maple.

Backwater flooding in the major tributaries of the Mississippi and Missouri Rivers has resulted in the formation of similar wetlands along their flood plains. The existence and continued survival of these forested, scrub-shrub, and emergent wetlands depends on whether these areas are able to undergo continued flooding and dewatering cycles. Disruption of this continual flooding/dewatering cycle results in (1) replacement of the existing trees by less water-tolerant trees and shrubs when periodic flooding is prevented (such as occurs when levees are built along a river and the flood plain is drained) or (2) lack of recruitment of new trees in areas that become permanently flooded (such as occurs when a river is dammed).

Water in fens is supplied by local shallow ground-water flow systems. These wetlands typically are associated with springs or seeps that discharge at the surface. In Missouri, fens occur in the Ozark Highlands ecoregion. The Ozark Highlands ecoregion is underlain by limestone and dolomite overlain by less easily erodible rock such as sandstone. If sinkholes (formed by the collapse of limestone and dolomite caves) become plugged, fens develop as the result of retention of ground-water discharge or stormwater runoff. Fens are sustained by water that has passed through highly mineralized soils (Mitsch and Gosselink, 1993).

TRENDS

Wetland losses and the land-use changes that have altered wetland functions and biota began at the time of settlement by Europeans. As of the 1980's, Missouri had only 643,000 acres of wetlands of an estimated 4,844,000 acres of wetlands existing in the 1780's (Dahl, 1990), an 87-percent loss. Large-scale wetland losses began after 1850, when the U.S. Congress passed the Swamp Land Act. The act granted to Missouri 3,432,481 acres of Federal forested wetlands and overflow lands considered unfit for cultivation. The object of the act was to promote flood control in the Mississippi River Valley (Shaw and Fredine, 1971). The remaining 1,410,000

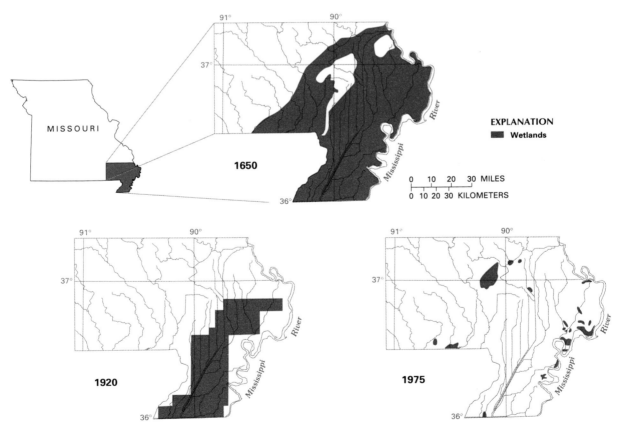

Figure 3. Palustrine forested-wetland loss in the Mississippi Alluvial Plain, southeastern Missouri, 1650–1975. (Source: Epperson, 1992.)

acres were transferred to the State during the next few years. Shortly thereafter, the land was transferred to the counties, which in turn sold large tracts at public auction (Epperson, 1992).

By 1912, about 3,500,000 acres of wetlands had been targeted for drainage statewide (Epperson, 1992). Stream channelization and damming also have significantly affected wetlands within Missouri. The primary cause of recent wetland loss, both nationally and state-wide, has been conversion of wetlands to agricultural use. Other causes include urban development, flood control, and timber harvesting (Frayer and others, 1983).

The most severe wetland loss has occurred in the southeastern part of the State in the Mississippi Alluvial Plain (fig. 3), where only about 60,000 acres (2.5 percent) of an estimated original 2,400,000 acres of forested wetlands remain intact (Vaught and Bowmaster, 1983). Wetland loss in the southeastern part of the State ranged from 257,000 acres from 1870 to 1890 to 595,000 acres from 1900 to 1920. In the 1930's, fearing that this magnificent wetland forest would be lost, businessmen, residents, and local school children contributed their nickels and dimes to purchase some of the last remnants of the once vast wetland forest. In 1938, more than 1,000 acres were purchased and became the Big Oak Tree State Park (Johnson and DeLano, 1990).

CONSERVATION

Many government agencies and private organizations participate in wetland conservation in Missouri. The most active agencies and organizations and some of their activities are listed in table 1.

Federal wetland activities.—Development activities in Missouri wetlands are regulated by several Federal statutory prohibitions and incentives that are intended to slow wetland losses. Some of the more important of these are contained in the 1899 Rivers and Harbors Act; the 1972 Clean Water Act and amendments; the 1985 Food Security Act; the 1990 Food, Agriculture, Conservation, and Trade Act; and the 1986 Emergency Wetlands Resources Act.

Section 10 of the Rivers and Harbors Act gives the U.S. Army Corps of Engineers (Corps) authority to regulate certain activities

in navigable waters. Regulated activities include diking, deepening, filling, excavating, and placing of structures. The related section 404 of the Clean Water Act is the most often-used Federal legislation protecting wetlands. Under section 404 provisions, the Corps issues permits regulating the discharge of dredged or fill material into wetlands. Permits are subject to review and possible veto by the U.S. Environmental Protection Agency, and the FWS has review and advisory roles. Section 401 of the Clean Water Act grants to States and eligible Indian Tribes the authority to approve, apply conditions to, or deny section 404 permit applications on the basis of a proposed activity's probable effects on the water quality of a wetland.

Most farming, ranching, and silviculture activities are not subject to section 404 regulation. However, the "Swampbuster" provision of the 1985 Food Security Act and amendments in the 1990 Food, Agriculture, Conservation, and Trade Act discourage (through financial disincentives) the draining, filling, or other alteration of wetlands for agricultural use. The law allows exemptions from penalties in some cases, especially if the farmer agrees to restore the altered wetland or other wetlands that have been converted to agricultural use. The Wetlands Reserve Program of the 1990 Food, Agriculture, Conservation, and Trade Act authorizes the Federal Government to purchase conservation easements from landowners who agree to protect or restore wetlands. The Consolidated Farm Service Agency (formerly the Agricultural Stabilization and Conservation Service) administers the Swampbuster provisions and Wetlands Reserve Program. The Natural Resources Conservation Service (formerly the Soil Conservation Service) (NRCS) determines compliance with Swampbuster provisions and assists farmers in the identification of wetlands and in the development of wetland protection, restoration, or creation plans.

The 1986 Emergency Wetlands Resources Act encourages wetland protection through funding incentives. The act requires States to address wetland protection in their Statewide Comprehensive Outdoor Recreation Plans to qualify for Federal funding for State recreational land; the National Park Service (NPS) provides guidance to States in developing the wetland component of their plans.

The Rivers and Harbors Act of 1899 requires a permit for construction or excavation in, over, or under "navigable waters" of the United States. The Corps is the lead agency for administration of this Act. The Lake of the Ozarks and the Osage, Mississippi, and Missouri Rivers are the major navigable waters in Missouri. The Flood Control Act of 1928 authorizes the Corps to construct and maintain levees, floodways, channel modifications, and various control structures for the lower Mississippi River Valley downstream from Cairo, Ill.

The FWS has section 404 responsibilities under the Fish and Wildlife Coordination Act of 1934, National Environmental Policy Act of 1969, and the Endangered Species Act of 1973. The FWS provides advisory comments to the Corps, during section 404 permit-application review on the potential effects on fish, wildlife, and related environmental resources. The FWS is mapping the Nation's wetlands under its National Wetlands Inventory project. Missouri has five National Wildlife Refuges that are managed by the FWS primarily for migratory birds and federally listed threatened and endangered species.

The NPS manages the Ozark National Scenic Riverways, which includes 134 miles of the Current and Jack Fork Rivers. Natural wetland communities are common in the riparian corridors (the area adjacent to a stream or river that is at least occasionally flooded) of these rivers and their tributaries.

State wetland activities.—Under section 401 of the Clean Water Act, the Missouri Department of Natural Resources must certify that a proposed federally permitted or licensed activity will not violate State water-quality standards. If section 401 water-quality certification is denied, the Corps must deny the section 404 permit

Table 1. Selected wetland-related activities of government agencies and private organizations in Missouri, 1993

[Source: Classification of activities is generalized from information provided by agencies and organizations. ●, agency or organization participates in wetland-related activity; ..., agency or organization does not participate in wetland-related activity. MAN, management; REG, regulation; R&C, restoration and creation; LAN, land acquisition; R&D, research and data collection; D&I, delineation and inventory]

Agency or organization	MAN	REG	R&C	LAN	R&D	D&I
FEDERAL						
Department of Agriculture						
Consolidated Farm Service Agency	...	●	...	...	...	...
Forest Service	●	...	...	●	...	●
Natural Resources Conservation Service	...	●	●	...	...	●
Department of Defense						
Army Corps of Engineers	...	●	...	●	●	●
Department of the Interior						
Fish and Wildlife Service	●	...	●	●	●	●
Geological Survey	...	...	...	...	●	...
National Biological Service	...	...	...	...	●	...
National Park Service	●	...	●	●	●	...
Environmental Protection Agency	...	●	...	...	...	...
STATE						
Department of Conservation	●	...	●	●	●	●
Department of Natural Resources	●	●	●	●	●	●
PRIVATE						
Ducks Unlimited	●	...	●	●	...	●
National Audubon Society	●	...	...	●	...	...
The Nature Conservancy	●	...	...	●	●	●

application. The Department's Division of State Parks is responsible for preserving, restoring, and managing natural wetland ecosystems through the State park system. The Department of Natural Resources, Division of Geology and Land Survey's Water Resources Program, with extensive public participation, has developed short- and long-term wetland goals for the State, as well as specific recommendations for achievement of the goals. Recently, the Missouri Departments of Natural Resources and Conservation, the FWS, and the NRCS have been working toward a common wetland data base for use by these agencies.

The Missouri Department of Conservation is the State's primary fish and wildlife agency. The Department's Natural Heritage Database is an inventory of wetlands and other natural features owned or managed by the Department, as well as of other wetlands considered by the State to be valuable. The Department also has developed a wetland-management plan to guide its efforts in the restoration and management of wetlands until the year 2000. The key elements of the plan are to (1) protect, restore, and improve wetland habitat, (2) acquire new wetland areas, (3) identify population goals and management strategies for waterfowl, wildlife, furbearer, and fish species, (4) address human use of wetland resources, and (5) identify future research needs.

Private wetland activities.—The Nature Conservancy is developing an integrated approach for the conservation and restoration of the Mississippi Alluvial Plain. The organization owns six properties containing wetlands, including ponds, fens, flood-plain forest, and wet prairies. Ducks Unlimited participates in wetland-protection efforts through its involvement in the North American Waterfowl Management Plan. The National Audubon Society conducts a considerable variety of public-education and wetland-preservation programs and projects.

References Cited

Cowardin, L.M., Carter, Virginia, Golet, F.C., and LaRoe, E.T., 1979, Classification of wetlands and deepwater habitats of the United States: U.S. Fish and Wildlife Service Report FWS/OBS–79/31, 131 p.

Dahl, T.E., 1990, Wetlands—Losses in the United States, 1780's to 1980's: Washington, D.C., U.S. Fish and Wildlife Service Report to Congress, 13 p.

Epperson, J.E., 1992, Missouri wetlands—A vanishing resource: Missouri Division of Geology and Land Survey Water Resources Report 39, 67 p.

Frayer, W.E., Monahan, T.J., Bowden, D.C., and Graybill, F.A., 1983, Status and trends of wetlands and deepwater habitats in the conterminous United States, 1950's to 1970's: Fort Collins, Colorado State University, 31 p.

Johnson, Cathy, and DeLano, Patti, 1990, Missouri—Off the beaten path: Chester, Conn., The Glope Pequot Press, 166 p.

Lower Mississippi Valley Joint Venture Management Board, 1990, Conserving waterfowl and wetlands—The Lower Mississippi Valley Joint Venture: Vicksburg, Miss., North American Waterfowl Management Plan, 32 p.

McCaig, Barbara, and Boyce, Chris, 1988, Missouri Parks Guide: Wauwatosa, Wis., Affordable Adventures, Inc., 43 p.

Mitsch, W.J., and Gosselink, J.G., 1993, Wetlands (2d ed.): New York, Van Nostrand Reinhold Co., 722 p.

Mohlenbrock, R.H., 1993, Slaughter Sink, Missouri: Natural History, v. 6, no. 93, p. 25–26.

Omernik, J.M., 1987, Ecoregions of the United States—Map supplement: Annals of the Association of American Geographers, v. 77, no. 1, scale 1:7,500,000.

Riley, Laura, and Riley, William, 1979, Guide to the National Wildlife Refuges: Garden City, N.Y., Anchor Press, p. 319–322, 335–341.

Shaw, S.P., and Fredine, C.G., 1971, Wetlands of the United States—Their extent and their value to waterfowl and other wildlife: U.S. Fish and Wildlife Service Circular 39, 67 p.

Vaught, Richard, and Bowmaster, J.T., 1983, Missouri wetlands and their management: Jefferson City, Missouri Department of Conservation, 23 p.

Waite, L.A., and Skelton, John, 1986, Missouri surface-water resources, *in* National water summary 1985—Hydrologic events and surface-water resources: U.S. Geological Survey Water-Supply Paper 2300, p. 301–308.

Winter, T.C., and Woo, Ming-Ko, 1990, Hydrology of lakes and wetlands, *in* Wolman, M.G., and Riggs, H.C., eds., Surface water hydrology: Boulder, Colo., Geological Society of America, The Geology of North America, v. O–1, chap. 8, p. 159–187.

FOR ADDITIONAL INFORMATION: District Chief, U.S. Geological Survey, 1400 Independence Road, Rolla, MO 65401; Regional Wetland Coordinator, U.S. Fish and Wildlife Service, BHW Federal Building, 1 Federal Drive, Fort Snelling, MN 55111

Prepared by
Charles R. Demas and Dennis K. Demcheck,
U.S. Geological Survey

Montana
Wetland Resources

Wetlands cover only a small part of Montana, but their ecological and economic importance far outweighs their relative size. Wetlands provide stopover feeding areas and breeding grounds for migratory waterfowl (fig. 1). The Nation's most valuable waterfowl production area, the prairie pothole region of the northern Great Plains, includes wetlands of north-central and northeastern Montana. Wetlands are highly productive and provide food for both aquatic and terrestrial animals. Several threatened or endangered species depend on Montana wetlands, including the whooping crane, least tern, bald eagle, piping plover, grizzly bear, and peregrine falcon. Many freshwater fish and upland game birds are wetland dependent, as are antelope, white-tailed and mule deer, elk, moose, and bear, as well as other nongame mammals.

Wetlands stabilize or improve environmental quality by trapping sediments, producing oxygen, recycling nutrients, absorbing chemicals and other pollutants, moderating water temperature, and storing carbon (Tiner, 1984). Many small cities and towns in Montana use sewage lagoons, which are constructed wetlands, for municipal wastewater treatment.

Socioeconomic benefits of Montana wetlands are well documented. Wetland vegetation stabilizes streambanks, reduces erosion and flooding, and provides windbreaks for crops and farmsteads. In some areas, wetlands augment streamflow, whereas in other areas they capture overland runoff and slowly release it to underlying aquifers. Because of their high level of productivity, wetlands are excellent providers of renewable resources, including timber, hay, and livestock water. Montana natives and pioneers highly regarded wetland plants such as cattails, willows, and black cottonwood for food, fuel, insulation, basket-making materials, and construction materials, and their use continues to some extent today (Hansen and others, 1991; R.M. Hazelwood, U.S. Fish and Wildlife Service, oral commun., 1993).

Finally, wetlands are valued for recreation, education, and esthetics. As Montana's tourism industry becomes increasingly important, so do wetlands for the extensive opportunities they provide for fishing, hunting, camping, and observing wildlife.

Figure 1. Freezout Lake Wildlife Management Area in west-central Montana. Wetlands associated with this natural lake receive irrigation return flow, furnish habitat for numerous waterfowl species, and provide a variety of recreational opportunities. *(Photograph by John H. Lambing, U.S. Geological Survey.)*

TYPES AND DISTRIBUTION

Wetlands are lands transitional between terrestrial and deepwater habitats where the water table usually is at or near the land surface or the land is covered by shallow water (Cowardin and others, 1979). The distribution of wetlands and deepwater habitats in Montana is shown in figure 2*A*; only wetlands are discussed herein.

Wetlands can be vegetated or nonvegetated and are classified on the basis of their hydrology, vegetation, and substrate. In this summary, wetlands are classified according to the system proposed by Cowardin and others (1979), which is used by the U.S. Fish and Wildlife Service (FWS) to map and inventory the Nation's wetlands. At the most general level of the classification system, wetlands are grouped into five ecological systems: Palustrine, Lacustrine, Riverine, Estuarine, and Marine. The Palustrine System includes only wetlands, whereas the other systems comprise wetlands and deepwater habitats. Wetlands of the systems that occur in Montana are described below.

System	Wetland description
Palustrine	Wetlands in which vegetation is predominantly trees (forested wetlands); shrubs (scrub-shrub wetlands); persistent or nonpersistent emergent, erect, rooted, herbaceous plants (persistent- and nonpersistent-emergent wetlands); or submersed and (or) floating plants (aquatic beds). Also, intermittently to permanently flooded open-water bodies of less than 20 acres in which water is less than 6.6 feet deep.
Lacustrine	Wetlands within an intermittently to permanently flooded lake or reservoir. Vegetation, when present, is predominantly nonpersistent emergent plants (nonpersistent-emergent wetlands), or submersed and (or) floating plants (aquatic beds), or both.
Riverine	Wetlands within a channel. Vegetation, when present, is same as in the Lacustrine System.

Dahl (1990), on the basis of unpublished data from the FWS, estimated that 840,300 acres, or 0.9 percent of the State, contained wetlands. However, the total wetland area of Montana has not yet been systematically inventoried. Since 1974, the FWS has been conducting a thorough inventory of the Nation's wetlands. That inventory will enable a more accurate estimate of Montana's wetland acreage.

Other investigators have made estimates of wetland acreage for various specific purposes. These estimates did not include all of the State's wetlands. On the basis of an inventory of 15 counties in northern Montana, the FWS (1954) concluded that 187,400 acres of wetlands statewide provide valuable waterfowl breeding habitat. R.J. King (U.S. Fish and and Wildlife Service, unpub. data, 1975) identified 159,608 wetland acres with significant waterfowl production capability (exclusive of constructed reservoirs and stock ponds) in 40 of Montana's 56 counties. The Water Quality Bureau of the Montana Department of Health and Environmental Sciences (1992) estimated that riparian areas comprise about 1,860,000 acres. Riparian areas include both wetlands and uplands.

Most Montana wetlands are palustrine. These include forested wetlands adjacent to rivers statewide; scrub-shrub wetlands such as willow carrs (thickets) in western Montana and greasewood

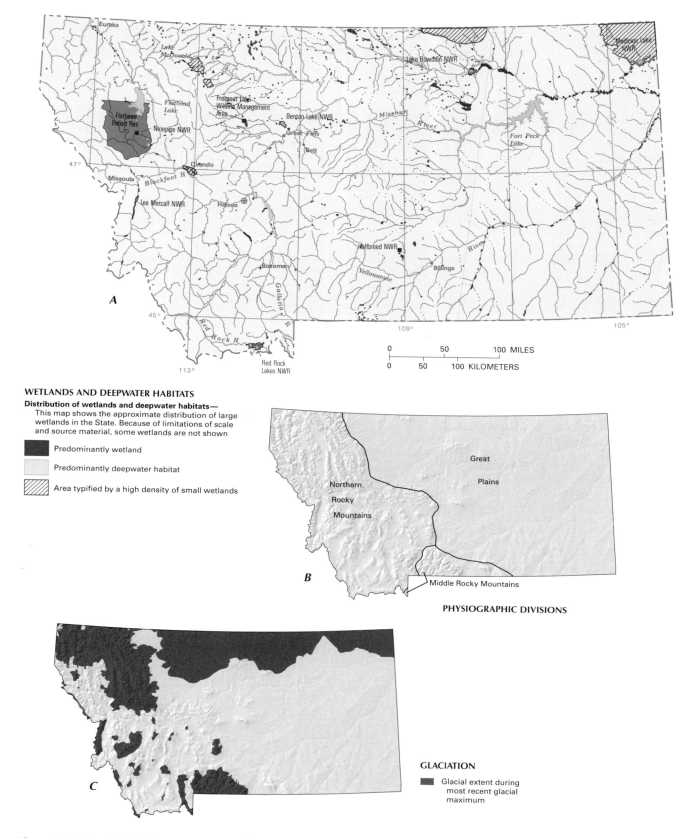

WETLANDS AND DEEPWATER HABITATS

Distribution of wetlands and deepwater habitats—
This map shows the approximate distribution of large wetlands in the State. Because of limitations of scale and source material, some wetlands are not shown

■ Predominantly wetland

▫ Predominantly deepwater habitat

▨ Area typified by a high density of small wetlands

PHYSIOGRAPHIC DIVISIONS

GLACIATION

■ Glacial extent during most recent glacial maximum

Figure 2. Wetland distribution in Montana and physical features that control wetland distribution in the State. *A*, Distribution of wetlands and deepwater habitats. *B*, Physiography. *C*, Extent of most recent glaciation. *(Sources: A, T.E. Dahl, U.S. Fish and Wildlife Service, unpub. data, 1991. B, Physiographic divisions from Fenneman, 1946; landforms data from EROS Data Center. C, Alden, 1932, 1953.)*

scrubland adjacent to rivers in eastern and southwestern Montana; persistent-emergent wetlands such as marshes, fens and wet meadows in western Montana, and fresh and saline marshes in eastern Montana; and aquatic-bed wetlands such as water-lily ponds in northwestern Montana (Tiner, 1984; Hansen and others, 1991; Windell and others, 1986). Palustrine wetlands also are associated with artificial lakes and ponds throughout the State.

The distribution of the different types of wetlands in Montana correlates with the State's physiography (fig. 2B). In glaciated areas of the Great Plains (fig. 2C), wetlands are primarily in topographic depressions commonly referred to as prairie potholes. In the Northern and Middle Rocky Mountains, wetlands are primarily in potholes of glaciated intermontane basins, in the flood plains of streams in unglaciated intermontane basins, and in high mountain valleys. In unglaciated areas of the Great Plains, wetlands occur in flood plains of streams in the Missouri and Yellowstone River basins and also are commonly associated with constructed livestock ponds.

HYDROLOGIC SETTING

Wetlands form where the soil or substrate is saturated with or covered by water for extended periods. The location and persistence of water are a function of interdependent climatic, topographic, hydrologic, and geologic factors. In Montana, except in the high mountains, annual potential evaporation exceeds precipitation, resulting in a moisture deficit that inhibits wetland formation. Therefore, topographic, hydrologic, and geologic factors are as important as climatic factors in creating and maintaining most Montana wetlands.

Glaciation in the northern Great Plains (fig. 2C) blanketed the landscape with dense, clayey glacial till (sediment) (Alden, 1932). As the overlying glacial ice melted, potholes (kettle lakes) remained where ice blocks had previously been embedded in the till. These potholes range in area from less than 1 acre to several square miles. The nearly impermeable till inhibits direct infiltration of snowmelt into the soil. Instead, meltwater flows overland into prairie potholes. Even though potential evaporation exceeds precipitation in this region, the high moisture-retention capacity of the clayey soil allows lush, diverse wetland vegetation to develop wherever water accumulates, resulting in highly productive wetlands (Winter, 1989). In terms of waterfowl production, the seven most productive counties in Montana are located in the prairie pothole region (R.J. King, U.S. Fish and Wildlife Service, unpub. data, 1975).

The hydrology and water quality of prairie pothole wetlands can vary over time. In some areas, ground-water flow reverses direction because of changing water levels in adjacent potholes. Prairie pothole wetlands can recharge ground-water aquifers in spring until evaporation and water uptake by plants cause the water level in the wetland to drop below the local water table. At that time, ground water begins to flow back into the wetland (Winter, 1989). Wetland salinity commonly increases as evaporation concentrates dissolved minerals in the water through the summer and freezing concentrates them through the winter (LaBaugh, 1989). In spring, snowmelt dilutes the salinity.

Water quality can differ between temporary and permanent prairie pothole wetlands, even within the same area. Some prairie pothole wetlands are sustained by ground-water inflow, which provides a constant, but commonly mineralized or saline, source of water. Other prairie pothole wetlands are sustained only by runoff and receive no ground-water inflow. In wet years, these wetlands generally have freshwater, but during most years the combination of evaporation and infiltration causes them to go dry. Still other prairie pothole wetlands have brackish (slightly to moderately salty) water resulting from a combination of ground-water and surface-water inflow (Winter, 1989).

The glaciated areas of the Great Plains typically have a small regional topographic gradient, no integrated drainage system, and soils that have low permeability. Consequently, the region is highly susceptible to flooding. The large storage capacity of prairie potholes makes them instrumental in controlling seasonal flooding and thus in protecting productive cropland and rural communities from damage. Furthermore, the slow infiltration afforded by compact, clayey soils allows the potholes to slowly augment ground-water supplies with water that otherwise would leave the area as overland flow.

Glaciation in the Northern Rocky Mountains (fig. 2C) also covered some intermontane basins with glacial till, allowing the formation of pothole wetlands such as the complexes near Ovando and the Ninepipe National Wildlife Refuge. Dams formed by glacial debris created other productive wetland areas, including those associated with Flathead Lake and Lake McDonald. Geologic characteristics play an important role in the water quality of these wetlands. The mountain ground water that interacts with intermontane wetlands generally is less mineralized than prairie ground water, so the water is fresher in intermontane wetlands than in prairie pothole wetlands. However, some intermontane pothole wetlands near Eureka are biologically sterile because slime deposits from glacial rock flour inhibit growth (Reichmuth, 1986).

Intermontane basins are drained by low-gradient, meandering streams and rivers that develop riparian (streamside) wetlands in slackwater deposits behind natural levees, in oxbow lakes formed by meander cutoffs, on islands, below diversions, along shorelines, and on deltas and fans (Reichmuth, 1986). Riparian wetlands are dependent on seasonal flooding for moisture. The frequency and duration of flooding depend on climate, flood-plain elevation, drainage area, channel slope, and soils. The magnitude of flooding and the resultant ground-water levels in the alluvium affect the type and productivity of vegetation in riparian areas. Floodwaters also deposit nutrient-rich sediments and promote anaerobic (oxygen-poor) conditions that make the nutrients available to plants.

Intermontane basins, particularly those in southwestern Montana, are seismically active. For example, regional northwest tilting elevated the northern Gallatin River above the streambeds of its western tributaries, and wetlands have developed in resulting areas of shallow ground water. Another example is a geologically recent uplift that reversed the direction of flow in the upper Red Rock River. The uplift occurred so rapidly that streams have not had sufficient time to cut and deepen channels in response to the new regional gradient. The lack of an integrated drainage system has created large waterlogged areas (Reichmuth, 1986). These areas receive additional inflow from geologic faults, which allow warm ground water to flow toward the land surface, providing excellent wetland habitat for waterfowl. Fault-controlled ground-water flow also is a primary moisture source for wetlands in other intermontane basins.

High-mountain wetlands form in response to geologic, climatic, and even biological forces. In alpine and subalpine zones, where precipitation exceeds evaporation, wetlands persist wherever natural impoundments prevent surface runoff. For example, alpine lakes fill cirques, which are scour holes that glaciers carved below mountain peaks. Below the subalpine zone, sinuous, low-velocity streams drain broad, U-shaped glaciated mountain valleys. Seasonal flooding and high water tables sustain wetlands behind glacial moraines and beaver dams and within low-lying depressions such as oxbow and kettle lakes. Downstream from glaciated valleys, running water has eroded steep, V-shaped valleys that have wetlands along streams and springs and within impoundments created by landslides and beaver dams (Windell and others, 1986).

A recent study of peat-fen (wetlands that have organic soils) hydrology in the headwaters of the Blackfoot River reveals the complexity of water flow through a mountain wetland. Not only does the flow velocity range markedly, from 1.8 to 880 feet per day, but ground water flows both into and out of the wetland. The large range of flow velocities was explained by the extreme variability of peat permeability (Morton and others, 1989).

Some eastern States have taken advantage of the natural filtering capacity of wetlands to mitigate acidic mine drainage. In an attempt to duplicate their success, three artificial wetlands have been constructed to treat acidic mine drainage from abandoned coal mines near Belt, Mont. The artificial wetlands have decreased the concentrations of toxic metals somewhat, but the concentrations still exceed State and Federal water-quality standards, and the discharge remains acidic. These shortcomings are attributable to mechanical problems, freezing in the winter, and, most significantly, extremely acidic, highly mineralized mine discharge that exceeds the treatment capacity of the wetlands. Therefore, wetlands might not provide a viable solution to acidic mine drainage problems in Montana (J.N. Koerth, Montana Department of State Lands, oral commun., 1992.)

TRENDS

Although wetland deterioration can be physical, chemical, or biological, the major concern in Montana is physical loss of wetlands (Montana Department of Health and Environmental Sciences, 1982, 1988, 1992). In its biennial report to the U.S. Environmental Protection Agency (EPA), the Water Quality Bureau stated that, "Precious little is known about Montana wetlands except that they are disappearing" (Montana Department of Health and Environmental Sciences, 1982, p. 3). The Montana Department of Fish, Wildlife and Parks (1992, p. 2) concurs, forecasting that "***a continuing general decline in the wetland base in the State appears most probable." The acreage of wetlands that have been lost is not precisely known, but one estimate is that only 73 percent of the State's predevelopment wetlands remain (Dahl, 1990).

Most losses have been due to conversion of wetlands to croplands, particularly in the prairie pothole region. As of the mid-1980's, about 20,000 acres of prairie in eastern Montana had been artificially drained for agricultural production (Dahl, 1990). Significant losses of wetlands are also attributable to the construction of highways, railroads, dams, large reservoirs, and irrigation systems; soil erosion and siltation; urbanization; recreational development; channelization; mining; logging; oil and gas production; and intensive grazing (Hansen and others, 1988; Montana Department of Fish, Wildlife and Parks, 1992; Windell and others, 1986). Montana wetland losses will become more critical as wetland habitat for breeding and migrating waterfowl diminishes in neighboring States.

Although the decline of wetland acreage continues, the national rate of wetland loss has slowed since protective legislation and educational programs were implemented in the mid-1980's (Dahl and others, 1991). Under that legislation, private organizations and government agencies have created, restored, and protected wetlands throughout Montana. In addition, the construction of reservoirs used for livestock watering, especially in eastern Montana, has improved waterfowl production and has contributed significantly to the wetland base (Montana Department of Fish, Wildlife and Parks, 1992).

Whereas the major wetland concern in Montana is the diminishing quantity, also important is the deteriorating quality of the wetlands that remain. Fertilizers, pesticides, sediments, and salts from farms and ranches, brine from oil-field activities, and saline seeps induced by agricultural practices adversely affect the quality of water in some Montana wetlands (Montana Department of Fish, Wildlife and Parks, 1992; Reiten, 1992; Miller and Bergantino, 1983). A recent drought in Montana also has adversely affected both the quantity and quality of the State's wetlands. Many wetlands have dried up, and evaporation has concentrated dissolved minerals in others.

CONSERVATION

Many government agencies and private organizations participate in wetland conservation in Montana. The most active agencies and organizations and some of their activities are listed in table 1.

Federal wetland activities.—Development activities in Montana wetlands are regulated by several Federal statutory prohibitions and incentives that are intended to slow wetland losses. Some of the more important of these are contained in the 1899 Rivers and Harbors Act; the 1972 Clean Water Act and amendments; the 1985 Food Security Act; the 1990 Food, Agriculture, Conservation, and Trade Act; and the 1986 Emergency Wetlands Resources Act.

Section 10 of the Rivers and Harbors Act gives the U.S. Army Corps of Engineers (Corps) authority to regulate certain activities in navigable waters. Regulated activities include diking, deepening, filling, excavating, and placing of structures. The related section 404 of the Clean Water Act is the most often-used Federal legislation protecting wetlands. Under section 404 provisions, the Corps issues permits regulating the discharge of dredged or fill material into wetlands. Permits are subject to review and possible veto by the EPA, and the FWS has review and advisory roles. Section 401 of the Clean Water Act grants to States and eligible Indian Tribes the authority to approve, apply conditions to, or deny section 404 permit applications on the basis of a proposed activity's probable effects on the water quality of a wetland.

Most farming, ranching, and silviculture activities are not subject to section 404 regulation. However, the "Swampbuster" provi-

Table 1. Selected wetland-related activities of government agencies and private organizations in Montana, 1993

[Source: Classification of activities is generalized from information provided by agencies and organizations. •, agency or organization participates in wetland-related activity; ..., agency or organization does not participate in wetland-related activity. MAN, management; REG, regulation; R&C, restoration and creation; LAN, land acquisition; R&D, research and data collection; D&I, delineation and inventory]

Agency or organization	MAN	REG	R&C	LAN	R&D	D&I
FEDERAL						
Department of Agriculture						
Consolidated Farm Service Agency	...	•	...	...	...	...
Forest Service	•	...	•	...	•	•
Natural Resources Conservation Service	...	•	...	...	•	•
Department of Defense						
Army Corps of Engineers	•	•	•	•	•	•
Military reservations	•	...	...	...	...	...
Department of the Interior						
Bureau of Land Management	•	...	•	•	•	•
Bureau of Reclamation	...	...	•	...	•	...
Fish and Wildlife Service	•	...	•	•	•	•
Geological Survey	...	...	...	...	•	...
National Biological Service	...	...	...	...	•	...
National Park Service	•	...	•	•	•	•
Environmental Protection Agency	...	•	...	...	•	...
TRIBAL						
Confederated Salish and Kootenai Tribes	•	•	•	•	•	•
STATE						
Department of Fish, Wildlife and Parks	•	•	•	•	...	...
Department of Environmental Quality						
Reclamation Division	...	•	•	...	•	•
Water Quality Division	•	•	•	...	•	•
Department of Natural Resources and Conservation						
Forestry Division	...	•	...	...	...	...
Trust Land Management Division	•	•	...	•	...	•
Department of Transportation	•	•	...	...	...	...
Montana Bureau of Mines and Geology	...	...	...	...	•	...
Montana Riparian Association	...	...	...	...	•	•
Natural Resource Information System	...	...	...	...	...	•
LOCAL ORGANIZATIONS						
Conservation Districts	...	•	...	...	...	...
PRIVATE ORGANIZATIONS						
Ducks Unlimited	...	...	•	...	•	...
The Nature Conservancy	•	...	...	•	...	•

sion of the 1985 Food Security Act and amendments in the 1990 Food, Agriculture, Conservation, and Trade Act discourage (through financial disincentives) the draining, filling, or other alteration of wetlands for agricultural use. The law allows exemptions from penalties in some cases, especially if the farmer agrees to restore the altered wetland or other wetlands that have been converted to agricultural use. The Wetlands Reserve Program of the 1990 Food, Agriculture, Conservation, and Trade Act authorizes the Federal Government to purchase conservation easements from landowners who agree to protect or restore wetlands. The Consolidated Farm Service Agency (CFSA) (formerly the Agricultural Stabilization and Conservation Service) administers the Swampbuster provisions and Wetlands Reserve Program. The Natural Resources Conservation Service (formerly the Soil Conservation Service) determines compliance with Swampbuster provisions and assists farmers in the identification of wetlands and in the development of wetland protection, restoration, or creation plans.

The 1986 Emergency Wetlands Resources Act encourages wetland protection through funding incentives. The act requires States to address wetland protection in their Statewide Comprehensive Outdoor Recreation Plans to qualify for Federal funding for State recreational land; the National Park Service provides guidance to States in developing the wetland component of their plans.

Federal agencies are responsible for the proper management of wetlands on public land under their jurisdiction. The Bureau of Land Management manages about 267,000 acres of wetlands and deepwater habitats in Montana, including 9,000 miles of streams (D.K. Hinckley, Bureau of Land Management, oral commun., 1992). The Corps manages the 408,591-acre Fort Peck Lake project area, which includes deepwater and upland habitats, palustrine and lacustrine wetlands, and 1,520 miles of shoreline (L.D. Krueger, U.S. Army Corps of Engineers, oral commun., 1992). The U.S. Forest Service manages 16,806,039 acres in 11 National Forests in Montana (U.S. Forest Service, 1991). The FWS manages 40,590 acres of waterfowl protection areas and 1,066,559 acres of National Wildlife Refuges in Montana, including major wetland complexes at Medicine Lake, Lake Bowdoin, Benton Lake, Lee Metcalf, Red Rock Lakes, Halfbreed, and Ninepipe National Wildlife Refuges. The FWS also holds perpetual easements on 32,100 acres of Montana wetlands. Finally, since 1988, the FWS has involved about 300 Montana landowners in the restoration, enhancement, and creation of about 7,500 wetland acres (J.W. Stutzman and P.H. Hartmann, U.S. Fish and Wildlife Service, oral commun., 1992, 1993). The CFSA administers a Water Bank program in which private landowners agree not to destroy wetlands in return for annual payments. In Montana, about 3,200 wetland acres are protected under this program (Montana Department of Health and Environmental Sciences, 1988).

Tribal wetland activities.—Indian tribes are becoming increasingly involved in wetland programs on reservation lands and ceded territories in Montana. For example, the Confederated Salish and Kootenai Tribes of the Flathead Indian Reservation in western Montana have enacted several ordinances directed at protecting and managing wetlands in their 1.2-million-acre reservation. These include a Tribal Water Quality Ordinance and Shoreline Protection and Aquatic Lands Conservation Ordinances, which enforce a "no net loss" policy. The tribes also have applied for treatment as a State under section 404 of the Clean Water Act and are awaiting action by EPA (S.K. Ball, Confederated Salish and Kootenai Tribes, written commun., 1993).

State wetland activities.—Four State interagency agreements pertain to wetland protection. The Montana Riparian Association is a statewide interagency cooperative that develops riparian ecological classifications to assist in the identification, description, and management of riparian communities, including wetlands (Hansen and others, 1991). The Montana Riparian Education Committee, which is composed of agricultural and conservation organizations

and State and Federal agencies, informs private landowners of the economic benefits and resource values of riparian areas (J.F. Schumaker, Montana Department of Natural Resources and Conservation, written commun., 1992). The Montana Interagency Wetlands Group cooperates to avoid, minimize, or mitigate damage to wetlands that might result from State highway construction. If none of those alternatives is feasible, the group operates a wetland-banking system, which creates new wetlands to replace those that are lost (Montana Department of Fish, Wildlife and Parks, 1992). The North American Waterfowl Management Plan is an agreement between Canada and the United States to reverse recent declines in waterfowl populations. Under the plan, wetlands can be purchased, leased, or protected by easements. Landowners are offered economic incentives for using farming practices that are beneficial to waterfowl. Another component of the plan is the joint venture—a partnership of public and private organizations working toward the common goal of wetland preservation. The U.S. Prairie Pothole Joint Venture is a coalition of Federal and State agencies and private organizations that researches, protects, and enhances prairie wetland and upland habitat in northeastern Montana and four other States that have prairie potholes. Joint ventures are also being planned for the northern Great Plains and the intermontane basins of Montana (Montana Department of Fish, Wildlife and Parks, 1992).

The Montana Department of Fish, Wildlife and Parks has a supporting technical role in all four interagency agreements. As a regulatory agency, the Department administers the Montana Stream Protection Act of 1963, which regulates construction by government agencies along streams, and the U.S. Fish and Wildlife Coordination Act, which regulates Federal activities that might adversely affect wetlands. Also, the Department determines wetland designations for Swampbuster enforcement and assists the FWS with its ongoing wetland inventory. The State Waterfowl Stamp program, with matching funds from Ducks Unlimited, supports the Department efforts to protect, develop, and enhance wetlands and associated upland areas on public and private land. Forty-five State Wildlife Management Areas, including 19 that contain wetlands, also are administered by the Department (Montana Department of Health and Environmental Sciences, 1982).

The Montana Department of Environmental Quality (a new State agency formed July 1, 1995, and composed of parts of the former Departments of Health and Environmental Sciences, Natural Resources and Conservation, and State Lands), administers and enforces State water-quality standards. Although none of the existing standards apply directly to wetlands, the Department is developing enforceable water-quality and biological standards that will be specific to Montana wetlands. This effort, funded by EPA, also includes the development of a State wetlands data base, water-quality and biological monitoring, education, river-corridor management, support for the Montana Riparian Association and wetland banking, and a wetland-protection coordinator. The coordinator is working with other agencies and organizations to develop a State wetland-protection plan (Montana Department of Health and Environmental Sciences, 1992). Until the new standards are approved, section 404 of the Clean Water Act continues to provide the most explicit protection for Montana wetlands. The Department is the State agency that reviews section 404 permit applications and certifies compliance with State water-quality standards. As the permitting agency for hardrock and coal mines, the Department of Environmental Quality enforces compliance with section 404 and requires mitigation of wetland loss in mining areas (S.J. Olsen and B.K. Lovelace, Montana Department of State Lands, oral commun., 1992).

The Montana Department of Natural Resources and Conservation (reorganized July 1, 1995, to include parts of the former Department of Natural Resources and Conservation and the Department of State Lands) manages 5.2 million acres statewide in addition to all land below the low-water level of navigable lakes and streams. An estimate of wetland acreage under Department management is not available. The Department leases about 80,000 acres to the Department of Fish, Wildlife and Parks, the FWS, and The Nature Conservancy; most of the remaining area is leased to individuals and corporations for logging, grazing, and agricultural activities. The Streamside Management Zone Act, which the Department administers, prohibits certain forestry practices along streams, lakes, other water bodies, and adjacent wetlands.

County and local wetland activities.—County conservation districts administer the Natural Streambed and Land Preservation Act of 1975. Districts review applications and issue permits to individuals and other private entities planning activities that may physically alter or modify the bed or immediate banks of a perennial stream. By educating the public and enforcing permit conditions, the Districts minimize impacts to riparian wetlands (J.F. Schumaker, Montana Department of Natural Resources and Conservation, written commun., 1992).

Private wetland activities.—Ducks Unlimited provides funds for State agencies to restore, enhance, and create wetlands in Montana and supports university research of waterfowl ecology (P.M. Bultsma, Ducks Unlimited, oral commun., 1992). The Nature Conservancy manages habitat for the preservation of rare species and ecosystems. Working with private landowners, the Conservancy has established more than 152,000 acres of conservation easements and has acquired more than 15,000 acres of critical habitat statewide. In addition, the Conservancy cooperates with government agencies to assist them in acquiring land. To complement its conservation efforts, the Conservancy coordinates the Natural Heritage Program of the Natural Resource Information System, which maintains a computerized inventory of biological resources (H.S. Zackheim, The Nature Conservancy, oral commun., 1992).

References Cited

Alden, W.C., 1932, Physiography and glacial geology of eastern Montana and adjacent areas: U.S. Geological Survey Professional Paper 174, 133 p.

———1953, Physiography and glacial geology of western Montana and adjacent areas: U.S. Geological Survey Professional Paper 231, 200 p.

Cowardin, L.M., Carter, Virginia, Golet, F.C., and LaRoe, E.T., 1979, Classification of wetlands and deepwater habitats of the United States: U.S. Fish and Wildlife Service Report FWS/OBS–79/31, 131 p.

Dahl, T.E., 1990, Wetlands—Losses in the United States, 1780's to 1980's: Washington, D.C., U.S. Fish and Wildlife Service Report to Congress, 13 p.

Dahl, T.E., Johnson, C.E., and Frayer, W.E., 1991, Wetlands—Status and trends in the conterminous United States, mid-1970's to mid-1980's: Washington, D.C., U.S. Fish and Wildlife Service Report to Congress, 22 p.

Fenneman, N.M., 1946, Physical divisions of the United States: Washington, D.C., U.S. Geological Survey special map, scale 1:7,000,000.

Hansen, P.L., Boggs, K.W., Pfister, R.D., and Joy, John, 1991, Classification and management of riparian and wetland sites in Montana, draft version 1: Missoula, Montana Riparian Association, Montana Forest and Conservation Experiment Station, School of Forestry, University of Montana, 478 p.

Hansen, P.L., Chadde, S.W., and Pfister, R.D., 1988, Riparian dominance types of Montana: University of Montana Miscellaneous Publication 49, p. 9–23.

LaBaugh, J.W., 1989, Chemical characteristics of water in northern prairie wetlands, *in* van der Valk, Arnold, ed., Northern prairie wetlands: Ames, Iowa State University Press, p. 56–91.

Miller, M.R., and Bergantino, R.N., 1983, Distribution of saline seeps in Montana: Montana Bureau of Mines and Geology Hydrogeologic Map 7, 7 p.

Montana Department of Fish, Wildlife and Parks, 1992, 1993 Montana statewide comprehensive outdoor recreation plan, draft section III, Montana wetlands: Helena, Montana Department of Fish, Wildlife and Parks, 8 p.

Montana Department of Health and Environmental Sciences, 1982, Montana water quality, 1982: Helena, Water Quality Bureau, Montana 305(b) Report, 116 p.

———1988, Montana water quality, 1988: Helena, Water Quality Bureau, Montana 305(b) Report, 80 p.

———1992, Montana water quality, 1992: Helena, Water Quality Bureau, Montana 305(b) Report, 42 p.

Morton, R.B., Goering, J.D., and Dollhopf, D.J., 1989, Hydrologic characteristics of a wetland using a bromide tracer, *in* Woessner, W.W., and Potts, D.F., eds., Proceedings of the Symposium on Headwaters Hydrology, Missoula, Mont.: American Water Resources Association Technical Publication Series TPS–89–1, p. 553–562.

Reichmuth, D.R., 1986, Fluvial systems in the wetland environment, *in* Sather, J.H., and Low, Jessop, eds., Proceedings of the Great Basin/ Desert and Montane Regional Wetland Functions Workshop, Logan, Utah, February 27–28, 1986: University of Massachusetts at Amherst, The Environmental Institute Publication 90–4, p. 23–59.

Reiten, J.C., 1992, Water quality of selected lakes in eastern Sheridan County, Montana: Montana Bureau of Mines and Geology Open-File Report MBMG 244, 44 p.

Tiner, R.W., Jr., 1984, Wetlands of the United States—Current status and recent trends: Newton Corner, Mass., U.S. Fish and Wildlife Service, National Wetlands Inventory, 59 p.

U.S. Fish and Wildlife Service, 1954, Wetlands inventory of Montana: Billings, Mont., U.S. Fish and Wildlife Service, Office of River Basin Studies, p. 20.

U.S. Forest Service, 1991, Land areas of the national forest system as of September 30, 1991: U.S. Forest Service Report FS–383, p. 25.

Windell, J.T., Willard, B.E., Cooper, D.J., and others, 1986, An ecological characterization of Rocky Mountain montane and subalpine wetlands: U.S. Fish and Wildlife Service Biological Report 86(11), 298 p.

Winter, T.C., 1989, Hydrologic studies of wetlands in the northern prairie, *in* van der Valk, Arnold, ed., Northern prairie wetlands: Ames, Iowa State University Press, p. 16–55.

FOR ADDITIONAL INFORMATION: District Chief, U.S. Geological Survey, 428 Federal Building, 301 South Park, Drawer 10076, Helena, MT 59626; Regional Wetland Coordinator, U.S. Fish and Wildlife Service, Fish and Wildlife Enhancement, P.O. Box 25486, Denver Federal Center, Denver, CO 80225

Prepared by
Eloise Kendy,
U.S. Geological Survey

Nebraska
Wetland Resources

Although wetlands occupy only 1.9 million acres in Nebraska, or about 4 percent of the State's area (Dahl, 1990), Nebraska's wetland resources are diverse in form, function, and value. Within the State, wetlands range from freshwater to saline and from acidic to alkaline. Many are sustained by ground water, whereas others depend on precipitation and the resulting runoff as a water source (Gersib, 1991).

Wetlands in Nebraska have many functions that are of value to humans. Wetlands control flooding, trap sediment, control erosion, retain nutrients, and sometimes recharge ground water. Wetlands are used recreationally for canoeing, fishing, hunting, and swimming. In addition to being of economic and social value to humans, wetlands are critical to the survival of certain wildlife.

Nebraska has three major wetland complexes of international importance (Gersib, 1991). The Rainwater Basin wetland complex (fig. 1) in south-central and southeastern Nebraska provides staging and migrational habitat for waterfowl and shore birds in the spring. The basins in this complex are focal points in the Central Flyway spring-migration corridor. The Big Bend Reach of the Platte River is a migrational habitat for sandhill cranes and the endangered whooping crane. This reach also is breeding habitat for the endangered least tern and the threatened piping plover. The Sandhills wetland complex in north-central and northwestern Nebraska provides migrational habitat for the whooping crane and bald eagle, as well as migrational and breeding habitat for other nongame birds and waterfowl (Gersib, 1991).

TYPES AND DISTRIBUTION

Wetlands are lands transitional between terrestrial and deepwater habitats where the water table usually is at or near the land surface or the land is covered by shallow water (Cowardin and others, 1979). The distribution of wetlands and deepwater habitats in Nebraska is shown in figure 2*A*; only wetlands are discussed herein.

Wetlands can be vegetated or nonvegetated and are classified on the basis of their hydrology, vegetation, and substrate. In this summary, wetlands are classified according to the system proposed by Cowardin and others (1979), which is used by the U.S. Fish and Wildlife Service (FWS) to map and inventory the Nation's wetlands. At the most general level of the classification system, wetlands are grouped into five ecological systems: Palustrine, Lacustrine, Riverine, Estuarine, and Marine. The Palustrine System includes only wetlands, whereas the other systems comprise wetlands and deepwater habitats. Wetlands of the systems that occur in Nebraska are described below.

System	Wetland description
Palustrine	Wetlands in which vegetation is predominantly trees (forested wetlands); shrubs (scrub-shrub wetlands); persistent or nonpersistent emergent, erect, rooted, herbaceous plants (persistent- and nonpersistent-emergent wetlands); or submersed and (or) floating plants (aquatic beds). Also, intermittently to permanently flooded open-water bodies of less than 20 acres in which water is less than 6.6 feet deep.
Lacustrine	Wetlands within an intermittently to permanently flooded lake or reservoir. Vegetation, when present, is predominantly nonpersistent emergent plants (nonpersistent-emergent wetlands), or submersed and (or) floating plants (aquatic beds), or both.
Riverine	Wetlands within a channel. Vegetation, when present, is same as in the Lacustrine System.

Although the FWS National Wetlands Inventory has wetland acreage statistics for most of the State, there is no statewide estimate of the wetland acreage within each of these systems. Gersib (1991) gives the approximate wetland acreage for six major wetland complexes in Nebraska: the Eastern Saline, the Rainwater Basin, the Missouri River, the Platte River Big Bend Reach, the North Platte River Lower Reach, and the Sandhills (fig. 2*B*). This estimate indicates that of the approximately 1.4 million acres of wetlands inventoried, 85 percent were palustrine, 13 percent were lacustrine, and 2 percent were riverine (Gersib, 1991). Documentation is not adequate for classification of other State wetlands.

HYDROLOGIC SETTING

The distribution of wetlands is determined by physiographic, climatic, and hydrologic factors. The eastern one-fourth of the State is generally characterized by low hills; the remainder is composed of dissected plains, high plains, and sandhills. Nebraska's climate is semiarid in the western part of the State and subhumid in the eastern part. Average annual precipitation from 1951 to 1980 ranged from less than 16 inches in the western panhandle to more than 32 inches in the southeastern corner of the State (Engel and Steele, 1986). Nebraska's average annual free-water-surface evaporation for 1956–70 ranged from about 42 inches in the northeastern part of the State to more than 52 inches in the southwest (Farnsworth and others, 1982). Average annual runoff differs considerably across the State, ranging from less than 1 inch in the west and southwest to about 6 inches in the southeast (Gebert and others, 1985).

Saline marshes (emergent wetlands) characterize the eastern saline wetland complex in southeastern Nebraska. These marshes have developed in areas where sandstone bedrock is at or near the land surface, and saline ground water seeps into streams or flood-

Figure 1. Waterfowl on a wetland in the Rainwater Basin wetland complex in south-central Nebraska at sunrise. This wetland complex is used by 5 to 7 million ducks and geese annually and has lost 78 percent of its original wetland acres. *(Photograph courtesy of the Nebraska Game and Parks Commission.)*

plain depressions (fig. 3A). Although seeps and springs contribute to the concentrations of dissolved solids in the saline marshes, surface runoff from precipitation and flooding along streams provide most of the wetlands' water supply and a substantial part of the dissolved solids (Farrar and Gersib, 1991). Most water loss is due to evapotranspiration, and this process has concentrated the dissolved minerals in the flood-plain soils and wetlands.

In south-central and southeastern Nebraska, overland runoff supplies nearly all water for wetlands within the Rainwater Basin wetland complex (Gilbert, 1989). This part of the State is characterized by nearly level to gently rolling loess plains; within these plains are depressions probably formed by wind erosion. Surface drainage is poorly developed, resulting in numerous closed basins in which all drainage is internal (Gersib, 1991). Most accumulated water is lost through evaporation, but some leaches through underlying materials and may produce chemical precipitates that result in a relatively impermeable layer below the land surface (Nebraska Game and Parks Commission, 1984) (fig. 3B). The water table generally is from 60 to 100 feet below the bottoms of most of these basins (Keech and Dreezen, 1968). The amount of water in the wetlands within the Rainwater Basin complex varies greatly and depends upon the rates of precipitation and evapotranspiration.

In the Missouri River wetland complex, wetlands form in and along the river (on alluvial islands, deep pools, marshes, and shallow-water areas), and isolated wetlands form within oxbows and sloughs that have resulted from high flows that have changed the course of the river. Although shallow aquifers are associated with the Missouri River, the river is fed primarily by overland runoff (Kuzelka and others, 1993). Some water loss in the Missouri River wetlands is the result of evapotranspiration and seepage to the adjacent aquifers; however, much of the wetland loss is due to channelization and flood control along the river.

Along the Platte and North Platte Rivers, wet meadows (emergent wetlands) result from a combination of ground-water seepage, runoff from precipitation and snowmelt, and surface-water diversions and return flows (Hurr, 1983). During spring and early summer, snowmelt supplies water to the river, raising the river stage and causing a corresponding rise in ground-water levels in the adjacent flood plain (fig. 3C). Because of the high water table and surface soils that generally are saturated, precipitation often pools in the wet meadows in sloughs and swales (Currier, 1989). During summer and early fall, river stage is lower because of decreased runoff. Water loss from the associated wet meadows occurs by evapotranspiration and as a result of ground-water withdrawals that lower the water table in the river valley and induce infiltration from the river to the aquifer. Concurrently, water levels within the wet meadows associated with the river decline.

The Sandhills region of north-central and northwestern Nebraska contains the largest sand-dune area in the Western Hemisphere and one of the largest grass-stabilized dune regions in the

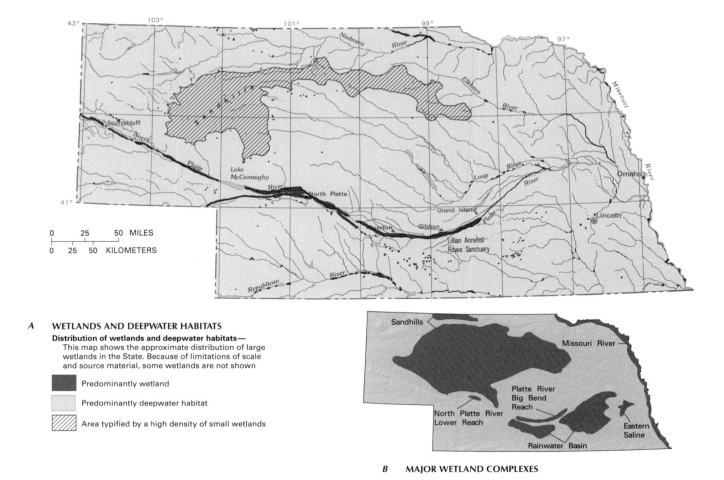

A   WETLANDS AND DEEPWATER HABITATS

Distribution of wetlands and deepwater habitats—
This map shows the approximate distribution of large wetlands in the State. Because of limitations of scale and source material, some wetlands are not shown

　　Predominantly wetland

　　Predominantly deepwater habitat

　　Area typified by a high density of small wetlands

B   MAJOR WETLAND COMPLEXES

Figure 2.   Distribution of wetlands and deepwater habitats and major wetland complexes in Nebraska. **A**, Distribution of wetlands and deepwater habitats. **B**, Major wetland complexes. *(Sources: A, T.E. Dahl, U.S. Fish and Wildlife Service, unpub. data, 1991. B, Gersib, 1991.)*

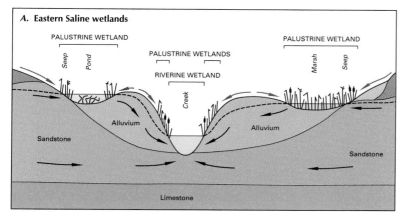

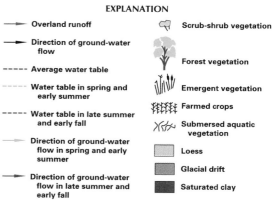

A. Eastern Saline wetlands

B. Rainwater Basin

C. Platte River wetlands

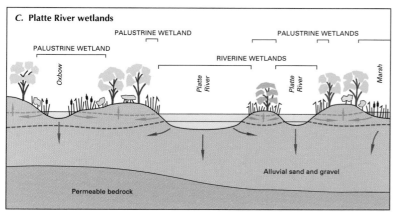

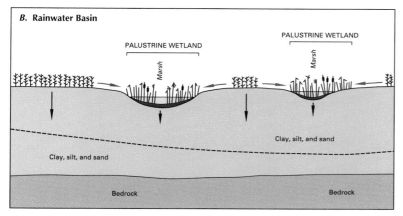

D. Sandhills

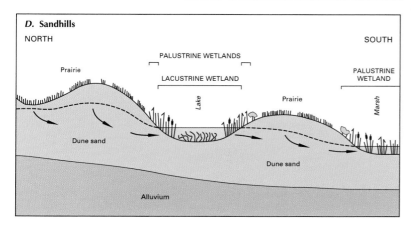

EXPLANATION

→ Overland runoff	Scrub-shrub vegetation
→ Direction of ground-water flow	Forest vegetation
----- Average water table	Emergent vegetation
----- Water table in spring and early summer	Farmed crops
----- Water table in late summer and early fall	Submersed aquatic vegetation
→ Direction of ground-water flow in spring and early summer	Loess
→ Direction of ground-water flow in late summer and early fall	Glacial drift
	Saturated clay

Figure 3. Generalized geohydrology of wetlands within Nebraska. *A*, Eastern Saline wetlands. *B*, Rainwater Basin. *C*, Platte River wetlands. *D*, Sandhills.

world (Bleed and Flowerday, 1990). Sandhill wetlands include wet meadows, where the water table is at or near the land surface, marshes that are associated with area lakes and often contain standing water, and permanent lakes. Most of the lakes are 10 acres or less in area, average about 5 feet in depth (McCarraher, 1977), and are considered palustrine wetlands according to the classification system used by the FWS.

In the central and eastern parts of the Sandhills, lakes and marshes typically are slightly alkaline, are in hydrologic connection with the ground water, and commonly have suface outlets (Ginsberg, 1985). Many wetlands in the western Sandhills are strongly alkaline and have little or no surface outflow. LaBaugh (1986) and Winter (1986) have shown that these lakes, in addition to being maintained by overland runoff, also are interconnected with the ground-water system (fig. 3*D*). Lakes that have high alkalinity are found in areas where the ground water becomes mineralized as it moves through the rock formations. Where water circulation is impeded and the water table intersects the land surface, the concentration of total dissolved solids is increased by the high rate of evaporation in this region (Hem, 1985). The physical, chemical, and biological interactions of the marshes and wet meadows are largely unknown (Bleed and Flowerday, 1990).

TRENDS

From 1780 to 1980, Nebraska lost about 1 million acres, or about 35 percent of the State's original wetlands (Dahl, 1990). Agricultural conversions that involved draining, clearing, leveling, and ground-water pumping were the principal causes of these losses. Losses also were caused by construction of impoundments and large reservoirs, urbanization, road construction, and other activities.

The Rainwater Basin, used by 5 to 7 million ducks and geese annually, has lost an estimated 78 percent of its original acreage (Nebraska Game and Parks Commission, 1984). In the Sandhills, agricultural conversions account for the loss of 28,000 acres, or 15 percent, of the original wetlands in that area

(Nebraska Game and Parks Commission, 1972).

Channelization of the Missouri River has enabled agricultural, urban, and industrial development of its flood plain, including the wetland areas. Wetland losses in the unchannelized reaches of the Missouri River also have been substantial owing to operation of dams on the main stem.

Williams (1978) showed that the North Platte and Platte Rivers have had channel-width decreases of 80 to 90 percent from the Wyoming–Nebraska State line to Overton between 1860 and 1965. From Overton to Grand Island, channel-width reductions of 60 to 70 percent have occurred.

CONSERVATION

Many government agencies and private organizations participate in wetland conservation in Nebraska. The most active agencies and organizations and some of their activities are listed in table 1.

Federal wetland activities.—Development activities in Nebraska wetlands are regulated by several Federal statutory prohibitions and incentives that are intended to slow wetland losses. Some of the more important of these are contained in the 1899 Rivers and Harbors Act; the 1972 Clean Water Act and amendments; the 1985 Food Security Act; the 1990 Food, Agriculture, Conservation, and Trade Act; and the 1986 Emergency Wetlands Resources Act.

Section 10 of the Rivers and Harbors Act gives the U.S. Army Corps of Engineers (Corps) authority to regulate certain activities in navigable waters. Regulated activities include diking, deepening, filling, excavating, and placing of structures. The related section 404 of the Clean Water Act is the most often-used Federal legislation protecting wetlands. Under section 404 provisions, the Corps issues permits regulating the discharge of dredged or fill material into wetlands. Permits are subject to review and possible veto by the U.S. Environmental Protection Agency (EPA), and the FWS has review and advisory roles. Section 401 of the Clean Water Act grants to States and eligible Indian Tribes the authority to approve, apply conditions to, or deny section 404 permit applications on the basis of a proposed activity's probable effects on the water quality of a wetland.

Most farming, ranching, and silviculture activities are not subject to section 404 regulation. However, the "Swampbuster" provision of the 1985 Food Security Act and amendments in the 1990 Food, Agriculture, Conservation, and Trade Act discourage (through financial disincentives) the draining, filling, or other alteration of wetlands for agricultural use. The law allows exemptions from penalties in some cases, especially if the farmer agrees to restore the altered wetland or other wetlands that have been converted to agricultural use. The Wetlands Reserve Program of the 1990 Food, Agriculture, Conservation, and Trade Act authorizes the Federal Government to purchase conservation easements from landowners who agree to protect or restore wetlands. The Consolidated Farm Service Agency (formerly the Agricultural Stabilization and Conservation Service) administers the Swampbuster provisions and Wetlands Reserve Program. The Natural Resources Conservation Service (formerly the Soil Conservation Service) determines compliance with Swampbuster provisions and assists farmers in the identification of wetlands and in the development of wetland protection, restoration, or creation plans.

The 1986 Emergency Wetlands Resources Act encourages wetland protection through funding incentives. The act requires States to address wetland protection in their Statewide Comprehensive Outdoor Recreation Plans to qualify for Federal funding for State recreational land; the National Park Service (NPS) provides guidance to States in developing the wetland component of their plans.

In addition to regulatory responsibilities, the EPA provides financial assistance for special studies, development of wetland in-

Table 1. Selected wetland-related activities of government agencies and private organizations in Nebraska, 1993

[Source: Classification of activities is generalized from information provided by agencies and organizations. •, agency or organization participates in wetland-related activity; ..., agency or organization does not participate in wetland-related activity. MAN, management; REG, regulation; R&C, restoration and creation; LAN, land acquisition; R&D, research and data collection; D&I, delineation and inventory]

Agency or organization	MAN	REG	R&C	LAN	R&D	D&I
FEDERAL						
Department of Agriculture						
Consolidated Farm Service Agency	...	•	...	...	...	...
Forest Service	•	...	•	•	•	•
Natural Resources Conservation Service	...	•	•	...	...	...
Department of Defense						
Army Corps of Engineers	•	•	•	•	•	•
Department of the Interior						
Bureau of Land Management	...	...	...	...	•	•
Bureau of Reclamation	...	...	•	•	•	•
Fish and Wildlife Service	...	...	•	•	•	•
Geological Survey	...	...	...	...	•	...
National Biological Service	...	...	...	...	•	...
National Park Service	...	...	...	...	•	...
Environmental Protection Agency	...	...	•	...	•	•
STATE						
Department of Environmental Quality	...	...	•	...	•	•
Department of Roads	...	...	•	•	•	...
Department of Water Resources	...	...	•	...	...	...
Forest Service	...	...	...	...	...	...
Game and Parks Commission	•	...	•	•	•	•
Natural Resources Commission	...	...	...	...	•	...
Water Resources Center	...	...	...	...	•	...
University of Nebraska						
Conservation and Survey Division	...	...	...	...	•	•
Other State-university programs	...	...	...	...	•	...
COUNTY AND LOCAL						
Some county and local governments	...	•	...	•	•	•
Natural Resources Districts	•	...	•	•	•	...
PRIVATE ORGANIZATIONS						
Ducks Unlimited	•	...	•	•	•	...
Nebraska Audubon Society	•	...	...	...	•	•
Platte River Whooping Crane Habitat Maintenance Trust, Inc.	•	...	•	•	•	•
Preserve Our Water Resources Association	...	...	...	...	•	•
The Nature Conservancy	•	...	•	•	•	•

ventories, and other resource-management tools. Technical assistance is available for wetland-delineation training, project consultation, and public education. The EPA oversees the development and implementation of water-quality standards that apply to surface waters, including wetlands, and a nonpoint-source pollution-control program that can include the restoration and maintenance of wetlands.

Other Federal agencies have active nonregulatory wetland policies. The U.S. Forest Service (FS) is involved primarily in research of riparian wetlands and in managing wetlands in the national forests in Nebraska. In addition, the FS is developing a program to integrate livestock grazing and wetland maintenance and is working with Ducks Unlimited, a private conservation organization, to develop habitat for waterfowl.

The Bureau of Land Management (BLM) manages 6,600 acres of public land in Nebraska. Some of these lands have been inventoried, and none have been identified as wetlands. If wetland areas are identified on BLM-administered lands, appropriate management actions and protective requirements for wetland habitats will be applied (Bureau of Land Management, 1992).

The Bureau of Reclamation (BOR) mitigates for degraded or destroyed wetlands through restoration of degraded wetlands and creation of new wetlands. The BOR, as stated in their wetland initiative, is responsible for the management of wetland resources that occur on Federal property purchased for project purposes.

State wetland activities. — Nebraska has no laws specifically for the protection of wetlands. The Nebraska Department of Environmental Quality is responsible for the Clean Water Act section 401 certification process, which considers the effects of dredge or fill activities on water quality to determine compliance with State water-quality standards. An antidegradation clause within the standards protects present water-quality conditions and has been applied to wetlands.

The Nebraska Department of Roads must identify wetlands that might be degraded by road construction. If wetland degradation or destruction is unavoidable, the Department must, through the process of mitigation, restore former wetlands or create new wetlands. A mitigation bank for use by the Nebraska Department of Roads is being developed with the Corps, the FWS, the EPA, the Nebraska Game and Parks Commission, and the Nebraska Department of Environmental Quality.

The Nebraska Game and Parks Commission's involvement in wetlands includes the acquisition, restoration, and management of State-owned wetlands. The Commission also provides technical assistance for wetlands management to private owners and sponsors the Wetland Initiative Program. The Commission acts as an advisory agency for the section 404 permit process administered by the Corps. As a nonregulatory agency, the Commission has inventoried wetlands within the State but is not involved with the delineation of wetlands. The Nebraska Natural Heritage data base, now administered by the Commission, is the only existing comprehensive system for identifying the ecologically significant components of Nebraska's natural diversity (Clausen and others, 1989).

The Nebraska Department of Water Resources regulates construction in wetland areas through the flood-plain permit process within counties that do not assert jurisdiction. The Department also conducts wetland research, data collection, and education. Other State agencies that are involved in these activities are the Nebraska Natural Resources Commission, the Nebraska Forest Service, the Nebraska Water Resources Center, and the Conservation and Survey Division of the University of Nebraska.

County and local wetland activities. — Some county and local governments regulate construction in wetlands through flood-plain permits. The Nebraska Natural Resources Districts also are involved in conservation at the local level. The roles of the Districts differ with location. Many participate in the Wildlife Habitat Improvement Program, a cooperative program with the Nebraska Game and Parks Commission. Other Districts are active in wetland acquisition, restoration, creation, and management.

Private wetland activities. — Within Nebraska, numerous private organizations are involved in wetlands. The Nebraska chapter of The Nature Conservancy has purchased 1,750 acres of land at four different sites in the Platte River Big Bend Reach wetlands complex and about 500 acres within the Rainwater Basin wetlands complex. The Nature Conservancy and the Platte River Whooping Crane Habitat Maintenance Trust, Inc., a private organization, cooperatively manage most of that land.

Between 1979 and 1992, the Platte River Whooping Crane Habitat Maintenance Trust, Inc., acquired 8,600 acres of habitat in and along the Platte River; 1,200 acres are under perpetual conservation easement. The Trust's principal charge is the acquisition and management of wildlife habitat, but it also has the authority to conduct research and acquire interests in water and has the responsibility to protect the biologic and hydrologic integrity of the habitat.

The National Audubon Society owns and manages wetlands in Nebraska, including the 1,200-acre Lillian Annette Rowe Sanctuary near Gibbon. Local chapters of the National Audubon Society have diversified involvement in wetlands. Many chapters have wetland-education and wetland-identification programs but generally do not own or manage wetlands.

Ducks Unlimited has cooperative programs with government agencies and private organizations and will provide as much as 50-percent cost-share funding for wetland acquisition and development. Ducks Unlimited also is active in the creation and restoration of wetlands on land owned by the organization.

The Preserve Our Water Resources Association promotes the restoration and creation of wetlands and monitors the success of mitigation. Other private organizations participating in wetland activities include the Nebraska Sierra Club, The Nebraska Wildlife Federation, and Pheasants Forever.

References Cited

Bleed, Ann, and Flowerday, Charles, eds., 1990, An atlas of the Sand Hills: University of Nebraska, Conservation and Survey Division, Resource Atlas No. 5a, 265 p.

Bureau of Land Management, 1992, Nebraska record of decision and approved resource management plan: Bureau of Land Management Report BLM/WY/ES–92/010+4410, 51 p.

Clausen, Mary, Fritz, Mike, and Steinauer, Gerry, 1989, The Nebraska natural heritage program—Two-year progress report: Lincoln, Nebraska Natural Heritage Program, 154 p.

Cowardin, L.M., Carter, Virginia, Golet, F.C., and LaRoe, E.T., 1979, Classification of wetlands and deepwater habitats of the United States: U.S. Fish and Wildlife Service Report FWS/OBS–79/31, 131 p.

Currier, P.J., 1989, Plant species composition and groundwater levels in a Platte River wet meadow, *in* Bragg, T.B. and Stubbendieck, James, eds., Proceedings of the 11th North American Prairie Conference, Lincoln, Nebr., August 7–11, 1988: Lincoln, University of Nebraska, p. 19–24.

Dahl, T.E., 1990, Wetlands—Losses in the United States, 1780's to 1980's: Washington, D.C., U.S. Fish and Wildlife Service Report to Congress, 13 p.

Engel, G.B., and Steele, E.K., Jr., 1986, Nebraska surface-water resources, *in* U.S. Geological Survey, National water summary 1985—Hydrologic events and surface-water resources: U.S. Geological Survey Water-Supply Paper 2300, p. 315–322.

Farnsworth, R.K., Thompson, E.S., and Peck, E.L., 1982, Evaporation atlas for the contiguous 48 United States: National Oceanic and Atmospheric Administration Technical Report NWS 33, 27 p.

Farrar, Jon, and Gersib, Richard, 1991, Nebraska salt marshes—Last of the least: Lincoln, Nebraska Game and Parks Commission, 23 p.

Gebert, W.A., Graczyk, D.J., and Krug, W.R., 1985, Average annual runoff in the United States, 1951–80: U.S. Geological Survey Open-File Report 85–627, scale 1:2,000,000.

Gersib, R.A., 1991, Nebraska wetlands priority plan for inclusion in The 1991–1995 Nebraska State Comprehensive Outdoor Recreation Plan: Lincoln, Nebraska Game and Parks Commission, 35 p.

Gilbert, M.C., 1989, Ordination and mapping of wetland communities in Nebraska's Rainwater Basin region, CEMRO Environmental Report 89–1: Omaha, U.S. Army Corps of Engineers, 105 p.

Ginsberg, Marilyn, 1985, Nebraska's sandhills lakes—A hydrogeologic overview: Water Resources Bulletin, v. 21, no. 4, p. 573–578.

Hem, J.D., 1985, Study and interpretation of the chemical characteristics of natural water (3d ed.): U.S. Geological Survey Water-Supply Paper 2254, 263 p.

Hurr, R.T., 1983, Ground-water hydrology of the Mormon Island Crane Meadows Wildlife Area near Grand Island, Hall County, Nebraska: U.S. Geological Survey Professional Paper 1277–H, 12 p.

Keech, C.F., and Dreezen, V.H., 1968, Geology and ground-water resources of Fillmore county, Nebraska: U.S. Geological Survey Water-Supply Paper 1839–L, 27 p.

Kuzelka, R.D., Flowerday, C.A., Manley, R.N., Rundquist, B.C., and Herrin, S.J., 1993, Flat water—A history of Nebraska and its water: University of Nebraska, Conservation and Survey Division, Resource Report No. 12, 292 p.

LaBaugh, J.W., 1986, Limnological characteristics of selected lakes in the Nebraska sandhills, U.S.A., and their relation to chemical characteristics of adjacent ground water: Journal of Hydrology, v. 86, no. 3/4, p. 279–298.

McCarraher, D.B., 1977, Nebraska's sandhills lakes: Lincoln, Nebraska

Game and Parks Commission, 67 p.

Nebraska Game and Parks Commission, 1972, Survey of habitat: Lincoln, Nebraska Game and Parks Commission, Workplan K–71, 78 p.

_____1984, Survey of habitat: Lincoln, Nebraska Game and Parks Commission Workplan K–83, 13 p.

Williams, G.P., 1978, The case of the shrinking channels—The North Platte and Platte Rivers in Nebraska: U.S. Geological Survey Circular 781, 48 p.

Winter, T.C., 1986, Effect of ground-water recharge on configuration of the water table beneath sand dunes and on seepage in lakes in the sandhills of Nebraska, U.S.A.: Journal of Hydrology, v. 86, no. 3/4, p. 221–237.

FOR ADDITIONAL INFORMATION: District Chief, U.S. Geological Survey, Room 406, Federal Building, 100 Centennial Mall North, Lincoln, NE 68508; Regional Wetland Coordinator, U.S. Fish and Wildlife Service, Fish and Wildlife Enhancement, P.O. Box 25486, Denver Federal Center, Denver, CO 80225

Prepared by
Jill D. Frankforter,
U.S. Geological Survey

Nevada
Wetland Resources

Wetlands cover less than 1 percent of Nevada but are some of the most economically and ecologically valuable lands in the State. Wetlands provide important habitat for the State's fish and wildlife. In Nevada, riparian (streamside) wetlands and large marshes provide stopover and breeding grounds for migratory waterfowl. Many of Nevada's threatened and endangered species inhabit wetlands. Other important functions of wetlands include flood attenuation, bank stabilization, and water-quality improvement (fig. 1). Economic benefits, such as recreational activities, are abundant in Nevada's wetland areas and include hunting, fishing, boating, bird watching, photography, and camping. Other economic benefits of wetlands and associated lands include grazing and mining. Wetland vegetation generally is more lush than that in surrounding uplands, so it is desirable for grazing of cattle or sheep. Mining of placer gold and silver deposits in riparian wetlands has been a profitable venture in parts of Nevada but not without negative effects on wetland resources. Economic-grade uranium deposits are present in alpine peat bogs and fens in the Sierra Nevada but have not been exploited.

TYPES AND DISTRIBUTION

Wetlands are lands transitional between terrestrial and deepwater habitats where the water table usually is at or near the land surface or the land is covered by shallow water (Cowardin and others, 1979). The distribution of wetlands and deepwater habitats in Nevada is shown in figure 2A; only wetlands are discussed herein.

Wetlands can be vegetated or nonvegetated and are classified on the basis of their hydrology, vegetation, and substrate. In this summary, wetlands are classified according to the system proposed by Cowardin and others (1979), which is used by the U.S. Fish and Wildlife Service (FWS) to map and inventory the Nation's wetlands. At the most general level of the classification system, wetlands are grouped into five ecological systems: Palustrine, Lacustrine, Riverine, Estuarine, and Marine. The Palustrine System includes only wetlands, whereas the other systems comprise wetlands and deepwater habitats. Wetlands of the systems that occur in Nevada are described below.

System	Wetland description
Palustrine	Wetlands in which vegetation is predominantly trees (forested wetlands); shrubs (scrub-shrub wetlands); persistent or nonpersistent emergent, erect, rooted, herbaceous plants (persistent- and nonpersistent-emergent wetlands); or submersed and (or) floating plants (aquatic beds). Also, intermittently to permanently flooded open-water bodies of less than 20 acres in which water is less than 6.6 feet deep.
Lacustrine	Wetlands within an intermittently to permanently flooded lake or reservoir. Vegetation, when present, is predominantly nonpersistent emergent plants (nonpersistent-emergent wetlands), or submersed and (or) floating plants (aquatic beds), or both.
Riverine	Wetlands within a channel. Vegetation, when present, is same as in the Lacustrine System.

Nevada had about 236,350 acres of wetlands in the mid-1980's, according to an inventory by the FWS (Dahl, 1990). However, wetland acreage available as bird and fish habitat varies considerably from wet years to dry years, as detailed by Hoffman and others

(1990) for wetlands in Lahontan Valley. Palustrine and lacustrine wetlands constitute most of the State's wetland acreage. Forested, scrub-shrub, and emergent wetlands are the most common types of palustrine wetlands. Riparian wetlands are mostly forested and scrub-shrub types.

The Bureau of Land Management (BLM) administers almost 48 million acres of land in Nevada, of which approximately 75,000 acres are riparian-wetland habitat (Bureau of Land Management, 1991). More than 2,100 miles of riparian-stream habitat are present on BLM land in Nevada. Some of the largest areas of riparian wetlands are along the Humboldt River and the upper part of the White River. Large marshes, such as Stillwater Marsh (33,400 acres) and Humboldt Marsh (58,000 acres) and those on Carson Lake (25,600 acres) and Ruby and Franklin Lakes (20,000 acres combined), are mostly scrub-shrub and emergent wetlands. Many of the basins in Nevada contain playa and wet-meadow wetlands; these are especially common in the northwestern part of the State. Some of the largest playas are in the Black Rock Desert in northwestern Nevada, Spring Valley in eastern Nevada, Railroad Valley in south-central Nevada, Smoke Creek Desert in northwestern Nevada, Carson Sink in west-central Nevada, Winnemucca Lake in northwestern Nevada, and Clayton Valley in southwestern Nevada. Pyramid Lake, Lake Tahoe, Walker Lake, Lake Mead (a reservoir), and many smaller reservoirs contain most of the nonplaya lacustrine wetlands. Riverine wetlands make up only a small percentage of the wetland acreage in the State.

HYDROLOGIC SETTING

Wetlands in Nevada are limited to areas where there is a persistent water supply at or near land surface. The location and persistence of water supply is a function of several interrelated factors, including climate, physiography, and hydrology.

In Nevada, precipitation (fig. 2B) and runoff (fig. 2C) have wide ranges in values annually, seasonally, and areally (Moosburner, 1986). Nevada, the most arid State in the Nation, has average annual precipitation values ranging from more than 16 inches in the Sierra Nevada and other high mountain ranges to less than 4 inches

Figure 1. Wetland in Carson Valley, about 5 miles south of Carson City. This wetland was constructed to receive treated sewage effluent from Incline Village in the Lake Tahoe Basin and to function as a nutrient-removal system for the effluent before discharge into the Carson River. View looking southwest, with Sierra Nevada in background, 1993. *(Photograph by Michael S. Lico, U.S. Geological Survey.)*

near Fallon and in the Las Vegas area. Runoff in the spring and early summer is mostly a result of snowmelt and is greatest in the mountain areas. Occasional summer thunderstorms can create large amounts of runoff, although these storms generally are localized.

Evaporation, which removes water that could potentially form wetlands, is greatest in the lower altitudes and southern part of the State (fig. 2D). The lowest yearly evaporation is in the Sierra Nevada and other high mountain ranges. Large tracts of land in the basin areas have high evaporation rates, as much as 80 inches per year in the lowlands near the Colorado River (Moosburner, 1986).

Potential evaporation exceeds precipitation in most of Nevada, the exceptions being in the high mountain areas, creating a water deficit that inhibits wetland development. The existence of fens (emergent wetlands that have organic soil) in high mountain valleys and the paucity of them in lower altitude basins attests to their dependence on abundant water from precipitation. However, steep topography and shifting stream channels prevent the formation of fens in many areas where adequate water is present.

In most of the basins in Nevada, wetlands are associated with discharge areas. Ground water commonly discharges from springs and seeps along the fault-bounded basins and creates wetlands. Water for the Ruby Lake wetlands (fig. 2A) is mostly from spring discharge. Playa lakes, where wetlands are maintained by water from the typically shallow water table, are another common setting for wetlands. Wetlands also are present at the discharge points of regional ground-water flow systems, where springs commonly

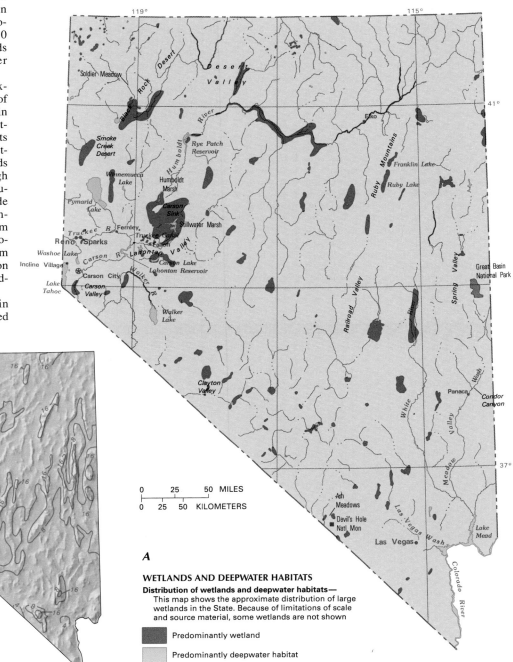

A

WETLANDS AND DEEPWATER HABITATS

Distribution of wetlands and deepwater habitats—
This map shows the approximate distribution of large wetlands in the State. Because of limitations of scale and source material, some wetlands are not shown

◾ Predominantly wetland

▢ Predominantly deepwater habitat

B

PRECIPITATION

—16— **Line of average annual precipitation — Interval, in inches, is variable**

Figure 2. Wetland distribution in Nevada and physical and climatological features that control wetland distribution in the State. *A*, Distribution of wetlands and deepwater habitats. *B*, Annual precipitation. *(Sources: A, T.E. Dahl, U.S. Fish and Wildlife Service, unpub. data, 1991; B, Moosburner, 1986.)*

discharge large volumes of ground water. An example of this hydrologic setting is the Ash Meadows wetlands (Winograd and Thordarson, 1975).

In the high mountain areas of the State, wetlands commonly form in glaciated valleys. Glacially scoured valleys commonly have large cirque basins where remnant glaciers or semipermanent snow fields supply water for wetlands. Many of these cirque basins have lakes (tarns) that provide wetland habitat. Below the cirque basins, the glaciated mountain valleys typically are steep sided, U-shaped, and have relatively flat floors with low-gradient streams. Wetlands form on the valley floors in cut-off meander channels (oxbows), behind glacial moraines, in small kettle holes, and behind beaver dams.

Riparian wetlands are present along most of the perennial streams in Nevada. These wetlands occur along natural streambanks and constructed channels. Annual flushing of stream channels and wetlands by spring floods has been attenuated largely by diversion for irrigation, stream channelization, and construction of dams. However, constructed water bodies such as reservoirs, canals, and agricultural drains are common settings for wetland formation. As an example of an artificially maintained wetland system, leakage from a canal near Fernley raised the water table until drainage ditches had to be dug to lower the water table for efficient crop growth. The water in these ditches flows to a State Wildlife Area where wetlands are present near the channels and impoundments.

Most wetlands are maintained by a shallow water table. The water-table altitude depends on several factors, among which are geology, topography, soil characteristics, water supply, pumpage, and local hydrology. Irrigation of land for agriculture commonly results in a rise of the water table, which can create wetlands. The Newlands (irrigation) Project near Fallon in western Nevada has caused the water table in parts of Lahontan Valley to rise by as much as 30 to 60 feet (Rush, 1972; R.L. Seiler, U.S. Geological Survey,

written commun., 1993); this water-table rise has resulted in the formation of small wetlands throughout the valley.

Wetlands can be formed by other human activities. Dewatering—more than 23,000 acre-feet in 1991—of a large open-pit mine in Desert Valley in northern Nevada has created a lush wetland of 3,500 acres that is being used by increasing numbers of waterfowl. In Carson Valley, about 900 acres of wetlands have been created by constructing cells (diked impoundments) and filling them with treated sewage effluent from the Lake Tahoe Basin (fig. 1). The area has become a popular duck-hunting site.

Stillwater Marsh is an important wetland complex in the Pacific Flyway. Archeological evidence indicates that as much as 5,000 years ago humans used the marsh for food resources (Hoffman and others, 1990). Because of the importance of Stillwater Marsh and other Lahontan Valley wetlands to migratory birds, the area has been classified as a Hemispheric Reserve within the Western Hemispheric Shorebird Reserve Network (WHSRN) by the WHSRN Council. Lahontan Valley supports about 75 percent of the ducks, 50 percent of the Canada geese, and 65 percent of the tundra swans in the State. Between 30 and 50 percent of the Pacific Flyway canvasback ducks stop in Lahontan Valley in the fall.

Stillwater Marsh is located at the terminus of the Carson River, which flowed freely to the wetlands until the Newlands Project was constructed in the early 1900's. Annual springtime floods flushed the wetlands and removed accumulated mineral salts, leaving a prime freshwater marsh. Currently, most of the water flowing to Stillwater Marsh is irrigation drainage that has high concentrations of arsenic, boron, selenium, and other toxic constituents (Lico, 1992). Owing to the highly regulated nature of the irrigation system, springtime floods are uncommon, and no mechanism exists to remove salts from the marsh. Presently, Stillwater Marsh would require large volumes of freshwater to reduce the salinity and concentrations of several toxic constituents that have been implicated

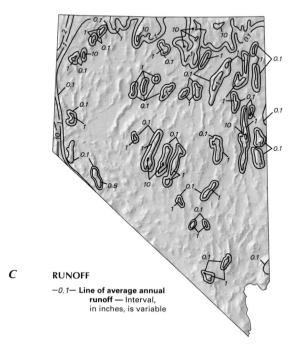

C   RUNOFF

—0.1— **Line of average annual
   runoff** — Interval,
   in inches, is variable

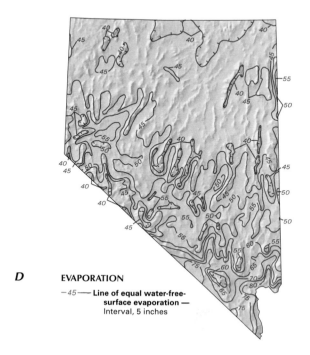

D   EVAPORATION

—45— **Line of equal water-free-
   surface evaporation** —
   Interval, 5 inches

Figure 2.   Continued.   Wetland distribution in Nevada and physical and climatological features that control wetland distribution in the State.   **C**, Annual runoff.   **D**, Annual free-water-surface (lake) evaporation.   *(Sources: C, Moosburner, 1986;   D, Farnsworth and others, 1982.)*

in the deaths and low reproduction rates of waterfowl (Hoffman and others, 1990; Lico, 1992). Volumes of irrigation return flow will be further reduced when the Newlands Project implements operating criteria adopted by the Bureau of Reclamation [(BOR)1987]. Recent drought has severely affected Stillwater Marsh, leaving only a few hundred acres of water surface for waterfowl use. In 1990, Public Law 101–618 was passed by Congress, authorizing the FWS to purchase water rights from willing sellers within the Newlands Project area and use the water for maintenance of wildlife habitat. The Nevada Department of Wildlife and The Nature Conservancy are assisting FWS in this "water-buyout program."

Ash Meadows wetlands, in southern Nevada, are administered by the FWS and are the sole habitat for 33 plant and animal species (U.S. Fish and Wildlife Service, 1990). The wetlands are home for three species of endangered pupfish and one species of speckled dace. These unique wetlands are a result of ground water from a regional carbonate-rock aquifer discharging through lake-bed deposits to a series of springs along a fault contact. More than 17,000 acre-feet of water discharges from these springs annually (Winograd and Thordarson, 1975). Devils Hole National Monument, administered by the National Park Service (NPS), is included in this group of wetlands but is unique in that it occupies a solution cavern in the carbonate-rock aquifer. The Devils Hole pupfish, an endangered species, is found only within this small pool (U.S. Fish and Wildlife Service, 1990).

Carson Valley, in western Nevada, is the setting for wetlands of a different nature. Incline Village, in the Lake Tahoe Basin, exports all of its treated sewage effluent to Carson Valley by way of a pipeline. Before 1984, the effluent was discharged into the Carson River at the northern end of the valley. In 1975, the U.S. Environmental Protection Agency (EPA) issued a more stringent discharge permit; as a result, several diked impoundments were constructed to hold the sewage effluent, creating a 900-acre site with 140 acres of permanent wetlands. The area now provides nesting habitat for waterfowl and recreational opportunities for residents of the area.

Ruby Lake wetlands are east of the Ruby Mountains in northeastern Nevada (fig. 2A). The FWS operates and maintains a 37,600-acre National Wildlife Refuge there, which includes the marsh and surrounding area. During a year of average precipitation, more than 13,000 acres of bird and fish habitat are present in the spring, declining to about 11,000 acres in the fall. Water for the wetlands is provided mostly by the discharge of many springs at the base of the Ruby Mountains. This discharge is proportional to the amount of snowpack in the mountains (Jeff Mackay, U.S. Fish and Wildlife Service, written commun., 1992). More than 200 species of birds regularly use the wetlands for nesting, feeding, or stopover during migration periods. In some years, more than 6,000 ducks, mostly redheads and canvasbacks, have hatched at the marsh.

TRENDS

The FWS has estimated that, from the 1780's to the 1980's, 52 percent of Nevada's wetlands were lost (Dahl, 1990). In terms of area, that represents a loss of about 251,000 acres of wetlands during settlement of the State. Conversion of wetlands to cropland and diversion of water for agricultural and urban purposes are the primary reasons for this loss of wetlands. A large part of the flow in major rivers within the State (Carson, Humboldt, Truckee, and Walker) has been diverted for irrigation, leaving insufficient quantities of water for wetland maintenance. Riparian wetlands have been drastically affected by a variety of human activities. The BLM, which administers approximately 2,100 miles of riparian stream habitat in the State, has reported that more than 80 percent of that habitat is in poor condition (Nevada Department of Conservation and Natural Resources, 1988). In the same report, the U.S. Forest Service (FS) estimated that 53 percent of the riparian wetlands under its jurisdiction are in fair to poor condition. The primary reason for

the poor quality of the riparian wetland habitat is overgrazing of cattle on Federal land (Bureau of Land Management, 1992). The BLM has formal plans for improving the condition of wetlands under its jurisdiction (Bureau of Land Management, 1991). Urban development, particularly near Reno, has adversely affected wetlands; detrimental activities include building directly on filled wetlands, draining of wetlands, channelization of creeks and rivers, and contamination of wetlands by inadequately treated sewage and industrial waste. Las Vegas Wash contains wetlands that are threatened by treated municipal sewage effluent, industrial chemicals, and erosion.

According to Thompson and Merritt (1988), 82 percent of wetlands have been lost in western Nevada. They document the loss of two National Wildlife Refuges and the decreasing quality of the remaining wetlands. Historical accounts by Captain J.H. Simpson in 1859 of conditions before irrigation read as follows: "Carson Lake beautifully blue; lake margined with rushes; the shores are covered with muscle-shells [sic]; pelicans and other aquatic fowl a characteristic." According to Simpson, "***the lake is filled with fish***"; he also observed that the local Indians had "***piles of fish lying about drying" (Simpson, 1876). Carson Lake no longer supports fish populations of any consequence. The loss of wetlands was mostly due to diversion of streamflow to irrigate crops in western Nevada and for urban uses in the Reno–Sparks area. The drought of the late 1980's to early 1990's further reduced the acreage of wetlands in western Nevada.

Some human activities have resulted in an increase in wetland acreage. Constructed wetlands in Carson Valley (fig. 1) utilize sewage effluent to provide habitat for waterfowl. In Desert Valley, a mine-dewatering operation has supplied water for constructed wetlands that have become important habitat for waterfowl and other wildlife. Wetlands were constructed by the Nevada Department of Transportation in Washoe Valley near Washoe Lake to offset losses from highway construction (John Nelson, Nevada Division of Environmental Protection, oral commun., 1993). Leakage from the Truckee Canal near Fernley has been used to create an extensive wetland operated and maintained by the Department of Wildlife. Agriculture-related activities, including construction of ponds, reservoirs (such as Lahontan and Rye Patch), drainage ditches, and canals, undoubtedly have added to wetland acreage throughout the State.

CONSERVATION

Many government agencies and private organizations participate in wetland conservation in Nevada. The most active agencies and organizations and some of their activities are listed in table 1.

Federal wetland activities.—Development activities in Nevada wetlands are regulated by several Federal statutory prohibitions and incentives that are intended to slow wetland losses. Some of the more important of these are contained in the 1899 Rivers and Harbors Act; the 1972 Clean Water Act and amendments; the 1985 Food Security Act; the 1990 Food, Agriculture, Conservation, and Trade Act; and the 1986 Emergency Wetlands Resources Act.

Section 10 of the Rivers and Harbors Act gives the U.S. Army Corps of Engineers (Corps) authority to regulate certain activities in navigable waters. Regulated activities include diking, deepening, filling, excavating, and placing of structures. The related section 404 of the Clean Water Act is the most often-used Federal legislation protecting wetlands. Under section 404 provisions, the Corps issues permits regulating the discharge of dredged or fill material into wetlands. Permits are subject to review and possible veto by the EPA, and the FWS has review and advisory roles. Section 401 of the Clean Water Act grants to States and eligible Indian Tribes the authority to approve, apply conditions to, or deny section 404 permit applications on the basis of a proposed activity's probable effects on the water quality of a wetland.

Table 1. Selected wetland-related activities of government agencies and private organizations in Nevada, 1993

[Source: Classification of activities is generalized from information provided by agencies and organizations. •, agency or organization participates in wetland-related activity; ..., agency or organization does not participate in wetland-related activity. MAN, management; REG, regulation; R&C, restoration and creation; LAN, land acquisition; R&D, research and data collection; D&I, delineation and inventory]

Agency or organization	MAN	REG	R&C	LAN	R&D	D&I
FEDERAL						
Department of Agriculture						
Consolidated Farm Service Agency	...	•	...	...	...	...
Forest Service	•	...	•	•	•	•
Natural Resources Conservation Service	...	•	•	...	•	•
Department of Defense						
Army Corps of Engineers	...	•	•	...	•	...
Military reservations	•	...	•	...	...	...
Department of the Interior						
Bureau of Land Management	•	...	•	•	•	•
Bureau of Reclamation	...	...	•	...	•	•
Fish and Wildlife Service	•	...	•	•	•	•
Geological Survey	...	...	...	...	•	...
National Biological Service	...	...	...	...	•	...
National Park Service	•	...	•	•	•	•
Environmental Protection Agency	...	•	...	...	•	...
STATE						
Department of Conservation and Natural Resources:						
Division of Environmental Protection	...	•	...	...	•	...
Division of State Lands	...	•	...	...	...	...
Division of State Parks	•	•	•	...	...	...
Division of Water Planning	...	•	...	...	...	...
Department of Transportation	...	...	•	...	...	...
Department of Wildlife	•	•	•	•	•	•
PRIVATE						
Ducks Unlimited	...	...	•	•	...	...
Environmental Defense Fund	...	...	•	•	...	...
The Nature Conservancy	•	...	•	•	...	...

Most farming, ranching, and silviculture activities are not subject to section 404 regulation. However, the "Swampbuster" provision of the 1985 Food Security Act and amendments in the 1990 Food, Agriculture, Conservation, and Trade Act discourage (through financial disincentives) the draining, filling, or other alteration of wetlands for agricultural use. The law allows exemptions from penalties in some cases, especially if the farmer agrees to restore the altered wetland or other wetlands that have been converted to agricultural use. The Wetlands Reserve Program of the 1990 Food, Agriculture, Conservation, and Trade Act authorizes the Federal Government to purchase conservation easements from landowners who agree to protect or restore wetlands. The Consolidated Farm Service Agency (formerly the Agricultural Stabilization and Conservation Service) administers the Swampbuster provisions and Wetlands Reserve Program. The Natural Resources Conservation Service (formerly the Soil Conservation Service) determines compliance with Swampbuster provisions and assists farmers in the identification of wetlands and in the development of wetland protection, restoration, or creation plans.

The 1986 Emergency Wetlands Resources Act encourages wetland protection through funding incentives. The act requires States to address wetland protection in their Statewide Comprehensive Outdoor Recreation Plans to qualify for Federal funding for State recreational land; the NPS provides guidance to States in developing the wetland component of their plans.

Federal agencies are responsible for the proper management of wetlands on public land under their jurisdiction. The BLM, FS, and the Department of Defense administer most of the Federal land in Nevada; BLM land (almost 48 million acres) alone contains about 75,000 acres of riparian wetlands (Bureau of Land Management,

1991). The BLM and FS have riparian-wetland management plans that include educating the public on the benefits and importance of healthy riparian areas; assessing acreage and condition of riparian wetlands; and restoring, maintaining, and protecting riparian wetlands. The BLM has acquired about 5,000 acres of wetlands in Soldier Meadow, Black Rock Desert, through land exchange. Military installations are responsible for preparing resource-management plans for fish and wildlife, recreation, and other natural and cultural resources. The plans provide policy and a framework for addressing wetland and other natural and cultural resource issues. The FWS manages seven National Wildlife Refuges, two National Wildlife Ranges, and two fish hatcheries in Nevada. National Wildlife Refuges total more than 220,000 acres and National Wildlife Ranges total more than 2 million acres. The NPS manages more than 77,000 acres of land (National Park Service, 1991) at two locations—Great Basin National Park and Devils Hole National Monument. An estimate of wetland acreages within National Parks in Nevada does not exist. The BOR is involved in the restoration and creation of wetlands in conjunction with some of their projects and has been instrumental in the construction of irrigation projects in Nevada. Inherently associated with these projects is the alteration of natural riparian and wet-meadow wetlands. The BOR has attempted either to minimize or to mitigate adverse effects on these wetlands.

State wetland activities.—Several State agencies are involved in wetland activities in Nevada (table 1). Nevada does not currently (1993) have a comprehensive wetlands-protection program but follows Federal policy and cooperates in many Federal programs.

Four agencies within the Nevada Department of Conservation and Natural Resources engage in wetland-related activities. The Division of Environmental Protection is the key regulatory agency and enforces provisions of the Clean Water Act within the State. Pursuant to section 305(b) of the act, the Division of Environmental Protection submits to the EPA and the U.S. Congress a biennial assessment of the State's surface-water quality (Nevada Department of Conservation and Natural Resources, 1992), including that of wetlands. The Division issues discharge permits, monitors water quality, and sets water-quality standards for Nevada. Reviews for subdivision permits also are under the jurisdiction of the Division of Environmental Protection. The Division of Water Planning is responsible for review of section 404 permit applications, and Division approval is necessary for the Corps to issue a permit. The Division of State Lands has legislative authority for wetlands protection on lands owned or managed by the State of Nevada; the Division issues permits for all activities associated with State lands. The Division of State Parks is responsible for management of State park land and reviews activities that may affect wetlands in parks. The Division of State Parks has been involved in the construction of wetlands on State park land and is responsible for Nevada's Statewide Comprehensive Outdoor Recreation Plans, which contain a summary of wetland-related activities within the State.

The Nevada Department of Transportation is responsible for assessing and mitigating impacts on wetlands that are a result of highway construction and maintenance. In cooperation with Department of State Parks, the Department of Transportation has constructed wetlands near Washoe Lake to mitigate losses of wetlands from construction of nearby highways.

The Department of Wildlife is responsible for day-to-day management of the State's 10 Wildlife Management Areas (comprising about 256,000 acres). These areas contain important wetlands and include areas such as Carson Lake in Lahontan Valley and Franklin Lake on the eastern side of the Ruby Mountains. The Department of Wildlife can require a Habitat Modification Permit before dredging in any river, stream, or lake if the Department determines that the activity will be harmful to fish. The Department of Wildlife has been monitoring the condition of wetlands by taking yearly population counts of waterfowl (Norman Saake, Nevada Department of Wildlife, oral commun., 1992). The Department of Wildlife has the authority to implement and manage a program for conserving, protecting, restoring, and propagating selected species of native fishes and other wildlife that are threatened with extinction. Wetlands have been constructed under the auspices of the Department of Wildlife; these wetlands, which are mostly for waterfowl, include most of the State Wildlife Management Areas and those constructed with the cooperation of private entities.

County and local wetland activities.—Most regulation of development activities in Nevada's wetlands is accomplished through Federal and State laws. However, some local activities, such as pond construction at local parks or river-enhancement projects, also can be beneficial to wetlands.

Private wetland activities.—Activities by private entities include purchasing wetlands and water rights, public education on wetland issues, and lobbying for wetland-enhancement legislation. The Nature Conservancy is perhaps the most active private organization involved in wetland protection in Nevada. The Nature Conservancy has one wetland holding in Condor Canyon, a part of Meadow Valley Wash near Panaca. Purchasing sensitive wetland areas has been a critical function of The Nature Conservancy in Nevada. The Nature Conservancy has purchased land containing wetlands at Franklin Lake and Ash Meadows and sold the properties to State or Federal agencies for management (Livermore, 1988). In Lahontan Valley, The Nature Conservancy has purchased water rights from farmers within the Newlands Project area, taking land out of agricultural production, and is reselling the water rights to the FWS for use at Stillwater Marsh. This action is providing freshwater to the marsh, which has received irrigation drainage as its only source of water in recent years. This effort by The Nature Conservancy will result in an improvement of the habitat in this important wetland on the Pacific Flyway. The Environmental Defense Fund has been actively assisting The Nature Conservancy in acquisition of water rights in Lahontan Valley. Ducks Unlimited also acquires wetlands for purposes of conservation. Private local and national organizations that participate in educational or lobbying activities in the State include gun and hunting clubs, the Sierra Club, the Lahontan Valley Wetlands Coalition, the National Audubon Society, and the Nevada Waterfowl Association.

References Cited

Bureau of Land Management, 1991, Riparian-wetland initiative for the 1990's: U.S. Bureau of Land Management Report BLM/WO/GI–91/ 001+4340, 50 p.

———1992, BLM—Meeting the challenge in 1991—Recreation 2000, fish and wildlife 2000, riparian-wetland initiative for the 1990's— Progress report on the implementation of three initiatives: U.S. Bureau of Land Management Report BLM–WO–GI–92–003–4333, 94 p.

Bureau of Reclamation, 1987, Final environmental impact statement for the Newlands Project, proposed operating criteria and procedures: Washington, D.C., U.S. Bureau of Reclamation, 332 p.

Cowardin, L.M., Carter, Virginia, Golet, F.C., and LaRoe, E.T., 1979, Classification of wetlands and deepwater habitats of the United States: U.S. Fish and Wildlife Service Report FWS/OBS–79/31, 131 p.

Dahl, T.E., 1990, Wetlands—Losses in the United States, 1780's to 1980's: Washington, D.C., U.S. Fish and Wildlife Service Report to Congress, 13 p.

Farnsworth, R.K., Thompson, E.S., and Peck, E.L., 1982, Evaporation atlas for the contiguous 48 United States: National Oceanic and Atmospheric Administration Technical Report NWS 33, 27 p.

Hoffman, R.J., Hallock, R.J., Rowe, T.G., Lico, M.S., Burge, H.L., and Thompson, S.P., 1990, Reconnaissance investigation of water quality, bottom sediment, and biota associated with irrigation drainage in and near Stillwater Wildlife Management Area, Churchill County, Nevada, 1986–87: U.S. Geological Survey Water-Resources Investigations Report 89–4105, 150 p.

Lico, M.S., 1992, Detailed study of irrigation drainage in and near wildlife management areas, west-central Nevada, 1987–90. Part A—Water quality, sediment composition, and hydrogeochemical processes in Stillwater and Fernley Wildlife Management Areas: U.S. Geological Survey Water-Resources Investigations Report 92–4024A, 65 p.

Livermore, David, 1988, Wetlands acquired in the Ruby Valley: The Nature Conservancy, Great Basin Newsletter, Spring 1988, unpaginated.

Moosburner, Otto, 1986, Nevada surface-water resources, *in* U.S. Geological Survey, National water summary 1985—Hydrologic events and surface-water resources: U.S. Geological Survey Water-Supply Paper 2300, p. 323–328.

National Park Service, 1991, Draft general management plan, development concept plans, and environmental impact statement, Great Basin National Park, White Pine County, Nevada: Denver, Colo., National Park Service, 274 p.

Nevada Department of Conservation and Natural Resources, 1988, Nevada's wetlands—An element of recreation in Nevada, 1987—Statewide comprehensive outdoor recreation plan: Carson City, Nevada Department of Conservation and Natural Resources, Division of State Parks, 78 p.

———1992, Nevada water quality assessment (305b) report: Carson City, Nevada Department of Conservation and Natural Resources, Division of Environmental Protection, unpaginated.

Rush, F.E., 1972, Hydrologic reconnaissance of Big and Little Soda Lakes, Churchill County, Nevada: Nevada Division of Water Resources, Information Report 11, 1 sheet.

Simpson, J.H., 1876, Report of explorations across the Great Basin of the territory of Utah for a direct wagon-route from Camp Floyd to Genoa, in Carson Valley, in 1859: Reno, University of Nevada Press, 518 p. (Reprinted in 1983.)

Thompson, S.P., and Merritt, K.L., 1988, Western Nevada wetlands—History and current status, *in* Blesse, R.E., and Goin, Peter, eds., Nevada public affairs review no. 1: Reno, University of Nevada, p. 40–45.

U.S. Fish and Wildlife Service, 1990, Recovery plan for the endangered and threatened species of Ash Meadows, Nevada: Portland, Oreg., U.S. Fish and Wildlife Service, 123 p.

Winograd, I.J., and Thordarson, William, 1975, Hydrogeologic and hydrochemical framework, south-central Great Basin, Nevada-California, *with special reference to* the Nevada Test Site: U.S. Geological Survey Professional Paper 712–C, 126 p.

FOR ADDITIONAL INFORMATION: District Chief, U.S. Geological Survey, 333 W. Nye Lane, Carson City, NV 89706; Regional Wetland Coordinator, U.S. Fish and Wildlife Service, Eastside Federal Complex, 911 NE. 11th Avenue, Portland, OR 97232

Prepared by
Michael S. Lico
U.S. Geological Survey

New Hampshire
Wetland Resources

Wetlands are an integral part of New Hampshire's natural resources. They provide essential habitat for wildlife and vegetation, including rare and endangered species and natural communities. Wetlands are a source of timber and provide opportunities for hunting and fishing, education and research, and bird, wildlife, and plant observation, all of which benefit the tourist industry and economy. Other benefits include flood control, bank- and shoreline-erosion control, sediment retention, water filtration, and nutrient uptake. In recognition of the importance of wetlands, many government agencies and private organizations have worked to preserve wetlands and educate the public about wetland values. For example, Lake Umbagog and its associated wetlands (fig. 1), which constitute one of the most productive wildlife areas in New Hampshire, are protected by the State and by the U.S. Fish and Wildlife Service (FWS) as a National Wildlife Refuge.

TYPES AND DISTRIBUTION

Wetlands are lands transitional between terrestrial and deep-water habitats where the water table usually is at or near the land surface or the land is covered by shallow water (Cowardin and others, 1979). The distribution of wetlands and deepwater habitats in New Hampshire is shown in figure 2A; only wetlands are discussed herein.

Wetlands can be vegetated or nonvegetated and are classified on the basis of their hydrology, vegetation, and substrate. In this summary, wetlands are classified according to the system proposed by Cowardin and others (1979), which is used by the FWS to map and inventory the Nation's wetlands. At the most general level of the classification system, wetlands are grouped into five ecological systems: Palustrine, Lacustrine, Riverine, Estuarine, and Marine. The Palustrine System includes only wetlands, whereas the other systems comprise wetlands and deepwater habitats. Wetlands of the systems that occur in New Hampshire are described below.

System	Wetland description
Palustrine	Nontidal and tidal-freshwater wetlands in which vegetation is predominantly trees (forested wetlands); shrubs (scrub-shrub wetlands); persistent or nonpersistent emergent, erect, rooted herbaceous plants (persistent- and nonpersistent-emergent wetlands); or submersed and (or) floating plants (aquatic beds). Also, intermittently to permanently flooded open-water bodies of less than 20 acres in which water is less than 6.6 feet deep.
Lacustrine	Nontidal and tidal-freshwater wetlands within an intermittently to permanently flooded lake or reservoir larger than 20 acres and (or) deeper than 6.6 feet. Vegetation, when present, is predominantly nonpersistent emergent plants (nonpersistent-emergent wetlands), or submersed and (or) floating plants (aquatic beds), or both.
Riverine	Nontidal and tidal-freshwater wetlands within a channel. Vegetation, when present, is same as in the Lacustrine System.
Estuarine	Tidal wetlands in low-wave-energy environments where the salinity of the water is greater than 0.5 part per thousand (ppt) and is variable owing to evaporation and the mixing of seawater and freshwater.
Marine	Tidal wetlands that are exposed to waves and currents of the open ocean and to water having a salinity greater than 30 ppt.

Rubin and others (1993) used LANDSAT (satellite) imagery to estimate wetland area at 396,246 acres, or about 6.7 percent of the State. That estimate probably underestimates the actual wetland area owing to similarities between evergreen forest in upland and wetland areas. Also, LANDSAT imagery cannot discern wetlands smaller than about 2 acres (Ken Kettenring, New Hampshire Wetlands Board, oral commun., 1993). Estimates of wetland area based on review of permits by the U.S. Environmental Protection Agency (EPA) and field checking during functional assessments by the Audubon Society of New Hampshire place New Hampshire's wetland area at about 10 percent of the State's total area (Mark Kern, Environmental Protection Agency, oral commun., 1993).

The distribution of wetlands in New Hampshire has been influenced by the State's physiography (fig. 2B). In the northern part of the White Mountain Section, glacial erosion and sediment deposits have created broad valleys in which large wetland complexes have formed. For example, many wetlands are present along tributaries to the Connecticut Lakes and Lake Francis near Pittsburg. Small wetlands in the White Mountains have formed mainly along small streams in river valleys or where streams flow over flat benches on hillsides. Wetlands in the New England Upland and Seaboard Lowland Sections are in many settings, such as in topographic depressions, around the margins of ponds and lakes, and in river valleys. In many areas of the State, small wetlands are interrelated and form large wetland complexes.

To date (1993) there is no published information concerning acreage of the different wetland types in New Hampshire. However, the similarities of the ecological, hydrologic, and physiographic settings of New Hampshire to those in the other New England States makes it likely that the predominant wetland types in the State are the same as in the remainder of the region—palustrine forested and scrub-shrub (Tiner, 1987, 1992; Widoff, 1988). Forested and scrub-shrub wetlands that have organic-rich mineral soils are commonly referred to as swamps, whereas wetlands that have organic soils over mineral soils are called peatlands. In southern New Hampshire and in the Connecticut River Valley, forested swamps in poorly drained basins typically are dominated by red maple or have mixtures of red maple, yellow birch, hemlock, and white pine. Swamps in the flood plains of major rivers typically are dominated by silver maple. Peatlands in southern and coastal New Hampshire commonly contain pitch pine or Atlantic white cedar (Dan Sperduto, New Hampshire Natural Heritage Inventory, written commun., 1993). A few

Figure 1. Wetlands along the mouth of Hampshire Brook and Lake Umbagog. *(Photograph courtesy of the Society for Protection of New Hampshire Forests.)*

swamps in southern New Hampshire contain black gum, which is a species near the northern extent of its range. In northern New Hampshire and at higher altitudes, forested swamps typically contain red spruce and balsam fir, and forested peatlands generally are dominated by black spruce, larch, or northern white cedar.

Peatlands are present throughout New Hampshire but are more common in the north. Most are small. The absence of extensive peatlands in New Hampshire is due largely to the State's mountainous terrain (Johnson, 1985). The terms bog and fen have been used to differentiate peatlands in some classification systems (Damman and French, 1987). Bogs (palustrine forested and scrub-shrub wet-

lands) are acidic, nutrient poor, and have a low diversity of plant species, whereas fens (palustrine forested, scrub-shrub, and persistent-emergent wetlands) are less acidic and have higher nutrient levels and plant diversity. The herbaceous-plant community in bogs generally is dominated by sphagnum moss, whereas in fens it typically is dominated by mosses and sedges.

Scrub-shrub vegetation grows in most wetlands, typically as a transitional community between emergent wetlands and forested wetlands or upland, or between open water and forested wetlands or upland. In general, shrub swamps are dominated by broad-leaved deciduous shrubs such as willow and alder; scrub-shrub commu-

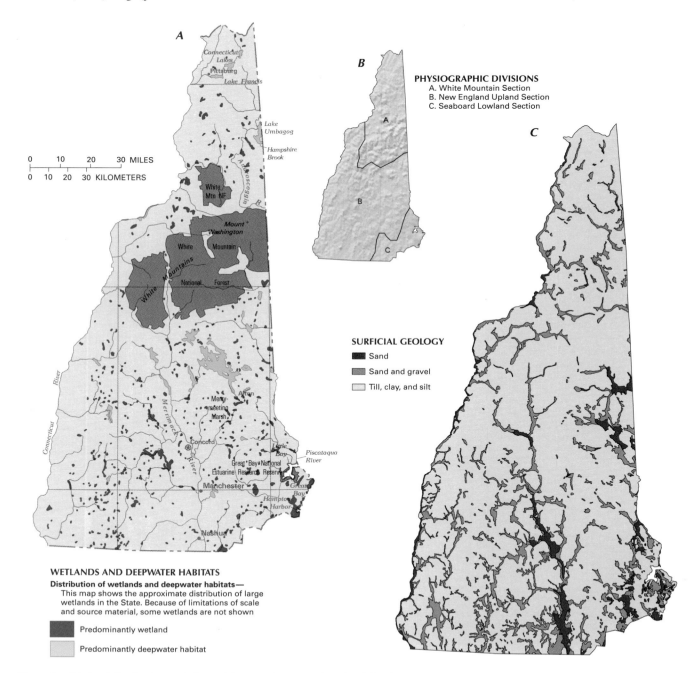

Figure 2. Wetland distribution and physical features that control wetland distribution in New Hampshire. ***A***, Distribution of wetlands and deepwater habitats. ***B***, Physiography. ***C***, Surficial geology. *(Sources: A, T.E. Dahl, U.S. Fish and Wildlife Service, unpub. data, 1991. B, Physiographic divisions from Fenneman, 1946; landforms data from EROS Data Center; C, Koteff, 1993).*

nities in bogs contain broad-leaved evergreen shrubs such as leatherleaf and labrador tea and stunted conifers such as black spruce and larch; and fens generally contain broad-leaved evergreen shrubs, broad-leaved deciduous shrubs, and northern white cedar. (Dan Sperduto, written commun., 1993).

Palustrine emergent wetlands, commonly referred to as marshes, are more common in southern New Hampshire. Most are small and associated with lacustrine or riverine wetlands. Marshes that have shallow water or saturated soils generally contain sedges, rushes, or grasses, whereas those in deeper water typically contain cattails.

Most of New Hampshire's lakes and rivers have areas of shallow water where aquatic vegetation has become established. These lacustrine and riverine wetlands are essential for the biological productivity of lakes and rivers. As a result of recent increases in beaver populations, many riparian (streamside) wetlands along smaller streams and rivers have been flooded behind beaver dams. Over time, this flooding promotes a cyclical change from riparian shrub swamps to small ponds and marshes to wet meadows and then back to shrub swamps (George Springston, Vermont Wetlands Office, written commun., 1993). Many State wildlife areas contain emergent wetlands in impoundments built for the improvement of waterfowl habitat. However, although flooding caused by beaver dams or manmade dams can create wetlands, it also can be detrimental to existing riparian wetlands.

Estuarine and marine wetlands along New Hampshire's 18-mile coastline are estimated at about 7,500 acres (New Hampshire Office of State Planning, 1989). Most of these wetlands are in or near Hampton Harbor, Great Bay, and Little Bay. Short (1992) determined that Great Bay estuary, which includes Great Bay, Little Bay, and the lower Piscataqua River, contains about 2,600 acres of aquatic beds, 1,200 acres of mud flats, and 1,000 acres of salt marsh. In general, salt marshes that are only occasionally flooded by tides are vegetated predominantly by saltmeadow cordgrass and black grass, whereas those that are regularly flooded are dominated by saltmarsh cordgrass.

HYDROLOGIC SETTING

Wetlands are hydrologic features that form where climate and physiography favor the retention of water. Wetlands are found along rivers, lakes, and estuaries where flooding occurs, in isolated depressions surrounded by upland where surface water collects, on slopes and surface drainageways, and where ground water discharges to the land surface in spring or seepage areas. Soil saturation favors the growth of wetland plants and development of hydric soils. Water either can flood wetlands, be present at the surface of wetlands, or keep underlying soils saturated near the surface with no surface water present (Tiner, 1991).

The timing and duration of the presence of water affects water chemistry, soil development, and plant-community structure in wetlands. Although degree of wetness is important in the determination of wetland type, many ecologic functions of wetlands also depend upon wetland size, position of the wetland in a drainage network, and sources of water (Brinson, 1993). Climate, physiography, and geology influence the hydrology and water quality of wetlands. The complex interactions of these variables with biotic factors and site history determine the type of wetland that develops in any particular setting.

New Hampshire's climate is conducive to wetland development. Precipitation exceeds potential evapotranspiration on an annual basis, and the excess moisture is available for formation and maintenance of wetlands. Climate varies with altitude and distance from the Atlantic Ocean. For example, from the coast to the White Mountains, average annual precipitation and average annual runoff increase, summer temperatures decrease, and the growing season

becomes shorter (Hammond and Cotton, 1986). Wetland vegetation is influenced by these climatic differences. Wetlands in southern New Hampshire are dominated by plant communities similar to those of southern New England wetlands, whereas wetlands in northern New Hampshire are dominated by communities similar to those in Canadian wetlands.

The distribution of wetlands in New Hampshire also is partly determined by physiography, distribution of glacially derived sediments, and the geologic character of the underlying bedrock. Areas of steep topography do not retain water long enough for wetlands to develop. However, given favorable hydrologic conditions, wetlands can form on drainage divides and near mountaintops. For example, several ridge-top subalpine bogs occur on Mount Washington (Johnson, 1985). Most of New Hampshire's wetlands, however, are in lowlands, valleys, and depressions that have more favorable hydrologic conditions for wetlands.

Many of the low-lying areas of New Hampshire are covered by stratified sand, gravel, clay, and silt deposited by glacial meltwater and by modern streams in the time since glaciation (fig. 2C). Most uplands are underlain by bedrock mantled by glacial till, a mixture of clay, silt, sand, gravel, and boulders. Both till and fine-grained sediments can restrict drainage and retain surface water. Wetlands form over till in many small depressions in New Hampshire uplands, over silty, clayey sands in some valleys in northern New Hampshire, over fine-grained glacial-lake deposits in parts of the Merrimack and Connecticut River valleys, and over fine-grained marine deposits along the coast. In seep areas near streams or depressions that intersect the water table, coarse-grained glacial deposits can transmit ground water to overlying wetlands (Motts and O'Brien, 1981). Some glacial landforms, such as ridges, hills, and depressions can create conditions favorable for wetland formation by attenuating runoff or retaining water. For example, kettles, which are depressions that formed when glacial ice that had been buried by outwash melted, have either filled with water to form ponds or passed through several successional stages of infilling to become bogs.

Contrasts in the interactions between hydrology and vegetation in different settings can be illustrated by peatlands and coastal pondshore wetlands. In peatlands, vegetation patterns are determined largely by water chemistry and movement (Damman and French, 1987). For example, bogs receive little input from runoff or ground water and rely on precipitation (including fog) and wind-blown dust as sources for water, nutrients, and minerals. Vegetation in bogs commonly grows in a concentric pattern because of the scarcity of nutrients and minerals in the center of the bog and the increased availability of nutrients and minerals along bog margins. Bogs are seldom flooded; even quaking (floating-mat) bogs surrounding open water in ponds are rarely flooded because the bog mat fluctuates with changes in water level. Fens also receive inputs from precipitation but rely principally on ground water and overland flow for inputs of minerals and nutrients; like bogs, fens seldom are flooded.

In contrast, flooding is the major hydrologic influence in pondshore wetlands. Coastal ponds occur largely in sandy glacial outwash, and pond water levels reflect seasonal and annual fluctuations in ground-water levels. Pondshore wetlands can be flooded or saturated for much of the year. Wetland plant communities are concentrically zoned around the pond along a gradient from the longest to the shortest duration of flooding (Dan Sperduto, written commun., 1993).

TRENDS

Wetlands once were much more extensive in New Hampshire. In the 1800's and early 1900's, timber harvesting and clearing and draining of wetlands for crops and grazing resulted in the loss or degradation of many wetlands, particularly in the major river valleys and along the coastline. Some of those areas reverted to wetlands as pasture land was abandoned. In some cases, the character of the wetlands has changed. For example, most of New Hampshire's Atlantic white cedar bogs were altered by logging or flooding, and many have revegetated with red maple. As much as 7,500 acres of tidal marsh have been lost since settlement by Europeans (New Hampshire Office of State Planning, 1989). Although several Federal and State regulations focus on minimizing wetland loss, many wetlands remain vulnerable.

Development in and near wetlands due to urbanization is a major cause of wetland loss or degradation. Other factors that can destroy wetlands or affect wetland functions include farming, peat harvesting, timber harvesting, road building, inadequate bridge-support spacing and culvert diameter, all-terrain vehicle use, reservoir construction, hydropower releases, navigation impoundments, ground-water pumping, and air or water pollution.

CONSERVATION

Many government agencies and private organizations participate in wetland conservation in New Hampshire. The most active agencies and organizations and some of their activities are listed in table 1.

Federal wetland activities.—Development activities in New Hampshire wetlands are regulated by several Federal statutory prohibitions and incentives that are intended to slow wetland losses. Some of the more important of these are contained in the 1899 Rivers and Harbors Act; the 1972 Clean Water Act and amendments; the 1985 Food Security Act; the 1990 Food, Agriculture, Conservation, and Trade Act; the 1986 Emergency Wetlands Resources Act; and the 1972 Coastal Zone Management Act.

Section 10 of the Rivers and Harbors Act gives the U.S. Army Corps of Engineers (Corps) authority to regulate certain activities in navigable waters. Regulated activities include diking, deepening, filling, excavating, and placing of structures. The related section 404 of the Clean Water Act is the most often-used Federal legislation protecting wetlands. Under section 404 provisions, the Corps issues permits regulating the discharge of dredged or fill material into wetlands. Permits are subject to review and possible veto by the EPA, and the FWS has review and advisory roles. Section 401 of the Clean Water Act grants to States and eligible Indian Tribes the authority to approve, apply conditions to, or deny section 404 permit applications on the basis of a proposed activity's probable effects on the water quality of a wetland.

Most farming, ranching, and silviculture activities are not subject to section 404 regulation. However, the "Swampbuster" provision of the 1985 Food Security Act and amendments in the 1990 Food, Agriculture, Conservation, and Trade Act discourage (through financial disincentives) the draining, filling, or other alteration of wetlands for agricultural use. The law allows exemptions from penalties in some cases, especially if the farmer agrees to restore the altered wetland or other wetlands that have been converted to agricultural use. The Wetlands Reserve Program of the 1990 Food, Agriculture, Conservation, and Trade Act authorizes the Federal Government to purchase conservation easements from landowners who agree to protect or restore wetlands. The Consolidated Farm Service Agency (formerly the Agricultural Stabilization and Conservation Service) administers the Swampbuster provisions and Wetlands Reserve Program. The Natural Resources Conservation Service (formerly the Soil Conservation Service) determines compliance with Swampbuster provisions and assists farmers in the identification of wetlands and in the development of wetland protection, restoration, or creation plans.

The 1986 Emergency Wetlands Resources Act and the 1972 Coastal Zone Management Act and amendments encourage wetland

Table 1. Selected wetland-related activities of government agencies and private organizations in New Hampshire, 1993

[Source: Classification of activities is generalized from information provided by agencies and organizations. •, agency or organization participates in wetland-related activity; ..., agency or organization does not participate in wetland-related activity. MAN, management; REG, regulation; R&C, restoration and creation; LAN, land acquisition; R&D, research and data collection; D&I, delineation and inventory]

Agency or organization	MAN	REG	R&C	LAN	R&D	D&I
FEDERAL						
Department of Agriculture						
Consolidated Farm Service Agency	...	•	...	...	...	...
Forest Service	...	•	...	•	•	•
Natural Resources Conservation Service	...	•	•	...	•	•
Department of Commerce						
National Oceanic and Atmospheric Administration	•	•	•	•	•	•
Department of Defense						
Army Corps of Engineers	•	•	•	•	•	•
Military reservations	•					
Department of the Interior						
Fish and Wildlife Service	•	...	•	•	•	•
Geological Survey					•	•
National Biological Service					•	•
National Park Service	•	...	•	•	•	•
Environmental Protection Agency		•	...		•	•
STATE						
Department of Environmental Services		•				
Waste Management	•	•				
Water Resources Division	•	•	•	•	•	•
Water Supply and Pollution Control	•	•				
Department of Resources and Economic Development		•				
Division of Forests and Lands	•	•		•		
Division of Parks and Recreation	•			•		
Natural Heritage Inventory	•	•				•
Department of Safety		•				
Department of Transportaiton		•		•		
Fish and Game Department	•	•	•	•		•
Office of State Planning	•	•	•	•		
State educational institutions					•	•
Wetlands Board		•				
COUNTY AND LOCAL						
Conservation Commissions	•		•	•		
Soil and Water Conservation Districts	...		•		•	
Some county and local governments	•	•	•	•		
PRIVATE ORGANIZATIONS						
Audubon Society of New Hampshire		•		•		
Ducks Unlimited		•				
New England Wildflower Society		•			•	
Private colleges and other educational institutions	•				•	•
Society for the Protection of New Hampshire Forests	•			•		•
The Nature Conservancy	•			•		...

protection through funding incentives. The Emergency Wetland Resources Act requires States to address wetland protection in their Statewide Comprehensive Outdoor Recreation Plans to qualify for Federal funding for State recreational land; the National Park Service (NPS) provides guidance to States in developing the wetland component of their plans. Coastal States that adopt coastal-zone management programs and plans approved by the National Oceanic and Atmospheric Administration (NOAA) are eligible for Federal funding and technical assistance through the Coastal Zone Management Act.

Some of New Hampshire's wetlands are managed by Federal agencies. The FWS manages wetlands in waterfowl-protection areas, National Fish Hatcheries, and National Wildlife Refuges. Also, the FWS administers wetland-acquisition programs such as the Partners for Wildlife Program, which helps restore wetlands on private lands, and the North American Waterfowl Management Plan, a cooperative program that provides funding for purchasing wetlands and associated uplands. The FWS also has funded research on peatland ecology (Damman and French, 1987). The NPS has designated 11 sites in New Hampshire as National Natural Landmarks, at least 4 of which contain significant wetlands. Some of these are owned by the State, and others are protected voluntarily by individual landowners. The U.S. Forest Service manages a small number of wetlands in the White Mountain National Forest. The Great Bay National Estuarine Research Reserve is supported by NOAA in cooperation with the New Hampshire Fish and Game Department. The EPA, through a grant program under the Clean Water Act, has provided funding to the New Hampshire Wetlands Board and the New Hampshire Department of Resources and Economic Development's Natural Heritage Inventory Program. The EPA also is providing additional funds through the Merrimack River Initiative to identify and protect important resources and habitats of the Merrimack River, including wetlands. The Corps is investigating the effectiveness of wetlands on storage and regulation of flood flows along the Connecticut River and the effect of development within the basin on natural valley storage. The U.S. Geological Survey, together with the New Hampshire Department of Environmental Services, is mapping marsh and peat deposits in the State.

State wetland activities.—New Hampshire regulates wetlands primarily through State law and the rules of the Wetlands Board. The Wetlands Board consists of 12 members who represent government and industry. Administrative support to the Wetlands Board is provided largely by the Wetlands Bureau of the Department of Environmental Services' Water Resources Division and by the New Hampshire Office of State Planning's Coastal Zone Management Program. In New Hampshire, wetland regulations require permits to dredge, fill, or place structures in tidal or nontidal wetlands and waterways. The highest value has been placed on coastal wetlands, which were first protected by State statute in 1967. To enhance habitat values in adjacent tidal wetlands and to protect tidal environments from potential sources of pollution, the Board also emphasizes the preservation of tidal buffer zones. For freshwater wetlands, emphasis is placed on bogs and marshes, with priority based on the rarity of the habitat type, the difficulty of restoration, and the wetland's functions (New Hampshire Wetlands Board, 1993).

Projects that will alter wetlands are categorized as major-, minor-, and minimum-impact projects and projects not requiring a permit. All wetlands are regulated regardless of size. In addition to the size and type of the disturbance allowed in each category, the evaluation criteria include (1) the history of disturbance at the site and related projects elsewhere in the wetland or wetland complex (cumulative impact), (2) whether the wetland has been identified by the Natural Heritage Inventory Program as an exemplary natural community or whether there are documented occurrences of State or federally listed endangered or threatened species, (3) the function and value of the area, and (4) whether the wetland is designated a "Prime Wetland" by the local community under State guidelines. The Wetlands Board may not grant a permit for projects in or adjacent to an area designated as "prime" without a public hearing and without evidence in the record that there will be no significant net loss of values as a result of the project or activity associated with the project. Because the State's regulations are more inclusive than section 404 of the Clean Water Act, the Corps has issued a New Hampshire State Programmatic General Permit that allows as much as 95 percent of the permit applications in New Hampshire that normally would require a Corps permit to be approved through the New Hampshire Wetlands Board permitting process after Corps review (K.N. Kettenring, written commun., 1993).

The Department of Environmental Services administers section 401 of the Federal Clean Water Act, which requires State wa-ter-quality certification before a section 404 permit may be issued. The Department of Environmental Services' Water Resources Division also protects some wetlands through regulations of activities in rivers and lakes. The New Hampshire Department of Resources and Economic Development's Division of Forests and Lands establishes and enforces acceptable management practices for logging and erosion control near surface-water bodies and wetlands.

Other legislation designed to protect ecologically sensitive habitats such as wetlands includes the New Hampshire Native Plant Protection Act of 1987, which requires all State agencies and departments to cooperate in preserving and protecting endangered and threatened plants. In addition, the New Hampshire Legislature has enacted a Current Use Taxation law to reduce development pressures on recreational, scenic, and ecologically important open spaces. This law uses a property tax abatement program on tracts of land larger than 10 acres to encourage preservation of open space, farm land, forest land, wild land, and recreation land, including wetlands and flood plains (New Hampshire Office of State Planning, 1989).

Several State agencies own or manage wetlands or are involved in other aspects of wetland protection. The Department of Fish and Game acquires and protects wetlands through wildlife-management programs. Wetlands are purchased with funds received from the sale of wildlife emblems and migratory-waterfowl stamps, as well as from accounts set up for management of nongame and endangered species (New Hampshire Office of State Planning, 1989). The Department owns about 35,000 acres, more than one-half of which is wetland. Most of these wetlands are part of wildlife-management areas. Merrymeeting Marsh is one example. The Natural Heritage Inventory Program has documented New Hampshire's natural communities and rare and endangered species and their habitats. The Program also develops plans for the protection of endangered and threatened plant species and reviews State projects and permit applications for activities that could affect wetlands. The Office of State Planning is responsible for producing the wetland component of the New Hampshire Statewide Comprehensive Outdoor Recreation Plan, which describes the State's wetland-protection plans. Wetland losses due to roadbuilding are minimized through close cooperation between the New Hampshire Department of Transportation, the Wetlands Board, and Federal agencies.

County and local wetland activities.—Local conservation commissions have an advisory role in local wetland protection through oversight of the designation of Prime Wetlands and review of wetland permit applications. Under the Prime Wetlands law, municipalities may adopt what resembles a zoning overlay district (New Hampshire Office of State Planning, 1989). The adoption of the Prime Wetlands designation allows for protection of wetlands that have high local value even if they are not regionally or nationally significant. Conservation commissions must use inventory and evaluation methods accepted by the Wetlands Board for this process, such as those of Ammann and Stone (1991) and Cook and others (1993). As of 1993, Prime Wetlands designations had been adopted and submitted to the Wetlands Board by 20 of New Hampshire's 234 towns, and many others are in process (Marjorie Swope, New Hampshire Association for Conservation Commissions, oral commun., 1993).

Private wetland activities.—During 1987–83, through a partnership between the privately funded Trust for New Hampshire Lands and the publicly funded New Hampshire Land Conservation Investment Program, New Hampshire spent $46.4 million to protect 385 parcels of land totaling 100,897 acres, including diverse wetlands. These lands were acquired through purchases and donations or protected through the use of conservation easements. The Society for the Protection of New Hampshire Forests is compiling an inventory of the wetland acreage acquired by the program, which will be available through the Complex Systems Research Center at the University of New Hampshire.

Private organizations provide complementary functions that cannot readily be accomplished by governmental agencies. For example, private organizations such as The Nature Conservancy can more easily purchase property. The Nature Conservancy manages 14 preserves in New Hampshire, 8 of which include wetlands, and has protected 12 additional wetland sites by easement, management agreement, legal assistance, or purchase and transfer. The Audubon Society of New Hampshire monitors threatened and endangered species that use wetlands and offers educational workshops to promote the use of the New Hampshire Method (Ammann and Stone, 1991; Cook and others, 1993) for the evaluation of wetlands. The New Hampshire chapter of Ducks Unlimited has worked in cooperation with the State to purchase about 354 acres of wetland and surrounding upland habitat. The Society for Protection of New Hampshire Forests owns 83 properties and holds conservation easements on 309 properties, many of which include wetlands. Other wetlands are owned or protected by local land trusts, The New England Wildflower Society, the Appalachian Mountain Club, and many others. Individuals, timber companies, towns, and other private landowners own most of New Hampshire's wetlands, and many actively pursue wetland conservation.

References Cited

Ammann, A.P., and Stone, A.L., 1991, Method for the comparative evaluation of nontidal wetlands in New Hampshire: Concord, New Hampshire Department of Environmental Services, variously paged.

Brinson, M.M., 1993, Changes in the functioning of wetlands along environmental gradients: Wetlands, v. 13, no. 2, p. 65–74.

Cook, R.A., Stone, A.L., and Ammann, A.P., 1993, Method for the evaluation and inventory of vegetated tidal marshes in New Hampshire: Concord, Audubon Society of New Hampshire, variously paged.

Cowardin, L.M., Carter, Virginia, Golet, F.C., and LaRoe, E.T., 1979, Classification of wetlands and deepwater habitats of the United States: U.S. Fish and Wildlife Service Report FWS/OBS–79/31, 131 p.

Damman, A.W.H., and French, T.W., 1987, The ecology and peat bogs of the glaciated northeastern United States—A community profile: U.S. Fish and Wildlife Service Biological Report 85(7.16), 114 p.

Fenneman, N.M., 1946, Physical divisions of the United States: Washington D.C., U.S. Geological Survey special map, scale 1:7,000,000.

Hammond, R.E., and Cotton, John, 1986, New Hampshire surface-water resources, *in* U.S. Geological Survey, National water summary 1985—Hydrologic events and surface-water resources: U.S. Geological Survey Water-Supply Paper 2300, p. 329–334.

Johnson, C.W., 1985, Bogs of the northeast: Hanover, N.H., The University Press of New England, 269 p.

Koteff, Carl, 1993, New Hampshire sand and gravel resources: Boston, New England Governors' Conference, Inc., 16 p.

Motts, W.S., and O'Brien, A.L., 1981, Geology and hydrology of wetlands in Massachusetts: University of Massachusetts Water Resources Research Center Publication 123, 147 p.

New Hampshire Office of State Planning, 1989, New Hampshire wetlands priority conservation plan: Concord, New Hampshire Office of State Planning, 95 p.

New Hampshire Wetlands Board, 1993, New Hampshire Code of Administrative Rules, Chapter Wt 100 through Wt 800: Concord, New Hampshire Wetlands Board, 118 p.

Rubin, F.A., Justice, D.G., and Vogelmann, J.E., 1993, Final report—New Hampshire statewide digital wetlands inventory: Durham, University of New Hampshire, Complex Systems Research Center, 30 p.

Short, F.T., ed., 1992, The ecology of the Great Bay estuary, New Hampshire and Maine—An estuarine profile and bibliography: Durham, University of New Hampshire, Jackson Estuarine Laboratory, 222 p.

Tiner, R.W., 1987, Preliminary National Wetlands Inventory report on Vermont's wetland acreage: Newton Corner, Mass., U.S. Fish and Wildlife Service, 5 p.

———1991, Maine wetlands and their boundaries—A guide for code enforcement officers: Augusta, Maine Department of Economic and Community Development, Office of Comprehensive Planning, 72 p.

———1992, Preliminary National Wetland Inventory report on Massachusetts' wetland acreage: Newton Corner, Mass., U.S. Fish and Wildlife Service, 5 p.

Widoff, Lissa, 1988, Maine wetlands conservation priority plan: Augusta, Maine State Planning Office, Bureau of Parks and Recreation, 117 p.

FOR ADDITIONAL INFORMATION: District Chief, U.S. Geological Survey, 525 Clinton Street, Bow, NH 03304; Regional Wetland Coordinator, U.S. Fish and Wildlife Service, 300 Westgate Center Drive, Hadley, MA 01035

Prepared by
David S. Armstrong,
U.S. Geological Survey

New Jersey
Wetland Resources

New Jersey's diverse wetlands are the result of the interaction of geologic events, human activities, and recent hydrologic conditions. The State's location on the East Coast has made it home to plants that include many threatened and endangered species (Tiner, 1985; Reyer and others, 1990). Of 338 rare plants identified in New Jersey by the U.S. Fish and Wildlife Service (FWS), 249 species grow in wetland or aquatic habitats. Major wetlands in the State include the Great Swamp (fig. 1) in the north and the wetlands of the New Jersey Pinelands and estuaries in the south (fig. 2A).

The wetlands of New Jersey are valuable for their fish and wildlife and their contribution to environmental quality, society, and the economy (Tiner, 1985). Wetlands provide spawning and nursery grounds for shellfish such as crabs, clams, oysters, and shrimp and for finfish species such as alewives, blueback herring, bass, white perch, American shad, menhaden, bluefish, sea trout, and mullet. Bird species that include peregrine falcons, snow and Canada geese, and pintail, canvasback, mallard, and black ducks use New Jersey's salt marshes for feeding, migration, and wintering grounds. Beaver and muskrat use wetlands for their homes, and other furbearers such as raccoons, mink, river otter, foxes, mice, and rabbits use wetlands for food and shelter (Tiner, 1985). Many reptile and amphibian species, including the endangered pine barrens tree frog, the blue-spotted salamander, and the endangered bog turtle, also live in the State's wetlands (Susan Lockwood, New Jersey Department of Environmental Protection and Energy, written commun., 1993).

The environmental quality of aquatic habitats is enhanced by wetlands. Wetland soils and vegetation filter or absorb nutrients and can remove heavy metals and other contaminants from waters moving through them (Tiner, 1985). Wetlands reduce turbidity and sediment loading, thereby slowing the rate of siltation of downstream harbors and navigable rivers and streams. The aquatic productivity of wetlands is very high. The net vegetative productivity of a salt marsh can exceed that of a tropical rain forest, and salt marshes support a diverse community of animals that inhabit estuarine waters.

Wetlands have socioeconomic as well as habitat and environmental-quality value (Tiner, 1985). They provide flood- and storm-damage protection, erosion control, and public water supply and allow for the production of economically important natural species such as blueberries, cranberries, wild rice, salt hay, and timber. Cranberry growing is a significant industry in New Jersey; more

than 3,000 acres of cranberry bog were under private management in 1992. Wetlands also provide many recreational and educational opportunities, including hunting and fishing, nature study, boating, painting and drawing, and photography.

TYPES AND DISTRIBUTION

Wetlands are lands transitional between terrestrial and deepwater habitats where the water table usually is at or near the land surface or the land is covered by shallow water (Cowardin and others, 1979). The distribution of wetlands and deepwater habitats in New Jersey is shown in figure 2A; only wetlands are discussed herein.

Wetlands can be vegetated or nonvegetated and are classified on the basis of their hydrology, vegetation, and substrate. In this summary, wetlands are classified according to the system proposed by Cowardin and others (1979), which is used by the U.S. Fish and Wildlife Service (FWS) to map and inventory the Nation's wetlands. At the most general level of the classification system, wetlands are grouped into five ecological systems: Palustrine, Lacustrine, Riverine, Estuarine, and Marine. The Palustrine System includes only wetlands, whereas the other systems comprise wetlands and deepwater habitats. Wetlands of the systems that occur in New Jersey are described below.

System	Wetland description
Palustrine	Nontidal and tidal-freshwater wetlands in which vegetation is predominantly trees (forested wetlands); shrubs (scrub-shrub wetlands); persistent or nonpersistent emergent, erect, rooted herbaceous plants (persistent- and nonpersistent-emergent wetlands); or submersed and (or) floating plants (aquatic beds). Also, intermittently to permanently flooded open-water bodies of less than 20 acres in which water is less than 6.6 feet deep.
Lacustrine	Nontidal and tidal-freshwater wetlands within an intermittently to permanently flooded lake or reservoir larger than 20 acres and (or) deeper than 6.6 feet. Vegetation, when present, is predominantly nonpersistent emergent plants (nonpersistent-emergent wetlands), or submersed and (or) floating plants (aquatic beds), or both.
Riverine	Nontidal and tidal-freshwater wetlands within a channel. Vegetation, when present, is same as in the Lacustrine System.
Estuarine	Tidal wetlands in low-wave-energy environments where the salinity of the water is greater than 0.5 part per thousand (ppt) and is variable owing to evaporation and the mixing of seawater and freshwater.
Marine	Tidal wetlands that are exposed to waves and currents of the open ocean and to water having a salinity greater than 30 ppt.

An FWS study indicated that, as of the mid-1980's, wetlands covered about 916,000 acres (19 percent) of New Jersey (Tiner, 1985). Although wetlands are present throughout the State, most are in New Jersey's coastal plain. Six of the 10 counties in the Coastal Plain are more than 25 percent wetland; 3 of the remaining 4 are between 10 and 25 percent wetland.

Nearly 99 percent (by area) of New Jersey's wetlands are palustrine or estuarine (Tiner, 1985). Palustrine wetlands generally

Figure 1. The Great Swamp National Wildlife Refuge near Meyersville. *(Photograph by Mark Hardy, U.S. Geological Survey).*

are swamps and freshwater lowlands, whereas estuarine wetlands are marshes and associated saltwater wetlands. Two-thirds of the State's wetland acreage is palustrine, and nearly one-third is estuarine. The remaining 1 percent is divided among the other wetland systems. New Jersey's most common palustrine wetland types are swamps (forested wetland), shrub swamps (scrub-shrub wetland), and freshwater marsh and wet meadow (emergent wetland). Bogs (wetlands that have organic soils) are less common and are found mainly in the northwestern part of the State. Palustrine forested wetlands are more abundant and more widely distributed in New Jersey than any other wetland type. They also have the most diverse vegetation. Of the palustrine category, about three-fifths (by area) is deciduous-forested (hardwood swamps), and about one-fifth is evergreen-forested (cedar swamps and pitch-pine lowlands). Nearly

three-fourths of New Jersey's estuarine wetlands is salt and brackish marsh distributed over four major drainage areas: Hudson River–Raritan Bay, Barnegat Bay, New Jersey inland bays, and Delaware Bay (Field and others, 1991).

The location of New Jersey's wetlands is closely related to the State's ecoregion distribution (fig. 2B), as defined by Omernik (1987). The ecoregional structure of the State is, in large part, defined by its physiography (fig. 2C), which is, in turn, determined primarily by its geology and glacial history. The northern part of the State is mostly in the Northern Piedmont Ecoregion and is underlain by sedimentary, igneous, and metamorphic rocks that have been modified in places by glacial action. During the last ice age, glaciation affected the northern one-third of the State, and this was a major factor in the creation of wetlands there. After the glaciers melted, wetlands formed in depressions left by glacial action. Three of the State's physiographic units—the Piedmont, New England, and Valley and Ridge Provinces—largely correspond to the sedimentary and igneous geological units of the northern part of the State and generally coincide with the Northern Piedmont Ecoregion.

The State's southern one-half lies in the Middle Atlantic Coastal Plain ecoregion and is in the Coastal Plain physiographic province, which is underlain by layered sedimentary rocks. Water in the well-drained sandy soils and aquifers of the southern part of the State discharges to the barrier-island embayments of the Atlantic coast and to the Delaware Bay, forming estuarine wetlands along those coasts. Also, freshwater wetlands have formed where water discharges to streams or to depressions in the low-relief landscape.

Human and animal activities also have created wetlands. Beaver have played an important role, creating impoundments behind their dams. Dam building, farm-pond construction, and construc-

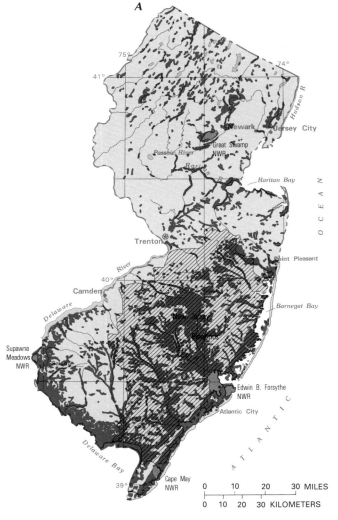

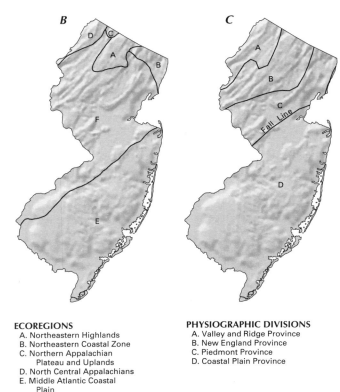

WETLANDS AND DEEPWATER HABITATS

Distribution of wetlands and deepwater habitats—
This map shows the approximate distribution of large wetlands in the State. Because of limitations of scale and source material, some wetlands are not shown

■ Predominantly wetland

▨ Predominantly deepwater habitat

ECOREGIONS
A. Northeastern Highlands
B. Northeastern Coastal Zone
C. Northern Appalachian Plateau and Uplands
D. North Central Appalachians
E. Middle Atlantic Coastal Plain
F. Northern Piedmont

PHYSIOGRAPHIC DIVISIONS
A. Valley and Ridge Province
B. New England Province
C. Piedmont Province
D. Coastal Plain Province

Figure 2. Wetland distribution in New Jersey and ecological and physical features that control wetland distribution in the State. *A*, Distribution of wetlands and deepwater habitats. *B*, Ecoregions. *C*, Physiography. *(Sources: A, T.E. Dahl, U.S. Fish and Wildlife Service, unpub. data, 1991. B, Omernik, 1987. C, Physiographic divisions from Fenneman, 1946; landforms data from EROS Data Center.)*

tion of artificially engineered wetlands are three of the ways that humans can create wetlands. Wetlands also can be formed by river action (Tiner, 1985).

HYDROLOGIC SETTING

New Jersey has two geohydrologic regimes—one south of the Fall Line in the Coastal Plain, and the other north of the Fall Line, associated with the State's remaining physiographic provinces. The aquifer system of the Coastal Plain in the southern one-half of the State is composed of alternating layers of unconsolidated clay, sand, and gravel. In contrast, north of the Fall Line, ground water flows through fractured rocks and glacial valley-fill deposits. Precipitation, which is the source of water to the State's hydrologic system, ranges from about 43 inches on the coast to about 47 inches in the northern part. About one-half of the precipitation that reaches the land surface is returned to the atmosphere by evaporation and plant transpiration.

South of the Fall Line.—About 95 percent of the State's estuarine wetlands and 75 percent of its marshes and swamplands are in the Coastal Plain. Coastal Plain wetlands constitute about 87 percent of the State's total wetland area (Tiner, 1985). The layered clay, sand, and gravel that make up New Jersey's Coastal Plain form a wedge that dips and thickens to the southeast. From a feather edge along the Fall Line and the Delaware River, the Coastal Plain sediments thicken to more than 1,000 feet at the Continental Shelf. Recharge to the region's shallow ground-water system occurs in interstream areas. Water entering the system flows toward areas of lower altitude, where it returns to the surface as base flow to streams, ponds, and lakes and as leakage to coastal water bodies. Aquifers that are overlain by relatively impermeable clay layers are recharged by precipitation entering outcrop areas near the Fall Line and by slow percolation downward through the confining clay.

Wetlands form where ground water discharges along rivers and streams and in low-lying coastal areas. Farther inland, wetlands form where clay or other impervious materials restrict vertical water movement and provide habitats for hydrophytic vegetation. The forested swamplands in the Coastal Plain are strongly associated with rivers and streams—many of them in the New Jersey Pinelands. Most estuarine wetlands in the Coastal Plain are located in the barrier-island complex that lies along the Atlantic coast south of Point Pleasant and on the coast of the Delaware Bay south of Salem.

North of the Fall Line.—Northern New Jersey is underlain by consolidated sedimentary and igneous rocks. In such geohydrologic systems, ground-water storage and flow occur in fractures in the rocks. In the northeastern part of the State, glacial valley-fill sediments also store and transport water. Most of the wetlands in the northern part of the State are palustrine and have formed around water in glacial lakes and depressions that formed at the end of the last ice age. These lakes are gradually filling in with organic matter and becoming emergent, scrub-shrub, or forested wetlands that have organic soils. Water for the wetlands is supplied by precipitation and by ground-water discharge from the surrounding glacial sediments and fractured crystalline rock. Where silt and clay locally confine the aquifers, freshwater wetlands such as the Great Swamp have formed (Vecchioli and others, 1962).

The location and composition of plant communities inhabiting New Jersey's wetlands—both north and south of the Fall Line—are affected by depth of water, water-level fluctuations, soil moisture, and salinity (Penfound, 1952), as well as by other soil properties, biological factors, and human activities.

TRENDS

The State's wetlands have been drained and filled since settlement by Europeans began in the 1600's. Dahl (1990) estimated that

New Jersey lost 39 percent of its wetlands between about 1780 and 1980. Filling increased markedly following World War II. Tiner (1987) estimates median losses of tidal marshes on a county-by-county basis from 1952 to 1973 at about 30 percent but reports losses of up to 100 percent in two counties. During that period, 2 of New Jersey's 15 counties that contain tidal marsh lost 100 percent of that marsh; 5 other counties lost about 50 percent of their tidal-marsh area. Ferrigno and others (1973) estimated that the loss in tidal-marsh acreage in New Jersey from 1953 to 1973 exceeded 24 percent. Since the enactment of the Wetlands Act of 1970 and the Freshwater Wetlands Protection Act of 1987 by the State, permitted wetland losses have fallen sharply to between 50 and 100 acres per year (Ernest Hahn, New Jersey Department of Environmental Protection and Energy, oral commun., 1992).

Wetlands have been drained primarily for crop production and pasturage. Wetlands have been filled for housing, transportation, industrialization, and landfills. Stream channelization, dredging for navigation, and reservoir, harbor, and marina construction also have adversely affected New Jersey's wetlands. In addition to quantitative changes caused by these activities, qualitative changes have resulted from point and nonpoint discharges to surface waters. The discharges are associated with agriculture, logging, industry, municipal sewage, and urban runoff, all of which add contaminants and silt to surface waters (Tiner, 1985). Although the trend has been toward a net loss of wetlands, some wetland area has been added through the construction of ponds and reservoirs and through planned wetland construction.

CONSERVATION

Many government agencies and private organizations participate in wetland conservation in New Jersey. The most active agencies and organizations and some of their activities are listed in table 1.

Federal wetland activities.—Development activities in New Jersey wetlands are regulated by several Federal statutory prohibitions and incentives that are intended to slow wetland losses. Some of the more important of these are contained in the 1899 Rivers and Harbors Act; the 1972 Clean Water Act and amendments; the 1985 Food Security Act; the 1990 Food, Agriculture, Conservation, and Trade Act; the 1986 Emergency Wetlands Resources Act; and the 1972 Coastal Zone Management Act.

Section 10 of the Rivers and Harbors Act gives the U.S. Army Corps of Engineers (Corps) authority to regulate certain activities in navigable waters. Regulated activities include diking, deepening, filling, excavating, and placing of structures. The related section 404 of the Clean Water Act is the most often-used Federal legislation protecting wetlands. Under section 404 provisions, the Corps issues permits regulating the discharge of dredged or fill material into wetlands. Permits are subject to review and possible veto by the U.S. Environmental Protection Agency, and the FWS has review and advisory roles. Section 401 of the Clean Water Act grants to States and eligible Indian Tribes the authority to approve, apply conditions to, or deny section 404 permit applications on the basis of a proposed activity's probable effects on the water quality of a wetland.

Most farming, ranching, and silvicultural activities are not subject to section 404 regulation. However, the "Swampbuster" provision of the 1985 Food Security Act and amendments in the 1990 Food, Agriculture, Conservation, and Trade Act discourage (through financial disincentives) the draining, filling, or other alteration of wetlands for agricultural use. The law allows exemptions from penalties in some cases, especially if the farmer agrees to restore the altered wetland or other wetlands that have been converted to agricultural use. The Wetlands Reserve Program of the 1990 Food, Agriculture, Conservation, and Trade Act authorizes the Federal Government to purchase conservation easements from landowners

Table 1. Selected wetland-related activities of government agencies and private organizations in New Jersey, 1993

[Source: Classification of activities is generalizexd from information provided by agencies and organizations. •, agency or organization participates in wetland-related activity; ..., agency or organization does not participate in wetland-related activity. MAN, management; REG, regulation; R&C, restoration and creation; LAN, land acquisition; R&D, research and data collection; D&I, delineation and inventory]

Agency or organization	MAN	REG	R&C	LAN	R&D	D&I
FEDERAL						
Department of Agriculture						
Consolidated Farm Service Agency	...	•	...	...	...	...
Forest Service	•	...	•	•	•	•
Natural Resources Conservation Service	...	•	•	...	•	•
Department of Commerce						
National Oceanic and Atmospheric Administration	•	•	•	...	...	...
Department of Defense						
Army Corps of Engineers	◦	•	•	...	•	•
Military reservations	•	...	...	...	...	...
Department of the Interior						
Fish and Wildlife Service	•	...	•	•	•	•
Geological Survey	...	...	...	...	•	...
National Biological Service	...	...	...	...	•	...
National Park Service	•	...	•	•	•	•
Environmental Protection Agency	•	...	...	...	•	•
STATE						
Department of Environmental Protection and Energy						
Bureau of Coastal Regulation	...	•	•	...	...	•
Bureau of Inland Regulation	...	•	•	...	...	•
The Natural Lands Trust	•	...	...	•	...	...
Pinelands Commission	•	•	...	•	•	•
Rutgers University Center for Coastal and Environmental Studies	...	...	...	...	•	...
PRIVATE						
Ducks Unlimited	•	...	•	...	•	•
The Nature Conservancy	•	...	•	•	•	...
The New Jersey Conservation Foundation	...	...	...	•	•	•
The Trust for Public Lands	...	...	...	•	...	...
Private cranberry growers	•	...	...	...	...	...

who agree to protect or restore wetlands. The Consolidated Farm Service Agency (formerly the Agricultural Stabilization and Conservation Service) administers the Swampbuster provisions and Wetlands Reserve Program. The Natural Resources Conservation Service (formerly the Soil Conservation Service) determines compliance with Swampbuster provisions and assists farmers in the identification of wetlands and in the development of wetland protection, restoration, or creation plans.

The 1986 Emergency Wetlands Resources Act and the 1972 Coastal Zone Management Act and amendments encourage wetland protection through funding incentives. The Emergency Wetland Resources Act requires States to address wetland protection in their Statewide Comprehensive Outdoor Recreation Plans to qualify for Federal funding for State recreational land; the National Park Service provides guidance to States in developing the wetland component of their plans. Coastal and Great Lakes States that adopt coastal-zone management programs and plans approved by the National Oceanic and Atmospheric Administration are eligible for Federal funding and technical assistance through the Coastal Zone Management Act.

Several wetlands in New Jersey have been specially designated for research, protection, education, or other purposes. The 13,080-acre Edwin B. Forsythe National Wildlife Refuge has been designated a wetland of international significance by the FWS under the Ramsar Convention. (The Ramsar Convention on Wetlands of International Importance, named for Ramsar, Iran, where the convention was held, is an intergovernmental treaty that forms the basis for international cooperation in conserving wetland habitats.) Also, Supawna Meadows on the Delaware Bay, Cape May, and the Great Swamp are National Wildlife Refuges. Many other New Jersey wetlands are in State Wildlife Management Areas. The New Jersey Pinelands extends across much of the eastern part of southern New Jersey. Most of the Pinelands, including its wetlands, is part of the Atlantic Coastal Plain Biosphere Reserve of the United Nations Man and the Biosphere program (Good and Good, 1984). In the Pinelands, the Mullica River estuary is part of the Experimental Ecological Reserve network. The Mullica River also is being considered as a site for a National Estuarine Research Reserve.

State Wetland Activities. — State laws governing wetlands are the Hackensack Meadowlands Reclamation and Development Act of 1969, the Wetlands Act of 1970, the Waterfront Development Act of 1914, the Coastal Area Facility Review Act of 1973, the Flood Hazard Area Control Act of 1979, the Pinelands Protection Act of 1979, and the Freshwater Wetlands Protection Act of 1987. State agencies that have a role in wetland conservation include the Delaware River Basin Commission, the New Jersey Department of Environmental Protection and Energy, and the Pinelands Commission. The Department of Environmental Protection and Energy administers the Wetlands Act of 1970, the Coastal Area Facility Review Act, the Waterfront Development Act of 1914, the Flood Hazard Control Act of 1979, and the Freshwater Wetlands Protection Act of 1987. The Pinelands Protection Act of 1979 is administered by the Pinelands Commission. A summary of these laws can be found in a publication by the Department of Environmental Protection and Energy (1992).

In addition to its wetland-management activities, New Jersey also is active in data collection and public education regarding wetlands. The State's Natural Heritage Program maintains a data base of rare plant, animal, and natural communities, and its Natural Areas program administers 42 areas that are set aside for public use and education. New Jersey also runs the Delaware Estuary Research Program and the Natural Lands Trust, a land-bank program. The Natural Lands Trust has protected between 6,000 and 7,000 acres of New Jersey wetlands, mostly salt marsh, and was active in obtaining designation of the Delaware Bay as a Ramsar site. The Rutgers University Center for Coastal and Environmental Studies performs research and data-collection activities.

Private wetland activities. — Several private organizations are active in New Jersey wetlands protection. The New Jersey Conservation Foundation has a wetland-acquisition program and was instrumental in obtaining passage of the New Jersey Freshwater Wetlands Protection Act. The Trust for Public Lands also administers a wetland-acquisition program. The Nature Conservancy and Ducks Unlimited acquire and manage wetlands, conduct research on the preservation of endangered species, and work to create and restore wetland areas. Cranberry growers also manage several thousand acres of wetlands.

References Cited

Cowardin, L.M., Carter, Virginia, Golet, F.C., and LaRoe, E.T., 1979, Classification of wetlands and deepwater habitats of the United States: U.S. Fish and Wildlife Service Report, FWS/OBS–79/31, 131 p.

Dahl, T.E., 1990, Wetlands—Losses in the United States, 1780's to 1980's: Washington, D.C., U.S. Fish and Wildlife Service Report to Congress, 13 p.

Fenneman, N.M., 1946, Physical divisions of the United States: U.S. Geological Survey special map, scale 1:7,000,000.

Ferrigno, Fred, Widjeskog, Lee, and Toth, Steve, 1973, Marsh destruction: Trenton, New Jersey Department of Environmental Protection, Division of Fish, Game, and Wildlife, 20 p.

Field, D.W., Reyer, A.J., Genovese, P.V., and Shearer, B.D., 1991, Coastal wetlands of the United States—An accounting of a valuable natural resource: Washington, D.C., National Oceanic and Atmospheric Administration and U.S. Fish and Wildlife Service cooperative report, 59 p.

Good, R.E., and Good, N.F., 1984, The Pinelands National Reserve—An ecosystem approach to management: BioScience, v. 34, no. 3, p. 169–173.

Hafner, C.L., Moore, C.R., and Day, C.G., 1992, An investigation and verification of draft national wetlands inventory maps for Cape May County, New Jersey: Pleasantville, N.J., U.S. Fish and Wildlife Service, 93 p.

New Jersey Department of Environmental Protection and Energy, 1992, The environmental manual for municipal officials: Trenton, New Jersey Department of Environmental Protection and Energy and The Association of New Jersey Environmental Commissions, 177 p.

Omernik, J.M., 1987, Ecoregions of the conterminous United States—Map supplement: Annals of the Association of American Geographers, v. 77, no. 1, scale 1:7,500,000.

Penfound, W.T., 1952, Southern swamps and marshes: Botanical Review, v. 18, p. 413–446.

Reyer, A.J., Shearer, B.D., Genovese, P.V., Holland, C.L., Cassells, J.E., Field, D.W., and Alexander, C.E., 1990, The distribution and areal extent of coastal wetlands in estuaries of the mid-Atlantic region: Washington, D.C., National Oceanic and Atmospheric Administration, 23 p.

Tiner, R.W., Jr., 1985, Wetlands of New Jersey: Newton Corner, Mass., U.S. Fish and Wildlife Service, 117 p.

_____1987, Mid-Atlantic wetlands—A disappearing natural treasure: Newton Corner, Mass., U.S. Fish and Wildlife Service, 28 p.

Vecchioli, John, Gill, H.E., and Lang, S.M., 1962, Hydrologic role of the Great Swamp and other marshland in the upper Passaic River basin: Journal of the American Water Works Association, v. 54, no. 6, p. 695–701.

FOR ADDITIONAL INFORMATION: District Chief, U.S. Geological Survey, 810 Bear Tavern Road, Suite 206, West Trenton, NJ 08628; Regional Wetland Coordinator, U.S. Fish and Wildlife Service, 300 Westgate Center Drive, Hadley, MA 01035

Prepared by
Thomas H. Barringer,
U.S. Geological Survey

New Mexico
Wetland Resources

Wetlands cover about 482,000 acres (0.6 percent) of New Mexico, a reduction of about 33 percent from the wetland acreage that existed about 200 years ago (Dahl, 1990). New Mexico's wetland acreage places the State 34th in total wetland acreage among the 48 conterminous States.

Wetlands are ecologically important and economically valuable to the State. Wetlands provide important wildlife habitat. For example, in the Rio Grande Valley, wetlands provide habitat for 246 species of birds, 10 species of amphibians, 38 species of reptiles, and 60 species of mammals (U.S. Fish and Wildlife Service, 1990). Wetlands also provide stopover, feeding, and breeding grounds for migratory waterfowl (fig. 1).

Riparian (streamside) wetlands along perennial streams are important as migration corridors for a variety of waterfowl and other wildlife. The playa lakes in eastern New Mexico are vital links in a chain of wetlands along the Central Flyway, which extends from central Canada to the coast of Texas. Areas of springs and marshes provide essential habitat for many rare and endangered species and for indigenous fish and wildlife in the western part of the State.

Wetlands contribute to flood attenuation, bank stabilization, and improved water quality. New Mexico's tourist industry benefits from the beauty of the State's diverse wetlands. These wetlands provide opportunities for recreational activities that include fishing, hunting, bird watching, nature photography, camping, and hiking.

TYPES AND DISTRIBUTION

Wetlands are lands transitional between terrestrial and deepwater habitats where the water table usually is at or near the land surface or the land is covered by shallow water (Cowardin and others, 1979). The distribution of wetlands and deepwater habitats in New Mexico is shown in figure 2A; only wetlands are discussed herein.

Wetlands can be vegetated or nonvegetated and are classified on the basis of their hydrology, vegetation, and substrate. In this summary, wetlands are classified according to the system proposed by Cowardin and others (1979), which is used by the U.S. Fish and Wildlife Service (FWS) to map and inventory the Nation's wetlands. At the most general level of the classification system, wetlands are grouped into five ecological systems: Palustrine, Lacustrine, Riverine, Estuarine, and Marine. The Palustrine System includes only

Figure 1. Bosque del Apache National Wildlife Refuge. These riparian wetlands provide habitat for migratory and resident waterfowl, fish, and other wildlife. *(Photograph by Lisa Carter, U.S. Geological Survey.)*

wetlands, whereas the other systems comprise wetlands and deepwater habitats. Wetlands of the systems that occur in New Mexico are described below.

System	Wetland description
Palustrine	Wetlands in which vegetation is predominantly trees (forested wetlands); shrubs (scrub-shrub wetlands); persistent or nonpersistent emergent, erect, rooted, herbaceous plants (persistent- and nonpersistent-emergent wetlands); or submersed and (or) floating plants (aquatic beds). Also, intermittently to permanently flooded open-water bodies of less than 20 acres in which water is less than 6.6 feet deep.
Lacustrine	Wetlands within an intermittently to permanently flooded lake or reservoir. Vegetation, when present, is predominantly nonpersistent emergent plants (nonpersistent-emergent wetlands), or submersed and (or) floating plants (aquatic beds), or both.
Riverine	Wetlands within a channel. Vegetation, when present, is same as in the Lacustrine System.

Although wetlands occur in all areas of New Mexico, they are most numerous in the eastern and northern areas of the State (fig. 2A). In the Southern Rocky Mountains (fig. 2B), wetlands are mostly in high mountain valleys and intermountain basins. In the Great Plains, wetlands occur along the flood plains of the Canadian and Pecos Rivers and in association with playa lakes. In the Colorado Plateaus and Basin and Range, wetlands are sparsely distributed, with the exception of wetlands associated with the San Juan, San Francisco, and Gila Rivers.

Palustrine wetlands are distributed statewide. In New Mexico, palustrine wetlands include forested wetlands in river flood plains and near springs and seeps; scrub-shrub wetlands such as bottomland shrubland; emergent wetlands, such as marshes, fens, alpine snow glades, and wet and salt meadows; aquatic bed wetlands in shallow ponds and small lakes; and sparsely or nonvegetated wetlands such as playa lakes. Palustrine wetlands along rivers, streams, springs, lakes, and ponds are called riparian wetlands. Riparian wetlands along the State's major rivers provide habitat for fish, wildlife, and diverse plant life. They also provide habitat for migrating, overwintering, and nesting waterfowl. One of the more notable riparian wetlands in New Mexico is in the Bosque del Apache National Wildlife Refuge. The 57,191-acre refuge lies along 9 miles of the Rio Grande in south-central New Mexico. Marshes within the refuge are ideal winter habitat for migratory birds, including ducks, geese, sandhill cranes, and whooping cranes. Efforts are being made to maintain and restore native riparian cottonwood habitat in the refuge for a variety of birds and other wildlife. Many western species of riparian trees and shrubs, such as willows and cottonwoods, have been lost because of nonnatural streamflow regimes (Howe and Knopf, 1991). The nonnatural flows followed the completion of water projects in the first half of the 20th century, resulting in rapid colonization and expansion of the exotic Russian-olive and salt cedar.

The playa lakes of eastern New Mexico provide habitat for migrating, overwintering, and nesting waterfowl in the Central Flyway (U.S. Fish and Wildlife Service, 1990). The estimated number of playa lakes in the State is 1,700, and they range in area from less than 1 acre to more than 600 acres (Nelson and others, 1983). The playa lakes range in wetness from dry lake bed to shallow lake and can be fresh or saline. The freshwater playas are numerous, small to medium in size, and serve as zones of recharge to the underlying aquifer (Osterkamp and Wood, 1987). The saline playas are larger and fewer than the freshwater playas and are areas of discharge from the underlying aquifer. Most playa lakes in New Mexico are palustrine. However, playa lakes larger than 20 acres are classified as lacustrine wetlands, as are the shallow areas of large reservoirs.

Riverine wetlands occur in the shallow river channels of perennial streams. There are about 3,500 miles of streams in New Mexico (Ong and others, 1993).

HYDROLOGIC SETTING

Wetlands form where a persistent water supply is at or near the land surface. The location and persistence of the supply of water is a function of precipitation and runoff patterns, evaporation potential, topography, and the presence of a shallow water table.

Precipitation and runoff rates differ annually and with location and season. Average annual precipitation in New Mexico (fig. 2C) ranges from about 8 inches in the northwestern corner of the State and in the southern Rio Grande Valley to 24 inches in the mountains of the northern and southern parts of the State. Runoff (fig. 2D) is greatest in the northern mountains and smallest in the desert areas of the southern and eastern parts of the State. Much of the runoff from the mountains occurs during concurrent snowmelt and rainfall in the spring and summer.

Average annual pan evaporation varies across the State and ranges from about 40 to 112 inches per year (Nelson and others, 1983). Most evaporation occurs from March through September and decreases with increasing altitude. Because annual evaporation exceeds annual rainfall, most of the State has a net annual moisture deficit. The moisture deficit is a limiting factor in the formation of wetlands and to the continued existence of some of the more fragile wetlands. Even those areas of the State having the highest precipitation and lowest evaporation (high mountain regions) can be unfavorable for development of wetlands because of steep topography, shifting stream channels, and unfavorable soil conditions (Cooper, 1986).

Shallow water tables and groundwater discharge into topographic depressions, streams, and springs maintain wetlands in many areas of New Mexico. These wetlands can be along small streams that have perennial flow in only short reaches or along larger, perennial streams. In intermountain basins, wetlands are maintained by a shallow water table and springs whose source is recharge from precipitation and runoff that occur during spring and summer.

Climatic, topographic, and hydrologic characteristics differ among and sometimes within the physiographic provinces. New Mexico's diverse physiography, climate, and topography result in diverse hydrologic settings for wetland formation.

In the Colorado Plateaus and Basin and Range Provinces (fig. 2B), wetlands occur in springs and seeps, around oxbow lakes, along streams and rivers, around reservoirs, and in other areas where the water table is near the land surface. The arid climate of this region results in a low density and acreage of wetlands. Wetlands, although few in number, are vital to wildlife of these physiographic provinces.

In the Great Plains, wetlands occur in riparian zones along perennial streams, around oxbow lakes, in isolated natural depressions with permanent or seasonal water supply, in playa lakes, and in association with other lakes, reservoirs, channelized streams, rivers, and irrigation ditches. Playa lakes make up the largest area of wetlands in this province.

The area of playa lakes has topography classified as either smooth plains, irregular plains, or tablelands (Nelson and others, 1983). Smooth plains are largely on upland terrain, and irregular plains and tablelands are mostly on lowland terrain. Because of the flatness of the terrain, there is generally little stream drainage, and playa lakes collect most of the surface runoff. The playa lakes are

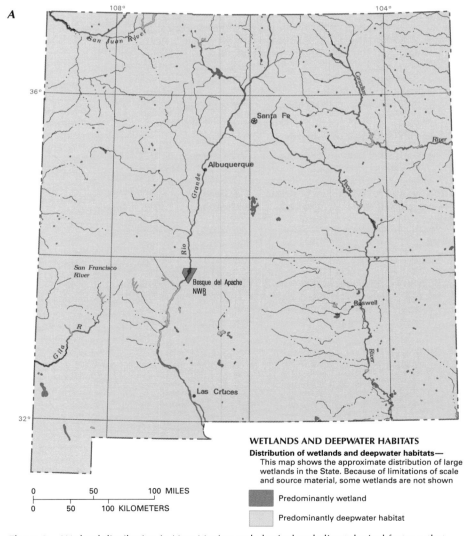

WETLANDS AND DEEPWATER HABITATS
Distribution of wetlands and deepwater habitats—
This map shows the approximate distribution of large wetlands in the State. Because of limitations of scale and source material, some wetlands are not shown

■ Predominantly wetland

▢ Predominantly deepwater habitat

Figure 2. Wetland distribution in New Mexico and physical and climatological features that control wetland distribution in the State. **A,** Distribution of wetlands and deepwater habitats. *(Sources: A, T.E. Dahl, U.S. Fish and Wildlife Service, unpub. data, 1991.)*

usually shallow depressions that have large surface area relative to the total volume of water contained in them. Consequently, most playa lakes have small storage capacities.

Studies by Osterkamp and Wood (1987) indicate that freshwater playa lakes in the Great Plains of New Mexico originate wherever surface depressions collect precipitation runoff. The lakes enlarge as a result of dissolution of carbonates by water infiltrating the unsaturated zone above the underlying aquifer and subsequent subsidence of the lake bed. Over time, the older central lake acquires a layer of clay-rich deposits that largely restricts water movement from the playa lake to the underlying aquifer. Water probably is removed from freshwater playa lakes primarily by recharge to the underlying aquifer from the areas around the lake where lake-bed sediments have not yet accumulated (Osterkamp and Wood, 1987) and by evaporation that in some years ranges as high as 96 to 112 inches per year (Nelson and others, 1983). There is no general agree-

ment on the origin of saline playa lakes; however, Wood and Jones (1990) propose that the source of the salinity is from the concentration by evaporation of runoff and shallow, fresh ground water that discharges from the underlying aquifer.

In the Southern Rocky Mountains, wetlands occur in two physiographically and climatically distinct settings, mountain valleys and intermountain basins. Generally, mountain valleys are geologically young and therefore steep. The valleys have been shaped over time either by running water throughout their entire length or by glaciers at higher altitudes and running water at lower altitudes. At high altitudes in some mountain valleys, glaciation formed large cirque basins in which remnant glaciers or late-melting snow maintains spring, seep, and snow-bed wetlands. Also, at these high altitudes, ponds form in depressions behind slumping saturated soils or in depressions caused by the weight of accumulated snow. Below the cirque basins, wetlands occur in the glaciated, U-shaped valleys, on saturated cliff faces, at the sloping floor near the sides of the valley, in glacial kettle ponds, in oxbow lakes, in depressions on glacial moraines, in lakes created by terminal or lateral moraines, in landslide-formed lakes, in seeps and springs, and in beaver ponds. In steep, V-shaped, nonglaciated areas of mountain valleys, wetlands occur as narrow riparian wetlands, near seeps and springs, and in beaver ponds (Windell and others, 1986).

Intermountain basins were filled by sediments derived from erosion of the surrounding mountains. The large, flat valleys are drained by low-gradient meandering streams and rivers. Intermountain-basin wetlands occur along these streams and rivers, in constructed and natural impoundments, around oxbow lakes, and in other areas where the water table is near the land surface. The shallow water table is maintained by underlying aquifers, impermeable substrates, or annual floods (Windell and others, 1986).

TRENDS

The FWS has estimated that from the 1780's to the 1980's, wetland acreage in New Mexico decreased by 33 percent—from about 720,000 to 482,000 acres (Dahl, 1990). Much of the decrease is attributable to the loss of native vegetation along streams because

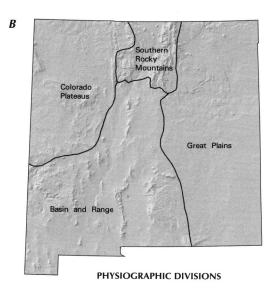

PHYSIOGRAPHIC DIVISIONS

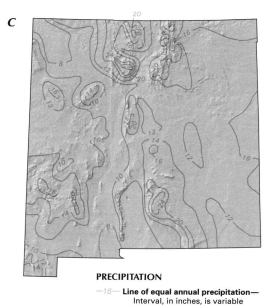

PRECIPITATION

—*16*— **Line of equal annual precipitation—**
Interval, in inches, is variable

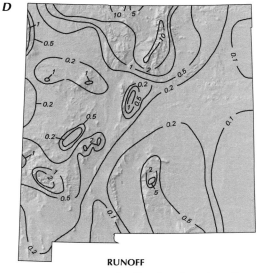

RUNOFF

— *2* — **Line of equal annual runoff—**
Interval, in inches, is variable

Figure 2. Continued. Wetland distribution in New Mexico and physical and climatological features that control wetland distribution in the State. ***B***, Physiography. ***C***, Average annual precipitation. ***D***, Average annual runoff. (*Sources: B, Physiographic divisions from Fenneman, 1946; landforms data from EROS Data Center. C and D, Gold and Denis, 1986.*)

of a change in streamflow resulting from reservoir construction or agricultural water diversions. The loss of native vegetation along streams alters riparian-wetland functions and allows the proliferation of nonnative vegetation (Howe and Knopf, 1991).

Wetland losses in rural areas can be attributed to conversion to cropland, dewatering or diverting water for irrigation, and overgrazing by livestock. Development of urban areas has caused wetland loss or degradation owing to encroachment of residential and commercial construction, dewatering for municipal and industrial water supply, channelization, and contamination from inadequately treated sewage and industrial waste. Other causes of wetland loss or degradation are clear cutting, burning, hard-rock mining and related activities that produce toxic acidic or alkaline runoff, placer mining, erosion and sedimentation, sand and gravel mining, road and railroad construction, and dam and reservoir construction in wetland areas (Windell and others, 1986).

Some human activities have helped to form wetlands or enlarge existing ones. The construction of reservoirs between 1916 and 1985, which provided for storage of more than 5.9 million acre-feet of surface water (Garrabrant and Garn, 1990), resulted in the formation of wetlands along the edge of those water bodies. However, such gains are at the expense of the original, natural riparian wetlands. Farm-pond construction also contributes to the formation of wetlands around the edge of the pond. More than one-half of the State's cropland is irrigated (Garrabrant and Garn, 1990), and leaking ditches and seeps and return flow associated with irrigation have contributed to the formation of wetlands.

CONSERVATION

Many government agencies and private organizations participate in wetland conservation in New Mexico. The most active agencies and organizations and some of their activities are listed in table 1.

Federal wetland activities. — Development activities in New Mexico wetlands are regulated by several Federal statutory prohibitions and incentives that are intended to slow wetland losses. Some of the more important of these are contained in the 1899 Rivers and Harbors Act; the 1972 Clean Water Act and amendments; the 1985 Food Security Act; the 1990 Food, Agriculture, Conservation, and Trade Act; and the 1986 Emergency Wetlands Resources Act.

Section 10 of the Rivers and Harbors Act gives the U.S. Army Corps of Engineers (Corps) authority to regulate certain activities in navigable waters. Regulated activities include diking, deepening, filling, excavating, and placing of structures. The related section 404 of the Clean Water Act is the most often-used Federal legislation protecting wetlands. Under section 404 provisions, the Corps issues permits regulating the discharge of dredged or fill material into wetlands. Permits are subject to review and possible veto by the U.S. Environmental Protection Agency, and the FWS has review and advisory roles. Section 401 of the Clean Water Act grants to States and eligible Indian Tribes the authority to approve, apply conditions to, or deny section 404 permit applications on the basis of a proposed activity's probable effects on the water quality of a wetland.

Most farming, ranching, and silviculture activities are not subject to section 404 regulation. However, the "Swampbuster" provision of the 1985 Food Security Act and amendments in the 1990 Food, Agriculture, Conservation, and Trade Act discourage (through financial disincentives) the draining, filling, or other alteration of wetlands for agricultural use. The law allows exemptions from penalties in some cases, especially if the farmer agrees to restore the altered wetland or other wetlands that have been converted to agricultural use. The Wetlands Reserve Program of the 1990 Food, Agriculture, Conservation, and Trade Act authorizes the Federal Government to purchase conservation easements from landowners who agree to protect or restore wetlands. The Consolidated Farm

Table 1. Selected wetland-related activities of government agencies and private organizations in New Mexico, 1993

[Source: Classification of activities is generalized from information provided by agencies and organizations. •, agency or organization participates in wetland-related activity; ..., agency or organization does not participate in wetland-related activity. MAN, management; REG, regulation; R&C, restoration and creation; LAN, land acquisition; R&D, research and data collection; D&I, delineation and inventory]

Agency or organization	MAN	REG	R&C	LAN	R&D	D&I
FEDERAL						
Department of Agriculture						
Consolidated Farm Service Agency	...	•	...	...	...	...
Forest Service	•	...	•	•	•	•
Natural Resources Conservation Service	...	•	•	...	•	•
Department of Defense						
Army Corps of Engineers	•	•	•	...	...	...
Military reservations	•	...	...	...	...	...
Department of the Interior						
Bureau of Land Management	•	...	•	•	•	•
Bureau of Reclamation	•	...	•	...	•	...
Fish and Wildlife Service	•	...	•	•	•	•
Geological Survey	...	...	...	...	•	...
National Biological Service	...	...	...	...	•	...
National Park Service	•	...	•	•	•	•
Environmental Protection Agency	...	•	...	...	•	...
STATE						
Department of Game and Fish	•	•	•	•	...	•
Energy, Mineral, and Natural Resources Department	...	...	•	...	...	...
Environment Department	•	•	•	...	...	•
State Engineer Office	•	•	...	...	...	•
University of New Mexico						
Natural Heritage Program	...	...	...	...	•	•
COUNTY AND LOCAL GOVERNMENTS						
Albuquerque Open Space Division	•	...	•	•	•	•
Santa Fe County	...	...	...	...	•	•
PRIVATE ORGANIZATIONS						
National Audubon Society	...	...	•	...	...	...
Sierra Club	...	...	•	...	•	...
The Nature Conservancy	...	...	•	...	...	...

Service Agency (formerly the Agricultural Stabilization and Conservation Service) administers the Swampbuster provisions and Wetlands Reserve Program. The Natural Resources Conservation Service (formerly the Soil Conservation Service) determines compliance with Swampbuster provisions and assists farmers in the identification of wetlands and in the development of wetland protection, restoration, or creation plans.

The 1986 Emergency Wetlands Resources Act encourages wetland protection through funding incentives. The act requires States to address wetland protection in their Statewide Comprehensive Outdoor Recreation Plans to qualify for Federal funding for State recreational land; the National Park Service provides guidance to States in developing the wetland component of their plans.

The U.S. Forest Service (FS) manages five National Forests in New Mexico that contain diverse wetlands and riparian ecosystems. The FS also coordinates with State agencies and private landowners on wetland-conservation activities.

The FWS manages six National Wildlife Refuges in New Mexico that provide habitat for migrating birds, endangered species, and other wildlife and wildlife-oriented public recreation. Under the 1986 Emergency Wetlands Resources Act, the FWS evaluated eight priority wetland sites in the State for acquisition (U.S. Fish and Wildlife Service, 1990).

A goal of the Bureau of Land Management (BLM) is to restore, maintain, and improve riparian wetland area conditions on public land in New Mexico. The BLM is responsible for the management of 12.8 million acres of public land in the tristate area of New Mexico,

Oklahoma, and Kansas, which includes 27,600 acres of riparian wetland (Bureau of Land Management, 1990).

State wetland activities.—The principal State agencies in New Mexico that regulate or manage wetlands are the Department of Game and Fish, Environment Department, and the State Engineer Office. Also involved is the State Park and Recreation Division of the Energy, Mineral, and Natural Resources Department, which developed the New Mexico Wetlands Priority Conservation Plan (New Mexico Energy, Minerals, and Natural Resources Department, 1988). This plan is a component of the 1986 Statewide Comprehensive Outdoor Recreation Plan. The goals of agencies managing wetlands in New Mexico are to provide habitat for fish and wildlife and for diverse plant species, to maintain wetlands for erosion and flood control, and to enhance wetlands as agricultural, recreational, and scenic resources.

State management of wetlands in New Mexico began with an assessment of State wetlands by the State Park and Recreation Division (New Mexico Energy, Minerals, and Natural Resources Department, 1988). The steps in the assessment were to locate wetlands, determine their types, assess their quality, prioritize them according to their value and benefit, and rate the probable effect on them of each of the major causes of wetland losses. The Division considers the seven major causes of loss or degradation of wetlands in New Mexico to be (1) municipal water development, (2) natural water-table fluctuation, (3) development of land surfaces, (4) pollution, (5) erosion, tree cutting, or siltation, (6) invasion by nonnative plant species, and (7) poor management. The assessment of the quality of wetlands is based on habitat conditions, the dominance of native or rare species, the presence of terrestrial animals, and the uniqueness of the wetland in New Mexico. State government acquisition of wetlands will be based on whether the public values and benefits of wetlands can be maintained or realized under present ownership (New Mexico Energy, Minerals, and Natural Resources Department, 1988).

County and local wetland activities.—The Open Space Division of the city of Albuquerque acquires, manages, and restores wetlands. The Division also conducts feasibility studies and inventories wetlands in areas under its jurisdiction. The county of Santa Fe is involved in research and inventory of wetlands in the county.

Private wetland activities.—Private organizations involved in wetland management and conservation in New Mexico include the National Audubon Society, the Sierra Club, and The Nature Conservancy. A principal activity of the National Audubon Society and the Sierra Club is the restoration and creation of wetlands. The Sierra Club also conducts research in wetlands. The Nature Conservancy acquires wetlands and other ecologically valuable habitats for conservation. A major goal of these private organizations is to inform the public about the value of wetlands.

References Cited

Bureau of Land Management, 1990, New Mexico riparian-wetland 2000— A management strategy: Santa Fe, N. Mex., Bureau of Land Management, 25 p.

Cooper, D.J., 1986, Ecological studies in wetland vegetation, Cross Creek Valley, Holy Cross Wilderness, Sawatch Range, Colorado: Boulder, Colo., Holy Cross Wilderness Defense Fund Technical Report 2, 25 p. (Available from Holy Cross Wilderness Defense Fund, 1130 Alpine, Boulder, Colo. 80304.)

Cowardin, L.M., Carter, Virginia, Golet, F.C., and LaRoe, E.T., 1979, Classification of wetlands and deepwater habitats of the United States: U.S. Fish and Wildlife Service Report FWS/OBS–79/31, 131 p.

Dahl, T.E., 1990, Wetlands—Losses in the United States, 1780's to 1980's: Washington, D.C., U.S. Fish and Wildlife Service Report to Congress, 13 p.

Fenneman, N.M., 1946, Physical divisions of the United States: Washington, D.C., U.S. Geological Survey special map, scale 1:7,000,000.

Garrabrant, L.A., and Garn, H.S., 1990, New Mexico water supply and use, *in* National water summary 1987—Hydrologic events and water supply and use: U.S. Geological Survey Water Supply Paper 2350, p. 375–382.

Gold, R.L., and Denis, L.P., Jr., 1986, New Mexico surface-water resources, *in* U.S. Geological Survey, National water summary 1985—Hydrologic events and surface-water resources: U.S. Geological Survey Water-Supply Paper 2300, p. 341–346.

Howe, W.H., and Knopf, F.L., 1991, On the imminent decline of Rio Grande cottonwoods in central New Mexico: The Southwestern Naturalist, v. 36, no. 2, p. 218–224.

Nelson, R.W., Logan, W.J., and Weller, E.C., 1983, Playa wetlands and wildlife on the southern great plains—A characterization of habitat: U.S. Fish and Wildlife Service Report FWS/OBS–83128, 163 p.

New Mexico Energy, Minerals, and Natural Resources Department, 1988, New Mexico wetlands priority conservation plan: Albuquerque, N. Mex., New Mexico Energy, Minerals and Natural Resources Department, State Park and Recreation Division, 78 p.

Ong, Kim, Lepp, R.L., and Piatt, Jim, 1993, New Mexico stream water quality, *in* U.S. Geological Survey, National water summary 1990–91—Hydrologic events and stream water quality: U.S. Geological Survey Water-Supply Paper 2400, p. 403–412.

Osterkamp, W.R., and Wood, W.W., 1987, Playa lake basins on the Southern High Plains of Texas and New Mexico—Part 1, Hydrologic, geomorphic, and geologic evidence for their development: Geologic Society of America Bulletin, v. 99, no. 2, p. 215–223.

U.S. Fish and Wildlife Service, 1990, Regional wetlands concept plan—New Mexico wetlands: Albuquerque, N. Mex., U.S. Fish and Wildlife Service, 185 p.

Windell, J.T., Willard, B.E., Cooper, D.J., and others, 1986, An ecological characterization of Rocky Mountain montane and subalpine wetlands: U.S. Fish and Wildlife Service Biological Report 86 (11), 298 p.

Wood, W.W., and Jones, B.F., 1990, Origin of saline lakes and springs on the southern High Plains of Texas and New Mexico, *in* Gustavson, T.C., ed., Geological framework and regional hydrology—Upper Cenozoic Blackwater Draw and Ogallala Formation, Great Plains: Austin, Tex., Bureau of Economic Geology, p. 193–208.

FOR ADDITIONAL INFORMATION: District Chief, U.S. Geological Survey, 4501 Indian School Rd., NE, Suite 200, Albuquerque, NM 87110; Regional Wetland Coordinator, U.S. Fish and Wildlife, Fish and Wildlife Enhancement, 500 Gold Ave., SW, Albuquerque, NM 87103

Prepared by
B.D. Jones,
U.S. Geological Survey

New York
Wetland Resources

The diverse wetlands of New York have formed from the interaction of geologic events, climate, and hydrology. New York's freshwater and saltwater wetlands are important for fish and wildlife, environmental quality, human society, and the economy. Estuarine wetlands provide habitat for clams and oysters, and they provide spawning and nursery grounds for commercially important fish species, including alewife, blueback herring, bass, white perch, American shad, menhaden, bluefish, sea trout, and mullet. Many bird species, including osprey, peregrine falcons, snow and Canada geese, and pintail, canvasback, mallard, and black ducks, use New York's salt marshes for feeding, migration, and wintering grounds. Nesting bald eagles and the largest colony of great blue herons in New York live in the Iroquois National Wildlife Refuge. Beavers, muskrat, raccoons, river otters, foxes, and rabbits use wetlands as a source of food and shelter. Many reptile and amphibian species also live in the State's wetlands.

New York's wetlands are home to many threatened and endangered plants and animals. Of the 160 threatened or endangered plant species identified by the State's Department of Environmental Conservation, 50 percent are wetland species, as are 10 species of vertebrates (Alvin Breisch, New York State Department of Environmental Conservation, oral commun., 1993).

The environmental quality of aquatic habitats is enhanced by wetlands. Wetlands filter or absorb nutrients, and they also remove heavy metals and other contaminants from waters moving through them. Wetlands reduce turbidity and sediment loading, thereby slowing the siltation of harbors and navigable rivers and streams. The aquatic productivity of wetlands is very high — the amount of plant material produced per acre annually by an estuarine wetland (gross primary productivity) has been estimated to be about the same as that of a tropical rain forest (Odum, 1971). Salt marshes support a diverse community of animals that inhabit estuarine waters.

In addition to the habitat and environmental benefits of wetlands, they also provide socioeconomic benefits, including flood and storm-damage protection, erosion control, and the production of plants such as blueberries, cranberries, wild rice, salt hay, and timber. Wetlands also provide many recreational and educational opportunities, including hunting and fishing, nature study, boating, painting and drawing, and photography. The Hudson River National Estuarine Research Reserve (fig. 1) is a wetland-upland complex of national significance that provides outstanding opportunities for research and education.

TYPES AND DISTRIBUTION

Wetlands are lands transitional between terrestrial and deepwater habitats where the water table usually is at or near the land surface or the land is covered by shallow water (Cowardin and others, 1979). The distribution of wetlands and deepwater habitats in New York is shown in figure 2A; only wetlands are discussed herein.

Wetlands can be vegetated or nonvegetated and are classified on the basis of their hydrology, vegetation, and substrate. In this summary, wetlands are classified according to the system proposed by Cowardin and others (1979), which is used by the U.S. Fish and Wildlife Service (FWS) to map and inventory the Nation's wetlands. At the most general level of the classification system, wetlands are grouped into five ecological systems: Palustrine, Lacustrine, Riverine, Estuarine, and Marine. The Palustrine System includes only wetlands, whereas the other systems comprise wetlands and deepwater habitats. Wetlands of the systems that occur in New York are described below.

System	Wetland description
Palustrine	Nontidal and tidal-freshwater wetlands in which vegetation is predominantly trees (forested wetlands); shrubs (scrub-shrub wetlands); persistent or nonpersistent emergent, erect, rooted herbaceous plants (persistent- and nonpersistent-emergent wetlands); or submersed and (or) floating plants (aquatic beds). Also, intermittently to permanently flooded open-water bodies of less than 20 acres in which water is less than 6.6 feet deep.
Lacustrine	Nontidal and tidal-freshwater wetlands within an intermittently to permanently flooded lake or reservoir larger than 20 acres and (or) deeper than 6.6 feet. Vegetation, when present, is predominantly nonpersistent emergent plants (nonpersistent-emergent wetlands), or submersed and (or) floating plants (aquatic beds), or both.
Riverine	Nontidal and tidal-freshwater wetlands within a channel. Vegetation, when present, is same as in the Lacustrine System.
Estuarine	Tidal wetlands in low-wave-energy environments where the salinity of the water is greater than 0.5 part per thousand (ppt) and is variable owing to evaporation and the mixing of seawater and freshwater.
Marine	Tidal wetlands that are exposed to waves and currents of the open ocean and to water having a salinity greater than 30 ppt.

Dahl (1990) has estimated that wetlands cover about 1.0 million acres of New York. Another estimate places the present-day acreage at 2.2 to 2.4 million acres (Patricia Riexinger, New York Department of Environmental Conservation, oral commun., 1993). Such estimates of wetland area are typically based on surveys that

Figure 1. Tivoli Bays, Hudson River National Estuarine Research Reserve. The reserve is managed cooperatively by the State of New York and the National Oceanic and Atmospheric Administration's Sanctuaries and Reserves Division. (*Photograph by E.A. Blair, Hudson River National Estuarine Research Reserve.*)

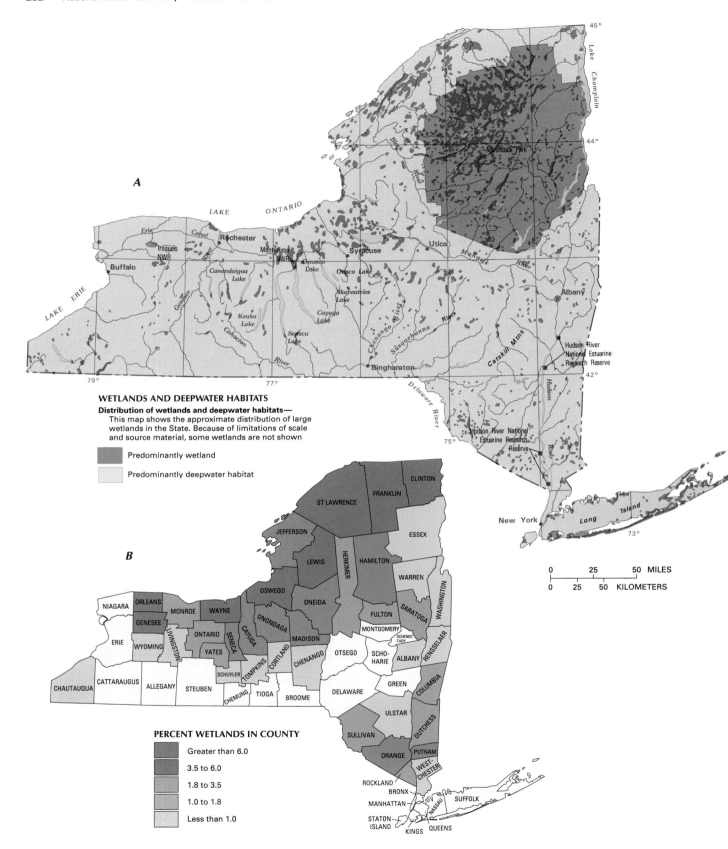

WETLANDS AND DEEPWATER HABITATS

Distribution of wetlands and deepwater habitats—
This map shows the approximate distribution of large wetlands in the State. Because of limitations of scale and source material, some wetlands are not shown

Predominantly wetland

Predominantly deepwater habitat

PERCENT WETLANDS IN COUNTY

Greater than 6.0

3.5 to 6.0

1.8 to 3.5

1.0 to 1.8

Less than 1.0

Figure 2. Wetland distribution in New York and physical and climatological features that affect wetland distribution in the State. **A**, Distribution of wetlands and deepwater habitats. **B**, Percentage area of New York counties that is wetland. *(Sources: A, T.E. Dahl, U.S. Fish and Wildlife Service, unpub. data, 1991. B, O'Connor and Cole, 1989.)*

have different minimum unit sizes, which could account, in part, for the disparity of these estimates.

About 75 percent of New York's wetlands occupy areas of less than 6 acres. O'Connor and Cole (1989) classified New York's freshwater wetlands of at least one-half acre into 14 cover types by use of aerial-photographic methods. Their study did not consider saltwater wetlands, which compose only a small percentage of the State's wetland acreage and are confined to the Long Island coast and the lower 30 miles of the Hudson River (Karl Schwartz, U.S. Fish and Wildlife Service, oral commun., 1993), but covers all other wetlands in the State. The five most common freshwater-wetland cover types in New York, in order of area, are flooded deciduous trees (palustrine forested wetland); flooded shrubs (palustrine scrub-shrub wetland); flooded coniferous trees (palustrine forested wetland); drained muckland, which is not considered wetland under the Cowardin and others (1979) classification system; and emergents (palustrine emergent wetlands or lacustrine or riverine nonpersistent-emergent wetlands). Together, these types constitute almost 88 percent of New York's freshwater wetland area.

The counties of upstate New York, including those in the Adirondack Mountains and the counties south and east of Lake Ontario, have the largest percentages of freshwater wetland area (fig. 2B). Among New York's counties, St. Lawrence County, which has about 21,000 acres of wetlands, has the largest area of freshwater wetland, and Wayne County, which contains 12 percent of the State's wetland acreage, has the highest percentage of wetland area. The urban counties of New York City and Long Island and the southern-tier counties along the State's border with Pennsylvania have the smallest percentage of wetland area. Counties in the Catskill Mountains also have relatively low areal percentages of wetlands.

Wetlands provide habitat for many threatened or endangered species. In New York, a species can be classified as threatened or endangered either by the State or by the Federal Government. Wetland plant species that are considered to be threatened or endangered in New York include heartleaf plantain, spreading globeflower, fringed gentian, and curlygrass fern. In addition to plants, a number of animal species are listed, including the red-shouldered hawk, osprey, bog turtle, and tiger salamander (Alvin Breisch, New York Department of Environmental Conservation, written commun., 1993).

HYDROLOGIC SETTING

New York's wetlands have formed primarily as the result of the interaction of geologic, physiographic, climatic, and hydrologic factors. Geologic history and climatic regime have influenced the State's physiography and hydrology, which largely determine the location and types of those wetlands.

During the last ice age, which ended about 18,000 years ago, glaciers covered most of New York. Erosion caused by movement of the glaciers and subsequent erosion and deposition by glacial meltwater and precipitation runoff shaped the present-day, topographically diverse landscape. The State's physiography (fig. 2C) ranges from lowlands to mountains, some having elevations higher than 5,000 feet in the Adirondack Mountains. Glacial drift (clay, sand, gravel, and boulders deposited by glaciers or transported by glacial meltwater) of varying thickness mantles the bedrock of most of the State and forms the floor of stream valleys and most other areas of low relief. Long Island is composed largely of glacial drift that was deposited at the edge of the glacier's farthest advance.

New York has 13.5 million acres of lakes (Zembrzuski and Gannon, 1986), which are most abundant in the St. Lawrence Valley, Adirondack, and Central Lowland physiographic provinces. These lakes were formed in three stages by glacial activity. First, the glaciers advanced, scouring the State's landscape. Then, as the glaciers retreated, large ice blocks were left behind and buried by glacial drift. These blocks subsequently melted, releasing their meltwater to form lakes. Other lakes, such as the Finger Lakes of west-central New York, are river valleys that have been deeply scoured by glaciers. Glacial lakes are most common in northern New York, especially in the Adirondack Mountains. Natural lakes of any kind are scarce in the Appalachian Plateaus of southwestern New York. There, rivers have cut deeply into the region's shale to form steep-sided valleys.

Noncoastal wetlands.—Most of New York's noncoastal wetlands have formed in and around glacial lakes. Some wetlands also occur along river and stream corridors and in other lowlands where deposits of fine-grained sediments provide an underlying impermeable layer that prevents water from percolating below the surface. Ground water and overland precipitation runoff are the principal sources of water for glacial-lake wetlands, and river flooding is an

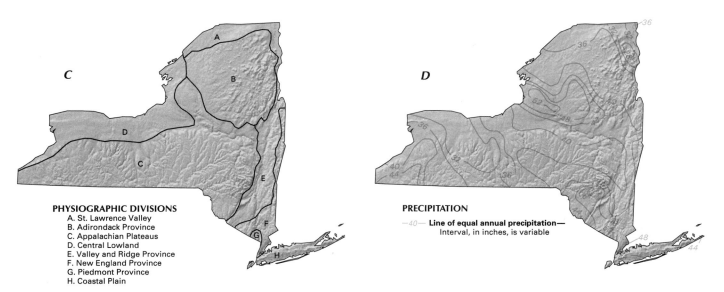

PHYSIOGRAPHIC DIVISIONS
A. St. Lawrence Valley
B. Adirondack Province
C. Appalachian Plateaus
D. Central Lowland
E. Valley and Ridge Province
F. New England Province
G. Piedmont Province
H. Coastal Plain

PRECIPITATION
—40— **Line of equal annual precipitation**—
Interval, in inches, is variable

Figure 2. Continued. Wetland distribution in New York and physical and climatological features that affect wetland distribution in the State. *C*, Physiography. *D*, Precipitation. *(Sources: C, Physiographic divisions from Fenneman, 1946; landforms data from EROS Data Center. D, Zembrzuski and Gannon, 1986.)*

additional source for wetlands along rivers and streams. Annual precipitation in the State ranges from 28 inches to the west of Lake Champlain to more than 50 inches in the Adirondack and Catskill Mountains (fig. 2D). Annual precipitation substantially exceeds annual evapotranspiration, resulting in an annual moisture surplus and ample water to maintain wetlands.

Ground water flows into wetlands from either glacial drift, fractures in crystalline bedrock, or solution cavities in carbonate bedrock, depending on local geological characteristics. Most recharge to ground-water systems occurs in upland areas, where precipitation percolates through the surficial sediments and into the underlying aquifers. In stream valleys containing valley-fill aquifers that are composed of glacial deposits, precipitation runoff from valley walls also is a common source of recharge. From recharge areas, ground water flows to areas of lower elevation, discharging to streams, ponds, lakes, and wetlands.

Vegetated wetlands formed in New York's glacial lakes when the lakes filled with sediment and organic material, providing a substrate for rooted plants. Partially decomposed wetland vegetation accumulates in the wetlands, forming a continually thickening layer of organic matter called peat. Such wetlands are known as peatlands (Mitsch and Gosselink, 1986), of which bogs (forested, scrub-shrub, or emergent wetlands) and fens (similar wetland classes to bogs but different vegetation composition) are common types in New York. Bogs receive most or all of their water from precipitation and have a characteristic plant community that is composed of peat (sphagnum) moss and other plants tolerant of acidic conditions. Fens receive at least some water from ground water and are less acidic than bogs. Peatlands can evolve into uplands through an ecological process called succession, wherein the vegetative composition of the wetland changes over time. The plant community gradually evolves from one in which wetland plants predominate to one having more upland species. Although succession of some kind occurs in most ecosystems, it is possible that a wetland will never reach a steady-state condition. It can instead cycle through forested, open-water, emergent, and shrub phases several times as the community evolves (Virginia Carter, U.S. Geological Survey, written commun., 1994). Lakes undergo a similar process, called eutrophication, in which they fill in with decaying organic matter, which then forms the substrate for plants that make up the next stage in the successional process.

Coastal wetlands.—Nearly all of New York's coastal wetlands are in the intertidal zone in the bays of Long Island and comprise mostly salt marshes, aquatic beds, and tidal flats. These wetlands receive their water from the ocean, streams, and ground-water seepage and are subject to hydrologic and salinity regimes that vary daily with the tides and seasonally with precipitation and streamflow. The bottom material of coastal wetlands in the Northeastern United States generally consists of peat and fine sediments derived from the glacial drift that covers upland areas. Salt-marsh plant communities contain species physiologically adapted to dynamic conditions of moisture and salinity. Plant-species composition changes along a gradient that corresponds to frequency of inundation and to salinity range. Production of plant material is high in coastal marshes owing to a constant supply of nutrients (mostly nitrogen and phosphorus). Much of the plant material in estuarine marshes is washed into the estuary during the high tides of winter and becomes part of the detrital food web of the estuary (Virginia Carter, U.S. Geological Survey, written commun., 1994).

TRENDS

New York's wetlands have been drained and filled since settlement by Europeans began in the 1600's. Filling of wetlands increased markedly following World War II. Between about the 1780's and the 1980's, New York lost an estimated 60 percent of its wetlands (Dahl, 1990).

Wetlands have been drained for crop production and pasturage, and they have been filled for transportation, industrialization, housing, and landfills (Tiner, 1984). Dredging for navigation and the construction of reservoirs, harbors, and marinas also have adversely affected New York's wetlands. In addition to the acreage losses caused by these activities, wetlands have been degraded by point and nonpoint discharges to surface waters from agriculture, logging, industry, municipal sewerage, and urban runoff, which add contaminants and silt to surface waters.

Some wetlands have been created as a result of the activities of beavers and humans. By impounding streams, beavers can create wetlands in areas that were formerly uplands. In the last century, beavers were trapped in some parts of the Northeast for their pelts. The reduction of the population led to deterioration of their dams and to subsequent wetland loss. In more recent times, beavers have reestablished their population and their impoundments and the associated wetlands. Humans also have created wetlands, intentionally through the construction of artificial wetlands and inadvertently through dam and farm-pond construction. These additions, however, probably have not compensated for the losses of natural wetlands (Tiner, 1984).

CONSERVATION

Many government agencies and private organizations participate in wetland conservation in New York. The most active agencies and organizations and some of their activities are listed in table 1.

Federal wetland activities.—Development activities in New York wetlands are regulated by several Federal statutory prohibi-

Table 1. Selected wetland-related activities of government agencies and private organizations in New York, 1993

[Source: Classification of activities is generalized from information provided by agencies and organizations. ●, agency or organization participates in wetland-related activity; ..., agency or organization does not participate in wetland-related activity. MAN, management; REG, regulation; R&C, restoration and creation; LAN, land acquisition; R&D, research and data collection; D&I, delineation and inventory]

Agency or organization	MAN	REG	R&C	LAN	R&D	D&I
FEDERAL						
Department of Agriculture						
Consolidated Farm Service Agency	...	●	...	...	...	...
Forest Service	●	...	●	●	●	●
Natural Resources Conservation Service	...	●	●	...	●	●
Department of Commerce						
National Oceanic and Atmospheric Administration	●	●	...	...	●	...
Department of Defense						
Army Corps of Engineers	●	●	●	●	...	●
Military reservations	●	...	...	...	...	...
Department of the Interior						
Fish and Wildlife Service	●	...	●	●	●	●
Geological Survey	...	...	...	...	●	...
National Biological Service	...	...	...	...	●	...
National Park Service	●	...	●	●	●	...
Environmental Protection Agency	...	●	...	...	●	●
STATE						
Adirondack Park Agency	...	●	...	●	...	...
Department of Environmental Conservation						
Division of Fish and Wildlife	...	●	●	...	●	●
Department of State	...	...	●	...	...	...
PRIVATE ORGANIZATIONS						
Ducks Unlimited	●	...	●	...	●	●
Finger Lakes Land Trust	...	...	...	●	...	...
The National Audubon Society	●	...	...	●	...	...
The Nature Conservancy	●	...	●	●	●	●
The Open Space Institute	...	...	...	●	...	...
Scenic Hudson	●	...	...	●	...	...

tions and incentives that are intended to slow wetland losses. Some of the more important of these are contained in the 1899 Rivers and Harbors Act; the 1972 Clean Water Act and amendments; the 1985 Food Security Act; the 1990 Food, Agriculture, Conservation, and Trade Act; the 1986 Emergency Wetlands Resources Act; and the 1972 Coastal Zone Management Act.

Section 10 of the Rivers and Harbors Act gives the U.S. Army Corps of Engineers (Corps) authority to regulate certain activities in navigable waters. Regulated activities include diking, deepening, filling, excavating, and placing of structures. The related section 404 of the Clean Water Act is the most often-used Federal legislation protecting wetlands. Under section 404 provisions, the Corps issues permits regulating the discharge of dredged or fill material into wetlands. Permits are subject to review and possible veto by the U.S. Environmental Protection Agency, and the FWS has review and advisory roles. Section 401 of the Clean Water Act grants to States and eligible Indian Tribes the authority to approve, apply conditions to, or deny section 404 permit applications on the basis of a proposed activity's probable effects on the water quality of a wetland.

Most farming, ranching, and silviculture activities are not subject to section 404 regulation. However, the "Swampbuster" provision of the 1985 Food Security Act and amendments in the 1990 Food, Agriculture, Conservation, and Trade Act discourage (through financial disincentives) the draining, filling, or other alteration of wetlands for agricultural use. The law allows exemptions from penalties in some cases, especially if the farmer agrees to restore the altered wetland or other wetlands that have been converted to agricultural use. The Wetlands Reserve Program of the 1990 Food, Agriculture, Conservation, and Trade Act authorizes the Federal Government to purchase conservation easements from landowners who agree to protect or restore wetlands. The Consolidated Farm Service Agency (formerly the Agricultural Stabilization and Conservation Service) administers the Swampbuster provisions and Wetlands Reserve Program. The Natural Resources Conservation Service (formerly the Soil Conservation Service) determines compliance with Swampbuster provisions and assists farmers in the identification of wetlands and in the development of wetland protection, restoration, or creation plans.

The 1986 Emergency Wetlands Resources Act and the 1972 Coastal Zone Management Act and amendments encourage wetland protection through funding incentives. The Emergency Wetland Resources Act requires States to address wetland protection in their Statewide Comprehensive Outdoor Recreation Plans to qualify for Federal funding for State recreational land; the National Park Service provides guidance to States in developing the wetland component of their plans. Coastal States that adopt coastal-zone management programs and plans approved by the National Oceanic and Atmospheric Administration (NOAA) are eligible for Federal funding and technical assistance through the Coastal Zone Management Act.

State wetland activities.—State laws governing New York's wetlands include the 1973 Tidal Wetlands Act, the 1975 Freshwater Wetlands Act, the Protection of Waters Act, and the Waterfront Revitalization and Coastal Resource Act. Of these, the first three are administered by the New York Department of Environmental Conservation, and the fourth is administered by the New York Department of State. Wetland activities in the Adirondack Park are regulated by the Adirondack Park Agency under the 1975 Freshwater Wetlands Act.

The State has extended protection to many wetlands within its borders. By far the largest protected area containing wetlands is the Adirondack Park in northern New York. The wetland acreage within the park is not precisely known because the Adirondack Park Agency wetlands inventory is not complete. In addition to park wetlands,

the State has protected a number of wetlands of unusual local importance (mostly in down-State areas). A major cooperative effort is underway among Federal and State agencies and private organizations to acquire more than 20,000 acres of wetlands and associated uplands to the north of the Montezuma National Wildlife Refuge. This area will be a major protected wetland resource for the State. Also, many State wildlife-management areas are wetland-upland complexes that are managed for wetland values. The Hudson River National Estuarine Research Reserve is a federally designated wetland system that is managed cooperatively by the New York Department of Environmental Conservation and NOAA. The reserve consists of four sites totaling 5,000 acres of mostly wetlands that are distributed along the salinity gradient of the Hudson River. The reserve's purposes are protection, research, and education.

County and local wetland activities.—Under the Freshwater Wetlands Act, a county, town, village, or municipality can take over responsibility for wetland management with oversight by the Department of Environmental Conservation. Under this provision, local governments review and process permit applications. The Department approves the local procedures and also reserves the right to oversee Class 1 wetlands, which are wetlands considered most in need of protection because they provide benefits that make them particularly valuable. Any municipality is allowed to pass regulations that are more restrictive than the Department's guidelines. When such regulations are passed, the Department defers to the local authority. To date, only two towns and one village have taken over wetland-management responsibility, and no county government has opted to preempt the Department's regulations (Russell Cole, New York State Department of Environmental Conservation, oral commun., 1993).

Counties may facilitate wetland acquisition through the funding of bond acts. Such acts have been used extensively on Long Island for this purpose (Sarah Davidson, The Nature Conservancy, Long Island Chapter, oral commun., 1993).

Private wetland activities.—Among the private organizations that are active in the conservation of New York's wetlands are Ducks Unlimited, The Nature Conservancy, the National Audubon Society, Scenic Hudson, the Open Space Institute, and the Finger Lakes Land Trust. Privately organized and funded land trusts exist in many New York counties, and these can enable wetland acquisition and protection (Peggy Olson, The Nature Conservancy, Eastern New York Chapter, oral commun., 1993).

References Cited

Cowardin, L.M., Carter, Virginia, Golet, F.C., and LaRoe, E.T., 1979, Classification of wetlands and deepwater habitats of the United States: U.S. Fish and Wildlife Service Report FWS/OBS–79/31, 131 p.

Dahl, T.E., 1990, Wetlands—Losses in the United States, 1780's to 1980's: Washington, D.C., U.S. Fish and Wildlife Service Report to Congress, 13 p.

Fenneman, N.M., 1946, Physical divisions of the United States: Washington, D.C., U.S. Geological Survey special map, scale 1:7,000,000.

Mitsch, W.J., and Gosselink, J.G., 1986, Wetlands: New York, Van Nostrand Reinhold, 539 p.

O'Connor, Sharon, and Cole, N.B., 1989, Freshwater wetlands inventory—Data analysis: Albany, New York State Department of Environmental Conservation, Division of Fish and Wildlife, 107 p.

Odum, E.P., 1971, Fundamentals of ecology: Philadelphia, Saunders, 574 p.

Tiner, R.W., Jr., 1984, Wetlands of the United States—Current status and recent trends: Washington, D.C., U.S. Fish and Wildlife Service, 59 p.

Zembrzuski, T.J., and Gannon, W.B., 1986, New York surface-water resources, *in* U.S. Geological Survey National water summary 1985—Hydrologic events and surface-water resources: U.S. Geological Survey Water-Supply Paper 2300, p. 347–354.

FOR ADDITIONAL INFORMATION: District Chief, U.S. Geological Survey, James T. Foley U.S. Courthouse, P.O. Box 1669, Room 343, 445 Broadway, Albany, NY 12201; Regional Wetland Coordinator, U.S. Fish and Wildlife Service, Regional Wetland Coordinator, 300 Westgate Center Dr., Hadley, MA 01035

Prepared by
Thomas H. Barringer, John S. Williams, and Deborah S. Lumia,
U.S. Geological Survey

North Carolina
Wetland Resources

Wetlands of North Carolina are diverse and widely distributed. About 5.7 million acres, or 17 percent, of the State is covered by wetlands (Dahl, 1990). About 95 percent of these wetlands are in the eastern part of the State (fig. 1).

Wetlands affect streamflow and water quality and provide critical habitat to a variety of plants and animals. Because of the large size of some eastern North Carolina wetlands and their proximity to coastal waters, these wetlands are important regulators of freshwater, nutrient, and sediment inputs to North Carolina estuaries. Almost one-half of North Carolina's wetlands are bottom-land hardwood forests, which are valuable habitats for waterfowl breeding and overwintering and for anadromous fish spawning (U.S. Fish and Wildlife Service, 1992). About 90 percent of the State's commercial fish harvest is derived from estuary-dependent species. Tidal and nontidal creeks surrounded by wetlands and vast beds of submersed aquatic vegetation function as nursery areas for larval and juvenile fish and provide critical finfish and shellfish habitats for adults. Small wetlands throughout the Piedmont and Blue Ridge Provinces of the State harbor at least 80 species of rare or endangered plants. Statewide, about 70 percent of the rare and endangered plants and animals depend on wetlands.

TYPES AND DISTRIBUTION

Wetlands are lands transitional between terrestrial and deepwater habitats where the water table usually is at or near the land surface or the land is covered by shallow water (Cowardin and others, 1979). The distribution of wetlands and deepwater habitats in North Carolina is shown in figure 2A; only wetlands are discussed herein.

Wetlands can be vegetated or nonvegetated and are classified on the basis of their hydrology, vegetation, and substrate. In this summary, wetlands are classified according to the system proposed by Cowardin and others (1979), which is used by the U.S. Fish and Wildlife Service (FWS) to map and inventory the Nation's wetlands. At the most general level of the classification system, wetlands are grouped into five ecological systems: Palustrine, Lacustrine, Riverine, Estuarine, and Marine. The Palustrine System includes only wetlands, whereas the other systems comprise wetlands and

Figure 1. Merchants Millpond, a forested wetland in northeastern North Carolina. *(Photograph by Virginia Carter, U.S. Geological Survey.)*

deepwater habitats. Wetlands of the systems that occur in North Carolina are described below.

System	Wetland description
Palustrine	Nontidal and tidal-freshwater wetlands in which vegetation is predominantly trees (forested wetlands); shrubs (scrub-shrub wetlands); persistent or nonpersistent emergent, erect, rooted herbaceous plants (persistent- and nonpersistent-emergent wetlands); or submersed and (or) floating plants (aquatic beds). Also, intermittently to permanently flooded open-water bodies of less than 20 acres in which water is less than 6.6 feet deep.
Lacustrine	Wetlands within an intermittently to permanently flooded lake or reservoir larger than 20 acres and (or) deeper than 6.6 feet. Vegetation, when present, is predominantly nonpersistent emergent plants (nonpersistent-emergent wetlands), or submersed and (or) floating plants (aquatic beds), or both.
Riverine	Nontidal and tidal-freshwater wetlands within a channel. Vegetation, when present, is same as in the Lacustrine System.
Estuarine	Tidal wetlands in low-wave-energy environments where the salinity of the water is greater than 0.5 part per thousand (ppt) and is variable owing to evaporation and the mixing of seawater and freshwater.
Marine	Tidal wetlands that are exposed to waves and currents of the open ocean and to water having a salinity greater than 30 ppt.

Palustrine system.—Palustrine wetlands account for most of the wetland acreage in North Carolina. Palustrine wetlands in the State include forested wetlands (bottom-land hardwood forests, fringe wooded swamps, wet pine flatwoods, pine savannas, and hardwood flats), wetlands that are classified as forested or scrub-shrub wetlands, depending on the characteristics of the dominant vegetation (Carolina bays, pocosins, and bogs), and emergent wetlands (nontidal and tidal fresh marshes).

Bottom-land hardwood forests cover about 2.7 million acres (U.S. Fish and Wildlife Service, 1992) and occur primarily in the Coastal Plain along the Roanoke, Tar, Neuse, and Cape Fear Rivers, as well as along other large interior streams (fig. 2A and 2B). The Roanoke River flood plain has one of the largest and least disturbed bottom-land hardwood forests in the mid-Atlantic region. Cypress, swamp gum, and black gum grow in the wetter areas of the flood plain, whereas temporarily or seasonally flooded bottom-land hardwood-forest wetlands are dominated by red maple, green ash, elm, sycamore, and sweet gum.

Fringe wooded swamps are the dominant shoreline type around Albemarle Sound; along the Alligator, Scuppernong, and lower Chowan Rivers; and in some locations along tributaries to Pamlico Sound. These swamps cover an area of about 400,000 acres (North Carolina Department of Environment, Health, and Natural Resources, 1994) and are vegetated primarily by cypress (Environmental Defense Fund, 1989).

Wet pine flatwoods possibly occupy more than 2 million acres, and pine savannas cover an area of about 28,000 acres (North Carolina Department of Environment, Health, and Natural Resources, 1994). Both ecosystems have a canopy of longleaf pine and occasional loblolly pine with an understory of wiregrass. Pine savannas have a greater density of trees than wet pine flatwoods, and pine savannas support orchids and various small vascular plants, such as pitcher plants, Venus flytrap, and sundews. Wet pine flatwoods are common throughout the western and middle regions of the Coastal Plain, except in the Sand Hills, whereas pine savannas are most common in the southeastern corner of the State (Schafale and Weakley, 1990).

Carolina bays are ovate depressions that occur across the Coastal Plain but are most common in the southeastern corner of the State (Sharitz and Gibbons, 1982). Most of the bays contain palustrine wetlands, but a few large Carolina bays, such as Lake Waccamaw, are lacustrine wetlands. The bays range in length from about 150 feet to more than 5 miles. Because of variability in size, depth, location, and substrate, Carolina bays are not characterized by a single vegetation type. These systems are unusual in their geographic orientation (northwest to southeast) and consistent shape (narrower at the southeast end).

About 700,000 acres of pocosins remain in North Carolina (Environmental Defense Fund, 1989)—about 70 percent of the Nation's pocosin wetlands (Richardson and others, 1981). Pocosins form in poorly drained basins, including interior depressions of Carolina bays (Ash and others, 1983). The typical pocosin is classified as a scrub-shrub wetland. However, a pocosin can be a forested wetland, depending on the successional stage of the pocosin, which is commonly determined by hydrology or by fire and other disturbances (Hefner and Moorhead, 1991). Scrub-shrub pocosins are dominated by dense, almost impenetrable, growths of evergreens such as titi and yaupon, thorny vines, and occasional taller pond pines projecting above the thicket. Forested pocosins are generally dominated by red bay, sweet bay, Atlantic white cedar, loblolly bay, and pond pine (Sharitz and Gibbons, 1982; Ash and others, 1983). Vegetation in large pocosins commonly grows in zones with shorter vegetation in the center.

Other types of palustrine wetlands include bogs and fresh marshes. Bogs, which occur throughout the Blue Ridge Province, have been subject to draining, impoundment, and clearing at lower elevation sites (Schafale and Weakley, 1990). Nontidal fresh marshes cover about 46,000 acres in the Coastal Plain (Field and others, 1991) and often grade upriver to cypress-gum swamps (forested wetlands). About 2,200 acres of tidal fresh marshes exist in North Carolina (Field and others, 1991).

Lacustrine and Riverine Systems.—Lacustrine wetlands comprise the shallows of natural lakes and reservoirs where there is no persistent emergent vegetation or trees. All of the State's natural lakes are located in the Coastal Plain, and many are associated with Carolina bays or peatlands. More than 100 water-supply and flood-control reservoirs have been constructed throughout the Piedmont and Blue Ridge Provinces (North Carolina Department of Environment, Health, and Natural Resources, 1992). Riverine wetlands constitute the entire channel of small, shallow streams and shallow areas near the banks in large, deep streams. The total area of lacustrine and riverine wetlands in the State is not known but is small relative to the area of palustrine wetlands.

Estuarine and Marine Systems.—North Carolina contains more than 3,000 miles of tidal (estuarine and ocean) shoreline (Clay

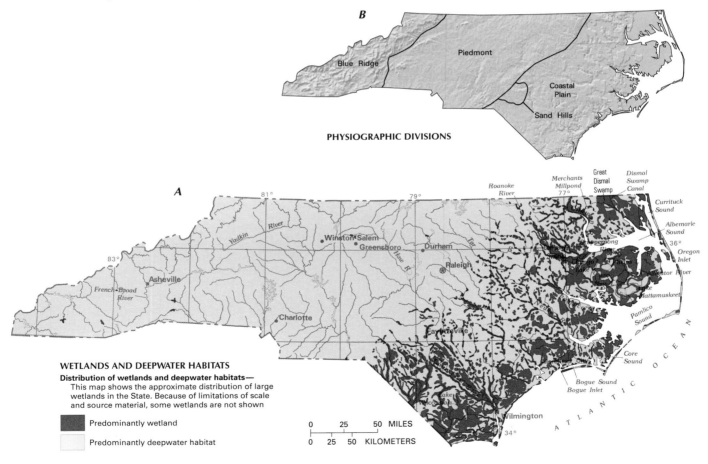

PHYSIOGRAPHIC DIVISIONS

WETLANDS AND DEEPWATER HABITATS

Distribution of wetlands and deepwater habitats—
This map shows the approximate distribution of large wetlands in the State. Because of limitations of scale and source material, some wetlands are not shown

⬛ Predominantly wetland

⬜ Predominantly deepwater habitat

0   25   50 MILES
0   25   50 KILOMETERS

Figure 2.   Wetland distribution in North Carolina and physiography of the State. ***A***, Distribution of wetlands and deepwater habitats. ***B***, Physiography. *(Sources: A, T.E. Dahl, U.S. Fish and Wildlife Service, unpub. data, 1991. B, Physiographic divisions from Fenneman, 1946; landforms data from EROS Data Center.)*

and others, 1975). Between 183,000 (Cashin and others, 1992) and 236,000 acres (Moorhead, 1992) of salt marsh (emergent wetlands) are present in the State, which constitutes about 11 percent of the tidal salt marshes of the southeastern Atlantic coast (Wiegert and Freeman, 1990). Salt marshes, also known as "low marshes," are generally covered by smooth cordgrass. "High marshes" typically contain mixtures of species, including needlerush and shrubs such as wax myrtle and marsh elder. About 30,000 acres of high marsh are present in the State (Moorhead, 1992).

Most seagrass beds (aquatic beds) are subtidal and, thus, are classified as deepwater habitats. However, some seagrass beds in North Carolina are intertidal and are classified as wetlands. The most extensive beds, which typically contain eelgrass, shoalgrass, and widgeon grass, are in Bogue Sound, Core Sound, and eastern Pamlico Sound; seagrass beds also grow in the Pamlico River, Neuse River, and Currituck Sound. Ferguson and others (1989) estimated that 200,000 acres of seagrass beds are present between Bogue Inlet and Oregon Inlet.

Tidal flats usually consist of sand, silt, or clay regularly exposed and flooded by tides. The vegetation on tidal flats is minimal because of the unstable sediments. About 44,000 acres of tidal flats are present in North Carolina (Field and others, 1991), which is about 4 percent of the national total.

HYDROLOGIC SETTING

Abundant precipitation and flat terrain in the Coastal Plain are the most important factors that contribute to the abundance of wetlands in North Carolina. Fifty-nine percent of the State's palustrine wetlands are headwater wetlands (on streams having an average flow of less than 5 cubic feet per second), and 11 percent of palustrine wetlands are hydrologically isolated (North Carolina Department of Environment, Health, and Natural Resources, 1991).

Bottom-land hardwood forests.—Water and sediment carried by rivers are responsible for the origin, character, and maintenance of bottom-land hardwood-forest wetlands. Erosional and depositional processes typically result in a sinuous river channel located within a broad flood plain (fig. 3A). Sources of water to the wetlands include overbank flow during seasonal flooding, precipitation, runoff from upland areas, ground water from regional and local aquifers, and tidal flow (Wharton and others, 1982). Seasonal flooding is the primary hydrologic factor responsible for the existence of these wetlands. At times, streamflow can actually decrease in the downstream direction because water spreads through the flood plain providing increased opportunity for evapotranspiration or loss to the shallow ground-water system.

Wet pine flatwoods and pine savannas.—Wet pine flatwoods and pine savannas occur on flat or nearly flat, wet organic or sandy soils. The soils are saturated seasonally by a high water table, although some sites are wet most of the year. These wetlands, particularly the savannas, also form on gently sloping hillsides where ground-water seepage occurs (Schafale and Weakley, 1990).

Pocosins.—Because pocosins generally are isolated from streams, direct precipitation is the primary moisture source. Pocosins having a thick layer of peat near the center of the wetland are nutrient poor, and

ground water seldom extends into the root zone. Under these conditions, vegetation generally consists of low shrubs and scattered trees (fig. 3B). Near the outer edges of the pocosin, where the peat layer is thinner, vegetation grades into a mixture of hardwoods and evergreens because of the increased availability of nutrients from

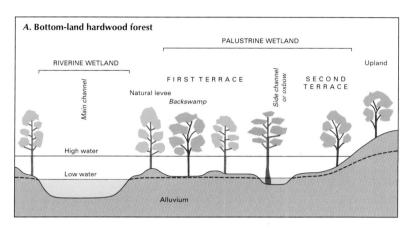

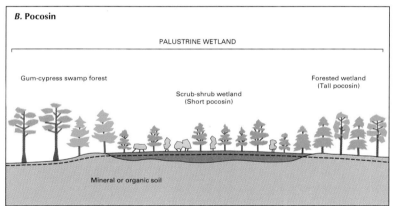

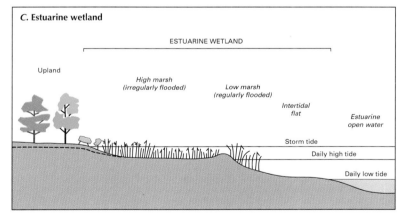

Figure 3. Cross-sectional diagrams of typical North Carolina wetlands. *A*, Bottom-land hardwood forest. *B*, Pocosin. *C*, Estuarine wetland. *(Sources: A, Wharton and others, 1982; Tiner, 1984. B, Ash and others, 1983. C, Tiner, 1984.)*

ground and surface water. In some cases, however, pocosins are entirely forested without the gradation from scrub-shrub to forested wetland. Vertical water movement through the peat is slight, resulting in little loss of water to the ground-water system. Lateral water movement also is typically slow, which accounts for the important role of pocosins in preventing rapid surface runoff and, thus, in filtering sediment and nutrients from runoff before it enters the estuary.

Tidal freshwater and salt marshes. — With the exception of the Cape Fear River, North Carolina's large coastal rivers drain to sounds rather than to the open ocean. Consequently, tides in these rivers are small in magnitude, resulting in limited tidal flooding and a small area of tidal fresh marsh in comparison to other Southeastern States.

Salt marshes in areas that have high tidal amplitudes can have natural berms or levees, which are formed by tidal sedimentation and consist of coarse-grained material. Water flows through the berms in small breaks or over the berms during extremely high tides (fig. 3*C*) to flood the area landward of the berm. Vegetation characteristics landward of the berm are determined by the periodicity of flooding, the salinity level in the soil, the frequency of occurrence of oxygen-poor conditions, and the contribution of ground water. In salt marshes with low tidal amplitudes, such as those in estuaries and sounds protected by barrier islands, berm formation is limited because of low sedimentation rates.

TRENDS

Before colonization by Europeans, the area that now is North Carolina contained about 11 million acres of wetlands (Dahl, 1990). Dahl estimated that in the mid-1980's, about one-half, or 5.7 million acres, remained.

Because of the absence of reliable historical data, wetland loss can be difficult to assess. Moreover, most surveys consider the alteration of a wetland from its natural condition to be a "loss," whereas many pine plantations and some agricultural lands on converted wetlands retain some of their original wetland functions and support limited wetland uses. North Carolina evaluates wetland resources in terms of use support rather than areal coverage (North Carolina Department of Environment, Health, and Natural Resources, 1991).

The first major alteration of wetlands in North Carolina was associated with the completion of a canal between Phelps Lake and the Scuppernong River in 1787 (17 years before the Dismal Swamp Canal) that lowered the lake level and permitted farming around the lake (Heath, 1975). The State Literary Board encouraged settlement on swamplands in the 1830's by providing funds for drainage canals around Lake Mattamuskeet, Pungo Lake, and New Lake. Several other large-scale wetland alteration projects, including the drainage of the 43,000-acre Lake Mattamuskeet, occurred in the late 1800's and early 1900's (Heath, 1975). Wilson (1962) estimated that more than 1 million miles of drainage ditches and canals were constructed throughout the Coastal Plain to drain wetlands.

About one-third of the wetland alteration in the Coastal Plain has occurred since the 1950's (Cashin and others, 1992). Cashin and others (1992) found that in the Coastal Plain, conversion to managed forests was responsible for 53 percent of the wetland alteration during that period, and conversion to agriculture was responsible for 42 percent.

About 2.5 million acres of pocosins existed before colonization (Richardson and others, 1981). Wilson (1962) reported that about 2.2 million acres of pocosins existed in the early 1960's and estimated that more than 100,000 acres of pocosins were drained between 1950 and 1960. Between 1962 and 1972, 33 percent of the State's remaining pocosin habitat was converted to agriculture or managed forests. About 700,000 acres of pocosins remain unaltered in North Carolina (Environmental Defense Fund, 1989).

Atlantic white cedar was once common in Coastal Plain wetlands, particularly in pocosins. However, as much as 200,000 acres of white cedar forest has been harvested from the Great Dismal Swamp and from the peninsula between Albemarle and Pamlico Sounds. Nonetheless, the area around the Alligator River still contains the most extensive white cedar forest in the world, including approximately 10,000 acres of high-quality cedar swamp forest protected as a North Carolina Natural Heritage Area (Laderman, 1989).

Estuarine wetlands have been altered less extensively than palustrine wetlands (Cashin and others, 1992). Stockton and Richardson (1987) reported that there was a decrease in the area of coastal wetland (salt marsh) alteration after the State adopted a strong coastal-wetland protection program.

Some land-use practices have created new wetlands or enlarged existing ones. Reservoir construction has increased the acreage of lacustrine wetlands, although usually at the expense of palustrine wetlands. Farm ponds constructed on previously upland areas in one Piedmont Province county account for about 1 percent of the total area of the county (Newcomb, 1993). Similar conditions likely exist throughout the Piedmont region of the State. Interest is increasing within the State for the use of created wetlands for treating wastewater.

CONSERVATION

Many government agencies and private organizations participate in wetland conservation in North Carolina. The most active agencies and organizations and some of their activities are listed in table 1.

Federal wetland activities. — Development activities in North Carolina wetlands are regulated by several Federal statutory prohibitions and incentives that are intended to slow wetland losses. Some of the more important of these are contained in the 1899 Rivers and Harbors Act; the 1972 Clean Water Act and amendments; the 1985 Food Security Act; the 1990 Food, Agriculture, Conservation, and Trade Act; the 1986 Emergency Wetlands Resources Act; and the 1972 Coastal Zone Management Act.

Section 10 of the Rivers and Harbors Act gives the U.S. Army Corps of Engineers (Corps) authority to regulate certain activities in navigable waters. Regulated activities include diking, deepening, filling, excavating, and placing of structures. The related section 404 of the Clean Water Act is the most often-used Federal legislation protecting wetlands. Under section 404 provisions, the Corps issues permits regulating the discharge of dredged or fill material into wetlands. Permits are subject to review and possible veto by the U.S. Environmental Protection Agency (EPA), and the FWS has review and advisory roles. Section 401 of the Clean Water Act grants to States and eligible Indian Tribes the authority to approve, apply conditions to, or deny section 404 permit applications on the basis of a proposed activity's probable effects on the water quality of a wetland.

Most farming, ranching, and silviculture activities are not subject to section 404 regulation. However, the "Swampbuster" provision of the 1985 Food Security Act and amendments in the 1990 Food, Agriculture, Conservation, and Trade Act discourage (through financial disincentives) the draining, filling, or other alteration of wetlands for agricultural use. The law allows exemptions from penalties in some cases, especially if the farmer agrees to restore the altered wetland or other wetlands that have been converted to agricultural use. The Wetlands Reserve Program of the 1990 Food, Agriculture, Conservation, and Trade Act authorizes the Federal Government to purchase conservation easements from landowners who agree to protect or restore wetlands. The Consolidated Farm Service Agency (formerly the Agricultural Stabilization and Conservation Service) administers the Swampbuster provisions and Wetlands Reserve Program. The Natural Resources Conservation Service (NRCS) (formerly the Soil Conservation Service) determines compliance with Swampbuster provisions and assists farmers in the

Table 1. Selected wetland-related activities of government agencies and private organizations in North Carolina, 1993

[Source: Classification of activities is generalized from information provided by agencies and organizations. •, agency or organization participates in wetland-related activity; ..., agency or organization does not participate in wetland-related activity. MAN, management; REG, regulation; R&C, restoration and creation; LAN, land acquisition; R&D, research and data collection; D&I, delineation and inventory]

Agency or organization	MAN	REG	R&C	LAN	R&D	D&I
FEDERAL						
Department of Agriculture						
Consolidated Farm Service Agency	...	•	...	...	...	...
Forest Service	•	...	•	•	•	•
Natural Resources Conservation Service	...	•	•	...	•	•
Department of Commerce						
National Oceanic and Atmospheric Administration	•	•	...	...	•	•
Department of Defense						
Army Corps of Engineers	•	•	•	...	•	•
Military reservations	•	...	...	...	...	...
Department of the Interior						
Fish and Wildlife Service	•	...	•	•	•	•
Geological Survey	...	...	...	...	•	...
National Biological Service	...	...	...	...	•	...
National Park Service	•	...	•	•	•	•
Environmental Protection Agency	...	•	...	...	•	•
STATE						
Department of Agriculture	...	...	...	...	...	•
Department of Environment, Health, and Natural Resources						
Division of Coastal Management	•	•	•	•	...	•
Division of Environmental Health	...	•	...	...	...	...
Division of Environmental Management	...	•	...	...	...	•
Division of Forestry Resources	...	...	...	...	•	•
Division of Marine Fisheries	•	...	...	...	•	...
Division of Parks and Recreation	•	...	•	•	•	•
Division of Planning and Assessment	...	...	...	•	...	...
Division of Soil and Water Conservation	...	...	...	...	...	•
Division of Water Resources	•	...	...	...	...	...
Department of Transportation	...	...	...	...	•	...
Museum of Natural Science	...	...	...	...	•	...
Wildlife Resources Commission	•	•	•	•	•	•
SOME COUNTY AND LOCAL GOVERNMENTS	•	•	•	•	...	•
PRIVATE ORGANIZATIONS	•	...	•	•	•	...

identification of wetlands and in the development of wetland protection, restoration, or creation plans.

The 1986 Emergency Wetlands Resources Act and the 1972 Coastal Zone Management Act and amendments encourage wetland protection through funding incentives. The Emergency Wetland Resources Act requires States to address wetland protection in their Statewide Comprehensive Outdoor Recreation Plans to qualify for Federal funding for State recreational land; the National Park Service (NPS) provides guidance to States in developing the wetland component of their plans. Coastal States that adopt coastal-zone management programs and plans approved by the National Oceanic and Atmospheric Administration are eligible for Federal funding and technical assistance through the Coastal Zone Management Act.

Large tracts of land, many containing wetlands, are managed by the FWS, the U.S. Forest Service, the U.S. Department of Defense, and the NPS. The management plans for these lands are subject to a review process that allows local groups and individuals to have input into the planning process.

North Carolina is one of nine States participating in the U.S. Department of Agriculture's (USDA) Pilot Wetlands Reserve Program. The purpose of the program is to restore 1 million acres of cultivated land to wetlands by 1995. Landowners receive easement payments from USDA, which pays 75 percent of the restoration costs. The NRCS and FWS assist in completion of the restoration plans.

About 15,000 acres of cultivated land in North Carolina were enrolled in the program in 1992 (Darby, 1993).

State wetland activities.—The State has adopted a strong coastal-wetlands program as part of a broader coastal zone management effort. The North Carolina Coastal Area Management Act of 1974 includes provisions for local land-use planning, regulation for Areas of Environmental Concern (including estuarine waters and coastal wetlands), and permit coordination within the 20 counties affected by the act. Uses that are not water dependent are not permitted in wetlands, but uses that are water dependent may be permitted. The Division of Coastal Management administers the act and also administers the National Estuarine Research Reserve and North Carolina Coastal Reserve systems in the State. About 32 percent of all Coastal Plain wetlands are publicly owned (North Carolina Department of Environment, Health, and Natural Resources, 1991).

No State regulations exist specifically to protect freshwater wetlands. Moreover, Clean Water Act Section 404 regulations allow up to 10 acres of headwater wetlands to be filled without a permit or public review. However, section 401 of the Clean Water Act requires that any applicant for a Federal permit or license first obtain certification that the proposed activity, including those in wetlands, will comply with water-quality standards in the affected State. The Division of Environmental Management has developed a preliminary rating system for freshwater wetlands to assist in making permitting decisions as part of the section 401 program (North Carolina Department of Environment, Health, and Natural Resources, 1993). Some additional measure of protection of wetlands is provided by other classifications and designations, including Outstanding Resource Waters, Nutrient Sensitive Waters, High Quality Waters, Shellfishing Waters, Primary Nursery Areas, and Secondary Nursery Areas.

In 1986, the North Carolina Department of Transportation, in cooperation with the North Carolina Wildlife Resources Commission, the FWS, and The Nature Conservancy, purchased Company Swamp, a 1,436-acre tract of bottom-land hardwood-forest wetland on the Roanoke River. The wetland is being used to mitigate unavoidable wetland losses associated with individually permitted section 404 activities that the Department conducts in bottom-land hardwood forests and that cannot be mitigated on site. This mitigation bank avoids the need to establish numerous small mitigation efforts and protects a valuable wetland resource.

County and local wetland activities.—Many local governments, particularly in the 20 counties affected by the Coastal Area Management Act, have wetland-protection policies in their land-use plans. Local governments also use the purchase of greenways through bond issues (for example, Mecklenburg County, which contains Charlotte) or as a required part of the development process (for example, Raleigh) to protect wetlands. Carteret County (which contains Morehead City) is participating in the Advanced Identification Program, an EPA program which attempts to identify wetland parcels inappropriate for disposal of fill material and, in some cases, wetlands that could serve as disposal sites.

Private wetland activities.—Private organizations in North Carolina are active in public education, lobbying for wetland protection, land acquisition, and public participation in permit review and policy development. The Nature Conservancy, North Carolina chapter, has purchased wetlands in North Carolina for preservation, and ownership of some of these lands has been transferred to Federal and State agencies. The North Carolina Coastal Federation, the Pamlico–Tar River Foundation, the Neuse River Foundation, the Sierra Club, the National Wildlife Federation, the Environmental Defense Fund, Ducks Unlimited, and others provide services to educate the public on wetland issues and provide input to State and Federal agencies on wetland issues.

References Cited

Ash, A.N., McDonald, C.B., Kane, E.S., and Pories, C.A., 1983, Natural and modified pocosins—Literature synthesis and management options: U.S. Fish and Wildlife Service Report FWS/OBS–83–04, 156 p.

Cashin, G.E., Dorney, J.R., and Richardson, C.J., 1992, Wetland alteration trends on the North Carolina Coastal Plain: Wetlands, v. 12, no. 2, p. 63–71.

Clay, J.W., Orr, D.M., Jr., and Stuart, A.W., eds., 1975, North Carolina atlas—Portrait of a changing southern state: Chapel Hill, University of North Carolina Press, 331 p.

Cowardin, L.M., Carter, Virginia, Golet, F.C., and LaRoe, E.T., 1979, Classification of wetlands and deepwater habitats of the United States: U.S. Fish and Wildlife Service Report FWS/OBS–79/31, 131 p.

Dahl, T.E., 1990, Wetlands—Losses in the United States, 1780's to 1980's: Washington, D.C., U.S. Fish and Wildlife Service Report to Congress, 13 p.

Darby, P.V., 1993, Protection and management options for wetlands in the Albemarle–Pamlico study area: Raleigh, N.C., U.S. Fish and Wildlife Service, 46 p.

Environmental Defense Fund, 1989, Carolina wetlands—Our vanishing resource: Raleigh, N.C., 89 p. and appendix.

Fenneman, N.M., 1946, Physical divisions of the United States: Washington, D.C., U.S. Geological Survey special map, scale 1:7,000,000.

Ferguson, R.L., Rivera, J.A., and Wood, L.L., 1989, Submerged aquatic vegetation in the Albemarle-Pamlico estuarine system: Beaufort, N.C., National Oceanic and Atmospheric Administration, National Marine Fisheries Service, Project No. 88–10, 68 p.

Field, D.W., Reyer, A.J., Genovese, P.V., and Shearer, B.D., 1991, Coastal wetlands of the United States—An accounting of a valuable national resource: Washington, D.C., National Oceanic and Atmospheric Administration and U.S. Fish and Wildlife Service cooperative publication, 59 p.

Heath, R.C., 1975, Hydrology of the Albemarle–Pamlico region, North Carolina—A preliminary report on the impact of agricultural developments: U.S. Geological Survey Water-Resources Investigations Report 9–75, 98 p.

Hefner, J.M., and Moorhead, K.K., 1991, Mapping pocosins and associated wetlands in North Carolina: Wetlands, v. 11, p. 377–389.

Laderman, A.D., 1989, The ecology of Atlantic white cedar wetlands—A community profile: U.S. Fish and Wildlife Service Biological Report 85(7.21), 89 p.

Moorhead, K.K., 1992, Wetland resources of coastal North Carolina: Wetlands, v. 12, no. 3, p. 184–191.

Newcomb, D.J., 1993, Positive effects on total wetland area by human activities in Alamance County, North Carolina: Chapel Hill, University of North Carolina, unpublished M.A. thesis, 72 p.

North Carolina Department of Environment, Health, and Natural Resources, 1991, Original extent, status, and trends of wetlands in North Carolina—A report to the N.C. Legislative Study Commission on wetlands protection: North Carolina Department of Environment, Health, and Natural Resources, Division of Environmental Management, Water Quality Section, Report 91–01, 33 p.

_____1992, North Carolina lake assessment report: North Carolina Department of Environment, Health, and Natural Resources, Division of Environmental Management, Water Quality Section, Report 92–02, 353 p.

_____1993, Indicators of freshwater wetland function and value for protection and management: North Carolina Department of Environment, Health, and Natural Resources, Division of Environmental Management, Water Quality Section, 50 p.

_____1994, Water quality progress in North Carolina—1992–1993 305(b) report: North Carolina Department of Environment, Health, and Natural Resources, Division of Environmental Management, Water Quality Section, 96 p. and appendix.

Richardson, C.J., Evans, R., and Carr, D., 1981, Pocosins—An ecosystem in transition, in Richardson, C.J., ed., Pocosin wetlands: Stroudsburg, Pa., Hutchinson Ross Publishing Company, p. 3–19.

Schafale, M.P., and Weakley, A.S., 1990, Classification of the natural communities of North Carolina, third approximation: North Carolina Department of Environment, Health, and Natural Resources, Division of Parks and Recreation, 325 p.

Sharitz, R.R., and Gibbons, J.W., 1982, The ecology of southeastern shrub bogs (pocosins) and Carolina Bays—A community profile: U.S. Fish and Wildlife Service Report FWS/OBS–82/04, 93 p.

Stockton, M.B., and Richardson, C.J., 1987, Wetland development trends in coastal North Carolina, USA, from 1970 to 1984: Environmental Management, v. 11, no. 5, p. 649–657.

Tiner, R.W., Jr., 1984, Wetlands of the United States—Current status and recent trends: Washington, D.C., U.S. Fish and Wildlife Service, 59 p.

U.S. Fish and Wildlife Service, 1992, Regional wetlands concept plan, Emergency Wetlands Resources Act, Southeast Region: Atlanta, Ga., U.S. Fish and Wildlife Service, 259 p.

Wharton, C.H., Kitchens, W.M., Pendleton, E.C., and Sipe, T.W., 1982, The ecology of bottomland hardwood swamps of the southeast—A community profile: U.S. Fish and Wildlife Service Report FWS/OBS–81/37, 126 p.

Wiegert, P.G., and Freeman, B.J., 1990, Tidal salt marshes of the southeastern Atlantic coast—A community profile: U.S. Fish and Wildlife Service Biological Report 85(7.29), 70 p.

Wilson, K.A., 1962, North Carolina wetlands—Their distribution and management: Raleigh, North Carolina Wildlife Resources Commission Project W–6–R, 169 p.

FOR ADDITIONAL INFORMATION: District Chief, U.S. Geological Survey, 3916 Sunset Ridge Road, Raleigh, NC 27607; Regional Wetland Coordinator, U.S. Fish and Wildlife Service, 1875 Century Building, Suite 200, Atlanta, GA 30345

Prepared by
Jerad D. Bales and Douglas J. Newcomb,
U.S. Geological Survey

North Dakota
Wetland Resources

Wetlands covered nearly 11 percent of North Dakota, about 4.9 million acres, in predevelopment times (Dahl, 1990). By the 1980's, wetlands covered about 6 percent of the State, or about 2.7 million acres, which represents a 45 percent reduction from the predevelopment acreage (North Dakota Parks and Recreation Department, 1987).

Wetlands are ecologically and economically valuable to the State. Wetlands trap, remove, and transform waterborne constituents by processes such as sedimentation, plant uptake, microbial transformation, and soil adsorption. Attenuation of runoff from snowmelt and rainfall by wetlands reduces the magnitude of potential flooding downstream. Riparian vegetation along watercourses reduces the potential for bank and channel erosion by stabilizing the banks and channels. In some areas, the water held in a wetland recharges the local ground-water system.

Wetlands provide habitat for furbearers, game species, and many nongame-wildlife species. Probably the best known function of wetlands in North Dakota is waterfowl production. The Prairie Pothole Region, which extends across much of the State, contains only 10 percent of the waterfowl breeding area in North America, yet it accounts for 50 percent of the duck crop in an average year (Smith and others, 1964). The hunting industry in States all along the Central Flyway benefit from North Dakota's prairie pothole wetlands. Aside from their value as breeding areas, North Dakota wetlands also provide resting and feeding habitat for migratory waterfowl and wading birds.

TYPES AND DISTRIBUTION

Wetlands are lands transitional between terrestrial and deepwater habitats where the water table usually is at or near the land surface or the land is covered by shallow water (Cowardin and others, 1979). The distribution of wetlands and deepwater habitats in North Dakota is shown in figure 2A; only wetlands are discussed herein.

Wetlands can be vegetated or nonvegetated and are classified on the basis of their hydrology, vegetation, and substrate. In this summary, wetlands are classified according to the system proposed by Cowardin and others (1979), which is used by the U.S. Fish and Wildlife Service (FWS) to map and inventory the Nation's wetlands. At the most general level of the classification system, wetlands are grouped into five ecological systems: Palustrine, Lacustrine, Riv-

erine, Estuarine, and Marine. The Palustrine System includes only wetlands, whereas the other systems comprise wetlands and deepwater habitats. Wetlands of the systems that occur in North Dakota are described below.

System	Wetland description
Palustrine	Wetlands in which vegetation is predominantly trees (forested wetlands); shrubs (scrub-shrub wetlands); persistent or nonpersistent emergent, erect, rooted, herbaceous plants (persistent- and nonpersistent-emergent wetlands); or submersed and (or) floating plants (aquatic beds). Also, intermittently to permanently flooded open-water bodies of less than 20 acres in which water is less than 6.6 feet deep.
Lacustrine	Wetlands within an intermittently to permanently flooded lake or reservoir. Vegetation, when present, is predominantly nonpersistent emergent plants (nonpersistent-emergent wetlands), or submersed and (or) floating plants (aquatic beds), or both.
Riverine	Wetlands within a channel. Vegetation, when present, is same as in the Lacustrine System

Currently (1993), no estimate of statewide wetland acreage in each of these ecological systems is available. Stewart and Kantrud (1973) estimated wetland acreages by using data collected in 1967; however, their classification system differed from that of Cowardin and others (1979). Stewart and Kantrud classified wetlands according to the following habitat types: natural basin wetlands, streams and oxbows, stock ponds and dugouts, and road ditches and drainage channels. Under the Cowardin and others (1979) classification system, natural basin wetlands would include wetlands classified mostly as palustrine and a small amount as lacustrine and are estimated to constitute about 91 percent, or about 2.5 million acres, of the wetlands in the State. Streams and oxbows would be classified as palustrine or riverine and constitute about 160,000 acres. Stock ponds and dugouts would be classified as palustrine or lacustrine and constitute about 50,000 acres. Road ditches and drainage channels would be classified as palustrine and constitute about 30,000 acres. The total acres of wetlands in Stewart and Kantrud's estimate for the late 1960's is about 2.7 million acres, slightly more than the 2.5 million acres estimated by the FWS using 1980's data (Dahl, 1990).

Stewart and Kantrud (1973) divided North Dakota into four biotic regions (fig. 2B). They estimated that 2.2 million acres of wetlands, or 81 percent of the wetlands in the State, are in the Prairie Pothole Region. Specific estimates were not available for the Agassiz Lake Plain, the Coteau Slope, or the Southwestern Slope Regions. The wetland types in the Prairie Pothole, Agassiz Lake Plain, and Coteau Slope Regions are similar; about 90 percent of the wetlands are in natural basins. The least amount of wetland acreage in the four regions is in the Southwestern Slope Region. About 95 percent of the wetlands in this region are riparian wetlands along streams and around stock ponds and dugouts.

More than 90 percent of the wetlands in the State are classified by Stewart and Kantrud (1973) as natural basin wetlands, commonly called prairie potholes. The prairie potholes primarily contain persistent-emergent wetlands, variously called wet meadows, marshes, and fens. The distinction among these different wetlands is based in part on vegetation. The species of plants found in a

Figure 1. Prairie pothole wetlands about 28 miles northwest of Jamestown. *(Photograph by T.C. Winter, U.S. Geological Survey.)*

wetland is a function of water availability in each year. Climatic fluctuations can cause emergent wetlands to change or revert to an open-water phase in some years (Stewart and Kantrud, 1972). Wet meadows are present in the shallow pond basins and around the deeper ponds and lakes. Flooding persists in wet meadows for only a few weeks following spring snowmelt or a few days following heavy rainstorms. Plant species that characterize wet meadows are fine-textured grasses, rushes, and low sedges. Marshes form in pond basins where water either persists throughout the year or persists for long periods and then evaporates or is transpired in late summer and fall. Marsh vegetation consists of grasses or grasslike plants, such as sedges, bulrushes, and cattails, that are coarser and taller than the plants in the wet meadow. Fen wetlands are quagmires that have floating mats of emergent vegetation. Fen wetlands are a result of ground-water seepage on sloping terrain, usually adjacent to a pond or lake. Plant species in fen wetlands can be the same as those in wet meadows and marshes. Fen wetlands are not common in North Dakota.

Prairie potholes that contain submerged or floating plants are called aquatic-bed wetlands. Aquatic-bed vegetation commonly grows in ponds and lakes that persist for weeks or longer. Most of the plant species are bottom-rooted plants, but free-floating plants also are common. The types of plant species present are closely correlated with water salinity. The plants that grow in fresh or slightly brackish ponds or lakes are not present in the saline waters of alkali ponds and lakes.

Other palustrine classes that exist but are not common in North Dakota are scrub-shrub wetlands and forested wetlands. Scrub-shrub wetlands contain willows, cottonwoods, and aspens. Forested wetlands have formed along rivers and contain mostly cottonwoods.

The distribution and abundance of wetlands in North Dakota are the result of the State's glacial history. The Coteau Slope, Prairie Pothole, and Agassiz Lake Plain Regions were glaciated during the most recent glacial period, whereas the Southwest Slope Region was not. Wetlands in the glaciated regions formed in depressions resulting from glacial and postglacial activity. Permanently flooded

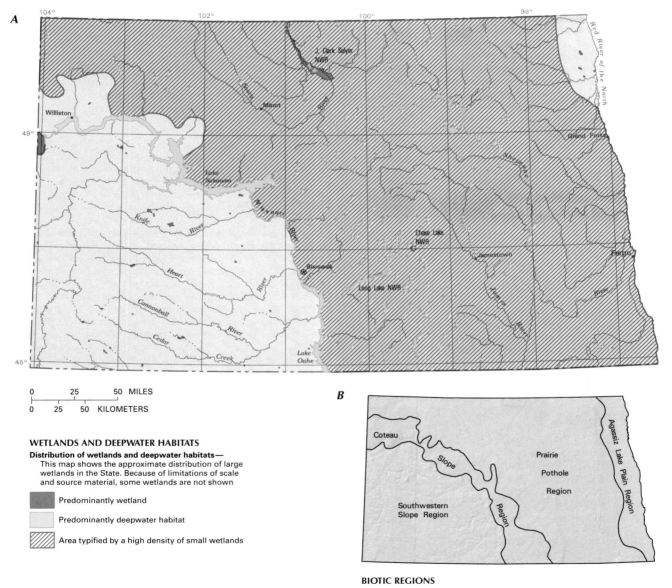

WETLANDS AND DEEPWATER HABITATS

Distribution of wetlands and deepwater habitats—
This map shows the approximate distribution of large wetlands in the State. Because of limitations of scale and source material, some wetlands are not shown

   Predominantly wetland

   Predominantly deepwater habitat

   Area typified by a high density of small wetlands

BIOTIC REGIONS

Figure 2.   Wetland distribution in North Dakota and biotic regions of the State. **A**, Distribution of wetlands and deepwater habitats. **B**, Biotic regions. *(Sources: A, T.E. Dahl, U.S. Fish and Wildlife Service, unpub. data, 1991. B, Modified from Stewart and Kantrud, 1973.)*

to semipermanently flooded wetlands generally are in areas of end moraines and stagnation moraines, which are most common in the Coteau Slope Region. Seasonally flooded to intermittently flooded wetlands generally form in areas of ground moraine and lake plains, which are most common in the Prairie Pothole and Agassiz Lake Plain Regions. Wetlands in the unglaciated Southwestern Slope Region are few and are present as riparian wetlands along watercourses and as artificially flooded wetlands around reservoirs, stock ponds, and dugouts.

The FWS National Wetlands Inventory is mapping the Nation's wetlands. Wetlands are identified on U.S. Geological Survey 7.5-minute quadrangle topographic maps, many of which are stored in digital format. Currently (1993), paper maps are available for 79 percent of North Dakota, and digital-format maps are available for 31 percent of the State.

HYDROLOGIC SETTING

Wetlands form where surface-water and ground-water flow patterns cause water to be near or above the soil surface for a significant period of time during the growing season. The location and persistence of the wetland is a function of climate, topography, ground-water flow patterns, surface-water flow patterns, and runoff characteristics in a basin.

The most common wetlands in North Dakota are prairie potholes. These wetlands formed in glacial deposits such as end moraines, stagnation moraines, ground moraines, outwash plains, and lake plains. The glacial deposits generally consist of silt and clay through which water moves slowly. Outwash plains, however, mostly consist of sorted sand, which transmits water readily. In the morainal areas, no natural surface-drainage network has developed, so many depressions are not connected to an integrated drainage system (fig. 3).

Figure 3. Prairie pothole wetlands near Chase Lake National Wildlife Refuge. Note the absence of a surface-drainage system. *(Photograph courtesy of U.S. Fish and Wildlife Service.)*

The interaction between ground water and a wetland affects the permanence and water quality of the wetland. Studies of the Prairie Pothole Region (Hubbard, 1988; Winter, 1989) indicate that ground-water flow among wetlands is complicated. Wetlands in the same area can discharge to different ground-water systems: one to a regional system, another to an intermediate system, and still another to a local system (fig. 4).

Generally, wetlands in the Prairie Pothole Region have three types of interaction with the ground-water system (Kantrud and others, 1989). Some wetlands recharge the underlying ground-water system. These wetlands tend to hold water for only a few months

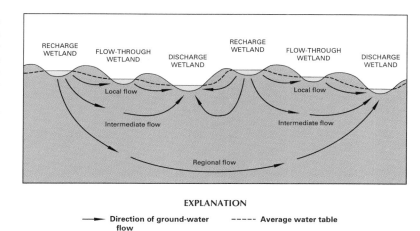

EXPLANATION

→ **Direction of ground-water flow**   ----- **Average water table**

Figure 4. Generalized ground-water flow in the Prairie Pothole Region. *(Source: Modified from Winter, 1989.)*

a year, and the water generally has low dissolved-solids concentrations. Other wetlands are flow-through systems; that is, ground water flows into parts of the wetland while other parts of the wetland recharge the ground-water system. Flow-through wetlands tend to hold water for longer periods and generally have higher dissolved-solids concentrations. A third type of wetland serves only as a discharge area for ground water. These wetlands are permanently flooded and typically saline.

Climate has a major effect on wetland formation and permanence. Most of North Dakota is dry; average precipitation ranges from about 13 inches in the western part of the State to about 20 inches along the eastern border. Average annual free-water-surface evaporation ranges from 32 inches in the northeastern part of the State to about 40 inches in the southwestern part (Winter and others, 1984). Because average annual free-water-surface evaporation is greater than average annual precipitation, there is an annual moisture deficit that inhibits wetland formation and permanence.

North Dakota's harsh winters also affect the hydrology of wetlands in the State. About 25 percent of the annual precipitation occurs as snow, which generally falls between October and March (Winter and others, 1984). Snow is blown off the unsheltered farmland and accumulates in sheltered areas and depressions, such as wetlands. When the snow begins to melt in the spring, the ground is still frozen, so snowmelt and spring rains do not readily infiltrate into the soil. As a result, snowmelt runoff and spring rains are the major source of water to the prairie potholes (Shjeflo, 1968).

Annual variations in climate affect the permanence of wetlands. Stewart and Kantrud (1973) estimated that 67 percent of the wetlands (by area) in the Prairie Pothole Region are seasonally flooded or temporarily flooded wetlands. Because these wetlands are filled in the spring by snowmelt runoff, the amount of snowpack accumulated in the winter determines to what extent a wetland is filled. Temperature and windspeed determine how long the water remains in the wetland. Standing water is present from about a week in the temporarily flooded wetlands to about 2 months in the seasonally flooded wetlands. All of these wetlands go dry before the growing season is complete. Following a winter of little snowfall, many wetlands do not receive any water for that year, and some of them are tilled. About 29 percent of the wetlands in the Prairie Pothole Region have been tilled.

Forested and scrub-shrub wetlands are present along creeks and rivers and around most of the dugouts and small reservoirs in the State. During runoff periods, particularly following snowmelt runoff, parts of the creek and river flood plains are inundated for short periods of time. The runoff also fills the dugouts and small reservoirs. During drier parts of the year, the existence of forested and scrub-shrub wetlands along the creeks and rivers and around dugouts and small reservoirs depends on ground water.

In some wildlife refuges, the FWS has attempted to stabilize the effects that climate has on the permanence of wetlands. An example is J. Clark Salyer National Wildlife Refuge. Five small dams that can maintain about 4 feet of water over parts of the flood plain were built on the Souris River. Water is regulated to sustain the desired emergent wetlands. If emergent vegetation, such as cattails, becomes too thick, the growth can be controlled by increasing the water level in the wetland or draining the wetland. Because the Souris River provides a reliable source of water, the variable climatic conditions will not greatly affect the management of the wetlands.

TRENDS

Predevelopment wetland acreage in North Dakota has been estimated to be about 4.9 million acres (North Dakota Parks and Recreation Department, 1987; Dahl, 1990). When settlers moved into the State, they noted in their journals many wet meadows, particularly along the Red River of the North. Farmers drained some of these wetlands to grow crops. The most recent and complete published wetland inventory was done in 1982 by the Natural Resources Conservation Service (formerly the Soil Conservation Service) (NRCS), which estimated that 2.7 million acres of wetlands remained in the State (North Dakota Parks and Recreation Department, 1987). The most extensive drainage has occurred in the Agassiz Lake Plain Region, where about 1.2 million acres of wet soils have been drained (North Dakota Parks and Recreation Department, 1987). To a lesser extent, wetlands have been drained for road construction, urban development, and surface mining. In addition to the loss of many wetlands due to drainage, others have been degraded by siltation and chemical contamination.

Agricultural drainage still poses the greatest threat to wetlands in the State. The wetlands that were the easiest and cheapest to drain already have been drained; therefore, economic factors limit current drainage trends. As small farms are consolidated into large commercial farms, drainage might not be as large a financial burden, and additional wetlands might be drained. Economists feel that if free-market prices remain low, Federal farm programs will have made wetland drainage unprofitable (North Dakota Parks and Recreation Department, 1987). However, if crop prices increase and Federal programs are eliminated, drainage will be profitable and political pressure could change the State's "no-net-loss" policy.

CONSERVATION

Many government agencies and private organizations participate in aspects of wetland management and conservation in North Dakota. The most active agencies and organizations and some of their activities are listed in table 1.

Federal wetland activities. — Development activities in North Dakota wetlands are regulated by several Federal statutory prohibitions and incentives that are intended to slow wetland losses. Some of the more important of these are contained in the 1899 Rivers and Harbors Act; the 1972 Clean Water Act and amendments; the 1985 Food Security Act; the 1990 Food, Agriculture, Conservation, and Trade Act; and the 1986 Emergency Wetlands Resources Act.

Section 10 of the Rivers and Harbors Act gives the U.S. Army Corps of Engineers (Corps) authority to regulate certain activities in navigable waters. Regulated activities include diking, deepening, filling, excavating, and placing of structures. The related section 404 of the Clean Water Act is the most often-used Federal legislation protecting wetlands. Under section 404 provisions, the Corps issues permits regulating the discharge of dredged or fill material into wetlands. Permits are subject to review and possible veto by the U.S.

Table 1. Selected wetland-related activities of government agencies and private organizations in North Dakota, 1993

[Source: Classification of activities is generalized from information provided by agencies and organizations. •, agency or organization participates in wetland-related activity; ..., agency or organization does not participate in wetland-related activity. MAN, management; REG, regulation; R&C, restoration and creation; LAN, land acquisition; R&D, research and data collection; D&I, delineation and inventory]

Agency or organization	MAN	REG	R&C	LAN	R&D	D&I
FEDERAL						
Department of Agriculture						
Consolidated Farm Service Agency	...	•	...	...	...	...
Forest Service	•	...	•	•	•	•
Natural Resources Conservation Service	...	•	...	...	•	•
Department of Defense						
Army Corps of Engineers	•	•	•	•	•	•
Military reservations	•	...	...	...	...	...
Department of the Interior						
Bureau of Land Management	•	...	•	...	•	•
Bureau of Reclamation	...	...	•	•	•	•
Fish and Wildlife Service	•	...	•	...	•	•
Geological Survey	...	...	...	...	•	...
National Biological Service	...	...	...	...	•	...
National Park Service	•	...	•	...	•	...
Environmental Protection Agency	...	•	...	...	•	•
STATE						
Department of Health and Consolidated Laboratories	•	•	...	•	•	...
Department of Transportation	...	...	•	•	...	•
Forest Service	•	...	...	...	•	•
Game and Fish Department	•	...	•	•	•	•
Parks and Tourism Department	•	...	•	...	•	•
Water Commission	...	•	...	...	•	•
PRIVATE						
Ducks Unlimited	...	...	•	•	...	...
The Nature Conservancy	•	...	•	•	...	...

Environmental Protection Agency (EPA), and the FWS has review and advisory roles. Section 401 of the Clean Water Act grants to States and eligible Indian Tribes the authority to approve, apply conditions to, or deny section 404 permit applications on the basis of a proposed activity's probable effects on the water quality of a wetland.

Most farming, ranching, and silviculture activities are not subject to section 404 regulation. However, the "Swampbuster" provision of the 1985 Food Security Act and amendments in the 1990 Food, Agriculture, Conservation, and Trade Act discourage (through financial disincentives) the draining, filling, or other alteration of wetlands for agricultural use. The law allows exemptions from penalties in some cases, especially if the farmer agrees to restore the altered wetland or other wetlands that have been converted to agricultural use. The Wetlands Reserve Program of the 1990 Food, Agriculture, Conservation, and Trade Act authorizes the Federal Government to purchase conservation easements from landowners who agree to protect or restore wetlands. The Consolidated Farm Service Agency (formerly the Agricultural Stabilization and Conservation Service) administers the Swampbuster provisions and Wetlands Reserve Program. The NRCS determines compliance with Swampbuster provisions and assists farmers in the identification of wetlands and in the development of wetland protection, restoration, or creation plans.

The 1986 Emergency Wetlands Resources Act encourages wetland protection through funding incentives. The act requires States to address wetland protection in their Statewide Comprehensive Outdoor Recreation Plans to qualify for Federal funding for State recreational land; the National Park Service (NPS) provides guidance to States in developing the wetland component of their plans.

Federal agencies are responsible for the proper management of wetlands on public land under their jurisdiction. In North Dakota, the FWS manages about 290,000 acres in 63 National Wildlife Refuges. The (FWS) manages about 240,000 acres in 1,000 Waterfowl Protection Units. In addition, the FWS has conservation easements to 700,000 acres of private wetlands. The Bureau of Land Management (BLM) manages about 6,800 acres of wetlands in 66,000 acres of BLM land. The U.S. Forest Service manages about 1.1 million acres of land in three National Grasslands that have an estimated riparian acreage of 16,000 acres. The NPS manages 71,000 acres in two National Historic Sites and one National Park but currently (1993) has no estimate of wetland acreage under its jurisdiction. The Bureau of Reclamation (BOR) has acquired land owing to mitigation of projects in the State. The BOR has transferred management responsibilities of about 17,000 acres to the FWS, of which 5,000 acres are wetlands. The BOR is still developing about 6,000 acres of mitigated land, of which 1,000 acres are wetlands. The BOR also is developing about 10,000 acres of land encompassed by its projects, of which 6,000 acres are wetlands. Eventually the management responsibilities of all land being developed by the BOR will be transferred to another Federal or State agency.

State wetland activities.—State programs for wetland protection are 80-acre drainage permits (North Dakota Century Code 61–01–22), Senate Bill No. 2035, and the State Water Bank Program. Since 1957, North Dakota has required landowners to obtain a permit to drain wetlands that have a drainage area larger than 80 acres. Permits are reviewed by the local Water Resources District and by the North Dakota State Water Commission State Engineer. Senate Bill No. 2035, commonly known as the "no-net-loss" bill, was passed in 1987. The bill maintains existing drainage regulations, but the bill also requires that the same acreage of wetlands will exist in the future as existed on January 1, 1987. The Water Commission State Engineer and the Game and Fish Department Director must jointly find that the wetland proposed to be destroyed will be replaced by an equal acreage of suitable wetland. A wetlands bank was established to keep track of the wetlands drained and restored. The wetlands bank is the responsibility of the Water Commission. Wetlands drained are reported as debits and wetlands created or restored are reported as credits. The "no-net-loss" bill mandates that the bank cannot carry a net debit greater than 2,500 acres. The State Water Bank Program was created in 1981 to give landowners financial incentive to set aside cropland to preserve the State's wetlands. The program is administered at the State and county levels and uses private donations.

The Department of Health and Consolidated Laboratories reviews section 404 permit applications to ensure compliance with water-quality regulations. Also, the Department submits a biennial assessment of the State's surface-water quality, including wetlands, to the EPA and the U.S. Congress, according to Clean Water Act Section 305(b) requirements.

State agencies also are responsible for the proper management of wetlands on public land under their jurisdiction. The North Dakota Game and Fish Department manages 80,000 acres in fee or title ownership, and many of these acres are wetlands. The North Dakota Department of Transportation manages 195,000 acres of right-of-ways along the highways in the State and uses best-management practices to avoid unnecessary disturbances of wetlands while maintaining or constructing highways. Unavoidable filling of wetlands is mitigated through wetland restoration or creation. The State Parks

and Tourism Department manages 16,000 acres of land in State Parks but currently (1993) has no estimate of wetland acreage. The North Dakota Forest Service manages 13,000 acres of land in five State Forests but currently (1993) has no estimate of wetland acreage.

Private wetland activities.—Ducks Unlimited works with Federal, State, and private landowners to restore and enhance lands for wildlife production, with emphasis on waterfowl production. The Nature Conservancy manages about 4,000 acres of land on two preserves, and about one-half of the acreage is wetlands. The Nature Conservancy's interest is to preserve habitat unique to endangered plant and animal species in the State, particularly species unique to alkali wetlands.

References Cited

Cowardin, L.M., Carter, Virginia, Golet, F.C., and LaRoe, E.T., 1979, Classification of wetlands and deepwater habitats of the United States: U.S. Fish and Wildlife Service Report FWS/OBS–79/31, 131 p.

Dahl, T.E., 1990, Wetlands—Losses in the United States, 1780's to 1980's: Washington, D.C., U.S. Fish and Wildlife Service Report to Congress, 13 p.

Hubbard, D.E., 1988, Glaciated prairie wetlands functions and values—A synthesis of the literature: U.S. Fish and Wildlife Service Biological Report 88(43), 50 p.

Kantrud, H.A., Krapu, G.L., and Swanson, G.A., 1989, Prairie basin wetlands of the Dakotas—A community profile: U.S. Fish and Wildlife Service Biological Report 85(7.28), 111 p.

North Dakota Parks and Recreation Department, 1987, North Dakota State comprehensive outdoor recreation plan addendum, wetlands priority plan: North Dakota Parks and Recreation Department, 82 p.

Shjeflo, J.B., 1968, Evapotranspiration and the water budget of prairie potholes in North Dakota: U.S. Geological Survey Professional Paper 585–B, 49 p.

Smith, A.G., Stoudt, J.H., and Gollop, J.B., 1964, Prairie potholes and marshes, *in* Linduska, J.P., ed., Waterfowl tomorrow: Washington D.C., U.S. Fish and Wildlife Service, p. 39–50.

Stewart, R.E., and Kantrud, H.A., 1972, Vegetation of prairie potholes, North Dakota, in relation to quality of water and other environmental factors: U.S. Geological Survey Professional Paper 585–D, 36 p.

———1973, Ecological distribution of breeding water fowl populations in North Dakota: Journal of Wildlife Management, v. 37, no. 1, p. 39–50.

Winter, T.C., 1989, Hydrologic studies of wetlands in the northern prairie, *in* Van Der Valk, A., ed., Northern prairie wetlands: Ames, Iowa State University Press, p. 16–54.

Winter, T.C., Benson, R.D., Engberg, R.A., and others, 1984, Synopsis of ground-water and surface-water resources of North Dakota: U.S. Geological Survey Open-File Report 84–732, 127 p.

FOR ADDITIONAL INFORMATION: District Chief, U.S. Geological Survey, 821 East Interstate Avenue, Bismarck, ND 58501; Regional Wetland Coordinator, U.S. Fish and Wildlife Service, Fish and Wildlife Enhancement, P.O. Box 25486, Denver Federal Center, Denver, CO 80225

Prepared by
Wayne R. Berkas,
U.S. Geological Survey

Ohio
Wetland Resources

Ohio's wetlands cover about 1.8 percent of the State (Dahl, 1990). Though greatly reduced in acreage since colonial times, these wetlands are an important economic and environmental resource. Wetlands can lessen the effects of floods by storing floodwater and releasing it gradually. Wetlands also help regulate water quality, and wetland vegetation can provide bank stabilization and reduce erosion. Wetlands provide habitat for migratory birds, waterfowl, and fish and are prominent attractions in a well-developed State system of nature areas, preserves, and parks (fig. 1). Ohio wetlands attract large numbers of hunters, fishermen, and naturalists. Historically, wetlands have provided timber and peat and have been converted into some of the most fertile farmland in the State.

TYPES AND DISTRIBUTION

Wetlands are lands transitional between terrestrial and deepwater habitats where the water table usually is at or near the land surface or the land is covered by shallow water (Cowardin and others, 1979). The distribution of wetlands and deepwater habitats in Ohio is shown in figure 2A; only wetlands are discussed herein.

Wetlands can be vegetated or nonvegetated and are classified on the basis of their hydrology, vegetation, and substrate. In this summary, wetlands are classified according to the system proposed by Cowardin and others (1979), which is used by the U.S. Fish and Wildlife Service (FWS) to map and inventory the Nation's wetlands. At the most general level of the classification system, wetlands are grouped into five ecological systems: Palustrine, Lacustrine, Riverine, Estuarine, and Marine. The Palustrine System includes only wetlands, whereas the other systems comprise wetlands and deepwater habitats. Wetlands of the systems that occur in Ohio are described below.

System	Wetland description
Palustrine	Wetlands in which vegetation is predominantly trees (forested wetlands); shrubs (scrub-shrub wetlands); persistent or nonpersistent emergent, erect, rooted, herbaceous plants (persistent- and nonpersistent-emergent wetlands); or submersed and (or) floating plants (aquatic beds). Also, intermittently to permanently flooded open-water bodies of less than 20 acres in which water is less than 6.6 feet deep.
Lacustrine	Wetlands within an intermittently to permanently flooded lake or reservoir. Vegetation, when present, is predominantly nonpersistent emergent plants (nonpersistent-emergent wetlands), or submersed and (or) floating plants (aquatic beds), or both.
Riverine	Wetlands within a channel. Vegetation, when present, is same as in the Lacustrine System.

There is no published comprehensive inventory of Ohio wetlands. Dahl (1990) provided the only recent estimate of total area—about 483,000 acres. Two inventories are presently (1993) in progress. The National Wetlands Inventory has been completed for northern and eastern Ohio. State and Federal agencies began the Ohio Wetland Inventory in 1991 and have located and classified wetlands in 50 of 88 Ohio counties. This inventory locates wetlands on LANDSAT satellite images and, in some cases, verifies wetland identification and classification by ground reconnaissance (Ohio Department of Natural Resources, 1992; Yi and others, 1994).

Palustrine wetlands such as swamps (forested wetlands), wet prairies (emergent wetlands), coastal and embayment marshes (emergent wetlands), peatlands (wetlands that have organic soils), and wetlands along stream margins and backwaters collectively are the most important Ohio wetlands. Lacustrine and riverine wetlands constitute only a small percentage of the State's wetland acreage. Many wetlands have formed on poorly drained soils that are of glacial origin. Remnants of once extensive forested wetlands and wet prairies are widely distributed across glaciated parts of northern, central, and western Ohio. Wetlands in these areas include the swamps, oak forests, and wet prairies that were part of a large wetland system known historically as the Great Black Swamp (Ohio Department of Natural Resources, 1988) and the wet prairies and wet mixed-oak forests of south-central Ohio (Forsyth, 1970).

Ohio peatlands comprise bogs and fens. Bogs receive moisture mostly from precipitation and typically contain large numbers of mosses that are tolerant of acidic conditions. Fens generally receive drainage from surrounding mineral soils and commonly support communities of grasses, sedges, or reeds (Mitsch and Gosselink, 1986). Bogs and fens are located in glaciated areas of northern and western Ohio (Andreas and Knoop, 1992). Bogs are concentrated in the Southern New York Section of the Appalachian Plateaus of northeastern Ohio, and fens are common in the Till Plains of the Central Lowland of western Ohio (fig. 2B) (Denny, 1979).

Large coastal marshes border the southwestern shore and Sandusky Bay of Lake Erie (fig. 2A). These marshes generally range from 1 to 2 miles in width and are interrupted by points of higher land and developed areas. Undisturbed shores of western Lake Erie have marshes fronted by low barrier beaches and interspaced with river mouths. These wetlands are protected by constructed earthen and rock dikes. Two sand spits separate Sandusky Bay from Lake Erie and protect extensive wetlands in the bay. East of Sandusky Bay, low, marshy backshores grade into low bluffs, and wetlands in this area are restricted to mouths of tributaries such as the Huron River and Old Woman Creek. A large wetland, Mentor Marsh, occupies the former valley and delta of the Grand River. Twelve bedrock islands in western Lake Erie have rocky shores, but small embayments on large islands contain wetlands (Herdendorf, 1992).

Figure 1. Cedar Run in Cedar Bog Nature Preserve. Cedar Run drains bog meadows and marl meadows of Cedar Bog, a relict alkaline fen. *(Photograph by Ralph E. Ramey, Columbus, Ohio).*

Numerous riverine and palustrine wetlands are located in the drainages of the Muskingum, Scioto, and Great Miami Rivers (fig. 2*A*). These wetlands extend from glaciated headwaters into unglaciated sections. To date, the hydrology and ecology of these wetlands have been little studied.

HYDROLOGIC SETTING

Wetlands form where ground water or surface water saturates poorly drained or impermeable soils. Wetlands typically develop in depressions or other low areas that are intermittently to permanently flooded by runoff, ground-water discharge, or precipitation. Water is removed primarily by runoff, evaporation, and transpiration. In areas that develop into wetlands, moisture is maintained at or near the surface by fine-grained, hydric soils. These water-saturated soils support the growth of specialized plants (hydrophytes) that are adapted to low oxygen concentrations and, in some cases, extreme acidity, alkalinity, or low nitrogen concentrations.

Many Ohio wetlands are located on fine-grained soils that were deposited by an extensive system of glacial lakes. These lakes were created as advancing glaciers blocked the flow of preglacial streams or when receding glaciers blocked the flow of meltwater. As the lakes drained, their beds became extensive deposits of fine-grained silts and clays known as till. These deposits cover extensive areas of northwestern Ohio (Spooner, 1982).

As ice of the most recent glaciation receded to the southern shore of Lake Erie, it blocked the northward drainage of meltwater and formed a large lake (Lake Maumee) in northwestern Ohio. As ice sheets continued to recede, Lake Maumee drained, and sand deposits from ancient dunes and flat deposits that formed the lakebed were left behind. Lake deposits contained large amounts of silt and clay and formed poorly drained soils that at one time supported extensive swamps (Forsyth, 1970).

Sand deposits left by Lake Maumee were inhabited by oak forests and wet prairies. Oak forests developed where precipitation drained through thick sand of ancient dunes and accumulated on underlying clay till. The surfaces of these sand deposits were relatively dry and supported only dry-tolerant, oak forests. Where sand deposits were thin, ground water saturated the sandy soil and created swamps or shallow lakes. These areas developed into wet prairies (Forsyth, 1970).

Lake deposits from early glaciation and glacial outwash from more recent glaciations have been deposited in valleys of the Kanawha Section of the Appalachian Plateaus of southeastern Ohio (fig. 2*B*). Following the retreat of the last glacier, wetlands have developed along streams that drain these deposits. These wetlands typically are located on saturated loam soils and include oak-maple associations on clays; elm, sycamore, and birch associations on alluvial bottoms; and American elm, ash, and maple associations in better drained and aerated soils (Spooner, 1982). Sedges, button-

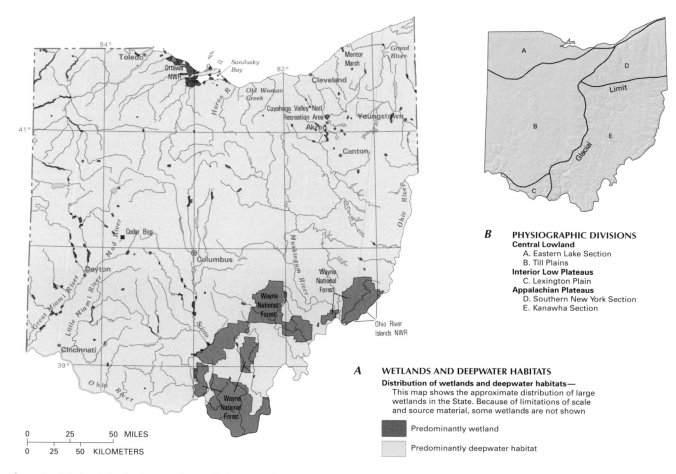

Figure 2. Wetland distribution in Ohio and physiography of the State. *A*, Distribution of wetlands and deepwater habitats. *B*, Physiography. *(Sources: A, T.E. Dahl, U.S. Fish and Wildlife Service, unpub. data, 1991. B, Physiographic divisions from Fenneman, 1946; landforms data from EROS Data Center.)*

bush, willow, alder, and maple grow in the wettest areas. Swamp forests consist of swamp white oak, black willow on wetter sites, and American elm, sycamore, and maple stands in less wet areas. Recent beaver activity has killed trees and created wetter and more open wetlands (Spooner, 1982).

In the glaciated part of Ohio, peatlands are located on lakebed deposits (Dachnowski, 1912) and in areas where glacial deposits formed topographic features that favor the retention of water (Andreas, 1985). These features provided the poorly drained soils and hydrologic setting necessary for the formation and maintenance of peatlands (Andreas, 1985; Andreas and Knoop, 1992). A common glacially derived feature, kettle holes, formed as ice was trapped in glacial deposits and then melted. As these ice pieces slowly thawed, meltwater eroded the surrounding deposits into funnel-shaped depressions (Goldthwait, 1959). Large kettle holes developed into lakes that eventually were filled by peat from accumulated and consolidated plant debris (Denny, 1979). The resultant wetlands developed plant communities dominated by mosses and evergreens.

Hydrologic and biological differences separate peatlands into acidic (pH 3.5–4.5) bogs and circumneutral (pH 5.5–8.0) fens. In Ohio, fens develop where springs emerge from glacial deposits and produce a continuous flow of cool, mineral-rich water. Primarily sedges and grasses, not sphagnum, are adapted to this environment and in fens form most of the peat. Bogs develop as water-saturated organic materials decay slowly at low pH and temperature to form thick peat deposits (Denny, 1979).

The relation of glacial geology to wetland hydrology has been thoroughly studied in Cedar Bog, a typical Ohio fen located in the Mad River Valley (figs. 1 and 2A). Cedar Bog developed in the Mad River Valley Train (fig. 3), an outwash made up of highly permeable, calcium carbonate gravel (Quinn, 1974). In the Mad River Valley, ground water generally is 10 feet below the land surface. However, Cedar Bog has developed on hydric soils that were produced where ground water discharges on the eastern side of the valley. The water that sustains Cedar Bog is derived mainly from glacial outwashes to the north and east (Forsyth, 1974). These outwashes consist of coarse calcium carbonate gravel and rise about 100 feet above the fen. Ground water flows through the outwashes until it reaches the base of an escarpment along the eastern border of Cedar Bog. Here, cool, alkaline ground water discharges in springs, saturates soils, and flows across the fen. The continuously seeping ground water produces a perpetually cool, moist microenvironment that maintains a flora composed of many species normally found much farther north (Frederick, 1974). As surface water accumulates, it is drained by Cedar Run and the Mad River (Hillman and Kenoyer, 1989).

Changing water levels are important in the formation and maintenance of Lake Erie wetlands. Water levels in Lake Erie and in bordering coastal marshes are subject to long-term and short-term fluctuations. Long-term fluctuations are caused by changes in inflow that result from extended periods of wet or dry weather in the upper Great Lakes drainage. Wind action produces short-term changes in water level called seiches. These changes can cause water and chemical exchanges similar to those in salt marshes during tidal flow (Mitsch, 1992). Fluctuating water levels promote wetland formation by producing barrier bars, deltas, beaches, spits, lagoons, and natural levees. Water-level fluctuations also rejuvenate existing coastal wetland communities and preclude the conversion of vegetated marshes into dry fields (Herdendorf, 1992). Water levels at Cleveland have fluctuated almost 5 feet during the past 130 years.

TRENDS

From the 1780's to the 1980's, wetland area in Ohio declined by 90 percent, from about 5,000,000 acres to about 483,000 acres (Dahl, 1990). For the conterminous 48 States, the percentage of wetland loss in Ohio is second only to that of California. Drainage of wetlands for agriculture has been the primary cause of wetland loss, but recreational use, fluctuating water levels, urban development, mining, logging, and fire also have contributed (Andreas and Knoop, 1992).

The swamps of the Great Black Swamp in northwestern Ohio and the marshes bordering Lake Erie were once the State's two largest wetland systems. Before European settlement of the area, the Great Black Swamp occupied nearly 900,000 acres. Beginning in 1859, a series of drainage projects converted the swamp into some of the most productive farmland in Ohio. Today only 5 percent of the original swamp forest remains (Andreas and Knoop, 1992).

Coastal wetlands along the Ohio shore of Lake Erie have been destroyed as agriculture, real-estate development, and recreational areas have expanded (Heath, 1992). From 1850 to 1993, about 951,000 of 988,000 acres of coastal wetlands were destroyed along the southwestern coast of Lake Erie (Herdendorf, 1992). Only 10 percent of the original marsh along Lake Erie exists today (Andreas and Knoop, 1992). Since 1988, public agencies and private organizations involved in the Lower Great Lakes Joint Venture of the North American Waterfowl Management Plan have purchased and restored about 5,240 acres of Lake Erie wetlands (Ohio Department of Natural Resources, 1992).

Before 1780, about 183,000 acres (0.5 percent of Ohio's total area) were covered by peatlands (Dachnowski, 1912). In 1912, Dachnowski conducted a comprehensive, county-by-county survey of glaciated parts of Ohio and located 206 peatlands that had a com-

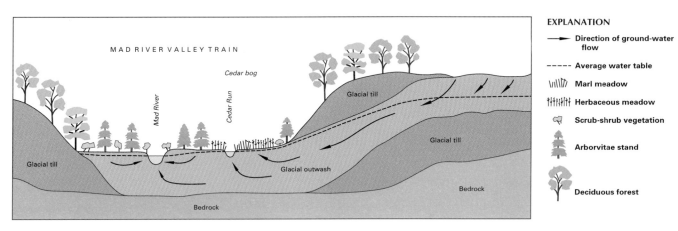

Figure 3. Generalized geohydrologic setting and vegetation of Cedar Bog. *(Sources: Forsyth, 1974; Frederick, 1974.)*

bined area of about 150,000 acres. Andreas and Knoop (1992) field-inventoried the flora of 125 peatlands and estimated that between 1900 and 1991, 76,500 of 79,500 acres of peatland were destroyed, and only 2 percent of these wetlands today contain plant communities associated with peatlands.

CONSERVATION

Many government agencies and private organizations participate in wetland conservation in Ohio. The most active agencies and organizations and some of their activities are listed in table 1.

Federal wetland activities.— Development activities in Ohio wetlands are regulated by several Federal statutory prohibitions and incentives that are intended to slow wetland losses. Some of the more important of these are contained in the 1899 Rivers and Harbors Act; the 1972 Clean Water Act and amendments; the 1985 Food Security Act; the 1990 Food, Agriculture, Conservation, and Trade Act; the 1986 Emergency Wetlands Resources Act; and the 1972 Coastal Zone Management Act.

Section 10 of the Rivers and Harbors Act gives the U.S. Army Corps of Engineers (Corps) authority to regulate certain activities in navigable waters. Regulated activities include diking, deepening, filling, excavating, and placing of structures. The related section 404 of the Clean Water Act is the most often-used Federal legislation protecting wetlands. Under section 404 provisions, the Corps issues permits regulating the discharge of dredged or fill material into wetlands. Permits are subject to review and possible veto by the U.S. Environmental Protection Agency, and the FWS has review and advisory roles. Section 401 of the Clean Water Act grants to States and eligible Indian Tribes the authority to approve, apply conditions to, or deny section 404 permit applications on the basis of a proposed activity's probable effects on the water quality of a wetland.

Most farming, ranching, and silviculture activities are not subject to section 404 regulation. However, the "Swampbuster" provision of the 1985 Food Security Act and amendments in the 1990 Food, Agriculture, Conservation, and Trade Act discourage (through financial disincentives) the draining, filling, or other alteration of wetlands for agricultural use. The law allows exemptions from penalties in some cases, especially if the farmer agrees to restore the altered wetland or other wetlands that have been converted to agricultural use. The Wetlands Reserve Program of the 1990 Food, Agriculture, Conservation, and Trade Act authorizes the Federal Government to purchase conservation easements from landowners who agree to protect or restore wetlands. The Consolidated Farm Service Agency (formerly the Agricultural Stabilization and Conservation Service) administers the Swampbuster provisions and Wetlands Reserve Program. The Natural Resources Conservation Service (formerly the Soil Conservation Service) (NRCS) determines compliance with Swampbuster provisions and assists farmers in the identification of wetlands and in the development of wetland protection, restoration, or creation plans.

The 1986 Emergency Wetlands Resources Act and the 1972 Coastal Zone Management Act and amendments encourage wetland protection through funding incentives. The Emergency Wetland Resources Act requires States to address wetland protection in their Statewide Comprehensive Outdoor Recreation Plans to qualify for Federal funding for State recreational land; the National Park Service (NPS) provides guidance to States in developing the wetland component of their plans. Coastal and Great Lakes States that adopt coastal-zone management programs and plans approved by the National Oceanic and Atmospheric Administration are eligible for Federal funding and technical assistance through the Coastal Zone Management Act.

Several Federal agencies have managerial and regulatory responsibilities for specific Ohio wetlands. The FWS is presently (1993) surveying Ohio wetlands located in Ohio River embayments

Table 1. Selected wetland-related activities of government agencies and private organizations in Ohio, 1993

[Source: Classification of activities is generalized from information provided by agencies and organizations. •, agency or organization participates in wetland-related activity; ..., agency or organization does not participate in wetland-related activity. MAN, management; REG, regulation; R&C, restoration and creation; LAN, land acquisition; R&D, research and data collection; D&I, delineation and inventory]

Agency or organization	MAN	REG	R&C	LAN	R&D	D&I
FEDERAL						
Department of Agriculture						
Consolidated Farm Service Agency	...	•	...	...	...	...
Natural Resources Conservation Service	...	•	...	...	•	•
Department of Defense						
Army Corps of Engineers	...	•	•	...	•	•
Department of the Interior						
Fish and Wildlife Service	•	...	•	•	•	•
Geological Survey	...	...	...	...	•	...
National Biological Service	...	...	...	...	•	...
National Park Service	•	...	•	•	•	...
Environmental Protection Agency	...	•	...	...	•	•
STATE						
Department of Highways	...	...	...	...	•	...
Department of Natural Resources						
Division of Natural Areas and Preserves	•	...	•	•	•	...
Division of Parks	•	...	•	•	...	...
Division of Soil and Water	...	...	...	...	...	•
Division of Wildlife	•	...	•	•	•	...
Environmental Protection Agency	...	•	...	...	...	...
PRIVATE ORGANIZATIONS						
Ducks Unlimited	...	...	•	•	...	...
The Nature Conservancy	•	...	•	•	...	...

and on Ohio River islands. Wetlands on designated islands and in embayments could become part of the Ohio River Islands National Wildlife Refuge. The FWS also manages wetlands along the Lake Erie shore in the Ottawa National Wildlife Refuge, surveys flora and fauna of Ohio wetlands, and reviews all section 404 permit applications and section 401 water-quality certifications. The U.S. Forest Service (FS) manages wetlands in the Wayne National Forest in cooperation with the Ohio Department of Natural Resources. The FS has obtained three wetlands as part of eight recent land acquisitions. In addition, three wetlands recently have been constructed. No specific inventories of wetland plants and animals have been initiated by the FS, but recent inventories of amphibians, reptiles, and fish have included wetland areas. The NPS manages wetlands in the Cuyahoga Valley National Recreation Area between Cleveland and Akron. The NPS also protects all wetlands on fee-purchased lands, allows wetlands to develop naturally on all acquired lands, and purchases easements that protect wetlands on adjacent properties. The NRCS confirms wetland boundaries for the Ohio Wetland Inventory and notifies farmers when they are not in compliance with the Food Security Act of 1985.

State wetland activities.—Ohio designates all wetlands as State Resource Waters. As such, wetland water quality is protected from any degradation that may interfere with designated uses. The designation of Ohio wetlands as State Resource Waters protects them from the addition of toxic substances and addition or removal of any earthen material. Any dredging or filling of an Ohio wetland requires a section 404 permit issued by the Corps and a section 401 water-quality certification issued by the Ohio Environmental Protection Agency (Ohio Environmental Protection Agency, 1992). Typical activities that might affect wetlands and, consequently, require a section 404 permit and section 401 water-quality certification are construction of boat ramps, placement of rip-rap for erosion protection, placing fill, construction of dams or dikes, and stream channelization or diversion.

The Division of Wildlife has worked with conservation groups and government groups such as the FWS and NRCS to purchase, restore, and construct wetlands for waterfowl and other migratory birds. An important part of this effort has been the Lower Great Lakes Joint Venture of the North American Waterfowl Management Plan. This program purchases and manages wetlands in five focus areas. The Division also has initiated an Ohio income tax check-off option that provides monies for a nongame-wildlife management program and the Habitat Restoration Program, which protects wildlife habitat. The Division regulates and manages wetlands in 46 public wildlife areas throughout the State.

The Ohio Natural Areas Act of 1970 established a statewide system of natural areas and nature preserves that are managed either by the Division of Natural Areas and Preserves or by a cooperating managing agency. Twenty-five natural areas and preserves in the State contain 4,505 acres of wetlands. Wetlands constitute approximately one-fourth of all natural-area and preserve acreage in Ohio (Ohio Department of Natural Resources, 1988). The Division of Parks and Recreation manages wetlands in 59 State parks. Management responsibilities are coordinated with the Division of Wildlife, the Corps, and other governmental agencies.

The Division of Soil and Water Conservation has initiated the Ohio Land Capability Analysis Program. The program provides information on wetlands in the form of computer-generated maps and data relating to soil types, mineral resources, vegetation, and land use to local governments and private landowners.

The Department of Highways recently initiated programs that identify wetlands likely to be affected by road construction. These programs provide for the purchase or development of wetlands to mitigate wetland loss.

Wetland management in the future will be coordinated by a statewide task force consisting of about 30 individuals from State, county, and municipal governments; environmental and advocacy organizations; and business and industry affiliates. The Commission on Dispute Resolution and Conflict Management will chair the task force. The task force will attempt to reach consensus on the public values of wetlands, wetlands assessment, wetlands regulation, and wetlands creation and restoration.

Private wetland activities. — The Nature Conservancy has established the following preserves that contain wetlands: 7 sites (3,240 acres of wetlands) in the Eastern Lakes Section of the Central Lowland Province; 6 sites (1,000 acres of wetlands) in the Till Plains Section; 11 sites (2,510 acres of wetlands) in the Southern New York Section of the Appalachian Plateaus; and 2 sites (125 acres of wetlands) in the Kanawha Section. Thirteen of these sites are managed by a cooperating public or private agency. Ducks Unlimited has been influential in developing and preserving wetlands, particularly coastal marshes along Lake Erie. The organization's activities have included the purchase, restoration, and enhancement of wetlands. The Oak Harbor Conservation Club, Wildlife Legislative Fund of America, Ohio Plan Clubs, Lake Erie Wildflowers, Maumee Valley Audubon Club, Ohio Historical Society, Izaak Walton League, Sierra Club, League of Ohio Sportsmen, and other conservation groups contribute significantly to wetland conservation.

References Cited

Andreas, B.K., 1985, The relationship between Ohio peatland distribution and buried river valleys: The Ohio Journal of Science, v. 85, no. 3, p. 116–125.

Andreas, B.K., and Knoop, J.D., 1992, 100 years of changes in Ohio peatlands: The Ohio Journal of Science, v. 92, no. 5, p. 130–138.

Cowardin, L.M., Carter, Virginia, Golet, F.C., and LaRoe, E.T., 1979, Classification of wetlands and deepwater habitats of the United States: U.S. Fish and Wildlife Service Report FWS/OBS–79/31, 131 p.

Dachnowski, Alfred, 1912, Peat deposits of Ohio—Their origin, formation and uses: Columbus, Ohio Geological Survey, 4th series, Bulletin 16, 424 p.

Dahl, T.E., 1990, Wetlands—Losses in the United States, 1780's to 1980's: Washington, D.C., U.S. Fish and Wildlife Service Report to Congress, 13 p.

Denny, G.L., 1979, Bogs, *in* Lafferty, M.B., ed., Ohio's natural heritage: Columbus, The Ohio Academy of Science and the Ohio Department of Natural Resources, p. 134–157.

Fenneman, N.M., 1946, Physical divisions of the United States: U.S. Geological Survey special map, scale 1:7,000,000.

Forsyth, J.L., 1970, A geologist looks at the natural vegetation map of Ohio: The Ohio Journal of Science, v. 70, no. 3, p. 180–191.

_____1974, Geologic conditions essential for the perpetuation of Cedar Bog, Champaign County, Ohio: The Ohio Journal of Science, v. 74, no. 2, p. 116–139.

Frederick, C.M., 1974, A natural history of the vascular flora of Cedar Bog, Champaign County, Ohio: The Ohio Journal of Science, v. 74, no. 2, p. 65–115.

Goldthwait, R.P., 1959, Scenes in Ohio during the last ice age: The Ohio Journal of Science, v. 59, no. 4, p. 193–216.

Heath, R.T., 1992, Nutrient dynamics in Great Lakes coastal wetlands—Future directions: Journal of Great Lakes Research, v. 18 no. 4, p. 590–602.

Herdendorf, C.E., 1992, Lake Erie coastal wetlands—An overview: Journal of Great Lakes Research, v. 18, no. 4, p. 533–551.

Hillman, D.L., and Kenoyer, Galen, 1989, An analysis of the Cedar Bog hydrologic system through the use of a three-dimensional groundwater flow model, *in* Glotzhober, R.C., Kochman, Anne, and Schultz, W.T., eds., Cedar Bog Symposium II: Columbus, Ohio Historical Society, p. 65–74.

Mitsch, W.J., 1992, Combining ecosystem and landscape approaches to Great Lakes wetlands: Journal of Great Lakes Research, v. 18, no. 4, p. 552–570.

Mitsch, W.J., and Gosselink, J.G., 1986, Wetlands: New York, Van Nostrand Reinhold, 539 p.

Ohio Department of Natural Resources, 1988, Ohio wetlands priority conservation plan: Columbus, Ohio Department of Natural Resources, Office of Outdoor Recreational Services, 67 p.

_____1992, North American Waterfowl Management Plan, Lower Great Lakes Joint Venture, 1988–1991: Columbus, Ohio Department of Natural Resources, 27 p.

Ohio Environmental Protection Agency, 1992, Fact sheet—Section 401 water quality certification: Columbus, Ohio Environmental Protection Agency, Division of Water Quality Planning and Assessment, 3 p.

Quinn, M.J., 1974, The late glacial history of the Cedar Bog area, *in* King, C.C., and Frederick, C.M., eds., Cedar Bog Symposium: Columbus, The Ohio State University, p. 7–12.

Spooner, D.M., 1982, Wetlands in Teays-stage valleys in extreme southeastern Ohio—Formation and flora, *in* McDonald, B.R., ed., Proceedings of the Symposium on Wetlands of the Unglaciated Appalachian Region, West Virginia University, Morgantown, May 26–28: Morgantown, West Virginia, p. 89–99.

Yi, Gi-Chul, Risley, David, Koneff, Mark, and Davis, Craig, 1994, Development of Ohio's GIS-based wetlands inventory: Journal of Soil and Water Conservation, v. 49, p. 23–28.

FOR ADDITIONAL INFORMATION: District Chief, U.S. Geological Survey, 975 West Third Avenue, Columbus, OH 43212; Regional Wetland Coordinator, U.S. Fish and Wildlife Service, BHW Building, 1 Federal Drive, Fort Snelling, MN 55111

Prepared by
Michael Little and Marcus C. Waldron,
U.S. Geological Survey

Oklahoma
Wetland Resources

Wetlands cover about 950,000 acres (2 percent) of Oklahoma— a decrease of about 67 percent over the last 200 years (Dahl, 1990). Oklahoma's wetland acreage places the State twenty-third in total wetland acreage among the 48 conterminous States.

Wetlands are environmentally and economically valuable to the State. They reduce flood peaks by dispersing water over a large area and releasing it gradually to downstream areas, thus reducing the severity of floods. Wetlands in flood plains (fig. 1) improve the quality of water in rivers and streams by trapping or absorbing sediment, nutrients, and toxins. Wetland vegetation helps stabilize streambanks and provides food for wildlife. The vegetation also reduces wind and water erosion.

Wetlands provide important wildlife habitat. Most of the State's fish and wildlife, during some part of their life cycle, depend on riparian (streamside) habitats that include wetlands. Wetlands also provide important stopover, feeding, overwintering, and breeding grounds for migratory waterfowl, wading birds, and shore birds. The tourist industry benefits from the scenic beauty of the State's diverse wetlands, which afford opportunities for recreational activities such as hunting, fishing, birdwatching, nature photography, camping, hiking, and boating.

TYPES AND DISTRIBUTION

Wetlands are lands transitional between terrestrial and deepwater habitats where the water table usually is at or near the land surface or the land is covered by shallow water (Cowardin and others, 1979). The distribution of wetlands and deepwater habitats in Oklahoma is shown in figure 2A; only wetlands are discussed herein.

Wetlands can be vegetated or nonvegetated and are classified on the basis of their hydrology, vegetation, and substrate. In this summary, wetlands are classified according to the system proposed by Cowardin and others (1979), which is used by the U.S. Fish and Wildlife Service (FWS) to map and inventory the Nation's wetlands. At the most general level of the classification system, wetlands are grouped into five ecological systems: Palustrine, Lacustrine, Riverine, Estuarine, and Marine. The Palustrine System includes only wetlands, whereas the other systems comprise wetlands and deepwater habitats. Wetlands of the systems that occur in Oklahoma are described below.

Palustrine wetlands constitute most of Oklahoma's wetland acreage. Palustrine wetlands in the State include forested wetlands such as bottom-land hardwood forests and swamps; emergent wetlands such as marshes and wet meadows; aquatic-bed wetlands characterized by submersed or floating plants in ponds, lakes, rivers, and sloughs; and sparsely vegetated wetlands such as small, intermittently flooded playa lakes.

Palustrine forested wetlands are most common on river flood plains and along some streams in the moist, eastern part of Oklahoma in the Ozark Plateaus, Ouachita, Coastal Plain, and eastern Central Lowland physiographic provinces (fig. 2B). A survey conducted in the early 1980's indicated that forested wetlands covered about 240,000 acres of the eastern one-third of the State at that time (Brabander and others, 1985). The degree and duration of river flooding generally influence which tree species predominate in a forested wetland and what common name is applied to the wetland. Commonly, forested wetlands that are deeply flooded for much of the year are termed "swamps," whereas those that are flooded intermittently or only during the wettest parts of the year are termed "bottom-land hardwood forests."

Riparian wetlands are palustrine wetlands that form along the banks of streams, rivers, and lakes. These wetlands can be dominated by herbaceous emergent plants (emergent wetland), shrubs and saplings (scrub-shrub wetland), or trees (forested wetland). Riparian wetlands are especially important to fish and wildlife in the grasslands of the plains and prairie regions because they provide shelter and moisture in a landscape that is otherwise sparsely vegetated by trees or shrubs and lacks year-round sources of water.

In Oklahoma, riparian wetlands range in area from about 10 to 2,000 acres (Oklahoma Tourism and Recreation Department, 1987). The largest expanses of riparian wetland are along the Cimarron, Canadian, Washita, and Red Rivers and their tributaries. Examples of these wetland are the numerous small marshes on river terraces along the Cimarron River. A recent study of riparian lands in western Oklahoma (Stinnett and others, 1987) indicated that riparian areas that are frequently flooded cover about 621,000 acres along 5,200 miles of streams west of about the longitude of Oklahoma City. Forests cover from 22 to 28 percent of the riparian flood plains.

System	Wetland description
Palustrine	Wetlands in which vegetation is predominantly trees (forested wetlands); shrubs (scrub-shrub wetlands); persistent or nonpersistent emergent, erect, rooted, herbaceous plants (persistent- and nonpersistent-emergent wetlands); or submersed and (or) floating plants (aquatic beds). Also, intermittently to permanently flooded open-water bodies of less than 20 acres in which water is less than 6.6 feet deep.
Lacustrine	Wetlands within an intermittently to permanently flooded lake or reservoir. Vegetation, when present, is predominantly nonpersistent emergent plants (nonpersistent-emergent wetlands), or submersed and (or) floating plants (aquatic beds), or both.
Riverine	Wetlands within a channel. Vegetation, when present, is same as in the Lacustrine System.

Figure 1. Stinchcomb Wildlife Refuge above Lake Overholser, Oklahoma. *(Photograph courtesy of U.S. Fish and Wildlife Service.)*

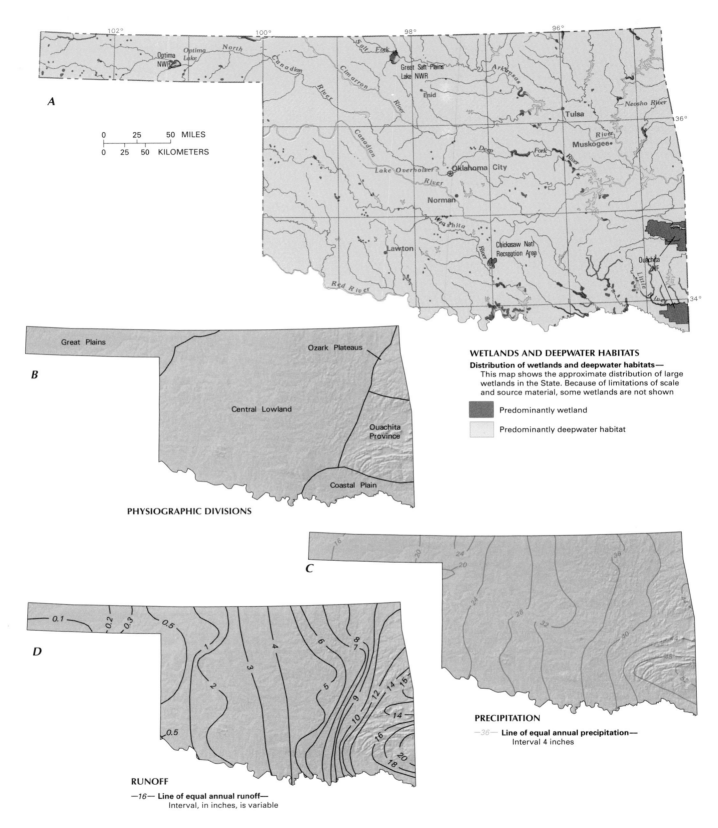

WETLANDS AND DEEPWATER HABITATS

Distribution of wetlands and deepwater habitats—
This map shows the approximate distribution of large wetlands in the State. Because of limitations of scale and source material, some wetlands are not shown

Predominantly wetland

Predominantly deepwater habitat

PHYSIOGRAPHIC DIVISIONS

PRECIPITATION

—36— **Line of equal annual precipitation—**
Interval 4 inches

RUNOFF

—16— **Line of equal annual runoff—**
Interval, in inches, is variable

Figure 2. Wetland distribution in Oklahoma and physical and climatological features that control wetland distribution in the State. *A*, Distribution of wetlands and deepwater habitats. *B*, Physiography. *C*, Average annual precipitation. *D*, Average annual runoff. *(Sources: A, T.E. Dahl, U.S. Fish and Wildlife Service, unpub. data, 1991. B, Physiographic divisions from Fenneman, 1946; landforms data from EROS Data Center. C and D, Blumer, 1986).*

Oklahoma's playa lakes are mostly in the panhandle region. They provide overwintering and resting habitat for waterfowl migrating along the Central Flyway (U.S. Fish and Wildlife Service, 1990). The number of playa lakes in the State is about 1,200, totaling about 9,000 acres, and the lakes range in area from less than 1 acre to more than 200 acres (Oklahoma Department of Wildlife Conservation, unpub. data, 1990). Playa lakes are sand- or mudbottomed lakes that receive most of their moisture from precipitation runoff and have little external drainage. They range from dry lakebeds to shallow lakes that can be freshwater or saline. Freshwater playas are numerous, small to medium in size, and serve as zones of recharge to the underlying aquifer (Osterkamp and Wood, 1987). Saline playas are larger in size and fewer in number than the freshwater playas and are areas of discharge from the underlying aquifer.

Playa lakes smaller than 20 acres typically are intermittently flooded, whereas larger playa lakes generally are continuously flooded. Small playas are classified as palustrine wetlands; the larger, more permanent playa lakes are lacustrine wetlands and bordered by palustrine emergent wetlands. Flooded playa lakes, especially those containing vegetation, provide optimum wildlife habitat.

Most lacustrine wetlands in Oklahoma are in the larger playa lakes and in the shallows of the many reservoirs on rivers statewide. Because of their depth, reservoirs typically contain more deepwater habitat than wetland; however, wetlands in the shallow margins of reservoirs can be extensive in areas of low relief. Siltation (as in Great Salt Plains Lake on the Arkansas River) or declining water levels caused by low streamflow in dry years or reservoir leakage (as in Optima Lake) can create additional wetland acreage in reservoirs. Lacustrine wetlands in reservoirs and large playa lakes and the adjacent palustrine marshes provide valuable habitat for resident and migratory waterfowl. Both Great Salt Plains Lake and Optima Lake are National Wildlife Refuges.

Riverine wetlands include beds of small streams and the shallows of rivers. Riverine wetlands are restricted to the channels of streams and undammed rivers and do not include wetlands in their flood plains. Because of the many miles of streams and rivers in Oklahoma, the State has extensive riverine wetlands. However, reservoir construction converted many formerly riverine wetlands into lacustrine wetlands or deepwater habitat.

HYDROLOGIC SETTING

Wetlands form where a persistent water supply is at or near the land surface. The location, abundance, and persistence of the water supply is a function of physiographic, climatic, and hydrologic factors, such as topography, precipitation and runoff patterns, evapotranspiration rate, and configuration of the water table.

Precipitation and runoff rates differ annually, with the seasons, and geographically. The average annual precipitation in Oklahoma ranges from about 16 inches in the western panhandle to more than 52 inches in southeastern Oklahoma (fig. 2C). Spring is the wettest season, and May is the wettest month. Runoff ranges widely across the State. The average annual runoff ranges from about 0.1 inch in the western panhandle to more than 20 inches in the southeastern corner of the State (fig. 2D). Evaporation is greatest in western Oklahoma and least in the eastern part of the State.

The forested wetlands (bottom-land hardwood forests) of eastern Oklahoma are primarily on flood plains in alluvial river valleys. Flood-plain wetlands generally depend on river flooding in spring for much of their moisture. Annual flooding of the rivers generally is confined to the main channel or lowlands that border a river, but floods of 5- to 100-year recurrence intervals typically overflow the banks, leaving residual water in backswamps, pools, sloughs, oxbows, and depressions. Rainfall is also a source of moisture to these wetlands. Flood-plain forests and swamps delay runoff and provide surface-water storage. Organic soils in the forested wetlands function somewhat like sponges, increasing water-storage capacity and retarding evapotranspiration (Wilkinson and others, 1987).

Riparian wetlands in south-central Oklahoma are in areas classified as rolling to gently rolling prairie and savannah. These wetlands have formed on flood plains of permanent streams and are maintained by frequent or seasonal flooding or by a high water table. Riparian-wetland vegetation typically consists of emergent herbaceous plants, shrubs, or trees. Soil types range from sandy loam to clay loam underlain by sandstone and shale. Average annual precipitation in the region ranges from 30 to 34 inches. Lake evaporation is about 63 inches annually (Barclay, 1980). Because of the extensive channelization of streams, which has lowered the water table, and the many impoundments, which have reduced flooding, a large percentage of the riparian wetlands once present in this part of the State have been lost (Barclay, 1980).

A study by Taylor and others (1984) describes the riparian wetlands along the north side of the Cimarron River in north-central Oklahoma as marshes and ponded water in surface depressions of terrace deposits along the river. The terrace surface is generally level to gently sloping, and sand dunes line the river. The wetlands began to appear in formerly dry depressions in 1975 because of a rise in the water table. The depressions have flat bottoms and are assumed to be formed by wind. The areal extent of these wetlands has increased since 1975, owing to a further rise in ground-water levels. The terrace and associated deposits consist of dune sands and alluvial and wind-blown sediments overlying bedrock. Soils in the nonwetland areas of the terrace are sandy loam or loamy sand, whereas soils in the wetlands are clayey with some characteristics of hydric soils.

The riparian wetlands in western Oklahoma are on the flood plains of perennial streams in an area of the State that is transitional between the arid lands of the west and the humid, temperate forests of the east (Stinnett and others, 1987). These wetlands are maintained by periodic flooding, ground water, and local precipitation. During drought, the wetlands can dry up, causing the riparian vegetation to disappear. Soil types in the area range from loamy fine sand to sandy clay loam. Average annual precipitation in this region ranges from 18 to 34 inches. Annual lake evaporation in western Oklahoma ranges from 56 to 64 inches. Evaporation is greatest in the panhandle (Stinnett and others, 1987).

The major perennial streams that have riparian wetlands in west-central Oklahoma are the Canadian and Washita Rivers, which flow southeasterly through rolling hills of mixed-grass and tall-grass prairie. The major perennial stream that has riparian wetlands in the southwestern part of the State is the Red River, which flows easterly through level to gently rolling topography that supports mixed-grass vegetative cover (Stinnett and others, 1987).

Historically, the area of playa lakes in the panhandle was shortgrass and mixed-grass prairie. However, much of the area of playa lakes is now under cultivation. The physiography of the playa lake area is characterized by relatively flat terrain. Because of the flatness of the terrain, there is generally little stream drainage; consequently, playa lakes collect most of the surface runoff. The playa lakes are shallow depressions that have large surface area relative to the total volume of water contained in them. Consequently, most playa lakes have small storage capacities. Osterkamp and Wood (1987) indicate that freshwater playa lakes in the Great Plains originate wherever surface depressions collect precipitation. The lakes enlarge as a result of dissolution of carbonates by water infiltrating the unsaturated zone above the underlying aquifer and subsequent subsidence of the lakebed. Over time, the older, central lakebeds acquire a layer of clay-rich deposits that largely restricts movement of water between the playa lake and the underlying aquifer. Water probably is removed from freshwater playa lakes primarily by recharge to the underlying aquifer from the outer areas of the lake, where lakebed sediments have not yet accumulated (Osterkamp and Wood, 1987) and by evaporation (Nelson and others, 1983). There is no general agreement on the origin of saline playa lakes; however, Wood and Jones (1990) propose that the source of the salinity is the concentration by evaporation of runoff and shallow, fresh ground water that discharges from the underlying aquifer.

TRENDS

The FWS has estimated that from the 1780's to the 1980's, the wetland area in Oklahoma decreased from about 2,840,000 acres to about 950,000 acres (Dahl, 1990). This decrease represents a change in wetland acreage from 6.4 percent of the State's surface area to 2.1 percent.

The major causes of bottom-land hardwood-forest loss in eastern Oklahoma have been the cutting of virgin timber and the conversion of flood plains to cropland and pasture. These practices have resulted in the loss of about 1,653,000 acres of bottom-land hardwood forest (Wilkinson and others, 1987), or about 75 percent of the original forested area, much of which contained wetlands. An area in east-central Oklahoma that has had considerable losses of bottom-land hardwood-forest wetlands is the flood plain of the Deep Fork River. In this river basin, the flood plain on the upper one-third of the river lost most of its wetlands because of channelization between 1912 and 1923. The flood plain on the lower two-thirds of the river was altered or degraded in some parts; however, much of the unchannelized area in the lower two-thirds of the river represents one of the few areas in the State where extensive strands of bottom-land hardwood forest remain (Alan Stacey, Oklahoma Department of Wildlife Conservation, written commun., 1994).

Another major cause of wetland loss in eastern Oklahoma has been reservoir construction. Twenty-eight major reservoirs in eastern Oklahoma have inundated about 240,000 acres, or about 10 percent of the bottom-land hardwood forests. Nine additional major reservoirs have been proposed, the construction of which would result in inundation of an additional 50,000 acres of bottom-land hardwood forest (Wilkinson and others, 1987).

The Canadian, Washita, and Red Rivers and their tributaries have undergone extensive channelization and impoundment, resulting in loss of many riparian wetlands. A study by Barclay (1980) of two prairie streams that are tributaries to the Washita River in south-central Oklahoma showed that channelization of these streams resulted in an 86-percent reduction in bottom-land forest and the loss of all the wetlands, about 1,800 acres, or 6.2 percent of the flood plain of the two streams. Other losses of wetlands in this area are attributable to reservoir construction and conversion of wetlands to agricultural use.

A rise in water levels beginning in 1975 in the terrace deposits along the Cimarron River (Taylor and others, 1984) resulted in the restoring of some riparian wetlands in north-central Oklahoma. These wetlands have increased in area since 1975 owing to a continuing rise in water levels and surface pooling. Activities that lower the water levels, such as channelization or drainage of land for cropping or pasture, could cause the loss of wetlands. Terrace wetlands are at risk from petroleum-production activities, timber harvesting, and farming and grazing (Taylor and others, 1984). However, Taylor and others (1984) indicate that with proper management practices, the terrace marshes and other riparian wetlands can be retained as a wildlife habitat and a water resource without significantly affecting landowners.

From the mid-1950's to the mid-1980's, wetlands associated with the Canadian River in western Oklahoma decreased in area by about 45 percent (Stinnett and others, 1987). Additionally, wetland types changed substantially. Results of aerial-photograph analysis indicate an increase from 1,145 acres to 10,873 acres in forested

wetlands, an increase from 12,975 acres to 24,210 acres in shrub wetland, an increase from 199 acres to 520 acres in open-water and mudflat wetlands, a decrease from 12,599 acres to 4,670 acres of emergent wetlands, and a decrease from 68,602 acres to 11,960 acres of river and sandbar wetlands during a 30-year period. Riverine wetlands decreased from 72 percent to 23 percent of the total wetland acreage and palustrine wetlands increased from 28 percent to 77 percent of the total wetland acreage. The changes probably were caused by lower streamflow resulting from the upstream construction of Lake Meredith Reservoir in the Texas panhandle.

The quality and number of playa lakes available to wetland wildlife in the Oklahoma panhandle has declined significantly. The decline has been attributed to cultivation of playa lake areas, field leveling, cattle grazing, and modification for irrigation and livestock watering (Oklahoma Department of Wildlife Conservation, unpub. data, 1990). About 61 percent of the playas are cultivated. The agricultural conversions in the playa lake area have resulted in a substantial change in land use from short-grass and mixed-grass prairie to cropland.

CONSERVATION

Many government agencies and private organizations participate in wetland conservation in Oklahoma. The most active agencies and organizations and some of their activities are listed in table 1.

Table 1. Selected wetland-related activities of government agencies and private organizations in Oklahoma, 1993

[Source: Classification of activities is generalized from information provided by agencies and organizations. ●, agency or organization participates in wetland-related activity; ..., agency or organization does not participate in wetland-related activity. MAN, management; REG, regulation; R&C, restoration and creation; LAN, land acquisition; R&D, research and data collection; D&I, delineation and inventory]

Agency or organization	MAN	REG	R&C	LAN	R&D	D&I
FEDERAL						
Department of Agriculture						
Consolidated Farm Service Agency	...	●	...	...	...	...
Forest Service	●	...	●	●	●	●
Natural Resources Conservation Service	...	●	...	●	...	●
Department of Defense						
Army Corps of Engineers	●	●	●	●	...	●
Military reservations	●	...	...	...	...	...
Department of the Interior						
Bureau of Land Management	●	...	●	●	●	●
Bureau of Reclamation	...	...	●	●	●	●
Fish and Wildlife Service	●	...	●	●	●	●
Geological Survey	...	...	...	...	●	...
National Biological Service	...	...	...	...	●	...
National Park Service	●	...	●	●	●	●
Environmental Protection Agency	...	●	...	...	●	●
STATE						
Oklahoma Conservation Commission	●	●	...	...	●	●
Oklahoma Water Resources Board	●	●	...	...	...	●
Oklahoma Department of Wildlife Conservation	●	●	●	●	...	...
SOME COUNTY AND LOCAL GOVERNMENTS	...	●	...	...	...	...
PRIVATE ORGANIZATIONS						
Ducks Unlimited	●	...	●	...	●	●
The Nature Conservancy	●	...	●	●	●	●

Federal wetland activities. —Development activities in Oklahoma wetlands are regulated by several Federal statutory prohibitions and incentives that are intended to slow wetland losses. Some of the more important of these are contained in the 1899 Rivers and Harbors Act; the 1972 Clean Water Act and amendments; the 1985 Food Security Act; the 1990 Food, Agriculture, Conservation, and Trade Act; and the 1986 Emergency Wetlands Resources Act.

Section 10 of the Rivers and Harbors Act gives the U.S. Army Corps of Engineers (Corps) authority to regulate certain activities in navigable waters. Regulated activities include diking, deepening, filling, excavating, and placing of structures. The related section 404 of the Clean Water Act is the most often-used Federal legislation protecting wetlands. Under section 404 provisions, the Corps issues permits regulating the discharge of dredged or fill material into wetlands. Permits are subject to review and possible veto by the U.S. Environmental Protection Agency, and the FWS has review and advisory roles. Section 401 of the Clean Water Act grants to States and eligible Indian Tribes the authority to approve, apply conditions to, or deny section 404 permit applications on the basis of a proposed activity's probable effects on the water quality of a wetland.

Most farming, ranching, and silviculture activities are not subject to section 404 regulation. However, the "Swampbuster" provision of the 1985 Food Security Act and amendments in the 1990 Food, Agriculture, Conservation, and Trade Act discourages (through financial disincentives) the draining, filling, or other alteration of wetlands for agricultural use. The law allows exemptions from penalties in some cases, especially if the farmer agrees to restore the altered wetland or other wetlands that have been converted to agricultural use. The Wetlands Reserve Program of the 1990 Food, Agriculture, Conservation, and Trade Act authorizes the Federal Government to purchase conservation easements from landowners who agree to protect or restore wetlands. The Consolidated Farm Service Agency (formerly the Agricultural Stabilization and Conservation Service) administers the Swampbuster provisions and Wetlands Reserve Program. The Natural Resources Conservation Service (formerly the Soil Conservation Service) determines compliance with Swampbuster provisions and assists farmers in the identification of wetlands and in the development of wetland protection, restoration, or creation plans.

The 1986 Emergency Wetlands Resources Act encourages wetland protection through funding incentives. The act requires States to address wetland protection in their Statewide Comprehensive Outdoor Recreation Plans to qualify for Federal funding for State recreational land; the National Park Service (NPS) provides guidance to States in developing the wetland component of their plans.

The wetland-related activities of the FWS in Oklahoma include acquiring bottom land along the Deep Fork River and along the Little River for the benefit of wetland-dependent wildlife (Oklahoma Conservation Commission, 1991). The FWS also has prepared an Oklahoma Wetlands Priority Plan that identifies 13 priority wetland areas in the State encompassing nearly 175,000 acres. The FWS, in 1990, enrolled 10 landowners in their program of providing technical and financial assistance for the restoration of wetlands on private lands in Oklahoma. Seven National Wildlife Refuges in Oklahoma are managed by the FWS.

The North American Waterfowl Management Plan is a joint effort by the U.S. and Canadian Governments to slow the rate of waterfowl-habitat loss. Mexico has signed an agreement to aid in the effort, which seeks to protect more then 6 million acres of wetlands. The FWS coordinates two joint venture projects of the North American Waterfowl Management Plan that includes two areas of Oklahoma. One is the Playa Lakes Joint Venture, which is intended to ensure the continual accommodation of waterfowl overwintering in, migrating through, and breeding in the panhandle region. A second is the Lower Mississippi Valley Joint Venture, which has the goal of protecting the bottom-land hardwood forests in eastern Oklahoma (Forsythe and Aldrich, 1989).

Other Federal Agencies in Oklahoma, such as the Bureau of Land Management (BLM), the Bureau of Reclamation (BOR), the U.S. Forest Service (FS), and the NPS, are charged with the responsible management of public lands, including wetlands, under their jurisdiction. The BLM's wetland-related goals are to protect, maintain,

and restore riparian-wetland areas on lands administered by the BLM in Oklahoma. The acreage of riparian wetlands on lands administered by the BLM in Oklahoma, Kansas, and New Mexico is 27,600 acres (Bureau of Land Management, 1990). The BOR's jurisdiction extends over their project areas. The FS manages lands and resources in the two National Grasslands in western Oklahoma and the Ouachita National Forest in eastern Oklahoma. The NPS manages the Chickasaw National Recreation Area in south-central Oklahoma to preserve the natural and cultural resources of the area.

State wetland activities. — The State agencies most involved in wetland conservation are the Oklahoma Conservation Commission, the Oklahoma Water Resources Board, and the Oklahoma Department of Wildlife Conservation. The Conservation Commission develops the strategy for wetland management. The strategy includes defining wetlands, enumerating the beneficial uses of wetlands, inventorying wetlands, and recommending measures to mitigate losses and protect wetlands. The Water Resources Board prepares the State's water-quality standards, and certifies that permits issued by the Corps to dredge and fill will not violate the State water-quality standards. The Department of Wildlife Conservation protects, enhances, and restores wetlands in wildlife-management areas for the benefit of wildlife. The Department also provides technical assistances to owners of wetlands and works cooperatively with other organizations on wetland programs.

Private wetland activities. — The Nature Conservancy provides leadership in the acquisition of land for the preservation of wildlife. The Conservancy has established 14 preserves in Oklahoma. The organization also participates in a program that enlists landowners to voluntarily protect rare species on their property. Ducks Unlimited and many other organizations in Oklahoma advocate the preservation and restoration of wildlife habitats.

References Cited

Barclay, J.S., 1980, Impact of stream alteration on riparian communities in southcentral Oklahoma: U.S. Fish and Wildlife Service Report FWS/OBS–80/17, 91 p.

Blumer, S.P., 1986, Oklahoma surface-water resources, *in* U.S. Geological Survey, National water summary 1985—Hydrologic events and surface-water resources: U.S. Geological Survey Water-Supply Paper 2300, p. 375–382.

Brabander, J.J., Masters, R.E., and Short, R.M., 1985, Bottomland hardwoods of eastern Oklahoma—A special study of their status, trends, and values: Tulsa, Okla., U.S. Fish and Wildlife Service, 147 p.

Bureau of Land Management, 1990, New Mexico riparian-wetland 2000—A management strategy: Santa Fe, N. Mex., Bureau of Land Management, 25 p.

Cowardin, L.M., Carter, Virginia, Golet, F.C., and LaRoe, E.T., 1979, Classification of wetlands and deepwater habitats of the United States: U.S. Fish and Wildlife Service Report FWS/OBS–79/31, 131 p.

Dahl, T.E., 1990, Wetlands—Losses in the United States, 1780's to 1980's: Washington, D.C., U.S. Fish and Wildlife Service Report to Congress, 13 p.

Fenneman, N.M., 1946, Physical divisions of the United States: Washington, D.C., U.S. Geological Survey special map, scale 1:7,000,000.

Forsythe, S.W., and Aldrich, J.W., 1989, Eastern Oklahoma wetland plan—A State implementation plan: Tulsa, Okla., U.S. Fish and Wildlife Service and Oklahoma Department of Wildlife Conservation cooperative publication, 20 p.

Nelson, W.R., Logan, W.J., and Weller, L.C., 1983, Playa wetlands and wildlife on the southern Great Plains—A characterization of habitat: U.S. Fish and Wildlife Service Report FWS/OBS–83/28, 99 p.

Oklahoma Conservation Commission, 1991, Background paper—Wetlands management in Oklahoma: Oklahoma City, Oklahoma Conservation Commission, 30 p.

Oklahoma Tourism and Recreation Department, 1987, Oklahoma statewide comprehensive outdoor recreation plan: Oklahoma City, Oklahoma Tourism and Recreation Department, 216 p.

Osterkamp, W.R., and Wood, W.W., 1987, Playa lake basins on the southern High Plains of Texas and New Mexico—Part 1, Hydrologic, geomorphic, and geologic evidence for their development: Geologic Society of America Bulletin, v. 99, no. 2, p. 215–223.

Stinnett, D.P., Smith, R.W., and Conrady, S.W., 1987, Riparian areas of western Oklahoma—A special study of their status, trends, and values: Tulsa, Okla., U.S. Fish and Wildlife Service, 80 p.

Taylor, T.J., Erickson, N.E., Tumlison, Renn, Ratzlaff, J.A., and Cunningham, K.D., 1984, Groundwater wetlands of the Cimarron Terrace, north-central Oklahoma: Stillwater, Oklahoma State University, 58 p.

U.S. Fish and Wildlife Service, 1990, Region II wetlands regional concept plan—Oklahoma wetlands: Albuquerque, N. Mex., U.S. Fish and Wildlife Service, 185 p.

Wilkinson, D.L., McDonald, K.S., Olson, R.W., and Auble, G.T., 1987, Synopsis of wetland functions and values—Bottomland hardwoods with emphasis on eastern Texas and Oklahoma: U.S. Fish and Wildlife Service Biological Report 87(12), 132 p.

Wood, W.W., and Jones, B.F., 1990, Origin of saline lakes and springs on the southern High Plains of Texas and New Mexico, *in* Gustavson, T.C., ed., Geological framework and regional hydrology—Upper Cenozoic Blackwater Draw and Ogallala Formation, Great Plains: Austin, Texas, Bureau of Economic Geology, p. 193–208.

FOR ADDITIONAL INFORMATION: District Chief, U.S. Geological Survey, Building 7, 202 W 66 St., Oklahoma City, OK 73116; Regional Wetland Coordinator, U.S. Fish and Wildlife, Fish and Wildlife Enhancement, 500 Gold Ave., SW, Albuquerque, NM 87102

Prepared by
B.D. Jones,
U.S. Geological Survey

Oregon
Wetland Resources

Oregon's diverse wetlands are the result of climate and physiography that range from wet and mountainous to dry and flat. Wetlands can be found statewide, even in the deserts of the central and southeastern parts of the State (fig. 1).

Although wetlands cover little more than 2 percent of Oregon, their ecological and economic benefits make them valuable to the State. Among the beneficial hydrologic functions of wetlands are flood attenuation, erosion and storm-damage reduction, water-quality maintenance, and water supply. Coastal and inland wetlands provide stopover, feeding, and breeding habitat to migratory waterfowl and shorebirds; habitat for native fish and wildlife; and outdoor recreation. About one-half of commercially harvested Pacific Ocean fish and shellfish species depend on wetlands for food, spawning, or nursery habitat during some stage of life (Oregon Division of State Lands and Oregon State Parks and Recreation Division, 1989).

TYPES AND DISTRIBUTION

Wetlands are lands transitional between terrestrial and deepwater habitats where the water table usually is at or near the land surface or the land is covered by shallow water (Cowardin and others, 1979). The distribution of wetlands and deepwater habitats in Oregon is shown in figure 2A; only wetlands are discussed herein.

Wetlands can be vegetated or nonvegetated and are classified on the basis of their hydrology, vegetation, and substrate. In this summary, wetlands are classified according to the system proposed by Cowardin and others (1979), which is used by the U.S. Fish and Wildlife Service (FWS) to map and inventory the Nation's wetlands. At the most general level of the classification system, wetlands are grouped into five ecological systems: Palustrine, Lacustrine, Riverine, Estuarine, and Marine. The Palustrine System includes only wetlands, whereas the other systems comprise wetlands and deepwater habitats. Wetlands of the systems that occur in Oregon are described below.

System	Wetland description
Palustrine	Nontidal and tidal-freshwater wetlands in which vegetation is predominantly trees (forested wetlands); shrubs (scrub-shrub wetlands); persistent or nonpersistent emergent, erect, rooted herbaceous plants (persistent- and nonpersistent-emergent wetlands); or submersed and (or) floating plants (aquatic beds). Also, intermittently to permanently flooded open-water bodies of less than 20 acres in which water is less than 6.6 feet deep.
Lacustrine	Nontidal and tidal-freshwater wetlands within an intermittently to permanently flooded lake or reservoir larger than 20 acres and (or) deeper than 6.6 feet. Vegetation, when present, is predominantly nonpersistent emergent plants (nonpersistent-emergent wetlands), or submersed and (or) floating plants (aquatic beds), or both.
Riverine	Nontidal and tidal-freshwater wetlands within a channel. Vegetation, when present, is same as in the Lacustrine System.
Estuarine	Tidal wetlands in low-wave-energy environments where the salinity of the water is greater than 0.5 part per thousand (ppt) and is variable owing to evaporation and the mixing of seawater and freshwater.
Marine	Tidal wetlands that are exposed to waves and currents of the open ocean and to water having a salinity greater than 30 ppt.

Oregon has between 1.2 and 1.5 million acres of wetlands (J.F. Watson, U.S. Fish and Wildlife Service, written commun., 1993). Palustrine, lacustrine, and estuarine wetlands constitute most of the State's wetland acreage. The area of marine and riverine wetlands is small relative to that in the other systems.

Coastal wetlands. — The steep slopes of Oregon's Coast Range mountains extend to the Pacific Ocean along much of the coast, leaving little area for wetland formation. Thus, coastal wetlands are confined mainly to areas of accumulated sediment near the mouths of rivers that have cut through the mountains and to the dune regions that have formed where the Coast Range front is distant from the ocean.

Estuarine wetlands have developed in the shallow, low-gradient reaches near the mouths of Oregon's coastal rivers and in their deltas. Estuarine wetlands cover about 55,600 acres, and there are about 10,000 acres of tidal fresh marsh, mostly in the Columbia River estuary (Oregon Division of State Lands and Oregon State Parks and Recreation Division, 1989). Akins and Jefferson (1973) identified three major types of estuarine wetlands in Oregon: tideflats, eelgrass beds, and salt marshes.

Tideflats (unconsolidated-shore wetlands) are mostly nonvegetated and exist where accumulations of sediment (sand, silt, clay, or gravel) are flooded and exposed daily by tides. Eelgrass-bed (aquatic-bed) wetlands are tideflats that have been extensively colonized by eelgrass, a plant that can tolerate high salinity and periods of exposure. Salt marshes (emergent wetlands) are regularly to irregularly flooded emergent wetlands vegetated by salt-tolerant plants such as rushes, sedges, glasswort, and arrowgrass. Most of Oregon's large estuaries also contain areas of diked marsh, former salt marshes that have been diked and drained. Diked wetlands are commonly used for cattle grazing.

Coastal nontidal fresh marshes, swamps, bogs, and ponds are palustrine wetlands that have formed around in lakes and wind-scoured depressions among sand dunes (Akins and Jefferson, 1973). The areas containing most of the coastal nontidal wetlands are the Clatsop Plains, which extend from the Columbia River to Gearhart, the broad dune sheet that extends from Haceta Head to Coos Bay, and the low dunes between Bandon and Cape Blanco. Isolated dune areas containing wetlands are present between Tillamook Bay and Waldport.

Figure 1. Wetlands in the Malheur National Wildlife Refuge. *(Photograph courtesy of the U.S. Fish and Wildlife Service.)*

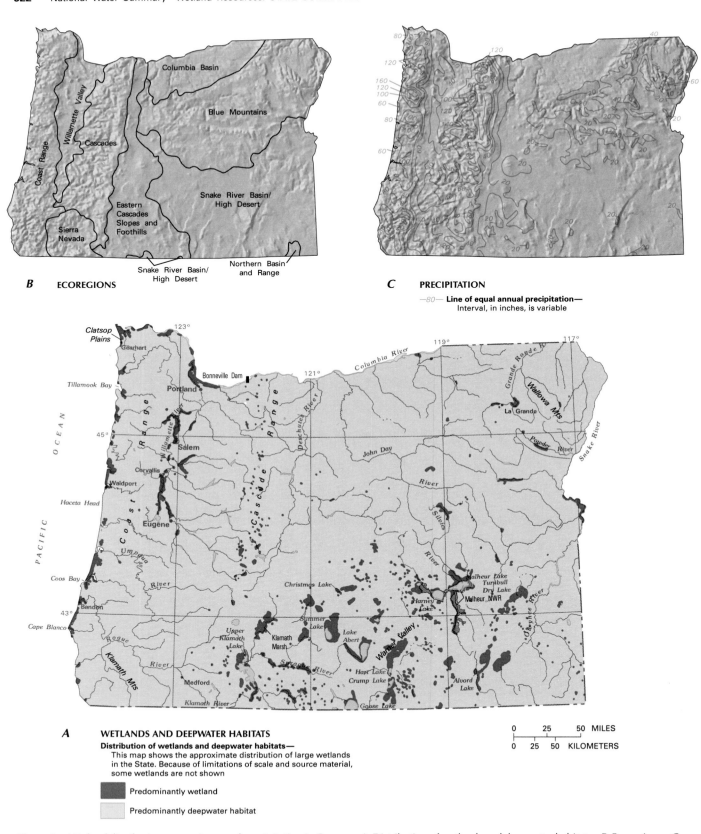

B   ECOREGIONS

C   PRECIPITATION

—80— **Line of equal annual precipitation—**
Interval, in inches, is variable

A   WETLANDS AND DEEPWATER HABITATS

Distribution of wetlands and deepwater habitats—
This map shows the approximate distribution of large wetlands
in the State. Because of limitations of scale and source material,
some wetlands are not shown

Predominantly wetland

Predominantly deepwater habitat

Figure 2.   Wetland distribution, ecoregions, and precipitation in Oregon. **A**, Distribution of wetlands and deepwater habitats. **B**, Ecoregions. **C**, Precipitation. *(Sources: A, T.E. Dahl, U.S. Fish and Wildlife Service, unpub. data, 1991. B, Ecoregions from Omernik, 1987; landforms data from EROS Data Center. C, Hubbard, 1986.)*

Coastal nontidal fresh marshes form in dune lake basins and along their tributary streams. Some shallow lakes are completely covered by marsh vegetation. Interdunal marshes form between dunes in wind-scoured depressions. Interdunal marshes are flooded seasonally or perennially and typically contain slough sedge, silver weed, bog St. Johnswort, creeping buttercup, and western lilaeopsis (Akins and Jefferson, 1973). Other coastal-zone freshwater wetlands—swamps, bogs, and ponds—constitute a small percentage of the coastal-zone wetland acreage, but they are of value to wildlife and also are of scientific interest.

Mountain wetlands.—The Coast Range and Klamath Mountains have few lakes, and the stream valleys (except near the coast) are steep sided and provide few places for wetlands to form; therefore, wetlands in the coastal mountains generally are small and scattered. However, glacial lakes are common in the Cascade Range and Wallowa Mountains. Such lakes can support marsh vegetation around their shores, and their shallow zones are themselves classified as wetlands. The wider mountain valleys in the Cascade Range also have areas of wetlands—predominantly marshes and wet meadows (emergent wetlands) vegetated by sedges and other herbaceous plants. Intermountain basins such as those on the Silvies, Powder, and Grande Ronde Rivers—all in the Blue Mountains Ecoregion (fig. 2B)—have or once had areas of marsh, wet prairie, and wet meadow.

Willamette River Valley wetlands.—The Willamette River Valley is an intermountain basin located between the Coast Range and the Cascade Range (fig. 2B). The flat valley floor once had vast areas of fresh marsh and wet prairie, and the flood plains of the Willamette River and the lower reaches of its tributaries contained extensive shrub swamps and swamp forests. However, drainage for agricultural and urban development and realignment of the river's main stem have eliminated much of the former wetland area. Although greatly reduced in area, valley wetlands provide stopover and overwintering habitat for thousands of migratory waterfowl (Loy, 1976).

Desert wetlands.—Oregon's desert wetlands are in the Snake River Basin/High Desert Ecoregion (fig. 2B). Many desert wetlands are valuable to wildlife because of the moisture they provide in an otherwise arid environment. Desert wetlands include saltwood and greasewood flats (scrub-shrub wetlands), shallow lakes (unconsolidated-shore wetlands), marshes, and riparian (streamside, typically scrub-shrub or emergent) wetlands.

Most of the area shown as wetland in figure 2A comprises shallow, slightly to very saline lakes that range from typically flooded to typically dry. Among lakes that contain water in many or most years are Malheur Lake (fig. 1), Harney Lake, Goose Lake, Lake Abert, Summer Lake, Crump Lake, and Hart Lake (Loy, 1976). These perennial lakes provide stopover and nesting habitat for migratory waterfowl. Lakes that are dry in most years include Alvord Lake, Christmas Lake, Turnbull Dry Lake, and the lakes north of Hart Lake in the Warner Valley. Vegetated areas of flooded desert lakes typically contain submersed and marsh vegetation.

Perennial or seasonal rivers that flow into desert lakes commonly have areas of riparian wetlands, which are vegetated predominantly by shrubs, trees, or herbaceous emergent vegetation. Riparian wetlands provide habitat for plants and animals that otherwise could not exist in the harsh desert environment.

Other wetlands.—The upper Klamath River Basin is in the Eastern Cascades Slopes and Foothills Ecoregion (fig. 2B). The basin contains vast areas of marsh—notably in Klamath Marsh, along the Sprague River, and in the upper part of Upper Klamath Lake—that supply stopover habitat for millions of ducks and geese migrating along the Pacific Flyway (Loy, 1976). Other wetlands important to waterfowl include marsh, scrub-shrub, and open-water wetlands on the Columbia and Snake Rivers. Croplands near those rivers contribute significantly to the birds' food supply.

HYDROLOGIC SETTING

Wetlands form where water persists at or near the land surface for extended periods. Depending on its hydrologic setting, a wetland receives moisture from direct precipitation; surface runoff; flooding from streams, rivers, or lakes; inundation by ocean tides; ground-water discharge; or a combination of those sources. The wide variety of hydrologic settings in Oregon has resulted in diverse wetland types statewide, but wetlands in each region have common hydrologic characteristics owing to common climatic, geologic, and topographic conditions.

Coastal wetlands.—Much of Oregon's coast is rocky, precipitous, and exposed to high-energy ocean waves. Wetlands in that environment are in the Marine System, as are ocean beaches. Those wetlands constitute only a small percentage of the State's wetland acreage. The most extensive coastal wetlands are estuarine or palustrine.

Estuarine wetlands develop where stream velocity and wave energy are low enough to permit sediment carried in streams to settle out of the water and accumulate to above the low-tide level, resulting in a tideflat (Akins and Jefferson, 1973). Tideflats are a transitional stage between deepwater habitat and salt marsh and thus are located between those areas. Tideflats typically are composed of silt and clay mixed with sand and gravel. Where they are sufficiently stable, tideflats are colonized by submersed vegetation, predominantly eelgrass and arrowgrass, which traps more sediment. As the tideflat becomes higher and more stable, marsh vegetation gradually becomes established, and the tideflat becomes a salt marsh.

Salt marshes are subject to a wide range of hydrologic conditions. For most of the year, tides alternately expose the marsh and then inundate it with brackish to very salty water. Winter flooding can inundate the marsh with freshwater. As sediment and dead vegetation accumulate, the substrate gradually rises until the marsh is subject to less frequent inundation by either tides or river flooding. In Oregon, such "high marsh" has commonly been altered by diking and draining to facilitate cattle grazing.

Tidal fresh marsh occurs inland from salt marshes in many estuaries. Some fresh marsh is present in coastal rivers upstream from the most upstream extent of saltwater at high tide. Other fresh marshes form in low-lying areas of flood plains that are flooded when rivers are, effectively, dammed by high tides.

Oregon's other major coastal wetlands have formed in the sand-dune regions that extend along about one-half the length of the coast. Inland marshes develop in and around dune lake basins and along the small, slow-flowing streams that feed the lakes. The lakes form when shifting sand dams the small coastal streams that are fed by ground water in the dunes. Flow in these streams is insufficient to wash away the sand dams, so most dune lakes are permanent. In shallow lakes, vegetation can extend from shore to shore.

Interdunal marshes form between sand dunes where wind has scoured the sand down to the water table. The process of wind scouring is known as deflation, and the scoured area is called a deflation plain. Interdunal marshes are sustained almost entirely by ground water. Because the water table declines to below the bottom of some deflation plains in the dry season (midsummer to early fall), some of these marshes are seasonal. Interdunal marshes are prone to filling by windblown sand and typically succeed to shrub swamp or upland habitat.

Willamette River Valley wetlands.—The physiography and climate of the Willamette River Valley are ideal for wetland formation. The wide valley floor, which is underlain primarily by alluvial deposits, is nearly flat, and the valley is surrounded by mountains that receive large amounts of precipitation (fig. 2C). Water from that precipitation, in the form of rainfall runoff or snowmelt, flows in streams and rivers into the valley, where it enters the ground-water system or remains in stream channels. The valley's wetlands are sustained by ground-water discharge, stream flooding, or both.

Because there is little elevation change from the valley margins to the Willamette River, the water table is at or near the land surface over large areas. Before widespread drainage for agricultural development (fig. 3), the saturated or flooded valley soils from the base of the surrounding mountains to the river flood plain sustained extensive marshes and wet prairies. Until the mid-1800's, the prairie landscape was maintained by fires regularly set by Native American inhabitants of the valley for game and food-plant management and for defense (Johannessen and others, 1971).

Figure 3. Drained agricultural land in the Willamette River Valley near Salem. Formerly a lakebed, this cropland is now farmed for onions. *(Photograph by Dennis A. Wentz, U.S. Geological Survey.)*

Owing to the gentle south-north gradient of the valley, the Willamette River is slow-flowing and meandering and has a wide flood plain. At one time, winter and spring flooding and the water table sustained a nearly continuous expanse of forested and shrub wetlands in the flood plain. However, drainage and flood control to facilitate agricultural and urban development have greatly reduced the extent of those wetlands.

Mountain wetlands.—Oregon's mountain wetlands are near seeps and springs, in and along rivers, and in lakes and small depressions. The State's mountains, especially the Coast and Cascade Ranges, receive large amounts of precipitation (fig. 2C). However, steep mountain slopes are not conducive to the long-term retention of water, so larger wetlands generally are present in river flood plains and lakes, where runoff, mostly from snowmelt, can accumulate as ground or surface water.

Flood-plain wetlands form where river flood plains are wide enough to sustain a water table at or near the land surface, generally in wide valleys and intermountain basins. Mountain-lake wetlands can be found in lakes of several origins. Some mountain lakes were formed when lava flowed across the stream and water ponded behind the lava dam (Phillips and others, 1965). Landslides also have dammed streams with similar results. Beavers impound streams, forming ponds and small lakes behind the dams. Most of the State's mountain lakes that contain wetlands, however, were formed by glaciers. The most common of Oregon's glacial lakes are cirque lakes, small lakes that are also known as tarns, which formed when water filled depressions scoured by a glacier.

Desert wetlands.—Oregon's desert basins contain large expanses of flat terrain from which water does not readily drain. Most desert basins are internally drained; that is, water that enters them can leave only through evaporation, transpiration, or discharge to the ground-water system rather than by way of surface drainage.

Deserts receive little direct precipitation because they are in the precipitation shadow of the Cascade Range. Basins collect snowmelt from the surrounding mountains, where precipitation amounts are higher than on the basin floor (fig. 2C). Water reaches the basin floor in streams or springs. The collected water forms shallow lakes, which can range in size from less than 1 acre to tens of thousands of acres and in wetness from flooded to nearly always dry, depending on climatic cycles and local hydrologic characteristics. Nonetheless, even a wetland that is temporarily dry probably will contain water at some time in the future unless the hydrologic setting is altered by human activities or long-term climate change. Some desert lakes, such as Lake Abert and the Warner Valley lakes, are the result of faulting; others, such as Malheur and Harney Lakes, are topographic depressions in the basin floor. Evaporation of water in the shallow lakes leaves mineral deposits in the lakebed sediments. These deposits make the lakebed less permeable, inhibiting infiltration into the subsurface.

Desert wetlands form along streams, around springs, and around and in the shallow lakes. The wetness of a desert wetland is controlled by several interrelated factors, including local topography, the depth to the water table, and the balance between water input and evaporation. In some flats near streams and lakes, the water table is at or near the land surface, but water generally does not pond on the land surface because shallow standing water quickly evaporates during most of the year. Soil in these wetlands commonly is saline because evaporation removes water but not the dissolved salts. The saturated soils of these flats commonly support salt-tolerant emergent and scrub vegetation. Most desert lakes that are flooded but that cannot overflow also are saline—some more so than seawater—because of evaporation. Lakes that can overflow, such as Malheur Lake, are not saline in most years and support extensive marsh vegetation.

Other major wetlands.—The upper Klamath River Basin, although it receives little precipitation, contains large areas of wetlands. Wetlands are widespread because the basin floor has little topographic relief and the natural water table is at or near the land surface over wide areas. Basin wetlands receive water from snowmelt, which reaches the basin floor either in streams or as springs. Drainage to facilitate agricultural development has lowered the water table in many areas, resulting in widespread conversion of wetlands to upland (fig. 4).

Figure 4. Grazing land, formerly wetland, in the upper Klamath River Basin. Much of the grazing land in the basin was once wetland. Drainage systems, consisting of ditches, sluice gates, and pumps, keep ground-water levels sufficiently below the land surface to allow the development of pasture. *(Photograph by Daniel T. Snyder, U.S. Geological Survey.)*

The Columbia and Snake River wetlands developed in the few areas where the flood plains are wide enough for sediment to accumulate and support emergent vegetation. The wetlands are sustained by ground-water discharge and river flooding; near the coast, marshes in the Columbia River are regularly flooded by saltwater as well. Flow in the Columbia River is affected by tides as far upstream as the Bonneville Dam, and wetlands commonly are flooded during high tides. In the Snake River Valley, irrigation recharges aquifers and sustains ground-water discharge to streams and wetlands during the summer-fall dry season (Kjelstrom, 1992).

TRENDS

Wetlands covered as much as 2.3 million acres (about 3.6 percent) of what is now Oregon as of the late 1700's (Dahl, 1990). Since that time, wetland acreage has decreased by more than one-third, mostly owing to conversion of wetlands to agricultural uses by diking, draining, or both. Other causes of wetland loss or degradation have been urbanization, industrial development, flood-control projects, surface-water diversion and ground-water pumping for irrigation, stream snagging, land clearing, grazing, and beaver trapping. The greatest losses were of estuarine marshes, eastern Oregon riparian wetlands, Willamette River Valley wet prairies and riparian wetlands, and upper Klamath River Basin marshes (Oregon Division of State Lands and Oregon State Parks and Recreation Division, 1989).

Recent evidence suggests that losses of estuarine wetlands have slowed substantially since the mid-1900's (Oregon Division of State Lands and Oregon State Parks and Recreation Division, 1989). Most continuing losses are due to conversion of tidal land to urban use. More than 90 percent of remaining estuarine wetlands are protected, commonly through local planning and zoning. The State and Federal governments have identified coastal wetlands, Willamette River Valley wetlands, riparian wetlands in eastern Oregon, desert-lake wetlands, and upper Klamath River Basin wetlands as priority areas for conservation.

CONSERVATION

Many government agencies and private organizations participate in wetland conservation in Oregon. The most active agencies and organizations and some of their activities are listed in table 1.

Federal wetland activities.— Development activities in Oregon wetlands are regulated by several Federal statutory prohibitions and incentives that are intended to slow wetland losses. Some of the more important of these are contained in the 1899 Rivers and Harbors Act; the 1972 Clean Water Act and amendments; the 1985 Food Security Act; the 1990 Food, Agriculture, Conservation, and Trade Act; the 1986 Emergency Wetlands Resources Act; and the 1972 Coastal Zone Management Act.

Section 10 of the Rivers and Harbors Act gives the U.S. Army Corps of Engineers (Corps) authority to regulate certain activities in navigable waters. Regulated activities include diking, deepening, filling, excavating, and placing of structures. The related section 404 of the Clean Water Act is the most often-used Federal legislation protecting wetlands. Under section 404 provisions, the Corps issues permits regulating the discharge of dredged or fill material into wetlands. Permits are subject to review and possible veto by the U.S. Environmental Protection Agency, and the FWS has review and advisory roles. Section 401 of the Clean Water Act grants to States and eligible Indian Tribes the authority to approve, apply conditions to, or deny section 404 permit applications on the basis of a proposed activity's probable effects on the water quality of a wetland.

Most farming, ranching, and silviculture activities are not subject to section 404 regulation. However, the "Swampbuster" provision of the 1985 Food Security Act and amendments in the 1990

Table 1. Selected wetland-related activities of government agencies and private organizations in Oregon, 1993

[Source: Classification of activities is generalized from information provided by agencies and organizations. •, agency or organization participates in wetland-related activity; ..., agency or organization does not participate in wetland-related activity. MAN, management; REG, regulation; R&C, restoration and creation; LAN, land acquisition; R&D, research and data collection; D&I, delineation and inventory]

Agency or organization	MAN	REG	R&C	LAN	R&D	D&I
FEDERAL						
Department of Agriculture						
Consolidated Farm Service Agency	...	•	...	...	...	...
Forest Service	•	...	•	•	•	•
Natural Resources Conservation Service	...	•	•	...	•	•
Department of Defense						
Army Corps of Engineers	•	•	•	...	•	•
Military reservations	•	...	...	...	...	...
Department of the Interior						
Bureau of Land Management	•	...	•	•	•	•
Bureau of Reclamation	•	...	...	•	•	...
Fish and Wildlife Service	•	...	•	•	•	•
Geological Survey	...	...	...	...	•	•
National Biological Service	...	...	...	...	•	•
National Park Service	•	...	...	...	...	...
Environmental Protection Agency	...	•	...	...	•	...
STATE						
Department of Agriculture	...	•	...	...	...	•
Department of Environmental Quality	...	•	...	...	•	...
Department of Fish and Wildlife	•	•	•	•	•	...
Department of Forestry	•	•	•	...	•	•
Department of Land Conservation and Development	...	•	...	...	...	...
Division of State Lands	•	•	•	•	...	•
Parks and Recreation Department	•	•	•	...	...	...
Water Resources Department	...	•	...	...	...	...
SOME COUNTY AND LOCAL GOVERNMENTS	•	•	...	•	...	...
PRIVATE ORGANIZATIONS						
Ducks Unlimited	•	...	•	•	...	...
Pacific Coast Joint Venture	...	...	•	•	...	...
The Nature Conservancy	•	...	•	•	...	...

Food, Agriculture, Conservation, and Trade Act discourage (through financial disincentives) the draining, filling, or other alteration of wetlands for agricultural use. The law allows exemptions from penalties in some cases, especially if the farmer agrees to restore the altered wetland or other wetlands that have been converted to agricultural use. The Wetlands Reserve Program of the 1990 Food, Agriculture, Conservation, and Trade Act authorizes the Federal Government to purchase conservation easements from landowners who agree to protect or restore wetlands. The Consolidated Farm Service Agency (formerly the Agricultural Stabilization and Conservation Service) administers the Swampbuster provisions and Wetlands Reserve Program. The Natural Resources Conservation Service (formerly the Soil Conservation Service) determines compliance with Swampbuster provisions and assists farmers in the identification of wetlands and in the development of wetland protection, restoration, or creation plans.

The 1986 Emergency Wetlands Resources Act and the 1972 Coastal Zone Management Act and amendments encourage wetland protection through funding incentives. The Emergency Wetlands Resources Act requires States to address wetland protection in their Statewide Comprehensive Outdoor Recreation Plans to qualify for Federal funding for State recreational land; the National Park Service provides guidance to States in developing the wetland component of their plans. Coastal States that adopt coastal-zone management programs and plans approved by the National Oceanic and Atmospheric Administration are eligible for Federal funding and technical assistance through the Coastal Zone Management Act.

Federal agencies are responsible for the proper management of wetlands on public land under their jurisdiction. The U.S. Forest Service (FS) manages 13 National Forests in Oregon and is developing a process to evaluate values and functions of wetlands in those forests. The Bureau of Land Management (BLM) manages about 16 million acres of rangeland, of which about 1.2 percent is riparian wetland (Bureau of Land Management, 1991). The BLM is assessing the status of riparian wetlands and has ongoing or planned projects to develop or enhance many of those wetlands. The FWS manages nine National Wildlife Refuges in Oregon that have extensive wetlands. The FWS funds wetland-restoration projects under the Partners for Wildlife Program. FWS National Wetlands Inventory maps are available for all of Oregon. The Corps manages wetlands within its project areas, researches ways to identify and enhance wetlands, and evaluates losses of wetland area and functions caused by filling and dredging. The Bureau of Reclamation conducts multipurpose wetland-restoration projects; all enhance waterfowl habitat in accordance with the 1986 North American Waterfowl Management Plan. The Environmental Protection Agency has awarded grants to State and local agencies to plan coordinated wetland-protection efforts, inventory wetlands, and conduct a watershed-protection pilot study. The BLM, Corps, FS, and FWS and several State agencies have developed a Memorandum of Understanding concerning the management and protection of Oregon's wetland resources on public lands (Oregon Division of State Lands, 1993).

State wetland activities.—To improve the effectiveness and efficiency of Oregon's efforts to conserve, restore, and protect wetlands, the State has developed a Wetland Conservation Strategy (Oregon Division of State Lands, 1993). The strategy provides the focus and framework for an integrated State wetland program designed to conserve, protect, and manage the State's wetland resources. The strategy is based on the recommendations of advisory committees representing Federal, State, and local agencies and interest groups.

In Oregon, the regulatory programs that are implemented at the State level are the State Removal-Fill Law, the Oregon Wetland Inventory and Wetland Conservation Plans, and the Clean Water Act Section 401 program. The Oregon Removal-Fill Law, administered by the Division of State Lands, is similar to section 404 of the Clean Water Act but in some respects is more comprehensive. Oregon has adopted the FWS National Wetlands Inventory as a basis for a State Wetland Inventory. The statewide inventory is being supplemented by detailed local information that is suitable for planning and regulatory purposes. The Wetland Conservation Plans program established a local planning process that provides local governments an opportunity to address wetland-resource decisions in a context with other land-use needs. Pursuant to section 401 of the Clean Water Act, the Department of Environmental Quality reviews Federal permits and licenses affecting wetlands for compliance with Oregon's water-quality standards. A section 404 permit is not issued by the Corps without certification of compliance by the Department.

Wetland mitigation is another important State regulatory function. The Division of State Lands has the authority to establish mitigation banks to be used when mitigation of unavoidable impacts caused by construction is not possible onsite; compensation may be made by the offsite creation, restoration, or enhancement of wetlands.

County and local wetland activities.—Oregon's Comprehensive Land Use Planning Act requires local governments to adopt planning and regulatory programs consistent with statewide planning goals. The State Wetland Conservation Plans program allows local governments to balance wetland protection with other land-use needs (Oregon Division of State Lands, 1993). Some county and city governments have regulatory or land-acquisition programs that provide additional wetland protection.

Private wetland activities.—The Oregon Coastal Wetlands Joint Venture, the State's part of the Pacific Coast Joint Venture of the North American Waterfowl Management Plan, is a cooperative effort of local citizens, conservation organizations, private companies, and State and Federal agencies. The primary goal of the joint venture is to reverse the downward trend in waterfowl populations in coastal areas and to address concerns about coastal wetlands. Land acquisition, wetland-habitat improvement, and small wetland-restoration projects are among the organization's activities. A concept plan for another joint venture that would include eastern Oregon has been prepared (Ratti and Kadlec, 1992).

The Nature Conservancy and Ducks Unlimited have participated in projects involving land acquisition and restoration of wetland habitat in Oregon. The Wetlands Conservancy owns and manages several small wetlands totaling about 60 acres, mainly in the Portland metropolitan area. These and many other conservation organizations provide information to the public on the values and functions of wetlands or promote wetland protection.

References Cited

Akins, G.J., and Jefferson, C.A., 1973, Coastal wetlands of Oregon: Florence, Oregon Coastal Conservation and Development Commission, 190 p.

Bureau of Land Management, 1991, Riparian wetland initiative for the 1990's: Bureau of Land Management Report BLM/WO/GI–91/001+4340, 50 p.

Cowardin, L.M., Carter, Virginia, Golet, F.C., and LaRoe, T.E., 1979, Classification of wetlands and deepwater habitats of the United States: U.S. Fish and Wildlife Service Report FWS/OBS–79/31, 131 p.

Dahl, T.E., 1990, Wetlands—Losses in the United States, 1780's to 1980's: Washington, D.C., U.S. Fish and Wildlife Report to Congress, 13 p.

Hubbard, L.L., Oregon surface-water resources, *in* National Water Summary 1985—Hydrologic events and surface-water resources: U.S. Geological Survey Water-Supply Paper 2300, p. 383–390.

Johannessen, C.L., Davenport, W.A., Millet, Artimus, and McWilliams, Steven, 1971, The vegetation of the Willamette Valley: Annals of the Association of American Geographers, v. 61, p. 286–302.

Kjelstrom, L.C., 1992, Streamflow gains and losses in the Snake River and ground-water budgets for the Snake River plain, Idaho and eastern Oregon: U.S. Geological Survey Open-File Report 90–172, 71 p.

Loy, W.G., 1976, Atlas of Oregon: Eugene, University of Oregon Books, 215 p.

Omernik, J.M, 1987, Ecoregions of the conterminous United States—Map supplement: Annals of the Association of American Geographers, v. 77, no. 1, scale 1:7,500,000.

Oregon Division of State Lands, 1993, Oregon's wetland conservation strategy: Salem, Oregon Division of State Lands, 100 p.

Oregon Division of State Lands and Oregon State Parks and Recreation Division, 1989, Oregon wetlands priority plan: Salem, Oregon Division of State Lands and Oregon State Parks and Recreation Division, 75 p.

Phillips, K.N., Newcomb, R.C., Swenson, H.A., and Laird, L.B., 1965, Water for Oregon: U.S. Geological Survey Water-Supply Paper 1649, 150 p.

Ratti, J.T., and Kadlec, J.A., 1992, Concept plan for the preservation of wetland habitat of the intermountain west—North American Waterfowl Management Plan: Portland, Oreg., U.S. Fish and Wildlife Service, 146 p.

FOR ADDITIONAL INFORMATION: District Chief, U.S. Geological Survey, 10615 S.E. Cherry Blossom Drive, Portland, OR 97216; Regional Wetland Coordinator, U.S. Fish and Wildlife Service, 911 N.E. 11th Avenue, Portland, OR 97232

Prepared by
Luther C. Kjelstrom and John S. Williams,
U.S. Geological Survey

Pennsylvania
Wetland Resources

Wetlands cover about 2 percent of Pennsylvania (Tiner, 1990). Although once regarded as wastelands, wetlands now are recognized as ecologically and economically valuable ecosystems. Fish and wildlife use these highly productive areas for feeding, breeding, nesting, and refuge. More than 80 percent of the animals on Pennsylvania's list of endangered and threatened species depend on wetlands during their life cycle (Brooks, 1990). Wetlands also are home to most of Pennsylvania's rare, threatened, or endangered plants (Pennsylvania Department of Environmental Resources, 1988). The Long Pond area of Tunkhannock Creek (fig. 1) has the State's largest known concentration of endangered species (Roger Latham, University of Pennsylvania, written commun., 1993).

Wetlands trap suspended sediments and organic and inorganic contaminants in soils and plant tissue, thus enhancing water quality. Wetland vegetation also retards erosion by decreasing water velocity and increasing soil stability. During floods, riparian (streamside) wetlands regulate streamflow by temporarily storing floodwater and then slowly releasing it to the stream or river, greatly reducing flooding downstream. Of particular interest in Pennsylvania is the use of constructed wetlands as an effective passive treatment of coal-mine drainage, which can be highly acidic and contain elevated concentrations of iron, manganese, sulfate, aluminum, and other trace elements (Hedin, 1989). Constructed wetlands also are used to reduce nutrient loads from agricultural drainage.

Figure 1. Wetland at Tunkhannock Creek near Long Pond. This wetland contains the State's largest known concentration of endangered plants and animals. *(Photograph by Annette C. Heist, U.S. Geological Survey.)*

Wetlands are productive ecosystems, yielding a large amount of plant material for both wildlife and human consumption. Products harvested from wetlands include cranberries, blueberries, and wild rice. Pennsylvania's tourist industry benefits from the recreational opportunities that wetlands provide, including hunting, fishing, boating, and camping. Many wetland areas throughout the State also provide educational opportunities for schools and the general public.

TYPES AND DISTRIBUTION

Wetlands are lands transitional between terrestrial and deepwater habitats where the water table usually is at or near the land surface or the land is covered by shallow water (Cowardin and others, 1979). The distribution of wetlands and deepwater habitats in Pennsylvania is shown in figure 2*A*; only wetlands are discussed herein.

Wetlands can be vegetated or nonvegetated and are classified on the basis of their hydrology, vegetation, and substrate. In this summary, wetlands are classified according to the system proposed by Cowardin and others (1979), which is used by the U.S. Fish and Wildlife Service (FWS) to map and inventory the Nation's wetlands. At the most general level of the classification system, wetlands are grouped into five ecological systems: Palustrine, Lacustrine, Riverine, Estuarine, and Marine. The Palustrine System includes only wetlands, whereas the other systems comprise wetlands and deepwater habitats. Wetlands of the systems that occur in Pennsylvania are described below.

System	Wetland description
Palustrine	Wetlands in which vegetation is predominantly trees (forested wetlands); shrubs (scrub-shrub wetlands); persistent or nonpersistent emergent, erect, rooted, herbaceous plants (persistent- and nonpersistent-emergent wetlands); or submersed and (or) floating plants (aquatic beds). Also, intermittently to permanently flooded open-water bodies of less than 20 acres in which water is less than 6.6 feet deep.
Lacustrine	Wetlands within an intermittently to permanently flooded lake or reservoir. Vegetation, when present, is predominantly nonpersistent emergent plants (nonpersistent-emergent wetlands), or submersed and (or) floating plants (aquatic beds), or both.
Riverine	Wetlands within a channel. Vegetation, when present, is same as in the Lacustrine System.

About 1.4 percent (404,000 acres) of Pennsylvania's land surface is covered by wetlands. About 97 percent of these wetlands are palustrine, about 2 percent are lacustrine, and 1 percent are riverine. Pennsylvania's 392,000 acres of palustrine wetlands consist of 178,000 acres of deciduous and evergreen forested wetlands, 62,000 acres of open water, 52,000 acres of emergent wetlands, 49,000 acres of deciduous and evergreen scrub-shrub wetlands, 25,000 acres of mixed deciduous scrub-shrub and emergent wetlands, and 26,000 acres of other types (Tiner, 1990). Pennsylvania wetlands are known by a variety of local names, the most common of which are swamp (forested wetland) and marsh (emergent wetland typically dominated by sedges and grasses). Many of Pennsylvania's palustrine wetlands line major rivers or surround lakes and reservoirs. Peatlands (wetlands that have organic soils, such as bogs and fens) are common in mountainous or glaciated areas and commonly contain sphagnum moss, tamarack or black spruce trees, a variety of low trees and shrubs, or sedges, grasses, and other herbaceous plants.

About 42 percent of Pennsylvania wetlands are in the glaciated parts of the northwestern and northeastern corners of the State (Tiner, 1990). Wetlands in the northwest are primarily deciduous forested and scrub-shrub wetlands. Those in the northeast are primarily deciduous and evergreen forested wetlands. Most of the central and southern parts of the State were not glaciated. In the nonglaciated parts of the State, wetlands are most commonly associated with the headwaters and flood plains of streams (Brooks and others, 1987). The largest area of lacustrine wetlands (5,650 acres) is along the Lake Erie shoreline. Minor amounts of tidal riverine wetlands are along the Delaware River in southeastern Pennsylvania.

HYDROLOGIC SETTING

Wetland characteristics are determined by the balance between inflow and outflow of water, surface contours of the land, soil type, and geology (Mitsch and Gosselink, 1986). Topographic depressions caused by glacial or stream-related processes, areas with impermeable substrates that prevent infiltration of water into the ground, and areas where the water table is near the surface provide ideal conditions for wetland formation. Wetlands commonly form at groundwater discharge sites where permeable rocks intersect the land surface or at the base of slopes where the water table intersects the land surface (Novitzki, 1989).

Wetlands are most densely distributed in the northwestern and northeastern parts of the State, which were glaciated at least twice and possibly three times (fig. 2B). The latest glaciation occurred between 18,000 and 22,000 years ago. Glacial scouring and deposition left surface depressions and impermeable soils that are ideal for wetland development (Bushnell, 1989). Outside the glaciated

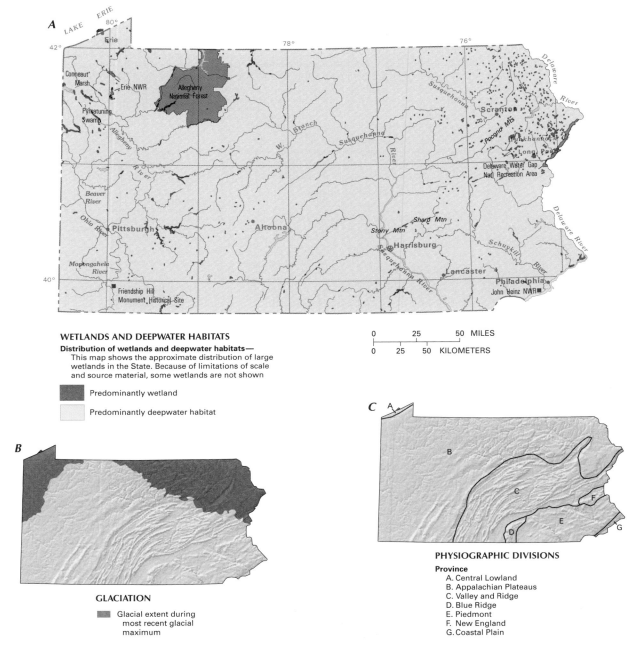

WETLANDS AND DEEPWATER HABITATS

Distribution of wetlands and deepwater habitats—
This map shows the approximate distribution of large wetlands in the State. Because of limitations of scale and source material, some wetlands are not shown

Predominantly wetland

Predominantly deepwater habitat

GLACIATION

Glacial extent during most recent glacial maximum

PHYSIOGRAPHIC DIVISIONS

Province
A. Central Lowland
B. Appalachian Plateaus
C. Valley and Ridge
D. Blue Ridge
E. Piedmont
F. New England
G. Coastal Plain

Figure 2.   Wetland distribution in Pennsylvania and physical features that control wetland distribution in the State. *A*, Distribution of wetlands and deepwater habitats. *B*, Extent of most recent glaciation. *C*, Physiography. *(Sources: A, T.E. Dahl, U.S. Fish and Wildlife Service, unpub. data, 1991. B, Pennsylvania Bureau of Topographic and Geologic Survey, 1989. C, Physiographic divisions from Fenneman, 1946; landforms data from EROS Data Center.)*

areas, wetlands typically are associated with streams and rivers. Some wetlands gain moisture from stream flooding, whereas others are fed by ground water and drain into streams. Riparian wetlands develop when lateral erosion and deposition widen a river valley or when accumulated sediment fills and flattens a valley. In riparian areas, a depositional substrate of silt, mud, and clay and the shallow water table near a river combine to create ideal conditions for the formation of small lakes and swamps. However, many of the large rivers in Pennsylvania are in deep, narrow valleys and lack extensive riparian areas (Bushnell, 1989).

Pennsylvania has abundant precipitation. Average annual precipitation ranges from about 36 inches in the north and west to about 48 inches in the east. Precipitation in eastern Pennsylvania is distributed evenly throughout the year, whereas the western part of the State receives most of the precipitation in the spring and summer. Statewide, an average of about 25 inches of the annual precipitation returns to the atmosphere by evaporation or transpiration (Wetzel, 1986).

Pennsylvania lies in parts of seven physiographic provinces (fig. 2C): the Central Lowland, Appalachian Plateaus, Valley and Ridge, New England, Blue Ridge, Piedmont, and Coastal Plain. Each province has unique characteristics that control the distribution and types of wetlands.

Central Lowland.—The Central Lowland is underlain mainly by sedimentary rocks, including sandstone, shale, dolomite, and limestone (Krothe and Kempton, 1988). The region includes areas of both thick and thin glacial till, which is a mixture of clay, sand, and boulders deposited by a melting glacier. The low permeability of the glacial till allows the formation of wetlands in depressions and low-lying areas. The region is flat to gently sloping except where cut by streams. Most of the streams in the Central Lowland of Pennsylvania flow northward to Lake Erie. The streams have steep gradients and flow over or have cut deeply into bedrock, resulting in few associated wetlands (Richards and others, 1987). Lacustrine wetlands associated with Lake Erie comprise nearly two-thirds of total wetland acreage in this part of the State (Tiner and Anderson, 1986).

Appalachian Plateaus.—The Appalachian Plateaus Province is underlain by interbedded shale, sandstone, and some limestone (Bushnell, 1989). The rocks of this province are gently folded to nearly flat-lying. Fracturing and jointing are common (Seaber and others, 1988). The northeastern and northwestern parts of the province have been glaciated.

In the nonglaciated areas, palustrine wetlands have formed in riparian areas along the major rivers and streams. Some wetlands also are present in and around impoundments. Locally, small wetlands are present on hilltops where clayey soils and shale support shallow water tables. Wetlands also form along the valley sides and heads of streams where erosion has exposed aquifers or where joints break the continuity of confined aquifers (Bushnell, 1989).

In the northwestern part of the province, before glaciation, rivers flowed north to Lake Erie (Leggette, 1936). Advancing ice blocked the north-flowing rivers, forming lakes and forcing drainage southward. Present drainage patterns were created as ice melted and glacial sediments were carried in south- and southeast-sloping channels. The largest wetlands in this area, including Conneaut Marsh and Pymatuning Swamp, developed on the glacial sediments that filled deep, preglacial valleys. Numerous smaller wetlands also formed in the irregular, hummocky topography of the end and ground moraines, which are landscape features formed by glacially formed sediments (Bushnell, 1989).

In the glaciated northeast, wetlands are associated mainly with end and ground moraines and have developed as lakes, swamps, and peatlands in glacially scoured depressions (Bushnell, 1989). Many wetlands also were formed by the damming of preglacial valleys by glacial debris. In addition, "kettle-hole" lakes were created where

large blocks of ice remained after glacial retreat and melted to form spring-fed lakes that have no surface inlet or outlet.

Peatlands in the Pocono Mountains of northeastern Pennsylvania are the southernmost peatlands of recent glacial origin and are considered rare habitats in Pennsylvania (Brooks and others, 1987). Peatlands can develop where drainage is slow and where precipitation normally exceeds evapotranspiration. Fens and bogs are two types of peatlands found in Pennsylvania. Fens are fed by mineral-rich ground water. Bogs are fed mostly or entirely by rainwater and, as a result, are mineral poor. The process of peat formation follows a general evolution. Clay from glacial tills accumulates on the bottom of ponds, trapping the organic material. Under the oxygen-poor conditions in the bottom substrate, slow decomposition allows the formation of peat. As peat accumulates, the pond shrinks and a marsh commonly forms. As more peat accumulates, the surface of the peatland rises to such an extent that the substrate is saturated, but there is little standing water. At that stage, trees, shrubs, and sphagnum moss become common. Eventually, as the accumulating peat brings the land surface above the water table, shrubs and trees advance until a scrub-shrub or forested wetland is formed. Flooding of the peatland by natural or artificial changes in drainage will cause the peatland to return to a marsh. If the water table is lowered for any sustained period of time, the soils will undergo aeration, and the organic content of the soil will decrease (Cameron, 1970).

Valley and Ridge Province.—The Valley and Ridge Province is underlain mainly by sedimentary rocks, including sandstone, conglomerate, shale, siltstone, dolomite, and limestone, that are tilted and folded (Seaber and others, 1988). The structure and weathering pattern of the rocks combine to yield the characteristic alternating valley and ridge topography. Some of the limestone valleys have an extensive karst or underground drainage system that precludes extensive wetland development (Bushnell, 1989). In contrast, limestone outcrops along the western edge of the province are the source of many springs and seeps that supports wetlands. Most wetlands are associated with the Susquehanna River and its tributaries (Bushnell, 1989), especially in the upper, glaciated regions of the river.

An unexpected wetland lies in a valley between the peaks of Sharp Mountain and Stony Mountain, about 15 miles northeast of Harrisburg. The wetland lies along the axis of a syncline that is underlain by resistant beds of rock that have low permeability (Bushnell, 1989). The wetland consists of forested and emergent wetlands that contain sphagnum moss, swamp azalea, red maple, and black gum.

New England Province.—The New England Province is an area of high hills and ridges that are composed principally of metamorphic rocks, and igneous rocks, and limestone (Wood and others, 1972). Because the province has steep topography and is well drained, few wetlands have formed there. Most wetlands are in riparian areas along the Delaware River.

Blue Ridge and Piedmont Provinces.—The Blue Ridge and Piedmont Provinces are underlain by fractured-rock, water-table aquifers. Deformed igneous and metamorphic rocks, commonly mantled with weathered rock and soil, characterize the bedrock of the region (LeGrand, 1988). The Piedmont Province also has gently dipping beds of sedimentary rock. The region has small ground-water units, each confined to a small basin in which a perennial stream flows. Ground water flows continuously toward streams and discharges as small springs and as channel seepage into the streams (LeGrand, 1988). Most wetlands are in stream valleys where the water table is near the land surface. Others are in upland areas where there are clayey, impermeable soils or local ground-water discharge (Bushnell, 1989).

Coastal Plain.—The Coastal Plain, limited to the southeastern edge of Pennsylvania, is underlain mainly by permeable soils composed of sand, silt, and clay (Meissler and others, 1988). Most wetlands in this area are associated with the Delaware River and its riparian areas. Approximately 19 percent of the freshwater tidal marshes and flats in the Delaware River Basin are in this province within Pennsylvania (Tiner and Wilen, 1988), including the largest freshwater tidal marsh in the State, the John Heinz National Wildlife Refuge at Tinicum.

TRENDS

The U.S. Fish and Wildlife Service has estimated that, from the 1780's to the 1980's, wetland area in Pennsylvania decreased by more than one-half (Dahl, 1990). Activities such as conversion to cropland, channelization, forestry, mining, urban development, and the construction of impoundments have contributed to widespread wetland loss or degradation.

Between 1956 and 1979, Pennsylvania lost about 28,000 acres (nearly 7 percent) of its vegetated wetlands. More than one-half of the vegetated wetland losses took place in the northeastern (9,700 acres) and northwestern (4,600 acres) parts of the State. The leading cause of losses was conversion to ponds, lakes, and reservoirs (46 percent); farmland (17 percent); urban land (14 percent); and other land uses, mostly by channelization and drainage (23 percent) (Tiner, 1990). Peat mining in the Pocono Mountains region also has contributed to the loss of wetlands (Timer, 1987). After peat has been removed from the wetland, the area commonly is converted to a pond or lake.

The loss of vegetated wetland by conversion to pond wetland cannot be interpreted as a simple "no net loss" exchange. The importance of the gain in pond acreage in terms of fish and wildlife species, as well as the impact on wetland functions such as flood and erosion control, has not been adequately assessed. In contrast, the loss of vegetated wetlands is known to cause the loss of valuable fish and wildlife species as well as of other ecological and economical benefits (Tiner and Finn, 1986).

The Delaware River estuary and Lake Erie coastal zones contain habitats that are rare in Pennsylvania, and small losses of wetlands there could be significant. In Pennsylvania, the Delaware River estuary coastal zone consists of approximately 50 square miles along the Delaware River south of Philadelphia. Although only 129 acres of emergent wetlands have been lost in the Delaware River estuary coastal zone since the mid-1970's, this represented a 22-percent loss for the area. Major causes were the construction of a sewage-treatment plant and highway construction (Tiner,1990).

The Lake Erie coastal zone consists of approximately 63 square miles in the Lake Erie area. There were no significant changes in wetland acreage in the Lake Erie coastal zone between the mid-1970's and 1986 (Tiner, 1990). However, between 1986 and 1989, approximately 50 acres of wetlands were lost. Most of those losses (91 percent) were due to housing construction (Smith and Tiner, 1992).

CONSERVATION

Many government agencies and private organizations participate in wetland conservation in Pennsylvania. The most active agencies and organizations and some of their activities are listed in table 1.

Federal wetland activities.—Development activities in Pennsylvania wetlands are regulated by several Federal statutory prohibitions and incentives that are intended to slow wetland losses. Some of the more important of these are contained in the 1899 Rivers and Harbors Act; the 1972 Clean Water Act and amendments; the 1985 Food Security Act; the 1990 Food, Agriculture, Conservation, and Trade Act; the 1986 Emergency Wetlands Resources Act; and the 1972 Coastal Zone Management Act.

Table 1. Selected wetland-related activities of government agencies and private organizations in Pennsylvania, 1993

[Source: Classification of activities is generalized from information provided by agencies and organizations. •, agency or organization participates in wetland-related activity; ..., agency or organization does not participate in wetland-related activity. MAN, management; REG, regulation; R&C, restoration and creation; LAN, land acquisition; R&D, research and data collection; D&I, delineation and inventory]

Agency or organization	MAN	REG	R&C	LAN	R&D	D&I
FEDERAL						
Department of Agriculture						
Federal						
Consolidated Farm Service Agency	...	•	...	...	...	...
Forest Service	•	...	•	•	•	•
Natural Resources Conservation Service	...	•	•	•	•	•
Department of Commerce						
National Oceanic and Atmospheric Administration	...	•	...	...	•	...
Department of Defense						
Army Corps of Engineers	•	•	...	...	•	...
Department of the Interior						
Bureau of Mines	...	...	•	...	•	...
Fish and Wildlife Service	...	•	•	•	•	•
Geological Survey	...	...	...	...	•	...
National Biological Service	...	...	...	...	•	...
National Park Service	•	...	•	•	•	•
Environmental Protection Agency	...	•	...	...	•	•
STATE						
Department of Environmental Resources						
Bureau of Dams, Waterways, and Wetlands	•	•	•	•	•	•
Bureau of Forestry	•	...	•	•	•	•
Bureau of Land and Water (Coastal Zone management)	•	...	...	...	•	•
Bureau of State Parks	•	...	...	...	•	•
Department of Transportation	...	...	•	...	•	•
Pennsylvania Fish and Boat Commission	•	...	...	...	•	...
Pennsylvania Game Commission	•	...	•	•	...	•
Pennsylvania State University	...	...	...	...	•	...
Other State universities	...	...	...	...	•	...
COUNTY AND LOCAL						
Some county and local governments	•	•	...	...	•	...
Some county conservation districts	•	•	...	...	•	...
PRIVATE ORGANIZATIONS						
The Nature Conservancy	•	...	...	•	...	...
Pennsylvania Academy of Natural Sciences	...	...	...	...	•	...
Western Pennsylvania Conservancy	•	...	•	•	•	•

Section 10 of the Rivers and Harbors Act gives the U.S. Army Corps of Engineers (Corps) authority to regulate certain activities in navigable waters. Regulated activities include diking, deepening, filling, excavating, and placing of structures. The related section 404 of the Clean Water Act is the most often-used Federal legislation protecting wetlands. Under section 404 provisions, the Corps issues permits regulating the discharge of dredged or fill material into wetlands. Permits are subject to review and possible veto by the U.S. Environmental Protection Agency (EPA), and the FWS has review and advisory roles. Section 401 of the Clean Water Act grants to States and eligible Indian Tribes the authority to approve, apply conditions to, or deny section 404 permit applications on the basis of a proposed activity's probable effects on the water quality of a wetland.

Most farming, ranching, and silviculture activities are not subject to section 404 regulation. However, the "Swampbuster" provision of the 1985 Food Security Act and amendments in the 1990 Food, Agriculture, Conservation, and Trade Act discourage (through financial disincentives) the draining, filling, or other alteration of wetlands for agricultural use. The law allows exemptions from penalties in some cases, especially if the farmer agrees to restore the altered wetland or other wetlands that have been converted to agricultural use. The Wetlands Reserve Program of the 1990 Food,

Agriculture, Conservation, and Trade Act authorizes the Federal Government to purchase conservation easements from landowners who agree to protect or restore wetlands. The Consolidated Farm Service Agency (formerly the Agricultural Stabilization and Conservation Service) administers the Swampbuster provisions and Wetlands Reserve Program. The Natural Resources Conservation Service (formerly the Soil Conservation Service) determines compliance with Swampbuster provisions and assists farmers in the identification of wetlands and in the development of wetland protection, restoration, or creation plans.

The 1986 Emergency Wetlands Resources Act and the 1972 Coastal Zone Management Act and amendments encourage wetland protection through funding incentives. The Emergency Wetland Resources Act requires States to address wetland protection in their Statewide Comprehensive Outdoor Recreation Plans to qualify for Federal funding for State recreational land; the National Park Service (NPS) provides guidance to States in developing the wetland component of their plans. Coastal and Great Lakes States that adopt coastal-zone management programs and plans approved by the National Oceanic and Atmospheric Administration are eligible for Federal funding and technical assistance through the Coastal Zone Management Act.

Federal agencies are responsible for the management of wetlands on public land under their jurisdiction. The FWS manages two wildlife refuges in Pennsylvania, the John Heinz National Wildlife Refuge at Tinicum and the Erie National Wildlife Refuge. The U.S. Forest Service manages about one-half million acres of land in the Allegheny National Forest. The NPS manages 11 sites in Pennsylvania, including the Delaware Water Gap National Recreation Area. Wetlands are inventoried on these lands as part of resource management plans developed for each park. The U.S. Bureau of Mines has been involved in research into the creation of wetlands for the passive treatment of acid-mine drainage. One such experimental wetland was created by the U.S. Bureau of Mines and the NPS on the Friendship Hill National Historic Site.

State wetland activities.—The Pennsylvania Department of Environmental Resources' Bureau of Dams, Waterways, and Wetlands, is the principal State agency responsible for wetland regulation. Wetlands are regulated as "bodies of water" under the Dam Safety and Encroachments Act of 1978. The wetland regulations are found at 25 Pa. code Chapter 105, Dam Safety and Waterway Management, amended October 31, 1991. Virtually any structure or activity that in any manner changes, expands, or diminishes the course, current, or cross section of any wetland requires a chapter 105 permit in addition to any Federal permits that are required for the project.

Pursuant to section 305(b) of the Clean Water Act, the Department of Environmental Resources submits to the EPA and the U.S. Congress a biennial assessment of the State's surface-water quality, including that of wetlands. The Department's Bureau of Land and Water Division of Coastal Zone Management conducts a yearly wetlands monitoring program in the Delaware River estuary and Lake Erie coastal zones.

The Bureau of State Parks and the Bureau of Forestry inventory wetlands as part of their resource-management plans. Monies from the Land and Water Conservation Fund are used by the Department of Community Affairs, the Department of Environmental Resources, the Fish and Boat Commission, the Game Commission, and the Historical and Museum Commission for planning, acquisition, and development of outdoor recreation areas, including wetlands. Land acquisition also is made possible through the Recreational Improvement and Rehabilitation Act and the Federal Land and Water Conservation Fund.

County and local wetland activities.—Most regulation of activities in wetlands is carried out through State and Federal laws. However, some county and local governments are involved in the protection of wetland resources through zoning, regulating, and land acquisition. Some county conservation districts manage public and private lands that contain wetlands.

Private wetland activities.—Private organizations in Pennsylvania are involved in wetland activities that include policy planning, land acquisition and management, research, and public education. Some of the organizations active in Pennsylvania are The Nature Conservancy and the Western Pennsylvania Conservancy (land acquisition and management), the Sierra Club and Chesapeake Bay Foundation (policy planning and education), and the Pennsylvania Academy of Natural Sciences (research). About 50 conservancy organizations throughout the State work to protect and preserve natural lands, including wetlands, on a local level.

References Cited

Brooks, R.P., 1990, Wetlands and deepwater habitats in Pennsylvania, *in* Majumdar, S.K., Miller, E.W., and Parizek, R.R., eds., Water resources in Pennsylvania—Availability, quality and management: Easton, The Pennsylvania Academy of Science, p. 71–79.

Brooks, R.P., Arnold, D.E., and Bellis, E.D., 1987, Wildlife and plant communities of selected wetlands—Pocono Region of Pennsylvania: National Wetlands Research Center Open File Report 87–02, 27 p.

Bushnell, Kent, 1989, Geology of Pennsylvania wetlands, *in* Majumdar, S.K., and others, eds., Wetlands ecology and conservation—Emphasis in Pennsylvania: Easton, The Pennsylvania Academy of Science, p. 39–46.

Cameron, C.C., 1970, Peat deposits of northeastern Pennsylvania: U.S. Geological Survey Bulletin 1317–A, 90 p.

Cowardin, L.M., Carter, Virginia, Golet, F.C., and LaRoe, E.T., 1979, Classification of wetlands and deepwater habitats of the United States: U.S. Fish and Wildlife Service Report FWS/OBS–79/31, 131 p.

Dahl, T.E., 1990, Wetlands—Losses in the United States, 1780's to 1980's: Washington, D.C., U.S. Fish and Wildlife Service Report to Congress, 13 p.

Fenneman, N.M., 1946, Physical divisions of the United States: Washington, D.C., U.S. Geological Survey special map, scale 1:7,000,000.

Hedin, R.S., 1989, Treatment of coal mine drainage with constructed wetlands, *in* Majumdar, S.K., and others, eds., Wetlands ecology and conservation—Emphasis in Pennsylvania: Easton, The Pennsylvania Academy of Science, p. 349–362.

Krothe, N.C., and Kempton, J.P., 1988, Region 14, central glaciated plains, *in* Back, William, Rosenshein, J.S., and Seaber, P.R., eds., The geology of North America, v. 0–2—Hydrogeology: Boulder, Colo., Geological Society of America, p. 129–132.

Leggette, R.M., 1936, Ground water in northwestern Pennsylvania: Pennsylvania Geological Survey, 4th series, Bulletin W3, 215 p.

LeGrand, H.E., 1988, Region 21, Piedmont and Blue Ridge, *in* Back, William, Rosenshein, J.S., and Seaber, P.R., eds., The geology of North America, v. 0–2—Hydrogeology: Boulder, Colo., Geological Society of America, p. 201–208.

Meissler, Harold, Miller, J.A., Knobel, L.L., and Wait, R.L., 1988, Region 22, Atlantic and eastern Gulf Coastal Plain, *in* Back, William, Rosenshein, J.S., and Seaber, P.R., eds., The geology of North America, v.–0–2—Hydrogeology: Boulder, Colo., Geological Society of America, p. 209–218.

Mitsch, W.J., and Gosselink, J.G., 1986, Wetlands: New York, Van Nostrand Reinhold Company, 539 p.

Novitzki, R.P., 1989, Wetland Hydrology, *in* Majumdar, S.K., and others, eds., Wetlands ecology and conservation—Emphasis in Pennsylvania: Easton, The Pennsylvania Academy of Science, p. 47–64.

Pennsylvania Bureau of Topographic and Geologic Survey, 1989, Physiographic provinces of Pennsylvania: Harrisburg, Pennsylvania Bureau of Topographic and Geologic Survey, scale 1:2,000,000.

Pennsylvania Department of Environmental Resources, 1988, Pennsylvania's recreation plan 1986–1990—Wetlands addendum: Harrisburg, Pennsylvania Department of Environmental Resources, 48 p.

Richards, D.B., McCoy, H.J., and Gallaher, J.T., 1987, Groundwater resources of Erie County, Pennsylvania: Pennsylvania Topographical and Geological Survey Water Resources Report 62, 59 p.

Seaber, P.R., Brahana, J.V., and Hollyday, E.F., 1988, Region 20, Appalachian Plateaus and Valley and Ridge, *in* Back, William, Rosenshein, J.S., and Seaber, P.R., eds., The geology of North America, v. 0–2—Hydrogeology: Boulder, Colo., Geological Society of America, p. 189–200.

Smith, G.S., and Tiner, R.W., Jr., 1992, Current status and recent trends in wetlands of the Lake Erie and Delaware Estuary coastal zones of Pennsylvania (1986–1989): Newton Corner, Mass., U.S. Fish and Wildlife Service, 7 p.

Tiner, R.W., Jr., 1987, Mid-Atlantic wetlands — A disappearing natural treasure: Newton Corner, Mass., U.S. Fish and Wildlife Service and U.S. Environmental Protection Agency cooperative publication, 28 p.

_____1990, Pennsylvania's wetlands — Current status and recent trends: Newton Corner, Mass., U.S. Fish and Wildlife Service, 104 p.

Tiner, R.W., Jr., and Anderson, J.C., 1986, Current status and recent trends in wetlands of the Lake Erie coastal zone of Pennsylvania: U.S. Fish and Wildlife Service, Newton Corner, Mass., p. 12.

Tiner, R.W., Jr., and Finn, J.T., 1986, Status and recent trends of wetlands in five Mid-Atlantic States — Delaware, Maryland, Pennsylvania, Virginia, and West Virginia: Newton Corner, Mass., U.S. Fish and Wildlife Service, 40 p.

Tiner, R.W., Jr., and Wilen, B.O., 1988, Wetlands of the Delaware River Basin, *in* Majumdar, S.K., Miller, E.W., and Sage, L.E., eds., Ecology and restoration of the Delaware River Basin: Easton, Pennsylvania Academy of Science, p. 187–201.

Wetzel, Kim, 1986, Pennsylvania surface-water resources, *in* U.S. Geological Survey, National water summary 1985 — Hydrologic events and surface-water resources: U.S. Geological Survey Water-Supply Paper 2300, p. 391–398.

Wood, C.R., Flippo, H.N., Jr., Lescinsky, J.B., and Barker, J.L., 1972, Water resources of Lehigh County, Pennsylvania: Pennsylvania Geological Survey, 4th series, Water Resource Report 31, 263 p.

FOR ADDITIONAL INFORMATION: District Chief, U.S. Geological Survey, 840 Market Street, Lemoyne, PA 17043; Regional Wetland Coordinator, U.S. Fish and Wildlife Service, 300 Westgate Center Drive, Hadley, MA 01035

Prepared by
Annette C. Heist and Andrew G. Reif,
U.S. Geological Survey

Puerto Rico
Wetland Resources

The island of Puerto Rico, located in the northern Caribbean Sea, and its principal offshore islands of Vieques, Culebra, and Mona have abundant wetland resources. The subtropical climate, abundant rainfall, and complex topographic and geologic features of these islands give rise to wetlands ranging from the rare and unusual cloud forests in the highlands to extensive mangrove forests, seagrasses, and coral reefs along the northern and southern coasts. However, wetland resources of Puerto Rico have declined during the last several hundred years as a result of an increase in agricultural development, population, and tourism. Some types of wetlands, such as the bloodwood (*Pterocarpus officinalis*) forests (fig. 1), have been reduced to only a few remnants.

Wetlands are among the most biologically productive areas in the islands. The wetlands associated with the rain forest in the interior highlands of Puerto Rico contain many rare plant and animal species not found in other parts of the island. Runoff from wetlands in the higher elevations of the island provides a source of water used for public supply by several cities. Coastal wetlands, such as mangrove forests, seagrass beds, and coral reefs, provide breeding grounds and nursery areas for a variety of juvenile fish, crustaceans, and other species in the food web (López and others, 1988). In this manner, coastal wetlands contribute to the biological productivity of shallow marine waters around the islands. Wetlands also stabilize shorelines by trapping and holding unconsolidated sediments and dampen potentially damaging storm surges and wave action.

The value of Puerto Rican wetlands to wildlife is well documented. For example, the salt flats of Cabo Rojo, on the southwestern coast, provide resting and feeding areas for thousands of migratory shorebirds en route between North and South America. Before the drainage of coastal wetlands for agricultural purposes, freshwater marshes like those of the Laguna Cartagena, Laguna Guánica, and Ciénaga El Anegado provided habitat for more than 100 species of resident and migratory birds. The wetlands of the central highlands are the last stronghold of the endangered Puerto Rican parrot. Even wetlands like those within metropolitan San Juan (Laguna La Torrecilla, Torrecilla Baja, Laguna de Piñones to Punta Vacia Talega) provide excellent wildlife habitat, support economically valuable fisheries, and provide recreation and educational opportunities for an urban populace. Thirty-eight species of finfish and shellfish and 46 bird species, some rare or endangered like the yellow-shouldered blackbird, brown pelican, masked duck, West Indian whistling duck, and white-crowned pigeon, have been ob-

served in the area. Also, the beaches associated with these urban wetlands provide nesting sites for the endangered hawksbill and leatherback turtles (del Llano and others, 1986).

TYPES AND DISTRIBUTION

Wetlands are lands transitional between terrestrial and deepwater habitats where the water table usually is at or near the land surface or the land is covered by shallow water (Cowardin and others, 1979). The distribution of wetlands and deepwater habitats in Puerto Rico is shown in figure 2A; only wetlands are discussed herein.

Wetlands can be vegetated or nonvegetated and are classified on the basis of their hydrology, vegetation, and substrate. In this summary, wetlands are classified according to the system proposed by Cowardin and others (1979), which is used by the U.S. Fish and Wildlife Service (FWS) to map and inventory the Nation's wetlands. At the most general level of the classification system, wetlands are grouped into five ecological systems: Palustrine, Lacustrine, Riverine, Estuarine, and Marine. The Palustrine System includes only wetlands, whereas the other systems comprise wetlands and deepwater habitats. Wetlands of the systems that occur in Puerto Rico are described below.

System	Wetland description
Palustrine	Nontidal and tidal-freshwater wetlands in which vegetation is predominantly trees (forested wetlands); shrubs (scrub-shrub wetlands); persistent or nonpersistent emergent, erect, rooted herbaceous plants (persistent- and nonpersistent-emergent wetlands); or submersed and (or) floating plants (aquatic beds). Also, intermittently to permanently flooded open-water bodies of less than 20 acres in which water is less than 6.6 feet deep.
Lacustrine	Nontidal and tidal-freshwater wetlands within an intermittently to permanently flooded lake or reservoir larger than 20 acres and (or) deeper than 6.6 feet. Vegetation, when present, is predominantly nonpersistent emergent plants (nonpersistent-emergent wetlands), or submersed and (or) floating plants (aquatic beds), or both.
Riverine	Nontidal and tidal-freshwater wetlands within a channel. Vegetation, when present, is same as in the Lacustrine System.
Estuarine	Tidal wetlands in low-wave-energy environments where the salinity of the water is greater than 0.5 part per thousand (ppt) and is variable owing to evaporation and the mixing of seawater and freshwater.
Marine	Tidal wetlands that are exposed to waves and currents of the open ocean and to water having a salinity greater than 30 ppt.

In Puerto Rico, the Lacustrine and Riverine Systems consist largely of deepwater habitats. Lacustrine wetlands are limited to shallow areas of lakes and reservoirs. Riverine wetlands are limited to the shallows of river channels and canals. Where the stream current is swift, these wetland areas typically are nonvegetated. When vegetated, lacustrine and riverine wetlands generally are characterized by plants that grow in aquatic beds on or below the surface of the water. Some of the more common plants in these wetlands

Figure 1. Bloodwood trees at Pterocarpus Forest near Humacao, Puerto Rico. *(Photograph courtesy of Conservation Trust of Puerto Rico.)*

are rooted aquatic plants, such as water lily, fanwort, pondweed, hornwort, and southern naiad, and floating aquatic plants such as duckweed, bladderwort, and water hyacinth.

Most of the wetlands in Puerto Rico and its principal offshore islands are palustrine or estuarine. One type of palustrine wetland that is of particular interest in Puerto Rico is the bloodwood forest. Bloodwood forests, which are common in parts of Central and South America, are now rare in Puerto Rico. Bloodwood trees tolerate low salinity and can grow in nearly pure stands at the brackish limits of the Estuarine System or form swamps (forested wetlands) in the interior. Bloodwood forests share numerous characteristics with cypress swamps of the Southeastern United States. Like cypress, bloodwood trees exist in nearly pure stands or mixed with a variety of other species of trees and shrubs. Epiphytes (plants that grow on other plants) are common on the trees, and typically ferns are the prevalent understory species (Alvarez-López, 1990). Growth forms of these two trees are similar; both cypress and bloodwood can develop buttressed trunks and commonly have modified surface

roots that form kneelike structures (Bacon, 1990). The largest of the remaining bloodwood forests in Puerto Rico is the Pterocarpus Forest (fig. 1), which has an area of 370 acres and is located near Humacao on the eastern coast. Much smaller stands of bloodwood trees exist in the Sierra de Luquillo Mountains (fig. 2B) and at sites near Dorado, Mayagüez, and Patillas (fig. 2A).

Three other important palustrine wetland types, the cloud forest, colorado forest, and palm forest (forested or scrub-shrub wetlands), exist throughout Puerto Rico on the high mountain slopes. On the highest mountaintops are the cloud forests, in which gnarled evergreen trees 15 to 20 feet tall predominate. The more common trees in these areas include roble de sierra, nemocá, jusillo, oreganillo, and guayabota (Ewel and Whitmore, 1973). Trees in the cloud forest stay moist from nearly continuous cloud cover and support an abundance of epiphytic growth. Palo colorado, called titi in the Southeastern United States, is the dominant tree species in colorado forests, which are most common at elevations greater than about 2,500 feet and below cloud forests. This species is shrublike in the

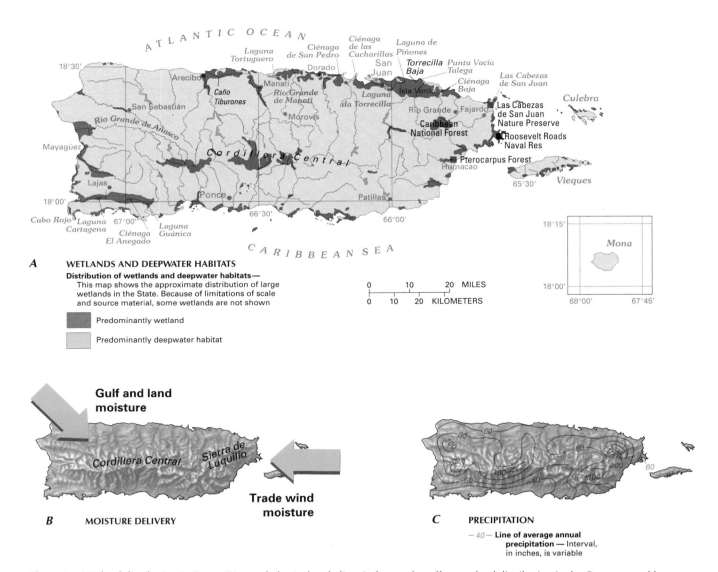

Figure 2. Wetland distribution in Puerto Rico and physical and climatic factors that affect wetland distribution in the Commonwealth. **A**, Distribution of wetlands and deepwater habitats. **B**, Principal sources and patterns of delivery of moisture into Puerto Rico. **C**, Average annual precipitation in Puerto Rico. (*Sources: A, T.E. Dahl, U.S. Fish and Wildlife Service, unpub. data, 1991. B, Colón-Dieppa and others, 1991. C, Colón-Dieppa, 1986.*)

United States, but in Puerto Rico it can grow to a height of more than 30 feet and have a trunk diameter of more than 6 feet (Lugo and Brown, 1988). At elevations between 1,500 and 3,000 feet, mountain slopes generally are covered by palm forests, where nearly pure stands of sierra palms predominate. The sierra palm is also an important component of flood-plain wetlands. Some investigators believe that these montane palm forests are an early successional stage in areas subject to landslides or other forms of severe erosion (Beard, 1955). Although the total acreage of Puerto Rico's montane wetlands is unknown, the Caribbean National Forest in the Cordillera Central supports an estimated 933 acres of cloud forest, 8,490 acres of colorado forest, and 5,088 acres of palm forest.

Freshwater marshes (palustrine emergent wetlands) are common throughout the island, especially along the northern coast. In some areas, these freshwater marshes have been drained for sugar cane cultivation and pasture. Among the largest freshwater marshes are Caño Tiburones near Arecibo, Laguna Cartagena at Lajas, Ciénaga de San Pedro and Ciénaga de las Cucharillas along the northern coast, and Ciénaga Baja near Río Grande. In the deeper marshes, cattail is the most common emergent plant, although sawgrass and giant sedge also are common. The shallower marshes have a more complex species composition and soils that are saturated for shorter periods during the year. Common plants in shallow marshes are swamp fern, sedges, river grass, spike rush, panic grass, joint grass, and beakrush (U.S. Army Engineer Environmental Laboratory, 1978). The large marsh complex at Laguna Tortuguero near Manatí is the only documented spring- and seep-fed marsh in Puerto Rico (Quiñones-Márquez and Fusté, 1978). Water that enters the limestone aquifers in the karstic region of the island's interior discharges upward in the form of springs and seeps and keeps the soil saturated. Nearly 700 plant species, many of which are rare, endangered, or endemic to Puerto Rico, have been identified in this marsh (Lugo and Brown, 1988).

The most extensive estuarine wetlands are the mangrove forests (forested or scrub-shrub wetlands) in which red, black, and white mangrove and buttonwood predominate. Mangroves stabilize nearshore overwash islands, fringe the coastal shoreline, form extensive forests along estuarine rivers, and grow in basins that trap saltwater (Lugo and Brown, 1988). The largest mangrove stand in Puerto Rico is located just east of metropolitan San Juan in an area that includes about 2,500 acres of wetlands, beaches, and associated open-water habitats. In areas along the southern coast of the island, which are subject to drier climatic conditions, salt flats or salinas wetlands (primarily unconsolidated-shore wetlands) commonly exist, generally in association with mangrove-dominated habitats. These extremely saline environments develop where tidal saltwater is trapped and evaporated. The high salt content of soils in the flats can be tolerated by only a few plants, and the most saline of the flats are nonvegetated. An excellent example of this wetland type is the wetland at Cabo Rojo, in the extreme southwestern part of Puerto Rico.

Estuarine marshes (emergent wetlands) are uncommon in Puerto Rico. They usually form a narrow transition zone between mangrove-dominated wetlands and adjacent freshwater wetlands. Plant species in estuarine marshes typically include sawgrass, cattails, and leather ferns.

Open-water areas of the Estuarine and Marine Systems contain deepwater habitats and wetlands. The substrate and associated plants, rocks, or coral of a permanently flooded area constitute deepwater habitat, whereas areas that are exposed during even the lowest spring tide are classified wetland. In Puerto Rico, open-water estuarine wetlands can be nonvegetated or vegetated. The non-vegetated estuarine wetlands are primarily beaches, sand bars, and tidal flats (unconsolidated-shore wetlands), and the vegetated wetlands are mostly seagrass beds (aquatic-bed wetlands). Similarly, Puerto Rico's marine wetlands include unconsolidated shore and aquatic-

bed wetlands, and in areas where coral reefs are exposed at extreme low tides, they too are considered wetlands.

HYDROLOGIC SETTING

The hydrologic setting of Puerto Rico is the major factor that controls the diversity and uniqueness of wetlands on the island. Local geohydrologic characteristics differ throughout the island largely because of variations in the geology, topography, and climate. In the mountainous Cordillera Central and Sierra de Luquillo (fig. 2B), which have peak elevations that exceed 4,300 feet above sea level, rainfall and runoff rates are high. The axis of the central mountain range, the Cordillera Central, trends east-west, and the core of the mountains is composed primarily of folded, faulted, intrusive volcanic rocks and sedimentary rocks. Along the northern flank of the mountains, a series of northward-dipping limestone formations dissected by streams and collapsed subterranean drainage features forms a band of mature karst topography that extends nearly to the coastline. These limestone formations constitute some of the most productive aquifers on the island. A flat coastal plain lies near the coast in many parts of the island. The coastal plain is particularly prominent along the southern coast where fan deltas from the southern drainages coalesce. In addition to alluvial fans, there are landslide, marine-terrace, coastal-dune, beach, swamp, and other recent deposits that overlie the older rocks on both the northern and southern coasts (P.G. Olcott, U.S. Geological Survey, written commun., 1993). On the eastern end of the island, the topography is characterized by steep-sided valleys and on the western end by broad, alluvial valleys that overlie volcanic rocks and limestone lenses.

The climate is classified as subtropical according to the life zone maps of the Holdridge classification system commonly used in Puerto Rico (Ewell and Whitmore, 1973). Winter is the coolest and driest season. During winter, there generally are at least 2 months of low precipitation when the region is under the influence of a subtropical high-pressure system. Precipitation in winter and spring generally is associated with moisture-laden frontal systems that approach the islands from the northwest (fig. 2B). Summers are hot and humid. During summer, the islands are no longer under the influence of high atmospheric pressure, and there is a steady westward flow of moist air from the Atlantic Ocean (the trade winds) that is the primary source of summer and fall precipitation.

Precipitation on Puerto Rico's main island varies geographically as well as seasonally. Average annual precipitation ranges from less than 35 inches in some southwestern coastal valleys to more than 200 inches in parts of the montane rain forests (fig. 2C) and averages about 70 to 72 inches per year islandwide. The geographic variation in precipitation is primarily the result of topography and the predominant weather patterns. The northern and southern parts of Puerto Rico's main island are separated by an east-west-trending mountain range, the Cordillera Central, which joins the southwest-northeast-trending Sierra de Luquillo in the eastern part of the island. Precipitation rates are high in the mountains because when atmospheric moisture in the weather systems is forced up the slopes into the cooler air of the higher elevations, the moisture condenses and falls as rain. Along much of the southern coast, annual rainfall totals are low relative to the rest of the island because this area lies in the rain shadow of the surrounding mountains, which intercept the prevailing westward- or southeastward-moving weather systems.

The ratio of precipitation to evapotranspiration also is a factor that affects the type and diversity of wetlands in Puerto Rico. As the ratio of precipitation to evaporation increases, the diversity of wetlands also increases. For example, on the leeward (southern) side of the island, where precipitation is low and evapotranspiration is high, estuarine wetlands predominate. On the windward (northern) side of the island, where precipitation is high, palustrine wetlands are more common. These freshwater wetlands extend along perennial streams from coastal basins inland to some of the mountain slopes and exist in the rain forests at higher elevations (Zack and Román-Más, 1988).

In the northern part of Puerto Rico, freshwater wetlands receive nearly continuous precipitation in the montane rain forests, and wetlands on the coastal plain receive overland runoff and ground-water discharge from the limestone aquifer system (fig. 3). Near the coast, estuarine wetlands receive water from both the ocean and inland sources. In the coastal wetlands on the northern side of the island, direct precipitation is insignificant relative to the other moisture sources. However, the farther inland a wetland is and the greater its elevation, the more important direct precipitation becomes (Lugo and others, 1980).

Because the southern part of Puerto Rico receives less precipitation and has higher evapotranspiration rates than the northern part of the island, it is considered arid in relation to other parts of the island. Even though precipitation is not abundant in this part of the island, it is important to coastal-plain wetlands. Precipitation produces surface runoff, fills the rivers, and recharges the ground-water system. Overland flow, streamflow, and ground water are major sources of moisture for the southern coast's freshwater wetlands and are important sources for its estuarine wetlands. The ground-water system of southern Puerto Rico is entirely contained in the sedimentary aquifers of the coastal plain. Recharge to the aquifers occurs where the coastal plain meets the southern flank of the mountains at river valleys. The southerly flowing rivers are generally ephemeral, reaching the Caribbean Sea and the estuarine wetlands only during periods of high flow in summer and fall. At other times of the year, ground water discharges to the sea and is the only major source of moisture for nontidal wetlands.

Ground water in the valleys on the eastern and western ends of Puerto Rico generally is limited to local alluvial aquifers and is eventually discharged to the ocean. This ground-water discharge supports narrow, discontinuous wetlands along the coast in these areas.

The principal types of wetlands in Puerto Rico and their distribution with respect to elevation are shown in figure 3. The almost continuous precipitation and thin soil layers over insoluble rocks in the higher mountain elevations assure water saturation of the root zone, as well as nearly continuous water-vapor saturation of the atmosphere surrounding the canopy of the montane wetlands. This abundance of water also provides high runoff volumes for the successional wetlands at lower elevations. The water moves downslope into rivers, where it recharges the limestone aquifers. Farther downgradient, the aquifers discharge to rivers and springs, providing water for the lowland and coastal wetlands.

TRENDS

Reliable estimates of Puerto Rico's original wetland acreage are not available, but the wetlands of the island have been greatly reduced in number and size as a result of agricultural development and the growth in population. Virtually every wetland, with the exception of those in the highlands, has been damaged to some extent by attempts to drain the land for other uses. The small size of many of the wetlands increases their susceptibility to destruction (Lugo and Brown, 1988).

More than one-half of the original 30,000 acres of mangrove forests in Puerto Rico has been destroyed. Although mangrove forests are protected by law (Lugo, 1988), mangrove wetlands continue to be filled for housing developments, transportation facilities, highways, and landfills. Some mangrove wetlands are also destroyed by excavation for marinas and canals. A proposed expansion of Luis Muñoz Marín International Airport at Isla Verde would destroy an additional 160 acres of mangrove forest (Fernando J. Rodriguez and Associates, 1991).

Only a few bloodwood forests remain in Puerto Rico. Cintrón (1983) estimated that by 1977, only 14 stands of bloodwood trees having a combined area of about 600 acres existed on the island. Although the species probably was, at one time, distributed throughout the highlands of the interior, it is now limited to the Sierra de

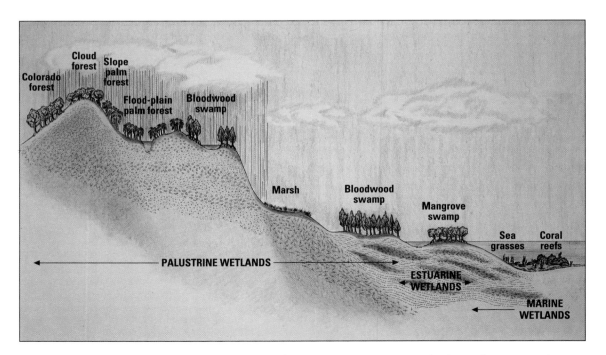

Figure 3. Generalized geohydrologic setting of wetlands in Puerto Rico. *(Source: Wetland types from Lugo and Brown, 1988.)*

Luquillo (Alvarez-López, 1990). A number of coastal stands that were documented earlier this century no longer exist. Although the large bloodwood forest at Humacao was recently brought under public ownership, most wetlands of this type are privately owned.

Over a period of several hundred years, large acreages of palustrine wetland were converted to agricultural use in the coastal-plain regions of Puerto Rico. For example, the Caño Tiburones wetland originally covered more than 6,000 acres but has, since 1917, been drained by pumping for land reclamation (Zack and Class-Cacho, 1984). The remaining mangrove swamp encompasses about 250 acres (A.L. Zack, U.S. Geological Survey, written commun., 1994). This trend has been reversed in recent years because of the declining profitability of sugar cane production. Agricultural areas that required intensive water management by draining and pumping are now being allowed to go fallow. Water levels in these areas have risen, and the abandoned farms are reverting to marsh. However, many of these areas are now subject to conversion for commercial development.

CONSERVATION

Many government agencies and private organizations participate in wetland conservation in Puerto Rico. The most active agencies and organizations and some of their activities are listed in table 1.

Federal wetland activities. — Development activities in Puerto Rico wetlands are regulated by several Federal statutory prohibitions and incentives that are intended to slow wetland losses. Some of the more important of these are contained in the 1899 Rivers and Harbors Act; the 1972 Clean Water Act and amendments; the 1985 Food Security Act; the 1990 Food, Agriculture, Conservation, and Trade Act; the 1986 Emergency Wetland Resources Act; and the 1972 Coastal Zone Management Act. In the following description of wetland-related Federal legislation, regulations that apply to States also apply to Puerto Rico.

Table 1. Selected wetland-related activities of government agencies and private organizations in Puerto Rico, 1993

[Source: Classification of activities is generalized from information provided by agencies and organizations. •, agency or organization participates in wetland-related activity; ..., agency or organization does not participate in wetland-related activity. MAN, management; REG, regulation; R&C, restoration and creation; LAN, land acquisition; R&D, research and data collection; D&I, delineation and inventory]

Agency or organization	MAN	REG	R&C	LAN	R&D	D&I
FEDERAL						
Department of Agriculture						
Consolidated Farm Service Agency	...	•	...	...	...	...
Forest Service	•	...	•	•	•	•
Natural Resources Conservation Service	...	•	•	...	•	•
Department of Commerce						
National Oceanic and Atmospheric Administration	•	•	...	...	•	...
Department of Defense						
Army Corps of Engineers	•	•	•	•	...	•
Military reservations	•	...	...	...	...	...
Department of the Interior						
Fish and Wildlife Service	•	...	•	•	•	•
Geological Survey	...	...	...	•	•	...
National Biological Service	...	...	...	...	•	...
National Park Service	•	...	•	•	•	•
Environmental Protection Agency	...	•	...	...	•	•
COMMONWEALTH						
Department of Environmental and Natural Resources	•	•	•	•	•	•
PRIVATE						
Conservation Trust of Puerto Rico	•	...	...	•	•	...

Section 10 of the Rivers and Harbors Act gives the U.S. Army Corps of Engineers (Corps) authority to regulate certain activities in navigable waters. Regulated activities include diking, deepening, filling, excavating, and placing of structures. The related section 404 of the Clean Water Act is the most often-used Federal legislation protecting wetlands. Under section 404 provisions, the Corps issues permits regulating the discharge of dredged or fill material into wetlands. Permits are subject to review and possible veto by the U.S. Environmental Protection Agency (EPA), and the FWS has review and advisory roles. Section 401 of the Clean Water Act grants to States and eligible Indian Tribes the authority to approve, apply conditions to, or deny section 404 permit applications on the basis of a proposed activity's probable effects on the water quality of a wetland.

Most farming, ranching, and silviculture activities are not subject to section 404 regulation. However, the "Swampbuster" provision of the 1985 Food Security Act and amendments in the 1990 Food, Agriculture, Conservation, and Trade Act discourage (through financial disincentives) the draining, filling, or other alteration of wetlands for agricultural use. The law allows exemptions from penalties in some cases, especially if the farmer agrees to restore the altered wetland or other wetlands that have been converted to agricultural use. The Wetlands Reserve Program of the 1990 Food, Agriculture, Conservation, and Trade Act authorizes the Federal Government to purchase conservation easements from landowners who agree to protect or restore wetlands. The Consolidated Farm Service Agency (formerly the Agricultural Staibilization and Conservation Service) administers the Swampbuster provisions and Wetlands Reserve Program. The Natural Resources Conservation Service (formerly the Soil Conservation Service) compliance with Swampbuster provisions and assists farmers in the identification of wetlands and in the development of wetland protection, restoration, or creation plans.

The 1986 Emergency Wetland Resources Act and the 1972 Coastal Zone Management Act and amendments encourage wetland protection through funding incentives. The Emergency Wetland Resources Act requires States to address wetland protection in their Statewide Comprehensive Outdoor Recreation Plans to qualify for Federal funding for State recreational land; the National Park Service provides guidance to States in developing the wetland component of their plans. Coastal and Great Lakes States that adopt coastal-zone management programs and plans approved by the National Oceanic and Atmospheric Administration are eligible for Federal funding and technical assistance through the Coastal Zone Management Act.

Federal agencies acquire and manage wetlands at numerous locations in Puerto Rico. The Caribbean National Forest, administrated by the U.S. Forest Service, encompasses the rain forest wetlands of El Yunque and the surrounding highlands. The FWS also actively manages wetlands as part of the National Wildlife Refuge system and has recently acquired the freshwater wetlands of Laguna Cartagena. Management and restoration plans for the lagoon are being developed cooperatively with the municipality of Lajas. The U.S. Navy manages wetlands on their reservations at Roosevelt Roads and on the island of Vieques.

Commonwealth wetland activities. — Many of Puerto Rico's wetlands are in public ownership. Theoretically, under the Spanish law still in effect, all mangrove forests are owned by the Commonwealth of Puerto Rico because they are within the maritime (intertidal) zone (Lugo, 1988). Large areas of mangrove forests, having been set aside years ago as a future source of fuel, are managed by the Puerto Rico Department of Environmental and Natural Resources as part of the Commonwealth forest system. Wetland management by the Department is not limited to estuarine habitats. Freshwater wetlands in the Pterocarpus Forest and Laguna Tortuguero are also under the Department's control.

Under the authority of the Coastal Zone Management Act, the

Commonwealth has developed a comprehensive management plan of which wetland protection, particularly of mangrove wetlands, is an integral part. Certification of consistency with the plan is required before any Federal permits or licenses are granted for activities in the coastal zone. The Planning Board of the Commonwealth is the primary agency responsible for administration of the plan.

A number of other planning documents have been developed to guide wetland-management activities. The Department of Environmental and Natural Resources, FWS, and EPA have independently prepared prioritized listings of important wetland-resource areas. The Natural Heritage Program within the Department of Environmental and Natural Resources has also developed restoration and management plans for wetlands of exceptional importance such as those at Caño Tiburones and Laguna Guánica.

Private wetland activities. — The Conservation Trust of Puerto Rico is the principal private organization actively involved in the preservation and management of wetlands in Puerto Rico. The Conservation Trust is a privately funded institution that acquires and manages wetlands and other historical properties of notable and cultural significance in Puerto Rico. For example, the Conservation Trust, in cooperation with the Puerto Rico Department of Environmental and Natural Resources, manages the Department's lands at Las Cabezas de San Juan Nature Reserve near Fajardo at the eastern end of the island.

References Cited

Alvarez-López, Migdalia, 1990, Ecology of *Pterocarpus officinalis* forested wetlands of Puerto Rico, *in* Lugo, A.E., Brinson, Marlo, and Brown, Sandra, eds., Forested wetlands, Ecosystems of the World, v. 15: New York, Elsevier, p. 251–265.

Bacon, P.R., 1990, Ecology and management of swamp forests in the Guianas and Caribbean region, *in* Lugo, A.E., Brinson, Marlo, and Brown, Sandra, eds., Forested wetlands — Ecosystems of the World, v. 15: New York, Elsevier, p. 213–225.

Beard, J.S., 1955, The classification of tropical American vegetation types: Ecology, v. 36, no. 1, p. 89–100.

Cintrón, B.B., 1983, Coastal freshwater swamp forests — Puerto Rico's most endangered ecosystem?, *in* Lugo, A.E., ed., Los Bosques de Puerto Rico: Río Piedras, Puerto Rico, U.S. Department of Agriculture Forest Service, Institute of Tropical Forestry, p. 249–282.

Colón-Dieppa, Eloy, 1986, Puerto Rico Surface-Water Resources, *in* U.S. Geological Survey, National water summary 1985 — Hydrologic events and surface water resources: U.S. Geological Survey Water-Supply Paper 2300, p. 399–406.

Colón-Dieppa, Eloy, Torres-Sierra, Heriberto, and Colón J.A., 1991, Puerto Rico floods and droughts, *in* U.S. Geological Survey, National water summary, 1988–89 — Hydrologic events and floods and droughts: U.S. Geological Survey Water-Supply Paper 2375, p. 475–481.

Cowardin, L.M., Carter, Virginia, Golet, F.C., and LaRoe, E.T., 1979, Classification of wetlands and deepwater habitats of the United States: U.S. Fish and Wildlife Service Report FWS/OBS –79/31, 131 p.

Dahl, T.E., 1991, Wetland Resources of the United States: St. Petersburg Fla., U.S. Fish and Wildlife Service special map, scale 1:3,168,000.

del Llano, Manuel, Colón, J.A., and Chabert, J.L., 1986, A directory of neotropical wetlands, *in* Scott, D.A., and Carbonell, Montserrat (compilers): Cambridge, U.K., International Union for Conservation of Nature and Natural Resources and Slimbridge, U.K., International Waterfowl Research Bureau, p. 559–571.

Ewel, J.J., and Whitmore, J.L., 1973, The ecological life zones of Puerto Rico and the U.S. Virgin Islands: U.S. Forest Service Research Paper ITF–18, 72 p.

Fernando J. Rodriguez and Associates, 1991, Environmental assessment, proposed master plan report improvements—Luis Muñoz Marín International Airport (prepared for Puerto Rico Ports Authority): San Juan, Puerto Rico, Fernando J. Rodriguez and Associates, Report No. 81.06 [Revised 1992], [400 p.].

López, J.M., Stoner, A.W., García, J.R., and García-Muñíz, Iván, 1988, Marine food webs associated with Caribbean islands mangrove wetlands: Acta Científica, v. 2, no. 2–3 p. 94–123.

Lugo, A.E., 1988, The mangroves of Puerto Rico are in trouble: Acta Científica, v. 2, no. 2–3, p. 124.

Lugo, A.E., and Brown, Sandra, 1988, The wetlands of the Caribbean Islands: Acta Científica, v. 2, no. 2–3, p. 48–61.

Lugo, A.E., Twilley, R.R., Patterson-Zucca, Carol, 1980, The role of black mangrove forests in the productivity of coastal ecosystems in South Florida — Report to the Southern Forest Experiment Station, U.S. Environmental Protection Agency: Gainesville, University of Florida, Center for Wetlands, 281 p.

Quiñones-Márquez, Ferdinand, and Fusté, L.A., 1978, Limnology of Laguna Tortuguero, Puerto Rico: U.S. Geological Survey Water-Resources Investigations Report 77–122, 84 p.

U.S. Army Engineer Environmental Laboratory, 1978, Preliminary guide to wetlands of Puerto Rico: U.S. Army Engineer Waterways Experiment Station Technical Report Y–78–3, 77 p.

Zack, A.L., and Class-Cacho, Angel, 1984, Restoration of freshwater in the Caño Tiburones area, Puerto Rico: U.S. Geological Survey Water-Resources Investigations Report 83–4071, 33 p., 1 plate.

Zack, Allen, and Román-Más, Angel, 1988, Hydrology of the Caribbean Islands Wetlands: Acta Científica, v. 2, no. 2–3 p. 65–73.

FOR ADDITIONAL INFORMATION: District Chief, U.S. Geological Survey, P.O. Box 364424, San Juan, PR 00936; Regional Wetland Coordinator, U.S. Fish and Wildlife Service, 1875 Century Building, Atlanta, GA 30345

Prepared by
D. Briane Adams, U.S. Geological Survey, and John M. Hefner, U.S. Fish and Wildlife Service

Rhode Island
Wetland Resources

Wetlands cover about 10 percent of Rhode Island's land surface (Tiner, 1989) and are an important component of the State's natural resources. Rhode Island's wetlands are valued for the environmental and economic benefits they provide, such as wildlife habitat, water-quality improvement, flood and erosion control, recreational activities, and esthetic beauty (fig. 1). Wetlands provide important food, shelter, breeding, and nursery habitats for shellfish, fish, birds and other wildlife. Undeveloped flood-plain wetlands along the rivers in the State provide natural storage that helps regulate floodwaters. Wetland vegetation can inhibit flood erosion when streams swell out of their banks. Acquiring flood-plain wetlands to protect them from development was found to be the most cost-effective approach to limit future flood damage along the Pawtuxet River near Warwick (U.S. Army Corps of Engineers, 1991).

TYPES AND DISTRIBUTION

Wetlands are lands transitional between terrestrial and deepwater habitats where the water table usually is at or near the land surface or the land is covered by shallow water (Cowardin and others, 1979). The distribution of wetlands and deepwater habitats in Rhode Island is shown in figure 2*A*; only wetlands are discussed herein.

Wetlands can be vegetated or nonvegetated and are classified on the basis of their hydrology, vegetation, and substrate. In this summary, wetlands are classified according to the system proposed by Cowardin and others (1979), which is used by the U.S. Fish and Wildlife Service (FWS) to map and inventory the Nation's wetlands. At the most general level of the classification system, wetlands are grouped into five ecological systems: Palustrine, Lacustrine, Riverine, Estuarine, and Marine. The Palustrine System includes only wetlands, whereas the other systems comprise wetlands and deepwater habitats. Wetlands of the systems that occur in Rhode Island are described below.

System	Wetland description
Palustrine	Nontidal and tidal-freshwater wetlands in which vegetation is predominantly trees (forested wetlands); shrubs (scrub-shrub wetlands); persistent or nonpersistent emergent, erect, rooted herbaceous plants (persistent- and nonpersistent-emergent wetlands); or submersed and (or) floating plants (aquatic beds). Also, intermittently to permanently flooded open-water bodies of less than 20 acres in which water is less than 6.6 feet deep.
Lacustrine	Nontidal and tidal-freshwater wetlands within an intermittently to permanently flooded lake or reservoir larger than 20 acres and (or) deeper than 6.6 feet. Vegetation, when present, is predominantly nonpersistent emergent plants (nonpersistent-emergent wetlands), or submersed and (or) floating plants (aquatic beds), or both.
Riverine	Nontidal and tidal-freshwater wetlands within a channel. Vegetation, when present, is same as in the Lacustrine System.
Estuarine	Tidal wetlands in low-wave-energy environments where the salinity of the water is greater than 0.5 part per thousand (ppt) and is variable owing to evaporation and the mixing of seawater and freshwater.
Marine	Tidal wetlands that are exposed to waves and currents of the open ocean and to water having a salinity greater than 30 ppt.

The most recent inventory of Rhode Island wetlands mapped about 65,000 acres of wetlands statewide (Tiner, 1989). Wetlands were mapped from aerial photographs taken from 1974 through 1977 for the FWS National Wetlands Inventory Project. Most of the State's wetlands were classified as palustrine (fig. 2*B*). Palustrine forested wetlands can be found throughout the State and are the most abundant wetland type, accounting for 73 percent of Rhode Island's wetlands (Tiner, 1989, table 5). Most of these forested wetlands are deciduous, red maple swamps. Red maple grows in most inland wetlands because it tolerates a wide range of flooding and soil saturation conditions (Metzler and Tiner, 1992). The vegetation found with red maple, in the understory and intermixed or codominating in the canopy, differs according to nutrient availability and water regime.

Atlantic white cedar wetlands, which are palustrine evergreen-forested wetlands, are most abundant in southwestern Rhode Island (Laderman and others, 1987). These freshwater wetlands contain a distinctive plant community that grows under conditions too extreme for most other northeastern trees: standing water for one-half of the growing season or longer, highly acidic waters, and low nutrient availability. Atlantic white cedar swamps were once more common in Rhode Island; many cedar swamps have changed over time to red maple and other types of swamps (Tiner, 1989).

Figure 1. Rhode Island's estuarine wetlands benefit both humans and wildlife. *(Photograph courtesy of the Audubon Society of Rhode Island.)*

Palustrine scrub-shrub wetlands account for 8 percent of the State's wetlands. Highbush blueberry, swamp azalea, sweet pepperbush, northern arrowwood, alder, willow, and young red maples are common. Bogs are palustrine scrub-shrub wetlands that are characterized by nutrient-poor, acidic water, constant saturation, and peaty soils. Organic matter decays slowly in bogs and forms deep peat accumulations that can seal off vegetation from direct contact with mineral soil or mineral-rich ground water (Damman and French, 1987). Bogs generally have a well-developed sphagnum mat that contains shrubs such as leatherleaf, sheep laurel, black huckleberry, and blueberry. Pitcher plants and sundews commonly are present — trapped insects provide an important source of nutrients to these plants. Trees are commonly the dominant plants at the outer borders of bogs, where nutrient-enriched seepage water is discharged from the adjacent upland, or they grow as stunted individuals scattered across the bog mat. Tree species may grade from those requiring high nutrient levels (hemlock, larch, and red maple) near the bog's outer border to those with lower nutrient requirements

(Atlantic white cedar) near the inner border (Damman and French, 1987).

Vernal pools are small, generally temporary palustrine wetlands that occur throughout Rhode Island. Because these wetlands dry up by late summer or earlier, they are devoid of fish and thus provide a safe breeding habitat for many amphibian and invertebrate species.

Lacustrine and riverine wetlands compose only a small percentage of Rhode Island's wetland acreage. Lacustrine wetlands in the State include aquatic-bed and nonpersistent-emergent wetlands. Riverine wetlands are present in all of the State's freshwater rivers and their tributaries. Most riverine wetlands in Rhode Island are nonvegetated, but nonpersistent emergent vegetation is visible in slow-flowing, shallow water in the lower reaches of many of the State's rivers and streams, and aquatic beds are established in the deeper water of some clear rivers and streams.

Estuarine wetlands account for 7,000 acres, or about 11 percent, of the State's wetland acreage. Estuarine wetlands have developed behind the barrier beaches of the State's southern coast, from the Connecticut border to Narragansett Bay, and in protected coves and embayments of Narragansett Bay and Block Island. Rhode Island's vegetated estuarine wetlands are primarily salt and brackish marshes (emergent wetlands) that are commonly vegetated by grasses, bulrushes, or cattails. Nonvegetated estuarine intertidal flats and beaches, alternately flooded by tide or exposed to air, also are an important wetland type in Rhode Island.

Marine wetlands account for only 1 percent of the State's total wetland acreage. Marine wetlands, composed primarily of intertidal beaches and rocky shores, are present along the shoreline of the State.

HYDROLOGIC SETTING

Wetlands occur in geologic, topographic, and hydrologic settings that enhance the accumulation and retention of ground water and surface water. Hydrologic processes are the primary factor determining the existence of wetlands; even if the geologic and topographic settings are favorable for wetland formation, unfavorable hydrologic conditions can inhibit wetland formation (Winter, 1988). On an annual basis, precipitation exceeds evapotranspiration losses in Rhode Island (Johnston, 1986). Hydrologic conditions, therefore, favor the formation and maintenance of wetlands throughout the

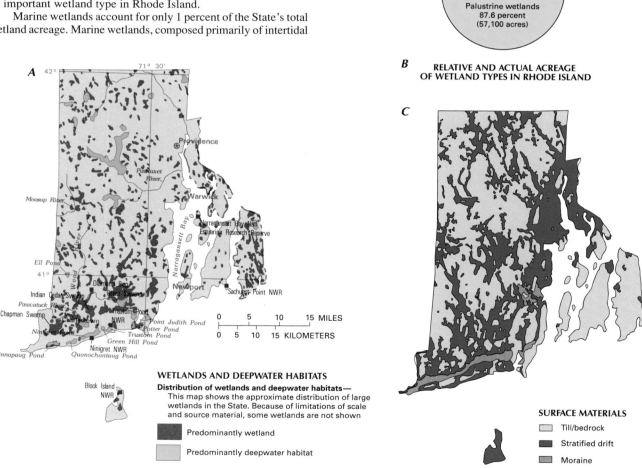

Figure 2. Wetland distribution and acreage in Rhode Island and distribution of surface materials across the State. *A*, Distribution of wetlands and deepwater habitats. *B*, Relative and actual acreage of the most common wetland types, mid-1970's. (No data are available for riverine wetlands.) *C*, Distribution of surface materials. *(Sources: A, T.E. Dahl, U.S. Fish and Wildlife Service, unpub. data, 1991. B, Tiner, 1989. C, Rhode Island Department of Environmental Management, Groundwater Division.)*

State, and wetland location is determined primarily by geologic and topographic controls.

Rhode Island was completely covered by ice during the last glaciation. Large quantities of glacial drift (sediment derived from glacial action) were produced and deposited over bedrock throughout the State (fig. 2C). Drift deposited directly by the ice is called unstratified drift or till. Till is exposed at the land surface in about two-thirds of the State (Johnston and Barlow, 1988), primarily on upland hilltops and slopes. Because till was deposited directly from glacial ice, it is a poorly sorted mixture of boulders, gravel, sand, and silt. Sediment that was eroded and reworked by glacial meltwater is called stratified drift. Because stratified drift was deposited by flowing water in either riverine or lake environments, it consists of well-sorted gravel, sand, and silt. Stratified drift is exposed at the land surface in the remaining one-third of the State and is commonly 75 to 125 feet thick. These deposits are present in topographically low areas, such as narrow stream and river valleys, or occur as broad, flat plains beyond former ice margin positions. Ice-contact stratified drift was deposited directly against ice by glacial-meltwater streams; often these deposits have higher relief due to the control of sedimentation by the ice or valley walls or both.

Wetlands occur throughout Rhode Island in topographic depressions within glacial drift or bedrock. Closed topographic depressions called kettle holes pit the surface of glacial drift. Kettle holes resulted from melting ice blocks that were embedded in glacial sediments. Surface runoff and ground-water discharge collect in small hollows, kettle holes, and other topographic depressions, leading to the formation and maintenance of wetlands. Retention of moisture occurs in depressions which have no outflow or have drainage controlled by bedrock sills, glacial drift, beaver dams, or manmade structures. Seepage wetlands commonly form where the ground-water table intersects the land surface—on concave slopes and at breaks in slope; however, the wetlands are perennial only if ground-water discharge is also perennial (Winter, 1988).

After the glaciers retreated, vegetation colonized the landscape in response to the warming climate; open-water depressions filled in with sediment and organic matter to become freshwater wetlands or remained lakes with wetlands fringing open water. The availability of nutrients determines the types of plants that grow in wetlands. As water moves through soil and surficial materials, it is enriched in nutrients that enhance plant growth. The longer the flow path beneath the surface, the more the water is enriched. Wetlands in upland till and bedrock depressions are primarily areas of discharge from nutrient-poor, local ground-water flow systems, whereas wetlands in lowland valleys underlain by stratified drift receive discharge from nutrient-enriched, longer ground-water flow systems.

Results from a 7-year study of water-table activity in Atlantic white cedar wetlands (Golet and Lowry, 1987) illustrate the effect of geologic setting on wetland hydrology. Water levels fluctuated primarily in response to variations in annual precipitation in all wetlands studied (Golet and Lowry, 1987). However, seasonal water-level activity differed between wetlands because of different sources and amounts of moisture input. Ell Pond and its associated wetlands overlie a deep bedrock fracture (Laderman and others, 1987). Water levels in this wetland fluctuated significantly in response to precipitation input and transpiration losses (Golet and Lowry, 1987). Diamond Bog is a deep kettle-hole wetland within permeable stratified drift, and it receives significant ground-water input. In contrast to Ell Pond, water levels within Diamond Bog remained relatively high even during periods of high evapotranspiration losses.

As the last glacier retreated northward, a succession of till ridges or moraines was deposited at the edge of each ice front. Moraines on Long Island in New York, Block Island in Rhode Island, and Martha's Vineyard and Nantucket Island in Massachusetts mark the maximum extent of the last ice front (Sirkin, 1982; Gold-

smith, 1982). The high topography of the Charlestown moraine, near Charlestown, roughly paralleling the coast, and the Old Saybrook moraine, just north of the Pawcatuck River, mark pauses in the retreat of the ice sheet (Goldsmith, 1982). Drainage of surface water in many valleys or lowland areas is blocked or slowed by the higher topography of glacial moraines or mounds of ice-contact stratified drift. Some of the largest stands of Atlantic white cedar in Rhode Island and also the State's largest wetlands—the 2,150-acre Chapman Swamp, the 960-acre Indian Cedar Swamp, and the 2,970-acre Great Swamp (Laderman, 1989)—occur in basins blocked by moraines. Many other large, shallow wetlands are present in valleys throughout the State owing to drainage blocked by ice-contact stratified drift.

Some of Rhode Island's palustrine wetlands are lowland areas modified by the recent erosion and deposition by rivers—in abandoned river channels, in flood-plain areas, behind levees and overbank sediments adjacent to rivers, and in backswamp areas. These wetlands receive moisture from river flooding and ground-water discharge.

Tidal wetlands form a narrow fringe along coastal areas of the State. Tidal wetlands receive freshwater from upland areas through ground-water discharge and surface-water runoff. Floodwater resulting from high tides or storm flows is temporarily stored on the wetland surface but drains into the tidal river or estuary as the river stage recedes. The drainage of floodwater and surface-water runoff from the wetland surface is slowed by the low slope of coastal areas.

As the last ice sheet melted and water stored as glacial ice returned to the sea, sea level rose and encroached upon land, flooding many stream and river valleys to form estuaries. Narragansett Bay is an estuary formed in such a "drowned" river valley. Tidal wetlands have either migrated inland along estuaries, river valleys, and coastal slopes, or the wetlands have been completely submerged by the rising sea. Some kettle holes were flooded by saltwater, resulting in a change from freshwater to tidal wetlands (Boothroyd and others, 1985). The interconnected Point Judith and Potter Ponds, located perpendicular to the State's southern coast, formed when the sea flooded a series of individual kettle holes. The shallow, elongate salt ponds paralleling the barrier beaches of the State's southern coast—Green Hill, Ninigret, Quonochontaug, Trustom, and Winnapaug Ponds—have formed through the gradual rise in sea level over low-slope outwash plains. Presently, tidal wetlands exist between rising sea level and expanding coastal development and have little area for future inland migration.

TRENDS

There are no statewide estimates of recent wetland losses or alteration; however, wetland losses and alterations continue in Rhode Island despite Federal and State regulation. In the first 5 months of 1993, more than 230 preliminary-determination applications were submitted to the Department of Environmental Management for work proposed in or near freshwater wetlands in the State (Chuck Horbert, Department of Environmental Management, oral commun., 1993). Of these applications for wetland alteration, 149 were approved because the projects would result in insignificant wetland alterations, 17 required formal applications because the projects would cause significant wetland alterations, and the remaining projects were not near wetlands. Generally, the functions for which wetlands are valued operate at a drainage basin or landscape scale, not at the permit site or single-wetland scale. The contribution of a single wetland to landscape functions can depend not only on the actual size of the wetland but also on its setting within a landscape system (Bedford and Preston, 1988). The cumulative impact of individually insignificant, but collectively significant, wetland losses could lead to serious impairment of beneficial wetland functions.

Studies of the sediments deposited in wetlands show that wetlands have been strongly affected by activities within their drainage basins. Postsettlement agricultural and industrial practices in the uplands of northeastern Connecticut were found to be the most important ecological influence on wetlands since glaciation (Thorson, 1990, 1992; Thorson and Harris, 1991). Both the frequency of transitions between wetland types and the rate of sediment accumulation increased by at least one order of magnitude after colonial settlement as compared to the thousands of years before settlement. Cores of bottom sediments from Narragansett Bay show a distinct increase in the percentage of organic accumulation 2 to 3 feet below the surface; the increase marks a change in wetland type from intertidal sand flats to salt marshes. This change in wetland type was caused when dams, built across upstream tributaries for power generation, decreased the downstream transport of sediment (Bricker-Urso and others, 1989). Other wetlands have formed as a result of the numerous dams and impoundments built along rivers throughout the State and the subsequent rise in local water tables; flood-plain wetlands along the Pawcatuck River are examples (Schafer, 1968). These studies indicate that even human activities not located directly within a wetland can affect wetlands owing to the response of wetlands to changing geologic and hydrologic conditions within the landscape system.

CONSERVATION

Many government agencies and private organizations participate in wetland conservation in Rhode Island. The most active agencies and organizations and some of their activities are listed in table 1.

Federal wetland activities.—Development activities in Rhode Island wetlands are regulated by several Federal statutory prohibitions and incentives that are intended to slow wetland losses. Some of the more important of these are contained in the 1899 Rivers and Harbors Act; the 1972 Clean Water Act and amendments; the 1985 Food Security Act; the 1990 Food, Agriculture, Conservation, and Trade Act; the 1986 Emergency Wetlands Resources Act; and the 1972 Coastal Zone Management Act.

Section 10 of the Rivers and Harbors Act gives the U.S. Army Corps of Engineers (Corps) authority to regulate certain activities in navigable waters. Regulated activities include diking, deepening, filling, excavating, and placing of structures. The related section 404 of the Clean Water Act is the most often-used Federal legislation protecting wetlands. Under section 404 provisions, the Corps issues permits regulating the discharge of dredged or fill material into wetlands. Permits are subject to review and possible veto by the U.S. Environmental Protection Agency, and the FWS has review and advisory roles. Section 401 of the Clean Water Act grants to States and eligible Indian Tribes the authority to approve, apply conditions to, or deny section 404 permit applications on the basis of a proposed activity's probable effects on the water quality of a wetland.

Most farming, ranching, and silviculture activities are not subject to section 404 regulation. However, the "Swampbuster" provision of the 1985 Food Security Act and amendments in the 1990 Food, Agriculture, and Trade Act discourage (through financial disincentives) the draining, filling, or other alteration of wetlands for agricultural use. The law allows exemptions from penalties in some cases, especially if the farmer agrees to restore the altered wetland or other wetlands that have been converted to agricultural use. The Wetlands Reserve Program of the 1990 Food, Agriculture, Conservation, and Trade Act authorizes the Federal Government to purchase conservation easements from landowners who agree to protect or restore wetlands. The Consolidated Farm Service Agency (formerly the Agricultural Stabilization and Conservation Service administers the Swampbuster provisions and Wet-

Table 1. Selected wetland-related activities of government agencies and private organizations in Rhode Island, 1993

[Source: Classification of activities is generalized from information provided by agencies and organizations. •, agency or organization participates in wetland-related activity; ..., agency or organization does not participate in wetland-related activity. MAN, management; REG, regulation; R&C, restoration and creation; LAN, land acquisition; R&D, research and data collection; D&I, delineation and inventory]

Agency or organization	MAN	REG	R&C	LAN	R&D	D&I
FEDERAL						
Department of Agriculture						
Consolidated Farm Service Agency	...	•	...	...	...	...
Forest Service	...	...	...	...	...	•
Natural Resources Conservation Service	...	...	•	•	...	•
Department of Commerce						
National Oceanic and Atmospheric Administration	•	•	...	•	•	...
Department of Defense						
Army Corps of Engineers	...	•	•	...	•	...
Military reservations	•	...	...	...	...	...
Department of the Interior						
Fish and Wildlife Service	•	...	•	•	•	•
Geological Survey	...	...	...	...	•	...
National Biological Service	...	...	...	...	•	...
Environmental Protection Agency	...	•	...	...	•	•
STATE						
Coastal Resources Management Council	•	•	...	•	...	•
Department of Environmental Management						
Fish, Wildlife, and Estuarine Resources Division	•	•	•	•	•	...
Freshwater Wetlands Division	•	•	...	...	...	•
Parks and Recreation Division	•	...	•	...	...	...
Water Resources Division	•	...	...	...	...	...
University of Rhode Island	•	...	•	...	•	...
PRIVATE ORGANIZATIONS						
Audubon Society of Rhode Island	•	...	...	•	•	•
Ducks Unlimited	•	...	•	•	...	•
The Champlin Foundation	...	...	...	•	•	...
The Nature Conservancy	•	...	...	•	•	•

lands Reserve Program. The Natural Resources Conservation Service (formerly the Soil Conservation Service) determines compliance with Swampbuster provisions and assists farmers in the identification of wetlands and in the development of wetland protection, restoration, or creation plans.

The 1986 Emergency Wetlands Resources Act and the 1972 Coastal Zone Management Act and amendments encourage wetland protection through funding incentives. The Emergency Wetland Resources Act requires States to address wetland protection in their Statewide Comprehensive Outdoor Recreation Plans to qualify for Federal funding for State recreational land; the National Park Service provides guidance to States in developing the wetland component of their plans. Coastal and Great Lakes States that adopt coastal-zone management programs and plans approved by the National Oceanic and Atmospheric Administration (NOAA) are eligible for Federal funding and technical assistance through the Coastal Zone Management Act.

Federal agencies are responsible for the proper management of wetlands on public lands under their jurisdiction. The FWS protects and manages salt marsh and freshwater wetlands in the Ninigret National Wildlife Refuge. Wetlands are also protected in the Block Island National Wildlife Refuge, the Trustom Pond National Wildlife Refuge, and Sachuest Point National Wildlife Refuge.

State wetland activities.—Wetlands are regulated primarily at the State level in Rhode Island; separate agencies regulate coastal and freshwater wetlands. The Coastal Resources Management Program requires that permits be obtained from the Coastal Resources Management Council for any dredging, filling, or other physical alteration of coastal wetlands and directly contiguous areas, including contiguous freshwater wetlands. Coastal wetlands are defined as any salt marsh that borders on tidal waters and contains certain plant species. Activities in coastal ponds and contiguous upland areas, extending no more than 200 feet inland, also are regulated in order to preserve the integrity of tidal wetlands. The Coastal Resources Management Council has regulatory, planning, and management powers within these specified coastal areas.

Under the Freshwater Wetlands Act, permits must be obtained from the Department of Environmental Management's Division of Freshwater Wetlands for any dredging, filling or other type of alteration to inland wetlands, including adjacent upland areas. Areas subject to regulation as freshwater wetlands include, but are not limited to, any swamp, marsh, bog, pond, vernal pool, river, stream, riverbank, flood plain (as defined by a 100-year-frequency storm), areas subject to flooding and storm flows, emergent and submerged plant communities in any body of water, and the area of land within 50 feet of any bog, swamp, marsh, or pond.

The Department of Environmental Management is the primary land-management agency in Rhode Island. The Department has responsibility for developing and operating some 87,000 acres of State-owned open space, including parks, beaches, water-supply areas, wildlife-habitat reserves, and conservation areas (Rhode Island Department of Administration, 1992). About 2,000 acres of land have recently been acquired on six of the islands in Narragansett Bay. This land is part of the State's Bay Island Park System and provides recreation, conservation, environmental education, and research opportunities. More than 2,000 acres of fish and wildlife habitat and wetlands along the Wood, Pawcatuck, and Moosup Rivers have been acquired by using State and Federal funds. The Department's Fish, Wildlife and Estuarine Resources Division is focusing on anadromous-fish restoration programs on these rivers.

The Narragansett Bay National Estuarine Research Reserve is cooperatively managed by the Department of Environmental Management and NOAA's Office of Ocean and Coastal Resource Management. The 4,950-acre reserve was created under section 315 of the Federal Coastal Zone Management Act and contains undisturbed salt marshes, tidal flats, and open-water habitats. The reserve serves as a natural laboratory and is the site of several interagency research projects.

The Rhode Island Natural Heritage Program compiles and updates rare and endangered animal and plant lists within the State. The program comments on State freshwater-wetlands permit applications, Clean Water Act Section 404 permit applications, and local comprehensive plans. Certain wetland types and rare biological communities are identified by the program for priority protection. The Natural Heritage program, along with nongame research and management projects, is funded by the nongame-wildlife fund, a voluntary contribution on State income tax forms.

The Department of Environmental Management's Freshwater Wetlands Division requires water-quality certification from the Department of Environmental Management's Water Resources Division before approval of any significant wetland alterations. Under section 401 of the Federal Clean Water Act, any activity that results in a discharge, including that of fill into wetlands or State waters, must obtain a section 401 water-quality certification stating that the activity will not result in violation of State surface-water-quality standards. Normal maintenance and improvement of agricultural lands are exempt from State and Federal authority under this program. However, any discharge from exempted activities that might convert open-water areas or wetlands to dry land, impede circulation, or reduce the size of a wetland or water body is subject to section 404 regulation. Enforcement of the antidegradation provisions of State surface-water-quality standards for wetlands provides enhanced wetland protection. Antidegradation provisions provide

for the protection of existing uses in wetlands and the level of water quality necessary to maintain those uses. No degradation is allowed in areas designated as "Outstanding National Resource Waters" such as National Wildlife Refuges, National Parks, State Parks, wildlife areas, and other areas of ecological significance.

Private wetland activities.—Regulation of wetlands in Rhode Island includes consideration of local concerns and issues. Local land-use controls are an additional wetland-protection measure. Fifteen of Rhode Island's 39 communities have established local land trusts (Rhode Island Department of Administration, 1992).

Many of Rhode Island's natural resources have been acquired and protected through cooperative efforts involving private organizations, local land trusts, and State and local governments. The Nature Conservancy, the Champlin Foundation, and State and local governments together have protected endangered-species habitats and unique areas on Block Island. Block Island contains some of the State's rarest ecosystems and most valuable natural habitats; the island has recently been designated as one of 12 bioreserves in the Western Hemisphere by The Nature Conservancy. The Champlin Foundation provides funds for land acquisition to the State, The Nature Conservancy, and The Audubon Society of Rhode Island. The GreenSpace 2000 Project is a statewide plan to protect critical open-space values and functions through a network of tracts and greenways; the plan establishes protection priorities and strategies to reach its goals (Rhode Island Department of Administration, 1992). Save The Bay, the State's largest private, nonprofit environmental group, the Conservation Fund, a national nonprofit group that promotes greenways, and State and local officials are cooperating to implement the plan's goals. Wetlands are identified as critical geographic-resource areas by the plan, and many are priority protection areas in the GreenSpace 2000 Project.

The Audubon Society of Rhode Island owns and manages more than 6,000 acres of land, containing many freshwater and saltwater wetlands, for recreational and educational purposes. Ducks Unlimited provides technical and financial assistance to Federal and State agencies to protect waterfowl habitat in Rhode Island.

References Cited

Bedford, B.L., and Preston, E.M., 1988, Developing the scientific basis for assessing cumulative effects of wetland loss and degradation on landscape functions—Status, perspectives, and prospects: Environmental Management, v. 12, p. 751–771.

Boothroyd, J.C., Friedrich, N.E., and McGinn, S.R., 1985, Geology of microtidal coastal lagoons—Rhode Island: Marine Geology, v. 63, p. 35–76.

Bricker-Urso, Suzanne, Nixon, S.W., Cochran, J.K., Hirschberg, D.J., and Hunt, C.D., 1989, Accretion rates and sediment accumulation in Rhode Island salt marshes: Estuaries, v. 12, p. 300–317.

Cowardin, L.M., Carter, Virginia, Golet, F.C., and LaRoe, E.T., 1979, Classification of wetlands and deepwater habitats of the United States: U.S. Fish and Wildlife Service Report FWS/OBS–79/31, 131 p.

Damman, A.W.H., and French, T.W., 1987, The ecology of peat bogs of the glaciated northeastern United States—A community profile: U.S. Fish and Wildlife Service Biological Report 85(7.16), 100 p.

Goldsmith, Richard, 1982, Recessional moraines and ice retreat in southeastern Connecticut, *in* Larson, G.J., and Stone, B.D., eds., Late Wisconsinan glaciation of New England: Dubuque, Iowa, Kendall/Hunt Publishing Company, p. 61–76.

Golet, F.C., and Lowry, D.J., 1987, Water regimes and tree growth in Rhode Island Atlantic white cedar swamps, *in* Laderman, A.D., ed., Atlantic white cedar wetlands: Boulder, Colo., Westview Press, p. 91–110.

Johnston, H.E., 1986, Rhode Island surface-water resources, *in* U.S. Geological Survey, National water summary 1985—Hydrologic events and surface-water resources: U.S. Geological Survey Water-Supply Paper 2300, p. 407–412.

Johnston, H.E., and Barlow, P.M., 1988, Rhode Island ground-water quality, *in* U.S. Geological Survey, National water summary 1986—Hydrologic events and ground-water quality: U.S. Geological Survey Water-Supply Paper 2325, p. 443–448.

Laderman, A.D., 1989, The ecology of Atlantic white cedar wetlands—A community profile: U.S. Fish and Wildlife Service Biological Report 85(7.21), 114 p.

Laderman, A.D., Golet, F.C., Sorrie, B.A., and Woolsey, H.L., 1987, Atlantic white cedar in the glaciated northeast, *in* Laderman, A.D., ed., Atlantic white cedar wetlands: Boulder, Colo., Westview Press, p. 19–33.

Metzler, K.J., and Tiner, R.W., 1992, Wetlands of Connecticut: Connecticut Geological and Natural History Survey Report of Investigations 13, 115 p.

Rhode Island Department of Administration, 1992, Ocean State outdoors—Rhode Island's comprehensive outdoor recreation plan: Rhode Island Department of Administration, Division of Planning Report 76.

Schafer, J.P., 1968, Surficial geologic map of the Ashaway quadrangle, Connecticut-Rhode Island: U.S. Geological Survey Geologic Quadrangle Map GQ–712, scale 1:24,000.

Sirkin, Les, 1982, Wisconsinan glaciation of Long Island, New York, to Block Island, Rhode Island, *in* Larson, G.J, and Stone, B.D., eds., Late Wisconsinan glaciation of New England: Dubuque, Iowa, Kendall/Hunt Publishing Company, p. 35–57.

Thorson, R.M., 1990, Development of small upland wetlands—A stratigraphic study in northeastern Connecticut: University of Connecticut, School of Engineering, Final Report JHR 90–191, 285 p.

_____1992, Remaking the wetlands in Lebanon, Connecticut—Cultural and natural changes in the postglacial epoch: University of Connecticut, School of Engineering, Final Report JHR 92–215, 157 p.

Thorson, R.M., and Harris, S.L., 1991, How "natural" are inland wetlands? An example from the Trail Wood Audubon Sanctuary in Connecticut, USA: Environmental Management, v. 15, p. 675–687.

Tiner, R.W., 1989, Wetlands of Rhode Island: Newton Corner, Mass., U.S. Fish and Wildlife Service, National Wetlands Inventory, 71 p., 1 app.

U.S. Army Corps of Engineers, 1991, Water resources development—The work of the U.S Army Corps of Engineers in Rhode Island 1991: Waltham, Mass., U.S. Army Corps of Engineers, 60 p.

Winter, T.C., 1988, A conceptual framework for assessing cumulative impacts on the hydrology of nontidal wetlands: Environmental Management, v. 12, p. 605–620.

FOR ADDITIONAL INFORMATION: Chief, Rhode Island Office, U.S. Geological Survey, 237 Pastore Federal Building, Providence, RI 02903; Regional Wetlands Coordinator, U.S. Fish and Wildlife Service, 300 Westgate Center, Hadley, MA 01035

Prepared by
Sandra L. Harris,
U.S. Geological Survey

South Carolina
Wetland Resources

South Carolina has about 4.6 million acres of wetlands, accounting for about 23.4 percent of the surface area of the State (Dahl, 1990). Only two other States, Florida and Louisiana, have a higher percentage of land area as wetlands. Freshwater forested wetlands (fig. 1) are the most common type of wetland in South Carolina.

The benefits of South Carolina's wetlands include enhanced water quality, fish and wildlife productivity, and socioeconomic values. Wetlands enhance water quality by intercepting upland runoff and filtering out nutrients, wastes, and sediment. Fish and wildlife benefit from the abundance of habitat and food that wetlands provide. For example, South Carolina wetlands serve as wintering areas for migrating waterfowl, supporting greater than 30 percent each of American green-winged teal, northern shovelers, mallards, northern pintails, American wigeon, and gadwall that traverse the Atlantic Flyway (Gordon and others, 1989). Socioeconomic values of wetlands include flood protection, erosion control, and groundwater recharge as well as opportunities for hunting, fishing, tourism, and other recreational activities that are economically important to the State.

TYPES AND DISTRIBUTION

Wetlands are lands transitional between terrestrial and deepwater habitats where the water table usually is at or near the land surface or the land is covered by shallow water (Cowardin and others, 1979). The distribution of wetlands and deepwater habitats in South Carolina is shown in figure 2A; only wetlands are discussed herein.

Wetlands can be vegetated or nonvegetated and are classified on the basis of their hydrology, vegetation, and substrate. In this summary, wetlands are classified according to the system proposed by Cowardin and others (1979), which is used by the U.S. Fish and Wildlife Service (FWS) to map and inventory the Nation's wetlands. At the most general level of the classification system, wetlands are grouped into five ecological systems: Palustrine, Lacustrine, Riverine, Estuarine, and Marine. The Palustrine System includes only wetlands, whereas the other systems comprise wetlands and deepwater habitats. Wetlands of the systems that occur in South Carolina are described below.

System	Wetland description
Palustrine	Nontidal and tidal-freshwater wetlands in which vegetation is predominantly trees (forested wetlands); shrubs (scrub-shrub wetlands); persistent or nonpersistent emergent, erect, rooted herbaceous plants (persistent- and nonpersistent-emergent wetlands); or submersed and (or) floating plants (aquatic beds). Also, intermittently to permanently flooded open-water bodies of less than 20 acres in which water is less than 6.6 feet deep.
Lacustrine	Nontidal and tidal-freshwater wetlands within an intermittently to permanently flooded lake or reservoir larger than 20 acres and (or) deeper than 6.6 feet. Vegetation, when present, is predominantly nonpersistent emergent plants (nonpersistent-emergent wetlands), or submersed and (or) floating plants (aquatic beds), or both.
Riverine	Nontidal and tidal-freshwater wetlands within a channel. Vegetation, when present, is same as in the Lacustrine System.
Estuarine	Tidal wetlands in low-wave-energy environments where the salinity of the water is greater than 0.5 part per thousand (ppt) and is variable owing to evaporation and the mixing of seawater and freshwater.
Marine	Tidal wetlands that are exposed to waves and currents of the open ocean and to water having a salinity greater than 30 ppt.

Ninety percent of South Carolina's wetlands are freshwater (palustrine, lacustrine, and riverine) wetlands and occur primarily in the Coastal Plain and the flood plains of rivers and streams in the Blue Ridge and Piedmont Provinces (fig. 2A and 2B). Palustrine forested wetlands encompass 3.7 million acres in South Carolina and constitute 80 percent of the wetlands in the State. Palustrine wetlands include areas commonly referred to as wet pine flatwoods, pocosins, Carolina bays, beaver ponds, bottom-land hardwood forests, swamps, and tidal-freshwater marshes.

Wet pine flatwoods (forested wetlands) are extensive flat areas that have a shallow water table and are dominated by pine (longleaf, loblolly, slash, and pond). These wetlands occur primarily in the Coastal Plain. Although acreage estimates are not available, extensive tracts of wet pine flatwoods occur in the Francis Marion National Forest.

Pocosins (scrub-shrub wetlands) are wetlands vegetated by evergreen shrubs or low-growing trees, such as sweet bay or pond pine. However, vegetation in severely burned pocosins may be dominated by herbaceous plants. The word pocosin is derived from an Indian word meaning low marshy ground or swamp. South Carolina pocosins can be found throughout the Coastal Plain.

Carolina bay wetlands are isolated freshwater wetlands formed in elliptical depressions. Because of their variability in size, depth, and substrate conditions, Carolina bays support plant communities ranging from grass-sedge prairies (emergent wetlands) to cypress-gum swamps (forested wetlands). Carolina bays are scattered throughout the Coastal Plain. The State Heritage Trust Program has identified 2,651 Carolina bays that are 2 acres or larger (Bennett and Nelson, 1991).

Beaver ponds are freshwater forested, scrub-shrub or emergent wetlands typically associated with river flood plains and can be found throughout the State. As beavers impound a stream and flood a bottom-land area, many of the trees are killed, thus opening the

Figure 1. A freshwater forested wetland at the upper end of Lake Marion in South Carolina.

canopy and allowing for growth of herbaceous vegetation. Plant communities associated with South Carolina beaver-pond wetlands include water oak, sweet gum, red maple, buttonbush, and rice cutgrass. The structure of the plant community is influenced by factors such as the age, topography, and substrate soil characteristics of the pond. Arner and Hepp (1989) reported that a 1976 survey revealed that beavers have created an estimated 4,400 acres of wetlands in South Carolina.

Bottom-land hardwood forests and swamps are woody communities that are found primarily on alluvial flood plains. These wetlands, found along the rivers of South Carolina, occur in the Piedmont Province and Coastal Plain. Bottom-land hardwood forests support a variety of tree species including oaks, ashes, maples, hackberries, cypress, and tupelo. The presence of extensive wetlands along a 45-mile segment of the Congaree River has resulted in consideration of the Congaree River for the State Scenic Rivers Program. Within this section of the Congaree River flood plain is the Congaree Swamp National Monument, a 15,000-acre wetland that contains one of the few remaining tracts of old-growth bottom-land hardwoods. The Sumter National Forest in the upper Savannah River Basin contains about 1,500 acres of bottom-land hardwood-forest wetlands, and the U.S. Department of Energy's Savannah River Site contains approximately 34,500 acres of bottom-land hardwood-forest wetlands (Bebber, 1988).

Tidal-freshwater marshes (emergent wetlands) occur along South Carolina's coast, where they are tidally influenced, but freshwater input from precipitation and rivers prevents significant saltwater intrusion from the ocean. Dominant plants in tidal-freshwater marshes include yellow pond lily, arrowheads, and sedges. There are an estimated 46,300 acres of tidal-freshwater marshes in South Carolina (Field and others, 1991), mostly occurring along the Santee River and the rivers that form Winyah Bay (the Sampit, Black, Pee Dee, and Waccamaw), Charleston Harbor (the Cooper and Ashley), and Saint Helena Sound (the Ashepoo, Edisto, and Combahee).

Lacustrine wetlands include the shallows of permanently flooded lakes and reservoirs and intermittent lakes. Common lacustrine wetland plants include American lotus, pickerelweed, duckweed, arrowheads, and sedges. Lacustrine wetlands occur throughout the State, most notably along major reservoirs and in association with ephemeral lakes such as Carolina bays. Along the shores of Lake Marion is the Santee National Wildlife Refuge, a 15,000-acre wetland used by migrating waterfowl.

The Riverine and Marine Systems contain mostly deepwater habitat. Riverine wetlands are limited to shallow freshwater river and stream channels or, in the case of deep rivers, to shallow areas near the bank. South Carolina riverine wetlands can contain floating aquatic plants, such as water lily and nonpersistent emergent plants such as pickerelweed. The Marine System is limited to the

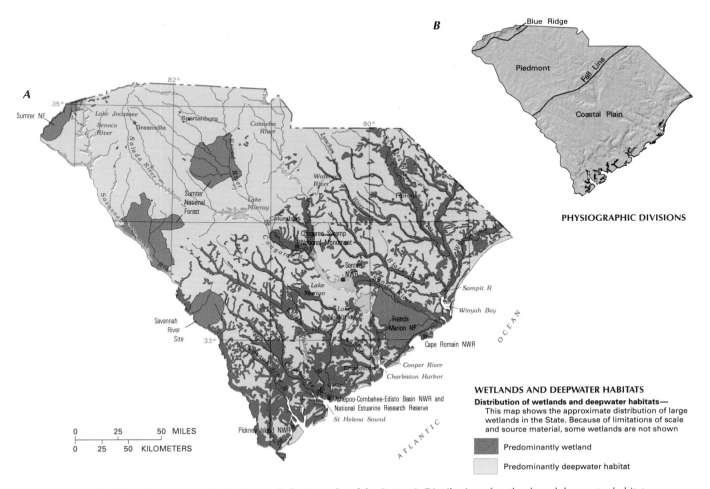

Figure 2. Wetland distribution in South Carolina and physiography of the State. *A*, Distribution of wetlands and deepwater habitats. *B*, Physiography. *(Sources: A, T.E. Dahl, U.S. Fish and Wildlife Service, unpub. data, 1991. B, Physiographic divisions from Fenneman, 1946; landforms data from EROS Data Center.)*

open ocean overlying the continental shelf and its associated coastline.

Estuarine wetlands include intertidal flats and irregularly and regularly tidally flooded salt marshes dominated by emergent vegetation such as saltmeadow cordgrass, black needlerush, and smooth cordgrass. Intertidal flats are generally devoid of vegetation as a result of unstable sand or mud sediments that are regularly exposed and flooded by tides. There are about 32,000 acres of intertidal flats and 366,000 acres of salt-marsh wetlands in South Carolina (Field and others, 1991). The Cape Romain National Wildlife Refuge, a 64,000-acre salt-marsh wetland, is located near the mouth of the Santee River. At the mouth of the Coosawhatchie River is Pickney Island National Wildlife Refuge, a 4,053-acre expanse of salt-marsh wetlands. Nearby are the Ashepoo–Combahee–Edisto Basin National Wildlife Refuge (18,000 acres of salt marsh), and the 144,000-acre Ashepoo–Combahee–Edisto National Estuarine Research Reserve.

HYDROLOGIC SETTING

Wetlands generally develop where the land surface is relatively flat and the water table is shallow. Most of South Carolina's wetlands occur in the Coastal Plain where alluvial, marginal-marine, and marine sediments have been deposited and sometimes reworked in lowland flats or upland depressions. Coastal Plain deposits consist of consolidated and unconsolidated sediments of continental and marine origin that range in thickness from a few feet at the Fall Line to more than 4,000 feet at the southern tip of the State. The gently rolling hills of the Piedmont Province and the mountains of the Blue Ridge Province are underlain by metamorphosed sedimentary, volcanic, and igneous rocks. Where hydric soils occur in the Blue Ridge and Piedmont Provinces, they are commonly overlain by 2 to 5 feet of loam and clay as a result of erosion from agricultural areas (Larry Robinson, Natural Resources Conservation Service, oral commun., 1993). Thus, identification of wetlands in the Blue Ridge and Piedmont Provinces based on the presence of hydric soils has been difficult.

The State's moist climate produces ample precipitation, which finds its way to the wetlands by way of overland runoff, periodic flooding by rivers, and ground-water discharge. Average annual precipitation is 80 inches in the Blue Ridge Province, decreasing to approximately 48 inches in the Piedmont Province and most of the Coastal Plain, and then increasing to about 50 inches near the coast (Purvis and others, 1990). Rainfall is greatest during spring and summer and least in fall. Average annual runoff ranges from 10 inches in the Coastal Plain Province to about 50 inches in the Blue Ridge Province. Annual potential evapotranspiration ranges from about 30 inches in the Blue Ridge Province to about 47 inches in the Coastal Plain. Most evaporation occurs during summer (about 3 to 5 inches per month) and the least occurs during winter (about 1 inch per month).

Pocosins and Carolina bays are examples of isolated wetlands that characteristically have no tributary streams, are not spring fed, and rely on direct precipitation and overland runoff to maintain water volume (Sharitz and Gibbons, 1982). Ground-water recharge has been suggested as an additional source in some situations (Schalles and Shure, 1989). Pocosins are typically characterized by poorly drained mineral soils and peats. Carolina bays, generally found in sandy terrain but typically having a clay layer, are aligned in a northwest-southeast direction.

The structure and function of South Carolina's bottom-land hardwood-forest wetlands are determined primarily by the hydrologic regime of the State's large rivers (Patterson and others, 1985). The principal river basins in South Carolina—the Pee Dee, Santee, Edisto, and Savannah—contain rivers that flow eastward through the Coastal Plain to the sea. They have broad flood plains that are flooded for several months during the winter and during storms. Near the coast, daily tides back up freshwater onto these flood plains. Bottom-land hardwood forests dominated by trees that are tolerant of a long dormant season and occasional flooding during the growing season are particularly well developed on these wide flood plains.

As the rivers flow into the sea, freshwater riverine flow mixes with daily tidal influxes from the ocean. The hydrology of the mixing area is poorly understood. However, a combination of factors including freshwater input, tidal influx, and wind direction and velocity create an environment suitable for tidal-freshwater wetlands.

The flood plains near the mouths of these large rivers and the bays behind the barrier island provide protection from destructive waves and storms. These protected areas allow for the accretion of clay and silt sediments and the establishment of vegetation. The extensive estuarine wetlands of South Carolina are formed and maintained by incursions of brackish water over these sediments.

TRENDS

Wetland losses in South Carolina have occurred as a result of both natural and human influences. Natural factors have included sea-level rise, natural succession, erosion and accretion, animal activity, droughts, and major storms. Human factors have included draining and clearing wetlands for agriculture, pond and reservoir construction, urban development, coastal impoundment construction, and pollution. Wetland loss in South Carolina from the 1780's to 1980's has been estimated to be 27 percent (Dahl, 1990). During the period from 1974 through 1983 alone, South Carolina had an estimated wetland loss of about 1.3 percent, approximately 61,000 acres of wetlands (John Hefner, U.S. Fish and Wildlife Service, oral commun., 1993).

Freshwater-wetland losses in South Carolina are not well documented but appear to be less extensive than in some other Southeastern States. However, studies conducted by the South Carolina Heritage Trust Program indicated that Carolina bay wetlands have been extensively disturbed and altered. Of the 2,651 Carolina bays that are 2 acres or larger identified by the State Heritage Trust Program in 1983 (Bennett and Nelson, 1991), more than 80 percent have been significantly altered and degraded. Many of South Carolina's tidal-freshwater marshes were diked, impounded, and converted to rice fields during the 18th and 19th centuries. Estimates of changes in wetland areas as a result of Hurricane Hugo are difficult to determine, but as much as 90 percent of the wet pine flatwoods of the Francis Marion National Forest may have been damaged by the wind.

Loss of freshwater wetlands has also been caused by changes in the hydrologic regime of South Carolina rivers. Alteration of the normal hydrologic regime by construction of dams on the upper Savannah, Santee, and Pee Dee Rivers has changed the natural pattern of annual flooding and has directly affected forested-wetland regeneration in South Carolina wetlands. Conversely, beaver-pond wetlands are thought to be increasing in South Carolina, though information on changes in beaver-pond wetland acreage is limited (Arner and Hepp, 1989).

CONSERVATION

Many government agencies and private organizations participate in wetland conservation in South Carolina. The most active agencies and organizations and some of their activities are listed in table 1.

Federal wetland activities.—Development activities in South Carolina wetlands are regulated by several Federal statutory prohibitions and incentives that are intended to slow wetland losses. Some of the more important of these are contained in the 1899 Rivers and Harbors Act; the 1972 Clean Water Act and amendments; the 1985 Food Security Act; the 1990 Food, Agriculture, Conservation, and Trade Act; the 1986 Emergency Wetlands Resources Act; and the 1972 Coastal Management Act.

Section 10 of the Rivers and Harbors Act gives the U.S. Army Corps of Engineers (Corps) authority to regulate certain activities in navigable waters. Regulated activities include diking, deepening, filling, excavating, and placing of structures. The related section 404 of the Clean Water Act is the most often-used Federal legislation protecting wetlands. Under section 404 provisions, the Corps issues permits regulating the discharge of dredged or fill material into wetlands. Permits are subject to review and possible veto by the U.S. Environmental Protection Agency, and the FWS has review and advisory roles. Section 401 of the Clean Water Act grants to States and eligible Indian Tribes the authority to approve, apply conditions to, or deny section 404 permit applications on the basis of a proposed activity's probable effects on the water quality of a wetland.

Most farming, ranching, and silviculture activities are not subject to section 404 regulation. However, the "Swampbuster" provision of the 1985 Food Security Act and amendments in the 1990 Food, Agriculture, Conservation, and Trade Act discourage (through financial disincentives) the draining, filling, or other alteration of wetlands for agricultural use. The law allows exemptions from penalties in some cases, especially if the farmer agrees to restore the altered wetland or other wetlands that have been converted to agricultural use. The Wetlands Reserve Program of the 1990 Food, Agriculture, Conservation, and Trade Act authorizes the Federal Government to purchase conservation easements from landowners who agree to protect or restore wetlands. The Consolidated Farm Service Agency (formerly the Agricultural Stabilization and Conservation Service) administers the Swampbuster provisions and Wetlands Reserve Program. The Natural Resources Conservation Service (formerly the Soil Conservation Service) determines compliance with Swampbuster provisions and assists farmers in the identification of wetlands and in the development of wetland protection, restoration, or creation plans.

The 1986 Emergency Wetlands Resources Act and the 1972 Coastal Zone Management Act and amendments encourage wetland protection through funding incentives. The Emergency Wetland Resources Act requires States to address wetland protection in their Statewide Comprehensive Outdoor Recreation Plans to qualify for Federal funding for State recreational land; the National Park Service provides guidance to States in developing the wetland component of their plans. Coastal and Great Lakes States that adopt coastal-zone management programs and plans approved by the National Oceanic and Atmospheric Administration are eligible for Federal funding and technical assistance through the Coastal Zone Management Act.

State wetland activities. — South Carolina regulates coastal wetlands under the South Carolina Coastal Management Act. The act authorizes the South Carolina Coastal Council to regulate any activities that fill, remove, dredge, drain, construct, or in any way alter any critical area within the eight coastal counties that are under its jurisdiction. The State Coastal Management Act provides 10 criteria to guide the Coastal Council in determining whether to issue a permit. Two of the key criteria are (1) a comparison of economic benefits to preservation benefits and (2) the extent to which all feasible safeguards to avoid adverse economic impact are considered. Under the Coastal Council regulations, dredging and filling wetlands is undertaken only if the activity is water dependent and no feasible alternatives exist. Applications are denied for purposes other than access, navigation, mining, or drainage unless an overriding public interest can be demonstrated. The Coastal Council regulates freshwater wetlands indirectly through review of other State or Federal permits required in coastal areas.

Table 1. Selected wetland-related activities of government agencies and private organizations in South Carolina, 1993

[Source: Classification of activities is generalized from information provided by agencies and organizations. •, agency or organization participates in wetland-related activity; ..., agency or organization does not participate in wetland-related activity. MAN, management; REG, regulation; R&C, restoration and creation; LAN, land acquisition; R&D, research and data collection; D&I, delineation and inventory]

Agency or organization	MAN	REG	R&C	LAN	R&D	D&I
FEDERAL						
Department of Agriculture						
Consolidated Farm Service Agency	...	•	...	...	...	...
Natural Resources Conservation Service	...	•	•	...	•	•
Department of Commerce						
National Oceanic and Atmospheric Administration	•	•	...	...	•	•
Department of Defense						
Army Corps of Engineers	•	•	•	...	•	•
Department of the Interior						
Fish and Wildlife Service	•	•	•	•	•	•
Geological Survey	...	...	...	...	•	•
National Biological Service	...	...	...	...	•	•
National Park Service	•	...	•	•	•	•
Environmental Protection Agency	...	•	...	...	•	•
STATE						
Belle W. Baruch Institute	...	...	...	...	•	...
Clemson University	...	...	...	...	•	...
Coastal Council	•	•	...	...	...	...
Department of Health and Environmental Control	...	•	...	...	...	...
Department of Highways and Public Transportation	...	•	...	...	...	...
Department of Parks, Recreation, and Tourism	•	...	•	...	•	...
Forestry Commission	...	•	...	...	...	...
Land Resources Commission	...	•	...	...	...	•
Soil and Water Conservation District	•	•	•	...	...	...
University of Georgia						
Savannah River Ecology Lab	...	...	...	...	•	...
University of South Carolina	...	...	...	...	•	...
Water Resources Commission	...	•	...	...	...	•
Department of Natural Resources	•	...	...	...	...	...
Heritage Trust Program	•	...	•	•	•	•
PRIVATE						
Ducks Unlimited	•	...	•	•	...	...
South Carolina Waterfowl Association	•	...	•	•	...	...
The Nature Conservancy	•	...	•	•	...	...

The South Carolina Department of Health and Environmental Control is active in wetland conservation through the section 401 and 402 requirements of the Clean Water Act. Section 401 requires that a permit applicant provide certification from the State that a discharge will comply with water-quality standards. The certification from the Department is necessary before a permit from the Corps can be obtained. Section 402 of the Clean Water Act requires that permits be obtained for discharges of treated wastewater to wetlands and other water bodies under the National Pollutant Discharge Elimination System program. The Department of Health and Environmental Control is the State agency delegated to administer this program.

Another State program that has relevance to wetlands is the South Carolina Navigable Waters Permitting Program administered by the South Carolina Water Resources Commission in association with the State Budget and Control Board. Under this program, a permit is required for any kind of construction or alteration activity in what the State considers navigable waters, similar to the requirements of Section 10 of the Federal Rivers and Harbors Act Program. However, most wetlands in the State are outside the jurisdiction of the Navigable Waters Permitting Program.

The Heritage Trust Program of the South Carolina Department of Natural Resources has been involved in the study and acquisition of Carolina bay wetlands. The Department manages about 42,000 acres of wetlands contained within Wildlife Management Areas. The Department of Parks, Recreation, and Tourism manages approximately 15,000 acres of wetlands included in the South Carolina State Park system. The South Carolina Forestry Commission and South Carolina Land Resources Commission have developed best-management practices for activities in forested wetlands. Under the South Carolina Scenic Rivers Act, the South Carolina Water Resources Commission and the Department of Natural Resources share responsibilities for planning, acquisition, regulation, and enforcement.

Private wetland activities.—The Nature Conservancy has acquired more than 35,000 acres of wetlands in South Carolina and currently manages about 9,000 acres of wetlands. Ducks Unlimited and the South Carolina Waterfowl Association are actively involved in wetland acquisition and management of waterfowl. One focus of the Association is to work with landowners who wish to flood former rice fields to increase tidal freshwater marsh acreage. The South Carolina Wildlife Federation promotes education concerning the importance of wetlands and also reviews permit applications.

References Cited

Arner, D.H, and Hepp, G.R., 1989, Beaver pond wetlands—A southern perspective, *in* Smith, L.M., Pederson, R.L., and Kaminski, R.M., Habitat management for migrating and wintering waterfowl in North America: Lubbock, Texas Tech University Press, p. 130–177.

Bebber, T.L., 1988, South Carolina wetlands study—A component of the State Comprehensive Outdoor Recreation Plan: Columbia, South Carolina Department of Parks, Recreation, and Tourism, 235 p.

Bennett, S.H., and Nelson, J.B., 1991, Distribution and status of Carolina bays in South Carolina: Columbia, South Carolina Wildlife and Marine Resources Department, 88 p.

Cowardin, L.M., Carter, Virginia, Golet, F.C., and LaRoe, E.T., 1979, Classification of wetlands and deepwater habitats of the United States: U.S. Fish and Wildlife Service Report FWS/OBS–79/31, 131 p.

Dahl, T.E., 1990, Wetlands—Losses in the United States, 1780's to 1980's: Washington, D.C., U.S. Fish and Wildlife Service Report to Congress, 13 p.

Fenneman, N.M., 1946, Physical divisions of the United States: Washington, D.C., U.S. Geological Survey special map, scale 1:7,000,000.

Field, D.W., Reyer, A.J., Genovese, P.V., and Shearer, B.D., 1991, Coastal wetlands of the United States: Washington, D.C., National Oceanic and Atmospheric Administration and U.S. Fish and Wildlife Service cooperative report, 59 p.

Gordon, D.H., Gray, B.T., Perry, R.D., Prevost, M.B., Strange, T.H., and Williams, R.K., 1989, South Atlantic coastal wetlands, *in* Smith, L.M., Pederson, R.L., and Kaminski, R.M., Habitat management for migrating and wintering waterfowl in North America: Lubbock, Texas Tech University Press, p. 57–92.

Patterson, G.G., Speiran, G.K., and Whetstone, B.H., 1985, Hydrology and its effects on distribution of vegetation in Congaree Swamp National Monument, South Carolina: U.S. Geological Survey Water-Resources Investigations Report 85–4256, 31 p.

Purvis, J.C., Tyler, Wes, and Sidlow, Scott, 1990, General characteristics of South Carolina's climate: Columbia, South Carolina Water Resources Commission, 22 p.

Schalles, J.F., and Shure, D.J., 1989, Hydrology, community structure, and productivity patterns of a dystrophic Carolina bay wetland: Ecological Monographs, v. 59, p. 365–385.

Sharitz, R.R., and Gibbons, J.W., 1982, The ecology of southeastern shrub bogs (pocosins) and Carolina bays—A community profile: U.S. Fish and Wildlife Service Report, FWS/OBS–82/04, 93 p.

FOR ADDITIONAL INFORMATION: District Chief, U.S. Geological Survey, 720 Gracern Road, Stephenson Center, Suite 129, Columbia, SC 29210; Regional Wetland Coordinator, U.S. Fish and Wildlife Service, 1875 Century Building, Suite 200, Atlanta, GA 30345

Prepared by
Michael R. Meador,
U.S. Geological Survey

South Dakota
Wetland Resources

Although wetlands cover only 3.6 percent of South Dakota (Dahl, 1990), they are of substantial ecological and economic importance to the State and Nation. Depressional wetlands in the glaciated eastern part of South Dakota, commonly referred to as prairie potholes, and wetlands associated with reservoirs provide important breeding and resting habitat for migratory and resident waterfowl (fig. 1). South Dakota wetlands also provide important habitat to many other nongame and game wildlife species, including pheasants (Sather-Blair and Linder, 1980; Soil Conservation Service, 1985) and whitetail deer (Kramlich, 1985), which are economically valuable to the State.

Hydrologic functions of wetlands include water retention and flood attenuation (Hubbard and Linder, 1986) and, on a local basis, ground-water recharge (Hubbard, 1988a). Hunting, trapping, fishing, bird watching, nature photography, camping, hiking, and boating are some of the recreational opportunities provided by wetlands, and the South Dakota tourist industry relies heavily on the recreational and esthetic value of the State's wetlands. Other important benefits of wetlands in South Dakota include livestock forage (Hubbard, 1988b), bait-fish production (Carlson and Berry, 1990), and mineral mining. These benefits are provided by diverse wetlands distributed across South Dakota's plains and the Black Hills.

TYPES AND DISTRIBUTION

Wetlands are lands transitional between terrestrial and deepwater habitats where the water table usually is at or near the land surface or the land is covered by shallow water (Cowardin and others, 1979). The distribution of wetlands and deepwater habitats in South Dakota is shown in figure 2A; only wetlands are discussed herein.

Wetlands can be vegetated or nonvegetated and are classified on the basis of their hydrology, vegetation, and substrate. In this summary, wetlands are classified according to the system proposed by Cowardin and others (1979), which is used by the U.S. Fish and Wildlife Service (FWS) to map and inventory the Nation's wetlands. At the most general level of the classification system, wetlands are grouped into five ecological systems: Palustrine, Lacustrine, Riverine, Estuarine, and Marine. The Palustrine System includes only wetlands, whereas the other systems comprise wetlands and deepwater habitats. Wetlands of the systems that occur in South Dakota are described below.

System	Wetland description
Palustrine	Wetlands in which vegetation is predominantly trees (forested wetlands); shrubs (scrub-shrub wetlands); persistent or nonpersistent emergent, erect, rooted, herbaceous plants (persistent- and nonpersistent-emergent wetlands); or submersed and (or) floating plants (aquatic beds). Also, intermittently to permanently flooded open-water bodies of less than 20 acres in which water is less than 6.6 feet deep.
Lacustrine	Wetlands within an intermittently to permanently flooded lake or reservoir. Vegetation, when present, is predominantly nonpersistent emergent plants (nonpersistent-emergent wetlands), or submersed and (or) floating plants (aquatic beds), or both.
Riverine	Wetlands within a channel. Vegetation, when present, is same as in the Lacustrine System.

There is no current (1993) estimate of statewide wetland acreage in each of the systems. Final mapping and digitizing for the FWS National Wetlands Inventory has been completed for eastern South Dakota, but only preliminary draft mapping has been completed for the remainder of the State (Chuck Elliot, U.S. Fish and Wildlife Service, oral commun., 1993). Final mapping and digitizing for the entire State may be completed within a few years.

An inventory of wetland and open-water areas conducted in 1973–74 estimated that 71 percent of South Dakota's wetlands were palustrine (Ruwaldt and others, 1979); 19 percent were mixed lacustrine and palustrine associated with prairie ponds and lakes and manmade stock ponds and dugouts; and 10 percent were riverine. Stock ponds are impoundments constructed by damming deep draws; dugouts are constructed by excavating a depression and do not have dams (Ruwaldt and others, 1979). Palustrine wetlands in South Dakota primarily include emergent wetlands such as marshes and sloughs, in which coarse, herbaceous vegetation like cattails and bulrushes are predominant; wet meadows, in which low, herbaceous vegetation like grasses and sedges are predominant; and vegetated, shallow-water zones of stock ponds and dugouts (Stewart and Kantrud, 1971). Lacustrine wetland areas occur in the numerous glacial lakes in the eastern part of the State and in artificial impoundments throughout the State. Submersed vegetation like widgeongrass and pondweed are common in lacustrine wetlands. Prairie potholes (a palustrine emergent wetland) that contain erect, rooted, herbaceous hydrophytes are by far the most common wetland type in South Dakota (Kantrud, Krapu, and Swanson, 1989).

Wetlands occupy about 1.8 million acres (3.6 percent) of South Dakota (Dahl, 1990). In the Great Plains (fig. 2B), the natural drainage system generally is well developed, and there are few natural wetlands. Wetlands in the Great Plains generally are associated with manmade stock ponds. The Central Lowland is entirely within the glaciated part of South Dakota (fig. 2C), and most wetlands are in depressions among ground moraines deposited by the glaciers.

HYDROLOGIC SETTING

Wetlands form where there is a persistent water supply at or near the land surface. The location and persistence of the supply is a function of interdependent climatic, physiographic, geologic, and

Figure 1. Palustrine wetland in the Sand Lake National Wildlife Refuge. This refuge encompasses about 22,000 acres (mostly palustrine and lacustrine wetlands) and is an important nesting and staging area for migratory waterfowl. *(Photograph by Bill Schultze, U.S. Fish and Wildlife Service.)*

hydrologic factors such as precipitation and runoff patterns, evaporation, topography, and configuration of the water table. In South Dakota, the dominant factors influencing the distribution of wetlands are moisture deficit, topography, and composition of surficial materials.

Precipitation and runoff rates in South Dakota differ annually and with season and location. The normal annual precipitation in South Dakota ranges from about 16 inches in the northwest to about 24 inches in the Black Hills and the southeast (Benson, 1986). About 70 percent of annual precipitation occurs during the growing sea-

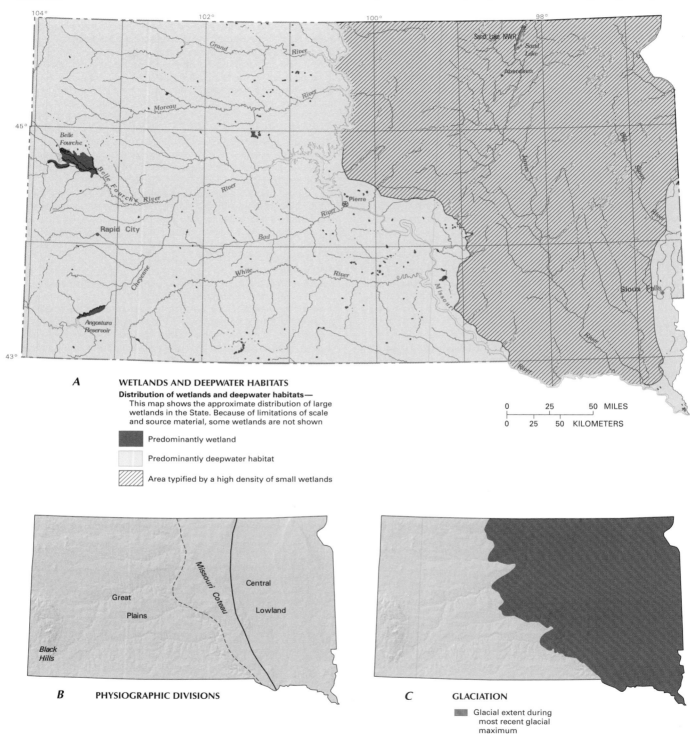

A   WETLANDS AND DEEPWATER HABITATS

Distribution of wetlands and deepwater habitats—
This map shows the approximate distribution of large wetlands in the State. Because of limitations of scale and source material, some wetlands are not shown

Predominantly wetland

Predominantly deepwater habitat

Area typified by a high density of small wetlands

B   PHYSIOGRAPHIC DIVISIONS

C   GLACIATION

Glacial extent during most recent glacial maximum

Figure 2. Wetland distribution in South Dakota and physical features that control wetland distribution in the State. **A**, Distribution of wetlands and deepwater habitats. **B**, Physiography. **C**, Extent of most recent glaciation. *(Sources: A, T.E. Dahl, U.S. Fish and Wildlife Service, unpub. data, 1991. B, Physiographic divisions from Fenneman, 1946; landform data from EROS Data Center. C, South Dakota Geological Survey, 1971).*

son (May through October). The average annual runoff ranges from about 0.2 inch in the northwest to about 2 inches in the Black Hills. A large percentage of runoff occurs as a result of snowmelt and rainfall in the spring and early summer. Precipitation and snowmelt runoff are the principal water sources for prairie pothole wetlands (Shjeflo, 1968).

Annual lake evaporation in South Dakota ranges from about 38 inches in the northeast to about 48 inches in the southwest (Benson, 1986). About 75 percent of the annual evaporation occurs during the growing season. In South Dakota, evaporation exceeds precipitation in most years, and there is a net statewide annual moisture deficit that ranges from about 20 inches along the eastern border of the State to about 32 inches in the southwest. Evaporation is the principal source of water loss from prairie pothole wetlands (Shjeflo, 1968).

Climatic, topographic, and hydrologic characteristics differ among and sometimes within physiographic provinces. The two major physiographic provinces in South Dakota (fig. 2B), the Great Plains and the Central Lowland, generally have very different hydrologic settings for wetland formation.

The Great Plains physiographic province generally is unglaciated, and the natural drainage system is well developed. Steeper topography, a better developed drainage system, and a generally more arid climate are factors that result in substantially fewer wetlands in the Great Plains than in the Central Lowland in eastern South Dakota. Wetlands in the Great Plains occur primarily in association with manmade stock ponds and perennial and ephemeral streams (Brewster and others, 1976; Ruwaldt and others, 1979). Most of the wetland areas associated with perennial streams are classified as riverine, whereas those associated with ephemeral streams generally are palustrine because of the presence of emergent plants (Hubbard, 1988a). Wetlands associated with stock ponds and dugouts generally are classified as palustrine or lacustrine. About 60 percent of the wetlands in the unglaciated western part of South Dakota occur in association with stock ponds. Although several studies have indicated that stock ponds do not equal natural wetlands in habitat quality, the stock ponds provide valuable habitat for plants and animals, especially during drought (Duebbert, 1972; Flake, 1979). A small part of the Great Plains lies east of the Missouri River in a glaciated region known as the Missouri Coteau. Prairie pothole wetlands are common in this region.

In the glaciated Central Lowland, several factors result in retention of water on the land surface and the occurrence of numerous prairie pothole wetlands: (1) the generally flat topography results in a poorly developed drainage system and low runoff velocities, (2) depressions in the glaciated topography result in retention of water on the surface and extensive ponding, (3) low permeability of the geologic materials (soils and fine-grained glacial till) results in minimal infiltration of water, and (4) in the spring, when most of the annual precipitation and runoff occurs, frozen soils further restrict infiltration of water and cause the water to pond (Winter, 1989). About 90 percent of the wetland area of the glaciated eastern part of South Dakota is associated with prairie ponds and lakes (primarily palustrine emergent wetlands); the remaining 10 percent is divided between riverine wetlands and those associated with stock ponds or dugouts (Ruwaldt and others, 1979).

Ground-water interactions with palustrine wetlands in the prairie region can be complex (Winter, 1989). The flat topography provides opportunity for infiltration, but the impermeable substrate inhibits infiltration. Because the glacial till in eastern South Dakota generally is composed of fine-grained materials and has a high smectite-clay content, it expands greatly on wetting and becomes impermeable (Hubbard and others, 1988). Water can flow through fractures in the till; but even where fractures occur, permeability is low (Winter, 1989; Grisak, 1975). Greater interaction between wetlands and ground water can exist in areas of glacial outwash where lenses of coarser grained, more permeable materials exist (Lewis Howells, U.S. Geological Survey, oral commun., 1993). However, interaction between wetlands and ground water in eastern South Dakota generally is small and typically accounts for about 5 to 25 percent of water exchange (Winter and Woo, 1990).

Hubbard (1988a) and Winter (1989) have discussed a general model of ground-water flow systems underlying prairie wetlands (fig. 3). A local flow system (of which most shallow ground water is a part) occurs where ground water moves from an adjacent upland into a wetland or between adjacent wetlands. Intermediate flow systems generally underlie local flow systems, and water flowing in intermediate flow systems may pass under some streams and wetlands. Regional flow systems underlie both local and intermediate systems and discharge at major topographic lows such as large rivers, lakes, and wetlands. Factors that determine which ground-water flow systems a prairie pothole wetland is interacting with include the topographic setting, position of the water table, thickness and hydraulic characteristics of the aquifer material, and the configuration of the underlying bedrock (Hubbard and others, 1988).

Depending on their location within the local, intermediate, and regional ground-water flow systems, individual wetlands can serve as discharge areas, recharge areas, or both (flow-through wetlands). In the prairie pothole region, wetland water quality is affected by the interaction between wetlands and ground water: recharge wetlands tend to have low dissolved-solids concentrations, discharge

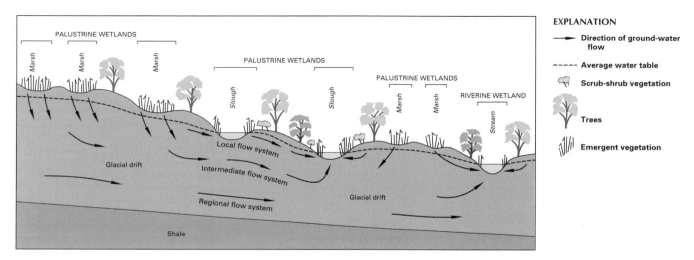

Figure 3. Generalized hydrologic setting of South Dakota wetlands. *(Source: Hydrologic concepts from Winter, 1989.)*

wetlands tend to have high dissolved-solids concentrations, and flow-through wetlands tend to have intermediate dissolved-solids concentrations (LaBaugh and others, 1987; Hubbard and others, 1988). There can be seasonal reversals in the direction of water exchange between a wetland and the ground water (Winter, 1989). In spring, water can seep from a wetland to the ground water when wetland water levels are high and can then reverse later in summer as evapotranspiration creates a discharge point for ground water. Although recharge of water from individual wetlands to the intermediate and regional ground-water flow system generally is small, on a regional basis the total contribution of recharge from prairie pothole wetlands to deep aquifers might be substantial (Winter, 1989).

Wetlands also significantly affect the surface-water hydrology of eastern South Dakota. The glacial depressions retain runoff, effectively reduce the contributing drainage area of a drainage basin, and result in attenuation of flood peaks (Hubbard, 1988a; Hubbard and Linder, 1986). Antecedent moisture conditions affect the capacity of prairie pothole wetlands to retain runoff.

TRENDS

The FWS has estimated that, from the 1780's to the 1980's, wetland area in South Dakota decreased by about 35 percent—from about 2.7 million to about 1.8 million acres (Dahl, 1990). Historically, agricultural conversions have accounted for most wetland losses in South Dakota. Kantrud, Millar, and van der Valk (1989) discussed the effects of agricultural disturbances in wetlands in the prairie pothole region. In cropland areas, wetland losses have resulted from tilling for crop production and from draining and filling to increase crop-producing land area and to avoid the inconvenience of maneuvering farm machinery around wet spots. High erosion rates in agricultural areas due to exposed soils in cropland areas and overgrazed parts of range and pastureland areas also have contributed to wetland degradation and loss.

Other practices that have had an adverse effect on South Dakota wetlands include inundation of wetlands during reservoir filling, timber harvesting, dugout construction (for livestock watering) in existing wetlands, and contamination from inadequately treated sewage and industrial waste. In urban areas, wetlands have been drained and filled for residential and commercial expansion. Stream channelization and road construction have adversely affected wetlands directly by draining wetlands within construction areas and indirectly by providing convenient drainage outlets that encourage unauthorized wetland drainage by adjacent landowners (Erickson and others, 1979; Smith and others, 1989).

Some land-use practices have created new wetlands or enlarged existing ones. Seepage associated with distribution and application of irrigation water has increased wetland acreage, especially on the large Bureau of Reclamation (BOR) irrigation projects in western South Dakota (primarily Belle Fourche and Angostura Reservoirs). In many parts of South Dakota, flowing artesian wells constructed for livestock watering or fish production have increased wetland area. Stock ponds and dugouts constructed for livestock watering constitute an important part of South Dakota wetlands, especially in the unglaciated western part of the State. Reservoir construction has undoubtedly increased the acreage of lacustrine wetlands.

CONSERVATION

Many government agencies and private organizations participate in wetland conservation in South Dakota. The most active agencies and organizations and some of their activities are listed in table 1.

Federal wetland activities. — Development activities in South Dakota wetlands are regulated by several Federal statutory prohi-

Table 1. Selected wetland-related activities of government agencies and private organizations in South Dakota, 1993

[Source: Classification of activities is generalized from information provided by agencies and organizations. •, agency or organization participates in wetland-related activity; ..., agency or organization does not participate in wetland-related activity. MAN, management; REG, regulation; R&C, restoration and creation; LAN, land acquisition; R&D, research and data collection; D&I, delineation and inventory]

Agency or organization	MAN	REG	R&C	LAN	R&D	D&I
FEDERAL						
Department of Agriculture						
Consolidated Farm Service Agency	...	•	...	...	...	...
Forest Service	•	...	•	...	•	•
Natural Resources Conservation Service	...	•	•	...	•	•
Department of Commerce						
National Oceanic and Atmospheric Administration	...	...	...	...	•	...
Department of Defense						
Army Corps of Engineers	•	•	...	...	...	•
Military reservations	•	...	...	...	...	...
Department of the Interior						
Bureau of Land Management	•	...	...	...	•	•
Bureau of Reclamation	•	...	•	...	•	•
Fish and Wildlife Service	•	...	•	...	•	•
Geological Survey	...	...	...	...	•	•
National Biological Service	...	...	•	...	•	•
National Park Service	•	...	•	•	•	...
Environmental Protection Agency	...	•	...	...	...	•
TRIBAL						
Cheyenne River Sioux Tribe	•	...	...	•	...	...
Crow Creek Sioux Tribe	•	...	...	•	...	...
Lower Brule Sioux Tribe	•	...	...	•	...	...
Oglala Sioux Tribe	•	...	...	•	...	...
Rosebud Sioux Tribe	•	...	...	•	...	...
Sisseton–Wahpeton Sioux Tribe	•	...	...	•	...	...
Standing Rock Sioux Tribe	•	...	...	•	...	...
Yankton Sioux Tribe	•	•	...	•	•	...
STATE						
Department of Agriculture	...	...	•	...	•	...
Department of Environment and Natural Resources	...	•	•	...	•	...
Department of Game, Fish and Parks	•	•	•	•	•	...
Department of Transportation	•	•	•	•	...	...
State universities	...	...	...	...	•	•
PRIVATE ORGANIZATIONS						
Ducks Unlimited	•	...	•	•	•	...
The National Wildlife Federation	...	•	•	•	...	...
The Nature Conservancy	•	...	•	•	...	...

bitions and incentives that are intended to slow wetland losses. Some of the more important of these are contained in the 1899 Rivers and Harbors Act; the 1972 Clean Water Act and amendments; the 1985 Food Security Act; the 1990 Food, Agriculture, Conservation, and Trade Act; and the 1986 Emergency Wetlands Resources Act.

Section 10 of the Rivers and Harbors Act gives the U.S. Army Corps of Engineers (Corps) authority to regulate certain activities in navigable waters. Regulated activities include diking, deepening, filling, excavating, and placing of structures. The related section 404 of the Clean Water Act is the most often-used Federal legislation protecting wetlands. Under section 404 provisions, the Corps issues permits regulating the discharge of dredged or fill material into wetlands. Permits are subject to review and possible veto by the U.S. Environmental Protection Agency (EPA), and the FWS has review and advisory roles. Section 401 of the Clean Water Act grants to States and eligible Indian Tribes the authority to approve, apply conditions to, or deny section 404 permit applications on the basis of a proposed activity's probable effects on the water quality of a wetland.

Most farming, ranching, and silviculture activities are not subject to section 404 regulation. However, the "Swampbuster" provision of the 1985 Food Security Act and amendments in the 1990 Food, Agriculture, Conservation, and Trade Act discourages (through financial disincentives) the draining, filling, or other alteration of wetlands for agricultural use. The law allows exemptions from penalties in some cases, especially if the farmer agrees to restore the altered wetland or other wetlands that have been converted to agricultural use. The Wetlands Reserve Program of the 1990 Food, Agriculture, Conservation, and Trade Act authorizes the Federal Government to purchase conservation easements from landowners who agree to protect or restore wetlands. The Consolidated Farm Service Agency (formerly the Agricultural Stabilization and Conservation Service) administers the Swampbuster provisions and Wet-lands Reserve Program. The Natural Resources Conservation Service (formerly the Soil Conservation Service) determines compliance with Swampbuster provisions and assists farmers in the identification of wetlands and in the development of wetland protection, restoration, or creation plans.

The 1986 Emergency Wetlands Resources Act encourages wetland protection through funding incentives. The act requires States to address wetland protection in their Statewide Comprehensive Outdoor Recreation Plans to qualify for Federal funding for State recreational land; the National Park Service (NPS) provides guidance to States in developing the wetland component of their plans.

Federal agencies are responsible for the proper management of wetlands on public land under their jurisdiction and also are involved in other wetland-enhancement and protection activities. With the mission to conserve, protect, and enhance fish and wildlife populations and their habitats, the FWS is perhaps the most active Federal agency in wetlands management and protection in South Dakota. The FWS manages about 47,000 acres in six National Wildlife Refuges that are predominantly wetlands, and about 146,000 acres in numerous waterfowl-production areas in the eastern part of the State. The FWS protects wetlands on private lands through its Wetlands Easement Program, in which private landowners agree not to drain, burn, level, or fill specified wetlands in exchange for monetary payment. About 500,000 acres of wetlands are protected by this program. The FWS also is involved in a program to construct 3,000 acres of new wetlands on private and Indian-reservation lands in South Dakota (Carl Madsen, U.S. Fish and Wildlife Service, written commun., 1993).

The U.S. Forest Service (FS) manages about 2.1 million acres in three National Forests and three National Grasslands in South Dakota. The FS is in the process of compiling estimates of wetlands and other riparian areas on their jurisdictional lands in South Dakota. A preliminary estimate is that about 1 percent of FS lands are wetlands or other riparian areas (Barry Parrish, U.S. Forest Service, oral commun., 1993). The FS also is involved in wetland-creation activities on their land.

The Bureau of Land Management (BLM) manages about 273,000 acres in South Dakota, of which about 1,560 acres are in riparian areas (Eric Luse, Bureau of Land Management, oral commun., 1993). The FS and the BLM have riparian-area management plans whose goals include restoring, maintaining, and protecting riparian areas; educating the public concerning the importance of healthy riparian areas; and cooperating with private landowners, resource users, and other Federal agencies in the protection of riparian areas (Bureau of Land Management, 1991). The NPS manages about 274,000 acres in two National Parks, one National Monument, and one National Memorial in South Dakota, but currently there are no estimates of wetland acreage on those lands.

The BOR has jurisdiction over about 63,500 acres in South Dakota, including land in existing irrigation projects and land in proposed, but not yet constructed, projects (Loren Hindbjorgen, Bureau of Reclamation, oral commun., 1993). Currently, there are no estimates of wetland acreage on BOR lands in the State. The BOR does not have a specific wetland-management plan, but a wetland and riparian-habitat element is being included in an initiative be-

ing developed by the BOR (Rick Nelson, Bureau of Reclamation, oral commun., 1993). The BOR has been involved in wetlands creation on its jurisdictional land, but there are no estimates of total acres involved.

Tribal wetland activities. — There are eight Indian reservations in South Dakota, and the different tribes have varying levels of involvement in wetland management and enhancement on their lands. Most of the tribes are developing wetland-management plans for their reservations, and four tribes are participating financially with the FWS in wetland-creation programs on tribal lands.

State wetland activities. — Although South Dakota currently (1993) has no comprehensive wetland-protection program, the State is developing a wetland policy. The State, with the assistance of an EPA grant, has created a wetlands-coordinator position whose responsibility it is to develop a wetland-protection program. The position is within the South Dakota Department of Agriculture under the oversight of a committee that has members from four State agencies: the Department of Agriculture; the Department of Game, Fish and Parks; the Department of Environment and Natural Resources; and the Department of Transportation.

Several State agencies participate in aspects of Federal programs, and wetlands are enhanced or protected under some State programs. The Department of Game, Fish and Parks has diverse wetland responsibilities under the mission statement of the Division of Wildlife: to manage South Dakota's wildlife and fisheries resources and their associated habitats for their sustained and equitable use and for the benefit, welfare, and enjoyment of the citizens of South Dakota and its visitors. Specific activities of the agency include providing technical advice regarding effects on fish, wildlife, and habitat for section 404 permit applications; providing technical expertise to the Department of Transportation to mitigate wetland impacts from road-construction activities; being actively involved in educational programs to teach landowners and school-age children the importance of wetland habitats; managing State-owned recreational and wildlife-production lands to protect and maintain wetland areas; and acquiring new land for wetland protection.

The Department of Environment and Natural Resources' Division of Environmental Regulation reviews section 404 permit applications to ensure compliance with State water-quality laws. A permit is not issued by the Corps without a Clean Water Act section 401 certification of such compliance. Pursuant to section 305(b) of the Clean Water Act, the Department's Division of Water Resources Management submits to the EPA and the U.S. Congress a biennial assessment of the State's surface-water quality, including that of wetlands. The Department's Division of Geological Survey and Division of Water Resources collects wetland hydrologic and water-quality data.

The Department of Transportation attempts to mitigate and minimize impacts to wetlands that result from its road-construction activities. The Department is the most frequent applicant for section 404 permits and avoids wetland alteration unless there is no feasible alternative. When wetland alteration is considerable, new wetland areas equal to or greater than the size of the losses typically are created within the project area. When onsite mitigation is not possible, a Wetlands Bank program is used to create new wetlands outside the project area that are equal to or greater than the size of the altered wetland.

State universities in South Dakota, including South Dakota State University, Northern State University, and the South Dakota School of Mines and Technology, are active in wetlands research. South Dakota State University participates in the National Wetlands Inventory program of the FWS and is coordinating an EPA-funded study of the effects of global climate change on wetlands in the United States (Carter Johnson, South Dakota State University, written commun., 1993).

Private wetland activities.—Ducks Unlimited owns about 2,000 acres and manages those lands for wetlands enhancement (Rick Warhurst, Ducks Unlimited, oral commun., 1993). The organization also has participated in cost-shared purchases of about 2,100 wetland acres with the Department of Game, Fish and Parks and has implemented wetland creation, restoration, and enhancement projects on about 9,500 acres of State or federally owned lands. The National Wildlife Federation is active in educating the public concerning wetland issues and has shared costs of land purchases with the Department of Game, Fish and Parks and the FWS (Dan Limmer, National Wildlife Federation, oral commun., 1993). The Nature Conservancy owns about 8,000 acres of wetlands in South Dakota and is active in monitoring and protecting endangered species on those lands (Joe Satrom, The Nature Conservancy, oral commun., 1993). Other organizations that participate in wetland-protection activities in the State include the Izaak Walton League, the National Audubon Society, and the Sierra Club. The South Dakota Association of Conservation Districts (an organization closely associated with the South Dakota Department of Agriculture) also has been involved in wetlands enhancement, with most of the 69 conservation districts in the State participating financially in wetland-creation programs of the FWS.

References Cited

Benson, R.D., 1986, South Dakota surface-water resources, *in* National water summary 1985—Hydrologic events and surface-water resources: U.S. Geological Survey Water-Supply Paper 2300, p. 419–424.

Brewster, W.G., Gates, J.M., Flake, L.D., 1976, Breeding waterfowl populations and their distribution in South Dakota: The Journal of Wildlife Management, v. 40, p. 50–59.

Bureau of Land Management, 1991, Riparian-wetland initiative for the 1990's: Bureau of Land Management Report BLM/WO/GI–91/001+4340, 50 p.

Carlson B.N., and Berry, C.R., 1990, Population size and economic value of aquatic bait species in palustrine wetlands of eastern South Dakota: Prairie Naturalist, v. 22, p. 119–128.

Cowardin, L.M., Carter, Virginia, Golet, F.C., and LaRoe, E.T., 1979, Classification of wetlands and deepwater habitats of the United States: U.S. Fish and Wildlife Service, FWS/OBS–79/31, 131 p.

Dahl, T.E., 1990, Wetlands—Losses in the United States, 1780's to 1980's: Washington, D.C., U.S. Fish and Wildlife Service Report to Congress, 13 p.

Duebbert, H.F., 1972, Ducks on stock ponds in north central South Dakota, *in* Miller, H.W., ed., Wildlife on man-made water areas—Reports and discussions at the second seminar, April 15–16, 1970, Jamestown, N. Dak.: U.S. Fish and Wildlife Service, Northern Prairie Wildlife Research Center, p. 33–35.

Erickson, R.E., Linder, R.L., and Harmon, K.W., 1979, Stream channelization (P.L. 83–566) increased wetland losses in the Dakotas: The Wildlife Society Bulletin, v. 7, p. 71–78.

Fenneman, N.M., 1946, Physical divisions of the United States: Washington, D.C., U.S. Geological Survey special map, scale 1:7,000,000.

Flake, L.D., 1979, Wetland diversity and waterfowl, *in* Greeson, P.E., Clark, J.R., and Clark, J.E., eds., Proceedings of the National Symposium on Wetlands, November 1978: Minneapolis, Minn., American Water Resources Association, p. 312–319.

Grisak, G.E., 1975, The fracture porosity of glacial till: Canadian Journal of Earth Science, v. 12, p. 513–515.

Hubbard, D.E., 1988a, Glaciated prairie wetlands functions and values—A synthesis of the literature: U.S. Fish and Wildlife Service Biological Report 88(43), 50 p.

_____1988b, Using your wetland for forage: South Dakota State University, Department of Wildlife and Fisheries Sciences, 4 p.

Hubbard, D.E., and Linder, R.L., 1986, Spring runoff retention in prairie pothole wetlands: Journal of Soil and Water Conservation, v. 41, p. 122–125.

Hubbard, D.E., Richardson, J.L., and Malo, D.D., 1988, Glaciated prairie wetlands — Soils, hydrology, and land-use implications *in* Kusler, J.A., and Brooks, eds., Proceedings of the National Wetland Hydrology Symposium, September, 1987: Chicago, Ill., Association of State Wetland Managers Technical Report 6, p. 137–143.

Kantrud, H.A., Krapu, G.L., and Swanson, G.A., 1989, Prairie basin wetlands of the Dakotas—A community profile: U.S. Fish and Wildlife Service Biological Report 85(7.28).

Kantrud, H.A., Millar, J.B., and van der Valk, A.G., 1989, Vegetation of wetlands in the prairie pothole region, *in* van der Valk, A.G., ed., Northern prairie wetlands: Ames, Iowa State University Press, p. 132–187.

Kramlich, T.J., 1985, Evaluation of seasonal habitat use by white-tailed deer in eastern South Dakota: Brookings, South Dakota State University, Masters thesis, 36 p.

LaBaugh, J.W., Winter, T.C., Adomaitis, V.A., and Swanson, G.A., 1987, Hydrology and chemistry of selected prairie wetlands in the Cottonwood Lake area, Stutsman County, North Dakota: U.S. Geological Survey Professional Paper 1431, 26 p.

Ruwaldt, J.J., Flake, L.D., and Gates, J.M., 1979, Waterfowl pair use of natural and man-made wetlands in South Dakota: Journal of Wildlife Management, v. 43, p. 375–383.

Sather-Blair, Signe, and Linder, R.L., 1980, Pheasant use of South Dakota wetlands during the winter: Proceedings of the South Dakota Academy of Sciences, v. 59, p. 147–155.

Shjeflo, J.B., 1968, Evapotranspiration and the water budget of prairie potholes in North Dakota: U.S. Geological Survey Professional Paper 585–B, 49 p.

Smith, B.J., Browers, H.W., Dahl, T.E., Nomsen, D.E., and Higgins, K.F., 1989, Indirect wetland drainage in association with Federal highway projects in the prairie pothole region: Wetlands, v. 9, p. 27–39.

Soil Conservation Service, 1985, Duck and pheasant use of water bank program agreement areas in east-central South Dakota: Soil Conservation Service, 67 p.

South Dakota Geological Survey, 1971, Generalized glacial map of South Dakota: South Dakota Geological Survey Educational Series, Map 2, 1 sheet.

Stewart, R.E., and Kantrud, H.A., 1971, Classification of natural ponds and lakes in the glaciated prairie region: U.S. Fish and Wildlife Service Resource Publication 92, 57 p.

Winter, T.C., 1989, Hydrologic studies of wetlands in the Northern Prairie, *in* van der Valk, A.G., ed., Northern prairie wetlands: Ames, Iowa State University Press, p. 16–54.

Winter, T.C., and Woo, M.K., 1990, Hydrology of lakes and wetlands, *in* Wolman M.G., and Riggs, H.C., eds., The Geology of North America, Surface water hydrology: Boulder, Colo., Geological Society of America, v. O–1, p. 159–187.

FOR ADDITIONAL INFORMATION: District Chief, U.S. Geological Survey, 1608 Mountain View Road, Rapid City, SD 57702; Regional Wetland Coordinator, U.S. Fish and Wildlife Service, Fish and Wildlife Enhancement, P.O. Box 25486, Denver Federal Center, Denver, CO 80225

Prepared by
Steven K. Sando,
U.S. Geological Survey

Tennessee
Wetland Resources

Recent surveys have indicated that Tennessee has between 640,000 and 787,000 acres of wetlands (Tennessee Department of Conservation, 1988; Dahl, 1990). Another recent, unpublished survey determined that the State might have as much as 1.4 million acres of wetlands (D.L. Porter, Tennessee Valley Authority, written commun., 1993). Although wetlands constitute a small percentage of Tennessee's total area, wetlands, such as the bottom-land hardwood forest shown in figure 1, are ecologically and economically important to the State.

The benefits of Tennessee's wetlands include enhanced water quality, fish and wildlife productivity, and socioeconomic values. Wetlands enhance water quality by filtering nutrients, wastes, and sediment from upland runoff. Fish and wildlife benefit from the abundance of habitat and food that wetlands provide. More than 95 plant, 65 mollusk, and 44 vertebrate species listed by the State as rare are found in Tennessee's wetlands (Tennessee Department of Conservation, 1988). Socioeconomic values of wetlands include flood-damage reduction through temporary storage of floodwaters, erosion control, and, in a few areas, ground-water recharge. Tennessee wetlands also provide economically important recreational opportunities, such as hunting, fishing, boating, wildlife photography, hiking, and bird watching for residents and tourists.

TYPES AND DISTRIBUTION

Wetlands are lands transitional between terrestrial and deep-water habitats where the water table usually is at or near the land surface or the land is covered by shallow water (Cowardin and others, 1979). The distribution of wetlands and deepwater habitats in Tennessee is shown in figure 2A; only wetlands are discussed herein.

Wetlands can be vegetated or nonvegetated and are classified on the basis of their hydrology, vegetation, and substrate. In this summary, wetlands are classified according to the system proposed by Cowardin and others (1979), which is used by the U.S. Fish and Wildlife Service (FWS) to map and inventory the Nation's wetlands. At the most general level of the classification system, wetlands are grouped into five ecological systems: Palustrine, Lacustrine, Riverine, Estuarine, and Marine. The Palustrine System includes only wetlands, whereas the other systems comprise wetlands and deepwater habitats. Wetlands of the systems that occur in Tennessee are described below.

System	Wetland description
Palustrine	Wetlands in which vegetation is predominantly trees (forested wetlands); shrubs (scrub-shrub wetlands); persistent or nonpersistent emergent, erect, rooted, herbaceous plants (persistent- and nonpersistent-emergent wetlands); or submersed and (or) floating plants (aquatic beds). Also, intermittently to permanently flooded open-water bodies of less than 20 acres in which water is less than 6.6 feet deep.
Lacustrine	Wetlands within an intermittently to permanently flooded lake or reservoir. Vegetation, when present, is predominantly nonpersistent emergent plants (nonpersistent-emergent wetlands), or submersed and (or) floating plants (aquatic beds), or both.
Riverine	Wetlands within a channel. Vegetation, when present, is same as in the Lacustrine System.

Palustrine System. — Palustrine wetlands are the predominant wetlands in Tennessee. Most of these wetlands are in the Coastal Plain in the western part of the State along alluvial flood plains of the Mississippi River and its tributaries (fig. 2A and 2B). Tennessee's palustrine wetlands include bottom-land hardwood forests and upland swamps (forested wetlands), scrub-shrub wetlands, beaver ponds (unconsolidated-bottom, aquatic-bed, or emergent wetlands), wet meadows and marshes (emergent wetlands), and highland bogs (forested, scrub-shrub, or emergent wetlands that have organic soils).

Bottom-land hardwood forests are the most common wetlands in Tennessee. These forests have formed primarily in the flat flood plains along streams that drain into the Mississippi and Tennessee Rivers in western Tennessee. Unaltered bottom-land hardwood-forest wetlands in western Tennessee typically contain bald cypress, water tupelo, oaks, sweet gum, red and silver maple, river birch, box elder, and green ash (Hupp, 1992). Scrub-shrub wetlands are present along downstream reaches of channelized streams in western Tennessee. These areas support dense thickets of buttonbush and alder.

Figure 1. Forested wetland along the Hatchie River in western Tennessee. *(Photograph by Cliff R. Hupp, U.S. Geological Survey.)*

Isolated forested wetlands known locally as upland swamps are found in the Highland Rim, Central Basin, Cumberland Plateau, Valley and Ridge, and Blue Ridge Provinces. The predominant trees in upland swamps are sweet gum, sycamore, and species of oak, willow, and maple. Anderson Pond (72 acres), Cedar Hill Swamp (207 acres), and Mingo Swamp (563 acres), located in the Highland Rim, are examples of upland swamps. Each represents land-forms that were once commonplace and have been recommended for consideration as National Natural Landmarks (Ellis and Chester, 1989).

Beaver ponds, typically associated with flood plains, are present throughout the State. As beavers impound water in a bottom-land area, many of the less flood-tolerant trees are killed, thus opening the canopy and allowing for growth of herbaceous vegetation. The vegetation, which is determined by factors such as the age of the pond, topography, and soil characteristics, commonly includes cattails and sedges. The acreage of Tennessee wetlands attributable to beaver activity is unknown (Arner and Hepp, 1989).

Wet meadows are most common in the western and central parts of Tennessee. Grasses, sedges, and rushes are the predominant plants. These wetlands typically are covered by shallow water for only short periods during the growing season, typically after heavy rains. In dry years, wet meadows may be grazed by cattle. Such grazing generally alters the vegetation community.

Freshwater marshes exist throughout Tennessee. Freshwater marshes, vegetated primarily by smartweed and southern wild rice, can be found along the shores of 15,500-acre Reelfoot Lake, a reservoir in northwestern Tennessee. Extensive freshwater marshes also are present along the shores of the Tennessee River.

Highland bogs have formed in the Valley and Ridge Province of eastern Tennessee. Sedges, ferns, and manna grass are typical examples of emergent vegetation in these bogs. Buttonbush and tag alder (scrub-shrub vegetation) commonly are prevalent, and under some conditions, red maple and river birch also are present.

Lacustrine and Riverine Systems. — In Tennessee, lakes (mainly reservoirs) and rivers contain mostly deepwater habitat. However, aquatic beds consisting of floating and submersed aquatic plants, such as water lily and coontail, and nonpersistent-emergent wetlands consisting of plants such as pickerelweed and American lotus are associated with Tennessee's rivers, lakes, and reservoirs.

HYDROLOGIC SETTING

Wetland hydrology is a complex interaction of local and regional factors, including topography, climate, soil characteristics, and geology. Wetlands typically form along the margins of rivers and lakes that are subject to flooding and in depressions where the water table is at or near the land surface. Some wetlands form on highland slopes and are associated with ground-water-discharge points such as springs or seeps.

Tennessee has a diverse topography, ranging from rolling hills and broad flood plains in the Coastal Plain in western Tennessee to the mountains and valleys in the east. Annual precipitation averages about 50 inches statewide and ranges from approximately 47 inches in the west to 80 inches in the mountains in the east. About 20 percent of the precipitation infiltrates into the ground to recharge the State's aquifers. Average annual runoff ranges from approximately 18 to 40 inches. During winter and spring, when evapotranspiration is low, flooding is common. The abundance of water in the State enhances the potential for wetland development and persistence.

The structure and function of Tennessee's bottom-land hard-wood-forest wetlands are determined primarily by the hydrologic regime of the State's rivers. Annual flooding for as long as 60 days in winter and early spring is typical of Tennessee's larger river systems such as the Tennessee, Hatchie, and Mississippi (Carter and Burbank, 1978). Rivers of western Tennessee lie almost entirely within the nearly flat Coastal Plain and include the Obion, Forked Deer, Hatchie, Loosahatchie, and Wolf. Low stream gradients, which contribute to the frequency and severity of flooding, and broad flood plains provide a suitable environment for bottom-land hardwood forests dominated by trees tolerant of a long dormant season and occasional growing-season flooding.

Many streams in western Tennessee have been channelized to enhance drainage of adjacent wetlands (fig. 3), making cultivation possible. However, these streams flow through unconsolidated and

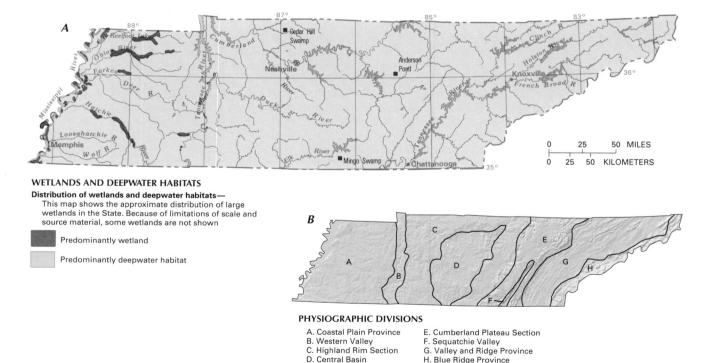

WETLANDS AND DEEPWATER HABITATS

Distribution of wetlands and deepwater habitats—
This map shows the approximate distribution of large wetlands in the State. Because of limitations of scale and source material, some wetlands are not shown

■ Predominantly wetland

☐ Predominantly deepwater habitat

PHYSIOGRAPHIC DIVISIONS

A. Coastal Plain Province
B. Western Valley
C. Highland Rim Section
D. Central Basin
E. Cumberland Plateau Section
F. Sequatchie Valley
G. Valley and Ridge Province
H. Blue Ridge Province

Figure 2. Wetland distribution in Tennessee and physiography of the State. **A,** Distribution of wetlands and deepwater habitats. **B,** Physiography. *(Sources: A, T.E. Dahl, U.S. Fish and Wildlife Service, unpub. data, 1991. B, Physiographic divisions from Fenneman, 1946, and Miller, 1974; landforms data from EROS Data Center.)*

Figure 3. Channelized creek in western Tennessee. *(Photograph by Cliff R. Hupp, U.S. Geological Survey.)*

erodible alluvial deposits, and channelization causes the streams to erode their channel beds and banks in some reaches, whereas other reaches fill with the material eroded from upstream (Robbins and Simon, 1983; Simon and Hupp, 1992). Thus, channelization has had a direct influence on wetland hydrologic processes in Tennessee by reducing flooding and lowering the water table in upper reaches of streams but increasing downstream deposition of sediment and contributing to downstream flooding (Shankman and Samson, 1991; Hupp, 1992).

Isolated wetlands, such as highland bogs and upland swamps, are not associated with streams and typically are formed in limestone sinkholes or depressions on stream terraces. These wetlands rely on direct precipitation and runoff, ground-water discharge, or both, to maintain water volume. Whereas water levels associated with these wetlands fluctuate and can be no more than a few inches deep during dry seasons, complete drying rarely occurs. Soils of these wetlands typically are poorly drained, organic, and acidic.

TRENDS

The FWS National Wetland Inventory has estimated that Tennessee lost as much as 59 percent of its wetland area in the 200 years before the 1980's (Dahl, 1990). Although wetland loss can occur as a result of natural ecological succession, human activities such as livestock grazing, draining, and clearing for agriculture, logging, pond and lake construction, and urban development are most often the cause. Losses have been particularly extensive in western Tennessee.

Logging of western Tennessee bottom lands proceeded rapidly after about 1880, and favorable agricultural prices provided an economic incentive to cultivate marginal lands in the area. Drainage districts were formed to establish dredging and channelization projects to drain the bottom lands to exploit their agricultural potential. By the 1930's, many dredged channels in western Tennessee were partially or completely filled by sediment from agricultural operations. This sedimentation has altered the hydrology of the bottom lands and caused changes in vegetation patterns and wetland types (Wolfe and Diehl, 1993). As much as 83 percent of the original bottom-land hardwood-forest wetlands in the Obion and Forked Deer River Basins alone have been lost (Tennessee Department of Conservation, 1988).

The Hatchie and Wolf Rivers are the remaining major rivers in western Tennessee that have not been channelized along substantial parts of their courses. Most other streams, including tributaries to the Hatchie River, have been repeatedly channelized from their mouths nearly to the drainage divides. Following channelization,

reestablishment of bottom-land hardwood forests takes at least 65 years (Hupp, 1992). Although agricultural conversions could be decreasing, future losses of wetlands might occur as a result of urban conversion, transportation construction, and channelization. Also, though wetland losses are most notable in the western part of the State, significant losses of upland swamps, freshwater marshes, and bottom-land hardwood forests have occurred and could continue to occur in middle and eastern Tennessee (Tennessee Department of Conservation, 1988).

In 1988, the Governor of Tennessee established the Interagency Wetlands Committee in response to concerns over the significant losses of wetlands. The purpose of this committee is to exchange information and coordinate programs of Federal, State, and local agencies, conservation organizations, and private landowners to manage, conserve, or restore wetlands for beneficial uses.

CONSERVATION

Many government agencies and private organizations participate in wetland conservation in Tennessee. The most active agencies and organizations and some of their activities are listed in table 1.

Federal wetland activities. — Development activities in Tennessee wetlands are regulated by several Federal statutory prohibitions and incentives that are intended to slow wetland losses. Some of the more important of these are contained in the 1899 Rivers and Harbors Act; the 1972 Clean Water Act and amendments; the 1985 Food Security Act; the 1990 Food, Agriculture, Conservation, and Trade Act; and the 1986 Emergency Wetlands Resources Act.

Section 10 of the Rivers and Harbors Act gives the U.S. Army Corps of Engineers (Corps) authority to regulate certain activities in navigable waters. Regulated activities include diking, deepening, filling, excavating, and placing of structures. The related section 404 of the Clean Water Act is the most often-used Federal legislation

Table 1. Selected wetland-related activities of government agencies and private organizations in Tennessee, 1993

[Source: Classification of activities is generalized from information provided by agencies and organizations. ●, agency or organization participates in wetland-related activity; ..., agency or organization does not participate in wetland-related activity. MAN, management; REG, regulation; R&C, restoration and creation; LAN, land acquisition; R&D, research and data collection; D&I, delineation and inventory]

Agency or organization	MAN	REG	R&C	LAN	R&D	D&I
FEDERAL						
Department of Agriculture						
Consolidated Farm Service Agency	...	●	...	...	...	...
Natural Resources Conservation Service	...	●	●	...	●	●
Department of Defense						
Army Corps of Engineers	●	●	●	●	●	●
Military reservations	●	...	...	...	...	...
Department of the Interior						
Fish and Wildlife Service	●	...	●	●	●	●
Geological Survey	...	...	...	...	●	...
National Biological Service	...	...	...	...	●	...
National Park Service	●	...	●	●	●	...
Environmental Protection Agency	...	●	●	...	●	●
Tennessee Valley Authority	●	...	●	...	●	...
STATE						
Department of Environment and Conservation	●	●	●	...	...	●
Department of Transportation	...	...	●	...	...	...
Tennessee Technological University	...	...	...	...	●	...
University of Tennessee	...	...	...	...	●	...
Wildlife Resources Agency	●	...	●	●	...	●
PRIVATE						
The Nature Conservancy	...	...	●	●	...	...
Ducks Unlimited	●	...	●	●	...	...
Farm Bureau Federation	...	...	●	...	...	...

protecting wetlands. Under section 404 provisions, the Corps issues permits regulating the discharge of dredged or fill material into wetlands. Permits are subject to review and possible veto by the U.S. Environmental Protection Agency, and the FWS has review and advisory roles. Section 401 of the Clean Water Act grants to States and eligible Indian Tribes the authority to approve, apply conditions to, or deny section 404 permit applications on the basis of a proposed activity's probable effects on the water quality of a wetland.

Most farming, ranching, and silviculture activities are not subject to section 404 regulation. However, the "Swampbuster" provision of the 1985 Food Security Act and amendments in the 1990 Food, Agriculture, Conservation, and Trade Act discourage (through financial disincentives) the draining, filling, or other alteration of wetlands for agricultural use. The law allows exemptions from penalties in some cases, especially if the farmer agrees to restore the altered wetland or other wetlands that have been converted to agricultural use. The Wetlands Reserve Program of the 1990 Food, Agriculture, Conservation, and Trade Act authorizes the Federal Government to purchase conservation easements from landowners who agree to protect or restore wetlands. The Consolidated Farm Service Agency (formerly the Agricultural Stabilization and Conservation Service) administers the Swampbuster provisions and Wetlands Reserve Program. The Natural Resources Conservation Service (formerly the Soil Conservation Service) determines compliance with Swampbuster provisions and assists farmers in the identification of wetlands and in the development of wetland protection, restoration, or creation plans.

The 1986 Emergency Wetlands Resources Act encourages wetland protection through funding incentives. The act requires States to address wetland protection in their Statewide Comprehensive Outdoor Recreation Plans to qualify for Federal funding for State recreational land; the National Park Service provides guidance to States in developing the wetland component of their plans.

The Tennessee Valley Authority (TVA) does not directly regulate wetland activities but conducts a wetlands review for any action affecting TVA-controlled properties. Through the review process, the TVA attempts to minimize the destruction, loss, or degradation of wetlands. In cooperation with the FWS, the TVA operates projects in western Tennessee that provide wetland habitat for migratory waterfowl. In addition, the TVA promotes the use of constructed wetlands as a means of wastewater treatment.

State wetland activities. — The Tennessee Department of Environment and Conservation was created in 1990 by combining the Department of Conservation and the Department of Health and Environment. The Department of Environment and Conservation regulates development activities in wetlands through sections 401 and 402 of the Clean Water Act. The section 401 program requires that a section 404 permit applicant provide certification from the State that a discharge will comply with State water-quality standards. The section 401 certification from the Department is necessary before a section 404 permit can be obtained from the Corps. Section 402 of the Clean Water Act requires that permits be obtained for discharges of treated wastewater to wetlands under the National Pollutant Discharge Elimination System Program. The Department of Environment and Conservation is the State agency delegated to administer this program. The Tennessee Water Quality Control Act of 1977 requires that a State permit be obtained if changes are proposed to an existing aquatic environment; agricultural and forestry activities are exempted.

Through the Tennessee Natural Areas Preservation Act of 1971, the Department of Environment and Conservation has assumed the former Department of Conservation's responsibility for acquiring wetlands that represent outstanding examples of the State's natural landscape. The Tennessee Oil and Gas Law enables the Department to regulate oil and gas drilling by placing special conditions on drilling activities near wetlands. As a result of the U.S. Land and

Water Conservation Act of 1965, the Department is active in wetland-program planning by amending and updating the Statewide Comprehensive Outdoor Recreation Plans to identify wetlands that have high recreation potential.

The Tennessee Wildlife Resources Agency administers the Wetlands Acquisition Fund. The Tennessee Wetlands Acquisition Act of 1986 sets aside a part of the State real estate transfer tax for acquisition of wetlands. The acquisition of wetlands through the Wetlands Acquisition Fund must be approved by the Director of the Wildlife Resources Agency and the Commissioner of Agriculture.

The Tennessee Department of Transportation conducts wetland restorations along its construction projects to mitigate unavoidable wetland destruction. The Department of Transportation also constructs wetlands as large as 450 acres to compensate for unavoidable losses.

County and local wetland activities. — There has been little involvement by county and local governments in wetlands issues in Tennessee. Notable exceptions include Knoxville, Nashville, Chattanooga, and Memphis. These metropolitan areas have developed plans for the construction of greenway recreational areas, some of which will contain wetlands. However, as of 1993, the only city that had begun implementing its plan was Chattanooga.

Private wetland activities. — Several private groups are actively involved in wetlands issues in Tennessee. The Farm Bureau Federation promotes funding and research concerning the use of constructed wetlands for water-quality improvement. The Nature Conservancy cooperates with the State in acquiring areas for preservation. The Tennessee Conservation League and the Sierra Club promote public use and conservation of wetlands. Through its national headquarters in Memphis, Ducks Unlimited cooperates with the Tennessee Wildlife Resources Agency in acquiring and managing wetlands and assists private landowners in constructing wetlands.

References Cited

Arner, D.H., and Hepp, G.R., 1989, Beaver pond wetlands—A southern perspective, *in* Smith, L.M., Pederson, R.L., and Kaminski, R.M., eds., Habitat management for migrating and wintering waterfowl in North America: Lubbock, Texas Tech University Press, p. 130–177.

Carter, Virginia, and Burbank, J.H., 1978, Wetland classification system for the Tennessee Valley Region: Tennessee Valley Authority Technical Note B24, 36 p.

Cowardin, L.M., Carter, Virginia, Golet, F.C., and LaRoe, E.T., 1979, Classification of wetlands and deepwater habitats of the United States: U.S. Fish and Wildlife Service Report FWS/OBS–79/31, 131 p.

Dahl, T.E., 1990, Wetlands—Losses in the United States, 1780's to 1980's: Washington, D.C., U.S. Fish and Wildlife Service Report to Congress, 13 p.

Ellis, W.H., and Chester, E.W., 1989, Upland swamps of the Highland Rim of Tennessee: Journal of the Tennessee Academy of Science, v. 64, no. 3, p. 97–101.

Fenneman, N.M., 1946, Physical divisions of the United States: Washington, D.C., U.S. Geological Survey special map, scale 1:700,000.

Hupp, C.R., 1992, Riparian vegetation recovery patterns following stream channelization: A geomorphic perspective: Ecology, v. 73, no. 4, p. 1,209–1,226.

Miller, R.A., 1974, The geologic history of Tennessee: Tennessee Division of Geology Bulletin 74, 63 p.

Robbins, C.H., and Simon, Andrew, 1983, Man-induced channel adjustment in Tennessee streams: U.S. Geological Survey Water-Resources Investigations Report 82–4098, 129 p.

Shankman, David, and Samson, S.A., 1991, Channelization effects on Obion River flooding, western Tennessee: Water Resources Bulletin, v. 27, no. 2, p. 247–254.

Simon, Andrew, and Hupp, C.R., 1992, Geomorphic and vegetative recovery processes along modified stream channels of western Tennessee: U.S. Geological Survey Open-File Report 91–502, 142 p.

Tennessee Department of Conservation, 1988, Tennessee wetlands plan: Nashville, Tennessee Department of Conservation, 118 p.

Wolfe, W.J., and Diehl, T.H., 1993, Recent sedimentation and surface-water flow patterns on the flood plain of the North Fork Forked Deer River, Dyer County, Tennessee: U.S. Geological Survey Water-Resources Investigations Report 92–4082, 22 p.

FOR ADDITIONAL INFORMATION: District Chief, U.S. Geological Survey, 810 Broadway, Suite 500, Nashville, TN 37203; Regional Wetland Coordinator, U.S. Fish and Wildlife Service, 1875 Century Building, Suite 200, Atlanta, GA 30345

Prepared by
Michael R. Meador,
U.S. Geological Survey

Texas
Wetland Resources

Wetlands cover about 7.6 million acres of Texas—a decrease of about 52 percent from the State's original wetland acreage (Dahl, 1990). Wetlands have considerable environmental and economic value. In river basins, wetlands provide flood attenuation, bank stabilization, and water-quality maintenance. The tourist industry benefits from the scenic beauty of the State's many and diverse wetlands, which afford opportunities for recreational activities that include hunting, fishing, bird watching, nature photography, camping, and hiking. Coastal wetlands (fig. 1) are essential to maintaining important fish and shellfish population and habitat, which in turn provide an economic benefit from the recreational and commercial harvesting of these resources (Tiner, 1984).

Wetlands provide important wildlife habitat. For example, about 90 percent of overwintering waterfowl in the High Plains inhabit playa lake wetlands (Nelson and others, 1983). Statewide riparian and coastal wetlands provide stopover, feeding, and breeding grounds to migratory waterfowl and habitat to nonmigrating wildlife. Among the migrants from Canada that stop at riparian wetlands and overwinter in wetlands along the Texas coast are snow geese, Canada geese, and whooping cranes (an endangered species). Some of the migratory ducks that reside on coastal marshes are American widgeon, mallard, green-winged teal, and blue-winged teal. The mottled duck is a common year-round resident on coastal marshes (Britton and Morton, 1989).

TYPES AND DISTRIBUTION

Wetlands are lands transitional between terrestrial and deepwater habitats where the water table usually is at or near the land surface or the land is covered by shallow water (Cowardin and others, 1979). The distribution of wetlands and deepwater habitats in Texas is shown in figure 2A; only wetlands are discussed herein.

Wetlands can be vegetated or nonvegetated and are classified on the basis of their hydrology, vegetation, and substrate. In this summary, wetlands are classified according to the system proposed by Cowardin and others (1979), which is used by the U.S. Fish and Wildlife Service (FWS) to map and inventory the Nation's wetlands. At the most general level of the classification system, wetlands are grouped into five ecological systems: Palustrine, Lacustrine, Riverine, Estuarine, and Marine. The Palustrine System includes only wetlands, whereas the other systems comprise wetlands and

Figure 1. Wetlands in Welder Flats Coastal Preserve. The preserve was established to manage sensitive and productive estuarine wetlands and protect the endangered whooping cranes that overwinter there. *(Photograph by B.D. Jones, U.S. Geological Survey.)*

deepwater habitats. Wetlands of the systems that occur in Texas are described below.

System	Wetland description
Palustrine	Nontidal and tidal-freshwater wetlands in which vegetation is predominantly trees (forested wetlands); shrubs (scrub-shrub wetlands); persistent or nonpersistent emergent, erect, rooted herbaceous plants (persistent- and nonpersistent-emergent wetlands); or submersed and (or) floating plants (aquatic beds). Also, intermittently to permanently flooded open-water bodies of less than 20 acres in which water is less than 6.6 feet deep.
Lacustrine	Nontidal and tidal-freshwater wetlands within an intermittently to permanently flooded lake or reservoir larger than 20 acres and (or) deeper than 6.6 feet. Vegetation, when present, is predominantly nonpersistent emergent plants (nonpersistent-emergent wetlands), or submersed and (or) floating plants (aquatic beds), or both.
Riverine	Nontidal and tidal-freshwater wetlands within a channel. Vegetation, when present, is same as in the Lacustrine System.
Estuarine	Tidal wetlands in low-wave-energy environments where the salinity of the water is greater than 0.5 part per thousand (ppt) and is variable owing to evaporation and the mixing of seawater and freshwater.
Marine	Tidal wetlands that are exposed to waves and currents of the open ocean and to water having a salinity greater than 30 ppt.

Most Texas wetlands are palustrine; estuarine wetlands are next in area. Lacustrine, riverine, and marine wetlands are ecologically significant but cover a smaller area. The most extensive wetlands are the bottom-land hardwood forests and swamps (forested and scrub-shrub wetlands) of East Texas (the part of the State east of about 96 degrees longitude); the marshes (emergent wetlands), swamps, and tidal flats (unconsolidated-shore wetlands) of the Gulf of Mexico coast; the playa lakes of the High Plains; and the small, shallow, inland depressional basins called potholes found in coastal areas from Brownsville to Port O'Connor.

Most of the State's wetlands are palustrine bottom-land hardwood forests and swamps, and most of these are in the flood plains of East Texas rivers. A recent inventory estimated that, as of the early 1980's, forested wetlands in the State consisted of about 6,068,000 acres, including 5,973,000 acres of bottom-land hardwood forest and other riparian vegetation and 95,000 acres of swamp (Frye, 1987). East Texas contains about 71 percent of the forested wetlands, and the remaining 29 percent is located along rivers and streams throughout the rest of the State.

Data from LANDSAT images taken from 1972 through 1980 provided the basis for the preceding acreage estimates. The use of the LANDSAT images enabled the Texas Parks and Wildlife Department to determine the distribution and types of forested wetlands. Five principal vegetative groups were determined. They include (1) cottonwood-hackberry-salt cedar brush/woods, (2) pecan-elm forest, (3) water oak-elm-hackberry forest, (4) willow oak-water oak-blackgum forest, and (5) bald cypress-water tupelo swamp (McMahan and others, 1984).

Texas coastal wetlands—wetlands that are either on the coast, in or adjacent to estuaries, or in or near the tidal reaches of the rivers—extend the entire length of the coast. Palustrine wetlands, such as swamps and fresh marshes, occupy the flood plains and line the shores of tidal freshwater reaches of sluggish coastal rivers. Pothole wetlands are small, circular bodies of water fringed by emergent vegetation. The pothole wetlands are found inland from the coast and generally contain freshwater. Estuarine wetlands such as salt marshes (emergent wetlands) and tidal flats (mostly unconsolidated-shore, unconsolidated-bottom, and aquatic-bed wetlands) form in tidal reaches of rivers and in sounds and bays, where the salinity of the water can range from slightly more salty than freshwater to nearly as salty as seawater.

A recent inventory of coastal wetlands performed by the National Oceanic and Atmospheric Administration (NOAA) (Field and others, 1991) estimated the area covered by fresh marsh to be 530,300 acres. Estuarine wetlands comprised most of the coastal acreage—710,300 acres. Of the estuarine wetlands, 432,100 acres

PHYSIOGRAPHIC DIVISIONS

WETLANDS AND DEEPWATER HABITATS

Distribution of wetlands and deepwater habitats—
This map shows the approximate distribution of large wetlands in the State. Because of limitations of scale and source material, some wetlands are not shown

Predominantly wetland

Predominantly deepwater habitat

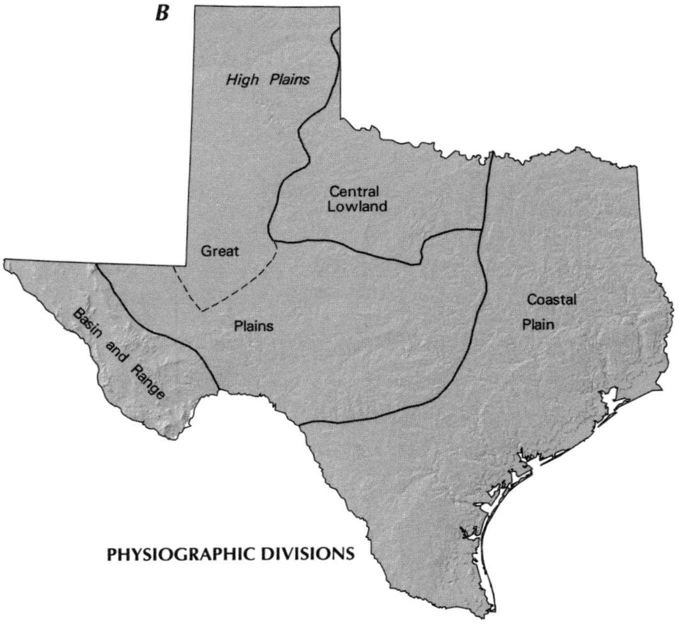

Area typified by a high density of small wetlands

Dams (storage capacity at least 5,000 acre/feet)

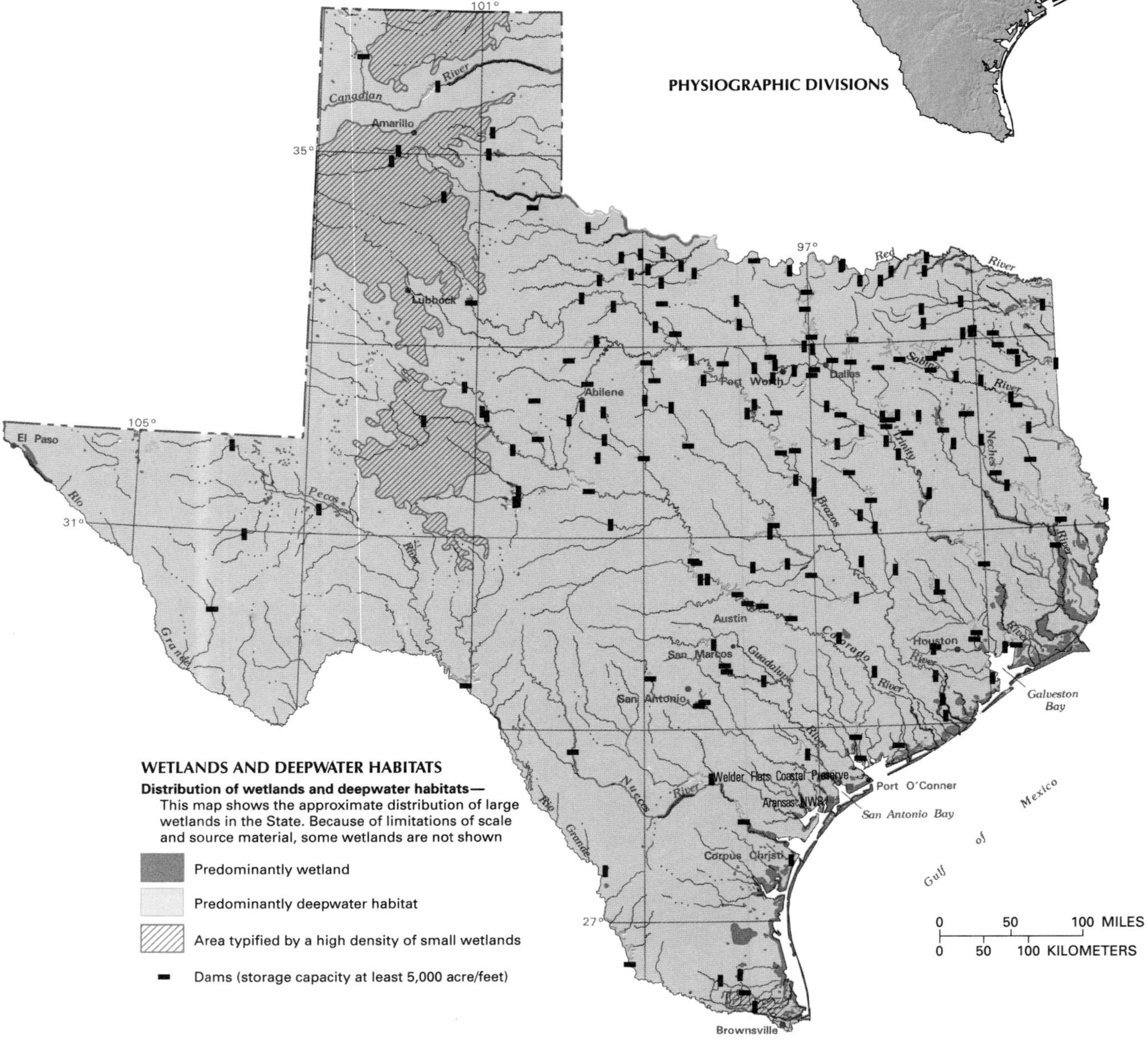

Figure 2. Wetland distribution in Texas and physical and climatological features that control wetland distribution in the State. **A**, Distribution of wetlands and deepwater habitats. **B**, Physiography. *(Sources: A, T.E. Dahl, U.S. Fish and Wildlife Service, unpub. data, 1991. B, Physiographic divisions from Fenneman, 1946; landforms data from EROS Data Center.)*

were salt marsh, 275,300 acres were tidal flats, and 2,900 acres were forested or scrub-shrub wetlands. The acreage summaries were produced using a grid-sampling procedure and wetland maps from the National Wetland Inventory project of the FWS (Tiner, 1984).

The Welder Flats Coastal Preserve (fig. 1) consists of approximately 1,400 acres of wetlands adjacent to San Antonio Bay (Texas Parks and Wildlife Department, 1990). These wetlands are a part of a dynamic estuarine system that has developed in response to the physical, chemical, and biological processes of the Guadalupe River–San Antonio Bay estuary. The wetlands consist of salt marshes, submersed vegetation known as seagrass beds (aquatic beds), nonvegetated mud and sand flats, and shallow saltwater ponds and lagoons. Welder Flats is near the Aransas National Wildlife Refuge, which provides critical shelter and plant food for a large variety of bay waterfowl, estuarine fishes, and bottom-dwelling organisms. It is also an overwintering area for endangered whooping cranes, a migration stopover for shorebirds, and a roosting and foraging area for nonmigrating wildlife.

The State's playa lakes are predominantly within the High Plains. The natural landscape is grassland except along the southeastern border of the area of playa lakes, where it becomes grassland and forest. The playa lakes, which range from dry lakebeds to shallow lakes, have been estimated to total 296,000 acres, or about 4 percent of Texas' wetland area (Guthery and Bryant, 1982). The estimated 20,000 or more playa lakes range in size from about 1 acre to more than 100 acres and in salinity from freshwater to saline. The freshwater playas are numerous, small to medium in size, and serve as zones of recharge to the underlying aquifer (Osterkamp and Wood, 1987). The saline playas are fewer, larger, and are areas of discharge from the underlying aquifer. The density of playa lakes is generally highest in the central part of the High Plains (Nelson and others, 1983).

The playas can be dry for extended periods. In wet conditions, the playa wetlands are either shallow lakes having little or no vegetation or lakes having aquatic vegetation (Nelson and others, 1983). Most of the playas are palustrine wetlands. However, playa lakes that exceed 20 acres are classified as lacustrine wetlands.

HYDROLOGIC SETTING

Wetlands form where there is a persistent water supply at or near the land surface. The location and persistence of the water supply is affected by many factors, such as climate, physiography, and hydrology.

Precipitation and runoff rates in Texas vary annually and with location and season. The average annual precipitation in the State ranges from about 8 inches at El Paso in the Basin and Range Province to about 56 inches in the lower Sabine River valley in the Coastal Plain of extreme eastern Texas (fig. 2B and 2C). The wettest seasons are spring and late summer (Jones, 1991). Evaporation is highest in West Texas and is lowest in East Texas (fig. 2D). In West Texas, annual lake evaporation is 4 to 5 times annual precipitation, whereas in East Texas, annual precipitation approaches annual evaporation. The areas with the highest annual precipitation and lowest evaporation are also the areas that have the most wetlands. East Texas contains more than one-half of the wetland acres in the State.

Bottom-land hardwood or flood-plain forests in East Texas are diverse wetland ecosystems dominated by woody vegetation (Wilkinson and others, 1987). These wetlands form in alluvial sediments deposited in flood plains when streams overflow their banks. The wetlands are maintained by fluctuating water levels resulting from flooding, by stream meanders that retard flow, and by the adaptation of woody vegetation to an environment in which the roots are in organic soils that are inundated or saturated during the growing season.

In East Texas, abundant precipitation and annual flooding in the seven major river basins cause fluctuation of water levels in stream channels, bottom lands, flood plains, and backwater areas, which promotes the development and maintenance of forested wetlands. Other conditions conducive to wetland development and maintenance in East Texas are low evaporation rates, shallow ground water, many springs, and nutrient-rich, clayey bottom-land soils.

The estuaries of the Gulf of Mexico coast were formed when water from melting glaciers caused sea level to rise and inundate

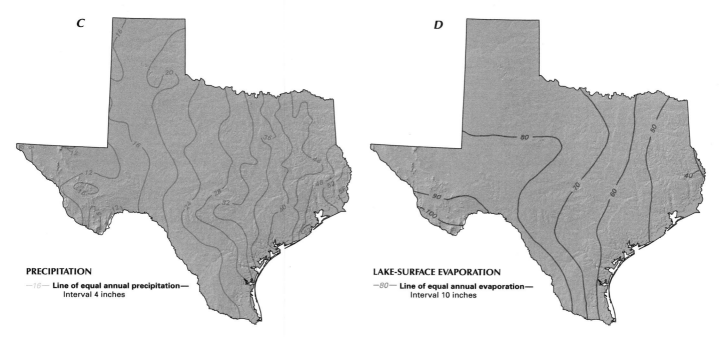

PRECIPITATION

—16— **Line of equal annual precipitation—** Interval 4 inches

LAKE-SURFACE EVAPORATION

—80— **Line of equal annual evaporation—** Interval 10 inches

Figure 2.   Continued.   Wetland distribution in Texas and physical and climatological features that control wetland distribution in the State. **C**, Average annual precipitation. **D**, Average annual gross lake-surface evaporation. *(Sources: C, Woodward, 1986. D, Kane, 1967.)*

coastal river valleys. These drowned valleys were separated from the open sea by barrier islands, forming the bays and lagoons of the present shoreline. The bays and lagoons became shallow as they received sediment from rivers and wind to form estuaries. A variety of habitats develop in an estuary. Each habitat's ecological characteristics are the result of the stability of the substrate, rates of sediment accumulation or erosion, water depth, current flow, and other variables (Britton and Morton, 1989). The salinity of coastal wetlands depends upon whether the source of most of the water entering the estuary is from ocean tides or inland streams.

The soils that support wetlands on the coast have level to depressed relief and low permeability. These soils typically are poorly drained and have a high clay content and a moderate to high water-holding capacity (Barrera and Kelly, 1990).

Rainfall along the coast ranges from 56 inches per year in the subhumid east to 26 inches per year in the semiarid south at the Mexico border. Other principal factors in the climate of the coast are windspeed and direction. Wind, in combination with rainfall, evaporation, humidity, and temperature, affects most of the natural coastal processes. Evaporation generally exceeds precipitation in summer owing to high winds and temperatures. During fall and winter, there is generally a water surplus because of lower temperatures and increased rainfall from tropical storms. Severe tropical storms cause flooding of tidal flats, streams, and hummocky, wind-blown depressions that have poor drainage. Flooding from these tropical storms also results in widespread ponding and development of a shallow water table in the wind-deposited sand overlying older deposits that have very low permeability.

The playa lakes of the High Plains typically are shallow depressions that have a large surface area relative to the volume of water contained in them. Consequently, most playa lakes have a small storage capacity. Osterkamp and Wood (1987) stated that playa lakes form in the Great Plains wherever surface depressions collect water. The lakes enlarge as a result of dissolution of carbonates by water infiltrating the unsaturated zone above the underlying aquifer and subsequent subsidence of the lakebed. There is no general agreement on the origin of saline lakes; however, the source of the salinity might be the concentration by evaporation of shallow ground water that discharges from the underlying aquifer (Wood and Jones, 1990).

The playa-lake area has topography classified as either smooth plains, irregular plains, or tablelands (Nelson and others, 1983). Smooth plains are largely on upland terrain, and irregular plains and tablelands are mostly on lowland terrain. Because of the flatness of the terrain, there is generally little stream drainage; consequently, playa lakes collect most of the surface runoff. Water probably is removed from playa lakes by evaporation that can range as high as 96 to 112 inches per year (Nelson and others, 1983) and by slow leakage to the ground-water system (Osterkamp and Wood, 1987). The playa-lake beds generally have a layer of clay that retards movement of water from the playa lakes to the underlying aquifer.

Annual precipitation in the playa-lake area ranges from 15 inches along the western edge of the High Plains to 21 inches along the eastern edge. On average, more than an inch of rain falls each month between April and October. Windspeeds can range between 40 and 60 miles per hour for as long as a day in March, April, and May. Extreme winter temperatures range from −8°F in the south to −18°F in the north. Extreme summer temperatures range from 109°F to 112°F (Nelson and others, 1983).

TRENDS

The FWS has estimated that from the 1780's to the 1980's, wetland acreage in Texas decreased by 52 percent—from about 16 million to about 7.6 million acres (Dahl, 1990). Wetlands of every type have been affected. Some of these losses can be attributed to natural causes, but a large percentage were caused by human activities. In rural agricultural areas, losses can be attributed to conversion to cropland, declining water levels due to pumpage for irrigation, and overgrazing of wetland vegetation by livestock, which can increase erosion and evaporation. In urban areas, wetland losses occur because of encroachment by residential and commercial construction and industrial development. Wetland degradation has resulted from the discharge of inadequately treated sewage and industrial waste into wetlands. Other activities that can cause wetland losses are filling, water diversion, drainage and river channelization, clearcutting, burning, lowering or disturbing the shallow water table, and the construction of dams, reservoirs, flood-control ditches, levees, irrigation canals, and barge and ship canals. In recent years, several State agencies have begun to develop wetland plans and strategies to reduce wetland losses (Texas Parks and Wildlife Department, 1988).

Bottom-land-hardwood-forest acreage has declined from about 16 million acres in early Texas history (Kier and others, 1977) to about 5.9 million acres (Frye, 1987), a 63 percent loss. A study by the Texas A&M University Remote Sensing Center conducted in the early 1980's indicated that some areas of eastern and southeastern Texas had wetland increases, and some areas had decreases (R.G. Frye, Texas Parks and Wildlife Department, written commun., 1985). The FWS has reported, on the basis of U.S. Forest Service (FS) statistics, that commercial bottom-land forests decreased by 18 percent between 1935 and 1975 and by 10 percent between 1975 and 1985 (U.S. Fish and Wildlife Service, 1984). Lake and reservoir construction, based on the Texas Water Plan to meet projected water needs, would further reduce these wetlands by about 262,000 acres if the 44 reservoirs proposed by the plan were constructed (Texas Department of Water Resources, 1984).

Some of the fresh and salt marshes along the Gulf of Mexico coast have been lost because of dredging, agricultural drainage, and industrialization and urbanization. On the basis of estimates of coastal-wetland area (fresh and salt marshes) made in 1956 and 1980 (Texas Parks and Wildlife Department, 1988), the estimated loss in wetland acreage was about 35 percent during that period. Seagrass beds in the Galveston Bay estuarine system decreased from about 2,500 acres in the 1950's to about 700 acres in 1989 (White and others, 1993). The decrease was attributed to Hurricane Carla, land-surface subsidence, and human activity. A study of six coastal counties found a 41 percent loss in pothole wetlands from 1955 to 1979 (Spiller and French, 1986). Most of the loss was attributed to conversion to agriculture. It also is probable that many of the remaining coastal wetlands have been degraded by land subsidence, saltwater intrusion, and pollution from industry, shipping, and urbanization (D.W. Moulton, Texas Parks and Wildlife Department, written commun., 1990).

The playa lakes of the High Plains have been affected by intense cultivation and irrigation for the last 50 years. It has been estimated that about 90 percent of the playas have been modified (W.W. Wood, U.S. Geological Survey, written commun., 1994), and that more than two-thirds of the larger playas (10 acres or more) have been modified drastically (Guthery and Bryant, 1982). However, no comprehensive estimates of acreage losses exist for the playa-lakes area. Losses of other types of wetlands, such as freshwater springs and riparian wetlands, have occurred throughout the State.

Some land-use practices have led to the creation of new wetlands or the enlargment of existing wetlands. Rice farming near the gulf coast might have contributed to increases in wetland acreage, and construction of lakes and reservoirs undoubtedly has increased the acreage of lacustrine wetlands. However, those gains cannot offset the losses of wetland acreage, function, and value that have occurred in the State.

Table 1. Selected wetland-related activities of government agencies and private organizations in Texas, 1993

[Source: Classification of activities is generalized from information provided by agencies and organizations. •, agency or organization participates in wetland-related activity; ..., agency or organization does not participate in wetland-related activity. MAN, management; REG, regulation; R&C, restoration and creation; LAN, land acquisition; R&D, research and data collection; D&I, delineation and inventory]

Agency or organization	MAN	REG	R&C	LAN	R&D	D&I
FEDERAL						
Department of Agriculture						
Consolidated Farm Service Agency	...	•	...	...	...	...
Forest Service	•	...	•	•	•	•
Natural Resources Conservation Service	...	•	•	...	•	•
Department of Commerce						
National Oceanic and Atmospheric Administration	•	...	...	...	•	•
Department of Defense						
Army Corps of Engineers	•	•	•	...	•	•
Military reservations	•	...	...	...	...	...
Department of the Interior						
Fish and Wildlife Service	•	...	•	•	•	•
Geological Survey	...	...	...	...	•	...
National Biological Service	...	...	...	...	•	...
National Park Service	•	...	•	•	•	•
Environmental Protection Agency	•	...	...	•	•	...
STATE						
Department of Agriculture	...	...	...	...	•	...
Department of Transportation	...	...	...	•	•	...
Forest Service	...	...	...	...	•	...
General Land Office	...	...	•	•	...	•
Parks and Wildlife Department	•	•	•	•	•	•
Railroad Commission	...	•	...	...	...	...
Water Development Board	...	•	...	...	...	...
SOME COUNTIES AND LOCAL GOVERNMENTS	•	•	...	...	...	...
PRIVATE ORGANIZATIONS						
Ducks Unlimited	•	...	•	...	•	•
National Audubon Society	...	...	•	...	...	...
The Conservation Fund	...	...	...	•	...	...
The Nature Conservancy	•	...	•	•	•	•
Trust for Public Land	...	...	...	•	...	...

CONSERVATION

Many government agencies and private organizations participate in wetland conservation in Texas. The most active agencies and organizations and some of their activities are listed in table 1.

Federal wetland activities.—Development activities in Texas wetlands are regulated by several Federal statutory prohibitions and incentives that are intended to slow wetland losses. Some of the more important of these are contained in the 1899 Rivers and Harbors Act; the 1972 Clean Water Act and amendments; the 1985 Food Security Act; the 1990 Food, Agriculture, Conservation, and Trade Act; the 1986 Emergency Wetlands Resources Act; and the 1972 Coastal Zone Management Act.

Section 10 of the Rivers and Harbors Act gives the U.S. Army Corps of Engineers (Corps) authority to regulate certain activities in navigable waters. Regulated activities include diking, deepening, filling, excavating, and placing of structures. The related section 404 of the Clean Water Act is the most often-used Federal legislation protecting wetlands. Under section 404 provisions, the Corps issues permits regulating the discharge of dredged or fill material into wetlands. Permits are subject to review and possible veto by the U.S. Environmental Protection Agency, and the FWS has review and advisory roles. Section 401 of the Clean Water Act grants to States and eligible Indian Tribes the authority to approve, apply conditions to, or deny section 404 permit applications on the basis of a proposed activity's probable effects on the water quality of a wetland.

Most farming, ranching, and silviculture activities are not subject to section 404 regulation. However, the "Swampbuster" provision of the 1985 Food Security Act and amendments in the 1990 Food, Agriculture, Conservation, and Trade Act discourage (through financial disincentives) the draining, filling, or other alteration of wetlands for agricultural use. The law allows exemptions from penalties in some cases, especially if the farmer agrees to restore the altered wetland or other wetlands that have been converted to agricultural use. The Wetlands Reserve Program of the 1990 Food, Agriculture, Conservation, and Trade Act authorizes the Federal Government to purchase conservation easements from landowners who agree to protect or restore wetlands. The Consolidated Farm Service Agency (formerly the Agricultural Stabilization and Conservation Service) administers the Swampbuster provisions and Wetlands Reserve Program. The Natural Resources Conservation Service (formerly the Soil Conservation Service) determines compliance with Swampbuster provisions and assists farmers in the identification of wetlands and in the development of wetland protection, restoration, or creation plans.

The 1986 Emergency Wetlands Resources Act and the 1972 Coastal Zone Management Act and amendments encourage wetland protection through funding incentives. The Emergency Wetland Resources Act requires States to address wetland protection in their Statewide Comprehensive Outdoor Recreation Plans to qualify for Federal funding for State recreational land; the National Park Service (NPS) provides guidance to States in developing the wetland component of their plans. Coastal and Great Lakes States that adopt coastal-zone management programs and plans approved by NOAA are eligible for Federal funding and technical assistance through the Coastal Zone Management Act.

Federal agencies that have public land under their jurisdiction are responsible for the proper management of any wetlands that exist on these lands. In Texas, the FS manages about 636,000 acres of forested land and riparian habitat and about 148,600 acres of grassland (Dallas Morning News, 1992). About 8,500 acres of this land is estimated to be wetlands. The FS goal is to provide for healthy, diverse, and productive ecosystems that will sustain a variety of public benefits now and in the future.

The FWS manages about 396,000 acres in 14 National Wildlife Refuges in Texas. About 228,000 acres of this land is estimated to be wetlands (D.W. Moulton, Texas Parks and Wildlife Department, written commun., 1990). The FWS mission is to conserve, protect, and enhance fish, wildlife, and their habitats.

The NPS manages about 260,000 acres of land in Texas, and more than 99,000 acres of this land is protected waterfowl habitat (D.W. Moulton, Texas Parks and Wildlife Department, written commun., 1990). Regional water-resource coordinators are responsible for wetlands programs within their respective regions. The mission of the NPS is to conserve, preserve, and manage resources of the lands in the National Park system.

State wetland activities.—Several State agencies participate in managing natural resources. Agencies whose responsibilities include some aspect of wetland conservation and a brief description of their activities follow:

The Texas Railroad Commission is responsible for the regulation of surface coal mining and oil and gas production and transport. The regulations are oriented toward production stabilization and include prevention of pollution of wetlands.

The Texas Department of Transportation is responsible for avoiding damage to wetlands while constructing roads and bridges. They also are responsible for acquiring upland disposal areas for maintenance material from the Gulf Intracoastal Waterway.

The Texas Forest Service and Texas Department of Agriculture are involved in wetlands primarily in an advisory capacity to landowners. The agencies assist private owners in the management of forested land and use of land in crop production, including land containing wetlands.

The Texas Water Development Board prepares the State Water Plan and administers funds for reservoir construction and flood control. The State Water Plan must consider the effect of upstream development on bays and estuaries.

The Texas Natural Resource Conservation Commission regulates the allocation of State waters. The effects on fish and wildlife must be considered in permit application for allocations of 5,000 acre-feet or more. The Commission is involved in the process for granting permits for draining, channelizing, levee improvement, construction of wastewater-treatment facilities, and wastewater discharge. The degradation of waters and wetlands in the State is considered in all permit applications.

The Texas General Land Office has management responsibility for 15 large bays totaling over 1.5 million acres. The Land Office manages State lands and leases and grants easements to these lands under rules and regulations that require protection of natural resources, including fish and wildlife habitats.

The Texas Parks and Wildlife Department manages the State Park system, which features many wetland habitats. The Department acquires lands for the preservation, management, and study of wildlife. It also conducts research on management practices for waters and wetlands necessary to promote and sustain fisheries. As the State agency responsible for fish and wildlife, it reviews permit applications submitted to Federal and other State permitting agencies and evaluates their impact on wildlife habitat.

Counties and local wetland activities.—Counties and cities in Texas differ greatly in their commitment to the protection of wetland resources. A few municipalities, such as Austin and San Marcos, have implemented watershed-development controls to protect water quality and riparian wetlands. Some counties and cities have acquired wetlands in order to protect them.

Private wetland activities.—Private organizations have an important function as advocates of wetland conservation and protection. Texas has many private groups that inform the public, organize citizen groups, and lobby governments for the protection of wetlands. The Conservation Fund, National Audubon Society, The Nature Conservancy, and Trust for Public Land have programs for the purchase of wetlands for preservation. These lands can be transferred to State or Federal ownership or, in some cases, may remain in private ownership. Groups that provide information, education, evaluation, and technical help to both public and private owners of wetlands include Ducks Unlimited, Galveston Bay Foundation, Sierra Club, and the Texas Committee on Natural Resources.

References Cited

Barrera, T.A., and Kelly, Nivra, 1990, Wetland creation and enhancement on private lands along the mid to lower gulf coast of Texas under the north American waterfowl management plan: U.S. Fish and Wildlife Service Report CCSU–9002–CCS, 62 p.

Britton, J.C., and Morton, Brian, 1989, Shore ecology of the Gulf of Mexico: Austin, University of Texas Press, 289 p.

Cowardin, L.M., Carter, Virginia, Golet, F.C., and LaRoe, E.T., 1979, Classification of wetlands and deepwater habitats of the United States: U.S. Fish and Wildlife Service Report FWS/OBS–79/31, 131 p.

Dahl, T.E., 1990, Wetlands—Losses in the United States, 1780's to 1980's: Washington, D.C., U.S. Fish and Wildlife Service Report to Congress, 13 p.

Dallas Morning News, 1992, 1990–91 Texas Almanac: Dallas, Texas Monthly Press, 607 p.

Fenneman, N.M., 1946, Physical divisions of the United States: Washington, D.C., U.S. Geological Survey special map, scale 1:7,000,000.

Field, D.W., Reyer, A.J., Genovese, P.V., and Shearer, B.D., 1991, Coastal wetlands of the United States—An accounting of a valuable national resource: Washington, D.C., National Oceanic and Atmospheric Administration and U.S. Fish and Wildlife Service cooperative publication, 59 p.

Frye, R.G., 1987, Current supply, status, habitat quality and future impacts from reservoirs, *in* McMahan, C.A., and Frye, F.G., eds., Bottomland hardwoods in Texas—Proceedings of an interagency workshop on status and ecology, May 6–7, 1986, Nacogdoches, Tex.: Texas Parks and Wildlife Report PWD–RP–7100–133–3/87, p. 24–28.

Guthery, F.S., and Bryant F.C., 1982, Status of playas in the southern Great Plains: Wildlife Society Bulletin, v. 10, no. 4, p. 309–317.

Jones, B.D., 1991, Texas floods and droughts, *in* U.S. Geological Survey, National water summary 1988–89—Hydrologic events and floods and droughts: U.S. Geological Survey Water-Supply Paper 2375, p. 513–520.

Kane, J.W., 1967, Monthly reservoir evaporation rates for Texas, 1940 through 1965: Texas Water Development Board Report 64, 111 p., 7 pls., scale 1:5,000,000.

Kier, R.S., Garner, L.E., and Brown, L.F., Jr., 1977, Land resources of Texas—A map of Texas lands classified according to natural suitability and use considerations: University of Texas at Austin, Bureau of Economic Geology, 42 p., 4 map sheets, scale 1:500,000.

McMahan, C.A., Frye, R.G., and Brown, K.L., 1984, The vegetation types of Texas—Including cropland: Texas Parks and Wildlife Department, PWD Bulletin 7000–120, 40 p., map, scale 1:1,000,000.

Nelson, R.W., Logan, W.J., and Weller, E.C., 1983, Playa wetlands and wildlife on the southern Great Plains—A characterization of habitat: U.S. Fish and Wildlife Service Report FWS/OBS–83/28, 163 p.

Osterkamp, W.R., and Wood, W.W., 1987, Playa lake basins on the southern High Plains of Texas and New Mexico—Part 1, hydrologic, geomorphic, and geologic evidence for their development: Geological Society of America Bulletin, v. 99, p. 215–223.

Spiller, S.F., and French, J.D., 1986, The value and status of inland pothole wetlands in the lower Rio Grande Valley, Texas: U.S. Fish and Wildlife Service Special Report, 18 p.

Texas Department of Water Resources, 1984, Water for Texas—A comprehensive plan for the future: Texas Department of Water Resources Report G–P–4–1, 2 volumes, 72 p.

Texas Parks and Wildlife Department, 1988, The Texas wetlands plan—Addendum to the 1985 Texas outdoor recreation plan: Austin, Texas Parks and Wildlife Department, 35 p.

_____1990, Welder Flats Coastal Preserve—Baseline studies report: Austin, Texas Parks and Wildlife Department [variously paged].

Tiner, R.W., Jr., 1984, Wetlands of the United States—Current status and recent trends: Washington, D.C., U.S. Fish and Wildlife Service, 59 p.

U.S. Fish and Wildlife Service, 1984, Texas bottomland hardwood preservation program: Albuquerque, N. Mex., U.S. Fish and Wildlife Service, 378 p.

White, W.A., Tremblay, T.A., Wermund, E.G., Jr., and Handley, L.R., 1993, Trends and status of wetland habitats in the Galveston Bay system, Texas: U.S. Fish and Wildlife Publication GBNEP–31, 225 p.

Wilkinson, D.L., Schneller-McDonald, Karen, Olson, R.W., and Auble, G.T., 1987, Synopsis of wetlands functions and values—Bottomland hardwoods with special emphasis on eastern Texas and Oklahoma: U.S. Fish and Wildlife Service Biological Report 87(12), 131 p.

Wood, W.W., and Jones, B.F., 1990, Origin of saline lakes and springs on the southern High Plains of Texas and New Mexico, *in* Gustavson, T.C., ed., Geological framework and regional hydrology—Upper Cenozoic Blackwater Draw and Ogallala Formation, Great Plains: Austin, Tex., Bureau of Economic Geology, p. 193–208.

Woodward D.G., 1986, Texas surface-water resources, *in* National water summary 1985—Hydrologic events and surface-water resources: U.S. Geological Survey Water-Supply Paper 2300, p. 431–440.

FOR ADDITIONAL INFORMATION: District Chief, U.S. Geological Survey, 8011 Cameron Road, Building A, Austin, TX 78754; Regional Wetland Coordinator, U.S. Fish and Wildlife Service, 500 Gold Avenue, SW, Room 4012, Albuquerque, NM 87103

Prepared by
B.D. Jones,
U.S. Geological Survey

U.S. Virgin Islands
Wetland Resources

The wetlands of the U.S. Virgin Islands, which comprise St. Croix, St. Thomas, St. John, and about 50 smaller islands, are limited in area but are an important natural resource. The U.S. Virgin Islands are located on the northeastern edge of the Caribbean Sea east of Puerto Rico's Vieques and Culebra islands in the arc of the Lesser Antilles, which curves southward toward South America. The wetlands of these islands generally are coastal wetlands such as mangrove forests and saltponds (fig. 1). Many of these valuable wetlands are threatened by development.

Wetlands on the U.S. Virgin Islands are biologically productive. They support food webs intricately linked to seagrasses and coral reefs of the nearshore waters of the Caribbean Sea by providing nursery and feeding habitat for marine fish and shellfish (Lopez and others, 1988). Seagrass beds provide foraging for the threatened green turtle and important nursery grounds for lobster and conch. Ninety percent of the U.S. Virgin Islands' resident and migratory bird species use wetlands (Philibosian and Yntema, 1977). One-hundred twenty-one species of birds have been observed in coastal wetlands (William Knowles, U.S. Virgin Islands Department of Planning and Natural Resources, written commun., 1994). Endangered species, such as the peregrine falcon and brown pelican, and other rare species, such as the white-cheeked pintail and white-crowned pigeon, nest and feed within the wetlands. Sandpipers, plovers, snipe, and other shorebirds depend on these areas during migration. The wetlands also maintain water quality by trapping sediments transported in runoff from the island interior, protect the shoreline from wave erosion, and dampen the effects of storm surges.

TYPES AND DISTRIBUTION

Wetlands are lands transitional between terrestrial and deepwater habitats where the water table usually is at or near the land surface or the land is covered by shallow water (Cowardin and others, 1979). The distribution of wetlands and deepwater habitats in the U.S. Virgin Islands is shown in figure 2; only wetlands are discussed herein.

Wetlands can be vegetated or novegetated and are classified on the basis of their hydrology, vegetation, and substrate. In this summary, wetlands are classified according to the system proposed by Cowardin and others (1979), which is used by the U.S. Fish and Wildlife Service (FWS) to map and inventory the Nation's wetlands. At the most general level of the classification system, wetlands are grouped into five ecological systems: Palustrine, Lacustrine, Riverine, Estuarine, and Marine. The Palustrine System includes only wetlands, whereas the other systems comprise wetlands and deepwater habitats. Wetlands of the systems that occur in the U.S. Virgin Islands are described below.

System	Wetland description
Palustrine	Nontidal and tidal-freshwater wetlands in which vegetation is predominantly trees (forested wetlands); shrubs (scrub-shrub wetlands); persistent or nonpersistent emergent, erect, rooted herbaceous plants (persistent- and nonpersistent-emergent wetlands); or submersed and (or) floating plants (aquatic beds). Also, intermittently to permanently flooded open-water bodies of less than 20 acres in which water is less than 6.6 feet deep.
Riverine	Nontidal and tidal-freshwater wetlands within a channel. Vegetation, when present, is same as in the Lacustrine System.
Estuarine	Tidal wetlands in low-wave-energy environments where the salinity of the water is greater than 0.5 part per thousand (ppt) and is variable owing to evaporation and the mixing of seawater and freshwater.
Marine	Tidal wetlands that are exposed to waves and currents of the open ocean and to water having a salinity greater than 30 ppt.

As a result of steep terrain, small drainage basins, and limited rainfall, freshwater wetlands and deepwater habitats are scarce on the U.S. Virgin Islands. St. Thomas, about 28 square miles in area, reaches an altitude of 1,556 feet above sea level and is very steep. St. John, about 19 square miles in area, reaches an altitude of 1,297 feet above sea level and is also steep. St. Croix, about 84 square miles in area, reaches an altitude of 1,165 feet above sea level and is less rugged—more than 50 percent of the landscape has a slope of less than 10 percent. No lacustrine habitats (large freshwater bodies) occur in the islands. Because nearly all streams are ephemeral, riverine wetlands are limited to channels of intermittent streams. Palustrine wetlands consist of a few small marshes. Constructed catchment basins fill with water during the wet season and may be vegetated by cattails or other wetland plants, depending on the time of year, age of the impoundment, and degree of maintenance. There are three small, natural freshwater marshes on St. Croix. One is a small emergent area at the interior edge of the Sugar Bay wetland complex. The second is a 7-acre, seasonally flooded marsh about 1 mile north of Frederiksted. The third is a small area owned and managed by the University of the Virgin Islands northeast of Krause Lagoon.

Most wetlands of the U.S. Virgin Islands are located along the coasts and are classified as estuarine or marine wetlands. The largest of the wetlands are on St. Croix, where the terrain is less steep and the drainage basins are larger than on St. Thomas or St. John.

Estuarine intertidal vegetated wetlands in the U.S. Virgin Islands are dominated by red, white, and black mangroves. Buttonwood also is common, particularly in hypersaline (salinity greater than seawater) environments. Mangroves grow in shallow lagoons,

Figure 1. Salt Pond near Saltpond Bay in Virgin Islands National Park on St. John, U.S. Virgin Islands. *(Photograph by D. Briane Adams, U.S. Geological Survey.)*

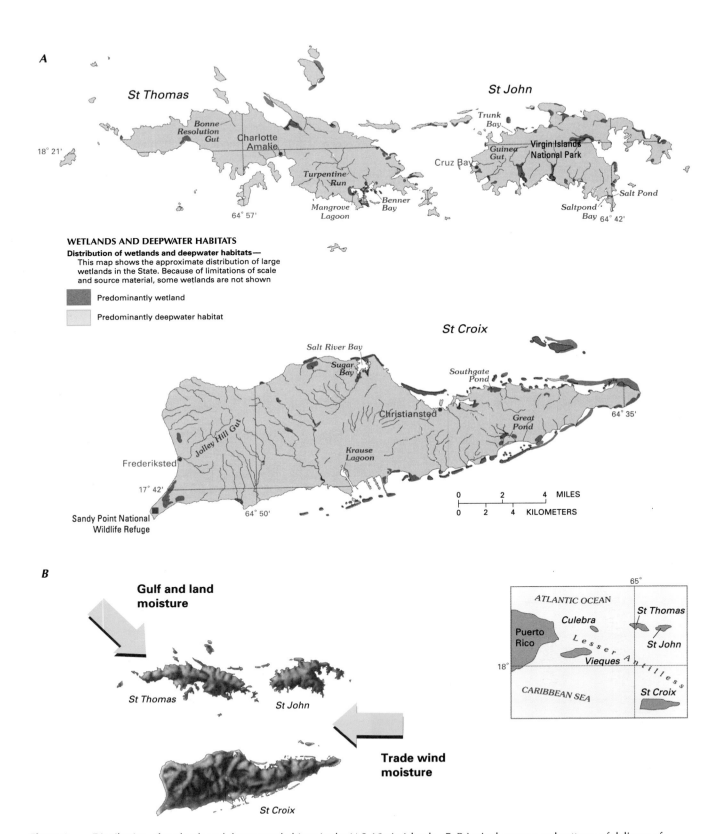

A

St Thomas

Bonne
Resolution
Gut

Charlotte
Amalie

18° 21'

Turpentine
Run

64° 57'

Mangrove
Lagoon

Benner
Bay

St John

Trunk
Bay

Guinea
Gut

Virgin Islands
National Park

Cruz Bay

Salt Pond

Saltpond
Bay 64° 42'

WETLANDS AND DEEPWATER HABITATS

Distribution of wetlands and deepwater habitats—
This map shows the approximate distribution of large
wetlands in the State. Because of limitations of scale
and source material, some wetlands are not shown

Predominantly wetland

Predominantly deepwater habitat

St Croix

Salt River Bay

Sugar
Bay

Southgate
Pond

Christiansted

Great
Pond

64° 35'

Jolley Hill Gut

Krause
Lagoon

Frederiksted

17° 42'

64° 50'

Sandy Point National
Wildlife Refuge

| 0 | | 2 | | 4 | MILES |
| 0 | | 2 | | 4 | KILOMETERS |

B

**Gulf and land
moisture**

St Thomas

St John

**Trade wind
moisture**

St Croix

65°

ATLANTIC OCEAN

Culebra

St Thomas

Puerto
Rico

St John

18°

Vieques

Lesser Antilles

CARIBBEAN SEA

St Croix

Figure 2. , Distribution of wetlands and deepwater habitats in the U.S. Virgin Islands. **B**, Principal sources and patterns of delivery of
moisture into the U.S. Virgin Islands. *(Sources: A, Digitized from USFWS–NWI, U.S. Fish and Wildlife Service, National Wetland Inventory,
unpub. data, 1994. B, Data from Douglas Clark and Andrea Lage, Wisconsin Geological and Natural History Survey.)*

such as Mangrove Lagoon on St. Thomas; ring "saltponds," such as Great Pond on St. Croix; or fringe bays and coves, such as the Salt River Bay–Sugar Bay estuary on St. Croix.

Saltponds are the predominant wetlands in the U.S. Virgin Islands. They are tidal flats or basins that are at least partially separated from direct contact to the sea by a beach berm. Saltponds range in size from less than 1 acre to more than 125 acres. An example of this wetland type is Salt Pond near Saltpond Bay in Virgin Islands National Park on St. John (fig. 1). Saltwater inputs to the ponds result from tidal or storm-surge overwash of the berm, seepage of seawater through the berm, or from subterranean connections to the sea. Ponds that have sporadic input of seawater go through an annual cycle of filling with freshwater runoff and rainfall during the rainy season and drawing down or drying during the remainder of the year. Consequently, saltponds are subject to extreme salinity variations during the annual cycle.

Coral reefs ring many of the U.S. Virgin Islands. Though most of the reefs and seagrass beds are submersed, at least some are exposed at low tide and thus are classified as wetlands. The most extensive of the reefs surround St. Croix. The reef in Trunk Bay in Virgin Islands National Park on St. John is the site of an underwater trail and has corals typical of those in the Caribbean area.

HYDROLOGIC SETTING

Wetlands form where the local hydrology makes possible a dependable water supply at or near the land surface. In the U.S. Virgin Islands, the type of wetland that exists at a particular location is determined by the local hydrologic setting. The components of that setting include the duration of inundation or saturation, the salinity of the water, and the nature of the substrate, which in turn are the result of climate, geology, and topography.

The climate of the U.S. Virgin Islands is classified as subtropical (Ewell and Whitmore, 1973). Winters are mild and dry, whereas summers are warm and humid. In the winter, precipitation generally comes from frontal systems from the northwest and is greatest during February and March, when the regional climate is influenced by a subtropical high pressure area. During summer, the regional climate is no longer influenced by high atmospheric pressure, and there is a steady westerly flow of moist air from the Atlantic Ocean (the trade winds) that is the primary source of summer and fall precipitation (fig. 2B).

Average annual precipitation ranges from about 30 inches in the lowlands of St. Croix to about 55 inches in the mountain peaks of St. John. Precipitation increases with altitude because moist air in the weather systems is forced up the slopes into the cooler air at the higher altitudes, causing the moisture to condense and fall as rain. However, because of the small size of the islands and brief time for passage of these systems over them, these effects are not

as pronounced as for larger Caribbean islands with higher mountain peaks. Clouds form as they pass over St. Thomas and St. Croix, but most resultant precipitation falls in the Caribbean Sea on the lee side of the islands.

The geology and topography of the U.S. Virgin Islands are major factors influencing the hydrology of the islands, which in turn controls the presence or absence of wetlands. The U.S. Virgin Islands are composed of volcanic rock that was uplifted by tectonic activity. The islands have steep slopes and irregular coastlines. Both St. Thomas and St. John have steep slopes throughout, but on St. Croix the mountains in the northwest give way to rolling hills that broaden to an expanse of relatively low flatland along the southern two-thirds of the island.

Ground water in the U.S. Virgin Islands is scarce. The most extensive ground-water source on the islands is the fractured volcanic rocks of which the islands are generally composed (Gómez-Gómez and others, 1985). Embayment aquifers occur near guts (stream drainages) along the coasts of the islands. These aquifers are composed principally of weathered rocks overlain by shallow alluvium. They are recharged by seepage from the surrounding volcanic rocks and by direct infiltration from ephemeral runoff and precipitation. Discharge from these aquifers to the oceans is a source of freshwater for estuarine wetlands, such as mangrove wetlands, in the coastal embayments. On St. Croix, an aquifer composed of limestone interbedded with sand and gravel and covered by alluvium exists throughout most of the lowlands. This aquifer discharges small amounts of ground water to coastal wetlands.

On an annual basis, surface runoff, which is a major factor in the formation of streamside and coastal wetlands, is low. There are no perennial streams, and most natural surface-water drainages are dry for long periods of time and flow only during periods of intense rainfall. Because of the impermeable underlying volcanic rocks, floodwaters accumulate and recede rapidly, generally in less than 1 day. During a year of average precipitation, annual runoff ranges from about 2 to 8 percent of the rainfall (Santiago-Rivera and Colón-Dieppa, 1986), which is about 0.5 to 2 inches, depending on conditions in a particular basin. Runoff is controlled by topography, soil moisture, local evaporation rates, and vegetation cover. On St. Croix, runoff is stored in ponds for agricultural uses. Commonly, total runoff from individual storms exceeds 10 percent of the rainfall and can be as high as 30 percent when rainfall is intense and soil moisture demands are low. As these floodwaters reach the coastal areas, they overflow saltponds and provide freshwater inflow to embayments that support mangrove stands and coral reefs (fig. 3).

A few streams are intermittent; that is, they flow year-round in some reaches. For Turpentine Run on St. Thomas, base flow is predominantly from sewage effluent, and about one-half to three-

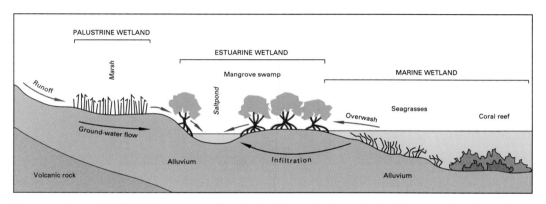

Figure 3. Generalized hydrologic setting of wetlands in the U.S. Virgin Islands. *(Source: Wetland types from Lugo and Brown, 1988.)*

fourths of total flow is from storm runoff (Santiago-Rivera and Colón-Dieppa, 1986). Turpentine Run discharges to Mangrove Lagoon (fig. 4A) on the southeastern side of the island. On St. Thomas, the only other intermittent stream is Bonne Resolution Gut. Guinea Gut on St. John, which has base flow from spring discharge, and Jolley Hill Gut on St. Croix, once reported to be perennial, are the only intermittent streams on those islands.

TRENDS

Wetlands in the U.S. Virgin Islands occupy less than 3 percent of the land area. On the basis of mapping by the FWS National Wetlands Inventory, there are 960 acres of wetlands on St. Croix, 320 acres of wetlands on St. Thomas, and 425 acres of wetlands on St. John.

The wetlands of the U.S. Virgin Islands have been adversely affected by both natural forces and human activities. Hurricane Hugo, which passed directly over St. Croix in September 1989, was the last major storm to significantly alter the wetlands of the islands. Hurricane winds defoliated mangroves to such an extent that many died. In addition, many black and white mangroves were uprooted (Knowles and Amrani, 1991). Although recovery might be slow, the wetland vegetation probably will become reestablished if it is not disturbed.

Human-caused wetland alterations have been severe and will likely be long lasting. Wetlands in the islands remained virtually untouched until the 1960's. During the economic growth period of the 1960's and 1970's, numerous wetlands were altered on St. Thomas and St. John (J.H. Farrelly, U.S. Virgin Islands Department of Planning and Natural Resources, written commun., 1992). The most extensive wetland alteration took place in St. Croix at Krause Lagoon, the largest of the U.S. Virgin Island wetlands. By the late 1970's, Krause Lagoon was virtually eliminated by dredging and filling for construction of port facilities for a major oil refinery, an aluminum plant, and a container manufacturer. An important large wetland complex, Mangrove Lagoon–Benner Bay (fig. 4A) on St. Thomas, has been similarly affected. Mangrove Lagoon is one of the U.S. Virgin Islands' largest wetland complexes, consisting of saltponds, a barrier reef, and fringe mangroves. Loss of mangroves and associated submersed seagrasses and corals has resulted from construction of marinas, recreation facilities, a wastewater treatment facility, and encroachment by a major landfill. Most of the adverse impacts, except for dredging, are the result of alterations that have disrupted the normal patterns of runoff to the bay.

Wetlands of the U.S. Virgin Islands remain susceptible to development. Their location along the shoreline make them particularly attractive as sites for tourist facilities and water-dependent developments. It is relatively easy to construct marinas from saltponds, as was done in Southgate Pond on the north shore of St. Croix and saltponds on St. Thomas (fig. 4B). The demand for such facilities is great; more than 4,000 vessels are registered in the U.S. Virgin Islands (J.H. Farrelly, U.S. Virgin Islands Department of Planning and Natural Resources, written commun., 1992).

Wetlands also are susceptible to degradation by sedimentation and septic tank leachate from upland areas. The extent to which this type of impact is occurring is unknown.

A

B

C

D

Figure 4. Selected U.S. Virgin Islands wetlands. **A**, Mangrove Lagoon–Benner Bay on St. Thomas. **B**, Saltpond on St. Thomas. **C**, Trunk Bay on St. John. **D**, Salt River Bay on St. Croix. *(Photographs by D. Briane Adams.)*

CONSERVATION

Many government agencies and private organizations participate in wetland conservation in the U.S. Virgin Islands. The most active agencies and organizations and some of their activities are listed in table 1.

Table 1. Selected wetland-related activities of government agencies and private organizations in the U.S. Virgin Islands, 1993

[Source: Classification of activities is generalized from information provided by agencies and organizations. •, agency or organization participates in wetland-related activity; ..., agency or organization does not participate in wetland-related activity. MAN, management; REG, regulation; R&C, restoration and creation; LAN, land acquisition; R&D, research and data collection; D&I, delineation and inventory]

Agency or organization	MAN	REG	R&C	LAN	R&D	D&I
FEDERAL						
Department of Agriculture						
Consolidated Farm Service Agency	...	•	...	...	...	...
Forest Service	•	...	•	•	•	•
Natural Resources Conservation Service	...	•	•	...	•	•
Department of Commerce						
National Oceanic and Atmospheric Administration	•	•	...	...	•	...
Department of Defense						
Army Corps of Engineers	•	•	•	•	•	•
Department of the Interior						
Fish and Wildlife Service	•	•	...	...	•	•
Geological Survey	...	...	...	...	•	...
National Biological Service	...	...	...	...	•	...
National Park Service	•	...	•	•	•	•
Environmental Protection Agency	...	•	...	...	•	...
TERRITORY OF THE U.S. VIRGIN ISLANDS						
Department of Planning and Natural Resources						
Department of Planning and Coastal Zone Management Program	•	•	•	...	•	•
Division of Fish and Wildlife	•	...	•	...	•	...
PRIVATE						
Island Resources Foundation	...	...	...	...	•	...

Federal wetland activities.—Development within or near wetlands is regulated by several Federal statutory prohibitions and incentives that are intended to slow wetland losses. Some of the more important of these are contained in the 1899 Rivers and Harbors Act; the 1972 Clean Water Act and amendments; the 1985 Food Security Act; the 1990 Food, Agriculture, Conservation, and Trade Act; the 1986 Emergency Wetlands Resources Act; and the 1972 Coastal Zone Management Act. In the following description of wetland-related Federal legislation, regulations that apply to States also apply to the U.S. Virgin Islands.

Section 10 of the Rivers and Harbors Act gives the U.S. Army Corps of Engineers (Corps) authority to regulate certain activities in navigable waters. Regulated activities include diking deepening, filling, excavating, and placing of structures. The related section 404 of the Clean Water Act is the most often-used Federal legislation protecting wetlands. Under section 404 provisions, the Corps issues permits regulating the discharge of dredged or fill material into wetlands. Permits are subject to review and possible veto by the U.S. Environmental Protection Agency, and the FWS has review and advisory roles. Section 401 of the Clean Water Act grants to States and eligible Indian Tribes the authority to approve, apply conditions to, or deny section 404 permit applications based on a proposed activity's probable effects on the water quality of a wetland.

Most farming, ranching, and silviculture activities are not subject to section 404 regulation, but the "Swampbuster" provision of the 1985 Food Security Act and amendments in the 1990 Food, Agriculture, Conservation, and Trade Act discourage (through financial disincentives) the draining, filling, or other alteration of wetlands for agricultural use. The law allows exemptions from penalties in some cases, especially if the farmer agrees to restore the altered wetland or other wetlands that have been converted to agricultural use. The Wetlands Reserve Program of the 1990 Food, Agriculture, Conservation, and Trade Act authorized the Federal Government to purchase conservation easements from landowners who agree to protect or restore wetlands. The Consolidated Farm Service Agency (formerly the Agricultural Stabilization and Conservation Service) administers the Swampbuster provisions and Wetlands Reserve Program. The Natural Resources Conservation Service (formerly the Soil Conservation Service) determines compliance with Swampbuster provisions and assists farmers in the identification of wetlands and in the development of wetland protection, restoration, or creation plans.

The 1986 Emergency Wetlands Resources Act and the 1972 Coastal Zone Management Act and amendments encourage wetland protection through funding incentives. The Emergency Wetlands Resources Act requires States to address wetland protection in their Statewide Comprehensive Outdoor Recreation Plans to quality for Federal funding for State recreational land; the National Park Service (NPS) provides guidance in developing the wetland component of their plans. Coastal States that adopt coastal-zone management programs and plans approved by the National Oceanic and Atmospheric Administration are eligible for Federal funding and technical assistance through the Coastal Zone Management Act.

Large tracts of land, many containing wetlands, are managed by the FWS and the NPS. The largest area managed by the FWS is the 326-acre Sandy Point National Wildlife Refuge in southwestern St. Croix. The NPS manages most of the Island of St. John, along with extensive offshore areas, such as the underwater trail at Trunk Bay in Virgin Islands National Park (fig. 4C). The NPS has received authorization to acquire lands around Salt River Bay on St. Croix (fig. 4D). Not only is the area one of the U.S. Virgin Islands' most important wetland complexes, but it is also a valuable historical resource believed to be the landing site of Christopher Columbus on his second voyage to the Americas in 1493.

Territorial wetland activities.—The Department of Planning and Natural Resources is the principal agency requiring permit application for construction activities in the coastal zone, where wetlands usually form. This responsibility was granted to the Department by the Coastal Zone Management Act passed in 1978. In addition to evaluating permit requests, the Department comments on Federal permit applications to ensure consistency with the Coastal Zone Management Plan. When wetland losses are unavoidable, the Department requires mitigation actions to ameliorate anticipated losses. The Department also monitors wetlands to ensure that unpermitted activities are not taking place and that authorized activities are in full compliance with permit requirements. The Territorial Legislature adopted the Indigenous and Endangered Species Act of 1990, in which section 104(e) establishes a policy of "no net loss of wetlands" to the maximum extent possible.

Private wetland activities.—The Island Resources Foundation is headquartered on St. Thomas. The Foundation is an important advocate for conservation of island wetlands and other natural resources unique to islands of the Caribbean and elsewhere. Through lobbying, organization of citizen networks, and development of educational materials and research, the Foundation promotes sound management of the area's natural resources.

References Cited

Cowardin, L.M., Carter, Virginia, Golet, F.C., and LaRoe, E.T., 1979, Classification of wetlands and deepwater habitats of the United States: U.S. Fish and Wildlife Service Report FWS/OBS–79/31, 131 p.

Ewell, J.J., and Whitmore, J.L., 1973, The ecological life zones of Puerto Rico and the U.S. Virgin Islands: U.S. Forest Service Research Paper ITF–18, 72 p.

Gómez-Gómez, Fernando, Guiñones-Márquez, Ferdinand, and Zack, A.L., 1985, U.S. Virgin Islands ground-water resources, *in* U.S. Geological Survey, National water summary 1984— Hydrologic events, selected water-quality trends, and ground-water resources: U.S. Geological Survey Water-Supply Paper 2275, p. 409–414.

Knowles, W.C., and Amrani, Cheri, 1991, Wildlife use of the Virgin Islands' wetlands: St. Thomas, U.S. Virgin Islands, Department of Planning and Natural Resources, Division of Fish and Wildlife, 220 p.

Lopez, J.M., Stoner, A.W., García, J.R., and García-Muñíz, Ivan, 1988, Marine food webs associated with Caribbean island mangrove wetlands: Acta Cientifica, v. 2, no. 2–3, p. 94–123.

Lugo, A.E., and Brown, Sandra, 1988, The wetlands of the Caribbean islands: Acta Cientifica, v. 2, no. 2–3, p. 48–61.

Philibosian, Richard, and Yntema, J.A., 1977, Annotated checklist of the birds, mammals, reptiles, and amphibians of the Virgin Islands and Puerto Rico: St. Croix, U.S. Virgin Islands, Information Services, 48 p.

Santiago-Rivera, Luis, and Colón-Dieppa, Eloy, 1986, U.S. Virgin Islands surface-water resources, *in* U.S. Geological Survey, National water summary 1985— Hydrologic events and surface-water resources: U.S. Geological Survey Water-Supply Paper 2300, p. 447–452.

FOR ADDITIONAL INFORMATION: District Chief, U.S. Geological Survey, P.O. Box 364424, San Juan, PR 00936; Regional Wetland Coordinator, U.S. Fish and Wildlife Service, 1875 Century Building, Suite 200, Atlanta, GA 30345

Prepared by
D. Briane Adams, U.S. Geological Survey, and John M. Hefner, U.S. Fish and Wildlife Service

Utah
Wetland Resources

Wetlands cover only a small part of Utah but provide critical aquatic habitat in an arid environment (fig. 1) as well as economic and other benefits. Utah's wetlands provide habitat for fish, fur-bearing wildlife, resident waterfowl, shorebirds, songbirds, and nearly 500 species of wetland plants (Reed, 1986). Wetlands also provide stopover and breeding habitat for migratory waterfowl, including an estimated 1 million ducks and 65,000 swans and geese that pass through the State during fall migration (Redelfs, 1980). Recreational activities associated with wetlands, such as hunting, bird watching, canoeing, fishing, and camping, provide considerable revenue to the State. Duck and goose hunting on wetlands adjacent to Great Salt Lake alone resulted in an estimated expenditure of $6.4 million dollars by hunters in 1974 (Rawley, 1974).

About 30 percent of the ducks migrating along the Pacific Flyway stop at marshes around Great Salt Lake (Rawley, 1980), and 74 percent of the waterfowl harvested in the State comes from this area (Rawley, 1974). Because of the importance of Great Salt Lake and its associated wetlands to migratory birds, in 1991 the lake was designated a Hemispheric Reserve in the Western Hemisphere Shorebird Reserve Network. At least 33 species of shorebirds use Great Salt Lake and its wetlands at some point in their life cycle; typically, 500,000 Wilson's phalaropes (about 80 percent of the world's population) visit the lake in the summer. From 2 to 5 million shorebirds use the lake annually (Utah Division of Wildlife Resources, 1992).

Wetlands aid in flood control by slowing water velocity and providing ponding areas, which in some places can function as recharge basins for ground water. Wetland vegetation along streams and rivers stabilizes banks and reduces erosion. Wetlands improve water quality by settling particulates, producing oxygen, recycling nutrients, and degrading many harmful compounds found in water. Mountain wetlands can reduce the concentration of trace metals in mine drainage (Owen and others, 1992), lessening the impact on receiving streams. Because wetlands commonly are associated with rich soils and dependable water sources, Utah's wetlands also are important grazing areas for cattle and sheep.

TYPES AND DISTRIBUTION

Wetlands are lands transitional between terrestrial and deepwater habitats where the water table usually is at or near the land surface or the land is covered by shallow water (Cowardin and oth-

ers, 1979). The distribution of wetlands and deepwater habitats in Utah is shown in figure 2A; only wetlands are discussed herein.

Wetlands can be vegetated or nonvegetated and are classified on the basis of their hydrology, vegetation, and substrate. In this summary, wetlands are classified according to the system proposed by Cowardin and others (1979), which is used by the U.S. Fish and Wildlife Service (FWS) to map and inventory the Nation's wetlands. At the most general level of the classification system, wetlands are grouped into five ecological systems: Palustrine, Lacustrine, Riverine, Estuarine, and Marine. The Palustrine System includes only wetlands, whereas the other systems comprise wetlands and deepwater habitats. Wetlands of the systems that occur in Utah are described below.

System	Wetland description
Palustrine	Wetlands in which vegetation is predominantly trees (forested wetlands); shrubs (scrub-shrub wetlands); persistent or nonpersistent emergent, erect, rooted, herbaceous plants (persistent- and nonpersistent-emergent wetlands); or submersed and (or) floating plants (aquatic beds). Also, intermittently to permanently flooded open-water bodies of less than 20 acres in which water is less than 6.6 feet deep.
Lacustrine	Wetlands within an intermittently to permanently flooded lake or reservoir. Vegetation, when present, is predominantly nonpersistent emergent plants (nonpersistent-emergent wetlands), or submersed and (or) floating plants (aquatic beds), or both.
Riverine	Wetlands within a channel. Vegetation, when present, is same as in the Lacustrine System.

Several studies of wetlands in Utah have determined wetland acreages and types throughout the State. An inventory done by the FWS in the 1950's (U.S. Fish and Wildlife Service, 1955) identified 1,200,000 acres of wetlands in Utah. Sixty-eight percent were salt flats (nonvegetated lacustrine and palustrine wetlands). In 1974, only 558,000 acres of wetlands were identified by Utah's Division of Wildlife Resources (Jensen, 1974). Wetlands were classified as first-, second-, and third-magnitude marshes, depending on their ability to support waterfowl. Because of the criteria for classification, many mountain wetlands and areas defined as "incidental waterfowl habitat," such as Sevier Lake, were not included in the total wetland acreage of the State. More recent National Wetlands Inventory data (Bob Freeman and Clark Johnson, U.S. Fish and Wildlife Service, written commun., 1993) indicate that there are 510,000 acres of emergent marshes and nonvegetated mud flats and salt flats along the eastern shore of Great Salt Lake, within an area that covers less than 2 percent of the State. (The inventory has not been completed for the rest of the State.) Wetland losses, naturally changing boundaries, different classification systems, changing ideas about functions and values of wetlands, and different study objectives are all partly responsible for the discrepancies in total acreage.

Wetlands in Utah include the shallows of small lakes, reservoirs, ponds, and streams (emergent and aquatic-bed wetlands); riparian wetlands (forested, scrub-shrub, and emergent wetlands); marshes and wet meadows (emergent wetlands); nonvegetated mudflats and salt flats; and playas (unconsolidated-shore wetlands). In the mountains of Utah, wetlands occur as open bodies of water or near them,

Figure 1. Pelicans at Bear River Migratory Bird Refuge, northeast shore of Great Salt Lake. *(Photograph courtesy of U.S. Fish and Wildlife Service.)*

near springs, and where snowmelt collects. The largest and most notable wetlands in the State, however, occur in western Utah adjacent to Great Salt Lake, where much of the mountain runoff eventually discharges. Wetlands in western Utah also occur as playas, near springs in tectonically active areas, and near freshwater bodies. In eastern Utah, wetlands are sparse but are present in the flood plains of some streams and rivers.

HYDROLOGIC SETTING

Wetlands form under conditions of continuous water supply at or near the land surface. The location and persistence of the water supply depends on physiographic features that control runoff and impoundment of water, climatic conditions such as precipitation and evaporation, and hydrologic factors such as location of the water table and discharge areas. Conditions in Utah differ greatly from one part of the State to another, but three principal physiographic provinces (fig. 2B) define areas with similarities. The Middle Rocky Mountains contain the Uinta Mountains and the Wasatch Range. The Basin and Range Province is characterized by a series of alternating north-south-trending ranges and valleys. The Colorado Plateaus consist of plateaus and mesas interspersed with deep canyons.

Middle Rocky Mountains.— Some of the highest mountain peaks in the Uinta Mountains and the Wasatch Range reach altitudes of 10,000 to 13,000 feet and receive more than 60 inches of precipitation per year (Cruff, 1986), mostly as snow. The large accumulation of snow in the mountains ultimately provides much of the water to wetlands throughout Utah. Mountain wetlands occur as small lakes (such as cirque and moraine lakes), reservoirs, ponds (such as beaver ponds), and streams; as marshes along flood plains; and as wet meadows below snow fields and dams, near springs, and along flood plains (fig. 3A). Some wetlands receive moisture only during periods of runoff, whereas others are recharged continuously by shallow ground water or by water impounded in lakes, rivers, and streams.

One of the few wetland studies conducted in Utah's mountains identified 200 acres of wetlands in Albion Basin (Jensen, 1993). Most of the wetlands are classified as scrub-shrub where willows predominate, but persistent-emergent and forested wetlands are also common where veratrum, sedges, and bluebells occur and where spruce and fir grow. These wetlands provide habitat for a diversity of wildlife including moose, beaver, and abundant nongame birds. Studies in a small part of the wetlands showed that, during runoff, 83 to 85 percent of the suspended solids and two trace metals were

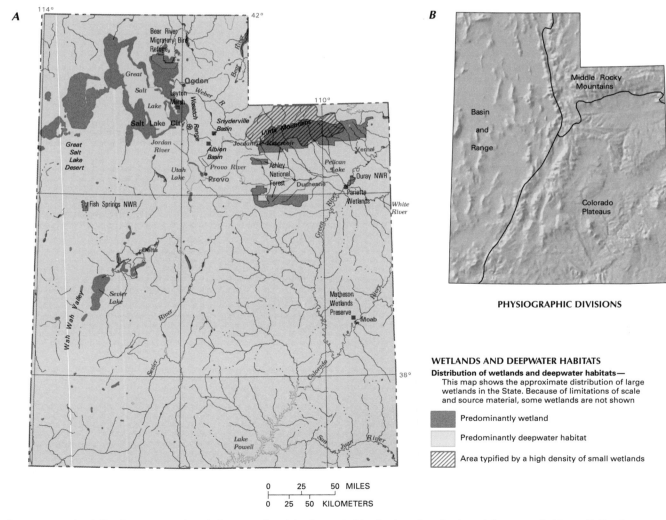

Figure 2. Wetland distribution in Utah and physiography of the State. **A**, Distribution of wetlands and deepwater habitats. **B**, Physiography. *(Sources: A, T.E. Dahl, U.S. Fish and Wildlife Service, unpub. data, 1991. B, Physiographic divisions from Fenneman, 1946; landforms data from EROS Data Center.)*

retained by the wetlands (Jensen, 1993), reducing the potential for downstream contamination.

Much of the runoff in the Uinta Mountains and Wasatch Range leaves the Middle Rocky Mountains as surface water in streams and rivers or as seepage into the ground that recharges basin aquifers. Much of the runoff from the Middle Rocky Mountains eventually reaches Great Salt Lake in the Basin and Range Province by way of the Bear, Weber, and Jordan Rivers or as ground-water discharge along the eastern shore of the lake.

Basin and Range Province. — Great Salt Lake is located at the base of the Wasatch Range and is a remnant of an ancient and much larger lake. It receives 66 percent of its annual water supply from surface runoff, 31 percent from direct precipitation, and 3 percent from ground-water inflow (Arnow and Stephens, 1990). Great Salt Lake is a terminal lake; that is, it has no outlets. It is the fourth largest lake of this type in the world (Arnow and Stephens, 1990). Because the lake is located in a discharge area (fig. 3*B*), where movement of confined ground water is upward (Clark and others, 1990), downward seepage of lake water is limited. Water remains in the lake until it evaporates or is used by plants. Wetlands adjacent to Great Salt Lake are abundant and include marshes, mud flats, and salt flats. Marshes occur where freshwater enters the lake along the eastern shore, including areas near springs and the mouths of rivers. Common vegetation includes cattails and bulrush. Mud and salt flats occur along flood plains, generally between upland or marshes and the lake itself. Mud and salt flats usually are barren, although emergent vegetation and plants adapted to alkali conditions, such as salt grass, grow nearby.

Above-average precipitation during the early 1980's resulted in flooding of rivers statewide, and Great Salt Lake reached its highest level on record. Transgression of the shorelines, inundation of areas that were normally dry, and the development of new wetlands served as a reminder of the functions of flood plains, which were slowly being developed. Sevier Lake, which covers 850 square miles near Delta, is a typical playa that flooded during the 1980's. It reached a depth of 13 feet (Wilberg, 1991).

"Playa" is a geologic term for very flat, and usually barren, areas of closed arid drainage basins that occasionally flood (Neal, 1975). Playas form in areas where evaporation exceeds precipitation, which is true of most of Utah. In western Utah, annual evaporation rates are as high as 65 inches per year (Farnsworth and others, 1982), and annual precipitation is as low as 5 inches (Cruff, 1986). Playa lakes like Great Salt Lake commonly are flooded by desert thunderstorms, receiving direct precipitation and runoff in washes and ephemeral stream channels from the ranges of western Utah.

Playas in valleys where ground water is at or near land surface, such as the Great Salt Lake Desert, can become flooded by a rising water table during periods of minimal evaporation and can remain wet throughout the year. Evaporites accumulate as a result of dissolution of lakebed material during flooding that is followed by continued evaporation and by capillary rise of saline ground water. A layer of white salt crystals commonly develops at the surface over mud and other evaporites (Snyder, 1975). Although the playa is usually devoid of vegetation, salt grass is common near the edges, and Nuttall alkali-grass, sea blight, and pickleweed also can be found (Vice and Messmer, 1993). Playas in valleys where ground water never reaches the surface, such as Wah Wah Valley, become flooded only after rains. The ponded water dissipates more rapidly because of downward seepage. The playa surface is dry and hard most of the time and consists of fine sand, silt, and clay; evaporites are absent (Snyder, 1975). Any vegetation near a dry playa is adapted to long periods of extreme dryness.

Great Salt Lake and playas provide critical habitat for resident wildlife and migrating waterfowl in an arid environment, but ground-water discharge from springs and freshwater bodies also

A. Middle Rocky Mountains

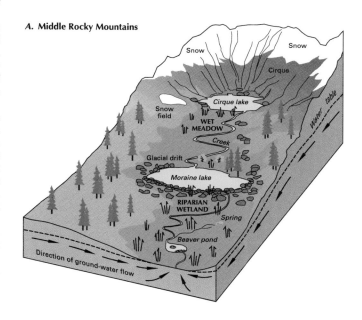

B. Basin and Range

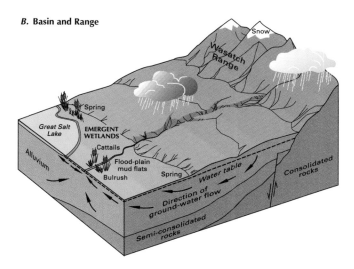

C. Colorado Plateaus

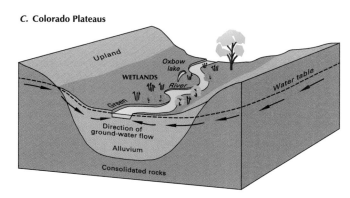

Figure 3. Generalized hydrologic setting of wetlands in Utah. *A*, Middle Rocky Mountains. *B*, Basin and Range Province. *C*, Colorado Plateaus.

maintain wetlands in the Basin and Range Province. Fish Springs National Wildlife Refuge, in Utah's western desert, is an example of a spring-fed wetland. Discharge from 10 springs maintains 12,000 acres of ponds and marsh habitat. Marshes and mud flats also occur in western Utah along flood plains of streams and rivers, and adjacent to freshwater lakes and reservoirs. Utah Lake covers more surface area than any other natural freshwater body in Utah and wetlands dot its shores.

Colorado Plateaus.—The Colorado Plateaus, south of the Middle Rocky Mountains and east of the Basin and Range Province, receive about 10 to 20 inches of precipitation per year. Three major rivers, the Colorado, Green, and San Juan, flow through the Colorado Plateaus and gouge deep canyons that do not provide conditions for development of large wetlands. Some emergent wetlands occur on river and tributary flood plains where the canyons widen and the terrain becomes less steep (fig. 3C). These wetlands provide oases for migrating and resident waterfowl and backwater habitat for fish. Common vegetation in these areas includes boxelder and cottonwood trees, willows and tamarisk (an introduced species), cattails, bulrush, and a variety of grasses.

Ouray National Wildlife Refuge, near Vernal, is an example of an emergent wetland on the flood plain of the Green River. The Green River provides the principal source of water, which reaches the wetlands by flooding and managed pumping. Since its development, supplemental water from Pelican Lake and seeps in uplands to the north has been required to help support the 2,100 acres of wetland habitat.

TRENDS

On the basis of unpublished U.S. Department of Agriculture records, Dahl (1990) estimated that 244,000 acres of Utah's wetlands had been lost from the 1780's to the 1980's, apparently from agricultural drainage alone. Large-scale water-development projects also have resulted in losses of wetland habitat. According to records filed with the Utah Division of Water Rights, at least 1,600 dams have been constructed in Utah since the mid-1800's. Of these dams, 445 impound 20 acre-feet of water or more (Joe Borgione, Utah Division of Water Rights, oral commun., 1993). Impounded water provides some wetland habitat but might not compensate for wetlands lost to dam construction, rising waters in reservoirs, or receding rivers. Because of dam construction, less than 10 percent of the original riparian area (uplands and wetlands associated with unimpounded water bodies) along the Colorado River still exists (Redelfs, 1980). The FWS has estimated that 50 to 60 percent of riparian wetlands in Utah have been lost (U.S. Fish and Wildlife Service, 1990). Expansion of agricultural areas, encroachment of residential developments, industrial growth, mining, ski-area development, and grazing also have resulted in wetland losses.

CONSERVATION

Many government agencies and private organizations participate in wetland conservation in Utah. The most active agencies and organizations and some of their activities are listed in table 1.

Federal wetland activities.—Development activities in Utah wetlands are regulated by several Federal statutory prohibitions and incentives that are intended to slow wetland losses. Some of the more important of these are contained in the 1899 Rivers and Harbors Act; the 1972 Clean Water Act and amendments; the 1985 Food Security Act; the 1990 Food, Agriculture, Conservation, and Trade Act; and the 1986 Emergency Wetlands Resources Act.

Section 10 of the Rivers and Harbors Act gives the U.S. Army Corps of Engineers (Corps) authority to regulate certain activities in navigable waters. Regulated activities include diking, deepening, filling, excavating, and placing of structures. The related section 404

Table 1. Selected wetland-related activities of government agencies and private organizations in Utah, 1993

[Source: Classification of activities is generalized from information provided by agencies and organizations. •, agency or organization participates in wetland-related activity; ..., agency or organization does not participate in wetland-related activity. MAN, management; REG, regulation; R&C, restoration and creation; LAN, land acquisition; R&D, research and data collection; D&I, delineation and inventory]

Agency or organization	MAN	REG	R&C	LAN	R&D	D&I
FEDERAL						
Department of Agriculture						
Consolidated Farm Service Agency	...	•	...	...	...	...
Forest Service	•	...	•	...	•	•
Natural Resources Conservation Service	...	•	...	...	•	•
Department of Defense						
Army Corps of Engineers	•	•	•	...	•	•
Department of the Interior						
Bureau of Land Management	•	•	•	•	•	•
Bureau of Reclamation	•	...	•	•	•	•
Fish and Wildlife Service	•	...	•	•	•	•
Geological Survey	...	...	...	...	•	...
National Biological Service	...	...	...	...	•	...
National Park Service	•	...	...	...	...	...
Environmental Protection Agency	...	•	...	...	•	•
STATE						
Department of Agriculture						
Environmental Quality Section	...	...	•	...	•	•
Department of Environmental Quality						
Division of Water Quality	...	•	...	...	•	•
Department of Natural Resources						
Division of Oil, Gas, and Mining	...	•	...	...	...	...
Division of Parks and Recreation	•	...	•	•	...	...
Division of State Lands and Forestry	•	•	...	...	...	...
Division of Water Resources	...	...	...	...	•	•
Division of Water Rights	...	•	...	...	•	•
Division of Wildlife Resources	•	...	•	•	•	•
Department of Transportation	•	...	•	•	•	•
University of Utah						
Department of Botany	...	...	...	...	•	...
Red Butte Garden and Arboretum	•	...	...	...	•	...
Utah State University						
Department of Fisheries and Wildlife	•	...	•	...	•	...
SOME COUNTY AND LOCAL GOVERNMENTS	•	...	•	...	•	•
PRIVATE ORGANIZATIONS						
National Audubon Society	...	...	•	•	...	...
Brigham Young University						
Department of Botany	...	...	...	...	•	...
Ducks Unlimited	•	...	•	•	...	•
The Nature Conservancy	•	...	•	•	•	•
Southern Utah Wilderness Alliance	...	...	•	...	...	...
Utah Riparian and Management Coalition	...	...	...	...	•	...
Utah Wetlands Foundation	...	...	•	•	...	...

of the Clean Water Act is the most often-used Federal legislation protecting wetlands. Under section 404 provisions, the Corps issues permits regulating the discharge of dredged or fill material into wetlands. Permits are subject to review and possible veto by the U.S. Environmental Protection Agency (EPA), and the FWS has review and advisory roles. Section 401 of the Clean Water Act grants to States and eligible Indian Tribes the authority to approve, apply conditions to, or deny section 404 permit applications on the basis of a proposed activity's probable effects on the water quality of a wetland.

Most farming, ranching, and silviculture activities are not subject to section 404 regulation. However, the "Swampbuster" provision of the 1985 Food Security Act and amendments in the 1990 Food, Agriculture, Conservation, and Trade Act discourage (through financial disincentives) the draining, filling, or other alteration of wetlands for agricultural use. The law allows exemptions from penalties in some cases, especially if the farmer agrees to restore the altered wetland or other wetlands that have been converted to agricultural use. The Wetlands Reserve Program of the 1990 Food,

Agriculture, Conservation, and Trade Act authorizes the Federal Government to purchase conservation easements from landowners who agree to protect or restore wetlands. The Consolidated Farm Service Agency (formerly the Agricultural Stabilization and Conservation Service) administers the Swampbuster provisions and Wetlands Reserve Program. The Natural Resources Conservation Service (formerly the Soil Conservation Service) (NRCS) determines compliance with Swampbuster provisions and assists farmers in the identification of wetlands and in the development of wetland protection, restoration, or creation plans.

The 1986 Emergency Wetlands Resources Act encourages wetland protection through funding incentives. The act requires States to address wetland protection in their Statewide Comprehensive Outdoor Recreation Plans to qualify for Federal funding for State recreational land; the National Park Service (NPS) provides guidance to States in developing the wetland component of their plans.

Federal land-management agencies provide for the protection and management of natural resources on land they administer, which includes wetlands. Most of the wetlands are not formally managed and are associated with riparian areas. Riparian acreages determined by agencies likely often include both uplands and wetlands. The Bureau of Land Management (BLM) manages 22,142,000 acres of land in Utah. An estimated 216,000 acres of this total are classified as riparian-wetland areas (Bureau of Land Management, 1991). Pariette Wetlands near Vernal is the largest wetland (3,000 acres) managed by the BLM.

The U.S. Forest Service manages 8,099,000 acres of land in six National Forests in Utah (Bruce Strom, U.S. Forest Service, oral commun., 1993). An estimated 250,000 acres of this total are riparian areas (Roland Leidy, Livia Crowley, Gil Garcia, Dennis Kelly, and Rick Patton, U.S. Forest Service, oral commun., 1993). The Ashley National Forest accounts for about 148,000 acres of the total, of which an estimated 70,000 acres have been identified as wet meadows (Roland Leidy, U.S. Forest Service, oral commun., 1993). The NPS manages 2,096,000 acres of land in Utah (Marty Ott, National Park Service, oral commun., 1993). Currently (1993), no estimates exist of wetland or riparian acres on land administered by the NPS.

Other Federal agencies also manage Utah wetlands. The FWS manages three refuges. Bear River Migratory Bird Refuge is the largest federally managed refuge in the State and the largest managed wetland near Great Salt Lake. It includes 63,000 acres of wetlands, but expansion plans will increase that to 93,500 acres. The Bureau of Reclamation mitigates sites affected by dam and reservoir construction and is creating new wetlands downstream from Jordanelle Reservoir along the Provo River. The Utah office of the NRCS prepares resource-management plans, which often address management of wetlands for landowners engaging in agricultural activities.

State wetland activities.—The Utah Department of Natural Resources, Division of Wildlife Resources, in cooperation with other State agencies, is developing a State wetland policy and plan under the EPA's Wetland Protection Program. The plan will serve as a management guide for all State-owned lands and will provide for consistency in actions taken on Utah's wetlands. The Division also is conducting an inventory to identify, classify, and develop a base map of Utah wetlands. The Division administers 20 designated Waterfowl Management Areas (87,000 acres) throughout Utah that include 64,000 acres of wetlands. The Division also participates in many cooperative efforts with private organizations to acquire wetland areas by using funds from the sale of State waterfowl stamps and from Ducks Unlimited marsh funds.

The Utah Department of Natural Resources, Division of Parks and Recreation, manages 46 parks that total more than 95,000 acres. This acreage includes an estimated 5,800 acres of wetlands (Terry Green, Utah Division of Parks and Recreation, written commun., 1993). In compliance with the requirements of the Emergency Wetlands Resources Act, Utah's 1992 Statewide Comprehensive Outdoor Recreation Plan (unpublished draft) identifies priority wetlands. The Division of Parks and Recreation also provides protection for wetlands by regulating development along the Jordan and Provo River corridors under the Utah River Enhancement Act. Other divisions of the Utah Department of Natural Resources participate in wetland-related activities: the Division of State Lands regulates wetlands through land-use permits; the Division of Oil, Gas, and Mining restores degraded habitat under the Abandoned Mine Reclamation Program; the Division of Water Resources addresses the State's future water needs and potential effects of proposed projects on water resources; and the Division of Water Rights issues some section 404 permits under the guidance of the Corps.

The Utah Department of Environmental Quality, Division of Water Quality, is responsible for Clean Water Act section 401 certification, which helps ensure that water quality will not be adversely affected by activities specified in a section 404 permit. The Division of Water Quality and the Environmental Quality Section of the Department of Agriculture evaluate riparian areas and potential nonpoint sources of pollution and develop plans for priority watersheds that include alternatives for water-quality improvement. The Utah Department of Transportation mitigates wetland loss when it cannot be avoided during construction of new highways or improvement of existing highways.

County and local wetland activities.—Several county and local agencies participate in the management of water resources. The EPA provides support and funding for Wetland Advance Identification Studies, which are usually collaborative efforts by local cooperating agencies. The data collected during these studies facilitate the section 404 permitting process. An Advance Identification of wetlands along the Jordan River was conducted by the Salt Lake City-County Health Department. Advance Identification Studies of wetlands also have been conducted in Albion and Snyderville Basins.

Private wetland activities.—The National Audubon Society promotes public awareness and educational programs concerning wetlands and provides physical assistance in wetland restoration and creation projects. Ducks Unlimited is dedicated to funding wetland acquisition. Seven wetland projects in Utah, funded cooperatively by Ducks Unlimited, have involved land acquisition and improved water-resource utilization. The Nature Conservancy seeks to protect plants and animals from extinction through acquisition of areas for critical habitat. They currently manage two notable wetlands in Utah: the Matheson Wetlands Preserve near Moab and the Layton Marsh near Ogden. Twenty-six private hunt clubs manage 46,000 acres of wetlands and uplands surrounding Great Salt Lake (Jensen, 1974). Other private organizations involved in wetland activities include the Utah Wetlands Foundation, the Southern Utah Wilderness Alliance, the Summit County Land Trust, and the Utah Riparian Management Coalition.

References Cited

Arnow, Ted, and Stephens, Doyle, 1990, Hydrologic characteristics of the Great Salt Lake, Utah—1847–1986: U.S. Geological Survey Water-Supply Paper 2332, 32 p.

Bureau of Land Management, 1991, Riparian-wetlands initiative for the 1990's: Bureau of Land Management Report BLM/WO/GI–91/001+4340, 50 p.

Clark, David W., Appel, Cynthia L., Lambert, Patrick M., Puryear, Robert L., 1990, Ground-water resources and simulated effects of withdrawals in the east shore area of Great Salt Lake, Utah: Utah Department of Natural Resources Technical Publication 93, 150 p., 1 pl.

Cowardin, L.M, Carter, Virginia, Golet, F.C., and LaRoe, E.T., 1979, Classification of wetlands and deepwater habitats of the United States: U.S. Fish and Wildlife Service Report FWS/OBS–79/31, 131 p.

Cruff, R.W., 1986, Utah surface-water resources, *in* U.S. Geological Survey, National water summary 1985—Hydrologic events and surface-water resources: U.S. Geological Survey Water-Supply Paper 2300, p. 453-460.

Dahl, T.E., 1990, Wetlands—Losses in the United States, 1780's to 1980's: Washington, D.C., U.S. Fish and Wildlife Service Report to Congress, 13 p.

Farnsworth, R.K., Thompson, E.S., and Peck, E.L., 1982, Evaporation atlas for the contiguous 48 United States: National Oceanic and Atmospheric Administration Technical Report NWS 33, 27 p.

Fenneman, N.M., 1946, Physical divisions of the United States: Washington, D.C., U.S. Geological Survey special map, scale 1:7,000,000.

Jensen, F.C., 1974, Evaluation of existing wetland habitat in Utah: Utah State Division of Wildlife Resources Publication 74–17, 219 p.

Jensen, S.F., 1993, Ecological characterization and functional evaluation of subalpine and lower montane wetlands in the Albion Basin region of Utah: Salt Lake City, Salt Lake County Commission Staff Office, 45 p., 4 apps.

Neal, J.T., 1975, Introduction, *in* Neal, J.T., ed., Benchmark papers in geology/20—Playas and dried lakes, occurrence and development: Stroudsburg, Pa., Dowden, Hutchinson, and Ross, Inc., p. 1–5.

Owen, D.E., Otton, J.K., Hills, F.A., and Schumann, R.R., 1992, Uranium and other elements in Colorado Rocky Mountain wetlands—A reconnaissance study: U.S. Geological Survey Bulletin 1992, 33 p.

Rawley, E.V., 1974, The Great Salt Lake biotic system: Utah Division of Wildlife Resources Publication 74–13, 431 p.

———1980, Wildlife of the Great Salt Lake, *in* Gwynn, J.W., ed., Great Salt Lake—A scientific, historical and economic overview: Utah Geological and Mineral Survey Bulletin 116, p. 287–304.

Redelfs, A.E., 1980, Wetlands values and losses in the United States: Stillwater, Oklahoma State University, M.S. thesis, 144 p.

Reed, P.B., Jr., 1986, Wetland plant list—Utah: U.S. Fish and Wildlife Service WELUT–86/W12.44, 26 unnumbered pages.

Snyder, C.T., 1975, A hydrologic classification of valleys, the Great Basin, Western United States, *in* Neal, J.T., ed., Benchmark Papers in Geology/20, Playas and dried lakes, occurrence and development: Stroudsburg, Pa., Dowden, Hutchinson, and Ross, Inc., p. 113–119.

U.S. Fish and Wildlife Service, 1955, Wetlands inventory—Utah: Albuquerque, N. Mex., U.S. Fish and Wildlife Service, 15 p., 7 pls.

———1990, Regional wetlands concept plan—Emergency wetlands resources act: Lakewood, Colo., U.S. Fish and Wildlife Service, 90 p., 4 apps.

Utah Division of Wildlife Resources, 1992, Wilson's phalarope: Utah Division of Wildlife Resources Wildlife Notebook Series No. 6, 4 p.

Vice, Daniel, and Messmer, Terry, 1993, Wetlands of Utah—A citizen's guide to the enjoyment and conservation of Utah's wetlands: Logan, Utah State University, 20 p.

Wilberg, D.E., 1991, Hydrologic reconnaissance of the Sevier Lake area, west-central Utah: Utah Department of Natural Resources Technical Publication 96, 51 p.

FOR ADDITIONAL INFORMATION: District Chief, U.S. Geological Survey, Administration Building Room 1016, 1745 West 1700 South, Salt Lake City, UT 84104; Regional Wetland Coordinator, U.S. Fish and Wildlife Service, Fish and Wildlife Enhancement, P.O. Box 25486, Denver Federal Center, Denver, CO 80225

Prepared by
Doyle W. Stephens and Linda J. Gerner,
U.S. Geological Survey

Vermont
Wetland Resources

$\mathbf{R}$ecent estimates of the area covered by wetlands in Vermont range from 4 to 6 percent of the State's total area. Many of the State's wetlands are small; about 80 percent are less than 10 acres (Parsons, 1988a). The largest wetlands are in the broad valleys of northeastern Vermont and in the flood plains and deltas of rivers that discharge into Lake Champlain (fig. 1).

Despite their small collective area, wetlands are an integral part of Vermont's natural resources. They provide essential habitat for certain types of wildlife and vegetation, including rare and endangered species. Wetlands provide timber and opportunities for hunting and fishing; education and research; and bird, wildlife, and plant observation that all boost the tourist industry and economy. Beneficial wetland functions include flood control, bank- and shoreline-erosion control, sediment retention, water filtration, and nutrient uptake. In recognition of the importance of wetlands, many government and private organizations have worked to preserve wetlands and educate the public about wetland values. For example, wetlands in the delta of the Missisquoi River contain one of the largest great blue heron colonies in the Northeastern United States (Wanner, 1979) and are protected as part of the Missisquoi National Wildlife Refuge.

TYPES AND DISTRIBUTION

Wetlands are lands transitional between terrestrial and deepwater habitats where the water table usually is at or near the land surface or the land is covered by shallow water (Cowardin and others, 1979). The distribution of wetlands and deepwater habitats in Vermont is shown in figure 2A; only wetlands are discussed herein.

Wetlands can be vegetated or nonvegetated and are classified on the basis of their hydrology, vegetation, and substrate. In this summary, wetlands are classified according to the system proposed by Cowardin and others (1979), which is used by the U.S. Fish and Wildlife Service (FWS) to map and inventory the Nation's wetlands. At the most general level of the classification system, wetlands are grouped into five ecological systems: Palustrine, Lacustrine, Riverine, Estuarine, and Marine. The Palustrine System includes only wetlands, whereas the other systems comprise wetlands and deepwater habitats. Wetlands of the systems that occur in Vermont are described below.

System	Wetland description
Palustrine	Wetlands in which vegetation is predominantly trees (forested wetlands); shrubs (scrub-shrub wetlands); persistent or nonpersistent emergent, erect, rooted, herbaceous plants (persistent- and nonpersistent-emergent wetlands); or submersed and (or) floating plants (aquatic beds). Also, intermittently to permanently flooded open-water bodies of less than 20 acres in which water is less than 6.6 feet deep.
Lacustrine	Wetlands within an intermittently to permanently flooded lake or reservoir. Vegetation, when present, is predominantly nonpersistent emergent plants (nonpersistent-emergent wetlands), or submersed and (or) floating plants (aquatic beds), or both.
Riverine	Wetlands within a channel. Vegetation, when present, is same as in the Lacustrine System.

The FWS National Wetlands Inventory estimated that Vermont contains approximately 243,000 acres of wetlands, including 218,600 acres of palustrine wetland, 800 acres of lacustrine wetland (exclusive of Lake Champlain), and less than 200 acres of riverine wetland, as well as 23,400 acres of lacustrine wetlands in Lake Champlain (Tiner, 1987). The 243,000-acre total represents about 4 percent of the State's area. The Wetlands Office in the Water Quality Division of the Vermont Agency of Natural Resources' Department of Environmental Conservation, considers the State's actual wetland acreage to be as much as 50 percent higher (George Springston, Vermont Agency of Natural Resources, written commun., 1993).

The distribution of wetlands in Vermont is influenced by physiography (fig. 2B). About one-half of the State's wetlands are in the Lake Champlain Valley (Tiner, 1987), either in river flood plains and low-lying areas in valleys, or in deltas, bayheads, and other areas of shallow water in Lake Champlain. Wetlands are sparse in the mountains and southern parts of the New England Upland, where they have formed primarily in river valleys. Several large wetlands are present in the Otter Creek Valley between the Taconic and Green Mountains. About one-third of the State's wetlands are in northeastern Vermont (Tiner, 1987), where they have formed in broad valleys over thick glacial deposits, such as in Victory Basin along the Moose River. Except in the headwaters and a few areas where dams have created backwater conditions along tributaries, wetlands are sparse in the lowlands of the Connecticut River Valley.

Palustrine forested wetlands constitute about 55 percent of Vermont's wetlands (Tiner, 1987). Forested wetlands that have mineral soils rich in organic material are commonly referred to as swamps, whereas wetlands that have organic soils over mineral soils are called peatlands. Forested wetlands in southern Vermont and in the Connecticut River and Lake Champlain Valleys contain hardwood communities similar to those in southern New England wetlands. For example, silver maple and swamp white oak predominate in swamps along Lake Champlain, silver maple and black ash

Figure 1. Fall foliage in a cattail marsh along East Creek, southwest of Middleburg. About two-thirds of the wetland has been protected by the Vermont chapter of The Nature Conservancy. *(Photograph courtesy of John Roe, The Nature Conservancy.)*

are common in flood plains of major rivers, and red maple-black ash swamps typically are present in poorly drained basins and along small streams (Thompson, 1989). Some red maple swamps, such as Cornwall Swamp near Middlebury, were northern white cedar swamps before they were logged. The distribution of northern white cedar in Vermont corresponds well to the distribution of calcareous soils (Meeks, 1986), which exist where the underlying bedrock is limestone, marble, or other rock that contains calcium carbonate. A few wetlands in extreme southwestern Vermont and in the Lake Champlain Valley contain black gum, a species at the northern extent of its range. Forested wetlands in northeastern Vermont and at higher altitudes elsewhere in the State are similar to those in Canadian wetlands. For example, swamps containing red spruce, balsam fir, and larch are most common in poorly drained basins and along streams, whereas black spruce, larch, and northern white cedar predominate in evergreen forested peatlands (Thompson, 1989).

Peatlands are present throughout Vermont but are less common in the southeastern part of the State. The terms "bog" and "fen" have been used to differentiate peatlands in some classification systems (Damman and French, 1987). Bogs (palustrine forested and scrub-shrub wetlands) are acidic, nutrient-poor peatlands that have a low species diversity; whereas fens (palustrine forested, scrub-shrub, and persistent-emergent wetlands) are less acidic and have higher nutrient levels and plant-species diversity. The herbaceous-plant community in bogs is generally dominated by sphagnum moss, whereas in fens it typically is dominated by sedges and mosses.

Palustrine scrub-shrub wetlands constitute about 29 percent of Vermont's wetlands (Tiner, 1987). Scrub-shrub vegetation grows in most wetlands, generally either as a transitional community between emergent wetlands and forested wetlands or upland, or between open water and forested wetlands or upland. Broad-leaved deciduous shrubs such as willow and alder typically predominate in shrub swamps (Thompson, 1989); stunted black spruce and larch and broad-leaved evergreen shrubs such as leatherleaf and labrador tea are characteristic of scrub-shrub communities in bogs; and broad-leaved evergreen shrubs, broad-leaved deciduous shrubs, and northern white cedar commonly grow in fens.

Palustrine emergent wetlands, commonly referred to as marshes, constitute about 11 percent of Vermont's wetlands (Tiner, 1987). Most of the State's largest marshes are in the Lake Champlain Valley in deltas and flood plains of rivers that flow into the lake. For

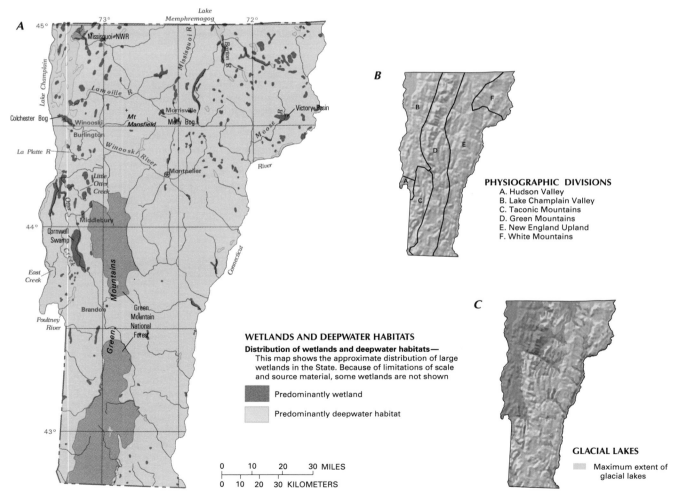

Figure 2. Wetland distribution and physical features that determine wetland distribution in Vermont. *A*, Distribution of wetlands and deepwater habitats. *B*, Physiography. *C*, Maximum extent of glacial lakes. *(Sources: A, T.E. Dahl, U.S. Fish and Wildlife Service, unpub. data, 1991. B, Physiographic divisions modified from Fenneman, 1946; landforms from EROS Data Center. C, Modified from Meeks, 1986; and Doll, 1970.)*

example, extensive marshes have formed near the mouths of the Missisquoi, Lamoille, and Winooski Rivers and also along several smaller rivers and creeks such as the La Platte and Poultney Rivers, and Otter, Little Otter, and East Creeks. A large marsh is in a similar setting at the mouth of the Barton River where it discharges into Lake Memphremagog. Several marshes line creeks and fringe bayheads in the islands and peninsulas of northern Lake Champlain. Elsewhere in Vermont, marshes are generally small and are associated with lacustrine and riverine wetlands. Marsh vegetation is largely determined by the wetland's hydrologic setting or soil type. Cattails and bulrushes are characteristic of semipermanently or permanently flooded marshes; grasses predominate in areas that have permanently saturated mineral soils, such as swales; and sedges are typical of permanently saturated or seasonally flooded peatlands or areas that have muck soils (Thompson, 1989).

Lacustrine wetlands in Vermont include about 600 acres of open water, 200 acres of aquatic-bed wetlands, less than 50 acres of emergent wetlands, and 23,400 acres of unclassified near-shore wetlands in Lake Champlain (Tiner, 1987). Riverine emergent wetlands cover about 174 acres. Many of the shores and bottoms of shallow lakes and rivers are unconsolidated gravel, sand, or rock. Although largely unvegetated, these habitats are classified as wetlands. Most of Vermont's lakes and rivers have areas of shallow water or slow reaches where aquatic-bed and nonpersistent-emergent vegetation is established. These wetlands and associated riparian wetlands are very important to the biological productivity of lakes and rivers.

As a result of recent increases in beaver populations, many riverine and riparian wetlands in smaller streams and rivers have been flooded behind beaver dams. Over time, this flooding promotes a cyclical change from shrub swamps to small ponds and marshes to wet meadows and then back to shrub swamps (George Springston, Vermont Wetlands Office, written commun., 1993). This flooding can be detrimental to existing wetlands but also can create wetlands that have high value to some wildlife, such as waterfowl.

HYDROLOGIC SETTING

Wetlands are hydrologic features that occur wherever climate and physiography favor the retention of water (Winter, 1992). Wetlands are found along rivers and lakes where flooding is likely to occur, in isolated depressions where surface water collects, and on slopes and surface drainageways where ground water discharges to the land surface in spring or seepage areas (Federal Interagency Committee for Wetland Delineation, 1989). Soil saturation favors the growth of wetland plants and the development of hydric soils. Water either can be present on the surface of wetlands or it can keep underlying soils saturated near the surface with no surface water present (Tiner, 1991).

The timing and duration of the presence of water affects water chemistry, soil development, and plant communities in wetlands. Although degree of wetness is important in the determination of wetland type, many ecological functions of wetlands also depend upon wetland size, position of the wetland in a drainage network, and sources of water (Brinson, 1993). Differences in climate, physiography, and geology influence the hydrology and water quality of wetlands. The complex interactions of these factors with biology, in combination with site history, determine the type of wetland that develops in any particular setting.

Although Vermont is the driest of the New England States, adequate moisture exists to support the development and maintenance of wetlands. Many climatic and hydrologic variables in Vermont are influenced by altitude and mirror the State's topography when mapped. For instance, from the lowlands of the Lake Champlain and Connecticut River Valleys to higher altitudes of the Taconic and Green Mountains, the average summer temperature and

length of the growing season decrease, and the average annual precipitation and runoff increase (Meeks, 1986; Hammond and Cotton, 1986). The structure of plant communities in Vermont's wetlands is influenced by these climatic differences.

The distribution of wetlands in Vermont is partly determined by physiography, glacial history, and characteristics of the underlying bedrock. Areas of steep topography do not retain water long enough for wetlands to form. However, given favorable hydrologic conditions, wetlands form on drainage divides and near mountain tops. For example, a small alpine bog lies near the summit of Mount Mansfield, the highest mountain in the State. Most of Vermont's wetlands, however, are in lowlands, valleys, and depressions that have more favorable hydrologic conditions for wetlands.

Many of the low-lying areas of Vermont are covered by stratified sand, gravel, clay, and silt deposited by glacial meltwater and by modern streams in the time since glaciation. Stratified deposits in the lowlands of the Lake Champlain Valley include marine clay deposited during glaciation when the land was depressed by the weight of glacial ice, allowing an arm of the Atlantic Ocean to occupy the valley (Meeks, 1986). Most mountains and uplands in Vermont are composed of bedrock mantled by glacial till, an unstratified mixture of clay, silt, sand, gravel, and boulders. Both till and fine-grained sediments can restrict drainage and retain surface water. Thus, wetlands occur over till in northeastern Vermont and at higher altitudes elsewhere, over fine-grained glacial-lake and marine deposits in the lowlands of the Lake Champlain Valley, over fine-grained glacial-lake deposits in the lowlands around Lake Memphremagog, and over fine-grained glacial-lake deposits in parts of the Missisquoi, Lamoille, Winooski, and Connecticut River Valleys (fig. 2C). A lack of clay exposures accounts in part for the scarcity of wetlands in parts of the Connecticut River Valley (Fred Larson, Norwich University, oral commun., 1993). In parts of northeastern Vermont, thick sand and till deposits (moraines) contain many poorly drained depressions favorable for wetlands. In a few areas, depressions called kettle holes formed when ice blocks buried by glacial outwash melted. These kettles either filled with water or passed through several successional stages of infilling to become kettle bogs. Molly Bog, near Morrisville, likely developed in this manner (Johnson, 1985). Most Vermont bogs are in small depressions, although some are in basins that also include open water, such as around the margins of small ponds or in lake-level basins cut off from the influence of lake water. The absence of extensive peatlands in northern Vermont is due to the mountainous terrain and the limited extent of glacial outwash and glacially derived surface features in Vermont (Johnson, 1985).

Differences in the interactions of hydrology and vegetation in different wetland types can be illustrated by peatlands and lakeside wetlands. In peatlands, vegetation patterns are determined largely by water chemistry and movement (Damman and French, 1987). For instance, bogs receive little input from runoff or ground water and rely on precipitation (including fog) and wind-blown dust as sources for water, nutrients, and minerals. Vegetation in bogs commonly grows in a concentric pattern because of the scarcity of nutrients and minerals in the center of the bog and the increased availability of nutrients and minerals along bog margins. In contrast, fens rely principally on ground-water discharge and runoff for inputs of water, minerals, and nutrients. Flooding is the major hydrologic influence in lakeside wetlands. The water level in Lake Champlain is unregulated and fluctuates by an average of 6 feet annually, but the range can be as much as 9 feet (Downer, 1971; Meeks, 1986). In response to these fluctuations, vegetation communities in lakeside wetlands grow in zones; wetlands nearest lake level have more flood-tolerant species. Furthermore, changes in lake level change the sediment and nutrient dynamics in lakeside wetlands. High water levels in spring can dilute nutrient and sediment concentrations (Clausen and Johnson, 1990). For example, wetlands at the mouth of the Lamoille

River and in nearby Colchester Bog receive floodwaters from Lake Champlain. However, Lamoille River wetlands support a large variety of vegetation largely owing to nutrient inputs from the river, whereas Colchester Bog, which receives no river input, remains nutrient poor and has low plant-species diversity.

TRENDS

Flood-plain forests and wetlands once were extensive in Vermont. In the 1800's and early 1900's, timber harvesting and clearing and draining of wetlands for crops and grazing resulted in the degradation or loss of many wetlands (Bulmer, 1988), particularly in the Connecticut River Valley. As much as 35 percent of Vermont's wetland resources have been lost since settlement by Europeans; much of the loss has been emergent and scrub-shrub wetlands (Parsons, 1988a). Although Federal and State regulations focus on minimizing wetland losses, many wetlands remain threatened. Before the adoption of the Vermont Wetland Rules in 1990, annual wetland losses were estimated to be 200 acres (Parsons, 1988a). Present losses are as much as 30 to 40 acres per year (George Springston, Vermont Wetlands Office, written commun., 1993). These losses commonly are in areas where pressure from population growth has resulted in development in and adjacent to wetlands, such as in the Lake Champlain Valley and in other seasonal residential and recreation areas (Parsons, 1988a). Other factors that can destroy wetlands or affect wetland functions include road building, reservoir construction, agricultural activities, peat harvesting, timber harvesting, hydropower releases, inadequate bridge and culvert sizing, navigation, and air or water pollution. The cumulative effect of loss or alteration of wetlands in Vermont is yet to be determined but is likely to be an important issue in the future.

CONSERVATION

Many government agencies and private organizations participate in wetland conservation in Vermont. The most active agencies and organizations and some of their activities are listed in table 1.

Federal wetland activities. — Development activities in Vermont wetlands are regulated by several Federal statutory prohibitions and incentives that are intended to slow wetland losses. Some of the more important of these are contained in the 1899 Rivers and Harbors Act; the 1972 Clean Water Act and amendments; the 1985 Food Security Act; the 1990 Food, Agriculture, Conservation, and Trade Act; and the 1986 Emergency Wetlands Resources Act.

Section 10 of the Rivers and Harbors Act gives the U.S. Army Corps of Engineers (Corps) authority to regulate certain activities in navigable waters. Regulated activities include diking, deepening, filling, excavating, and placing of structures. The related section 404 of the Clean Water Act is the most often-used Federal legislation protecting wetlands. Under section 404 provisions, the Corps issues permits regulating the discharge of dredged or fill material into wetlands. Permits are subject to review and possible veto by the U.S. Environmental Protection Agency (EPA), and the FWS has review and advisory roles. Section 401 of the Clean Water Act grants to States and eligible Indian Tribes the authority to approve, apply conditions to, or deny section 404 permit applications on the basis of a proposed activity's probable effects on the water quality of a wetland.

Most farming, ranching, and silviculture activities are not subject to section 404 regulation. However, the "Swampbuster" provision of the 1985 Food Security Act and amendments in the 1990 Food, Agriculture, Conservation, and Trade Act discourage (through financial disincentives) the draining, filling, or other alteration of wetlands for agricultural use. The law allows exemptions from penalties in some cases, especially if the farmer agrees to restore the altered wetland or other wetlands that have been converted to agricultural use. The Wetlands Reserve Program of the 1990 Food,

Table 1. Selected wetland-related activities of government agencies and private organizations in Vermont, 1993

[Source: Classification of activities is generalized from information provided by agencies and organizations. •, agency or organization participates in wetland-related activity; ..., agency or organization does not participate in wetland-related activity. MAN, management; REG, regulation; R&C, restoration and creation; LAN, land acquisition; R&D, research and data collection; D&I, delineation and inventory]

Agency or organization	MAN	REG	R&C	LAN	R&D	D&I
FEDERAL						
Department of Agriculture						
Consolidated Farm Service Agency	...	•	...	...	...	...
Forest Service	•	...	•	•	•	•
Natural Resources Conservation Service	...	•	•	...	•	•
Department of Commerce						
National Oceanic and Atmospheric Administration	...	•	...	...	•	...
Department of Defense						
Army Corps of Engineers	•	•	•	•	...	•
Military reservations	•	...	...	...	...	...
Department of the Interior						
Fish and Wildlife Service	•	...	•	•	•	•
Geological Survey	...	...	...	...	•	•
National Biological Service	...	...	...	...	•	•
National Park Service	•	...	...	...	•	•
Environmental Protection Agency	...	•	...	...	•	•
STATE						
Agency of Natural Resources						
Department of Environmental Conservation	•	•	•	...	•	•
Department of Fish and Wildlife	•	•	•	•	•	•
Department of Forests, Parks, and Recreation	•	•	...	...	•	•
Vermont Geological Survey	...	...	...	...	•	•
Vermont Housing and Conservation Board	...	...	...	•	...	...
State universities	...	...	...	...	•	•
COUNTY AND LOCAL						
District environmental commissions	...	•	...	...	...	•
Soil and water conservation districts	...	...	•	...	•	•
Some county, town, and city governments	•	•	...	•	...	...
Winooski Valley Park District	•	•	...	...	...	...
PRIVATE ORGANIZATIONS						
Ducks Unlimited	...	...	...	•	...	...
Private colleges and universities	...	...	...	...	•	•
The Nature Conservancy	•	...	...	•	...	...
Vermont Land Trust	...	...	...	•	...	...

Agriculture, Conservation, and Trade Act authorizes the Federal Government to purchase conservation easements from landowners who agree to protect or restore wetlands. The Consolidated Farm Service Agency (formerly the Agricultural Stabilization and Conservation Service) administers the Swampbuster provisions and Wetlands Reserve Program. The Natural Resources Conservation Service (formerly the Soil Conservation Service) determines compliance with Swampbuster provisions and assists farmers in the identification of wetlands and in the development of wetland protection, restoration, or creation plans.

The 1986 Emergency Wetlands Resources Act encourages wetland protection through funding incentives. The act requires States to address wetland protection in their Statewide Comprehensive Outdoor Recreation Plans to qualify for Federal funding for State recreational land; the National Park Service (NPS) provides guidance to States in developing the wetland component of their plans.

Federal agencies manage many wetlands in Vermont. The FWS manages wetlands in waterfowl protection areas, National Fish Hatcheries, and National Wildlife Refuges. For example, the FWS is responsible for about 5,800 acres of wetlands in the Missisquoi National Wildlife Refuge. Also, the FWS administers wetland-acquisition programs such as the Partners for Wildlife Program, which helps restore wetlands on private lands, and the North American

Waterfowl Management Plan, a cooperative program that provides funding for purchasing wetlands and contiguous uplands. In addition, the FWS has funded research on peatland ecology (Damman and French, 1987). The NPS has designated 11 sites in Vermont as National Natural Landmarks, 5 of which contain significant wetlands. Some of these are protected voluntarily by individual landowners. The U.S. Forest Service manages about 3,750 acres of wetlands in the Green Mountain National Forest. The Corps owns and manages several impoundments that have an undetermined amount of wetland acreage (Parsons, 1988a). The EPA has funded several wetland studies in Vermont, including the study of wetlands of outstanding ecological significance in Chittenden County (which contains Burlington, Vermont's largest city) and Grand Isle County (Vermont Department of Fish and Wildlife, 1992), the study of threats to wetlands in the Lake Champlain region (Borre, 1989), and the study of calcareous fens. The EPA has provided partial funding to the Lake Champlain Basin Program, which has included wetland-acquisition study (Jon Binhammer, The Nature Conservancy, written commun., 1993).

State wetland activities. — Vermont protects wetlands primarily through the Vermont Wetland Rules and Act 250 (Vermont's Land Use and Development Law) permit process and review. The Vermont Wetland Rules are administered by the Wetlands Office of the Vermont Agency of Natural Resources' Department of Environmental Conservation. The Vermont Wetland Rules establish three classes of wetlands (Vermont Department of Environmental Conservation, 1990a). Class One wetlands are those determined to provide an exceptional and irreplaceable contribution to Vermont's natural heritage in addition to providing other functions and have the highest level of protection. Class Two wetlands provide valuable ecologic, hydrologic, water-quality, cultural, or economic functions. Class Two wetlands include most wetlands shown on the National Wetland Inventory maps for Vermont and wetland areas contiguous to those wetlands but do not include seven categories of riverine and lacustrine open-water, beach, or bar wetlands. Class One and Two wetlands are protected by 100-foot and 50-foot buffer zones, respectively, unless otherwise ruled by the Water Resources Board. Under certain guidelines, activities such as logging and agriculture are allowed in Class One and Two wetlands. Class Three wetlands are those wetlands not designated as Class One or Two wetlands but which may still be protected under other Federal, State, or local regulations (Vermont Department of Environmental Conservation, 1990).

Act 250 requires a permit for every major land development and subdivision in Vermont. Administrative support for Act 250 is provided by nine District Environmental Commissions and an Environmental Board. Each Act 250 permit must comply with Vermont Wetland Rules, and all permit applications are reviewed by the Wetlands Office (Vermont Department of Environmental Conservation, 1990b). Some Class Three wetlands not protected under Vermont Wetland Rules may be protected under several criteria of Act 250.

The Department of Environmental Conservation administers sections 305(b) and 401 of the Federal Clean Water Act. Section 305(b) requires States to submit biennial water-quality-assessment reports to Congress and the EPA, a part of which specifically addresses water quality in wetlands. Section 401 requires State water-quality certification before a section 404 permit may be issued. A number of other programs, acts, and laws protect Vermont's wetlands. For example, a lake- and pond-management law protects wetlands below the average water level of lakes and ponds. A stream-alteration law protects wetlands within and along streambanks. Act 200, Vermont's growth bill, encourages local, regional, and State agency planning and has established broad goals for quality of wetlands and other resources. Through a grant from the EPA, the Department of Environmental Conservation is undertaking the Vermont Wetlands Conservation Strategy, a comprehensive review of

wetland conservation programs that will analyze the strengths and weaknesses of wetland conservation at the Federal, State, municipal, and private levels and recommend and rank actions to improve wetland conservation in Vermont (George Springston, Vermont Wetlands Office, written commun., 1993).

Several other State agencies own wetlands or have jurisdiction in wetland protection. The Vermont Department of Fish and Wildlife comments on projects that arise during Act 250 permit process and review (Parsons, 1988a). The Department has compiled a list of wetland-acquisition priorities (Parsons, 1988b) and has purchased wetlands and surrounding uplands for waterfowl habitat through administration of a duck-stamp program and through implementation of the Matching Aid to Restore States' Habitat program in cooperation with the Vermont chapter of Ducks Unlimited. The Department protects over 9,000 acres of wetlands within its waterfowl and wildlife management areas. The Vermont Department of Forests, Parks, and Recreation has established and enforces acceptable timber-management practices near surface waters and wetlands. The Vermont Nongame and Natural Heritage Program has inventoried natural wetland communities and rare and endangered species of wetlands and their habitats. This program also helps administer the Fragile Areas Registry and, along with the Department of Forests, Parks, and Recreation, administers State Natural Areas. There are more than 30 designated Natural Areas in Vermont, comprising more than 14,000 acres, some of which include wetlands. Designation as a Fragile Area does not provide direct protection but encourages landowners to conserve sensitive areas. The Department of Forests, Parks, and Recreation also is responsible for producing the wetlands component of the Vermont Statewide Comprehensive Outdoor Recreation Plan (Parsons, 1988a), which is the primary document guiding wetland acquisition with some Federal funding. The Vermont Housing and Conservation Board administers the Housing and Conservation Trust Fund. Approximately $10 million is appropriated annually to this fund by the State legislature. Part of these funds is granted to State agencies and nonprofit organizations for the purchase of easements and fee title acquisition of conservation lands, including wetlands, and of farm and forest lands, which sometimes include wetlands. For instance, the Vermont office of The Nature Conservancy has received grants to acquire wetland and upland buffers along East Creek, a tributary to Lake Champlain (fig. 1).

County and local wetland activities. — More than 20 towns in the State have adopted zoning bylaws to provide additional protection to wetlands (George Springston, Vermont Wetlands Office, written commun., 1993). Several intermunicipal districts in Vermont protect wetland areas. For example, the Winooski Valley Park District, a consortium of several towns in Chittendon County near Burlington, owns and manages several hundred acres of wetlands along the lower Winooski River (Parsons, 1988a). Vermont statutes authorize municipalities to acquire conservation easements as a land-protection tool, but few wetlands have been protected this way.

Private wetland activities. — Private organizations provide complementary functions that cannot readily be accomplished in governmental agencies. Private organizations, such as The Nature Conservancy, can provide rapid action in the purchase of property. The Nature Conservancy manages nine sites in Vermont that include significant wetlands and has assisted in the protection or purchase and transfer of nine additional sites. In 1993, The Nature Conservancy received a $600,000 grant from the FWS North American Wetlands Conservation Council for easements and fee title acquisition of approximately 1,500 acres of Lake Champlain wetlands. The Vermont chapter of Ducks Unlimited has worked in cooperation with the Department of Fish and Wildlife to purchase about 430 acres of waterfowl habitat, much of which is wetland. The Vermont Land Trust is a private organization that negotiates conservation easements with landowners to protect productive agricultural and forest lands. The Trust's holdings include several properties that have wetlands. Other organizations involved in wetland protection include the National Audubon Society, the New England Wildflower Society, the Izaak Walton League, the Sierra Club, the Appalachian Mountain Club, and others. Individuals, timber companies, towns, and other private landowners own most of Vermont's wetlands, and many actively pursue wetland conservation.

References Cited

Borre, M.A., 1989, Threats to wetlands in the Lake Champlain region of Vermont—Boundary determination for the EPA's proposed advance identification: New Haven, Conn., Yale University, School of Forestry and Environmental Studies, 51 p.

Brinson, M.M., 1993, Changes in the functioning of wetlands along environmental gradients: Wetlands, v. 13, no. 2, p. 65–74.

Bulmer, S.K., 1988, 1988 Vermont recreation plan: Waterbury, Vt., Agency of Natural Resources, Department of Forests, Parks, and Recreation, 128 p.

Clausen, J.C., and Johnson, G.D., 1990, Lake level influences on sediment and nutrient retention in a lakeside wetland: Journal of Environmental Quality, v. 19, no. 1, p. 83–88.

Cowardin, L.M., Carter, Virginia, Golet, F.C., and LaRoe, E.T., 1979, Classification of wetlands and deepwater habitats of the United States: U.S. Fish and Wildlife Service Report FWS/OBS–79/31, 131 p.

Damman, A.W.H., and French, T.W., 1987, The ecology of peat bogs of the glaciated northeastern United States—A community profile: U.S. Fish and Wildlife Service Biological Report 85(7.16), 114 p.

Doll, C.G., comp., 1970, Surficial geologic map of Vermont: Waterbury, Vermont Geological Survey Division, scale 1:250,000.

Downer, R.N., 1971, Extreme mean daily annual water levels of Lake Champlain: University of Vermont, Vermont Water Resources Research Report 3, 18 p.

Federal Interagency Committee for Wetland Delineation, 1989, Federal manual for identifying and delineating jurisdictional wetlands: Washington, D.C., U.S. Army Corps of Engineers, U.S. Environmental Protection Agency, U.S. Fish and Wildlife Service, and U.S. Department of Agriculture Soil Conservation Service Cooperative Technical Publication, 76 p.

Fenneman, N.M., 1946, Physical divisions of the United States: Washington D.C., U.S. Geological Survey special map, scale 1:7,000,000.

Hammond, R.E., and Cotton, J.E., 1986, Vermont surface-water resources, *in* U.S. Geological Survey, National water summary 1985—Hydrologic events and surface-water resources: U.S. Geological Survey Water-Supply Paper 2300, p. 461–466.

Johnson, C.W., 1985, Bogs of the northeast: Hanover, N.H., The University Press of New England, 269 p.

Meeks, H.A., 1986, Vermont's land and resources: Shelburne, Vt., The New England Press, 332 p.

Parsons, Jeffrey, 1988a, Wetlands component, 1988 Vermont recreation plan: Waterbury, Vermont Department of Forests, Parks, and Recreation, Recreation Division, 43 p.

———1988b, A characterization of Vermont's more important wetlands: Waterbury, Vermont Department of Forests, Parks, and Recreation, 23 p.

Thompson, Liz, 1989, Natural communities of Vermont: Waterbury, Vermont Department of Fish and Wildlife, Nongame and Heritage Program, 12 p.

Tiner, R.W., 1987, Preliminary National Wetlands Inventory report on Vermont's wetland acreage: Newton Corner, Mass., U.S. Fish and Wildlife Service, 5 p.

———1991, Maine wetlands and their boundaries—A guide for code enforcement officers: Augusta, Maine Department of Economic and Community Development, Office of Comprehensive Planning, 72 p.

Vermont Department of Environmental Conservation, 1990a, Wetland fact sheet number 4, wetland rules summary: Waterbury, Vermont Department of Environmental Conservation, Water Quality Division, Wetlands Office, 2 p.

———1990b, Wetland fact sheet number 1, Act 250 review guidelines: Waterbury, Vermont Department of Environmental Conservation, Water Quality Division, Wetlands Office, 2 p.

Vermont Department of Fish and Wildlife, 1992, Wetlands of outstanding ecological significance in Chittenden County, Vermont: Waterbury, Vermont Department of Fish and Wildlife, Nongame and Natural Heritage Program, 122 p.

Wanner, R., 1979, Wetlands in Vermont, their identification and protection: Montpelier, Vermont Natural Resources Council, 71 p.

Winter, T.C., 1992, A physiographic and climatic framework for hydrologic studies of wetlands, *in* Robarts, R.D., and Bothwell, M.L., eds., Aquatic ecosystems in semi-arid regions—Implications for resource management, 1992: National Hydrologic Research Institute Symposium Series 7, Environment Canada, Saskatoon, p. 127–148.

FOR ADDITIONAL INFORMATION: District Chief, U.S. Geological Survey, 525 Clinton Street, Bow, NH 03304; Regional Wetland Coordinator, U.S. Fish and Wildlife Service, 300 Westgate Center Drive, Hadley, MA 01035

Prepared by
David S. Armstrong,
U.S. Geological Survey

Virginia
Wetland Resources

Wetlands cover about 4 percent of Virginia (Dahl, 1990). These wetlands support rich biotic communities in freshwater, saltwater, and brackish-water settings across the State. Well-known Virginia wetlands include the extensive estuarine marshes behind the coastal barrier islands and the forested wetlands along tidal rivers and in the Great Dismal Swamp (fig.1).

Wetlands have many chemical, physical, and biological functions. They benefit entire ecosystems, including resident human populations (Hershner, 1992). Wetlands trap waterborne sediments and retain nutrients and toxic chemicals by filtering them out of inflowing water and storing or transforming them. Wetlands also can recharge ground-water supplies or serve as points of ground-water discharge to the surface. Coastal-zone and flood-plain wetlands mitigate the effects of flooding caused by tides and runoff by reducing flow velocity, storing water temporarily, and releasing it gradually. Vegetation in riparian wetlands maintains stream channels by stabilizing the banks, and vegetated tidal wetlands act as buffers against storm tides and waves, thus impeding erosion. One of the most important functions of wetlands is to provide habitat for waterfowl, terrestrial and aquatic animals, and a wide variety of plant life. Wetlands in Virginia provide food, shelter, and resting places for migratory birds, as well as breeding areas and nurseries for many animals, including those of particular economic interest in Virginia such as blue crabs, muskrat, fish, ducks, and geese. Many rare and endangered plant species are adapted to hydrologic conditions present only in wetlands.

Virginia's wetlands have considerable esthetic, historic, archeological, recreational, and economic value (Hershner, 1992). Humans have inhabited the coastal wetlands of Virginia for thousands of years, and unique cultures have developed there. Wetlands provide outdoor educational and recreational opportunities such as birdwatching, hiking, and canoeing. They also support the hunting, fur trapping, commercial and sport fishing, lumbering, and tourist industries, which benefit the economy of the State.

TYPES AND DISTRIBUTION

Wetlands are lands transitional between terrestrial and deepwater habitats where the water table usually is at or near the land surface or the land is covered by shallow water (Cowardin and oth-

ers, 1979). The distribution of wetlands and deepwater habitats in Virginia is shown in figure 2A; only wetlands are discussed herein.

Wetlands can be vegetated or nonvegetated and are classified on the basis of their hydrology, vegetation, and substrate. In this summary, wetlands are classified according to the system proposed by Cowardin and others (1979), which is used by the U.S. Fish and Wildlife Service (FWS) to map and inventory the Nation's wetlands. At the most general level of the classification system, wetlands are grouped into five ecological systems: Palustrine, Lacustrine, Riverine, Estuarine, and Marine. The Palustrine System includes only wetlands, whereas the other systems comprise wetlands and deepwater habitats. Wetlands of the systems that occur in Virginia are described below.

System	Wetland description
Palustrine	Nontidal and tidal-freshwater wetlands in which vegetation is predominantly trees (forested wetlands); shrubs (scrub-shrub wetlands); persistent or nonpersistent emergent, erect, rooted herbaceous plants (persistent- and nonpersistent-emergent wetlands); or submersed and (or) floating plants (aquatic beds). Also, intermittently to permanently flooded open-water bodies of less than 20 acres in which water is less than 6.6 feet deep.
Lacustrine	Nontidal and tidal-freshwater wetlands within an intermittently to permanently flooded lake or reservoir larger than 20 acres and (or) deeper than 6.6 feet. Vegetation, when present, is predominantly nonpersistent emergent plants (nonpersistent-emergent wetlands), or submersed and (or) floating plants (aquatic beds), or both.
Riverine	Nontidal and tidal-freshwater wetlands within a channel. Vegetation, when present, is same as in the Lacustrine System.
Estuarine	Tidal wetlands in low-wave-energy environments where the salinity of the water is greater than 0.5 part per thousand (ppt) and is variable owing to evaporation and the mixing of seawater and freshwater.
Marine	Tidal wetlands that are exposed to waves and currents of the open ocean and to water having a salinity greater than 30 ppt.

Palustrine wetlands comprise about 72 percent of the wetland area of Virginia (Tiner and Finn, 1986). Estuarine wetlands comprise about 23 percent of the State's wetlands. Lacustrine wetlands in freshwater ponds comprise most of the remaining 5 percent. Only a few hundred acres of marine and riverine wetlands exist in Virginia. Palustrine forested wetlands (swamps) are the most abundant type of wetland in Virginia, accounting for about 60 percent of the total wetland area in the State. Estuarine emergent wetlands (tidal marshes) are the second-most abundant type of wetland, comprising about 8 percent of the wetlands in the State (Tiner and Finn, 1986).

Virginia has many different types of wetlands. Salt marshes include the extensive estuarine wetlands along the Chesapeake Bay that are characterized by vegetation tolerant of brackish to salty water. Other tidal marshes include estuarine wetlands located along freshwater parts of tidal rivers. Interdunal swales are topographic depressions among sand dunes on the Atlantic coast that contain palustrine emergent or scrub-shrub wetlands. Virginia's Atlantic

Figure 1. Wetlands in the Great Dismal Swamp, a palustrine forested wetland. *(Photograph by Virginia Carter, U.S. Geological Survey.)*

white cedar swamps, red spruce swamps, and cypress-tupelo swamps and its nontidal flood-plain forests are palustrine forested wetlands that have seasonally occurring standing water and flood-tolerant trees. Pocosins are palustrine scrub-shrub wetlands that are slightly elevated above the surrounding landscape and have flat topography and poor natural drainage. Virginia's bogs, fens, and wet meadows are palustrine emergent wetlands that are often underlain by organic soils. The presence and composition of plant communities in the wetlands of Virginia are determined by factors such as the extent and duration of flooding, climate, type of soil, and ground- and surface-water chemistry.

About 72 percent of the wetland area in Virginia, including all the estuarine wetlands and most of the large nontidal wetlands, is in the Coastal Plain (fig. 2A and 2B) (Tiner and Finn, 1986). Extensive estuarine wetlands have developed in low-lying areas along the shores of the Chesapeake Bay and its tributaries and behind the barrier beaches of the Atlantic coast. Palustrine wetlands are distributed throughout the State and are located primarily in bottom lands and in flood plains along stream channels, especially in headwater areas. About 22 percent of the wetlands in Virginia are in the Piedmont, and most of the remaining wetland area is in the Appalachian Plateaus (Tiner and Finn, 1986; Harlow and LeCain, 1991).

HYDROLOGIC SETTING

Virginia's wetlands (fig. 3A–3C) are formed and maintained by water supplied by precipitation, overland runoff from precipitation, local and regional ground-water flow, and tides. Precipitation

supplies adequate moisture for wetland formation and maintenance and ranges statewide from 36 to 52 inches per year (Prugh and Scott, 1986). Precipitation does not have a strong seasonal pattern during the year, but 80 to 85 percent of evaporation from open bodies of water occurs from April to October. That period coincides with the higher transpiration rates of the growing season.

Annual and seasonal fluctuations in local precipitation and evapotranspiration rates combine with local differences in geology, topography, and soil characteristics to create short- or long-term changes in the interactions of ground water and surface water in wetlands. These changes can result in alternating flooded and dry conditions, especially in small wetlands (Winter, 1992; Phillips and Shedlock, 1993). Additionally, larger wetlands (tidal and nontidal) can interact with regional ground-water flow systems. In tidal wetlands, a major source of water is tidal inundation. Overland runoff and ground-water discharge can be important secondary sources. The major sources of water in nontidal wetlands are precipitation and ground-water discharge.

Virginia includes five physiographic provinces: the Coastal Plain, Piedmont, Blue Ridge, Valley and Ridge, and Appalachian Plateaus (fig. 2B). Each province is characterized by geologic features, landforms, and soils that directly affect the hydrology of wetlands.

Coastal Plain. — The Coastal Plain is relatively flat, rising from below sea level to about 50 feet above sea level on the Delmarva Peninsula east of the Chesapeake Bay and to about 200 feet above sea level on the upper Coastal Plain west of the Chesapeake Bay. This province is underlain by an extensive and locally complex

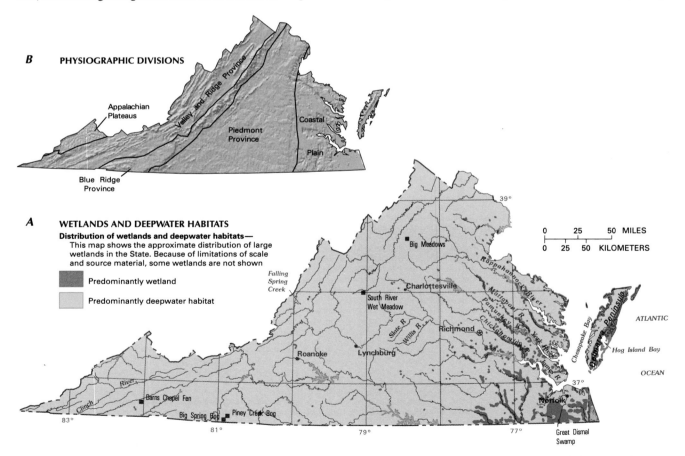

Figure 2. Wetland distribution in Virginia and physiography of the State. **A,** Distribution of wetlands and deepwater habitats. **B,** Physiography. (*Sources: A, T.E. Dahl, U.S. Fish and Wildlife Service, unpub. data, 1991. B, Physiographic divisions from Fenneman, 1946; landforms data from EROS Data Center.*)

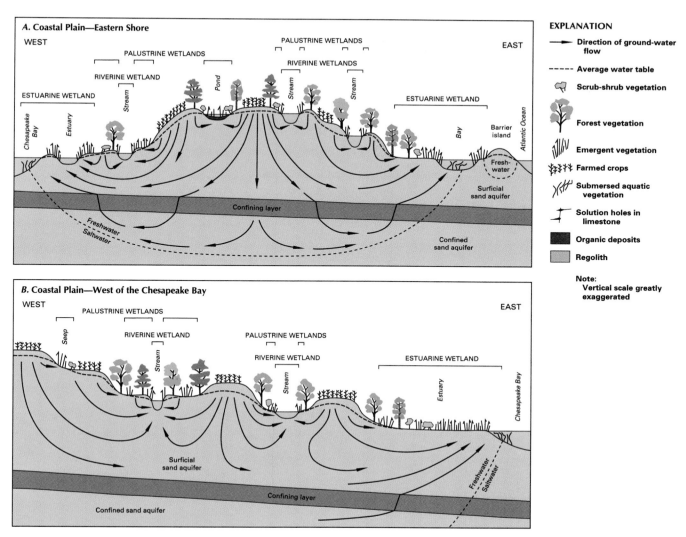

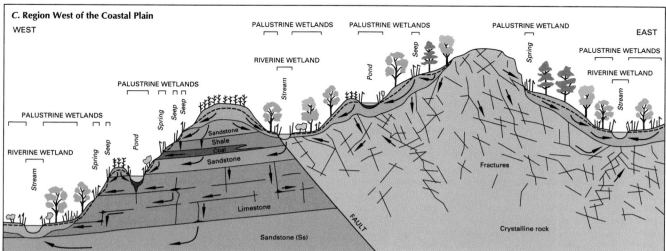

Figure 3. Generalized geohydrology of wetlands in Virginia. **A**, Coastal Plain—Eastern Shore. **B**, Coastal Plain—west of the Chesapeake Bay. **C**, Region west of the Coastal Plain. *(Sources: A, Based on information in Harsh and Laczniak, 1986; Richardson, 1992; and M.J. Focazio, written commun., 1993. B, Based on information in Back, 1966; Harsh and Laczniak, 1986; and Winter, 1992. C, Based on information in Heath, 1984.)*

surficial aquifer composed primarily of unconsolidated sediments. Below the surficial aquifer are several confined aquifers and confining layers.

Coastal Plain wetlands are maintained by precipitation, overland runoff, flooding from streams, and ground-water discharge. Wetlands in the Coastal Plain generally intersect the water table of the surficial aquifer. Recharge of the surficial aquifer in the Coastal Plain is mainly by infiltration of precipitation in interstream areas (Heath, 1984). Discharge occurs by evapotranspiration and by seepage to wetlands, streams, estuaries, wells, ditches, and the ocean.

Many Coastal Plain wetlands are in local and regional ground-water discharge areas of coastal and riparian zones. Low-lying areas of the Coastal Plain contain extensive wetlands in the form of seagrass beds, salt and brackish marshes, and tidal freshwater marshes and swamps. These wetlands have complex hydrology; streamflow, local and regional ground-water flow, and tidal flow all are components. Nontidal wetlands of the Coastal Plain are maintained by local and regional ground-water flow systems and storm-related flooding. The area of forested wetlands in flood plains often is reduced by artificial draining and conversion of the land for agricultural and urban uses.

The Coastal Plain can be divided into two subregions of differing geohydrology: the Eastern Shore, on the Delmarva Peninsula (fig. 3A) and the area of the Coastal Plain west of the Chesapeake Bay (fig. 3B). On the Eastern Shore, the surficial sand aquifer overlies eastward-dipping confined aquifers and confining layers. The center of the Delmarva Peninsula is poorly drained and has small depressional palustrine wetlands (Delmarva bays) and narrow bands of palustrine wetlands along ditches and streams. Extensive brackish and saline estuarine wetlands are located along the eastern shore of the peninsula behind a barrier-island complex and on the western shore of the peninsula.

West of the Chesapeake Bay, several major aquifers crop out and dip to the east under the bay and the Delmarva Peninsula. In this region, large freshwater swamps dominated by cypress, red maple, black gum, and tupelo gum trees are located along the many tidal rivers (Virginia Sea Grant College Program, 1989). Numerous nontidal freshwater forested wetlands also are in the region, especially along the boundary between the sediments of the Coastal Plain and the higher altitude crystalline rocks of the Piedmont.

The Coastal Plain of Virginia has many notable wetlands. They include the extensive tidal freshwater marshes and swamps along the Chickahominy River, the salt marshes behind the coastal barrier islands that protect Hog Island Bay, and the forested wetlands along the Mattaponi, Pamunkey, James, and York Rivers, as well as those in the Great Dismal Swamp. This swamp (fig. 1) is the largest nontidal freshwater wetland in the State.

West of the Coastal Plain. — West of the Coastal Plain, there is considerably more topographic relief. The gently rolling hills of the Piedmont are generally less than 800 feet above sea level. The mountains of the Blue Ridge rise to more than 1,600 feet. Altitudes in the Valley and Ridge range from about 400 feet in the valleys to about 1,500 feet on the ridges. The valleys and mountains of the Appalachian Plateaus range from 1,500 to more than 3,000 feet above sea level. The aquifers west of the Coastal Plain generally are unconfined; in highly fractured, saturated crystalline or sedimentary bedrock; and overlain by regolith of irregular thickness (Meng and others, 1985). Regolith, which forms the land surface nearly everywhere, is a layer of unconsolidated, mostly fine-grained material composed of fragmented, weathered bedrock and alluvium overlying unweathered bedrock.

Wetlands west of the Coastal Plain are generally small and localized (fig. 3C). Their location and size are controlled mainly by topography, precipitation, and ground-water availability. Much of the precipitation in this province is transported to surface depressions and streams by overland runoff (Heath, 1984). Much of the

ground water available to wetlands is held in the regolith (Powell and Abe, 1985; Wright, 1990; Harlow and LeCain, 1991). Topographically high areas (ridges) function as aquifer recharge areas (Harlow and LeCain, 1991). Water infiltrates the surface, seeps into the regolith, and flows downward and laterally through fractures and solution cavities in the shallow bedrock. If the vertical hydraulic conductivity of the bedrock is negligible, water is discharged wherever the water table intersects the land surface, forming springs or seeps on hill slopes and fens in closed topographic depressions. If the conductivity is appreciable, ground water follows a stairstep path through the regolith, fractures, bedding planes, and coal seams, eventually discharging to streams. With increasing depth, ground water flows primarily in a lateral direction. Deep, regional ground-water flow is not a significant source of moisture for wetlands in this region.

Wetlands west of the Coastal Plain are commonly found along riparian valleys and other low areas of the ground surface, which typically overlie fracture zones in the bedrock. Water is more likely to discharge into these depressions than into other areas because fracture zones are major pathways of ground-water movement (Heath, 1984).

Types of wetland west of the Coastal Plain include flood-plain marshes and swamps, seeps, fens, and excavated farm ponds. Notable wetlands in this region include the Slate River and Willis River wetlands in the Piedmont; Big Spring Bog, Piney Creek Bog, Big Meadows and South River Wet Meadow in the Blue Ridge; and Barns Chapel Fen, Falling Spring Creek, and the Clinch River flood-plain wetlands in the Valley and Ridge (U.S. Fish and Wildlife Service, 1990; T.J. Rawinski, Virginia Department of Conservation and Recreation, written commun., 1993).

TRENDS

In the 1780's, wetlands covered about 1,849,000 acres (more than 7 percent) of Virginia (Dahl, 1990). By the mid-1980's, about 1,075,000 wetland acres remained in Virginia—a loss of about 42 percent in 200 years (Dahl, 1990). Inventories published in 1989 by the Virginia Institute of Marine Science and the FWS estimated that there were approximately 215,000 acres of vegetated tidal wetlands and 673,192 acres of vegetated nontidal wetlands remaining in Virginia (Virginia Department of Conservation and Recreation, 1989).

Agriculture, industrial and urban development, and recreation have led to the draining, dredging and ditching, filling, diking, and damming of wetlands in Virginia. These practices—combined with human activities that affect water quality and natural phenomena that result in erosion, saltwater inundation, and botanical succession—have contributed to the widespread wetland loss and degradation and some wetland generation. The estimated annual loss of all wetland types between 1955 and 1977 was about 3,000 acres (Tiner, 1987), amounting to a total wetland loss of about 6 percent during that period. Eighty percent of estimated losses of freshwater vegetated wetlands (mostly palustrine forested systems) occurred in the Coastal Plain.

Major causes of nontidal wetland loss have been direct conversion to agriculture (about 45 percent), channelization and ditching (about 27 percent), and lake and pond creation (about 25 percent) (Tiner, 1987). Between 1955 and 1977, pond construction and beaver impoundment resulted in an estimated 170-percent (35,000 acres) increase in freshwater pond acreage across the State, mostly in upland areas. Major causes of tidal wetland loss have been urbanization (about 43 percent), inundation by submersion, dredging, or impoundment (about 36 percent), agricultural conversion (about 5 percent), and pond creation (about 5 percent).

Small areas of wetland have been created in recent times, especially by flooding during road, lake, and pond construction and, most recently, by the establishment of compensatory wetland-mitigation sites. New wetlands also have formed on sediments deposited by storms and dredging activities in coastal areas.

Management policies and rationales generally reflect the latest technical understanding within the field but not necessarily the latest scientific understanding. For example, up to the early years of the 20th century, wetlands were considered to be habitat for noxious pests and management policies focused on eliminating the undesirable habitat value or the wetland itself. In the last 25 years, numerous other wetland functions of significant potential value to natural and human systems have been identified (Hershner, 1992), and regulations have been changed to reflect this understanding. Implementation of the 1972 Virginia Wetlands Act and the 1972 Federal Clean Water Act markedly reduced the rate of human-induced tidal wetland loss. Between 1972, when the Wetlands Act was enacted, and 1977, the annual rate of tidal wetland loss decreased from between 400 and 600 acres to 20 acres or less (Dawes, 1978). Still, however important wetlands may be environmentally, they present a volatile issue because of development pressure (Virginia Sea Grant College Program, 1989), and the demand for space for an expanding human population has resulted in increasing conversion of wetlands into developed landscapes (Hershner, 1992).

CONSERVATION

Many government agencies and private organizations participate in wetland conservation in Virginia. The most active agencies and organizations and some of their activities are listed in table 1.

Federal wetland activities. — Development activities in Virginia wetlands are regulated by several Federal statutory prohibitions and incentives that are intended to slow wetland losses. Some of the more important of these are contained in the 1899 Rivers and Harbors Act; the 1972 Clean Water Act and amendments; the 1985 Food Security Act; the 1990 Food, Agriculture, Conservation, and Trade Act; the 1986 Emergency Wetlands Resources Act; and the 1972 Coastal Zone Management Act.

Section 10 of the Rivers and Harbors Act gives the U.S. Army Corps of Engineers (Corps) authority to regulate certain activities in navigable waters. Regulated activities include diking, deepening, filling, excavating, and placing of structures. The related section 404 of the Clean Water Act is the most often-used Federal legislation protecting wetlands. Under section 404 provisions, the Corps issues permits regulating the discharge of dredged or fill material into wetlands. Permits are subject to review and possible veto by the U.S. Environmental Protection Agency, and the FWS has review and advisory roles. Section 401 of the Clean Water Act grants to States and eligible Indian Tribes the authority to approve, apply conditions to, or deny section 404 permit applications on the basis of a proposed activity's probable effects on the water quality of a wetland.

Most farming, ranching, and silviculture activities are not subject to section 404 regulation. However, the "Swampbuster" provision of the 1985 Food Security Act and amendments in the 1990 Food, Agriculture, Conservation, and Trade Act discourage (through financial disincentives) the draining, filling, or other alteration of wetlands for agricultural use. The law allows exemptions from penalties in some cases, especially if the farmer agrees to restore the altered wetland or other wetlands that have been converted to agricultural use. The Wetlands Reserve Program of the 1990 Food, Agriculture, Conservation, and Trade Act authorizes the Federal Government to purchase conservation easements from landowners who agree to protect or restore wetlands. The Consolidated Farm Service Agency (formerly the Agricultural Stabilization and Conservation Service) administers the Swampbuster provisions and Wetlands Reserve Program. The Natural Resources Conservation Service (NRCS) (formerly the Soil Conservation Service) determines compliance with Swampbuster provisions and assists farmers in the

Table 1. Selected wetland-related activities of government agencies and private organizations in Virginia, 1993

[Source: Classification of activities is generalized from information provided by agencies and organizations. •, agency or organization participates in wetland-related activity; ..., agency or organization does not participate in wetland-related activity. MAN, management; REG, regulation; R&C, restoration and creation; LAN, land acquisition; R&D, research and data collection; D&I, delineation and inventory]

Agency or organization	MAN	REG	R&C	LAN	R&D	D&I
FEDERAL						
Department of Agriculture						
Consolidated Farm Service Agency	...	•	...	...	...	...
Natural Resources Conservation Service	...	•	•	...	•	•
Department of Commerce						
National Oceanic and Atmospheric Administration	•	•	...	...	•	•
Department of Defense						
Army Corps of Engineers	...	•	•	...	•	...
Department of the Interior						
Fish and Wildlife Service	•	...	•	•	•	•
Geological Survey	...	...	...	...	•	...
National Biological Service	...	...	...	...	•	...
National Park Service	•	...	•	•	•	...
Environmental Protection Agency	...	•	•	...	•	•
STATE						
College of William and Mary						
Virginia Institute of Marine Science	...	...	...	...	•	•
Department of Conservation and Recreation						
Division of Natural Heritage	•	...	...	•	...	•
Division of State Parks	•	...	...	•	...	...
Department of Environmental Quality	•	•	•	...	•	•
Department of Game and Inland Fisheries	•	•	...	•	...	•
Department of Transportation	•	...	•	...	•	•
Virginia Joint Venture Board	...	...	•	•	...	...
Virginia Marine Resources Commission	•	•	•	...	•	•
Virginia Outdoors Foundation	...	...	...	•	...	...
Virginia Polytechnic Institute and State University	...	...	...	...	•	...
SOME COUNTY AND LOCAL GOVERNMENTS	•	•	...	...	•	•
PRIVATE ORGANIZATIONS						
Chesapeake Bay Foundation	•	...	...	...	•	...
Ducks Unlimited	•	...	•	•	•	...
Friends of the Rivers of Virginia	•	...	...	...	•	...
The Lower James River Association	•	...	...	...	...	...
The Nature Conservancy	•	...	...	•	•	...

identification of wetlands and in the development of wetland protection, restoration, or creation plans.

The 1986 Emergency Wetlands Resources Act and the 1972 Coastal Zone Management Act and amendments encourage wetland protection through funding incentives. The Emergency Wetlands Resources Act requires States to address wetland protection in their Statewide Comprehensive Outdoor Recreation Plans to qualify for Federal funding for State recreational land; the National Park Service provides guidance to States in developing the wetland component of their plans. Coastal and Great Lakes States that adopt coastal-zone management programs and plans approved by the National Oceanic and Atmospheric Administration are eligible for Federal funding and technical assistance through the Coastal Zone Management Act.

State wetland activities. — Activities in both tidal and nontidal wetlands in the State of Virginia are regulated through the Department of Environmental Quality's Water Division by means of the Virginia Water Protection Permit. This permit is issued to ensure compliance with the State Water Control Law and serves as the certification of Virginia's compliance with section 401 of the Federal Clean Water Act. To obtain this permit and other permits showing compliance with the Virginia Wetlands Act and section 404 of the Federal Clean Water Act, a Joint Permit Application is submitted to the Virginia Marine Resources Commission.

The Virginia Marine Resources Commission has ultimate regulatory authority for the coastal resources included in the State Wetlands Act, the Federal Chesapeake Bay Preservation Act, and the State Coastal Primary Sand Dune Protection Act (Bradshaw, 1991). Local governments have the option of adopting prescribed zoning ordinances and forming citizen wetlands boards to regulate their own tidal wetlands. The Commission retains an oversight and appellate role in those localities, and the Virginia Institute of Marine Science has an advisory role in the permitting process. Virginia has no laws that apply specifically to nontidal wetlands. However, the Water Control Board (now called the Department of Environmental Quality, Water Division) adopted a wetlands policy in 1974 (revised in 1982) that covers both nontidal and tidal wetlands. In addition, the Scenic Rivers Act of 1970 prevents certain activities in designated riparian areas that include wetlands, and the Endangered Species Act of 1972 provides habitat preservation and protection in wetlands and elsewhere. The Chesapeake Bay Preservation Act, which is implemented by local governments, calls for establishment of protective buffers around tidal and nontidal wetlands adjacent to surface waters or tidal wetlands in Virginia's coastal plain.

In 1990, the Division of Soil and Water Conservation of the Virginia Department of Conservation and Recreation began to gather and update all existing data on the wetlands of Virginia with the goal of creating a single, comprehensive data base (Virginia Department of Conservation and Recreation, 1990). This project has been designed to conform with the standards of the FWS National Wetland Inventory project. National Wetland Inventory data for about three-fourths of the State have been digitized. Information for the eastern part of the State is older and less detailed than the western part, and about one-fourth of the eastern inland part of the State is currently (1993) being reinventoried and digitized. Another comprehensive project to map wetland locations was conducted by the NRCS, which inventoried wetlands down to less than one-fourth of an acre at different scales. This information has not been standardized or published collectively but is available through county NRCS offices.

Private wetland organization activities. — Private organizations with interests in wetlands in Virginia are active in policy planning, the development of regulations, advocacy, land acquisition and management, environmental education, and research. A few of the many such organizations in the State are The Nature Conservancy, the Chesapeake Bay Foundation, the Friends of the Rivers of Virginia, The Lower James River Foundation, and Ducks Unlimited. The State and The Nature Conservancy jointly administer the Virginia Natural Heritage Program, which identifies natural areas, including wetlands, for conservation planning.

References Cited

Back, William, 1966, Hydrochemical facies and ground-water flow patterns in northern part of Atlantic Coastal Plain—Hydrology of aquifer systems: U.S. Geological Survey Professional Paper 498–A, 42 p.

Bradshaw, J.G., 1991, Coastal resources and the permit process—Definitions and jurisdictions: Virginia Institute of Marine Science Technical Report no. 91–2, 7 p.

Cowardin, L.M., Carter, Virginia, Golet, F.C., and LaRoe, E.T., 1979, Classification of wetlands and deepwater habitats of the United States: U.S. Fish and Wildlife Service Report FWS/OBS–79/31, 131 p.

Dahl, T.E., 1990, Wetlands—Losses in the United States, 1780's to 1980's: Washington, D.C., U.S. Fish and Wildlife Service Report to Congress, 13 p.

Dawes, G.M., 1978, Implementation of the Virginia Wetland Act of 1972, *in* Proceedings of the 1978 National Wetland Protection Symposium: Gloucester Point, Virginia Institute of Marine Science, p. 53–56.

Fenneman, N.M., 1946, Physical divisions of the United States: Washington, D.C., U.S. Geological Survey special map, scale 1:7,000,000.

Harlow, G.E., Jr., and LeCain, G.D., 1991, Hydraulic characteristics of, and ground-water flow in, coal-bearing rocks of southwestern Virginia: U.S. Geological Survey Open-File Report 91–250, 48 p.

Harsh, J.F., and Laczniak, R.J., 1986, Conceptualization and analysis of the ground-water system in the Coastal Plain aquifers of Virginia: U.S. Geological Survey Professional Paper 1404–E, 107 p.

Heath, R.C., 1984, Ground-water regions of the United States: U.S. Geological Survey Water-Supply Paper 2242, 78 p.

Hershner, Carl, 1992, Ecological functions and values of nontidal wetlands, *in* Perspectives on Chesapeake Bay, 1992—Advances in Estuarine Sciences: Chesapeake Research Consortium Publication 143, p. 1–16.

Meng, A.A., Harsh, J.F., and Kull, T.K., 1985, Virginia ground-water resources, *in* U.S. Geological Survey, National water summary 1984—Hydrologic events and selected water-quality trends and ground-water resources: U.S. Geological Survey Water-Supply Paper 2275, p. 427–432.

Phillips, P.J., and Shedlock, R.J., 1993, Hydrology and chemistry of ground-water and seasonal ponds in the Atlantic Coastal Plain in Delaware, USA: Journal of Hydrology, v. 141, p. 157–178.

Powell, J.D., and Abe, J.M., 1985, Availability and quality of ground water in the Piedmont Province of Virginia: U.S. Geological Survey Water-Resources Investigations Report 85–4235, 33 p.

Prugh, B.J., and Scott, W.B., 1986, Virginia surface-water resources, *in* U.S. Geological Survey, National water summary 1985—Hydrologic events and surface-water resources: U.S. Geological Survey Water-Supply Paper 2300, p. 467–472.

Richardson, D.L., 1992, Hydrogeology and analysis of the ground-water-flow system of the Eastern Shore, Virginia: U.S. Geological Survey Open-File Report 91–490, 117 p.

Tiner, R.W., 1987, Mid-Atlantic wetlands—A disappearing natural treasure: Newton Corner, Mass., U.S. Fish and Wildlife Service and U.S. Environmental Protection Agency cooperative publication, 28 p.

Tiner, R.W., and Finn, J.T., 1986, Status and recent trends of wetlands in five mid-Atlantic states—Delaware, Maryland, Pennsylvania, Virginia, and West Virginia: Newton Corner, Mass., U.S. Fish and Wildlife Service, National Wetlands Inventory project technical report, 40 p.

U.S. Fish and Wildlife Service, 1990, Regional wetlands concept plan, emergency wetlands resources act, Northeast Region: Newton Corner, Mass., U.S. Fish and Wildlife Service, app. A.

Virginia Department of Conservation and Recreation, 1989, The 1989 Virginia outdoors plan: Richmond, Virginia Department of Conservation and Recreation, 289 p.

———1990, The Virginia nontidal wetlands inventory: Richmond, Virginia Department of Conservation and Recreation, 19 p., 3 app.

Virginia Sea Grant College Program, 1989, Marine resource bulletin: Virginia Graduate Marine Science Consortium, v. 21, no. 1, 21 p.

Winter, T.C., 1992, A physiographic and climatic framework for hydrologic studies of wetlands, *in* Robarts, R.D., and Bothwell, M.L., eds., Proceedings of the Symposium on Aquatic Ecosystems in Semi-Arid Regions, 1990—Implications for resource management: Saskatoon, Saskatchewan, Environment Canada, The National Hydrology Research Institute Symposium Series no. 7, p. 127–147.

Wright, W.G., 1990, Ground-water hydrology and quality in the Valley and Ridge and Blue Ridge physiographic provinces of Clarke County, Virginia: U.S. Geological Survey Water-Resources Investigations Report 90–4134, 61 p.

FOR ADDITIONAL INFORMATION: District Chief, U.S. Geological Survey, 3600 West Broad Street, Room 606, Richmond, VA 23230; Regional Wetland Coordinator, U.S. Fish and Wildlife Service, 300 Westgate Center Drive, Hadley, MA 01035

Prepared by
Martha A. Hayes,
U.S. Geological Survey

Washington
Wetland Resources

Washington's wetlands are remarkably diverse, each having a unique combination of ecological characteristics such as altitude, seasonality, chemistry, and species composition. Although wetlands cover only about 2 percent of the State, they are a valuable and important resource.

Wetlands perform many important hydrologic functions, such as maintaining streamflows, slowing and storing floodwaters, stabilizing streambanks, and reducing the erosion of shorelines. Although usually thought of as areas of ground-water discharge, some wetlands serve as areas of ground-water recharge (Washington State Department of Ecology, 1992a). Wetlands also improve water quality by filtering out sediments, excessive nutrients, and toxic chemicals. By serving these and other functions, wetlands can sometimes reduce or eliminate the need for the costly engineering and construction of control, treatment, and retention facilities (Puget Sound Water Quality Authority, 1990).

For a vast and diverse array of wildlife, including invertebrates, fish, amphibians, reptiles, birds, and mammals, wetlands are essential habitats for feeding, nesting, cover, or breeding. More than 315 species of wildlife use the State's wetlands as primary feeding or breeding habitat. Wetlands are vital nursery and feeding areas for anadromous fish such as salmon and steelhead trout (Washington State Department of Wildlife, undated). Wetlands are critical habitats for at least one-third of the State's threatened or endangered species of wildlife (Puget Sound Water Quality Authority, 1990).

Wetlands furnish many opportunities for education and scientific research. The numbers and diversity of plants and animals found in wetlands make these habitats excellent locations for teaching and research in biology, botany, ornithology, environmental science, and ecology.

Washington's wetlands provide many quality-of-life benefits. As scenic areas, wetlands present a visually pleasing contrast to upland areas, open water, and forests (fig. 1). In addition, the State's wetlands support a wide range of recreational activities, including

bird watching, nature appreciation, camping, boating, fishing, and hunting.

TYPES AND DISTRIBUTION

Wetlands are lands transitional between terrestrial and deepwater habitats where the water table usually is at or near the land surface or the land is covered by shallow water (Cowardin and others, 1979). The distribution of wetlands and deepwater habitats in Washington is shown in figure 2A; only wetlands are discussed herein.

Wetlands can be vegetated or nonvegetated and are classified on the basis of their hydrology, vegetation, and substrate. In this summary, wetlands are classified according to the system proposed by Cowardin and others (1979), which is used by the U.S. Fish and Wildlife Service (FWS) to map and inventory the Nation's wetlands. At the most general level of the classification system, wetlands are grouped into five ecological systems: Palustrine, Lacustrine, Riverine, Estuarine, and Marine. The Palustrine System includes only wetlands, whereas the other systems comprise wetlands and deepwater habitats. Wetlands of the systems that occur in Washington are described below.

System	Wetland description
Palustrine	Nontidal and tidal-freshwater wetlands in which vegetation is predominantly trees (forested wetlands); shrubs (scrub-shrub wetlands); persistent or nonpersistent emergent, erect, rooted herbaceous plants (persistent- and nonpersistent-emergent wetlands); or submersed and (or) floating plants (aquatic beds). Also, intermittently to permanently flooded open-water bodies of less than 20 acres in which water is less than 6.6 feet deep.
Lacustrine	Nontidal and tidal-freshwater wetlands within an intermittently to permanently flooded lake or reservoir larger than 20 acres and (or) deeper than 6.6 feet. Vegetation, when present, is predominantly nonpersistent emergent plants (nonpersistent-emergent wetlands), or submersed and (or) floating plants (aquatic beds), or both.
Riverine	Nontidal and tidal-freshwater wetlands within a channel. Vegetation, when present, is same as in the Lacustrine System.
Estuarine	Tidal wetlands in low-wave-energy environments where the salinity of the water is greater than 0.5 part per thousand (ppt) and is variable owing to evaporation and the mixing of seawater and freshwater.
Marine	Tidal wetlands that are exposed to waves and currents of the open ocean and to water having a salinity greater than 30 ppt.

According to a 1988 FWS inventory, wetlands cover about 939,000 acres in Washington (D.D. Peters, U.S. Fish and Wildlife Service, unpub. data, 1990). That inventory, part of the FWS National Wetlands Inventory, used color-infrared aerial photographs taken from 1980 to 1984 combined with field inventories of selected wetlands. Owing to the limitations of this process, a small percentage of wetlands might not have been included in the acreages.

Palustrine wetlands cover about 709,000 acres, about 75 percent of the total wetland acreage in Washington (D.D. Peters, U.S. Fish and Wildlife Service, unpub. data, 1990). These wetlands ex-

Figure 1. Wetland in the Nisqually National Wildlife Refuge, Washington. Mount Rainier is in the distance. *(Photograph by James Lyles, U.S. Geological Survey.)*

ist throughout the State in coastal sand dunes; in lowlands adjacent to estuaries, rivers, and lakes; in the backwaters of reservoirs and irrigation wasteways; adjacent to springs or seeps; and in isolated depressions. Extensive tracts of palustrine wetlands cover the sand spits of Grays Harbor and Willapa Bay and the banks of the Columbia, Chehalis, Yakima, and Pend Oreille Rivers (Canning and Stevens, 1989; Washington State Department of Ecology, 1992b).

Palustrine forested wetlands commonly are referred to as swamps or coastal swamps. Their predominant vegetation includes red alder, thin-leafed alder, black cottonwood, western red cedar, Sitka spruce, and hemlock. Palustrine scrub-shrub wetlands commonly are referred to as swamps or bogs. Their predominant vegetation includes willows, red Osier dogwood, Douglas spiraea, snowberry, hawthorn, wild rose, and gooseberry. Palustrine emergent wetlands are also known as freshwater marshes, wet meadows, fens, bogs, prairies, potholes, vernal pools, and playas. Predominant emergent vegetation includes cattail, bulrush, and reed canary grass. Predominant aquatic-bed vegetation includes duckweed, water lilies, and water buttercup (Canning and Stevens, 1989).

Lacustrine wetland acreage in Washington is not addressed in this summary because the acreage has not yet been separated from the acreage for lacustrine deepwater habitat (D.D. Peters, U.S. Fish and Wildlife Service, unpub. data, 1990). Lacustrine emergent wetlands and aquatic beds exist in the shallows of lakes throughout Washington. Predominant emergent vegetation includes duckweed, water lilies, water buttercup, arrowhead, water plantain, smartweed, yellow water lily, common mare's tail, and pondweed. Predominant lacustrine aquatic-bed vegetation is the same as noted for palustrine aquatic beds (Canning and Stevens, 1989).

Riverine wetlands cover about 700 acres in Washington (D.D. Peters, U.S. Fish and Wildlife Service, unpub. data, 1990) and consist of the areas of river channels that are occasionally to permanently flooded. These areas can be nonvegetated or vegetated by submersed and nonpersistent emergent aquatic plants. Areas of the river channel that typically are exposed commonly are referred to as river bars, gravel bars, or unconsolidated shorelines. They commonly become vegetated by pioneering terrestrial species such as dandelion and fireweed during periods of low flow. Plant species commonly found in the flooded areas of the channel include true watercress, yellowcress, yellow water lily, arrowhead, water plantain, and smartweed (Canning and Stevens, 1989).

Estuarine wetlands cover about 202,000 acres, about 22 percent of the total wetland acreage in Washington (D.D. Peters, U.S. Fish and Wildlife Service, unpub. data, 1990). These wetlands are present on the deltas and in the lower reaches of most of the rivers in western Washington (the part of the State west of the crest of the Cascade Range [fig. 2B]). Broad expanses of estuarine wetlands exist around Grays Harbor and Willapa Bay on the coast, at the mouth of the Columbia River, and around Skagit and Padilla Bays on Puget Sound (Canning and Stevens, 1989; Washington State Department of Ecology, 1992b).

Predominant forest and scrub-shrub vegetation bordering estuaries includes western crabapple, Hooker's willow, Sitka willow, red Osier dogwood, Pacific ninebark, red alder, western red cedar, and Sitka spruce. Predominant herbaceous emergent vegetation includes pickleweed, salt grass, seaside arrowgrass, Jaumea, salt-marsh sandspurry, Olney's Three Square, Lyngby's sedge, redtop, hardstem bulrush, and cattail. Estuarine aquatic beds are vegetated

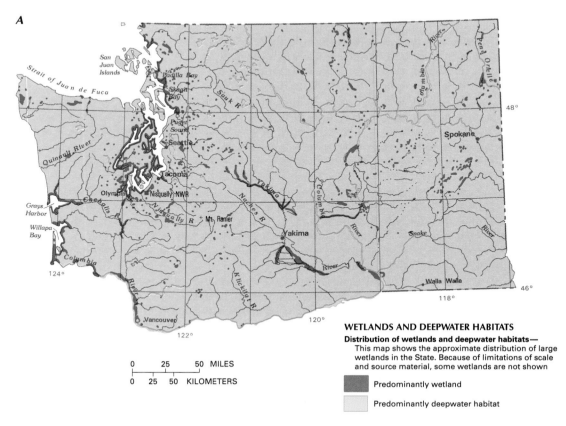

WETLANDS AND DEEPWATER HABITATS

Distribution of wetlands and deepwater habitats—
This map shows the approximate distribution of large wetlands in the State. Because of limitations of scale and source material, some wetlands are not shown

Predominantly wetland

Predominantly deepwater habitat

Figure 2.   Wetland distribution in Washington and physical and climatological factors that control wetland distribution in the State. **A**, Distribution of wetlands and deepwater habitats. *(Sources: A, T.E. Dahl, U.S. Fish and Wildlife Service, unpub. data, 1991.)*

rocky, sandy, or muddy substrates adjacent to tidal zones. Predominant aquatic-bed vegetation includes eelgrass, kelp, and green algae. Estuarine unconsolidated shores consist of gravel, sand, or mud exposed by tides and commonly are known as tideflats or tidal flats. Large tidal fluctuations discourage most plant communities from colonizing these sites. However, extensive mats of green and blue-green algae can develop during the summer months (Canning and Stevens, 1989).

Marine wetlands cover about 27,000 acres, about 3 percent of the total wetland acreage in Washington (D.D. Peters, U.S. Fish and Wildlife Service, unpub. data, 1990) and consist of beaches and rocky shores. The high-energy tidal environment of these wetlands keeps them unvegetated except for algae. Marine wetlands exist along the Pacific coast and the Strait of Juan de Fuca, on some offshore rocky islands, and in the San Juan Islands (Canning and Stevens, 1989).

HYDROLOGIC SETTING

Western Washington has a predominantly marine climate with cool, dry summers and mild, wet winters (Phillips, 1960). Precipitation ranges from less than 20 inches per year to about 200 inches per year (fig. 2C). Evaporation ranges from about 20 inches per year to about 25 inches per year (fig. 2D) and generally is less than annual precipitation.

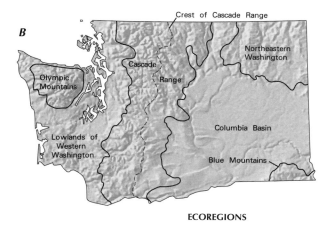

B

ECOREGIONS

Although many wetlands in western Washington are associated with ponds, lakes, estuaries, or rivers, many more are isolated from bodies of surface water and owe their existence to saturated soil conditions caused by precipitation or ground-water seepage (Canning and Stevens, 1989; Washington State Department of Ecology, 1992b,c). Wetlands that are isolated from bodies of surface water typically occupy depressions in the land surface that are of glacial origin. In the lowlands of western Washington, these depressions generally are elongated troughs cut by continental glaciers, circular kettles left by the melting of blocks of glacial ice embedded in glacial deposits, or simply shallow depressions on an irregular surface of glacial deposits. In the Olympic Mountains and the Cascade Range, the depressions generally have been cut into bedrock by local alpine glaciers (Dion, 1978).

Eastern Washington (the part of the State east of the crest of the Cascade Range) has characteristics of both continental and marine climates with hot, dry summers and cold, wet winters (Phillips, 1960). Precipitation ranges from less than 10 inches per year to about 40 inches per year (fig. 2C). Evaporation ranges from about 25 inches per year to more than 45 inches per year (fig. 2D) and generally exceeds annual precipitation.

As in western Washington, most wetlands on the eastern slope of the Cascade Range and in Northeastern Washington (fig. 2B) are associated either with bodies of surface water or with depressions in the land surface that are of glacial origin (Dion, 1978; Washington State Department of Ecology, 1992b). Most wetlands in the Columbia Basin (fig. 2B) were created by human activities, such as large hydroelectric and irrigation projects, and typically owe their existence to shallow water tables caused by the importation and use of surface water for irrigation (Washington State Department of Ecology, 1992b). Almost 85 percent of the wetlands in the area are in isolated depressions in the land surface that were created by catastrophic floods resulting from the collapse of glacial ice dams and the ensuing rapid emptying of large glacial lakes in what is now Montana (Weis and Newman, 1989; Dion, 1978; Washington State Department of Ecology, 1992b). Many of the other wetlands in the Columbia River Basin are associated with reservoirs and irrigation wasteways (Canning and Stevens, 1989; Washington State Department of Ecology, 1992b).

TRENDS

Estimates of presettlement wetland acreage in Washington range from 1.17 to 1.53 million acres, depending on the historical

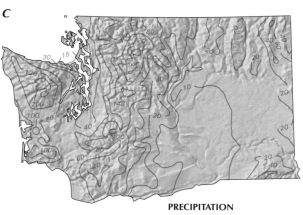

PRECIPITATION

—*80*— **Line of equal annual precipitation—** Interval, in inches, is variable

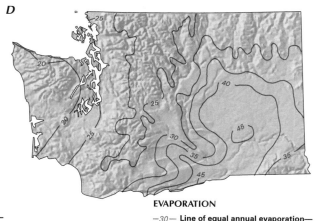

D

EVAPORATION

—*30*— **Line of equal annual evaporation—** Interval, in inches, is variable

Figure 2. Continued. Wetland distribution in Washington and physical and climatological factors that control wetland distribution in the State. *B*, Generalized physiographic areas. *C*, Precipitation. *D*, Free-water-surface evaporation. *(Sources: B, C, and D, Landforms data from EROS Data Center. B, Generalized physiographic areas modified from Dion, 1978. C, Williams, 1986. D, Farnsworth and others, 1982.)*

information and research assumptions used (Canning and Stevens, 1989; Dahl, 1990; Washington State Department of Ecology, 1992b). Based on a 1988 estimate by the FWS, about 20 to 39 percent of Washington's wetlands, have been lost during the past two centuries. Other estimates place the total loss as great as 50 percent, and some urbanized areas of the Puget Sound area have experienced losses of from 70 to 100 percent. Estimates of continuing wetland loss range from 700 to 2,000 acres per year. In addition, most of the State's remaining wetlands have been significantly degraded (Washington State Department of Ecology, 1992b,d).

The principal historical causes of wetland loss and degradation are the expansion of agriculture and the siting of ports and industrial facilities. The major causes of continuing loss and degradation of wetlands are urban expansion, forestry and agricultural practices, and the invasion of exotic plants and animals (Canning and Stevens, 1989; Washington State Department of Ecology, 1992b,d).

CONSERVATION

Many government agencies and private organizations participate in wetland conservation in Washington. The most active agencies and organizations and some of their activities are listed in table 1.

Federal wetland activities. — Development activities in Washington wetlands are regulated by several Federal statutory prohibitions and incentives that are intended to slow wetland losses. Some of the more important of these are contained in the 1899 Rivers and Harbors Act; the 1972 Clean Water Act and amendments; the 1985 Food Security Act; the 1990 Food, Agriculture, Conservation, and Trade Act; the 1986 Emergency Wetlands Resources Act; and the 1972 Coastal Zone Management Act.

Section 10 of the Rivers and Harbors Act gives the U.S. Army Corps of Engineers (Corps) authority to regulate certain activities in navigable waters. Regulated activities include diking, deepening, filling, excavating, and placing of structures. The related section 404 of the Clean Water Act is the most often-used Federal legislation protecting wetlands. Under section 404 provisions, the Corps issues permits regulating the discharge of dredged or fill material into wetlands. Permits are subject to review and possible veto by the U.S. Environmental Protection Agency, and the FWS has review and advisory roles. Section 401 of the Clean Water Act grants to States and eligible Indian Tribes the authority to approve, apply conditions to, or deny section 404 permit applications on the basis of a proposed activity's probable effects on the water quality of a wetland.

Most farming, ranching, and silviculture activities are not subject to section 404 regulation. However, the "Swampbuster" provision of the 1985 Food Security Act and amendments in the 1990 Food, Agriculture, Conservation, and Trade Act discourage (through financial disincentives) the draining, filling, or other alteration of wetlands for agricultural use. The law allows exemptions from penalties in some cases, especially if the farmer agrees to restore the altered wetland or other wetlands that have been converted to agricultural use. The Wetlands Reserve Program of the 1990 Food, Agriculture, Conservation, and Trade Act authorizes the Federal Government to purchase conservation easements from landowners who agree to protect or restore wetlands. The Consolidated Farm Service Agency (formerly the Agricultural Stabilization and Conservation Service) administers the Swampbuster provisions and Wetlands Reserve Program. The Natural Resources Conservation Service (formerly the Soil Conservation Service) determines compliance with Swampbuster provisions and assists farmers in the identification of wetlands and in the development of wetland protection, restoration, or creation plans.

The 1986 Emergency Wetlands Resources Act and the 1972

Table 1. Selected wetland-related activities of government agencies and private organizations in Washington, 1993

[Source: Classification of activities is generalized from information provided by agencies and organizations. •, agency or organization participates in wetland-related activity; ..., agency or organization does not participate in wetland-related activity. MAN, management; REG, regulation; R&C, restoration and creation; LAN, land acquisition; R&D, research and data collection; D&I, delineation and inventory]

Agency or organization	MAN	REG	R&C	LAN	R&D	D&I
FEDERAL						
Department of Agriculture						
Consolidated Farm Service Agency	...	•	...	...	...	...
Forest Service	•	...	•	•	•	•
Natural Resources Conservation Service	...	•	•	...	•	•
Department of Commerce						
National Oceanic and Atmospheric Administration	•	•	...	...	•	•
Department of Defense						
Army Corps of Engineers	•	•	•	•	•	•
Military reservations	•	...	...	...	...	...
Department of the Interior						
Bureau of Land Management	•	...	•	...	•	•
Bureau of Reclamation	•	...	•	•	...	•
Fish and Wildlife Service	•	...	•	•	•	•
Geological Survey	...	...	...	...	•	...
National Biological Service	...	...	...	...	•	...
National Park Service	•	...	•	•	•	•
Environmental Protection Agency	...	•	...	...	•	•
STATE						
Department of Agriculture	...	•	•	...	•	...
Department of Community Development	•	•	...	•	...	...
Department of Ecology	•	•	•	•	•	•
Department of Fisheries	•	•	•	...	•	•
Department of Health	•	•	...	...	•	...
Department of Natural Resources	•	•	•	•	•	•
Department of Parks and Recreation	•	•	•	•	...	•
Department of Transportation	•	•	•	...	•	•
Department of Wildlife	•	•	•	•	•	•
REGIONAL						
Puget Sound Water Quality Authority	•	...	...	...	•	...
COUNTY AND LOCAL						
All counties and local governments	...	•	...	...	...	•
Some counties and local governments	•	•	•	•	•	•
PRIVATE						
Local chapters of the National Audubon Society	•	...	...	•	•	•
Ducks Unlimited	...	...	•	•	•	•
Friends of the Earth	...	...	...	...	•	•
The Nature Conservancy	•	...	•	•	•	...
Trust for Public Lands	...	...	...	•	...	...
Urban Wildlife Coalition	...	...	•	...	•	...
Washington Environmental Council	...	...	...	...	•	...

Coastal Zone Management Act and amendments encourage wetland protection through funding incentives. The Emergency Wetlands Resources Act requires States to address wetland protection in their Statewide Comprehensive Outdoor Recreation Plans to qualify for Federal funding for State recreational land; the National Park Service provides guidance to States in developing the wetland component of their plans. Coastal and Great Lakes States that adopt coastal-zone management programs and plans approved by the National Oceanic and Atmospheric Administration are eligible for Federal funding and technical assistance through the Coastal Zone Management Act.

Federal agencies own about 1.3 million acres of land in Washington, 30 percent of the total land area of the State. However, there is no reliable estimate of the total acreage of wetlands owned by the Federal Government. The major causes of this situation are budget constraints; differences in the missions, goals, and needs of the various agencies; and variations in the use and definitions of wetlands.

State wetland activities. —Wetland protection and management activities in Washington are almost as diverse as the State's wetlands. The State uses the FWS classification system (Cowardin and others, 1979) for inventory purposes but uses the Federal Clean Water Act definition of wetlands as vegetated sites for regulatory purposes. Nonvegetated wetlands are regulated as marine waters, lakes, or other special aquatic sites (Canning and Stevens, 1989; Perry Lund, Washington State Department of Ecology, written commun., 1993). The Washington State Department of Ecology is the lead agency for wetland activities in the State and has established a Wetlands Section to provide technical assistance and guidance to other Federal and State agencies and to local governments. In addition, all State agencies are required to exercise their authority to the maximum extent in order to achieve the goal of "no overall net loss of wetlands" in the State. The primary State regulations affecting wetlands include the Shoreline Management Act of 1971, the Hydraulic Procedures Act of 1949, the State Environmental Policy Act of 1983, the Growth Management Act of 1991, and the Floodplain Management Program. However, none of these regulations has the protection of the wetlands as its main purpose (Washington State Department of Ecology, 1988, 1990, 1991, 1992b, 1993).

Regional wetland activities. —The Puget Sound Water Quality Authority is charged with the development of a comprehensive plan for the protection of water quality in the Puget Sound Basin. The wetlands-protection element of the plan is designed to ensure that the most valuable wetlands in the basin are preserved in perpetuity and that degradation of other valuable wetlands is minimized (Puget Sound Water Quality Authority, 1990; Washington State Department of Ecology, 1988, 1992b,c).

County and local wetland activities. —The State's Growth Management Act requires counties and local governments to protect wetlands within each government's jurisdiction. The most common means of protecting wetlands is through Shoreline Master Programs developed under the State's Shoreline Management Act and the State Environmental Policy Act. Under these programs, policies and regulations limit certain disruptive activities such as dredging and filling. Other local ordinances may establish sensitivity areas, regulate clearing and grading practices, or require special analysis and review for projects affecting wetlands covered by the master program. In many cases, these programs and ordinances are more restrictive than, and include wetlands not covered by, Federal or State regulations. However, the degree to which programs and ordinances have been adopted and enforced varies greatly across the State (Washington State Department of Ecology, 1988; Granger, 1989).

Private wetland activities. —More than 400 private organizations are active in the preservation and protection of wetlands in Washington (Seattle Audubon Society, 1993). These organizations keep the public informed on wetland issues, organize citizen networks, and lobby for wetland-protection measures. Local chapters of the Audubon Society, The Nature Conservancy, and the Trust for Public Lands have purchased wetlands and associated buffer areas in the State for preservation.

References Cited

Canning, D.J., and Stevens, Michelle, 1989, Wetlands of Washington—A resource characterization: Olympia, Washington State Department of Ecology, 45 p.
Cowardin, L.M., Carter, Virginia, Golet, F.C., and LaRoe, E.T., 1979, Classification of wetlands and deepwater habitats of the United States: U.S. Fish and Wildlife Report FWS/OBS–79/31, 131 p.
Dahl, T.E., 1990, Wetlands—Losses in the United States, 1780's to 1980's: Washington D.C., U.S. Fish and Wildlife Service, 13 p.
Dion, N.P., 1978, Primer on lakes in Washington: Washington State Department of Ecology Water-Supply Bulletin 49, 55 p.
Farnsworth, R.K., Thompson, E.S., and Peck, E.L., 1982, Evaporation atlas for the contiguous 48 United States: National Oceanic and Atmospheric Administration Technical Report NWS 33, 26 p.
Granger, Teri, 1989, A guide to conducting wetlands inventories: Washington State Department of Ecology Publication 89–60, 59 p.
Phillips, E.L., 1960, Climate of Washington: U.S. Department of Commerce, Climatography of the United States no. 60–45, 26 p. [Reprint 1972.]
Puget Sound Water Quality Authority, 1990, 1991 Puget Sound Water Quality Management Plan: Olympia, Puget Sound Water Quality Authority, 344 p.
Seattle Audubon Society, 1993, WETNET citizen's directory—A guide to Washington organizations concerned with wetlands protection: Seattle, Wash., Seattle Audubon Society, 59 p.
Washington State Department of Ecology, 1988, Wetland regulations guidebook: Washington State Department of Ecology publication 88–5, 46 p.
_____1990, Focus—Wetlands law: Olympia, Washington State Department of Ecology, 2 p.
_____1991, Focus—Ecology's wetlands section: Washington State Department of Ecology publication F–S–91–107, 2 p.
_____1992a, Washington's wetlands: Washington State Department of Ecology publication 92–105, 12 p.
_____1992b, 1992 Statewide water quality assessment, 305(b) report: Washington State Department of Ecology publication 92–04, 245 p.
_____1992c, Focus—Puget Sound wetland preservation: Washington State Department of Ecology publication F–S–92–112, 2 p.
_____1992d, Focus—Wetlands in Washington State: Washington State Department of Ecology publication F–S–92–108, 2 p.
_____1993, Focus—Wetlands technical assistance to local government: Olympia, Washington State Department of Ecology, 2 p.
Washington State Department of Wildlife, undated, Washington wetlands—Time is running out: Olympia, Washington State Department of Wildlife, 11 p.
Weis, P.L., and Newman, W.L., 1989, The Channeled Scablands of eastern Washington—The geologic story of the Spokane flood (2d ed.): Cheney, Eastern Washington University Press, 24 p.
Williams, J.R., 1986, Washington surface-water resources, in U.S. Geological Survey, National water summary 1985—Hydrologic events and surface-water resources: U.S. Geological Survey Water-Supply Paper 2300, p. 473–478.

FOR ADDITIONAL INFORMATION: District Chief, U.S. Geological Survey, 1201 Pacific Avenue, Suite 600, Tacoma, WA 98402; Regional Wetland Coordinator, U.S. Fish and Wildlife Service, 911 NE. 11th Avenue, Portland, OR 97232

Prepared by
R.C. Lane and William A. Taylor,
U.S. Geological Survey

West Virginia
Wetland Resources

Wetlands constitute less than 1 percent of West Virginia's surface area but contribute significantly to the State's economic development and ecological diversity (Tiner, 1987). Most of the State's wetlands are in highlands that extend along a north-south axis near the eastern State boundary and in the lower elevations of the Potomac River drainage basin to the east and the Ohio River drainage basin to the west. The plants and animals of upland West Virginia bogs and marshes include species that are distinctly northern in range and distribution (Fortney, 1977). Some of these species may be ice age relicts that migrated southward during the last glacial period and became established in the cool, moist environment of the central Appalachian Mountains when the glaciers retreated. Wetlands that contain this unusually diverse assemblage of plants and wildlife draw large numbers of tourists to the State and provide educational and recreational opportunities.

The State's two largest wetlands and other wetlands associated with river main stems provide habitat for waterfowl and other game and nongame animals and support many rare and endangered plant species. Natural and constructed wetlands in West Virginia have been used to mitigate the effects of road construction, to increase habitat of nongame animals, and to treat both active- and abandoned-mine drainage and municipal wastewater.

TYPES AND DISTRIBUTION

Wetlands are lands transitional between terrestrial and deepwater habitats where the water table usually is at or near the land surface or the land is covered by shallow water (Cowardin and others, 1979). The distribution of wetlands and deepwater habitats in West Virginia is shown in figure 2A; only wetlands are discussed herein.

Wetlands can be vegetated or nonvegetated and are classified on the basis of their hydrology, vegetation, and substrate. In this summary, wetlands are classified according to the system proposed by Cowardin and others (1979), which is used by the U.S. Fish and Wildlife Service (FWS) to map and inventory the Nation's wetlands. At the most general level of the classification system, wetlands are

Figure 1. Canaan Valley, West Virginia. The valley's extensive upland bogs and marshes were designated a National Natural Landmark by the Secretary of the Interior in 1974. *(Photograph by Stephen J. Shaluta, Jr., West Virginia Department of Commerce, Labor and Environmental Resources, Division of Tourism and Parks.)*

grouped into five ecological systems: Palustrine, Lacustrine, Riverine, Estuarine, and Marine. The Palustrine System includes only wetlands, whereas the other systems comprise wetlands and deepwater habitats. Wetlands of the systems that occur in West Virginia are described below.

System	Wetland description
Palustrine	Wetlands in which vegetation is predominantly trees (forested wetlands); shrubs (scrub-shrub wetlands); persistent or nonpersistent emergent, erect, rooted, herbaceous plants (persistent- and nonpersistent-emergent wetlands); or submersed and (or) floating plants (aquatic beds). Also, intermittently to permanently flooded open-water bodies of less than 20 acres in which water is less than 6.6 feet deep.
Lacustrine	Wetlands within an intermittently to permanently flooded lake or reservoir. Vegetation, when present, is predominantly nonpersistent emergent plants (nonpersistent-emergent wetlands), or submersed and (or) floating plants (aquatic beds), or both.
Riverine	Wetlands within a channel. Vegetation, when present, is same as in the Lacustrine System.

West Virginia's wetlands were inventoried by the West Virginia Division of Natural Resources (formerly the West Virginia Department of Natural Resources) as part of a State survey initiated in 1975 and more recently by FWS as part of the National Wetlands Inventory. The Division surveyed all wetlands larger than 5 acres and listed them by class, location, size, source, and vulnerability to destruction. A total of 22,490 stream miles and 45,542 acres of wetlands were identified from ground and map searches. Palustrine and lacustrine wetlands constituted 0.3 percent of the State's total land and water surface area (West Virginia Department of Natural Resources, 1988).

The FWS National Wetlands Inventory identified West Virginia wetlands on high-resolution aerial photographs and listed location, type, and distribution of all wetlands 1 acre or larger. The results of the inventory indicated that West Virginia has about 102,000 acres of wetlands, including 42,000 acres of forested wetlands, 24,000 acres of scrub-shrub wetlands, 20,000 acres of emergent wetlands, and 16,000 acres of ponds (Tiner, 1987). The difference in acreage reported by the two surveys reflects the large number of wetlands in the State that are smaller than 5 acres and the inventory techniques used.

The Canaan Valley and Meadow River wetland complexes contain about 14 percent of the State's wetlands. The Canaan Valley wetland complex includes palustrine forested, scrub-shrub, and emergent wetlands and, with an area of 6,740 acres, is the largest wetland complex in the central Appalachian Mountains. The Meadow River wetland complex is the second-largest wetland complex in the State and, in terms of acreage, contains about one-fourth of the State's swamps (forested and scrub-shrub wetlands) and one-third of the State's wet meadows (emergent wetlands).

Other wetlands, commonly located along streams and rivers, are mostly of small to moderate size and are distributed widely across the State (West Virginia Department of Natural Resources, 1988). Forested wetlands are the most common type, with interspersed scrub-shrub, emergent, and open-water wetlands (ponds). West Virginia also has many small wetlands located on islands and flood plains and along embayments adjacent to large rivers. Embayments are backwater zones that form at the mouths of tributaries where main-stem navigation dams raise upstream pool levels. The FWS is inventorying the flora and fauna of Ohio River island wetlands and 79 West Virginia embayments between Ohio River miles 47.5 and 312. Embayments and wetlands on islands are important stopover areas for migrating waterfowl, nurseries for riverine fish, and habitat for beaver, bald eagles, herons, sandpipers, and ospreys (Patti Morrison, U.S. Fish and Wildlife Service, oral commun., 1993). Ely (1993) surveyed the vascular plants in eight Ohio River embayments and identified 259 species in 169 genera and 76 families. Thirteen plant species are on the State Endangered Species list.

HYDROLOGIC SETTING

The distribution of wetlands in West Virginia is determined by the interaction of climatic and orographic factors, local topography, and geologic setting. The State is in three physiographic provinces—the Appalachian Plateaus, Valley and Ridge, and Blue Ridge (fig. 2B). Eastern West Virginia is in the Valley and Ridge Province and contains a small section of the Blue Ridge Province. The region is drained by Potomac River tributaries to the north and by Kanawha River tributaries to the south. The Appalachian Plateaus physiographic province of southern and western West Virginia contains the Allegheny Mountain and Kanawha Sections.

Most of the State's wetlands are located in the Allegheny Mountain Section and along the Eastern Divide. The Eastern Divide is located along the boundary between the Appalachian Plateaus and the Valley and Ridge Province and separates the Ohio River drainage basin to the west from the Potomac River drainage basin to the east. The highest point on the Eastern Divide has an altitude of 4,860 feet. Predominantly westerly winds carry gulf, subtropical Atlantic, and land-recycled moisture across the State. Air masses rise and cool in the higher altitudes of the Eastern Divide, releasing moisture on the western slope. After crossing the Eastern Divide, the air masses sink and warm and release little moisture, creating a "rain shadow" to the east. Consequently, annual precipitation increases eastward from about 40 inches along the State's western boundary to about 60 inches in the higher altitudes of the Eastern Divide and then decreases to about 36 inches in the eastern panhandle. The abundance of precipitation along the western slopes of the Eastern Divide supplies moisture needed to support wetlands and is the most important determinant of wetland formation and maintenance in West Virginia.

Where ample water is available, wetland formation depends primarily on local topography and geologic setting. Diehl and Behling (1982) examined 49 wetlands in the Appalachian Plateaus and identified geologic settings that affect wetland formation and maintenance. Stream valleys with low gradients (less than 5 feet per

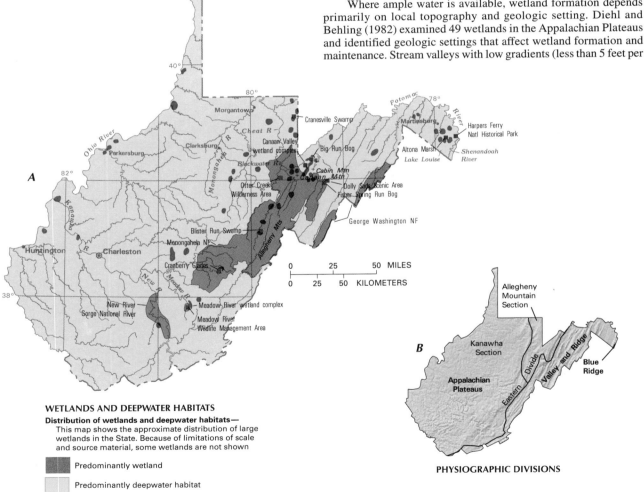

WETLANDS AND DEEPWATER HABITATS

Distribution of wetlands and deepwater habitats—
This map shows the approximate distribution of large wetlands in the State. Because of limitations of scale and source material, some wetlands are not shown

Predominantly wetland

Predominantly deepwater habitat

PHYSIOGRAPHIC DIVISIONS

Figure 2. Wetland distribution in West Virginia and physiography of the State. *A*, Distribution of wetlands and deepwater habitats. *B*, Physiography. (*Sources: A, T.E. Dahl, U.S. Fish and Wildlife Service, unpub. data, 1991. B, Physiographic divisions from Fenneman, 1946; landforms data from EROS Data Center.*)

mile) and poorly drained alluvial plains were found to be conducive to wetland formation. Wetlands develop on the alluvial plain, but because the stream channel typically has cut into the alluvial material, the water table can be several feet beneath the alluvial plain; the wetlands are thus highly dependent on seasonal flooding. In mountain valleys, where streams have steeper gradients and rapid rates of flow, wetlands form near the slopes and receive abundant ground-water discharge (Winter, 1992).

Most wetlands in the Allegheny Mountain Section are upstream from where layers of erosion-resistant sedimentary rock intersect streambeds at an acute angle (Diehl and Behling, 1982). Erosion of less resistant rock layers upstream and downstream from the point of intersection causes a widening of the stream channel upstream and an increase in stream gradient downstream. Ponding and settling-out of fine sediments in the upstream area reduce permeability and favor formation of wetlands. Cranesville Swamp on the West Virginia–Maryland border is an example of a wetland formed in this type of geologic setting.

Anticlines are formed when stratified rock is folded downward in opposite directions from a crest. Erosion of the crest produces a valley (a "breached" anticline) surrounded by mountains and exited by a water gap at the downstream end. Canaan Valley (fig. 3) is an example of a breached anticline in which weathering of the valley floor is proceeding at a faster rate than that of the downstream water gap (Diehl and Behling, 1982). Ponding of water over poorly drained erosional sediments has produced conditions favorable to wetland formation.

Highlands consisting of flat, or nearly flat, rock layers that have been dissected by streams occur throughout the Allegheny Mountain Section. These settings are conducive to wetland formation because water ponds on the flat topography. An example of a wetland in this type of geologic setting is Big Run Bog, near Canaan Valley in north-central West Virginia.

Embayments have formed in the mouths of many small tributaries of the Ohio and Kanawha Rivers because of higher pool levels upstream from main-stem navigation dams. These embayments support wetland communities that did not exist along the rivers before construction of the dams. Although embayment-wetland communities have not been studied in detail, plant-species diversity in some is high (Koryak, 1978; Ely, 1993).

West Virginia wetlands of special interest include marl wetlands in the eastern panhandle and sphagnum-dominated peatlands situated along the Eastern Divide. Marl is a calcium carbonate precipitate combined with lesser amounts of clay and organic material. The precipitate forms when carbon dioxide is removed from shallow bodies of water by photosynthesis. Marl wetlands in the Shenandoah and Potomac River valleys of eastern West Virginia have near-neutral pH (6.8–7.2), widely fluctuating amounts of surface water, and a 16- to 28-inch-thick bottom layer of organic material underlain by about 10 feet of marl (Bartgis and Lang, 1984). West Virginia marl wetlands contain unique assemblages of calciphilic plants (plants adapted to alkaline conditions). Bartgis and Lang (1984) inventoried the flora of 10 marl wetlands in eastern West Virginia and recorded 12 vascular-plant species that are restricted to eastern West Virginia marl wetlands and 15 vascular-plant species that are found in only a few sites other than marl wetlands. Five marl wetlands in eastern West Virginia, including Lake Louise and Altona Marsh, have been designated as National Natural Landmarks and are listed on the National Registry of Natural Landmarks (National Park Service, 1992).

In West Virginia, sphagnum-dominated peatlands occur mainly in the mountainous, higher altitudes of the Eastern Divide. Few peatlands occur south of West Virginia (Wieder, 1985). Southern peatlands, such as those in West Virginia, have higher annual net primary production (Wieder and Lang, 1983) and higher annual organic-matter decomposition (Lang and McDonald, 1982) than those to the north. In West Virginia, peatlands range in size from widely distributed bogs of less than 1 acre to large areas of the State's largest wetland, the Canaan Valley wetland complex. Several peatlands in the Monongahela National Forest—notably Cranberry Glades, Blister Run Swamp, Big Run Bog, and Fisher Spring Run Bog—contain unique plant associations such as cranberry glades interspaced with bog forests and shrub thickets, high-altitude balsam fir swamps, and sphagnum-red spruce bogs (National Park Service, 1992).

The sphagnum-dominated peatlands of the Canaan Valley wetland complex occupy the largest intermontane valley east of the Mississippi River. The valley floor is about 14 miles long and 5 miles wide. With an average altitude of 3,200 feet, it is the highest valley of its size east of the Rocky Mountains. The valley is flanked by Canaan and Cabin Mountains and is drained by the Blackwater River, a tributary of the Cheat River, through a narrow water gap at the northwest end (fig. 2A). Once densely forested, the area was logged and burned in the late 1800's and early 1900's. The valley now supports extensive wetlands resulting from abundant precipitation (53 inches per year) and a blanket of poorly drained soils derived from the erosion of underlying limestone. Water enters the wetland by discharge from the surrounding mountain slopes and by ground-water flow (fig. 3). Springs emanate from the contacts of alternating layers of shale and sandstone. The wetland complex in-

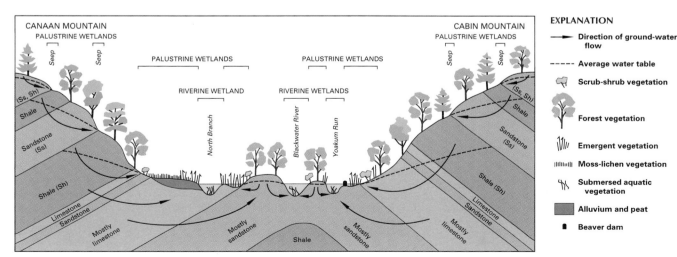

Figure 3. Geohydrologic setting of the Canaan Valley wetland complex in north-central West Virginia.

cludes wet meadows dominated by sedges and grasses, dense thickets of alder and spiraea (scrub-shrub wetlands), and extensive peat bogs (moss-lichen wetlands) consisting of sphagnum and haircap mosses, sedges, and heaths. Beavers have constructed dams on the Blackwater River and many of its tributaries, flooding stream margins and forming ponds and marshes.

TRENDS

Of the wetlands present in West Virginia in the 1780's, about three-fourths remain today (Dahl, 1990). Most of the loss was caused by agricultural drainage of wetlands in flood plains of the Ohio, Kanawha, and Monongahela Rivers (West Virginia Department of Natural Resources, 1988). Agricultural drainage, channelization, pond construction, urbanization, and reservoir construction are the primary causes of wetland loss in West Virginia (Tiner, 1987). From 1957 to 1980, West Virginia gained 10,900 acres of forested and scrub-shrub wetlands and lost 5,800 acres of emergent wetlands (West Virginia Department of Natural Resources, 1988). Much of the increase in wetland acreage was caused either by beaver activity, which through flooding converted uplands into forested and scrub-shrub wetlands, or by plant succession.

Residential, commercial, industrial, and highway-development projects could threaten West Virginia wetlands (West Virginia Department of Natural Resources, 1988). These developments often are associated with inundation, filling, or drainage of large and small wetland areas. In 1990 the Canaan Valley Task Force, composed of Federal, State, and local government agencies, business concerns, and environmental groups, was organized to define and implement strategies to protect the unique natural resources of Canaan Valley while considering local community needs. Current activities of the task force include surveying and modeling water quality in the valley and producing materials designed to inform the public of the ecological and economic significance of the area (Canaan Valley Task Force, 1992).

A section of Interstate Highway 64 has been constructed through the Meadow River wetland complex. The West Virginia Department of Highways is mitigating the impact of construction by purchasing or developing additional wetlands. Because future urbanization associated with the highway might further threaten this wetland, the Division of Natural Resources has made long-term acquisition of Meadow River wetlands the State's foremost acquisition priority. A large section of this wetland that has been purchased comprises the Meadow River Wildlife Management Area (West Virginia Department of Natural Resources, 1988).

The West Virginia Department of Transportation, Division of Highways, and the U.S. Department of Transportation commissioned a study of wetlands created by or contiguous with 511 miles of limited-access highways. The area contained 96 wetlands, 60 of which were produced by highway construction. The Division mitigates wetland losses resulting from road construction by acquiring additional wetlands or enhancing existing wetlands with sandbags, dikes, and drainage structures (Ben Hark, West Virginia Department of Transportation, Division of Highways, oral commun., 1993). The Division is mitigating losses of wetlands from construction of limited-access highways and Federal facilities. The losses include about 48 acres of wetlands in the Meadow River Wildlife Management Area that have been disturbed by construction of secondary highways and about 10 acres of wetlands affected by construction of a Federal facility near Clarksburg. Effects of these activities on wetlands have been mitigated by purchase and enhancement of existing wetlands and by wetland construction (Ben Hark, West Virginia Department of Transportation, Division of Highways, oral commun., 1993).

Federal and State agencies and private organizations are working to preserve a diverse group of West Virginia wetlands. The FWS

has purchased 8 Ohio River islands that contain important wetlands, is acquiring 38 additional islands, and is inventorying the flora and fauna of several islands and embayments. These wetlands would become part of the proposed Ohio River Islands National Wildlife Refuge (Patti Morrison, U.S. Fish and Wildlife Service, oral commun., 1993).

CONSERVATION

Many government agencies and private organizations participate in wetland conservation in West Virginia. The most active agencies and organizations and some of their activities are listed in table 1.

Federal wetland activities.—Development activities in West Virginia wetlands are regulated by several Federal statutory prohibitions and incentives that are intended to slow wetland losses. Some of the more important of these are contained in the 1899 Rivers and Harbors Act; the 1972 Clean Water Act and amendments; the 1985 Food Security Act; the 1990 Food, Agriculture, Conservation, and Trade Act; and the 1986 Emergency Wetlands Resources Act.

Section 10 of the Rivers and Harbors Act gives the U.S. Army Corps of Engineers (Corps) authority to regulate certain activities in navigable waters. Regulated activities include diking, deepening, filling, excavating, and placing of structures. The related section 404 of the Clean Water Act is the most often-used Federal legislation protecting wetlands. Under section 404 provisions, the Corps issues permits regulating the discharge of dredged or fill material into wetlands. Permits are subject to review and possible veto by the U.S. Environmental Protection Agency, and the FWS has review and advisory roles. Section 401 of the Clean Water Act grants to States and eligible Indian Tribes the authority to approve, apply conditions to, or deny section 404 permit applications on the basis of a proposed activity's probable effects on the water quality of a wetland.

Most farming, ranching, and silviculture activities are not subject to section 404 regulation. However, the "Swampbuster" provi-

Table 1. Selected wetland-related activities of government agencies and private organizations in West Virginia, 1993

[Source: Classification of activities is generalized from information provided by agencies and organizations. •, agency or organization participates in wetland-related activity; ..., agency or organization does not participate in wetland-related activity. MAN, management; REG, regulation; R&C, restoration and creation; LAN, land acquisition; R&D, research and data collection; D&I, delineation and inventory]

Agency or organization	MAN	REG	R&C	LAN	R&D	D&I
FEDERAL						
Department of Agriculture						
Consolidated Farm Service Agency	...	•	...	...	...	...
Forest Service	•	...	...	...	...	...
Natural Resources Conservation Service	...	•	...	...	...	•
Department of Defense						
Army Corps of Engineers	...	•	...	...	•	•
Department of the Interior						
Fish and Wildlife Service	•	...	•	•	•	•
Geological Survey	...	...	...	...	•	...
National Biological Service	...	...	...	...	•	...
National Park Service	•	...	...	•	...	...
Environmental Protection Agency	...	•	...	...	•	•
STATE						
Department of Labor, Commerce, and Environment						
Division of Natural Resources	•	•	•	•	•	•
Division of Environmental Protection	...	•	•	•	•	•
Department of Transportation						
Division of Highways	•	...	•	•	•	...
PRIVATE ORGANIZATIONS						
Ducks Unlimited	...	...	•	•	...	...
The Nature Conservancy	•	...	...	•	•	...

sion of the 1985 Food Security Act and amendments in the 1990 Food, Agriculture, Conservation, and Trade Act discourages (through financial disincentives) the draining, filling, or other alteration of wetlands for agricultural use. The law allows exemptions from penalties in some cases, especially if the farmer agrees to restore the altered wetland or other wetlands that have been converted to agricultural use. The Wetlands Reserve Program of the 1990 Food, Agriculture, Conservation, and Trade Act authorizes the Federal Government to purchase conservation easements from landowners who agree to protect or restore wetlands. The Consolidated Farm Service Agency (formerly the Agricultural Stabilization and Conservation Service) administers the Swampbuster provisions and Wetlands Reserve Program. The Natural Resources Conservation Service (formerly the Soil Conservation Service) determines compliance with Swampbuster provisions and assists farmers in the identification of wetlands and in the development of wetland protection, restoration, or creation plans.

The 1986 Emergency Wetlands Resources Act encourages wetland protection through funding incentives. The act requires States to address wetland protection in their Statewide Comprehensive Outdoor Recreation Plans to qualify for Federal funding for State recreational land; the National Park Service (NPS) provides guidance to States in developing the wetland component of their plans.

In addition to the regulatory responsibilities described above, Federal agencies are involved in other conservation activities. The FWS surveys wetlands in and around the Ohio River, assists the Division of Natural Resources in the evaluation of applications for Clean Water Act Section 401 (water-quality) certification, and cooperates with other agencies in the mitigation of wetland losses. Through the Partners for Wildlife program, the FWS is cooperating with landowners to restore wetlands on privately owned land. The program provides total funding for wetland restoration. To be eligible for the program, landowners must agree to maintain restored wetlands in their natural state for 10 years. The FWS is using this program to restore wetlands in the Potomac and Ohio River drainages. In the Potomac River drainage, a 25- to 50-foot buffer strip of riparian (streamside) wetlands is being developed. These protected wetlands will prevent damage from grazing cattle and allow riparian vegetation to develop along streambanks (John Schmidt, U.S. Fish and Wildlife Service, written commun., 1993).

The U.S. Forest Service (FS) manages wetlands in the Monongahela and George Washington National Forests. The FS regulates access to important wetlands. These include four wetlands that are registered as National Natural Landmarks (Cranberry Glades, Blister Run Swamp, Big Run Bog, and Fisher Spring Run Bog) and small bogs in the Monongahela National Forest, particularly in the Dolly Sods Scenic and Otter Creek Wilderness Areas. The FS restricts activities that might directly affect or indirectly alter the water table near those wetlands. In addition, before any sale of timber resources in national forests, the FS requires an inventory of all affected wetlands.

The Abandoned Mine Lands Section of the Office of Surface Mining (OSM) has oversight over wetlands that have developed as a result of surface mining. Wetlands that have developed in and adjacent to mining impoundments commonly are liabilities to landowners, who might seek to drain and fill the wetland. The OSM enforces Clean Water Act Section 404 regulations, which require that new wetlands be constructed to mitigate wetland loss.

The NPS manages wetlands in Harpers Ferry National Historical Park and the New River Gorge National River. The NPS has recently completed an inventory of wetlands along the New River Gorge National River.

State wetland activities.—West Virginia State water-quality standards define wetlands as "***such areas as swamps, marshes, bogs, and other land subject to frequent saturation or inundation,

and which normally support a prevalence of vegetation typically found where wet soil conditions prevail" (West Virginia Code, Chapter 20, Section 5A–2: Definitions). West Virginia does not have specific legislation protecting wetlands, but statutes under Chapter 20 of the West Virginia Code allow State involvement in section 404 permitting through section 401 of the Clean Water Act (West Virginia Department of Natural Resources, 1989). Presently, the State does not approve of all section 404 nationwide exemptions and requires application for section 401 certification to fill any wetland, regardless of size or location. Applications for section 401 certification are evaluated by the Division of Natural Resources and Division of Environmental Protection of the State Department of Labor, Commerce, and Environment. Applications are made directly to the Division of Environmental Protection, which has signatory authority for section 401 certification. However, through memoranda of understanding, the Division of Environmental Protection certifies wetland filling associated with coal mining, and the Division of Natural Resources certifies wetland filling for projects other than mining.

Private wetland activities.—Through the Matching Aid to Restore State Habitat (MARSH) program, Ducks Unlimited has provided funding for the purchase and restoration of West Virginia wetlands. Thirteen Ohio River islands that were purchased by Ducks Unlimited and deeded to the FWS contain wetlands. These wetlands will be managed by the FWS as part of the proposed Ohio River Islands National Wildlife Refuge (Jerry Thomas, Ducks Unlimited, oral commun., 1993). Ducks Unlimited also matches funds that the Division of Natural Resources obtains from the sale of Duck Stamps. These funds are used to restore wetland habitat. In West Virginia, The Nature Conservancy has established the preservation of plant and animal diversity in eastern West Virginia marl wetlands as its first priority. The Nature Conservancy has secured a conservation easement that is used to protect and manage large areas of Altona Marsh and Cranesville Swamp, an important peatland in the north-central part of the State. These easements restrict development in the area and guarantee public access for educational and scientific purposes.

References Cited

Bartgis, R.L., and Lang, G.E., 1984, Marl wetlands in eastern West Virginia—Distribution, rare plant species, and recent history: Castanea, v. 49, p. 17–25.

Canaan Valley Task Force, 1992, Canaan Valley—A national treasure: Elkins, W. Va., Canaan Valley Task Force, 10 p.

Cowardin, L.M., Carter, Virginia, Golet, F.C., and LaRoe, E.T., 1979, Classification of wetlands and deepwater habitats of the United States: U.S. Fish and Wildlife Service, Report FWS/OBS–79/31, 131 p.

Dahl, T.E., 1990, Wetlands—Losses in the United States, 1780's to 1980's: Washington, D.C., U.S. Fish and Wildlife Service Report to Congress, 13 p.

Diehl, J.W., and Behling, R.E., 1982, Geologic factors affecting formation and presence of wetlands in the north central section of the Appalachian Plateaus Province of West Virginia, *in* McDonald, B.R., ed., Proceedings of the Symposium on Wetlands of the Unglaciated Appalachian Region, May 26–28, 1982: Morgantown, West Virginia University, p. 3–9.

Ely, J.S., 1993, The vegetation of selected embayments along the upper to mid-upper Ohio River floodplain: Huntington, W. Va., Marshall University, M.S. thesis, 86 p.

Fenneman, N.M., 1946, Physical divisions of the United States: Washington, D.C., U.S. Geological Survey special map, scale 1:7,000,000.

Fortney, R.H., 1975, The vegetation of Canaan Valley, West Virginia—A taxonomic and ecological study: Morgantown, West Virginia University, Ph.D. dissertation, 210 p.

———1977, A bit of Canada gone astray: Wonderful West Virginia, v. 41, no. 5, p. 24–31.

Koryak, Michael, 1978, Emergent and aquatic plants in the upper Ohio River and major tributaries, West Virginia and Pennsylvania: Castanea, v. 43, no. 4, p. 228–237.

Lang, G.E., and McDonald, B.R., 1982, Loss of mass and elemental changes in decomposing sedge and alder leaves, *in* McDonald, B.R., ed., Proceedings of the Symposium on Wetlands of the Unglaciated Appalachian Region, May 26–28, 1982: Morgantown, West Virginia University, p. 31–41.

National Park Service, 1992, National registry of natural landmarks: Washington, D.C., National Park Service, Wildlife and Vegetation Division, 35 p.

Tiner, R.W., Jr., 1987, Mid-Atlantic wetlands—A disappearing natural treasure: Newton Corner, Mass., U.S. Fish and Wildlife Service and U.S. Environmental Protection Agency cooperative publication, 28 p.

West Virginia Department of Natural Resources, 1988, West Virginia wetlands conservation plan: Charleston, West Virginia Department of Natural Resources, Wildlife Resources Division, 22 p.

———1989, West Virginia water quality status assessment 1987–1989: West Virginia Department of Natural Resources, Wildlife Resources Division, 131 p.

Wieder, R.K., 1985, Peat and water chemistry at Big Run Bog, a peatland in the Appalachian mountains of West Virginia, USA: Biogeochemistry, v. 1, p. 277–302.

Wieder, R.K., and Lang, G.E., 1983, Net primary production of the dominant bryophytes in a sphagnum-dominated wetland in West Virginia: The Bryologist, v. 86, no. 3, p. 280–286.

Winter, T.C., 1992, A physiographic and climatic framework for hydrologic studies of wetlands, *in* Robarts, R.D., and Bothwell, M.L., eds., Aquatic ecosystems in semi-arid regions—Implications for resource management: Saskatoon, Saskatchewan, Environment Canada, The National Hydrology Research Institute Symposium Series 7, p. 127–148.

FOR ADDITIONAL INFORMATION: District Chief, U.S. Geological Survey, 11 Dunbar Street, Charleston, WV 25301; Regional Wetland Coordinator, U.S. Fish and Wildlife Service, 300 Westgate Center Drive, Hadley, MA 01035

Prepared by
Michael Little and Marcus C. Waldron,
U.S. Geological Survey

Western Pacific Islands
Wetland Resources

The western Pacific Ocean contains thousands of small volcanic islands and coral atolls, many of which are now or were formerly under the jurisdiction of the United States. Herein, those islands are called the Western Pacific Islands. Wetlands are of great economic importance on many of these islands because of the wetland cultivation of taro, a staple food crop. Wetlands also provide important wildlife habitat on the larger islands (fig. 1) (U.S. Army Corps of Engineers, 1981; Guam Department of Parks and Recreation, 1988). Despite the economic importance of wetlands in the western Pacific region, not much information is available concerning wetland resources on most of the islands. This summary, therefore, is restricted to several major islands for which some published information is available.

TYPES AND DISTRIBUTION

Wetlands are lands transitional between terrestrial and deepwater habitats where the water table usually is at or near the land surface or the land is covered by shallow water (Cowardin and others, 1979). The distribution of wetlands and deepwater habitats in the Western Pacific Islands is shown in figure 2A; only wetlands are discussed herein.

Wetlands can be vegetated or nonvegetated and are classified on the basis of their hydrology, vegetation, and substrate. In this summary, wetlands are classified according to the system proposed by Cowardin and others (1979), which is used by the U.S. Fish and Wildlife Service (FWS) to map and inventory wetlands. At the most general level of the classification system, wetlands are grouped into five ecological systems: Palustrine, Lacustrine, Riverine, Estuarine, and Marine. The Palustrine System includes only wetlands, whereas the other systems comprise wetlands and deepwater habitats. Wetlands of the systems that occur in the Western Pacific Islands are described below.

System	Wetland description
Palustrine	Nontidal and tidal-freshwater wetlands in which vegetation is predominantly trees (forested wetlands); shrubs (scrub-shrub wetlands); persistent or nonpersistent emergent, erect, rooted herbaceous plants (persistent- and nonpersistent-emergent wetlands); or submersed and (or) floating plants (aquatic beds). Also, intermittently to permanently flooded open-water bodies of less than 20 acres in which water is less than 6.6 feet deep.
Lacustrine	Nontidal and tidal-freshwater wetlands within an intermittently to permanently flooded lake or reservoir larger than 20 acres and (or) deeper than 6.6 feet. Vegetation, when present, is predominantly nonpersistent emergent plants (nonpersistent-emergent wetlands), or submersed and (or) floating plants (aquatic beds), or both.
Riverine	Nontidal and tidal-freshwater wetlands within a channel. Vegetation, when present, is same as in the Lacustrine System.
Estuarine	Tidal wetlands in low-wave-energy environments where the salinity of the water is greater than 0.5 part per thousand (ppt) and is variable owing to evaporation and the mixing of seawater and freshwater.
Marine	Tidal wetlands that are exposed to waves and currents of the open ocean and to water having a salinity greater than 30 ppt.

The FWS has mapped wetlands on Guam, Rota, Tinian, Aguijan, and Saipan in the Mariana Islands (fig. 2). With the exception of Guam, estimates of total wetland areas are not available for these islands.

Wetlands on Guam were inventoried by the Guam Department of Parks and Recreation (1988). Using the FWS wetland maps, the Department of Parks and Recreation estimated a total of about 14,000 acres of wetland. Most of this total, about 9,000 acres, consists of marine coral reefs. Palustrine wetlands cover about 3,500 acres, equivalent to less than 3 percent of the land area of Guam. Most of the palustrine wetlands are forested with mangroves.

Figure 1. Lake Susupe, a lacustrine wetland on Saipan in the Commonwealth of the Northern Mariana Islands. *(Photograph by S.K. Izuka, U.S. Geological Survey.)*

Wetlands mapped by the FWS on Saipan are primarily marine and palustrine wetlands. Marine wetlands include coral reefs along most of the shoreline and in the lagoons on the west side of the island. Palustrine wetlands are located mostly near the western shore at altitudes below 30 feet. The largest freshwater wetland is the Lake Susupe wetland near Chalan Kanoa in the southwestern part of the island (fig. 2); this wetland includes lacustrine, palustrine emergent, and palustrine scrub-shrub wetlands. Small estuarine, lacustrine, and riverine wetlands have been mapped along the western and eastern shores of the island. A few small and isolated riverine and palustrine wetlands have been mapped in the mountainous interior.

Wetlands on Tinian are marine and palustrine. The marine wetlands are predominantly coral reefs and rocky shores around much of the coast. The palustrine wetlands are mostly emergent and are concentrated in two closed depressions that resulted from the collapse of limestone solution cavities. These wetlands are known as the Magpo and Lake Hagoi wetlands. Tinian has no streams and, therefore, no riverine or estuarine wetlands. Several small marine and palustrine wetlands also have been mapped on the nearby small island of Aguijan.

Numerous marine, palustrine, and riverine wetlands were mapped on Rota. The marine wetlands include reefs and rocky shores. Reefs surround almost the entire island. Palustrine wetlands are mainly emergent and are concentrated in the southwestern end of the island, where collapse of limestone solution cavities has created several closed depressions on the plateau known as the Sabana. Riverine wetlands are confined to the few steep streams that flow over volcanic terrain in the south of the island.

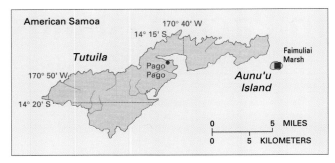

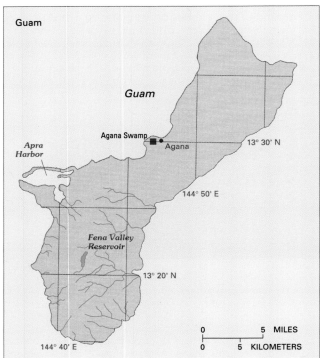

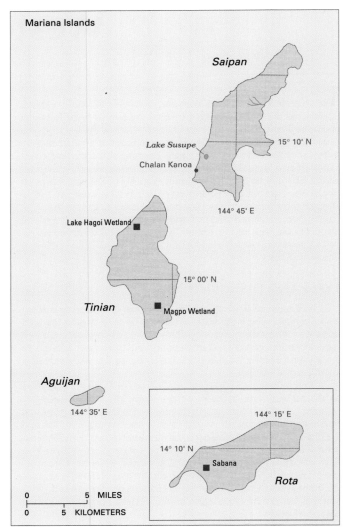

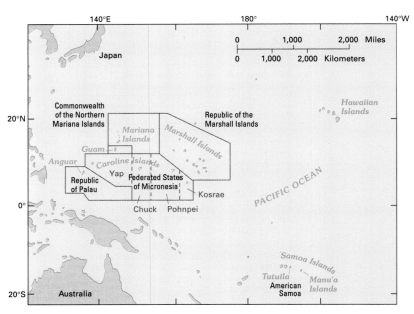

Figure 2. Locations of selected wetlands in the Western Pacific Islands. *(Source: U.S. Fish and Wildlife Service, National Wetlands Inventory maps.)*

Wetlands in American Samoa (fig. 2) were inventoried for the American Samoa Department of Parks and Recreation by Ridings (1987) on the basis of surveys by the FWS. Total wetland area was estimated to be 240 acres, which is less than 1 percent of the land area of American Samoa. Wetlands were classed as coastal marshes or as mangrove forests. American Samoa's coastal marshes, as described by Ridings (1987), are palustrine (freshwater) emergent wetlands. The total area of coastal marshes was estimated to be 89 acres. Mangrove forests are estuarine forested and scrub-shrub wetlands and comprise a total of 131 acres.

A second inventory of wetlands in American Samoa, based on field surveys and aerial-photograph interpretation, gave an estimate of 463 acres of wetlands in 1991 on Tutuila and Aunu'u Island (fig. 2) (BioSystemsAnalysis, Inc., 1991). Wetland areas were listed for 10 wetlands on Tutuila and 4 wetlands on Aunu'u Island.

The difference between the estimates of Ridings (1987) and BioSystems Analysis, Inc. (1991) may be due to differences in methodology and classification. Marine wetlands and wetlands on the Manu'a Islands were not included in either survey.

HYDROLOGIC SETTING

The Western Pacific Islands have a tropical climate that is affected by prevailing northeasterly trade winds north of the equator and southeasterly trade winds south of the equator. The islands have distinct dry and wet (monsoon) seasons. On the islands discussed in this report, rainfall ranges from 80 to 250 inches annually, depending on location, and annual runoff ranges from 26 to 200 inches (Aldridge, 1986).

Bedrock of the Western Pacific Islands consists mainly of limestone and two types of volcanic rocks (Detay and others, 1989). The Mariana Islands have cores of low-permeability, andesitic volcanic rocks covered in most places by high-permeability limestone (Valenciano, 1985). Atolls in the Caroline and Marshall Islands (fig. 2) are formed of coral sand and limestone (Anthony and others, 1989; Detay and others, 1989). The islands of American Samoa are predominantly steep, volcanic edifices formed of low- to high-permeability basaltic lava flows rimmed with narrow coastal benches formed of wave-deposited sediments (Bentley, 1975).

Most of the wetlands in the Western Pacific Islands are marine, estuarine, or palustrine wetlands in coastal areas. Both the land surface and the water table in these areas are near sea level owing to the proximity of the ocean and discharge of ground water from fresh to brackish basal ground-water lenses (Valenciano, 1985). The balance between rainfall and evaporation, generally steep slopes, and the high permeability of limestone and basaltic bedrock does not favor the retention of water near the land surface in upland areas except where collapse of limestone caves has created closed depressions or where less-permeable volcanic rocks crop out.

Mariana Islands. — The largest coastal wetlands, such as Agana Swamp on Guam and Lake Susupe on Saipan (fig. 2), probably originated as marine embayments or lagoons (Ayers and Clayshulte, 1983). These wetlands were isolated from the ocean when sea level declined and were subsequently filled with carbonate and organic sediments. Tidal effects on water levels in these coastal wetlands apparently are small (U.S. Army Corps of Engineers, 1981; Ayers and Clayshulte, 1983).

The hydrogeology of Agana Swamp on Guam was investigated by Ayers and Clayshulte (1983). They inferred that the water level in the swamp was maintained largely by rainfall and surface-water runoff. They also found that the swamp was hydraulically connected to the basal freshwater lens that forms the primary ground-water source for the island, and they hypothesized that the swamp functioned as a ground-water recharge zone during wet periods and a discharge zone during dry periods.

Lake Susupe on Saipan (figs. 1 and 2) is a lacustrine wetland, about 3 feet above sea level, surrounded by palustrine emergent and forested wetlands. The lake is shallow, and the lake bottom is mostly below sea level. Except during major storms, surface water does not flow into the lake from the surrounding uplands or into the sea from the lake. Apparently, the lake surface is continuous with the water table. The lake gains water from rainfall and runoff and loses water owing to ground-water recharge and evaporation (U.S. Army Corps of Engineers, 1981).

The Magpo wetland on Tinian (fig. 2) is a major source of water for that island. The land surface and water table of this wetland are at or near sea level. The wetland was considered to be a ground-water recharge zone for the principal aquifer in a recent proposal for a watershed protection plan by the Coastal Resource Management Office of the Commonwealth of the Northern Mariana Islands (J.P. Villagomez, Coastal Resource Management Office, written commun., 1992).

Samoan Islands. — Coastal marshes in American Samoa occur inland from beach berms and lack surface-water connections to the sea. Marsh sediments generally are poorly permeable, and marsh water levels are only slightly affected by tides (Ridings, 1987). The soil of these marshes is almost always saturated (Ridings, 1987). Mangrove forests in American Samoa grow mainly at the mouths of streams (Ridings, 1987).

Caroline Islands. — Templin and others (1949) described a large freshwater swamp (palustrine forested wetland) on the island of Anguar in the Republic of Palau (fig. 2). The water table was reported to be within a few inches of the land surface most of the time and 2 to 4 feet below the surface during the driest periods. During some severe storms, the swamp was inundated by seawater. The swamp was noted to be favorable for cultivation of taro. Wetland taro cultivation in Palau (Belau) was described by Gressitt (1952).

Artificial wetlands used for cultivation of taro and other crops in the Caroline Islands were described by Niering (1956). These wetlands consist of pits dug below the water table and partially filled with decayed vegetation. The size of these pits ranged from a few square feet to 11 acres. The number of artificial wetlands created for taro cultivation in the Caroline Islands was reported to be increasing because of increases in population (Niering, 1956).

Marshall Islands. — Wetlands in the Marshall Islands were described by Hatheway (1953). These included mangrove swamps and freshwater swamps. Mangrove swamps (estuarine forested wetlands) occurred in areas of saline or brackish water where ocean waves had created closed depressions owing to successive deposition of dunes or boulder ridges. Freshwater swamps (palustrine forested and scrub-shrub wetlands) and marshes (emergent wetlands) include pits dug for taro cultivation as well as naturally formed peat bogs that contain organic soils.

Wetlands on atolls in the Marshall Islands were briefly described by Fosberg (1953). Most of these wetlands were artificial marshes consisting of pits dug below the water table, partially filled with decayed vegetation, and planted in taro. Natural marshes and a peat bog also were noted. Fosberg (1953) distinguished these two wetland types on the basis of substrate; marshes have a muck bottom and bogs consist of fibrous peat. Both of these wetland types are palustrine emergent wetlands.

TRENDS

Very little information concerning trends in wetland conditions is available for the Western Pacific Islands. Information available from published sources is mostly qualitative but does provide some indications of wetland changes in historic times.

A large part of Agana Swamp on Guam was filled to provide room for expansion of the town of Agana (Ayers and Clayshulte,

1983). The swamp was also affected by dredging in 1933–34, when a channel was cut through the swamp. Dredging resulted in considerable drying of the swamp surface, decreased ground-water levels near the swamp, and increased flow in the Agana River, which flows through the swamp (Ayers and Clayshulte, 1983).

Lake Susupe on Saipan also was subject to filling and draining during the Japanese occupation (1914–44) (U.S. Army Corps of Engineers, 1981). Much of the wetland was used for cultivation of sugarcane during this period. The lake and surrounding wetlands were considered for use as a flood-control basin in 1981 and are presently (1993) being evaluated as a source of municipal water supply.

Wetland losses in American Samoa were assessed by Ridings (1987). Only one-third to one-half of the total area of coastal marsh was reported to be in its natural condition. Faimulivai Marsh on Aunuʻu Island was considered the only coastal marsh not disturbed by taro cultivation or other agricultural uses. However, Ridings (1987) considered further disturbance of coastal marshes for agricultural purposes unlikely as a result of demographic and economic shifts (Ridings, 1987). About one-third of the original area of mangrove forest was reported lost due to firewood cutting, land clearing, and filling for home sites and government land (Ridings, 1987). Contamination of streams flowing into wetland areas was also considered a threat to mangrove forests. Continued decrease in mangrove forests was predicted.

Trends in wetlands between 1961 and 1991 on Tutuila and Aunuʻu Island in American Samoa were recently evaluated by BioSystems Analysis, Inc. (1991). Their report indicated a net loss of 137 acres. On the basis of their estimates from aerial photography, this loss represents a 28-percent reduction in area (BioSystems Analysis, Inc., 1991).

CONSERVATION

Wetland management in the western Pacific is complex because many islands of the former U.S. Trust Territory of the Pacific are now governed by independent national governments. The Federated States of Micronesia and the Republic of the Marshall Islands (fig. 2) are now independent nations governing most of the Caroline and Marshall Islands. Guam and American Samoa are U.S. territories, and the Northern Mariana Islands are a U.S. commonwealth. The Republic of Palau (Belau) remains at present (1993) a U.S. trust territory. Only islands under the jurisdiction of the United States are discussed below.

Many government agencies and private organizations participate in wetland conservation in the Western Pacific Islands. The most active agencies and organizations and some of their activities are listed in table 1.

Federal wetland activities. — Development activities in wetlands of the Western Pacific Islands that are under the jurisdiction of the United States are regulated by several Federal statutory prohibitions and incentives that are intended to slow wetland losses. Some of the more important of these are contained in the 1899 Rivers and Harbors Act; the 1972 Clean Water Act and amendments; the 1985 Food Security Act; the 1990 Food, Agriculture, Conservation, and Trade Act; the 1986 Emergency Wetlands Resources Act; and the 1972 Coastal Zone Management Act.

Section 10 of the Rivers and Harbors Act gives the U.S. Army Corps of Engineers (Corps) authority to regulate certain activities in navigable waters. Regulated activities include diking, deepening, filling, excavating, and placing of structures. The related section 404 of the Clean Water Act is the most often-used Federal legislation protecting wetlands. Under section 404 provisions, the Corps issues permits regulating the discharge of dredged or fill material into wetlands. Permits are subject to review and possible veto by the U.S.

Table 1. Selected wetland-related activities of government agencies and private organizations in the Western Pacific Islands, 1993

[Source: Classification of activities is generalized from information provided by agencies and organizations. ●, agency or organization participates in wetland-related activity; ..., agency or organization does not participate in wetland-related activity. MAN, management; REG, regulation; R&C, restoration and creation; LAN, land acquisition; R&D, research and data collection; D&I, delineation and inventory]

Agency or organization	MAN	REG	R&C	LAN	R&D	D&I
FEDERAL						
Department of Agriculture						
Consolidated Farm Service Agency	...	●	...	...	...	...
Natural Resources Conservation Service	...	●	●	...	...	●
Department of Commerce						
National Oceanic and Atmospheric Administration	●	●	...	...	●	...
Department of Defense						
All military reservations	...	●	...	...	...	...
Army Corps of Engineers	...	●	●	...	●	●
Navy (Guam)	...	●	●	...	●	...
Department of the Interior						
Fish and Wildlife Service	...	●	●	●	●	●
Geological Survey	...	...	...	...	●	...
Environmental Protection Agency	...	●	...	...	...	...
TERRITORIAL AND COMMONWEALTH						
American Samoa						
Department of Marine and Wildlife Resources	...	●	●	...	●	...
Department of Parks and Recreation	...	●	●	...	...	...
Department of Public Works	...	●	●	...	...	...
Economic Development Planning Office	...	●	...	...	...	●
Environmental Protection Agency	...	●	...	...	...	...
Village leaders and councils	...	...	●	...	...	...
Zoning Board	...	...	●	...	...	...
Commonwealth of the Northern Mariana Islands						
Coastal Resource Management Office	...	●	...	...	...	...
Commonwealth Utilities Commission	...	●	...	...	...	...
Department of Commerce and Labor	...	●	...	...	...	...
Department of Health	...	●	...	...	...	...
Department of Natural Resources	...	●	...	...	●	...
Historical Preservation Commission	...	●	...	...	...	...
Public Works Department	...	●	...	...	...	...
Guam						
Bureau of Planning	...	●	...	...	...	...
Department of Agriculture	...	●	...	...	●	...
Environmental Protection Agency	...	●	...	...	...	●
Territorial Land Use Commission	...	●	...	...	...	...
PRIVATE ORGANIZATIONS						
The Nature Conservancy	...	...	●	...	●	...

Environmental Protection Agency (EPA), and the FWS has review and advisory roles. Section 401 of the Clean Water Act grants to States, eligible Indian Tribes, U.S. Trust Territories, Commonwealths, and other U.S. territories the authority to approve, apply conditions to, or deny section 404 permit applications on the basis of a proposed activity's probable effects on the water quality of a wetland.

Most farming, ranching, and silviculture activities are not subject to section 404 regulation. However, the "Swampbuster" provision of the 1985 Food Security Act and amendments in the 1990 Food, Agriculture, Conservation, and Trade Act discourage (through financial disincentives) the draining, filling, or other alteration of wetlands for agricultural use. The law allows exemptions from penalties in some cases, especially if the farmer agrees to restore the altered wetland or other wetlands that have been converted to agricultural use. The Wetlands Reserve Program of the 1990 Food, Agriculture, Conservation, and Trade Act authorizes the Federal Government to purchase conservation easements from landowners who agree to protect or restore wetlands. The Consolidated Farm Service Agency (formerly the Agricultural Stabilization and Conservation Service) administers the Swampbuster provisions and Wetlands Reserve Program. The Natural Resources Conservation Service (formerly the Soil Conservation Service) determines compliance with Swampbuster provisions and assists farmers in the identification of wetlands and in the development of wetland protection, restoration, or creation plans.

The 1986 Emergency Wetlands Resources Act and the 1972 Coastal Zone Management Act and amendments encourage wetland protection through funding incentives. The Emergency Wetlands Resources Act requires States and U.S. territories to address wetland protection in their Statewide Comprehensive Outdoor Recreation Plans to qualify for Federal funding for recreational land; the National Park Service provides guidance in developing the wetland component of their plans. Coastal States and U.S. territories that adopt coastal-zone management programs and plans approved by the National Oceanic and Atmospheric Administration are eligible for Federal funding and technical assistance through the Coastal Zone Management Act.

The FWS is planning a National Wildlife Refuge on Guam. This refuge will include wetlands as well as terrestrial habitats. There are no existing National Wildlife Refuges under United States jurisdiction in the western Pacific.

The U.S. Navy manages wetlands on Guam in the vicinity of Apra Harbor. The Navy is planning a wetlands-enhancement project in cooperation with FWS (Stephanie Aschmann, U.S. Navy, written commun., 1992).

The U.S. Geological Survey collects hydrologic data in wetlands in the Mariana Islands. A bathymetric survey of Fena Valley Reservoir on Guam was completed in 1990 (Nakama, 1992). Water-quality samples were collected in Lake Susupe on Saipan in 1990. Monitoring wells are being drilled in the Magpo wetland on Tinian.

Territorial and Commonwealth activities. — Guam has at present (1993) no laws specifically protecting wetlands, but Executive Order 90–13 in June 1990 established the Guam Environmental Protection Agency as the lead agency for wetland protection in Guam. The Guam Environmental Protection Agency is responsible for the inventory and classification of wetlands and development of rules and regulations for wetland uses. The Agency provides water-quality certification for permits issued by the Corps. The Agency also has established water-quality standards specific to wetlands and instituted a wetlands education program. Fish and Wildlife Service wetland maps are used to identify wetland areas, but Guam Environmental Protection Agency staff revise wetland delineations for specific development sites. Development projects on Guam require permits from the Territorial Land Use Commission in addition to federally required permits. The commission may require mitigation of wetland losses. The Guam Environmental Protection Agency, the Bureau of Planning, and the Department of Agriculture, Division of Aquatic Resources and Wildlife, act as advocates before the commission for wetland concerns.

Wetland regulation in the Commonwealth of the Northern Mariana Islands (fig. 2) is coordinated by the Coastal Resource Management Office under the authority of the Federal Coastal Zone Management Act. The Office issues consolidated permits for wetland developments and may require mitigation. The Office consists of the directors of the Division of Environmental Quality, the Department of Natural Resources, the Commonwealth Utility Corporation, the Historical Preservation Commission, the Public Works Department, and the Department of Commerce and Labor. The Office has produced its own wetland maps. The Department of Environmental Quality is responsible for section 401 water-quality certification of projects under the Clean Water Act and monitors streams and coastal waters weekly. The Department of Health, under which the Department of Environmental Quality operates, has established local water-quality standards.

In American Samoa, wetlands are protected by the land-use permit system administered by the Economic Development Planning Office, which is developing a wetland-management plan under the authority of the Coastal Zone Management Act (BioSystems Analysis, Inc., 1991). As part of this plan, wetlands were mapped for all islands in American Samoa (Sheila Wiegman, American Samoa Environmental Protection Agency, written commun., 1993). The American Samoa Environmental Protection Agency acts in an advisory role in the Economic Development Planning Office permitting process and also provides section 401 water-quality certification for Corps permits. The American Samoa Environmental Protection Agency also develops water-quality standards and issues permits for activities affecting wetland water quality. The Department of Marine and Wildlife Resources also acts in an advisory role for Economic Development Planning Office permits affecting wetlands and conducts habitat improvement and wetland-research projects. The Department of Parks and Recreation has jurisdiction over all areas between mean high tide and a depth of 60 feet and enforces rules protecting these areas. The Department of Public Works reviews permit applications for dredging, filling, and excavation. The Zoning Board defines zones, which may include wetlands, where some land-use activities are prohibited. Local leaders and village councils also have authority to enforce regulations pertaining to public health and natural resources.

The Republic of Palau has at present (1993) no wetland-protection program. The Palau Environmental Quality Protection Board is cooperating with the EPA in an effort to initiate a wetlands program.

Private organizations. — The Nature Conservancy has a project in the Republic of Palau to protect freshwater marshes for crocodile habitat. The Nature Conservancy is also working with local governments on Pohnpei and Kosrae in the Federated States of Micronesia to protect wetlands.

References Cited

Aldridge, B.N., 1986, Surface-water resources of the Trust Territory of the Pacific Islands, Saipan, Guam, and American Samoa, *in* U.S. Geological Survey, National water summary 1985 — Hydrologic events and surface-water resources: U.S. Geological Survey Water-Supply Paper 2300, p. 441–446.

Anthony, S.S., Peterson, F.L., Mackenzie, F.T., and Hamlin, S.N., 1989, Geohydrology of the Laura fresh-water lens, Majuro Atoll — A hydrogeochemical approach: Geological Society of America Bulletin, v. 101, no. 8, p. 1,066–1,075.

Ayers, J.F., and Clayshulte, R.N., 1983, Hydrogeologic investigation of Agana Swamp, Northern Guam: University of Guam, Water and Energy Research Institute of the western Pacific, Technical Report 40, 25 p.

Bentley, C.B., 1975, Ground-water resources of American Samoa with emphasis on Tafuna–Leone Plain, Tutuila Island: U.S. Geological Survey Water-Resources Investigations Report 29–75, 32 p.

BioSystems Analysis, Inc., 1991, A comprehensive wetlands management plan for the islands of Tutuila and Aunu'u, American Samoa (preliminary draft): [available from BioSystems Analysis, Inc., 3152 Paradise Drive, Tiburon, CA 94920].

Cowardin, L.M., Carter, Virginia, Golet, F.C., and LaRoe, E.T., 1979, Classification of wetlands and deepwater habitats of the United States: U.S. Fish and Wildlife Service Report FWS/OBS–79/31, 131 p.

Detay, M., Alessandrello, E., Come, P., and Groom, I., 1989, Groundwater contamination and pollution in Micronesia: Journal of Hydrology, v. 112, p. 149–170.

Fosberg, F.R., 1953, Vegetation of central Pacific atolls, a brief summary: Washington, D.C., National Academy of Sciences, Pacific Science Board, Atoll Research Bulletin 23, 26 p.

Gressitt, J.L., 1952, Description of Kayangel Atoll, Palau Islands: Washington, D.C., National Academy of Sciences, Pacific Science Board, Atoll Research Bulletin 14, 5 p.

Guam Department of Parks and Recreation, 1988, Guam wetlands priority plan—1988 addendum to 1986 Guam Comprehensive Outdoor Recreation Plan: Agana, Guam Department of Parks and Recreation, 24 p.

Hatheway, W.H., 1953, The land vegetation of Arno Atoll, Marshall Islands: Washington, D.C., National Academy of Sciences, Pacific Science Board, Atoll Research Bulletin 16, 68 p.

Nakama, L.Y., 1992, Storage capacity of Fena Valley Reservoir, Guam, Mariana Islands, 1990: U.S. Geological Survey Water-Resources Investigations Report 92–4114, 17 p.

Niering, W.A., 1956, Bioecology of Kapingamarangi Atoll, Caroline Islands—Terrestrial aspects: Washington, D.C., National Academy of Sciences, Pacific Science Board, Atoll Research Bulletin 49, 32 p.

Ridings, P.J., 1987, American Samoa Territorial comprehensive outdoor recreation plan 1987–1992—Addendum—Wetlands priority plan: Pago Pago, American Samoa Department of Parks and Recreation, 11 p.

Templin, E.H., Vessel, A.J., and McCracken, R.J., 1949, Land classification of Anguar, Palau Islands: U.S. Army Corps of Engineers, Office of the Engineer, Far East Command, 16 p.

U.S. Army Corps of Engineers, 1981, Final detailed project report and environmental statement, Susupe–Chalan Kanoa flood control study, Saipan, Commonwealth of the Northern Mariana Islands: U.S. Army Engineer District, Honolulu, Hawaii [variously paged].

Valenciano, Santos, 1985, Ground-water resources of the Trust Territory of the Pacific Islands, Saipan, Guam, and American Samoa, *in* U.S. Geological Survey, National water summary 1984—Hydrologic events, selected water-quality trends, and ground-water resources: U.S. Geological Survey Water-Supply Paper 2275, p. 403–408.

FOR ADDITIONAL INFORMATION: District Chief, U.S. Geological Survey, 677 Ala Moana Boulevard, Suite 415, Honolulu, HI 96813; Regional Wetland Coordinator, U.S. Fish and Wildlife Service, 911 NE. 11th Avenue, Portland, OR 97232

Prepared by
B.R. Hill,
U.S. Geological Survey

Wisconsin
Wetland Resources

Wetlands cover more than 5 million acres of Wisconsin. Although once regarded as wastelands, wetlands are now recognized as ecologically and economically valuable ecosystems. The preservation of wetlands is important for the continued survival of much of Wisconsin's plant and wildlife resources. Many fish and wildlife species, including endangered and threatened species, depend on wetlands for survival at one time or another during their life cycles. Animals that depend on wetlands include muskrats, ducks, water snakes, and leopard frogs. Ducks, geese, and other migratory birds depend on wetlands for resting and feeding during migration. Fish, including northern pike, walleye, and muskellunge, use wetlands for spawning and feeding.

Wetlands (such as that shown in figure 1) help maintain water quality by acting as filters that trap suspended sediments and organic and inorganic contaminants suspended or dissolved in the waters that reach them. These trapped pollutants are stored in the wetland soils and plants. Wetlands help to regulate streamflow by temporarily storing floodwater and then slowly releasing it to the stream or river, reducing the magnitude of flooding downstream. Flood peaks in watersheds (drainage basins) containing a large area of wetlands can be as much as 80 percent lower than in watersheds that have few or no wetlands (Novitzki, 1982). Wetlands also protect the shorelines and banks of lakes and rivers from erosion by absorbing wave energy, decreasing water velocity, and increasing soil stability.

Wetlands are productive ecosystems, yielding a large amount of plant material for wildlife and human consumption. Products that are harvested from wetlands include cranberries, wild rice, and sphagnum moss. Wisconsin's tourist industry benefits from the recreational opportunities that wetlands provide, including hunting, fishing, boating, hiking, camping, and bird watching. Many wetland areas throughout the State also provide educational opportunities for schools and the general public.

TYPES AND DISTRIBUTION

Wetlands are lands transitional between terrestrial and deepwater habitats where the water table usually is at or near the land surface or the land is covered by shallow water (Cowardin and others, 1979). The distribution of wetlands and deepwater habitats in Wisconsin is shown in figure 2A; only wetlands are discussed herein.

Figure 1. Constructed wetland near Tomah in southwestern Wisconsin. *(Photograph by Randall J. Hunt, U.S. Geological Survey.)*

Wetlands can be vegetated or nonvegetated and are classified on the basis of their hydrology, vegetation, and substrate. In this summary, wetlands are classified according to the system proposed by Cowardin and others (1979), which is used by the U.S. Fish and Wildlife Service (FWS) to map and inventory the Nation's wetlands. At the most general level of the classification system, wetlands are grouped into five ecological systems: Palustrine, Lacustrine, Riverine, Estuarine, and Marine. The Palustrine System includes only wetlands, whereas the other systems comprise wetlands and deepwater habitats. Wetlands of the systems that occur in Wisconsin are described below.

System	Wetland description
Palustrine	Wetlands in which vegetation is predominantly trees (forested wetlands); shrubs (scrub-shrub wetlands); persistent or nonpersistent emergent, erect, rooted, herbaceous plants (persistent- and nonpersistent-emergent wetlands); or submersed and (or) floating plants (aquatic beds). Also, intermittently to permanently flooded open-water bodies of less than 20 acres in which water is less than 6.6 feet deep.
Lacustrine	Wetlands within an intermittently to permanently flooded lake or reservoir. Vegetation, when present, is predominantly nonpersistent emergent plants (nonpersistent-emergent wetlands), or submersed and (or) floating plants (aquatic beds), or both.
Riverine	Wetlands within a channel. Vegetation, when present, is same as in the Lacustrine System.

About 15 percent (5,300,000 acres) of Wisconsin's land surface is covered by wetlands (fig. 2A) (Wisconsin Department of Natural Resources, 1992a). The Wisconsin Department of Natural Resources completed an inventory of Wisconsin's wetland locations, sizes, and types in 1984. The information from the inventory is being used by the FWS as part of its National Wetlands Inventory project. Currently, this information is available only in map form, and the statewide total acreages for specific wetland types have not yet been computed.

The classification system used by the Department of Natural Resources to map Wisconsin wetlands recognizes seven major classes of wetlands: aquatic bed, moss (moss-lichen wetland), wet meadow (emergent wetland), scrub-shrub, forested, flats/unvegetated wet soils (unconsolidated-shore wetland), and open water (Wisconsin Department of Natural Resources, 1992b). Common types of wetlands in Wisconsin include swamps, marshes, and peatlands. Swamps and marshes are most common in southern Wisconsin, and peatlands are most common in northern Wisconsin (Yanggen and others, 1976). Swamps are palustrine forested wetlands. Marshes are palustrine emergent wetlands dominated by grass, rush, and sedge species. Peatlands, including bogs and fens, are wetlands that accumulate organic material owing to limited inflow and outflow. Peatlands can be forested, scrub-shrub, or emergent wetlands. Scrub-shrub wetlands (wetlands dominated by woody vegetation less than 20 feet tall) are common in Wisconsin and include both deciduous and evergreen vegetation. Many Wisconsin wetlands are riparian (streamside) wetlands adjacent to rivers or streams that periodically flood.

Wetland distribution in Wisconsin is related to the extent of the most recent glaciation. The southwestern part of the State (fig.

2*B*) was not affected by the latest glaciation, and wetlands are uncommon there except in stream valleys filled with glacial drift (Novitzki, 1982). The rest of the State contains glacial deposits and numerous wetlands.

HYDROLOGIC SETTING

Hydrology is the single most important determinant for establishing and maintaining wetlands (Mitsch and Gosselink, 1986). Wetland formation is determined by the balance among the inflows and outflows of water, surface contours of the land, soil type, geology, and ground-water conditions. Topographic depressions caused by glacial and erosional processes, areas underlain by impermeable substrates that prevent infiltration of water into the ground, and areas where the water table is near the land surface provide ideal conditions for wetland formation.

Wisconsin's wetlands generally are in depressions, poorly drained areas, and, rarely, on slopes. All receive surface water, but a large proportion also receive ground water. Wisconsin's wetlands

can be divided into four hydrologic classes: surface-water depression, surface-water slope, ground-water depression, and ground-water slope (Novitzki, 1982).

Surface-water-depression wetlands form where overland flow and precipitation collect in a depression. Water leaves this type of wetland by infiltrating through the substrate, evaporating, or being transpired by plants. The water level in surface-water-depression wetlands can fluctuate greatly, depending on surface-water flow.

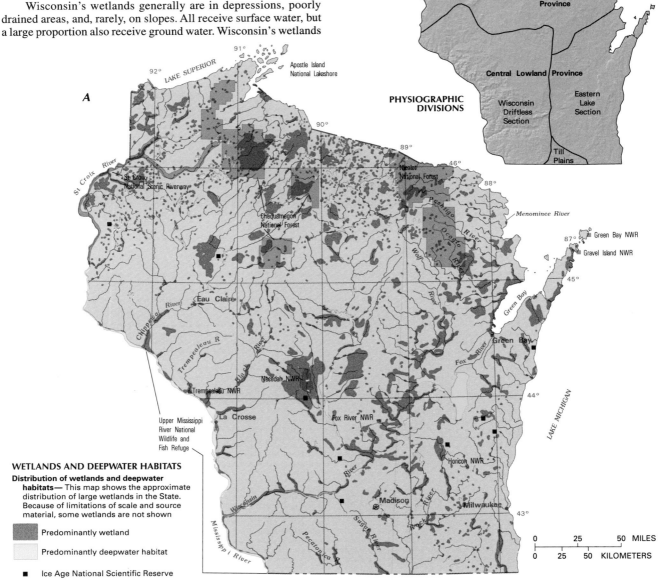

Figure 2. Wetland distribution in Wisconsin and physical features that control wetland distribution in the State. *A*, Distribution of wetlands and deepwater habitats. *B*, Physiography. *(Sources: A, T.E. Dahl, U.S. Fish and Wildlife Service, unpub. data, 1991. B, Physiographic divisions from Fenneman, 1946; landforms data from EROS Data Center.)*

Water levels rise during periods of high streamflow and fall during low streamflow. The bottom of the wetland is above the local water table most of the time (Novitzki, 1982). Surface-water depressions typically support ponds, marshes, swamps, and wet meadows (emergent wetlands).

Surface-water-slope wetlands form on or near the margins of lakes and streams. Included in this type of wetland are the shallow part of a lake or river and the bank to the point that is subject to flooding. This type of wetland is generally above the local water table, and floodwaters from the lake or river drain quickly. These wetlands are fed by precipitation, overland flow, and flooding from lakes and rivers (Novitzki, 1982). Surface-water-slope wetlands typically support shrub swamps (scrub-shrub wetland) and shallow marshes.

Ground-water-depression wetlands are located where a depression is below the water table. Water enters the wetland as precipitation, overland flow, and ground-water discharge. There generally is a lack of surface drainage away from this type of wetland. Although ground-water flow can be a small part of the total inflow, it can be an important water source during drought (Novitzki, 1982). Ground-water-depression wetlands typically support forested and shrub bogs, fens, and marshes.

Ground-water-slope wetlands form at ground-water-discharge sites, such as springs and seeps, typically on hillsides or at the bottom of hills where the water table intersects the land surface. These wetlands receive continuous ground-water inflow, but drainage away from the site reduces the ponding of water. The drainage commonly is the headwater of a small stream (Novitzki, 1982). Ground-water-slope wetlands typically support marshes, swamps, and wet meadows.

Wetlands are most numerous in areas that were covered by glaciers during the most recent glacial period (fig. 2C). Glacial erosion and deposition commonly create surface depressions and deposits of impermeable tills (sediments of glacial origin) that are ideal for wetland development (Bushnell, 1989). The unglaciated part of southwestern Wisconsin contains rugged terrain that is conducive to overland runoff, leaving little water for wetland development. Wetlands in the unglaciated areas are most commonly in riparian areas where glacial sediments have been deposited. Riparian wetlands develop either as lateral erosion widens a river valley or as deposition fills and flattens a valley. In riparian wetlands, a depositional substrate of silt, mud, and clay combines with the shallow water table near a river to create ideal conditions for the formation of small lakes and swamps (Bushnell,1989).

Wisconsin has about 43,000 miles of streams and about 15,000 lakes. Statewide, the annual average precipitation is 31 inches and annual evapotranspiration is 20 inches (Krohelski and others, 1990), so there is a moisture surplus on an annual basis. Many of Wisconsin's wetlands are supported by precipitation, either directly by surface-water runoff or indirectly by ground-water flow (Novitzki, 1979). A wetland's water supply is determined by the balance between precipitation and evapotranspiration. In northern Wisconsin, precipitation exceeds evaporation, whereas in the southern and western parts of the State, precipitation and evaporation are about equal (Novitzki, 1982). Therefore, more water is available for wetland formation in northern Wisconsin than in the southern and western parts of the State.

Annual and seasonal variations in precipitation can affect the amount of water available for wetlands. In years when snowmelt produces surface runoff and rain is frequent during the summer, surface-water wetlands have large quantities of water available. If the snowmelt recharges the ground-water system, ground-water wetlands have large amounts of water available to them. In general, water levels are highest in the spring and early summer when snowmelt has collected; levels then decline throughout the rest of the summer when evapotranspiration is at its highest. Ground-water wetlands are more stable than surface-water wetlands during drought because ground-water flow replaces some of the water lost to evapotranspiration (Novitzki, 1982). These natural fluctuations in precipitation quantity cause wetland vegetation to change in response to changes in moisture availability. Natural climatic changes are cyclical, whereas manmade changes, such as draining, cause a more permanent change in hydrology and vegetative types (Novitzki, 1979).

In most of the State, except the southwestern part, basement rocks are covered by unconsolidated glacial deposits, in which formed the kettles and potholes that contain many of the lakes and wetlands in the State. The Wisconsin Driftless Section in the southwestern part of the State is a region over which the most recent continental ice sheets did not pass. This region differs from the surrounding areas in topography and soil (Atwood, 1940). The topography is rugged, and few wetlands exist.

Wisconsin is in the Central Lowland and Superior Upland physiographic provinces (fig. 2B). The major surface-water drainage basins in the Central Lowland province are the Trempealeau– Black, Central Wisconsin, Lower Wisconsin, Fox– Wolf, Rock–Fox, and Pecatonica–Sugar River Basins, and the Lake Michigan Basin. The Wisconsin River, the largest in the State, drains the central part

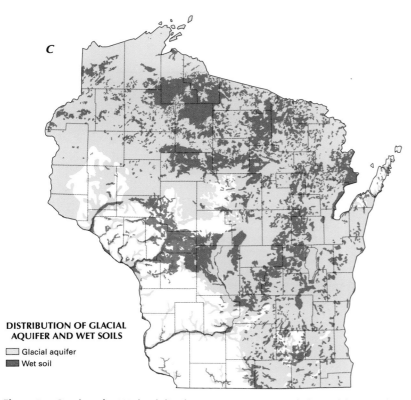

C

**DISTRIBUTION OF GLACIAL
AQUIFER AND WET SOILS**

☐ Glacial aquifer
■ Wet soil

Figure 2. Continued. Wetland distribution in Wisconsin and physical features that control wetland distribution in the State. *C*, Distribution of glacial aquifers and wet soils. *(Sources: C, Wet soils map from Frazier and Kiefer, 1974; limit of glacial aquifer from Devaul, 1975.)*

of the State from its headwaters at the Michigan border to its confluence with the Mississippi River. The Rock–Fox River Basin drains the southern part of the State and contains a large number of wetlands, including the 30,000-acre Horicon Marsh, which is located in the headwaters of the Rock River. The marsh is on a major flyway and provides habitat for large numbers of migrating geese and ducks. Flooding is reduced along the Rock River because of runoff detention by the large number of wetlands in the basin (Gebert, 1986). The Upper Mississippi River Basin drains west-central Wisconsin and includes numerous wetlands associated with the headwaters of the Trempealeau and Black Rivers. The area drained by tributaries to Lake Michigan contains wetlands that are the headwaters for the streams that flow into the lake (Gebert, 1986).

The major surface-water drainage basins in the Superior Upland province are the St. Croix, Chippewa, Upper Wisconsin, and Menominee–Oconto–Peshtigo River Basins, and the Western Lake Superior Basin. The St. Croix River drains northwestern Wisconsin. This area has numerous wetlands, many of which are cranberry bogs. The Chippewa River Basin in north-central Wisconsin contains wetlands around the headwaters of most streams. The Upper Wisconsin River Basin has one of the largest concentrations of lakes in the world (Gebert, 1986). The Western Lake Superior Basin contains many small streams, many inland lakes, and the Lake Superior shore, all of which support wetlands.

Wisconsin has coastal wetlands along the Lake Michigan and Lake Superior shorelines. Most of the coastal wetlands are just landward of the shoreline in shallow depressions called lagoons or flood ponds. Barriers created by multiple cycles of deposition and erosion reduce wave energy and allow sediments to accumulate and vegetation to become rooted. The upland boundaries of these wetlands are formed by glacial features (Geis, 1985). Water-level fluctuations in coastal wetlands increase the area and diversity of shoreline vegetation. Periods of high water prevent woody plants from establishing and also prevent aggressive plants, such as cattails, from overtaking a site. When the high water drains away, emergent plants regenerate from buried seeds, creating a wetland high in vegetative diversity (Keddy and Reznicek, 1985).

TRENDS

Dahl (1990) estimated that from the 1780's to the 1980's, wetland acreage in Wisconsin decreased from 9.8 million acres to 5.3 million acres—a 46-percent loss of the State's original wetlands. Wetlands were converted to upland or to other types of wetlands primarily for agricultural, residential, commercial, and industrial development. Agricultural development in wetlands was the major cause of wetland losses. Agricultural uses of Wisconsin wetlands include cranberry cultivation, sphagnum moss harvesting, and feed-crop production. Cranberry cultivation and sphagnum moss harvesting severely alter wetlands but do not drain them. Feed-crop production necessitates wetland drainage.

Urban development also destroyed or altered many wetlands in Wisconsin. Many cities were established in and around wetlands because of a reliance on water for transportation. Milwaukee was built over what was a large, marshy river delta. Riverbanks were established and the wetland was filled as the city grew (Wisconsin Department of Natural Resources, undated).

Two studies of wetland losses were conducted by the Department of Natural Resources. One study tracked wetland losses in seven counties in the southeastern part of the State from 1970 to 1985 (Wisconsin Department of Natural Resources, 1992a). The area is highly developed, so study results cannot be extrapolated to the entire State. Losses were 154 acres per year during 1970–75, 320 acres per year during 1975–80, and 328 acres per year during 1980–85. The Department of Natural Resources also conducted a study of wetland losses associated with projects that received U.S.

Army Corps of Engineers (Corps) section 404 permits. A review of permit decisions from 1982 to August 1990 indicated that permitted wetland losses were about 11,800 acres statewide. Annual losses during 1989–90 increased by 220 percent over annual wetland losses during the period 1982–89. That figure understates actual losses because it does not include activities preauthorized by general or nationwide permits or activities not regulated by section 404 (Wisconsin Department of Natural Resources, 1992a).

The Partners for Wildlife Program administered by the FWS is working to reverse these losses by restoring wetlands on private lands and providing technical assistance to Federal and State agencies and private landowners. As part of the program, 1,071 wetland restorations totaling 3,580 acres took place in Wisconsin in 1992 (Moriarty, 1992).

CONSERVATION

Many government agencies and private organizations participate in wetland conservation in Wisconsin. The most active agencies and organizations and some of their activities are listed in table 1.

Federal wetland activities.—Development activities in Wisconsin wetlands are regulated by several Federal statutory prohibitions and incentives that are intended to slow wetland losses. Some of the more important of these are contained in the 1899 Rivers and Harbors Act; the 1972 Clean Water Act and amendments; the 1985 Food Security Act; the 1990 Food, Agriculture, Conservation, and

Table 1. Selected wetland-related activities of government agencies and private organizations in Wisconsin, 1993

[Source: Classification of activities is generalized from information provided by agencies and organizations. •, agency or organization participates in wetland-related activity; ..., agency or organization does not participate in wetland-related activity. MAN, management; REG, regulation; R&C, restoration and creation; LAN, land acquisition; R&D, research and data collection; D&I, delineation and inventory]

Agency or organization	MAN	REG	R&C	LAN	R&D	D&I
FEDERAL						
Department of Agriculture						
Consolidated Farm Service Agency	...	•	...	...	...	...
Forest Service	•	...	•	•	...	•
Natural Resources Conservation Service	•	•	...	...	•	•
Rural Economic and Community Development	•	•	...	...	...	•
Department of Commerce						
National Oceanic and Atmospheric Administration	...	•	...	...	•	...
Department of Defense						
Army Corps of Engineers	•	•	•	•	...	•
Department of the Interior						
Fish and Wildlife Service	•	...	•	•	•	•
Geological Survey	...	...	...	...	•	...
National Biological Service	...	...	...	...	•	...
National Park Service	•	...	...	...	...	•
Environmental Protection Agency	...	•	...	...	...	•
STATE						
Department of Natural Resources						
Bureau of Water Regulation and Zoning	•	•	•	•	•	•
Department of Transportation	•	...	•	•	•	•
Regional planning commissions	...	•	...	•	•	•
State universities	...	...	...	...	•	...
SOME COUNTY AND LOCAL GOVERNMENTS	•	•	...	...	...	...
PRIVATE ORGANIZATIONS						
Audubon Society	...	...	•	...	...	...
Ducks Unlimited	...	...	•	•	...	...
Pheasants Forever	...	...	•	•	...	...
The Nature Conservancy	•	...	•	•	•	•
Wisconsin Waterfowl Association	...	...	•	•	...	...
Wisconsin Wildlife Federation	...	...	•	...	...	...

Trade Act; the 1986 Emergency Wetlands Resources Act; and the 1972 Coastal Zone Management Act.

Section 10 of the Rivers and Harbors Act gives the Corps authority to regulate certain activities in navigable waters. Regulated activities include diking, deepening, filling, excavating, and placing of structures. The related section 404 of the Clean Water Act is the most often-used Federal legislation protecting wetlands. Under section 404 provisions, the Corps issues permits regulating the discharge of dredged or fill material into wetlands. Permits are subject to review and possible veto by the U.S. Environmental Protection Agency (EPA), and the FWS has review and advisory roles. Section 401 of the Clean Water Act grants to States and eligible Indian Tribes the authority to approve, apply conditions to, or deny section 404 permit applications on the basis of a proposed activity's probable effects on the water quality of a wetland.

Most farming, ranching, and silviculture activities are not subject to section 404 regulation. However, the "Swampbuster" provision of the 1985 Food Security Act and amendments in the 1990 Food, Agriculture, Conservation, and Trade Act discourage (through financial disincentives) the draining, filling, or other alteration of wetlands for agricultural use. The law allows exemptions from penalties in some cases, especially if the farmer agrees to restore the altered wetland or other wetlands that have been converted to agricultural use. The Wetlands Reserve Program of the 1990 Food, Agriculture, Conservation, and Trade Act authorizes the Federal Government to purchase conservation easements from landowners who agree to protect or restore wetlands. The Consolidated Farm Service Agency (formerly the Agricultural Stabilization and Conservation Service) administers the Swampbuster provisions and Wetlands Reserve Program. The Natural Resources Conservation Service (NRCS) (formerly the Soil Conservation Service) determines compliance with Swampbuster provisions and assists farmers in the identification of wetlands and in the development of wetland protection, restoration, or creation plans.

The 1986 Emergency Wetlands Resources Act and the 1972 Coastal Zone Management Act and amendments encourage wetland protection through funding incentives. The Emergency Wetlands Resources Act requires States to address wetland protection in their Statewide Comprehensive Outdoor Recreation Plans to qualify for Federal funding for State recreational land; the National Park Service (NPS) provides guidance to States in developing the wetland component of their plans. Coastal and Great Lakes States that adopt coastal-zone management programs and plans approved by the National Oceanic and Atmospheric Administration (NOAA) are eligible for Federal funding and technical assistance through the Coastal Zone Management Act.

Federal agencies are responsible for the management of wetlands on public lands under their jurisdiction. There are approximately 300,000 acres of wetlands in federally managed forests and wildlife refuges in Wisconsin. The FWS manages seven sites in Wisconsin: the Trempealeau, Necedah, Upper Mississippi, Horicon, Fox River, Green Bay, and Gravel Island National Wildlife Refuges. The FWS also has two wetland-management districts that cover about 11,000 acres. The U.S. Forest Service manages more than 1 million acres of land in the Chequamegon National Forest and almost 1 million acres of land in the Nicolet National Forest. Both National Forests contain numerous wetlands. The NPS has jurisdiction over wetlands in the Apostle Island National Lakeshore, St. Croix National Scenic Riverway, and Ice Age National Scientific Reserve, which is administered by the Department of Natural Resources. Apostle Island National Lakeshore is made up of 21 islands and 12 miles of shoreline that support many coastal wetlands. The St. Croix National Scenic Riverway flows through undeveloped parts of northwestern Wisconsin. The Ice Age National Scientific Reserve is made up of nine units spread across the State. The Rural Economic and Community Development service manages farms that the Federal

Government has acquired by loan default. Wetlands on these lands are delineated, and the land is sold with wetland easements on it. These wetland easements are then managed by the FWS. The EPA is involved in wetlands planning projects including the Green Bay Special Wetlands Inventory Study and Advanced Identification wetland projects in southeast Wisconsin.

State wetland activities.—Wisconsin has about 400,000 acres of wetlands in county forests and 300,000 acres of wetlands in State forests, parks, wildlife areas, and natural areas. The Department of Natural Resources is the principal State agency responsible for wetland management and regulation. Applications for section 404 permits are reviewed by the Department. Permit applications approved by the Department are then reviewed by the Corps. Approval of both the Department and the Corps is required for a section 404 application to be approved. In August 1991, Wisconsin became the first State to adopt water-quality standards for wetlands. Wisconsin's wetland water-quality standards allow the State to control wetland development under section 401 of the Clean Water Act. The Department of Natural Resources maintains an antidegradation policy to ensure that no adverse effects will occur from human activities. Projects must be water dependent and have no practicable alternatives. The project must also have no significant adverse effect on wetland function, values, or water quality or have other environmental consequences (Wisconsin Department of Natural Resources, 1992a).

The Department of Natural Resources, in cooperation with the FWS, has restored 1,252 acres of historic wetlands on Conservation Reserve Program lands. The Department also is working in cooperation with the FWS, the EPA, and NOAA on an Advanced Identification Project in the Green Bay area.

The Wisconsin Department of Transportation follows a policy of avoiding wetlands in its construction projects. When a wetland is disturbed, the Department mitigates the impacts of the road construction by enhancing and creating additional wetlands.

County and local activities.—Local governments are required to protect wetlands that are within 1,000 feet of navigable lakes and 300 feet of navigable streams. Wetland protection is achieved through shoreland-wetland zoning ordinances overseen by the Department of Natural Resources. All counties currently have shoreland ordinances to protect their wetlands. Adoption of shoreland-wetland ordinances is taking place in cities and villages.

Private wetland activities.—Private organizations in Wisconsin participate in wetland activities that include policy planning, land acquisition and management, restoration and creation, research, and public education. Some of the organizations active in Wisconsin are The Nature Conservancy (land acquisition and management), the Sierra Club, Wisconsin Wetland Association, and Wisconsin Environmental Decade (policy planning and education). Organizations including Ducks Unlimited, the Audubon Society, Pheasants Forever, Wisconsin Waterfowl Association, and the Wisconsin Wildlife Federation, in cooperation with the FWS, the NRCS, and the Department of Natural Resources, are involved in projects that create, restore, and enhance wetlands.

References Cited

Atwood, W.W., 1940, The physiographic provinces of North America: Boston, Ginn and Company, 536 p.
Bushnell, Kent, 1989, Geology of Pennsylvania Wetlands, *in* Majumdar, S.K., and others, eds., Wetlands ecology and conservation—Emphasis in Pennsylvania: Easton, The Pennsylvania Academy of Science, p. 39–46.
Cowardin, L.M., Carter, Virginia, Golet, F.C., and LaRoe, E.T., 1979, Classification of wetlands and deepwater habitats of the United States: U.S. Fish and Wildlife Service Report FWS/OBS–79/31, 131 p.

Dahl, T.E., 1990, Wetlands—Losses in the United States, 1780's to 1980's: Washington, D.C., U.S. Fish and Wildlife Service Report to Congress, 13 p.

Devaul, R.W., 1975, Probable yields of wells in the sand-and-gravel aquifer, Wisconsin: Madison, Wisconsin Geological and Natural History Survey map.

Fenneman, N.M., 1946, Physical divisions of the United States: Washington, D.C., U.S. Geological Survey special map, scale 1:7,000,000.

Frazier, B.E., and Kiefer, R.W., 1974, Generalized land cover interpreted from ERTS—1 satellite imagery: Madison, University of Wisconsin, Institute for Environmental Studies, LRAP Map No. 7.

Gebert, W.A.,1986 Wisconsin surface-water resources, *in* U.S. Geological Survey, National water summary 1985—Hydrologic events and surface-water resources: U.S. Geological Survey Water-Supply Paper 2300, p. 485–492.

Geis, J.W., 1985, Environmental influences on the distribution and composition of wetlands in the Great Lakes Basin, *in* Prince, H.H., and D'Itri, F.M., eds., Coastal wetlands: Chelsea, Mich., Lewis Publishers, Inc., p. 15–27.

Keddy, P.A., and Reznicek, A.A., 1985, Vegetation dynamics, buried seeds, and water level fluctuations on the shorelines of the Great Lakes, *in* Prince, H.H., and D'Itri, F.M., eds., Coastal wetlands: Chelsea, Mich., Lewis Publishers, Inc., p. 33–51.

Krohelski, J.T., Ellefson, B.R., and Rury, K.S., 1990, Wisconsin water supply and use, *in* U.S. Geological Survey, National water summary 1987—Water supply and use: U.S. Geological Survey Water-Supply Paper 2350, p. 531–538.

Mitsch, W.J., and Gosselink, J.G., 1986, Wetlands: New York, Van Nostrand Reinhold Company, 539 p.

Moriarty, M.E., 1992, Partners for Wildlife Program—Region 3 final report, fiscal year 1992: Washington D.C., U.S. Fish and Wildlife Service, 11 p.

Novitzki, R.P., 1979, An Introduction to Wisconsin wetlands—Plants, hydrology and soils: Wisconsin Geological and Natural History Survey Educational Information Series 22, 19 p.

_____1982, Hydrology of Wisconsin wetlands: Wisconsin Geological and Natural History Survey Information Circular 40, 22 p.

Wisconsin Department of Natural Resources, 1992a, Wisconsin water quality assessment report to Congress 1992: Madison, Wisconsin Department of Natural Resources, 220 p.

_____1992b, Wisconsin Wetland Inventory Classification Guide: Madison, Wisconsin Department of Natural Resources Publication W2–W2023, 3 p.

_____undated, Wisconsin wetlands priority plan—An addendum to Wisconsin's 1986–91 statewide comprehensive outdoor recreation plan: Madison, Wisconsin Department of Natural Resources, 22 p.

Yanggen, D.A., Johnson, C.D., Lee, G.B., Massie, L.R., Mulcahy, L.F., Ruff, R.L., and Schoenemann, J.A., 1976, Wisconsin wetlands: University of Wisconsin, Extension Publication G2818, 28 p.

FOR ADDITIONAL INFORMATION: District Chief, U.S. Geological Survey, 6417 Normandy Lane, Madison, WI 53719; Regional Wetland Coordinator, U.S. Fish and Wildlife Service, BHW Building, 1 Federal Drive, Fort Snelling, MN 55111

Prepared by
Annette C. Heist and Andrew G. Reif,
U.S. Geological Survey

Wyoming
Wetland Resources

Wetlands cover approximately 1.25 million acres of Wyoming according to estimates made in the 1980's (Dahl, 1990; University of Wyoming, 1990). Although wetlands comprise only about 2 percent of the State's area (Dahl, 1990), their ecologic and economic value is greater than their surface area might indicate. Wetlands are the most diverse ecosystems in Wyoming's semiarid environment. About 90 percent of the State's wildlife use wetlands daily (University of Wyoming, 1990). Wyoming wetlands support large numbers of breeding birds and many species of spring and fall migrants (fig. 1). Some waterfowl species, such as Canada geese, mallards, redheads, and the interior populations of trumpeter swans, use open water in the wetlands during the winter. Wetlands are the focus of varied recreational and tourist activities such as hunting, fishing, bird watching, camping, and hiking. Water and forage for Wyoming's livestock are provided by wetland areas.

Wetlands function as water reservoirs, linking surface and ground water, and as modulators of water quality (Odum, 1979). Their hydrologic functions include flood attenuation, water-quality improvement, water storage, and aquifer recharge and discharge. In the spring, wetlands usually receive flood waters, thereby attenuating flood peaks and reducing erosion. Wetlands can modulate water quality (Odum, 1979); water is stored in the wetlands, sediment settles out, and nutrients and heavy metals can be removed through biological and chemical processes. Depending on hydrologic conditions, aquifers may be recharged from wetland areas. Some wetlands slowly release water, augmenting streamflow and extending the period of flow later into the summer and fall.

Figure 1. American avocet at the Laramie Plain Lakes wetland complex. *(Photograph by LuRae Parker, Wyoming Game and Fish Department.)*

TYPES AND DISTRIBUTION

Wetlands are lands transitional between terrestrial and deepwater habitats where the water table usually is at or near the land surface or the land is covered by shallow water (Cowardin and oth-

ers, 1979). The distribution of wetlands and deepwater habitats in Wyoming is shown in figure 2*A*; only wetlands are discussed herein.

Wetlands can be vegetated or nonvegetated and are classified on the basis of their hydrology, vegetation, and substrate. In this summary, wetlands are classified according to the system proposed by Cowardin and others (1979), which is used by the U.S. Fish and Wildlife Service (FWS) to map and inventory the Nation's wetlands. At the most general level of the classification system, wetlands are grouped into five ecological systems: Palustrine, Lacustrine, Riverine, Estuarine, and Marine. The Palustrine System includes only wetlands, whereas the other systems comprise wetlands and deepwater habitats. Wetlands of the systems that occur in Wyoming are described below.

System	Wetland description
Palustrine	Wetlands in which vegetation is predominantly trees (forested wetlands); shrubs (scrub-shrub wetlands); persistent or nonpersistent emergent, erect, rooted, herbaceous plants (persistent- and nonpersistent-emergent wetlands); or submersed and (or) floating plants (aquatic beds). Also, intermittently to permanently flooded open-water bodies of less than 20 acres in which water is less than 6.6 feet deep.
Lacustrine	Wetlands within an intermittently to permanently flooded lake or reservoir. Vegetation, when present, is predominantly nonpersistent emergent plants (nonpersistent-emergent wetlands), or submersed and (or) floating plants (aquatic beds), or both.
Riverine	Wetlands within a channel. Vegetation, when present, is same as in the Lacustrine System.

There is no recent estimate for Wyoming of statewide wetland acreage in each of the three ecological systems; however, the FWS National Wetlands Inventory Program currently (1993) is mapping the State at a 1:24,000 scale. As of April 1993, only Yellowstone National Park (about 4 percent of the State) remained unmapped. Inventories of wetlands and permanent water areas significant to waterfowl were conducted in the 1950's by the FWS (U.S. Fish and Wildlife Service, 1955a,b). Those studies found 26 percent of Wyoming's wetlands to be palustrine, 35 percent mixed palustrine and lacustrine, 9 percent lacustrine, and 30 percent riverine. The inventories did not include many shallow plains basins and high mountain wetlands (C.R. Elliott, written commun., 1993); thus, it is not known if the percentages approximate the overall distribution of Wyoming's wetlands.

Wetlands are distributed throughout Wyoming (U.S. Fish and Wildlife Service, 1955a,b). Palustrine wetlands occur throughout Wyoming and include emergent wetlands such as seasonally flooded basins or flats, fresh marshes, fresh meadows, saline marshes, and playas; forested wetlands such as swamps; scrub-shrub wetlands such as shrub swamps and bogs; unconsolidated shore wetlands such as saline flats; and unconsolidated bottom wetlands such as small stock ponds. Freshwater wetlands are more concentrated in the mountainous areas, whereas the saline wetlands and stock ponds occur in greater density in the basins and plains (fig. 2*A*). Lacustrine wetlands discussed herein are limited to the shallows of reservoirs and naturally occurring lakes. Riverine wetlands associated with high-gradient streams are concentrated in the mountainous areas, whereas wetlands associated with low-gradient streams and intermittent streams are more prevalent in basins and plains.

Wetlands also are distributed throughout the State in areas not delineated in figure 2A. On a map of the scale of figure 2A, many of the smaller wetlands do not appear because of their size. However, these small wetlands are ecologically significant because they sometimes are the only source of water and specialized habitat in a large area. Ratti and Kadlec (1992) noted that wetlands, as all resources, gain value from scarcity. The presence of wetlands allows much broader use of the upland areas in arid or semiarid climates. Ratti and Kadlec (1992) stated that wetlands in arid and semiarid areas are used far more extensively than wetlands in humid regions, where wetlands are more abundant. An example of the distribution of these small wetlands is shown in figure 2B, an area near Ocean Lake.

HYDROLOGIC SETTING

Wetlands form where there is a water supply at or near the land surface. The location and persistence of the supply is a function of interdependent climatic, physiographic, and hydrologic factors including precipitation and runoff patterns, evaporation potential, topography, and ground-water discharge. There have been few, if

any, studies that examine the influence of those factors on the distribution of wetlands in Wyoming. However, published reports indicate that combinations of those factors create conditions that support wetlands in Wyoming in four settings: mountain ranges, river drainages, closed basins, and areas of human activity.

Wetlands exist in all the major mountain ranges in Wyoming. The Wyoming Basin separates the Middle Rocky Mountains from the Southern Rocky Mountains, which reach into southeastern Wyoming, and the Great Plains extend to the east (fig. 2C). The mountain ranges force air masses to rise to higher altitudes, where cooling causes increased precipitation (fig. 2D). The average annual precipitation ranges from more than 60 inches in mountainous areas to less than 6 inches in the Wyoming Basin (Martner, 1986). High precipitation and runoff in the mountains, coupled with low evaporation, create a net moisture surplus that allows wetlands to form. Ground-water storage at higher altitude, due to such factors as frequent storms, bedrock depressions, and shallow soils, keeps the water table close to land surface and enhances the development of the mountain wetlands (Skinner, 1986).

Semipermanently and permanently flooded palustrine and riverine wetlands are associated with river drainages throughout Wyoming. Many of these wetlands exist because water storage in moun-

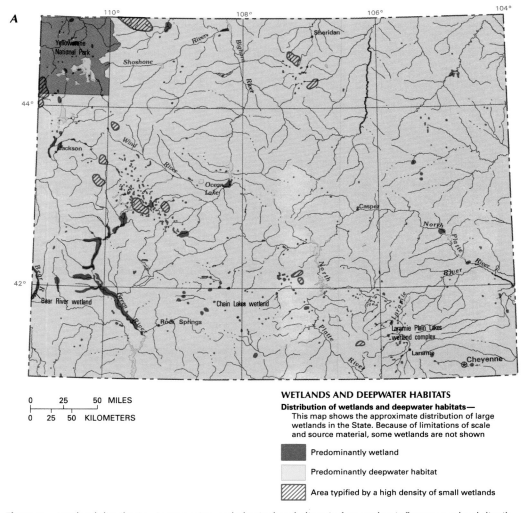

WETLANDS AND DEEPWATER HABITATS

Distribution of wetlands and deepwater habitats—
This map shows the approximate distribution of large wetlands in the State. Because of limitations of scale and source material, some wetlands are not shown

▓ Predominantly wetland

☐ Predominantly deepwater habitat

▨ Area typified by a high density of small wetlands

Figure 2.   Wetland distribution in Wyoming and physical and climatic factors that influence wetland distribution in the State. **A**, Distribution of wetlands and deepwater habitats. (*Sources: A, T.E. Dahl, U.S. Fish and Wildlife Service, unpub. data, 1991.*)

tainous areas, reservoirs, or aquifers extends the season of flow beyond the spring snowmelt period. In mountainous areas, water is stored in snowpack, lakes, bogs, riparian areas, and aquifers and then is gradually released from spring through fall. Runoff is higher in the mountains than in the basin and plains areas (fig. 2*E*). Several large reservoirs on the North Platte River, the Wind–Bighorn River system, and the Green River control streamflow by storing spring runoff and, later in the year, releasing the water to downstream users. The extended streamflow provides water to the associated wetlands over a longer period of time, but it limits overbank flooding, thus reducing spring flood moisture to riparian wetlands. Ground-water discharge supplies much of the base flow to rivers and wetlands on the plains of Wyoming. This base flow comes either from water stored in alluvial aquifers or discharged from deeper, bedrock aquifers. These different types of water storage provide the moisture necessary for the existence of wetlands along Wyoming's major drainages.

Playa wetlands exist in closed basins of various sizes throughout Wyoming. These wetlands may be saline or fresh, depending on local factors such as the hydrology and soils. Examples of saline playa wetlands can be found in the Chain Lakes of the Wyoming Basin. The Chain Lakes contain saline, shallow, palustrine emergent wetlands; palustrine and lacustrine unconsolidated shore wetlands; and seasonally flooded depressions. These wetlands lie within a salt-desert shrub- and sagebrush-covered basin that is one of the driest areas in Wyoming. Owing to the high evapotranspiration potential, the area has a net average annual water deficit of from 10 to 17 inches per year. The Chain Lakes wetlands are maintained by ground-water discharge where the land surface intersects with the water table, but their water level changes in response to precipitation and runoff (Charles Reed, Bureau of Land Management, oral commun., 1993). One attribute of such wetlands is their attenuation of the variability in the hydrologic cycle. In the arid and semiarid West, variability rather than stability may actually be the norm in the hydrologic cycle (Ratti and Kadlec, 1992). The cycle of wet and dry years causes constant fluctuations of water levels in lakes and streams. Playas that are dry in drought years take on special importance in wet years because many other wetlands are deeply

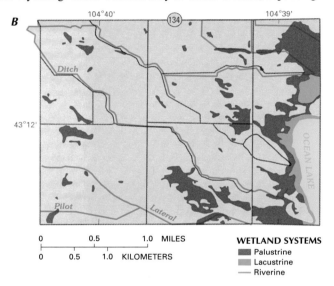

WETLAND SYSTEMS
■ Palustrine
▨ Lacustrine
— Riverine

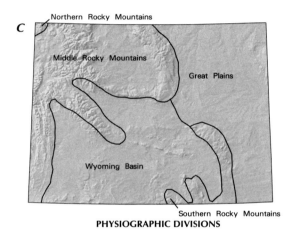

PHYSIOGRAPHIC DIVISIONS

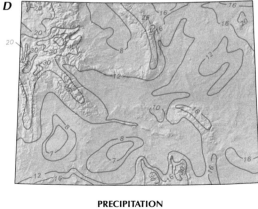

PRECIPITATION
—20— **Line of equal annual precipitation—**
Interval, in inches, is variable

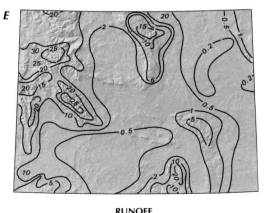

RUNOFF
—10— **Line of equal annual runoff—**
Interval, in inches, is variable

Figure 2.   Continued   Wetland distribution in Wyoming and physical and climatic factors that influence wetland distribution in the State. ***B***, Detail of wetlands west of Ocean Lake in the Wind River Basin. ***C***, Physiography. ***D***, Average annual precipitation. ***E***, Average annual runoff. *(Sources: B, Modified from U.S. Fish and Wildlife Service, 1987. C, Physiographic divisions from Fenneman, 1946; landforms data from EROS Data Center. D and E, Schuetz and others, 1986.*

flooded and their submersed vegetation is less available and productive. Ecologically, the fluctuation of water levels has interactive effects with the vegetation's germination, establishment, and competition, adding to the diversity or productivity of these sites (Ratti and Kadlec, 1992). Osterkamp and Wood (1987) found that water fluctuation also may aid in the development and enlargement of these playas through carbonate-rock dissolution, piping, and weathering.

The Laramie Plain Lakes wetland complex (fig. 3) consists of 5,500 acres of riverine, palustrine, and lacustrine wetlands associated with the Laramie River and small, closed basins (University of Wyoming, 1990). Many of the closed basins containing playa lakes in this complex are the result of blowouts (Kolm, 1982) caused by high winds funneled across the more than 7,000-foot-high plain between mountain ranges. Some lakes are fresh and others are saline. In addition to being significant habitat for many bird species (fig. 1), this complex of wetlands provides habitat for the Wyoming toad, an endangered species (fig. 3). When the glaciers retreated about 17,000 years ago, a population of Wyoming toad was stranded in the basin, where it adapted to a grassier, less forested environment (Johnson, 1985).

Some small wetlands result from human activities. Irrigation of farm lands, mining, and stock ponds associated with ranching have changed or created wetlands. An example of the interactive

effects of human activities and natural wetlands associated with a stream is the Bear River wetland, the most productive and diverse bird habitat in Wyoming. The area contains 23,000 acres of continuous wetlands; 97 percent are palustrine and 3 percent are riverine (D.C. Lockman and Leonard Serdiuk, Wyoming Game and Fish Department, written commun., 1984). These wetlands were enhanced by agricultural diversion of water during the spring high flows into the low-gradient flood-plain areas adjacent to the Bear River. The original purpose of the diversions was to flush salts and increase hay-meadow production. The complex hydrology of the Bear River system resulted in lengthening the wetland production period from the original spring runoff period of late May to mid-June to an extended period of late April to early July (D.C. Lockman and Leonard Serdiuk, written commun., 1984). The low gradient of the Bear River and the existence of old oxbows allowed a mosaic of marshes, other wet areas, and dry nesting areas to develop.

Wetlands have developed in stock ponds and in pits and depressions resulting from mining. Stock ponds generally receive only surface-water runoff and are concentrated in arid and semiarid basins. The wetlands associated with mining are scattered throughout the State and generally are the result of intersecting the water table during the excavation of the pit, although the wetlands can also

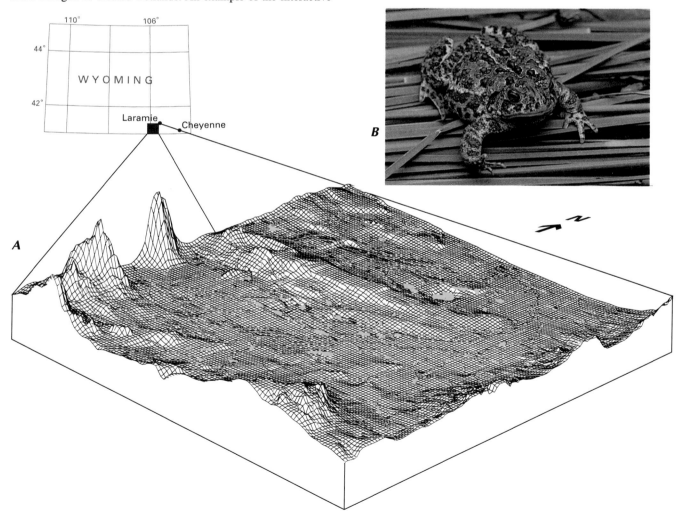

Figure 3.   Laramie Plain Lakes wetland complex and the resident endangered Wyoming toad. *A*, Laramie Plain Lakes wetland complex. *B*, Wyoming toad. *(Sources: A, Compiled by C.A. Eshelman, U.S. Geological Survey. B, Photograph by LuRae Parker, Wyoming Game and Fish Department.)*

receive surface-water runoff. Wetlands created during reclamation of bentonite-mine pits in northeastern Wyoming were designed to reduce water turbidity from colloids by settlement of sediment and establishment of vegetation (P.R. Ogle, Mariah Associates, oral commun., 1993). Some studies have compared strip-mine and stock-pond wetlands. Olson (1979) found that the concentration of chemical constituents in the water was inversely related to water levels and that strip-mine ponds had different chemical concentrations than stock ponds. Wangsness (1977) discovered that dissolved-oxygen concentrations were smaller, major-ion concentrations were larger, biological communities were less diverse, and chemical fluctuations were more pronounced in strip-mine ponds than in natural ponds in northwestern Wyoming near Sheridan.

TRENDS

Trends in the acreage and types of wetlands in Wyoming are the subject of controversy. Dahl (1990) estimated that between the 1780's and 1980's Wyoming lost 38 percent (by area) of its wetlands. Skinner (1986), in an examination of historic journals of Lewis and Clark, Captain John C. Fremont, and Osborne Russell, cites observations of changing hydrologic and riparian conditions over the 1804–1986 period that indicate a change in the type of wetlands along some major streams but do not necessarily support reports of large losses in wetland acreage.

Palustrine wetlands, particularly those created and maintained by seasonal flooding, have decreased in area, owing to agricultural and urban activities, although the loss has not been quantified (U.S. Fish and Wildlife Service, 1990). Knight (1991) reported that, in the Bighorn River flood plain between 1938 and 1986, woodlands decreased, shrublands increased, the area of meadow and marshes fluctuated before 1961 but stabilized since that time, and salt cedar increased. Knight (1991) suggests that some of these changes might have been related to the construction of dams on the Bighorn River.

Approximately 230,000 acres of deepwater reservoir habitat have been created in Wyoming. The operation of reservoirs for irrigation and power production can cause downstream water-level fluctuations that are unfavorable to the regeneration of riparian and other wetland vegetation (U.S. Fish and Wildlife Service, 1990). Conversely, flood-irrigation systems have created wetlands as a result of canal and dam seepage. Urban development, especially in the Jackson area, has resulted in both direct wetland loss and decline in wetland quality (U.S. Fish and Wildlife Service, 1990). Shallow pond acreage, primarily stock ponds, has increased substantially in Wyoming.

CONSERVATION

Many government agencies and private organizations participate in wetland conservation in Wyoming. The most active agencies and organizations and some of their activities are listed in table 1.

Federal wetland activities. — Development activities in Wyoming wetlands are regulated by several Federal statutory prohibitions and incentives that are intended to slow wetland losses. Some of the more important of these are contained in the 1899 Rivers and Harbors Act; the 1972 Clean Water Act and amendments; the 1985 Food Security Act; the 1990 Food, Agriculture, Conservation, and Trade Act; and the 1986 Emergency Wetlands Resources Act.

Section 10 of the Rivers and Harbors Act gives the U.S. Army Corps of Engineers (Corps) authority to regulate certain activities in navigable waters. Regulated activities include diking, deepening, filling, excavating, and placing of structures. The related section 404 of the Clean Water Act is the most often-used Federal legislation protecting wetlands. Under section 404 provisions, the Corps issues

Table 1. Selected wetland-related activities of government agencies and private organizations in Wyoming, 1993

[Source: Classification of activities is generalized from information provided by agencies and organizations. •, agency or organization participates in wetland-related activity; ..., agency or organization does not participate in wetland-related activity. MAN, management; REG, regulation; R&C, restoration and creation; LAN, land acquisition; R&D, research and data collection; D&I, delineation and inventory]

Agency or organization	MAN	REG	R&C	LAN	R&D	D&I
FEDERAL						
Department of Agriculture						
Consolidated Farm Service Agency	...	•	...	...	...	...
Forest Service	•	...	•	...	•	•
Natural Resources Conservation Service	...	•	...	...	•	•
Department of Commerce						
National Oceanic and Atmospheric Administration	...	...	...	...	•	...
Department of Defense						
Army Corps of Engineers	•	•	•	...	...	•
Military reservations	•	...	...	...	...	...
Department of the Interior						
Bureau of Land Management	•	...	•	...	•	•
Bureau of Reclamation	...	...	•	...	•	...
Fish and Wildlife Service	•	...	•	•	•	•
Geological Survey	...	...	...	...	•	...
National Biological Service	...	...	...	...	•	•
National Park Service	•	...	•	•	•	...
Environmental Protection Agency	...	•	...	...	...	•
NORTHERN ARAPAHO AND EASTERN SHOSHONE TRIBES	•	•	•	•	•	•
STATE						
Department of Agriculture	...	•	...	...	...	...
Department of Commerce						
Economic and Community Development	•	...	•	•	...	...
Department of Environmental Quality						
Abandoned Mine Land Division	...	•	•	...	...	•
Industrial Siting	...	•	...	...	...	...
Land Quality Division	...	•	...	...	...	•
Solid and Hazardous Waste	...	•	...	...	...	•
Water Quality Division	...	•	...	...	...	•
Department of Transportation	...	•	...	...	...	...
Game and Fish Department	•	•	•	...	•	•
Geological Survey	...	...	...	...	•	...
Oil and Gas Commission	...	•	...	...	•	...
State Engineer's Office	...	•	...	...	•	...
State Land and Farm Loan Board	•	...	...	...	...	...
University of Wyoming	...	...	...	...	•	...
Water Development Commission	•	...	•	...	...	•
COUNTY AND LOCAL	...	...	•	...	...	•
PRIVATE ORGANIZATIONS						
Ducks Unlimited	•	...	•	•	...	•
Powder River Resource Council	...	...	...	...	•	...
The National Audubon Society	•	...	•	...	•	•
The Nature Conservancy	•	...	•	•	•	•
Pheasants Forever	•	•	•	•	...	...
Trout Unlimited	•	...	•	•	•	...
Wyoming Association of Conservation Districts	•	...	•	...	...	...
Wyoming Riparian Association	...	...	...	...	•	...
Wyoming Stockgrowers Association	...	•	...	...	...	...
Wyoming Wildlife Federation	...	•	...	...	...	...

permits regulating the discharge of dredged or fill material into wetlands. Permits are subject to review and possible veto by the U.S. Environmental Protection Agency, and the FWS has review and advisory roles. Section 401 of the Clean Water Act grants to States and eligible Indian Tribes the authority to approve, apply conditions to, or deny section 404 permit applications on the basis of a proposed activity's probable effects on the water quality of a wetland.

Most farming, ranching, and silviculture activities are not subject to section 404 regulation. However, the "Swampbuster" provision of the 1985 Food Security Act and amendments in the 1990 Food, Agriculture, Conservation, and Trade Act discourage (through financial disincentives) the draining, filling, or other alteration of wetlands for agricultural use. The law allows exemptions from penalties in some cases, especially if the farmer agrees to restore the altered wetland or other wetlands that have been converted to agricultural use. The Wetlands Reserve Program of the 1990 Food, Agriculture, Conservation, and Trade Act authorizes the Federal Government to purchase conservation easements from landowners who agree to protect or restore wetlands. The Consolidated Farm Service Agency (formerly the Agricultural Stabilization and Conservation Service) administers the Swampbuster provisions and Wetlands Reserve Program. The Natural Resources Conservation Service (formerly the Soil Conservation Service) determines compliance with Swampbuster provisions and assists farmers in the identification of wetlands and in the development of wetland protection, restoration, or creation plans.

The 1986 Emergency Wetlands Resources Act encourages wetland protection through funding incentives. The act requires States to address wetland protection in their Statewide Comprehensive Outdoor Recreation Plans to qualify for Federal funding for State recreational land; the National Park Service provides guidance to States in developing the wetland component of their plans.

State wetland activities. — The Wyoming Wetlands Act is the basis for wetland program development by the State. The act designates the Wyoming Department of Environmental Quality's Water Quality Division as the lead agency for developing guidance for the evaluation of wetland ecological functions and values and for establishment of a statewide wetland-mitigation bank. Section 35–11–309(d) of Wyoming Statutes and the Legislative Policy and Intent of the Wyoming Wetlands Act differentiates between naturally occurring wetlands and wetlands resulting from human activities. As part of the Wyoming Wetlands Act, the State is considering the use of a wetland bank for tracking and mitigation of wetland disturbance and for creation management. Use of water, an essential part of any wetland, also is regulated by State laws, seven interstate compacts, and various U.S. Supreme Court decrees (Wolfe, 1986).

County and local wetland activities. — Wetland activities at county and local government levels differ throughout the State. Wetland considerations commonly are addressed as part of the county zoning or land-use plans in Wyoming's 23 counties. Conservation Districts often are active in implementing wetland projects.

Private wetland activities. — Ducks Unlimited and The Nature Conservancy are active in the acquisition and management of wetland areas. Other organizations participating in wetland-protection activities in Wyoming include Trout Unlimited, the National Audubon Society, the Powder River Resource Council, the Wyoming Wildlife Federation, the Wyoming Stockgrowers Association, the Wyoming Riparian Association, and the Sierra Club.

References Cited

Cowardin, L.M., Carter, Virginia, Golet, F.C., and LaRoe, E.T., 1979, Classification of wetlands and deepwater habitats of the United States: U.S. Fish and Wildlife Service Report FWS/OBS–79/31, 131 p.

Dahl, T.E., 1990, Wetlands—Losses in the United States, 1780's to 1980's: Washington, D.C., U.S. Fish and Wildlife Service Report to Congress, 13 p.

Fenneman, N.M., 1946, Physical divisions of the United States: Washington, D.C., U.S. Geological Survey special map, scale 1:7,000,000.

Johnson, Kevin, 1985, More time for the Wyoming toad: Wyoming Wildlife, v. 1L, no. 5, p. 28–33.

Knight, Dennis, 1991, Riparian vegetation dynamics, *in* Proceedings of the Riparian Workshop, August 20–22, 1991: Laramie, University of Wyoming, p. 24–32.

Kolm, K.E., 1982, Predicting the surface wind characteristics of southern Wyoming from remote sensing and eolian geomorphology, *in* Marrs, R.W., and Kolm, K.E., eds., Interpretation of windflow characteristics from eolian landforms: Geological Society of America Special Paper 192, p. 25–53.

Martner, B.E., 1986, Wyoming climate atlas: Lincoln, University of Nebraska Press, 432 p.

Odum, E.P., 1979, The value of wetlands—A hierarchical approach, *in* Greeson, P.E., and others, eds., Wetland functions and values—The state of our understanding—Proceedings of the National Symposium on Wetlands, November 1978, Minneapolis, Minn.: American Water Resources Association, p. 16–25.

Olson, R.A., 1979, Ecology of wetland vegetation on selected strip mine ponds and stockdams in the northern Great Plains: Fargo, North Dakota State University, Ph.D. thesis, 476 p.

Osterkamp, W.R., and Wood, W.W., 1987, Playa-lake basins on the southern High Plains of Texas and New Mexico—Part 1, Hydrologic, geomorphic, and geologic evidence for their development: Geological Society of America Bulletin, v. 99, p. 215–223.

Ratti, J.T., and Kadlec, J.A., 1992, Concept plan for the preservation of wetland habitat of the intermountain West, North American waterfowl management plan: U.S. Fish and Wildlife Service Region 1, Portland, Oreg., 146 p.

Schuetz, J.R., Trefren, D.A., and Lowham, H.W., 1986, Wyoming surface-water resources, *in* U.S. Geological Survey, National water summary 1985—Hydrologic events and surface-water resources: U.S. Geological Survey Water-Supply Paper 2300, p. 493–498.

Skinner, Q.D., 1986, Riparian zones then and now, *in* Proceedings of the Wyoming Water 1986 and Streamside Zone Conference, Casper, April 28–30, 1986: Casper, Wyoming Water Research Center and University of Wyoming Agricultural Extension Service, p. 8–22.

U.S. Fish and Wildlife Service, 1955a, Wetlands inventory of Wyoming: Billings, Mont., U.S. Fish and Wildlife Service, 33 p.

_____1955b, Permanent water inventory—Wyoming: Billings, Mont., U.S. Fish and Wildlife Service, 9 p.

_____1987, U.S. Fish and Wildlife Service National Wetlands Inventory map—Pavillion, Wyo., quadrangle: St. Petersburg, Fla., U.S. Fish and Wildlife Service, scale 1:24,000.

_____1990, Regional wetlands concept plan—Emergency Wetlands Resources Act: Lakewood, Colo., U.S. Fish and Wildlife Service, Mountain-Prairie Region, 90 p.

University of Wyoming, 1990, Wyoming State comprehensive outdoor recreation plan: Cheyenne, Wyo., Department of Commerce, 274 p.

Wangsness, D.J., 1977, Physical, chemical, and biological relations of four ponds in the Hidden Water Creek strip-mine area, Powder River Basin, Wyoming: U.S. Geological Survey Water-Resources Investigations Report 77–72, 48 p.

Wolfe, L.J., 1986, Federal/State water laws, *in* Proceedings of the Wyoming Water 1986 and Streamside Zone Conference, Casper, April 28–30, 1986: Casper, Wyoming Water Research Center and University of Wyoming Agricultural Extension Service, p. 24–32.

FOR ADDITIONAL INFORMATION: District Chief, U.S. Geological Survey, 2617 East Lincolnway, Suite B, Cheyenne, WY 82001; Regional Wetland Coordinator, U.S. Fish and Wildlife Service, Fish and Wildlife Enhancement, P.O. Box 25486, Denver Federal Center, Denver, CO 80225

Prepared by
Kathy Muller Ogle,
U.S. Geological Survey

Conversion Table and Glossary

Sunset on the San Joaquin Delta near Stockton, California. *(Photograph by Steve Van Denburgh, U.S. Geological Survey.)*

Conversion Factors

The following list provides the necessary factors for converting U.S. Customary (inch-pound) units used in this National Water Summary to International System (metric) and other commonly used U.S. Customary units. Units, which are written in abbreviated form below, are spelled out in parentheses the first time that they appear. Most of the quantities listed are rounded to five significant figures. However, quantities shown in italics are exact equivalents—no rounding was necessary. To convert the unit in the left-hand column to that in the right, multiply by the number in the right-hand column, except for temperature. For temperature, use the equation provided.

The data in this list were adapted largely from information found in the following publications:
Chisholm, L.J., 1967, Units of weight and measure—International (Metric) and U.S. Customary:
    U.S. National Bureau of Standards Miscellaneous Publication 286, 251 p.
U.S. Geological Survey, 1919, Hydraulic conversion tables and convenient equivalents (2d ed.): U.S.
    Geological Survey Water-Supply Paper 425–C, p. C71–C94.

U.S. CUSTOMARY (INCH-POUND)		U.S. CUSTOMARY (INCH-POUND) OR INTERNATIONAL SYSTEM (METRIC)
LENGTH		
1 in (inch)	=	*25.4* mm (millimeters)
1 ft (foot)	=	*0.3048* m (meter)
1 mi (mile)	=	*5,280.* ft
	=	*1,609.344* m
	=	*1.609344* km (kilometers)
AREA		
1 ft^2 (square foot)	=	*0.09290304* m^2 (square meter)
1 acre	=	*43,560.* ft^2 (square feet)
	=	*0.0015625* mi^2 (square mile)
	=	0.40469 ha (hectare)
	=	4,046.9 m^2
1 mi^2	=	*640.* acres
	=	259.00 ha
	=	2.5900 km^2 (square kilometers)
VOLUME OR CAPACITY (liquid measure)		
1 gal (gallon, U.S.)	=	*231.* in^3 (cubic inches)
	=	0.13368 ft^3 (cubic foot)
	=	3.7854 L (liter)
	=	0.0037854 m^3 (cubic meter)
1 Mgal (million gallons)	=	3.0689 acre-ft (acre-feet)
1 ft^3	=	*1,728.* in^3
	=	7.4805 gal
	=	28.317 L
	=	0.028317 m^3
1 acre-ft*	=	*43,560.* ft^3
	=	0.32585 Mgal
	=	*1,233.5* m^3
SPEED		
1 mi/hr (mile per hour)	=	1.4667 ft/s (feet per second)
	=	*0.44704* m/s (meter per second)
VOLUME PER UNIT OF TIME		
1 ft^3/s (cubic foot per second)	=	448.83 gal/min
	=	0.64632 Mgal/d
	=	1.9835 acre-ft/d (acre-feet per day)
	=	28.317 L/s (liters per second)
TEMPERATURE [°F (degrees, Fahrenheit) to °C (degrees, Celsius)]		
(°F − 32) x 5/9 = °C		

* Volume of water 1 foot deep covering an area of 1 acre.

Glossary

Absorption—the process by which substances in gaseous, liquid, or solid form are assimilated or taken up by other substances.

Acid—pH of water less than 5.5; pH modifier used in the U.S. Fish and Wildlife Service wetland classification system.

Acidic—has a pH of less than 7.

Acidic deposition—the transfer of acidic or acidifying substances from the atmosphere to the surface of the Earth or to objects on its surface. Transfer can be either by wet-deposition processes (rain, snow, dew, fog, frost, hail) or by dry deposition (gases, aerosols, or fine to coarse particles).

Acre-foot (acre-ft)—the volume of water needed to cover an acre of land to a depth of one foot; equivalent to 43,560 cubic feet or 325,851 gallons.

Adsorption—the adherence of gas molecules, ions, or molecules in solution to the surface of solids.

Aerate—to supply air to water, soil, or other media.

Aerobic—pertaining to or caused by the presence of oxygen.

Algal bloom—the rapid proliferation of passively floating, simple plant life, such as blue-green algae, in and on a body of water.

Alkaline—has a pH greater than 7; pH modifier in the U.S. Fish and Wildlife Service wetland classification system; in common usage, a pH of water greater than 7.4.

Alluvium—general term for sediments of gravel, sand, silt, clay, or other particulate rock material deposited by flowing water, usually in the beds of rivers and streams, on a flood plain, on a delta, or at the base of a mountain.

Alpine snow glade—a marshy clearing between slopes above the timberline in mountains.

Anadromous fish—migratory species that are born in freshwater, live mostly in estuaries and ocean water, and return to freshwater to spawn.

Anaerobic—pertaining to or caused by the absence of oxygen.

Anthropogenic—having to do with or caused by humans.

Anticline—a fold in the Earth's crust, convex upward, whose core contains stratigraphically older rocks.

Aquatic—living or growing in or on water.

Aquaculture—the science of farming organisms that live in water, such as fish, shellfish, and algae.

Aquifer—a geologic formation, group of formations, or part of a formation that contains sufficient saturated permeable material to yield significant quantities of water to springs and wells.

Arroyo—a small, deep, flat-floored channel or gully of an ephemeral or intermittent stream, usually with nearly vertical banks cut into unconsolidated material—term commonly used in the arid and semiarid regions of the Southwestern United States.

Atmospheric pressure—the pressure exerted by the atmosphere on any surface beneath or within it; equal to 14.7 pounds per square inch at sea level.

Backwater—a body of water in which the flow is slowed or turned back by an obstruction such as a bridge or dam, an opposing current, or the movement of the tide.

Bacteria—single-celled microscopic organisms.

Bank storage—the change in the amount of water stored in an aquifer resulting from a change in stage of an adjacent surface-water body.

Barrier bar—an elongate offshore ridge submerged at least at high tide, built up by the action of waves or currents.

Barrier beach—a narrow, elongate sandy ridge rising slightly above the high-tide level and extending generally parallel with the mainland shore, but separated from it by a lagoon.

Base flow—the sustained low flow of a stream, usually ground-water inflow to the stream channel.

Basic—the opposite of acidic; has a pH of greater than 7.

Bed material—sediment composing the streambed.

Bedrock—a general term used for solid rock that underlies soils or other unconsolidated material.

Benthic organism—a form of aquatic life that lives on the bottom or near the bottom of streams, lakes, or oceans.

Bind—to exert a strong chemical attraction.

Biochemical-oxygen demand (BOD)—the amount of oxygen, in milligrams per liter, that is removed from aquatic environments by the life processes of micro-organisms.

Biochemical process—a process characterized by, produced by, or involving chemical reactions in living organisms.

Biomass—the amount of living matter, in the form of organisms, present in a particular habitat, usually expressed as weight-per-unit area.

Biota—all living organisms of an area.

Blowout—a small saucer or trough-shaped hollow or depression formed by wind erosion on a pre-existing dune or other sand deposit.

Bog—a nutrient-poor, acidic wetland dominated by a waterlogged spongy mat of sphagum moss that ultimately forms a thick layer of acidic peat; generally has no inflow or outflow; fed primarily by rain water.

Bolson—an extensive, flat, saucer-shaped, alluvium-floored basin or depression, almost or completely surrounded by mountains and from which drainage has no surface outlet; a term used in the desert regions of the Southwestern United States.

Boreal—a climatic zone having a definite winter with snow and a short summer that is generally hot, and which is characterized by a large annual range of temperature.

Bosque—a dense growth of trees and underbrush.

Bottom land—See flood plain.

Bottom-land forest—low-lying forested wetland found along streams and rivers, usually on alluvial flood plains.

Brackish water—water with a salinity intermediate between seawater and freshwater (containing from 1,000 to 10,000 milligrams per liter of dissolved solids).

Braided river—a river that divides into or follows an interlacing or tangled network of several small branching and reuniting shallow channels.

Brine—water that contains more than 35,000 milligrams per liter of dissolved solids.

Calcareous—formed of calcium carbonate or magnesium carbonate by biological deposition or inorganic precipitation in sufficient quantities to effervesce when treated with cold hydrochloric acid.

Caldera—a large, more or less circular, basin-shaped volcanic depression whose diameter is many times greater than the volcanic vent.

Channel scour—erosion by flowing water and sediment on a stream channel; results in removal of mud, silt, and sand on the outside curve of a stream bend and the bed material of a stream channel.

Channelization—the straightening and deepening of a stream channel to permit the water to move faster or to drain a wet area for farming.

Cienaga—a marshy area where the ground is wet due to the presence of seepage or springs.

Circumneutral—pH of water between 5.5 and 7.4; pH modifier used in the U.S. Fish and Wildlife Service wetland classification system.

Cirque—a deep, steep-walled half-bowllike recess or hollow situated high on the side of a mountain and commonly at the head of a glacial valley and produced by the erosive activity of mountain glaciers.

Concentration—the ratio of the quantity of any substance present in a sample of a given volume or a given weight compared to the volume or weight of the sample.

Confining layer—a body of impermeable or distinctly less permeable material stratigraphically adjacent to one or more aquifers that restricts the movement of water into and out of the aquifers.

Conglomerate—a coarse-grained sedimentary rock composed of fragments larger than 2 millimeters in diameter.

Contact recreation—recreational activities where there is prolonged or intimate contact with water and in which there is a likelihood of ingesting water.

Contributing area—the area in a drainage basin that contributes water to streamflow or recharge to an aquifer.

Coral reef—a ridge of limestone, composed chiefly of coral, coral sands, and solid limestone resulting from organic secretion of calcium carbonate; occur along continents and islands where the temperature is generally above 18° C.

Core sample—a sample of rock, soil, or other material obtained by driving a hollow tube into the undisturbed medium and withdrawing it with its contained sample.

Cypress dome—small, isolated, circular, depressional, forested wetlands, in which cypress predominates, that have convex silhouettes when viewed from a distance.

Deciduous—shedding foliage at the end of the growing season.

Deepwater habitat—permanently flooded lands lying below the deepwater boundary of wetlands.

Degraded—condition of the quality of water that has been made unfit for some specified purpose.

Delta—the low, nearly flat tract of land at or near the mouth of a river, resulting from the accumulation of sediment supplied by the river in such quantities that it is not removed by tides, waves, or currents. Commonly a triangular or fan-shaped plain.

Direct runoff—the runoff entering stream channels promptly after rainfall or snowmelt.

Discharge—the volume of fluid passing a point per unit of time, commonly expressed in cubic feet per second, million gallons per day, gallons per minute, or seconds per minute per day.

Discharge area (ground water)—area where subsurface water is discharged to the land surface, to surface water, or to the atmosphere.

Dissolved oxygen—oxygen dissolved in water; one of the most important indicators of the condition of a water body. Dissolved oxygen is necessary for the life of fish and most other aquatic organisms.

Dissolved solids—minerals and organic matter dissolved in water.

Dolomite—a sedimentary rock consisting chiefly of magnesium carbonate.

Dominant plant—the plant species controlling the environment.

Drainage basin—the land area drained by a river or stream.

Drought—a prolonged period of less-than-normal precipitation such that the lack of water causes a serious hydrologic imbalance.

Ecosystem—a community of organisms considered together with the nonliving factors of its environment.

Emergent plants—erect, rooted, herbaceous plants that may be temporarily to permanently flooded at the base but do not tolerate prolonged inundation of the entire plant.

Endangered species—a species that is in imminent danger of becoming extinct.

Environment—the sum of all conditions and influences affecting the life of organisms.

Ephemeral stream—a stream or part of a stream that flows only in direct response to precipitation; it receives little or no water from springs, melting snow, or other sources; its channel is at all times above the water table.

Erosion—the process whereby materials of the Earth's crust are loosened, dissolved, or worn away and simultaneously moved from one place to another.

Estuarine wetlands—tidal wetlands in low-wave-energy environments where the salinity of the water is greater than 0.5 part per thousand and is variable owing to evaporation and the mixing of seawater and freshwater; tidal wetlands of coastal rivers and embayments, salty tidal marshes, mangrove swamps, and tidal flats.

Estuary—area where the current of a stream meets the ocean and where tidal effects are evident; an arm of the ocean at the lower end of a river.

Eutrophication—the process by which water becomes enriched with plant nutrients, most commonly phosphorus and nitrogen.

Evaporation—the process by which water is changed to gas or vapor; occurs directly from water surfaces and from the soil.

Evaporites—a class of sedimentary rocks composed primarily of minerals precipitated from a saline solution as a result of extensive or total evaporation of water.

Evapotranspiration—a term that includes water discharged to the atmosphere as a result of evaporation from the soil and surface-water bodies and by plant transpiration.

Exotic species—plants or animals not native to the area.

Fall line—imaginary line marking the boundary between the ancient, resistant crystalline rocks of the Piedmont province of the Appalachian Mountains, and the younger, softer sediments of the Atlantic Coastal Plain province in the Eastern United States. Along rivers, this line commonly is reflected by waterfalls.

Fallow—cropland, tilled or untilled, allowed to lie idle during the whole or greater part of the growing season.

Fen—peat-accumulating wetland that generally receives water from surface runoff and (or) seepage from mineral soils in addition to direct precipitation; generally alkaline; or slightly acid.

Filtrate—liquid that has been passed through a filter.

Flood—any relatively high streamflow that overflows the natural or artificial banks of a stream.

Flood attenuation—a weakening or reduction in the force or intensity of a flood.

Flood plain—a strip of relatively flat land bordering a stream channel that is overflowed at times of high water.

Fluvial—pertaining to a river or stream.

Flyway—a specific air route taken by birds during migration.

Freshwater—water with less than 1,000 milligrams per liter of dissolved solids.

Friable—descriptive of a rock or mineral that crumbles naturally or is easily broken, pulverized, or reduced to powder.

Geomorphic—pertaining to the form of the Earth or of its surface features.

Geomorphology—the science that treats the general configuration of the Earth's surface; the description of landforms.

Glacial—of or relating to the presence and activities of ice or glaciers.

Glacial drift—a general term for rock material transported by glaciers or icebergs and deposited directly on land or in the sea.

Glacial lake—a lake that derives its water, or much of its water, from the melting of glacial ice; also a lake that occupies a basin produced by glacial erosion.

Glacial outwash—stratified detritus (chiefly sand and gravel) "washed out" from a glacier by meltwater streams and deposited in front of or beyond the end moraine or the margin of an active glacier.

Ground water—in the broadest sense, all subsurface water; more commonly that part of the subsurface water in the saturated zone.

Ground-water flow system—the underground pathway by which ground water moves from areas of recharge to areas of discharge.

Growing season—the frost-free period of the year.

Habitat—the part of the physical environment in which a plant or animal lives.

Hardpan—a relatively hard, impervious, and usually clayey layer of soil lying at or just below land surface—produced as a result of cementation by precipitation of insoluble minerals.

Herbaceous—with characteristics of an herb; a plant with no persistent woody stem above ground.

Herbicide—a type of pesticide designed to kill plants.

Hydraulic head—the height of the free surface of a body of water above a given point beneath the surface.

Hydraulic gradient—the change of hydraulic head per unit of distance in a given direction.

Hydric soil—soil that is wet long enough to periodically produce anaerobic conditions, thereby influencing the growth of plants.

Hydrologic cycle—the circulation of water from the sea, through the atmosphere, to the land, and thence back to the sea by overland and subterranean routes.

Hydrology—the science that deals with water as it occurs in the atmosphere, on the surface of the ground, and underground.

Hydrophyte—any plant growing in water or on a substrate that is at least periodically deficient in oxygen as a result of excessive water content.

Hydrostatic pressure—the pressure exerted by the water at any given point in a body of water at rest.

Hydrologic regime—the characteristic behavior and total quantity of water involved in a drainage basin.

Igneous rocks—rocks that have solidified from molten or partly molten material.

Immobilize—to hold by a strong chemical attraction.

Impaired—condition of the quality of water that has been adversely affected for a specific use by contamination or pollution.

Indurated—cemented, hardened, or a rocklike condition.

Infiltration—the downward movement of water from the atmosphere into soil or porous rock.

Inorganic—containing no carbon; matter other than plant or animal.

Inorganic soil—soil with less than 20 percent organic matter in the upper 16 inches.

Integrated drainage—drainage developed during maturity in an arid region, characterized by coalescence of drainage basins as a result of headward erosion in the lower basins or spilling over from the upper basins.

Interface—in hydrology, the contact zone between two fluids of different chemical or physical makeup.

Intermittent stream—a stream that flows only when it receives water from rainfall runoff or springs, or from some surface source such as melting snow.

Intermontane—situated between or surrounded by mountains, mountain ranges, or mountainous regions.

Internal drainage—surface drainage whereby the water does not reach the ocean, such as drainage toward the lowermost or central part of an interior basin.

Intertidal—alternately flooded and exposed by tides.

Ion—a positively or negatively charged atom or group of atoms.

Irrigation—controlled application of water to arable land to supply requirements of crops not satisfied by rainfall.

Karst—a type of topography that results from dissolution and collapse of carbonate rocks such as limestone, dolomite, and gypsum, and that is characterized by closed depressions or sinkholes, caves, and underground drainage.

Kettle—a steep-sided hole or depression, commonly without surface drainage, formed by the melting of a large detached block of stagnant ice that had been buried in the glacial drift.

Kettle lake—a body of water occupying a kettle, as in a pitted outwash plain or in a kettle moraine.

Lacustrine—pertaining to, produced by, or formed in a lake.

Lacustrine wetlands—wetlands within a lake or reservoir greater than 20 acres or within a lake or reservoir less than 20 acres if the water is greater than 2 meters deep in the deepest part of the basin; ocean-derived salinity is less than 0.5 part per thousand.

Lagoon—a shallow stretch of seawater (or lakewater) near or communicating with the sea (or lake) and partly or completely separated from it by a low, narrow, elongate strip of land.

Latent heat—the amount of heat given up or absorbed when a substance changes from one state to another, such as from a liquid to a solid.

Lateral moraine—a low ridgelike moraine carried on, or deposited near, the side margin of a mountain glacier.

Leachate—a liquid that has percolated through soil containing soluble substances and that contains certain amounts of these substances in solution.

Life zone—major area of plant and animal life; region characterized by particular plants and animals and distinguished by temperature differences.

Limestone—a sedimentary rock consisting chiefly of calcium carbonate, primarily in the form of the mineral calcite.

Limnetic—the deepwater zone (greater than 2 meters deep); a subsystem of the Lacustrine System of the U.S. Fish and Wildlife Service wetland classification system.

Littoral—the shallow-water zone (less than 2 meters deep); a subsystem of the Lacustrine System of the U.S. Fish and Wildlife Service wetland classification system.

Load—material that is moved or carried by streams, reported as weight of material transported during a specified time period, such as tons per year.

Loess—a widespread, homogeneous, commonly nonstratified, porous, friable, slightly coherent, fine-grained blanket deposit of wind-blown and wind-deposited silt and fine sand.

Main stem—the principal trunk of a river or a stream.

Marine wetland—wetlands that are exposed to waves and currents of the open ocean and to water having a salinity greater than 30 parts per thousand; present along the coastlines of the open ocean.

Marsh—a water-saturated, poorly drained area, intermittently or permanently water covered, having aquatic and grasslike vegetation.

Maturity—a stage in the evolutionary erosion of land areas where the flat uplands have been widely dissected by deep river valleys.

Maturity (stream)—the stage in the development of a stream at which it has reached its maximum efficiency, when velocity is just sufficient to carry the sediment delivered to it by tributaries; characterized by a broad, open, flat-floored valley having a moderate gradient and gentle slope.

Mean low tide—the average altitude of all low tides recorded at a given place over a 19-year period.

Mean high tide—the average altitude of all high tides recorded at a given place over a 19-year period.

Mesophyte—any plant growing where moisture and aeration conditions lie between the extremes of "wet" and "dry."

Metamorphic rocks—rocks derived from preexisting rocks by mineralogical, chemical, or structural changes (essentially in a solid state) in response to marked changes in temperature, pressure, shearing stress, and chemical environment at depth in the Earth's crust.

Mineral soil—soil composed predominantly of mineral rather than organic materials; less than 20 percent organic material.

Mitigation—actions taken to avoid, reduce, or compensate for the effects of human-induced environmental damage.

Montane—of, pertaining to, or inhabiting cool upland slopes below the timber line; characterized by the dominance of evergreen trees.

Moraine—a mound, ridge, or other distinct accumulation of unsorted, unstratified glacial drift, predominantly till, deposited chiefly by direct action of glacier ice.

Muck—dark, finely divided, well-decomposed, organic matter forming a surface deposit in some poorly drained areas.

Muskeg—large expanses of peatlands or bogs that occur in subarctic zones.

National Geodetic Vertical Datum of 1929—geodetic datum derived from a general adjustment of first-order level nets of the United States and Canada—formerly called "Sea Level Datum of 1929."

Natural levee—a long, broad, low ridge built by a stream on its flood plain along one or both banks of its channel in time of flood.

Navigable water—in the context of the Clean Water Act, all surface water.

Noncontact water recreation—recreational activities, such as fishing or boating, that do not include direct contact with the water.

Nonpersistent emergent plants—emergent plants whose leaves and stems break down at the end of the growing season from decay or by the physical forces of waves and ice; at certain seasons, there are no visible traces of the plants above the surface of the water.

Nonpoint source—a source (of any water-carried material) from a broad area, rather than from discrete points.

Nuisance species—undesirable plants and animals, commonly exotic species.

Nutrient—any inorganic or organic compound needed to sustain plant life.

Organic—containing carbon, but possibly also containing hydrogen, oxygen, chlorine, nitrogen, and other elements.

Organic soil—soil that contains more than 20 percent organic matter in the upper 16 inches.

Orographic—pertaining to mountains, in regard to their location and distribution; said of the precipitation caused by the lifting of moisture-laden air over mountains.

Overland flow—the flow of rainwater or snowmelt over the land surface toward stream channels.

Oxbow—a bow-shaped lake formed in an abandoned meander of a river.

Palustrine wetlands—freshwater wetlands including open water bodies of less than 20 acres in which water is less than 2 meters deep; includes marshes, wet meadows, fens, playas, potholes, pocosins, bogs, swamps, and shallow ponds; most wetlands are in the Palustrine system.

Pathogen—any living organism that causes disease.

Peat—a highly organic soil, composed of partially decomposed vegetable matter.

Perched ground water—unconfined ground water separated from an underlying main body of ground water by an unsaturated zone.

Percolation—the movement, under hydrostatic pressure, of water through interstices of a rock or soil (except the movement through large openings such as caves).

Periphyton—micro-organisms that coat rocks, plants, and other surfaces on lake bottoms.

Perennial stream—a stream that normally has water in its channel at all times.

Permafrost—any frozen soil, subsoil, surficial deposit, or bedrock in arctic or subarctic regions where below-freezing temperatures have existed continuously from two to tens of thousands of years.

Permeability—the capacity of a rock for transmitting a fluid; a measure of the relative ease with which a porous medium can transmit a liquid.

Pesticide—any substance used to kill plant or animal pests; major categories of pesticides include herbicides and insecticides.

pH—a measure of the acidity (less than 7) or alkalinity (greater than 7) of a solution; a pH of 7 is considered neutral.

Photosynthesis—the synthesis of compounds with the aid of light.

Physiographic province—a region in which the land-forms differ significantly from those of adjacent regions.

Physiography—a description of the surface features of the Earth, with an emphasis on the mode or origin.

Pioneer plant—herbaceous annual and perennial seedling plants that colonize bare areas as a first stage in secondary succession.

Piping—erosion by percolating water in a layer of subsoil, resulting in caving and in the formation of narrow conduits, tunnels, or "pipes" through which soluble or granular soil material is removed.

Placer—a surficial mineral deposit formed by mechanical concentration of mineral particles from weathered debris.

Playa—a dry, flat area at the lowest part of an undrained desert basin in which water accumulates and is quickly evaporated; underlain by stratified clay, silt, or sand and commonly by soluble salts; term used in Southwestern United States.

Playa lake—a shallow, temporary lake in an arid or semiarid region, covering or occupying a playa in the wet season but drying up in summer; temporary lake that upon evaporation leaves or forms a playa.

Pocosin—a local term along the Atlantic coastal plain, from Virginia south, for a shrub-scrub wetland located on a relatively flat terrain, often between streams.

Point source—originating at any discrete source.

Population—a collection of individuals of one species or mixed species making up the residents of a prescribed area.

Porosity—the ratio of the volume of voids in a rock or soil to the total volume.

Potential evapotranspiration—the amount of moisture which, if available, would be removed from a given land area by evapotranspiration, expressed in units of water depth.

Prairie pothole—a shallow depression, generally containing wetlands, occurring in an outwash plain, a recessional moraine, or a till plain; usually the result of melted blocks of covered glacial ice; occur most commonly in the North-Central United States and in States west of the Great Lakes from Wisconsin to eastern Montana.

Precipitation—any or all forms of water particles that fall from the atmosphere, such as rain, snow, hail, and sleet. The act or process of producing a solid phase within a liquid medium.

Pristine—the earliest condition of the quality of a water body; unaffected by human activities.

Rain shadow—a dry region on the lee side of a topographic obstacle, usually a mountain range, where rainfall is noticeably less than on the windward side.

Reach—a continuous part of a stream between two specified points.

Reaeration—the replenishment of oxygen in water from which oxygen has been removed.

Recessional moraine—an end moraine built during a temporary but significant pause in the final retreat of a glacier.

Recharge (ground water)—the process involved in the absorption and addition of water to the zone of saturation; also, the amount of water added.

Recharge area (ground water)—an area in which water infiltrates the ground and reaches the zone of saturation.

Recurrence interval—the average interval of time within which the magnitude of a given event, such as a storm or flood, will be equaled or exceeded once.

Regolith—the layer or mantle of fragmented and unconsolidated rock material, residual or transported, that nearly everywhere forms the surface of the land and overlies or covers the bedrock.

Regulation (of a stream)—artificial manipulation of the flow of a stream.

Return flow—that part of irrigation water that is not consumed by evapotranspiration and that returns to its source or another body of water.

Riparian—pertaining to or situated on the bank of a natural body of flowing water.

Riverine wetlands—wetlands within river and stream channels; ocean-derived salinity is less than 0.5 part per thousand.

Runoff—that part of precipitation or snowmelt that appears in streams or surface-water bodies.

Salina—an area where deposits of crystalline salt are formed, such as a salt flat; a body of saline water, such as a saline playa or salt marsh.

Saline water—water that is considered generally unsuitable for human consumption or for irrigation because of its high content of dissolved solids; generally expressed as milligrams per liter (mg/L) of dissolved solids; seawater is generally considered to contain more than 35,000 mg/L of dissolved solids. A general salinity scale is—

Description	Dissolved solids, in milligrams per liter
Slightly	1,000–3,000
Moderately	3,000–10,000
Very	10,000–35,000
Brine	More than 35,000

In the U.S. Fish and Wildlife Service wetland classification system, a general term for waters containing various dissolved salts; applied specifically to inland waters where the ratio of salts often vary; the term haline is applied to coastal waters where the salts are roughly in the same proportion as found in sea water.

Salinity—the concentration of dissolved salts in a body of water; commonly expressed as parts per thousand.

Salt flat—the level, salt-encrusted bottom of a dried up lake or pond.

Salt meadow—a meadow subject to overflow by salt water.

Saltwater—water with a high concentration of salt; sometimes used synonymously with seawater or saline water.

Sandstone—a medium-grained sedimentary rock composed of abundant fragments of sand that are more or less firmly united by a cementing material.

Saturated zone—generally the zone within sediment and rock formations where all voids are filled with water under pressure greater than atmospheric.

Savanna—a plain characterized by coarse grasses and scattered tree growth.

Scrub-shrub wetland—wetlands dominated by woody vegetation less than 6 meters tall.

Sea level—the long-term average position of the sea surface; in this volume, it refers to the National Geodetic Vertical Datum of 1929.

Secondary succession—an association of plants that develops after the destruction of all or part of the original plant community.

Sediment—particles derived from rocks or biological materials that have been transported by, suspended in, or deposited by air, water, or ice or that are accumulated by other natural agents, such as chemical precipitation from solution or secretion by organisms.

Sedimentary rocks—rocks resulting from the consolidation of loose sediment that has accumulated in layers.

Sedimentation—the act or process of forming or accumulating sediment in layers; the process of deposition of sediment.

Seep—a small area where water percolates slowly to the land surface.

Seiche—a sudden oscillation of the water in a moderate-size body of water, caused by wind.

Shale—a fine-grained sedimentary rock formed by the consolidation of clay, silt, or mud.

Shallows—a term applied to a shallow place or area in a body of water; a shoal.

Shoal—a relatively shallow place in a stream, lake, or sea.

Shrubland—land covered predominantly with shrubs.

Siltation—the deposition or accumulation of silt (or small-grained material) in a body of water.

Siltstone—an indurated silt having the texture and composition of shale but lacking its fine lamination.

Silviculture—the cultivation of forest trees.

Sinkhole—a depression in an area underlain by limestone. Its drainage is subterranean.

Slough—a small marshy tract lying in a swale or other local shallow undrained depression; a sluggish creek or channel in a wetland.

Soil horizon—a layer of soil that is distinguishable from adjacent layers by characteristic physical and chemical properties.

Soil moisture—water occurring in the pore spaces between the soil particles in the unsaturated zone from which water is discharged by the transpiration of plants or by evaporation from the soil.

Spit—a small point or low tongue or narrow embankment of land having one end attached to the mainland and the other terminating in open water.

Specific conductance—a measure of the ability of a substance to conduct an electrical current.

Spoil—overburden or other waste material removed

in mining, quarrying, dredging, or excavating.

Spring—area where there is a concentrated discharge of ground water that flows at the ground surface.

Stage—height of the water surface above an established datum plane, such as in a river above a predetermined point that may (or may not) be near the channel floor.

Storm surge—an abnormal and sudden rise of the sea along a shore as a result of the winds of a storm.

Streamflow—the discharge of water in a natural channel.

Submersed plant—a plant which lies entirely beneath the water surface, except for flowering parts in some species.

Subsidence—the gradual downward settling or sinking of the Earth's surface with little or no horizontal motion.

Substrate—the surface beneath a wetland in which organisms grow or to which organisms are attached.

Subtidal—continuously submerged; an area affected by ocean tides.

Surface runoff—runoff which travels over the land surface to the nearest stream channel.

Surface water—an open body of water such as a lake, river, or stream.

Suspended sediment—sediment that is transported in suspension by a stream.

Swale—a slight depression, sometimes filled with water, in the midst of generally level land.

Swamp—an area intermittently or permanently covered with water, and having trees and shrubs.

Tarn—a relatively small and deep, steep-sided lake or pool occupying an ice-gouged basin amid glaciated mountains.

Tectonic activity—movement of the Earth's crust resulting in the formation of ocean basins, continents, plateaus, and mountain ranges.

Terrestrial—pertaining to, consisting of, or representing the Earth.

Terminal moraine—the end moraine extending across a glacial plain or valley as an arcuate or crescent ridge that marks the farthest advance or maximum extent of a glacier.

Terrain—physical features of a tract of land.

Terrane—area or surface over which a particular rock type or group of rock types is prevalent.

Thermokarst—an irregular land surface formed in a permafrost region by melting ground ice and a subsequent settling of the ground.

Tidal flat—an extensive, nearly horizontal, tract of land that is alternately covered and uncovered by the tide and consists of unconsolidated sediment.

Tide—the rhythmic, alternate rise and fall of the surface (or water level) of the ocean, and connected bodies of water, occurring twice a day over most of the Earth, resulting from the gravitational attraction of the Moon, and to a lesser degree, the Sun.

Till—predominantly unsorted and unstratified drift, deposited directly by and underneath a glacier without subsequent reworking by meltwater, and consisting of a heterogeneous mixture of clay, silt, sand, gravel, and boulders.

Tinaja—a pocket of water developed below a waterfall; a term used in the Southwestern United States; used loosely to mean a temporary pool.

Topography—the general configuration of a land surface or any part of the Earth's surface, including its relief and the position of its natural and man-made features.

Trace element—a chemical element that occurs in minute quantities in a substance.

Trade winds—a system of easterly winds that dominate most of the tropics. A major component of the general circulation of the atmosphere.

Transpiration—the process by which water passes through living organisms, primarily plants, into the atmosphere.

Tundra—a vast, nearly level, treeless plain of the arctic and subarctic regions. It usually has a marshy surface which supports mosses, lichens, and low shrubs, underlain by mucky soils and permafrost.

Turbidity—the state, condition, or quality of opaqueness or reduced clarity of a fluid due to the presence of suspended matter.

Unconfined aquifer—an aquifer whose upper surface is a water table free to fluctuate under atmospheric pressure.

Understory—a foliage layer lying beneath and shaded by the main canopy of a forest.

Unsaturated zone—a subsurface zone above the water table where the pore spaces may contain a combination of air and water.

Upland—a general term for nonwetland; elevated land above low areas along streams or between hills; any elevated region from which rivers gather drainage.

Vascular plant—a plant composed of or provided with vessels or ducts that convey water or sap. A fern is an example of this type of plant.

Vernal pool—a small lake or pond that is filled with water for only a short time during the spring.

Water budget—an accounting of the inflow to, outflow from, and storage changes of water in a hydrologic unit.

Water column—an imaginary column extending through a water body from its floor to its surface.

Water gap—a deep, narrow pass in a mountain ridge, through which a stream flows.

Watershed—same as drainage basin.

Water table—the top water surface of an unconfined aquifer at atmospheric pressure.

Weathering—process whereby earthy or rocky materials are changed in color, texture, composition, or form (with little or no transportation) by exposure to atmospheric agents.

Wetland function—a process or series of processes that take place within a wetland that are beneficial to the wetland itself, the surrounding ecosystems, and people.

Willow carr—a pool, or wetland dominated by willow trees or shrubs.

Xerophyte—a plant adapted for growth under dry conditions.

National water summary on
wetland resources